COMPETITION LAW

Seventh Edition

RICHARD WHISH

BA BCL (Oxon)

Professor of Law at King's College London

DAVID BAILEY

LLB (King's College London), LLM (Harv)

Senior Lecturer at King's College London

OXFORD
UNIVERSITY PRESS

OXFORD
UNIVERSITY PRESS

Great Clarendon Street, Oxford OX2 6DP

Oxford University Press is a department of the University of Oxford.
It furthers the University's objective of excellence in research, scholarship,
and education by publishing worldwide in

Oxford New York

Auckland Cape Town Dar es Salaam Hong Kong Karachi
Kuala Lumpur Madrid Melbourne Mexico City Nairobi
New Delhi Shanghai Taipei Toronto

With offices in

Argentina Austria Brazil Chile Czech Republic France Greece
Guatemala Hungary Italy Japan Poland Portugal Singapore
South Korea Switzerland Thailand Turkey Ukraine Vietnam

Oxford is a registered trade mark of Oxford University Press
in the UK and in certain other countries

Published in the United States
by Oxford University Press Inc., New York

© Oxford University Press 2012

Fourth edition 2003, published by Butterworths

Fifth edition 2003

Sixth edition 2008

British Library Cataloguing in Publication Data

Data available

Library of Congress Control Number: 2011939968

Typeset by Newgen Imaging Systems (P) Ltd., Chennai, India
Printed in Great Britain
on acid-free paper by
Ashford Colour Press Ltd, Gosport, Hampshire

ISBN 978-0-19-958655-4

3 5 7 9 10 8 6 4 2

Preface to the seventh edition

It has become customary for Richard Whish to begin the preface to successive editions of this book by remarking upon how much has changed since the previous edition. For this edition there is a significant change of a different kind, which is the addition of David Bailey as a co-author of the book. David worked as a research assistant on the fifth edition, contributed significantly to the sixth, and now shares responsibility, and credit(!), for the seventh. Richard is delighted that David has become party to what is now a joint venture.

Of course, it is also true to say that there has been an enormous amount of change to the law, even in the three years between the last edition and this one.

The most important development, though not involving any change of the law as such, is probably the publication of the *Guidance on the Commission's enforcement priorities in applying Article [102 TFEU] to abusive exclusionary conduct by dominant undertakings*. The preface to the sixth edition predicted that the Commission would not publish guidelines setting out the law: that proved to be a correct prediction. It speculated that instead the Commission might make a statement as to the 'principles' it would apply when deciding which types of abuse, or which economic sectors, to investigate: that was almost correct, except that the document in question explains the Commission's 'enforcement priorities', not quite the same as 'principles'. The publication of these *Enforcement priorities* has provoked a huge amount of debate, not always supportive of the Commission's approach. We are supportive. The *Enforcement priorities* do not state the law: it is for the EU Courts to decide what the law is. But they do shed light on what a 'more economic approach' to the application of Article 102 TFEU might look like in practice, and it is not unreasonable to suppose that they will have a subtle influence on the future orientation of the law. This is all work-in-progress: it will be for the ninth edition of this book (probably not the eighth) to reflect on what influence the *Enforcement priorities* will have had in practice. We have tried very hard to weave the *Enforcement priorities* into the text, but without in any sense treating them as a statement of the law: we repeatedly tell our students at King's not to fall into error by treating the *Enforcement priorities* as guidelines setting out the law; the two should not be elided.

There have been many other developments. The regime in the EU for vertical agreements under Article 101 TFEU has been refreshed, with the adoption of Regulation 330/2010 and the publication of new Guidelines. The same is true for horizontal cooperation agreements: chapter 15 has been rewritten. The European Commission has introduced a system of settlements in cartel cases, and three decisions have so far been adopted under this procedure. There has been an enormous amount of case law from the Courts in Luxembourg, often dealing with procedural issues and the level of fines, in particular in cartel cases; but also exploring some of the most basic issues under Articles 101 and 102 TFEU such as the meaning of 'object' restrictions under Article 101(1) (*Beef Industry Development Society v Competition Authority, GlaxoSmithKline v Commission, T-Mobile v NMa*) and the nature of 'abuse' under Article 102 (see in particular *AstraZeneca v Commission*). *Deutsche Telekom v Commission* and *TeliaSonera v Konkurrensverket* are notable not only for their recognition of margin squeeze as an independent type of abuse under Article 102 but also for their emphasis on the 'as efficient' competitor approach to that provision. The Court of Justice would appear to want to contradict the common accusation that Article 102 is used to protect competitors rather than the process of competition: it actually protects competition between *efficient* firms.

Much has been happening in UK competition law and policy as well. The OFT has imposed significant fines in a number of cases in recent years, for example in *Construction bid rigging*, *Recruitment agencies*, *Royal Bank of Scotland*, *Tobacco* and *Reckitt Benckiser*. The fines in the first two of these were reduced on appeal, but there is no doubt that the law is being enforced more vigorously now than previously. There have been many new guidelines on matters such as leniency, OFT investigation procedures and merger control: a welcome development has been the adoption of joint guidelines on substantive merger assessment by the OFT and Competition Commission.

At the time of writing, a consultation on the reform of UK competition law, initiated by the Department for Business, Innovation and Skills, has just closed: this is likely to lead to the OFT and Competition Commission being merged into a new Competition and Markets Authority. In writing this book we are constrained by a word limit (this edition is the same length as the sixth). We have chosen to say little about the possibilities for reform in the text of this edition, as it is likely that anything we write now will soon be overtaken by events. We intend, therefore, to keep readers informed of the position by updating the Online Resource Centre that accompanies this book. The cut-off date for this text is 20 June 2011, although a few minor updates have been included at the stage of correcting proofs.

We have made many changes to the text to reflect the entry into force of the Lisbon Treaty. In particular we have used the terms 'General Court' and 'Court of Justice' throughout, and have deleted all references to the 'CFI' and 'ECJ'. We have usually changed Articles 81 and 82 to Articles 101 and 102, except that we have not altered the titles of books and articles, in deference to their authors.

The book contains numerous tables of cases and decisions, for example of commitment decisions of the European Commission under Article 9 of Regulation 1/2003 (chapter 7), decisions of the competition authorities in the UK under the Chapter I and II prohibitions in the Competition Act 1998 and Articles 101 and 102 (chapter 9) and Phase II merger investigations under the EU Merger Regulation (chapter 21). In some cases fuller tables containing details of older decisions will be found on the Online Resource Centre: for example we have posted there tables of all Phase II merger cases under the EU Merger Regulation and the UK Enterprise Act 2002 since they entered into force.

Many people have been very helpful to us with their comments, and we thank them hugely. In particular we would like to mention Carole Begent, Margaret Bloom, Leo Flynn, Jackie Holland, Deborah Jones, Adrian Majumdar, Sheldon Mills, David Rawlings, Chris Townley and Wouter Wils. If we have forgotten anyone, we apologise profusely! A very special 'thank you' goes to Dimitris Mourkas, who was also Richard's research assistant for the sixth edition: his contribution was terrific, and he is also a very good friend. We are very grateful to the Centre of European Law at King's College London, which provided the funding for Dimitris' research assistance. We also thank OUP for their support throughout, including their understanding of our difficulties in complying with what would have been their ideal deadlines.

The development of competition law today is ceaseless, and updating a book that attempts to explain the EU rules as well as the UK ones (which in several ways are quite different) within a broader international context inevitably takes its toll on social and family life. For this edition Anil Sinanan was unable to provide any Bollywood blockbusters to provide respite (sadly a lean period musically), but at least there was always some Pinot Grigio to encourage original thinking.

Richard Whish
Marshfield, June 2011
David Bailey
London, June 2011

Contents

Table of treaties and conventions

Table of EU legislation

Table of statutes

Table of statutory instruments

Table of competition commission reports

Table of OFT reports, decisions and publications

Table of cases

List of abbreviations

AAC	Average Avoidable Cost
AEC	Adverse Effect on Competition
Am Ec Rev	American Economic Review
ATC	Average Total Cost
AVC	Average Variable Cost
Bell J Ec	Bell Journal of Economics
BIS	Department for Business, Innovation and Skills
CAA	Civil Aviation Authority
CAT	UK Competition Appeal Tribunal
CC	UK Competition Commission
CDDA	UK Company Directors Disqualification Act 1986
CDO	Competition Disqualification Order
Cm	Command Papers
CML Rev	Common Market Law Review
CMLR	Common Market Law Reports
CompAR	Competition Appeal Reports
Comp Law	Competition Law Journal
Cong Rec	Congressional Record
CRM	Case Review Meeting
CSOH	Scottish Court of Session Outer House
CWP	Concurrency Working Party
DG COMP	Directorate General for Competition
DoJ	US Department of Justice
DTI	Department of Trade and Industry
Ec J	Economic Journal
ECLR	European Competition Law Review
ECOSOC	Economic and Social Committee
ECN	European Competition Network
ECPR	Efficient Component Pricing Rule
ECR	European Court Reports
ECSC	European Coal and Steel Community
EEA	European Economic Area
EFTA	European Free Trade Association
EIPR	European Intellectual Property Review
EL Rev	European Law Review

ESA	EFTA Surveillance Authority
ETSI	European Telecommunications Standards Institute
EUMR	European Union Merger Regulation
EWCA	England and Wales Court of Appeal
EWHC	England and Wales High Court
FRAND	Fair, Reasonable and Non-discriminatory
FSA	Financial Services Authority
FTC	US Federal Trade Commission
GEMA	Gas and Electricity Markets Authority
HHI	Herfindahl-Hirschman Index
ICB	UK Independent Commission on Banking
ICLQ	International and Comparative Law Quarterly
ICN	International Competition Network
ICPAC	International Competition Policy Advisory Committee
IPR	Intellectual Property Rights
J Ind Ec	Journal of Industrial Economics
J Pol Ec	Journal of Political Economics
LRAIC	Long-run Average Incremental Cost
LRIC	Long-run Incremental Cost
MLR	Modern Law Review
NCAs	National Competition Authorities
NIAER	Northern Ireland Authority for Energy Regulation
OECD	Organisation for Economic Co-operation and Development
OFCOM	Office of Communications
OFGEM	Office of Gas and Electricity Markets
OFT	Office of Fair Trading
OFTEL	Office of Telecommunications
OFWAT	Office of Water Services
OJ	Official Journal of the European Union
OJLS	Oxford Journal of Legal Studies
ORR	Office of Rail Regulation
PACE	UK Police and Criminal Evidence Act 1984
PRS	Performing Rights Society
Qu J Ec	Quebec Journal of Economics
RAND	Reasonable and Non-discriminatory
Rev Ec Stud	Review of Economic Studies
RPI	Retail Price Index
SFO	Serious Fraud Office
SI	Statutory Instrument
SIEC	Significant Impediment to Effective Competition

SLC	Substantial Lessening of Competition
SMEs	Small and Medium-sized Enterprises
SSNIP	Small but Significant Non-transitory Increase in Price
SWIFT	Society for Worldwide International Finanical Telecommunications
TEU	Treaty on European Union
TFEU	Treaty on the Functioning of the European Union
UKCLR	United Kingdom Competition Law Reports
UKHL	UK House of Lords
UNCTAD	United Nations Conference on Trade and Development
WSRA	Water Services Regulation Authority
WTO	World Trade Organization

1

Competition policy and economics

1. Introduction

As a general proposition competition law consists of rules that are intended to protect the process of competition in order to maximise consumer welfare. Competition law has grown at a phenomenal rate in recent years in response to the enormous changes in political thinking and economic behaviour that have taken place around the world. There are now more than 120 systems of competition law in the world[1]. In recent years competition laws have entered into force in both China and in India, potentially bringing the benefits of competitive markets to an additional two and a half billion citizens of the world; a competition law will come into effect in Malaysia in 2012. There are several other new competition laws in contemplation, for example in Hong Kong and the Philippines. Competition laws will be found in all continents and in all types of economies – large, small, continental, island, advanced, developing, industrial, trading, agricultural, liberal and post-communist. Quite apart from its geographical growth, competition law is now applied to many economic activities that once were regarded as natural monopolies or the preserve of the state: telecommunications, energy, transport, broadcasting and postal services, to name a few obvious examples, have become the subject of competition law scrutiny. Other sectors, such as the liberal professions, sport and the media, are also within the scope of the subject.

The global reach of competition laws is reflected in the creation of the International Competition Network, a virtual organisation which brings together more than 100 of the world's competition authorities. It has enormous influence in building consensus and convergence towards sound competition policy principles. Its work is considered in chapter 12[2].

A central concern of competition policy is that a firm or firms with market power are able, in various ways, to harm consumer welfare, for example by reducing output, raising prices, degrading the quality of products on the market, suppressing innovation and

---

[1] A helpful way of accessing the competition laws of the world is through the website of the International Bar Association's Global Competition Forum, at www.globalcompetitionforum.org; other useful sources are the websites of the International Competition Network, www.internationalcompetitionnetwork.org; the OECD, www.oecd.org; and UNCTAD, www.unctad.org.

[2] See ch 12, 'International competition network', p 508.

depriving consumers of choice. These concerns cannot be expressed in a codified table of rules capable of precise application in the way, for example, that laws on taxation or the relationship of landlord and tenant can. The analysis of competition issues invariably requires an assessment of market power, and such an assessment cannot be conducted without an understanding of the economic concepts involved. The same is true of the types of behaviour – for example cartelisation, predatory pricing, discrimination, mergers – with which competition law is concerned. Competition lawyers must understand economic concepts, and competition economists must understand legal processes. It is common practice today – and much to be welcomed – that competition lawyers attend courses on economics and vice versa. Complex cases require both legal and economic input. A (possibly apocryphal) story is that a competition lawyer once remarked at a competition law conference that, in his view, in any competition law case the lawyer should be in the driving seat; and that a competition economist readily agreed, since he always preferred to have a chauffeur. To the extent that this suggests that there is inevitably a conflict between lawyers and economists is, hopefully, outdated: it is better to think of the two as co-pilots of an aeroplane, each understanding the contribution to be made by the other[3].

In the early days of competition law in the European Union the role of economics was not particularly strongly emphasised; the same was true in the US in the early years of antitrust law there. Competition law developed in a fairly formalistic manner, and there were many more 'rules' of a legalistic nature than is the case today. The position – from the middle of the 1990s onwards – has changed dramatically, not least as a result of eminent economists being appointed to some of the most influential positions in institutions entrusted with the application of competition law[4]. An attempt will be made throughout this book to place the competition law of the EU and the UK in its economic context.

This chapter will begin with a brief description of the types of behaviour that competition law is concerned with. It will then attempt to explain why competition policy is considered to be so important to modern economies based on the market mechanism: first it will explore the theory of competition itself and then the various functions that a system of competition law might be expected to fulfil. The chapter will then introduce two key economic concepts – market definition and, more importantly, market power – that are of fundamental importance to understanding competition policy, and that are central to all competition analysis in practice. The chapter will conclude with a table of market share figures that have significance in the application of EU and UK competition law, while reminding the reader that market shares are only ever a proxy for market power and can never be determinative of market power in themselves.

2. Overview of the Practices Controlled by Competition Law

Systems of competition law are concerned with practices that are harmful to the competitive process. In particular competition law is concerned with:

- **anti-competitive agreements**: agreements that have as their object or effect the restriction of competition are unlawful, unless they have some redeeming virtue

---

[3] For discussion see Kovacic and Shapiro 'Antitrust Policy: A Century of Economic and Legal Thinking' (2000) 14(1) Journal of Economic Perspectives 43.

[4] Obvious examples are the appointment of Mario Monti as European Commissioner for Competition, Sir Derek Morris as Chairman of the UK Competition Commission and Sir John Vickers as Chairman and Chief Executive of the UK Office of Fair Trading.

such as the enhancement of economic efficiency. In particular agreements between competitors, for example to fix prices, to share markets or to restrict output – often referred to as horizontal agreements – are severely punished, and in some systems of law can even lead to the imprisonment of the individuals responsible for them. Agreements between firms at different levels of the market – known as vertical agreements – may also be struck down when they could be harmful to competition: an example would be where a supplier of goods instructs its retailers not to resell them at less than a certain price, a practice often referred to as resale price maintenance. As a general proposition, vertical agreements are much less likely to harm competition than horizontal ones

- **abusive behaviour**: abusive behaviour by a monopolist, or by a dominant firm with substantial market power which enables it to behave as if it were a monopolist, can also be condemned by competition law. An example would be where a dominant firm reduces its prices to less than cost in order to drive a competitor out of the market or to deter a competitor from entering the market so that it can subsequently charge higher prices, a phenomenon known as predatory pricing

- **mergers**: many systems of competition law enable a competition authority to investigate mergers between firms that could be harmful to the competitive process: clearly if one competitor were to acquire its main competitor the possibility exists that consumers would be deprived of choice and may have to pay higher prices as a result. Many systems of competition law provide that certain mergers cannot be completed until the approval of the relevant competition authority has been obtained

- **public restrictions of competition**: the State is often responsible for restrictions and distortions of competition, for example as a result of legislative measures, regulations, licensing rules or the provision of subsidies. Some systems of competition law give a role to competition authorities to scrutinise 'public' restrictions of competition and to play a 'competition advocacy' role by commenting on, and even recommending the removal of, such restrictions.

3. The Theory of Competition

Competition means a struggle or contention for superiority, and in the commercial world this means a striving for the custom and business of people in the market place: competition has been described as 'a process of rivalry between firms... seeking to win customers' business over time'[5]. The ideological struggle between capitalism and communism was a dominant feature of the twentieth century. Many countries had the greatest suspicion of competitive markets and saw, instead, benefits in state planning and management of the economy. However enormous changes took place as the millennium approached, leading to widespread demonopolisation, liberalisation and privatisation. These phenomena, coupled with rapid technological changes and the opening up of international trade, unleashed unprecedentedly powerful economic forces. These changes impact upon individuals and societies in different ways, and sometimes the effects can be uncomfortable. Underlying them, however, is a growing consensus that, on the whole, markets deliver

[5] See para 4.1.2 of the *Merger Assessment Guidelines* of the UK Office of Fair Trading and Competition Commission, CC2 revised and OFT 1254, September 2010, available at www.competition-commission. org.uk.

better outcomes than state planning; and central to the idea of a market is the process of competition.

The important issue therefore is to determine the effect which competition can have on economic performance. To understand this one must first turn to economic theory and consider what would happen in conditions of perfect competition and compare the outcome with what happens under monopoly, recognising as one does so that a theoretical analysis of perfect competition does not adequately explain business behaviour in the 'real' world.

(A) The benefits of perfect competition

At its simplest – and it is sensible in considering competition law and policy not to lose sight of the simple propositions – the benefits of competition are lower prices, better products, wider choice and greater efficiency than would be obtained under conditions of monopoly. According to neo-classical economic theory, social welfare is maximised in conditions of perfect competition[6]. For this purpose 'social welfare' is not a vague generalised concept, but instead has a more specific meaning: that allocative and productive efficiency will be achieved; the combined effect of allocative and productive efficiency is that society's wealth overall is maximised. Consumer welfare, which is specifically concerned with gains to consumers as opposed to society at large, is also maximised in perfect competition[7]. A related benefit of competition is that it may have the dynamic effect of stimulating innovation as competitors strive to produce new and better products for consumers: this is a particularly important feature of high technology markets.

(i) Allocative efficiency

Under perfect competition economic resources are allocated between different goods and services in such a way that it is not possible to make anyone better off without making someone else worse off; consumer surplus – the net gain to a consumer when buying a product – is at its largest. Goods and services are allocated between consumers according

---

[6] See Asch *Industrial Organization and Antitrust Policy* (Wiley, revised ed, 1983), ch 1; Scherer and Ross *Industrial Market Structure and Economic Performance* (Houghton Mifflin, 3rd ed, 1990), chs 1 and 2; Lipsey and Chrystal *Economics* (Oxford University Press, 12th ed, 2011), ch 7; on industrial economics and competition generally see Tirole *The Theory of Industrial Organization* (MIT Press, 1988); Hay and Morris *Industrial Economics: Theory and Evidence* (Oxford University Press, 1991); Peeperkorn and Mehta 'The Economics of Competition', ch 1 in Faull and Nikpay *The EC Law of Competition* (Oxford University Press, 2nd ed, 2007); Sullivan and Harrison *Understanding Antitrust and Its Economic Implications* (LexisNexis, 4th ed, 2003); Hylton *Antitrust Law: Economic Theory and Common Law Evolution* (Cambridge University Press, 2003); Motta *Competition Policy: Theory and Practice* (Cambridge University Press, 2004); Carlton and Perloff *Modern Industrial Organisation* (Addison Wesley, 4th ed, 2005); Van den Bergh and Camesasca *European Competition Law and Economics: A Comparative Perspective* (Sweet & Maxwell, 2nd ed, 2006); Bishop and Walker *The Economics of EC Competition Law* (Sweet & Maxwell, 3rd ed, 2010), ch 2; Niels, Jenkins and Kavanagh *Economics for Competition Lawyers* (Oxford University Press, 2011); on the psychology of competition from the business manager's perspective, see Porter *Competitive Strategy: Techniques for Analyzing Industries and Competitors* (Macmillan, 1998). Readers may find helpful, in coping with the terminology of the economics of competition law, the *Glossary of Industrial Organisation, Economics and Competition Law* (OECD, 1993); Black *Oxford Dictionary of Economics* (Oxford University Press, 3rd ed, 2003); and the European Commission's *Glossary of Terms used in Competition related matters*, available at www.ec.europa.eu/competition/publications/glossary_en.pdf.

[7] See *Bishop and Walker*, paras 2.17–2.19; *Van den Bergh and Camesasca*, pp 62–69; Cseres 'The Controversies of the Consumer Welfare Standard' (2007) 3(2) Competition Law Review 121; Orbach 'The Antitrust Consumer Welfare Paradox' (2011) 7(1) Journal of Competition Law and Economics 133.

to the price they are prepared to pay, and, in the long run, price equals the marginal cost[8] of production (cost for this purpose including a sufficient profit margin to have encouraged the producer to invest his capital in the industry in the first place, but no more).

The achievement of allocative efficiency, as this phenomenon is known[9], can be shown analytically on the economist's model[10]. Allocative efficiency is achieved under perfect competition because the producer, assuming he is acting rationally and has a desire to maximise his profits, will expand his production for as long as it is privately profitable to do so. As long as he can earn more by producing one extra unit of whatever he produces than it costs to make it, he will presumably do so. Only when the cost of producing a further unit (the 'marginal cost') exceeds the price he would obtain for it (the 'marginal revenue') will he cease to expand production. Where competition is perfect, a reduction in a producer's own output cannot affect the market price and so there is no reason to limit it; the producer will therefore increase output to the point at which marginal cost and marginal revenue (the net addition to revenue of selling the last unit) coincide. This means that allocative efficiency is achieved, as consumers can obtain the amounts of goods or services they require at the price they are prepared to pay: resources are allocated precisely according to their wishes. A monopolist however can restrict output and increase his own marginal revenue as a consequence of doing so[11].

(ii) Productive efficiency

Apart from allocative efficiency many economists consider that under perfect competition goods and services will be produced at the lowest cost possible, which means that as little of society's wealth is expended in the production process as necessary. Monopolists, free from the constraints of competition, may be high cost producers. Thus competition is said to be conducive to productive efficiency[12]. Productive efficiency is achieved because a producer is unable to sell above cost (if he did his customers would immediately desert him) and he will not of course sell below it (because then he would make no profit). In particular, if a producer were to charge above cost, other competitors would move into the market in the hope of profitable activity[13]. They would attempt to produce on a more efficient basis so that they could earn a greater profit. In the long run the tendency will be to force producers to incur the lowest cost possible in order to be able to earn any profit at all: an equilibrium will be reached where price and the average cost of producing goods necessarily coincide. This in turn means that price will never rise above cost. If on the other hand price were to fall below cost, there would be an exit of capital from the industry and, as output would therefore decrease, price would be restored to the competitive level.

(iii) Dynamic efficiency

A further benefit of competition, albeit one that cannot be proved scientifically and is not captured by the theory of perfect competition, is that producers will be more likely to innovate and develop new products as part of the continual battle of striving for consumers' business. Thus competition may have the desirable dynamic effect of stimulating important technological research and development. This assumption has been

---

[8] That is to say, the cost of producing an additional unit of output.

[9] Allocative efficiency is also sometimes referred to as 'Pareto efficiency'.

[10] *Scherer and Ross*, pp 19ff; *Lipsey and Chrystal*, pp 153–155.

[11] See 'The harmful effects of monopoly', pp 6–7 below.

[12] For discussion see Vickers 'Concepts of Competition' (1995) 47 Oxford Economic Papers 1.

[13] As will be seen, determining what is meant by 'cost' is, in itself, often a complex matter in competition law: see ch 18, 'Cost concepts', pp 716–718.

questioned. Some argue that only monopolists enjoy the wealth to innovate and carry out expensive research[14]. Schumpeter was a champion of the notion that the motivation to innovate was the prospect of monopoly profits and that, even if existing monopolists earned such profits in the short term, outsiders would in due course enter the market and displace them[15]. A 'perennial gale of creative destruction' would be sufficient to protect the public interest, so that short-term monopoly power need not cause concern. Empirical research tends to suggest that neither monopolists nor fierce competitors have a superior track record in this respect, but it would seem clear that the assertion that only monopolists can innovate is incorrect[16].

It is important to acknowledge that in certain industries, particularly where technology is sophisticated and expensive, one firm may, for a period of time, enjoy very high market shares; however, in due course, a competitor may be able to enter that market with superior technology and replace the incumbent firm. In cases such as this, high market shares over a period of time may exaggerate the market power of the firm that is currently the market leader, but vulnerable to dynamic entry.

(B) **The harmful effects of monopoly**

The theoretical model just outlined suggests that in perfect competition any producer will be able to sell his product only at the market price. The producer is a price-taker, with no capacity to affect the price by his own unilateral action. The consumer is sovereign. The reason why the producer cannot affect the price is that any change in his own individual output will have only a negligible effect on the aggregate output of the market as a whole, and it is aggregate output that determines price through the 'law' of supply and demand.

Under conditions of monopoly the position is very different[17]. The monopolist is in a position to affect the market price. Since he is responsible for all the output, and since it is aggregate output that determines price through the relationship of supply to demand, he will be able either to increase price by reducing the volume of his own production or to reduce sales by increasing price: the latter occurs in the case of highly branded products which are sold at a high price, such as luxury perfumes. Furthermore, again assuming a motive to maximise profits, the monopolist will see that he will be able to earn the largest profit if he refrains from expanding his production to the level that would be attained under perfect competition. The result will be that output is lower than would be the case under perfect competition and that therefore consumers will be deprived of goods and services that they would have been prepared to pay for at the competitive market price. There is therefore allocative inefficiency in this situation: society's resources are not distributed in the most efficient way possible. The inefficiency is accentuated by the fact that consumers, deprived of the monopolised product they would have bought, will spend their money on products which they wanted less. The economy to this extent is performing below its potential. The extent of this allocative inefficiency is sometimes referred to as the 'deadweight loss' attributable to monopoly.

The objection to monopoly does not stop there. There is also the problem that productive efficiency may be lower because the monopolist is not constrained by competitive forces to reduce costs to the lowest possible level. Instead the firm becomes 'X-inefficient'. This term, first used by Liebenstein[18], refers to a situation in which resources are used to

---

[14] Galbraith *American Capitalism: The Concept of Countervailing Power* (Houghton Mifflin, 1952).

[15] *Capitalism, Socialism and Democracy* (Taylor & Francis Books, 1976).

[16] *Scherer and Ross*, ch 17.   [17] See *Scherer and Ross*, ch 2; *Lipsey and Chrystal*, ch 8.

[18] 'Allocative Efficiency vs X-Efficiency' (1966) 56 Am Ec Rev 392–415.

make the right product, but less productively than they might be: management spends too much time on the golf course, outdated industrial processes are maintained and a general slackness pervades the organisation of the firm. Furthermore the monopolist may not feel the need to innovate, because he does not experience the constant pressure to go on attracting custom by offering better, more advanced, products. Thus it has been said that the greatest benefit of being a monopolist is the quiet life he is able to enjoy. However it is important to bear in mind that inefficient managers of a business may be affected by pressures other than those of competition. In particular their position may be undermined by uninvited takeover bids on stock exchanges from investors who consider that more efficient use could be made of the firm's assets[19]. Competition may be felt in capital as well as product markets: this is sometimes referred to as 'the market for corporate control'.

A final objection to the monopolist is that, since he can charge a higher price than in conditions of competition (he is a price-maker), wealth is transferred from the hapless consumer to him. This may be particularly true where he is able to discriminate between customers, charging some more than others: however it is important to recognise that price discrimination in some circumstances may be welfare-enhancing, or at least neutral in terms of social welfare, in particular where it allows firms to recover fixed expenditure that would otherwise not have been recovered[20]. While it is not the function of competition authorities themselves to determine how society's wealth should be distributed, it is manifestly a legitimate matter for Governments to take an interest in economic equity, and it may be that one of the ways in which policy is expressed on this issue is through competition law[21].

Thus runs the theory of perfect competition and monopoly. It indicates that there is much to be said for the 'invisible hand' of competition which magically and surreptitiously orders society's resources in an optimal way, as opposed to the lumbering inefficiency of monopoly. However, we must now turn from the models used in the economist's laboratory to the more haphazard ways of commercial life before rendering a final verdict on the desirability of competition.

(C) Questioning the theory of perfect competition

(i) The model of perfect competition is based on assumptions unlikely to be observed in practice

The first point which must be made about the theory of perfect competition is that it is only a theory; the conditions necessary for perfect competition are extremely unlikely to be observed in practice. Perfect competition requires that on any particular market there is an infinite number of buyers and sellers, all producing identical (or 'homogeneous') products; consumers have perfect information about market conditions; resources can flow freely from one area of economic activity to another: there are no 'barriers to entry' which might prevent the emergence of new competition, and there are no 'barriers to exit' which might hinder firms wishing to leave the industry[22]. Of course a market structure

---

[19] See eg Hall 'Control Type and the Market for Corporate Control in Large US Corporations' (1977) 25 J Ind Ec 259–273; this issue is discussed further in ch 20, 'Management efficiency and the market for corporate control', pp 814–815.

[20] See *Lipsey and Chrystal*, pp 289–291; on abusive pricing by dominant firms generally see ch 18.

[21] See 'Goals of competition law', pp 19–24 below on the various functions of competition law.

[22] See 'Potential competitors', pp 44–45 below for further discussion of barriers to entry and exit.

satisfying all these conditions is unlikely, if not impossible: we are simply at this stage considering theory, and the theory is based upon a number of assumptions.

Between the polar market structures, of perfect competition on the one hand and monopoly on the other, there are many intermediate positions. Many firms sell products which are slightly differentiated from those of their rivals or command some degree of consumer loyalty, so that there will not be the homogeneity required for perfect competition. This means that an increase in price will not necessarily result in a substantial loss of business. It is unlikely that a customer will have such complete information of the market that he will immediately know that a lower price is available elsewhere for the product he requires, yet the theory of perfect competition depends on perfect information being available to consumers. This is why legislation sometimes requires that adequate information must be made available to consumers about prices, terms and conditions[23]. There are often barriers to entry and exit to and from markets; this is particularly so where a firm that enters a market incurs 'sunk costs', that is to say costs that cannot be recovered when it ceases to operate in the future.

Just as perfect competition is unlikely to be experienced in practice, monopoly in its purest form is also rare. There are few products where one firm is responsible for the entire output: normally this happens only where a state confers a monopoly, for example to deliver letters. Most economic operators have some competitors; and even a true monopolist may hoist prices so high that customers cease to buy: demand is not infinitely inelastic[24]. In practice, most cases involve not a monopolist, in the etymological sense of one firm selling all the products on a particular market. Rather, competition law concerns itself with firms that have a dominant position, which in competition law terms is equated with significant market power. The economic concept of market power is key to understanding and applying competition law. When assessing whether a firm or firms have market power it is normal to begin by defining the relevant product and geographical markets; then the competitive constraints upon firms both from within and from outside those markets are considered, as well as countervailing buyer power. These issues are considered further in section 5 of this chapter.

(ii) Other problems with the theory of perfect competition

Apart from the fact that perfect competition and pure monopoly are inherently unlikely, there are other problems with the theory itself. It depends on the notion that all businessmen are rational and that they always attempt to maximise profits, but this is not necessarily the case. Directors of a company may not think that earning large profits for their shareholders is the most important consideration they face: they may be more interested to see the size of their business empire grow or to indulge themselves in the quiet life that monopolists may enjoy[25].

A further problem with the theory of perfect competition is that its assertion that costs are kept to an absolute minimum is not necessarily correct. It is true that the private costs of the producer will be kept low, but that says nothing about the social costs or 'externalities' which arise for society at large from, for example, the air pollution that a factory

---

[23] This is a possible remedy under UK law following a market or merger investigation: see Enterprise Act 2002, Sch 8, paras 15–19; the CC has imposed remedies requiring the provision of clearer information to consumers on a number of occasions: see ch 11, 'The Market Investigations Provisions in Practice', pp 479–485.

[24] Demand is inelastic when a 1 per cent change in price leads to a fall in quantity of less than 1 per cent; it is elastic when a 1 per cent change in price leads to a reduction in quantity of a greater percentage.

[25] *Scherer and Ross*, pp 44–46; see also *Bishop and Walker*, p 21, n 17.

causes, or the severed limbs that must be paid for because cheap machinery is used which does not include satisfactory safeguards against injury. It has been argued that competition law should not concern itself with these social costs[26], and perhaps it is true that this is a matter best left to specific legislation on issues such as conservation, the environment and health and safety at work; also it would be wrong to suppose that monopolists do not themselves produce social costs. However it is reasonable to be at least sceptical of the argument that in perfect competition the costs of society overall will inevitably be kept at a minimal level. Lastly, there is the difficulty with the theory of perfect competition that it is based on a static model of economic behaviour which may fail to account for the dynamic nature of markets and the way in which they operate over a period of time[27]. Firms such as Xerox and IBM, that may have dominated their industries at a particular time in history, nevertheless have found themselves to be engulfed subsequently by competitive forces in the market; it is possible that the same fate might befall Microsoft as cloud technology diminishes the importance of personal computers as a place to store data. Schumpeter's gale of perennial destruction may affect even the most powerful economic operators.

Given these doubts it might be wondered whether pursuit of an unattainable ideal of perfect competition is worthwhile at all. Indeed some theoreticians have asserted that it might be positively harmful to aspire to a 'second-best solution' in which something similar to, but falling short of, perfect competition is achieved[28]. A second-best solution may actually compound allocative inefficiency and harm consumer welfare, as one distortion in the market inevitably affects performance in other parts of the economy. Where competition is imperfect and monopoly exists, attacking individual vulnerable monopolies while leaving other ones intact might simply exacerbate the pre-existing allocative inefficiency. One should guard against the assumption that tinkering with individual sectors of the economy will necessarily improve performance in the economy as a whole.

Apart from the issue of 'second-best', there is the further problem that if perfect competition cannot be attained, some alternative model is needed to explain how imperfect markets work or should work. In particular it will be necessary to decide how monopolists or dominant firms should be treated, and an adequate theory will be needed to deal with oligopoly, a common industrial phenomenon which exists where a few firms between them supply most of the products within the relevant market without any of them having a clear ascendancy over the others. Some economists would argue that, as the most common market form is oligopoly, competition policy ought to be designed around an analytical model of this phenomenon rather than the theory of perfect competition[29].

(D) **Questioning competition itself**

The comments just made question various aspects of the theory of perfect competition. A second line of inquiry considers whether competition is so obviously beneficial anyway. There are some arguments that suggest that competition may not yield the best outcome for society.

---

[26] Bork *The Antitrust Paradox* (The Free Press, 1993), pp 114–115.

[27] See eg Evans and Hylton 'The Lawful Acquisition and Exercise of Monopoly Power and Its Implications for the Objectives of Antitrust' (2008) 4(2) Competition Policy International 203.

[28] Lipsey and Lancaster 'The General Theory of Second Best' (1956–57) 24 Rev Ec Stud 11–32; see also *Scherer and Ross*, pp 33–38 and *Asch*, pp 97–100.

[29] On tacit collusion, oligopoly and parallel behaviour see ch 14.

(i) Economies of scale and scope and natural monopolies

The first relates to economies of scale, scope and the phenomenon of 'natural monopoly'[30]. In some markets there may be significant economies of scale, meaning that the average cost per unit of output decreases with the increase in the scale of the outputs produced; economies of scope occur where it is cheaper to produce two products together than to produce them separately. In some markets a profit can be made only by a firm supplying at least one quarter or one third of total output; it may even be that the 'minimum efficient scale' of operation is achieved only by a firm with a market share exceeding 50 per cent, so that monopoly may be seen to be a natural market condition[31]. Similarly, economies of scope may be essential to profitable behaviour. Natural monopoly means a situation in which scale economies are so great that having two or more competing producers would not be viable and so efficiency dictates that a single firm serves the entire market. Natural monopoly is an economic phenomenon, to be contrasted with statutory monopoly, where the right to exclude rivals from the market is derived from law. Where natural monopoly exists, it is inappropriate to attempt to achieve a level of competition which would destroy the efficiency that this entails. This problem may be exacerbated where the 'natural monopolist' is also required to perform a 'universal service obligation', such as the daily delivery of letters to all postal addresses at a uniform price; performance of such an obligation may not be profitable in normal market conditions, so that the state may confer a statutory monopoly on the undertaking entrusted with the task in question. The lawfulness under EU and UK competition law of 'special or exclusive rights' conferred by the state is one of the more complex issues to be considered in this book[32].

Where the minimum efficient scale is very large in relation to total output, a separate question arises as to how that industry can be made to operate in a way that is beneficial to society as a whole. It may be that public ownership is a solution, or that a system of regulation should be introduced while leaving the producer or producers in the private sector[33]. A further possibility is that firms should be allowed to bid for a franchise to run the industry in question for a set period of time, at the end of which there will be a further round of bidding. In other words there will be periodic competition to run the industry, although no actual competition within it during the period of the franchise[34]: this happens in the UK, for example, when companies bid for television or rail franchises or to run the national lottery. The 100 per cent share of the market that a firm might have after it has won the bid does not accurately reflect its market power if it was subject to effective competition when making its bid[35].

---

[30] *Lipsey and Chrystal*, pp 291–293; *Scherer and Ross*, pp 97–141.

[31] See Schmalensee *The Control of Natural Monopolies* (Lexington, 1979); Sharkey *The Theory of Natural Monopoly* (Cambridge University Press, 1982).

[32] See ch 6, 'Article 106', pp 222–224 and ch 9, 'Services of general economic interest', pp 352–353.

[33] See ch 23, 'Regulated Industries', pp 977–980.

[34] See Demsetz 'Why Regulate Utilities?' (1968) 11 J L Ec 55–66; for criticism of the idea of franchise bidding see Williamson 'Franchise Bidding for Natural Monopolies in General and with respect to CATV' (1976) 7 Bell J Ec 73–104.

[35] For further discussion of so-called 'bidding markets' see 'Market shares', p 43 below.

(ii) Network effects and two-sided markets[36]

(A) Network effects

Certain markets are characterised by 'network effects'. A direct network effect arises where the value of a product increases with the number of other customers consuming the same product. A simple example of a direct network effect is a telecommunications network. Suppose that Telcom has 100 subscribers to its network; suppose further that it is impossible for the users of Telcom's network to communicate with subscribers to competing networks. If a new consumer subscribes to the Telcom system the 100 original subscribers can now make contact with an additional person, without having incurred any additional cost themselves: for this reason the benefit to those subscribers is sometimes described as a network externality. In the same way users of a particular computer software system will benefit as more people use the same system, since it becomes possible to share documents, images and music with more people. Where this occurs computer programmers will increasingly write new software that is compatible with the system, so that the system becomes even more valuable to the consumers that use it (an indirect network effect).

(B) Two-sided markets[37]

In the simple example given above of subscribers joining a telecommunications network, the value of the network increased because of the number of consumers joining it. However there are some markets, often referred to as 'two-sided markets', where two or more groups of customers are catered for, and where a network effect arises as more consumers join one or the other side of the market. A simple example is a newspaper. A newspaper publisher sells advertising space; it also supplies newspapers to citizens, sometimes at a cover price and sometimes free of charge. The publisher's ability to sell advertising space increases according to the number of citizens expected to read the newspaper. Exactly the same is true of commercial television stations: advertising slots during the football World Cup final will be hugely expensive because of the opportunity that exists to advertise products to a large number of people. The same phenomenon can be seen at play in the case of credit cards: the more merchants that accept a particular card, the more consumers will use that card; and the more consumers that use that card, the more merchants will accept it.

(C) Network effects and competition policy

Network effects may have positive effects on competition, since consumers become better off as a product becomes more popular. The increased utility of a telecommunications network is of value both to the operator and to the subscribers. In the case of a successful credit card system, merchants, the card issuer and consumers benefit. However network

---

[36] See OFT Economic Discussion Paper 3 (OFT 377) *Innovation and Competition Policy* (Charles River Associates, March 2002), paras 1.6–1.8; *Merger Assessment Guidelines* of the UK Office of Fair Trading and Competition Commission (CC2 revised and OFT 1254, September 2010), paras 5.2.20, 5.7.16 and 5.8.6; see further Salop and Romaine 'Preserving Monopoly: Economic Analysis, Legal Standards, and Microsoft' (1999) 7 George Mason Law Review 617; Cass and Hylton 'Preserving Competition: Economic Analysis, Legal Standards and Microsoft' (1999) 8 George Mason Law Review 1; Posner 'Antitrust in the New Economy' (2001) 68 Antitrust Law Journal 925.

[37] For discussion of two-sided markets see the contributions at a symposium on two-sided markets, specifically concerned with payment cards, at (2006) 73 Antitrust Law Journal 571ff and the series of essays in (2007) 3(1) Competition Policy International 147ff; see also *Bishop and Walker*, paras 3.042–3.045; and the OECD Roundtable on *Two-sided markets* of December 2009, available at www.oecd.org.

effects also give rise to the possibility of one firm dominating a market, in particular because there may be 'tipping effects' where all the customers in a particular market decide to opt for the product of one firm or for one particular technology. Many years ago, when video cassettes and video recorders were first introduced to the market, there were two competing technologies, Betamax and VHS; many people considered that the Betamax technology was superior, and yet the market tipped in favour of VHS. In the same way the market can be seen to have tipped in favour of Microsoft's Windows operating system[38]. If tipping does take place, or if it is a likely consequence of a merger, a question for competition policy is to determine how the issue should be addressed. Various possibilities exist, including remedies in merger cases[39] and the possibility that third parties should be allowed to have access to the product of the successful firm in whose favour the tipping has occurred: however, mandatory access to the successful products of innovative firms risks chilling the investment that created the product in the first place[40].

A specific point about two-sided markets is that pricing practices that, at first sight, appear to be anti-competitive might have an objective justification in their specific context. For example in the case of free-to-air television the broadcaster, in one sense, could be seen to be acting in a predatory manner by supplying a service at below the cost of production, which would be abusive if it was in a dominant position; but in a two-sided market this analysis may be wrong if the free-to-air broadcasting is paid for by the sale of advertising; the same is true of the 'free' newspapers that are now so prevalent, for example, in London and other major cities.

(iii) Particular sectors

As well as the complexity of introducing competition into markets that might be regarded as natural monopolies, it is possible that social or political value-judgments may lead to the conclusion that competition is inappropriate in particular economic sectors. Agriculture is an obvious example. Legislatures have tended to the view that agriculture possesses special features entitling it to protection from the potentially ruthless effects of the competitive system. An obvious illustration of this is the Common Agricultural Policy of the EU[41]. Similarly it might be thought inappropriate (or politically impossible) to expose the labour market to the full discipline of the competitive process; this point is demonstrated by the judgment of the European Court of Justice in *Albany International BV v Stichting Begrijfspensioenfonds Textielindustrie*[42] which concluded that collective bargaining between organisations representing employers and employees is outside Article 101 TFEU. Defence industries may be excluded from competition law scrutiny[43]. Systems of competition law have often shown a tendency to refrain from insisting that the liberal professions should have to sully their hands with anything as offensive as price competition or advertising, although the European Commission has taken a stricter line

---

[38] The Commission discussed tipping effects in *Microsoft*, Commission decision of 24 March 2004, paras 448–472.

[39] See eg Case M 1069 *WorldCom/MCI*, decision of 8 July 1998; the Commission subsequently prohibited the merger in Case M 1741 *MCIWorldCom/Sprint*, decision of 28 June 2000 where it had network concerns, but this decision was annulled on appeal for procedural reasons, Case T-310/00 *MCI Inc v Commission* [2004] ECR II-3253, [2004] 5 CMLR 1274.

[40] See in particular ch 17, 'Refusal to Supply', pp 697–711 on the law of refusal to supply and the so-called 'essential facilities' doctrine.

[41] On the (non-)application of EU competition law to the agricultural sector see ch 23, 'Agriculture', pp 963–967; leading texts on the common agricultural policy are cited at ch 23 n 7, p 963.

[42] Case C-67/96 [1999] ECR I-5751, [2000] 4 CMLR 446; see ch 3, 'Employees and trades unions', pp 90–91.

[43] See ch 23, 'Military Equipment', p 963 for the position in EU law.

in recent years[44]; however the Court of Justice has held that restrictive professional rules that are proportionate and ancillary to a regulatory system that protects a legitimate public interest fall outside Article 101(1) TFEU[45]. The Court of Justice in 2006 established that the competition rules are capable of application to sport[46], overturning a judgment of the General Court to the contrary[47].

(iv) Beneficial restrictions of competition

Another line of argument is that in some circumstances restrictions of competition can have beneficial results. This may manifest itself in various ways. One example is the suggestion that firms which are forced to pare costs to the minimum because of the pressures of competition will skimp on safety checks. This argument is particularly pertinent in the transport sector, where fears are sometimes expressed that safety considerations may be subordinated to the profit motive: an example would be where airlines compete fiercely on price. It may be that specific safety legislation can be used to overcome this anxiety; and monopolists seeking to enlarge their profits may show the same disregard for safety considerations as competing firms, a charge levelled against Railtrack (since replaced by Network Rail) in the UK following a series of serious rail accidents in the late 1990s and 2000. Safety was an important issue in the debate in the UK as to whether National Traffic Control Services (now known as National Air Traffic Services), responsible for the control of air navigation, should be privatised, provision for which was made in sections 41 to 65 of the Transport Act 2000. A related argument is that higher alcohol prices – and a restriction of price competition between suppliers of alcohol – might save drinkers, and the rest of society, from the harmful effects of excess drinking; the same argument can be applied to smoking.

Another possibly beneficial restriction of competition could arise where two or more firms, by acting in concert and restricting competition between themselves, are able to develop new products or to produce goods or services on a more efficient scale: the benefit to the public at large may be considerable; both Article 101(3) TFEU and section 9 of the UK Competition Act 1998 recognise that, in some cases, agreements may be tolerated which, though restrictive of competition, produce beneficial effects[48]. A further example of the same point is that a producer might impose restrictions on his distributors in order to ensure that they promote his products in the most effective way possible; although this might diminish competition in his own goods (intra-brand competition), the net effect may be to enhance the competitive edge of them as against those produced by his competitors (inter-brand competition)[49]. These examples suggest that a blanket prohibition of agreements that restrict competition would deprive the public of substantial advantages.

(v) Ethical and other objections

A more fundamental objection to competition might be that it is considered in some sense to be inherently objectionable. The very notion of a process of rivalry whereby firms strive for superiority may be considered ethically unsound. One argument (now largely

---

[44] See ch 13, 'Advertising Restrictions', pp 547–550.

[45] Case C-309/99 *Wouters v Algemene Raad van de Nederlandse Orde van Advocaten* [2002] ECR I-1577, [2002] 4 CMLR 913: see ch 3, 'Regulatory ancillarity: the judgment of the Court of Justice in *Wouters*', pp 130–133.

[46] Case C-519/04 P *David Meca-Medina v Commission* [2006] ECR I-6991, [2006] 5 CMLR 1023; see ch 3, 'The application of Article 101(1) to sporting rules', pp 133–134.

[47] Case T-313/02 *David Meca-Medina v Commission* [2004] ECR II-3291, [2004] 3 CMLR 1314.

[48] On horizontal cooperation agreements generally see ch 15.

[49] On vertical agreements generally see ch 16.

discredited) is that 'cut-throat' competition means that firms are forced to charge ever lower prices until in the end the vicious cycle leads them to charge below marginal cost in order to keep custom at all; the inevitable effect of this will be insolvency. The prevailing attitude in much of UK industry during the first half of the twentieth century was that competition was 'harmful' and even destructive and it was this entrenched feeling that led to the adoption of a pragmatic and non-doctrinaire system of control in 1948[50]. It was not until the Competition Act 1998 – 50 years later – that the UK finally adopted legislation that gave the Office of Fair Trading ('the OFT') effective powers to unearth and penalise pernicious cartels[51]. Economically the argument that competition is a cut-throat business that leads to insolvency is implausible, but industrialists do use it.

Another argument is that competition should be arrested where industries enter cyclical recessions – or even long-term decline – in order that they do not disappear altogether[52]. Again competition might be thought undesirable because of its wasteful effects. The consumer may be incapable of purchasing a tin of baked beans in one supermarket because of the agonising fear that at the other end of town a competitor is offering them more cheaply. He will waste his time (a social cost) and money 'shopping around': such an argument once commended itself to the (now abolished) Restrictive Practices Court in the UK[53]. Meanwhile competitors will be wasting their own money by paying advertising agencies to think up more expensive and elaborate campaigns to promote their products[54].

(vi) Industrial policy

One practical objection to promoting competition is that it may be considered to be inimical to the general thrust of industrial policy. Admittedly the suggestion has been made that, in conditions of perfect competition, firms will innovate in order to keep or attract new custom. However Governments often encourage firms to collaborate where this would lead to economies of scale or to more effective research and development; and they may adopt a policy of promoting 'national champions' which will be effective as competitors in international markets[55]. There are certainly circumstances in which the innovator, the entrepreneur and the risk-taker may require some immunity from competition if they are to indulge in expensive technological projects. This is recognised in the law of intellectual property rights which provides an incentive to firms to innovate by preventing the appropriation of commercial ideas which they have developed[56]. A patentee in the UK is given the exclusive right for 20 years to exploit the subject-matter of his patent[57]. A similar incentive and/or reward is given to the owners of copyright, registered designs and analogous rights[58]. This is a recognition of the fact that in some circumstances competition suppresses innovation and an indication of the vacuity of relentlessly pursuing the ideal of perfect competition. The relationship between competition law and the law of intellectual property is a fascinating one, in particular the

---

[50] See Allen *Monopoly and Restrictive Practices* (George Allen & Unwin, 1968).

[51] On these powers see ch 10, 'Inquiries and Investigations', pp 394–402 and 'Penalties', 410–414.

[52] *Scherer and Ross*, pp 294–306; see also ch 15, 'Restructuring agreements', pp 612–613 on restructuring agreements.

[53] See *Re Black Bolt and Nut Association of Great Britain's Agreement* (1960) LR 2 RP 50, [1960] 3 All ER 122.

[54] *Scherer and Ross*, pp 404–407.

[55] This can be an important issue in some merger cases: see ch 20, 'National champions', p 814.

[56] See generally Cornish, Llewellyn and Aplin *Intellectual Property Law* (Sweet & Maxwell, 7th ed, 2010); see also speech by Vickers 'Competition Policy and Innovation' 27 June 2001, available at www.oft.gov.uk.

[57] Patents Act 1977, s 25.   [58] Copyright, Designs and Patents Act 1988, ss 12–15, 191, 216, 269.

apparent tension between on the one hand the desire to keep markets open and free from monopoly and on the other the need to encourage innovation precisely by granting monopoly rights; in fact, however, this tension is more apparent than real[59]. These issues will be considered in chapter 19.

(vii) The economic crisis and competition policy

The global economic crisis that commenced in the late 2000s led to loud calls in some quarters for a relaxation, or even the abandonment, of competition law in order to provide relief to firms facing an uncertain financial future. Competition authorities globally resisted such calls, arguing that competition remained as important in harsh economic times as in benign ones[60].

(viii) Competitions are there to be won

The last point that should be made in this brief survey of objections to competition is that the competitive process contains an inevitable paradox. Some competitors win. By being the most innovative, the most responsive to customers' wishes, and by producing goods or services in the most efficient way possible, one firm may succeed in seeing off its rivals. It would be strange, and indeed harmful, if that firm could then be condemned for being a monopolist. As Judge Learned Hand opined in *US v Aluminum Co of America*[61]:

> [A] single producer may be the survivor out of a group of active companies, merely by virtue of his superior skill, foresight and industry ... The successful competitor, having been urged to compete, must not be turned upon when he wins.

(E) Empirical evidence

A separate issue is whether there is any empirical evidence to support, or indeed to contradict, the case for competition and, if so, what the evidence can tell us. It is notoriously difficult to measure such things as allocative efficiency or the extent to which innovation is attributable to the pressure of competition upon individual firms. Economists have often suggested that there is some direct causal relationship between industrial structure, the conduct of firms on the market and the quality of their economic performance[62]: this is often referred to as the 'structure-conduct-performance paradigm'. A monopolistic structure can be expected to lead to a restriction of output and a loss of economic efficiency: a natural consequence of this view would be that competition law should be watchful for any acts or omissions that could be harmful to the structure of the market, and in particular for conduct that could foreclose access to it and mergers that lead to fewer players. Others argue that this schematic presentation is too simplistic. In particular it is said to be unsound because it is uni-directional and fails to indicate the extent to

---

[59] See ch 19, 'Is there an inevitable tension between intellectual property rights and competition law?', pp 769–770.

[60] Innumerable speeches to this effect can be found: as examples see Kroes 'Competition Policy, growth and consumer purchasing power' 13 October 2008, available at www.ec.europa.eu/competition/speeches/index_2008.html; Fingleton 'Competition Policy in Troubled Times' 20 January 2009, available at www.oft.gov.uk.

[61] 148 F 2d 416 (2nd Cir 1945).

[62] This schematic model of industrial behaviour was first suggested by Mason 'Price and Production Policies of Large-Scale Enterprise' (1939) 29 Am Ec Rev Supplement 61–74; see *Scherer and Ross*, chs 3 and 4.

which performance itself can influence structure and conduct[63]. Good performance, for example, may in itself affect structure by attracting new entrants into an industry.

Other economists have attempted to measure the extent to which monopoly results in allocative inefficiency and leads to a deadweight loss to society[64]. There are of course formidable difficulties associated with this type of exercise, and many of the studies that have been published have been criticised for their methodology. Scherer and Ross devote a chapter of their book to this problem[65] and point out that there has been a dramatic expansion in the range and intensity of empirical research into industrial organisation in recent years. Their conclusion is that, despite the theoretical problems of such research, important relationships do exist between market structure and performance, and that the research should continue[66]. These issues are considered further in an Economic Discussion Paper, published by the OFT in June 2002, which contains literature reviews looking in turn at the deadweight welfare loss attributable to monopoly, at competition and efficiency and at price fixing and cartels[67]. More prosaically it might be added that, even if there are difficulties in measuring scientifically the harmful effects of monopoly in liberalised market economies, the economic performance of the Soviet Union and its neighbours in the second half of the twentieth century suggests that the effects of state planning and monopoly can be pernicious.

(F) **Workable competition**

The discussion so far has presented a model of perfect competition, but has acknowledged that it is based upon a set of assumptions that are unlikely to be observed in practice; it has also been pointed out that there are some arguments that can be made against competition, although some of them are less convincing than others. If perfect competition is unattainable, the question arises whether there is an alternative economic model to which it would be reasonable to aspire. Some economists have been prepared to settle for a more prosaic theory of 'workable competition'[68]. They recognise the limitations of the theory of perfect competition, but nonetheless consider that it is worthwhile seeking the best competitive arrangement that is practically attainable. Quite what workable competition should consist of has caused theoretical difficulties[69]; however a workably competitive structure might be expected to have a beneficial effect on conduct and performance, and therefore be worth striving for and maintaining.

---

[63] Phillips 'Structure, Conduct and Performance – and Performance, Conduct and Structure' in Markham and Papanek (eds) *Industrial Organization and Economic Development* (Houghton Mifflin Co, 1970); Sutton *Sunk Costs and Market Structure: Price Competition, Advertising and the Evolution of Concentration* (MIT Press, 1991).

[64] Weiss 'Concentration-Profit Relationship' in *Industrial Concentration: the New Learning* (eds Goldschmid and others, 1974); Gribbin *Postwar Revival of Competition as Industrial Policy*; Cowling and Mueller 'The Social Costs of Monopoly Power' (1978) 88 Ec J 724–748, criticised by Littlechild at (1981) 91 Ec J 348–363.

[65] *Industrial Market Structure and Economic Performance*, ch 11.   [66] Ibid, p 447.

[67] OFT Economic Discussion Paper 4 (OFT 386) *The development of targets for consumer savings arising from competition policy* (Davies and Majumdar, June 2002), available at www.oft.gov.uk.

[68] Clark 'Toward a Concept of Workable Competition' (1940) 30 Am Ec Rev 241–256; Sosnick 'A Critique of Concepts of Workable Competition' (1958) 72 Qu J Ec 380–423 (a general review of the literature); see also *Scherer and Ross* pp 52–55.

[69] See Asch *Industrial Organization and Antitrust Policy* (Wiley, revised ed, 1983), pp 100–104.

(G) Contestable markets

Some economists have advanced a theory of 'contestable markets' upon which competition law might be based[70]. According to this theory, firms will be forced to ensure an optimal allocation of resources provided that the market on which they operate is 'contestable', that is to say provided that it is possible for firms easily to enter the market without incurring sunk costs[71] and to leave it without loss. While this theory aims to have general applicability, it has been particularly significant in discussion of the deregulation of industries in the US. In a perfectly contestable market, entry into an industry is free and exit is costless. The emphasis on exit is important as firms should be able to leave an industry without incurring a loss if and when opportunities to profit within it disappear. A perfectly *contestable* market need not be perfectly *competitive*: perfect competition requires an infinite number of sellers on a market; in a perfectly contestable market an economically efficient outcome can be achieved even where there are only a few competitors, since there is always the possibility of 'hit and run' entry into the market. Even an industry in which only one or two firms are operating may be perfectly contestable where there are no impediments to entry or exit, so that intervention by the competition authorities is unnecessary. The theory shifts the focus of competition policy, as it is more sanguine about markets on which few firms operate than the 'traditional' model of perfect competition; having said this, it is questionable whether the theory of contestability really adds a great deal to traditional thinking on industrial economics or whether it simply involves a difference of emphasis.

As far as the specific issue of deregulation is concerned, the theory of contestability suggests, for example, that the existence within the air transport sector of only a few airlines need not have adverse economic effects provided that the conditions for entry and exit to and from the market are not disadvantageous. It is not clear how significant the theory of contestable markets is likely to be in the formulation of EU and UK competition policy, other than in the particular area of deregulation. In the UK Competition Commission's investigation of *CHC Helicopter Corpn/Helicopter Services Group ASA*[72] the Commission cleared a merger that would create a duopoly in helicopter services where the market was found to be contestable. The European Commission was less impressed by contestable market theory in *Far East Trade Tariff Charges and Surcharges Agreement (FETTCSA)*[73].

(H) Effective competition

On some occasions, legal provisions and regulators use the expression 'effective competition'. For example it is found in Article 2(3) of the European Union Merger Regulation ('the EUMR'), as part of the test for determining when a merger is incompatible with the common market: 'effective competition' must not be significantly impeded. In the UK the Office of Telecommunications (now the Office of Communications) published a strategy statement in January 2000, one of the objectives of which would be to achieve 'effective

---

[70] See Baumol, Panzar and Willig *Contestable Markets and the Theory of Industry Structure* (Harcourt Brace Jovanovich, revised ed, 1988); Bailey 'Contestability and the Design of Regulatory and Antitrust Policy' (1981) 71 Am Ec Rev 178–183.

[71] See 'The model of perfect competition is based on assumptions unlikely to be observed in practice', pp 7–8 above.

[72] Cm 4556 (2000); for comment see Oldale 'Contestability: The Competition Commission Decision on North Sea Helicopter Services' (2000) 21 ECLR 345.

[73] OJ [2000] L 268/1, [2000] 5 CMLR 1011, para 119.

competition in all main UK telecoms markets'[74], and the same expression can be found in recital 27 of the EU Framework Directive on electronic communications[75]. The UK Utilities Act 2000 provides that the Gas and Electricity Markets Authority should have, as one of its tasks, the promotion of effective competition in the gas and electricity sectors[76]. Case law of the EU Courts and Commission communications also use the term[77]. The idea of effective competition does not appear to be the product of any particular theory or model of competition – perfect, workable, contestable or any other. Indeed, given the number of theories and assumptions already discussed in this chapter, and the many others not discussed, the idea of effective competition, free from theoretical baggage, may have much to commend it. Effective competition does connote the idea, however, that firms should be subject to a reasonable degree of competitive constraint, from actual and potential competitors and from customers, and that the role of a competition authority is to see that such constraints are present on the market[78].

(I) **Conclusion**

What can perhaps be concluded at the end of this discussion is that, despite the range of different theories and the difficulties associated with them, competition does possess sufficient properties to lead to a strong policy choice in its favour. Competitive markets seem, on the whole, to deliver better outcomes than monopolistic ones, and there are demonstrable benefits for consumers[79]. The UK Government, in its White Paper *Productivity and Enterprise: A World Class Competition Regime*[80], stated that:

> Vigorous competition between firms is the lifeblood of strong and effective markets. Competition helps consumers get a good deal. It encourages firms to innovate by reducing slack, putting downward pressure on costs and providing incentives for the efficient organisation of production[81].

This is why competition policy has been so widely embraced in recent years; there is probably a greater global consensus on the desirability of competition and free markets today than at any time in the history of human economic behaviour. In particular monopoly does seem to lead to a restriction in output and higher prices; there is a greater incentive to achieve productive efficiency in a competitive market; the suggestion that only monopolists can innovate is unsound; and competition provides the consumer with a greater degree of choice. Furthermore, in markets such as electronic communications, energy and transport competition has been introduced where once there was little, if any, and this seems to have produced significant benefits for consumers.

---

[74] *OFTEL strategy statement: Achieving the best deal for telecoms consumers*, January 2000, available at www.ofcom.org.uk.

[75] Directive 2002/21/EC, OJ [2002] L 108/33; Directive 2009/140/EC, OJ [2009] L 337/37, which amended the Framework Directive, also refers to effective competition in recitals 54–55.

[76] Utilities Act 2000, ss 9 and 13, amending the Gas Act 1986 and the Electricity Act 1989 respectively.

[77] See eg Case T-168/01 *GlaxoSmithKline Services v Commission* [2006] ECR II-2969, [2006] 5 CMLR 1623, para 109; Case T-321/05 *AstraZeneca v Commission* [2010] ECR II-000, [2010] 5 CMLR 1585, para 175; the Commission's *Guidelines on Vertical Restraints* OJ [2010] C 130/1, para 107; the Commission's *Guidance on the Commission's Enforcement Priorities in Applying Article [102] to abusive exclusionary conduct by dominant undertakings* OJ [2009] C 45/7, paras 5–6 and 19.

[78] For further discussion see *Bishop and Walker*, ch 2, 'Effective Competition'.

[79] See speech by Vickers 'Competition is for Consumers' 21 February 2002, available at www.oft.gov.uk.

[80] Cm 5233 (2001).   [81] Ibid, para 1.1.

It may be helpful to summarise the benefits that are expected to be derived from effective competition:

- competition promotes allocative and productive efficiency
- competition leads to lower prices for consumers
- competition means that firms will be innovative in order to win business: innovation and dynamic efficiency mean that there will be better products available on the market
- where there is effective competition, consumers have a choice as to the products that they buy.

4. The Function of Competition Law

(A) **Goals of competition law**[82]

In recent years many competition authorities have stressed the central importance of consumer welfare when applying competition law[83]. A very clear statement to this effect can be found in a speech of the former European Commissioner for competition policy, Neelie Kroes, given in London in October 2005:

> Consumer welfare is now well established as the standard the Commission applies when assessing mergers and infringements of the Treaty rules on cartels and monopolies. Our aim is simple: to protect competition in the market as a means of enhancing consumer welfare and ensuring an efficient allocation of resources[84].

This does not mean that EU competition law is applicable only where a specific increase in prices to end consumers can be demonstrated. EU law has recognised from the early days that consumers can be indirectly harmed by action that harms the competitive structure of the market[85], and it continues to do so today[86]: there is no inconsistency between these statements and the proposition that EU competition law is oriented around the promotion of consumer welfare[87].

However it would be reasonable to point out that, although the consumer welfare standard is currently in the ascendancy, many different policy objectives have been pursued in the name of competition law over the years; some of these were not rooted in notions of consumer welfare in the technical sense at all, and some were plainly inimical to the pursuit of allocative and productive efficiency. The result has sometimes been inconsistency and contradiction, but it is as well for the reader to be aware of this before coming to the law itself. Historically there has not been one single, unifying, policy that bound the

[82] See Odudu 'The Wider Concerns of Competition Law' (2010) 30(3) OJLS 599.

[83] For discussion see the Symposium on 'Welfare Standards in Competition Policy' (2006) Competition Policy International; Pittman 'Consumer Surplus as the Appropriate Standard for Antitrust Enforcement' (2007) 3(2) Competition Policy International 205.

[84] SPEECH/05/512 of 15 September 2005, available at www.ec/europa/eu/competition.

[85] See eg Case 6/72 *Europemballage and Continental Can v Commission* [1973] ECR 215, [1973] CMLR 199, paras 20–26.

[86] See eg Cases C-501/06 P etc *GlaxoSmithKline Services Unlimited v Commission* [2009] ECR I-9291, [2010] 4 CMLR 50, para 63; Case C-8/08 *T-Mobile Netherlands BV and others v Raad van bestuur van de Nederlandse Mededingingsautoriteit* [2009] ECR I-4529, [2009] 5 CMLR 1701, para 38.

[87] For arguments to the contrary see Andriychuk 'Rediscovering the Spirit of Competition: On the Normative Value of the Competition Process' (2010) 6(3) European Competition Journal 575.

development of EU and UK law together. In particular competition policy does not exist in a vacuum: it is an expression of the current values and aims of society and is as susceptible to change as political thinking generally. Because views and insights shift over a period of time, competition law is infused with tension. Different systems of competition law reflect different concerns, an important point when comparing the laws of the US, the EU and the UK[88]. As already noted, competition law has now been adopted in more than 100 countries, whose economies and economic development may be very different from one another. It is impossible to suppose that each system will have identical concerns[89]. The debate at the time of the negotiation of the Lisbon Treaty of 2007 demonstrated that some Member States are less enthusiastic about the process of competition than others[90].

(i) Consumer protection

Several different objectives other than the maximisation of consumer welfare in the technical sense can be ascribed to competition law. The first is that its essential purpose should be to protect the interests of consumers, not by protecting the competitive process itself, but by taking direct action against offending undertakings, for example by requiring dominant firms to reduce their prices. It is of course correct in principle that competition law should be regarded as having a 'consumer protection' function: ultimately the process of competition itself is intended to deliver benefits to consumers. However the possibility exists that competition law might be invoked in a more 'populist' manner; this appeared to happen in the UK in 1998 and 1999, at a time when the Government wished to be seen to be doing something about so-called 'rip-off Britain', where Ministers suggested that excessive prices were being charged by both monopolists and non-monopolists[91]. A problem with using competition law to assume direct control over prices, however, is that competition authorities are ill-placed to determine what price a competitive market would set for particular goods or services, and indeed by fixing a price they may further distort the competitive fabric of the market. The UK Competition Commission declined to recommend price control following its report in 2000 on *Supermarkets*[92] where it found that, in general, the market was working well for consumers and that such intervention would be disproportionate and unduly regulatory. Populist measures taken to have electoral appeal may ultimately be more harmful than the high prices themselves.

Similarly the consumer may be harmed – or at least consider himself to be harmed – where a producer insists that all his goods should be sold by dealers at maintained prices, or that dealers should provide a combined package of goods plus after-sales service. Here the consumer's choice is restricted by the producer's decision. Competition law may proscribe resale price maintenance or tie-in sales for this reason, although there are those who argue that this intervention is undesirable: the producer is restricting intra-brand competition, but inter-brand competition may be enhanced as a result[93]. The obsession with protecting the consumer can also be considered short-sighted since, in the longer run, the producer

---

[88] On the differences between the policies of competition law in the US and the EU see eg Jebsen and Stevens 'Assumptions, Goals and Dominant Undertakings; the Regulation of Competition under Article 86 of the European Union' (1996) 64 Antitrust Law Journal 443.

[89] See Fox 'The Kaleidoscope of Antitrust and its Significance in the World Economy: Respecting Differences' [2001] Fordham Corporate Law Institute (ed Hawk), 597.

[90] See ch 2, 'The competition chapter in the TFEU', pp 50–51.

[91] See ch 18, pp 725–728 on the control of exploitative pricing practices under UK law.

[92] Cm 4842 (2000); see similarly paras 2.11–2.18 of the CC's Report on *Groceries*, 30 April 2008, available at www.competition-commission.org.uk.

[93] See in particular ch 16 on vertical agreements.

might choose to abandon the market altogether rather than comply with an unreasonable competition law; short-term benefits will then be outweighed by long-term harm to consumer welfare[94].

(ii) Redistribution

A second possible objective of competition law might be the dispersal of economic power and the redistribution of wealth: the promotion of economic equity rather than economic efficiency[95]. Aggregations of resources in the hands of monopolists, multinational corporations or conglomerates could be considered a threat to the very notion of democracy, individual freedom of choice and economic opportunity. This argument was influential in the US for many years at a time when there was a fundamental mistrust of big business. President Roosevelt warned Congress in 1938 that:

> The liberty of a democracy is not safe if the people tolerate the growth of a private power to a point where it becomes stronger than the democratic state itself… Among us today a concentration of private power without equal in history is growing[96].

It was under the US antitrust laws that the world's largest corporation at the time, AT&T, was dismembered. Some critics of the action brought by the Department of Justice against Microsoft were concerned that it amounted to an attack on a spectacularly successful business[97], while others welcomed the attempt to restrain its undoubted economic muscle[98].

(iii) Protecting competitors

Linked to the argument that competition law should be concerned with redistribution is the view that competition law should be applied in such a way as to protect small firms against more powerful rivals: the competition authorities should hold the ring and ensure that the 'small guy' is given a fair chance to succeed. To put the point another way, there are some who consider that competition law should be concerned with competitors as well as the process of competition. This idea has at times had a strong appeal in the US, in particular during the period when Chief Justice Warren led the Supreme Court. However it has to be appreciated that the arrest of the Darwinian struggle, in which the most efficient succeed and the weak disappear, for the purpose of protecting small business can run directly counter to the idea of consumer welfare in the technical economic sense. It may be that competition law is used to preserve the inefficient and to stunt the performance of the efficient. In the US the 'Chicago School' of economists has been particularly scathing of the 'uncritical sentimentality' in favour of the small competitor, and in the 1980s, in particular, US law developed in a noticeably less sentimental way[99]. To the Chicago School, the essential question in an antitrust case should be whether the conduct

---

[94] This is one of Bork's most pressing arguments in *The Antitrust Paradox* (The Free Press, 1993).

[95] See Odudu 'The Distributional Consequences of Antitrust' in Marsden (ed) *Handbook of Research in Trans-Atlantic Antitrust* (Edward Elgar, 2007) ch 23.

[96] 83 Cong Rec 5992 (1938).

[97] For a highly critical view of the Microsoft case generally see McKenzie *Antitrust on Trial: How the Microsoft Case Is Reframing the Rules of Competition* (Perseus Publishing, 2nd ed, 2001).

[98] See 'Now Bust Microsoft's Trust' *The Economist* 13 November 1999; 'Bill Rockefeller?' *The Economist* 29 April 2000.

[99] See Fox 'The New American Competition Policy – from Anti-Trust to Pro-Efficiency' (1981) 2 ECLR 439 where the author traces the change in the policy of the Supreme Court from judgments such as *Brown Shoe Co v US* 370 US 294 (1962) to the position in *Continental TV Inc v GTE Sylvania Inc* 433 US 36 (1977); Fox 'What's Harm to Competition? Exclusionary Practices and Anticompetitive Effect' (2002) 70 Antitrust

under investigation could lead to consumers paying higher prices, and whether those prices could be sustained against the forces of competition; antitrust intervention to protect competitors from their more efficient rivals is harmful to social and consumer welfare. Even firms with high market shares are subject to competitive constraints provided that barriers to entry and exit are low, so that intervention on the part of the competition authority is usually uncalled for.

There seems little doubt that EU competition law has, in some cases, been applied with competitors in mind: this is particularly noticeable in some decisions under Article 102, and some commentators have traced this phenomenon back to the influence of the so-called 'Freiburg School' of ordoliberalism[100]. Scholars of the Freiburg School, which originated in Germany in the 1930s, saw the free market as a necessary ingredient in a liberal economy, but not as sufficient in itself. The problems of Weimar and Nazi Germany were attributable in part to the inability of the legal system to control and, if necessary, to disperse private economic power. An economic constitution was necessary to constrain the economic power of firms, but without giving Government unrestrained control over their behaviour: public power could be just as pernicious as private. Legal rules could be put in place which would achieve both of these aims. It is not surprising that the beneficiaries of such thinking would be small and medium-sized firms, the very opposite of the monopolists and cartels feared by the members of the Freiburg School. There is no doubt that ordoliberal thinking had a direct influence on the leading figures involved in the establishment of the three European Communities in the 1950s[101]. This may have led to decisions and judgments in which the law was applied to protect competitors rather than the process of competition, although it may be that the role of ordoliberalism in competition law cases has been exaggerated: some commentators assert that economic efficiency was a key goal of competition policy from the outset[102]. However, without questioning the appropriateness of decisions taken in the early years of the EU, it can be questioned whether it is appropriate in the new millennium to maintain this approach: there is much to be said for applying competition rules to achieve economic efficiency rather than economic equity. The two ideas sit awkwardly together: indeed they may flatly contradict one another, since an efficient undertaking will inevitably be able to defeat less efficient competitors, whose position in the market ought not to be underwritten by a competition authority on the basis of political preference or, as Bork might say, sentimentality. This is an issue that will be considered further in later chapters, and in particular in chapters 5, 17, and 18 on abusive practices on the part of dominant firms where, in particular, we will see that the European Commission is clear that Article 102 is an instrument for the protection of competition and not of competitors as such.

Law Journal 371; Kolasky 'North Atlantic Competition Policy: Converging Toward What?' 17 May 2002, available at www.justice.gov/atr.

[100] See Gerber *Law and Competition in Twentieth Century Europe: Protecting Prometheus* (Clarendon Press Oxford, 1998), ch VII; see also Gerber 'Constitutionalising the Economy: German Neo-liberalism, Competition Law and the New Europe' (1994) 42 American Journal of Comparative Law 25; Eucken 'The Competitive Order and Its Implementation' (2006) 2(2) Competition Policy International 219; Ahlborn and Grave 'Walter Eucken and Ordoliberalism: An Introduction from a Consumer Welfare Perspective' (2006) 2(2) Competition Policy International 197.

[101] See Gerber, pp 263–265; ch IX.

[102] See Akman 'Searching for the long-lost soul of Article 82 EC' (2009) 29(2) OJLS 267.

(iv) Other issues

In some cases, particularly involving mergers, the relevant authorities might find that other issues require attention: whether they can be taken into account will depend on the applicable law[103]. For example, unemployment and regional policy are issues which arise in the analysis of mergers and cooperation agreements; the ability of competition to dampen price-inflation may be considered to be important; merger controls may be used to prevent foreign takeovers of domestic companies; the UK Government permitted a merger between LloydsTSB and HBOS which might otherwise have been prohibited or subject to modification because of the economic crisis in the banking sector in the late 2000s[104]; and South African law specifically provides that in certain circumstances the position of historically disadvantaged people – that is to say the victims of apartheid – should be taken into account[105].

(v) The single market imperative

Lastly it is important to understand that competition policy in the context of the EU fulfils an additional but quite different function from those just described (although EU law may be applied with them in mind as well). This is that competition law plays a hugely important part in the overriding goal of achieving single market integration[106]. The very idea of the single market is that internal barriers to trade within the EU should be dismantled and that goods, services, workers and capital should have complete freedom of movement. Firms should be able to outgrow their national markets and operate on a more efficient, transnational, scale throughout the EU. This remains as important in 2011 as it ever was[107]. Competition law has both a negative and a positive role to play in the integration of the single market. The negative one is that it can prevent measures which attempt to maintain the isolation of one domestic market from another: for example national cartels, export bans and market-sharing will be seriously punished[108]. For example a fine of €149 million was imposed on Nintendo for taking action to prevent exports of game consoles and related products from the UK to the Netherlands and Germany[109].

The positive role is that competition law can be moulded in such a way as to encourage trade between Member States, partly by 'levelling the playing fields of Europe' as one contemporary catchphrase puts it, and partly by facilitating cross-border transactions and integration. Horizontal collaboration between firms in different Member States may be permitted in some circumstances[110]; and a producer in one Member State can be permitted to appoint an exclusive distributor in another and so penetrate a market which

---

[103] On the relevant tests to be applied to mergers under EU and UK law see respectively ch 21, 'Substantive Analysis', pp 861–864 and ch 22, 'The "Substantial Lessening of Competition" Test', pp 932–940.

[104] See ch 22, 'Public interest cases', pp 956–958.

[105] South African Competition Act 1998, section 2(f).

[106] See Ehlermann 'The Contribution of EC Competition Policy to the Single Market' (1992) 29 CML Rev 257; the Commission's XXIXth *Report on Competition Policy* (1999), point 3.

[107] For recent pronouncements on the importance of market integration see the Commission's *Guidelines on Vertical Restraints* OJ [2010] C 130/1, para 7; Monti *A New Strategy for the Single Market: At the Service of Europe's Economy and Society* (2010), Report to the President of the European Commission, available at www.ec.europa.eu/bepa/pdf/monti_report_final.

[108] See ch 7, 'Chapter VI: penalties', pp 275–282 on the powers of the European Commission to impose fines for infringements of Articles 101 and 102.

[109] OJ [2003] L 255/33, [2004] 4 CMLR 421; on appeal to the General Court the fine imposed on Nintendo was reduced to €119 million: Case T-13/03 *Nintendo v Commission* [2009] ECR II-975, [2009] 5 CMLR 1421; for further discussion of the single market imperative see ch 2, 'Single market imperative', p 51.

[110] See generally ch 15.

individually he could not have done[111]. Unification of the single market is an obsession of the EU authorities; this has meant that decisions have sometimes been taken prohibiting behaviour which a competition authority elsewhere, unconcerned with single market considerations, would not have reached. Faced with a conflict between the narrow interests of a particular firm and the broader problem of integrating the market, the tendency has been to subordinate the former to the latter.

(B) **Who decides?**

A further issue that should be mentioned is that competition law may not be so much about any particular policy – for example the promotion of consumer welfare or protection of the weak – but about who actually should make decisions about the way in which business should be conducted. The great ideological debate of the twentieth century was between capitalism and communism: whether to have a market or not. For the most part that debate has been concluded in favour of the market mechanism. But competition law and policy by their very nature envisage that there may be situations in which some control of economic behaviour in the marketplace may be necessary in order to achieve a desirable outcome. To some the market, and the vast rewards it brings to successful operators, remains an object of suspicion; to others, the spectre of the state as regulator is more alarming. These matters have been eloquently discussed by Amato[112]:

> It is a fact that within liberal society itself one of the key divisions of political identity (and hence identification) is between these two sides: the side that fears private power more, and in order to fight it is ready to give more room to the power of government; and the side that fears the expansion of government more, and is therefore more prepared to tolerate private power.

In Europe there seems little doubt that, notwithstanding the demonopolisation and liberalisation of economic behaviour and the promotion of free enterprise that occurred in the late twentieth century, there remains a scepticism about the market, and that this results in 'active' enforcement of the competition rules by the European Commission and by the national competition authorities[113].

This in turn raises an additional, complex, issue: if there are to be competition authorities to decide on what is and what is not acceptable business behaviour, what type of institution should be asked to make these decisions (a court, a commission, an individual?); how should individuals be appointed to those institutions (by ministerial appointment, by election, by open competition?); and how should those institutions themselves be controlled (by judicial review, or by an appellate court?). Here we leave law and economics and move into the world of political science which, though fascinating, is beyond the scope of this book[114].

---

[111] See generally ch 16.

[112] Amato *Antitrust and the Bounds of Power: The Dilemma of Liberal Democracy in the History of the Market* (Hart Publishing, 1997), p 4.

[113] See Gerber *Law and Competition in Twentieth Century Europe* (Clarendon Press, 1998), pp 421ff.

[114] On these issues see generally Doern and Wilks (eds) *Comparative Competition Policy: National Institutions in a Global Market* (Clarendon Press, 1996) and, in particular, chs 1 and 2; Cini and McGowan *Competition Policy in the European Union* (Macmillan, 1998); Craig *Administrative Law* (Sweet & Maxwell, 6th ed, 2008), ch 11.

(C) Competition advocacy and public restrictions of competition

A final point about the function of competition law is that competition authorities can usefully be given a different task, which is to scrutinise legislation that will bring about, or is responsible for, a distortion of competition in the economy. The reality is that states and international regulatory authorities are capable of harming the competitive process at least as seriously as private economic operators on the market itself, for example by granting legal monopolies to undertakings, by limiting in other ways the number of competitors in the market, or by establishing unduly restrictive rules and regulations. Some competition authorities are specifically mandated to scrutinise legislation that will distort competition[115]. Some developing countries might more usefully deploy their resources on this issue rather than adopting their own competition rules[116]. In the UK the OFT, acting under section 7 of the Enterprise Act 2002, can bring to the attention of Ministers laws or proposed laws that could be harmful to competition[117]. The International Competition Network (an association of various national competition authorities), through the work originally of its competition advocacy working group and now of its competition policy implementation group, is seeking to develop best practices in promoting competition law and policy[118].

5. Market Definition and Market Power

This section will discuss the issues of market definition and market power. As has been noted above competition law is concerned, above all, with the problems that occur where one or more firms possess, or will possess after a merger, market power. Market power presents undertakings with the possibility of profitably raising prices over a period of time; the expression 'raising price' here includes, and is a shorthand for, other ways in which competition can be restricted, for example by limiting output, suppressing innovation, reducing the variety or quality of goods or services or by depriving consumers of choice, all of which are clearly inimical to consumer welfare[119]. In a perfectly competitive market no firm has market power; in a pure monopoly one firm has absolute control over it. There is a continuum between these two extremes, and many degrees of market power lie along it. Competition law attaches particular significance to 'substantial market power', often equated with 'a dominant position', since the prohibition of certain unilateral practices, for example in Article 102 TFEU and the Chapter II prohibition of the Competition Act 1998 in the UK, applies only where an undertaking or undertakings have this amount of market power. The International Competition Network Working

---

[115] See eg s 21(1)(k) of the South African Competition Act 1998, which requires the Competition Commission to 'review legislation and public regulations and report to the Minister concerning any provision that permits uncompetitive behaviour'; and s 49(1) of the Indian Competition Act 2002 which provides that the Competition Commission of India can review legislation, but only if a reference is made to it by either the Central or the State governments.

[116] Rodriguez and Coate 'Competition Policy in Transition Economies: the Role of Competition Advocacy' (1997) 23 Brooklyn Journal of International Law 365.

[117] See ch 2, 'Functions of the OFT', pp 65–66.

[118] See www.internationalcompetitionnetwork.org/working-groups/current/advocacy.aspx; see also Emberger 'How to strengthen competition advocacy through competition screening' (2006) (Spring) Competition Policy Newsletter 28.

[119] See Landes and Posner 'Market power in antitrust cases' (1981) 94 Harvard Law Review 937; Vickers 'Market power in competition cases' (2006) 2 European Competition Journal 3.

Group on Unilateral Behaviour has produced 'Recommended Practices' for the assessment of dominance/substantial market power in the context of unilateral conduct laws. They contain ten recommendations for competition authorities when applying their domestic law in this difficult area[120]. In particular they stress that determinations of substantial market power should not be based on market shares alone; rather a comprehensive analysis should be undertaken of all factors affecting competitive conditions in the market under investigation.

There are numerous ways in which this key concern – the exercise of market power – is manifested, by implication if not expressly, in EU and UK competition law. A variety of legal tests and expressions will be found, but in essence they all express a concern about the misuse of market power:

- there are rules that firms should not enter into agreements to restrict competition (Article 101 TFEU; Chapter I prohibition, Competition Act 1998): however any such restriction must be appreciable, and there are various '*de minimis*' exceptions where the parties lack market power[121]

- block exemption is not available to parties to agreements where the parties' market share exceeds a certain threshold[122]

- firms should not abuse a dominant position (Article 102 TFEU; Chapter II prohibition, Competition Act 1998)

- concentrations can be prohibited under the EUMR that would significantly impede effective competition, in particular by creating or strengthening a dominant position

- mergers can be prohibited under UK law that would substantially lessen competition (Part 3 of the Enterprise Act 2002)

- 'market investigations' can be conducted by the Competition Commission where features of a market could have an adverse effect on competition (Part 4 of the Enterprise Act)

- other variants can be found: for example in the electronic communications sector regulatory obligations can be imposed upon firms that have 'significant market power', which has the same meaning for this purpose as 'dominance' under Article 102 TFEU[123].

Each of these provisions reflects a concern about the abuse or potential abuse of market power. Throughout this book and throughout competition law and practice generally, therefore, two key issues recur: first, the definition of the relevant product and geographic (and sometimes the temporal) markets in relation to which market power may be found to exist; secondly, and more importantly, the identification of market power itself.

---

[120] Available at www.internationalcompetitionnetwork.org.

[121] See eg ch 3, 'The *De Minimis* Doctrine', pp 140–144.

[122] See eg Article 3 of Regulation 772/2004, OJ [2004] L 123/11, on technology transfer agreements: 20 per cent market share cap in the case of horizontal agreements and 30 per cent cap in the case of vertical agreements; Article 3 of Regulation 330/2010, OJ [2010] L 102/1, on vertical agreements: 30 per cent market share cap; Article 4 of Regulation 1217/2010, OJ [2010] L 335/36, on research and development agreements: 25 per cent market share cap; and Article 3 of Regulation 1218/2010, OJ [2010] L 335/43, on specialisation agreements: 20 per cent market share cap.

[123] See ch 23, 'Legislation', pp 980–981.

(A) **Market definition**

Pure monopoly is rare, but a firm or firms collectively may have sufficient power over the market to enjoy some of the benefits available to the true monopolist. If the notion of 'power over the market' is key to analysing competition issues, it becomes immediately obvious that it is necessary to understand what is meant by 'the market' or, as will be explained below, the 'relevant market' for this purpose. The concept is an economic one, and in many cases it may be necessary for lawyers to engage the services of economists to assist in the proper delineation of the market, as highly sophisticated economic and econometric analysis is sometimes called for.

In the last 20 years the 'science' of market definition has evolved considerably. There are numerous sources of information on how to define markets. A useful document is the International Competition Network's *Recommended Practices for Merger Analysis*, Part II of which contains useful discussion of market definition issues[124]. One particular comment in the *Recommended Practices* is worth stressing: that the boundaries of relevant markets may not be precise. Some products may be 'in the market' while others may be 'out of the market'; however products that lie outside the market can still provide a competitive constraint, and should not be excluded from competition analysis simply because of the market definition.

Of particular importance in the EU is the European Commission's *Notice on the Definition of the Relevant Market for the Purposes of [EU] Competition Law*[125] which adopts the so-called 'hypothetical monopolist' test (also known as the 'SSNIP test') for defining markets. This *Notice* provides a conceptual framework within which to think of market definition, and then explains some of the techniques that may be deployed when defining markets. The Commission's *Notice* adopts the approach taken by the antitrust authorities in the US in the analysis of horizontal mergers[126]; the OFT in the UK has adopted a guideline which adopts a similar approach to that of the Commission[127]. Other competition authorities also apply the hypothetical monopolist test[128].

Paragraph 2 of the Commission's *Notice* explains why market definition is important:

Market definition is a tool to identify and define the boundaries of competition between firms. It serves to establish the framework within which competition policy is applied by the Commission. The main purpose of market definition is to identify in a systematic way the competitive constraints that the undertakings involved face. The objective of defining a market in both its product and geographic dimension is to identify those actual competitors of the undertakings involved that are capable of constraining those undertakings' behaviour and of preventing them from behaving independently of effective competitive pressure.

---

[124] Available at www.internationalcompetitionnetwork.org.

[125] OJ [1997] C 372/5; more specific guidance on market definition can be found in the Commission's *Guidelines on the application of Article [101 TFEU] to technology transfer agreements* OJ [2004] C 101/2, paras 19–25; *Guidelines on Vertical Restraints* OJ [2010] C 130/1, paras 86–95 and *Guidelines on the applicability of Article 101 of the Treaty on the Functioning of the European Union to horizontal co-operation agreements* OJ [2011] C 11/1, paras 112–126, 155–156, 197–199, 229 and 261–262.

[126] See 'Demand-side substitutability', pp 31–32 below.

[127] *Market Definition*, OFT 403, December 2004, available at www.oft.gov.uk.

[128] See eg the *Merger Guidelines* of the Australian Competition and Consumer Commission, available at www.accc.gov.au; the *Mergers and Acquisitions Guidelines* of the New Zealand Commerce Commission, available at www.comcom.govt.nz; and the *Merger Enforcement Guidelines* of the Canadian Competition Bureau, available at www.competitionbureau.gc.ca.

This paragraph contains a number of important points. First, market definition is not an end in itself[129]. Rather it is an analytical tool that assists in determining the competitive constraints upon undertakings: market definition provides a framework within which to assess the critical question of whether a firm or firms possess market power. Secondly, both the product and geographic dimensions of markets must be analysed. Thirdly, market definition enables the competitive constraints only from *actual* competitors to be identified: it tells us nothing about *potential* competitors. However, as paragraph 13 of the *Notice* points out, there are three main sources of competitive constraint upon undertakings: demand substitutability, supply substitutability and potential competition. As will be explained below, demand substitutability is the essence of market definition. In some, albeit fairly narrow, circumstances supply substitutability may also be part of the market definition; however normally supply substitutability lies outside market definition and is an issue of potential competition. It is also necessary, when assessing a supplier's market power, to take into account any countervailing power on the buyer's side of the market. It is very important to understand that factors such as potential entry and buyer power are relevant, since this means that a particular share of a market cannot, in itself, indicate that a firm has market power; an undertaking with 100 per cent of the widget market would not have market power if there are numerous potential competitors and no barriers to entry into the market. Lawyers must not be seduced by numbers when determining whether a firm has market power; market shares, of course, are helpful; indeed there are circumstances in which they are very important: a share of 50 per cent or more of a market creates a rebuttable presumption of dominance in a case under Article 102[130], and a market share of 30 per cent or more will prevent the application of the block exemption in Regulation 330/2010 on vertical agreements[131]. However, calculating an undertaking's market share is only one step in determining whether it has market power.

(B) Circumstances in which it is necessary to define the relevant market

The foregoing discussion may be rendered less abstract by considering the circumstances in EU and UK competition law in which it may be necessary to define the relevant market.

(i) EU competition law

- under Article 101(1), when considering whether an agreement has the effect of restricting competition[132]
- under Article 101(1), when considering whether an agreement *appreciably* restricts competition. In particular there are market share tests in the *Notice on Agreements of Minor Importance*: a horizontal agreement, that is one between competitors, will usually be *de minimis* where the parties' market share is 10 per cent or less; and an agreement between non-competitors that operate at different levels of the market will usually be *de minimis* where their market share is 15 per cent or less[133]

---

[129] For an interesting discussion of the limits of market definition see Carlton 'Market Definition: Use and Abuse' (2007) 3(1) Competition Policy International 3.

[130] See ch 5, 'The *AKZO* presumption of dominance where an undertaking has a market share of 50 per cent or more', pp 182–183.

[131] See ch 16, 'Article 3: the market share cap', pp 660–662.

[132] See eg Case C-234/89 *Delimitis v Henninger Bräu* [1991] ECR I-935, [1992] 5 CMLR 210; para 27 of the Commission's *Guidelines on the application of Article [101(3)]* OJ [2004] C 101/97.

[133] OJ [2001] C 368/13, para 7.

- under the Commission's guidelines on the application of Article 101(1) to horizontal cooperation agreements, where various market share thresholds will be found[134]

- under Article 101(1), when considering whether an agreement has an *appreciable* effect on trade between Member States[135]

- under Article 101(3)(b), when considering whether an agreement would substantially eliminate competition[136]

- under numerous block exemptions containing market share tests, for example Regulation 330/2010 on vertical agreements[137], Regulation 1217/2010 on research and development agreements[138] and Regulation 1218/2010 on specialisation agreements[139]

- under Article 102, when considering whether an undertaking has a dominant position[140]

- under the EUMR when determining whether a merger would significantly impede effective competition, in particular by creating or strengthening a dominant position[141].

(ii) UK law

- when applying the Chapter I and Chapter II prohibitions of the Competition Act 1998, which are based on the provisions in Articles 101 and 102[142]

- when determining the level of a penalty under the Competition Act 1998[143]

- when scrutinising mergers under Part 3 of the Enterprise Act 2002[144]

- when conducting 'market investigations' under Part 4 of the Enterprise Act 2002[145].

Market definition, therefore, plays an important part in much competition law analysis. The table at the end of this chapter captures some of the important market share thresholds that may be relevant in competition law cases.

(C) **The relevant product market**

The Court of Justice, when it heard its first appeal on the application of Article 102 in *Europemballage Corpn and Continental Can Co Inc v Commission*[146], held that when identifying a dominant position the delimitation of the relevant product market was of crucial importance. This has been repeated by the Court of Justice on numerous occasions[147]. In *Continental Can Co Inc*[148] it was the Commission's failure to define the relevant product market that caused the Court of Justice to quash its decision. The Commission had held that Continental Can and its subsidiary SLW had a dominant position in three different product markets – cans for meat, cans for fish and metal tops – without giving a

---

[134] See ch 15, 'Purchasing Agreements', p 604.   [135] OJ [2004] C 101/97, para 55.
[136] See ch 4, 'Fourth condition of Article 101(3): no elemination of competition in a substantial part of the market', pp 164–165.
[137] See ch 16, 'Article 3: the market share cap', pp 660–662.
[138] See ch 15, 'Article 4: duration of exemption and the market share threshold and duration of exemption', p 597.
[139] See ch 15, 'Article 3: the market share threshold', p 602.
[140] See ch 5, 'Dominant position', pp 179–189.   [141] See ch 21, 'Market definition', pp 862–863.
[142] See ch 9, generally.   [143] *Guidance as to the Appropriate Amount of a Penalty*, OFT 423, para 2.3.
[144] See ch 22, 'Market definition', p 934.
[145] See ch 11, 'The Market Investigation Provisions on Practice', p 479.
[146] Case 6/72 [1973] ECR 215, [1973] CMLR 199, para 32.
[147] See eg Case 27/76 *United Brands v Commission* [1978] ECR 207, [1978] 1 CMLR 429, para 10.
[148] JO [1972] L 7/25, [1972] CMLR D11.

satisfactory explanation of why these markets were separate from one another or from the market for cans and containers generally. The Court of Justice in effect insisted that the Commission should define the relevant product market and support its definition in a reasoned decision.

(i) The legal test

The judgments of the Court of Justice show that the definition of the market is essentially a matter of interchangeability. Where goods or services can be regarded as interchangeable, they are within the same product market. In *Continental Can* the Court of Justice enjoined the Commission, for the purpose of delimiting the market, to investigate:

> [those] characteristics of the products in question by virtue of which they are particularly apt to satisfy an inelastic need and are only to a limited extent interchangeable with other products[149].

Similarly in *United Brands v Commission*, where the applicant was arguing that bananas were in the same market as other fresh fruit, the Court of Justice said that this depended on whether the banana could be:

> singled out by such special features distinguishing it from other fruits that it is only to a limited extent interchangeable with them and is only exposed to their competition in a way that is hardly perceptible[150].

(ii) Measuring interchangeability

Conceptually, the idea that a relevant market consists of goods or services that are interchangeable with one another is simple enough. In practice, however, the measurement of interchangeability can give rise to considerable problems for a variety of reasons: for example there may be no data available on the issue, or the data that exist may be unreliable, incomplete or deficient in some other way. A further problem is that, in many cases, the data will be open to (at least) two interpretations. It is often the case therefore that market definition is extremely difficult; this is why the EU Courts have conducted a fairly 'light touch' review of the Commission's conclusions on market definition, recognising that this involves a 'complex economic assessment'[151].

(iii) Commission Notice on the Definition of the Relevant Market for the Purposes of [EU] Competition Law[152]

Useful guidance on market definition is provided by the Commission's *Notice*; the *Notice* has received the approval of the EU Courts[153]. The introduction of the EUMR in 1990 had, as an inevitable consequence, that the Commission was called upon to define markets in a far larger number of situations than previously. Whereas it may have had to deal with complaints under Article 102, say, 20 times a year in the 1980s, by the 1990s it was having to deal with 100 or more notifications under the EUMR each year, and it now receives at

---

[149] Case 6/72 [1973] ECR 215, [1973] CMLR 199, para 32; for a definition of inelastic demand see ch 1, n 24 above.

[150] Case 27/76 [1978] ECR 207, [1978] 1 CMLR 429, para 22.

[151] See eg Case T-201/04 *Microsoft Corpn v Commission* [2007] ECR II-3601, [2006] 4 CMLR 311, para 482.

[152] OJ [1997] C 372/5.

[153] See eg Case T-321/05 *AstraZeneca v Commission* [2010] ECR II-000, [2010] 5 CMLR 1585, para 86; Case T-427/08 *Confédération européenne des associations d'horlogers-réparateurs (CEAHR) v Commission* [2010] ECR II-000, [2010] 5 CMLR 1585, paras 68–70.

least 250 notifications a year: indeed in 2007 the number reached 402[154]. Furthermore, an Article 102 case would normally require the definition of just one market – the one in which the dominant firm was alleged to have abused its position; or perhaps two, for example where the abuse produces effects in a neighbouring market[155]. However – a case under the EUMR might be quite different, since the merging parties might conduct business in a number of different markets giving rise to competition considerations[156]. This necessarily meant that the Commission was called upon to develop more systematic methods for defining the market.

(iv) Demand-side substitutability

As mentioned above, the Commission explains at paragraph 13 of the *Notice* that firms are subject to three main competitive constraints: demand substitutability, supply substitutability and potential competition. It continues that, for the purpose of market definition, it is demand substitutability that is of the greatest significance; supply substitutability may be relevant to market definition in certain special circumstances, but normally this is a matter to be examined when determining whether there is market power; potential competition in the market is always a matter of market power rather than market definition.

Paragraph 14 of the *Notice* states that the assessment of demand substitution entails a determination of the range of products which are viewed as substitutes by the consumer. It proposes a test whereby it becomes possible to determine whether particular products are within the same market. The SSNIP test, first deployed by the Department of Justice and the Federal Trade Commission under US competition law when analysing horizontal mergers[157], works as follows: suppose that a producer of a product – for example a widget – were to introduce a Small but Significant Non-transitory Increase in Price. In those circumstances, would enough customers be inclined to switch their purchases to other makes of widgets, or indeed even to blodgets, to make the price rise unprofitable? If the answer is yes, this would suggest that the market is at least as wide as widgets generally and includes blodgets as well[158]. The same test can be applied to the delineation of the geographic market: if the price of widgets were to be raised in France by a small but significant amount, would customers switch to suppliers in Germany? If a firm could raise its price by a significant amount and retain its customers, this would mean that the market would be worth monopolising: prices could be raised profitably, since there would be no competitive constraint. For this reason, the SSNIP test is also – and more catchily – referred to sometimes as the 'hypothetical monopolist test'. The hypothetical monopolist test is given formal expression in paragraph 17 of the Commission's *Notice*, where it states that:

> The question to be asked is whether the parties' customers would switch to readily available substitutes or to suppliers located elsewhere in response to a hypothetical small (in the

[154] See www.ec.europa.eu/comm/competition/mergers/statistics.pdf.

[155] See ch 5, 'The dominant position, the abuse and the effects of the abuse may be in different markets', pp 205–208.

[156] Case COMP/M 2547 *Bayer Crop Science/Aventis* concerned a merger in which there were no fewer than 130 affected markets.

[157] *Horizontal Merger Guidelines* (issued in 1992); the current Guidelines were issued in 2010, available at www.justice.gov/atr/public/guidelines/hmg-2010.html; see Shapiro 'The Horizontal Merger Guidelines: From Hedgehog to Fox in Forty Years' (2010) 77 Antitrust LJ 701.

[158] It should be noted in passing that the possibility exists that consumers might switch from widgets to blodgets, but not the other way: in other words a phenomenon exists of 'one-way substitutability': see Case T-340/03 *France Télécom v Commission* [2007] ECR II-107, [2007] 4 CMLR 919, paras 88–90.

range 5 per cent to 10 per cent) but permanent relative price increase in the products and areas being considered. If substitution were enough to make the price increase unprofitable because of the resulting loss of sales, additional substitutes and areas are included in the relevant market.

This formulation of the test takes the 'range' of 5 per cent to 10 per cent to indicate 'significance' within the SSNIP test[159].

(v) The 'Cellophane Fallacy'[160]

It is necessary to enter a word of caution on the hypothetical monopolist test when applied to abuse of dominance cases. A monopolist may already be charging a monopoly price: if it were to raise its price further, its customers may cease to buy from it at all. In this situation the monopolist's 'own-price elasticity' – the extent to which consumers switch from its products in response to a price rise – is high. If a SSNIP test is applied in these circumstances between the monopolised product and another one, this might suggest a high degree of substitutability, since consumers are already at the point where they will cease to buy from the monopolist; the test therefore would exaggerate the breadth of the market by the inclusion of false substitutes. This error was committed by the US Supreme Court in *United States v EI du Pont de Nemour and Co*[161] in a case concerning packaging materials, including cellophane, since when it has been known as the 'Cellophane Fallacy'.

In the US the SSNIP test was devised in the context of merger cases, and is usually applied only in relation to them. In the European Commission's *Notice*, it states in the first paragraph that the test is to be used for cases under Articles 101, 102 and the EUMR; the Cellophane Fallacy is briefly acknowledged at paragraph 19 of the *Notice*, where it says that in cases under Article 102 'the fact that the prevailing price might already have been substantially increased will be taken into account'[162]. In DG COMP's *Discussion Paper on the application of [Article 102 TFEU] to exclusionary abuses*[163] it acknowledged that the SSNIP test needs to be particularly carefully considered in Article 102 cases, and that it is necessary in such cases to rely on a variety of methods for checking the robustness of alternative market definitions[164]. The Commission's *Guidance on the Commission's Enforcement Priorities in Applying Article [102 TFEU] to Abusive Exclusionary Conduct by Dominant Undertakings*[165] is silent on the issue of the Cellophane Fallacy.

In the UK the OFT's Guideline on *Market Definition* notes the problem of the Cellophane Fallacy, and states that the possibility that market conditions are distorted by the presence of market power will be accounted for 'when all the evidence on market

---

[159] In the UK the Competition Commission and the OFT have said that they will usually postulate a price rise of 5 per cent when applying the hypothetical monopolist test in merger cases: see *Merger Assessment Guidelines* CC2 (Revised), OFT 1254, September 2010, para 5.2.12, available at www.competition-commission.org.uk.

[160] For discussion see Glick, Cameron and Mangum 'Importing the Merger Guidelines Market Test in Section 2 Cases: Potential Benefits and Limitations' (1997) 42 Antitrust Bulletin 121.

[161] 351 US 377 (1956).

[162] It is worth pointing out that the Cellophane Fallacy can also occur where a SSNIP is applied to an unreasonably low (for example a predatory) price: the SSNIP test requires the hypothetical price rise to be applied to the *competitive* price.

[163] December 2005, available at www.ec.europa.eu/competition/antitrust/art82/discpaper2005.pdf.

[164] Ibid, paras 13–19.　　　[165] OJ [2009] C 45/7.

definition is weighed in the round'[166]. The OFT's decisions in *Aberdeen Journals II*[167] and *BSkyB*[168] both acknowledged the problem of the Cellophane Fallacy in defining the relevant markets in circumstances where competition may already have been distorted: in each case the OFT concluded that it was necessary to find alternative ways of determining whether the firms under consideration had market power and/or were guilty of abuse. In *BSkyB* the OFT looked at the physical characteristics of premium sports pay-TV channels and consumers' underlying preferences and in *Aberdeen Journals II* it looked at the conduct and statements of the allegedly dominant firm. In the appeal against the latter decision the Competition Appeal Tribunal ('the CAT') specifically stated that, in a case concerning an alleged abuse of a dominant position, the market to be taken into consideration means the market that would exist in normal competitive conditions, disregarding any distortive effects that the conduct of the dominant firm has itself created[169]. The CAT rejected arguments that the Cellophane Fallacy had been perpetrated in both *National Grid plc v Gas and Electricity Markets Authority*[170] and *Barclays Bank v Competition Commission*[171].

(vi) Supply-side substitutability

In most cases interchangeability will be determined by examining the market from the customer's perspective. However it is helpful in some situations to consider the degree of substitutability on the supply side of the market. Suppose that A is a producer of widgets and that B is a producer of blodgets: if it is a very simple matter for B to change its production process and to produce widgets, this might suggest that widgets and blodgets are part of the same market, even though consumers on the demand side of the market might not regard widgets and blodgets as substitutable. Dicta of the Court of Justice in *Continental Can v Commission*[172] indicate that the supply side of the market should be considered for the purpose of defining the market. Among its criticisms of the decision the Court of Justice said that the Commission should have made clear why it considered that producers of other types of containers would not be able to adapt their production to compete with Continental Can. The Commission has specifically addressed the issue of supply-side substitutability in subsequent decisions[173]. A good example is *Tetra Pak 1 (BTG Licence)*[174], where it took into account the fact that producers of milk-packaging machines could not readily adapt their production to make aseptic packaging machines and cartons in arriving at its market definition.

In paragraphs 20 to 23 of the *Notice on Market Definition* the Commission explains the circumstances in which it considers that supply-side substitutability is relevant to market definition. At paragraph 20 the Commission says that where suppliers are able

---

[166] *Market Definition*, OFT 403, December 2004, paras 5.4–5.6; see also OFT Economic Discussion Paper 2 (OFT 342) *The Role of Market Definition in Monopoly and Dominance Inquiries* (National Economic Research Associates, July 2001).

[167] *Aberdeen Journals (remitted case)*, OFT decision of 25 September 2002, paras 94–99, available at www. oft.gov.uk.

[168] *BSkyB investigation*, OFT decision of 30 January 2003, paras 88–97, available at www.oft.gov.uk.

[169] Case No 1009/1/1/02 *Aberdeen Journals Ltd v OFT* [2003] CAT 11, [2003] CompAR 67, para 276.

[170] Case No 1099/1/2/08 [2009] CAT 14, [2009] CompAR 282, paras 41–43.

[171] Case No 1109/6/8/09 [2009] CAT 27, [2009] CompAR 381, paras 53–55.

[172] Case 6/72 [1973] ECR 215, [1973] CMLR 199, paras 32ff.

[173] See eg *Eurofix-Bauco v Hilti* OJ [1988] L 65/19, [1989] 4 CMLR 677, para 55, upheld on appeal to the General Court Case T-30/89 *Hilti AG v Commission* [1991] ECR II-1439, [1992] 4 CMLR 16 and on appeal to the Court of Justice Case C-53/92 P [1994] ECR I-667, [1994] 4 CMLR 614.

[174] OJ [1988] L 272/27, [1988] 4 CMLR 47, upheld on appeal to the General Court Case T-51/89 *Tetra Pak Rausing SA v Commission* [1990] ECR II-309, [1991] 4 CMLR 334.

to switch production to other products and to market them 'in the short term' without incurring significant additional costs or risks in response to small and permanent changes in relative prices, then the market may be broadened to include the products that those suppliers are already producing. A footnote to paragraph 20 suggests that the short term means 'such a period that does not entail a significant adjustment of existing tangible and intangible assets'. A practical example is given in paragraph 22 of an undertaking producing a particular grade of paper: if it could change easily to producing other grades of paper, they should all be included in the market definition. However, where supply substitution is more complex than this, it should be regarded as a matter of determining market power rather than establishing the market[175].

While it may seem unimportant whether the issue of supply-side substitution is dealt with at the stage of market definition or of market power, where competition law deploys a market share test, as for example in Article 3 of Regulation 330/2010[176], the possibility of broadening the market definition through the inclusion of supply-side substitutes may have a decisive effect on the outcome of a particular case.

(vii) Evidence relied on to define relevant markets

The SSNIP test establishes a conceptual framework within which markets should be defined. In practice, however, the critical issue is to know what evidence can be adduced to determine the scope of the relevant market. If the world were composed of an infinite number of market research organisations devoted to asking SSNIP-like questions of customers and consumers, market definition would be truly scientific. But of course the world is not so composed, and a variety of techniques, some of considerable sophistication, are deployed by economists and econometrists in order to seek solutions. The Commission's *Notice*, from paragraph 25 onwards[177], considers some of the evidence that may be available, but it quite correctly says that tests that may be suitable in one industry may be wholly inappropriate in another. A moment's reflection shows that this must be so: for example, the demand-substitutability of one alcoholic beverage for another in the ordinary citizen's mind is likely to be tested by different criteria than an airline choosing whether to purchase aeroplanes from Boeing or Airbus. In *Aberdeen Journals Ltd v OFT*[178] the CAT has said that there is no 'hierarchy' of evidence on issues such as market definition that would require, for example, objective economic evidence to be given greater weight than subjective evidence such as the statements or conduct of the parties[179].

---

[175] Recommended Practice F of the ICN's *Recommended Practices for Merger Analysis* recommends that supply-side substitution should be taken into account when firms could produce or sell in the relevant market 'within a short time frame and without incurring significant sunk costs'; the *Recommended Practices* are available at www.internationalcompetitionnetwork.org.

[176] OJ [2010] L 102/1; on market definition under this block exemption see the Commission's *Guidelines on Vertical Restraints* OJ [2010] C 130/1, Section V, paras 86–92.

[177] See also *Bishop and Walker*, chs 9–14 and 16, which considers techniques that may be relevant to market definition; also OFT Research Paper 17 (OFT 266) *Quantitative techniques in competition analysis* (LECG Ltd, October 1999): this can be obtained from the OFT's website at www.oft.gov.uk.

[178] Case No 1009/1/1/02 [2003] CAT 11, [2003] CompAR 67.   [179] Ibid, para 127.

Both DG COMP[180] and the UK Competition Commission[181] have issued best practices on how economic evidence should be submitted.

(viii) Examples of evidence that may be used in defining the relevant product market

As far as definition of the product market is concerned the *Notice* suggests that the following evidence may be available.

(A) Evidence of substitution in the recent past

There may recently have been an event – such as a price increase or a 'shock', perhaps a failure of the Brazilian coffee crop due to a late frost – giving rise to direct evidence of the consequences that this had for consumers' consumption (perhaps a large increase in the drinking of tea).

(B) Quantitative tests

Various econometric and statistical tests have been devised which attempt to estimate own-price elasticities and cross-price elasticities for the demand of a product, based on the similarity of price movements over time, the causality between price series and the similarity of price levels and/or their convergence. Own-price elasticities measure the extent to which demand for a product changes in response to a change in its price. Cross-price elasticities measure the extent to which demand for a product changes in response to a change in the price of some other product. Own-price elasticities provide more information about the market power that an undertaking possesses than cross-price elasticities; however cross-price elasticities help more with market definition, since they provide evidence on substitutability.

(C) Views of customers and competitors

The Commission will contact customers and competitors in a case that involves market definition and will, where appropriate, specifically ask them to answer the SSNIP question. This happens routinely, for example, when it seeks to delineate markets under the EUMR.

(D) Marketing studies and consumer surveys

The Commission will look at marketing studies as a useful provider of information about the market, although it specifically states in paragraph 41 of the *Notice* that it will scrutinise 'with utmost care' the methodology followed in consumer surveys carried out *ad hoc* by the undertakings involved in merger cases or cases under Articles 101 and 102. Its concern is that the selection of questions in the survey may be deliberately made in order to achieve a favourable outcome[182].

---

[180] *Best Practices for the Submission of Economic Evidence and Data Collection in Cases Concerning the Application of Articles 101 and 102 TFEU and in Merger Cases* (2010), available at www.ec.europa.eu/competition/antitrust/legislation/legislation.html.

[181] *Suggested Best Practice for the Submission of Technical Economic Analysis from Parties to the Competition Commission*, available at www.competition-commission.org.uk/rep_pub/corporate_documents/other_guidance_documents.htm.

[182] Note that in the UK the Competition Commission and OFT have jointly published guidance on *Good Practice in the Design and Presentation of Consumer Survey Evidence in Merger Inquiries* OFT 1230 and CC2com1, March 2011, available at www.oft.gov.uk.

(E) Barriers and costs associated with switching demand to potential substitutes

There may be a number of barriers and/or costs that result in two apparent demand substitutes not belonging to one single product market. The Commission deals with these in paragraph 42 of the *Notice*, and gives as examples regulatory barriers, other forms of state intervention, constraints occurring in downstream markets, the need to incur capital investment and other factors. The OFT has published an Economic Discussion Paper that specifically considers the issue of switching costs[183].

(F) Different categories of customers and price discrimination

At paragraph 43 the Commission states that the extent of the product market might be narrowed where there exist distinct groups of customers for a particular product: the market for one group may be narrower than for the other, if it is possible to identify which group an individual belongs to at the moment of selling the relevant products and there is no possibility of trade between the two categories of customer[184].

(ix) A word of caution on the *Notice*

It is important to point out a few words of caution about the *Notice on Market Definition*. The problem of the Cellophane Fallacy has already been mentioned[185]. There are three other points about the *Notice*.

First, it is 'only' a Commission Notice: it does not have the force of law, and ought not to be treated as a legislative instrument. However the EU Courts have referred to it on various occasions with apparent approval[186].

A second point about the *Notice* is that, no matter how well it explains the SSNIP test and the evidence that may be used when applying it, the fact remains that in some sectors actual price data about substitutability may not be available: the information that can be captured varies hugely from one sector to another, and in some cases one will be thrown back on fairly subjective assessments of the market for want of hard, scientific evidence. In this situation it may be necessary to predict the likely effect of a SSNIP on customers by looking at various factors such as the physical characteristics of the products concerned or their intended use. In some cases it may not be possible to apply the SSNIP test at all. An example is the Commission's decision in *British Interactive Broadcasting*[187]: there the Commission stated that it could not delineate the markets for interactive broadcasting services by applying a SSNIP test since no data were available in relation to a product that had yet to be launched. In several broadcasting cases the fact that public-sector broadcasting is available 'free-to-air' to end users meant that a SSNIP test was inapplicable[188]. Clearly this is always likely to be a problem in relation to products introduced into the 'new' economy[189].

A third point about the *Notice* is that there are by now very many cases – in particular under the EUMR – in which the Commission has been called upon to define the

---

[183] OFT Economic Discussion Paper 5 (OFT 655) *Switching Costs* (National Economic Research Associates, April 2003).

[184] See also *Market Definition* OFT 403, December 2004, paras 3.8–3.10; Hausman, Leonard and Vellturo 'Market Definition Under Price Discrimination' (1996) 64 Antitrust LJ 367.

[185] See 'The "Cellophane Fallacy"', pp 32–31 above.   [186] See ch 1 n 153 above.

[187] OJ [1999] L 312/1, [2000] 4 CMLR 901.

[188] See eg Case M 553 *RTL/Veronica/Endemol* OJ [1996] L 134/32, upheld on appeal Case T-221/95 *Endemol Entertainment Holding BV v Commission* [1999] ECR II-1299, [1999] 5 CMLR 611.

[189] On the issue of market definition in cases involving e-commerce see OFT Economic Discussion Paper 1 (OFT 308) *E-commerce and its implications for competition policy* (Frontier Economics Group, August 2000), ch 4.

market. With more than 4,000 mergers having been notified to the Commission under the EUMR by the end of 2010, there are few sectors in which it has not been called upon to analyse relevant markets. As a consequence of this there is a very considerable 'decisional practice' of the Commission in which it has opined – from cars, buses and trucks to pharmaceuticals and agrochemicals, from banking and insurance services to international aviation and deep-sea drilling[190]. Not unnaturally, an undertaking in need of guidance on the Commission's likely response to a matter of market definition will wish to find out what it has had to say in the past in actual decisions; however the caveat should be entered that the General Court has established that the market must always be defined in any particular case by reference to the facts prevailing at the time and not by reference to precedents[191].

(x) **Spare parts and the aftermarket**[192]

There are numerous sectors in which a consumer of one product – for example a car – will need to purchase at a later date complementary products such as spare parts. The same can be true where a customer has to buy 'consumables', such as cartridges to be used in a laser printer, or maintenance services. In such cases one issue is to determine how the relevant product market should be defined. If there is a separate market for the complementary product, it may be that an undertaking that has no power over the 'primary' market may nevertheless be dominant in the 'secondary' one. An illustration is *Hugin v Commission*[193], where the Court of Justice upheld the Commission's finding that Hugin was dominant in the market for spare parts for its own cash machines. Liptons, a firm which serviced Hugin's machines, could not use spare parts produced by anyone else for this purpose because Hugin would have been able to prevent this by relying on its rights under the UK Design Copyright Act 1968. Therefore, although for other purposes it might be true to say that there is a market for spare parts generally, in this case, given the use to which Liptons intended to put them, the market had to be more narrowly defined. Liptons was 'locked in', as it was dependent on Hugin, and this justified a narrow market definition. This case, and the judgments of the Court of Justice in *AB Volvo v Erik Veng*[194] and *CICRA v Régie Nationale des Usines Renault*[195], establish that spare parts can form a market separate from the products for which they are needed.

---

[190] See ch 21, 'Access to the Commission's decisions', pp 832–833 on how to access the Commission's decisions under the EUMR.

[191] In Joined Cases T-125/97 etc *Coca-Cola v Commission* [2000] ECR II-1733, [2000] 5 CMLR 467, para 82, the General Court stated that in the course of any decision applying Article 102, 'the Commission must define the relevant market again and make a fresh analysis of the conditions of competition which will not necessarily be based on the same considerations as those underlying the previous finding of a dominant position': see similarly, in the UK, the CAT in Case No 1109/6/8/09 *Barclays Bank plc v Competition Commission* [2009] CAT 27, [2009] CompAR 381, para 36; examples of how market definitions can change over a period of time are afforded by cross-channel ferry services between the UK and continental Europe, where the Channel Tunnel has altered the market: see *The Peninsular and Oriental Steam Navigation Corpn and Stena Line AB* Cm 4030 (1998); and the market for betting shops in the UK: see *Ladbroke Group plc and The Coral Betting Business* Cm 4030 (1998); in the UK the OFT, pursuant to the *Coca-Cola* judgment, conducted a fresh market analysis in its *BSkyB* decision, 17 December 2002, paras 29ff, available at www.oft.gov. uk; see also *Market Definition*, OFT 403, December 2004, paras 5.7–5.9.

[192] See *Bishop and Walker*, paras 4.045–4.046 and 6.020–6.046; this issue often arises in cases concerning alleged 'tie-in transactions', as to which see ch 17, 'Tying', pp 688–696.

[193] Case 22/78 [1979] ECR 1869, [1979] 3 CMLR 345; the Commission's decision was quashed in this case as it had failed to establish the necessary effect on inter-state trade.

[194] Case 238/87 [1988] ECR 6211, [1989] 4 CMLR 122.

[195] Case 53/87 [1988] ECR 6039, [1990] 4 CMLR 265.

Likewise consumables, such as nails for use with nail-guns[196] and cartons for use with filling-machines[197], have been held to be a separate market from the product with which they are used.

However, as a matter of economics, it would be wrong to conclude that the primary and secondary markets are necessarily always discrete. It may be that a consumer, when deciding to purchase the primary product, will also take into account the price of the secondary products that will be needed in the future: this is sometimes referred to as 'whole life costing'. Where this occurs high prices in the secondary market may act as a competitive constraint when the purchaser is making his initial decision as to which primary product to purchase. It is an empirical question whether there is a separate aftermarket. The Commission has stated that it regards the issue as one that needs to be examined on a case-by-case basis[198], and that it will look at all important factors such as the price and life-time of the primary product, the transparency of the prices for the secondary product and the proportion of the price of the secondary product to the value of the primary one. In its investigation of *Kyocera/Pelikan*[199] the Commission concluded that Kyocera was not dominant in the market for toner cartridges for printers, since consumers took the price of cartridges into account when deciding which printer to buy. In the UK both the Office of Telecommunication (OFTEL, now the Office of Communications (OFCOM)) and the OFT have reached similar conclusions[200], and the OFT's guideline on *Market Definition* adopts the same approach[201]. However in *Confédération européenne des associations d'horlogers-réparateurs (CEAHR) v Commission*[202] the General Court disagreed with the Commission's view that the repairing and maintenance of Swiss watches was part of the market generally for prestige and luxury watches[203].

(xi) Procurement markets

In some cases the business behaviour under scrutiny is that of buyers rather than sellers. For example where supermarkets merge[204], or where their procurement policies are under investigation[205], the market must be defined from the demand rather than the supply side of the market. In the case of vertical agreements Article 3 of Regulation 330/2010, which contains a market share threshold of 30 per cent for the application of that block exemption, requires that the market be defined from the demand as well as the supply side of the market[206].

---

[196] Case T-30/89 *Hilti AG v Commission* [1990] ECR II-163, [1992] 4 CMLR 16, upheld on appeal Case C-53/92 P *Hilti AG v Commission* [1994] ECR I-667, [1994] 4 CMLR 614.

[197] *Tetra Pak II* OJ [1992] L 72/1, [1992] 4 CMLR 551, upheld on appeal to the General Court Case T-83/91 *Tetra Pak International SA v Commission* [1994] ECR II-755, [1997] 4 CMLR 726, and on appeal to the Court of Justice Case C-333/94 P *Tetra Pak International SA v Commission* [1996] ECR I-5951, [1997] 4 CMLR 662.

[198] XXVth *Report on Competition Policy* (1995), point 86; see also the *Notice on Market Definition* (p 30, ch 1, n 152 above), para 56; the *Guidelines on Vertical Restraints* (p 34, ch 1, n 176 above), para 91; DG COMP's *Discussion paper on the application of [Article 102 TFEU] to exclusionary abuses* paras 243–265.

[199] XXVth *Report on Competition Policy* (1995), point 87.

[200] See *Swan Solutions Ltd/Avaya ECS Ltd*, OFT decision of 6 April 2001 and OFT decision of, *ICL/Synstar*, 26 July 2001; both decisions are available on the OFT's website: www.oft.gov.uk.

[201] OFT 403, December 2004, paras 6.1–6.7.   [202] Case T-427/08 [2010] ECR II-000.

[203] Ibid, paras 65–121.   [204] See eg Case M 1221 *Rewe/Meinl* OJ [1999] L 274/1, [2000] 5 CMLR 256.

[205] See the reports of the UK Competition Commission on *Supermarkets* Cm 4842 (2000) and *Groceries*, 30 April 2008.

[206] See ch 16, 'The *Vertical guidelines*', p 662.

(xii) Innovation markets[207]

In the US a 'market for innovation', separate from products already on the market, has been found in some cases involving high technology industries[208]. The Commission's decision in *Shell/Montecatini*[209] suggested that it would be prepared to define a market for innovation, although in other cases it has made use of the more conventional idea of 'potential competition' to deal with the situation[210]. The Commission's *Guidelines on Horizontal Cooperation Agreements*[211] provide some guidance on this issue.

(D) The relevant geographic market

It is also necessary, when determining whether a firm or firms have market power, that the relevant geographic market should be defined. The definition of the geographic market may have a decisive impact on the outcome of a case, as in the *Volvo/Scania* decision[212] under the EUMR: the Commission's conclusion that there were national, rather than pan-European, markets for trucks and buses led to an outright prohibition of that merger[213]. Some products can be supplied without difficulty throughout the Union or even the world. In other cases there may be technical, legal or practical reasons why a product can be supplied only within a narrower area. The delineation of the geographic market helps to indicate which other firms impose a competitive constraint on the one(s) under investigation. The cost of transporting products is an important factor: some goods are so expensive to transport in relation to their value that it would not be economic to attempt to sell them on distant markets. Another factor might be legal controls which make it impossible for an undertaking in one Member State to export goods or services to another. This problem may be dealt with by the Commission bringing proceedings against the Member State to prevent restrictions on the free movement of goods (under Articles 34 to 36 TFEU) or of services (under Articles 56 to 62 TFEU). With the completion of the internal market, there should be fewer claims that fiscal, technical and legal barriers to inter-state trade exist.

(i) The legal test

That the geographic market should be identified is clear from the Court of Justice's judgment in *United Brands v Commission*[214]. The Court said that the opportunities for competition under Article 102 must be considered:

> with reference to a clearly defined geographic area in which [the product] is marketed and where the conditions are sufficiently homogeneous for the effect of the economic power of the undertaking concerned to be able to be evaluated.

---

[207] See Rapp 'The Misapplication of the Innovative Market Approach to Merger Analysis' (1995) 64 Antitrust LJ 19; Glader *Innovation Markets and Competition Analysis: EU Competition Law and US Antitrust Law* (Edward Elgar, 2006).

[208] See eg *United States v Flow International Corpn* 6 Trade Reg Rep (CCH) ¶ 45,094; US Department of Justice and Federal Trade Commission *Antitrust Guidelines for the Licensing of Intellectual Property* available at www.justice.gov/atr/public/guidelines/0558.htm.

[209] OJ [1994] L 332/48.

[210] See Temple Lang 'European Community Antitrust Law: Innovation Markets and High Technology Industries' [1996] Fordham Corporate Law Institute (ed Hawk), ch 23; Landman 'Innovation Markets in Europe' (1998) 19 ECLR 21; OFT Economic Discussion Paper 3 (OFT 377) *Innovation and Competition Policy* (Charles River Associates, March 2002), Annex B.

[211] OJ [2011] C 11/1, paras 119–126.

[212] Case M 1672, OJ [2001] L 143/74, [2001] 5 CMLR 11.

[213] See ch 21, 'Outright prohibitions', pp 902–904.

[214] Case 27/76 [1978] ECR 207, [1978] 1 CMLR 429, paras 10–11.

In that case the Commission had excluded the UK, France and Italy from the geographic market since in those countries special arrangements existed as to the importing and marketing of bananas. United Brands argued that, even so, the Commission had drawn the geographic market too widely, since competitive conditions varied between the remaining six Member States[215]; the Court of Justice however concluded that the Commission had drawn it correctly. The significance of the geographic market in determining dominance was emphasised by the Court of Justice in *Alsatel v Novasam SA*[216]. There the Court of Justice held that the facts before it failed to establish that a particular region in France rather than France generally constituted the geographic market, so that the claim that Novasam had a dominant position failed in the absence of evidence of power over the wider, national, market.

(ii) The Commission's Notice on Market Definition

The Commission provides helpful guidance on the definition of the geographic market in its *Notice on Market Definition*[217]. At paragraph 28 it says that its approach can be summarised as follows:

> it will take a preliminary view of the scope of the geographic market on the basis of broad indications as to the distribution of market shares between the parties and their competitors, as well as a preliminary analysis of pricing and price differences at national and [EU] or EEA level. This initial view is used basically as a working hypothesis to focus the Commission's enquiries for the purposes of arriving at a precise geographic market definition.

In the following paragraph the Commission says that it will then explore any particular configuration of prices or market shares in order to test whether they really do say something about the possibility of demand substitution between one market and another: for example it will consider the importance of national or local preferences, current patterns of purchases of customers and product differentiation. This survey is to be conducted within the context of the SSNIP test outlined above, the difference being that, in the case of geographic market definition, the question is whether, faced with an increase in price, consumers located in a particular area would switch their purchases to suppliers further away. Further relevant factors are set out in paragraphs 30 and 31 of the *Notice*, and at paragraph 32 the Commission points out that it will take into account the continuing process of market integration in defining the market, the assumption here being that, over time, the single market should become more of a reality, with the result that the geographic market should have a tendency to get wider. There is no reason in principle why the relevant geographic market should not extend to the entire world, and there have been decisions in which this has been so[218].

---

[215] This decision was reached before the accession of Greece, Spain and Portugal etc.

[216] Case 247/86 [1988] ECR 5987, [1990] 4 CMLR 434; other cases in which the General Court has upheld the Commission's definition of the geographic market include Case T-151/05 *Nederlandse Vakbond Varkenshouders v Commission* [2009] ECR II-1219, [2009] 5 CMLR 1613 paras 69–78 and Case T-57/01 *Solvay v Commission* [2009] ECR II-4621, paras 239–260, on appeal to the Court of Justice Case C-109/10 P *Solvay SA v Commission*, not yet decided.

[217] See p 29, ch 1, n 152 above.

[218] For example the Commission found global markets for top-level internet connectivity in Case M 1069 *WorldCom/MCI* OJ [1999] L 116/1, [1999] 5 CMLR 876, para 82 and Case M 1741 *MCI WorldCom/Sprint*, decision of 28 June 2000, para 97, available at www.europa.eu.int/comm/competition/mergers/cases.

(iii) Examples of evidence that may be used in defining the relevant geographic market

As far as definition of the geographic market is concerned, the Commission suggests that the following evidence may be available.

(A) Past evidence of diversion of orders to other areas

It may be that direct evidence is available of changes in prices between areas and consequent reactions by customers. The Commission points out that care may be needed in comparing prices where there have been exchange rate movements, where taxation levels are different and where there is significant product differentiation between one area and another.

(B) Basic demand characteristics

The scope of the geographic market may be determined by matters such as national preferences or preferences for national brands, language, culture and life style, and the need for a local presence.

(C) Views of customers and competitors

As in the case of defining the product market, the Commission will take the views of customers and competitors into account when determining the scope of the geographic market.

(D) Current geographic pattern of purchases

The Commission will examine where customers currently purchase goods or supplies. If they already purchase across the European Union, this would indicate an EU-wide market.

(E) Trade flows/patterns of shipments

Information on trade flows may be helpful in determining the geographic market, provided that the trade statistics are sufficiently detailed for the products in question.

(F) Barriers and switching costs associated with the diversion of orders to companies located in other areas

Barriers that isolate national markets, transport costs and transport restrictions may all contribute to the isolation of national markets.

(E) **The temporal market**

It may also be necessary to consider the temporal quality of the market[219]. Competitive conditions may vary from season to season, for example because of variations of weather or of consumer habits. A firm may find itself exposed to competition at one point in a year but effectively free from it at another. In this situation it may be that it has market power during one part of the year but not others.

The issue arose in *United Brands v Commission*[220]. There was evidence in that case which suggested that the cross-elasticity of demand for bananas fluctuated from season to season. When other fruit was plentiful in summer, demand for bananas dropped:

---

[219] The temporal market is discussed briefly in the OFT Guideline on *Market Definition*, OFT 403, December 2004, paras 5.1–5.3.
[220] Case 27/76 [1978] ECR 207, [1978] 1 CMLR 429.

this suggests that the Commission might have considered that there were two seasonal markets, and that United Brands had no market power over the summer months. The Commission however identified just the one temporal market and held that UBC was dominant within it. On appeal the Court of Justice declined to deal with this issue. In *ABG*[221] on the other hand the Commission did define the temporal market for oil more narrowly by limiting it to the period of crisis which followed the decision of OPEC to increase dramatically the price of oil in the early 1970s. The Commission held that during the crisis companies had a special responsibility to supply existing customers on a fair and equitable basis; the Court of Justice quashed the Commission's decision on the issue of abuse, but not on the definition of the market[222].

The fact that electricity as a product is not capable of being stored means that there may be different temporal markets in this sector[223].

(F) **Market power**

As has been stressed, market definition is not an end in itself. The really important question in competition law cases is whether a firm or firms have, or will have after a merger, market power. It will be recalled that market power exists where a firm has the ability profitably to raise prices over a period of time, or to behave analogously for example by restricting output or limiting consumer choice[224]. Three issues are relevant to an assessment of market power: these are usefully summarised in paragraph 12 of the Commission's *Guidance on the Commission's Enforcement Priorities in Applying Article [102 TFEU] to Abusive Exclusionary Conduct by Dominant Undertakings* ('*Guidance on Article 102 Enforcement Priorities*')[225]:

- constraints imposed by the existing supplies from, and the position on the market of, *actual competitors* (the market position of the dominant undertaking and its competitors),
- constraints imposed by the credible threat of future expansion by actual competitors or entry by *potential competitors* (expansion and entry),
- constraints imposed by the bargaining strength of the undertaking's customers (*countervailing buyer power*) (emphasis added).

It will require only a moment's reflection to appreciate that market share figures cannot provide any insights into the influence of potential competitors on the market power of existing ones, since a figure cannot be ascribed to someone not already in the market; nor, for the same reason, can market shares provide information about the extent of any countervailing buyer power. This is why market share figures are, at best, simply a proxy for market power, and cannot be determinative in themselves.

---

[221] OJ [1977] L 117/1, [1977] 2 CMLR D1.

[222] Case 77/77 *BP v Commission* [1978] ECR 1513, [1978] 3 CMLR 174.

[223] See eg *Application in the Energy Sector* OFT 428, January 2005, para 3.13; DG COMP's *Report on Energy sector Inquiry* SEC(2006)1724, para 398.

[224] See ch 1 n 119 above.

[225] OJ [2009] C 45/7; although this document is specifically concerned with market power of sufficient scale to earn the adjective 'substantial' for the purposes of Article 102 TFEU, the three criteria set out in para 12 of the *Guidance* are relevant to any assessment of market power; for further guidance on the assessment of market power see *Assessment of market power* OFT 415, December 2004.

(i) Actual competitors

(A) Market shares[226]

As paragraph 13 of the Commission's *Guidance on Article 102 Enforcement Priorities* says, market shares provide a useful first indication of the structure of any particular market and of the relative importance of the various undertakings active on it. However the Commission adds that it will interpret market shares in the light of the relevant market conditions, and in particular of the dynamics of the market and of the extent to which products are differentiated. It will also look at the development of market shares over time in the case of volatile markets or bidding markets, where firms bid *for* the market, often in auctions[227].

As noted earlier in this chapter, there are varying degrees of market power – from none, to 'non-appreciable', to 'substantial', to pure monopoly. Clearly market share figures tell us something about where an undertaking is along this continuum. The Table of Market Share Thresholds at the end of this chapter lists a (large) number of thresholds that have some significance in the application of EU and UK competition law, for example by providing a 'safe harbour' for firms below a certain threshold, or by indicating a fairly stormy sea for firms above a different one. Specific market share rules – such as the presumption of dominance where an undertaking has a market share of 50 per cent or more or the application of the block exemption for vertical agreements provided that the parties' market shares are below 30 per cent – are examined in later chapters of this book.

(B) Market concentration and the Herfindahl-Hirschman Index

In some cases market share figures may be used in order to determine how concentrated a market is, or how concentrated it will be following a merger or the entry into force, for example, of a cooperation agreement. Competition concerns may be greater as the market becomes more concentrated. One way of determining the level of concentration in the market is to use the so-called 'Herfindahl-Hirschman Index' ('the HHI'). This sums up the squares of the individual market shares of all the competitors in a market: the higher the total, the more concentrated the market. According to paragraph 16 of the European Commission's *Guidelines on the assessment of horizontal mergers*[228] the concentration level will be low where the total is below 1,000; moderate if between 1,000 and 1,800; and high where it is above 1,800. This is a relatively simple way of calculating market concentration, and its effectiveness is demonstrated by the following three examples:

Example 1
In the widget industry there are 15 competitors: 5 of them each has a market share in the region of 10 per cent, and 10 of them each has a market share in the region of 5 per cent

$$\text{HHI} = 5 \times 10^2 + 10 \times 5^2 = 500 + 250 = 750$$

The market concentration is low

---

[226] For a critical discussion of the use of market shares in competition analysis see Kaplow 'Market Share Thresholds: On the Conflation of Empirical Assessments and Legal Policy Judgments' (2011) 7 Journal of Competition Law and Economics 243.

[227] A helpful discussion of the types of auction that may be held and the decisional practice in the EU and the UK can be found in Szilági Pál 'Bidding Markets and Competition Law in the European Union and the United Kingdom' (2008) 29 ECLR 16 and (2008) 29 ECLR 89.

[228] [2004] OJ C 31/5; see also the Commission's *Guidelines on the assessment of non-horizontal mergers* OJ [2008] C 265/6, para 25.

Example 2
In the blodget industry there are 8 competitors: 2 of them each has a market share in the region of 20 per cent, and 6 of them each has a market share in the region of 10 per cent

$$HHI = 2 \times 20^2 + 6 \times 10^2 = 800 + 600 = 1400$$

The market concentration is moderate

Example 3
In the sprocket industry there are 4 competitors: 2 of them each has a market share in the region of 30 per cent and the other 2 each has a market share in the region of 20 per cent

$$HHI = 2 \times 30^2 + 2 \times 20^2 = 1800 + 800 = 2600$$

The market concentration is high

The same approach can be used to work out the consequences for the concentration of the market of any of the competitors merging or entering into an agreement with one another. For example if, in Example 2, the two firms with 20 per cent were to merge, the HHI after the agreement would be:

$$40^2 + 6 \times 10^2 = 1600 + 600 = 2200$$

The market concentration will have moved from moderate to high. The difference in the pre- and post-merger concentration levels – that is to say the increase of 800 from 1400 to 2200, is referred to as the 'Delta', represented by the symbol Δ.

If however, in Example 2, two of the firms with 10 per cent had entered into an agreement with one another, the HHI after the agreement would be:

$$2 \times 20^2 + 1 \times 20^2 + 4 \times 10^2 = 800 + 400 + 400 = 1600$$

The market concentration will remain moderate, and the Delta would be merely 200.

The HHI provides some insights into the competitive condition of markets; however it is fairly unsophisticated, not least since it adopts a static view of markets based on market share figures, and is unable to reflect dynamism and innovation. Its role, therefore, is fairly limited: it is at its most useful when screening out mergers that do not give rise to competitive concerns[229]; however little if any reliance would be placed on HHIs at the stage of deciding to prohibit an agreement, conduct or a merger, where much more sophisticated analysis would be undertaken.

(ii) Potential competitors[230]

Recommendation 7 of the International Competition Network's Working Group on *Unilateral Conduct Laws* is that 'The Assessment of durability of market power, with a focus on barriers to entry or expansion, should be an integral part of the analysis of dominance/substantial market power'. As paragraph 16 of the Commission's *Guidance on Article 102 Enforcement Priorities* points out, competition is a dynamic process and an assessment of competitive constraints cannot be based solely on the existing market situation: potential entry by new firms and expansion by existing ones must also be taken into account. This is why it is necessary to take barriers to entry and barriers to expansion into account. In the Commission's view, an

---

[229] See ch 21, 'Market shares and concentration levels', p 868 and ch 22, 'Measures of concentration', p 934.
[230] See further the OECD's *Best Practices Roundtable on Barriers to Entry*, 2005, available at www.oecd.org.

undertaking would be deterred from raising its prices if expansion is 'likely, timely and sufficient'; in particular paragraph 16 says that to be 'sufficient', entry cannot be simply on a small-scale basis, for example into a market niche, but must be of such a magnitude as to be able to deter any attempt by an undertaking already in the market to increase prices.

Paragraph 17 of the *Guidance* provides examples of such barriers:

- legal barriers, such as tariffs or quotas
- advantages specifically enjoyed by dominant undertakings such as economies of scale and scope; privileged access to essential inputs or natural resources; important technologies; or an established distribution and sales network
- costs and other impediments, for example resulting from network effects, faced by customers in switching to a new supplier
- the conduct of a dominant undertaking, such as long-term exclusive contracts that have appreciably foreclosing effects.

Barriers to entry and expansion will be considered further in specific chapters of this book[231].

(iii) Countervailing buyer power

Paragraph 18 of the Commission's *Guidance on Article 102 Enforcement Priorities* explains that competitive constraints may be exerted not only by actual or potential competitors, but also by customers if they have sufficient bargaining strength; such power may result from a customer's size or its commercial significance for a dominant firm. However buyer power may not amount to an effective competitive constraint where it ensures only that a particular or limited segment of customers is shielded from the market power of the supplier.

Buyer power will be considered further in specific chapters of this book[232].

(iv) Summary

The discussion above has explained the key features involved in the determination of whether a firm or firms have market power. In particular it was explained that:

- **market definition** is an important part of the analysis of market power, but it is not an end in itself and is simply one stage in the overall process
- **market shares** provide us with important information about the state of existing competition within the market, but they cannot, in themselves, be determinative, since they tell us nothing about barriers to expansion and entry, nor about buyer power
- **barriers to expansion and entry** are important, since they provide us with information about the existence of potential competition, something which cannot be captured by a market share figure, precisely because the competition is potential only
- **buyer power** is also an important part of the analysis of market power.

---

[231] See eg ch 5, 'Potential competitors', pp 184–187 on Article 102 TFEU and ch 21, 'Entry', p 874 on the EUMR.

[232] See eg ch 21, 'Countervailing buyer power', p 874 and ch 22, 'Countervailing buyer power', p 940.

(G) **A final reflection on market shares**

It has been said several times in this chapter that market share does not, in itself, determine whether an undertaking possesses market power; assessing market power is not and cannot be reduced simply to numbers. This having been said, however, it is interesting to consider the large range of situations in which EU and UK competition law require competition lawyers and their clients to consider market share figures for the purpose of deciding how to handle a particular case. This arises partly from numerous pieces of legislation and guidelines which contain a market share threshold; and partly from case law which has attributed significance to particular market share figures. The following table sets out a series of market share thresholds that should be embedded in the mind of in-house counsel to *DoItAll*, a diversified conglomerate company conducting business in the EU. The list is not exhaustive, and was compiled in a more light-hearted mood than the rest of this chapter: it does nevertheless reveal how influential market share figures can be in analysing competition law cases in the EU and the UK.

1.1 Table of market share thresholds

0%	With a market share of 0% even the most zealous of competition authorities is unlikely to take action against you
	With a market share of less than 5% your agreements are unlikely to have an appreciable effect on trade between Member States provided that certain other criteria are satisfied[1]
5%	At 5% or more your agreements with undertakings that are not actual or potential competitors may significantly contribute to any 'cumulative' foreclosure effect of parallel networks of similar agreements[2]
	Agreements with undertakings that concern imports and exports have been found to have an effect on trade between Member States where your market share is around the 5% level[3]
	When notifying mergers under the EU Merger Regulation you will be required to provide information about competitors that have more than 5% of the relevant geographic market[4]
10%	At 10% or more your agreements with actual or potential competitors are no longer *de minimis* under the European Commission's *Notice on Agreements of Minor Importance*[5]
15%	It is unlikely that your joint purchasing agreements[6] or your commercialisation[7] agreements infringe Article 101(1) where your market share is below 15%
	At 15% or more your agreements with undertakings that are not actual or potential competitors are no longer *de minimis* under the *Notice on Agreements of Minor Importance*[8]
	Under the EU Merger Regulation, in the case of horizontal mergers, markets in which your market share exceeds 15% are 'affected markets', necessitating the provision of substantial information on Form CO to DG COMP[9]
	With more than 15% of the market you are no longer eligible to take advantage of the 'simplified procedure' for certain horizontal mergers under the EU Merger Regulation[10]
20%	At 20% or more block exemption for certain co-insurance agreements ceases to be available[11]; some marginal relief is provided up to a market share cap of 25%[12] and even, exceptionally, beyond 25%[13]
	Block exemption ceases to be provided for specialisation agreements under Regulation 1218/2010 where the parties' market share exceeds 20%[14]; some marginal relief is available up to a market share cap of 25%[15]
	Block exemption ceases to be available for technology transfer agreements between competing undertakings where their combined market share exceeds 20%[16]
25%	At 25% or more block exemption ceases to be available for research and development agreements under Regulation 1217/2010[17]; some marginal relief is provided up to a market share cap of 30%[18] and even, exceptionally, beyond 30%[19]
	At 25% or more block exemption for certain co-reinsurance, as opposed to co-insurance, agreements ceases to be available[20]; some marginal relief is provided up to a threshold of 30%[21] and even, for a limited period, beyond 30%[22]

Under the EU Merger Regulation at 25% you cease to benefit from a presumption that your merger will not significantly impede effective competition[23]

Under the EU Merger Regulation you do not benefit from the simplified procedure in the case of vertical mergers where your market share exceeds 25%[24]

Under the EU Merger Regulation, in the case of vertical mergers, markets in which your market share exceeds 25% are affected markets[25]

Under UK law you could be referred to the Competition Commission under the merger provisions of the Enterprise Act 2002[26] where you supply or are supplied with 25% or more of the goods or services of a certain description[27]

30%   At 30% your agreements with undertakings that are not actual or potential competitors cease to benefit from the EU block exemption for vertical agreements[28], although there is some marginal relief up to 35%[29]

Your liner consortia agreements run into problems under Commission Regulation 906/2009 if your market share exceeds 30%, with some marginal relief of up to 10% (that is to say up to a market share of 33%)[30]

Block exemption ceases to be available for technology transfer agreements between non-competing undertakings where their combined market share exceeds 30%

At less than 30% your non-horizontal mergers are unlikely to give rise to any problems under the EU Merger Regulation; and there is no presumption against them where your market share is more than 30%[31]

40%   You may be dominant under Article 102 with a market share of 40% or more (there has been only one finding by the European Commission of dominance under Article 102 below 40%)[32]; if you are dominant, you have a special responsibility not to harm competition[33]

If your market share is below 40% the OFT considers it 'unlikely' that you are dominant[34]; the same point is made in the European Commission's *Guidance on the Commission's Enforcement Priorities in Applying Article [102 TFEU] to Abusive Exclusionary Conduct by Dominant Undertakings*[35]

There is unlikely to be a cumulative foreclosure effect arising from your exclusive purchasing agreements where all the companies at the retail level have market shares below 30% and the total tied market share is less than 40%[36]

45%

50%   There is a rebuttable presumption that, with 50% or more of the market, you have a dominant position[37]; this presumption applies in the case of collective dominance as well as single-firm dominance[38]

Where the market share of the 5 largest suppliers in a market is below 50%, and the market share of the largest supplier is below 30%, there is unlikely to be a single or cumulative anti-competitive effect arising from their agreements[39]

There is unlikely to be such an effect where the share of the market covered by selective distribution systems is less that 50%[40]

55%

60%

65%

70%

75%

80%   At 80% you may now be approaching a position of 'super-dominance', where you have a particularly special responsibility not to indulge in abusive behaviour[41]

85%

90%   At 90% you are approaching 'quasi-monopoly'[42]

In the European Commission's view it is unlikely that conduct that maintains, creates or strengthens a market position 'approaching that of monopoly' can normally be justified on the ground that it also creates efficiency gains[43]

95%

100%   At 100% you are a monopolist.

(Continued)

1 *Guidelines on the effect on trade concept* OJ [2004] C 101/81, para 52.

2 *Notice on agreements of minor importance* OJ [2001] C 368/13, para 8; the Commission's *Guidelines on Vertical Restraints* OJ [2010] C 130/1, paras 134 and 179; OFT Guideline *Agreements and concerted practices*, OFT 401, December 2004, para 2.16.

1.1 Table of market share thresholds (*Continued*)

3 *Guidelines on the effect on trade concept* OJ [2004] C 101/81, para 46.

4 Regulation 802/2004, OJ [2004] L 133/1, section 7.3.

5 OJ [2001] C 368/13, para 7; OFT Guideline *Agreements and concerted practices*, OFT 401, December 2004, para 2.16.

6 Commission's *Guidelines on Horizontal Cooperation Agreements* OJ [2011] C 11/1, para 208.

7 Ibid, para 240.

8 OJ [2001] C 368/13, para 7; OFT Guideline *Agreements and concerted practices*, OFT 401, December 2004, para 2.16.

9 See ch 21, 'Market Definition', pp 862–863.

10 See ch 21, 'Notifications', p 857.

11 Regulation 267/2010, OJ [2010] L 83/1, Article 6(2)(a).

12 Ibid, Article 6(5).

13 Ibid, Article 6(6).

14 Regulation 1218/2010, OJ [2010] L 335/43, Article 3.

15 Ibid, Article 5.

16 Regulation 772/2004, OJ [2004] L 123/11, Article 3(1).

17 Regulation 1217/2010, OJ [2010] L 335/36, Article 4.

18 Ibid, Article 7(d).

19 Ibid, Article 7(e).

20 Regulation 267/2010, OJ [2010] L 83/81, Article 6(2)(b).

21 Ibid, Article 6(8).

22 Ibid, Article 6(9).

23 Regulation 139/2004, OJ [2004] L 24/1, recital 32.

24 Ch 21, 'Notifications', p 857.

25 Ch 21, 'Market definition', pp 862–863.

26 See ch 22, 'The share of supply test', pp 922–923.

27 Note that the 'share of supply' test for referring a merger to the Competition Commission is not technically a market share test: see ch 22, 'The share of supply test', pp 922–933.

28 Regulation 330/2010, Article 3.

29 Ibid, Article 7(d)–(e).

30 Regulation 906/2009, OJ [2009] L 256/31, Articles 5(1) and 5(3).

31 *Guidelines on the assessment of non-horizontal mergers* OJ [2008] C 265/6, para 25.

32 See *Virgin/British Airways* OJ [2000] L 30/1, [2000] 4 CMLR 999: dominance at 39.7 per cent of the market, upheld on appeal Case T-219/99 *British Airways v Commission* [2003] ECR II-5917, [2004] 4 CMLR 1008.

33 On the special responsibility of dominant firms see ch 5, 'The "special responsibility" of dominant firms', pp 192–193.

34 OFT Guideline *Abuse of a dominant position*, OFT 402, December 2004, para 4.18 and *Assessment of market power*, OFT 415, para 2.12.

35 OJ [2009] C 45/7.

36 Commission's *Guidelines on Vertical Restraints* (p 34, n 176), para 141.

37 See Case C-62/86 *AKZO Chemie v Commission* [1991] ECR I-3359, [1993] 5 CMLR 215, para 60.

38 Case T-191/98 *Atlantic Container Line AB v Commission* [2003] ECR II-3275, [2005] 4 CMLR 1283, paras 931–932.

39 Commission's *Guidelines on Vertical Restraints*, para 135.

40 Ibid, para 179.

41 See ch 5, 'The emergence of super-dominance', pp 187–189.

42 Ibid, pp 187–189.

43 *Guidance on Article 102 Enforcement Priorities* OJ [2009] C 45/7, para 30.

2

Overview of EU and UK competition law

1. Introduction

This chapter will provide a brief overview of EU and UK competition law and the relevant institutions; it will also explain the relationship between EU competition law and the domestic competition laws of the Member States, in particular in the light of Article 3 of Regulation 1/2003[1]. The rules of the European Economic Area are briefly referred to, and the trend on the part of Member States to adopt domestic competition rules modelled on those in the EU is noted. Three diagrams at the end of the chapter explain the institutional structure of EU and UK competition law.

2. EU Law

(A) The Treaty on the Functioning of the European Union

The Rome Treaty of 1957[2] established what is now known as the European Union[3]. There are currently 27 Member States[4]. The Rome Treaty was renamed the Treaty on the Functioning

---

[1] Council Regulation 1/2003 on the implementation of the rules on competition laid down in Articles [101 and 102 TFEU] OJ [2003] L 1/1, available at www.ec.europa.eu.

[2] The Treaty of Paris of 1951 had earlier established a special regime for coal and steel which contained provisions dealing specifically with competition; this Treaty expired on 23 July 2002: it is discussed briefly in ch 23, 'Coal and Steel', p 967.

[3] The original name 'European Economic Community' was replaced by the 'European Community' by the Maastricht Treaty of 1992, which, in turn, was subsumed into the European Union by the Lisbon Treaty of 2009; it follows that references are now to EU, not to EC, competition law.

[4] As to the position of territories such as the Isle of Man and Gibraltar under EU Law see Murray *EU & Member State Territories – The Special Relationship under Community Law* (Palladian Law Publishing, 2004).

of the European Union ('TFEU') by the Lisbon Treaty[5] with effect from 1 December 2009. The Lisbon Treaty also renumbered the Treaty Articles and renamed various institutions; for example the Court of First Instance is now known as the General Court; as with the rest of this book, this chapter will use the post-Lisbon terminology.

The TFEU consists of 358 Articles. It is a complex document, the predecessors of which have generated a considerable body of jurisprudence[6]. Much of EU law is concerned with the elimination of obstacles to the free movement of goods, services, persons and capital; the removal of these obstacles in itself promotes competition within the Union. Initiatives such as the establishment of a public procurement regime[7], the creation of the Euro[8] and the 'EU 2020 Strategy'[9] with its emphasis on 'smart, sustainable and inclusive growth' also contribute substantially to greater competition within the European economy. However, quite apart from this 'macro' effect on competition, the TFEU also contains specific competition rules that apply to undertakings and to the Member States themselves.

(i) The competition chapter in the TFEU

EU competition law is contained in Chapter 1 of Title VII of Part Three of the TFEU, which consists of Articles 101 to 109. It is necessary to read these provisions in conjunction with the objectives and principles laid down in the TFEU and also the Treaty on European Union ('TEU'). Article 3(3) TEU provides that one of the EU's objectives is a highly competitive social market economy. Article 3(3) TEU also states that the EU is to establish an internal market, which, in accordance with Protocol 27 on the internal market and competition, annexed to the TEU and the TFEU, is to include a system ensuring that competition is not distorted. The Protocol has the same force as a Treaty provision[10]. The Lisbon Treaty repealed Article 3(1)(g) of the EC Treaty that established as one of the activities of the European Community the achievement of a system of undistorted competition. In *Konkurrensverket v TeliaSonera Sverige AB*[11] the Court of Justice referred to Article 3(3) TEU and Protocol 27 as though there was no difference from Article 3(1)(g) EC[12].

Article 3(1)(b) TFEU provides that the EU shall have exclusive competence in establishing the competition rules necessary for the functioning of the internal market. Article 119(1) TFEU provides that the activities of the Member States and the EU shall be conducted in accordance with the principle of an open market economy with free competition.

These references to competition in the TEU and the TFEU have a significant effect on the decisions of the European Commission ('the Commission'), and judgments of the General

---

[5] [2007] OJ C 306/1; on the Treaty reform process that led up to the Lisbon Treaty and its legal effects see Craig 'The Treaty of Lisbon, process, architecture and substance' (2008) 33 EL Rev 137.

[6] For comprehensive analysis of EU law in general see Wyatt and Dashwood's *European Union Law* (Hart Publishing, 6th ed, 2011, eds Dashwood, Dougan, Rodger, Spaventa and Wyatt); Chalmers, Hadjiemmanuil, Monti and Tomkins *European Union Law* (Cambridge University Press, 2006); Craig and de Búrca *EU Law: Texts, Cases, and Materials* (Oxford University Press, 4th ed, 2007).

[7] On public procurement see Bovis *EC Public Procurement: Case Law and Regulation* (Oxford University Press, 2005); Arrowsmith *The Law of Public and Utilities Procurement* (Sweet & Maxwell, 2nd ed, 2005); Trepte *Public Procurement in the EU* (Oxford University Press, 2nd ed, 2007); Graells *Public Procurement and the EU Competition Rules* (Hart Publishing, 2011).

[8] On the Euro see Herdegen 'Price Stability and Budgetary Restraints in Economic and Monetary Union: the Law as Guardian of Economic Wisdom' (1998) 35 CML Rev 9; Louis 'A Legal and Institutional Approach for Building a Monetary Union' (1998) 35 CML Rev 33; Swann *The Economics of Europe* (Penguin Books, 9th ed, 2000), ch 7; see further 'Economic and monetary union', p 52 below.

[9] See *Europe 2020* COM(2010) 2020 final; see also *A Pro-active Competition Policy for a Competitive Europe* COM(2004)293 final, both available at www.ec.europa.eu.

[10] See Article 51 TEU.

[11] Case C-52/09 [2011] ECR I-000.   [12] Ibid, paras 20–22.

Court and the Court of Justice (together, 'the EU Courts'), which have often interpreted the specific competition rules teleologically from the starting point of what are now Articles 3(3) TEU and Protocol 27[13]. Within Chapter 1 of Title VII of Part Three of the TFEU, Article 101(1) prohibits agreements, decisions by associations of undertakings and concerted practices that have as their object or effect the restriction of competition[14], although this prohibition may be declared inapplicable where the conditions in Article 101(3) are satisfied[15]. Article 102 prohibits the abuse by an undertaking or undertakings of a dominant position[16]. Article 106(1) imposes obligations on Member States in relation to the Treaty generally and the competition rules specifically, while Article 106(2) concerns the application of the competition rules to public undertakings and private undertakings to which a Member State entrusts particular responsibilities[17]. Articles 107 to 109 prohibit state aid to undertakings by Member States which might distort competition in the internal market[18]. An important additional instrument of EU competition law is the EU Merger Regulation ('the EUMR') which applies to concentrations between undertakings that have a Community dimension[19].

(ii) The single market imperative

As mentioned in chapter 1[20], it is important to stress that EU competition law is applied by the Commission and the EU Courts very much with the issue of single market integration in mind. The single market has been described by the Commission as one of the 'EU's biggest assets'[21] which it is determined to protect[22]. Agreements and conduct which might have the effect of dividing the territory of one Member State from another will be closely scrutinised and may be severely punished. The existence of 'single market' competition rules as well as 'conventional' competition rules is a unique feature of EU competition law. The fact that ten further countries acceded to the European Union on 1 May 2004 and two more on 1 January 2007, together with the possibility of future accessions, for example by some of the Balkan states and Turkey, means that single market integration is likely to remain a key feature of competition policy[23]. The arrival of the economic crisis in 2008 reinforced the Commission's determination to act as guardian of the single market; or, to put the point another way, to prevent a retreat into economic nationalism[24]. The Court of Justice reaffirmed the importance of the single market imperative in *GlaxoSmithKline Services Unlimited v Commission*[25].

---

[13] For examples of teleological interpretation of the competition rules see Cases C-68/94 and 30/95 *France v Commission* [1998] ECR I-1375, [1998] 4 CMLR 829, paras 169–178; Case T-102/96 *Gencor v Commission* [1999] ECR II-753, [1999] 4 CMLR 971, paras 148–158; Case T-99/04 *AC-Treuhand AG v Commission* [2008] ECR II-1501, [2008] 5 CMLR 962, paras 124–150.

[14] On Article 101(1) see ch 3.   [15] On Article 101(3) see ch 4.

[16] On Article 102 see chs 5, 17 and 18.   [17] On Article 106 see ch 6, 'Article 106', pp 222–244.

[18] Articles 107–109 are briefly discussed in ch 6, 'Articles 107 to 109 TFEU – State Aids', pp 246–247.

[19] Council Regulation 139/2004 on the control of concentrations between undertakings, OJ [2004] L 24/1; on the EUMR see ch 21.

[20] See ch 1, 'The single market imperative', pp 23–24.

[21] See the Commission's *Report on Competition Policy* (2009), para 9, available at www.ec.europa.eu.

[22] See eg Commission's *Guidelines on Vertical Restraints* OJ [2010] C 130/1, para 7; on the Commission's approach to vertical agreements see ch 16, 'The methodology for the analysis of vertical agreements in the Commission's *Vertical guidelines*', pp 631–637.

[23] For details of the progress of talks on future enlargement of the Union see www.ec.europa.eu/enlargement.

[24] See eg Speech of Commissioner Kroes of 11 May 2007 and Monti *A New Strategy for the Single Market – Report to the European Commission*, 9 May 2010, available at www.ec.europa.eu.

[25] Cases C-501/06 P etc [2009] ECR I-9291, [2010] 4 CMLR 50, paras 59–61.

(iii) Economic and monetary union

The creation of the Euro has an important influence on competition within the EU[26]. As explained in chapter 1 the competitive process depends, amongst other things, on consumers having adequate information to enable them to make rational choices[27]. Price comparisons are difficult when the same goods and services are sold in different, variable currencies; the problem is compounded by the cost of exchanging money. The Euro brings a transparency to price information that fundamentally transforms the position, and has a considerable impact on the way in which business is conducted. There are also moves towards the establishment of a 'Single Euro Payments Area' which would improve the efficiency of Euro payments[28].

(iv) The modernisation of EU competition law

During the course of the 1990s it became apparent that many aspects of EU competition law were in need of modernisation; in particular the law on vertical agreements, on horizontal cooperation agreements and on the obtaining of 'individual exemptions' under Article 101(3) TFEU were perceived by many people, including Commission officials, to be in need of radical reform. Proposals for reform were set out in 1998[29], and the modernisation programme gathered pace in 1999 and 2000[30]. There followed the reform of the vertical agreements regime[31], which involved a major repositioning of the law and economics of the subject and which has worked well in practice. Numerous other policy initiatives followed: a transformation of the Commission's approach to horizontal cooperation agreements[32], a new regime for technology transfer agreements[33], and considerable reform of the EUMR[34]. Even more radically, with effect from 1 May 2004 the way in which Articles 101 and 102 are applied in practice was fundamentally changed as a result of the entry into force of Regulation 1/2003[35]; in particular this Regulation abolished the system of notifying agreements to the Commission for individual exemption under Article 101(3), and removed the Commission's monopoly over the application of that provision to individual agreements[36]. This was followed, in 2009, by the publication of *Guidance on the Commission's Enforcement Priorities in Applying Article [102 TFEU] to Abusive Exclusionary Conduct by Dominant Undertakings*[37], an important contribution to an understanding of that difficult subject. There is no question that these are major changes in the direction of competition law and policy in the EU.

---

[26] See eg the Commission's XXVIIth *Report on Competition Policy* (1997), pp 7–8 and XXVIIIth *Report on Competition Policy* (1998), pp 24–25.

[27] See ch 1, 'The model of perfect competition is based on assumptions unlikely to be observed in practice', p 7.

[28] See Directive 2007/64/EC of the European Parliament and of the Council on payment services in the internal market, OJ [2007] L 319/1, available at www.ec.europa.eu/internal_market; see also the Staff Working Paper accompanying the Commission's *Report on Competition Policy* (2009), paras 229–233.

[29] See eg Schaub 'EC Competition System – Proposals for Reform' [1998] Fordham Corporate Law Institute (ed Hawk), ch 9; see also Ehlermann 'The Modernisation of EC Antitrust Policy: A Legal and Cultural Revolution' (2000) 37 CML Rev 537.

[30] See the Commission's XXIXth *Report on Competition Policy* (1999), points 8–42.

[31] See ch 16, 'Vertical Agreements: Regulation 330/2010', pp 649–672.

[32] See ch 15, 'Research and Development Agreements', pp 592–599.

[33] See ch 19, 'Technology Transfer Agreements: Regulation 772/2004', pp 781–791.

[34] See ch 21 generally.

[35] See ch 2, n 1 above; Regulation 1/2003 is discussed at 'Regulation 1/2003', pp 76–79 below, and further in ch 4, 'Regulation 1/2003', pp 166–168 and in ch 7 generally.

[36] The system of block exemptions continues: see ch 4, 'Block Exemptions', pp 168–172.

[37] OJ [2009] C 45/7; see ch 5, 'The Commission's *Guidance on Article 102 Enforcement Priorities*', pp 174–177.

(B) **Institutions**[38]

(i) Council of the European Union

The supreme legislative body of the European Union is the Council of the European Union, often referred to as the Council of Ministers[39]. The Council is not involved in competition policy on a regular basis. However, acting under powers conferred by Articles 103 and 352 TFEU, the Council has adopted several major pieces of legislation, including the EUMR; it has delegated important powers to the Commission through regulations to enforce the competition rules in the TFEU, in particular Regulation 1/2003[40]; and it has given the Commission power to grant block exemptions in respect of certain agreements caught by Article 101(1) but which satisfy the criteria of Article 101(3)[41].

(ii) European Commission

The European Commission in Brussels is at the core of EU competition policy[42] and is responsible for fact-finding, taking action against infringements of the law, imposing penalties, adopting block exemption regulations, conducting sectoral inquiries, investigating mergers and state aids, and for developing policy and legislative initiatives. The Commission is also involved in the international aspects of competition policy, including cooperation with competition authorities around the world[43]. One of the Commissioners takes special responsibility for competition matters; this is regarded as one of the most important portfolios within the Commission, and confers upon the incumbent a high public profile. Certain decisions can be taken by the Commissioner for Competition rather than by the College of Commissioners. There are two Hearing Officers[44], directly responsible to the Commissioner, who are responsible for ensuring that the rights of the defence are respected in proceedings under Articles 101 and 102 and the EUMR and that draft decisions of the Commission take due account of the relevant facts[45].

DG COMP is the Directorate of the Commission specifically responsible for competition policy. DG COMP's website is an invaluable source of material. From the index page it is possible to navigate to a series of policy areas, including antitrust (that is to say Articles 101 and 102, though there is a specific area for cartels), mergers, state aid, liberalisation, and international matters[46]. Within each policy area there is a 'What's new' section as well as relevant legislation, draft legislation and details of current and decided cases; there is also useful statistical information. The website also leads to information about specific sectors such as agriculture and food, consumer goods, energy and financial services. The website also has a page dedicated to providing consumers with information about competition policy[47]. There is information about the Commissioner for Competition Policy, the composition of DG COMP and the European Competition Network ('the ECN'), which consists of the Commission and the 27 national competition authorities of the Member

---

[38] The institutional structure of EU and UK law is set out in diagrammatic form at the end of this chapter: see Figs 2.1, 2.2 and 2.3, pp 79–81 below.

[39] See Article 16 TEU and Articles 237–243 TFEU.

[40] On the Commission's powers of enforcement see ch 7.

[41] See ch 4, '*Vires* and block exemptions currently in force', pp 169–171.

[42] See Article 17(1) TEU; see also Case C-344/98 *Masterfoods Ltd v HB Ice Cream Ltd* [2001] ECR I-11369, [2001] 4 CMLR 449, para 46.

[43] On the international dimension of competition policy see ch 12.

[44] See www.ec.europa.eu/competition/hearing_officers/index_en.html.

[45] On the role of the Hearing Officers see ch 7, 'The conduct of proceedings', pp 284–285.

[46] See www.ec.europa.eu/comm/competition/index_en.html.

[47] See www.ec.europa.eu/competition/consumers/index_en.html.

States who are jointly responsible for the enforcement of Articles 101 and 102[48]. The ECN publishes an *ECN Brief*, which is published five times a year, summarising its work and that of its members[49]. Press Releases about competition policy matters can be accessed through the website, as can speeches of the Commissioner and officials of DG COMP, policy documents and the *Competition Policy Newsletter*, which is published three times a year. It is easy to follow the progress of public consultations through the website, and forthcoming Commission events of relevance to competition policy are announced there.

DG COMP publishes an *Annual Management Plan* in which it sets out its key objectives for the year ahead[50]. The Commission's *Annual Report on Competition Policy* provides essential information on matters of both policy and enforcement, as well as a statistical review of DG COMP's activities[51]. DG COMP's website also has links to other important sites, including those of the EU Courts and the national competition authorities.

DG COMP has a Director General and three Deputy Directors General. There is also a Chief Competition Economist who reports directly to the Director General. DG COMP is divided into nine administrative units. Directorate A is responsible for policy and strategy, including the ECN, for international relations and for consumer liaison. Directorates B to F are the operational units, each with responsibility for particular sectors, which conduct cases under Articles 101 and 102 and the EUMR, other than cartel cases, from start to finish; they also deal with state aid cases. Directorate G is exclusively concerned with cartels, the detection and eradication of which is a major priority of the Commission[52]. Directorate H is responsible for cohesion and enforcement issues arising in relation to state aid. Directorate R is responsible for the registry and for resources. Formal decisions of the Commission must be vetted by the Legal Service of the Commission, with which DG COMP works closely. The Legal Service represents the Commission in proceedings before the EU Courts[53]. An organigramme showing the composition of DG COMP can be accessed on its website[54].

(iii) General Court[55]

Actions for annulment of Commission decisions in competition cases (including cases on state aid) are brought in the first instance before the General Court[56]. The General Court must assess the legality of decisions according to the provisions of the TFEU[57]. Member States' actions used to be taken to the Court of Justice as happened, for example, in the case of *France v Commission*[58], an important judgment which established, amongst other things, that the EUMR was capable of application to collective dominance[59]; however since the Nice Treaty all actions for annulment of Commission decisions, including those

---

[48] See ch 7, 'Case allocation under Regulation 1/2003', p 289.

[49] See www.ec.europa.eu/competition/ecn/brief/index.html.

[50] See www.ec.europa.eu/dgs/competition/index_en.htm.

[51] This can be found at www.ec.europa.eu/comm/competition/annual_reports.

[52] On cartels see ch 13 generally.

[53] For details of the Legal Service see www.ec.europa.eu/dgs/legal_service/index_en.htm.

[54] See www.ec.europa.eu/dgs/competition/directory/organi_en.pdf.

[55] See the *Codified version of the Rules of Procedure of the General Court* OJ [2010] C 177/37; on the General Court see Kerse and Khan *EC Antitrust Procedure* (Sweet & Maxwell, 5th ed, 2005), paras 1.58–1.60

[56] On the types of action that can be brought see ch 7, 'Judicial Review', pp 290–294.

[57] See Article 261 (penalties); Article 263 (actions for annulment); Article 265 (failures to act) for a general account see Vesterdorf 'Judicial Review in EC Competition Law: Reflections on the Role of the Community Courts in the EC System of Competition Law Enforcement' (2005) 1 Competition Policy International 3.

[58] Cases C-68/94 and 30/95 [1998] ECR I-1375, [1998] 4 CMLR 829; on collective dominance see ch 14, 'Article 102 and Collective Dominance', pp 571–582 and ch 21, 'The dominance/SLC debate', p 864.

[59] See further ch 21, 'The dominance/SLC debate', p 864.

brought by Member States, are taken to the General Court. It can happen that substantially similar matters are before both the General Court and the Court of Justice simultaneously, in which case it is likely that the General Court will suspend its proceedings pending the judgment of the Court of Justice: this happened, for example, in the case of the 'Irish ice-cream war', where the General Court stayed the appeal of Van den Bergh Foods Ltd against the Commission's decision finding infringements of Articles 101 and 102[60] pending the outcome of the Article 267 reference from the Irish Supreme Court in the case of *Masterfoods Ltd v HB Ice Cream Ltd*[61].

The website of the General Court (and of the Court of Justice) is an invaluable source of material where, for example, recent judgments of the Courts, opinions of the Advocates General of the Court of Justice and information about pending cases can be found; statistics on judicial activity; and there is also an Annual Report and a bibliography listing literature on the case law of the EU Courts[62]. The rules of the General Court were amended in December 2000 to provide for the possibility of a 'fast-track' or 'expedited' procedure for appeals in certain cases[63]; the expedited procedure has been used in several cases under the EUMR[64] and in an appeal against a commitment decision adopted by the Commission under Article 9 of Regulation 1/2003[65].

(iv) Court of Justice[66]

The Court of Justice hears appeals from the General Court on points of law only. The Court of Justice has been strict about what is meant by an appeal on a point of law, and it will not get drawn into factual disputes[67]. The Court also deals with points of law referred to it by national courts under Article 267 TFEU[68]. As mentioned above, the Court's website contains much useful material. The Court of Justice is assisted by an Advocate General, drawn from a panel of eight, who delivers an opinion on each case that comes before it. Although not binding, this opinion is frequently followed by the Court of Justice, and is often more cogent than the judgment of the Court of Justice itself which may be delphic, particularly where it represents a compromise between the judges (no dissenting judgments are given by the EU Courts). Anyone interested in competition law is strongly recommended to read the opinions of the Advocates General in competition cases, which are frequently of very high quality and contain a large amount of invaluable research material.

---

[60] *Van den Bergh Foods Ltd* OJ [1998] L 246/1, [1998] 5 CMLR 530, on appeal Case T-65/98 *Van den Bergh Foods v Commission* [2003] ECR II-4653, [2004] 4 CMLR 14; the final Order disposing of this issue was made by the Court of Justice in 2006: Case C-552/03 P, [2006] ECR I-9091, [2006] 5 CMLR 1494.

[61] Case C-344/98 [2000] ECR I-11369, [2001] 4 CMLR 449.   [62] See www.curia.europa.eu.

[63] OJ [2000] L 322/4, Article 76(a); the expedited procedure came into force on 1 February 2001.

[64] See ch 21, 'Appeals against the Commission's refusal to take jurisdiction', p 895.

[65] See ch 7, 'Article 9: practical considerations', p 258.

[66] See the *Codified version of the Rules of Procedure of the Court of Justice* OJ [2010] C 177/1; on the Court of Justice see *Kerse and Khan* (ch 2, n 55 above), paras 1.55–1.57; Arnull *The European Union and its Court of Justice* (Oxford EC Law Library, 2nd ed, 2006); Neville Brown and Kennedy *The Court of Justice of the European Communities* (Sweet & Maxwell, 5th ed, 2000); Lasok *The European Court of Justice: Practice and Procedure* (Butterworths, 3rd ed, 2003); Barents 'The Court of Justice after the Treaty of Lisbon' (2010) 47 CML Rev 709.

[67] See eg Case C-7/95 P *John Deere v Commission* [1998] ECR I-3111, [1998] 5 CMLR 311, paras 17–22; Case C-551/03 P *General Motors BV v Commission* [2006] ECR I-3173, [2006] 5 CMLR 1, paras 50–51.

[68] On the Article 267 reference procedure see Anderson *References to the European Court* (Sweet & Maxwell, 2nd ed, 2002); *Kerse and Khan* (ch 2, n 55 above) para 1.57; Collins *European Community Law in the United Kingdom* (Butterworths, 5th ed, 2003); Hartley *The Foundations of European Community Law* (Oxford University Press, 7th ed, 2010), ch 9.

The EU Courts are sometimes over-stretched, and there can be considerable delays in some cases[69]. The Court of Justice published a document in May 1999 setting out proposals to deal with some of the problems it experiences[70]. Article 257 TFEU provides that the European Parliament and the Council may establish specialised courts attached to the General Court to deal with specific types of cases. However, in March 2011, the Court of Justice concluded that an increase in the number of judges of the General Court was 'clearly preferable' to the establishment of a specialised court[71]. This conclusion chimes with that of the House of Lords European Union Committee[72].

(v) Advisory Committee on Restrictive Practices and Dominant Positions

The Advisory Committee on Restrictive Practices and Dominant Positions consists of officials from the national competition authorities of the Member States[73]. They attend oral hearings, consider draft decisions of the Commission and comment on them[74]; they also discuss draft legislation and the development of policy generally. This Committee also deals with certain matters in the maritime and air transport sectors and in relation to the insurance sector[75].

(vi) Advisory Committee on Concentrations

The Advisory Committee on Concentrations consists of officials from the national competition authorities of the Member States; they attend oral hearings and must be consulted on draft decisions of the Commission under the EUMR[76].

(vii) National courts

National courts are increasingly asked to apply the EU competition rules, which are directly applicable and may be invoked by natural and legal persons (both as defendant and as claimant)[77]. The Commission maintains on its website a database of some of the judgments given by the courts of the Member States on the application of Articles 101 and 102 TFEU in the original language arranged in a chronological order[78]. An Association

---

[69] See Case C-385/07 P *Duales System Deutschland v Commission* [2009] ECR I-6155, [2009] 5 CMLR 2215, paras 180–195 (competition proceedings before the General Court did not satisfy the principle that cases should be dealt with within a reasonable time).

[70] Press Release 36/99, 28 May 1999; see also the discussion paper of the President of the Court of Justice 'The Future of the Judicial System of the European Union' and 'The EC Court of Justice and the Institutional Reform of the European Union' (April 2000), both of which can be found at www.curia.europa.eu; see Vesterdorf 'The Community Court System Ten Years from Now and Beyond: Challenges and Possibilities' (2003) 28 EL Rev 303.

[71] See draft *Amendments to the Statute of the Court of Justice of the European Union and to Annex I thereto* (proposing to increase the number of General Court judges from 27 to 39), available at www.curia.europa.eu.

[72] See 14th Report of Session 2010–11 *The Workload of the Court of Justice of the European Union*, HL Paper 128, paras 135–136; see also 15th Report of Session 2006–2007, *An EU Competition Court*, HL Paper 75, recommending against the creation of a specialist competition court, a recommendation with which the UK Government agreed, available at www.parliament.uk.

[73] Provision is made for this Committee by Article 14 of Regulation 1/2003; on this Committee see ch 7, 'Article 14: Advisory Committee', p 264.

[74] On consulting the Advisory Committee see Case T-66/01 *Imperial Chemical Industries v Commission* [2010] ECR II-000, paras 163–171.

[75] See Regulation 1/2003, Articles 38, 41 and 42.

[76] See Council Regulation 139/2004, Article 19(3)–(7); on this Committee see ch 21, 'Close and constant liaison with Member States', pp 885–886.

[77] On the position of national courts see ch 8 generally.

[78] See www.ec.europa.eu/competition/elojade/antitrust/nationalcourts/.

of European Competition Law Judges has been established aimed at bringing together members of the judiciary of the Member States[79].

(viii) Parliament and ECOSOC

The European Parliament – in particular its Standing Committee on Economic and Monetary Matters – and the Economic and Social Committee ('ECOSOC'), are consulted on matters of competition policy and may be influential, for example, in the legislative process or in persuading the Commission to take action in relation to a particular issue.

(C) European Economic Area

On 21 October 1991 what is now the EU and its Member States and the Member States of the European Free Trade Association ('EFTA') signed an Agreement to establish the European Economic Area ('the EEA')[80]; it consists of the Member States of the EU, Norway, Iceland and Liechtenstein. The referendum in Switzerland on joining the EEA led to a 'no' vote, so that that signatory country remains outside. The EEA Agreement entered into force in 1994. It includes rules on competition which follow closely the TFEU and the EUMR. Article 101 on anti-competitive agreements appears as Article 53 of the EEA Agreement; Article 102 on the abuse of a dominant position is mirrored in Article 54; the EUMR is reflected in Article 57; and Article 106 on public undertakings and Article 107 on state aids appear as Articles 59 and 61 of the Agreement respectively.

The EEA Agreement and its associated texts establish a 'twin pillar' approach to jurisdiction: there are two authorities responsible for competition policy, the European Commission and the EFTA Surveillance Authority ('the ESA')[81], but any particular case will be investigated by only one of them. Article 108 of the EEA Agreement established the ESA; it mirrors the European Commission and is vested with similar powers. The ESA is subject to review by the EFTA Court of Justice[82], which sits in Luxembourg. Article 55 of the Agreement provides that the European Commission or the ESA shall ensure the application of Articles 53 and 54; Article 56 of the Agreement deals with the attribution of jurisdiction between these two bodies in cases caught by these Articles[83]; Article 57 provides for the division of competence in respect of mergers.

An important principle of the EEA Agreement is that there should be cooperation between the European Commission and the ESA, in order to develop and maintain uniform surveillance throughout the EEA and in order to promote a homogeneous implementation, application and interpretation of the provisions of the Agreement. Article 58

---

[79] The website of the AECLJ is www.aeclj.com.

[80] OJ [1994] L 1/1; the agreement entered into force on 1 January 1994; see Stragier 'The Competition Rules of the EEA Agreement and Their Implementation' (1993) 14 ECLR 30; Diem 'EEA Competition Law' (1994) 15 ECLR 263; see also Blanchet, Piiponen and Wetman-Clément *The Agreement on the European Economic Area (EEA)* (Clarendon Press, 1999); Forman 'The EEA Agreement Five Years On: Dynamic Homogeneity in Practice and Its Implementation by the Two EEA Courts' (1999) 36 CML Rev 751; Blanco *EC Competition Procedure* (Oxford University Press, 2nd ed, 2006), ch 28; Broberg *The European Commission's Jurisdiction to Scrutinise Mergers* (Kluwer International, 3rd ed, 2006), ch 7.

[81] The website of the ESA is www.eftasurv.int.

[82] The EFTA States signed an *Agreement on the Establishment of a Surveillance Authority and a Court of Justice* on 2 May 1992: it is reproduced in (1992) 15 Commercial Laws of Europe, Part 10; the Court of Justice delivered two Advisory Opinions on these arrangements: Opinion 1/91 [1991] ECR I-6079, [1992] 1 CMLR 245; and Opinion 1/92 [1992] ECR I-2821, [1992] 2 CMLR 217; the website of the EFTA Court is www.eftacourt.int.

[83] The division of competences between the European Commission and the ESA was considered in Cases T-67/00 etc *JFE Engineering Corp v Commission* [2004] ECR II-2501, [2005] 4 CMLR 27, paras 482–493.

requires the authorities to cooperate, in accordance with specific provisions contained in Protocol 23 (dealing with restrictive practices and the abuse of market power) and Protocol 24 (dealing with mergers). Similarly Article 106 of the Agreement establishes a system for the exchange of information between the two courts with a view to achieving a uniform interpretation of its terms.

(D) Modelling of domestic competition law on Articles 101 and 102[84]

The Member States of the EU and the EEA now have systems of competition law modelled to a greater or lesser extent upon Articles 101 and 102[85]. An easy way of accessing the websites, and the national laws, of the national competition authorities is through a hyperlink provided by DG COMP[86]. Another simple way of doing so is through the website of the Global Competition Forum[87].

The so-called 'Europe Agreements' between the EU and the countries of central and eastern Europe were part of the framework for implementation of the accession process towards full membership of the EU. Since the accessions of many of those countries in 2004 and 2006 there are no remaining Europe Agreements[88]. The establishment of the 'Union for the Mediterranean' means that countries on the Mediterranean coast from Algeria to Turkey are parties to Euro-Mediterranean Association Agreements containing provisions based on the EU competition rules[89].

3. UK Law

The Competition Act 1998 and the Enterprise Act 2002 fundamentally changed both the substantive provisions and the institutional architecture of the domestic competition law

---

[84] See generally Gerber *Law and Competition in Twentieth Century Europe: Protecting Prometheus* (Clarendon Press, 1998), ch X; Maher 'Alignment of Competition Laws in the European Community' (1996) 16 Oxford Yearbook of European Law 223; *European Competition Laws: A Guide to the EC and its Member States* (Matthew Bender, 2002, ed Fine); Geradin and Henry 'Competition Law in the new Member States: Where do we come from? Where do we go?' in *Modernisation and Enlargement: Two Major Challenges for EC Competition Law* (Intersentia, 2005); *A Practical Guide to National Competition Rules Across Europe* (Kluwer, 2nd ed, 2007, eds Holmes and Davey).

[85] For some sceptical comments on the alignment of the domestic competition laws of the Member States see Ullrich 'Harmonisation within the European Union' (1996) 17 ECLR 178.

[86] www.ec.europa.eu/comm/competition/nca/index_en.html.

[87] www.globalcompetitionforum.org/europe.htm.

[88] See www.ec.europa.eu/enlargement/glossary/terms/europe-agreement_en.htm; it is possible in principle for agreements between the EU and third countries to have direct effect: see Case 104/81 *Hauptzollamt Mainz v Kupferburg* [1982] ECR 3641, [1983] 1 CMLR 1; Case C-192/89 *Sevince v Staatssecretaris van Justitie* [1990] ECR I-3461, [1992] 2 CMLR 57 and Wyatt and Dashwood's *European Union Law*, pp 953–955; however there has yet to be a judgment on whether the competition rules in the Europe Agreements themselves have direct effect; on one occasion the Commission required amendments to Chanel's distribution agreements to remove restrictions on exports to countries with which the EU had negotiated 'Free Trade Agreements', but this was done by agreement and without a reasoned decision on the part of the Commission: *Chanel* OJ [1994] C 334/11, [1995] 4 CMLR 108.

[89] See Communication from the Commission to the European Parliament and the Council *Barcelona Process: Union for the Mediterranean* COM(2008) 319 final, 20 May 2008, available at www.ec.europa.eu/euromed/index_en.htm; Hakura 'The Extension of EC Competition Law to the Mediterranean Region' (1998) 19 ECLR 204; Geradin and Petit 'Competition Policy and the Euro-Mediterranean Partnership' (2003) 8 European Foreign Affairs Review 153; Geradin *Competition Law and Regional Integration: An Analysis of the Southern Mediterranean Countries* (The World Bank, 2004).

of the UK; in the course of this reform a raft of old legislation[90] was swept away. A further key piece of legislation is the Competition Act 1998 and Other Enactments (Amendment) Regulations 2004[91] which brought UK law into conformity with the principles of Regulation 1/2003. In March 2011 the Government began a consultation exercise considering the case for introducing further changes to various aspects of domestic law and in particular the institutional architecture: it is possible that the Office of Fair Trading ('the OFT') and the Competition Commission ('the CC') will be merged to create a new Competition and Markets Authority[92]. Developments following this consultation will be explained on the Online Resource Centre[93].

(A) Competition Act 1998

The Competition Act 1998 received the Royal Assent on 9 November 1998; the main provisions entered into force on 1 March 2000. The Act contains two prohibitions. The so-called 'Chapter I prohibition' is modelled on Article 101 TFEU, and forbids agreements, decisions by associations of undertakings and concerted practices that have as their object or effect the restriction of competition[94]. The Chapter II prohibition in the Competition Act is modelled on Article 102 TFEU and forbids the abuse of a dominant position[95]. The Act gives to the OFT wide powers to obtain information, to carry out on-the-spot investigations, to adopt decisions and to impose penalties on undertakings[96]. In relation to certain sectors such as electronic communications and energy the powers of the OFT are shared concurrently with the relevant regulator, such as the Office of Communications[97]. As 'public authorities' the bodies invested with powers to enforce the Competition Act are obliged under section 6 of the Human Rights Act 1998 (which received the Royal Assent on the same day as the Competition Act) to apply the legislation in a manner that is compatible with the European Convention for the Protection of Human Rights and Fundamental Freedoms of 1950. In competition law the right to a fair trial (Article 6(1) of the Convention), the presumption of innocence (Article 6(2)), the right to respect for private life (Article 8) and the right to peaceful enjoyment of possessions (Article 1 of the First Protocol) are of particular significance[98]. Section 60 of the Competition Act contains provisions designed to maintain consistency between the application of EU and domestic competition law; however this is subject to limitations, in particular with the result that judgments of the EU Courts motivated by single market considerations will not necessarily be followed in the UK[99].

---

[90] In particular the competition provisions in the Fair Trading Act 1973, the Restrictive Trade Practices Act 1976, the Resale Prices Act 1976 and the Competition Act 1980; note that section 11 of the Competition Act 1980, which provides for 'efficiency audits' of public-sector bodies, remains in force but has not been used for many years.

[91] SI 2004/1261.

[92] See *A Competition Regime for Growth: A Consultation on Options for Reform*, available at www.bis.gov.uk.

[93] www.oxfordtextbooks.co.uk/orc/whishandbailey7e.

[94] See ch 9, 'The Chapter I Prohibition', pp 327–353.

[95] See ch 9, 'The Chapter II Prohibition', pp 353–362.

[96] On the enforcement powers under the 1998 Act see ch 10.

[97] On concurrency see ch 10, 'Concurrency', pp 424–426.

[98] See further ch 10, 'Human Rights Act 1998 and Police and Criminal Evidence Act 1984', pp 400–401.

[99] See ch 9, '"Governing Principles Clause": Section 60 of the Competition Act 1998', pp 362–367.

(B) Enterprise Act 2002

The Enterprise Act 2002 received the Royal Assent on 7 November 2002; the main provisions entered into force on 20 June 2003. The Enterprise Act is a major piece of legislation that amends domestic competition law in a number of ways[100].

First, the Act effected a number of reforms to the institutional architecture of the domestic system. It abolished the office of Director General of Fair Trading[101] and created a new corporate body, the OFT[102]: the OFT has a variety of functions under the Competition Act and the Enterprise Act, including those formerly exercised by the Director General of Fair Trading[103]. The Act conferred on the CC the final decision-making role in relation to merger and market investigations[104]. The Act created the Competition Appeal Tribunal ('the CAT'), that has appellate and judicial review functions[105]. The Act also diminished substantially the powers of the Secretary of State to make decisions in competition law cases[106].

Secondly, the Act contained new provisions for the investigation of mergers and markets[107]. Thirdly, the Enterprise Act supplemented and reinforced the Competition Act 1998 in various ways, in particular by introducing a new and separate criminal 'cartel offence' which, on indictment, can lead to the imprisonment of individuals for up to five years and/or a fine of an unlimited amount[108]; by providing for company director disqualification for directors who knew or ought to have known of competition law infringements committed by their companies[109]; and by facilitating private competition law actions[110].

(C) Changes to domestic law as a result of Regulation 1/2003

The adoption of Regulation 1/2003 required or made desirable a number of changes to the Competition Act 1998. Section 209 of the Enterprise Act 2002, in conjunction with section 2(2) of the European Communities Act 1972, gave the Secretary of State power, by statutory instrument, to make such modifications as may be appropriate for the purpose of eliminating or reducing any differences between the Competition Act and EU competition law. The Competition Act 1998 and Other Enactments (Amendment) Regulations 2004[111] effected a number of changes to the Competition Act and to various other enactments pursuant to Regulation 1/2003; in particular they repealed the provisions in the Competition Act on the notification to the OFT of agreements and/or conduct for guidance and/or a decision. In December 2004 the OFT reissued most of the Competition Act

---

[100] A summary of the main provisions in the Enterprise Act can be found in an OFT publication *Overview of the Enterprise Act: the competition and consumer provisions* OFT 518, June 2003; it is available on the OFT's website, www.oft.gov.uk; see also Graham 'The Enterprise Act 2002 and Competition Law' (2004) 67 MLR 273.

[101] Enterprise Act 2002, s 2(2).   [102] Ibid, s 1(1).

[103] Ibid, s 2(1); see 'Functions of the OFT', pp 65–66 below.

[104] See further 'Competition Commission', pp 69–72 below and ch 22 (merger investigations) and ch 11 (market investigations).

[105] See further 'Competition Appeal Tribunal', pp 72–74 below; note that, prior to the Enterprise Act, the Competition Act 1998 had created a Competition Commission Appeals Tribunal within the CC: its functions were transferred by the 2002 Act to the CAT.

[106] See further ch 22, '"Public Interest Cases", "Other Special Cases" and Mergers in the Water Industry', pp 956–961.

[107] See further ch 22 (merger investigations) and ch 11 (market investigations); these provisions replaced the merger and monopoly provisions formerly contained in the Fair Trading Act 1973.

[108] See ch 10, 'Penalties', pp 410–424.

[109] See ch 10, 'Grounds for disqualification', p 435.

[110] See ch 8, 'Damages Actions in the UK Courts', pp 306–319.   [111] SI 2004/1261.

guidelines that had originally been published in 2000 in order to reflect the changes in law and practice flowing from Regulation 1/2003[112]. The OFT's Rules were also amended in 2004[113]; and the exclusion of vertical agreements from the Chapter I prohibition of the Competition Act was repealed in order to bring domestic law into line with EU law[114].

(D) Institutions[115]

Competition law in the UK assigns roles to the Secretary of State for Business, Innovation and Skills, the Lord Chancellor, the OFT, the Serious Fraud Office (or, in Scotland, the Lord Advocate), the sectoral regulators, the CC, the CAT and to the civil and criminal courts. The competition authorities are also subject to scrutiny by the National Audit Office and by parliamentary bodies, including the Treasury Committee, the Business Innovations and Skills Committee and the Public Accounts Committee of the House of Commons and the European Union Committee of the House of Lords.

(i) Secretary of State and the Department for Business, Innovation and Skills

The Secretary of State for Business, Innovation and Skills has various functions under the Competition Act 1998 and the Enterprise Act 2002. In the exercise of these functions he is assisted by a Parliamentary Under-Secretary of State for Employment Relations, Consumer and Postal Affairs whose portfolio includes competition issues. Within the Department for Business, Innovation and Skills there is a Consumer and Competition Policy Directorate. The Department's website provides information and guidance on aspects of competition law and policy, including public consultations[116].

(A) Appointments

The Secretary of State for Business, Innovation and Skills makes most of the senior appointments in competition law, for example of the chairman and other members of the Board of the OFT[117]; the members of the CAT[118]; the Registrar of the CAT[119]; the 'appointed members' of the Competition Service within the CAT[120]; the Chairman, Deputy Chairmen and members of the CC[121]; and members of the CC Council[122]. The Secretary of State can also designate bodies which represent consumers to make 'super-complaints' under section 11 of the Enterprise Act 2002[123].

(B) Amendment of legislation, the adoption of delegated legislation and the making or approval of guidance

The Secretary of State is given various powers to amend primary legislation, to adopt delegated legislation and to make or approve rules under the Competition Act 1998 and

---

[112] On the implications of Regulation 1/2003 for UK law see the OFT's guidance *Modernisation* OFT 442, December 2004.

[113] Competition Act 1998 (Office of Fair Trading's Rules) Order 2004, SI 2004/2751.

[114] Competition Act 1998 (Land Agreements Exclusion and Revocation) Order 2004, SI 2004/1260, art 2.

[115] The institutional structure of EU and UK competition law is set out in diagrammatic form at the end of this chapter: see Figs 2.1, 2.2 and 2.3, pp 79–81 below.

[116] The website will be found at www.bis.gov.uk.

[117] Enterprise Act 2002, s 1 and Sch 1, para 1.

[118] Ibid, s 12(2)(c); note that the President of the Tribunal and the members of the panel of chairmen are appointed by the Lord Chancellor upon the recommendation of the Judicial Appointments Commission: ibid, s 12(2)(a) and (b).

[119] Ibid, s 12(3).   [120] Ibid, Sch 3, para 1(2).

[121] Ibid, Sch 7, para 3 (Chairman) and para 2 (members).   [122] Ibid, Sch 7, para 5(2).

[123] Ibid, s 11(5); see further ch 11, 'Super-Complaints', pp 454–455.

the Enterprise Act 2002. For example under the Competition Act the Secretary of State has power to amend (and has amended) Schedules 1 and 3[124]; to adopt block exemptions from the Chapter I prohibition[125]; to make provision for the determination of turnover for the purpose of setting the level of penalties[126]; to approve the guidance of the OFT as to the appropriate amount of penalties under the Chapter I and Chapter II prohibitions and Articles 101 and 102 TFEU[127]; to determine the criteria for conferring limited immunity on 'small agreements' and 'conduct of minor significance'[128]; to vary the application of the Competition Act to vertical and land agreements[129]; to approve the procedural rules of the OFT[130]; to make regulations on the concurrent application of the Competition Act by the OFT and the sectoral regulators[131]; and to amend the list of appealable decisions in section 46 of the Act[132]. The Secretary of State also has power under paragraph 7 of Schedule 3 to the Competition Act to order that the Chapter I and Chapter II prohibitions do not apply to particular agreements or conduct where there are exceptional and compelling reasons of public policy for doing so[133].

Under the Enterprise Act the Secretary of State has power to make rules or to amend primary legislation in relation to a variety of matters: these include the procedural rules of the CAT[134]; the determination of turnover for the purpose of domestic merger control[135]; the maximum penalties that the CC can impose for procedural infringements[136]; the payment of fees for merger investigations[137]; for the alteration of the 'share of supply' test applicable to merger cases[138]; and for shortening the period within which merger inquiries should be completed[139]. The Act also enables the Secretary of State to extend the 'super-complaint' system to include sectoral regulators[140] and to designate consumer bodies for the purposes of bringing claims under section 47B of the Competition Act[141]; to modify Schedule 8 to the Act, which sets out the provisions that can be contained in enforcement orders[142]; and to make such modifications to the Competition Act 1998 as

---

[124] Competition Act 1998, s 3(2), s 19(2) (Sch 1, dealing with mergers and concentrations) and s 3(3), s 19(3) (Sch 3, dealing with general exclusions): see ch 9, 'The Chapter I prohibition: excluded agreements', pp 348–356 and 'Exclusions', p 369 respectively.

[125] Competition Act 1998, ss 6–8: see ch 9, 'Block Exemptions', p 359.

[126] Ibid, s 36(8): see ch 10, 'Maximum amount of a penalty', p 410.

[127] Ibid, s 38(4): see ch 10, 'The OFT's *Guidance as to the appropriate amount of a penalty*', p 411.

[128] Ibid, s 39 (small agreements) and s 40 (conduct of minor significance): see ch 10, 'Immunity for small agreements and conduct of minor significance', pp 413–414.

[129] Ibid, s 50: see ch 9, 'Section 50: land agreements', p 356 and ch 16, 'Repeal of the exclusion for vertical agreements', p 678.

[130] Competition Act 1998, s 51.

[131] Ibid, s 54(4)–(5); see also Enterprise Act 2002, s 204, which creates a power for the Secretary of State to make regulations in relation to concurrency functions as to company director disqualification: for a discussion of the rules on concurrency see ch 10, 'Concurrency', pp 437–439.

[132] See the Competition Act 1998 (Notification of Excluded Agreements and Appealable Decisions) Regulations 2000, SI 2000/263, reg 10.

[133] See ch 9, 'Public policy', p 354.

[134] Enterprise Act 2002, s 15 and Sch 4, Part 2; see 'Establishment of the Competition Commission', pp 69–70 below.

[135] Ibid; see ch 22, 'The turnover test', p 921.

[136] Ibid, s 111(4); see ch 22, 'Investigation powers and penalties', p 949.

[137] Ibid, s 121; see ch 22, 'Fees', pp 928–929.

[138] Ibid, s 123; see ch 22, 'The share of supply test', pp 922–923.   [139] Enterprise Act 2002, s 40(8).

[140] Ibid, s 205; on super-complaints, see ch 10.

[141] Ibid, s 19; see ch 8, 'Claims brought on behalf of consumers', pp 318–319.

[142] Ibid, s 206; see ch 22, 'Schedule 8 of the Enterprise Act' and following sections, pp 945–948.

are appropriate for the purpose of eliminating or reducing any differences between that Act and EU law as a result of Regulation 1/2003[143].

(C) Receipt of reports

The Secretary of State receives Annual Reports from the OFT[144] and from the CC[145].

(D) Involvement in individual cases

The Secretary of State has little involvement in individual competition cases. Prior to the Enterprise Act 2002 the Secretary of State had an important role in merger and monopoly investigations. However the provisions of the Enterprise Act confer upon the CC the final decision-making role in relation to merger and market investigations[146]. The Secretary of State retains powers in relation to such investigations only in strictly limited circumstances[147]; one such case was *BSkyB/News Corp*[148].

(ii) The Lord Chancellor

The Lord Chancellor is responsible for appointing the President of the CAT and the panel of chairmen, pursuant to a recommendation from the Judicial Appointments Commission[149]. He is also given power to make provision for civil courts in England and Wales to transfer to the CAT cases based on an infringement decision of the European Commission or of the OFT or sectoral regulators under Articles 101 and/or 102 TFEU or the Chapter I and II prohibitions[150]. There is also provision to make rules for the receipt of cases by the civil courts that are transferred to them by the CAT[151]. As of 20 June 2011 these powers had not been exercised.

(iii) The OFT

(A) Establishment of the OFT

The OFT is established by section 1 of the Enterprise Act 2002. Section 1 of the Fair Trading Act 1973 had established the office of Director General of Fair Trading, and many of the most important functions in competition law were carried out in the name of the individual appointed by the Secretary of State to this position. Similarly in the regulated sectors individuals, such as the Director General of Telecommunications, were given a wide variety of responsibilities[152]. However there was a growing acceptance that it was not appropriate that such significant powers should be invested in an individual office-holder as opposed to a group of people. The Enterprise Act therefore created the OFT[153], and abolished the office of Director General of Fair Trading[154]; his functions were transferred to the OFT[155]. The Board of the OFT consists of a (non-executive) Chairman and no fewer than

---

[143] Ibid, s 209; see further 'Changes to domestic law as a result of Regulation 1/2003', pp 60–61 above.

[144] Ibid, s 4; see 'Annual plan and annual report', pp 64–65 below.

[145] Competition Act 1998, Sch 7, para 12A, inserted by Enterprise Act 2002, s 186; see 'Corporate plan and annual report', p 70 below.

[146] See ch 22, 'Determination of references by the CC', pp 929–931 (merger investigations) and ch 11, 'Market Investigation References', pp 466–477 (market investigations).

[147] Ibid, explaining ss 42–68, s 132, ss 139–153 and Sch 7 Enterprise Act 2002.

[148] See ch 22, 'Public interest cases', pp 956–958.

[149] Enterprise Act 2002, s 12(2)(a) and (b) and Sch 2, para 1; the Judicial Appointments Commission was established by the Constitutional Reform Act 2005; its website is www.jac.judiciary.gov.uk.

[150] Ibid, s 16(1)–(4).

[151] Ibid, s 16(5); on s 16 see further ch 8, 'Which court to see in: the jurisdiction of the High Court and the Competition Appeal Tribunal', p 307.

[152] See further 'Sectoral regulators', pp 68–69 below.   [153] Enterprise Act 2002, s 1(1).

[154] Ibid, s 2(2).   [155] Ibid, s 2(1); the transfer took place on 1 April 2003.

four other members, appointed by the Secretary of State[156]. The Secretary of State must also appoint a Chief Executive of the OFT, who may or may not be a member of the OFT Board[157]; since 2005 the Chief Executive may not be the same person as the Chairman[158]. On 20 June 2011 there were ten members of the Board, of whom four (the Chief Executive and three executive directors) were executive members and six non-executive[159]. The Rules of Procedure of the Board of the OFT are available on its website, and minutes of its meetings will also be found there[160]. The Board is responsible for the strategic direction, priorities, plans and performance of the OFT, including the adoption of the Annual Plan[161]. It also makes the decision whether to make market investigation references to the CC; other operational decisions are delegated by the Board to the executive of the OFT[162].

Many of the decisions of the OFT under the Competition Act can be appealed on the merits to the CAT[163]. In cases where the OFT's behaviour is not subject to the scrutiny of the CAT it may, nevertheless, be subject to judicial review by the Administrative Court of the Queen's Bench Division of the High Court. Decisions under the Enterprise Act 2002 in relation to mergers and market investigations are subject to review by the CAT[164].

(B) The staff of the OFT

The Chief Executive of the OFT is responsible for the day-to-day running of the organisation. There are three further Executive Directors who sit on the Board of the OFT, one responsible for Corporate Services and two for Markets and Projects. The General Counsel's office, the office of the Chief Economist and Competition Policy and the Procedural Adjudicator report directly to the Chief Executive. Operational matters such as the investigation of mergers and cases under the Competition Act are handled by staff who work in the Markets and Projects area of the OFT; its project and enforcement work is conducted in two market groupings, one covering goods and consumer and the other services, infrastructure and public markets. There are also specific enforcement teams for mergers and for cartel and criminal investigations[165]. The total number of permanent staff of the OFT in the year 2009–2010 was 597[166].

(C) Annual plan and annual report

The OFT is required, following a public consultation, to publish an annual plan containing a statement of its main objectives and priorities for the year; both the annual plan and the consultation document must be laid before Parliament[167]. The most recent annual plan was published in March 2011 explaining that the OFT's work will have two overarching themes, the first of which is high-impact enforcement and the second is to make markets work well by changing the behaviour of businesses, consumers and Government[168]. The OFT must also make an annual report to the Secretary of State containing an assessment of the extent to which the objectives and priorities set out in the annual plan have been met and a summary of significant decisions, investigations and other activities in the

---

[156] Ibid, Sch 1(1).   [157] Ibid, Sch 1(5)(1).   [158] Ibid, Sch 1(5)(2).
[159] Details of the members of the OFT Board are available at www.oft.gov.uk.
[160] See www.oft.gov.uk.   [161] See 'Annual plan and annual report', p 64 below.
[162] Enterprise Act 2002, Sch 1, para 12.   [163] See ch 10, 'Appeals', pp 439–449.
[164] See ch 11, 'Review of decisions under Part 4 of the Enterprise Act', pp 478–479 and ch 22, 'Review of decisions under Part 3 of the Enterprise Act', pp 950–951.
[165] An organisational diagram of the structure of the OFT is available at www.oft.gov.uk.
[166] *Annual Report and Resource Accounts 2009–2010*, p 73.   [167] Enterprise Act 2002, s 3.
[168] *Annual Plan 2011–12*, OFT 1294, available at www.oft.gov.uk.

year[169]. The report must be laid before Parliament and must be published[170]. The report for 2009-10 was published in July 2010[171].

(D) Functions of the OFT

The OFT has stated that its mission is to make markets work well for consumers[172]. In order to achieve this end the OFT's activities are to enforce the competition and consumer protection rules, to investigate how well markets are working and to explain and improve public awareness and understanding. The *OFT Prioritisation Principles*[173] are used to decide which projects and cases the OFT will take on across its areas of responsibility. The general functions, as opposed to the enforcement functions, of the OFT include obtaining, compiling and keeping under review information relating to the exercise of its functions; making the public aware of ways in which competition may benefit consumers and the economy; providing information and advice to Ministers[174]; and promoting good consumer practice[175].

It is important to understand (but often overlooked by competition lawyers) that the OFT is not only a competition authority, but also has numerous consumer protection responsibilities under a variety of legal provisions, including:

- the Consumer Credit Act 1974
- the Estate Agents Act 1979
- the Consumer Protection (Cancellation of Contracts concluded away from Business Premises) Regulations 1987[176]
- the Control of Misleading Advertisements Regulations 1988[177]
- the Consumer Credit (Advertisements) Regulations 1989[178]
- the Package Travel, Package Holidays and Package Tours Regulations 1992[179]
- the Timeshare Regulations 1997[180]
- the Unfair Terms in Consumer Contracts Regulations 1999[181]
- the Consumer Protection (Distance Selling) Regulations 2000[182]
- the Stop Now Orders (EC Directive) Regulations 2001[183]
- the Enterprise Act 2002
- the Consumer Protection Cooperation Regulation[184]
- the Consumer Credit Act 2006
- the Consumers, Estate Agents and Redress Act 2007
- Consumer Protection from Unfair Trading Regulations 2008[185].

---

[169] Enterprise Act 2002, s 4(1) and (2).   [170] Ibid, s 4(3).

[171] *Annual Report and Resource Accounts 2009–10*, HC 301.

[172] Ibid, p 9; see further Whish 'The Role of the OFT in UK Competition Law' in Rodger (ed) *Ten Years of UK Competition Law Reform* (Dundee University Press, 2010), ch 1.

[173] OFT 953, October 2008; see further ch 10, 'Inquiries and Investigations', pp 394–402.

[174] The OFT's website includes a page on 'advocacy and guidance for policy makers': www.oft.gov.uk/OFTwork/cartels-and-competition/advocacy-guidance/.

[175] Enterprise Act 2002, ss 5–8.   [176] SI 1987/2117.   [177] SI 1988/915.

[178] SI 1989/1125.

[179] SI 1992/3288.   [180] SI 1997/1081.   [181] SI 1999/2083.

[182] SI 2000/2334, as amended by SI 2005/689.   [183] SI 2001/1422.

[184] Regulation 2006/2004, OJ [2004] 364/1; see also the Enterprise Act 2002 (Amendment) Regulations, SI 2006/3363 and the Enterprise Act 2002 (Part 8 Community Infringements Specified UK Laws) Order 2006, SI 2006/3372.

[185] SI 2008/1277.

The OFT manages Consumer Direct, a national telephone and online consumer advice scheme[186]; and it also provides a national voice for, and strategic leadership to, local Trading Standards Services. The OFT also has functions under the Money Laundering Regulations 2007[187]. The Regulatory Enforcement and Sanctions Act 2008 provides for the reduction and removal of regulatory burdens and requires the OFT to keep its regulatory functions under review[188].

The competition and consumer protection functions of the OFT are legally distinct. However in practice they are closely related since they are used collectively by the OFT with the aim of ensuring that markets work well for consumers[189]. As far as competition law is concerned the OFT has considerable powers under the Competition Act 1998: it plays the principal role in enforcing the Chapter I and Chapter II prohibitions, and has significant powers to obtain information, enter premises to conduct investigations, make interim and final decisions and impose financial penalties; it also has the power to enforce Articles 101 and 102 TFEU[190]. The OFT has an important role in relation to merger and market investigations under the Enterprise Act 2002[191], and works with the Serious Fraud Office in the case of a prosecution for commission of the 'cartel offence' under that Act[192]. The OFT has specific responsibilities in relation to competition as a result of provisions in the Courts and Legal Services Act 1990, the Law Reform (Miscellaneous Provisions) (Scotland) Act 1990, the Water Industry Act 1991, the Financial Services and Markets Act 2000[193], the Transport Act 2000, the Transport (Scotland) Act 2001, the Legal Services Act 2007 and the Payment Services Regulations 2009[194]. The OFT also has a duty to keep under review undertakings given as a result of investigations conducted under the monopoly and merger provisions of the now-repealed Fair Trading Act 1973[195]. The OFT liaises on competition matters with the European Commission in Brussels and is a member of the European Competition Network that brings together the Commission and the national competition authorities of the Member States pursuant to Regulation 1/2003[196]. The OFT attends meetings on competition policy on behalf of the UK at the Organisation for Economic Co-Operation and Development and the United Nations Conference on Trade and Development, and is an active participant in the International Competition Network[197].

The OFT has published details of arrangements that have been put in place for cooperation and constructive communication between it and the Co-operation and Competition Panel, established by the Secretary of State for Health, where cases arise involving the provision of healthcare services in England[198].

---

[186] The website of Consumer Direct is www.consumerdirect.gov.uk.

[187] SI 2007/2157.

[188] The OFT's regulatory functions consist of its powers to enforce consumer law, to license consumer credit businesses and to supervise anti-money laundering.

[189] See *Joining up Competition and Consumer Policy: The OFT's approach to building an integrated agency* OFT 1151, December 2009, available at www.oft.gov.uk; note however that in June the Department for Business, Innovation and Skills began a consultation on institutional changes in relation to the enforcement of consumer law: see www.bis.gov.uk for further information.

[190] See ch 10 generally.

[191] See ch 22, 'The OFT's duty to make references', pp 912–929 (merger investigations) and ch 11, 'Market Investigation References', pp 466–473 (market investigations).

[192] On the cartel offence see ch 10, 'The cartel offence', pp 425–434.

[193] See ch 9, 'Financial Services and Markets Act 2000', pp 351–352.   [194] SI 2009/209, Part 8.

[195] See further ch 11, 'Orders and undertakings under the Fair Trading Act 1973', pp 485–486 and ch 22, 'Enforcement functions of the OFT', pp 948–949.

[196] See ch 7, 'Regulation 1/2003 in Practice', pp 288–290.

[197] On the work of these bodies see ch 12, 'The Internationalisation of Competition Law', pp 506–511.

[198] Details of these arrangements can be found at www.oft.gov.uk/oft_at_work/partnership_working/CCP/; see also www.copanel.org.uk.

(E) Rules

Section 51 of and Schedule 9 to the Competition Act 1998 make provision for the adoption of procedural rules by the OFT, which require the approval of the Secretary of State[199]; the *Competition Act 1998 (Office of Fair Trading's Rules)* were adopted under this provision in 2004[200].

(F) Publications, information, guidance etc

The OFT is required by sections 6 and 7 of the Enterprise Act 2002 to provide information to the public and to Ministers. The OFT has published a statement setting out its approach to improving the transparency of its work[201]. The OFT's website is a vital source of information on UK competition law and policy and includes, among other things, a Public Register of its decisions and the decisions of the sectoral regulators under the Competition Act and the OFT's decisions under the Enterprise Act, the numerous guidelines on these Acts, Press Releases, the Annual Plan and the Annual Report of the OFT, consultations, speeches and articles[202].

The OFT has published a number of research papers on important issues in competition policy, for example on market definition, barriers to entry and exit and predatory behaviour, which are available on its website. Since the sixth edition of this book was published in 2008 the OFT has published the following 'economic discussion papers' by 20 June 2011:

- *An evaluation of the impact upon productivity of ending resale price maintenance on books*[203]
- *Interactions between competition and consumer policy*[204]
- *The economics of self-regulation in solving consumer quality issues*[205]
- *Road testing of consumer remedies*[206]
- *An assessment of discretionary penalties regimes*[207]
- *Behavioural Economics as Applied to Firms: A Primer*[208]
- *Minority interests in competitors*[209]
- *What does Behavioural Economics mean for Competition Policy?*[210]
- *The impact of price frames on consumer decision making*[211]

The OFT's Economic Discussion Paper Series is available on the OFT website[212].

The OFT has increasingly sought to carry out an evaluation of its work, both as a matter of external accountability, so that it can attempt to demonstrate that it provides value for money to the taxpayers that pay for it, and as a matter of internal management, in order to test whether it is prioritising its work effectively. The OFT has agreed to a performance target of delivering benefits to consumers worth more than five times the organisation's spending on competition enforcement[213]. In July 2010 the OFT published guidance on the way in which it calculates the direct customer benefits of its work[214]. The OFT has estimated that it saved consumers on average £359 million per year in the years from 2007

---

[199] Competition Act 1998, s 51(5).　　[200] SI 2004/2751, replacing the earlier rules in SI 2000/293.
[201] OFT 1234, June 2010.　　[202] See www.oft.gov.uk.　　[203] OFT 981, March 2008.
[204] OFT 991, April 2008.　　[205] OFT 1059, March 2009.　　[206] OFT 1099, July 2009.
[207] OFT 1132, October 2009.
[208] OFT 1213, March 2010.　　[209] OFT 1218, March 2010.　　[210] OFT 1224, March 2010.
[211] OFT 1226, May 2010.
[212] See www.oft.gov.uk/OFTwork/publications/publication-categories/reports/Economic-research/.
[213] OFT 962, November 2007, p 71.　　[214] Available at www.oft.gov.uk.

to 2010 as a result of its work in enforcing the Competition Act, reviewing mergers and taking action under its consumer powers against scams[215].

The OFT has published guidance explaining how it deals with requests for information under the Freedom of Information Act 2000[216].

(iv) Serious Fraud Office

Section 188 of the Enterprise Act 2002 introduced a criminal cartel offence for individuals responsible for 'hard-core' cartels[217]. Serious penalties – of up to five years in prison – can be imposed upon those found guilty of this offence. Prosecutions may be brought by or with the consent of the OFT[218], or by the Serious Fraud Office[219], working in close liaison with the OFT[220]. In Scotland the prosecution of the criminal offence is the responsibility of the Lord Advocate. Quite apart from the cartel offence, there are some rare circumstances in which some cartel agreements might be illegal under the common law criminal offence of conspiracy to defraud; the Serious Fraud Office is the prosecutor for this offence as well[221].

(v) Sectoral regulators

Various industries in the UK are subject to specific regulatory control, in particular utilities such as telecommunications and water. Originally the regulatory powers were vested in individuals such as the Director General of Telecommunications. Just as the position of Director General of Fair Trading has been superseded by the creation of an OFT Board, so too the individual regulators have been replaced by corporate boards, each supported by an office: these are the Gas and Electricity Markets Authority (supported by the Office of Gas and Electricity Markets (OFGEM))[222], the Office of Communications (OFCOM)[223], the Water Services Regulation Authority (OFWAT)[224], the Office of Rail Regulation (ORR)[225] and the Northern Ireland Authority for Energy Regulation (NIAER)[226]. These sectoral regulators, together with the Civil Aviation Authority[227], have concurrent power to enforce the Competition Act 1998, and Articles 101 and 102 TFEU, with the OFT. The Government intends to give Monitor, the regulator for health and social care, competition law functions[228]. Arrangements are in place for coordination of the performance of the concurrent functions under the Act[229]. Appeals against 'appealable decisions' of the sectoral regulators under the Competition

---

[215] See *Positive Impact 09/10* OFT 1251, July 2010, available at www.oft.gov.uk/OFTwork/publications/publication-categories/reports/Evaluating/.

[216] *Freedom of Information Act 2000 publication scheme* OFT 622, January 2005, available at www.oft.gov.uk/advice_and_resources/publications/corporate/general/oft622.

[217] See ch 10, 'The cartel offence', pp 425–434 below.　　　　　[218] Enterprise Act 2002, s 190(2)(b).

[219] The website of the SFO is www.sfo.gov.uk.

[220] Enterprise Act 2002, s 190(1); see ch 10, 'Prosecution and penalty', pp 430–431.

[221] See ch 10, 'Conspiracy to defraud at common law', pp 436–437.

[222] Utilities Act 2000, s 1.　　　　　[223] Office of Communications Act 2002, s 1.

[224] Water Act 2003, s 34.

[225] Railway and Transport Safety Act 2003, s 15.

[226] See the Energy Order 2003, SI 2003/419, art 3.

[227] See Airports Act 1986, s 41, which deals with anti-competitive practices at regulated airports, and Chapter V of the Transport Act 2000, which gives the Civil Aviation Authority ('the CAA') concurrent powers to enforce the Chapter I and II prohibitions in relation to air traffic services; the Government proposes to give the CAA concurrent powers to enforce the Chapter I and II prohibitions in relation to airport operator services; further details of these powers can be found at www.dft.gov.uk.

[228] See Chapter 2 of Part 3 of the Health and Social Care Bill introduced into Parliament on 19 January 2011.

[229] On concurrency see ch 10, 'Concurrency', pp 437–439.

Act lie to the CAT[230]; references in relation to the licensing functions of the sectoral regulators[231] and market investigations may be made to the CC[232]. Super-complaints may be made to the sectoral regulators under the provisions set out in section 11 of the Enterprise Act 2002[233]. The Government published, in March 2011, its proposals to make the sectoral regulators' exercise of their Competition Act powers less burdensome and to improve the practice of concurrency[234].

The OFT also works closely with the Financial Services Authority ('the FSA') across a range of matters; the OFT and the FSA have published a *Memorandum of Understanding* establishing a framework for cooperation between them[235].

As a separate matter, all economic regulators should consider whether their decisions might be called into question under Article 106 TFEU on the basis that they might result in infringements of Articles 101 and/or 102[236].

(vi) Competition Commission

(A) Establishment of the Competition Commission

The CC is an independent public body which was established by section 45(1) of the Competition Act 1998 and came into existence on 1 April 1999. Section 45(3) of the Act dissolved the Monopolies and Mergers Commission, which had been in existence under various names since 1948, and transferred its functions to the new CC[237]. Schedule 7 to the Competition Act, as amended by Schedule 11 to the Enterprise Act 2002, makes detailed provision in relation to the CC. It has a Chairman and some Deputy Chairmen. The Chairman is appointed on a full-time basis, as may be the Deputy Chairmen.

On 20 June 2011 there were 33 'reporting panel' members of the CC[238]. Members are appointed by the Secretary of State, following an open competition, for a single period of eight years; all members (other than the Chairman and some of the Deputy Chairmen) are part time. They are appointed for their diversity of background, individual experience and ability, not as representatives of particular organisations, interests or political parties. In each case referred to the CC a group will be appointed to conduct the investigation[239]. The Chairman appoints between three to six members to serve on an inquiry group[240]. In 2009/10 most of the investigations completed were conducted by groups of four[241].

---

[230] On the meaning of appealable decisions see ch 10, 'Appealable decisions', pp 440–443.

[231] On licence modification references see ch 23, 'Regulatory systems in the UK for utilities', pp 978–979.

[232] Enterprise Act 2002, Sch 9, Part 2.

[233] The Enterprise Act 2002 (Super-complaints to Regulators) Order 2003, SI 2003/1368; on super-complaints, see ch 11, 'Super-Complaints', pp 454–455.

[234] *A Competition Regime for Growth: A Consultation on Options for Reform*, March 2011, ch 7, available at www.bis.gov.uk; see also National Audit Office Report, *Review of the UK's Competition Landscape*, March 2010, available at www.nao.org.uk.

[235] December 2009; see also the OFT's *Financial Services Plan* OFT 1106, July 2009, both available at www.oft.gov.uk.

[236] See ch 6 generally, and in particular the reference at 'Introduction', p 215 to a decision of the UK National Lottery Commission not to authorise Camelot, the operator of the National Lottery, to provide 'ancillary services', available at www.natlotcomm.gov.uk.

[237] For an account of the work of the Monopolies and Mergers Commission in the 50 years from 1948 to 1998 see Wilks *In the Public Interest: Competition Policy and the Monopolies and Mergers Commission* (Manchester University Press, 1999).

[238] See the CC's *Annual Report and Accounts* 2009/2010, p 49.

[239] Provision is made for this by the Competition Act 1998, Sch 7, Part II, as amended by the Enterprise Act 2002, Sch 11, paras 10–12.

[240] Competition Act 1998, Sch 7, para 15(2).

[241] Details of the groups will be found in the short discussions of each investigation in the CC's *Annual Report and Accounts*.

There is a utilities panel from which the Chairman must appoint at least one member when conducting an investigation concerned with the regulation of the water, electricity or gas sectors or an energy code modification appeal. There is also a newspaper panel and a Communications Act panel. The Chairman of the CC has published *Guidance to Groups* on the procedures to be adopted when conducting inquiries[242]: the *Guidance* must be read in conjunction with the *Competition Commission Rules of Procedure*[243].

The CC has a Council through which some of its functions, such as the appointment of staff and the keeping of accounts, must be performed; the Council consists of the Chairman, the Deputy Chairmen, such other members as the Secretary of State may appoint[244] and the Chief Executive (referred to in the legislation as the Secretary) of the CC[245]. Management of the CC and its policy development are taken forward through five key groups: the Senior Management Team, an Analysis Group, a Procedures and Practices Group, a Remedies Standing Group and a Finance and Regulation Group; each of the groups reports to the Council.

The CC is subject to review by the CAT under provisions contained in the Enterprise Act 2002[246]; it is also subject to judicial review by the Administrative Court of the Queen's Bench Division of the High Court.

(B) The staff of the CC

The most senior member of staff of the CC is the chief executive, referred to in the legislation as the Secretary, who is a member of the CC Council. At the end of March 2010 the CC had a permanent staff of 122 officials, including administrators and specialists such as accountants, economists, business advisers and lawyers[247].

(C) Business plan and annual report

The CC publishes its Business Plan on its website; it is required to make an Annual Report to the Secretary of State[248].

(D) Functions of the CC

The CC has no power to conduct investigations on its own initiative. Rather it conducts market investigations under the Enterprise Act 2002 referred to it by either the OFT, one of the sectoral regulators or the Secretary of State and merger inquiries referred to it by the OFT or the Secretary of State. The CC can be asked to conduct 'efficiency audits' of public sector bodies under the Competition Act 1980: this provision has not been used for many years[249].

The CC has various regulatory functions in relation to privatised utilities as a result of provisions in:

- the Airports Act 1986 and the Airports (Northern Ireland) Order 1994
- the Gas Act 1986 and the Gas (Northern Ireland) Order 1996
- the Electricity Act 1989 and the Electricity (Northern Ireland) Order 1992

---

[242] CC6, March 2006, available at www.competition-commission.org.uk.

[243] CC1, March 2006.   [244] At 20 June 2011 the Council had three non-executive members.

[245] Competition Act 1998, Sch 7, para 5(3), as amended by Enterprise Act 2002, Sch 11, para 4 and Sch 26.

[246] See further 'Functions of the CAT', pp 72–73 below and ch 11, 'Review of decisions under Part 4 of the Enterprise Act', pp 478–479 (market investigations) and ch 22, 'Review of decisions under Part 3 of the Enterprise Act', pp 950–951 (merger investigations) respectively.

[247] See the *CC's Annual Report and Accounts 2009–10*, p 52.

[248] Competition Act 1998, Sch 7, para 12A, inserted by the Enterprise Act 2002, s 186.

[249] On efficiency audits see *Halsbury's Laws of England*, Vol 47, (4th ed reissue, 2001), paras 143–145.

- the Water Industry Act 1991 and the Water Services (Scotland) Act 2005 (Consequential Provisions and Modifications) Order 2005 and the Water and Sewerage Services (Northern Ireland) Order 2006
- the Railways Act 1993
- the Postal Services Act 2000
- the Transport Act 2000.

The CC has seldom been called upon to exercise these regulatory functions[250]. The CC has a role under the Financial Services and Markets Act 2000 to ensure that the rules and practices of the FSA do not impede competition. It also has a role under the Legal Services Act 2007 in relation to possible distortions on competition arising from regulatory rules applicable to the legal profession. The CC has an appellate function in relation to price control matters under the Communications Act 2003[251]. The CC also hears appeals in respect of modifications to the codes covering the energy industry by virtue of sections 173 to 177 of the Energy Act 2004[252].

The CC is not a designated competition authority for the purposes of Article 35 of Regulation 1/2003, with the result that it does not have the power to enforce Articles 101 and 102 TFEU[253]. The CC participates in the activities of the OECD, the United Nations Conference on Trade and Development ('UNCTAD') and the International Competition Network ('ICN').

(E) Rules

Schedule 7A to the Competition Act, inserted by Schedule 12 to the Enterprise Act 2002, makes provision for the adoption of procedural rules for the conduct of merger and market references by the CC. The current *Competition Commission Rules of Procedure* were adopted in March 2006 and are available on its website[254]. The CC has also published a series of guidance documents describing its approach to, and procedures for, merger and market investigations[255] and on several other matters, including *General Advice and Information*[256], a *Statement of Policy on Penalties*[257] and *Guidance on Disclosure of Information in Merger and Market Inquiries*[258].

(F) Publications, information, guidance etc

The CC has a website that contains a wide variety of information, for example on current inquiries, completed inquiries, press releases, evaluation reports and occasional papers, speeches, texts from the CC's lectures series, the *Annual Report and Accounts*,

---

[250] In 2007 the CC carried out the mandatory quinquennial review of airport charges; in August 2009 it rejected an appeal by Sutton and East Surrey Water plc against the price limits imposed on it by OFWAT, but an appeal by Bristol Water was partially successful in 2010. The CC's determinations are available at www.competition-commission.org.uk.

See the *Annual Report and Accounts 2006–2007*, p 6.

[251] See *Price control appeals under section 193 of the Communications Act 2003*, CC13, April 2011, available at www.competition-commission.org.uk.

[252] As amended by the Electricity and Gas Appeals (Designation and Exclusion) Order 2009 SI 2009/648; see further the *Energy Modification Rules*, CC10, July 2005, available at www.competition-commission.org.uk.

[253] See reg 3 of the Competition Act 1998 and Other Enactments (Amendment) Regulations 2004, SI 2004/1261 which designates the OFT and the sectoral regulators for this purpose.

[254] CC1, March 2006, available at www.competition-commission.org.uk.

[255] *Merger Assessment Guidelines* CC2 (Revised), September 2010 (jointly with the OFT) and *Market Investigation References* CC3, June 2003.

[256] CC4, March 2004.

[257] CC5, June 2003.

[258] CC7, July 2003.

the Business Plan and the way in which the CC is organised[259]. The CC has estimated that customers would have paid an extra £424 million for goods and services but for the decisions it took during the period from 1 April 2009 to 31 March 2010[260].

(vii) Competition Appeal Tribunal

(A) Establishment of the CAT

The CAT is established by section 12(1) of the Enterprise Act 2002[261]. It consists of a President[262], a panel of Chairmen appointed by the Lord Chancellor following a recommendation from the Judicial Appointments Commission[263] (the judges of the Chancery Division of the High Court have been appointed to this panel) and a panel of ordinary members appointed by the Secretary of State[264]. Cases are heard by a Tribunal of three persons, chaired by the President or one person from the panel of Chairmen. Procedural matters can be dealt with either by the President or by one of the Chairmen sitting alone. The CAT has a Registrar, also appointed by the Secretary of State[265]. Schedule 2 to the Enterprise Act contains provisions on such matters as eligibility for appointment as President or chairman of the Tribunal. Section 14 of the Act and Part I of Schedule 4 deal with the constitution of the Tribunal. Section 13 and Schedule 3 establish the Competition Service, the purpose of which is to fund and provide support services to the Tribunal[266]. The CAT's website provides details of decided and pending cases, and all of its judgments will be found there[267]. The CAT may sit outside London[268]. The CAT publishes an Annual Review and Accounts[269]. On 20 June 2011 the CAT had a staff of 13, including the Registrar and three referendaires. The CAT has established a User Group, which meets twice a year, to discuss its practical operation[270].

(B) Functions of the CAT

The CAT, which is an independent judicial body, has four functions under the Enterprise Act[271]; it also has some functions in relation to regulatory matters (see below). The first function under the Enterprise Act is to hear appeals from 'appealable decisions' of the OFT and the sectoral regulators under the Competition Act 1998 and Articles 101 and 102 TFEU[272]. Appeals on a point of law or as to the amount of a penalty lie from decisions of the

---

[259] The website of the CC is www.competition-commission.org.uk.

[260] See *Estimated benefits to consumers from the CC's actions in mergers and market investigations between April 2009 and March 2010*, available at www.competition-commission.org.uk.

[261] The Competition Act 1998 had established, within the CC, appeal tribunals which could hear appeals under that Act; these tribunals have been abolished, and the Competition Appeal Tribunal inherited their functions on 1 April 2003; s 21 of and Sch 5 to the Enterprise Act amend various provisions of the Competition Act 1998 in relation to proceedings of the Tribunal.

[262] Enterprise Act 2002, s 12(2)(a).

[263] Ibid, s 12(2)(b).

[264] Ibid, s 12(2)(c).

[265] Ibid, s 12(3).

[266] Ibid, s 13(2).

[267] The website of the CAT is www.catribunal.org.uk.

[268] See the Competition Appeal Tribunal Rules 2003, SI 2003/1372, rule 18; the CAT has sat in Belfast, in the *BetterCare* case and in Edinburgh in the *Aberdeen Journals* and *Claymore* cases: for details of these cases see the CAT's website.

[269] Available at www.catribunal.org.uk.

[270] The most recent minutes of the User Group meetings are available at www.catribunal.org.uk.

[271] See Bailey 'The early case law of the Competition Appeal Tribunal' in Rodger (ed) *Ten Years of UK Competition Law Reform* (Dundee University Press, 2010), ch 2.

[272] On appealable decisions see ch 10, 'Appealable decisions', pp 440–443; it is also possible that an application for judicial review of the OFT and sectoral regulators may be brought before the Administrative Court: ch 10, 'Appealable decisions', p 440.

CAT with permission to the Court of Appeal in England and Wales, to the Court of Session in Scotland and to the Court of Appeal of Northern Ireland in Northern Ireland[273]. From the Court of Appeal a further appeal may be taken, with permission, to the Supreme Court (formerly the House of Lords). It is also possible for the CAT to refer a matter of EU law to the Court of Justice[274]. The second function of the CAT is to hear monetary claims arising from infringement decisions made by the UK competition authorities or the European Commission under the Competition Act or the TFEU[275]. The third function is to deal with applications for review of decisions of the OFT, the Secretary of State or other Minister or the CC in relation to mergers[276] and market investigations[277]. The fourth function of the CAT under the Enterprise Act is to hear appeals against penalties imposed by the CC for failure to comply with notices requiring the attendance of witnesses or the production of documents in the course of a market or merger investigation[278].

The Communications Act 2003 provides that the CAT will hear appeals on the merits against certain decisions taken by OFCOM or the Secretary of State (as the case may be) under its provisions; the CAT must refer price control matters to the CC and decide the appeal on those matters in accordance with the CC's determination, unless it decides that the determination would be set aside on an application for judicial review[279]. The CAT has also been given certain functions under the Electricity (Single Wholesale Market)(Northern Ireland) Order 2007[280], the Mobile Roaming (European Communities) Regulations 2007[281], Schedule 2A to the Electricity Act 1989 in relation to determinations by OFGEM in respect of property schemes, and the Payment Services Regulations 2009[282].

Provision is made by section 16 of the Enterprise Act 2002 for the Lord Chancellor to adopt regulations enabling the transfer of cases between the civil courts and the CAT for it to determine whether there has been an infringement of Articles 101 and/or 102 TFEU or of the Chapter I and II prohibitions in the Competition Act. These provisions had not been activated as at 20 June 2011.

(C) Rules

Section 15 of the Enterprise Act 2002 and Part 2 of Schedule 4 provide for the Secretary of State to make rules with respect to proceedings before the CAT. The Competition Appeal Tribunal Rules 2003[283] entered into force in June 2003. The 2003 rules have been amended by the Competition Appeal Tribunal (Amendment and Communications Act Appeals) Rules 2004[284]. Following an Introduction in Part I, Part II of the 2003 Rules deals with appeals to the CAT respectively under the Competition Act and Communications Act[285];

[273] Competition Act 1998, s 49: see the Competition Appeal Tribunal Rules 2003, SI 2003/1372, rules 58 and 59 and ch 10, 'Appeals from the CAT to the Court of Appeal', p 449.

[274] See The Competition Appeal Tribunal Rules 2003, SI 2003/1372, rule 60 and ch 10, 'Which courts or tribunals in the UK can make an Article 267 reference in a case under the Competition Act 1998?', p 450; the CAT was asked to make a reference but declined to do so in Case No 1100/3/3/08 *The Number (UK) Ltd v OFCOM* [2008] CAT 33, paras 159–173; the Court of Appeal subsequently made a reference for a preliminary ruling, [2009] EWCA Civ 1360 which the Court of Justice gave on 17 February 2011 in Case C-16/10 *The Number (UK) and Conduit Enterprises* [2011] ECR I-000.

[275] See ch 8, 'Follow-on actions in the CAT and the High Court', pp 317–319.

[276] Enterprise Act 2002, s 120: see ch 22, 'Review of decisions under Part 3 of the Enterprise Act', pp 950–951.

[277] Enterprise Act 2002, s 179: see ch 11, 'Review of decisions under Part 4 of the Enterprise Act', pp 478–479.

[278] See further ch 11, 'Powers of investigation', p 477 and ch 22, 'Investigation powers and penalties', p 949.

[279] Communications Act 2003, s 193 and rule 3 of the Competition Appeal Tribunal (Amendment and Communications Act Appeals) Rules 2004, SI 2004/2068; see Case No 1146/3/3/09 *British Telecommunications Plc v OFCOM* [2010] CAT 15, paras 9–53.

[280] SI 2007/913.   [281] SI 2007/1933.   [282] SI 209/2009.   [283] SI 2003/1372.

[284] SI 2004/2068.

[285] On appeals under the Competition Act see ch 10, 'Appeals', pp 439–449.

Part III is concerned with proceedings under the Enterprise Act, that is appeals against penalties in merger and market investigations[286] and reviews of merger and market investigation references[287]. Part IV of the Rules deals with claims for damages under section 47A and 47B of the Competition Act[288], and Part V contains provisions on matters such as hearings, confidentiality, decisions of the CAT, appeals to the Court of Appeal and Article 267 references to the Court of Justice[289]. The CAT published a *Guide to Proceedings* in October 2005 which provides guidance for parties and their legal representatives as to its procedures in relation to all cases which it is competent to entertain and which has the status of a Practice Direction under Rule 68(2) of the 2003 Rules. Dissenting judgments are possible: this had happened on three occasions by 20 June 2011[290].

(viii) Civil courts

Where a warrant is required to enter premises under section 28, section 28A or section 62A of the Competition Act 1998, this must be obtained from a judge of the High Court[291]. The High Court may also issue warrants to enter premises in relation to investigations under the EU competition rules[292].

Actions may be brought in the High Court where there are infringements of Articles 101 and 102 TFEU or the Chapter I and II prohibitions[293]; such actions are usually brought in the Chancery Division, but sometimes may be dealt with by the Commercial Court[294]. Where the OFT or the CAT has already found such an infringement its decisions are binding in proceedings before the ordinary courts[295]. As noted above, the Enterprise Act makes provision for the Lord Chancellor to adopt regulations for the transfer of cases to and from the CAT[296].

(ix) Criminal courts

The Competition Act 1998 and the Enterprise Act 2002 create a number of criminal offences. Most notably, the Enterprise Act establishes the 'cartel offence', the commission of which could attract a prison sentence of up to five years as well as a fine[297]. The cartel offence is described in detail in chapter 10[298], as is the possibility that some cartel behaviour may, in exceptional circumstances, be criminal at common law as a conspiracy to defraud[299]. Under the Competition Act various criminal offences may also be committed

---

[286] See ch 11, 'Powers of investigation', p 477 and ch 22, 'Investigation powers and penalties', p 949.

[287] See ch 22, 'Review of decisions under Part 3 of the Enterprise Act', pp 937–938 (mergers) and ch 11, 'Review of decisions under Part 4 of the Enterprise Act', pp 478–479 (market investigations).

[288] See ch 8, 'Follow-on actions in the CAT and the High Court', pp 317–319.

[289] On Article 267 references see ch 10, 'Article 267 References', pp 449–450.

[290] Case No 1061/1/1/06 *Makers UK Ltd v OFT* [2007] CAT 11, [2007] CompAR 699, paras 172–173; Case No 1085/3/3/07 *British Telecommunications Plc v OFCOM* [2009] CAT 1, paras 91–107; and Case No 1154/3/3/10 *Telefónica O2 UK Ltd v OFCOM* [2010] CAT 25, paras 106–175.

[291] Competition Act 1998, s 28(1) and s 59; in Scotland the relevant court is the Court of Session: ibid.

[292] Ibid, ss 62 and 63.

[293] On the enforcement of Articles 101 and 102 TFEU and the Competition Act in the civil courts see ch 8 generally.

[294] *Practice Direction – Competition Law – Claims Relating to the Application of Articles [101 and 102 TFEU] and Chapters I and II of Part I of the Competition Act 1998*, available at www.justice.gov.uk.

[295] Competition Act 1998, s 58A; the ordinary courts are also bound by findings of fact made by the OFT in the course of its investigation, unless the court directs otherwise: ibid, s 58.

[296] Claims which may be made under sections 47A and 47B of the Competition Act may be transferred between the civil courts and the CAT: see rules 48 and 49 of the Competition Appeal Tribunal Rules 2003, SI 2003/1372, and CPR Part 30 Practice Direction, 30PD.8, available at www.justice.gov.uk.

[297] Enterprise Act 2002, s 190.   [298] See ch 10, 'The cartel offence', pp 425–434.

[299] See ch 10, 'Conspiracy to defraud at common law', p 436.

where investigations are obstructed, documents are destroyed or falsified or where false or misleading information is provided[300]. It is also a criminal offence to obstruct investigations conducted under the EU competition rules[301].

4. The Relationship Between EU Competition Law and National Competition Laws

(A) Introduction

All the Member States of the EU have systems of competition law, in large part modelled upon Articles 101 and 102. Some Member States require that domestic law should be interpreted consistently with the EU rules, thereby reinforcing the alignment of EU and domestic law[302]. It follows that many cases will have the same outcome whether they are investigated under EU or under domestic law: for example, a horizontal price-fixing agreement would infringe Article 101(1), and would normally also be caught by any domestic system of competition law in the EU unless, for example, it occurred in a sector which was not subject to the domestic rules. Even though there is a high degree of convergence between EU and domestic competition law, nevertheless the possibility remains that there could be different outcomes depending on which system of law is applied. In some cases domestic law may be more generous than EU law; in other cases the possibility exists that domestic law could have a stricter effect than EU law.

Much thought has gone into the issue of conflicts between EU and domestic competition law over the years[303]. The starting point is that EU law takes precedence over national law, so that where a clash occurs it is the former which must be applied[304]: in *Walt Wilhelm v Bundeskartellamt*[305] the Court of Justice held that conflicts between the rules of the EU and national rules on cartels must be resolved by applying the principle that EU law takes precedence. However the *Walt Wilhelm* judgment did not provide answers to all the situations that could arise: for example, could a Member State prohibit an agreement which benefited from an EU block exemption[306]? These matters are now dealt with by Article 3 of Regulation 1/2003.

---

[300] Competition Act 1998, ss 42–44, ss 65L–65N and s 72: see ch 10, 'Offences', pp 401–402.

[301] Competition Act 1998, s 65.

[302] Section 60 of the Competition Act 1998 is an example of this in the UK: see ch 9, '"Governing Principles Clause": Section 60 of the Competition Act 1998', pp 362–367.

[303] See eg Markert 'Some Legal and Administrative Problems of the Co-existence of Community and National Competition Law in the EC' (1974) 11 CML Rev 92; Stockmann 'EC Competition Law and Member State Competition Laws' [1987] Fordham Corporate Law Institute (ed Hawk), pp 265–300; Bellamy and Child *European Community Law of Competition* (Sweet & Maxwell, 5th ed, 2001, ed Roth), paras 10–074 to 10–080; Whish *Competition Law* (Butterworths, 4th ed, 2001), pp 322–329; Goyder *EC Competition Law* (Oxford EC Law Library, 4th ed, 2003), pp 440–445; Kerse and Khan *EC Antitrust Procedure* (Sweet & Maxwell, 5th ed, 2005), para 5.56.

[304] See Case 6/64 *Costa v ENEL* [1964] ECR 585, [1964] CMLR 425; Case 106/77 *Amministrazione delle Finanze dello Stato v Simmenthal* [1978] ECR 629, [1978] 3 CMLR 263; Case C-213/89 *R v Secretary of State for Transport, ex p Factortame Ltd (No 2)* [1991] 1 AC 603, [1990] 3 CMLR 1; Case C-221/89 *R v Secretary of State for Transport, ex p Factortame Ltd (No 3)* [1991] ECR I-3905, [1991] 3 CMLR 589; note also that NCAs have an obligation to disapply national law that involves an infringement of EU competition law: Case C-198/01 *Consorzio Industrie Fiammiferi* [2003] ECR I-8055, [2003] 5 CMLR 829.

[305] Case 14/68 [1969] ECR 1, [1969] CMLR 100.

[306] The Court of Justice declined to give an answer to this question in Case C-70/93 *Bayerische Motoren Werke AG v ALD Auto-Leasing* [1995] ECR I-3439, [1996] 4 CMLR 478 and Case C-266/93 *Bundeskartellamt v Volkswagen ACT and VAG Leasing GmbH* [1995] ECR I-3477, [1996] 4 CMLR 478, since it concluded that

(B) **Regulation 1/2003**[307]

Under the regime introduced by Regulation 1/2003[308] the Commission shares the competence to apply Articles 101 and 102 with national competition authorities ('NCAs') and national courts; of course NCAs and national courts can also apply domestic law. Member States are required by Article 35 of the Regulation to designate the authorities responsible for the application of Articles 101 and 102[309]: in the UK the OFT and the sectoral regulators have been designated as NCAs[310]. Recitals 8 and 9 and Article 3 of the Regulation deal with the relationship between Articles 101 and 102 and national competition laws.

(i) **Obligation to apply Articles 101 and 102**

Recital 8 states that, in order to ensure the effective enforcement of EU competition law, it is necessary to oblige NCAs and national courts, where they apply national competition law to agreements or practices, to also apply Article 101 or 102 where those provisions are applicable. Article 3(1) therefore provides that, where NCAs or national courts apply national competition law to agreements, decisions by associations of undertakings or concerted practices that may affect trade between Member States, they shall also apply Article 101; similarly they must apply Article 102 to any behaviour prohibited by that provision[311]. In its *Report on the functioning of Regulation 1/2003*[312] the Commission reported that Article 3(1) had led to a very significant increase in the application of Articles 101 and 102, 'making a single legal standard a reality on a very large scale'[313].

It is the concept of 'trade between Member States' that triggers the obligation to apply Articles 101 and 102, which is why the Commission published guidance on it in 2004[314]. The OFT's view is that the prosecution of *individuals* for commission of the cartel offence contained in section 188 of the Enterprise Act 2002 does *not* trigger the obligation to apply Article 101, since Article 101 is aimed at the anti-competitive agreements of *undertakings* rather than individuals[315]. The Court of Appeal concurred with this view, albeit on different grounds. In *IB v The Queen* the Court held that the cartel offence is not a 'national competition law' in the sense of Article 3 of Regulation 1/2003 and rejected the argument that the Crown Court, which is not a designated competition authority for the purposes of

---

the agreements under consideration in those cases were not covered by the block exemption for motor car distribution in force at that time.

[307] For further discussion of Article 3 of Regulation 1/2003 see Faull and Nikpay *The EC Law of Competition* (Oxford University Press, 2nd ed, 2007), paras 2.28–2.73; O'Neill and Saunders *UK Competition Procedure* (Oxford University Press, 2007), paras 3.08–3.93; see also the OFT's guidance *Modernisation* OFT 442, December 2004, paras 4.1–4.30.

[308] See ch 2, n 1 above.

[309] Designated national authorities have the right to participate in judicial proceedings against a decision that they have taken in relation to Articles 101 and/or 102: Case C-439/08 *VEBIC v Raad voor de Mededinging*, [2011] 4 CMLR 635.

[310] Competition Act 1998 and Other Enactments (Amendment) Regulations 2004, SI 2004/1261, reg 3.

[311] The temporal effect of this provision is under examination in Case C-17/10 *Toshiba Corporation v Úřad pro ochranu hospodářské soutěže*, not yet decided.

[312] SEC(2009) 574; see also the Commission Staff Working Paper accompanying the Report on the functioning of Regulation 1/2003, COM(2009) 206 final, paras 139–181 which contains detailed analysis of the operation of Article 3 between 2004 and 2009; both documents are available at www.ec.europa.eu/competition/antitrust/legislation.html.

[313] SEC(2009) 574, para 25.

[314] *Guidelines on the effect on trade concept contained in Articles [101 and 102 TFEU]* OJ [2004] C 101/81; the *Guidelines* are discussed in ch 3, 'The Effect on Trade between Member States', pp 142–146.

[315] See the OFT's guidance *Modernisation* OFT 442, December 2004, paras 4.21–4.22; see also Dekeyser's comments during a roundtable discussion at [2004] Fordham Corporate Law Institute (ed Hawk), pp 734–735.

that Regulation, did not have jurisdiction to try an indictment alleging the cartel offence[316]. The Court added that, even if the cartel offence were part of national competition law, it is a part of it which is not concerned with directly applying Article 101[317]. The position is not free from doubt, however[318]. In practice the reality is that the OFT, when proceeding against individuals under the Enterprise Act, would probably also conduct an investigation against the undertakings involved in the cartel under domestic and/or EU law[319]: whether it would be doing so as a result of an obligation arising from Article 3(1) may be a merely academic question.

In certain circumstances the use by sectoral regulators of their sector-specific regulatory powers might amount to the application of national competition law, with the consequence that the obligation to apply Articles 101 and 102 TFEU would arise in the event that the agreement or behaviour in question had an effect on trade between Member States[320].

(ii) Conflicts: Article 101

Recital 8 of Regulation 1/2003 states that it is necessary to create a 'level playing field' for agreements within the internal market. What this means is that, if an agreement is not prohibited under EU competition law, it should not be possible for an NCA or national court to apply stricter national competition law to it; this may be termed a 'convergence rule'[321]. Article 3(2) therefore provides that the application of national competition law may not lead to the prohibition of agreements, decisions by associations of undertakings or concerted practices which may affect trade between Member States but which do not restrict competition within the meaning of Article 101(1) or which fulfil the conditions of Article 101(3) or which are covered by a block exemption. There appear to have been no major difficulties with the application of the convergence rule between 2004 and 2009[322]. In terms of UK law it follows that, in so far as agreements affect trade between Member States but do not infringe Article 101(1) or do satisfy the criteria set out in Article 101(3), it would not be possible to take action against them under the market investigation provisions of the Enterprise Act 2002[323].

(iii) Conflicts: Article 102

The position in relation to Article 102 is different, since Regulation 1/2003 does not demand convergence in relation to unilateral behaviour. Recital 8 of the Regulation states that Member States should not be precluded from adopting and applying on their territory stricter national competition laws which prohibit or impose sanctions on unilateral conduct. Article 3(2) therefore makes provision to this effect. An example of a stricter national law on unilateral behaviour would be one that is intended to protect economically

---

[316] [2009] EWCA Crim 2575, [2010] 2 All ER 728, paras 21–37.

[317] Ibid, para 38; if an OFT investigation into an alleged cartel offence were considered to be 'acting under Article 101 or Article 102' for the purposes of Article 11(3) of Regulation 1/2003, the European Commission would have power under Article 11(6), by commencing its own proceedings, to relieve the OFT of the power to proceed.

[318] See eg Wils *Principles of European Antitrust Enforcement* (Hart Publishing, 2005), paras 153–157 and Wils 'Is Criminalization of EC Competition Law the Answer?' (2005) 28(2) World Competition 117, pp 130–133.

[319] *Modernisation* OFT 442, December 2004, paras 4.23–4.27.   [320] Ibid, paras 4.28–4.30.

[321] See the European Commission's *Guidelines on the application of Article [101(3) TFEU]* OJ [2004] C 101/8, para 14; *Faull and Nikpay*, para 2.30.

[322] See Commission Staff Working Paper accompanying the Report on the functioning of Regulation 1/2003, COM(2009) 206 final, para 159.

[323] See further ch 11, 'Relationship with Regulation 1/2003', pp 469–470.

dependent undertakings: several Member States have laws to this effect[324]. In terms of UK law it follows from Article 3(2) that it would be possible to take action under the market investigation provisions of the Enterprise Act 2002 against unilateral behaviour, such as refusal to supply or the imposition of unfair prices or other trading conditions, to stricter effect than the position under Article 102[325]. In so far as legislation such as the UK Gas Act 1986, the Electricity Act 1989 or the Communications Act 2003 provides for the imposition of *ex ante* regulatory controls on the unilateral behaviour of regulated undertakings, and in so far as those controls could be regarded as provisions of competition law, Article 3(2) would allow them to be applied to achieve a stricter outcome than under Article 102. In the event that they were intended to protect some other legitimate interest than the protection of competition they could be applied by virtue of Article 3(3) (below).

In its *Report on the functioning of Regulation 1/2003*[326] the Commission noted that the business and legal communities had criticised the divergence of legal standards on unilateral conduct across the Member States. The Commission considers that the exclusion of unilateral conduct from the scope of the convergence rule is a matter which warrants further reflection.

(iv) Protection of 'other legitimate interests'

Recital 9 of Regulation 1/2003 states that its provisions should not preclude Member States from applying national legislation that protects legitimate interests other than the protection of competition on the market, provided that such legislation is compatible with the general principles and other provisions of EU law[327]. Article 3(3) therefore provides that the Regulation does not preclude the application of provisions of national law that 'predominantly pursue an objective different from that pursued by Articles [101 and 102 TFEU]'. Recital 9 of the Regulation says that Articles 101 and 102 have as their objective 'the protection of competition on the market', which provides a benchmark against which to measure whether a particular national provision pursues an objective different from the EU competition rules. The recital specifically says that a Member State could apply legislation intended to combat unfair trading practices, for example a law that prevents the imposition on customers of terms and conditions that are unjustified, disproportionate or without consideration.

There may be situations in which it will be unclear whether a particular national provision is predominantly concerned with matters other than the protection of competition. Certain regulatory rules – for example requiring the provision of a universal service or the protection of vulnerable consumers – clearly pursue objectives other than the protection of competition and so could be applied by virtue of Article 3(3)[328]. Consumer laws which provide protection against, for example, unfair contract terms, misleading advertising or sharp selling practices would also seem to pursue a predominantly different objective from

---

[324] The Commission Staff Working Paper accompanying the Report on the functioning of Regulation 1/2003 SEC(2009) 574 final, paras 162–169 provides examples of national rules concerning economic dependence and similar situations, available at www.ec.europa.eu.

[325] See further ch 11, 'Relationship with Regulation 1/2003', p 469–470.

[326] SEC(2009) 574, para 27; see also Commission Staff Working Paper accompanying the Report on the functioning of Regulation 1/2003, COM(2009) 206 final, paras 160–179.

[327] See, to similar effect, Article 21(4) of the EUMR, discussed in ch 21, 'Article 21(4): legitimate interest clause', pp 851–852.

[328] See further *Concurrent application to regulated industries* OFT 405, December 2004, para 4.7.

Articles 101 and 102 TFEU[329]. However a national rule that was dependent, for example, on a prior finding of significant market power would look more like a rule whose concern was the protection of competition[330]. In that case the derogation provided by Article 3(3) would not be applicable, so that the position would be governed by Article 3(2): a stricter national rule in relation to agreements could not be applied, but a stricter rule on unilateral behaviour could be.

In *Days Medical Aids Ltd v Pihsiang*[331] the High Court suggested that the common law doctrine of restraint of trade could not be said predominantly to pursue an objective different from Articles 101 and 102 TFEU, with the result that it could not be applied to invalidate an agreement that did not infringe Article 101.

5. The Institutional Structure of EU and UK Competition Law

The following diagrams set out the institutional architecture of EU and UK competition law.

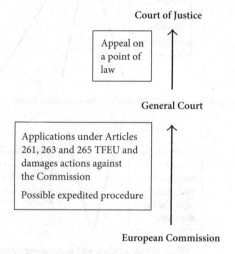

Court of Justice

Appeal on a point of law

General Court

Applications under Articles 261, 263 and 265 TFEU and damages actions against the Commission

Possible expedited procedure

European Commission

Fig. 2.1   Articles 101 and 102 TFEU; EU Merger Regulation

---

[329] For discussion on this point see Commission Staff Working Paper accompanying the Report on the functioning of Regulation 1/2003, COM(2009) 206 final, para 181.

[330] See eg Communications Act 2003, s 45.

[331] [2004] EWHC 44, paras 254–266; see also *Jones v Ricoh UK Ltd* [2010] EWHC 1743, para 49.

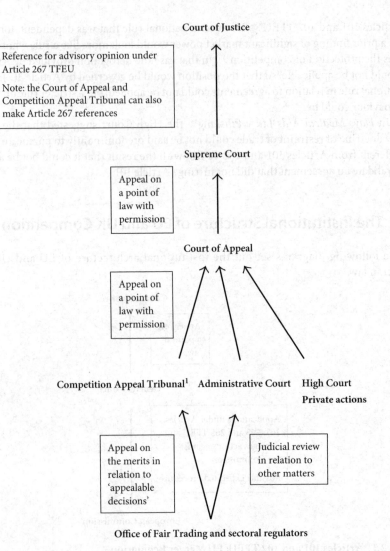

Fig. 2.2 Articles 101 and 102 TFEU; Competition Act 1998, Chapter I and II Prohibitions

[1] The Competition Appeal Tribunal also hears 'follow-on' actions for damages under sections 47A and 47B of the Competition Act 1998.

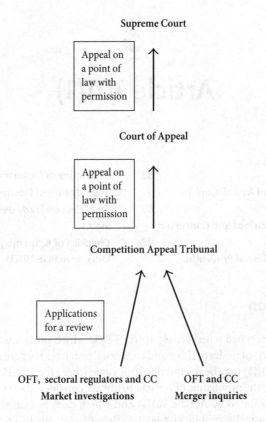

Fig. 2.3 Market investigations and merger investigations

3

Article 101(1)[1]

1. Introduction

This chapter is concerned with Article 101(1) TFEU which prohibits agreements, decisions by associations of undertakings and concerted practices that are restrictive of competition. Article 101(1) may be declared inapplicable where the criteria set out in Article 101(3) are satisfied: the provisions of Article 101(3) are considered in chapter 4. An agreement which is prohibited by Article 101(1) and which does not satisfy Article 101(3) is stated to be automatically void by virtue of Article 101(2)[2]. The full text of Article 101 is as follows:

1. The following shall be prohibited as incompatible with the internal market: all agreements between undertakings, decisions by associations of undertakings and concerted practices which may affect trade between Member States and which have as their object or effect the prevention, restriction or distortion of competition within the internal market, and in particular those which:

   (a) directly or indirectly fix purchase or selling prices or any other trading conditions;

   (b) limit or control production, markets, technical development, or investment;

   (c) share markets or sources of supply;

   (d) apply dissimilar conditions to equivalent transactions with other trading parties, thereby placing them at a competitive disadvantage;

   (e) make the conclusion of contracts subject to the acceptance by other parties of supplementary obligations which, by their nature or according to commercial usage, have no connection with the subject of such contracts.

---

[1] For further reading on Article 101(1) readers are referred to Faull and Nikpay *The EC Law of Competition* (Oxford University Press, 2nd ed, 2007), ch 3, paras 3.01–3.392; Bellamy & Child *European Community Law of Competition* (Oxford University Press, 6th ed, 2008, eds Roth and Rose), ch 3.

[2] See ch 8, 'The sanction of voidness', pp 319–325 on the implications of the sanction of voidness in Article 101(2).

2. Any agreements or decisions prohibited pursuant to this Article shall be automatically void.

3. The provisions of paragraph 1 may, however, be declared inapplicable in the case of:
    - any agreement or category of agreements between undertakings;
    - any decision or category of decisions by associations of undertakings;
    - any concerted practice or category of concerted practices;

    which contributes to improving the production or distribution of goods or to promoting technical or economic progress, while allowing consumers a fair share of the resulting benefit, and which does not:

    (a) impose on the undertakings concerned restrictions which are not indispensable to the attainment of these objectives;

    (b) afford such undertakings the possibility of eliminating competition in respect of a substantial part of the products in question.

Many aspects of the basic prohibition in Article 101(1) require elaboration. First, the meaning of 'undertakings' and 'associations of undertakings' and then the terms 'agreements', 'decisions' and 'concerted practices' will be explained. The fourth section of this chapter will consider what is meant by agreements that 'have as their object or effect the prevention, restriction or distortion of competition'. The fifth section deals with the *de minimis* doctrine. Section six explains the requirement of an effect on trade between Member States. The chapter concludes with a checklist of agreements that, for a variety of reasons, normally fall outside Article 101(1).

2. Undertakings and Associations of Undertakings[3]

Five issues must be considered in respect of this term: first, its basic definition for the purpose of Articles 101 and 102[4]; second, the meaning of 'associations of undertakings'; third, whether two or more legal persons form a single economic entity – and therefore comprise one undertaking – and the significance of such a finding; fourth, whether two or more entities may be treated as one undertaking where there is a corporate reorganisation; and fifth which undertaking is liable for an infringement of competition law when one business is sold to another.

The Treaty does not define an 'undertaking'[5]: it has been a task for the EU Courts to clarify its meaning[6]. However it is a critically important term, since only agreements and concerted practices *between undertakings* are caught by Article 101; similarly, Article 102 applies only to abuses committed by dominant *undertakings*. There is no doubt that organs of the Member States (for example public authorities, municipalities, communes, the health service) and entities entrusted by the Member States with regulatory or other

---

[3] For a particularly interesting discussion of this expression see Odudu 'The meaning of undertaking within Article 81 EC' in *The Boundaries of EC Competition Law: The Scope of Article 81* (Oxford University Press, 2006), ch 3.

[4] The term undertaking has the same meaning under Article 102, and this section discusses cases decided under both Article 101 and Article 102.

[5] Article 80 of the former ECSC Treaty and Article 80 of the Euratom Treaty do contain definitions of an undertaking for their respective purposes, as does Article 1 of Protocol 22 of the EEA Agreement.

[6] See Case T-99/04 *AC-Treuhand v Commission* [2008] ECR II-1501, [2008] 5 CMLR 962, para 144: 'the gradual clarification of the notions of "agreement" and "undertaking" by the Community judicature is of decisive importance in assessing whether their application in practice is definite and foreseeable'.

functions are capable of distorting competition. The competition law question is whether the distortion of competition is the responsibility of an *undertaking*: if it is, the behaviour in question may infringe Articles 101 and/or 102, subject to the availability of various defences such as state compulsion[7] or Article 106(2)[8]. However where the behaviour that distorts competition is not that of an undertaking, it will not be subject to competition law scrutiny at all. As will be seen, there have been many cases in which the EU Courts have been asked whether a particular entity, accused of anti-competitive behaviour, qualified as an undertaking for the purpose of the competition rules. The question often arises in the case of so-called 'mixed markets', where the state and private firms are both present on a market and where, typically, the latter complain of anti-competitive conduct on the part of the former. In so far as it is thought that there should be 'competitive neutrality' – more colloquially a level playing field – there would seem to be an attraction in treating all the operators on such markets as undertakings, with the responsibilities that that entails[9]; however this is not the inevitable outcome, as will be seen in the case law discussed below.

A separate question, considered in chapter 6, is whether Member States themselves may be liable for the anti-competitive behaviour of public undertakings and undertakings that have 'special or exclusive rights'.

(A) **Basic definition**

The Court of Justice held in *Höfner and Elser v Macrotron GmbH*[10] that:

> the concept of an undertaking encompasses every entity engaged in an economic activity regardless of the legal status of the entity and the way in which it is financed.

In *Pavlov*[11] the Court added that:

> It has also been consistently held that any activity consisting in offering goods or services on a given market is an economic activity.

In *Wouters v Algemene Raad van de Nederlandsche Orde van Advocaten*[12] the Court said that the competition rules in the Treaty:

> do not apply to activity which, by its nature, its aim and the rules to which it is subject does not belong to the sphere of economic activity … or which is connected with the exercise of the powers of a public authority.

These statements are a helpful starting point in understanding the meaning of the term undertaking and will be considered in the text that follows.

(i) Need to adopt a functional approach

It is important to understand at the outset that the same legal entity may be acting as an undertaking when it carries on one activity but not when it is carrying on another. A 'functional approach' must be adopted when determining whether an entity, when

---

[7] See 'State compulsion and highly regulated markets', pp 137–138 below.
[8] See ch 6, 'Article 106(2)', pp 235–242.
[9] For discussion see *Competition in mixed markets: ensuring competitive neutrality* OFT 1242, July 2010, available at www.oft.gov.uk.
[10] Case C-41/90 [1991] ECR I-1979, [1993] 4 CMLR 306, para 21.
[11] Cases C-180/98 etc [2000] ECR I-6451, [2001] 4 CMLR 30, para 75.
[12] Case C-309/99 [2002] ECR I-1577, [2002] 4 CMLR 913, para 57.

engaged in a particular activity, is doing so as an undertaking for the purpose of the competition rules[13]. As the Court of Justice said in *MOTOE*[14]:

> The classification as an activity falling within the exercise of public powers or as an economic activity must be carried out separately for each activity exercised by a given entity[15].

Thus, for example, a local authority in the UK may (a) have powers to adopt bye-laws specifying where cars can and cannot be parked and (b) own land which it operates commercially as a car park. When performing function (a) the authority would, in the language of *Wouters*, be exercising the powers of a public authority and therefore would not be acting as an undertaking; the behaviour in (b), however, would be economic, and therefore that of an undertaking[16]. In *SELEX Sistemi Integrati SpA v Commission*[17] the General Court had to decide whether Eurocontrol, an entity created by Member States of the EU for the purpose of establishing navigational safety in the airspace of Europe, was acting as an undertaking for the purpose of the EU competition rules. The Court concluded that some of Eurocontrol's activities – for example setting technical standards, procuring prototypes and managing intellectual property rights – were not economic; however it also concluded that some other activities – for example the provision of technical assistance to national administrations – could be separated from its other functions[18] and be characterised as economic[19]. An appeal by SELEX to the Court of Justice against the former ruling was dismissed; and in the course of its judgment the Court held that the General Court had erred in concluding that the latter activities were economic[20].

(ii) 'Engaged in an economic activity'

The sentence quoted from the *Höfner and Elser* judgment states that every entity engaged in economic activity does so as an undertaking: it is the idea of economic activity, therefore, that needs to be explored.

(A) *Offering goods or services on a given market is an economic activity*

As noted above the Court of Justice stated in *Pavlov* that activity consisting in offering goods or services on a market is an economic activity. The Commission held in *Spanish Courier Services*[21] that the Spanish Post Office, in so far as it was providing services on the market, was acting as an undertaking; in *Höfner and Elser* the Court of Justice reached the same conclusion in respect of the German Federal Employment Office. In *Ambulanz Glöckner v Landkreis Südwestpfalz*[22] the Court of Justice held that medical aid organisations providing ambulance services for remuneration were acting as undertakings for the purpose of the competition rules[23]. A legal entity that acts as a 'facilitator' to a cartel can be an undertaking, even though it does not itself produce the goods or services that are

---

[13] On this point see the Opinion of Advocate General Jacobs in Cases C-67/96 etc *Albany International BV v SBT* [1999] ECR I-5751, [2000] 4 CMLR 446, para 207; this Opinion contains an invaluable discussion of the meaning of undertakings in Article 101(1).

[14] Case C-49/07 [2008] ECR I-4863, [2008] 5 CMLR 790.   [15] Ibid, para 25.

[16] See eg *Eco-Emballages* OJ [2001] L 233/37, [2001] 5 CMLR 1096, para 70: French local authorities were acting as undertakings when entering into contracts in relation to the collection of household waste.

[17] Case T-155/04 [2006] ECR II-4797, [2007] 4 CMLR 372.

[18] Ibid, para 86.   [19] Ibid, para 92.

[20] Case C-113/07 P *SELEX Sistemi Integrati SpA v Commission* [2009] ECR-I 2207, [2009] 4 CMLR 1083, paras 77–79.

[21] OJ [1990] L 233/19, [1991] 4 CMLR 560.

[22] Case C-475/99 [2001] ECR I-8089, [2002] 4 CMLR 726.   [23] Ibid, paras 19–22.

cartelised[24]. The mere holding of shares in an undertaking does not, in itself, mean that the owner of the shares is itself an undertaking engaged in economic activity; however the position would be different where the shareholder actually exercises control by involving itself in the management of the undertaking[25].

(B) No need for a profit-motive or economic purpose

The fact that an organisation lacks a profit-motive[26] or does not have an economic purpose[27] does not, in itself, mean that an activity is not economic. On this basis the Commission held in *Distribution of Package Tours During the 1990 World Cup*[28] that FIFA, the body responsible for the 1990 Football World Cup in Italy, as well as the Italian football association and the local organising committee, were undertakings subject to Article 101[29]. In *Piau*[30] the General Court held that the practice of football by football clubs is an economic activity[31], and that national associations that group the clubs together are associations of undertakings; the position does not alter because the national associations group amateur clubs alongside professional ones[32]. The General Court also held in this case that FIFA was an association of undertakings[33].

(C) 'Regardless of the legal status of the entity and the way in which it is financed'

The Court of Justice in *Höfner and Elser* held that an assessment of whether an entity was acting as an undertaking was to be determined 'regardless of the legal status of the entity and the way in which it is financed'. An entity can be found to be acting as an undertaking only as a result of the activity it is engaged in; its legal form is irrelevant. Companies and partnerships of course can qualify as undertakings, but so too can other entities such as agricultural cooperatives[34], P and I clubs[35] and trade associations: it follows that agreements between trade associations may themselves be caught by Article 101(1)[36]. Natural persons have often been held to qualify as undertakings[37], although an individual acting

---

[24] *Organic peroxides*, Commission decision of 10 December 2003, paras 331–349, upheld on appeal to the General Court Case T-99/04 *AC-Treuhand v Commission* [2008] ECR II-1501, [2008] 5 CMLR 962; see further ch 13, 'Price fixing in any form is caught', p 525.

[25] Case C-222/04 *Cassa di Risparmio di Firenze* [2006] ECR I-289, [2008] 1 CMLR 705, paras 111–113.

[26] See eg Cases 209/78 etc *Van Landewyck v Commission* [1980] ECR 3125, [1981] 3 CMLR 134, para 88; *P & I Clubs* OJ [1985] L 376/2, [1989] 4 CMLR 178; *P & I Clubs* OJ [1999] L 125/12, [1999] 5 CMLR 646; Case C-244/94 *Fédération Française des Sociétés d'Assurance* [1995] ECR I-4013, [1996] 4 CMLR 536, para 21; Cases C-67/96 etc *Albany International BV v SBT* [1999] ECR I-5751, [2000] 4 CMLR 446, para 85.

[27] Case 155/73 *Italy v Sacchi* [1974] ECR 409, [1974] 2 CMLR 177, paras 13–14; Case C-222/04 *Cassa di Risparmio di Firenze* [2006] ECR I-289, [2008] 1 CMLR 705, para 123.

[28] OJ [1992] L 326/31, [1994] 5 CMLR 253, para 43.

[29] Ibid, paras 44–57; see similarly *UEFA's Broadcasting Regulations* OJ [2001] L 171/12, [2001] 5 CMLR 654, para 47.

[30] Case T-193/02 [2005] ECR I-209, [2005] 5 CMLR 42; see also Case C-519/04 P *Meca-Medina v Commission* [2006] ECR I-6991, [2006] 5 CMLR 1023: the IOC was held to be an undertaking and an association of undertakings.

[31] Case T-193/02 [2005] ECR I-209, [2005] 5 CMLR 42, para 69.

[32] Ibid, para 70.　　　[33] Ibid, para 72.

[34] See eg Case 61/80 *Coöperative Stremsel- en Kleurselfabriek v Commission* [1981] ECR 851, [1982] 1 CMLR 240; *MELDOC* OJ [1986] L 348/50, [1989] 4 CMLR 853.

[35] *P & I Clubs* OJ [1985] L 376/2, [1989] 4 CMLR 178; *P & I Clubs* OJ [1999] L 125/12, [1999] 5 CMLR 646, paras 50–51.

[36] See eg Case 71/74 *FRUBO v Commission* [1975] ECR 563, [1975] 2 CMLR 123; Case 96/82 *IAZ International Belgium NV v Commission* [1983] ECR 3369, [1984] 3 CMLR 276; *Algemene Schippersvereniging v ANTIB* OJ [1985] L 219/35, [1988] 4 CMLR 698, upheld on appeal Case 272/85 *ANTIB v Commission* [1987] ECR 2201, [1988] 4 CMLR 677.

[37] See eg *AOIP v Beyrard* OJ [1976] L 6/8, [1976] 1 CMLR D14 where a patent licence between an individual and a company was held to fall within Article 101(1); *Reuter/BASF* OJ [1976] L 254/40, [1976] 2 CMLR D44;

as an employee would not be[38]; nor would an individual purchasing goods or services as an end user/consumer, since that behaviour is not economic[39].

Public authorities, such as the Federal Employment Office in *Höfner and Elser* or the Autonomous Administration of State Monopolies in *Banchero*[40], have been held to be engaged in activities of an economic nature with regard to employment procurement and the offering of goods and services on the market for manufactured tobacco respectively. State-owned corporations may act as undertakings[41], as may bodies entrusted by the state with particular tasks[42] and quasi-governmental bodies which carry on economic activities[43]. Aéroports de Paris, responsible for the planning, administration and development of civil air transport installations in Paris, the Portuguese Airports Authority, ANA and the Finnish Civil Aviation Administration were all found by the Commission to constitute undertakings[44]. In *Aluminum Products*[45] foreign trade organisations in east European countries were regarded as undertakings, even though they had no existence separate from the state under their domestic law: claims of sovereign immunity should be confined to acts which are those of government and not of trade. The same point was made by the Commission in its decision in *Amministrazione Autonoma dei Monopoli di Stato*[46].

(iii) Activities that are not economic

Activities provided on the basis of 'solidarity' are not economic; nor is the exercise of public power. Procurement pursuant to a non-economic activity is not economic.

(A) Solidarity[47]

There have been several cases in which the question has arisen whether entities providing social protection, for example social security, pensions, health insurance or health care, did so as undertakings. The case law makes a distinction between situations in which

---

RAI v UNITEL OJ [1978] L 157/39, [1978] 3 CMLR 306 where opera singers were undertakings; *Vaessen BV v Moris* OJ [1979] L 19/32, [1979] 1 CMLR 511; Case 35/83 *BAT v Commission* [1985] ECR 363, [1985] 2 CMLR 470; Case 42/84 *Remia BV and Verenigde Bedrijven Nutricia NV v Commission* [1985] ECR 2545, [1987] 1 CMLR 1; *Breeders' Rights: Roses* OJ [1985] L 369/9, [1988] 4 CMLR 193: *French Beef* OJ [2003] L 209/12, paras 104–108, upheld on appeal to the General Court Cases T-217/03 and T-245/03 *FNCBV v Commission* [2006] ECR II-4987, [2008] 5 CMLR 406 and again on appeal to the Court of Justice Cases C-101/07 P and C-110/07 P *FNCBV v Commission* [2008] ECR I-10193, [2009] 4 CMLR 743; see also Case C-172/03 *Wolfgang Heiser v Finanzamt Innsbruck* [2005] ECR I-1627, [2005] 2 CMLR 402, a case on state aid in which a self-employed dentist was held to be acting as an undertaking.

[38] See 'Employees and trades unions', pp 90–91 below.

[39] On this point see Cases C-180/98 etc *Pavel Pavlov v Stichting Pensioenfonds Medische Specialisten* [2000] ECR I-6451, [2001] 4 CMLR 30, paras 78–81.

[40] Case C-387/93 [1995] ECR I-4663, [1996] 1 CMLR 829, para 50.

[41] See eg Case 155/73 *Sacchi* [1974] ECR 409, [1974] 2 CMLR 177; Case 41/83 *Italy v Commission* [1985] ECR 873, [1985] 2 CMLR 368.

[42] Such bodies have a limited dispensation from the competition rules by virtue of Article 106(2) TFEU: see ch 6, 'Article 106(2)', pp 235–242.

[43] Case 258/78 *Nungesser KG v Commission* [1982] ECR 2015, [1983] 1 CMLR 278.

[44] See respectively *Alpha Flight Services/Aéroports de Paris* OJ [1998] L 230/10, [1998] 5 CMLR 611, paras 49–55, upheld on appeal Case T-128/98 [2000] ECR II-3929, [2001] 4 CMLR 1376, paras 120–126 and by the Court of Justice in Case C-82/01 P [2002] ECR I-9297, [2003] 4 CMLR 609, paras 78–82; *Portuguese Airports* OJ [1999] L 69/31, [1999] 5 CMLR 103, para 12, upheld on appeal Case C-163/99 *Portugal v Commission* [2001] ECR I-2613, [2002] 4 CMLR 1319; *Ilmailulaitos/Luftfartsverket* OJ [1999] L 69/24, [1999] 5 CMLR 90, paras 21–23.

[45] OJ [1985] L 92/1, [1987] 3 CMLR 813: see the Commission's XIVth *Report on Competition Policy* (1984), point 57; see similarly *Re Colombian Coffee* OJ [1982] L 360/31, [1983] 1 CMLR 703.

[46] OJ [1998] L 252/47, [1998] 5 CMLR 786, para 21.

[47] See Winterstein 'Nailing the Jellyfish: Social Security and Competition Law' (1999) 20 ECLR 324.

such protection is provided in a market context on the one hand, or on the basis of 'solidarity' on the other. Solidarity was defined by Advocate General Fennelly in *Sodemare v Regione Lombardia*[48] as 'the inherently uncommercial act of involuntary subsidisation of one social group by another'[49]. Where social protection is provided on the basis of solidarity, it is not provided by an undertaking. The cases in which this issue has had to be examined are very fact-specific. As Advocate General Jacob said in his Opinion in *AOK Bundesverband*[50]:

> Schemes come in a wide variety of forms, ranging from State social security schemes at one end of the spectrum to private individual schemes operated by commercial insurers at the other. Classification is thus necessarily a question of degree[51].

In *Poucet v Assurances Générales de France*[52] the Court of Justice concluded that French regional social security offices administering sickness and maternity insurance schemes to self-employed persons were not acting as undertakings, but it reached the opposite conclusion in relation to a differently-constituted scheme in *Fédération Française des Sociétés d'Assurance*[53]. The difference was that in *Poucet* the benefits payable were identical for all recipients, contributions were proportionate to income, the pension rights were not proportionate to the contributions made and schemes that were in surplus helped to finance those which had financial difficulties; the schemes were based on the principle of solidarity. In *Fédération Française*, on the other hand, the benefits payable depended on the amount of the contributions paid by recipients and the financial results of the investments made by the managing organisation; the manager of the scheme was carrying on an economic activity in competition with life assurance companies. In *Albany International BV v Stichting Bedrijfspensioenfonds Textielindustrie*[54] the Court of Justice held that the pension fund in that case was acting as an undertaking, since it was carrying on an economic activity: its function was to make investments, the result of which determined the amount of benefits that the fund could pay to its members[55]; as such, this fund was different from the one in *Poucet*.

In *Cisal di Battistello Venanzio & C Sas v INAIL*[56] the Court of Justice held that INAIL, entrusted by law with management of a scheme providing insurance against accidents at work, was not acting as an undertaking for the purposes of the competition rules because it fulfilled an exclusively social function based on the principle of solidarity. Similarly in *AOK Bundesverband*[57] the Court of Justice held that German sickness funds were involved in the management of the social security system, fulfilling an exclusively social function founded on the principle of solidarity; it followed that they were not acting as undertakings. The same conclusion was reached in *Kattner Stahlbau GmbH v Maschinenbau- und Metal- Berufsgenossenschaft*[58] where MMB fulfilled an exclusively social function in providing insurance against accidents at work and occupational diseases, proceeded on the basis of solidarity and was subject to state supervision. In *AG2R Prévoyance v Beaudort*

[48] Case C-70/95 [1997] ECR I-3395, [1997] 3 CMLR 591.

[49] [1997] ECR I-3395, [1997] 3 CMLR 591, para 29.

[50] Cases C-264/01 etc [2004] ECR I-2493, [2004] 4 CMLR 1261.   [51] Ibid, para 36.

[52] Cases C-159/91 and 160/91 [1993] ECR I-637.

[53] Case C-244/94 [1995] ECR I-4013, [1996] 4 CMLR 536.

[54] Cases C-67/96 etc [1999] ECR I-5751, [2000] 4 CMLR 446: for commentary on this case see Gyselen (2000) 37 CML Rev 425; see also Cases C-180/98 etc *Pavel Pavlov v Stichting Pensioenfonds Medische Specialisten* [2000] ECR I-6451, [2001] 4 CMLR 30, paras 102–119.

[55] Ibid, paras 71–87.   [56] Case C-218/00 [2002] ECR I-691, [2002] 4 CMLR 833.

[57] Cases C-264/01 etc [2004] ECR I-2493, [2004] 4 CMLR 1261; see also, under Article 107 TFEU on state aid, Cases C-266/04 *Casino France* [2005] ECR I-9481, paras 45–55.

[58] Case C-350/07 [2009] ECR I-1513, [2009] CMLR 1339, paras 33–68.

Père et Fils SARL[59] the Court of Justice suggested that AG2R, which operated a scheme for supplementary reimbursement of healthcare costs that was 'characterised by a high degree of solidarity'[60], might nevertheless be acting as an undertaking where it enjoyed a degree of autonomy, that is to say was relatively free from state control[61].

(B) Activities connected with the exercise of the powers of a public authority are not economic

Although it is clear that state-owned corporations or public authorities may qualify as undertakings when engaged in economic activity, the *Wouters* judgment says they would not do so when their behaviour 'is connected with the exercise of the powers of a public authority'[62]. In *Corinne Bodson v Pompes Funèbres des Régions Libérées SA*[63] a French law entrusted the performance of funeral services to local communes; many of the communes in turn awarded concessions to provide those services to private undertakings. The Court of Justice held that Article 101 did not apply to 'contracts for concessions concluded between communes *acting in their capacity as public authorities* and undertakings entrusted with the provision of a public service' (emphasis added)[64]. An entity acts in the exercise of official authority where the activity in question is 'a task in the public interest which forms part of the essential functions of the State' and where that activity 'is connected by its nature, its aim and the rules to which it is subject with the exercise of powers...which are typically those of a public authority'[65]. For the same reason, in *SAT Fluggesellschaft v Eurocontrol*[66] the Court of Justice concluded that Eurocontrol was not acting as an undertaking when it created and collected route charges from users of air navigation services on behalf of the States that had created it[67]. In *Calì e Figli*[68] the Court of Justice held that a private company engaged in anti-pollution surveillance in Genoa harbour would not be acting as an undertaking when discharging that particular responsibility, since this was a task in the public interest, forming part of one of the essential functions of the state in protecting the maritime environment: this judgment is of particular interest as the public duty was being carried out by a private body.

(C) Procurement that is ancillary to a non-economic activity is not economic

In *FENIN v Commission*[69] a complaint was made to the Commission that 26 public bodies in Spain responsible for the operation of the Spanish national health system were abusing their dominant buyer power by delaying unreasonably the payment of invoices. The Commission rejected the complaint on the basis that the public bodies were not acting as undertakings. FENIN, an association representing most undertakings marketing medi-

[59] Case C-437/09 [2011] ECR I-000, [2011] 4 CMLR 1029; see also the judgment of the EFTA Court in Case E-5/07 *Private Barnehagers Landsforbund v EFTA Surveillance Authority* [2008] 2 CMLR 818, paras 82–83: Norwegian State not acting as an undertaking when funding municipal kindergartens.

[60] Case C-437/09 [2011] ECR I-000, [2011] 4 CMLR 1029, para 52.   [61] Ibid, paras 53–65.

[62] See to the same effect Case C-343/95 *Calì e Figli* [1997] ECR I-1547, [1997] 5 CMLR 484, paras 16–17.

[63] Case 30/87 [1988] ECR 2479, [1989] 4 CMLR 984.   [64] Ibid, para 18.

[65] Case C-343/95 *Calì e Figli* [1997] ECR I-1547, [1997] 5 CMLR 484, para 23.

[66] Case C-364/92 [1994] ECR I-43, [1994] 5 CMLR 208, para 30; different activities of Eurocontrol were held not to be economic in the *SELEX* case, ch 3 n 20 above.

[67] A similar conclusion had earlier been reached by the Commercial Court in London in *Irish Aerospace (Belgium) NV v European Organisation for the Safety of Air Navigation* [1992] 1 Lloyd's Rep 383.

[68] Case C-343/95 [1997] ECR I-1547, [1997] 5 CMLR 484.

[69] Case T-319/99 [2003] ECR II-357, [2003] 5 CMLR 34; it is interesting to compare this judgment with that of the UK Competition Appeal Tribunal in Case No 1006/2/1/01 *BetterCare Group Ltd v Director General of Fair Trading* [2002] CAT 7, [2002] Comp AR 299, a judgment which preceded that in *FENIN* and which came to a different view in relation to the procurement activities of the Health Trust in that case: see ch 9, 'The *BetterCare* case', pp 336–337.

cal goods and equipment used in Spanish hospitals, appealed to the General Court. The General Court dismissed the appeal. Its reasoning was that, when providing health care to citizens, the public bodies did so on the basis of solidarity: that behaviour therefore was not economic. The General Court then held that the activity of purchasing goods should not be dissociated from the purpose to which they would be put. Since the provision of health care was not economic, the ancillary behaviour of procurement for that purpose was not economic either[70]. This judgment was upheld on appeal to the Court of Justice[71]. The General Court's judgment did not say what the position would be where a health organisation purchasing goods uses them partly for the provision of state-sponsored health care on the basis of solidarity, but also charges certain patients, for example tourists from overseas, according to market principles: as the point had not been raised in the original complaint to the Commission, the General Court held that it did not need to adjudicate upon it[72]. The reasoning in *FENIN* was subsequently applied in *SELEX Sistemi Integrati SpA v Commission*[73].

(iv) The professions

Abundant case law has established that members of the professions can be undertakings for the purposes of the competition rules. In *Commission v Italy*[74] the Court of Justice held that customs agents in Italy, who offered for payment services consisting of the carrying out of customs formalities in relation to the import, export and transit of goods, were undertakings; it rejected the Italian Government's argument that the fact that the activity of customs agents is intellectual and requires authorisation and compliance with conditions meant that they were not undertakings. Self-employed medical specialists have been held to be undertakings[75], including when they are making contributions to their own supplementary pension scheme[76].

(v) Employees and trades unions

In *Jean Claude Becu*[77] the Court of Justice held that workers are, for the duration of their employment relationship, incorporated into the undertakings that employ them and thus form part of an economic unit with them; as such they do not constitute undertakings within the meaning of EU competition law[78]. Nor should the dock workers in that case, taken collectively, be regarded as constituting an undertaking[79]. However an ex-employee who carries on an independent business would be[80].

In *Albany*[81] the Court of Justice was concerned with a case where organisations representing employers and employees collectively agreed to set up a single pension fund

---

[70] Ibid, paras 35–36.

[71] Case C-205/03 P [2006] ECR I-6295, [2006] 5 CMLR 559, paras 25–26; Advocate General Maduro's Opinion in this case contains an extensive review of the law and literature on the issues raised.

[72] Case T-319/99 [2003] ECR II-357, [2003] 5 CMLR 34, paras 41–44.   [73] See ch 3 n 20 above.

[74] Case C-35/96 [1998] ECR I-3851, [1998] 5 CMLR 889; see similarly Case T-513/93 *CNSD v Commission* [2000] ECR II-1807, [2000] 5 CMLR 614, upholding the Commission's decision in *CNSD* OJ [1993] L 203/27, [1995] 5 CMLR 889; *Coapi* OJ [1995] L 122/37, [1995] 5 CMLR 468; *EPI code of conduct* OJ [1999] L 106/14, [1999] 5 CMLR 540, partially annulled on appeal to the General Court Case T-144/99 *Institut des Mandataires Agréés v Commission* [2001] ECR II-1087, [2001] 5 CMLR 77.

[75] Cases C-180/98 etc *Pavel Pavlov v Stichting Pensioenfonds Medische Specialisten* [2000] ECR I-6451, [2001] 4 CMLR 30, para 77.

[76] Ibid, paras 78–82; the Commission, intervening, had argued that, when making such contributions, the specialists were acting as consumers rather than as undertakings.

[77] Case C-22/98 [1999] ECR I-5665, [2001] 4 CMLR 968.

[78] Ibid, para 26.   [79] Ibid, para 27.

[80] See eg *Reuter/BASF* OJ [1976] L 254/40, [1976] 2 CMLR D44.   [81] See ch 3 n 54 above.

responsible for managing a supplementary pension scheme and requested the public authorities to make affiliation to the fund compulsory. One of the issues in the case was whether an agreement between such organisations was an agreement between undertakings. The Court of Justice's answer was that it was not. The Treaty's activities include not only the adoption of a competition policy, but also a policy in the social sphere: this is stated in Article 4(2)(b) TFEU and revealed, for example, in Article 153 TFEU, the purpose of which is to promote close cooperation between Member States in the social field, particularly in matters relating to the right of association and collective bargaining between employers and workers. The Court of Justice's view was that the social objectives pursued by collective agreements would be seriously undermined if they were subject to Article 101 and that therefore they fall outside it[82]. However the same exclusion does not apply in relation to a decision taken by members of the liberal professions, since it is not concluded in the context of collective bargaining between employers and employees[83]. In *Norwegian Federation of Trade Unions v Norwegian Association of Local and Regional Authorities*[84] the EFTA Court took a similar view of collective labour agreements under Article 53 of the European Economic Area ('EEA') Agreement, but noted that provisions in such agreements which pursue objectives extraneous to that of improving conditions of work and employment could amount to an infringement[85].

In *FNCBV v Commission*[86] the General Court rejected an argument that the application of Article 101 to agreements between associations of farmers to fix prices and to prevent imports of beef into France restricted the freedom of trade union activity[87].

(B) 'Associations of undertakings'

Article 101 applies not only to agreements and concerted practices between undertakings; it also applies to the decisions of 'associations of undertakings'[88]. A trade association does not have to have a commercial or economic activity of its own to be subject to Article 101(1)[89]; it follows that Article 101(1) may be applicable to the *decisions* of a trade association, even if it does not apply to its *agreements* because the association does not enter into the agreements as an undertaking[90]. Where an association is an undertaking, an agreement between it and other undertakings may be caught by Article 101(1)[91]. Article 101(1)

---

[82] Ibid, para 59; for critical comment see Van den Bergh and Camesasca 'Irreconcilable Principles? The Court of Justice Exempts Collective Labour Agreements from the Wrath of Antitrust' (2000) 25 EL Rev 492; Boni and Manzini 'National Social Legislation and EC Antitrust Law' (2001) 24 World Competition 239; see also Case C-222/98 *Van der Woude v Stichting Beatrixoord* [2000] ECR I-7111, [2001] 4 CMLR 93; Case C-437/09 *AG2R Prévoyance v Beaudort Père et Fils SARL* [2011] ECR I-000, [2011] 4 CMLR 1029, paras 28–36.

[83] Cases C-180/98 etc *Pavel Pavlov v Stichting Pensioenfonds Medische Specialisten* [2000] ECR I-6451, [2001] 4 CMLR 30, paras 67–70.

[84] Case E-8/00 [2002] 5 CMLR 160, paras 33–46.

[85] Ibid, paras 33–46 and 47–59.

[86] Cases T-217/03 and T-245/03 [2006] ECR II-4987, [2008] 5 CMLR 406, upheld on appeal Cases C-101/07 P and C-110/07 P *FNCBV v Commission* [2008] ECR I-10193, [2009] 4 CMLR 743.

[87] Ibid, paras 97–103.

[88] In *SEL-Imperial Ltd v The British Standards Institution* [2010] EWHC 854 (Ch) Roth J pointed out, at paras 36 and 41, that this expression is a term of art rather than one with a colloquial meaning.

[89] Cases T-25/95 etc *Cimenteries CBR SA v Commission* [2000] ECR II-491, [2000] 5 CMLR 204, para 1320, citing many earlier judgments of the Court of Justice and General Court to similar effect; *MasterCard*, Commission decision of 19 December 2007, para 342.

[90] See the Opinion of Advocate General Slynn in Case 123/85 *BNIC v Clair* [1985] ECR 391, p 396, [1985] 2 CMLR 430, p 442.

[91] Cases T-25/95 etc *Cimenteries CBR SA v Commission* [2000] ECR II-491, [2000] 5 CMLR 204, paras 1325 and 2622.

also applies to decisions by associations of trade associations[92]. A decision does not acquire immunity because it is subsequently approved and extended in scope by a public authority[93], nor does a trade association fall outside Article 101(1) because it is given statutory functions or because its members are appointed by the Government[94]. The Court of Justice has specifically stated that the public law status of a national body (for example an association of customs agents) does not preclude the application of Article 101[95].

In *Wouters v Algemene Raad van de Nederlandsche Orde van Advocaten*[96] the Court of Justice held that the General Council of the Dutch Bar was an association of undertakings, and rejected the argument that this was not so in so far as it was exercising its regulatory functions; the position might have been different if a majority of the members of the Council had been appointed by the state, rather than by members of the profession, and if the state had specified the public interest criteria to be taken into account by the Council[97]. Just as a 'functional' approach should be taken to the concept of an undertaking[98], so too it may be that a body can qualify as an association of undertakings when carrying out some of its tasks, but not when performing others (for example regulatory supervision on behalf of the state)[99].

(C) The 'single economic entity' doctrine

Article 101(1) does not apply to agreements between two or more legal persons that form a single economic entity: collectively they comprise a single undertaking, and so there is no agreement *between* undertakings. The most obvious example of this is an agreement between a parent and a subsidiary company, though the relationship between a principal and agent[100] and between a contractor and sub-contractor[101] is analogous. Numerous important consequences flow from the single economic entity doctrine, as will be seen below: one is that a parent company can be held liable for infringement of the competition rules by a subsidiary[102].

(i) Parent and subsidiary: the basic rule

Firms within the same corporate group can enter into legally enforceable agreements with one another. However such an agreement will not fall within Article 101 if the relationship

---

[92] See eg *Cematex* JO [1971] L 227/26, [1973] CMLR D135 and *Milchförderungsfonds* OJ [1985] L 35/35, [1985] 3 CMLR 101.

[93] *AROW v BNIC* OJ [1982] L 379/1, [1983] 2 CMLR 240; *Coapi* OJ [1995] L 122/37, [1995] 5 CMLR 468, para 32.

[94] Ibid and *Pabst and Richarz KG v BNIA* OJ [1976] L 231/24, [1976] 2 CMLR D63.

[95] Case C-35/96 *Commission v Italy* [1998] ECR I-3851, [1998] 5 CMLR 889, para 40; Cases C-180/98; C-184/98 *Pavel Pavlov v Stichting Pensioenfonds Medische Specialisten* [2000] ECR I-6451, [2001] 4 CMLR 30, para 85.

[96] Case C-309/99 [2002] ECR I-1577, [2002] 4 CMLR 913; the Opinion of Advocate General Léger deals with the meaning of 'association of undertakings' at length: see paras 56–87.

[97] Case C-309/99 [2002] ECR I-1577, [2002] 4 CMLR 913, paras 50–71.

[98] See 'Need to adopt a functional approach', pp 84–85 above.

[99] On this point see the Opinion of Advocate General Jacobs in Cases C-67/96 etc *Albany International BV v SBT* [1999] ECR I-5751, [2000] 4 CMLR 446, para 214 and Case C-309/99 *Wouters* [2002] ECR I-1577, [2002] 4 CMLR 913, para 64.

[100] See ch 16, 'Commercial Agents', pp 621–623 and, in particular, the Commission's *Guidelines on Vertical Restraints* OJ [2010] C 130/1, paras 12–21.

[101] See ch 16, 'Sub-Contracting Agreements', pp 676–677 and, in particular, the Commission's *Notice on Sub-contracting Agreements* OJ [1979] C 1/2, [1979] 1 CMLR 264.

[102] See 'Implications of the economic entity doctrine', pp 95–97 below; note that the same principle means that a principal may be found guilty of participating in a cartel if it was represented at cartel meetings by a commercial agent: see eg *Candle Waxes*, Commission decision of 1 October 2008, paras 399–409, on appeal to the General Court Cases T-543/08 etc *RWE and RWE Dea v Commission*, not yet decided.

between them is so close that economically they form a single economic entity, that is to say that they 'consist of a unitary organisation of personal, tangible and intangible elements, which pursue a specific economic aim on a long-term basis, and can contribute to the commission of an infringement of the kind referred to in [Article 101 TFEU]'[103]. Where this is the case the agreement is regarded as the internal allocation of functions within an economic group rather than a restrictive agreement between independent undertakings.

(ii) The *Viho* judgment

The proposition that agreements between entities in the same economic group fall outside Article 101 can be traced back to 1971[104]. The issue was revisited in *Viho v Commission*[105]. Parker Pen had established an integrated distribution system for Germany, France, Belgium, Spain and the Netherlands, where it used subsidiary companies for the distribution of its products. The Commission concluded that Article 101 had no application to this allocation of tasks within the Parker Pen group. This finding was challenged by a third party, Viho, which had been trying to obtain supplies of Parker Pen's products and which considered that the agreements between Parker Pen and its subsidiaries infringed Article 101. The General Court and the Court of Justice upheld the decision of the Commission, that Article 101 had no application. At paragraph 15 of its judgment the Court of Justice noted that Parker Pen held 100 per cent of the shares in the subsidiary companies, it directed their sales and marketing activities and it controlled sales, targets, gross margins, sales costs, cash flow and stocks:

> Parker and its subsidiaries thus form a single economic unit within which the subsidiaries do not enjoy real autonomy in determining their course of action in the market, but carry out the instructions issued to them by the parent company controlling them[106].

The Court of Justice went on to say that in those circumstances the fact that Parker Pen could divide national markets between its subsidiaries was outside Article 101, although it pointed out that such unilateral conduct could fall foul of Article 102 where the requirements for its application were satisfied[107]. In its *Guidelines on the applicability of Article 101 of the Treaty on the Functioning of the European Union to horizontal co-operation agreements*[108] the Commission relies on the *Viho* judgment for the proposition that '[w]hen a company exercises decisive influence over another company they form a

---

[103] See Case T-112/05 *Akzo Nobel NV v Commission* [2007] ECR II-5049, [2008] 4 CMLR 321, paras 57–58.

[104] See Case 22/71 *Béguelin Import v GL Import Export* [1971] ECR 949, [1972] CMLR 81; Case 15/74 *Centrafarm BV v Sterling Drug Inc* [1974] ECR 1147, [1974] 2 CMLR 480; Case 30/87 *Corinne Bodson v Pompes Funèbres des Régions Libérées SA* [1988] ECR 2479, [1989] 4 CMLR 984, para 19; the Commission reached a similar conclusion in *Re Christiani and Nielsen NV* JO [1969] L 165/12, [1969] CMLR D36 and in *Re Kodak* JO [1970] L 147/24, [1970] CMLR D19; see also *TFI/France 2 and France 3*, Commission's XXIXth *Report on Competition Policy* (1999), p 167.

[105] Case T-102/92 [1995] ECR II-17, [1995] 4 CMLR 299, upheld by the Court of Justice in Case C-73/95 P [1996] ECR I-5457, [1997] 4 CMLR 419: in his Opinion Advocate General Lenz discusses the case law on the economic entity doctrine referred to in footnote 104 ('an inconsistent picture') at paras 48–73; see also Case T-198/98 *Micro Leader Business v Commission* [1999] ECR II-3989, [2000] 4 CMLR 886, para 38 (agreements within the Microsoft group not subject to Article 101); on the similar position in US law see *Copperweld Corpn v Independence Tube Corpn* 467 US 752 (1984); *American Needle, Inc v National Football League et al* 560 US __ (2010).

[106] Case C-73/95 P [1996] ECR I-5457, [1997] 4 CMLR 419, para 16.

[107] Ibid, para 17; as to the possible application of Article 102 see *Interbrew*, Commission's XXVIth *Report on Competition Policy* (1996), pp 139–140.

[108] OJ [2011] C 11/1.

single economic entity and, hence, are part of the same undertaking'; it adds that the same would be true of 'sister companies, that is to say, companies over which decisive influence is exercised by the same parent company'[109].

(iii) The test of control

The crucial question, therefore, is whether parties to an agreement are independent in their decision-making or whether one is able to exercise decisive influence over the other with the result that the latter does not enjoy 'real autonomy' in determining its commercial policy on the market. For these purposes it is necessary to examine various factors such as the shareholding that a parent company has in its subsidiary, the composition of the board of directors, the extent to which the parent influences the policy of or issues instructions to the subsidiary and similar matters[110].

In *Akzo Nobel NV v Commission*[111] the issue before the Court of Justice was not whether an agreement between a parent and subsidiary infringed Article 101, but whether the Commission could address a decision to a parent company that it was liable for infringing Article 101 where it was a subsidiary company that was actually involved in the cartel. The Court held, referring to earlier judgments such as *Imperial Chemical Industries v Commission*[112], that where the parent has a 100 per cent shareholding in a subsidiary the parent exercises decisive influence over the subsidiary, and there is a rebuttable presumption that the parent does in fact exercise such influence[113]. In those circumstances the Commission may regard the parent as jointly and severally liable for any fine imposed on its subsidiary unless the parent can adduce sufficient evidence that the subsidiary acts independently on the market[114]. The Court added that, where the presumption applies, the Commission is not required to find additional evidence that the parent controlled the subsidiary: the presumption suffices unless rebutted[115]. In *Akzo Nobel* the General Court[116] had concluded that the parent had failed to rebut the presumption, and that judgment was upheld by the Court of Justice on appeal. There have been numerous other cases, before and since *Akzo*, in which a parent company has attempted to rebut the presumption: such attempts usually, though not inevitably, fail[117].

What is not clear is whether a minority shareholder might be held to have sufficient control to negate autonomy on the part of the subsidiary. Clearly the *Akzo* presumption would not apply, since that arises where a parent owns the totality, or almost the totality, of the shares of the subsidiary. Under Article 3(2) of the EU Merger Regulation ('the EUMR') a minority shareholder that would have the 'possibility of exercising decisive influence' over the affairs of another undertaking would have sufficient control for there to be a concentration[118]. The case law has yet to explain whether the notion of control in

---

[109] Ibid, para 11.

[110] See eg Case 107/82 *AEG-Telefunken v Commission* [1983] ECR 3151, [1984] 3 CMLR 325, paras 47–53.

[111] Case C-97/08 P [2009] ECR I-8237, [2009] 5 CMLR 2633.

[112] Case 48/69 [1972] ECR 619, [1972] CMLR 557.

[113] Case C-97/08 P [2009] ECR I-8237, [2009] 5 CMLR 2633, para 60; the presumption was also held to apply where Elf Aquitaine owned more than 97 per cent of the shares in Arkema France: Cases T-299/08 and T-343/08 *Elf Aquitaine v Commission* [2011] ECR II-000, on appeal to the Court of Justice Case C-401/11 P, not yet decided.

[114] Case C-97/08 P [2009] ECR I-8237, [2009] 5 CMLR 2633, para 61.

[115] Ibid, para 62; in saying this the Court was trying to avoid any possible confusion caused by its judgment in Case C-286/98 P *Stora Kopparbergs v Commission* [2000] ECR I-9925, [2001] 4 CMLR 370, which appeared to suggest that further indicia of control were needed even where the presumption applies.

[116] Case T-112/05 *Akzo Nobel NV v Commission* [2007] ECR II-5049, [2008] 4 CMLR 321.

[117] See 'Implications of the economic entity doctrine', pp 95–97 below.

[118] See ch 21, 'The concept of control', pp 834–836; note the more formalistic test of control for the purpose of calculating the turnover of 'undertakings concerned' in Article 5(4) of the EUMR: 'Turnover', pp 842–843.

the EUMR should be applied to the 'single economic entity' doctrine under Article 101(1), or whether the notions of control differ as between these two provisions. There are arguments for the adoption of a consistent approach[119]; however the notion of control under the EUMR includes negative control, and has the jurisdictional function of determining which transactions have to be scrutinised under that Regulation; the language of the cases under Article 101 suggest that there the requirement is for positive rather than negative control, where the test has substantive, as opposed to jurisdictional, consequences.

(iv) Decisions where the economic entity doctrine did not apply

In *Ijsselcentrale*[120] the Commission rejected the argument that four Dutch electricity generating companies and the joint venture that they controlled formed a single economic entity, and that therefore Article 101 did not apply to agreements between them. The fact that the generators formed part of an indivisible system of public electricity supply did not mean that they were one unit, for they were separate legal persons, not controlled by a single natural or legal person, and were able to determine their own conduct independently. In *Gosmé/Martell-DMP*[121] DMP was a joint subsidiary of Martell and Piper-Hiedsieck. Each parent held 50 per cent of the capital of DMP and the voting rights; half of the supervisory board members represented Martell shareholders and half Piper-Hiedsieck shareholders; DMP distributed brands not belonging to its parent companies; Martell and Piper-Hiedsieck products were invoiced to wholesalers on the same document; DMP had its own sales force and it alone concluded the contracts of sale with buying syndicates in France. In these circumstances the Commission concluded that Martell and DMP were independent undertakings, so that an agreement between them to identify and prevent parallel exports infringed Article 101 and attracted fines of €300,000 in the case of Martell and €50,000 in the case of DMP[122].

If a subsidiary becomes independent of its parent, for example by being sold off, an agreement between the two companies could be caught by Article 101 once the parent–subsidiary relationship ends. In *Austin Rover/Unipart*[123] the relationship between those undertakings following the privatisation of British Leyland and the selling off of Unipart was investigated by the Commission under Article 101, but was found to satisfy the criteria of Article 101(3).

(v) Implications of the economic entity doctrine

Numerous consequences flow from the economic entity doctrine.

First, although an agreement between connected firms may not infringe Article 101, the manipulation of a subsidiary company by a parent might mean that the competition rules are broken in other ways; for example a parent might order its subsidiaries to impose export bans on their distributors: the agreements containing such restrictions could themselves infringing Article 101[124].

---

[119] See Wils 'The Undertaking as Subject of EC Competition Law and the Imputation of Infringements to Natural or Legal Persons' (2000) 25 EL Rev 99, pp 104–108.

[120] OJ [1991] L 28/32, [1992] 5 CMLR 154, paras 22–24.

[121] OJ [1991] L 185/23, [1992] 5 CMLR 586, para 30.

[122] Note, however, the General Court's judgment in Case T-314/01 *Coöperatieve Verkoop- en Productievereniging van Aardappelmeel en Derivaten Avebe BA* [2006] ECR II-3085, [2007] 4 CMLR 9, where the General Court held that the parents of a joint venture were responsible for its participation in a cartel and could therefore be fined: see in particular paras 135–142.

[123] OJ [1988] L 45/34, [1988] 4 CMLR 513.

[124] See eg *Re Kodak* JO [1970] L 147/24, [1970] CMLR D 19.

Secondly, as already noted in *Akzo Nobel*, the economic entity doctrine means that a parent company can be liable for the activities of its subsidiaries. Whereas Article 101 applies to agreements between *undertakings*, Commission decisions must be addressed to *legal entities*, and one undertaking can consist of many entities. The Commission regularly addresses infringement decisions to both a parent and its subsidiary, each of which is then jointly and severally liable for the infringement[125]; the parents of a joint venture can also be the addressees of a decision where their joint venture has infringed Article 101[126]. In *Bananas*[127] the Commission concluded that Del Monte was jointly and severally liable with Weichert for infringing Article 101 as a result of the combination of a partnership agreement and a distribution agreement between them that enabled Del Monte to exercise decisive influence over Weichert[128]. There have been many appeals in which parents have argued that the presumption that 100 per cent ownership of a subsidiary confers decisive influence has been successfully rebutted: such appeals usually fail. However the General Court held in *Alliance One International v Commission*[129] that the presumption had been rebutted by one member of the Standard Group of companies, Trans-Continental Leaf Tobacco Corp, although not by two others, Alliance One International and Standard Commercial Tobacco[130].

Thirdly, where a parent and a subsidiary (or subsidiaries) form a single economic entity, the maximum fine permitted by Article 23(2) of Regulation 1/2003 of 10 per cent of an undertaking's worldwide turnover refers to the entire group's turnover, not just the turnover of the entity that actually committed the infringement: clearly this means that the maximum fine that can be imposed – for example where the subsidiary is part of a large conglomerate group – may be vastly greater than would otherwise be the case[131]. Fourthly, it may be that an action for damages can be brought either against a parent of a subsidiary company, or even against a subsidiary of a parent company; this can have significant implications for jurisdictional issues in civil litigation, potentially increasing the range of countries in which the action may be brought[132]. Fifthly, from a competition authority's point of view, it is desirable to attribute responsibility for infringements of the competition rules to the highest possible entity within a corporate group, not least in the hope that the board of directors of the parent company will take responsibility for eradicating anti-competitive behaviour from the entire organisation. Sixthly, the economic entity doctrine means that a parent company may bear responsibility for any infringements committed by subsidiaries within the corporate group, and this may lead to the imposition of higher fines because of recidivism[133].

A seventh point is that the Commission can carry out a surprise inspection of a legal entity that is part of an economic unit even though the alleged infringement of the competition rules was the responsibility of another part of it[134]. A further point is that the

---

[125] Recent examples include *Power transformers*, Commission decision of 7 October 2009, paras 175ff; *Heat stabilisers*, Commission decision of 11 November 2009, paras 500ff.

[126] See ch 3 n 122 above.   [127] Commission decision of 15 October 2008.

[128] The decision is on appeal to the General Court in Case T-587/08 *Fresh Del Monte Produce v Commission*, not yet decided.

[129] Case T-24/05 [2010] ECR II-000, [2011] 4 CMLR 545; see also Case T-185/06 *Air Liquide SA v Commission* [2011] ECR II-000, paras 63–64.

[130] Both the Commission and the two unsuccessful applicants have appealed to the Court of Justice in Cases C-628/10 P and C-14/11 P, not yet decided.

[131] See Case T-112/05 *Akzo Nobel NV v Commission* [2007] ECR II-5049, [2008] 4 CMLR 321, paras 90–91.

[132] See *Provimi Ltd v Aventis Animal Nutrition SA* [2003] EWHC 961 (Comm), [2003] All ER (D) 59 (May), a case arising out of the *Vitamins Cartel*, paras 31–36; see further ch 8, 'Private international law', pp 308–309.

[133] On the significance of recidivism to the level of fines see ch 7, 'Adjustments to the basic amount', pp 277–280.

[134] Case T-66/99 *Minoan Lines v Commission* [2003] ECR II-5515, [2005] 5 CMLR 1597.

logical consequence of the economic entity doctrine is that, when counting the number of undertakings that are party to an agreement for the purpose of applying one of the block exemptions, the legal and natural persons that form a single economic entity are counted as one[135]. Lastly, the immunity of agreements from Article 101 is in a sense a double-edged weapon: the EU Courts and the Commission have held that EU law can be applied to a parent company not present within the EU because of the conduct of its subsidiaries carried on there[136].

(D) Corporate reorganisation

Separate legal entities may be treated as one and the same undertaking where there is a corporate reorganisation in which one entity succeeds another: the liabilities of the latter may be attributed to the former[137]. In *Compagnie Royale Asturienne des Mines SA and Rheinzink GmbH v Commission*[138] the Court of Justice held that:

> a change in the legal form and name of an undertaking does not create a new undertaking free of liability for the anticompetitive behaviour of its predecessor when, from an economic point of view, the two are identical.

In *PVC*[139] the Commission held that it is a matter of EU law whether one undertaking can be liable for the past conduct of another: changes in organisation under national company law are not decisive. In order to decide whether there is 'undertaking identity', the expression used by the Commission in the *PVC* decision, the determining factor 'is whether there is a functional and economic continuity between the original infringer and the undertaking into which it was merged'[140]. It repeated this formulation in the second *PVC* decision[141]. In *All Weather Sports Benelux BV v Commission*[142] the General Court held that the Commission must adequately explain its reasoning when it imposes a fine on a successor to the entity that committed the infringement.

---

[135] Case 170/83 *Hydrotherm Gerätebau v Andreoli* [1984] ECR 2999, [1985] 3 CMLR 224; this is relevant, for example, under Regulation 330/2010, which requires that, for the block exemption to apply, there must not be two undertakings to a vertical agreement operating at the same level of the market: see ch 16, 'Article 2(4): agreements between competing undertakings', pp 658–659; and under Regulation 772/2004 on technology transfer agreements, which confers block exemption only on bilateral agreements: see ch 19, 'The exempted agreement must be bilateral', p 783.

[136] See Case 48/69 *ICI v Commission* [1972] ECR 619, [1972] CMLR 557; Case 6/72 *Europemballage Corpn and Continental Can Co Inc v Commission* [1973] ECR 215, [1973] CMLR 199; see ch 12 on extraterritoriality generally.

[137] See Garzaniti and Scassellati-Sforzolini 'Liability of Successor Undertakings for Infringements of EC Competition Law Committed Prior to Corporate Reorganisations' (1995) 16 ECLR 348; Dyekjær-Hansen and Hoegh 'Succession for Competition Law Infringements with Special Reference to Due Diligence and Warranty Claims' (2003) 24 ECLR 203; Chandler 'Successor Liability for Competition Law Infringements and How to Avoid It' (2006) 5 Competition Law Journal 63.

[138] Cases 29 and 30/83 [1984] ECR 1679, [1985] 1 CMLR 688, para 9; see also Case T-134/94 *NMH Stahlwerke GmbH v Commission* [1999] ECR II-239, [1997] 5 CMLR 227, paras 122–141; Case C-297/98 P *SCA Holdings Ltd v Commission* [2000] ECR I-10101, [2001] 4 CMLR 413, paras 23–32; Cases C-204/00 P etc *Aalborg Portland A/S v Commission* [2004] ECR I-123, [2005] 4 CMLR 251, para 59.

[139] OJ [1989] L 74/1, [1990] 4 CMLR 345, para 42.

[140] OJ [1989] L 74/1, [1990] 4 CMLR 345, para 43; see similarly *LdPE* OJ [1989] L 74/21, paras 49–54; other decisions of the Commission dealing with this point are *Peroxygen Products* OJ [1985] L 35/1, [1985] 1 CMLR 481, *Polypropylene* OJ [1986] L 230/1, [1988] 4 CMLR 347 and *Welded Steel Mesh* OJ [1989] L 260/1, [1991] 4 CMLR 13, para 194.

[141] OJ [1994] L 239/14, paras 14–43.

[142] Case T-38/92 [1994] ECR II-211, [1995] 4 CMLR 43, paras 26–36.

In *Autoritá Garante della Concurrenza e del Mercato v Ente tabacchi italiani – ETI SpA*[143] the Amministrazione autonoma del monopoli di Stato ('AAMS') was an organ of the Italian state that had responsibility for managing the tobacco monopoly in that country. In 1999 its activities were transferred by law to a newly-created public body, Ente tabacchi italiani ('ETI'). ETI was subsequently transformed into a public company and was then privatised, coming under the control of British American Tobacco plc. The Italian competition authority adopted a decision that the Philip Morris group of companies had implemented a cartel in Italy in conjunction with AAMS and, subsequently, with ETI. A fine of €20 million was imposed on ETI. In its decision the Italian competition authority attributed AAMS's conduct prior to 1999 to ETI. An Italian court held that it was wrong to have done so; on appeal the Italian Council of State referred the matter to the Court of Justice under Article 267 TFEU. The Court of Justice held that it was legitimate for the Italian competition authority to have imposed the fine on ETI: AAMS and ETI were answerable to the same public authority, and the same unlawful conduct was carried out first by AAMS and then by its successor, ETI; the Court applied the reasoning of the *Rheinzink* case, and said that it made no difference that the activity transferred to ETI occurred not as a result of individuals but through the action of the legislature preparing ETI for privatisation[144].

(E) Liability for competition law infringements when one business is sold to another

An important question arises where one undertaking commits an infringement of the competition rules, but then sells the business that was responsible for the infringement to a third party. Clearly the purchaser will need to know whether it bears the risk of a future fine in the event of a competition authority adopting a decision. The basic rule of personal responsibility is that, if the undertaking that was responsible for the business is still in existence, it remains liable for the infringement rather than the acquirer[145]. For example in *Zinc Phosphate*[146] the Commission decided that, where an undertaking commits an infringement of Article 101 and then disposes of the assets that were the vehicle of the infringement and withdraws from the market, it will still be held responsible if it is still in existence[147]. However the liability may pass to a successor where the corporate entity which committed the violation has ceased to exist in law after the infringement was committed[148]; or where the initial participant in the cartel still has a legal existence but no longer carries on an economic activity on the relevant market and where there are structural links between the initial entity and the new operator of the undertaking[149]. In *Hoechst GmbH v Commission*[150] Hoechst failed to establish that its liability in relation to a monochloroacetic acid cartel had passed to the purchaser of that business under either of these two exceptions[151]. In *Conex Bänninger Ltd v European Commission*[152] the purchaser of assets from an undertaking that had been fined for infringing Article 101 in the *Copper*

---

[143] Case C-280/06 [2007] ECR I-10893, [2008] 4 CMLR 277.   [144] Ibid, paras 38–52.

[145] See eg Case C-279/98 P *Cascades v Commission* [2000] ECR I-9693, para 78.

[146] OJ [2003] L 153/1.

[147] Ibid, para 238, relying, *inter alia*, on Case T-80/89 *BASF v Commission* [1995] ECR II-729.

[148] Case C-49/92 *Commission v Anic Partecipazioni SpA* [1999] ECR I-4125, [2001] 4 CMLR 602, para 145.

[149] Cases C-204/00 P etc *Aalborg Portland A/S v Commission* [2004] ECR I-123, [2005] 4 CMLR 251, para 359.

[150] Case T-161/05, [2009] ECR II-3555, [2009] 5 CMLR 2728.   [151] Ibid, paras 50–67.

[152] [2010] EWHC 1978 (Ch).

fittings decision[153] faced the uncertainty of not knowing whether the Commission would seek to enforce the fines against it; however Conex failed in its attempt to obtain a declaration from the High Court in England and Wales that it was not liable and/or to have the matter referred to the Court of Justice in Luxembourg.

3. Agreements, Decisions and Concerted Practices

The policy of Article 101 is to prohibit cooperation between undertakings which prevents, restricts or distorts competition. In particular Article 101 is concerned with the eradication of cartels: chapter 13 will examine this subject in detail. However it is important to bear in mind that Article 101 can also apply to vertical agreements: the difficulties in establishing the existence of a vertical agreement are discussed below[154].

The application of Article 101(1) is not limited to legal contracts: this would make evasion of the law simple. Article 101 applies also to cooperation achieved through informal agreements, decisions of trade associations and concerted practices. The Chapter I prohibition in the UK Competition Act 1998 has the same scope[155]. As will be seen, a broad interpretation has been given to each of the terms 'agreement', 'decision' and 'concerted practice'. A difficult issue is whether parallel behaviour by firms in an oligopolistic industry is attributable to an agreement or concerted practice between them, in which case Article 101(1) would be applicable; or whether it is a natural effect of the structure of the market, in which case a different competition law response might be needed. Chapter 14 will consider the issue of oligopoly, tacit collusion and so-called 'collective dominance' under Article 102 and the Chapter II prohibition in the Competition Act.

(A) **Agreements**

In *Bayer AG v Commission*[156] the General Court reviewed the case law on the meaning of agreement and stated that the concept:

> centres around the existence of a concurrence of wills between at least two parties, the form in which it is manifested being unimportant so long as it constitutes the faithful expression of the parties' intention[157].

In this section examples will be given of fact patterns that have been characterised as agreements for the purposes of Article 101. Consideration will then be given to the way in which the term 'agreement' applies to complex cartels. Discussion will follow on the steps that should be taken by an undertaking that wishes to 'publicly distance' itself from a cartel agreement. The final part of this section will look at the problems of proving that undertakings are party to a vertical agreement; the Court of Justice has stated specifically that the standard of proof on the Commission to prove the existence of an agreement contrary to Article 101(1) is the same whether the case is a horizontal or a vertical one[158].

---

[153] Commission decision of 20 September 2006.

[154] See '"Unilateral" conduct and Article 101(1) in vertical cases', pp 105–110 below.

[155] See ch 9, 'Agreements', pp 337–340.

[156] Case T-41/96 [2000] ECR II-3383, [2001] 4 CMLR 176.

[157] Ibid, para 69; this paragraph was quoted, apparently with approval, by the Court of Justice in the appeal against the General Court's judgment in the *Bayer* case in Cases C-2/01 P and C-3/01 P *Bundesverband der Arzneimittel-Importeure eV v Bayer AG* [2004] ECR I-23, [2004] 4 CMLR 653, at para 97; for discussion see Black 'Agreement: Concurrence of Wills, or Offer and Acceptance?' (2008) 4 European Competition Journal 103.

[158] Case C-260/09 P *Activision Blizzard Germany GmbH v Commission* [2011] ECR I-000, [2011] 4 CMLR 964, para 71.

(i) Examples of agreements

A legal contract of course qualifies as an agreement, including a compromise of litigation such as a trade mark delimitation agreement[159] or the settlement of a patent action[160]. 'Gentleman's agreements'[161] and simple understandings[162] have been held to be agreements, though neither is legally binding; there is no requirement that an agreement should be supported by enforcement procedures[163]. A 'protocol' which reflects a genuine concurrence of will between the parties constitutes an agreement within the meaning of Article 101(1)[164]. Connected agreements may be treated as a single one[165]. An agreement may be oral[166]. The Commission will treat the contractual terms and conditions in a standard-form contract as an agreement within Article 101(1)[167]. An agreement which has expired by effluxion of time but the effects of which continue to be felt can be caught by Article 101(1)[168]. The constitution of a trade association qualifies as an agreement[169]. An agreement entered into by a trade association might be construed as an agreement on the part of its members[170]. An agreement to create a European Economic Interest Grouping, or the bye-laws establishing it, may be caught by Article 101(1)[171]. There may be 'inchoate understandings and conditional or partial agreement' during a

---

[159] See eg *Re Penney's Trade Mark* OJ [1978] L 60/19, [1978] 2 CMLR 100; *Re Toltecs and Dorcet* OJ [1982] L 379/19, [1983] 1 CMLR 412, upheld on appeal Case 35/83 *BAT v Commission* [1985] ECR 363, [1985] 2 CMLR 470; it is not entirely clear what effect embodiment of the compromise in an order of a national court has on the applicability of Article 101(1): see Case 258/78 *LC Nungesser KG v Commission* [1982] ECR 2015, [1983] 1 CMLR 278, paras 80–91, where the Court of Justice was delphic on this issue; the tenor of the Court of Justice's judgment in *BAT v Commission* would suggest that the agreement would be caught even where sanctioned by a national court. On trade mark delimitation agreements, see further ch 19, 'Settlements of litigation', pp 795–796.

[160] See eg Case 65/86 *Bayer v Süllhofer* [1988] ECR 5249, [1990] 4 CMLR 182; see further ch 19, 'Settlements of litigation', pp 795–796.

[161] See Case 41/69 *ACF Chemiefarma NV v Commission* [1970] ECR 661, [1970] CMLR 43 and Case T-53/03 *BPB plc v Commission* [2008] ECR II-1333, [2008] 5 CMLR 1201, para 72.

[162] *Re Stichting Sigarettenindustrie Agreements* OJ [1982] L 232/1, [1982] 3 CMLR 702 (an 'understanding' between trade associations held to be an agreement); *National Panasonic* OJ [1982] L 354/28, [1983] 1 CMLR 497, where there was no formal agreement between Panasonic and its dealers, but the Commission still held that there was an agreement as opposed to a concerted practice between them; *Viho/Toshiba* OJ [1991] L 287/39, [1992] 5 CMLR 180, where the Commission found an understanding between Toshiba's German subsidiary and certain distributors that an export prohibition should apply, even though the standard distribution agreements had been amended to remove an export prohibition clause.

[163] *Soda-ash/Solvay, CFK* OJ [1991] L 152/16, [1994] 4 CMLR 645, para 11; *PVC* OJ [1994] L 239/14, para 30; *CISAC*, Commission decision of 16 July 2008 [2009] 4 CMLR 577, para 130.

[164] *HOV SVZ/MCN* OJ [1994] L 104/34, para 46.

[165] *ENI/Montedison* OJ [1987] L 5/13, [1988] 4 CMLR 444.

[166] Case 28/77 *Tepea v Commission* [1978] ECR 1391, [1978] 3 CMLR 392; Cases T-25/95 etc *Cimenteries CBR SA v Commission* [2000] ECR II-491, [2000] 5 CMLR 204, para 2341.

[167] *Putz v Kawasaki Motors (UK) Ltd* OJ [1979] 1 16/9, [1979] 1 CMLR 448; *Sandoz* OJ [1987] L 222/28, [1989] 4 CMLR 628, upheld on appeal Case 277/87 *Sandoz Prodotti Farmaceutici SpA v Commission* [1990] ECR I-45.

[168] Case T-7/89 *SA Hercules NV v Commission* [1991] ECR II-1711, [1992] 4 CMLR 84, para 257; Case 51/75 *EMI Records Ltd v CBS UK Ltd* [1976] ECR 811, pp 848–849, [1976] 2 CMLR 235, p 267; Case T-48/98 *Acerinox v Commission* [2001] ECR II-3859, para 63; *E.ON/GDF*, Commission decision of 8 July 2009, on appeal to the General Court Cases T-360/09 and T-370/09, not yet decided.

[169] *Re Nuovo CEGAM* OJ [1984] L 99/29, [1984] 2 CMLR 484.

[170] Cases 209/78 etc *Heintz Van Landewyck v Commission* [1980] ECR 3125, [1981] 3 CMLR 134.

[171] *Orphe* Commission's XXth *Report on Competition Policy* (1990), point 102; *Tepar* [1991] 4 CMLR 860; *Twinning Programme Engineering Group* OJ [1992] C 148/8, [1992] 5 CMLR 93.

bargaining process sufficient to amount to an agreement in the sense of Article 101(1)[172]. Guidelines issued by one person that are adhered to by another can amount to an agreement[173]; and circulars and warnings sent by a manufacturer to its dealers may be treated as part of the general agreement that exists between them, although the Commission lost a case of this kind in *Volkswagen*[174]. The exchange of correspondence can amount to an agreement[175]. The fact that formal agreement has not been reached on all matters does not preclude a finding of an agreement[176], and there can be an agreement or concerted practice notwithstanding the fact that only one of the participants at a meeting reveals its intentions[177]. Undertakings cannot justify infringement of the competition rules by claiming that they were forced into an agreement by the conduct of other traders[178]. Where an agreement is entered into unwillingly, this may be significant in influencing the Commission to mitigate a fine[179], not to impose a fine[180] or not to institute proceedings at all. The fact that one party accepts that it was party to an agreement does not preclude the other(s) from challenging the existence of the same agreement[181]. The fact that the natural person who entered into the agreement did not have authority to do so does not mean that the undertaking that employs him or her is not liable[182].

(ii) Complex cartels

Many cartels are complex and of long duration. Over a period of time some firms may be more active than others in the running of a cartel; some may 'drop out' for a while but subsequently re-enter; others may attend meetings or communicate in other ways in order to be kept informed, without necessarily intending to fall in line with the agreed plan; there may be few occasions on which all the members of a cartel actually meet or behave precisely in concert with one another. This presents a problem for a competition authority: where the shape and active membership of a cartel changes over a period of time, must the authority prove a series of discrete agreements or concerted practices, and identify each of the parties to each of those agreements and concerted practices? This would require a considerable amount of evidence and impose a very high burden on the competition authority. It might also mean that it would not be possible to impose fines in relation to 'old' agreements and concerted practices, in relation to which infringement

---

[172] *Pre-Insulated Pipe Cartel* OJ [1999] L 24/1, [1999] 4 CMLR 402, para 133, substantially upheld on appeal Cases T-9/99 etc *HFB Holding v Commission* [2002] ECR II-1487, [2002] 5 CMLR 571.

[173] *Anheuser-Busch Incorporated/Scottish & Newcastle* OJ [2000] L 49/37, [2000] 5 CMLR 75, para 26.

[174] See 'Judgments since *Bayer v Commission* annulling Commission findings of an agreement', pp 109–110 below.

[175] *Nintendo* OJ [2003] L 255/33, para 196, substantially upheld on appeal to the General Court Case T-18/03 *CD-Contact Data v Commission* [2009] ECR II-1021, [2009] 5 CMLR 1469, paras 52–69 and on appeal to the Court of Justice Case C-260/09 P *Activision Blizzard Germany GmbH v Commission* [2011] ECR I-000, [2011] 4 CMLR 964.

[176] *Pre-Insulated Pipe Cartel* OJ [1999] L 24/1, [1999] 4 CMLR 402, para 134.

[177] Cases T-202/98 etc *Tate & Lyle v Commission* [2001] ECR II-2035, [2001] 5 CMLR 859, para 54.

[178] Case 16/61 *Modena v High Authority* [1962] ECR 289, [1962] CMLR 221; *Musique Diffusion Française v Commission* [1983] ECR 1825, [1983] 3 CMLR 221, paras 90 and 100; Cases T-25/95 etc *Cimenteries CBR SA v Commission* [2000] ECR II-491, [2000] 5 CMLR 204, para 2557.

[179] *Hasselblad* OJ [1982] L 161/18, [1982] 2 CMLR 233; *Wood Pulp* OJ [1985] L 85/1, [1985] 3 CMLR 474, para 131.

[180] *Burns Tractors Ltd v Sperry New Holland* OJ [1985] L 376/21, [1988] 4 CMLR 306; *Fisher-Price/Quaker Oats Ltd—Toyco* OJ [1988] L 49/19, [1989] 4 CMLR 553.

[181] Case T-18/03 *CD-Contact Data v Commission* [2009] ECR II-1021, [2009] 5 CMLR 1469, para 51.

[182] Case T-53/03 *BPB plc v Commission* [2008] ECR II-1333, [2008] 5 CMLR 1201, para 360.

proceedings had become time-barred[183]: precisely this issue arose, for example, in *BASF AG v Commission*[184], an appeal in the *Choline Chloride* case.

The Commission, upheld by the EU Courts, has addressed these problems in two ways: first, by developing the idea that it is not necessary to characterise infringements of Article 101(1) specifically as an agreement on the one hand or a concerted practice on the other; and secondly by establishing the concept of a 'single overall agreement' for which all members of a cartel bear responsibility, irrespective of their precise involvement from day to day[185].

(A) Agreement 'and/or' concerted practice

The Commission has stated that agreements and concerted practices are conceptually distinct[186]. However Advocate General Reischl has said that there is little point in defining the exact point at which agreement ends and concerted practice begins[187]. It may be that, in a particular case, linguistically it is more natural to use one term than the other, but legally nothing turns on the distinction: the important distinction is between collusive and non-collusive behaviour[188]. Sometimes the Commission will say that, even if contacts between competitors do not amount to an agreement, they can still be characterised as a concerted practice[189]. In *PVC*[190] the Commission reached the conclusion that the parties to the cartel had participated in an agreement 'and/or' a concerted practice. On appeal to the General Court Enichem argued that the Commission was not entitled to have made this 'joint classification'. In its judgment the General Court rejected this argument and upheld the Commission[191]. It held that:

> In the context of a complex infringement which involves many producers seeking over a number of years to regulate the market between them the Commission cannot be expected to classify the infringement precisely, for each undertaking and for any given moment, as in any event both those forms of infringement are covered by Article [101] of the Treaty[192].

The General Court went on to say that joint classification was permissible where the infringement includes elements both of an agreement and of a concerted practice, with-

---

[183] Under Article 26 of Regulation 1/2003, OJ [2003] L 1/1, the Commission cannot impose fines in relation to an infringement that ended five years or more before it initiated proceedings: see Kerse and Khan *EC Antitrust Procedure* (Sweet & Maxwell, 5th ed, 2005), paras 7.82–7.85.

[184] Cases T-101/05 and T-111/05 [2007] ECR II-4949, [2008] 4 CMLR 347, paras 132–223.

[185] See generally Joshua 'Attitudes to Anti-Trust Enforcement in the EU and US: Dodging the Traffic Warden, or Respecting the Law' [1995] Fordham Corporate Law Institute (ed Hawk), 85.

[186] See *Polypropylene* OJ [1986] L 230/1, [1988] 4 CMLR 347, para 86.

[187] See Cases 209/78 etc *Van Landewyck v Commission* [1980] ECR 3125, p 3310, [1981] 3 CMLR 134, p 185.

[188] *Polypropylene* OJ [1986] L 230/1, [1988] 4 CMLR 347, para 87, substantially upheld on appeal Case T-7/89 *SA Hercules NV v Commission* [1991] ECR II-1711, [1992] 4 CMLR 84, upheld on appeal to the Court of Justice Case C-51/92 P *Hercules Chemicals v Commission* [1999] ECR I-4235, [1999] 5 CMLR 976; *Soda-ash/Solvay, ICI* OJ [1991] L 152/1, [1994] 4 CMLR 645, para 55.

[189] See eg *Candle Waxes*, Commission decision of 1 October 2008, para 239, on appeal to the General Court, Cases T-543/08 etc *RWE and RWE Dea v Commission*, not yet decided.

[190] OJ [1994] L 239/14, paras 30–31; this decision was taken by the Commission after its earlier decision, OJ [1989] L 74/1, had been annulled by the Court of Justice for infringement of essential procedural requirements: Cases C-137/92 P etc *Commission v BASF* [1994] ECR I-2555.

[191] Cases T-305/94 etc *NV Limburgse Vinyl Maatschappij v Commission* [1999] ECR II-931, [1999] 5 CMLR 303, paras 695–699; the General Court had noted the possibility of a joint classification in its earlier judgments in the *Polypropylene* case: see eg Case T-1/89 *Rhône-Poulenc v Commission* [1991] ECR II-867, paras 125–127 and Case T-8/89 *DSM v Commission* [1991] ECR II-1833, paras 234–235.

[192] Cases T-305/94 etc *NV Limburgse Vinyl Maatschappij v Commission* [1999] ECR II-931, [1999] 5 CMLR 303, para 696.

out the Commission having to prove that there was both an agreement and a concerted practice throughout the period of the infringement. This approach has been confirmed by the Court of Justice in *Commission v Anic*[193] and in *Asnef-Equifax*[194] where, in the case of cooperation between competitors in the form of an indirect exchange of information, it concluded that there was no need to characterise the cooperation at issue specifically as a concerted practice, an agreement or a decision of an association of undertakings.

The Commission has adopted a joint classification approach in many decisions, for example *Cartonboard*[195] and *Pre-Insulated Pipe Cartel*[196] and, more recently, *Car Glass*[197] and *Marine Hoses*[198]; it has taken this approach in vertical cases as well as horizontal ones[199]. As one former Commission official has put it: the search should not be for an agreement on the one hand or a concerted practice on the other; rather for a 'partnership for unlawful purposes with all the possible disagreements about methods that may occur in such a venture without affecting the cohesion of the shared purpose and design'[200].

(B) *The concept of a 'single, overall agreement'*[201]

In a series of decisions from the mid-1980s the Commission has developed the concept of a 'single, overall agreement' for which undertakings bear responsibility, even though they may not be involved in its operation on a day-to-day or a continuing basis. For example in *Polypropylene*[202] the Commission investigated a complex cartel agreement in the petrochemicals sector involving 15 firms over many years. It held that the detailed arrangements whereby the cartel operated were all part of a single, overall agreement: this agreement was oral, not legally binding, and there were no sanctions for its enforcement. Having established that there was a single agreement, the Commission concluded that all 15 firms were guilty of infringing Article 101, even though some had not attended every meeting of the cartel and had not been involved in every aspect of its decision-making: participation in the overall agreement was sufficient to establish guilt. Furthermore, the fact that some members of the cartel had reservations about whether to participate – or indeed intended to cheat by deviating from the agreed conduct – did not mean that they were not party to an agreement. The Commission reached similar conclusions in other cases, for example *PVC*[203], *LdPE*[204], in its second decision on *PVC*[205], in *Amino Acids*[206] and in *Dutch Bitumen*[207].

---

[193] Case C-49/92 [1999] ECR I-4125 [2001] 4 CMLR 602, paras 132 and 133: for critical comment on the Court of Justice's judgment in *Anic* see Wessely (2001) 38 CML Rev 739, 762–764; see also Case T-62/98 *Volkswagen AG v Commission* [2000] ECR II-2707, [2000] 5 CMLR 853, para 237

[194] Case C-238/05 [2006] ECR I-11125, [2007] 4 CMLR 224, para 32.

[195] OJ [1994] L 243/1, [1994] 5 CMLR 547, para 128.

[196] OJ [1999] L 24/1, [1999] 5 CMLR 402, paras 131–132.

[197] Commission decision of 12 November 2008, paras 121 and 486.

[198] Commission decision of 28 January 2009, para 272.

[199] See *Nintendo* OJ [2003] L 255/33, paras 261ff.

[200] Joshua 'Attitudes to Anti-Trust Enforcement in the EU and US: Dodging the Traffic Warden, or Respecting the Law?' [1995] Fordham Corporate Law Institute (ed Hawk), 85.

[201] For discussion of this concept see Seifert 'The Single Complex and Continuous Infringement – "Effet Utilitarianism?"' [2008] 29 ECLR 546; Joshua 'Single Continuous Infringement of Article 81 EC: Has the Commission Stretched the Concept Beyond the Limit of its Logic?' (2009) 5(2) European Competition Journal 451; Bailey 'Single, overall agreement in EU Competition Law' (2010) 47 CML Rev 473.

[202] OJ [1986] L 230/1, [1988] 4 CMLR 347.   [203] OJ [1989] L 74/1, [1990] 4 CMLR 345.

[204] OJ [1989] L 74/21, [1990] 4 CMLR 382, paras 49–54.   [205] OJ [1994] L 239/14, paras 30–31.

[206] OJ [2001] L 152/24, [2001] 5 CMLR 322, paras 237–238.

[207] Commission decision of 13 December 2006, paras 138–141.

The General Court has confirmed the concept of a 'single overall agreement'[208]. In the appeal against the second *PVC* decision the General Court upheld the Commission's view that an undertaking can be held responsible for an overall cartel, even though it participated in only one or some of its constituent elements, 'if it is shown that it knew, or must have known, that the collusion in which it participated...was part of an overall plan intended to distort competition and that the overall plan included all the constituent elements of the cartel'[209]. However the General Court has also said, in the *Cement* cases, that where there are numerous bilateral and multilateral agreements between a large number of undertakings, it cannot be *presumed* from this that they form part of a single, overall agreement: it is necessary for the Commission to prove that this is the case[210]. In *BASF v Commission*[211] the General Court annulled a Commission finding of a single overall agreement: the global and the European cartels were separate from one another, and the Commission was time-barred from imposing a fine in respect of the global cartel, which had ended in 1994[212]. The Court also annulled a finding of a single and continuous agreement in *Verhuizingen Coppens NV v Commission*[213], one of the appeals in the *International Removal Services* case, as the Commission had failed to show that Verhuizingen knew, or ought to have known, about the offending conduct of the other participants in the cartel[214].

It is not impossible that an undertaking might want to argue that it *did* participate in a single, overall agreement: for example the Commission imposed a series of fines on undertakings involved in four different infringements of Article 101 involving various graphite products[215]. The aggregated fines amounted to more than 10 per cent of SGL Carbon's turnover; the General Court held that the Commission was permitted to impose four fines, since each decision involved a different infringement; if it had decided that there was a single, overall agreement affecting all graphite products, the 10 per cent ceiling would have been applicable and the fines on SGL would have been subject to a cap[216].

The cumulative effect of these judgments is clearly beneficial to the Commission in its anti-cartel policy, since the EU Courts seem to have deliberately refrained from construing the expressions 'agreement' and 'concerted practice' in a legalistic or formalistic manner: what emerges, essentially, is that any contact between competitors that touches upon business behaviour such as pricing, markets, customers and volume of output is risky in the extreme.

(iii) 'Public distancing' from a cartel

In *Tréfileurope v Commission*[217], one of the appeals in the *Welded Steel Mesh* case, the General Court held that the fact that an undertaking does not abide by the outcome of meetings which have a manifestly anti-competitive purpose does not relieve it of full

---

[208] See Case T-1/89 *Rhône-Poulenc v Commission* [1991] ECR II-867, para 126.

[209] Cases T-305/94 etc *NV Limburgse Vinyl Maatschappij v Commission* [1999] ECR II-931, [1999] 5 CMLR 303, para 773.

[210] Cases T-25/95 etc *Cimenteries CBR SA v Commission* [2000] ECR II-491, [2000] 5 CMLR 204, paras 4027, 4060, 4109 and 4112.

[211] Cases T-101/05 and T-111/05 [2007] ECR II-4949, [2008] 4 CMLR 347.

[212] Ibid, paras 157–210.

[213] Case T-210/08 [2011] ECR II-000, [2011] 5 CMLR 333.   [214] Ibid, paras 28–32.

[215] See *Graphite electrodes* Commission decision of 18 July 2001; *Speciality graphite* Commission decision of 17 December 2002 (note that in that decision the Commission fined SGL Carbon twice for participating in two separate price-fixing cartels); and *Electrical and mechanical carbon and graphite products* Commission decision of 3 December 2003.

[216] Case T-68/04 *SGL Carbon AG v Commission* [2008] ECR II-2511, [2009] 4 CMLR 7, paras 122–134.

[217] Case T-141/89 [1995] ECR II-791, para 85.

responsibility for its participation in the cartel, if it has not publicly distanced itself from what was agreed in the meetings[218]. This has been repeated on numerous occasions, for example in *BPB de Eendracht NV v Commission*[219], an appeal in the *Cartonboard* case, in the *Cement* cases[220] and in *Steel Beams*[221]: the reason for this rule is that, having participated in the meeting without publicly distancing itself from what was discussed, the undertaking has given the other participants to believe that it subscribed to what was decided there and that it would comply with it[222]. In *Westfalen Gassen Nederland BV*[223], an appeal in the *Industrial and medical gases* case, the General Court said that the notion of 'public distancing' as a means of excluding liability must be interpreted narrowly[224]; the Court did not go so far as to say that, in order to do so, the undertaking concerned should have blown the whistle to a competition authority, but it did suggest that, at the least, it should have written to its competitors and to the secretary of the trade association responsible for the meetings to say that it did not wish to be considered to be a member of the cartel nor to participate in meetings that were a cover for unlawful concerted action[225].

(iv) 'Unilateral' conduct and Article 101(1) in vertical cases[226]

The scheme of the EU competition rules is that Article 101 applies to conduct by two or more undertakings which is consensual and that Article 102 applies to unilateral action by a dominant firm. It follows that unilateral conduct by a firm that is not dominant is not caught at all. In a number of vertical cases the Commission has held that conduct which at first sight appeared to be unilateral fell within Article 101(1) as an agreement or a concerted practice; these were cases in which the Commission was concerned either that exports from one Member State to another were being inhibited or that resale prices were being maintained. Several of these decisions were upheld on appeal by the EU Courts; however in a number of cases, beginning with *Bayer AG/Adalat*[227] in 1996, findings of the Commission that there were agreements between a supplier and its distributors have been annulled on appeal[228].

(A) *AEG Telefunken v Commission; Ford v Commission*

Two judgments of the Court of Justice in the 1980s provide an important starting point when considering this issue. In *AEG-Telefunken v Commission*[229] the Court of Justice rejected a claim that refusals to supply retail outlets which were objectively suitable to handle AEG's goods were unilateral acts falling outside Article 101(1). The Court of Justice held that the refusals arose out of the contractual relationship between AEG and

[218] See Bailey 'Publicly Distancing Oneself from a Cartel' (2008) 32 World Competition 177.

[219] Case T-311/94 [1998] ECR II-1129, para 203.

[220] Cases T-25/95 etc *Cimenteries CBR SA v Commission* [2000] ECR II-491, [2000] 5 CMLR 204, paras 1353, 1389 and 3199.

[221] Cases T-141/94 etc *Thyssen Stahl v Commission* [1999] ECR II-347, [1999] 4 CMLR 810; see similarly Cases T-202/98 etc *Tate & Lyle v Commission* [2001] ECR II-2035, [2001] 5 CMLR 859, paras 64–65 and Case T-48/98 *Acerinox v Commission* [2001] ECR II-3859, paras 29–46.

[222] See eg Case C-403/04 P *Sumitomo Metal Industries Ltd v Commission* [2007] ECR I-729, [2007] 4 CMLR 650, para 48.

[223] Case T-302/02 [2006] ECR II-4567, [2007] 4 CMLR 334.   [224] Ibid, para 103.

[225] Ibid.

[226] See Lianos 'Collusion in Vertical Relations under Article 81 EC' (2008) 45 CML Rev 1027.

[227] OJ [1996] L 201/1, [1996] 5 CMLR 416.

[228] See 'Judgments since *Bayer v Commission* annulling Commission findings of an agreement', pp 109–110 below.

[229] Case 107/82 [1983] ECR 3151, [1984] 3 CMLR 325.

the established distributors within its selective distribution system and their mutual acceptance, tacit or express, of AEG's intention to exclude from the network distributors who, though qualified technically, were not prepared to adhere to its policy of maintaining a high level of prices and excluding modern channels of distribution[230]. The frequency of AEG's refusals to supply precluded the possibility that they were isolated cases not forming part of systematic conduct[231]. The AEG case suggested that it may be relatively easy to infer an agreement and/or concerted practice between the participants in a selective distribution system who have a strong mutual interest in excluding firms willing to undercut the prevailing retail price[232].

In *Ford v Commission*[233] the Court of Justice held that a refusal by Ford's German subsidiary to supply right-hand drive cars to German distributors was attributable to the contractual relationship between them; at the time right-hand drive cars were sold in Germany to British military forces stationed there: they could then bring them back to the UK, having bought them in Germany at prices considerably below those in the UK. The *Ford* judgment appeared to be a considerable extension of *AEG*. In *AEG* there was an obvious community of interest between participants in the selective distribution system in excluding discounters. In *Ford*, however, the German distributors with whom Ford had entered into contracts did not themselves benefit from the refusal to supply right-hand drive cars: the beneficiaries of this policy were distributors in the UK, who would be shielded from cheaper parallel imports. In *Ford* the 'unilateral' act held to be attributable to the agreements between the supplier and its distributors was not an act for the benefit of those very distributors. However, the main issue in *Ford* was not whether there were agreements between Ford and its German distributors: of course there were. Rather the issue with which the Court of Justice was concerned was whether the agreements, as implemented in practice, satisfied the criteria of Article 101(3), and the Court decided that they did not[234]. This is how the Court distinguished the *Ford* judgment in its 2004 judgment in the *Bayer* case[235], and is an important limiting principle.

(B) *Subsequent cases prior to* **Bayer**

In a number of decisions after AEG and Ford the Commission successfully applied Article 101(1) to apparently unilateral conduct. In *Sandoz*[236] it held that, where there was no written record of agreements between a producer and its distributors, unilateral measures, including placing the words 'export prohibited' on all invoices, were attributable to the continuing commercial relationship between the parties and were within Article 101(1). On appeal the Court of Justice upheld the Commission's decision[237]. In *Vichy*[238] the Commission specifically applied paragraph 12 of the *Sandoz* judgment, and its decision finding an agreement was upheld on appeal[239]. In *Tipp-Ex*[240] the Commission applied the

---

[230] On selective distribution systems see ch 16, 'Selective distribution agreements', pp 641–645.

[231] Case 107/82 [1983] ECR 3151, [1984] 3 CMLR 325, paras 31–39.

[232] Note also the two UK cases, *Football Shirts* and *Toys and Games*, in which it was found that there could be a multilateral agreement between a supplier and its distributors, having both horizontal and vertical characteristics, that comes about as a result of contact between each distributor and the supplier, though without necessarily there being any contact between the distributors themselves (a so-called 'hub and spoke' arrangement in which the supplier is the hub and the vertical agreement with each distributor are spokes): see ch 9, 'Agreements', pp 337–340.

[233] Cases 25/84 and 26/84 [1985] ECR 2725, [1985] 3 CMLR 528.

[234] Ibid, para 12.   [235] See '*Bayer v Commission*', pp 107–109 below.

[236] OJ [1987] L 222/28, [1989] 4 CMLR 628.

[237] Case C-277/87 *Sandoz Prodotti Farmaceutici SpA v Commission* [1990] ECR I-45.

[238] OJ [1991] L 75/57.   [239] Case T-19/91 *Vichy v Commission* [1992] ECR II-415.

[240] OJ [1987] L 222/1, [1989] 4 CMLR 425.

Court of Justice's judgments in *AEG* and *Ford*, holding that there was an infringement of Article 101 consisting of agreements between Tipp-Ex and its authorised dealers regarding the mutual protection of territories; again the Commission's decision was upheld on appeal[241]. In *Konica*[242] the Commission held that the sending of a circular to its distributors requiring them not to export Konica film from the UK to Germany was an offer by Konica, and that by complying with the circular the distributors had accepted it, with the result that there was an agreement or at least a concerted practice within Article 101; there was no appeal in this case. In *Bayo-n-ox*[243] goods were supplied at a special price, on condition that customers use them for their own requirements: they could not resell them; this stipulation was contained in circulars sent by the supplier to the customers. The Commission said that by accepting the products at the special price the customers had tacitly agreed to abide by the 'own requirements' condition. The Commission has said that the fact that a customer is acting contrary to its own best interests in agreeing to its supplier's terms does not mean that it is not party to a prohibited agreement under Article 101(1)[244]. In *Volkswagen AG v Commission*[245] the General Court rejected Volkswagen's argument that it had acted unilaterally as opposed to by agreement with its distributors to restrict parallel trade from Italy to Germany and Austria[246]. These cases clearly demonstrated the considerable risks borne by suppliers that attempt to control the resale activities of their distributors; however the *Bayer* case discussed in the next section revealed that the notion of an agreement in Article 101(1) is not infinitely elastic, and that the Commission will be successful on appeal before the EU Courts only where it can adduce convincing evidence of a meeting of minds between a supplier and its distributor(s).

(C) *Bayer v Commission*

In *Bayer AG/Adalat*[247] the Commission adopted a decision that Bayer and its wholesalers were parties to an agreement to restrict parallel trade in a pharmaceutical product, Adalat, from France and Spain to the UK. On this occasion, however, the General Court annulled the decision since, in its view, the Commission had failed to prove the existence of an agreement[248]; an appeal by the Commission and a parallel importer to the Court of Justice to reverse the General Court's judgment failed[249].

In order to prevent its French and Spanish wholesalers from supplying to parallel exporters to the UK, and thereby to protect its UK pricing strategy, Bayer had reduced the volume of its supplies of Adalat to France and Spain. An important feature of the case was that wholesalers in France and Spain were required to maintain sufficient stocks to enable them to supply local pharmacies with their requirements for drugs: clearly this

---

[241] Case C-279/87 *Tipp-Ex GmbH v Commission* [1990] ECR I-261.

[242] OJ [1988] L 78/34, [1988] 4 CMLR 848.

[243] OJ [1990] L 21/71, [1990] 4 CMLR 930; see also *Bayer Dental* OJ [1990] L 351/46, [1992] 4 CMLR 61.

[244] See eg *Gosmé/Martell-DMP* OJ [1991] L 185/23, [1992] 5 CMLR 586.

[245] Case T-62/98 [2000] ECR II-2707, [2000] 5 CMLR 853, upheld on appeal to the Court of Justice Case C-338/00 P *Volkswagen AG v Commission* [2003] ECR I-9189, [2004] 4 CMLR 351, paras 60–69.

[246] Ibid, paras 236–239.

[247] OJ [1996] L 201/1, [1996] 5 CMLR 416; for criticism of the Commission's decision see Kon and Schoeffer 'Parallel Imports of Pharmaceutical Products: a New Realism or Back to Basics?' (1997) 22 EL Rev 123; Lidgard 'Unilateral Refusal to Supply: an Agreement in Disguise?' (1997) 18 ECLR 352; Jakobsen and Broberg 'The Concept of Agreement in Article 81(1) EC: On the Manufacturer's Right to Prevent Parallel Trade within the European Community' (2002) 23 ECLR 127.

[248] Case T-41/96 [2000] ECR II-3383, [2001] 4 CMLR 176.

[249] Cases C-2/01 P and C-3/01 P *Bundesverband der Arzneimittel-Importeure eV v Bayer* AG [2004] ECR I-23, [2004] 4 CMLR 653.

meant that, if Bayer assessed the level of domestic demand correctly, it could limit the volumes of Adalat supplied to the point where there would be none available for export. Prices for pharmaceuticals in France and Spain were as much as 40 per cent lower than in the UK, so that the market was ripe for parallel trade. The Commission concluded that a tacit agreement existed between Bayer and its wholesalers not to export to the UK that was contrary to Article 101(1): in its view the agreement was evidenced by the fact that the wholesalers had ceased to supply the UK in response to Bayer's tactic of reducing supplies. It has to be said that this would appear to be counter-intuitive, given that the wholesalers had tried every means possible to defy Bayer and to obtain extra supplies for the purpose of exporting to the UK: there was no 'common interest' in this case between Bayer and its wholesalers, whose respective needs were diametrically opposed. To put the point another way, this case was certainly not like *AEG*; if anything it was like *Ford*, where the beneficiary of Ford's restriction of supplies was not the German distributors deprived of suppliers, but the UK distributors protected from parallel trade. Bayer did not deny that it had reduced the quantities delivered to France and Spain, but it argued that it had acted unilaterally rather than pursuant to an agreement.

On appeal the General Court held that there was no agreement and annulled the Commission's decision. The Court acknowledged that there could be an agreement where one person tacitly acquiesces in practices and measures adopted by another[250]; however it concluded that the Commission had failed both to demonstrate that Bayer had intended to impose an export ban[251] and to prove that the wholesalers had intended to adhere to a policy on the part of Bayer to reduce parallel imports[252]. The General Court was satisfied that earlier judgments, including *Sandoz, Tipp-Ex* and *AEG*, were distinguishable[253]. It also rejected the argument that the wholesalers, by maintaining their commercial relations with Bayer after the reduction of supplies, could thereby be held to have agreed with it to restrain exports[254]. The General Court was not prepared to extend the scope of Article 101(1), acknowledging the importance of 'free enterprise' when applying the competition rules[255].

The Commission and a parallel importer appealed to the Court of Justice, which upheld the General Court's judgment[256]. At paragraph 88 of its judgment the Court of Justice held that:

> The mere fact that the unilateral policy of quotas implemented by Bayer, combined with the national requirements on the wholesalers to offer a full product range, produces the same effect as an export ban does not mean either that the manufacturer imposed such a ban or that there was an agreement prohibited by Article [101(1)] of the Treaty.

The Court of Justice noted that the Commission's analysis risked confusing the respective roles of Articles 101 and 102[257], and that the *AEG* and *Ford* cases were distinguishable[258].

---

[250] Ibid, para 71.
[251] Ibid, paras 78–110.   [252] Ibid, paras 111–157.   [253] Ibid, paras 158–171.
[254] Ibid, paras 172–182.   [255] Ibid, para 180.
[256] Cases C-2/01 P and C-3/01 P *Bundesverband der Arzneimittel-Importeure eV v Bayer AG* [2004] ECR I-23, [2004] 4 CMLR 653; the Court of Appeal in England and Wales applied the Court of Justice's judgment in *Bayer* in *Unipart Group Ltd v O2 (UK) Ltd* [2004] EWCA 1034, [2004] UKCLR 1453, in deciding that Unipart was not the victim of a margin squeeze imposed upon it by a co-contractor, O2: since O2 was not dominant Unipart could not proceed against it on the basis of Article 102 and therefore tried to argue that the margin squeeze arose from its contractual relationship with O2.
[257] Cases C-2/01 P and C-3/01 P *Bundesverband der Arzneimittel-Importeure eV v Bayer AG* [2004] ECR I-23, [2004] 4 CMLR 653, para 101.
[258] Ibid, paras 107–108.

The importance of the judgments of the General Court and Court of Justice in *Bayer* cannot be overstated. Had the Commission's decision been upheld, the notion that an agreement for the purpose of Article 101(1) requires consensus between the parties would have been virtually eliminated; while this would have given the Commission greater control over restrictions of parallel trade within the EU, it would have done so at the expense of the integrity of the competition rules, which clearly apprehend unilateral behaviour only where a firm has a dominant position in the sense of Article 102.

(D) Judgments since Bayer v Commission *annulling Commission findings of an agreement*[259]

There have been several cases since *Bayer* in which decisions of the Commission that vertical agreements existed between a supplier and its distributors have been annulled on appeal. For example in *JCB* the Commission imposed fines on JCB for various infringements of Article 101, including for entering into agreements with distributors to fix discounts and resale prices[260]. On appeal the General Court annulled the Commission's decision on this point: it was true that JCB had recommended prices to its distributors, and that the prices that it charged to them would influence their own resale prices; however this was not sufficient in itself to show that there was an agreement between JCB and the distributors[261]. In *General Motors Nederland BV v Commission*[262] the General Court heard an appeal from a Commission decision, *Opel Nederland* BV[263], in which it had imposed fines of €43 million on Opel, a subsidiary of General Motors. The General Court annulled one of the Commission's findings: the Commission had argued that Opel's policy was to limit the number of cars that would be supplied to its Dutch dealers in order to prevent exports, and that this policy had been communicated to the dealers and agreed to by them; the General Court held that there was no direct proof in the decision that there had been any such communication, and even less that that measure had entered into the contractual relations between Opel and its dealers[264]. As a consequence the fine was reduced from €43 million to €35 million. A separate finding in this case – that a bonus system that the dealers had undoubtedly agreed to had as its object the restriction of competition – was updated by the General Court[265].

In a second decision involving Volkswagen[266] the Commission fined that company €30.96 million for agreeing to fix prices with its distributors for the VW Passat car. Volkswagen had sent circulars and letters to its distributors urging them not to sell the Passat at discounted prices. In the Commission's view the objectives set out in these circulars or letters became integral parts of the dealership agreement that the distributors had entered into; relying on cases such as *AEG* and others on selective distribution

---

[259] The Commission's decisions finding vertical agreements were upheld in *Nintendo* OJ [2003] L 255/33, upheld on appeal Case T-13/03 *Nintendo v Commission* [2009] ECR II-975, [2009] 5 CMLR 1421 and Case T-18/03 *CD-Contact Data GmbH v Commission* [2009] ECR II-1021, [2009] 5 CMLR 1469, paras 46–75: the latter case was also upheld on appeal to the Court of Justice in Case C-260/09 P *Activision Blizzard Germany GmbH v Commission* [2011] ECR I-000, [2011] 4 CMLR 964, and in *SEP et autres/Peugeot SA* Commission decision of 5 October 2005, upheld on appeal Case T-450/05 *Automobiles Peugeot and Peugeot Nederland v Commission* [2009] ECR II-2533.

[260] OJ [2002] L 69/1, [2002] 4 CMLR 148, paras 138–149.

[261] Case T-67/01 *JCB Service v Commission* [2004] ECR II-49, [2004] 4 CMLR 1346, paras 121–133.

[262] Case T-368/00 [2003] ECR II-4491, [2004] 4 CMLR 1302.

[263] OJ [2001] L 59/1, [2001] 4 CMLR 1441.

[264] Case T-368/00 [2003] ECR II-4491, [2004] 4 CMLR 1302, paras 78–89.

[265] Ibid, paras 97–106; upheld on appeal Case C-551/03 P [2006] ECR I-3173, [2006] 5 CMLR 9.

[266] *Volkswagen* OJ [2001] L 262/14, [2001] 5 CMLR 1309, paras 61–69.

systems[267] the Commission argued that, within a selective distribution system, calls by a supplier such as Volkswagen of the type set out in the circulars and letters became part of the contractual relationship, without the need to prove any acquiescence on the part of the distributors. The General Court rejected the Commission's arguments and annulled the decision in *Volkswagen v Commission*[268]: the General Court did not accept the Commission's analysis of the case law on selective distribution, especially given that this would mean that the distributors, who had signed perfectly lawful dealership agreements in the first place, would be taken to have agreed to subsequent calls from Volkswagen that would make the implementation of the agreements illegal. On appeal the Court of Justice set aside the judgment of the General Court[269] in so far as it had suggested that a lawful clause in an agreement could never authorise a call contrary to Article 101[270]; nevertheless the Court of Justice still reached the same substantive conclusion, that the Commission had failed to establish an agreement[271].

(E) Comment

Clearly the judgments in the previous section in which Commission findings of agreements in vertical relationships were annulled mean that it must be particularly careful to adduce evidence that there exists 'a concurrence of wills between at least two parties', in the words of the General Court's judgment in *Bayer*. However it would be dangerous for suppliers, wishing to suppress exports or to maintain resale prices, to suppose that this case law means that this is something that can be achieved without risk. In so far as they can achieve their intended purpose on a purely unilateral basis, *Bayer* shows that Article 101 can be avoided. However it should be stressed that, in that case, if it were not for the stock-holding obligations to supply French and Spanish pharmacies with Adalat, the wholesalers in question could have decided to sell all the Adalat that they acquired to parallel traders: in other words Bayer's unilateral reduction of suppliers was not enough, in itself, to staunch the parallel trade. In *General Motors* the Commission lost on the point about Opel's export policy because it had failed to show that the policy had been communicated to its distributors or that they had reacted to a policy known to them: if one reverses the facts – suppose that Opel had communicated the policy and the distributors had changed their behaviour accordingly – there would have been an agreement. As far as *Volkswagen* is concerned, the Commission appears to have argued its case in much too legalistic a manner, basing itself on the terms of the standard-form dealership agreement and the inferences to be drawn from it. Had the Commission argued that the distributors knew of Volkswagen's intentions and altered their pricing practices accordingly, it might have succeeded. These cases are highly fact-specific, and it would be wrong for suppliers and their distributors to draw too comforting a conclusion from the Commission's succession of defeats.

(B) Decisions by associations of undertakings

Coordination between independent undertakings may be achieved through the medium of a trade association. A trade association may have a particularly important role where the cartel consists of a large number of firms, in which case compliance with the rules of the cartel needs to be monitored: where only a few firms collude, it is relatively easy for

---

[267] See the cases cited in paras 18 and 19 of the General Court's judgment.
[268] Case T-208/01 [2003] ECR I-5141, [2004] 4 CMLR 727, paras 30–68.
[269] Case C-74/04 P *Commission v Volkswagen* [2006] ECR I-6585, [2008] 4 CMLR 1297.
[270] Ibid, paras 43–44.   [271] Ibid, para 54.

each firm to monitor what the others are doing[272]. The possibility that trade associations may play a part in cartel activity is explicitly recognised in Article 101(1) by the proscription of 'decisions by associations of undertakings' that could restrict competition. The application of Article 101(1) to decisions means that the trade association itself may be held liable and be fined[273]; where the Commission intends to impose a fine on the association as well as, or in addition to, its members, this must be made clear in the statement of objections[274]. In *FNCBV v Commission*[275] the General Court upheld a decision of the Commission in which it had held that, as farm operators, farmers and breeders were engaged in economic activities, they were acting as undertakings; and that it followed that their trade unions and the federations that grouped those unions together were associations of undertakings. The federations, rather than the individual undertakings, were fined in this case[276]: the General Court reduced the fines slightly. Further appeals to the Court of Justice were rejected[277]; the Court confirmed that, in determining the maximum fine that could be imposed on the federations, the Commission was entitled to take into account the members' turnover; even though they had no power to bind their members, they had been engaged in practices directly for the benefit of their members and in co-operation with them[278].

It has been held that the constitution of a trade association is itself a decision[279], as well as regulations governing the operation of an association[280]. An agreement entered into by an association might also be a decision. A recommendation made by an association has been held to amount to a decision: the fact that the recommendation is not binding upon its members does not prevent the application of Article 101(1)[281], nor that it is not unanimously accepted by the members[282]. In such cases it is necessary to consider whether members in the past have tended to comply with recommendations that have

---

[272] See ch 14, 'The theory of oligopolistic interdependence', pp 560–567 on tacit collusion in oligopolistic markets.

[273] See eg *AROW v BNIC* OJ [1982] L 379/1, [1983] 2 CMLR 240 where BNIC was fined €160,000; *Fenex* OJ [1996] L 181/28, [1996] 5 CMLR 332 where Fenex was fined €1,000; *Belgian Architects Association* Commission decision of 24 June 2004 OJ [2005] L 4/10, where the association was fined €100,000.

[274] Cases T-25/95 etc *Cimenteries CBR SA v Commission* [2000] ECR II-491, [2000] 5 CMLR 204, para 485.

[275] Cases T-217/03 and T-245/03 [2006] ECR II-4987, [2008] 5 CMLR 406.

[276] Note that the association is obliged to ask for contributions from its members in the event that the association is insolvent: Article 23(4) of the Modernisation Regulation.

[277] Cases C-101/07 P and Case C-110/07 P *Coop de France bétail et viande v Commission* [2008] ECR I-10193, [2009] 4 CMLR 743.

[278] Ibid, para 97.

[279] See eg *Re ASPA* JO [1970] L 148/9, [1970] CMLR D25; *National Sulphuric Acid Association* OJ [1980] L 260/24, [1980] 3 CMLR 429.

[280] *Publishers' Association – Net Book Agreements* OJ [1989] L 22/12, [1989] 4 CMLR 825, upheld on appeal Case T-66/89 *Publishers' Association v Commission (No 2)* [1992] ECR II-1995, [1992] 5 CMLR 120, partially annulled on appeal to the Court of Justice in Case C-360/92 P *Publishers' Association v Commission* [1995] ECR I-23, [1995] 5 CMLR 33; *Sippa* OJ [1991] L 60/19; *Coapi* OJ [1995] L 122/37, [1995] 5 CMLR 468, para 34; *Nederlandse Federatieve Vereniging voor de Grootlandel op Elektrotechnisch Gebied and Technische Unie (FEG and TU)* OJ [2000] L 39/1, [2000] 4 CMLR 1208, para 95; *Visa International* OJ [2001] L 293/24, [2002] 4 CMLR 168, para 53; *Visa International – Multilateral Interchange Fee* OJ [2002] L 318/17, [2003] 4 CMLR 283, para 55.

[281] Case 8/72 *Vereeniging van Cementhandelaren v Commission* [1972] ECR 977, [1973] CMLR 7; Case 71/74 *FRUBO v Commission* [1975] ECR 563; [1975] 2 CMLR 123; Cases 209/78 etc *Van Landewyck v Commission* [1980] ECR 3125, [1981] 3 CMLR 134; Case 45/85 *VDS v Commission* [1987] ECR 405, [1988] 4 CMLR 264, para 32; see also *Distribution of railway tickets by travel agents* OJ [1992] L 366/47, paras 62–69, partially annulled on appeal Case T-14/93 *UIC v Commission* [1995] ECR II-1503, [1996] 5 CMLR 40; *Fenex* OJ [1996] L 181/28, [1996] 5 CMLR 332, paras 32–42.

[282] See *MasterCard*, Commission decision of 19 December 2007, para 384; the decision is on appeal to the General Court, Case T-111/08 *MasterCard Inc v Commission*, not yet decided.

been made, and whether compliance with the recommendation would have a significant influence on competition within the relevant market. In *IAZ International Belgium NV v Commission*[283] an association of water-supply undertakings recommended its members not to connect dishwashing machines to the mains system which did not have a conformity label supplied by a Belgian association of producers of such equipment. The Court of Justice confirmed the Commission's view that this recommendation, though not binding, could restrict competition, since its effect was to discriminate against appliances produced elsewhere in the EU.

In its decision in *MasterCard*[284] the Commission concluded that the rules of the MasterCard organisation remained a 'decision' of an association of undertakings even after MasterCard Inc was floated on the New York Stock Exchange[285].

(C) **Concerted practices**

The inclusion of concerted practices within Article 101 means that conduct which is not attributable to an agreement or a decision may nevertheless amount to an infringement. While it can readily be appreciated that loose, informal understandings to limit competition must be prevented as well as agreements, it is difficult both to define the type or degree of coordination within the mischief of the law and to apply that rule to the facts of any given case. In particular there is the problem that parties to a cartel may do all they can to destroy incriminating evidence of meetings, emails, faxes and correspondence, in which case the temptation of the competition authority may be to infer the existence of an agreement or concerted practice from circumstantial evidence such as parallel conduct on the market. This can be dangerous, for it may be that firms act in parallel not because of an agreement or concerted practice, but because their individual appreciation of market conditions tells them that a failure to match a rival's strategy could be damaging or even disastrous. The problem of parallel behaviour in oligopolistic markets will be examined in chapter 14.

It is necessary to consider first the legal meaning of a concerted practice; secondly the question of whether a concerted practice must have been put into effect for Article 101(1) to have been infringed; and lastly the burden of proof in such cases.

(i) **Meaning of concerted practice**[286]

ICI v Commission[287] (usually referred to as the *Dyestuffs* case) was the first important case on concerted practices to come before the Court of Justice. The Commission had fined several producers of dyestuffs which it considered had been guilty of price fixing through concerted practices[288]. The Commission's decision relied upon various pieces of evidence, including the similarity of the rate and timing of price increases and of instructions sent out by parent companies to their subsidiaries and the fact that there had been informal contact between the firms concerned. The Court of Justice upheld the Commission's

---

[283] Cases 96/82 etc [1983] ECR 3369, [1984] 3 CMLR 276.

[284] Commission decision of 19 December 2007.

[285] Ibid, paras 3 and 397–398.

[286] For stimulating discussion of the complexity of the notion of a concerted practice see Black 'Communication and Obligation in Arrangements and Concerted Practices' (1992) 13 ECLR 200; Black 'Concerted Practices, Joint Action and Reliance' (2003) 24 ECLR 219; Odudu *The Boundaries of EC Competition Law* (Oxford University Press, 2006), pp 71–91; for the treatment of concerted practices under the UK Competition Act 1998 see ch 9, 'Concerted practices', p 341.

[287] Case 48/69 [1972] ECR 619, [1972] CMLR 557.

[288] *Re Aniline Dyes Cartel* JO [1969] L 195/11, [1969] CMLR D23.

decision. It said that the object of bringing concerted practices within Article 101 was to prohibit:

> a form of coordination between undertakings which, without having reached the stage where an agreement properly so-called has been concluded, knowingly substitutes practical cooperation between them for the risks of competition[289].

In *Suiker Unie v Commission*[290] (the *Sugar Cartel* case) the Court of Justice elaborated upon this test. The Commission had held[291] that various sugar producers had taken part in concerted practices to protect the position of two Dutch producers on their domestic market. The producers denied this as they had not worked out a plan to this effect. The Court of Justice held that it was not necessary to prove that there was an actual plan. Article 101 strictly precluded:

> any direct or indirect contact between such operators, the object or effect whereof is either to influence the conduct on the market of an actual or potential competitor or to disclose to such a competitor the course of conduct which they themselves have decided to adopt or contemplate adopting on the market[292].

These two cases provide the legal test of what constitutes a concerted practice for the purpose of Article 101: there must be a mental consensus whereby practical cooperation is *knowingly* substituted for competition; however the consensus need not be achieved verbally, and can come about by direct or indirect contact between the parties.

The European Commission has provided guidance on the meaning of a concerted practice in the section of its *Guidelines on Horizontal Cooperation Agreements* that deals with the exchange of information[293]. It says that the exchange of information between competitors can amount to a concerted practice where it reduces 'strategic uncertainty' in the market, thereby facilitating collusion[294]. In paragraph 62 of those *Guidelines* it refers to the *Cement* appeals[295], where the General Court found that Lafarge was party to a concerted practice when it received information at a meeting about the future conduct of a competitor: it could not argue that it was merely the passive recipient of such information[296]. The Commission then cites the Court of Justice's judgment in *T-Mobile*[297] and says that mere attendance at a meeting where an undertaking discloses its pricing plans to its competitors is likely to be caught by Article 101, even in the absence of an explicit agreement to raise prices, adding, in support of this proposition, the presumption in the *Hüls* judgment cited below that contact between competitors leads to common conduct on the market.

(ii) Must a concerted practice have been put into effect?: the need for a 'causal connection'

The Court of Justice held in *Hüls*, one of the *Polypropylene* cases, that 'a concerted practice...is caught by Article [101(1) TFEU], even in the absence of anti-competitive effects on the market'[298]; however, in the *Cement* cases the General Court said that there would

---

[289] Case 48/69 [1972] ECR 619, [1972] CMLR 557, para 64; see similarly Case C-8/08 *T-Mobile Netherlands BV v Raad van bestuur van de Nederlandse Mededingingsautoriteit* [2009] ECR I-4529, [2009] 5 CMLR 1701, para 26 and the cases cited therein.

[290] Cases 40/73 etc [1975] ECR 1663, [1976] 1 CMLR 295.

[291] *Re European Sugar Cartel* OJ [1973] L 140/17, [1973] CMLR D65.

[292] [1975] ECR 1663, p 1942, [1976] 1 CMLR 295, p 425.

[293] OJ [2011] C 11/1, paras 60–63.　　　[294] Ibid, para 61.

[295] Cases T-25/95 etc *Cimenteries CBR SA v Commission* [2000] ECR II-491, [2000] 5 CMLR 204.

[296] Ibid, para 1849.　　　[297] Ch 3 n 289 above.

[298] Cases C-199/92 P etc *Hüls AG v Commission* [1999] ECR I-4287, [1999] 5 CMLR 1016, para 163.

be no infringement if the parties can prove to the contrary[299]. In reaching its conclusion in *Hüls* the Court of Justice stated that, as established by its own case law[300], Article 101(1) requires that each economic operator must determine its policy on the market independently. At paragraph 161 the Court acknowledged that the concept of a concerted practice implies that there will be common conduct on the market, but added that there must be a presumption that, by making contact with one another, such conduct will follow. In *T-Mobile*[301] the Court of Justice held that this presumption of a 'causal connection' between competitor contact and conduct on the market forms an integral part of EU law, in consequence of which a national court[302] applying Article 101 would be bound to apply the same presumption[303]; to put the point a different way, the national court would not be permitted to apply stricter evidential rules of national law than the EU presumption. The Court also held that the presumption in *T-Mobile* could apply even in the event of a single meeting between competitors[304]. In *Bananas*[305] the Commission held that three producers of bananas were party to a concerted practice by which they coordinated quotation prices for bananas in the north of Europe over a period of nearly three years[306]; in doing so it said that the presumption of a causal connection was stronger where the undertakings concert together on a regular basis over a long period[307].

(iii) The burden of proof

An important issue is to consider who bears the burden of proof in a concerted practice case. It is clear that the overall burden is on the Commission to establish that there has been a concerted practice; the EU Courts have annulled decisions where they were not convinced by the evidence on which the Commission relied[308]. However, the evidential burden of proof may be reversed, for example where the presumption of a causal connection between competitor contact and market conduct discussed in the previous paragraph applies: in that situation it will be for the parties to adduce evidence to rebut the presumption. Where the parties are able to produce evidence that appears to prove the innocence of their behaviour, the overall burden on the Commission requires it to demonstrate why that evidence is unpersuasive. For example in *Compagnie Royale Asturienne des Mines SA and Rheinzink GmbH v Commission*[309] the Commission had concluded that the simultaneous cessation of deliveries to a Belgian customer, Schlitz, by CRAM and

---

[299] Cases T-25/95 etc *Cimenteries CBR SA v Commission* [2000] ECR II-491, [2000] 5 CMLR 204, para 1865.

[300] Cases 40/73 etc *Suiker Unie v Commission* [1975] ECR 1663, [1976] 1 CMLR 295, para 73; Case 172/80 *Züchner v Bayerische Vereinsbank AG* [1981] ECR 2021, [1982] 1 CMLR 313, para 13; Cases 89/85 etc *Ahlström v Commission* [1993] ECR I-1307, [1993] 4 CMLR 407, para 63; Case C-7/95 P *John Deere v Commission* [1998] ECR I-3111, [1998] 5 CMLR 311, para 86.

[301] See ch 3 n 289 above.

[302] And also, one can assume, a national competition authority, though that was not the issue under consideration in *T-Mobile*.

[303] Case C-8/08 *T-Mobile Netherlands BV v Raad van bestuur van de Nederlandse Mededingingsautoriteit* [2009] ECR I-4529, [2009] 5 CMLR 1701, paras 44–53.

[304] Ibid, paras 54–62

[305] Commission decision of 15 October 2008, on appeal Case T-587/08 *Fresh Del Monte Produce v Commission*, not yet decided.

[306] Commission decision of 15 October 2008, paras 212–240.   [307] Ibid, para 218.

[308] See eg Cases 40/73 etc *Suiker Unie v Commission* [1975] ECR 1663, [1976] 1 CMLR 295; Cases 29/83 and 30/83 *Compagnie Royale Asturienne des Mines SA and Rheinzink GmbH v Commission* [1984] ECR 1679, [1985] 1 CMLR 688; and Cases T-68/89 etc *Società Italiano Vetro v Commission* [1992] ECR II-1403, [1992] 5 CMLR 302, in each of which the EU Courts quashed some or all of the findings of concerted practices.

[309] Cases 29/83 and 30/83 [1984] ECR 1679, [1985] 1 CMLR 688.

Rheinzink of Germany was attributable to a concerted practice to protect the German market. The Court of Justice held that there was a possible alternative explanation of the refusal to supply, which was that Schlitz had been failing to settle its accounts on the due date; as the Commission had not dealt with this possible explanation of the conduct in question its decision should be quashed. On the other hand in *CISAC*[310] the Commission was of the opinion that the only explanation for the fact that collecting societies restricted the grant of licences to licensees domiciled within their national territories was the existence of a concerted practice between them[311].

4. The Object or Effect of Preventing, Restricting or Distorting Competition

Article 101(1) prohibits agreements that have as their object or effect the prevention, restriction or distortion of competition[312]. It contains an illustrative list of agreements that may be caught such as price fixing and market sharing, but this is insufficient in itself to explain the numerous intricacies involved in understanding how this provision works. Judgments of the General Court and, at the top of the hierarchy, the Court of Justice contain the most authoritative statements of the law, and some of the best analyses will be found in Opinions of the Advocates General; the Commission's decisions, Notices and Guidelines provide important insights of its views on the application of Article 101(1), as do its *Annual Report on Competition Policy* and the quarterly *Competition Policy Newsletter*[313].

The application of Article 101(1) to agreements, in particular by the Commission, was for many years controversial. In essence the complaint of many commentators was that Article 101(1) was applied too broadly, catching many agreements that were not detrimental to competition at all[314]. Agreements that are caught by Article 101(1) are void and unenforceable[315], and may attract a fine, unless they satisfy the criteria set out in Article 101(3). Under Regulation 17[316], which conferred upon the Commission the power to enforce Articles 101 and 102, only it could grant a so-called 'individual exemption'

---

[310] Commission decision of 16 July 2008, on appeal to the General Court Cases T-398/08 etc, not yet decided.

[311] Ibid, paras 156–222.

[312] In the text that follows the term 'restriction' of competition is taken to include the prevention and distortion of competition.

[313] All of these materials are available on DG COMP's website at www.europa.eu.int/comm/competition/publications/cpn.

[314] See eg Bright 'EU Competition Policy: Rules, Objectives and Deregulation' (1996) 16 Oxford Journal of Legal Studies 535; there is a considerable amount of academic literature criticising the 'over'-application of Article 101(1): see eg Joliet *The Rule of Reason in Antitrust Law; American, German and Common Market Laws in Comparative Perspective* (1967), pp 77–106, 117 to the end; Korah 'The Rise and Fall of Provisional Validity' (1981) 3 NJILB 320; Schechter 'The Rule of Reason in European Competition Law' [1982(2)] Legal Issues in European Integration 1; Forrester and Norall 'The Laicization of Community Law: Self-help and the Rule of Reason' (1984) 21 CML Rev 11; Korah 'EEC Competition Policy – Legal Form or Economic Efficiency' (1986) 39 CLP 85; Venit 'Pronuptia: Ancillary Restraints or Unholy Alliances?' (1986) 11 EL Rev 213; Holley 'EEC Competition Practice; a Thirty-Year Retrospective' in [1992] Fordham Corp L Inst (ed Hawk), 669, p 689; Nazzini 'Article 81 EC Between Time Present and Time Past: A Normative Critique of 'Restriction of Competition' in EU Law (2006) 43 CML Rev 497; Marquis 'O2 (Germany) v Commission and the Exotic Mysteries of Article 81(1) EC' (2007) 32 EL Rev 29.

[315] See further ch 8, 'Competition law as a defence', pp 319–325.

[316] JO 204/62, OJ (Special Edition 1959–62) p 57.

to an agreement under Article 101(3); individual exemptions were rarely given, and
the procedure for obtaining one was time-consuming, costly and cumbersome. A consequence was that many firms would ensure that they satisfied the terms of one of the
'block exemptions' under Article 101(3) in order to be certain that their agreements
were legally enforceable[317]; where no block exemption was available firms that did not
notify their agreements to the Commission for an individual exemption ran the risk of
voidness and fines. An obvious solution proposed by critics of this situation was that
Article 101(1) should be applied to fewer agreements: only those agreements that posed a
real threat to competition should be caught in the net of competition law; others should
not be ensnared by the competition rules at all.

These criticisms were loud and persistent throughout the 1980s and 1990s. However
it is important to note that the advent of Regulation 1/2003[318] in May 2004 changed
this position significantly. Under this Regulation the Commission no longer enjoys a
'monopoly' over individual exemptions under Article 101(3) – indeed there is no longer
any such thing as an individual exemption; and the procedure of notifying agreements to
the Commission for such an exemption has been abolished[319]. Instead the Commission
now shares with national courts and national competition authorities ('NCAs') the power
to make decisions on the application of Article 101 in its entirety. It follows that it is no
longer necessary to argue that an agreement falls outside Article 101(1) for the procedural
reason that it is not block exempted and has not been notified to the Commission for an
individual exemption. Since Regulation 1/2003 it is always possible to argue that an agreement that is restrictive of competition under Article 101(1) satisfies the terms of Article
101(3), whether a case is being decided by the Commission, a national court or an NCA:
there is no longer a procedural tail to wag the substantive dog[320]. Coupled with the introduction of Regulation 1/2003 is the undoubted fact that the Commission, for many years,
has taken a more realistic approach both to Article 101(1) and Article 101(3), in particular
to ensure that Article 101 as a whole is applied in accordance with sound economic principles. The Commission today takes a much narrower view of what is meant by a restriction
of competition for the purpose of Article 101(1); and it also has a narrower approach to the
circumstances in which Article 101(3) is satisfied[321]. Since Regulation 1/2003 the precise
sphere of application of Article 101(1) on the one hand and Article 101(3) on the other does
not have the significance that it did in the days of notification for individual exemption[322];
today the real question is whether an agreement infringes Article 101 as a whole.

(A) **Three preliminary comments**

The text that follows will examine the meaning of agreements having as their 'object or
effect' the prevention, restriction or distortion of competition. However, a few preliminary comments may be helpful.

---

[317] On block exemptions see ch 4, 'Block Exemptions', pp 168–172.   [318] OJ [2003] L 1/1.

[319] See ch 4, 'The end of the system of notification for individual exemption', p 167.

[320] See Wils *Principles of European Antitrust Enforcement* (Hart Publishing, 2005), para 35.

[321] See ch 4, 'First condition of Article 101(3): an improvement in the production or distribution of goods
or in technical or economic progress', pp 156–162 for a discussion of the 'narrow' and the 'broad' interpretations of Article 101(3).

[322] Note however that the burden of proof rests with different persons under Article 101(1) and
Article 101(3): see ch 4, 'The burden of proving that the conditions of Article 101(3) are satisfied',
pp 152–153.

First, there are many judgments of the EU Courts that demonstrate that a contractual restriction does not necessarily result in a restriction of competition[323]. It is essential to understand this key point: the concept of a restriction of competition is an economic one, and as a general proposition economic analysis is needed to determine whether an agreement could have an anti-competitive effect. A relatively small class of agreements are considered by law to have as their object the restriction of competition[324]; in the case of all other agreements anti-competitive effects must be demonstrated for there to be an infringement of Article 101(1)[325].

Secondly, in several judgments the EU Courts have made clear that the Commission must adequately demonstrate that an agreement is restrictive of competition, and that they will not simply 'rubber-stamp' its analysis: a particularly good example is *European Night Services v Commission*[326], where the General Court exposed the thorough inadequacy of the Commission's reasoning in its decision in that case[327].

Thirdly, the General Court has said that in a case under Article 101(1) the definition of the market is relevant at the stage of determining whether there has been an impairment of competition or an effect on trade between Member States; it is not something that must be undertaken as a preliminary matter, as in the case of Article 102 where it is a necessary precondition to a finding of abuse of a dominant position[328].

(B) Horizontal and vertical agreements

One point is absolutely clear: Article 101 is capable of application both to horizontal agreements (between undertakings at the same level of the market) and to vertical agreements (between undertakings at different levels of the market). It was at one time thought that Article 101 might have no application at all to vertical agreements, but that idea was firmly contradicted by the Court of Justice's judgment in *Consten and Grundig v Commission*[329]; it remains the case that undertakings must carry out a careful assessment of whether their vertical agreements are compliant with the law. The application of Article 101 to vertical agreements will be considered in detail in chapter 16.

(C) The 'object or effect' of preventing, restricting or distorting competition

Article 101(1) prohibits agreements 'which have as their *object or effect* the prevention, restriction or distortion of competition' (emphasis added). It is important to understand the significance of the words 'object or effect' in Article 101(1).

---

[323] See the cases discussed at 'Cases in which agreements containing contractual restrictions were found not to have anti-competitive effects', pp 128–129 below.

[324] See 'Agreements that have as their object the prevention, restriction or distortion of competition', pp 121–125.

[325] See 'Agreements that have as their effect the prevention, restriction or distortion of competition', pp 125–137 below.

[326] Cases T-374/94 etc [1998] ECR II-3141, [1998] 5 CMLR 718.

[327] *European Night Services Ltd* OJ [1994] L 259/20, [1995] 5 CMLR 76.

[328] Case T-29/92 *SPO v Commission* [1995] ECR II-289, para 75; Cases T-25/95 etc *Cimenteries CBR SA v Commission* [2000] ECR II-491, [2000] 5 CMLR 204, para 833; Case T-62/98 *Volkswagen AG v Commission* [2000] ECR II-2707, [2000] 5 CMLR 853, paras 230–232; Case T-213/00 *CMA CGM v Commission* [2003] ECR II-913, [2003] 5 CMLR 268, para 206.

[329] Cases 56 and 58/64 [1966] ECR 299, [1966] CMLR 418.

(i) 'Object or effect' to be read disjunctively

It is clear that these are alternative, and not cumulative, requirements for a finding of an infringement of Article 101(1). In *Société Technique Minière v Maschinenbau Ulm*[330] the Court of Justice stated that the words were to be read disjunctively. This means that where an agreement has as its object the restriction of competition, it is unnecessary to prove anti-competitive effects; only if it is not clear that the object of an agreement is to restrict competition is it necessary to consider whether it might have the effect of doing so. This has been regularly repeated by the Court of Justice, in recent years for example in *Competition Authority v Beef Industry Development Society Ltd*[331], *T-Mobile Netherlands*[332] and in *GlaxoSmithKline Services Unlimited v Commission*[333]. Advocate General Kokott has pointed out that a law that forbids people from driving cars when under the influence of alcohol does not require, for a conviction, that the driver has caused an accident – that is to say proof of an effect; in the same way Article 101(1) prohibits certain agreements that have the object of restricting competition, irrespective of whether they produce adverse effects on the market in an individual case[334].

(ii) 'Object'

Case law has established that there are some types of agreement[335] the anti-competitiveness of which can be determined simply from their object. In *GlaxoSmithKline Services Unlimited v Commission*[336] the Court of Justice, citing earlier cases, said that in order to decide whether an agreement restricts by object:

> regard must be had inter alia to the content of its provisions, the objectives it seeks to attain and the economic and legal context of which it forms part[337].

In *T-Mobile Netherlands*[338] the Court said that, in order to ascribe an anti-competitive object to a concerted practice[339], it is sufficient that it has the *potential* to have a negative impact on competition: the effects of such a practice would be relevant only to the level of any fine or the award of damages to victims of the harm[340]. The Court also said that, in order to find a restriction by object, it was not necessary to demonstrate a direct effect on prices to end users: Article 101 is designed to protect the structure of the market and competition as such[341].

The text below will examine which types of agreement have been found to restrict by object[342]. However it may be helpful to begin with some general comments about object restrictions. The first is that the word 'object' in this context does not mean the

---

[330] Case 56/65 [1966] ECR 235, p 249, [1966] CMLR 357, p 375.

[331] Case C-209/07, [2008] ECR I-8637, [2009] 4 CMLR 310, paras 15 and 16.

[332] Case C-8/08 [2009] ECR I-4529, [2009] 5 CMLR 1701, paras 28 and 30.

[333] Cases C-501/06 P etc [2009] ECR I-9291, [2010] 4 CMLR 50, para 55.

[334] Case C-8/08 *T-Mobile Netherlands* [2009] ECR I-4529, [2009] 5 CMLR 1701, para 47.

[335] The Court of Justice has confirmed that a concerted practice can also have the object of restricting competition: see eg Cases C-199/92 P etc *Hüls AG v Commission* [1999] ECR I-4287, [1999] 5 CMLR 1016, para 164; Case C-8/08 *T-Mobile Netherlands* [2009] ECR I-4529, [2009] 5 CMLR 1701, paras 28–30.

[336] Case C-501/06 P [2009] ECR I-9291, [2010] 4 CMLR 50.   [337] Ibid, para 58.

[338] Case C-8/08 [2009] ECR I-4529, [2009] 5 CMLR 1701.

[339] The *T-Mobile* case concerned a concerted practice, but the Court would presumably have said the same if it had been dealing with an agreement.

[340] Case C-8/08 *T-Mobile* [2009] ECR I-4529, [2009] 5 CMLR 1701, para 31; see eg *Amino Acids* OJ [2001] L 154/24, [2001] 5 CMLR 322, paras 261–298.

[341] Case C-8/08 *T-Mobile* [2009] ECR I-4529, [2009] 5 CMLR 1701, paras 36–39.

[342] See also the Commission's *Guidelines on the application of Article [101(3)] of the Treaty* OJ [2004] C 101/8, paras 21–23 and its *Guidelines on Horizontal Cooperation Agreements* OJ [2011] C 11/1, paras 24–25.

subjective intention of the parties when entering into the agreement, but the objective meaning and purpose of the agreement considered in the economic context in which it is to be applied[343]. This does not mean that subjective intention is altogether irrelevant: in *T-Mobile*[344] the Court of Justice said that

> while the intention of the parties is not an essential factor in determining whether a concerted practice is restrictive, there is nothing to prevent the Commission of the European Communities or the competent Community judicature from taking it into account.[345]

It follows from the proposition that subjective intention is not a *necessary* condition to characterise an agreement as restrictive by object that the Court of Justice has held that it is irrelevant that the agreement was not in the commercial interest of some of the participants[346]; and that, where an agreement has an anti-competitive object, it does not cease to be characterised as such because it had an alternative, lawful, purpose[347].

A second point about object restrictions is that, from a competition authority's point of view, the fact that it does not need to demonstrate, for example, that horizontal price-fixing agreements produce adverse economic effects relieves it of some of the burden that would otherwise rest upon it. In her Opinion in *T-Mobile*[348] Advocate General Kokott said that the classification of certain types of agreement as restrictive by object 'sensibly conserves resources of competition authorities and the justice system'[349]. She also pointed out that the existence of object restrictions 'creates legal certainty and allows all market participants to adapt their conduct accordingly'[350] adding that, although the concept of restriction by object should not be given an unduly broad interpretation, nor should it be interpreted so narrowly as to deprive it of its practical effectiveness[351].

The third point is that, where the parties to an agreement that is restrictive by object wish to assert that it could produce efficiency-enhancing effects, they can do so only by proving that it satisfies the criteria of Article 101(3), the burden of proof being on them to prove that this is so[352]. Having decided in *Competition Authority v Beef Industry Development Society Ltd*[353] that an agreement between beef processors in Ireland to reduce overcapacity by encouraging some of them to withdraw from the market restricted competition by object, the Court of Justice said that the agreement could be defended only under Article 101(3)[354].

---

[343] Cases 29/83 and 30/83 *Compagnie Royale Asturienne des Mines SA and Rheinzinc GmbH v Commission* [1984] ECR 1679, [1985] 1 CMLR 688, paras 25–26; Case C-277/87 *Sandoz Prodotti Farmaceutici v Commission* [1990] ECR I-45; Case T-148/89 *Tréfilunion v Commission* [1995] ECR II-1063, para 79; Case C-551/03 P *General Motors v Commission* [2006] ECR II-3173, [2006] 5 CMLR 4491, paras 77–78.

[344] Case C-8/08 [2009] ECR I-4529, [2009] 5 CMLR 1701.

[345] Ibid, para 27; on the relevance of subjective intention see Odudu 'Interpreting Article 81(1): Object as Subjective Intention' (2001) 26 EL Rev 60 and Odudu 'Interpreting Article 81(1): the Object Requirement Revisited' (2001) 26 EL Rev 379.

[346] See eg Case C-403/04 P *Sumitomo Metal Industries Ltd v Commission* [2007] ECR I-729, [2007] 4 CMLR 650, paras 45–46.

[347] Case C-551/03 P [2006] ECR I-3173, [2006] 5 CMLR 9, para 64; Case C-209/07 *Competition Authority v Beef Industry Development Society Ltd* [2008] ECR I-8637, [2009] 4 CMLR 310, para 21; the same point was made by the General Court in Cases T-49/02 etc *Brasserie Nationale SA v Commission* [2005] ECR II-3033, [2006] 4 CMLR 266, para 85.

[348] Case C-8/08 [2009] ECR I-4529, [2009] 5 CMLR 1701.   [349] Ibid, para 43.   [350] Ibid.

[351] Ibid, para 44.

[352] See ch 4 generally on Article 101(3), including the burden of proof and the nature of the evidence required to succeed in showing that that provision is satisfied.

[353] Case C-209/07 [2008] ECR I-8637, [2009] 4 CMLR 310; for comment on this judgment see Odudu 'Restrictions of Competition by Object – What's the Beef?' (2009) 8(1) Competition Law Journal 11.

[354] Ibid, paras 21 and 39; the case was remitted to the High Court in Ireland to consider whether the criteria of Article 101(3) were satisfied; however BIDS withdrew its defence before the Court had made

A fourth point is that the fact that there is no need to prove anti-competitive effects in the case of object restrictions does not mean that there is no quantitative component to object analysis at all. There is a rule that any restriction of competition must be *appreciable*: even a restriction of competition by object could fall outside Article 101(1) if its likely impact on the market is minimal[355]. Furthermore, as a jurisdictional matter, an agreement infringes Article 101(1) only if it has an *appreciable* effect on trade between Member States: again, therefore, some quantitative analysis may be required before determining that Article 101(1) is infringed[356]. Because of the need to prove appreciability, it is necessary for the Commission to define the relevant market even in a case involving an object restriction[357].

(iii) 'Effect'

Where an agreement does not have as its object the restriction of competition, it is necessary to demonstrate that it would have a restrictive effect; this is a much more onerous task for the Commission or the person wishing to establish an infringement of Article 101(1). The position was stated clearly by the General Court in *European Night Services v Commission*[358]:

> it must be borne in mind that in assessing an agreement under Article [101(1)] of the Treaty, account should be taken of the actual conditions in which it functions, in particular the economic context in which the undertakings operate, the products or services covered by the agreement and the actual structure of the market concerned ... *unless it is an agreement containing obvious restrictions of competition such as price-fixing, market-sharing or the control of outlets.* ... In the latter case, such restrictions may be weighed against their claimed pro-competitive effects only in the context of Article [101(3)] of the Treaty, with a view to granting an exemption from the prohibition in Article [101(1)] (emphasis added).

(iv) Comment on the 'object or effect' distinction

Clearly it is important to know which agreements can be classified as having as their object the restriction of competition since in such cases it is not necessary to prove that anti-competitive effects would follow.

It may be helpful to think of the position in terms of two boxes, as follows:

OBJECT	EFFECT
Agreements that have as their object the restriction of competition	Agreements that have as their effect the restriction of competition

a decision on the matter: see Irish Competition Authority, Press Release of 25 January 2011, available at www.tca.ie/default.aspx.

[355] For discussion of this rule see 'The *De Minimis* Doctrine', pp 140–144 below.

[356] See 'The Effect on Trade between Member States', pp 144–149 below on the requirement of an appreciable effect on trade between Member States.

[357] See eg Case T-199/08 *Ziegler SA v Commission* [2011] ECR II-000, [2011] 5 CMLR 261, paras 41–45 (one of the appeals in the *International Removal Services* case).

[358] Cases T-374/94 etc [1998] ECR II-3141, [1998] 5 CMLR 718, para 136.

Article 101(1), as interpreted by the EU Courts, allocates particularly pernicious types of agreement that are overwhelmingly likely to harm consumer welfare to the object box, with the consequences just described. This is done as a matter of policy: certain agreements are so clearly inimical to the objectives of the EU that they can be permitted only where they can be shown to satisfy the requirements of Article 101(3). In all other cases, however, the lawfulness of an agreement under Article 101(1) must be tested according to its anti-competitive effects and this, as we shall see, requires a wide-ranging analysis of the market[359].

There is clearly an analogy here with the position under section 1 of the Sherman Act 1890 in the US, which characterises some agreements as *per se* infringements of the Act, whereas others are subject to so-called 'rule of reason' analysis[360]. Where there is a *per se* infringement, it is not open to the parties to the agreement to argue that it does not restrict competition: it belongs to a category of agreement that has, by law, been found to be restrictive of competition. However, there is an important difference in EU law in that, even if an agreement has as its object the restriction of competition, that is to say that it infringes Article 101(1) *per se*, the parties can still argue that the agreement satisfies the terms of Article 101(3). This possibility does not exist in US law, since there is no equivalent of Article 101(3) in that system. For this reason a judgment such as that of the US Supreme Court in *Leegin*[361], in which that Court determined that minimum resale price maintenance should be analysed under a rule of reason standard, rather than being subjected to a *per se* rule, brings US law into alignment with that of the EU: it has always been possible for an undertaking to argue that resale price maintenance satisfies Article 101(3), even though it is classified as having as its object the restriction of competition for the purpose of Article 101(1). Paragraph 46 of the Commission's *Guidelines on the application of Article [101(3)] of the Treaty*[362] cites the General Court's judgment in *Matra Hachette v Commission*[363], which established that there is no type of agreement that, on *a priori* grounds, can be said to be incapable of satisfying the criteria of Article 101(3): even agreements that restrict competition by object can do so, provided that probative evidence in support of efficiency gains can be adduced.

(D) **Agreements that have as their object the prevention, restriction or distortion of competition**

In *European Night Services v Commission*[364] the General Court referred to agreements 'containing obvious restrictions of competition such as price-fixing, market-sharing or the control of outlets'; without using the terminology used in this chapter, it seems clear that the General Court considered that agreements of this nature should be allocated to

---

[359] See 'Agreements that have as their effect the prevention, restriction or distortion of competition', pp 125–137 below.

[360] For an interesting discussion of this topic see Black 'Per Se Rules and Rules of Reason: What Are They?' (1997) 18 ECLR 145: this article contains extensive citation of the literature on the position under US law; see also Jones 'Analysis of agreements under US and EC antitrust law – Convergence or divergence?' (2006) 51 Antitrust Bulletin 691; Andreangeli 'From Mobile Phones to Cattle: How the Court of Justice Is reframing the Approach to Article 101 of the EU Treaty' (2011) 34 World Competition 215.

[361] *Leegin Creative Leather Products Inc v PSKS Inc* 551 US 877 (2007).

[362] OJ [2004] C 101/97.

[363] Case T-17/93 [1994] ECR II-595.

[364] Cases T-374/94 etc [1998] ECR II-3141, [1998] 5 CMLR 718.

the 'object' box. Advocate General Trstenjak said in her Opinion in *Competition Authority v Beef Industry Development Society Ltd*[365] that the notion of restriction of competition by object cannot be reduced to an exhaustive list, and that it should not be limited just to the examples of anti-competitive agreements given in Article 101(1) itself[366]. It is for the EU Courts to determine which agreements restrict competition by object; over a period of time the contents of the object box may expand or contract[367].

(i) Price fixing and exchanges of information in relation to future prices

Price fixing is specifically cited as an example of an anti-competitive agreement in Article 101(1)(a) of the Treaty, and it is unsurprising that it is characterised as having as its object the restriction of competition, whether horizontal[368] or vertical[369]. In *T-Mobile*[370] the Court of Justice said that the exchange of information between competitors 'is tainted with an anti-competitive object if the exchange is capable of removing uncertainties concerning the intended conduct of the participating undertakings'[371]; in that case mobile telephone operators exchanged information about the remuneration that they intended to pay to their dealers for the services that they provided. In its *Guidelines on Horizontal Cooperation Agreements*[372] the Commission says that it considers the exchange of information between competitors of individualised data regarding intended future prices or quantities to be restrictive of competition by object[373]. In *Bananas*[374] the Commission held that 'pre-pricing communications' in which undertakings discussed price-setting factors relevant to the setting of future quotation prices amounted to object restrictions[375]. Other information exchanges require effects analysis[376].

(ii) Market sharing, quotas, collective exclusive dealing

Market-sharing agreements are specifically mentioned in Article 101(1)(c), and again their treatment as restrictive by object is to be expected, in particular because they are likely to be harmful to the internal market[377].

The General Court did not refer in *European Night Services* to agreements to limit output when discussing 'obvious' restrictions of competition, but they must also be allo-

---

[365] Case C-209/07 [2008] ECR I-8637, [2009] 4 CMLR 310.

[366] Ibid, para 48; the Court of Justice's judgment appears to agree with this, although paragraph 23 of its judgment says only that Article 101 does not constitute an exhaustive list of prohibited collusion: the context of the statement suggests that it meant that it is not an exhaustive list of collusion *by object*.

[367] See 'Refinement of the range of agreements within the object box', pp 124–125 below; for criticism of the current lack of clarity in determining whether a restriction is one by object see Jones 'Left Behind my Modernisation? Restrictions by Object Under Article 101(1)' (2010) European Competition Journal 649; King 'The Object Box: Law, Policy or Myth?' (2011) 7(2) European Competition Journal 269.

[368] See ch 13, 'Horizontal Price Fixing', pp 522–530.

[369] See ch 16, 'Article 4(a): resale price maintenance', pp 664–665.

[370] Case C-8/08 [2009] ECR I-4529, [2009] 5 CMLR 1701.   [371] Ibid, para 43.

[372] OJ [2011] C 11/1.

[373] Ibid, para 74.

[374] *Bananas* Commission decision of 15 October 2008, paras 263–277, on appeal Case T-587/08 *Fresh Del Monte Produce v Commission*, not yet decided.

[375] Ibid, paras 263–277.

[376] See eg Case C-238/05 *Asnef-Equifax v Asociación de Usuarios de Servcicios Bancarios (Ausbanc)* [2006] ECR I-11125, [2007] 4 CMLR 224 and the Commission's *Guidelines on Horizontal Cooperation Agreements* OJ [2011] C 11/1, paras 75–94; information agreements are discussed in ch 13, 'Exchanges of Information', pp 539–547.

[377] See ch 13, 'Horizontal Market Sharing', pp 530–533.

cated to the object box on the basis that they clearly restrict competition, and they are specifically referred to in Article 101(1)(b); analogous agreements, for example to limit sales, must also be included[378]. In *Competition Authority v Beef Industry Development Society Ltd*[379] the Court of Justice held that arrangements to enable several undertakings to implement a common policy of encouraging some of them to withdraw from the market in order to reduce overcapacity had the object of restricting competition[380]. The Commission has also characterised collective exclusive dealing as restricting competition by object[381].

(iii) Controlling outlets; export bans

The General Court in *European Night Services* referred to agreements to control outlets as containing obvious restrictions of competition; the control of outlets is not specifically referred to in Article 101(1), but the Court presumably had in mind the imposition on distributors of export bans from one Member State to another, which have consistently been found to have as their object the restriction of competition[382]: nothing could be more obviously inimical to the goal of market integration than restrictions of this kind. The judgment of the General Court in *GlaxoSmithKline v Commission*[383] somewhat muddied this apparently simple point by suggesting that, in the specific and unusual conditions in which pharmaceutical products are bought and sold, an indirect export ban did not have its object the restriction of competition[384], although it did restrict competition by effect[385]. However the Court of Justice reversed the judgment of the General Court, repeating that an agreement aimed at prohibiting or limiting parallel trade has as its object the restriction of competition, and that that principle applies to the pharmaceutical sector as it does to any other[386]; the Court added that, in order to be found to restrict by object, it was not necessary to show that the agreement entailed disadvantages for final consumers[387].

The Court of Justice has also held that the imposition of fixed or minimum resale prices on distributors is restrictive of competition by object[388].

---

[378] See ch 13, 'Anti-Competitive Horizontal Restraints', pp 550–552.

[379] Case C-209/07 [2008] ECR I-8637, [2009] 4 CMLR 310.   [380] Ibid, paras 33–34.

[381] See eg *Nederlandse Federatieve Vereniging voor de Grootlandel op Elektrotechnisch Gebied and Technische Unie (FEG and TU)* OJ [2000] L 39/1, [2000] 4 CMLR 1208, para 105, and the further examples given in footnote 120 of that decision; the Commission's decision was upheld on appeal, Cases T-5/00 and 6/00 [2003] ECR II-5761, [2004] 5 CMLR 962.

[382] See eg Case 19/77 *Miller International Schallplaten v Commission* [1978] ECR 131, [1978] 2 CMLR 334, paras 7 and 18; see similarly Case C-551/03 P *General Motors BV v Commission* [2006] ECR I-3173, [2006] 5 CMLR 9, in particular paras 64–80; Cases T-175/95 and T-176/95 *BASF v Commission* [1999] ECR II-1581, [2000] 4 CMLR 33, para 133; Case T-176/95 *Accinauto SA v Commission* [1999] ECR II-1635, [2000] 4 CMLR 67, para 104.

[383] Case T-168/01 *GlaxoSmithKline Services v Commission* [2006] ECR II-2969, [2006] 5 CMLR 1623.

[384] Ibid, paras 114–147.

[385] Ibid, paras 148–192.

[386] Cases C-501/06 P etc *GlaxoSmithKline Services Unlimited v Commission* [2009] ECR I-9291, [2010] 4 CMLR 50, paras 59 and 60.

[387] Ibid, paras 62–64.

[388] Case 161/84 *Pronuptia de Paris GmbH v Schillgalis* [1986] ECR 353, [1986] 1 CMLR 414, paras 23 and 25.

Following the order of the text above, it seems that the contents of the 'object' box can be depicted as follows:

The object box[389]

Horizontal agreements:

- to fix prices
- to exchange information that reduces uncertainty about future behaviour
- to share markets
- to limit output, including the removal of excess capacity
- to limit sales
- for collective exclusive dealing

Vertical agreements:

- to impose fixed or minimum resale prices
- to impose export bans

(iv) Refinement of the range of agreements within the object box

An important qualification must be made. This presentation of the position slightly over-simplifies the position in so far as it suggests that the content of the object box is capable of precise definition: it is not; furthermore the content of the object box is capable of change over a period of time, as the EU Courts are called upon to consider, or perhaps to reconsider, the restrictive nature of particular types of agreements. This process of categorisation and recategorisation is natural and to be expected, and has a parallel in the US where the courts are from time to time called upon to determine whether a particular type of agreement should be tested according to a *per se* or a rule of reason standard[390]. However the fact that a particular type of agreement might be characterised as not having as its object the restriction of competition does *not* mean that an agreement that is found to restrict by object ceases to do so if it can be proven in an individual case that it does not have a restrictive effect: in that case all object cases would, in reality, be converted into effects ones, thereby undermining the very distinction between the two[391].

---

[389] It will be seen that the contents of the object box correspond to a large extent with the provisions that are blacklisted in Articles 4(a) and 4(b) of Regulation 330/2010 on vertical agreements (ch 16, 'Article 4(a): resale price maintenance', pp 664–665, and ch 16, 'Article 4(b): territorial and customer restrictions', pp 665–668), Article 5 of Regulation 1217/2010 on research and development agreements (ch 15, 'Article 4: the market share threshold and duration of exemption', p 597) and Article 4 of Regulation 1218/2010 on specialisation agreements (ch 15, 'Article 4: hardcore restrictions', p 602).

[390] In the US see *Continental TV v GTE Sylvania* 433 US 36 (1977), where the Supreme Court overruled an earlier judgment, *US v Arnold Schwinn & Co* 388 US 365 (1967), that had subjected non-price vertical restraints to a *per se* rule; *National Society of Professional Engineers v US* 435 US 679 (1978), where a trade association's rules prohibiting competitive bidding by members were tested under the rule of reason rather than a *per se* rule; *Broadcast Music Inc v CBS* 441 US 1 (1979), where the rule of reason was applied to the rules of a copyright collecting society: the Supreme Court accepted that the agreement was a price fixing agreement 'in the literal sense', but concluded that it was not a 'naked restraint', but instead enabled copyright owners to market their product more efficiently; *State Oil Co v Khan* 522 US 3 (1997), where the Supreme Court held that maximum resale price maintenance should be tested under the rule of reason and not a *per se* standard; and *Leegin Creative Leather Products, Inc v PSKS, Inc* 551 US 877 (2007) where the Supreme Court decided that agreements on *minimum* resale prices should be transferred from *per se* to rule of reason analysis.

[391] See on this Advocate General Kokott in Case C-8/08 *T-Mobile* [2009] ECR I-4529, [2009] 5 CMLR 1701, paras 45–46; see also Kolstad 'Object contra effect in Swedish and European competition law', Swedish Competition Authority, 2009, available at www.kkv.se/.

A few examples can be given of agreements that might have been considered to be restrictive by object, and yet in which the Commission or Court analysed them on the basis of effects instead. In *Visa International – Multilateral Interchange Fee*[392] participants in the Visa system agreed on the level of the 'multilateral interchange fee' that 'acquiring banks' (which act for merchants) pay to 'issuing banks' (which issue Visa cards to consumers) for each transaction with a Visa card; the Commission concluded that this did restrict the freedom of banks to decide their own pricing policies[393], but that this did not amount to a restriction of competition by object[394], but by effect[395]; the Commission decided that the agreement satisfied the criteria of Article 101(3)[396]. In *MasterCard*[397] the Commission left open the question of whether the interchange fee restricted by object since it considered that it clearly had an anti-competitive effect[398].

There have been a few occasions on which the Court of Justice has concluded that an export ban, in the context of a specific type of agreement, did not have as its object the restriction of competition. An example can be found in *Erauw-Jacquery Sprl v La Hesbignonne Société Coopérative*[399], where the Court of Justice held that a provision preventing a licensee from exporting so-called 'basic' seeds protected by plant breeders' rights could fall outside Article 101(1) where it was necessary to protect the right of the licensor to select his licensees. In *Javico v Yves St Laurent*[400], where an export ban was imposed on distributors in Russia and the Ukraine, the Court of Justice held that:

> In the case of agreements of this kind stipulations of the type mentioned in the question must be construed not as being intended to exclude parallel imports and marketing of the contractual product within the [EU] but as being designed to enable the producer to penetrate a market outside the [EU] by supplying a sufficient quantity of contractual products to that market. That interpretation is supported by the fact that, in the agreements at issue, the prohibition of selling outside the contractual territory also covers other non-member countries[401].

Having concluded that the agreement in *Javico* did not have as its object the restriction of competition, the Court of Justice went on to consider whether it might have this effect. The *Javico* judgment is easy to understand, given that the export ban was not imposed on a distributor within the EU, but rather concerned exports from Russia and the Ukraine.

(E) Agreements that have as their effect the prevention, restriction or distortion of competition

(i) Extensive analysis of an agreement in its market context is required to determine its effect[402]

Where it is not possible to say that the object of an agreement is to restrict competition, it is necessary to conduct an extensive analysis of its effect on the market before it can be

---

[392] OJ [2002] L 318/17, [2003] 4 CMLR 283.   [393] Ibid, paras 64–66.
[394] Ibid, para 69.   [395] Ibid, para 68.
[396] Ibid, paras 74–110; see further ch 13, 'Article 101(3)', pp 529–530.
[397] Commission decision of 19 December 2007.   [398] Ibid, paras 401–407.
[399] Case 27/87 [1988] ECR 1919, [1988] 4 CMLR 576; see similarly the Commission's decision in *Sicasov* OJ [1999] L 4/27, [1999] 4 CMLR 192, paras 53–61.
[400] Case C-306/96 [1998] ECR I-1983, [1998] 5 CMLR 172.   [401] Ibid, para 19.
[402] On the issue of anti-competitive effect see Odudu 'Interpreting Article 81(1): Demonstrating Restrictive Effect' (2001) 26 EL Rev 261 and Odudu 'A New Economic Approach to Article 81(1)?' (2001) 26 EL Rev 100.

found to infringe Article 101(1)[403]. This has been stressed by the EU Courts on a number of occasions. For example, in *Brasserie de Haecht v Wilkin*[404] the Court of Justice said that:

> it would be pointless to consider an agreement, decision or practice by reason of its effect if those effects were to be taken distinct from the market in which they are seen to operate, and could only be examined apart from the body of effects, whether convergent or not, surrounding their implementation. Thus in order to examine whether it is caught by Article [101(1)] an agreement cannot be examined in isolation from the above context, that is, from the factual or legal circumstances causing it to prevent, restrict or distort competition. The existence of similar contracts may be taken into consideration for this objective to the extent to which the general body of contracts of this type is capable of restricting the freedom of trade[405].

An important case which demonstrates the depth of analysis required in determining whether an agreement has the effect of restricting competition is *Delimitis v Henninger Bräu AG*[406]. There the Court of Justice considered a provision in an agreement between a brewery and a licensee of a public house owned by the brewery, whereby the licensee was required to purchase a minimum amount of beer each year. The litigation in the German courts concerned the refusal by the brewery, on termination, to return the full deposit to the licensee that he had paid when entering into the agreement: the brewery had deducted sums that it considered it was entitled to. The licensee claimed that the agreement was void and unenforceable under Article 101; an appeal court in Germany referred the case to the Court of Justice under Article 267 TFEU. The Court of Justice said that beer supply agreements of the type under consideration do not have as their object the restriction of competition[407]. Instead it stressed that the agreement had to be considered in the context in which it occurred[408]. To begin with it was necessary to define the relevant product and geographic markets[409]: these were defined as the sale of beer in licensed premises (as opposed to beer sold in retail outlets) in Germany. Having defined the markets, the Court then said that it was necessary to determine whether access to the market was impeded: could a new competitor enter the market, for example by buying an existing brewery together with its network of sales outlets or by opening new public houses[410]? If the answer was that access to the market was impeded, it was necessary to ask whether the agreements entered into by Henninger Bräu contributed to that foreclosure effect, for example because of their number and duration[411]. Only if the answer to both of these questions was yes could it be held that Article 101(1) was infringed. The analysis suggested in this case was specific to the issues raised by beer supply agreements, and is not

---

[403] Helpful guidance on the Commission's approach to the establishment of anti-competitive effects can be found in the Commission's *Guidelines on the application of Article [101(3)] of the Treaty* OJ [2004] C 101/8, paras 24–27 and in its *Guidelines on Horizontal Cooperation Agreements* OJ [2011] C 11/1, paras 26–47.

[404] Case 23/67 [1967] ECR 407, [1968] CMLR 26.

[405] Case 23/67 [1967] ECR 407, p 415, [1968] CMLR 26, p 40; see similarly Cases C-7/95 P and C-8/95 P *John Deere v Commission* [1998] ECR I-3111, [1998] 5 CMLR 311, paras 76 and 91 respectively and Cases C-215/96 and C-216/96 *Carlo Bagnsaco v BPN* [1999] ECR I-135, [1999] 4 CMLR 624, para 33.

[406] Case C-234/89 [1991] ECR I-935, [1992] 5 CMLR 210, para 13; see Korah 'The Judgment in *Delimitis*: A Milestone Towards a Realistic Assessment of the Effects of an Agreement – or a Damp Squib' (1992) 14 EIPR 167; there is a longer version in (1998) 8 Tulane European and Civil Law Forum 17; Lasok 'Assessing the Economic Consequences of Restrictive Agreements: A Comment on the Delimitis Case' (1991) 12 ECLR 194; see similarly Case C-214/99 *Neste Markkinointi Oy v Yötuuli* [2000] ECR I-11121, [2001] 4 CMLR 993; Case T-65/98 *Van den Bergh Foods Ltd v Commission* [2003] ECR II-4653, [2004] 4 CMLR 14, paras 75–119.

[407] Case C-234/89 [1991] ECR I-935, [1992] 5 CMLR 210, para 13.   [408] Ibid, para 14.

[409] Ibid, paras 16–18; on market definition see ch 1, 'Market definition', pp 27–42.

[410] Ibid, paras 19–23.   [411] Ibid, paras 24–27.

necessarily the same to be applied, for example, to restrictive covenants taken on the sale of a business[412] or to the rules of a group purchasing association[413]. However the important point about the judgment is its requirement that a full analysis of the agreement in its market context must be carried out before it is possible to determine whether its effect is to restrict competition.

(ii) The need to establish a 'counter-factual'

In determining whether an agreement has a restrictive effect on competition, it is necessary to consider what the position would have been in the absence of the agreement[414]: by comparing the two situations it should be possible to form a view as to whether the agreement could restrict competition. The need to examine the 'counter-factual' was stressed by the General Court in *O2 (Germany) GmbH & Co, OHG v Commission*[415], where it annulled a Commission decision[416] finding that a roaming agreement in the mobile telephony sector had the effect of restricting competition: the Commission had failed to show what the position would have been in the absence of the agreement, or that the agreement could have restrictive effects on competition[417].

(iii) Actual and potential competition

In deciding whether Article 101 is infringed the Commission and the EU Courts will not limit their consideration to whether existing competition will be restricted by the agreement; they will also take into account the possibility that an agreement might affect potential competition in a particular market. Following criticism of its overly interventionist approach in the 1980s the Commission shifted its perception of 'potential competition' under Article 101(1), and it now adopts a more realistic view of the expression so that fewer agreements are caught than previously[418]. The General Court in *European Night Services v Commission*[419] rejected in its entirety a finding of the Commission that the establishment of the joint venture European Night Services Ltd could restrict actual or potential competition between its parents: the Court considered this to be:

> a hypothesis unsupported by any evidence or any analysis of the structure of the relevant market from which it might be concluded that it represented a real, concrete possibility[420].

However, the Commission would be erring in law if it were to disregard altogether the impact of an agreement on potential competition[421]; while in *Visa Europe Ltd v*

---

[412] On agreements of this kind see *Remia BV and Vereenigde Bedrijven and Nutricia v Commission*, 'Cases in which agreements containing contractual restrictions were found not to have anti-competitive effects', p 129 below.

[413] On agreements of this kind see *Gøttrup-Klim Grovvareforeninger v Dansk Landburgs Grovvareselskab AmbA*, see 'Cases in which agreements containing contractual restrictions were found not to have anti-competitive effects', p 129 below.

[414] See Case 56/65 *Société Technique Minière v Maschinendau Ulm* [1966] ECR 235, pp 249–250, [1966] CMLR 357, p 375; 'Purpose and scope of Guidelines on Horizontal Cooperation Agreements', pp 588–589; see also the Commission's *Guidelines on Horizontal Cooperation Agreements* OJ [2011] C 11/1, para 29.

[415] Case T-328/03 [2006] ECR II-1231, [2006] 5 CMLR 258.

[416] *T-Mobile Deutschland/O2 Germany: Network Sharing Rahmenvertrag* OJ [2004] L 75/32.

[417] See in particular paras 65–117 of the General Court's judgment.

[418] See eg *Konsortium ECR 900* OJ [1990] L 228/31, [1992] 4 CMLR 54; *Elopak/Metal Box—Odin* OJ [1990] L 209/15, [1991] 4 CMLR 832; Commission's *Guidelines on Horizontal Cooperation Agreements* OJ [2011] C 11/1, para 10 and footnotes 3 and 4; see further ch 15, 'Potential competitors', p 576.

[419] Cases T-374/94 etc [1998] ECR II-3141, [1998] 5 CMLR 718.

[420] Ibid, paras 139–147.

[421] See Case T-504/93 *Tiercé-Ladbroke v Commission* [1997] ECR II-923, [1997] 5 CMLR 309, where the General Court annulled a Commission decision which failed to take into account a possible restriction of potential competition.

Commission[422] the General Court upheld the Commission's decision in *Morgan Stanley/ Visa International*[423] that Morgan Stanley was a potential entrant into the acquiring market for payment cards and had been illegally excluded from that market[424].

(iv) Cases in which agreements containing contractual restrictions were found not to have anti-competitive effects

The point was made earlier that a contractual restriction does not necessarily result in a restriction of competition. There have been many judgments in which the EU Courts have concluded that agreements containing contractual restrictions did not have the effect of restricting competition. Several of these cases were Article 267 references, where one party was trying to avoid a contractual restriction freely entered into by invoking Article 101(2) TFEU – which says that agreements that infringe Article 101 are void – in litigation in a national court.

The first case of note was as long ago as 1966: in *Société Technique Minière v Maschinenbau Ulm*[425] the Court of Justice said that a term conferring exclusivity on a distributor might not infringe Article 101(1) where this seemed to be 'really necessary for the penetration of a new area by an undertaking'. Two weeks later, the Court of Justice in *Consten and Grundig v Commission*[426] reached the conclusion that an agreement conferring absolute territorial protection on a distributor had as its object the restriction of competition and did not satisfy the criteria of Article 101(3). These two judgments are highly instructive. *Société Technique Minière* shows that simply granting exclusive rights to a territory, without export bans, may not infringe Article 101(1) at all: it is an empirical question whether such an agreement, assessed in its market context, has a restrictive effect; *Consten and Grundig*, however, shows that where an agreement goes further, imposing export bans and preventing the possibility of parallel trade, it is considered by law to have as its object the restriction of competition. There is no better illustration of the impact of the 'single market imperative'[427] than this.

In *Metro SB–Grossmärkte v Commission*[428] the Court of Justice held that restrictive provisions in a selective distribution system may fall outside Article 101(1) where they satisfy objective, qualitative criteria and are applied in a non-discriminatory manner[429]. In *LC Nungesser KG v Commission*[430] the Court of Justice held that an open exclusive licence of plant breeders' rights would not infringe Article 101(1) where, on the facts of the case, the licensee would not have risked investing in the production of maize seeds at all without some immunity from intra-brand competition[431]. In *Coditel v Ciné Vog Films SA (No 2)*[432] the Court of Justice held that an exclusive copyright licence to exhibit a film in a Member State would not necessarily infringe Article 101(1), even where this might prevent transmission of that film by cable broadcasting from a neighbouring Member State, where this was necessary to protect the investment of the licensee. Restrictive covenants may fall outside Article 101(1), provided that they are duly limited in time, space and subject-matter; in other words that they satisfy the principle of proportionality. This

---

[422] Case T-461/07 [2011] ECR II-000, [2011] 5 CMLR 74.

[423] Commission decision of 3 October 2007.

[424] Case T-461/07 [2011] ECR II-000, [2011] 5 CMLR 74, paras 162–197.

[425] Case 56/65 [1966] ECR 235, p 250, [1966] CMLR 357, p 375.

[426] Cases 56 and 58/64 [1966] ECR 299, [1966] CMLR 418.

[427] See ch 1, 'The single market imperative', pp 23–24 and ch 2, 'The single market imperative', p 51.

[428] Case 26/76 [1977] ECR 1875, [1978] 2 CMLR 1.

[429] See ch 16, 'Selective distribution agreements', pp 641–645.

[430] Case 258/78 [1982] ECR 2015, [1983] 1 CMLR 278.

[431] See ch 19, 'Territorial exclusivity and the *Maize Seeds* case', pp 774–775.

[432] Case 262/81 [1982] ECR 3381, [1983] 1 CMLR 49.

was established by the Commission in *Reuter/BASF*[433], and confirmed by the Court of Justice in *Remia BV and Verenidge Bedrijven and Nutricia v Commission*[434]; there the Court recognised that, in order to effect the sale of a business together with its associated goodwill, it may be necessary that the vendor should be restricted from competing with the purchaser; in the absence of such a covenant it may not be possible to sell the business at all. In *Métropole télévision v Commission*[435] the General Court held that an ancillary restriction is one that is 'directly related and necessary to the implementation of a main operation'[436], and said that this is a 'relatively abstract' matter that does not require a full market analysis[437].

In *Pronuptia de Paris v Schillgalis*[438] the Court of Justice held that many restrictive provisions in franchising agreements designed to protect the intellectual property rights of the franchisor and to maintain the common identity of the franchise system fall outside Article 101(1). In *Erauw-Jacquery Sprl v La Hesbignonne Société Coopérative*[439] the Court of Justice held that a provision preventing a licensee from exporting basic seeds protected by plant breeders' rights could fall outside Article 101(1) where it was necessary to protect the right of the licensor to select his licensees. In *Gøttrup-Klim Grovvareforeninger v Dansk Landburgs Grovvareselskab AmbA*[440] the Court of Justice held that a provision in the statutes of a cooperative purchasing association, forbidding its members from participating in other forms of organised cooperation which were in direct competition with it, did not necessarily restrict competition, and may even have beneficial effects on competition[441]; it was necessary to consider the effect of the provision on the market, and it would not be caught by Article 101(1) if it was restricted to what was necessary to ensure that the cooperative could function properly and maintain its contractual power in relation to the suppliers with which it had to deal[442].

(v) Commercial ancillarity

These judgments of the EU Courts show that, when considering whether an agreement has the effect of restricting competition, it is possible to argue successfully that restrictions which are necessary to enable the parties to an agreement to achieve a legitimate commercial purpose fall outside Article 101(1)[443]. The legitimate purposes under consideration were of various kinds: for example the penetration of a new market, the sale of a business and the successful establishment of a group purchasing association. An idea

---

[433] OJ [1976] L 254/40, [1976] 2 CMLR D44.

[434] Case 42/84 [1985] ECR 2545, [1987] 1 CMLR 1.

[435] Case T-112/99 [2001] ECR II-2459, [2001] 5 CMLR 1236.

[436] Ibid, para 104, citing the Commission's *Notice on Ancillary Restraints* OJ [1990] C 203/5, which has since been replaced by the *Notice on restrictions directly related and necessary to concentrations* OJ [2005] C 56/24; ancillary restraints are discussed further in the context of the EU Merger Regulation: see ch 21, 'Contractual restrictions directly related and necessary to a merger: "ancillary restraints"', pp 882–884.

[437] [2001] ECR II-2459, [2001] 5 CMLR 1236, para 109; on ancillary restraints under Article 101 see the Commission's *Guidelines on the application of Article [101(3] of the Treaty* OJ [2004] C 101/97, paras 28–31.

[438] Case 161/84 [1986] ECR 353, [1986] 1 CMLR 414.

[439] Case 27/87 [1988] ECR 1919, [1988] 4 CMLR 576, see similarly the Commission's decision in *Sicasov* OJ [1999] L 4/27, [1999] 4 CMLR 192, para 53–61.

[440] Case C-250/92 [1994] ECR I-5641, [1996] 4 CMLR 191.   [441] Ibid, para 34.

[442] Ibid, paras 35–45; the Court of Justice subsequently applied *Gøttrup-Klim* in Cases 319/93 etc *Dijkstra v Friesland Coöperatie BA* [1995] ECR I-4471, [1996] 5 CMLR 178 and in Case C-399/93 *Luttikhuis v Verenigde Coöperatieve Melkindustrie Coberco BA* [1995] ECR I-4515, [1996] 5 CMLR 178, paras 14 and 18; so did the Commission in *P and I Clubs* OJ [1999] L 125/12, [1999] 5 CMLR 646, paras 66ff.

[443] These issues are interestingly discussed in an English case, *Bookmakers' Afternoon Greyhound Services Ltd v Amalgamated Racing Ltd* [2008] EWHC 1978 (Ch), upheld on appeal [2009] EWCA Civ 750.

that unifies these judgments is that the restrictions found to fall outside Article 101(1) were ancillary to a legitimate commercial operation, and the expression 'commercial ancillarity' might be helpful in understanding that group of cases[444]; they can be distinguished from the judgment of the Court of Justice in *Wouters*, discussed in the next section, which recognises the idea of 'regulatory ancillarity'.

(vi) Regulatory ancillarity: the judgment of the Court of Justice in *Wouters*

In the cases discussed in the previous section the Court of Justice concluded that restrictions in agreements fell outside Article 101(1) where they were necessary to facilitate a commercial activity. In *Wouters v Algemene Raad van de Nederlandsche Orde van Advocaten*[445] the Court of Justice dealt with a rather different situation. In that case Mr Wouters challenged a rule adopted by the Dutch Bar Council which prohibited lawyers in the Netherlands from entering into partnership with non-lawyers: Mr Wouters wished to practise as a lawyer in a firm of accountants. A number of questions were referred to the Court of Justice as to the compatibility of such a rule with EU competition law. In its judgment the Court, consisting of 13 judges, stated that a prohibition of multi-disciplinary partnerships 'is liable to limit production and technical development within the meaning of Article [101(1)(b)] of the Treaty'[446]; it also considered that the rule had an effect on trade between Member States[447]. However, at paragraph 97 of its judgment the Court stated:

> However, not every agreement between undertakings or any decision of an association of undertakings which restricts the freedom of action of the parties or of one of them necessarily falls within the prohibition laid down in Article [101(1)] of the Treaty. For the purposes of application of that provision to a particular case, account must first of all be taken of the overall context in which the decision of the association of undertakings was taken or produces its effects. More particularly, account must be taken of its objectives, which are here connected with the need to make rules relating to organisation, qualifications, professional ethics, supervision and liability, in order to ensure that the ultimate consumers of legal services and the sound administration of justice are provided with the necessary guarantees in relation to integrity and experience... It has then to be considered whether the consequential effects restrictive of competition are inherent in the pursuit of those objectives[448].

This is a most interesting, and controversial, judgment. The early part of the judgment reads as though the Court would conclude that Article 101(1) was infringed, whereas from paragraph 97 onwards it explains why Article 101(1) would not be infringed if the rule in question could 'reasonably be considered to be necessary in order to ensure the proper

---

[444] The term 'commercial ancillarity' is used here to connote a broader concept than the narrowly-focused 'ancillary restraints doctrine' considered in the *Métropole* judgment discussed above and in ch 21, 'Contractual restrictions directly related and necessary to a merger: "ancillary restraints"', pp 882–884.

[445] Case C-309/99 [2002] ECR I-1577, [2002] 4 CMLR 913; for comment on this case see Vossestein (2002) 39 CML Rev 841; Monti 'Article 81 EC and Public Policy' (2002) 39 CML Rev 1057; O'Loughlin 'EC Competition Rules and Free Movement Rules: An Examination of the Parallels and their Furtherance by the Court of Justice *Wouters* Decision' (2003) 24 ECLR 62; Loozen 'Professional ethics and restraints of competition' (2006) 31 EL Rev 28; see also the judgment of the High Court in Ireland that the Medical Council of Ireland was not subject to competition law when making and applying professional rules in *Hemat v The Medical Council*, [2006] IEHC 187; the case is noted by Ahern at (2007) 28 ECLR 366.

[446] [2002] ECR I-1577, [2002] 4 CMLR 913, para 90; see also paras 86 and 94.

[447] Ibid, para 95.

[448] To similar effect see Case T-144/99 *Institut des Mandataires Agréés v Commission* [2001] ECR II-1087, [2001] 5 CMLR 77, para 78.

practice of the legal profession, as it is organised in [the Netherlands]'[449]. The judgment means that, in certain cases, it is possible to balance *non-competition* objectives against a restriction of competition, and to conclude that the former outweigh the latter, with the consequence that there is no infringement of Article 101(1). The Court does not make findings of fact in an Article 267 reference; rather it gives a preliminary ruling which the domestic court must apply to the case before it. However, it is clear that the judgment provides a basis on which the Dutch court could decide that the rule in question did not infringe Article 101(1). It also would seem from paragraphs 107 and 108 of the *Wouters* judgment that the Court of Justice was disinclined to interfere with the Bar Council's assessment of the need for, and content of, the rules in question; the position should be contrasted with Article 101(3), where the burden of proof rests on the undertaking(s) defending the agreement and where the Commission insists on convincing evidence of economic efficiencies[450].

Numerous questions arise from the judgment in *Wouters*. First, why did the Court of Justice decide that Article 101(1) was not applicable? Secondly, how does this judgment fit with those discussed in section (iv) above? Thirdly, how broad is the rule in *Wouters*? Finally, could the Court have decided the case in a different way, but still have come to the conclusion that the rule in question did not infringe Article 101?

(A) Why was Article 101(1) not applicable?

On the first point, the Court of Justice must have felt that it was appropriate to establish that 'reasonable' regulatory rules fall outside Article 101(1). Furthermore, it is possible that the Court was deliberately trying to reach a similar outcome under Article 101 to that which would have been achieved under Article 56 TFEU had the case been argued under the provisions on the free movement of services. It might have been the case that the rule in question had been adopted by the Dutch Government itself, if the regulatory regime for the legal profession in the Netherlands had been different: in that case the rule could not have been challenged under Article 101(1), but might have been under Article 56. Under that provision a Member State may adopt rules which restrict the free movement of services to the extent that they are necessary to achieve a legitimate public interest[451]; the judgment in *Wouters* effectively applies the same reasoning to a case in which the regulatory function was not carried out by a Member State, and so was not susceptible to challenge under Article 56, but by a private body empowered by the state to adopt regulatory rules, subject to control, if at all, under the competition rules[452].

(B) The relationship between the judgment in Wouters and earlier case law of the EU Courts

On the second point, the judgment in *Wouters* does have a conceptual similarity to the cases discussed in section (iv) above, in that they all are concerned with the idea

---

[449] [2001] ECR I-1577, [2002] 4 CMLR 913, para 107.

[450] See ch 4, 'The burden of proving that the conditions of Article 101(3) are satisfied', pp 152–153.

[451] See eg Case 33/74 *Van Binsbergen v Bestuur Van de Bedrijfsvereniging voor de Metaalnijverheid* [1974] ECR 1299, [1975] 1 CMLR 298, para 14.

[452] The Court cited Case 107/83 *Klopp* [1984] ECR 2971, para 17 and Case C-3/95 *Reisebüro Broede* [1996] ECR I-6511, para 37, cases on Article 56 TFEU, in para 99 of its judgment in *Wouters*: in these cases it had held that, in the absence of specific EU rules in the field, each Member State is in principle free to regulate the exercise of the legal profession in its territory; on the point discussed in the text see Monti 'Article 81 EC and Public Policy' (2002) 39 CML Rev 1057, in particular at pp 1086–1090, and Mortelmans 'Towards Convergence in the Application of the Rules on Free Movement and on Competition?' (2001) 38 CML Rev 613; see also O'Loughlin 'EC Competition Rules and Free Movement Rules: An Examination of the Parallels and their Furtherance by the Court of Justice *Wouters* Decision' (2003) 24 ECLR 62.

of ancillarity: restrictions on conduct, even ones that, in a colloquial sense, appear to restrict competition, do not infringe Article 101(1) where they are ancillary to some other legitimate purpose. What is of interest about *Wouters*, however, is that the restriction in that case was not necessary for the execution of a commercial transaction or the achieve-ment of a commercial outcome on the market; instead it was ancillary to a regulatory function 'to ensure that the ultimate consumers of legal services and the sound adminis-tration of justice are provided with the necessary guarantees in relation to integrity and experience'[453]. This seems to be a different application of the concept of ancillarity from that in the earlier case law: the *Wouters* case is concerned with what could be described as 'regulatory ancillarity', whereas earlier judgments were concerned with 'commercial ancillarity'; perhaps the use of these two terms would be useful in, first, demonstrating a continuity with the earlier case law, through the common use of the idea of ancillarity, while also capturing the difference between the two situations, by distinguishing com-mercial and regulatory cases.

(C) How broad is the rule in Wouters?

On the third point, that is the breadth of the rule in *Wouters*, there is nothing in the judgment itself that expressly limits its application to so-called 'deontological' (that is to say professional ethical) rules for the regulation of the legal profession, nor to the liberal professions generally. The Court of Justice's judgment in *Meca-Medina v Commission*[454] confirms that the *Wouters* doctrine can apply to other regulatory rules. In *Meca-Medina* the Court of Justice concluded that the anti-doping rules of the International Swimming Federation had a legitimate objective: to combat drugs in order for competitive sport to be conducted fairly, including the need to safeguard equal chances for athletes, athletes' health, the integrity and objectivity of competitive sport and ethical values in sport[455]; the Court went on to decide that the restrictions of competition inherent in the rules were proportionate[456]. The *Meca-Medina* judgment justifies the way in which the Commission had dismissed a complaint about rules of UEFA, the body responsible for the Champions League football tournament, which restricted the ownership of shares in more than one football team competing in the Champions League: the rules were necessary to protect the integrity of the tournament and were therefore, pursuant to *Wouters*, outside Article 101(1)[457]: spectators would not be confident that the results of football matches were genu-ine if the same person controlled opposing teams[458].

In *Wouters* the rules under scrutiny undoubtedly had a public law character: Dutch legislation provided for the regulation of the legal profession, albeit that the rule-making function belonged to a private law association of undertakings. In *Meca-Medina* the International Olympic Committee ('IOC') was responsible for the regulatory system: the IOC is a creature of public international law, which may explain the Court of Justice's willingness to apply the *Wouters* doctrine in that case. An intriguing question for the future is whether *Wouters* could be extended yet further, to a purely private regulatory system where there is no public component at all. Many sporting organisations have a purely private law character, such as the Football Association in the UK: the Court of Justice may be prepared to extend the *Wouters* case to such bodies. However other cases

---

[453] Case C-309/99 *Wouters v Algemene Raad van de Nederlandsche Orde van Advocaten* [2002] ECR I-1577, [2002] 4 CMLR 913, para 97.
[454] Case C-519/04 P [2006] ECR I-6991, [2006] 5 CMLR 1023; see Weatherill 'Anti-doping revisited – the demise of the rule of "purely sporting interest"?' (2006) 27 ECLR 645.
[455] Case C-519/04 P [2006] ECR I-6991, [2006] 5 CMLR 1023, paras 42–45.
[456] Ibid, paras 47–56.   [457] Commission Press Release IP/02/942, 27 June 2002.
[458] See further 'The application of Article 101(1) to sporting rules', pp 133–134 below.

are less easy to predict: for example, suppose that firms in a particular sector were to adopt rules for the protection of the environment on their own initiative, without any encouragement by the kind cognisable under Article 101(3): it remains to be seen whether *Wouters* could be invoked in such a case. In *Hilti v Commission*[459] the General Court said that, where there is a public authority with powers, for example, in relation to product safety, it is not for private undertakings to take private initiatives to eliminate products that they consider to be unsafe[460].

(D) Could the Court of Justice in Wouters have reached the same conclusion by a different route?

On the fourth point, it is interesting to consider whether the Court of Justice could have reached the conclusion that there was no infringement of the competition rules in *Wouters* by some other route than the one it adopted. Perhaps the most obvious alternative solution would have been to hold that the rules did infringe Article 101(1) – as noted, the Court did say that the prohibition on multi-disciplinary partnerships was liable to limit production and technical development within the meaning of Article 101(1)(b) – but that they satisfied the terms of Article 101(3)[461]. However this approach was not available in *Wouters* since, at the relevant time, a decision under Article 101(3) could be made only by the Commission pursuant to a notification under Article 4 of Regulation 17 and no notification had been made. It was not open to the Court of Justice to apply the provisions of Article 106(2) TFEU, since the Bar Council itself was not an entrusted undertaking[462]. The Court could have concluded that there was no effect on trade between Member States, so that Article 101(1) did not apply, thereby in effect referring the matter back to the Netherlands for the application of Dutch competition law; however it expressly held that trade between Member States was affected[463].

(vii) The application of Article 101(1) to sporting rules[464]

This discussion of the *Wouters* judgment provides an opportunity for a brief diversion, to discuss the application of Article 101(1) to sporting rules. All sports have rules: footballers, with the exception of goalkeepers, cannot handle the ball; boxers must not hit 'below the belt'; javelin throwers should not throw the javelin at other javelin throwers. These are 'the rules of the game', and self-evidently do not infringe Article 101(1). Similarly, all sports have disciplinary rules: violent conduct can lead to suspension; taking prohibited drugs may lead to bans. Again, football clubs that belong to one league will be prohibited

---

[459] Case T-30/89 [1991] ECR II-1439, [1992] 4 CMLR 16.   [460] Ibid, para 118.

[461] On this point see Case No 1003/2/1/01 *Institute of Independent Insurance Brokers v Director General of Fair Trading* [2001] CAT 4, [2001] CompAR 62, paras 168–178, in which the UK Competition Appeal Tribunal considered that the regulatory rules of the General Insurance Standards Council infringed s 2 of the Competition Act 1998 (the domestic equivalent of Article 101(1)), and should have been examined under ss 4 and 9 of that Act (the equivalent of Article 101(3)): see further ch 9, 'Object or effect the prevention, restriction or distortion of competition within the UK', p 342.

[462] See ch 6, 'Article 106(2)', pp 235–242 on the derogation from the application of Articles 101 and 102 provided by Article 106(2).

[463] Case C-309/99 [2002] ECR I-1577, [2002] 4 CMLR 913, para 95.

[464] For a general discussion of EU law and sport see Weatherill ' "Fair Play Please": Recent Developments in the Application of EC law to Sport' (2003) 40 CML Rev 51; Van den Bogaert and Vermeersch 'Sport and the EC Treaty: a Tale of Uneasy Bedfellows?' (2006) 31 ECLR 821; Szyszczak 'Competition and sport' (2007) 32 EL Rev 95; Kienapfel and Stein 'The application of Articles 81 and 82 EC in the sport sector' (2007) 3 *Competition Policy Newsletter* 6; the Opinion of Advocate General Kokott in Case C-49/07 *MOTOE*, [2008] ECR I-4863, [2008] 5 CMLR 790; note also the Commission's *Declaration on Sport*, annexed to the final act of the Treaty of Amsterdam, OJ [1997] C 340/136. For the position in the US see *National Collegiate Athletic Association v Board of Regents of University of Oklahoma* 468 US 85 (1984).

from belonging to another one. A conundrum for EU competition law has been to determine whether, and if so when, sporting rules might infringe Article 101 or 102. It is clear that some rules could have restrictive effects on competition in the market, for example where they go beyond 'the rules of the game' and instead distort competition in neighbouring broadcasting markets[465].

In *Meca-Medina* the General Court had held that a sporting rule that 'has nothing to do with any economic consideration'[466] falls entirely outside Articles 101 and 102. On appeal the Court of Justice held that this was an error of law on the General Court's part and therefore set the judgment aside[467]. The Court of Justice's approach is clearly preferable to that of the General Court: the latter's judgment would mean that sporting rules could not be scrutinised at all under the competition provisions, whereas the Court of Justice's means that they can be tested for anti-competitive effects, albeit that they might be permissible by virtue of the *Wouters* doctrine.

(viii) Have the EU Courts embraced the 'rule of reason'?

As mentioned above, critics of Article 101(1) complain that it is applied to too many agreements; they argue for the application of a 'rule of reason', which would result in fewer agreements being caught. The judgments that have just been discussed raise the question of whether the EU Courts have adopted a rule of reason under Article 101(1). Discussion of the rule of reason under Article 101(1) is often very imprecise. It is sometimes used as little more than a slogan by opponents of the judgments of the Courts and, in particular, decisions of the Commission. In so far as the call for a rule of reason is a request for good rather than bad, or reasonable rather than unreasonable, judgments and decisions, no one could disagree with it. However, if proponents of the rule of reason mean that US jurisprudence on the rule of reason under the Sherman Act 1890 should be incorporated into EU competition law, this seems to be misplaced: EU law is different in many ways from US law, not least in that it has the 'bifurcation' of Article 101(1) and Article 101(3), which does not exist in the Sherman Act, and that it is concerned with the promotion of a single market as well as with 'conventional' competition law concerns[468].

(A) The rule of reason in US law

In US law the rule of reason has a particular meaning. In *Continental TV Inc v GTE Sylvania* the Supreme Court defined the rule of reason as calling for a case-by-case evaluation 'that is, the factfinder weighs all the circumstances of a case in deciding whether a restrictive practice should be prohibited as imposing an unreasonable restraint on competition'[469]. In particular this means that, when determining whether an agreement restrains trade in the sense of section 1 of the Sherman Act, it is necessary to balance the agreement's pro- and anti-competitive effects; where the latter outweigh the former, the agreement will be unlawful. However US and EU competition law are materially different in numerous respects, and terminology should not be imported from US law that could

---

[465] On the joint selling of sporting rights see ch 13, 'Joint selling agencies', p 526.

[466] Case T-313/02 [2004] ECR II-3291, [2004] 3 CMLR 1314, para 47.

[467] Case C-519/04 P [2006] ECR I-6991, [2006] 5 CMLR 1023, paras 33 and 34.

[468] See ch 1, 'The single market imperative', pp 23–24 and ch 2, 'The single market imperative', p 51.

[469] 433 US 36, 49 (1977); see also *National Collegiate Athletic Association v Board of Regents of University of Oklahoma* 468 US 85 (1984); *California Dental Association v Federal Trade Commission* 526 US 756 (1999); for discussion of the rule of reason in US law see Areeda and Hovenkamp *Antitrust Law* Vol VII, ch 15 (2nd ed, 2003); Hovenkamp *Federal Antitrust Policy: The Law of Competition and its Practice* (West Publishing Company, 2nd ed, 2000), paras 6.4, 11.1, 11.2 and 11.6.

blur this significant fact[470]. The fact that the Court of Justice has handed down reasonable judgments does not mean that it has adopted the rule of reason in the sense in which that expression is used in the US. Various commentators have argued against incorporation into EU law of a rule of reason modelled upon US experience[471]. In its *White Paper on Modernisation*[472] the Commission said that it did not see the adoption of the rule of reason as a solution to the problems of enforcement and procedure that it had identified. In particular, it said that it would 'be paradoxical to cast aside Article [101(3)] when that provision in fact contains all the elements of a "rule of reason"' and that the adoption of the rule of reason under Article 101(1) would 'run the risk of diverting Article [101(3)] from its purpose, which is to provide a legal framework for the economic assessment of restrictive practices and not to allow application of the competition rules to be set aside because of political considerations'[473].

(B) *The judgment of the General Court in* Métropole

In *Métropole Télévision v Commission*[474] the General Court expressly rejected the suggestion that a rule of reason existed under Article 101(1). Six television companies in France had established a joint venture, Télévision par Satellite ('TPS'), to devise, develop and broadcast digital pay-TV services in French in Europe: TPS would be a competitor to the dominant pay-TV company, Canal+. The parties notified a number of agreements to the Commission. In 1999 the Commission adopted a decision that the creation of TPS was not caught by Article 101(1); however it concluded that a non-competition clause, preventing the parents of TPS from becoming involved in other digital pay-TV satellite companies, could be cleared (that is, found not to infringe Article 101(1)) for a period of three years; and that clauses giving TPS rights of pre-emption in relation to certain channels and services offered by its parents and exclusive rights to other channels infringed Article 101(1) but could be exempted under Article 101(3) for three years. Four of the shareholders in TPS applied to the General Court requesting that the Commission's decision should be annulled. They argued that the Commission should have applied the rule of reason, according to which 'an anti-competitive practice falls outside Article [101(1)] of the Treaty if it has more positive than negative effects on competition on a given market'[475]; in particular the clauses in the agreements giving TPS rights of pre-emption and exclusivity would enable it to enter the market dominated by Canal+, and therefore would 'favour' new competition[476]. Several well-known judgments of the Court of Justice and General Court were cited in support of this version of the rule of reason[477]. What is of interest is the explicit way in which the General Court's judgment rejected the applicants' argument:

72. According to the applicants, as a consequence of the existence of a rule of reason in Community competition law, when Article [101(1)] of the Treaty is applied it is necessary to weigh the pro and anti-competitive effects of an agreement in order to determine

---

[470] See Whish and Sufrin 'Article 85 and the Rule of Reason' (1987) 7 Ox YEL 1.

[471] *Whish and Sufrin* (1987) 7 Ox YEL 1; Waelbroeck 'Vertical Agreements: is the Commission Right not to Follow the US Policy?' (1985) 25 Swiss Rev ICL; Schröter 'Antitrust Analysis and Article [81(1)] and (3)' [1987] Fordham Corp L Inst (ed Hawk), ch 27; Caspari (formerly Director General of DG COMP at the Commission) [1987] Fordham Corp L Inst (ed Hawk), p 361.

[472] OJ [1999] C 132/1, [1999] 5 CMLR 208.   [473] OJ [1999] C 132/1, [1999] 5 CMLR 208, para 57.

[474] Case T-112/99 [2001] ECR II-2459, [2001] 5 CMLR 1236: for comment on this case see Manzini 'The European Rule of Reason – Crossing the Sea of Doubt' (2002) 23 ECLR 392.

[475] Case T-112/99 [2001] ECR II-2459 [2001] 5 CMLR 1236, para 68.

[476] Ibid, para 69.

[477] Ibid, paras 68 and 70, referring, *inter alia*, to Case 258/78 *Nungesser and Eisele v Commission (Maize Seeds)* [1982] ECR 2015; Case 262/81 *Coditel v Ciné Vog Films* [1982] ECR 3381 and Cases T-374/94 etc *European Night Services v Commission* [1998] ECR II-3141.

whether it is caught by the prohibition laid down in that article. It should, however, be observed, first of all, that contrary to the applicant's assertions the existence of such a rule has not, as such, been confirmed by the Community courts. Quite to the contrary, in various judgments the Court of Justice and the Court of First Instance have been at pains to indicate that the existence of a rule of reason in Community competition law is doubtful[478].

The General Court went on to say that the pro- and anti-competitive aspects of a restriction of competition should be weighed at the stage of considering whether an agreement satisfies the terms of Article 101(3)[479]: in the General Court's view:

Article [101(3)] would lose much of its effectiveness if such an examination had to be carried out already under Article [101(1)] of the Treaty[480].

The General Court acknowledged that in various judgments the EU Courts have been 'more flexible' in their interpretation of Article 101(1), but concluded that this did not mean that they had adopted the 'rule of reason' in the sense argued for by the applicants[481]. Rather, the more flexible judgments of the Courts demonstrate that they are not willing to find a restriction 'wholly abstractly'; instead a full market analysis is required[482]. The General Court came to the same conclusion in *Van den Bergh Foods Ltd v Commission*[483] and in *O2 (Germany) GmbH & Co, OHG v Commission*[484]. The Commission cites the *Métropole* judgment in paragraph 11 of its *Guidelines on the application of Article [101(3) TFEU]* in support of its proposition that '[t]he balancing of anti-competitive and pro-competitive effects is conducted exclusively within the framework laid down by Article [101(3)]'[485].

(C) Comment

In the authors' view the judgment in *Métropole* was correct to reject the US-style rule of reason in Article 101(1). Of course, the Commission and the Courts should be 'reasonable' when applying Article 101(1), but that does not mean that they should import the method of analysis adopted in the quite different context of the Sherman Act. An interesting question is whether the judgment of the Court of Justice in *Wouters* should be read as importing a rule of reason under Article 101(1)[486]. The doctrine of regulatory ancillarity in that case provides for a balancing of any restriction of competition against the reasonableness of regulatory rules adopted for non-competition reasons; as such, it appears to these authors that the *Wouters* judgment does not apply a US-style rule of reason, and it is preferable not to use this expression in order to explain it[487].

---

[478] Case T-112/99 [2001] ECR II-2459 [2001] 5 CMLR 1236, para 72.

[479] [2001] ECR II-2459 [2001] 5 CMLR 1236, para 74.   [480] Ibid, para 74.

[481] Ibid, paras 75–76.   [482] Ibid, para 76.

[483] Case T-65/98 [2003] ECR II-4653, [2004] 4 CMLR 14, para 106.

[484] Case T-328/03 [2006] ECR II-1231, [2006] 5 CMLR 258, para 69; for discussion of this case see Marquis 'O2(Germany) v Commission and the Exotic Mysteries of Article 81(1) EC' (2007) 21 ELR 29.

[485] OJ [2004] C 101/97.

[486] See Korah 'Rule of reason: apparent inconsistency in the case law under Article 81' (2002) 1 Competition Law Insight 24.

[487] An alternative would be to refer to the rule in *Wouters* as a 'European style rule of reason': see Monti 'Article 81 EC and Public Policy' (2002) 39 CML Rev 1057.

(ix) Joint ventures

Article 101(1) does not apply to full-function joint ventures, which are dealt with under the provisions on merger control: this is explained in chapter 21[488].

(F) Article 106(2)

Article 106(2) precludes the application of the competition rules to undertakings in so far as compliance with them would obstruct them in the performance of a task entrusted to them by a Member State. This subject is dealt with in chapter 6[489].

(G) State compulsion and highly regulated markets

The competition rules do not apply to undertakings in so far as they are compelled by law to behave in a particular way: this is sometimes referred to as the 'state compulsion' defence; nor do they apply where a legal framework leaves no possibility for competitive activity on the part of undertakings, that is to say where they operate on highly regulated markets. These two defences have often been invoked, but they are narrowly applied and almost invariably fail[490]. Where undertakings genuinely have no room for autonomous behaviour they would not be liable for infringing Article 101[491]; however the position would alter if a decision to disapply the national legislation has been taken and become definitive[492]. An argument that the Italian sugar market was so highly regulated that there was no scope for competition succeeded in *Suiker Unie v Commission*[493]. In *DaimlerChrysler AG v Commission*[494] the General Court annulled a decision of the Commission that DaimlerChrysler had infringed Article 101 by prohibiting its Spanish dealers from supplying cars to leasing companies in the absence of an identified customer

---

[488] Ch 21, 'Joint ventures – the concept of full-functionality', pp 837–838.

[489] See ch 6, 'Article 106(2)', pp 235–242.

[490] The 'state compulsion' defence was rejected in *Wood Pulp* OJ [1985] L 85/1, [1985] 3 CMLR 474; *ENI/Montedison* OJ [1987] L 5/13, [1988] 4 CMLR 444, para 25; *Aluminum Products* OJ [1985] L 92/1, [1987] 3 CMLR 813; *SSI* OJ [1982] L 232/1, [1982] 3 CMLR 702, upheld on appeal to the Court of Justice Cases 240/82 etc *SSI v Commission* [1985] ECR 3831, [1987] 3 CMLR 661; *French-West African Shipowners' Committee* OJ [1992] L 134/1, [1993] 5 CMLR 446, paras 32–38; and in *CNSD v Commission* Case T-513/93 [2000] ECR II-1807, [2000] 5 CMLR 614, paras 58–59; see also Cases C-359/95 and 379/95 P *Commission v Ladbroke Racing* [1997] ECR I-6265, [1998] 4 CMLR 27, para 33; Case T-228/97 *Irish Sugar v Commission* [1999] ECR II-2969, [1999] 5 CMLR 1300, para 130; the 'highly regulated markets' defence was rejected in Cases 209/78 etc *Van Landewyck v Commission* [1980] ECR 3125, [1981] 3 CMLR 134, paras 126–134 ; Cases 240/82 etc *SSI v Commission* [1985] ECR 3831, [1987] 3 CMLR 661, paras 13–37 and Case 260/82 *NSO v Commission* [1985] ECR 3801, [1988] 4 CMLR 755, paras 18–27; *Greek Ferry Services Cartel* OJ [1999] L 109/24, [1999] 5 CMLR 47, paras 98–108, upheld on appeal Cases T-56/99 etc *Marlines SA v Commission* [2003] ECR II-5225, [2005] 5 CMLR 1761; *French-West Africa Shipowners' Committees* OJ [1992] L 134/1, [1993] 5 CMLR 446; Cases T-202/98 etc *Tate & Lyle plc v Commission* [2001] ECR II-2035, [2001] 5 CMLR 859, paras 44–45; *Spanish Raw Tobacco* Commission decision of 20 October 2004, paras 349–356; *Raw Tobacco Italy* Commission decision of 20 October 2005, paras 315–324; *Bananas* Commission decision of 15 October 2008, on appeal to the General Court, Cases T-587/08 etc *Fresh Del Monte Produce v Commission*, not yet decided; *E.ON/GDF Suez* Commission decision of 8 July 2009, on appeal to the General Court, Cases T-360/09 etc *E.ON Ruhrgas and E.ON v Commission*, not yet decided.

[491] See eg Case T-387/94 *Asia Motor France v Commission* [1996] ECR II-961, [1996] 5 CMLR 537, paras 78–100; Case No 1027/2/3/04 *VIP Communications v OFCOM* [2009] CAT 28, [2010] CompAR 13, paras 17–27 (a judgment of the UK Competition Appeal Tribunal).

[492] See Case C-198/01 *CIF* [2003] ECR I-8055, [2003] 5 CMLR 829, paras 54ff.

[493] Cases 40/73 etc [1975] ECR 1663, [1976] 1 CMLR 295.

[494] Case T-325/01 [2005] ECR II-3319, [2007] 4 CMLR 559.

for a leasing contract: since it was a requirement of Spanish law that there should be an identified customer, the DaimlerChrysler agreements were not themselves restrictive of competition[495].

The law was helpfully summarised by the Court of Justice in *Deutsche Telekom AG v Commission*[496], where Deutsche Telekom argued (in an Article 102 case) that it was not guilty of an illegal margin squeeze because its behaviour was approved by the German regulator of the electronic communications sector. The Court rejected the defence because Deutsche Telekom ('DT') retained the right to adjust its prices for the retail sale of broadband internet access services and thereby bring the margin squeeze to an end: approval by the regulator did not deprive DT of its ability to behave autonomously. The Court of Justice summarised the law at paragraph 80 of its judgment[497]:

> According to the case-law of the Court of Justice, it is only if anti-competitive conduct is required of undertakings by national legislation, or if the latter creates a legal framework which itself eliminates any possibility of competitive activity on their part, that Articles [101 TFEU and 102 TFEU] do not apply. In such a situation, the restriction of competition is not attributable, as those provisions implicitly require, to the autonomous conduct of the undertakings. Articles [101 TFEU and 102 TFEU] may apply, however, if it is found that the national legislation leaves open the possibility of competition which may be prevented, restricted or distorted by the autonomous conduct of undertakings.

The Court's judgment cited several earlier judgments, in particular pointing out that there is no defence where national law merely encourages or makes it easier for undertakings to engage in autonomous anti-competitive conduct[498].

(H) Commission Notices

There are a number of Commission Notices in which it has provided guidance on the application of Article 101(1) to various types of agreement; it might be helpful to provide a checklist of these Notices, arranged chronologically.

(i) Notice on sub-contracting agreements[499]

Article 101(1) does not apply to some sub-contracting agreements.

(ii) Notice on the application of the competition rules to cross-border credit transfers[500]

This *Notice* has specific application in the banking sector.

(iii) Notice on the application of the competition rules to the postal sector[501]

This *Notice* has specific application in the postal sector.

(iv) Notice on the application of the competition rules to access agreements in the telecommunications sector[502]

This *Notice* has specific application in the telecommunications sector.

---

[495] Ibid, para 156.

[496] Case C-280/08 P [2010] ECR I-000, [2010] 5 CMLR 1495.

[497] The law is also usefully summarised in paragraph 22 of the Commission's *Guidelines on the applicability of Article 101 TFEU to horizontal co-operation agreements* OJ [2011] C 11/1.

[498] The Court cites Cases 40/73 etc *Suiker Unie v Commission* [1975] ECR 1663, [1976] 1 CMLR 295, paras 36–73 and Case C-198/01 *CIF* [2003] ECR I-8055, [2003] 5 CMLR 829, para 56 for this proposition.

[499] OJ [1979] C1/2.

[500] OJ [1995] C 251/3.   [501] OJ [1998] C 39/2; see ch 23, 'Post', pp 984–988.

[502] OJ [1998] C 265/2; see ch 23, 'Application of EU competition law', pp 982–983.

(v) Notice regarding restrictions directly related and necessary to the concentration[503]

Article 101(1) does not apply to ancillary restrictions; this *Notice* is specifically of relevance to the analysis of concentrations under the EUMR, but it provides useful insights into the Commission's thinking more generally[504].

(vi) Notice on agreements of minor importance[505]

This *Notice* is concerned with the *de minimis* doctrine and is examined below.

(vii) Guidelines on the effect on trade concept contained in Articles [101 and 102 TFEU][506]

These *Guidelines* are important in determining the jurisdictional scope of Article 101 and are examined below.

(viii) Guidelines on the application of Article [101(3) TFEU][507]

Although these *Guidelines* are predominantly concerned with the application of Article 101(3), paragraphs 13 to 37 contain useful discussion of the principles behind Article 101(1).

(ix) Guidelines on the application of Article [101 TFEU] to technology transfer agreements[508]

These *Guidelines* deal at length with the application of Article 101(1) and Article 101(3) to technology transfer agreements. They also examine matters such as technology pools.

(x) Commission Consolidated Jurisdictional Notice[509]

Article 101 does not apply to full-function joint ventures. Paragraphs 91 to 109 examine the concept of full-functionality.

(xi) Guidelines on the application of Article [101 TFEU] to maritime transport services[510]

These *Guidelines* set out the principles to be applied when assessing cooperation agreements in the maritime transport sector; in particular they consider the extent to which the exchange of information between competing undertakings may infringe Article 101.

(xii) Communication from the Commission on the application of Article 101(3) in the insurance sector[511]

This *Communication* has specific application in the insurance sector[512].

(xiii) Guidelines on vertical restraints[513]

These *Guidelines* deal with the application of Article 101(1) and Article 101(3) to vertical agreements. Paragraphs 12 to 21 of these *Guidelines* provide specific guidance on the application of Article 101(1) to agreements between principal and agent.

---

[503] OJ [2005] C 56/244.
[504] The Notice is discussed in ch 21, 'Jurisdiction', pp 833–844.
[505] OJ [2001] C 368/13.   [506] OJ [2004] C 101/81.   [507] OJ [2004] C 101/97.
[508] OJ [2004] C 101/2: see ch 19, 'Technology Transfer Agreements: Regulation 772/2004', pp 781–791.
[509] OJ [2008] C 95/1.
[510] OJ [2008] C 245/2.   [511] OJ [2010] C 82/20.
[512] See ch 15, 'The Commission's *Guidelines on Horizontal Cooperation Agreements*', pp 588–591.
[513] OJ [2010] C 130/1; see ch 16, 'Vertical agreements: competition policy considerations', pp 623–628.

(xiv) Guidelines on horizontal cooperation agreements[514]

These *Guidelines* deal with the application of Article 101(1) and Article 101(3) to horizontal cooperation agreements, that is to say agreements other than hard-core cartels.

5. The *De Minimis* Doctrine

(A) Introduction

Some agreements that affect competition within the terms of Article 101(1) may nevertheless not be caught because they do not have an appreciable impact either on competition or on inter-state trade[515]. This *de minimis* doctrine was first formulated by the Court of Justice in *Völk v Vervaecke*[516]. A German producer of washing machines granted an exclusive distributorship to Vervaecke in Belgium and Luxembourg and guaranteed it absolute territorial protection against parallel imports. Volk's market share was negligible[517]. In an Article 267 reference the Court of Justice held that:

> an agreement falls outside the prohibition in Article [101(1)] where it has only an insignificant effect on the market, taking into account the weak position which the persons concerned have on the market of the product in question.

The Commission has provided guidance on the issue of whether an agreement does not have an appreciable effect on competition[518] in a series of Notices, the most recent of which appeared in 2001 and is discussed below[519]. This Notice will in many cases give a reasonably clear idea of whether an agreement is *de minimis*. However in some circumstances an agreement might be held to fall within Article 101(1) even though it is below the quantitative criteria established by it; and an agreement may be found not to have an appreciable effect on competition even where the thresholds in the Notice are exceeded[520].

(B) The Commission's Notice on Agreements of Minor Importance

(i) Part I of the Notice: introductory paragraphs

Part I of the Notice contains important statements on the application of the *de minimis* doctrine. Paragraph 1 refers to the case law of the Court of Justice on appreciability. Paragraph 2 states that the Notice sets out the market share thresholds for determining when a restriction of competition is not appreciable. It points out that this 'negative' definition of appreciability (that is to say the explanation of what is *not* an appreciable restriction of competition) does not imply that agreements above the thresholds are caught by Article 101(1): agreements above the thresholds may have only a negligible effect on

---

[514] OJ [2011] C 11/1; see ch 15, 'The Commission's *Guidelines on Horizontal Cooperation Agreements*', pp 588–591.

[515] Note that an agreement that does not infringe Article 101 may nevertheless infringe the law of one (or more) of the Member States.

[516] Case 5/69 [1969] ECR 295, [1969] CMLR 273.

[517] 0.2 per cent and 0.5 per cent of production in Germany in 1963 and 1966 respectively.

[518] The issue of whether an agreement produces an appreciable effect on trade between Member States is dealt with in the Commission's *Guidelines on the effect on trade concept contained in Articles [101 and 102 TFEU]* which are discussed below.

[519] *Notice on Agreements of Minor Importance* OJ [2001] C 368/13, [2002] 4 CMLR 699, replacing the previous Notice OJ [1997] C 372/13, [1998] 4 CMLR 192; on the 2001 Notice see Peeperkorn 'Revision of the 1997 Notice on Agreements of Minor Importance' (2001) (June) *Competition Policy Newsletter* 4.

[520] See the text below.

competition and so not be caught[521]; another way of putting this point is that the Notice establishes a 'safe harbour' for agreements below the thresholds, but does not establish a dangerous one for agreements above it. Paragraph 3 makes the important point that the *de minimis* Notice does *not* deal with the concept of an appreciable effect on trade between Member States: this is dealt with in the Commission's *Guidelines on the effect on trade concept contained in Articles [101 and 102 TFEU]*[522]. Paragraph 3 adds, however, that agreements between small and medium-sized enterprises ('SMEs') are unlikely to affect trade between Member States: such undertakings are currently defined as those having fewer than 250 employees and with an annual turnover not exceeding €50 million or an annual balance-sheet total not exceeding €43 million[523].

Paragraph 4 of the Notice is important: it states that the Commission will not institute proceedings either upon application or upon its own initiative in respect of agreements covered by the Notice; and that, where undertakings assume in good faith that an agreement is covered by the Notice, the Commission will not impose fines. Paragraph 4 of the Notice adds that, although not binding on them, it is intended to provide guidance to national courts and NCAs. Paragraph 5 explains that the Notice also applies to decisions by associations of undertakings and to concerted practices. Paragraph 6 states that the Notice is without prejudice to any interpretation of Article 101 by the EU Courts.

(ii) Part II of the Notice: the threshold

The main provision in the Notice is contained in Part II, at paragraph 7. It provides as follows:

> The Commission holds the view that agreements between undertakings which affect trade between Member States do not appreciably restrict competition within the meaning of Article [101(1)]:
>
> (a) if the aggregate market share held by the parties to the agreement does not exceed 10 per cent on any of the relevant markets affected by the agreement, where the agreement is made between undertakings[524] which are actual or potential competitors on any of these markets (agreements between competitors); or
>
> (b) if the market share held by each of the parties to the agreement does not exceed 15 per cent on any of the relevant markets affected by the agreement, where the agreement is made between undertakings which are not actual or potential competitors on any of these markets (agreements between non-competitors).
>
> In cases where it is difficult to classify the agreement as either an agreement between competitors or an agreement between non-competitors the 10 per cent threshold is applicable.

---

[521] The Notice refers to Cases C-215/96 etc *Bagnasco* [1999] ECR I-135, [1999] 4 CMLR 624, paras 34–35 in support of this proposition; the same point will be found in two General Court judgments, Case T-7/93 *Langnese-Iglo GmbH v Commission* [1995] ECR II-1533, [1995] 5 CMLR 602, para 98; Case T-374/94 etc *European Night Services v Commission* [1998] ECR II-3141, [1998] 5 CMLR 718, paras 102–103; see also para 9 of the Commission's *Guidelines on Vertical Restraints* OJ [2010] C 130/1.

[522] See 'The Effect on Trade between Member States', pp 144–149 below.

[523] See Commission Recommendation 2003/361/EC, OJ [2003] L 124/36; note also para 11 of the Commission's *Guidelines on Vertical Restraints* OJ [2010] C 130/1 which says that vertical agreements between SMEs would rarely produce an appreciable restriction on competition or on trade between Members States and that where, exceptionally, they do so the Commission would be unlikely to take enforcement action unless those undertakings individually or collectively hold a dominant position in a substantial part of the internal market.

[524] Throughout the Notice the expression 'undertakings' includes 'connected undertakings' such as parents and subsidiaries: see para 12.

As can be seen the Notice treats vertical agreements more generously than horizontal ones, by providing a higher threshold.

A particular problem arises in some sectors where the cumulative effect of many vertical agreements may lead to foreclosure of the market[525]. The Notice provides guidance on appreciability in this situation (a) by indicating when a cumulative foreclosure effect is likely and (b) by providing a market share threshold indicating whether particular agreements contribute to that effect. Paragraph 8 provides that a cumulative foreclosure effect is unlikely to exist if less than 30 per cent of the relevant market is covered by parallel agreements having similar effects; where there is a foreclosure effect, individual suppliers or distributors will not be considered to contribute to that effect where their market share does not exceed 5 per cent.

A problem that may arise in application of the Notice is that firms may outgrow the market share thresholds established by paragraphs 7 and 8; marginal relief is provided by paragraph 9 where the thresholds (of 10 per cent, 15 per cent and 5 per cent respectively) are exceeded by no more than two percentage points during two successive years.

It is not clear what happens to an agreement when it has outgrown the Notice, including the provisions for marginal relief: one possibility is that it becomes retrospectively void; a second is that it becomes unenforceable from the moment that the Notice ceases to apply. The second suggestion appears to be consistent with the scheme of Article 101 TFEU. In the UK the Court of Appeal held in *Passmore v Morland plc*[526] that an agreement can infringe Article 101(1) at some times and at other times not do so, depending on the surrounding facts: in other words it can drift into and out of voidness.

Paragraph 10 of the Notice notes that guidance on market definition is provided by the Commission's *Notice on the Definition of Relevant Market for the Purpose of [EU] Competition Law*[527] and adds that market shares are to be calculated on the basis of sales value data or, where appropriate, purchase value data; where value data are not available, other criteria, including volume data, may be used.

A different point introduced in paragraph 44 of the Commission's *Guidelines on Horizontal Cooperation Agreements*[528] is the suggestion that, where the parties to a horizontal cooperation agreement have a high combined market share, but one of them has only an insignificant one and does not possess important resources, the agreement would be considered unlikely to have a restrictive effect on competition in the market.

(iii) Part II of the Notice: the treatment of 'hard-core' restrictions

The judgment of the Court of Justice in *Völk v Vervaecke*[529], that Article 101 applies only where competition is *appreciably* restricted, concerned a hard-core restriction: the distributor was granted absolute territorial protection; much more recently the Court said in *Pedro IV Servicios SL v Total España SA*[530] that a resale price maintenance provision would infringe Article 101 only if it 'perceptibly' restricts competition within the internal market. As a matter of law, therefore, it seems clear that even hard-core restrictions might fall outside Article 101 because they have no appreciable

---

[525] See ch 16, 'Factors to be considered in determining whether single branding agreements infringe Article 101(1)', pp 638–639.

[526] [1999] EWCA Civ 696, [1999] 1 CMLR 1129; see to similar effect para 44 of the Commission's *Guidelines on the application of Article [101(3) TFEU]* OJ [2004] C 101/97.

[527] OJ [1997] C 372/5, [1998] 4 CMLR 177; see ch 1, 'Market definition', p 27ff.

[528] OJ [2011] C 11/1; see ch 15, 'The Commission's *Guidelines on Horizontal Cooperation Agreements*', pp 588–591.

[529] See ch 3 n 516 above.

[530] Case C-260/07 [2009] ECR I-2437, [2009] 5 CMLR 1291, para 82, citing earlier case law.

impact. However the Commission specifically says in paragraph 11 of the Notice that the safe harbour provided by paragraph 7 does not apply to certain restrictions: horizontal agreements to fix prices, limit output or sales and to allocate markets or customers[531]; vertical agreements, for example to fix prices, impose export bans and to restrict sales within a selective distribution system[532]; and vertical agreements between competitors[533]. Thus there is no assurance that the Commission would not proceed against a hard-core cartel where the market share of the parties was less than 10 per cent; even SMEs might be investigated: in *Greek Ferries*[534] the Commission imposed fines on Marlines and Ventouris, which were SMEs as defined in an earlier Notice of 1997, since they were party to price-fixing agreements, a particularly serious infringement[535].

Of course the Commission is bound by the jurisprudence of the Court of Justice, and there would appear to be a conflict between judgments such as *Völk v Vervaecke* and *Pedro IV Servicios SL v Total España SA* and paragraph 11 of the Commission's Notice; furthermore the General Court has said that agreements that restrict competition by object infringe Article 101 only if they have an appreciable effect on competition and on trade between Member States[536]. Equally, however, it is understandable that the Commission does not wish to be seen to be giving a 'green light' to hard-core restrictions of any kind, irrespective of the market share of the undertakings that are party to an agreement. In practice the conflict is more apparent than real, since the Commission, as a matter of administrative priority, would be highly unlikely to proceed against hard-core restrictions below the thresholds set out in the Notice.

(C) Limitations of the Notice

It is important to note some limitations of this Notice. The Court of Justice has indicated that it is wrong to adopt a purely quantitative approach to the issue of *de minimis* agreements; in *Distillers Co Ltd v Commission*[537] it concluded that an agreement affecting the distribution of Pimms was of importance, notwithstanding the very small proportion of the market held by that drink, because Distillers was a major producer occupying an important position on the market for drinks generally. In *Musique Diffusion Française v Commission*[538] the Court of Justice held that a concerted practice was not within the *de minimis* doctrine where the parties' market shares were small but the market was a

---

[531] *De minimis Notice*, para 11(1).

[532] *De minimis Notice*, para 11(2); the list is the same as in Article 4 of Regulation 330/2010, as to which see ch 16, 'Article 4: hard-core restrictions', pp 663–669; on this point note *Volkswagen* OJ [2001] L 262/14, [2001] 5 CMLR 1309, para 79 (resale price maintenance could infringe Article 101(1) even where the parties' market share was below the *de minimis* threshold); see also para 10 of the Commission's *Guidelines on Vertical Restraints* OJ [2010] C 130/1 and the cases referred to in footnote 4 of the *Guidelines*.

[533] *De minimis Notice*, para 11(3).

[534] *Greek Ferry Services Cartel* OJ [1999] L 109/24, [1999] 5 CMLR 47, upheld on appeal Case T-59/99 *Ventouris Group Enterprises v Commission* [2003] ECR II-5257, [2005] 5 CMLR 1781, paras 167–170.

[535] OJ [1999] L 109/24, [1999] 5 CMLR 121, para 151.

[536] See eg Case T-199/08 *Ziegler SA v Commission* [2011] ECR II-000, [2011] 5 CMLR 261, paras 41–45 (one of the appeals in the *International Removal Services* case), see also Case T-49/01 *Brasserie Nationale v Commission* [2005] ECR II-3033, [2006] 4 CMLR 266, para 140.

[537] Case 30/78 [1980] ECR 2229, [1980] 3 CMLR 121; see similarly Case 19/77 *Miller International v Commission* [1978] ECR 131, [1978] 2 CMLR 334; Case 107/82 *AEG-Telefunken v Commission* [1983] ECR 3151, [1984] 3 CMLR 325, para 58.

[538] Cases 100/80 etc [1983] ECR 1825, [1983] 3 CMLR 221; see also *Yves Saint Laurent Parfums* OJ [1992] L 12/24, [1993] 4 CMLR 120.

fragmented one, their market shares exceeded those of most competitors and their turn-over figures were high.

(D) **Other examples of non-appreciability**

The *de minimis* doctrine described in the preceding sections stems from the judgment in *Völk v Vervaecke*[539], which referred to the 'weak position' that the persons had on the market in question; this is why the Commission's Notice giving expression to the doctrine does so in terms of market share thresholds, which are used as a proxy for undertakings' market power, or rather lack of market power. It should be noted however that appreciability may be relevant to the application of Article 101(1) in a different way: judgments of the EU Courts and decisions of the Commission can be found in which it was concluded that a restriction of competition was not appreciable, not because the parties to an agreement lacked market power, but because the restriction itself was insignificant in a qualitative sense. For example in *Pavel Pavlov v Stichting Pensioenfonds Medische Specialisten*[540] the Court of Justice concluded that a decision by medical specialists to set up a pension fund entrusted with the management of a supplementary pension scheme did not appreciably affect competition within the common market: the cost of the scheme had only a marginal and indirect influence on the final cost of the services that they offered. This finding was not linked in any way to the market power of the specialists[541].

6. **The Effect on Trade Between Member States**

The application of Article 101 is limited to agreements, decisions or concerted practices *which may affect trade between Member States*. The scope of Article 102 is similarly limited. The inter-Member State trade clause is very important in EU competition law, since it defines 'the boundary between the areas respectively covered by [EU] law and the law of the Member States'[542].

Historically both the Commission and the EU Courts have adopted a liberal interpretation of the inter-state trade clause, thereby enlarging the scope of Articles 101 and 102[543]. This was of particular significance at a time when many Member States had no competition laws

---

[539] See ch 3 n 516 above.

[540] Cases C-180/98 etc [2000] ECR I-6451, [2001] 4 CMLR 30, paras 90–97.

[541] Similar conclusions, where the non-appreciability of restrictions was not related to the parties' market power, can be found in *Irish Banks' Standing Committee* OJ [1986] L 295/28, [1987] 2 CMLR 601, para 16 (an agreement on the opening hours of Irish banks did not appreciably restrict competition); *Visa International* OJ [2001] L 293/24, [2002] 4 CMLR 168, para 65 (a rule of the Visa card system which required a bank to issue a certain number of Visa cards before contracting with retailers for processing credit card payments did not appreciably restrict competition since it improved the utility of the card system for traders and did not create significant barriers to entry: the same conclusion was reached in relation to the 'no-discrimination' rule: ibid, paras 54–58 and the principle of territorial licensing: ibid, paras 63–64); *UEFA's broadcasting regulations* OJ [2001] L 171/12, [2001] 5 CMLR 654, paras 49–58 (regulations preventing the live transmission of football matches at certain times on a Saturday or Sunday afternoon, in order to protect amateur participation in sport and to encourage live attendance at football matches, did not result in an appreciable restriction of competition); and *Identrus* OJ [2001] L 249/12, paras 54–55 (a prohibition on the members of Identrus selling their equity interest in it to third parties without first offering to sell the interest to Identrus itself or its other members did not amount to an appreciable restriction of competition).

[542] Case 22/78 *Hugin Kassaregister AB v Commission* [1979] ECR 1869, p 1899, [1979] 3 CMLR 345, p 373.

[543] Cf the position in the US where the inter-state commerce clause has also been construed flexibly: see eg *Manderville Island Farms v American Crystal Sugar Co* 334 US 219, 237 (1948); see also *United States v Lopez* 514 US 549, 560 (1995) and *United States v Morrison* 529 US 598, 610 (2000): these are not competition law cases, but each deals with the inter-state commerce clause.

of their own, or competition laws that were weak in terms of powers of investigation and sanctions. This point does not have the same significance today, since all the Member States have effective competition laws, and for the most part these are modelled upon Articles 101 and 102[544]. It follows that a cartel and/or abusive behaviour by a dominant firm will be illegal either under domestic or EU law, and to this extent it matters little whether the infringement occurs under one system or the other (or both). However the concept of inter-state trade is of central importance since the entry into force of Regulation 1/2003[545], and the creation of the European Competition Network. Determining whether an agreement or practice has an effect on trade between Member States is important for a series of reasons[546]:

- where there is an effect on trade between Member States, national courts and NCAs that apply national competition law to agreements or practices have an *obligation* to also apply Articles 101 and 102[547]

- where there is an effect on trade between Member States, national courts and NCAs cannot apply stricter national competition law to agreements, although they can apply stricter national law to unilateral conduct[548]

- NCAs that apply Articles 101 and 102 have an obligation to inform the Commission of the fact no later than 30 days before the adoption of the decision[549]. Clearly an NCA could avoid this obligation by reaching the conclusion that there is no effect on trade between Member States

- when the Commission is informed that an NCA intends to adopt a decision on the basis of EU competition law, the Commission has the power to initiate its own proceedings and thereby to terminate the proceedings of the NCA[550]

- the Commission and the NCAs have the right to exchange information for the purpose of applying Articles 101 and 102[551]

- there are cooperation provisions in place that facilitate the enforcement of Articles 101 and 102 by national courts, as well as an obligation for Member States to inform the Commission of court cases deciding on the application of those provisions[552]

- NCAs and national courts that apply Articles 101 and 102 must not take decisions that conflict with decisions adopted by the Commission[553].

Clearly these rules mean that it remains important to know whether an agreement or practice has an effect on trade between Member States. This is why the Commission has published *Guidelines on the effect on trade concept contained in Articles [101 and 102 TFEU]* ('the *Guidelines on inter-state trade*')[554]. They draw substantially on the case law of the EU Courts, going back to *Consten and Grundig v Commission* in 1966[555]. In the account of the *Guidelines on inter-state trade* that follows this case law will not be cited, but the reader should be aware that references to the relevant cases will be found in the footnotes of the *Guidelines*.

Part 1 of the *Guidelines on inter-state trade* contain a brief introduction explaining, in particular, that they deal with the issue of what is meant by an appreciable effect on inter-state trade, but not with the separate question of what is meant by an appreciable

---

[544] See ch 2, 'Modelling of domestic competition law on Articles 101 and 102', p 58.
[545] OJ [2003] L 1/1.
[546] For discussion of Regulation 1/2003 see ch 2, 'The modernisation of EU competition law', p 52 and ch 7 generally.
[547] Regulation 1/2003, Article 3(1).
[548] Ibid, Article 3(2).   [549] Ibid, Article 11(4).
[550] Ibid, Article 11(6).   [551] Ibid, Article 12.
[552] Ibid, Article 15.   [553] Ibid, Article 16.   [554] OJ [2004] C 101/81.
[555] Cases 56/64 and 58/64 [1966] ECR 299, [1966] CMLR 418.

restriction of competition[556]. Part 2 of the *Guidelines* explains the effect on trade criterion, and is divided into four parts: general principles, the concept of 'trade between Member States', the notion 'may affect', and the concept of appreciability. Part 3 considers the application of the effect on trade criterion to particular examples of agreements and practices.

(A) The effect on trade criterion

(i) General principles

Articles 101 and 102 are applicable only where any effect on trade between Member States is appreciable[557]. In the case of Article 101 the question is whether the agreement affects trade: it is not necessary that each part of the agreement does so[558]; and if the agreement affects trade between Member States it is irrelevant that a particular undertaking that is party to the agreement does not itself produce such an effect[559]. In the case of Article 102 the abuse must have an effect on trade between Member States, but this does not mean that each element of the behaviour must be assessed in isolation to determine its effect: the conduct must be assessed in terms of its overall impact[560].

(ii) The concept of 'trade between Member States'

The concept of 'trade' is not limited to traditional exchanges of goods and services across borders: it is a wider concept and covers all cross-border activity, including the establishment by undertakings of agencies, branches or subsidiaries in other Member States[561]. The concept of trade also covers situations where the competitive structure of the market is affected by agreements and/or conduct[562]. There can be an effect on trade between Member States where parts only of those States are affected: the effect does not need to extend to their entire territories[563]. The question of whether trade between Member States is affected is separate from the issue of the relevant geographical market: trade could be affected even though the geographical market is national or even smaller than national[564].

(iii) The notion 'may affect'

The Court of Justice has often said that the notion that an agreement or practice 'may affect' trade between Member States means that it must be possible to foresee, with a sufficient degree of probability on the basis of a set of objective factors of law or fact, that the agreement or practice may have an influence, direct or indirect, actual or potential, on the pattern of trade between Member States[565]. Subjective intent to affect trade is not required[566]; and it is sufficient that the agreement or practice is capable of having an effect: it is not necessary to prove that it actually will do so[567]. In determining whether the pattern of trade is influenced it is not necessary to show that trade is or would be restricted or reduced: an increase in trade also means that it has been influenced[568]: the effect on trade criterion is simply jurisdictional, determining whether an examination of an agreement or conduct under the EU competition rules is warranted[569].

The fact that the influence on trade may be 'direct *or indirect*, actual *or potential*' clearly means that the jurisdictional reach of Articles 101 and 102 can be extensive[570]. However, in the case of indirect and potential influence the analysis must not be based on remote

---

[556] *Guidelines on inter-state trade*, para 4.
[557] Ibid, para 13.   [558] Ibid, para 14.   [559] Ibid, para 15.   [560] Ibid, para 17.
[561] Ibid, paras 19 and 30.   [562] Ibid, para 20.   [563] Ibid, para 21.
[564] Ibid, para 22.   [565] Ibid, para 23, citing relevant case law.   [566] Ibid, para 25.
[567] Ibid, para 26.   [568] Ibid, para 34.   [569] Ibid, para 35.   [570] See ibid, paras 36–42.

or hypothetical effects: a person claiming that trade is affected in this way must be able to explain how and why this is the case[571].

(iv) The concept of appreciability

Any effect on trade must be appreciable. The stronger the market position of the undertakings concerned, the likelier it is that any effect will be appreciable[572]. An undertaking's market share, and the value of its turnover in the products concerned, are relevant to the appreciability of any effect[573]. An assessment of appreciability must be considered in the legal and economic context of any agreement or practice including, in the case of vertical agreements, the cumulative effect of parallel networks[574].

The *Guidelines on inter-state trade* do not provide general quantitative rules on when trade is appreciably affected; however they do provide two examples of situations where trade is normally *not* capable of being appreciably affected.

(A) Small and medium-sized businesses

The *Guidelines* state that agreements between small and medium-sized businesses, as defined in Commission Recommendation 2003/361/EC[575], would not normally affect trade between Member States; however they might do so where they engage in cross-border activity[576]. The point is repeated in paragraph 11 of the Commission's *Guidelines on Vertical Restraints*[577].

(B) A negative rebuttable presumption of non-appreciability

The *Guidelines* also set out a negative rebuttable presumption of non-appreciability. This arises where:

- the aggregate market share of the parties on any relevant market within the EU affected by the agreements does not exceed 5 per cent and

- the parties' turnover is below €40 million: turnover is calculated differently according to whether the agreement is horizontal or vertical[578].

The presumption continues to apply where the turnover threshold is exceeded during two successive calendar years by no more than 10 per cent and the market share threshold by no more than 2 per cent.

(C) A positive rebuttable presumption of appreciability

The *Guidelines* also set out a positive rebuttable presumption of appreciability in the case of agreements which 'by their very nature' are capable of affecting trade between Member States, such as agreements on imports and exports. This arises where:

- the turnover thresholds set out above are exceeded and

- the parties' market shares exceed 5 per cent.

This positive presumption does not apply where the agreement covers part only of a Member State[579].

---

[571] Ibid, para 43.   [572] Ibid, para 45.
[573] Ibid, paras 46–47.   [574] Ibid, para 49.
[575] OJ [2003] L 124/36: see 'Part I of the Notice: introductory paragraphs', p 140 above for the definition of SMEs in the Recommendation.
[576] *Guidelines on inter-state trade*, para 50.   [577] OJ [2010] C 130/1.
[578] Ibid, para 52.
[579] Ibid, para 53.

(B) The application of the effect on trade criterion to particular agreements and conduct

The *Guidelines on inter-state trade* proceed to examine how the effect on trade criterion applies in relation to particular types of agreement and conduct. They do so by reference to three categories: first, agreements and abuse covering or implemented in several Member States[580]; secondly, cases covering a single, or only part of a, Member State[581]; and thirdly, cases involving undertakings located in third countries[582]. It is important to understand that Articles 101 and 102 are capable of application irrespective of where the undertakings concerned are located, provided that the agreement or practice is implemented or has effects within the EU[583]. It is also possible that an export ban imposed by an EU supplier on a distributor in a third country, which prevents the latter from re-importing into the EU, could have an effect on trade between Member States in certain circumstances, for example where there is a significant price differential between prices in the different territories, where that differential would not be eroded by customs duties and transport costs, and where significant volumes of a product could be exported from the third country to the EU[584].

There have been some judgments of the EU Courts since the *Guidelines* were published. The General Court held in *Raiffeisen Zentralbank Österreich AG v Commission*[585] that a banking cartel in Austria had an effect on trade between Member States. In that case there was a series of regional committees within Austria; the Court held that it was not necessary to consider whether each individual committee had an affect on trade: rather it was necessary to look at the cumulative effect of all the committees[586]. The overall cartel in Austria affected the entire country, and the Court said that this raised a strong presumption that trade between Member States was affected[587]. The Court noted that there had been cases in which this presumption had been rebutted[588], but held that it was not rebutted on the facts of this case[589]. In *Ziegler SA v Commission*[590] (one of the appeals in the *International Removal Services* case) the General Court rejected an argument that the Commission had failed to demonstrate an appreciable effect on trade between Member States[591].

In *Emanuela Sbarigia v Azienda USL RM/A*[592] Ms Sbarigia, who operated a pharmacy in a pedestrianised part of Rome heavily used by tourists in the summer season, was challenging legislation, on the basis of both the free movement and the competition rules of the TFEU, that limited the maximum number of hours that she could trade, required her to close on Sundays, to close one half day per week and on public holidays and to take a minimum number of holidays each year. The Court of Justice concluded, as far as the application of the competition rules was concerned, that it was 'quite obvious' that the legislation in question could not affect trade between Member States, with the result that

---

[580] Ibid, paras 61–76.
[581] Ibid, paras 77–99.
[582] Ibid, paras 100–109.
[583] See further ch 12, 'The Extraterritorial Application of EU Competition Law', pp 495–500.
[584] *Guidelines on inter-state trade*, paras 108–109.
[585] Cases T-259/02 [2006] ECR II-5169, [2007] 5 CMLR 1142.
[586] Ibid, para 177.
[587] Ibid, para 181.
[588] See eg Cases C-215/96 and C-216/96 *Bagnasco and others* [1999] ECR I-135; *Netherlands Bank II* OJ [1999] L 271/28.
[589] Case T-259/02 [2006] ECR II-5169, [2007] 5 CMLR 1142, paras 182–186; the appeal to the Court of Justice in this case was dismissed, Case C-125/07 P *Erste Bank der Österreichischen Sparkassen AG v Commission* [2009] ECR I-8681, [2010] 5 CMLR 443, paras 36–70.
[590] Case T-199/08 [2011] ECR II-000, [2011] 5 CMLR 261.   [591] Ibid, paras 51–74.
[592] Case C-393/08 [2010] ECR I-000.

the reference of the matter under Article 267 TFEU by the Tribunale amministrativo regionale per il Lazio was inadmissible[593]. It is noticeable in this case that the referring court had itself expressed dissatisfaction with the relevant legislation, as had the Italian competition authority[594]; however the lack of an effect on inter-state trade meant that this matter could not be addressed under the TFEU.

7. Checklist of Agreements That Fall Outside Article 101(1)

At the end of this chapter it may be helpful to set out a checklist of the circumstances in which an agreement might be found not to infringe Article 101(1): the list follows the order of the text of this chapter:

- Article 101(1) does not apply to an agreement that is not between undertakings[595]
- Article 101(1) does not apply to collective agreements between employers and workers[596]
- Article 101(1) does not apply to an agreement between two or more persons that form a single economic entity[597]
- Article 101(1) normally does not apply to agreements between a principal and agent[598]
- Article 101(1) normally does not apply to an agreement between a contractor and a sub-contractor[599]
- Article 101(1) does not apply to unilateral conduct that is not attributable to a con-currence of wills between two or more undertakings[600]
- Article 101(1) does not apply to an agreement that has neither the object nor the effect of preventing, restricting or distorting competition[601]
- Article 101(1) does not apply to contractual restrictions that enable undertakings to achieve a legitimate purpose and which are not disproportionate[602]
- Article 101 does not apply to full-function joint ventures[603]
- a realistic view must be taken of potential competition[604]
- Article 101(1) does not apply to an agreement if this would obstruct an undertaking or undertakings in the performance of a task of general economic interest entrusted to them by a Member State[605]
- Article 101(1) does not apply to an agreement which undertakings were compelled to enter into by law[606]

---

[593] Ibid, paras 29–33.   [594] Ibid, paras 13–15.

[595] See 'Undertakings', pp 83–92 above.

[596] See 'Employees and trades unions', pp 90–91 above.

[597] See 'The "single economic entity" doctrine', pp 92–97 above.

[598] See p 92 above and ch 16, pp 621–623.

[599] See 'The single economic entity doctrine', p 92 above and ch 16, 'Sub-Contracting Agreements', pp 676–677.

[600] See '"Unilateral" conduct and Article 101(1) in vertical cases', pp 105–110 above.

[601] See 'The Object or Effect of Preventing, Restricting or Distorting Competition', pp 115–130 above.

[602] See 'Regulatory ancillarity: the judgment of the Court of Justice in *Wouters*', pp 130–134 above.

[603] See ch 21, 'Joint ventures – the concept of full-functionality', pp 837–838.

[604] See 'Actual and potential competition', pp 127–128 above.

[605] See 'Article 106(2)', p 137 above and ch 6, 'Article 106(2)', pp 235–242.

[606] See 'State compulsion and high regulated markets', pp 137–138 above.

- Article 101(1) does not apply to an agreement in a market that is so highly regulated that there is no latitude left for competition[607]

- Article 101(1) does not apply to an agreement that has no appreciable effect on competition[608]

- Article 101(1) does not apply to an agreement that does not have an appreciable effect on trade between Member States[609]

- Article 101(1) does not apply to an agreement that satisfies the criteria of Article 101(3)[610].

---

[607] See 'State compulsion and highly regulated markets', pp 137–138 above.
[608] See 'The *De Minimis* Doctrine', pp 140–144 above.
[609] See 'The Effect on Trade between Member States', pp 144–149 above.   [610] See ch 4.

4

Article 101(3)[1]

1. Introduction

An agreement that falls within Article 101(1) of the Treaty is not necessarily unlawful. Article 101(3) provides a 'legal exception' to the prohibition in Article 101(1) by providing that it may be declared inapplicable in respect of agreements, decisions or concerted practices[2], or of categories[3] of agreements, decisions or concerted practices, that satisfy four conditions, the first two positive and the last two negative. To satisfy Article 101(3) an agreement:

- must contribute to improving the production or distribution of goods or to promoting technical or economic progress
- while allowing consumers a fair share of the resulting benefit.

Furthermore the agreement[4]:

- must not impose on the undertakings concerned restrictions which are not indispensable to the attainment of these objectives nor
- afford such undertakings the possibility of eliminating competition in a substantial part of the products in question[5].

---

[1] For further reading on Article 101(3) readers are referred to Faull and Nikpay *The EC Law of Competition* (Oxford University Press, 2nd ed, 2007), ch 3, paras 3.395–3.460; Bellamy & Child *European Community Law of Competition* (Oxford University Press, 6th ed, 2008, eds Roth and Rose), ch 3.

[2] The reference to decisions is useful since it means eg that the rules of a trade association may satisfy Article 101(3); it will only be rarely that Article 101(3) is applied to a concerted practice, but this can happen: see eg *Re International Energy Agency* OJ [1983] L 376/30, [1984] 2 CMLR 186; renewed in 1994, OJ [1994] L 68/35; in *CISAC*, Commission decision of 16 July 2008, the Commission concluded that Article 101(3) was not applicable to a concerted practice between a number of copyright collecting societies which amounted to a systematic delineation of the market between them along territorial lines; the decision is on appeal Cases T-401/08 etc *Teosto v Commission*, not yet decided.

[3] The inclusion of 'categories' of agreements is important since it paves the way for block exemptions: see 'Block Exemptions', pp 168–172 below.

[4] The term 'agreement' should be taken to include decisions and concerted practices in the rest of this chapter.

[5] Note that the UK Competition Act 1998 contains a similar provision in s 9: see ch 9, 'The Chapter I prohibition: exemptions', pp 356–360.

Under Regulation 17 of 1962[6] the Commission had the exclusive right to grant so-called 'individual exemption' under Article 101(3) to agreements notified to it[7]. However the system of notification of agreements to the Commission and the grant of individual exemption was abolished with effect from 1 May 2004 by Council Regulation 1/2003[8]; since then Article 101(3) has been directly applicable[9], and the Commission shares the competence to apply Article 101(3) with the national competition authorities ('the NCAs')[10] and national courts[11]. It is no longer correct to say that agreements are given individual exemption: they either do, or do not, satisfy Article 101(3).

In order to provide guidance to national courts and NCAs, as well as to undertakings and their professional advisers, the Commission has published *Guidelines on the application of Article [101(3)] of the Treaty* ('the *Article [101(3)] Guidelines*' or 'the *Guidelines*')[12]. The *Guidelines* should be applied 'reasonably and flexibly' rather than in a mechanical manner[13]. The Commission has cited the *Guidelines* in several of its decisions since 2004[14]. Additional guidance on the application of Article 101(1) and (3) to agreements is provided by the Commission's guidelines on technology transfer agreements[15], on vertical restraints[16] and on horizontal cooperation agreements[17].

An alternative way of satisfying Article 101(3) is to draft an agreement to satisfy one of the so-called 'block exemptions' issued by the Council of the European Union ('the Council') or by the Commission under powers conferred on it by the Council; the system of block exemptions is unaffected by Regulation 1/2003.

After discussing the burden of proof under Article 101(3) and the implications of the General Court's important judgment in *Matra Hachette v Commission*, section 2 of this chapter will discuss the criteria in Article 101(3). It will then consider the implications of Regulation 1/2003 for undertakings and their professional advisers, and in particular their need to 'self-assess' the application of Article 101(3) to their agreements. The final section in this chapter describes the system of block exemptions.

(A) The burden of proving that the conditions of Article 101(3) are satisfied

Article 2 of Regulation 1/2003 confirms well-settled case law that the burden of proof is on the Commission, the NCAs or the person opposing an agreement in a national court to show that it infringes Article 101(1), but that it is on the undertaking or undertakings seeking to defend an agreement to demonstrate that it satisfies the four conditions in Article 101(3)[18]. The Commission must examine the arguments and evidence put forward by the undertakings relying on Article 101(3); if it is unable to refute them it may be that the undertakings will be taken to have discharged the burden of proof upon

---

[6] JO [1962] 204/62, OJ Sp Ed [1962] p 87.   [7] Ibid, Article 9(1).

[8] OJ [2003] L 1/1; see 'Regulation 1/2003', pp 166–168 below for discussion of the implications of Regulation 1/2003.

[9] Ibid, Article 1(1) and (2).   [10] Ibid, Article 5.   [11] Ibid, Article 6.

[12] OJ [2004] C 101/97.   [13] Ibid, para 6.

[14] See eg *MasterCard* Commission decision of 19 December 2007, paras 670–672 and 734; *Morgan Stanley/Visa* Commission decision of 3 October 2007, paras 311, 313 and 322–324.

[15] *Guidelines on the application of [Article 101 TFEU] to technology transfer agreements* OJ [2004] C 101/2.

[16] *Guidelines on Vertical Restraints* OJ [2010] C 130/1.

[17] *Guidelines on the applicability of [Article 101 TFEU] to horizontal co-operation agreements* OJ [2011] C 11/1.

[18] See similarly s 9(2) of the UK Competition Act 1998, see ch 9, 'Exemption criteria', p 357.

them[19]. National rules on the standard of proof apply in Article 101(3) cases before the NCAs and national courts[20].

All four of the conditions must be satisfied if an agreement is to benefit from Article 101(3): the Court of Justice has stressed this on a number of occasions[21], and paragraph 42 of the *Article [101(3)] Guidelines* contains a statement to the same effect. For example the General Court annulled a Commission decision that an agreement satisfied Article 101(3) in *Métropole télévision SA v Commission*[22] because the Commission had failed to demonstrate that restrictions in the agreement were indispensable[23]. Paragraph 35 of the *Article [101(3)] Guidelines* points out, however, that parties to an agreement covered by a block exemption do not have to show that each of the conditions of Article 101(3) is satisfied: there is a rebuttable presumption that agreements falling within the scope of a block exemption satisfy all four conditions.

Paragraph 44 of the *Article [101(3)] Guidelines* explains that Article 101(3) applies only for as long as the four conditions contained in it are satisfied; however when applying this rule due consideration must be given to the time that it will take, and the restrictions that may be needed, when firms make sunk investments to realise economic efficiencies.

(B) *Matra Hachette v Commission*

A very important point about Article 101(3) is that, as the General Court stated in *Matra Hachette v Commission*[24], there are no anti-competitive agreements which, *as a matter of law*, could never satisfy the four conditions set out in that provision: it is possible for the parties to any type of agreement to argue that the conditions of Article 101(3) are satisfied. Even an agreement that has as its *object* the restriction of competition in the sense of Article 101(1) is capable, in principle, of satisfying the conditions of Article 101(3): in this sense EU law differs from US law, since there are no agreements that are irredeemably, or *'per se'*, illegal in the EU system[25]. An example of a case in which an agreement restrictive of competition by object satisfied the terms of Article 101(3) can be found in *Société Air France/Alitalia Linee Aeree Italiane SpA*[26] where the Commission authorised an extensive strategic alliance between those two airlines. Of course it would require extremely convincing evidence to satisfy the Commission, an NCA or a national court that restrictions of competition by object such as horizontal price-fixing and market-sharing satisfy Article 101(3)[27], but in exceptional circumstances even this may be possible: indeed

[19] Cases 56/64 and 58/64 *Consten and Grundig v Commission* [1966] ECR 299, p 347, [1966] CMLR 418, p 478; Cases C-204/00 P etc *Aalborg Portland v Commission* [2004] ECR I-123, [2005] 4 CMLR 251, para 55; Cases C-501/06 P etc *GlaxoSmithKline Services Unlimited v Commission* [2009] ECR I-9291, [2010] 4 CMLR 50, paras 82–83.

[20] Regulation 1/2003, recital 5.

[21] See eg Cases 43/82 and 63/82 *VBVB and VVVB v Commission* [1984] ECR 19, para 61; Case C-238/05 *Asnef-Equifax v Asociación de Usuarios de Servicios Bancarios (Ausbanc)* [2006] ECR I-11125, [2007] 4 CMLR 6, para 65.

[22] Cases T-528/93 etc [1996] ECR II-649, [1996] 5 CMLR 386, para 93.

[23] The General Court did so again in Case T-185/00 *M6 v Commission* [2002] ECR II-3805, [2003] 4 CMLR 707, para 86, where it considered that the Commission had incorrectly concluded that an agreement would not substantially eliminate competition.

[24] Case T-17/93 [1994] ECR II-595, para 85; see also Case T-168/01 *GlaxoSmithKline Services Unlimited v Commission* [2006] ECR II-2969, [2006] 5 CMLR 29, para 233, and para 46 of the *Article [101(3)] Guidelines*.

[25] See further ch 3, 'Have the EU Courts embraced the "rule of reason"?', pp 134–136.

[26] Commission decision of 7 April 2004, OJ [2004] L 362/17.

[27] See the *Article [101(3)] Guidelines*, para 46.

for many years Articles 3 to 5 of Council Regulation 4056/86 on maritime transport[28] provided block exemption for horizontal price-fixing in the case of containerised cargo carried by international liner conferences due to the particular characteristics of that industry, though this exemption was ended in October 2008[29].

There have been two recent cases in which the possibility of an Article 101(3) defence for an agreement that restricted competition by object has been explored[30]. In *Competition Authority v Beef Industry Development Society Ltd* ('BIDS')[31] the Court of Justice concluded that an agreement between beef processors in Ireland to reduce capacity for beef processing there (some firms would stay in the market, and would pay other firms to exit and to agree not to re-enter for several years) had the object of restricting competition. Any justification for the agreement would have to be made out under Article 101(3)[32]. The Supreme Court of Ireland, which had referred the matter to the Court of Justice, subsequently asked the Irish High Court to consider whether the Society had produced evidence to support a finding on the basis of Article 101(3)[33]. However it was announced on 25 January 2011 that BIDS had withdrawn its claim under Article 101(3), with the result that the Court was not required to reach a conclusion on the matter.

In *GlaxoSmithKline Services Unlimited v Commission*[34] the Court of Justice considered that a term in a vertical agreement, whereby wholesale purchasers of pharmaceutical products from Glaxo in Spain were charged a higher price if the products were exported from Spain to higher-priced countries such as the UK, restricted competition by object; however the Court was not satisfied that the Commission was correct to dismiss Glaxo's arguments in support of the agreement under Article 101(3). Unfortunately the Commission did not subsequently give a view as to whether Article 101(3) was, in fact, satisfied, so that the parties must determine the issue for themselves.

There have been decisions in which the Commission was satisfied that the fixing of prices satisfied the requirements of Article 101(3). These were far from being classic cartel cases: rather they concerned network industries in which prices were 'fixed' between participants in a network that supplied services to one another (the price fixing was business to business, or 'B to B'), whereas 'hard-core' price fixing involves the fixing of prices to customers (business to customer, or 'B to C')). It is interesting to note that, in these decisions, the Commission considered that the agreements restricted competition *by effect* rather than *by object*: in other words it did not treat the restrictions as hard-core. In *Reims II*[35] the Commission considered that an agreement between the public postal operators in Europe as to the amount that one operator would pay to another for the onward delivery of letters in the latter's territory satisfied the terms of Article 101(3). The agreement did entail the 'fixing' of prices, in that participants in the scheme were committed to its principles; but this was price fixing of an 'unusual' nature[36], and the Commission could identify a number of economic efficiencies that would follow from it[37]. Similarly in *Visa International – Multilateral Interchange Fee*[38] the Commission stated that it is not the case that an agree-

---

[28] OJ [1986] L 378/1.

[29] The exemption was repealed by Article 1 of Regulation 1419/2006, OJ [2006] L 269/1: see ch 23, 'Legislative regime', pp 970–972.

[30] See also the Opinion of the UK Office of Fair Trading in *Newspaper and magazine distribution* OFT 1025, October 2008, paras 4.29–4.132, available at www.oft.gov.uk.

[31] Case C-209/07 [2008] ECR I-8637, [2009] 4 CMLR 310.   [32] Ibid, paras 21 and 39.

[33] [2009] IESC 72.   [34] Cases C-501/06 P etc [2009] ECR I-9291, [2010] 4 CMLR 50.

[35] OJ [1999] L 275/17, [2000] 4 CMLR 704.   [36] Ibid, para 65.

[37] Ibid, paras 69–76; this was a decision where the Commission granted individual exemption under the old procedure in Regulation 17 of 1962: the exemption was renewed in 2003 and expired on 31 December 2006, OJ [2004] L 56/76, [2004] 5 CMLR 2.

[38] OJ [2002] L 318/17, [2003] 4 CMLR 283.

ment concerning prices is always to be classified as a cartel and therefore as inherently incapable of satisfying Article 101(3)[39]: in that decision, adopted under the old procedure in Regulation 17, the Commission granted individual exemption to a 'multilateral interchange fee' agreed upon between 'acquiring' and 'issuing' banks within the Visa system[40].

2. The Article 101(3) Criteria

Each of the four requirements of Article 101(3) will now be examined. It is essential to consider them in conjunction with the *Article [101(3)] Guidelines*. The text that follows will emulate the *Guidelines* by reversing the treatment of the second and third conditions set out in Article 101(3) (a fair share to consumers and indispensability): the Commission's view is that consideration of whether consumers would obtain a fair share of any resulting benefit does not arise in the event that any restrictions fail the indispensability test, so that it is logical to consider the latter first[41].

(A) First condition of Article 101(3): an improvement in the production or distribution of goods or in technical or economic progress

The 'benefit' produced by an agreement must be something of objective value to the EU as a whole, not a private benefit to the parties themselves; cost savings that arise simply from the exercise of market power, for example by fixing prices or sharing markets, cannot be taken into account[42]. Any advantages claimed of the agreement must outweigh the detriments it might produce[43]; the Commission has declined to accept that an agreement produces an improvement if, in practice, its effect is a disproportionate distortion of competition in the market in question[44]. An agreement must be examined in the light of all the factual arguments and evidence put forward by the parties in support of their argument that Article 101(3) is satisfied[45]. The Commission requires the parties to found their argument that Article 101(3) applies 'on a detailed, robust and compelling analysis that relies in its assumptions and deductions on empirical data and facts': it will not be persuaded 'by economic theory alone'[46]. In *Groupement des Cartes Bancaires* the Commission concluded that the Groupement had provided no empirical evidence that the restrictive fees

---

[39] Ibid, para 79; the Commission's suggestion in this paragraph that some agreements are inherently incapable of satisfying Article 101(3) is clearly wrong given the judgment of the General Court in the *Matra Hachette* case.

[40] The individual exemption expired on 31 December 2008; subsequently the Commission accepted commitments from Visa Europe under Article 9 of Regulation 1/2003 that involved a significant reduction of the interchange fee for debit cards: see Commission Press Release IP/10/1684, 8 December 2010.

[41] *Article [101(3)] Guidelines*, para 39.

[42] See Cases 56/64 and 58/64 *Consten and Grundig v Commission* [1966] ECR 299, p 348, [1966] CMLR 418, p 478; Cases C-501/06 P etc *GlaxoSmithKline Services Unlimited* [2009] ECR I-9291, [2010] 4 CMLR 50, paras 89–96; and para 49 of the *Article [101(3)] Guidelines*.

[43] Cases 56/64 and 58/64 *Consten and Grundig v Commission* [1966] ECR 299, p 348, [1966] CMLR 418, p 478; Case T-65/98 *Van den Bergh Foods Ltd v Commission* [2003] ECR II-4563, para 139, upheld on appeal Case C-552/03 P *Unilever Bestfoods (Ireland) Ltd v Commission* [2006] ECR I-9091, [2006] CMLR 5 1494, paras 102–106.

[44] *Screensport/EBU* OJ [1991] L 63/32, [1992] 5 CMLR 273, para 71.

[45] Cases C-501/06 P etc *GlaxoSmithKline Services Unlimited* [2009] ECR I-9291, [2010] 4 CMLR 50, paras 102–104.

[46] See *MasterCard*, Commission decision of 19 December 2007, para 690: see also paras 694–701; the decision is on appeal to the General Court, Case T/111/08 *MasterCard and others v Commission*, not yet decided.

for membership of the CB payment card system were necessary to prevent new entrants from free riding on investment by the other members[47].

The benefits that may be claimed are specified in Article 101(3): the restrictions in the agreement must either contribute to an improvement in the production or distribution of goods[48] or promote technical or economic progress. These concepts overlap, and in many cases the Commission has considered that more than one – or even that all – the heads were satisfied[49]. In other cases a particular type of benefit may be obviously appropriate for the agreement in question. When permitting specialisation agreements, which can lead to economies of scale and other efficiencies, the Commission has considered that there would be an improvement in the production of goods[50], while it has often held that research and development projects would lead to technical and economic progress[51]. Vertical agreements between suppliers and distributors naturally come under the head of improvements in distribution[52]. The Commission has recognised network externalities as contributing to technical and economic progress from which consumers derive a benefit[53].

An important question is to determine how broad the criteria in the first condition of Article 101(3) are: to use an analogy from many card games, in what circumstances can a 'benefit' under Article 101(3) 'trump' a restriction of competition under Article 101(1), with the result that an agreement which would have been prohibited under Article 101(1) is in fact permitted as a result of the legal exception provided by Article 101(3)? The issue of the breadth of Article 101(3) has attracted considerable attention in recent years for various reasons. First, the abolition of the Commission's 'monopoly' over decision-making in individual cases under Article 101(3) as a result of the adoption of Regulation 1/2003 means that Article 101(3) decisions can now be made by NCAs and national courts as well as the Commission: concern was expressed when Regulation 1/2003 was in gestation that the criteria in Article 101(3) were so broad that they were not appropriate to be decided upon by NCAs and national courts; and that there was a risk that the criteria would be applied inconsistently from one Member State to another. A second point is that Governments increasingly find that social policies that they would like to pursue – for example encouraging undertakings in the drinks industry to restrict the sale of 'cheap' alcohol to young people, or supermarkets to impose a charge for providing environmentally unfriendly plastic bags – may infringe competition law, in particular if a 'narrow' rather than a 'broad' view of Article 101(3) is taken. A third point is that the global financial crisis that erupted in 2008 led to many calls for undertakings to be allowed to enter into cooperative agreements to enable them to survive, supported by an indulgent application of Article 101(3). These factors have led to urgent and lively debate about the 'true meaning' of Article 101(3).

---

[47] Commission decision of 17 October 2008, on appeal to the General Court in Case T-491/07 *CB v Commission*, not yet decided.

[48] Note that services are not explicitly referred to here; however para 48 of the *Article [101(3)] Guidelines* states that Article 101(3) applies, by analogy, to services; in the UK s 9 of the Competition Act 1998 specifically includes improvements in the production or distribution of goods *or services*.

[49] See eg *Re United Reprocessors GmbH* OJ [1976] L 51/7, [1976] 2 CMLR D1.

[50] On specialisation agreements see ch 15, 'The application of Article 101(1) to production agreements', pp 600–603.

[51] On research and developments agreements see ch 15, 'Research and Development Agreements', pp 592–599.

[52] On vertical agreements see ch 16 generally.

[53] *Visa International – Multilateral Interchange Fee* OJ [2002] L 318/17, [2003] 4 CMLR 283, para 83; on network effects see ch 1, 'Network effects and two-sided markets', pp 11–12; see similarly, under UK law, *LINK Interchange Network Ltd*, OFT decision of 16 October 2001 [2002] UKCLR 59, available at www.oft.gov.uk.

(i) A narrow view of Article 101(3)

A narrow view of Article 101(3) is that it permits only agreements that would bring about improvements in economic efficiency: the very wording of Article 101(3), which speaks of improvements to production and distribution and to technical and economic progress, is clearly suggestive of an efficiency standard. Article 101(3), therefore, simply allows a balancing of the restrictive effects of an agreement under Article 101(1) against the enhancement of efficiency under Article 101(3); in striving to achieve the right balance the other criteria of Article 101(3) – a fair share to consumers, no dispensable restrictions and no substantial elimination of competition – are there to ensure that a reasonable outcome in terms of consumer welfare is achieved. The Commission's *White Paper on Modernisation*[54], which began the process that culminated in the adoption of Regulation 1/2003, explained Article 101(1) and (3) in precisely this way[55]; and the *Article [101(3)] Guidelines* are drafted explicitly in terms of economic efficiency[56]. An attractive way of thinking of Article 101 as a whole is that Article 101(1) is concerned to establish whether an agreement could lead to allocative inefficiency, and that Article 101(3) permits such an agreement where there would be a compensating enhancement of productive efficiency[57].

(ii) A broader approach to Article 101(3)

However an alternative, and broader, view of Article 101(3) is possible: that it allows policies other than economic efficiency to be taken into account when deciding whether to allow agreements that are restrictive of competition. There are many important policies in the Union, for example on industry[58], the environment[59], employment[60], the regions[61] and culture[62], which go beyond the simple enhancement of economic efficiency. According to a broad view of Article 101(3) a benefit in terms of any of these policies may be able to 'trump' a restriction of competition under Article 101(1)[63]; another way of putting the point is to suggest that *non*-economic criteria can be taken into account under Article 101(3) as well as economic ones[64].

   Some of these broader considerations do seem to have had an influence on the application of Article 101(3) during the years when the Commission enjoyed a monopoly over decision-making under that provision[65]. For example industrial policy can be detected

---

[54] [1999] C 132/1, [1999] 5 CMLR 208.   [55] Ibid, para 57.

[56] See 'The Commission's approach in the *Article [101(3)] Guidelines*', pp 160–162 below.

[57] See Odudu *The Boundaries of EC Competition Law: The Scope of Article 81* (Oxford University Press, 2006), in particular ch 6; Odudu 'The Wider Concerns of Competition Law' (2010) 30 OJLS 1.

[58] On industry under the TFEU see Article 173 (ex Article 157 EC).

[59] On environmental protection under the TFEU see Article 11 (ex Article 6 EC) and Articles 191–193 (ex Articles 174–176 EC).

[60] On employment under the TFEU see Articles 145–159 (ex Articles 125–130 EC).

[61] On economic and social cohesion under the TFEU note Articles 174–178 (ex Articles 158–162 EC).

[62] On culture under the TFEU see Article 167 (ex Article 151 EC); several appellants in the *CISAC* case are relying on Article 167: see Cases T-392/08 etc *AEPI v Commission*, not yet decided.

[63] For powerful argument as to why these broader issues should not be brought within the internal regime of competition law see Odudu *The Boundaries of EC Competition Law: The Scope of Article 81* (Oxford University Press, 2006), ch 7; see also Kjolbye 'The new Commission guidelines on the application of Article 81(3): an economic approach to Article 81' (2004) 25 ECLR 566.

[64] For an interesting review of the issues see the OFT's discussion note 'Article 101(3) – A discussion of narrow versus broad definition of benefits' and the notes of the roundtable discussion held at the OFT on 12 May 2010, available at www.oft.gov.uk.

[65] For discussion of the policies under consideration in this section see Monti *EC Competition Law* (Cambridge University Press, 2007), ch 4; Jones and Sufrin *EU Competition Law: Text, Cases, and Materials* (Oxford University Press, 4th ed, 2010), pp 244–247.

in some competition law developments[66]: Amato suggests that the block exemption for specialisation agreements, with its acceptance that rationalisation in production fulfils the Article 101(3) criteria, reflects industrial policy rather than competition thinking[67]. In *Metro v Commission*[68] the Court of Justice considered that employment was a relevant factor under the first condition in Article 101(3), saying that the agreement under consideration was 'a stabilising factor with regard to the provision of employment which, since it improves the general conditions of production, especially when market conditions are unfavourable, comes within the framework of the objectives to which reference may be had pursuant to Article [101(3)]'. When considering whether an exemption might be given to a joint venture to produce a 'multi-purpose vehicle' in Portugal in *Ford/Volkswagen*[69] the Commission 'took note' of 'exceptional circumstances' in that it would bring a large number of jobs and substantial foreign investment to one of the poorest regions of the EU, promoting harmonious development, reducing regional disparities and furthering European market integration[70]. The Commission emphasised, however, that this would not be enough in itself to make an exemption possible unless the other conditions of Article 101(3) were fulfilled[71]. In its submissions to the General Court when the decision was unsuccessfully challenged by a third party on appeal, the Commission argued that it was possible to take into account factors other than those expressly mentioned in Article 101(3) including, for example, the maintenance of employment[72]. The General Court concluded that, since the Commission would have granted an individual exemption anyway, its decision could not be impugned for having taken into account improper criteria[73].

In *UEFA*, when granting an individual exemption to the sale of the media rights to the UEFA Champions League, the Commission took note of the financial solidarity that supports the development of European football (citing the Court of Justice's judgments in *Metro* and *Remia*)[74]. In *Laurent Piau v Commission*[75] the General Court seems to have accepted that rules of FIFA, the body that controls football worldwide, that required football players' agents to comply with a mandatory licensing system, could contribute to economic progress by raising professional and ethical standards for players' agents in order to protect football players who have a short playing career[76]. In *Stichting Baksteen*[77] the Commission considered that the restructuring of the Dutch brick industry, involving coordinated closures 'carried out in acceptable social conditions, including the redeployment of employees', promoted technical and economic progress[78]. In *CECED*[79] the Commission granted an individual exemption to an agreement between manufacturers

---

[66] Note however that Article 173 TFEU provides that the Union's industrial policy is to be conducted 'in accordance with a system of open and competitive markets'; see further OECD Roundtable on Competition Policy, 'Industrial Policy and National Champions' (2009), available at www.oecd.org/competition.

[67] Amato *Antitrust and the Bounds of Power* (Hart Publishing, 1997), pp 63–64; the relevant block exemption is now Regulation 1218/2010, OJ [2010] L 335/43.

[68] Case 26/76 [1977] ECR 1875, [1978] 2 CMLR 1, para 43; see similarly Case 42/84 *Remia BV and Verenigde Bedrijven Nutricia NV v Commission* [1985] ECR 2545, [1987] 1 CMLR 1, para 42.

[69] OJ [1993] L 20/14, [1993] 5 CMLR 617.

[70] OJ [1993] L 20/14, [1993] 5 CMLR 617, paras 23, 28 and 36; see also the Commission Press Release IP/92/1083, 23 December 1992.

[71] OJ [1993] L 20/14, [1993] 5 CMLR 617, para 36.

[72] Case T-17/93 *Matra Hachette v Commission* [1994] ECR II-595, para 96; on this case generally see Swaak (1995) 32 CML Rev 1271.

[73] [1994] ECR II-595, para 139.

[74] *Joint selling of the commercial rights of the UEFA Champions League* OJ [2003] L 291/25, [2004] 4 CMLR 9.

[75] Case T-193/02 [2005] ECR II-209, [2005] 5 CMLR 42, upheld on appeal Case C-171/05 P *Piau v Commission* [2006] ECR I-37.

[76] Ibid, paras 100–106.   [77] OJ [1994] L 131/15, [1995] 4 CMLR 646.

[78] Ibid, paras 27–28.   [79] OJ [2000] L 187/47, [2000] 5 CMLR 635.

of domestic appliances (washing machines etc) which would lead to energy efficiencies, and in doing so noted not only individual economic benefits to consumers from lower energy bills but also the 'collective environmental benefits' that would flow from the agreement[80], referring specifically to the Union's environmental policy in its decision. The Commission reached a similar conclusion when it informally settled cases relating to 'environmental' agreements for water heaters and dishwashers[81].

It is clear, therefore, that a number of factors appear to have been influential in decisions under Article 101(3), not all of which can be considered to be 'narrow' improvements in economic efficiency. There are significant proponents of the view that Article 101(3) does admit broad, non-competition considerations[82], and the General Court, in *Métropole télévision SA v Commission*[83], said that 'in the context of an overall assessment, the Commission is entitled to base itself on considerations *connected with the pursuit of the public interest* in order to grant exemption under Article [101(3)]' (emphasis added)[84]. It is also worth mentioning in passing that 'public interest' criteria may also be relevant when deciding whether Article 101(1) is infringed in the first place, as the Court of Justice's judgment in *Wouters*[85] has demonstrated: indeed the suppression of non-economic considerations under Article 101(3) might result in their re-emergence under the *Wouters* case law. Public interest issues are also relevant when deciding whether Article 106(2) permits a derogation from the application of Article 101(1)[86].

(iii) Comment

This discussion shows that, over a number of years, there has been uncertainty – even confusion – as to the proper application of Article 101(3). As long as the Commission enjoyed a monopoly over decision-making under Regulation 17 this may not have been too serious a problem: the Commission undoubtedly enjoyed a 'margin of appreciation' when applying Article 101(3)[87] under Regulation 17 and it would hardly be surprising if, when making decisions in individual cases over the period from 1962 to 2004, it was influenced, at least sometimes, by issues other than 'pure' economic efficiency. However Regulation 1/2003 makes it necessary to decide on the true content of Article 101(3) be-

---

[80] Ibid, paras 55–57; see similarly paras 268–271 of the Commission's decision in *ARA, ARGEV* Commission decision of 17 October 2003, upheld on appeal Case T-419/03 *Altstoff Recycling Austria AG v Commission* [2011] ECR II-000.

[81] Commission Press Release IP/01/1659, 26 November 2001; see also the Commission's *Competition Policy Newsletter*, February 2002, 50.

[82] See eg Siragusa in *European Competition Law Annual 1997: Objectives of Competition Policy* (Hart Publishing, 1998, eds Ehlermann and Laudati), p 39; Ehlermann 'The Modernization of EC Antitrust Policy: A Legal and Cultural Revolution' (2000) 37 CML Rev 537; Wesseling 'The Draft Regulation Modernising the Competition Rules: the Commission is Married to One Idea' (2001) 26 EL Rev 357; Monti 'Article 101 EC and Public Policy' (2002) 39 CML Rev 1057; Faull, giving the Burrell Lecture in London, 21 February 2000, said that social policy can 'reasonably credibly' be brought within Article 101(3); Lugard and Hancher 'Honey, I shrunk the Article! A Critical Assessment of the Commission's Notice on Article 81(3)' (2004) 25 ECLR 410; Townley *Article 81 and Public Policy* (Hart Publishing, 2009); for discussion of the issues see Sufrin 'The Evolution of Article 81(3) of the EC Treaty' (2006) 51 Antitrust Bulletin 915, pp 952–967.

[83] Cases T-528/93 etc [1996] ECR II-649, [1996] 5 CMLR 386; see similarly Case T-168/01 *GlaxoSmithKline Services Unlimited v Commission* [2006] ECR II-2969, [2006] 5 CMLR 29, para 244.

[84] Ibid, para 118.

[85] Case C-309/99 [2002] ECR I-1577, [2002] 4 CMLR 27; see also Case C-519/04 P *Meca-Medina and Majcen v Commission* [2006] ECR I-6991, [2006] 5 CMLR 1023; this case law is discussed in ch 3, 'Regulatory ancillarity: the judgment of the Court of Justice in *Wouters*', pp 130–133.

[86] See ch 6, 'Article 106(2)', pp 235–241.

[87] See Cases 56/64 and 58/64 *Consten and Grundig v Commission* [1966] ECR 299, p 347, [1966] CMLR 418, p 477.

cause decisions since 1 May 2004 can be made by NCAs and national courts as well as by the Commission itself. These institutions, and the undertakings that enter into agreements that might be challenged under Article 101, need to know the limits of what can be justified under Article 101(3); and the NCAs and national courts, unlike the Commission, are not well placed to balance a restriction of competition under Article 101(1) against a variety of European Union policies ranging from industrial and environmental policy to social and cultural issues under Article 101(3). It seems reasonable to suppose that NCAs and national courts would have less difficulty in applying a 'narrow' interpretation of Article 101(3), limited to a consideration of economic efficiencies. These considerations suggest that, in the post-Regulation 1/2003 world, Article 101(3) should be interpreted in a narrow rather than a broad manner, according to standards and by reference to principles that are justiciable in courts of law. This is borne out by the Commission's report of April 2009 on the functioning of Regulation 1/2003 during its first five years[88], in which it noted that 'neither the case practice of the Commission and the national enforcers, nor the experience reported by the business and legal community, indicate major difficulties with the direct application of Article [101(3)] which has been widely welcomed by stakeholders'[89].

(iv) The Commission's approach in the Article [101(3)] Guidelines

It is absolutely clear from the Commission's *Article [101(3)] Guidelines* that it intends Article 101(3) to be applied according to the narrow approach based on economic efficiency[90]. Paragraph 11 of the *Guidelines* states that Article 101(3) allows 'pro-competitive benefits' to be taken into account under Article 101(3), and that these may outweigh any 'anti-competitive effects' under Article 101(1). Paragraph 32 of the *Guidelines* again speaks of the 'positive economic effects' of agreements that can be taken into consideration under Article 101(3). Paragraph 33 refers to the achievement of 'pro-competitive effects by way of efficiency gains', explaining that efficiencies may create additional value by lowering the cost of producing an output, improving the quality of the product or creating a new product. Significantly paragraph 42 of the *Guidelines* explicitly states that '[g]oals pursued by other Treaty provisions can be taken into account only to the extent that they can be subsumed under the four conditions of Article 101(3)'. When the *Guidelines*, at paragraphs 48 to 72, reach the point of discussing the first condition of Article 101(3) – an improvement in production or distribution or in technical or economic progress – they do so specifically under the heading of 'efficiency gains', thereby removing any lingering doubt that might still remain that the Commission considers that other, non-economic, considerations could be relevant to the assessment. Similarly paragraph 20 of the Commission's *Guidelines on Horizontal Cooperation Agreements*[91] says that Article 101(3) asks whether any pro-competitive effects of an agreement outweigh its restrictive effects on competition.

It would not be unreasonable to expect that NCAs and national courts will take – and will be happy to take – a strong lead from the *Article [101(3)] Guidelines*, although it is obviously open to undertakings to argue that they do not fully reflect the jurisprudence

---

[88] Regulation 1/2003, Article 44.

[89] *Report on the functioning of Regulation 1/2003* COM(2009) 206 final, para 12.

[90] It is also noticeable that the recitals to the various block exemptions (as to which see 'Block Exemptions', pp 168–172 below) explain the reasons for permitting certain agreements under Article 101(3) purely in terms of economic efficiency; and that the approach taken in the *Guidelines* is consistent with the Commission's *Guidelines on the assessment of horizontal mergers* OJ [2004] C 31/5, paras 76–90 and its *Guidance on the Commission's enforcement priorities in applying Article [102 TFEU] to abusive exclusionary conduct by dominant undertakings* OJ [2009] C 45/7, paras 28–31, 46, 62, 74 and 89–90.

[91] OJ [2011] C 11/1.

of the General Court and the Court of Justice. There may be litigation in the future in which those Courts will have to reconsider some of the statements in cases such as *Metro*[92] and *Remia and Nutricia*[93] (both decided when the Commission had a 'monopoly' over decision-making under Article 101(3)) and to decide whether to allow a broader approach to Article 101(3) than the *Guidelines* envisage; or whether to adopt the narrower, and more justiciable, approach suggested by the Commission. In *GlaxoSmithKline Services Unlimited v Commission* the General Court's analysis of whether GSK had satisfied the first condition of Article 101(3) was conducted under the heading 'Evidence of a gain in efficiency', suggesting that it was comfortable with a narrow approach to that provision[94].

Paragraph 51 of the *Article [101(3)] Guidelines* stresses that all efficiency claims must be substantiated in order to verify:

- the *nature* of the claimed efficiencies, so that it is possible for the decision-maker to verify that they are objective in nature[95]
- the *link* between the agreement and the efficiencies which, as a general proposition, should be direct rather than indirect[96]
- the *likelihood* and *magnitude* of each claimed efficiency and
- *how* and *when* each claimed efficiency would be achieved.

The decision-maker must be able to verify the value of the claimed efficiencies in order to be able to balance them against the anti-competitive effects of the agreement[97]. The Commission's requirement that undertakings must substantiate their claims is an important feature of the *Article [101(3)] Guidelines* and its decisional practice since May 2004. Mere speculation or conjecture will be insufficient: there must be 'convincing arguments and evidence'[98] that the agreement will lead to the efficiencies claimed, the burden being on the parties seeking to defend it.

The Commission identifies two broad categories of efficiencies in the *Guidelines*, while acknowledging that it is not appropriate to draw clear and firm distinctions between the various categories[99].

(A) Cost efficiencies

Paragraphs 64 to 68 consider cost efficiencies which may result, for example, from the development of new production technologies and methods[100], synergies arising from the integration of existing assets[101], from economies of scale[102], economies of scope[103] and from better planning of production[104].

(B) Qualitative efficiencies

Paragraphs 69 to 72 consider qualitative efficiencies as opposed to cost reductions: research and development agreements are particularly cited in this respect[105], as are

---

[92] Case 26/76 [1977] ECR 1875, [1978] 2 CMLR 1.

[93] Case 42/84 [1985] ECR 2545, [1987] 1 CMLR 1.

[94] Case T-168/01 [2006] ECR II-2969, [2006] 5 CMLR 29, paras 247–308; the General Court's judgment in relation to Article 101(3) was upheld on appeal to the Court of Justice, Cases C-501/06 P etc *GlaxoSmithKline Services Unlimited v Commission* [2009] ECR I-9291, [2010] 4 CMLR 50, paras 68–168.

[95] *Article [101(3)] Guidelines*, para 52.

[96] Ibid, paras 53 and 54.   [97] Ibid, paras 55–58.

[98] See Case T-168/01 *GlaxoSmithKline Services Unlimited v Commission* [2006] ECR II-2969, [2006] 5 CMLR 29, para 235, upheld on appeal Cases C-501/06 P etc *GlaxoSmithKline Services Unlimited v Commission* [2009] ECR I-9291, [2010] 4 CMLR 50, para 82.

[99] *Article [101(3)] Guidelines*, para 59.   [100] Ibid, para 64.   [101] Ibid, para 65.

[102] Ibid, para 66.   [103] Ibid, para 67.   [104] Ibid, para 68.   [105] Ibid, para 70.

licensing agreements and agreements for the joint production of new or improved goods or services[106]; there is also a reference to the possibility of distribution agreements delivering qualitative efficiencies[107].

(B) Third condition of Article 101(3): indispensability of the restrictions

The *Article [101(3)] Guidelines* deal with the indispensability of restrictions before the question of a fair share for consumers, since the latter issue would not arise if the restrictions are not indispensable[108]. Paragraph 73 of the *Guidelines* states that the indispensability condition implies a two-fold test: first, whether the restrictive agreement itself is reasonably necessary in order to achieve the efficiencies; and secondly whether the individual restrictions of competition flowing from the agreement are reasonably necessary for the attainment of the efficiencies. Paragraph 30 of the *Guidelines* explains that the requirement of indispensability in Article 101(3) is conceptually distinct from the ancillary restraints doctrine: Article 101(3) involves a balancing of pro- and anti-competitive effects, which is not the case when determining whether a restraint is ancillary.

(i) The efficiencies must be specific to the agreement

Paragraphs 75 to 77 consider the first part of the two-fold test: the requirement that the efficiencies are specific to the agreement or, to put the point another way, that there are no other economically practicable and less restrictive means of achieving them[109]. The parties should explain, for example, why they could not have achieved the same efficiencies acting alone[110].

(ii) The indispensability of individual restrictions

Paragraphs 78 to 82 consider whether any individual restrictions of competition flowing from the agreement are indispensable. The parties must demonstrate both that the nature of any restriction and that its 'intensity' are reasonably necessary to produce the claimed efficiencies[111]. A restriction is indispensable if its absence would eliminate or significantly reduce the efficiencies that follow from the agreement or make it significantly less likely that they will materialise; restrictions of the kind 'blacklisted' in any of the block exemptions – for example horizontal price-fixing and market-sharing and the imposition of export bans in vertical agreements – would be unlikely to be considered indispensable[112]. A restriction may be indispensable only for a certain period of time; once that time has expired, it will cease to be so[113].

(C) Second condition of Article 101(3): fair share for consumers

The undertakings concerned must show that a fair share of the benefit that results from an agreement will accrue to consumers if Article 101(3) is to apply: it is helpful to think

---

    [106] Ibid, para 71.   [107] Ibid, para 72.   [108] Ibid, para 39.
    [109] Ibid, para 75; note that under para 85 of the Commission's *Guidelines on the assessment of horizontal mergers* OJ [2004] C 31/5 efficiencies are recognised in the assessment of mergers only where they can be shown to be merger-specific.
    [110] *Article [101(3)] Guidelines*, para 76.   [111] Ibid, para 78.
    [112] Ibid, para 79; for 'blacklisted' clauses in block exemptions see ch 15, 'Article 4: hard-core restrictions', p 602 (specialisation agreements) and 'Article 5: hard-core restrictions', pp 597–598 (research and development agreements); ch 16, 'Article 4: hard-core restrictions', pp 663–669 (vertical agreements); and ch 19, 'Article 4: hard-core restrictions', pp 786–789 (technology transfer agreements).
    [113] Ibid, para 81.

of this as the 'pass-on' requirement. Paragraph 84 of the *Article [101(3)] Guidelines* states that the concept of consumers in Article 101(3) encompasses all direct or indirect users of the products covered by the agreement, including producers that use the products as an input, wholesalers, retailers and final consumers; 'undertakings', in the competition law sense of the term[114], can be consumers for this purpose just as much as a natural person who purchases as a consumer in the lay sense. It is the beneficial nature of the effect on all consumers in the relevant markets that must be taken into consideration under this part of Article 101(3), not the effect on each member of that category of consumers[115]. Negative effects on consumers in one geographic or product market cannot normally be balanced against and compensated by positive effects for consumers in unrelated markets, although this may be possible where markets are related provided that the consumers affected by the restriction and benefiting from the efficiency gains are substantially the same[116].

If an agreement would leave consumers worse off than they would otherwise have been the pass-on condition of Article 101(3) will not have been satisfied[117]; however consumers do not have to gain from each and every efficiency achieved provided that they receive a fair share of the overall benefits[118]. It could be the case that an agreement, for example to produce a new product more quickly than if the parties had proceeded alone, might also lead to greater market power and therefore higher prices; the Commission does not rule out that early access to the new products might amount to a 'fair share' for consumers, notwithstanding the higher prices[119]. In its *MasterCard* decision the Commission said that if an agreement is likely to lead to higher prices, consumers must be compensated through increased quality or other benefits[120]. The greater the restriction of competition under Article 101(1), the greater must be the efficiency and the pass-on under Article 101(3)[121]; and where an agreement has substantial anti-competitive and substantial pro-competitive effects paragraph 92 of the *Guidelines* states that the decision-maker should take into account that competition is an important long-term driver of efficiency and innovation. The *Guidelines* proceed to discuss the pass-on requirement in relation to cost efficiencies and qualitative efficiencies respectively.

(i) Cost efficiencies

Paragraphs 95 to 101 consider pass-on and the balancing of cost efficiencies. Paragraph 96 notes that cost efficiencies may lead to increased output and lower prices for consumers: in assessing whether this is likely the following factors should be taken into account:

- the characteristics and structure of the market
- the nature and magnitude of the efficiency gains
- the elasticity of demand and
- the magnitude of the restriction of competition.

Paragraph 98 points out that consumers are more likely to benefit from a reduction in the parties' variable costs than in their fixed costs, since pricing and output

[114] See ch 3, 'Undertakings and Associations of Undertakings', pp 83–99.

[115] Case C-238/05 *Asnef-Equifax v Asociación de Usuarios de Servicios Bancarios (Ausbanc)* [2006] ECR I-11125, [2007] 4 CMLR 6, para 70.

[116] *Article [101(3)] Guidelines*, para 43.

[117] Ibid, para 85.   [118] Ibid, para 86.   [119] Ibid, para 89.

[120] Commission decision of 19 December 2007, para 734, on appeal Case T-111/08 *MasterCard v Commission*, not yet decided; see further Repa, Malczewska, Teixeira and Martinez Rivero 'Commission prohibits MasterCard's multilateral interchange fees for cross-border card payments in the EEA' (2008) 1 *Competition Policy Newsletter* 1.

[121] *Article [101(3)] Guidelines*, para 90.

decisions are determined predominantly by variable costs and demand conditions. Paragraph 99 explains that the actual rate of any pass-on to consumers will depend on the extent to which consumers will expand their demand in response to a lowering of price; this will depend, among other things, on the extent to which sellers are able to discriminate in price between different categories of customers. Paragraph 101 cautions that any reduction in costs, and therefore any prospect of lower prices for consumers, must be balanced against the fact that an agreement being considered under Article 101(3) must necessarily involve a restriction of competition under Article 101(1), which in itself is likely to mean that the parties have the ability to raise their prices as a result of their increased market power: these 'opposing forces' must be balanced against one another.

(ii) Qualitative efficiencies

Paragraphs 102 to 104 consider pass-on and the balancing of other types of efficiencies: for example the emergence of a new and improved product might compensate for the fact that an agreement leads to higher prices. Paragraph 103 concedes that this involves a value judgment and that it is difficult to assign precise values to a balancing exercise of this nature. Paragraph 104 acknowledges that new and improved products are an important source of consumer welfare; it continues that, where prices will be higher as a result of the restrictive effect of the agreement on competition, it is necessary to consider whether the claimed efficiencies will create 'real value' for consumers that will compensate for this.

(D) Fourth condition of Article 101(3): no elimination of competition in a substantial part of the market

Paragraph 105 of the *Article [101(3)] Guidelines* states that ultimately the protection of rivalry and the competitive process is given priority over pro-competitive efficiency gains that result from restrictive agreements.

(i) The relationship between Article 101(3) and Article 102

Paragraph 106 of the *Guidelines* explains that the concept of elimination of competition in a substantial part of the market is an autonomous EU concept specific to Article 101(3). Paragraph 106 then considers the relationship between Article 101(3) and Article 102. It refers to case law that establishes that Article 101(3) cannot prevent the application of Article 102[122] and that Article 101(3) cannot apply to agreements that constitute an abuse of a dominant position[123]. Paragraph 106 goes on to explain, however, that not all restrictive agreements concluded by a dominant undertaking necessarily constitute an abuse of a dominant position. The fact that most block exemptions contain market share caps means that dominant firms will rarely be in a position to rely on them[124].

---

[122] See Cases C-395/96 P etc *Compagnie Maritime Belge Transports SA v Commission* [2000] ECR I-1365, [2000] 4 CMLR 1076, para 130.

[123] Case T-51/89 *Tetra Pak Rausing SA v Commission* [1990] ECR II-309, [1991] 4 CMLR 334, para 28, and Cases T-191/98 etc *Atlantic Container Line v Commission* [2003] ECR II-3275, [2005] 4 CMLR 20, para 1456; in *Decca Navigator System* OJ [1989] L 43/27, [1990] 4 CMLR 627, para 122, the Commission refused individual exemption to an agreement that involved an abuse of a dominant position.

[124] See 'The format of block exemptions', pp 171–172 below.

(ii) Determining whether competition will be substantially eliminated

Paragraphs 107 to 116 explain how to assess whether an agreement will substantially eliminate competition. Paragraph 107 states that it is necessary to evaluate the extent to which competition will be reduced as a result of the agreement: the more that competition is already weakened in the market before the agreement, and the more that the agreement will reduce competition in the market, the more likely it is that the agreement will be considered to eliminate competition substantially. Both actual and potential competition should be taken into account when making the assessment[125]. The degree of actual competition in the market should not be assessed on the basis of market shares alone, but should be based on more extensive qualitative and quantitative analysis[126]. The *Article [101(3)] Guidelines* set out a series of factors that should be taken into account when assessing entry barriers and the possibility of entry into the market on a significant scale, including, for example, the cost of entry including sunk costs, the minimum efficient scale within the industry and the competitive strengths of potential entrants[127].

(E) Judicial review by the General Court[128]

The Commission's decisions on the application of Article 101(3) are subject to judicial review by the General Court and (on a point of law) by the Court of Justice. In *Consten and Grundig v Commission*[129] the Court of Justice indicated that it would not adopt an interventionist stance on applications for review; Article 101(3) involves complex evaluations of economic issues, and the Court of Justice considered that this task is essentially one for the Commission: the Court would confine itself to examining the relevant facts and the legal consequences deduced therefrom; it would not substitute its decision for the Commission's. The EU Courts have maintained this approach, emphasising the extent of the margin of appreciation available to the Commission when applying Article 101(3) and (by implication) their unwillingness to interfere with the exercise of this appreciation[130]. However it is essential that the Commission's decision should be adequately reasoned[131], and where there is a defect in this respect the Courts will be prepared to annul the decision in question[132]. Similarly the General Court will annul a Commission decision where it has seriously misapprehended the facts of a particular case[133]. The General Court summed up the position in *GlaxoSmithKline Services Unlimited v Commission*[134] as follows:

> 241 ...the Court dealing with an application for annulment of a decision applying Article 101(3) EC carries out, in so far as it is faced with complex economic assessments, a review confined, as regards the merits, to verifying whether the facts have been accurately stated, whether there has been any manifest error of appraisal and whether the legal consequences deduced from those facts were accurate.
>
> 242 It is for the Court to establish not only whether the evidence relied on is factually accurate, reliable and consistent, but also whether it contains all the information which

---

[125] *Article [101(3)] Guidelines*, paras 108 and 114. [126] Ibid, para 109.
[127] Ibid, para 115.
[128] See generally Bailey 'Scope of Judicial Review under Article 81 EC' (2004) 41 CMLRev 1327.
[129] Cases 56/64 and 58/64 [1966] ECR 299, [1966] CMLR 418.
[130] See eg Case 26/76 *Metro SB-Grossmärkte v Commission* [1977] ECR 1875, [1978] 2 CMLR 1, paras 45 and 50; Case T-7/93 *Langnese-Iglo GmbH v Commission* [1995] ECR II-1533, [1995] 5 CMLR 602, para 178.
[131] Article 296 TFEU provides that decisions by the Commission shall state the reasons on which they are based.
[132] See eg Case C-360/92 P *Publishers' Association v Commission* [1995] ECR I-23, [1995] 5 CMLR 33.
[133] Cases T-79/95 R etc *SNCF and BRB v Commission* [1996] ECR II-1491, [1997] 4 CMLR 334.
[134] Case T-168/01 [2006] ECR II-2969, [2006] 5 CMLR 29.

must be taken into account for the purpose of assessing a complex situation and whether it is capable of substantiating the conclusions drawn from it.

243 On the other hand, it is not for the Court to substitute its own economic assessment for that of the institution which adopted the decision the legality of which it is requested to review.

In the *Glaxo* case the General Court annulled the Commission's decision that GSK's standard conditions of sale, which were intended to prevent parallel trade from the low-priced Spanish pharmaceutical market to the higher-priced UK one, did not satisfy the criteria of Article 101(3): GSK argued that the restriction of trade was necessary to promote investment into research and development in the sector. The General Court held that the Commission had failed to carry out a proper examination of the factual arguments and evidence put forward by GSK or to refute its arguments[135]. On appeal the Court of Justice held that the General Court had stated the position accurately and dismissed the Commission's argument that it had misapplied the case law on the burden and standard of proof in an Article 101(3) case[136].

Despite their recognition of the margin of appreciation enjoyed by the Commission, the Courts have intervened on some occasions, as in the *Glaxo* case just discussed. Other cases in which the Commission's findings under Article 101(3) have been overturned include the Court of Justice's judgment in *Publishers' Association v Commission*[137] and the judgments of the General Court in *Métropole télévision SA v Commission*[138], *European Night Services v Commission*[139], and *Métropole télévision SA (M6) v Commission*[140].

3. Regulation 1/2003

(A) The Commission's former monopoly over the grant of individual exemptions

Under Regulation 17 of 1962 the Commission had sole power (subject to review by the General Court and the Court of Justice) to grant individual exemptions to agreements on the basis of the criteria in Article 101(3)[141]. This monopoly over the grant of individual exemptions meant that the Commission had the opportunity to develop its policy towards various types of agreement over a period of time, and in some cases to give expression to this policy in its block exemption regulations. However the monopoly had many drawbacks: the Commission never had sufficient staff to deal with the enormous volume of agreements that were notified to it: the result was that severe delays were experienced; considerable business time was spent collecting the data and preparing the so-called 'Form A/B' on which notifications had to be submitted; substantial expense was incurred, not least on legal and other professional fees; and businesses faced a long period of uncertainty as to the lawfulness of their agreements. The Commission was overburdened with notifications, many of which concerned agreements that had no seriously anti-competitive effect, with the consequence

[135] Ibid, paras 247–308.
[136] Cases C-501/06 P etc *GlaxoSmithKline Services Unlimited v Commission* [2009] ECR I-9291, [2010] 4 CMLR 50, paras 78–88.
[137] Case C-360/92 P [1995] ECR I-23, [1995] 5 CMLR 33.
[138] Cases T-528/93 etc [1996] ECR II-649, [1996] 5 CMLR 386.
[139] Cases T-374/94 etc [1998] ECR II-3141, [1998] 5 CMLR 718 at paras 205–221.
[140] Cases T-185/00 etc [2002] ECR II-3805, [2003] 4 CMLR 707.   [141] Regulation 17, Article 9(1).

that it was distracted from other tasks, such as the pursuit of cartels and abusive behaviour, which are of much greater significance for the public interest: as recital 3 of Regulation 1/2003 says, 'the system of notification...prevents the Commission from concentrating its resources on curbing the most serious infringements. It also imposes considerable costs on undertakings.' The problems associated with the process of notification for individual exemption were ameliorated to some extent, for example by the adoption of block exemption regulations and by the informal settlement of some cases. However the 'problem' of the monopoly over the grant of individual exemptions was a real one, and this led the Commission, in the White Paper of 1999, to propose abolition of the process of notification altogether; this policy was carried into effect by Regulation 1/2003.

(B) The end of the system of notification for individual exemption

Regulation 1/2003 ended the system of notification for individual exemption with effect from 1 May 2004. Previous editions of this book explained in detail how the system of individual exemptions operated[142].

(C) Self-assessment

The fact that undertakings and their lawyers can no longer notify agreements to the Commission and await an administrative 'stamp of approval' certifying that the criteria of Article 101(3) are satisfied means that they must now be self-reliant and conduct their own 'self-assessment' of the application of that provision. This caused some consternation in the business and legal communities at the time that Regulation 1/2003 was being debated. However, since Regulation 1/2003 entered into effect, there has been nothing to suggest that the direct applicability of Article 101(3) is causing difficulties in practice: it would appear to be the case that lawyers and their business clients are able to deal with self-assessment. This was the conclusion reached by the Commission in its *Report on the functioning of Regulation 1/2003*[143]. A helpful Report, *Practical methods to assess efficiency gains in the context of Article [101(3) of the TFEU]*[144], provides a structured framework on how to conduct a self-assessment of efficiency claims under Article 101(3); and DG COMP's *Best Practices for the Submission of Economic Evidence and Data Collection in Cases Concerning the Application of Articles 101 and 102 TFEU and in Merger Cases* set out best practices concerning the generation as well as the presentation of relevant economic and empirical evidence that may be taken into account in the assessment of competition cases.

Of course there may be cases in which there is genuine uncertainty whether an agreement infringes Article 101(1) and/or satisfies Article 101(3). Regulation 1/2003 provides three ways in which cases might be resolved following Commission intervention: the acceptance of legally-binding commitments under Article 9; a finding of inapplicability under Article 10; and the provision of informal guidance. Each of these possibilities is discussed in chapter 7[145]. The provisions on findings of inapplicability and informal guidance in certain cases of uncertainty, have

---

[142] See the fourth edition, ch 4, pp 136–141; see also Bellamy and Child *European Community Law of Competition* (Sweet & Maxwell, 6th ed, 2008, eds Roth and Rose), paras 13-004–13-016.

[143] COM(2009) 206 final, para 12; see further the accompanying Staff Working Paper, SEC(2009) 574 final, para 11; both documents are available at www.ec.europa.eu.

[144] Available at www.ec.europa.eu/enterprise/library/lib-competition/doc/efficiency_guidance.pdf; note that this Report was commissioned by DG Enterprise and Industry rather than DG COMP.

[145] See ch 7, 'Article 9: commitments', pp 255–262; in the UK the OFT has issued an Opinion in relation to the distribution of newspapers and magazines, and it has also introduced a practice of providing 'short-form Opinions': see ch 10, 'Opinions', p 404.

yet to be used[146]. However there have been Article 9 decisions in cases concerning the possible application of Article 101. A notable example is *British Airways, American Airlines and Iberia*[147] where the Commission accepted commitments, in particular to make landing and take-off slots available at Heathrow, Gatwick and JFK-New York airports, in order to facilitate entry and/or expansion by competitors on various aviation routes from and to the US.

Article 9 decisions lead to the Commission closing the case, without any finding that Article 101 (or Article 102) has been infringed, and as such are conceptually different from individual exemption decisions of the kind that used to be adopted under Regulation 17: under that Regulation the Commission would find that Article 101(1) was inapplicable because Article 101(3) was satisfied. Nevertheless there is a certain resemblance between an Article 9 decision, where the parties formally commit to change their behaviour and could be punished if they were to deviate from that commitment, and an individual exemption under the old system granted subject to conditions and obligations. Another important Article 9 commitment decisions was *Visa Europe*[148].

(D) Notification and individual exemptions under domestic law

Regulation 1/2003 does not *require* Member States to abolish systems of notification for exemption under *domestic* law; however it would seem in principle to be undesirable to maintain a domestic system of notification following the reforms at EU level. The provisions in the UK Competition Act 1998 on notification and individual exemption were repealed by the Competition Act 1998 and Other Enactments (Amendment) Regulations 2004[149]; and paragraph 36 of the Staff Working Paper accompanying the Commission's *Report on the functioning of Regulation 1/2003*[150] stated that more than 20 Member States now operate without a system of notification.

4. Block Exemptions[151]

(A) Role of block exemptions

Article 101(3) foreshadowed the advent of block exemptions by providing that the prohibition in Article 101(1) could be declared inapplicable both in relation to agreements and to *categories* of agreements; in other words the Treaty itself envisaged the generic authorisation of agreements as well as pursuant to individual assessment. Most block exemptions are adopted by the Commission, acting under powers conferred upon it by regulations of the Council[152].

---

[146] On findings of inapplicability and informal guidance see ch 7, 'Article 10: finding of inapplicability' and 'Informal guidance', p 261; in the UK the OFT has issued an Opinion in relation to the distribution of newspapers and magazines, and it has also introduced a practice of providing 'short-form Opinions': see ch 10, 'Opinions and Informal Advice', pp 403–404.

[147] Commission decision of 14 July 2010.

[148] See ch 7, 'Article 9: commitments', pp 255–261.

[149] SI 2004/1261; see ch 10, 'Opinions and Informal Advice', pp 403–404.

[150] See ch 4 n 143 above.

[151] The terms 'bloc' and 'group' exemptions are also used: the expression 'block exemption' is used here as it is the most common one, and the one normally used by the Commission.

[152] See '*Vires* and block exemptions currently in force', pp 169–171 below. There have been two exceptions to this, where the Council itself granted the block exemption: the block exemption for certain agreements in the road and inland waterway sectors was originally provided by Article 4 of Council Regulation 1017/68, OJ [1968] L 175/1, and is now to be found in Article 3 of Council Regulation 169/2009; and block exemption

Agreements within the terms of a block exemption have never needed, and do not need to be, notified to the Commission: they are valid without specific authorisation. The block exemptions therefore provide desirable legal certainty for firms and their professional advisers. In practice there is much to be said for drafting, for example, a vertical agreement or a transfer of technology licence so that it satisfies the terms of the relevant block exemption as this provides a 'safe harbour' for it; if an agreement satisfies a block exemption, there may be little point is determining whether it infringes Article 101(1) in the first place[153]. In the days of notification for individual exemption the block exemptions were also important from the Commission's point of view since, without them, there would have been hundreds, if not thousands, of notifications for individual exemption[154].

As paragraph 2 of the Commission's *Article [101(3)] Guidelines* points out, the system of block exemptions remains in effect, notwithstanding the abolition of individual exemptions as a result of Regulation 1/2003. Paragraph 2 of the *Guidelines* also points out that an agreement that is covered by a block exemption cannot be declared invalid by a national court. Article 29 of that Regulation provides the Commission and NCAs, in certain circumstances, with a power to withdraw the benefit of a block exemption in an individual case[155]. However paragraph 31 of the *Guidelines* explains that a national court cannot withdraw the benefit of a block exemption.

(B) **Vires and block exemptions currently in force**

The Commission requires authority from the Council to issue block exemptions[156]. The Council has published a number of empowering Regulations; these are listed below, along with the Commission Regulations currently in force (if any) under each Council Regulation.

(i) **Council Regulation 19/65**

Regulation 19/65[157], as amended by Regulation 1215/99[158], authorises the Commission to grant block exemption to vertical agreements and to bilateral licences of intellectual property rights. The following Commission Regulations are in force under Council Regulation 19/65:

- Regulation 772/2004 on technology transfer agreements[159]; Regulation 772/2004 is discussed in chapter 19[160]

- Regulation 330/2010 on vertical agreements[161]; Regulation 330/2010 is discussed in chapter 16[162]

---

for various agreements in the containerised shipping segment of the maritime transport sector was granted by Articles 3 to 6 of Council Regulation 4056/86, OJ [1986] L 378/1: this block exemption was repealed with effect from October 2008 by Regulation 1419/2006, OJ [2006] L 269/1.

[153] See Case C-260/07 *Pedro IV Servicios SL v Total España SA* [2009] ECR I-2247, [2009] 5 CMLR 1291, para 36.

[154] Indeed the adoption of block exemptions was a device used by the Commission to overcome the flood of notifications that it received pursuant to the notification provisions of Regulation 17 of 1962: for discussion see Goyder and Albors *Goyder's EC Competition Law* (Oxford University Press, 5th ed, 2009), pp 59–60.

[155] See 'The format of block exemptions', pp 171–172 below.

[156] The Council has power to confer such *vires* by virtue of Article 103(2)(b) TFEU.

[157] JO [1965] p 533, OJ [1965–66] p 35.   [158] OJ [1999] L 148/1.

[159] OJ [2004] L 123/11; this Regulation replaced Regulation 240/96, OJ [1996] L 31/2.

[160] See ch 19, 'Transfer Technology Agreements: Regulation 772/2004', pp 781–791.

[161] OJ [2010] L 102/1; this Regulation replaced Regulation 2790/99, OJ [1999] L 336/21.

[162] See ch 16, 'Vertical Agreements: Regulation 330/2010', pp 649–672.

- Regulation 461/2010[163] on vertical agreements in the motor vehicle sector; Regulation 461/2010 is discussed in chapter 16[164].

(ii) Council Regulation 2821/71

Regulation 2821/71[165] authorises the Commission to grant block exemption in respect of standardisation agreements, research and development agreements and specialisation agreements. The following Commission Regulations are in force under Council Regulation 2821/71:

- Regulation 1217/2010[166] on research and development agreements; Regulation 1217/2010 is discussed in chapter 15[167]

- Regulation 1218/2010[168] on specialisation agreements; Regulation 1218/2010 is discussed in chapter 15[169].

(iii) Council Regulation 1534/91

Regulation 1534/91[170] authorises the Commission to grant block exemption in the insurance sector. In March 2010 the Commission adopted Regulation 267/2010[171], replacing Regulation 358/2003[172], under the powers conferred upon it by Regulation 1534/91. Regulation 267/2010 is discussed in chapter 15[173].

(iv) Council Regulation 169/2009

Council Regulation 169/2009[174] itself provides block exemption for certain agreements between small and medium-sized undertakings in the road and inland waterway sectors[175]. There are no Commission Regulations granting block exemption under Regulation 169/2009.

(v) Council Regulation 246/2009

Council Regulation 246/2009[176] authorises the Commission to provide block exemption to consortia between liner shipping companies. In September 2009 the Commission adopted Regulation 906/2009[177], under the powers conferred upon it by Regulation 246/2009.

(vi) Council Regulation 487/2009

Regulation 487/2009[178] authorises the Commission to grant block exemptions for certain agreements in the air transport sector. There are no Commission Regulations currently in force under Regulation 487/2009[179].

---

[163] OJ [2010] L 129/52; Regulation 461/2010 replaced Regulation 1400/2002, OJ [2002] L 203/30.

[164] See ch 16, 'Regulation 461/2010 on Motor Vehicle Distribution', pp 674–676.

[165] JO [1971] L 285/46, OJ [1971] p 1032.

[166] OJ [2010] L 335/36; this Regulation replaced Regulation 2659/2000, OJ [2000] L 304/7.

[167] See ch 15, 'The block exemption for research and development agreements: Regulation 1217/2010', pp 595–599.

[168] OJ [2010] L 335/43; this Regulation replaced Regulation 2658/2000, OJ [2000] L 304/3.

[169] See ch 15, 'The block exemption for specialisation agreements: Regulation 1218/2010', pp 601–603.

[170] OJ [1991] L 143/1.   [171] OJ [2010] L 83/1.   [172] OJ [2003] L 53/8, [2003] 4 CMLR 734.

[173] See ch 15, 'Insurance sector', pp 220–221.

[174] OJ [2009] L 61/1; this Regulation replaced Council Regulation 1017/68, OJ [1968] L 175/1.

[175] See Article 3.

[176] OJ [2009] L 79/1; this Regulation replaced Regulation 479/92, OJ [1992] L 55/3.

[177] OJ [2009] L 256/31; this Regulation replaced Regulation 823/2000, OJ [2000] L 100/24; on Regulation 906/2009 see Prisker 'Commission adopts new block exemption regulation for liner shipping consortia' (2010) 1 *Competition Policy Newsletter* 8.

[178] OJ [2009] L 148/1; this Regulation replaced Regulation 3976/87, OJ [1987] L 374/9.

[179] See ch 23, 'Air transport', pp 974–977.

(C) **The format of block exemptions**

The typical format of block exemptions is that they begin with a series of recitals which explain the policy of the Commission in adopting the regulation in question; these recitals may themselves be of legal significance, as they may be referred to for the purpose of construing the substantive provisions of the regulation itself where there are problems of interpretation. Each regulation will then confer block exemption upon a particular category of agreements: for example Article 2 of Regulation 330/2010 block exempts vertical agreements, as defined in Article 1(1)(a) thereof. The older block exemptions were very specific as to the clauses that could benefit from block exemption: only those set out in the so-called 'white list' would do so. This was considered by many critics to be too prescriptive and formalistic, and the current block exemptions do not contain white lists. They do, however, contain black lists (as did all earlier regulations), setting out provisions that must not be included if an agreement is to enjoy block exemption.

Most block exemptions have market share thresholds. For example Article 3 of Regulation 330/2010 provides that an agreement will not qualify for block exemption where the supplier's or the buyer's market share exceeds 30 per cent; however where the parties' market shares exceed this threshold, an agreement may still be able to satisfy the conditions of Article 101(3) when assessed individually. Article 4 of the Regulation for research and development agreements has one of 25 per cent and Article 3 of the Regulation for specialisation agreements one of 20 per cent. Article 3 of the Regulation for technology transfer agreements has a 20 per cent cap for agreements between competitors and a 30 per cent cap for those between non-competitors.

Article 29(1) of Regulation 1/2003 confers power on the Commission to withdraw the benefit of a block exemption where it finds, in a particular case, that an agreement covered by a block exemption regulation has certain effects that are incompatible with Article 101(3). Block exemption has been withdrawn from an agreement on only one occasion, in *Langnese-Iglo GmbH v Commission*[180]; the Commission's decision to do so was upheld on appeal by the General Court[181].

Article 29(2) of Regulation 1/2003 gives to each NCA a power to withdraw the benefit of a block exemption from agreements which have effects incompatible with the conditions of Article 101(3) within its territory or a part thereof, where that territory has all the characteristics of a distinct geographical market. Paragraph 36 of the *Article [101(3)] Guidelines* explains that in such a situation the Member State must demonstrate both that the agreement infringes Article 101(1) and that it does not fulfil the conditions of Article 101(3). Withdrawal of the benefit of a block exemption applies only from the date of the decision.

Article 6 of Regulation 330/2010 gives power to the Commission, by regulation, to withdraw the benefit of the block exemption from an entire sector, where parallel networks of similar vertical restraints cover more than 50 per cent of a relevant market; Article 7 of Regulation 772/2004 contains a similar provision. These provisions have yet to be used.

(D) **Expiry of block exemptions**

Each block exemption regulation contains an expiry date. For example, Regulation 330/2010 will expire on 31 May 2022. This means that a vertical agreement that will endure

---

[180] OJ [1993] L 183/19, [1994] 4 CMLR 51.
[181] Case T-7/93 [1995] ECR II-1533, [1995] 5 CMLR 602.

beyond that date cannot be said, with certainty, to be exempt from 1 June 2022 onwards. Clearly this may present the parties with difficulty. The Commission is well aware of the need for legal certainty and so, if it subsequently adopts a new regulation, it will normally include transitional provisions for agreements already in force. Obviously it is necessary to examine the provisions of each particular regulation to find out what the position is on transition. It is also possible that, even if an agreement does not satisfy the terms of a new block exemption that replaces an old one, the agreement may either fall outside Article 101(1) or satisfy Article 101(3) on an individual basis.

Typically the Commission reviews and consults on the functioning of a block exemption regulation which is about to expire. When so doing the Commission goes back to 'first principles' and will ask whether a block exemption is necessary and, if it is, on what terms it should be renewed. There is no presumption in favour of renewing a block exemption. The Commission will consider possible alternatives to renewal, including the publication of guidelines; the provision of informal guidance[182]; and/or the adoption of Commission decisions pursuant to Article 9 or Article 10 of Regulation 1/2003[183]. The Commission decided not to renew the block exemptions for certain agreements in the insurance, maritime and motor vehicle sectors in the light of changed market conditions, considering that it would be more appropriate that they be subject to 'self-assessment'. At the same time the Commission has published sector-specific guidance on certain agreements in each of these sectors[184]. The block exemptions on vertical agreements and horizontal cooperation agreements were found to have worked well in practice and should be retained; however they were both updated to take account of recent market developments, such as, in the case of the block exemption for vertical agreements, the evolution of sales via the Internet[185].

---

[182]   See ch 7, 'Informal guidance', pp 261–262.

[183]   See ch 7, 'Article 9: commitments', pp 255–261.

[184]   *Guidelines on the application of Article [101 TFEU] to maritime transport services* OJ [2008] C 245/2; *Explanatory Communication on the application of Article 101(3) to certain agreements in the insurance sector* OJ [2010] C 82/20; *Supplementary guidelines on vertical restraints in agreements for the sale and repair of motor vehicles and for the distribution of spare parts for motor vehicles* OJ [2010] C 138/16.

[185]   See ch 16, 'Article 4(b): territorial and customer restrictions', pp 665–668.

5

Article 102[1]

1. Introduction

Article 102 TFEU is an important companion of Article 101. Whereas Article 101 is concerned with agreements, decisions and concerted practices which are harmful to competition, Article 102 is directed towards the unilateral conduct of dominant firms which act in an abusive manner. Article 102 provides as follows:

> Any abuse by one or more undertakings of a dominant position within the internal market or in a substantial part of it shall be prohibited as incompatible with the internal market in so far as it may affect trade between Member States. Such abuse may, in particular, consist in:
>
> (a) directly or indirectly imposing unfair purchase or selling prices or unfair trading conditions;
>
> (b) limiting production, markets or technical development to the prejudice of consumers;

---

[1] For further reading on Article 102 readers are referred to O'Donoghue and Padilla *The Law and Economics of Article 82* (Hart Publishing, 2006); *European Competition Law Annual: What is an Abuse of a Dominant Position?* (Hart Publishing, 2006, eds Ehlermann and Atanasiu); Faull and Nikpay *The EC Law of Competition* (Oxford University Press, 2nd ed, 2007), ch 4; Bellamy and Child *European Community Law of Competition* (Oxford University Press, 6th ed, 2008, eds Roth and Rose), ch 10; *Article 82 EC: Reflections on Its Recent Evolution* (Hart Publishing, 2009, ed Ezrachi); Rousseva *Rethinking Exclusionary Abuses in EU Competition Law* (Hart Publishing, 2010); Nazzini *The Foundations of European Union Competition Law: Objectives and Principles of Article 102* (Oxford University Press, 2011); Niels, Jenkins and Kavanagh *Economics for Competition Lawyers* (Oxford University Press, 2011), ch 4; see also *Dominance: the regulation of dominant firm conduct in 35 jurisdictions worldwide* (Global Competition Review, 2011, eds Janssens and Wessely).

(c) applying dissimilar conditions to equivalent transactions with other trading parties, thereby placing them at a competitive disadvantage;

(d) making the conclusion of contracts subject to acceptance by the other parties of supplementary obligations which, by their nature or according to commercial usage, have no connection with the subject of such contracts.

The purpose of this chapter is to describe the main features of Article 102. Section 2 introduces the Commission's *Guidance on the Commission's enforcement priorities in applying Article [102 TFEU] to abusive exclusionary conduct by dominant undertakings* ('the *Guidance on Article 102 Enforcement Priorities*' or 'the *Guidance*')[2], an important document that will be referred to at several points in the text that follows and in later chapters of this book. Section 3 briefly discusses the meaning of undertaking and section 4 examines the requirement of an effect on trade between Member States: concepts that have already been discussed in the context of Article 101. Section 5 considers what is meant by a dominant position under Article 102. Section 6 looks at the requirement that any dominant position should be held in a substantial part of the internal market. Section 7 makes the point that quite small firms might find themselves the subject of an Article 102 investigation; not least because of the possibility that relevant markets might be narrowly defined. Section 8 looks at the central – and most complex – issue in this chapter, the meaning of abuse: more detailed analysis of individual abusive practices will be found in later chapters of this book, in particular chapters 17, 18 and 19, which examine, first, non-pricing abuses, then pricing abuses, and finally abuses that can arise in relation to the exercise, or sometimes the non-exercise, of intellectual property rights. Section 9 considers defences to allegations of abuse, and section 10 briefly considers the consequences of infringing Article 102.

2. The Commission's *Guidance on Article 102 Enforcement Priorities*

(A) Introduction

Many of the most controversial competition law decisions of the Commission have been taken under Article 102, the most notable being the finding in 2004 of two abuses on the part of Microsoft, a refusal to supply interoperability information to competitors and the tying of a media player with its operating software, for which Microsoft was fined €497.2 million[3]. Another controversial decision involved the imposition by the Commission in 2009 of a fine of €1.06 billion on Intel for various exclusionary practices including the offering of loyalty rebates to customers who purchased all or most of their microprocessor chips from that undertaking; this decision is currently on appeal to the General Court[4].

---

[2] OJ [2009] C 45/7.

[3] *Microsoft* Commission decision of 24 March 2004, upheld on appeal Case T-201/04 *Microsoft Corpn v Commission* [2007] ECR II-3601, [2007] 5 CMLR 846; the *Microsoft* decision is discussed at various places in this book: see in particular ch 17, '*Microsoft*', pp 693–694 on the tying abuse and ch 19, 'The *Microsoft* case', pp 800–802 on the refusal to provide interoperability information; for further reading on the *Microsoft* case see Beckner and Gustafson *Trial and Error: United States v. Microsoft* (Citizens for a Sound Economy Foundation, 2nd ed, 2002); McKenzie *Trust on Trial: How the Microsoft case is reframing the rules of competition* (Perseus Publishing, 2000); *Microsoft on Trial: Legal and Economic Analysis of a Transatlantic Antitrust Case* (Edward Elgar Publishing, 2010, ed Luca Rubini).

[4] *Intel* Commission decision of 13 May 2009, on appeal Case T-286/09 *Intel v Commission*, not yet decided; the decision is discussed in ch 18, 'The *Intel* case', pp 732.

A frequent complaint against the Commission has been that it tends, when applying Article 102 in cases such as *Microsoft* and *Intel*, not to concern itself with the maintenance of the competitive process but, instead, with the protection of competitors, a quite different matter. To put the point another way, in any competition, whether economic, sporting or of some other kind, the most efficient or the fittest person will win: this is an inevitable part of the competitive process. This would suggest that, if a firm ends up as a monopolist simply by virtue of its superior efficiency, this should be applauded, or at the very least not be condemned. A more specific criticism of the Commission (and of the EU Courts) has been that they adopt a formalistic (as opposed to an economics-based) approach to the application of Article 102 and that as a consequence business practices of dominant firms have been condemned that did not have, or could not have, any harmful effect on consumer welfare; and which, indeed, may have been pro-competitive. Clearly it would be a strange paradox if it were to transpire that the application of competition law resulted in the condemnation of competitive behaviour that benefits consumers.

(B) **DG COMP's Discussion Paper on exclusionary abuses**

Aware of these concerns, in 2004 the Commission launched a review of the law and practice of Article 102 as it applied to exclusionary (as opposed to exploitative) abuses (this distinction is discussed later in this chapter[5]), leading to the publication, in December 2005, of a *Discussion Paper on the application of Article [102] of the Treaty to exclusionary abuses*[6]. This was a working paper produced by the staff of DG COMP: it was **not** an official document of the Commission itself, nor was it a set of draft guidelines on the application of Article 102, although many commentators erroneously treated it as such. The *Discussion Paper* led to feverish debate as to the proper application of Article 102, in which a broad spectrum of views was expressed, ranging from a staunch defence of the status quo, on the one hand, to demands, on the other, for a radical reorientation of the law of Article 102 that would leave dominant firms substantially freer from the risk of surveillance by competition authorities and hostile litigation in domestic courts. Between these extremes there was a fair degree of consensus that Article 102 ought not to be applied simply to protect competitors as such; that a dominant firm that is able to defeat its rivals as a result of its greater efficiency ought not to be condemned as acting abusively; that the economics of abuse are sufficiently complex that this is not an area in which formalistic, or '*per se*', rules are appropriate; and that (to put the point another way) behaviour should be condemned as abusively exclusionary under Article 102 only where it could be demonstrated that the conduct in question has had, or was likely to have, a seriously anti-competitive effect on the market.

However, even if there was some consensus in favour of a 'more economic approach' or an 'effects-based approach' to the application of Article 102 to exclusionary abuses, this still left the Commission with a formidable problem of how to 'operationalise' such a consensus: how could the principle of an effects-based approach to Article 102 be converted into administrable rules, capable of being applied by competition authorities, courts, lawyers and economists and their business clients? The task was not made easier by the fact that it was clear that there were disagreements as to the best way forward at several levels: within the Commission; between Member States and different competition authorities; at the private bar; and among undertakings, some of which considered themselves to be the victims of outrageously abusive behaviour, on the one hand, and others of which believed that they were the subject of outrageous accusations of abuse,

---

[5] See 'Exploitative, exclusionary and single market abuses', pp 201–202 below.
[6] Available at www.ec.europa.eu/competition/antitrust/art82/index.html.

on the other. A further difficulty lay in the fact that, even if the Commission were to consider that the law of Article 102 needed to change, this was not within its prerogative: the
EU Courts determine what is and what is not an abuse of a dominant position, and the
Commission cannot contradict established jurisprudence (although it can hope to shape
its future development, a quite different matter).

(C) Adoption of the Commission's *Guidance on Article 102 Enforcement Priorities*

The outcome of this process was that, in February 2009, the Commission published its
Guidance on Article 102 Enforcement Priorities. It is important to understand that this
document is **not** a set of guidelines on the law of Article 102; the document is what it says it
is: guidance on the Commission's enforcement priorities. The *Guidance* does not purport
to state the law of exclusionary abuse under Article 102: for that, interested stakeholders
must consult the jurisprudence of the EU Courts. Some commentators consider that this
gives rise to legal uncertainty, the Commission apparently taking a more lenient (less
interventionist) approach to the application of Article 102 to exclusionary abuses than
the case law: an example of this is the Court of Justice's judgment in *Konkurrensverket v
TeliaSonera Sverige AB*[7], where its interpretation of the abuse of margin squeeze is clearly
stricter than the Commission's approach in paragraph 80 of the *Guidance*[8]. It has even
been suggested that this dissonance between the jurisprudence of the EU Courts and the
Guidance on Article 102 Enforcement Priorities is so serious that the Commission should
withdraw it[9]; a less extreme view is that the Commission's *Guidance* fails to establish priorities, and may leave undertakings more confused about the law in this area than they
were before[10].

To the authors of this book these criticisms are unconvincing. To repeat: the *Guidance*
is not a set of guidelines that slavishly describe the existing law. Rather it explains why
the Commission, with its finite resources, would have a greater interest in prosecuting
some cases than others; in particular it explains that it is the likelihood that particular
conduct could cause seriously anti-competitive foreclosure effects on markets, thereby,
ultimately, causing harm to consumers, that legitimates intervention by the Commission[11].

---

[7] Case C-52/09 [2011] ECR I-000, [2011] 4 CMLR 982.

[8] For discussion see ch 18, 'The Commission's decisional practice', p 757.

[9] See Gormsen 'Why the European Commission's enforcement priorities on Article 82 EC should be
withdrawn' (2010) 31(2) ECLR 45.

[10] See Akman 'The European Commission's Guidance on Article 102 TFEU: From *Inferno* to *Paradiso*?'
(2010) 73(4) Modern Law Review 605; for further commentary on the debate leading to the *Guidance* and
the *Guidance* itself see *European Competition Law Annual 2007: A Reformed Approach to Article 82 EC*
(Hart Publishing, 2008, eds Ehlermann and Marquis); Ezrachi 'The European Commission Guidance on
Article 82 EC – The Way in Which Institutional Realities Limit the Potential for Reform' [2009] Oxford
Legal Research Paper Series (No 27/2009), available at www.ssrn.com; Petit 'From Formalism to Effects? –
The Commission's Communication on Enforcement Priorities in Applying Article 82 EC' (2009) 32 World
Competition 485; Kellerbauer 'The Commission's New Enforcement Priorities in Applying Article 82 EC to
Dominant Companies' Exclusionary Conduct: A Shift Towards a More Economic Approach?' (2010) 31(5)
ECLR 175 (the author is a member of the Commission's Legal Service); Geradin 'Is the Guidance Paper on
the Commission's Enforcement Priorities in Applying Article 102 TFEU to Abusive Exclusionary Conduct
Useful?', available at www.ssrn.com; *European Competition Law: The Impact of the Commission's Guidance
on Article 102* (Edward Elgar, 2011, ed Pace).

[11] An interesting question is what the legal position would be if the Commission were to refuse to con-
sider a complaint about conduct that clearly infringes Article 102 according to the jurisprudence of the EU
Courts on the basis that it does not comply with the *Guidance on Article 102 Enforcement Priorities*: see Wils
'Discretion and Prioritisation in Public Antitrust Enforcement' (2011) 34(3) World Competition 353.

The *Guidance* does not 'rewrite' the law of Article 102; it does not and cannot bind the EU Courts, nor the domestic courts of the Member States. On the other hand it is not unreasonable to suppose that competition authorities and courts, faced with competing arguments as to the proper scope of Article 102, will, at the least, be aware of the Commission's approach to certain business behaviour – for example pricing below cost, refusals to supply, the offering of discounts and rebates – and that, over a period of time, the *Guidance* will have an influence on the future orientation of Article 102 in its application to exclusionary behaviour. In his Opinion in *TeliaSonera*[12] Advocate General Mazák said that the *Guidance* could not bind the Court, but that it did provide a 'useful point of reference'[13]. The relationship of the *Guidance* to the existing law, and its potential for influencing future enforcement of the law, will be discussed throughout this book[14].

Whatever the merits of the criticism that has surrounded Article 102 over the years, it is undoubtedly the case that a dominant firm (or one that fears that it might be characterised as dominant) must behave on the market with great caution. A transgression of Article 102 may have serious consequences. Not only can the Commission (or a national competition authority) impose a very large fine, as occurred in *Microsoft* and *Intel*; an injured third party may also bring an action for an injunction and/or damages in a national court[15]. Furthermore the Commission has explicit power to impose structural remedies, albeit subject to limitations, as a result of Article 7 of Regulation 1/2003; it has yet to impose such a remedy in an infringement decision, although several cases have been closed as a result of undertakings offering structural commitments under Article 9 of Regulation 1/2003[16].

3. Undertakings

The term 'undertaking' has the same meaning in Article 102 as in Article 101, and reference should be made to the relevant section of chapter 3[17]. It may be worth pointing out in passing that several of the cases on the meaning of an undertaking have arisen in the context of Article 102, for example where complaints were made to the Commission about the monopsonistic power of the Spanish Health Service[18] or the standard-setting power of Eurocontrol[19]: it was held that neither of those entities was acting as an undertaking, with the consequence that the competition rules did not apply to them.

---

[12] See ch 5 n 7 above.

[13] In Case T-201/11 *Si.mobil v Commission*, not yet decided, an applicant to the General Court is complaining that the Commission failed to apply its *Guidance* when rejecting a complaint of abuse of dominance contrary to Article 102.

[14] See in particular 'Recent case law and decisions do require effects analysis', pp 200–201 below and chs 17 and 18 generally.

[15] It was reported in the media that out-of-court settlements were reached between Microsoft and various of the complainants against it for the payment of damages: a report in the *Financial Times* of October 2005 suggested that Microsoft had paid a total of $3.73 billion; it was similarly reported that Intel had agreed to pay damages to AMD, the complainant in that case, amounting to $ 1.25 billion: see *Financial Times*, 13 November 2009.

[16] See ch 7, 'Article 9: commitments', pp 255–261.

[17] See ch 3, 'Undertakings and Associations of Undertakings', pp 83–91.

[18] Case T-319/99 *FENIN v Commission* [2003] ECR II-357, [2003] 5 CMLR 34, upheld on appeal to the Court of Justice Case C-205/03 P *FENIN v Commission* [2006] ECR I-6295, [2006] 5 CMLR 559.

[19] Case T-155/04 *SELEX Sistemi Integrati v Commission* [2006] ECR II-4797, [2007] 4 CMLR 372, upheld on appeal to the Court of Justice Case C-113/07 P *SELEX Sistemi Integrati v Commission* [2009] ECR I-2207, [2009] 4 CMLR 1083.

The issue of the application of the competition rules to public undertakings or to undertakings entrusted with exclusive or special rights will be discussed in chapter 6[20]; a few particular points about Article 102 and the public sector should, however, be noted here. First, the fact that an undertaking has a monopoly conferred upon it by statute does not, in itself, remove it from the ambit of Article 102[21]. Secondly, Member States have a duty under Article 4(3) TEU not to do anything 'which could jeopardise the attainment of the Union's objectives', one of which is expressed in Protocol 27 to the Treaties to be the institution of a system ensuring that competition is not distorted[22]. This means that a Member State cannot confer immunity on undertakings from Article 102, except to the limited extent provided for in Article 106(2)[23]. Thirdly, the provisions in Article 106(2) permitting derogation from the competition rules to the extent that their application would 'obstruct the performance, in law or in fact, of the particular tasks assigned to them' have consistently been interpreted narrowly by both the Commission and the EU Courts[24]. Lastly, it is important in this context to bear in mind Article 37 TFEU, the function of which is to prevent Member States from discriminating in favour of their own state monopolies of a commercial character. This provides the Commission with a useful alternative weapon for dealing with some monopolies in the public sector[25].

4. **The Effect on Inter-State Trade**

The meaning of this phrase was analysed in chapter 3, to which reference should be made[26]. For the purpose of Article 102 particular attention should be paid to the Court of Justice's judgment in *Commercial Solvents v Commission*[27] in which it held that the requirement of an effect on trade between Member States would be satisfied where conduct brought about an alteration in the structure of competition in the common market[28]. This test, which has been applied by both the EU Courts and the Commission on subsequent occasions[29], is of particular importance in Article 102 cases: Article 102 can be applied only where

---

[20] See ch 6, 'Article 106 TFEU – compliance with the Treaties', pp 222–244.

[21] Case 311/84 *Centre Belge d'Etudes de Marché Télémarketing v CLT* [1985] ECR 3261, [1986] 2 CMLR 558, para 16; see also Case 26/75 *General Motors v Commission* [1975] ECR 1367, [1976] 1 CMLR 95; Case 41/83 *Italy v Commission* [1985] ECR 873, [1985] 2 CMLR 368; Case 226/84 *British Leyland v Commission* [1986] ECR 3263, [1987] 1 CMLR 185; Case C-41/90 *Höfner v Macrotron* [1991] ECR I–1979, [1993] 4 CMLR 306, para 28; Case C-18/93 *Corsica Ferries* [1994] ECR I–1783, para 43; Case C-242/95 *GT-Link v De Danske Statsbaner (DSB)* [1997] ECR I-4349, [1997] 5 CMLR 601, para 35; see also the Commission's decision in *French-West African Shipowners' Committees* OJ [1992] L 134/1, [1993] 5 CMLR 446, para 64.

[22] See eg Case C-260/89 *Elliniki Radiophonia Tiléorassi-Anonimi Etairia (ERT) v Dimotiki Etairia Pliroforissis (DEP)* [1991] ECR I-2925, [1994] 4 CMLR 540, para 27; note also that, under Article 119(1) TFEU, Member States (and the EU) are required to observe the principle of an 'open market economy with free competition'.

[23] Case 13/77 *INNO v ATAB* [1977] ECR 2115, [1978] 1 CMLR 283; see ch 6, 'Article 4(3) TEU – duty of sincere cooperation', pp 216–222.

[24] See ch 6, 'Article 106(2)', pp 235–242.

[25] See ch 6, 'Article 37 TFEU – state monopolies of a commercial character', pp 245–246.

[26] See ch 3, 'The Effect on Trade between Member States', pp 144–149.

[27] Cases 6/73 and 7/73 [1974] ECR 223, [1974] 1 CMLR 309, para 33; see also Cases T-24/93 etc *Compagnie Maritime Belge v Commission* [1996] ECR II-1201, [1997] 4 CMLR 273, para 203.

[28] The Commission refers to the 'competitive structure' test at para 20 of its *Guidelines on the effect on trade concept contained in Articles [101] and [102] of the Treaty* OJ [2004] C 101/81.

[29] See eg Case 27/76 *United Brands v Commission* [1978] ECR 207, [1978] 1 CMLR 429; *Tetra Pak 1 (BTG Licence)* OJ [1988] L 272/27, [1988] 4 CMLR 881, para 48; *Napier Brown – British Sugar* OJ [1988] L 284/41, [1990] 4 CMLR 196, paras 77–80; *London European – Sabena* OJ [1988] L 317/47, [1989] 4 CMLR 662, para 33.

there is already a dominant position – that is to say substantial market power – and it is unsurprising that the Commission will be concerned with the structure of the market in such cases. In the *Soda-ash* decisions under Article 102[30] the Commission held that rebates offered by ICI and Solvay in their respective markets had the effect of reinforcing the structural rigidity of the EU market as a whole and its division along national lines. What is of interest about these decisions is that it was US exporters who were excluded from the EU market, but the Commission still held that there was an effect on inter-state trade: imports would have helped to undermine the dominant positions of ICI and Solvay in their respective markets.

The Commission's *Guidelines on the effect on trade concept contained in Articles [101] and [102] of the Treaty*[31] contain paragraphs that give specific consideration to the circumstances in which abusive behaviour – for example exploitative abuses that harm downstream trading partners and exclusionary abuses that harm competitors – might have an effect on trade between Member States[32].

Under Regulation 1/2003[33] national courts and national competition authorities have an obligation to apply Article 102 where an abuse of a dominant position has an effect on trade between Member States[34]. This, however, does not preclude them from adopting or applying on their own territories stricter national laws which prohibit or sanction unilateral conduct engaged in by undertakings[35]; and the obligation is without prejudice to the application of provisions of national law that predominantly pursue an objective different from those pursued by Articles 101 and 102[36].

5. Dominant Position

Article 102 applies only where one undertaking has a 'dominant position' or where two or more undertakings are 'collectively dominant'[37]. The Court of Justice in *United Brands v Commission*[38] laid down the following test of what is meant by a dominant position:

> 65 The dominant position thus referred to by Article [102] relates to a position of economic strength enjoyed by an undertaking which enables it to prevent effective competition being maintained on the relevant market by affording it the power to behave to

---

[30] *Soda-ash/Solvay* OJ [1991] L 152/21 and *Soda-ash/ICI* OJ [1991] L 152/1; these decisions were annulled on procedural grounds by the General Court: Cases T-30/91 etc *Solvay SA v Commission* [1995] ECR II-1775, [1996] 5 CMLR 57; the Commission's appeal to the Court of Justice failed, Cases C-286/95 P etc [2000] ECR I-2341, [2000] 5 CMLR 413 and 454; the Commission readopted the decisions in December 2000: OJ [2003] L 10/1, which were substantially upheld in Case T-57/01 *Solvay SA v Commission* [2009] ECR II-4621, [2011] 4 CMLR 9, and Case T-66/01 *Imperial Chemical Industries Ltd v Commission* [2010] ECR II-000, [2011] 4 CMLR 162, the second *Solvay* judgment is now on appeal to the Court of Justice, Case C-109/10 P *Solvay SA v Commission*, not yet decided.

[31] OJ [2004] C 101/81.

[32] Ibid, paras 73–76 (dealing with abuses covering several Member States); paras 93–96 (abuses covering a single Member State); paras 97–99 (abuses covering part only of a Member State); and paras 106–109 (abuses involving undertakings located in third countries).

[33] OJ [2003] L 1/1.

[34] Regulation 1/2003, Article 3(1); see ch 2, 'Obligation to apply Articles 101 and 102', pp 76–77.

[35] Regulation 1/2003, Article 3(2).   [36] Ibid, Article 3(3).

[37] The issue of whether any dominance is *collective* is discussed in ch 14 of this book, which considers in general terms the issues of oligopoly and tacit coordination between independent undertakings.

[38] Case 27/76 [1978] ECR 207, [1978] 1 CMLR 429; it has used the same formulation on several other occasions, eg in Case 85/76 *Hoffmann-La Roche v Commission* [1979] ECR 461, [1979] 3 CMLR 211, para 38.

an appreciable extent independently of its competitors, customers and ultimately of its consumers[39].

The expression 'dominant position' will not be found in textbooks on economics; economists would ask whether a firm or firms have substantial market power. Paragraph 65 of the Court's judgment in *United Brands* can be understood to equate dominance with substantial market power; the Commission does so in paragraph 10 of its *Guidance on Article 102 Enforcement Priorities* where it says that the notion of independence referred to by the Court is related to the degree of competitive constraint exerted on the undertaking under investigation. Where competitive constraints are ineffective, the undertaking in question enjoys 'substantial market power over a period of time'; in paragraph 11 of the *Guidance* the Commission considers that an undertaking has substantial market power if it is 'capable of profitably increasing prices above the competitive level for a significant period of time'[40]. The same definition of dominance is used in the ICN's *Unilateral Conduct Workbook*[41].

An important point to bear in mind about Article 102 is that, as a matter of economics, there are degrees of market power: at one end of the spectrum would be a firm with no or only imperceptible market power; at the other end a firm which is a true monopolist. Between these two extremes could be found firms with 'some', or 'appreciable', or 'significant', or 'substantial' market power. However the legal expression 'dominant position' is a binary term: either an undertaking is dominant and therefore subject to Article 102 and the 'special responsibility' that this entails; or it is not, in which case its unilateral behaviour is not subject to competition law scrutiny at all. This is why a finding of dominance is so important; and why some commentators would like there to be a fairly generous 'safe harbour' for market shares below a certain percentage[42].

A finding of dominance – whether individual or collective – involves a two-stage assessment. The first is to determine the relevant market: market definition has been discussed in detail in chapter 1, in particular the 'hypothetical monopolist' or 'SSNIP' test; the problem of the 'Cellophane Fallacy' in Article 102 cases which might lead to the inclusion of false substitutes in the market definition; and the types of evidence that may be of assistance when defining relevant product, geographical and temporal markets[43].

Having defined the market, it is necessary in an Article 102 case to determine what is meant by a dominant position. This cannot be determined purely by reference to an

---

[39] This definition does not adequately reflect (what is undoubtedly true) that Article 102 also applies to market power on the buying as well as the selling side of the market, since that was not in issue in *United Brands*; a powerful purchaser may be able to behave independently of its sellers who are not 'customers' in the normal sense of that word; for action taken against undertakings with buyer power see *Re Eurofima* [1973] CMLR D217; *Re GEMA* OJ [1971] L 134/15, [1971] CMLR D35; Case 298/83 *CICCE v Commission* [1985] ECR 1105, [1986] 1 CMLR 486; *UK Small Mines* Commission's XXIst *Report on Competition Policy* (1991), point 107; *Virgin/British Airways* OJ [2000] L 30/1, [2000] 4 CMLR 999, upheld on appeal to the General Court, Case T-219/99 *British Airways plc v Commission* [2003] ECR II-5917, [2004] 4 CMLR 1008: the Court stated specifically at para 101 of its judgment that Article 102 can apply to undertakings with a dominant position on either side of the market; see also ch 1, 'Procurement markets', p 38.

[40] The Commission goes on in this paragraph to explain that 'increase in prices' is a short-hand term which includes other ways of influencing competition to the advantage of the dominant undertaking, for example by decreasing output, innovation, variety or quality of goods or services; on the same point see ch 1, 'Market Definition and Market Power', pp 25–48.

[41] Chapter 3 of the *Workbook* on the 'assessment of dominance' is available on the ICN website at www.internationalcompetitionnetwork.org.

[42] See 'Findings of dominance below the 50 per cent threshold', p 183 below.

[43] See further ch 1, 'Market definition' and following sections, pp 27–42.

undertaking's market share. Rather it is necessary to examine three issues, as set out in paragraph 12 of the *Guidance*:

- constraints imposed by the existing supplies from, and the position on the market of, *actual competitors* (the market position of the dominant undertaking and its competitors)
- constraints imposed by the credible threat of future expansion by actual competitors or entry by *potential competitors* (expansion and entry)
- constraints imposed by the bargaining strength of the undertaking's customers (*countervailing buyer power*) (emphasis added).

Each of these three criteria has already been discussed in chapter 1[44]. Some additional commentary will be provided here based on the judgments of the EU Courts and the decisional practice of the Commission in Article 102 cases. In paragraph 11 of its *Guidance* the Commission, citing case law of the EU Courts such as *United Brands*, points out that a finding of a dominant position derives from a combination of several factors which, taken separately, are not necessarily determinative.

(A) **Actual competitors**

True monopoly is rare, except where conferred by the state. The majority of cases are therefore concerned with the problem of deciding at what point an undertaking, though not a true monopolist, has sufficient power over the market to fall within the ambit of Article 102.

(i) **Statutory monopolies**

Various cases have concerned undertakings with a statutory monopoly in the provision of goods or services[45]. The Court of Justice has rejected the argument that, because a monopoly is conferred by statute, this immunises the undertaking from Article 102[46]; where an undertaking has a statutory monopoly it must comply with Article 102, its only special privilege being that conferred by Article 106(2)[47]. A different point is that the fact that an undertaking has a dominant position as a result of rights derived from national legislation does not in itself mean that it has exclusive rights in the sense of Article 106[48].

(ii) **The relevance of market shares**

In cases where there is no statutory monopoly, market shares provide valuable information about the structure of the market and of the relative importance of the undertakings active on it; however, as the Commission says in paragraph 13 of its *Guidance on Article 102 Enforcement Priorities*, market shares are only a 'useful first indication', and an assessment of market power requires that market conditions generally should be taken into account, including the dynamics of the market, the extent to which products are differentiated and the trend or development of market shares over time.

As far as Article 102 is concerned, it is obvious that the larger the market share, the more likely a finding of dominance. A market share of 100 per cent is rare in the absence

---

[44] See ch 1, 'Market power', pp 42–45.
[45] See eg Case T-229/94 *Deutsche Bahn AG v Commission* [1997] ECR II-1689, [1998] 4 CMLR 220, para 57.
[46] See the cases cited at ch 5 n 21 above.   [47] See ch 6, 'Article 106(2)', pp 235–241.
[48] See ch 6, 'Exclusive rights', pp 224–225.

of statutory privileges, although not unheard of[49]. However some firms have been found to have very large market shares. For example in *Tetra Pak 1 (BTG Licence)*[50] Tetra Pak's market share in the market for machines capable of filling cartons by an aseptic process was 91.8 per cent; and in *BPB Industries plc*[51] BPB was found to have a market share in plasterboard of 96 per cent, although the Commission had excluded wet plastering from the market definition. In the *Microsoft* decision[52] the Commission concluded that Microsoft had over 90 per cent of the market for personal computer operating software systems and at least 60 per cent of the market for work group server operating systems[53].

(A) The Court of Justice's judgment in Hoffmann-La Roche v Commission

In *Hoffmann-La Roche v Commission*[54] the Court of Justice said:

> 41…Furthermore although the importance of the market shares may vary from one market to another the view may legitimately be taken that very large shares are in themselves, and save in exceptional circumstances, evidence of the existence of a dominant position. An undertaking which has a very large market share and holds it for some time…is by virtue of that share in a position of strength…

(B) The AKZO presumption of dominance where an undertaking has a market share of 50 per cent or more

In *AKZO v Commission*[55] the Court of Justice referred to the passage from *Hoffmann-La Roche* quoted above and continued that a market share of 50 per cent could be considered to be very large so that, in the absence of exceptional circumstances pointing the other way, an undertaking with such a market share will be presumed dominant; that undertaking will bear the evidential burden of establishing that it is not dominant. The General Court applied this test in *Hilti AG v Commission*[56]. Clearly this is a very significant rule, which means that firms are at risk of being found to be dominant where they fall considerably short of being monopolists in the strict sense of that term. Some critics of Article 102, who believe that it is applied in too intrusive a manner, would like to see the 50 per cent threshold in *AKZO* raised: perhaps to 75 per cent; the binary effect of Article 102, whereby conduct that is legal when practised by a non-dominant firm becomes illegal when the firm is dominant, would be less pronounced if the presumption of dominance was set at a higher market share threshold. However the EU Courts have shown no inclination to discard or revise the *AKZO* presumption; recent judgments of the General Court such as *France*

[49] In *GVL* OJ [1981] L 370/49, [1982] 1 CMLR 221 that body had a 100 per cent market share in the market in Germany for the management of performing artists' rights of secondary exploitation; see also *Amministratzione Autonoma del Monopoli di Stato ('AAMS')* OJ [1998] L 252/47, [1998] 5 CMLR 786, para 31, where the Commission found AAMS held a *de facto* monopoly of the Italian market for the wholesale distribution of cigarettes, upheld on appeal to the General Court Case T-139/98 *AAMS v Commission* [2001] ECR II-3413, [2002] 4 CMLR 302, para 52.

[50] OJ [1988] L 272/27, [1988] 4 CMLR 881, para 44, upheld on appeal to the General Court Case T-51/89 *Tetra Pak Rausing SA v Commission* [1990] ECR II-539, [1991] 4 CMLR 334.

[51] OJ [1989] L 10/50, [1990] 4 CMLR 464, upheld on appeal to the General Court Case T-65/89 *BPB Industries Plc and British Gypsum Ltd v Commission* [1993] ECR II-389, [1993] 5 CMLR 33 and to the Court of Justice Case C-310/93 P *BPB Industries Plc and British Gypsum Ltd v Commission* [1995] ECR I-865, [1997] 4 CMLR 238.

[52] *Microsoft* Commission decision of 24 March 2004.   [53] Ibid, paras 430–435 and 473–499.

[54] Case 85/76 [1979] ECR 461, [1979] 3 CMLR 211; the Commission specifically referred to this paragraph in *Van den Bergh Foods Ltd* OJ [1998] L 246/1, [1998] 5 CMLR 530, para 258.

[55] Case C-62/86 [1991] ECR I-3359, [1993] 5 CMLR 215, para 60.

[56] Case T-30/89 [1991] ECR II-1439, [1992] 4 CMLR 16, para 92; see similarly Cases T-191/98 etc *Atlantic Container Line v Commission* [2003] ECR II-3275, [2005] 4 CMLR 1283, para 907.

Télécom v Commission[57], *Solvay SA v Commission*[58] and *AstraZeneca AB v Commission*[59] have continued to stress that high market shares can in themselves be indicative of dominance and to cite the *AKZO* presumption of dominance; indeed in *AstraZeneca* the Court went so far as to say that the Commission could not disregard the importance to be attached to AZ's very large market share throughout the relevant period of alleged abuse[60].

Interestingly the Commission does not refer to the *AKZO* presumption in its *Guidance on Article 102 Enforcement Priorities*, perhaps suggesting that it is not keen on a legal presumption that attaches such weight to a market share figure. Instead it notes at paragraph 15 that the higher the market share, and the longer the period of time over which it is held, the more likely it is that it constitutes an important preliminary indication of the existence of a dominant position; however the Commission concludes the paragraph by saying that it would come to a final conclusion on dominance only after examining all the relevant factors that may be relevant to constraining the behaviour of the undertaking under investigation.

(C) Findings of dominance below the 50 per cent threshold

The Court of Justice held in *United Brands* that that firm, with a market share in the range of 40 per cent to 45 per cent, was dominant. In that case other factors were considered to be significant: the market share alone would not have been sufficient to sustain a finding of dominance; however the case shows that a firm supplying less than 50 per cent of the market may be held to have a dominant position. In *United Brands* the Court said that, even though there was lively competition on the market at certain periods of the year, United Brands could still be held to be dominant for the purposes of Article 102; the Commission notes this point in paragraph 10 of its *Guidance*.

The decision in *Virgin/British Airways*[61] marked the first (and only) occasion on which an undertaking with a market share of less than 40 per cent has been found by the Commission to be in a dominant position under Article 102. BA was held to be dominant in the UK market for the procurement of air travel agency services with a market share of 39.7 per cent. When the Commission's decision was challenged before the General Court the Court agreed that BA was dominant, noting that its market share was considerably larger than its rivals, and that this was reinforced by the world rank held by BA in terms of international scheduled passenger-kilometres flown, the extent of the range of its transport services and its hub network; the General Court also considered that BA was an obligatory business partner for travel agents[62]. The General Court stated specifically that the fact that BA's market share was in decline could not, in itself, constitute proof that it was not dominant[63].

Some commentators would like there to be a 'safe harbour' below which a firm could not be found to be dominant. However the case law of the EU Courts does not provide one, and the Commission is not in a position to create one in the absence of jurisprudence enabling it to do so. In paragraph 14 of its *Guidance on Article 102 Enforcement Priorities* the Commission says that dominance is 'not likely' if the undertaking's market share is below 40 per cent; however it goes on to say that there could be some cases below that figure that may deserve its attention. Clearly this falls short of a safe harbour.

---

[57] Case T-340/03 [2007] ECR II-107, [2007] 4 CMLR 919, paras 99–101.

[58] Case T-57/01 [2009] ECR II-4621, [2011] 4 CMLR 9, paras 275–305.

[59] Case T-321/05 [2010] ECR II-000, [2010] 5 CMLR 1585, paras 242–254.

[60] Ibid, para 245.

[61] OJ [2000] L 30/1.

[62] Case T-219/99 *British Airways plc v Commission* [2003] ECR II-5917, [2004] 4 CMLR 1008, paras 189–225, upheld on appeal to the Court of Justice Case C-95/04 P *British Airways plc v Commission* [2007] ECR I-2331, [2007] 4 CMLR 982.

[63] Ibid, para 224.

(B) **Potential competitors**

As was stressed in chapter 1 and earlier in this chapter, market shares do not in themselves determine whether a firm has a dominant position; in particular they cannot indicate the competitive pressure exerted by firms not yet operating on the market but with the capacity to enter it in a timely manner. Paragraphs 16 and 17 of the Commission's *Guidance on Article 102 Enforcement Priorities* explain the importance of the impact of expansion by existing competitors and entry by potential ones to any assessment of dominance. In particular paragraph 17 provides examples of various barriers, such as legal barriers; economic advantages enjoyed by the dominant undertaking; costs and network effects that impede customers from switching from one supplier to another; and the dominant firm's own conduct.

(i) **Legal barriers**

The ownership of patents, trade marks and other intellectual property rights may constitute barriers to entry, depending on their strength and duration[64], although they do not, in themselves, confer dominance. In *Tetra Pak 1 (BTG Licence)*[65] the acquisition by Tetra Pak of a company that had the benefit of an exclusive patent and know-how licence was regarded as a factor indicating dominance, as it made entry to the market more difficult for other firms that would be unable to gain access to the licensed technology. In *Hugin v Commission*[66] the Court of Justice seems to have accepted that Hugin was dominant in the market for spare parts for its cash registers because other firms could not produce spares for fear of being sued by Hugin in the UK under the Design Copyright Act 1968. Other obvious legal barriers to entry are Government licensing requirements and planning regulations, governmental control of frequencies for the transmission of radio signals[67], statutory monopoly power[68] and tariffs and non-tariff barriers.

(ii) **Economic advantages**

Various economic advantages have been considered to be barriers to entry or expansion:

- the Court of Justice considered economies of scale to be a relevant factor in *United Brands v Commission*[69], and the Commission referred to this matter specifically in *BPB Industries plc*[70]; economies of scope would no doubt be treated in the same way[71]

- the control of an essential facility could confer an economic advantage on an incumbent undertaking[72], as could preferential access to natural resources, innovation or R&D

---

[64] See eg *Eurofix-Bauco v Hilti* OJ [1988] L 65/19, [1989] 4 CMLR 677, para 66; *Magill TV Guide/ITP, BBC and RTE* OJ [1989] L 78/43, [1989] 4 CMLR 757, para 22 (copyright protection of TV listings relevant to finding of dominance), upheld on appeal to the General Court Cases T-69/89 etc *RTE v Commission* [1991] ECR II-485, [1991] 4 CMLR 586, and further on appeal to the Court of Justice Cases C-241 and C-242/91 P [1995] ECR I-743, [1995] 4 CMLR 718.

[65] OJ [1988] L 272/27, [1988] 4 CMLR 881, para 44, upheld on appeal Case T-51/89 *Tetra Pak Rausing SA v Commission* [1990] ECR II-309, [1991] 4 CMLR 334.

[66] Case 22/78 [1979] ECR 1869, [1979] 3 CMLR 345.

[67] *Decca Navigator System* OJ [1989] L 43/27, [1990] 4 CMLR 627.

[68] Case 311/84 *Centre Belge d'Etudes de Marché Télémarketing v CLT* [1985] ECR 3261, [1986] 2 CMLR 558; see Marenco 'Legal Monopolies in the case law of the Court of Justice of the European Communities' [1991] Fordham Corp L Inst (ed Hawk), pp 197–222.

[69] Case 27/76 [1978] ECR 207, [1978] 1 CMLR 429.

[70] See ch 5 n 65 above, para 116.

[71] Economies of scale and scope are discussed in ch 1, 'Economies of scale and scope and natural monopolies', pp 10–11.

[72] On essential facilities see ch 17, 'Is the product to which access is sought indispensable to someone wishing to complete in the downstream market?', pp 701–707.

- the Court of Justice has considered an undertaking's superior technology to be an indicator of dominance in several cases, including *United Brands v Commission*[73], *Hoffmann-La Roche v Commission*[74] and *Michelin v Commission*[75]

- in *Continental Can*[76] the Commission regarded that firm's access to the international capital market as significant, and this factor was stressed in *United Brands v Commission*[77]

- in *United Brands v Commission*[78] the Court of Justice described the extent to which UBC's activities were integrated – it owned banana plantations and transport boats and it marketed its bananas itself – and said that this provided that firm with commercial stability which was a significant advantage over its competitors

- in *Hoffmann-La Roche v Commission*[79] the Court of Justice pointed to Roche's highly developed sales network as a relevant factor conferring upon it commercial advantages over its rivals. The Commission has treated both vertical integration and the benefit of well-established distribution systems as a barrier to entry in several other decisions[80], since this could impede access for a would-be entrant to the market

- in *United Brands v Commission*[81] the Court of Justice considered that United Brand's advertising campaigns and brand image were significant factors indicating dominance: it had spent considerable resources establishing the Chiquita brand name which was well protected by trade marks. In its second *Michelin* decision the Commission relied upon the 'indisputable' quality and reputation of the Michelin tyre brand in its finding of dominance[82]. The Commission has often noted (in cases under the EU Merger Regulation ('the EUMR')) that advertising expenditure could make entry difficult into the market for fast-moving consumer goods such as soft drinks[83], sanitary protection[84], and toilet tissue[85].

(iii) Costs and network effects

Network effects may be a barrier to expansion or entry[86]. This was a relevant consideration in *Microsoft*[87]: the Commission said that the ubiquity of Microsoft in the personal computer operating systems market meant that nearly all commercial applications software was written first and foremost to be compatible with the Microsoft platform. This gave

---

[73] Case 27/76 [1978] ECR 207, [1978] 1 CMLR 429, paras 82–84.

[74] Case 85/76 [1979] ECR 461, [1979] 3 CMLR 211, para 48.

[75] Case 322/81 [1983] ECR 3461, [1985] 1 CMLR 282; see also *Eurofix-Bauco v Hilti* (ch 5 n 64 above), para 69 and *Tetra Pak 1 (BTG Licence)* (n 65 above), para 44; *Michelin* OJ [2002] L 143/1, [2002] 5 CMLR 388, paras 182–183.

[76] JO [1972] L 7/25, [1972] CMLR D11.

[77] Case 27/76 [1978] ECR 207, [1978] 1 CMLR 429, para 122.   [78] Ibid, paras 69–81, 85–90.

[79] Case 85/76 [1979] ECR 461, [1979] 3 CMLR 211, para 48; see similarly Case 322/81 *Michelin v Commission* [1983] ECR 3461, [1985] 1 CMLR 282, para 58.

[80] See eg *Eurofix-Bauco v Hilti* OJ [1988] L 65/19, [1989] 4 CMLR 677, para 69; *Napier Brown – British Sugar* OJ [1988] L 284/41, [1990] 4 CMLR 196, para 56; *PO-Michelin* OJ [2002] L 143/1, [2002] 5 CMLR 388, paras 191–195.

[81] Case 27/76 [1978] ECR 207, [1978] 1 CMLR 429, paras 91–94.

[82] *Michelin* OJ [2002] L 143/1, [2002] 5 CMLR 388, para 184.

[83] See eg Case M.190 *Nestlé/Perrier* OJ [1992] L 356/1, [1993] 4 CMLR M17.

[84] See eg Case M.430 *Procter & Gamble/VP Schickendanz* OJ [1994] L 352/32.

[85] See eg Case M.623 *Kimberly-Clark/Scott Paper* OJ [1996] L 183/1.

[86] On network effects see ch 1, 'Network effects and two-sided markets', pp 11–12.

[87] Commission decision of 24 March 2004.

rise to a self-reinforcing dynamic: the more users there were of the Microsoft platform, the more software was written for it, and vice versa[88].

(iv) Conduct

The Court of Justice in *United Brands v Commission*[89] agreed with the idea that the conduct of an alleged dominant firm could be taken into account in deciding whether it is dominant. This means, for example, that it might be legitimate to take into account the fact that a firm has offered discriminatory rebates to certain customers in deciding whether it is dominant: the rebates may themselves prevent competitors entering the market and so constitute a barrier to entry. In *Michelin v Commission*[90] the Commission had relied on Michelin's price discrimination as an indicator of dominance. Michelin argued before the Court of Justice that this approach was circular: the Commission was saying that because it had offered discriminatory prices, it was dominant, and because it was dominant its discriminatory prices were an abuse. The Court of Justice did not explicitly deal with this issue in its judgment, but in affirming the Commission's decision there is at least tacit approval of considering conduct as a factor indicating dominance.

Despite criticism of the circularity of this approach, the Commission has continued to regard conduct as a relevant factor indicating dominance: for example in *Eurofix-Bauco v Hilti*[91] it regarded that firm's behaviour as 'witness to its ability to act independently of, and without due regard to, either competitors or customers…'[92]; in *AKZO* it found that that undertaking's ability to weaken or eliminate troublesome competitors was an indicator of dominance[93]; and in *Michelin II* it considered that Michelin's conduct was strong evidence that a dominant position existed[94]. There is increasing recognition that there are types of behaviour that may deter entry[95], and it would be wrong to discount such conduct from the consideration of whether an undertaking is dominant.

(v) Evidence of managers

In *BBI/Boosey and Hawkes: Interim Measures*[96] the Commission regarded internal documents of Boosey and Hawkes, in which it had described its instruments as 'automatically first choice' of all the top brass bands, as significant in its finding that Boosey and Hawkes was dominant. In *Prokent-Tomra*[97] the Commission referred to several documents found during its inspection of Tomra's premises containing statements such as that Tomra's overall goal was to 'maintain market dominance and market share'[98]. Statements of this

---

[88]　Ibid, paras 448–459.

[89]　Case 27/76 [1978] ECR 207, [1978] 1 CMLR 429, paras 67–68.

[90]　Case 322/81 [1983] ECR 3461, [1985] 1 CMLR 282.

[91]　OJ [1988] L 65/19, [1989] 4 CMLR 677.

[92]　Ibid, para 71; the objection to the 'circularity' argument may be met if the Commission uses conduct as an indicator only in clear cases, and provided that it is not relied on exclusively to support a finding of dominance.

[93]　*ECS/AKZO* OJ [1985] L 374/1, [1986] 3 CMLR 273, para 56, upheld on appeal Case 62/86 *AKZO Chemie BV v Commission* [1991] ECR I-3359, [1993] 5 CMLR 215, para 61.

[94]　*PO-Michelin* OJ [2002] L 143/1, [2002] 5 CMLR 388, paras 197–199.

[95]　See eg Ordover and Salonen 'Predation, Monopolisation and Antitrust' in *The Handbook of Industrial Organisation* (North-Holland, 1989, eds Schmalensee and Willig); OFT Research Paper 2 *Barriers to Entry and Exit in UK Competition Policy* (London Economics, 1994) and *Assessment of Market Power* OFT 415, December 2004, paras 5.23–5.28.

[96]　OJ [1988] L 286/36, [1988] 4 CMLR 67, para 18.

[97]　Commission decision of 29 March 2006, upheld on appeal to the General Court Case T-155/06 *Tomra Systems ASA v Commission* [2010] ECR II-000, [2011] 4 CMLR 416.

[98]　Commission decision of 29 March 2006, para 91; see also *Wanadoo Interactive* Commission decision of 16 July 2003, paras 229–230 (referring to Wanadoo's stock exchange listing prospectus noting the synergies it derived from being part of the France Télécom group).

kind could not be probative of dominance in themselves. However it is clearly advisable for in-house lawyers to exercise restraint over hawkish commercial personnel, given to describing their position in the global widget market in memoranda and advertising copy as 'world-beating', 'the strongest' or 'clearly the dominant player'. Whilst shareholders might like to hear this, and whilst no doubt individuals' bonuses may be linked to their performance, it is not always easy to convince Commission officials that one's market power is insignificant in the face of such assertions.

(C) **Countervailing buyer power**

As has been explained in chapter 1, a further issue of significance is whether a supplier or suppliers are confronted with buyer power[99].

(D) **Previous findings of dominance**

In *Coca-Cola Co v Commission*[100] the General Court held that, whenever the Commission adopts a decision applying Article 102 (or the EUMR), it must define the relevant market and make a fresh analysis of the conditions of competition within it on the basis of the available evidence at the appropriate time; this may lead to a determination of the market which is different from a previous finding[101]. Furthermore a national court (or a national competition authority) would not be bound in a later case by a previous finding of dominance by the Commission in a different case[102]. However the actual decision in an Article 102 case may serve as a basis for an action for damages brought by a third party before a national court in relation to the same facts, even where the Commission's decision did not impose a fine[103].

(E) **The emergence of super-dominance**

It may be the case[104] that the responsibility of a dominant firm becomes greater, so that a finding of abuse becomes more likely, where the firm under investigation is not merely dominant, but rather 'enjoys a position of dominance approaching a monopoly'[105]. The Court of Justice has said that the scope of the special responsibility of a dominant firm must be considered in the light of the special circumstances of each case[106]. It follows that behaviour may be considered not to be abusive when carried out by some dominant firms but to be abusive when carried out by others. An example of the distinction is afforded by the practice of a dominant firm which selectively cuts its prices to some customers, but

---

[99] See ch 1, 'Countervailing buyer power', p 45.

[100] Cases T-125/97 etc [2000] ECR II-1733, [2000] 5 CMLR 467; the Commission defined the relevant product and geographic market afresh in its second *Michelin* decision: OJ [2002] L 143/1, [2002] 5 CMLR 388, paras 109–171.

[101] [2000] ECR II-1733, [2000] 5 CMLR 467, para 82.   [102] Ibid, para 85.

[103] Ibid, para 86; see also Case C-344/98 *Masterfoods Ltd v HB Ice Cream Ltd* [2000] ECR I-11369, [2001] 4 CMLR 449 and Article 16(1) of Regulation 1/2003, discussed in ch 8, 'Article 16: uniform application of EU competition law', pp 304–305 and ch 8, 'Article 16(1) of Regulation 1/2003', pp 313–314.

[104] Note that the Court of Justice's judgment in Case C-52/09 *Konkurrensverket v TeliaSonera Sverige AB* [2011] ECR I-000, paras 78–82 casts some doubt on the text that follows: see 'The emergence of super-dominance', pp 187–189 below.

[105] See para 136 of the Opinion of Advocate General Fennelly in Cases C-395/96 P etc *Compagnie Maritime Belge Transports SA v Commission* [2000] ECR I-1365, [2000] 4 CMLR 1076.

[106] Case C-334/94 P *Tetra Pak v Commission* [1996] ECR I-5951, [1997] 4 CMLR 662, para 24; Cases C-395/96 P etc *Compagnie Maritime Belge Transports SA v Commission* [2000] ECR I-1365, [2000] 4 CMLR 1076, para 114.

not to below cost in the sense of the law on predatory pricing[107], whilst charging higher prices to others. There are strong arguments for not condemning this practice: if the dominant firm is not losing money, it would appear to be competing on the basis of efficiency, which competition law should encourage[108]. In *Compagnie Maritime Belge Transports SA v Commission*[109] the Court of Justice refrained from deciding generally on the practice of selective price cutting[110]; however, at paragraph 119 it said that:

> It is sufficient to recall that the conduct at issue here is that of a conference having a share of over 90 per cent of the market in question and only one competitor. The appellants have, moreover, never seriously disputed, and indeed admitted at the hearing, that the purpose of the conduct complained of was to eliminate G&C from the market.

On this basis the Court of Justice upheld the finding that there had been an abuse of a dominant position, whilst leaving open the possibility that the same conduct on the part of an undertaking with less than 90 per cent of the market and facing more competition would not have been found to be unlawful.

The idea that the obligations on dominant firms become more onerous depending on the special circumstances of the case (to use the language of the Court of Justice in *Tetra Pak II*), finds expression in decisions and judgments that seem to have turned on the degree of market power that the dominant undertaking enjoys. For example Tetra Pak's market share in the market for aseptic cartons and carton-filling machines was in the region of 90 to 95 per cent, and it was found to have abused a dominant position where its conduct did not take place in the market in which it was dominant, and was not intended to benefit its position in that market[111]. In *Compagnie Maritime Belge* the conference's market share was 90 per cent or more[112], and in the *IMS* case[113] the Commission, when ordering IMS to grant a licence of its copyright to third parties on the market on a non-discriminatory basis, noted that IMS was in a 'quasi-monopoly situation'[114].

In *Deutsche Post AG – Interception of cross-border mail*[115] the Commission noted that:

> [t]he actual scope of the dominant firm's special responsibility must be considered in relation to the degree of dominance held by that firm and to the special characteristics of the market which may affect the competitive situation[116].

In *Microsoft*[117] the Commission said that Microsoft, with a market share above 90 per cent, had an 'overwhelmingly' dominant position'[118]. The Commissioner for Competition said after the General Court's judgment upholding the Commission's decision that the Court's judgment 'sends a clear signal that super-dominant companies cannot abuse

---

[107] See ch 18, 'Selective price cutting but not below cost', pp 748–752.

[108] It is possible that this pricing policy may amount to a different type of abuse, namely price discrimination (see ch 18, 'Price Discrimination', pp 759–764), but the issue here is whether the selective price cutting, but not to below cost, *in itself* amounts to an abuse.

[109] Cases C-395/96 P etc [2000] ECR I-1365, [2000] 4 CMLR 1076.

[110] Ibid, para 118.

[111] See 'The dominant position, the abuse and the effects of the abuse may be in different markets', pp 205–208 below.

[112] See similarly, on the responsibility of a monopolist, Case 7/82 *GVL v Commission* [1983] ECR 483, [1983] 3 CMLR 645, para 56; this was cited by the Commission in *1998 Football World Cup* OJ [2000] L 5/55, [2000] 4 CMLR 963, para 85.

[113] *NDC Health/IMS Health: Interim Measures* OJ [2002] L 59/18, [2002] 4 CMLR 111; see also *Deutsche Post AG – Interception of cross-border mail* OJ [2001] L 331/40, [2002] 4 CMLR 598, paras 103 and 124.

[114] OJ [2002] L 59/18, [2002] 4 CMLR 111, para 58; this decision was subsequently withdrawn by the Commission: see Commission Press Release IP/03/1159, 13 August 2003.

[115] OJ [2001] L 331/40, [2002] 4 CMLR 598.   [116] Ibid, para 103, citing the *Tetra Pak II* case.

[117] Commission decision of 24 March 2004.   [118] Ibid, para 435.

their position to hurt consumers and dampen innovation by excluding competition in related markets'[119].

The idea that firms with a position of dominance approaching a monopoly may be subject to particularly onerous responsibilities would also help to explain why firms that control 'essential facilities' have an obligation in certain circumstances to provide access to them, since their market power is particularly strong[120]. It may be helpful, therefore, to identify a concept over and above dominance, that we might call 'super-dominance', where the risks of being found to be acting abusively are correspondingly higher: if a dominant undertaking has a 'special' responsibility, a super-dominant has one that is even greater.

The Commission does not use the expression 'super-dominance' in its *Guidance on Article 102 Enforcement Priorities*. However in paragraph 20, discussing factors that it will take into account when deciding whether to intervene on the basis that certain conduct may be having an anti-competitive foreclosure effect on the market, it says that the stronger the dominant position of the undertaking under investigation, the higher the likelihood that conduct protecting that position would have such an effect. Interestingly the Court of Justice's judgment in *Konkurrensverket v TeliaSonera*[121] seems to endorse this approach: whilst acknowledging that some of its judgments had referred to 'super-dominance' and 'quasi-monopoly', it said that, as a general rule, the degree of market strength of a dominant firm was relevant to the assessment of the effects of its conduct rather than to the question of whether an abuse as such exists[122].

6. A Substantial Part of the Internal Market

Once it has been established that a firm has a dominant position on the market, one further jurisdictional question must be answered before going on to the issue of abuse: is that dominant position held in the whole or a substantial part of the internal market? If not Article 102, by its own terms, does not apply. This issue is not the same as the delimitation of the relevant geographic market: that concept is used as part of the investigation into a firm's market power. The requirement that market power should exist over a substantial part of the internal market is in a sense the equivalent of the *de minimis* doctrine under Article 101, according to which agreements of minor importance are not caught[123].

Obviously there is no problem with the issue of substantiality where it is decided that an undertaking is dominant throughout the EU. The position may be less obvious where dominance is more localised than this. Suppose that a firm is dominant in just one Member State, or even in a part of one Member State: when will that area be considered to constitute a substantial part of the EU? Four points must be noted.

The first is that the issue is not solely a geographic one. In *Suiker Unie v Commission*[124] the Court of Justice said that for this purpose:

> the pattern and volume of the production and consumption of the said product as well as the habits and economic opportunities of vendors and purchasers must be considered[125].

---

[119] See SPEECH/07/539, 17 September 2007.
[120] On essential facilities see ch 17, 'Is the product to which access is sought indispensable to someone wishing to complete in the downstream market?', pp 701–707.
[121] Case C-52/09 [2011] ECR I-000, [2011] 4 CMLR 982.   [122] Ibid, paras 78–82.
[123] See ch 3, 'The *De Minimis* Doctrine', pp 140–144.
[124] Cases 40/73 etc [1975] ECR 1663, [1976] 1 CMLR 295.
[125] Ibid, para 371.

This indicates that substantiality is not simply a question of relating the *physical* size of the geographic market to the EU as a whole. In *Suiker Unie* the Court of Justice considered the ratio of the volume of Belgian and South German production of sugar to EU production overall and concluded on this basis that each of those markets could be considered to be substantial.

The second point is that it is likely that each Member State would be considered to be a substantial part of the internal market, in particular where an undertaking enjoys a statutory monopoly[126], and *Suiker Unie* further established that parts of a Member State can be[127].

The third point is that neither the EU Courts nor the Commission have laid down that any particular percentage of the internal market as a whole is critical in determining what is substantial. In *BP v Commission*[128] Advocate General Warner took the view that sole reliance should not be placed on percentages in such cases and was of the opinion that the Dutch market for petrol, which represented only about 4.6 per cent of the EU market as a whole, could be considered substantial. The Court of Justice did not comment on this issue, as it quashed the Commission's finding of abuse on other grounds.

There are numerous examples of the test of substantiality having been satisfied in relation to a single facility: in each of *Merci Convenzionali Porto di Genova v Siderugica Gabriella*[129], *Sealink/B and I – Holyhead: Interim Measures*[130], *Sea Containers v Stena Sealink – Interim Measures*[131], *Flughaven Frankfurt/Main*[132], *Corsica Ferries*[133], *Portuguese Airports*[134], *Ilmailulaitos/Luftfartsverket*[135] and *Spanish Airports*[136] ports or airports have been found to be sufficiently substantial. Furthermore the Court of Justice has held that, where national law confers a contiguous series of monopolies within a Member State which, taken together, cover the entire territory of that State, that law creates a dominant position in a substantial part of the internal market[137].

The fourth point is that, in the event that an undertaking is found not to be dominant in a substantial part of the internal market, the possibility remains that it might be guilty of infringing the domestic equivalent of Article 102, a variant of which will be found in all the Member States of the EU.

7. Small Firms and Narrow Markets

(A) Small firms

It might be assumed that Article 102 is applicable only to large undertakings. It is certainly true that the Commission has used it to investigate some of the industrial giants of the world such as Roche, Commercial Solvents, United Brands, IBM, Microsoft and

---

[126] Case 127/73 *BRT v SABAM* [1974] ECR 313, [1974] 2 CMLR 238, para 5; Case T-229/94 *Deutsche Bahn AG v Commission* [1997] ECR II-1689, [1998] 4 CMLR 220; Case T-228/97 *Irish Sugar v Commission* [1999] ECR II-2969, [1999] 5 CMLR 1300, para 99.

[127] It is important to remember however that the abuse must also have an effect on trade between Member States to fall within Article 102: see 'The Effect on Inter-State Trade', pp 178–179 above.

[128] Case 77/77 [1978] ECR 1513, [1978] 3 CMLR 174.

[129] Case C-179/90 [1991] ECR I-5889, [1994] 4 CMLR 422, para 15.

[130] [1992] 5 CMLR 255, para 40.   [131] OJ [1994] L 15/8, [1995] 4 CMLR 84.

[132] OJ [1998] L 72/30, [1998] 4 CMLR 779.   [133] Case C-18/93 [1994] ECR I-1783.

[134] OJ [1999] L 69/31, [1999] 5 CMLR 103, upheld on appeal Case C-163/99 *Portugal v Commission* [2001] ECR I-2613, [2002] 2 CMLR 1319.

[135] OJ [1999] L 69/24, [1999] 5 CMLR 90.   [136] OJ [2000] L 208/36, [2000] 5 CMLR 967.

[137] Case C-323/93 *La Crespelle* [1994] ECR I-5077, para 17; this reasoning was applied by the Commission in, for example, *Portuguese Airports* OJ [1999] L 69/31, [1999] 5 CMLR 103, paras 21–22.

Intel. However it would be wrong to suppose that only firms such as these fall within the risk of Article 102. The significant issue under Article 102 is market power, not the size of an undertaking. Given that the relevant market may be drawn very narrowly, small firms may be found guilty of an abuse of Article 102. In *Hugin*[138] that firm was fined by the Commission for refusing to supply its spare parts to Liptons, the market for these purposes being spare parts for Hugin machines; Hugin's share of the cash register market was 12 to 14 per cent, but its share of the spare parts market for its machines was 100 per cent. On appeal[139] the Court of Justice quashed the Commission's decision because it considered there to be no effect on inter-state trade, but it upheld the finding on dominance. A vivid illustration of the vulnerability of small firms under Article 102 is afforded by *BBI/Boosey and Hawkes: Interim Measures*[140]. Boosey and Hawkes was found by the Commission, in an interim decision, to have abused its dominant position when it refused to supply musical instruments to customers who were threatening to enter into competition with it. Boosey and Hawkes' worldwide sales in all products were worth £38 million in 1985, and the market it was accused of dominating was defined as instruments for British-style brass bands, in which its market share was 80 to 90 per cent.

(B) Narrow markets

In the *Hugin* case a small part of Hugin's activities, the supply of spare parts, constituted the relevant market within which it was dominant. Similarly in *General Motors v Commission*[141], where the Belgian Government had given General Motors the exclusive power to grant test certificates to second-hand imports of Opel cars, this function was held to constitute a separate market, and General Motors' exclusive right meant that it was in a dominant position. The decision in *British Leyland v Commission*[142] was similar, that firm being held to have a dominant position in the provision of national type-approval certificates for its vehicles. Two further cases illustrate how narrowly a market can be defined. In *Porto di Genova v Siderurgica Gabrielli*[143] the Court of Justice held that the organisation of port activities at a single port could constitute a relevant market; and in *Corsica Ferries*[144] it reached the same conclusion in relation to the provision of piloting services at the same port. Similarly narrow markets have been found by the Commission in a series of decisions on services linked to access to airports[145].

The *1998 Football World Cup*[146] decision epitomises the possibility of narrow market definitions. The Commission proceeded on the basis of abuse in the market for 574,300 'blind pass' tickets to matches at the 1998 World Cup, a blind pass consisting of a ticket where the consumer does not know, at the time of purchase, what game he or she will be seeing[147]. The CFO, responsible for the ticketing arrangements, was found to have abused its dominant position by selling tickets only to customers having a postal address in

---

[138] OJ [1978] L 22/23, [1978] 1 CMLR D19.

[139] Case 22/78 *Hugin v Commission* [1979] ECR 1869, [1979] 3 CMLR 345.

[140] OJ [1987] L 286/36, [1988] 4 CMLR 67.

[141] OJ [1975] L 29/14, [1975] 1 CMLR D20; the decision was quashed by the Court of Justice on the issue of whether General Motors was guilty of excessive pricing issue: Case 26/75 *General Motors Continental NV v Commission* [1975] ECR 1367, [1976] 1 CMLR 95: see ch 18, '*General Motors* and *United Brands*', pp 721–722.

[142] Case 226/84 [1986] ECR 3263, [1987] 1 CMLR 185.

[143] Case C-179/90 [1991] ECR I-5889, [1994] 4 CMLR 422.

[144] Case C-18/93 [1994] ECR I-1783.

[145] See 'A Substantial Part of the Internal Market', pp 189–190 above.

[146] OJ [2000] L 5/55, [2000] 4 CMLR 963.

[147] For example, the third place play-off between, as yet, unidentified teams.

France: this had caused complaints, not surprisingly, that it was guilty of discrimination in favour of French nationals. A token fine of €1,000 was imposed.

8. Abuse

(A) Introduction

It is not controversial to say that Article 102 is controversial. In the case of Article 101 undertakings are liable only where they enter into agreements or concerted practices that restrict competition; a great deal of the Commission's (and of the national competition authorities') attention is focused on the deliberate and secret cartelisation of markets, and there are few apologists today for this kind of behaviour[148]. Article 102, on the other hand, bears upon the individual behaviour of dominant firms[149]; by its nature the application of Article 102 involves a competition authority or a court having to decide whether that behaviour deviates from 'normal' or 'fair' or 'undistorted' competition, or from 'competition on the merits', none of which expressions is free from difficulty. It should be added that the controversy surrounding Article 102 is not unique to the EU: all systems of competition law contain provisions on the unilateral conduct of firms with substantial market power, and competition authorities and courts worldwide have had to grapple with the issues under consideration in this chapter. Significant work has been undertaken under the auspices of the International Competition Network on this topic: in particular in May 2007 the Unilateral Conduct Working Group produced a *Report on the Objectives of Unilateral Conduct Laws, Assessment of Dominance/Substantial Market Power, and State-Created Monopolies* which contains a useful discussion of this complex area[150].

(i) The 'special responsibility' of dominant firms

It is clear that it is not an offence in itself for a firm to have a dominant position; what is offensive is to abuse the position of dominance. However the Court of Justice in *Michelin v Commission*[151] stated that a firm in a dominant position has a 'special responsibility not to allow its conduct to impair undistorted competition' on the internal market[152]. This statement is routinely repeated in the judgments of the EU Courts and the decisions of the Commission on Article 102[153]. In a sense it is a statement of the obvious: it is clear that Article 102 imposes obligations on dominant firms that non-dominant firms do not bear. Unilateral behaviour is not controlled under Article 101, which applies only to conduct which is attributable to a concurrence of wills; unilateral

---

[148] See ch 13 generally on cartels.

[149] Article 102 can also apply to the abuse of collective dominance, although this is not a concept that has been explored in much detail in the case law: see ch 14, 'Abuse of collective dominance under Article 102', pp 579–582.

[150] Available at www.internationalcompetitionnetwork.org; many other interesting work products on unilateral conduct laws will be found on this site, along with the current and long-term work plans of the ICN in this area; see also the OECD Roundtable on *Competition on the Merits* of 2005, available at www.oecd.org.

[151] Case 322/81 [1983] ECR 3461, [1985] 1 CMLR 282.

[152] Ibid, para 57.

[153] For recent statements to the same effect see Case C-280/08 P *Deutsche Telekom AG v Commission* [2010] ECR I-000, [2010] 5 CMLR 1495, para 176 and Case C-52/09 *Konkurrensverket v TeliaSonera Sverige AB* [2011] ECR I-000, [2011] 4 CMLR 982, para 24.

acts can however amount to an infringement of Article 102[154]. However the conundrum for anyone interested in Article 102 is to determine what, precisely, is meant by an abuse of a dominant position.

(ii) Article 102 does not contain an exhaustive list of what amounts to abusive behaviour

Article 102 gives examples of conduct that is abusive – such as charging unfair prices, limiting production and discrimination that places certain trading parties at a competitive disadvantage – but this list is not exhaustive[155]; the Commission's decisions and the case law of the EU Courts have applied Article 102 to numerous practices not specifically mentioned in it. A recent example of this is the General Court's judgment in *AstraZeneca AB v Commission*[156] in which it held that a pattern of making misleading misrepresentations to national patent offices in various Member States that led to the extension of patent protection for pharmaceutical products to which AZ was not, in fact, entitled amounted to an abuse of a dominant position; the same was true of the submission of requests to public authorities to deregister market authorisations for particular drugs, thereby impeding entry to the market by generic manufacturers. A reading of the list of examples of abusive behaviour in Article 102 would not prepare any but the most imaginative reader to suppose that these practices were abusive; but the Court appears to have had no hesitation in finding them to be illegal. Examples of practices found to be abusive will be given later in this chapter and will be considered in depth in chapter 17 (non-pricing abuses) and chapter 18 (pricing abuses).

(iii) False positives and false negatives

A difficulty with Article 102 is that the line between pro- and anti-competitive conduct is not always an easy one to draw, and there is an obvious danger that, if Article 102 is applied too aggressively, firms might refrain from conduct that is in fact pro-competitive. Clearly it would be the ultimate paradox if a law designed to promote competition in fact were to have the effect of diminishing it[157].

A more stylised way of presenting this problem is to consider the difference between what are sometimes referred to as 'false positives' and 'false negatives'[158].

A **false positive** occurs where a competition authority incorrectly concludes that pro-competitive behaviour is abusive: a harm to the firm(s) found guilty, and also to consumers, since the pro-competitive behaviour will be prohibited. The problem here is that the law is over-inclusive.

A **false negative** occurs where a competition authority incorrectly concludes that anti-competitive behaviour is not illegal and therefore permits it: a harm to consumers. Here the law is under-inclusive.

---

[154] The respective roles of Articles 101 and 102 are spelt out particularly clearly in the judgment of the General Court in Case T-41/96 *Bayer v Commission* [2000] ECR II-3383, [2001] 4 CMLR 126, paras 175–176.

[155] Case 6/72 *Continental Can v Commission* [1973] ECR 215, [1973] CMLR 199, para 26; Cases C-395/96 P etc *Compagnie Maritime Belge Transports SA v Commission* [2000] ECR I-1365, [2000] 4 CMLR 1076, para 112; Case C-280/08 P *Deutsche Telekom AG v Commission* [2010] ECR I-000, [2010] 5 CMLR 1495, para 173.

[156] Case T-321/05 [2010] ECR II-000, [2010] 5 CMLR 1585; the judgment is on appeal to the Court of Justice, Case C-457/10 P *AstraZeneca AB v Commission*, not yet decided.

[157] A series of essays on the question of whether (mis)application of laws dealing with unilateral conduct have a chilling effect on competition, by Bougeois, Fingleton and Nikpay, Lewis and Lugard respectively, will be found in chs 15–18 of [2008] Fordham Corporate law Institute (ed Hawk).

[158] Economics literature sometimes uses the expressions 'Type I errors' and 'Type II errors', but the tendency to confuse which error is of which type (sometimes referred to jocularly as a 'Type III' error) argues in favour of the language of false positives and false negatives.

Given the inherent difficulty of determining which unilateral acts are anti-competitive and which are pro-competitive, it is inevitable that competition authorities will sometimes make errors; a policy question when framing rules on unilateral behaviour is to decide which of the two errors is preferable. There is an undoubted perception that the enforcement authorities and the courts in the US today are more concerned about false positives than false negatives: that is to say that they err on the side of non-intervention under section 2 of the Sherman Act 1890, which forbids the monopolisation of markets[159], whereas the Commission and the EU Courts perhaps tend the other way[160]. In *Verizon Communications Inc v Law Offices of Curtis Trinko*[161] the US Supreme Court, in a refusal to supply case, was explicit about its fear of false positives:

> Against the slight benefits of antitrust intervention here, we must weigh a realistic assessment of its costs...Mistaken inferences and the resulting false condemnations are 'especially costly, because they chill the very conduct the antitrust laws are designed to protect'...The cost of false positives counsels against an undue expansion of s. 2 liability[162].

The same attitude helps to explain the conclusion of the Supreme Court in *Pacific Bell v linkLine*[163], where it held that a margin squeeze is not an independent infringement of section 2 of the Sherman Act[164]. In contrast one might note that on many occasions when the EU Courts have been invited to expand Article 102 liability they have done so: for example when apparently establishing *per se* infringements[165]; when establishing that Article 102 could apply to mergers[166]; when deciding that there did not need to be any causation between the market power held by a dominant firm and its abusive behaviour[167]; when accepting that the dominance, abuse and effects of the abuse can be in different markets[168]; when extending the application of Article 102 to collective, as well as to individual, dominance[169]; and when acknowledging the possibility of an individual abuse of a collective dominant position[170]. This record does not suggest the same reticence as that of the Supreme Court in *Verizon*.

---

[159] For discussion of section 2 of the Sherman Act see Sullivan and Harrison *Understanding Antitrust and Its Economic Implications* (LexisNexis, 4th ed, 2003), ch 6; Sullivan and Hovenkamp *Antitrust Law, Policy and Procedure: Cases, Materials, Problems* (LexisNexis, 5th ed, 2004), ch 6; Fox, Sullivan and Peritz *Cases and Materials on US Antitrust in Global Context* (Thomson/West, 2nd ed, 2004), ch 3; Hovenkamp *Federal Antitrust Policy: The Law of Competition and Its Practice* (Thomson/West, 3rd ed, 2005), chs 6–10; Kovacic 'The Intellectual DNA of Modern US Competition Law for Dominant Firm Conduct: The Chicago/Harvard Double Helix' (2007) Columbia Business Law Review 1; for a critique of the 'vacuous standards and conclusory labels that provide no meaningful guidance about which conduct will be condemned as exclusionary' under section 2 of the Sherman Act see Elhauge 'Defining Better Monopolization Standards' (2003) 56 Stanford Law Review 253.

[160] For an interesting discussion of the differences in approach in the US and the EU, suggesting that the position in the US can lead to anti-competitive behaviour escaping sanction, see Fox 'A Tale of Two Jurisdictions and an Orphan Case: Antitrust, Intellectual Property, and Refusals to Deal' (2005) 28 Fordham International Law Journal 952.

[161] 540 US 398 (2004).   [162] Ibid, p 414.   [163] 555 US 438 (2009).

[164] See ch 18, 'The economic phenomenon', p 756.

[165] See 'Are there or should there be any *per se* rules under Articles 102?', pp 199–201 below.

[166] See '*Continental Can v Commission*', p 203 below.

[167] See 'Causation', pp 203–204 below.

[168] See 'The dominant position, the abuse and the effects of the abuse may be in different markets', pp 205–208 below.

[169] See ch 14, 'Article 102 and Collective Dominance', pp 571–579.

[170] See ch 14, 'Abuse of collective dominance under Article 102', pp 579–582.

(B) What is the purpose of Article 102?

Before considering the jurisprudence of the EU Courts and the practice of the Commission on the meaning of abuse of dominance, it is necessary to give some consideration to the underlying purpose of Article 102. The various possible objectives of competition law have been discussed in chapter 1 of this book[171]. There it was pointed out that competition authorities today stress the central importance of consumer welfare when applying competition law, but that other matters such as the redistribution of wealth and the protection of small firms against more powerful rivals have also been influential at various points in time.

(i) Protection of competitors or protection of competition?

A specific criticism of Article 102 is that it is used to protect competitors, including inefficient ones, rather than the process of competition, which is a quite different matter. According to this view Article 102, in effect, subjects dominant firms to a handicap: competitive acts, such as price reductions or the bundling of different products, that are perfectly legal for non-dominant firms, become illegal when a firm is dominant. The complaint is that this means that firms that possess superior efficiency are restrained in order to provide a place in the competitive arena for less efficient ones. This characteristic of Article 102 would be exacerbated if it is, indeed, the case that institutions in the EU have a tendency to be more concerned about false negatives than false positives.

The criticism that Article 102 protects competitors rather than competition brings to mind Robert Bork's attack on the antitrust rules as they were applied in the US in the 1960s and 1970s, and in particular what he regarded as the 'uncritical sentimentality in favour of the small guy' of the enforcement authorities and the courts there at that time[172]. The most high-level accusation of the EU's supposed predilection for protecting competitors rather than competition came from the Assistant Attorney General for Antitrust at the US Department of Justice in response to the judgment of the General Court of the EU in September 2007 upholding the European Commission's decision that Microsoft had abused its dominant position[173]. After expressing 'concern' about the standard applied to unilateral conduct in Europe, Mr Barnett said that:

> In the United States, the antitrust laws are enforced to protect consumers by protecting competition, not competitors[174].

Without saying more, his meaning could hardly have been clearer: that in the EU the prime concern is not with the protection of consumers through competition, but with the protection of competitors.

Some commentators lay the blame for what they see as an unduly interventionist application of Article 102 at the door of the school of ordoliberalism which, through its concern to protect economic freedom, including the right of access to markets unconstrained by barriers such as exclusive agreements or rebating and discounting practices having analogous effects, led to the adoption of formalistic rules capable of having perverse consequences[175].

---

[171] See ch 1, 'Goals of competition law', pp 19–24.

[172] Bork *The Antitrust Paradox* (The Free Press, 1993).

[173] Case T-201/04 *Microsoft Corpn v Commission* [2007] ECR II-3601, [2007] 5 CMLR 846.

[174] See Press Release of 17 September 2007, available at www.justice.gov.atr.

[175] For a discussion of ordoliberalism see ch 1, 'Protecting competitors', pp 21–22; for an example of criticism of the impact of ordoliberalism see eg Kallaugher and Sher 'Rebates Revisited: Anti-Competition Effects and Exclusionary Abuse Under Article 82' (2004) 25 ECLR 263; Venit 'Article 82: The Last Frontier – Fighting Fire with Fire' (2005) 28 Fordham International Law Journal 1157; Ahlborn and Padilla 'From Fairness to Welfare: Implications for the Assessment of Unilateral Conduct under EC Competition Law' in

However, in the opinion of the authors of this book the assertion that the fingerprints of the ordoliberal school are to be found on the case law of Article 102, and that this has led to a systematic bias in favour of competitors and against efficient dominant firms, is at best a misdescription of the true position and at worst little more than a slogan by protagonists of minimalist intervention. One commentator has examined the *travaux préparatoires* of Article 102 and suggested that its drafters were mainly concerned with increasing economic efficiency; their intention was not to protect competitors, but their customers[176]. This explains why the language of Article 102 is predominantly focused on exploitative behaviour, such as the imposition of unfair selling prices, terms and conditions and the limitation of markets to the prejudice of consumers, rather than exclusionary abuses[177]. It also tends to refute the widely-held belief in the English-language literature that Article 102 is based on ordoliberal foundations.

(ii) Article 102 protects competition; and competition is for the benefit of consumers

Numerous statements to the effect that Article 102 is actually concerned with the protection of competition rather than the protection of competitors can be found. Many of these come from the Commission (or from Commission officials), but they can also be found in judgments of the EU Courts, particularly in recent years in judgments such as *Deutsche Telekom* and *TeliaSonera* (see below).

A clear statement to this effect was made by Neelie Kroes, the former Commissioner for Competition, when discussing the Commission's review of exclusionary abuses at the annual conference at Fordham in September 2005[178]:

> My own philosophy on this is fairly simple. First, it is competition, and not competitors, that is to be protected. Second, ultimately the aim is to avoid consumers harm.
>   I like aggressive competition – including by dominant companies – and I don't care if it may hurt competitors – as long as it ultimately benefits consumers. That is because the main and ultimate objective of Article 102 is to protect consumers, and this does, of course, require the protection of an undistorted competitive process on the market.

That was a statement by one individual, but the same idea is stated more formally at several points in the Commission's *Guidance on Article 102 Enforcement Priorities*[179]. A few examples illustrate the point. In paragraph 5 the Commission says that:

> The Commission...will direct its enforcement to ensuring that markets function properly and that consumers benefit from the efficiency and productivity which result from effective competition between undertakings.

In paragraph 6 it says that:

> [T]he Commission is mindful that *what really matters is protecting an effective competitive process and not simply protecting competitors.* This may well mean that competitors

---

European Competition Law Annual 2007: A Reformed Approach to Article 82 EC (Hart Publishing, 2008, eds Ehlermann and Marquis).

[176] See Akman 'Searching for the Long-Lost Soul of Article 82 EC' (2009) 29(2) OJLS 267.

[177] See 'Exploitative, exclusionary and single market abuses', pp 201–202 below on the distinction between exploitative and exclusionary abuses.

[178] SPEECH/05/537, 23 September 2005; numerous statements to the same effect can be found: see eg speech by Lowe 'Innovation and Regulation of Dominant Firms', 23 September 2008 and speech by Commissioner Alumnia 'Converging paths in unilateral conduct', 3 December 2010, available at www.ec.europa.eu.

[179] OJ [2009] C 45/7.

who deliver less to consumers in terms of price, choice, quality and innovation will leave the market (emphasis added).

The Commission adds, in paragraph 23, that:

[T]he Commission will normally only intervene where the conduct concerned has already been or is capable of hampering competition from competitors *which are considered to be as efficient* as the dominant undertaking (emphasis added).

Sceptics might argue that these are merely statements of the Commission that lack the force of law, and that the *Guidance* simply sets out its enforcement policy: it does not describe the jurisprudence of the EU Courts. However judgments of the Court of Justice themselves stress the importance of protecting the process of competition for the benefit of consumers[180]; and in both *Deutsche Telekom AG v Commission*[181] and *Konkurrensverket v TeliaSonera Sverige AB*[182] it seemed to go out of its way to stress that Article 102 protects only 'as efficient' competitors, and not inefficient ones. At paragraph 177 of its judgment in *Deutsche Telekom* the Court said that:

Article [102 TFEU] prohibits a dominant undertaking from, inter alia, adopting pricing practices which have an exclusionary effect *on its equally efficient actual or potential competitors* (emphasis added)[183].

The same language occurs repeatedly throughout the judgment[184]; the same is true of the *TeliaSonera* judgment[185].

Collectively these various utterances reveal a consistent tendency on the part of both the Court of Justice and the Commission, at least in recent times, to stress competition, efficiency and consumer welfare as the key objectives of Article 102. It is difficult, therefore, to sustain the argument that the EU institutions today have an active policy of protecting competitors rather than the process of competition.

(C) Jurisprudence on the meaning of abuse

As already noted, Article 102 does not contain an exhaustive list of all the practices that can amount to an abuse. Nor is there one particular judgment of the Court of Justice or the General Court that provides an all-encompassing definition of what is meant by abuse. This is understandable: cases on abuse of dominance very much turn on their own particular facts – a point stressed on numerous occasions[186] – and the EU Courts have refrained from broad theoretical statements, preferring instead to decide each case on

---

[180] See eg (in a case on Article 101 rather than Article 102) the Court of Justice in Cases C-501/06 P etc *GlaxoSmithKline Services Unlimited v Commission* [2009] ECR I-9291, [2010] 4 CMLR 50, para 63; see also the General Court in Case T-340/03 *France Télécom v Commission* [2007] ECR II-107, [2007] 4 CMLR 919, para 266 and Case T-321/05 *AstraZeneca AB v Commission* [2010] ECR II-000, [2010] 5 CMLR 1585, para 353.

[181] Case C-280/08 P [2010] ECR I-000, [2010] 5 CMLR 1495; note also that the Court's judgment in Case C-7/97 *Oscar Bronner GmbH* [1998] ECR I-7791, [1999] 4 CMLR 112 presaged the 'as efficient competitor' test: see ch 17, 'Is the product to which access is sought indispensable to someone wishing to compete in the downstream market?', pp 701–703.

[182] Case C-52/09 [2011] ECR I-000, [2011] 4 CMLR 982.

[183] Case C-280/08 P [2010] ECR I-000, [2010] 5 CMLR 1495, para 177.

[184] Ibid, paras 203, 234, 236, 240, 252–255 and 259.

[185] Case C-52/09 *Konkurrensverket v TeliaSonera Sverige AB* [2011] ECR I-000, [2011] 4 CMLR 982, paras 31–33, 39–40, 43, 63–64, 67, 70 and 73.

[186] See eg Case C-95/04 P *British Airways plc v Commission* [2007] ECR I-2331, [2007] 4 CMLR 9(64; see also para 68 of the Opinion of Advocate General Jacobs in Case C-53/03 *Syfait* [2005] ECR [2005] 5 CMLR 7.

its merits (albeit taking into account earlier judgments). As Philip Lowe, at the time the Director General of DG COMP, said in his remarks on unilateral conduct in Washington in September 2006:

> [J]ust as physicists strive to find the theory that unifies Newtonian physics and quantum mechanics, so economists strive to find the theory that unifies the various aspects of anti-competitive unilateral conduct. And the economists, just as the physicists, have not yet found it[187].

One paragraph that is regularly cited on the meaning of abuse of dominance will be found in the judgment of the Court of Justice in *Hoffmann-La Roche v Commission*[188]. At paragraph 91 it said that abuse is:

> An objective concept relating to the behaviour of an undertaking in a dominant position which is such as to influence the structure of a market where, as a result of the very presence of the undertaking in question the degree of competition is weakened and which, through recourse to methods different from those which condition normal competition in products or services on the basis of the transaction of commercial operators, has the effect of hindering the maintenance of the degree of competition still existing in the market or the growth of that competition.

This is an important paragraph, but it does not provide an overarching definition of abuse. For example it does not capture the idea of exploitative, as opposed to exclusionary, practices of a dominant firm, such as charging customers excessively high prices: such conduct cannot be said to *hinder* competition, and yet it can undoubtedly amount to an abuse of a dominant position, as Article 102 explicitly states. However the Court's judgment in *Hoffmann-La Roche* does introduce the idea that dominant undertakings must refrain from 'methods different from those which condition normal competition'. Of course this begs the question: what is 'normal' competition, a vague and indeterminate word[189]. However the idea of 'normal' competition comes more clearly into focus if slightly different language is used: namely that dominant firms should 'compete on the merits', and that competition that is not on the merits is 'abnormal' competition. The EU Courts do use the language of competition on the merits, noticeably so in recent judgments. For example in *Deutsche Telekom v Commission*[190] it said, after quoting from paragraph 91 of *Hoffmann-La Roche*, that a dominant firm must not strengthen its dominant position:

> By using methods other than those which come within the scope of competition on the merits[191].

It used the same language in paragraph 43 of its judgment in *TeliaSonera*[192], as did the General Court in two judgments in 2010, *AstraZeneca AB v Commission*[193] and *Tomra*

---

[187] See speech of 11 September 2006, available at www.ec.europa.eu.

[188] Case 85/76 [1979] ECR 461, [1979] 3 CMLR 211; for a more recent statement to the same effect see eg Case C-280/08 P *Deutsche Telekom AG v Commission* [2010] ECR I-000, [2010] 5 CMLR 1495, para 174 and the case law cited therein.

[189] In *National Grid Plc v Gas & Electricity Markets Authority* [2010] EWCA Civ 114, [2010] UKCLR 386, the English Court of Appeal said that 'normal' competition is not 'a sufficiently hard-edged concept that it can be determined as a matter of law'; it is a 'question of expert appreciation': ibid, para 41.

[190] Case C-280/08 P [2010] ECR I-000, [2010] 5 CMLR 1495.

[191] Ibid, para 177; see similarly Case T-201/04 *Microsoft Corpn v Commission* [2007] ECR II-3601, [2007] 5 CMLR 846, para 1070.

[192] Case C-52/09 [2011] ECR I-000, [2011] 4 CMLR 982.

[193] Case T-321/05 [2010] II-ECR 000, [2010] 5 CMLR 1585, paras 354–355, 672 and 824.

Systems ASA v Commission[194]. There are a number of Article 102 cases pending before the EU Courts at the moment[195], and it will be of interest to see if they continue to use the language of 'competition on the merits', and whether they will attempt to explain in greater depth what this term means.

The Commission has given examples of what it considers to be competition on the merits in paragraph 5 of its *Guidance on Article 102 Enforcement Priorities*: offering lower prices, better quality and a wider choice of new and improved goods and services. When compared to business behaviour of this kind, it is not difficult to see that other acts – such as a margin squeeze, the misleading of patent authorities leading to the award of additional patent protection from generic producers of pharmaceutical products and the grant of rebates in return for exclusivity or near-exclusivity – do not amount to competition on the merits, and are therefore capable of being found to be abusive.

(D) Are there or should there be any *per se* rules under Article 102?

The discussion so far suggests that Article 102, as applied today, is concerned to protect consumer welfare; it does not protect competitors as such; and that dominant firms should compete on the merits and refrain from 'abnormal' competition. However, even if this is the case, there remains a problem: can these ideas be expressed in administrable rules capable of being applied by competition authorities, courts, professional advisers and dominant undertakings themselves? More specifically, is it possible to avoid the problem of false positives and false negatives, both of which are undesirable in principle?

One of the most common complaints about Article 102 is that the Commission and the EU Courts apply it in too formalistic a manner. This criticism can be articulated in various ways. One is the argument that some practices appear to be unlawful *per se*, but that *per se* rules are inappropriate for behaviour such as price cutting and refusals to deal which may, depending on the facts of a particular case, be pro-competitive, anti-competitive, or neutral. Another way of voicing the same criticism is to argue that the Commission and the Courts often fail to demonstrate how a particular practice could have significant effects on the market: too often they fail to articulate a convincing theory of economic harm and/or to produce evidence that adverse effects would follow from the practice under investigation.

(i) Are there any per se rules under Article 102?

Historically there has been a tendency on the part of both the Courts and the Commission to apply *per se* rules, at least to some abuses; however the undoubted trend, which the authors of this book expect to continue, is away from a *per se* standard towards effects-based analysis. There is no doubt that language can be found in some judgments that suggests that at least some unilateral practices are *per se* illegal. A few extracts from the General Court's judgment in *Michelin v Commission*, summarising earlier case law, illustrate this[196]:

> [I]t is apparent from a consistent line of decisions that a loyalty rebate, which is granted in return for an undertaking by the customer to obtain his stock exclusively or almost exclusively from an undertaking in a dominant position, is contrary to Article [102 TFEU][197].

[194] Case T-155/06 [2010] ECR II-000, [2011] 4 CMLR 416, paras 206 and 241.
[195] See eg Case T-336/07 *Telefónica v Commission*; Case T-286/09 *Intel v Commission*; Case T-201/11 *Si.mobil v Commission*; Case C-209/10 *Post Danmark A/S v Konkurrencerådet*; Case C-549/10 P *Tomra ASA v Commission*; Case C-109/10 P *Solvay SA v Commission*.
[196] Case T-203/01 [2003] ECR II-4071, [2004] 4 CMLR 923; for comment see Waelbroeck 'Michelin II: A *per-se* rule against rebates by dominant companies?' (2005) 1 Journal of Competition Law and Economics 149.
[197] Case T-203/01 [2003] ECR II-4071, [2004] 4 CMLR 923, para 56.

Later the General Court says that:

> [I]t may be inferred generally from the case law that any loyalty-inducing rebate system applied by an undertaking in a dominant position has foreclosure effects prohibited by Article [102 TFEU][198].

Later again the General Court says that:

> [D]iscounts granted by an undertaking in a dominant position must be based on a countervailing advantage which may be economically justified[199].

If these statements are correct, then it would seem that there are, indeed, *per se* rules under Article 102, at least for some types of rebates and discounts. In particular it is noticeable that the General Court says here that foreclosure effects can be *inferred*: that is to say that they do not need to be proved; in the language of Article 101(1), this would suggest that a loyalty-inducing rebate system abuses *by object*, so that there is no need to prove effects.

The General Court has repeated this kind of language on several occasions: recent examples are its judgments in *Solvay v Commission*[200] and *ICI v Commission*[201]. A further illustration can be found in *Tomra Systems ASA v Commission*[202] in which the General Court seemed to regard the rebates and exclusive agreements under consideration as unlawful *per se*[203]; however the General Court went on to accept a finding of the Commission that Tomra's practices were capable of having anti-competitive effects[204], suggesting an ambiguity on its part as to the desirability of *per se* rules in this area.

(ii) Recent case law and decisions do require effects analysis

Judgments of the kind just discussed make it difficult to say that the Courts have never tolerated *per se* rules under Article 102. However, as noted earlier in this chapter, there is an increasing intellectual consensus against the application of *per se* rules in the law and practice on unilateral behaviour; the Commission in its *Guidance on Article 102 Enforcement Priorities* considers that it should concentrate its enforcement activity on practices likely to have seriously anti-competitive effects on the market; and, in its recent decisions under Article 102, the Commission has sought evidence of anti-competitive effects, even where it considered that it was not legally obliged to do so. For example in *Microsoft*[205] the Commission decided that Microsoft was guilty of tying the provision of its Windows Media Player to its operating software only after demonstrating that the tying would restrict competition[206]. Similarly, in *Telefónica*[207] the Commission noted that, although it was not formally obliged to do so, it had demonstrated that Telefónica's pricing practices would harm competition and consumers[208]. The Commission adopted the same approach in its *Intel* decision[209]. When

---

[198] Ibid, para 65.
[199] Ibid, para 100.   [200] Case T-57/01 [2009] ECR II-4621.
[201] Case T-66/01 [2010] ECR II-000, [2011] 4 CMLR 162.
[202] Case T-155/06 [2010] ECR II-000, [2011] 4 CMLR 416, on appeal to the Court of Justice, Case C-549/10 P, not yet decided.
[203] Ibid, para 208–210.
[204] Commission decision of 29 March 2006, paras 331–346, upheld on appeal Case T-155/06 *Tomra Systems ASA v Commission* [2010] ECR II-000, [2011] 4 CMLR 416, paras 215–230.
[205] Commission decision of 24 March 2004.
[206] Ibid, paras 835–954, upheld on appeal to the General Court, Case T-201/04 *Microsoft Corpn v Commission* [2007] ECR II-3601, [2007] 5 CMLR 846, paras 1031–1090.
[207] Commission decision of 4 July 2007, on appeal to the General Court, Case T-336/07 *Telefónica v Commission*, not yet decided and Case T-398/07 *Spain v Commission*, not yet decided.
[208] Ibid, paras 543–618.
[209] Commission decision of 13 May 2009, paras 1597–1616; the Commission carried out an extensive 'as efficient competitor' analysis in paras 1002–1576 of its decision; this decision is on appeal Case T-286/09 *Intel v Commission*, not yet decided.

adopting its *Guidance on Article 102 Enforcement Priorities* the Commission stressed that it now adopts an effects-based approach to its decision-making under Article 102[210]. Of course the Commission does not establish what the law is (although it can help to influence it): the law is determined by the EU Courts. As pointed out, some judgments have applied Article 102 in a formalistic manner. However it is noticeable that other judgments have stressed the need for a demonstration of anti-competitive effects. For example in two recent judgments, *Deutsche Telekom v Commission*[211] and in *TeliaSonera*[212], the Court of Justice stated that potential anti-competitive effects must be demonstrated before a margin squeeze is condemned as unlawful[213]. For example in *TeliaSonera* it said that:

> in order to establish whether [a margin squeeze] is abusive, that practice must have an anti-competitive effect on the market.[213a]

It has been noted above that these same judgments stressed that Article 102 protects 'as efficient' competitors, rather than competitors as such; and that they both invoked the idea that dominant undertakings should compete 'on the merits'. These ideas, together with the insistence that anti-competitive effects should be demonstrated in these cases, are consistent with the position outlined in the Commission's *Guidance on Article 102 Enforcement Priorities*. It is for these reasons that the authors of this book consider that the trend towards effects analysis under Article 102 is clearly established, both on the part of the Courts and the Commission, and is unlikely to be reversed. It may be that the task of 'improving' the application of Article 102 remains 'work-in-progress', but the direction of travel seems to be clear and consistent.

(E) Exploitative, exclusionary and single market abuses

When reviewing the decisional practice of the Commission and the jurisprudence of the EU Courts, it is possible to identify at least two, and perhaps three, types of abuse. The first consists of **exploitative abuses**. The most obvious objection to a monopolist is that it is in a position to reduce output and increase the price of its products above the competitive level, thereby exploiting customers[214]. However in the absence of barriers to entry a monopolist earning monopoly profits would be expected to attract new entrants to the market: in other words exploitation of a monopoly position may in itself increase competition over time.

Of greater long-term significance is behaviour by a dominant firm designed to, or which might have the effect of, preventing the development of competition, and much of the case law of the EU Courts and the decisional practice of the Commission has been concerned with **exclusionary abuses** of this kind. The Commission's *Guidance on Article 102 Enforcement Priorities* recognises the distinction between exploitative and exclusionary abuses, and paragraph 7 explicitly states that it is limited to exclusionary conduct. Neelie Kroes, the former Commissioner for Competition, said in September 2005 that:

> We think that it is sound for our enforcement policy to give priority to so-called exclusionary abuses[215].

---

[210] Commission Press Release IP/08/1877, 3 December 2008.

[211] Case C-280/08 P *Deutsche Telekom AG v Commission* [2010] ECR I-000, [2010] 5 CMLR 1495.

[212] Case C-52/09 *Konkurrensverket v TeliaSonera Sverige AB* [2011] ECR I-000, [2011] 4 CMLR 982.

[213] Case C-280/08 P *Deutsche Telekom AG v Commission* [2010] ECR I-000, [2010] 5 CMLR 1495, paras 250–261; Case C-52/09 *Konkurrensverket v TeliaSonera Sverige AB* [2011] ECR I-000, [2011] 4 CMLR 982, paras 60–77.

[213a] Ibid, para 64.

[214] See the analysis of price theory in ch 1, 'The Theory of Competition', pp 3–7.

[215] SPEECH/05/537, 23 September 2005, available at www.ec.europa.eu.

In order to illustrate the kind of behaviour which falls within the mischief of Article 102 it is therefore helpful to consider exploitative and exclusionary abuses separately, although this is not to suggest that there is a rigid demarcation between these two categories: the same behaviour may exhibit both characteristics. For example a dominant firm that refuses to supply may have an exploitative purpose (for example where it is threatened or effected in order to make a customer pay a higher price) and/or an exclusionary one (where it is intended to remove a competitor from the market).

A possible third category of cases under Article 102 is concerned with **single market abuses**. For example excessive pricing, as well as being exploitative, may be a ploy to impede parallel imports and to limit intra-brand competition, as in the case of *British Leyland v Commission*[216].

(F) **Exploitative abuses**

It is clear from its very wording that Article 102 is capable of application to exploitative behaviour: Article 102(2)(a) gives as an example of an abuse the imposition of unfair purchase or selling prices or other unfair trading conditions. Exploitative pricing practices are considered further in chapter 18[217]. There have also been cases on the activities of collecting societies in which their rules have been scrutinised in order to ensure that they do not act in a way that unfairly exploits the owner of the copyright or the would-be licensee of it; collecting societies are considered in chapter 19[218]. Unfair trading conditions were condemned by the Commission in *AAMS*[219] and in *1998 Football World Cup*[220], where it considered that the arrangements for the sale of tickets were unfair to consumers resident outside France.

In its colloquial sense, exploitation suggests the earning of monopoly profits at the expense of the customer. One of the other 'benefits' of the monopolist is the 'quiet life' and the freedom from the need to innovate and improve efficiency in order to keep up with or ahead of competitors[221]. This raises the question whether inefficiency or inertia could be considered to be an abuse under Article 102. Article 102(2)(b) gives as an example of abuse the limitation of production, markets or technical development to the prejudice of the consumer, and in *British Telecommunications*[222] the Commission objected to behaviour on BT's part which, among other things, meant that the possible use of new technology was impeded. This is dealt with in chapter 6[223].

(G) **Exclusionary abuses**

Article 102 has most frequently been applied to behaviour which the Commission and EU Courts consider to be exclusionary. The Commission's *Guidance on Article 102 Enforcement Priorities* contains useful insights into the considerations that it considers

[216] Case 226/84 [1986] ECR 3263, [1987] 1 CMLR 185; see 'Abuses that are harmful to the single market', pp 205–206 below and ch 18, 'Pricing Practices That are Harmful to the Single Market', pp 764–766.

[217] See ch 18, 'Exploitative Pricing Practices', pp 718–728.

[218] See ch 19, 'Collecting societies', pp 803–804.

[219] OJ [1998] L 252/47, [1998] 5 CMLR 786, paras 33–46, upheld on appeal to the General Court Case T-139/98 *Amministratzione Autonoma dei Monopoli di Stato v Commission* [2001] ECR II-3413, [2002] 4 CMLR 302, paras 73–80.

[220] OJ [2000] L 5/55, [2000] 4 CMLR 963, para 91; see also paras 99–100.

[221] See ch 1, 'The harmful effects of monopoly', pp 6–7.

[222] OJ [1982] L 360/36, [1983] 1 CMLR 457, upheld on appeal Case 41/83 *Italy v Commission* [1985] ECR 873, [1985] 2 CMLR 368.

[223] Ch 6, 'Manifest inability to meet demand', pp 231–232.

to be important when deciding whether to investigate a possible exclusionary abuse; however the reader is reminded that this document does not contain a statement of the law, but rather an indication of the Commission's enforcement priorities.

(i) *Continental Can v Commission*[224]

The Court of Justice established in *Continental Can v Commission* that Article 102 was capable of application to exclusionary abuses as well as exploitative ones. The specific question before the Court was whether mergers could be prohibited under Article 102. One argument against this was that Article 102 was concerned only with the direct exploitation of consumers and not with the more indirect adverse effects that might be produced by harming the competitive process[225]; according to this argument structural changes in the market could not be caught. The Court of Justice rejected this. It was not possible to draw a distinction between direct and indirect effects on the market; instead it was necessary to interpret Article 102 in the light of the spirit of the Treaty generally. Article 3(3) TEU provides that the EU shall establish an internal market which, as explained in Protocol 27 to the Treaties, includes 'a system ensuring that competition is not distorted'[226]. Articles 101 and 102 had to be interpreted with this aim in mind: it would be futile to prevent agreements which distort competition under Article 101 but then to allow mergers which resulted in the elimination of competition. The adoption in 1989 of the EUMR means that Article 102 is now largely redundant in respect of mergers[227]; however *Continental Can* remains immensely important to the law on Article 102, since it confirmed that it could be applied to exclusionary abuses as well as to exploitative ones.

(ii) Causation

One of the arguments raised by Continental Can was that, even if mergers were caught by Article 102, it had not *used* its market power to effect the merger in question; thus there was a break in the chain of causation between its position on the market and the behaviour alleged to amount to an abuse. It had not, for example, threatened to drive the target firm out of the market by predatory price cutting if it refused to merge. The Court of Justice rejected this argument as well. It was possible to abuse a dominant position without actually exercising or relying on market power. It was an abuse simply for a dominant firm to strengthen its position and substantially to eliminate competition by taking over a rival. Abuse is an objective concept, and the conduct of an undertaking may be regarded as abusive in the absence of any fault and irrespective of the intention of the dominant undertaking. The scope of Article 102 would obviously be reduced if the Commission could apply it only to practices which were attributable to the exercise of

---

[224] Case 6/72 *Europemballage Corpn and Continental Can Co Inc Commission* [1973] ECR 215, [1973] CMLR 199; the impact of the judgment is discussed in Vogelenzang 'Abuse of a Dominant Position in Article 86: the Problem of Causality and Some Applications' (1976) 13 CML Rev 61.

[225] See eg Joliet *Monopolisation and Abuse of Dominance* (Martinus Nijhoff, 1970); it was also argued in *Continental Can* that mergers were not caught by Article 102 as Article 66(1) of the former ECSC Treaty dealt with them explicitly so that, by inference, the EC Treaty (now TFEU), which was silent on the issue, could not apply to them; and that anyway behaviour could not be abusive unless it was attributable to and caused by the use of the position of dominance (see below).

[226] This objective was previously contained in Article 3(1)(g) of the EC Treaty and, at the time of the *Continental Can* judgment, in Article 3(f) of the EEC Treaty: see ch 2, 'The competition chapter in the TFEU', pp 50–51.

[227] See ch 21 n 127, p 845.

market power that a dominant undertaking enjoys[228]. In *Hoffmann-La Roche* the Court of Justice said that:

> The interpretation suggested by the applicant that an abuse implies that the use of the economic power bestowed by a dominant position is the means whereby the abuse has been brought about cannot be accepted[229].

In *Tetra Pak II*[230] the Court of Justice stated at paragraph 27 of its judgment that 'application of Article [102] presupposes a link between the dominant position and the alleged abusive conduct'. This may appear to contradict the causation point in *Continental Can*. However, the issue in *Tetra Pak* was whether it is possible for the abuse to take place in a market different from the one in which an undertaking is dominant[231]; the Court was not concerned with the issue of whether the market power had to have been used in order to bring about the abuse.

It is interesting to note in passing that some systems of law – for example Australia and New Zealand – do require a causal connection between the position of dominance and the abusive behaviour: the majority judgment of the UK Privy Council in *Carter Holt Harvey Building Products Group Ltd v The Commerce Commission*[232] contains an interesting discussion of the case law in those two countries. Clearly such an approach will result in fewer findings of abuse; however the *Continental Can* judgment is clear that causation is not required under Article 102. The General Court relied on the judgments of the Court of Justice in *Continental Can* and *Hoffmann-La Roche* in *AstraZeneca AB v Commission*[233], where it said that 'an abuse of a dominant position does not necessarily have to consist in the use of the economic power conferred by the dominant position'[234].

(iii) Horizontal and vertical foreclosure

The concern about exclusionary abuses is that a dominant firm is able to behave in a way that forecloses competitors in an anti-competitive way[235] from entering the market, or prevents existing competitors from growing within it. The foreclosure might occur 'upstream' or 'downstream' in the market. Suppose that a firm is vertically integrated: it extracts a raw material, widgets, from its widget mines and processes widgets into widget dioxide: the upstream market is raw widgets, the downstream one is widget dioxide. Harm to competition could occur at either level of the market:

- **horizontal foreclosure**[236] arises where the dominant firm takes action to exclude a competitor that supplies widgets.

---

[228] See Vogelenzang 'Abuse of a Dominant Position in Article [102]: the Problem of Causality and Some Applications' (1976) 13 CML Rev 61; the Commission relied specifically on this aspect of the *Continental Can* judgment in para 46 of its decision in *Tetra Pak 1 (BTG Licence)* OJ [1988] L 272/27, [1988] 4 CMLR 881.

[229] Case 85/76 [1979] ECR 461, [1979] 3 CMLR 211, at para 91; note the suggestion by Advocate General Reischl at para 7c of his Opinion in *Hoffmann-La Roche* that causation might be treated differently according to the nature of the abuse in question.

[230] Case C-333/94 P *Tetra Pak International v Commission* [1996] ECR I-5951, [1997] 4 CMLR 662.

[231] See 'Horizontal and vertical foreclosure', pp 204–205 below.   [232] [2004] UKPC 37.

[233] Case T-321/05 [2010] ECR II-000, [2010] 5 CMLR 1585.   [234] Ibid, para 354.

[235] If a competitor is foreclosed by the superior efficiency of the dominant firm, the foreclosure would not be anti-competitive or abusive.

[236] The language of 'horizontal' and 'vertical' foreclosure is taken from paras 69–73 of DG COMP's *Discussion paper on the application of Article [102] of the Treaty to exclusionary abuses*; the Commission's *Guidance on Article 102 Enforcement Priorities* does not use the same language, while the Commission's *Guidelines on the assessment of non-horizontal mergers* OJ [2008] C 265/6, paras 30–59, distinguish between 'customer' and 'input' foreclosure, which are synonymous for horizontal and vertical foreclosure respectively.

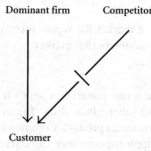

Fig. 5.1 **Horizontal foreclosure**

- **vertical foreclosure** arises where the dominant firm takes action to exclude a competitor in the downstream market for widget dioxide.

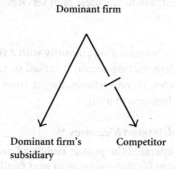

Fig. 5.2 **Vertical foreclosure**

Many exclusionary abuses are concerned with horizontal foreclosure: for example exclusive purchasing agreements, rebates and predatory pricing. Others however, for example refusal to supply and margin squeezing, are predominantly[237] concerned about harm to competition in the downstream market.

(iv) The dominant position, the abuse and the effects of the abuse may be in different markets

It is not necessary for the dominance, the abuse and the effects of the abuse all to be in the same market. In a simple case, X may be dominant in the market for widgets and charge high prices to exploit its customers or drop its prices in order to eliminate competitors from the widget market: clearly Article 102 can apply to this behaviour. However more complex situations may occur. X might be present on both the widget market and the downstream widget dioxide market, and may act on one of those markets in order to derive a benefit in the other: as we have just seen, there may be a horizontal or a vertical foreclosure of the market.

Some examples will illustrate the range of possibilities.

---

[237] A refusal to supply may sometimes have a horizontal effect: see ch 17, 'Horizontal foreclosure', p 708.

(A) Michelin v Commission[238]

Michelin was dominant in the market for replacement tyres and committed various abuses in order to protect its position in that market.

(B) Commercial Solvents[239]

Commercial Solvents supplied a raw material in which it was dominant to a customer which used it to make an anti-tuberculosis drug. The raw material was the upstream product; the drug was the downstream product. Commercial Solvents decided to produce the drug itself and ceased to supply the customer. Commercial Solvents was found to have abused its dominant position: it refused to supply the raw material in relation to which it was dominant, but this was done to benefit its position in the drug market, where it was not yet present at all.

(C) De Poste-La Poste[240]

The Belgian Post Office, dominant in the market for the delivery of 'normal' letters, abused its dominant position in that market in order to eliminate a competitor in the neighbouring market for business-to-business mail services.

(D) Télémarketing[241]

The dominant undertaking, a broadcasting authority with a statutory monopoly, decided to enter the downstream telemarketing sector. It ceased to supply broadcasting services to the only other telemarketer, thereby eliminating it from the market and effectively reserving the telemarketing business to itself.

(E) Sealink/B&I – Holyhead: Interim Measures[242]

Sealink, which owned and operated the port at Holyhead, was considered to have committed an abuse on the market for the provision of port facilities for passenger and ferry services, in which it was dominant, by structuring the sailing schedules there to the advantage of its own downstream ferry operations and to the disadvantage of its competitor at that level of the market, B&I. The same point can be noted in *Sea Containers v Stena Sealink – Interim Measures*[243].

(F) British Gypsum v Commission[244]

British Gypsum was dominant in the plasterboard market, but not dominant in the neighbouring plaster market (these markets were horizontally, rather than vertically, related). Among its abuses, British Gypsum gave priority treatment to customers for plaster who remained loyal to it in relation to plasterboard. This differs from the above examples, since in *British Gypsum* the abuse was committed in the non-dominated market in order to protect British Gypsum's position in its dominated market.

---

[238] Case 322/81 [1983] ECR 3461, [1985] 1 CMLR 282.
[239] Cases 6/73 etc [1974] ECR 223, [1974] 1 CMLR 309.
[240] OJ [2002] L 61/32, [2002] 4 CMLR 1426, paras 36–51.
[241] Case 311/84 *Centre Belge d'Etudes de Marché Télémarketing v CTL* [1985] ECR 3261, [1986] 2 CMLR 558.
[242] [1992] 5 CMLR 255.
[243] OJ [1994] L 15/8, [1995] 4 CMLR 84.
[244] Case C-310/93 P [1995] ECR I-865, [1997] 4 CMLR 238.

(G) Tetra Pak II[245]

The Court of Justice concluded that Tetra Pak had infringed Article 102 by tying practices and predatory pricing in the market for non-aseptic liquid repackaging machinery and non-aseptic cartons. It was not dominant in this market, but the abusive conduct was intended to benefit its position in that market. Tetra Pak was dominant in the (horizontally) associated market for aseptic machinery and cartons. The Court of Justice, after citing *Commercial Solvents*, *Télémarketing* and *British Gypsum*, held that 'in special circumstances'[246], there could be an abuse of a dominant position 'where conduct on a market distinct from the dominated market produces effects on that distinct market'[247]. The Court of Justice then went on to describe the 'close associative links' between the aseptic and non-aseptic markets which amounted to sufficiently special circumstances to engage Article 102: for example Tetra Pak had or could have customers in both markets, it could rely on having a favoured status in the non-dominated market because of its position in the dominated one, and it could concentrate its efforts on the non-aseptic market independently of other economic operators because of its position in relation to the aseptic market. This case extends the scope of application of Article 102 beyond, even, *British Gypsum*.

A table may help to explain the propositions set out in this paragraph.

5.3 Dominance, abuse and neighbouring markets

Case	Market A	Market B
Michelin v Commission	Dominance	
	Abuse	
	Benefit	
Commercial Solvents	Dominance	Benefit
Télémarketing	Abuse	
De Poste-La Poste		
Sealink decisions		
British Gypsum	Dominance	Abuse
	Benefit	
Tetra Pak v Commission	Dominance	Abuse
		Benefit

---

[245] Case C-333/94 P [1996] ECR I-5951, [1997] 4 CMLR 662; the Court of Justice's approach to the issue of abuse was different from that of the Commission's in its decision.

[246] Case C-333/94 P [1996] ECR I-5951, [1997] 4 CMLR 662, paras 25–31.

[247] Ibid, para 27.

Many of the Commission's decisions under Article 102 in recent years have involved two rather than one markets[248]. Obvious examples are *Deutsche Telekom v Commission*[249], *Microsoft v Commission*[250] and *Konkurrensverket v TeliaSonera*[251]; in the latter judgment the Court said that Article 102 gives no explicit guidance as to the market in which the abuse takes place: each case must be decided in the light of its specific circumstances[252]. Footnote 39 of the Commission's *Guidance on Article 102 Enforcement Priorities* says that the Commission may pursue predatory practices by dominant firms on markets on which they are not yet dominant.

The Commission could presumably apply the reasoning just described in the context of neighbouring product markets to dominance, abuse and benefits in neighbouring geographical markets[253].

(v) Effects analysis

It was pointed out above that there has been much criticism that the law and practice of Article 102 has been insufficiently aligned with sound economic principles. In recent years there have been several occasions on which the Commission has accepted that, where unilateral behaviour of a dominant firm is in issue, something more than proving the existence of that behaviour is needed to determine whether it is abusive[254]. There is much to be said for condemning alleged exclusionary conduct as abusive only where it can convincingly be demonstrated that there have been or will be adverse effects on the market[255]. Judgments such as *Deutsche Telekom* and *TeliaSonera* endorse this approach.

An important issue to consider is the standard of proof required: if every case were to require the demonstration of anti-competitive effects, to a high standard of proof, the enforcement of Article 102 might become all but impossible, which would bring one back to the problem of false negatives (as opposed to false positives)[256]. The text that follows will consider how the Commission seeks to deploy a realistic effects analysis when deciding which cases to bring under Article 102.

The Commission's *Guidance on Article 102 Enforcement Priorities* explains, at paragraph 19, that the aim of its enforcement activity in relation to exclusionary abuses is to ensure that dominant undertakings do not impair effective competition by foreclosing their competitors in an anti-competitive way: the concern is that such behaviour would have an adverse effect on consumer welfare, whether in the form of higher price levels than would otherwise have prevailed, or in some other form such as limiting the quality of goods or services or reducing consumer choice. 'Anti-competitive foreclosure' differs from 'mere foreclosure', which occurs where the dominant undertaking wins business on the merits as a result of its superior efficiency. Paragraph 20 of the *Guidance* sets out a series of factors which the Commission will take into account when deciding whether to intervene in relation to an alleged exclusionary abuse under Article 102: these factors will enable it to determine whether the conduct in question is likely to lead to an anti-competitive foreclosure

---

[248] Case T-219/99 *British Airways plc v Commission* [2003] ECR II-5917, [2004] 4 CMLR 1008, paras 127–135.

[249] Case C-280/08 P [2010] ECR I-000, [2010] 5 CMLR 1495.

[250] Case T-201/04 [2007] ECR II-3601, [2007] 5 CMLR 846.

[251] Case C-52/09 [2011] ECR I-000, [2011] 4 CMLR 982.

[252] Ibid, paras 84–89.

[253] See eg *Interbrew* in the Commission's XXVIth *Report on Competition Policy* (1996), point 53, where Interbrew was considered to have acted in non-dominated geographical markets to protect its dominant position in Belgium.

[254] See 'Recent case law and decisions do require effects analysis', pp 200–201 above.

[255] Ibid.

[256] See 'False positives and false negatives', pp 193–194 above.

of the market. The Commission adds that it would want there to be cogent and compelling evidence before it would intervene. The factors include:

- **the position of the dominant undertaking**: in general, the stronger the dominant position, the higher the likelihood that conduct protecting that position leads to anti-competitive foreclosure

- **the conditions on the relevant market**: these include the conditions of entry and expansion, such as the existence of economies of scale and/or scope and network effects

- **the position of the dominant undertaking's competitors**: even a fairly small competitor may play a significant competitive role where it is the closest competitor to the dominant undertaking, is particularly innovative or has the reputation of systematically cutting prices

- **the position of the customers or input suppliers**: this may include the possible selectivity of the conduct in question, for example where the dominant undertaking applies the practice only to selected customers or input suppliers who may be of particular importance for the entry or expansion of competitors, thereby enhancing the likelihood of anti-competitive foreclosure

- **the extent of the allegedly abusive conduct**: in general, the higher the percentage of total sales in the relevant market affected by the conduct, the longer its duration, and the more regularly it has been applied, the greater is the likely anti-competitive foreclosure effect

- **possible evidence of actual foreclosure**: where the conduct in question has already been taking place, there may be actual evidence of the dominant undertaking's market share having increased, or of competitors having exited the market; and

- **direct evidence of any exclusionary strategy**: there may be direct evidence – for example internal documents – of a strategy to exclude competitors, and this may be helpful in interpreting the dominant undertaking's conduct.

Paragraph 21 of the *Guidance* explains that, when pursuing a case, the Commission will develop its analysis, that is to say whether particular conduct is likely to have an anti-competitive foreclosure effect, using the general factors set out in paragraph 20, and the specific factors set out in later sections of the *Guidance*. This is a very important point to note. Later paragraphs of the *Guidance* discuss particular issues that are relevant to the assessment of the likelihood of anti-competitive foreclosure arising from individual practices. These specific points should always be understood within the broader context of the general factors discussed in paragraph 20 of the *Guidance*: they are a complement to, and not a substitute for, that paragraph.

The effects analysis described in the *Guidance* can be expected to have a positive influence on the future application of Article 102 to exclusionary behaviour. One must assume that the Commission will, in practice, apply its *Guidance* when deciding which cases to bring. This will mean that future cases brought by the Commission will concern conduct which it considers to have had, or to be likely to have, a significant anti-competitive foreclosing effect. It remains to be seen whether, over time, the EU Courts will follow the lead suggested by the Commission for a more detailed effects analysis under Article 102. What will also be interesting to observe is the extent to which the *Guidance* in practice has an influence on the decisions reached by national competition authorities and national courts. While they, of course, are bound by the jurisprudence of the EU Courts, it is not impossible to imagine that there might be occasions when, faced with an 'old' judgment lacking in sophisticated economic analysis, and analysis in the Commission's

Guidance that seems to be more convincing, the *Guidance* will play some part in the final decision[257].

(vi) Examples of exclusionary abuses

The Commission and the EU Courts have condemned many practices which could have anti-competitive effects. These will be examined in detail in chapters 17 to 19, which will consider in turn the following abuses:

- exclusive dealing agreements[258]
- tying[259]
- refusals to supply[260]
- miscellaneous other non-pricing abuses[261]
- rebates and other practices having effects similar to exclusive dealing agreements[262]
- bundling[263]
- predatory pricing[264]
- margin squeezing[265]
- price discrimination[266]
- refusals to license intellectual property rights or to provide proprietary information[267].

(H) Abuses that are harmful to the single market

As one would expect, abuses that are harmful to the single market are condemned[268]. Examples will be found later in this book of non-pricing[269] and pricing[270] abuses in which this was an obvious concern.

9. Defences

The term 'abuse' bears great intellectual strain, particularly as there is no equivalent in Article 102 to Article 101(3) whereby an agreement that restricts competition can nevertheless be permitted because it produces economic efficiencies. Over a number of years the Commission and the EU Courts came to recognise that there was some conduct which, although presumptively abusive, in fact did not amount to a violation of Article 102 because

---

[257] See eg in the UK *Alleged abuse of a dominant position by Flybe Limited* OFT decision of 5 November 2010, OFT 1286 (relying on the *Guidance* in support of its approach to predatory pricing).
[258] Ch 17, 'Exclusive Dealing Agreements', pp 682–688.   [259] Ch 17, 'Tying', pp 688–696.
[260] Ch 17, 'Refusal to Supply', pp 697–711.
[261] Ch 17, 'Miscellaneous Other Non-Pricing Abuses', pp 712–714.
[262] Ch 18, 'Rebates That Have Effects Similar to Exclusive Dealing Agreements', pp 728–737.
[263] Ch 18, 'Bundling', pp 737–739.   [264] Ch 18, 'Predatory Pricing', pp 739–754.
[265] Ch 18, 'Margin Squeezing', pp 754–759.   [266] Ch 18, 'Price Discrimination', pp 759–764.
[267] Ch 19, 'Article 102 and Intellectual Property Rights', pp 796–803.
[268] See ch 1, 'The single market imperative', pp 23–24 and ch 2, 'The single market imperative', p 51.
[269] See ch 17, 'Non-Pricing Abuses That are Harmful to the Internal Market', pp 711–712.
[270] See ch 18, 'Pricing Practices That are Harmful to the Single Market', pp 764–766.

it had an 'objective justification'[271]. For example in *Sot. Lélos*[272] the Court of Justice stated that the fact that an undertaking is in a dominant position cannot deprive it of its entitlement to protect its own commercial interests when they are attacked; however the Court added that such behaviour cannot be allowed if its purpose is to strengthen the dominant position and thereby abuse it. In its *Guidance on Article 102 Enforcement Priorities*, from paragraphs 28 to 31, the Commission says that it will take into account claims put forward by a dominant undertaking that its behaviour is objectively necessary or produces substantial efficiencies that outweigh any anti-competitive effects on consumers.

This section will examine what is meant by objective justification; it will briefly consider the question of whether a defence can be based on the principle of non-interference with property rights; and will conclude with a discussion of the burden of proving a defence.

(A) Objective justification[273]

The language of objective justification can be found in many judgments and decisions, coupled with the proposition that, to be objectively justified, the conduct in question must be proportionate. For example in *Centre Belge d'Etudes de Marché Télémarketing v CLT*[274] the Court of Justice held that an undertaking in a dominant position in television broad-casting which entrusted 'telemarketing' to its own subsidiary, thereby excluding other firms from entering this market, would be guilty of an abuse where there was no objective necessity for such behaviour[275]. The principles of objective justification and proportionality have been invoked on other occasions[276] and are firmly part of Article 102 analysis.

At paragraph 29 of the *Guidance on Article 102 Enforcement Priorities* the Commission says that a claim to objective necessity would have to be based on factors external to the dominant undertaking: for example, health or safety considerations. The Commission points out that it is normally the task of the public authorities to set and enforce public health and safety standards: this is based on judgments of the General Court in the *Hilti*[277] and *Tetra Pak II*[278] cases.

At paragraph 30 of the *Guidance* the Commission says that it will also consider arguments to the effect that conduct which apparently forecloses competitors can be defended

---

[271] For an interesting discussion of the concept of objective justification see the Opinion of Advocate General Jacobs in Case C-53/03 *Syfait* [2005] ECR I-4609, [2005] 5 CMLR 7, paras 71–72.

[272] Cases C-468/06 etc *Sot. Lélos kai Sia EE v GlaxoSmithKline AEVE Farmakeftikon Proionton* [2008] ECR I-7139, [2008] 5 CMLR 1382, para 50.

[273] For discussion see Loewenthal 'The Defence of "Objective Justification" in the Application of Article 82 EC' (2005) 28(4) World Competition 455; Albors-Llorens 'The Role of Objective Justification and Efficiencies in the Application of Article 82 EC' (2007) 44 CML Rev 1727; Rousseva 'Objective Justification and Article 82 EC in the Era of Modernisation' in *EC Competition Law: A Critical Assessment* (Hart Publishing, 2007, eds Amato and Ehlermann).

[274] Case 311/84 [1985] ECR 3261, [1986] 2 CMLR 558.

[275] Ibid, para 26; see also Case C-95/04 P *British Airways plc v Commission* [2007] ECR I-2331, [2007] 4 CMLR 982, para 69.

[276] See eg *BBI/Boosey and Hawkes* OJ [1987] L 286/36, [1988] 4 CMLR 67; *BPB Industries plc* OJ [1989] L 10/50, [1990] 4 CMLR 464, para 132, upheld on appeal Case T-65/89 *BPB Industries plc and British Gypsum v Commission* [1993] ECR II-389, [1993] 5 CMLR 32 and further on appeal to the Court of Justice Case C-310/93 P *BPB Industries plc and British Gypsum v Commission* [1995] ECR I-865, [1997] 4 CMLR 238; *Napier Brown – British Sugar* OJ [1988] L 284/41, [1990] 4 CMLR 196, paras 64 and 70; *NDC Health/IMS Health: Interim Measures* OJ [2002] L 59/18, [2002] 4 CMLR 111, paras 167–174; *Portuguese Airports* OJ [1999] L 69/31, [1999] 5 CMLR 103, para 29; *Prokent-Tomra* Commission decision of 29 March 2006, paras 347–390.

[277] Case T-30/89 *Hilti AG v Commission* [1991] ECR II-1439, [1992] 14 CMLR 16, paras 102–119.

[278] Case T-83/91 *Tetra Pak International SA v Commission* [1994] ECR II-755, [1997] 4 CMLR 726, paras 136–140, upheld on appeal to the Court of Justice Case C-333/94 P *Tetra Pak International SA v Commission* [1996] ECR I-5951, [1997] 4 CMLR 662, para 37.

on efficiency grounds. The Commission explains that four cumulative conditions would have to be fulfilled before an efficiency 'defence' could succeed:

- the efficiencies would have to be realised, or be likely to be realised, as a result of the conduct in question
- the conduct would have to be indispensable to the realisation of those efficiencies
- the efficiencies would have to outweigh any negative effects on competition and consumer welfare in the affected markets; and
- the conduct must not eliminate all effective competition.

In its decision in *Wanadoo de España v Telefónica*[279] the Commission included a lengthy discussion of possible defences including, from paragraphs 641 to 663, efficiencies, which it rejected on the facts of the case. In the opinion of the authors the Commission's approach seems reasonable, in that efficiency considerations can be taken into account under Article 101(3)[280] and in EU merger control[281]: it would seem odd if efficiency had no part to play in Article 102 analysis.

(B) **Abuse of dominance and property rights**

In a number of cases under Article 102 a particular issue has been the extent to which a dominant undertaking could be held to have acted abusively in relation to the way in which it chose to use, or not to use, its own property. Article 345 TFEU provides that:

> The Treaties shall in no way prejudice the rules in Member States governing the system of property ownership.

If it is possible for the Commission, under Article 102, to order the owner, for example, of an essential facility to provide access to it to a third party[282], this clearly affects that undertaking's property rights; but has it affected them to the point where the rules on property ownership in Member States have been prejudiced? The issue arose in relation to *Frankfurt Airport*[283] where the Commission required FAG, the owner and operator of that airport, to allow competition in the market for ground-handling services there. The Commission rejected the argument that this would interfere with the property rights of FAG. The Commission noted that the Court of Justice in *Hauer v Land Rheinland Pfalz*[284] had acknowledged the existence of a fundamental right to property in the EU legal order; however it had also noted that the constitutions of the Member States recognised that the exercise of property rights may be restricted in the public interest. In the *Frankfurt Airport* decision the Commission said that it followed from the *Hauer* judgment that the competition rules in the Treaty may be considered to constitute restrictions on the right of property which correspond to objectives of general interest pursued by the EU[285]. In the Commission's view, allowing the provision of ground-handling services within the airport would not constitute an excessive or intolerable interference

---

[279] Commission decision of 4 July 2007, on appeal to the General Court Case T-336/07 *Telefónica v Commission*, not yet decided and Case T-398/07 *Spain v Commission*, not yet decided.

[280] See ch 4, 'First condition of Article 101(3): an improvement in the production or distribution of goods or in technical or economic progress', pp 155–162.

[281] See ch 21, 'Efficiencies', pp 874–876.

[282] See ch 17, 'Refusal to Supply', pp 697–708.

[283] *Flughafen Frankfurt* OJ [1998] L 72/30, [1998] 4 CMLR 779.

[284] Case 44/79 [1979] ECR 3727, [1980] 3 CMLR 42, para 17.

[285] OJ [1998] L 72/30, [1998] 4 CMLR 779, para 90.

with FAG's rights as owner of the airport; it would not interfere with FAG's own ability to provide these services, and FAG could charge a reasonable fee to third parties for their right to do so.

In his Opinion in *Masterfoods Ltd v HB Ice Cream Ltd*[286] Advocate General Cosmas had no doubt that:

> it is perfectly comprehensible for restrictions to be placed on the right to property owner-ship pursuant to Articles [101 and 102 TFEU], to the degree to which they might be neces-sary to protect competition[287].

In *Van den Bergh Foods Ltd v Commission*[288] the General Court rejected an argument that the Commission's decision in *Van den Bergh Foods Ltd*[289], requiring that space be made available in Van den Bergh's freezer cabinets for the ice-cream of competitors, amounted to a disproportionate interference with its property rights[290]. In *Microsoft v Commission* the General Court rejected the argument that Microsoft was entitled to refuse to sup-ply interoperability information to competitors because it was protected by intellectual property rights: this would be inconsistent with the rule, derived from the *Magill* and *IMS Health* cases, that, in exceptional circumstances, there can be an obligation to grant licences to third parties[291].

(C) Burden of proof

In *Microsoft v Commission*[292] the General Court stated that:

> it is for the dominant undertaking concerned, and not for the Commission, before the end of the administrative procedure, to raise any plea of objective justification and to support it with arguments and evidence. It then falls to the Commission, where it proposes to make a finding of an abuse of a dominant position, to show that the arguments and evi-dence relied on by the undertaking cannot prevail and, accordingly, that the justification cannot be accepted[293].

The General Court went on to state that it was not sufficient for the dominant undertaking to put forward 'vague, general and theoretical arguments' in support of its objective jus-tification[294]. Paragraph 31 of the Commission's *Guidance on Article 102 Enforcement Priorities* adopts the same approach to the burden of proof.

---

[286] Case C-344/98 [2000] ECR I-11369, [2001] 4 CMLR 449; see also Case C-163/99 *Portugal v Commission* [2001] ECR I-2613, [2002] 2 CMLR 1319, paras 58–59.

[287] Ibid, para 105.

[288] Case T-65/98 [2003] ECR II-4653, [2004] 4 CMLR 14.

[289] OJ [1998] L 246/1, [1998] 5 CMLR 530.

[290] Case T-65/98 [2003] ECR II-4653, [2004] 4 CMLR 14, paras 170–171.

[291] Case T-201/04 [2007] ECR II-3601, [2007] 5 CMLR 846, paras 690–691; see ch 19, 'Microsoft', pp 800–802.

[292] Case T-201/04 [2007] ECR II-3601, [2007] 5 CMLR 846.

[293] Ibid, para 688; the General Court adopted the same approach in Case T-301/04 *Clearstream Banking AG v Commission* [2009] ECR II-3155, [2009] 5 CMLR 2677, para 185.

[294] Ibid, para 698; for discussion of proof generally in Article 102 cases see Paulis 'The burden of proof in Article 82 cases' [2006] Fordham Corporate Law Institute (ed Hawk), ch 20; Nazzini 'The wood began to move: an essay on consumer welfare, evidence and burden of proof in Article 82 EC cases' (2006) 31 ELRev 518.

10. The Consequences of Infringing Article 102

(A) Public enforcement[295]

Where the Commission finds an abuse of a dominant position it has power, pursuant to Article 23 of Regulation 1/2003, to impose a fine[296], and to order the dominant under-taking to cease and desist from the conduct in question[297]; where necessary, it may also order a dominant undertaking to adopt positive measures in order to bring an infringe-ment to an end[298]. It is even possible for the Commission to order the divestiture of an undertaking's assets, or to break an undertaking up, under the powers conferred by Article 7 of the Regulation 1/2003[299], provided it is proportionate and necessary to bring the infringement to an end and provided that there is no equally effective behavioural remedy or that such a remedy would be more burdensome[300]. The Commission has not, to date, imposed a structural remedy under Article 7, although such remedies have been accepted as legally-binding commitments under Article 9 of that Regulation[301].

(B) Private enforcement

The civil law consequences of infringing Article 102 are discussed in chapter 8[302].

---

[295] See the OECD Roundtable on *Remedies and Sanctions in Abuse of Dominance Cases* of 2006 for a general discussion of this topic, available at www.oecd.org.

[296] See ch 7, 'Article 23: Fines', pp 275–282.

[297] See ch 7, 'Behavioural remedies', p 253.

[298] See ch 7, 'Behavioural remedies', pp 253–254.

[299] OJ [2003] L 1/1; see ch 7, 'Structural remedies', p 254.

[300] See ch 7, 'Past infringements', pp 254–255.

[301] See ch 9, 'Article 9: commitments', pp 255–261.

[302] See ch 8, 'Article 102', p 324.

6

The obligations of Member States under the EU competition rules

1. Introduction

This chapter will examine the obligations of Member States in relation to EU competition law. Specifically it will consider the obligations that Article 4(3) TEU and Articles 37 and 106 TFEU place upon Member States; Articles 107 to 109 TFEU on state aid will be briefly mentioned at the end of the chapter. The expression 'Member State' for these purposes includes all organs of the state, of which a national competition authority[1] and an economic regulator[2] would be examples. Article 4(3) imposes a general duty of 'sincere cooperation' or 'loyalty' on Member States; Article 37 deals specifically with state monopolies of a commercial character; and Article 106 is concerned with measures that are contrary to the Treaty. In *France v Commission*[3] Advocate General Tesauro spoke of the 'obscure clarity' of Article 37 as opposed to the 'clear obscurity' of Article 106. These provisions are complex and the law has taken a long time to develop: the encroachment of EU law on national monopolies and state activity is inevitably political and contentious.

Article 3(3) TEU provides that the EU shall establish an internal market which, as explained in Protocol 27 to the Treaties, includes 'a system ensuring that competition is not distorted'[4]. Article 3(3) also provides that one of the EU's objectives is a highly competitive social market economy. Article 119 TFEU provides that the activities of the Member States and the EU shall be conducted in accordance with the principle of an open market economy with free competition[5]. State involvement in economic activities may work against this goal;

---

[1] See eg Case C-198/01 *Consorzio Industrie Fiammiferi* [2003] ECR I-8055, [2003] 5 CMLR 829, discussed at '*Consorzio Industrie Fiammiferi*', pp 219–220 below.

[2] See the decision of the National Lottery Commission of 3 March 2011 in which it refused consent to Camelot UK Lotteries Ltd, the operator of the UK Lottery, to provide commercial services such as over-the-counter cash bill payment and mobile phone top-up through its National Lottery terminals as this gave rise to 'serious concerns' about a possible infringement of Article 106 in conjunction with Articles 101 and/or 102.

[3] Case C-202/88 [1991] ECR I-1223, [1992] 5 CMLR 552, at para 11 of his Opinion.

[4] This objective was previously contained in Article 3(1)(g) of the EC Treaty: see ch 2, 'The competition chapter in the TFEU', pp 50–51.

[5] Note that the Court of Justice stressed the importance of Article 119 TFEU in its judgment in Case C-198/01 *Consorzio Industrie Fiammiferi (CIF)* [2003] ECR I-8055, [2003] 5 CMLR 829, para 47.

however Member States may take offence at too much interference at an EU level in domestic economic and social policy. Articles 101 and 102 are essentially private law provisions, conferring rights and imposing obligations on undertakings; many other Articles in the TFEU are primarily of a public law nature, imposing obligations on Member States. The extent to which Member States and undertakings which enjoy special or exclusive rights are subject to Articles 101 and 102 is an issue that is still being explored by the Commission and the EU Courts.

EU law is neutral on the issue of public ownership of industry in itself. Article 345 TFEU provides that the Treaties 'shall in no way prejudice the rules in Member States governing the system of property ownership'. This means that Member States may confer legal monopolies on organs of the state or on undertakings that are not publicly owned, and in cases under Article 106(1) such as *Sacchi*[6], *ERT v Dimotiki*[7] and *Höfner & Elser v Macrotron GmbH*[8] the Court of Justice has held that the conferment of special or exclusive rights on an undertaking is not, in itself, an infringement of EU law. However there is a tension between this principle and the obligation imposed on Member States by Article 106(1) not to enact nor to maintain in force measures contrary to the competition rules, with the result that property rights are not as inviolable as the wording of Article 345 suggests[9].

2. Article 4(3) TEU – Duty of Sincere Cooperation

Article 4(3) TEU provides that the EU and the Member States shall assist each other in carrying out tasks which flow from the Treaties. Article 4(3) also imposes positive and negative duties on Member States: it requires them to take all appropriate measures to ensure fulfilment of the obligations arising out of the Treaties and to refrain from any measure which could jeopardise the attainment of the EU's objectives. There have been many cases in which individuals and undertakings have invoked Article 4(3) in proceedings in the criminal and civil courts of Member States, both as plaintiff and defendant, to claim that a particular law of a Member State is unenforceable because of its incompatibility with the competition rules in the Treaty; many of these cases have led to references to the Court of Justice under Article 267 TFEU, and will be discussed in this section of the chapter. The Court has established that the obligation of Member States to disapply national legislation that contravenes EU law attaches not only to national courts but also to administrative bodies, including national competition authorities[10]. Where a Member State is in breach of its obligations under Article 4(3) it would also be possible for the Commission to take action against it, either under Article 258 TFEU, as in the case of *Commission v Italy*[11], or, where there is an infringement of Article 106(1), under Article 106(3)[12].

---

[6] Case 155/73 [1974] ECR 409, [1974] 2 CMLR 177, para 14.

[7] Case C-260/89 [1991] ECR I-2925, [1994] 4 CMLR 540, para 16.

[8] Case C-41/90 [1991] ECR I-1979, [1993] 4 CMLR 306, para 29.

[9] See further 'Making sense of the case law on Article 102 in conjunction with Article 106(1)', pp 229–235.

[10] See Case C-198/01 *Consorzio Industrie Fiammiferi (CIF)* [2003] ECR I-8055, [2003] 5 CMLR 829, paras 49–50.

[11] Case C-35/96 [1998] ECR I-3851, [1998] 5 CMLR 889; see 'Article 106(3)', pp 242–244 below.

[12] See further 'Article 106(3)', pp 242–244.

(A) The relationship between Article 4(3) TEU and Articles 101 and 102 TFEU

The case law on Article 4(3) is complex, for reasons that are not difficult to understand[13]. It is obvious that measures adopted by Member States may distort competition: they might do so for example by imposing minimum or maximum prices for goods or services; by adopting discriminatory measures of taxation; by imposing regulatory rules that make it difficult for undertakings to enter markets; or by operating restrictive licensing regimes for particular economic activities. Each of these measures might have serious implications for the competitiveness of markets. However the issue that arises in relation to Article 4(3), when read in conjunction with Articles 101 and 102, is the extent to which those measures can be challenged, and be found to be unlawful, under EU law.

Article 4(3) is addressed to Member States; Articles 101 and 102 are directed to under-takings. The conundrum is to decide when a Member State can be held liable for behaviour of undertakings that infringes the competition rules. On the one hand Member States are naturally jealous of their sovereignty, and do not welcome the use of Article 4(3) to under-mine national laws, delegated legislation, regulatory regimes and other measures because they happen to have an effect on the competitiveness of markets; a broad use of Article 4(3) would be particularly objectionable given that there are clear legal bases for proceeding against Member States under other parts of the Treaty dealing, for example, with the free movement of goods and services. On the other hand the full effectiveness of Articles 101 and 102 could be seriously undermined if Member States could act as the agent of cartels and dominant undertakings that act abusively by adopting measures that have the same effect on the market as the undertakings would have achieved themselves. The case law of the Court of Justice has sought to achieve a balance and to identify those infringements of Articles 101 and 102 for which Member States must bear responsibility.

(B) The case law predominantly concerns Article 4(3) TEU in conjunction with Article 101 TFEU

It is noticeable that state measures that raise issues in relation to abusive behaviour under Article 102 usually arise in the context of Article 106(1), which imposes a specific duty on Member States not to enact nor to maintain in force measures in the case of 'pub-lic undertakings and undertakings to which Member States grant special or exclusive rights' which infringe the Treaty and, specifically, the competition rules[14]. The case law on Article 4(3) therefore has been predominantly concerned with the liability of Member States for infringements of Article 101. Before considering the cases themselves it may be helpful to illustrate the type of problem that arises. Suppose the following:

- in Member State A all lawyers belong to a privately-established bar association and agree to comply with the fees that it recommends for legal services
- in Member State B the state itself fixes legal fees

---

[13] For interesting discussions of the issues involved see Bacon 'State Regulation of the Market and EC Competition Rules: Articles 85 and 86 Compared' (1997) 18 ECLR 283; Ehle 'State Regulation under the US Antitrust State Action Doctrine and under EC Competition Law: a Comparative Analysis' (1998) 19 ECLR 380; Neergaard *Competition Competences: The Tensions between European Competition Law and Anti-competitive Measures by the Member States* (DJØF Publishing, 1998); Gagliardi 'United States and European Union Antitrust Versus State Regulation of the Economy: Is There a Better Test?' (2000) 25 EL Rev 353; Schepel 'Delegation of Regulatory Powers to Private Powers under EC Competition Law: Towards a Procedural Public Interest' (2002) 39 CML Rev 31; on the position in the US in relation to state regulatory measures see *Parker v Brown* 317 US 341 (1943) and Delacourt and Zywicki 'The FTC and State Action: Evolving Views on the Proper Role of Government' (2005) 72(3) Antitrust LJ 1075.

[14] See 'Article 106(1)', pp 223–235 below.

- in Member State C the bar association is established by law but the association is free to decide whether to recommend fees and, if so, to determine the level of those fees
- in Member State D the state requires the bar association to fix fees but leaves it to determine what they should be
- in Member State E a Government Minister has the power, by order, to decree that all lawyers will comply with a draft tariff of fees prepared by the bar association.

In each of these cases the likely outcome will be that there is little competition in relation to legal fees: the effect is that of a horizontal cartel. However in EU competition law the important question is which, if any, of these situations is unlawful; and, specifically in the case of Article 4(3), whether there is a state measure that violates EU law with the consequence that it is void and unenforceable. These questions will be considered after the case law has been analysed.

(C) The case law of the Court of Justice on Article 4(3) and the competition rules

(i) The *INNO* doctrine

In *INNO v ATAB*[15] the Court, dealing in that case with the taxation of tobacco in Belgium, held that the combined effect of Article 4(3) TEU and Articles 101 and 102 TFEU[16] meant that a Member State could infringe EU law by maintaining in force legislation which could deprive the competition rules of their effectiveness. Subsequent cases have had to search out the implications of this judgment[17]. A challenge to French legislation requiring retailers of books to comply with minimum resale prices imposed by publishers failed since the Court of Justice was not certain that this practice was unlawful under Article 101 anyway[18]; a challenge to fixed minimum prices for petrol also failed, since this was a pure state measure unrelated to any agreement between undertakings[19]. Opposition to a French law forbidding the undercutting of tariffs for air fares approved by the Minister for Civil Aviation and made binding upon all traders also failed since, at the time, there was no implementing regulation for the application of the competition rules to the air transport sector; this meant that there was no mechanism in place for determining whether any agreements satisfied the terms of Article 101(3)[20]. In *BNIC v Clair*[21] a French trade association, BNIC, sued Clair for undercutting minimum prices established by it, but then extended by Ministerial decree to the entire industry. Under French law these 'extension orders' became binding on everyone in the industry, and BNIC was given the right to

---

[15] Case 13/77 [1977] ECR 2115, [1978] 1 CMLR 283.

[16] The Court also referred to Article 3(1)(g) EC but this provision was repealed by the Lisbon Treaty with effect from 1 December 2009; on Article 3(1)(g) and Protocol 27 to the Treaties see ch 2, 'The competition chapter in the TFEU', pp 50–51.

[17] The Opinion of AG Maduro in Case C-94/04 *Cipolla* [2006] ECR I-11421, [2007] 4 CMLR 286, paras 31–40 contains a useful review of the case law.

[18] See Case 229/83 *Association des Centres Distributeurs Edouard Leclerc v Au Ble Vert* [1985] ECR 1, [1985] 2 CMLR 286; Case 254/87 *Syndicat des Libraires de Normandie v L'Aigle Distribution SA* [1988] ECR 4457, [1990] 4 CMLR 37.

[19] Case 231/83 *Cullet v Centre Leclerc, Toulouse* [1985] ECR 305, [1985] 2 CMLR 524.

[20] Cases 209/84 etc *Ministère Public v Asjes* [1986] ECR 1425, [1986] 3 CMLR 173, paras 46–69; however the Court continued that, if an adverse finding had been made under Article 104 or 105(2), it would have been contrary to Article 4(3) TEU for France to have reinforced the effects of an unlawful agreement: ibid, paras 70–77; on the application of the competition rules to air transport: see ch 23, 'Air Transport', pp 974–977.

[21] Case 123/83 [1985] ECR 391, [1985] 2 CMLR 430.

bring an action against anyone selling at less than the fixed price. The Court of Justice, in an Article 267 reference from a French court, held that the involvement of the Minister did not deprive the activities of BNIC of illegality under Article 101(1). This confirmed the Commission's decisions in *BNIA*[22] and *BNIC*[23]; however the Court was not asked in this reference to consider the legality of the French legislation or of the Ministerial order themselves, so that Article 4(3) was not discussed.

(ii) Successful application of the INNO doctrine

(A) BNIC v Yves Aubert

The *INNO* doctrine was successfully applied in a similar case, *BNIC v Yves Aubert*[24]. There the Court of Justice held that the Minister's extension order, which in this case fixed quotas for wine-growers and permitted fines to be imposed on anyone who exceeded them, was itself unlawful. The order had the effect of strengthening the impact of the prior agreement made within the membership of BNIC and was a breach of France's obligations under the Treaty; it followed that an action brought against Yves Aubert by BNIC for infringement of the extension order failed.

(B) Vlaamse Reisbureaus v Sociale Dienst

In *Vlaamse Reisbureaus v Sociale Dienst*[25] a tour operator in Belgium brought an action against an association of travel agents which was passing on to its customers the commission it received from tour operators. By Belgian law the tour operator was permitted in these circumstances to bring an action for unfair competition against the price-cutter. The defendant raised the incompatibility of this law with Article 101(1). The Court of Justice held that there was a constellation of agreements in the industry between tour operators and agents intended to dampen price competition and which infringed Article 101(1); the Belgian legislation buttressed this anti-competitive system by giving it permanent effect, extending it to non-participating undertakings, and by providing penalties for firms which passed on their commission. Therefore the legislation infringed EU law and the claimant's action for unfair competition should fail.

(C) Ahmed Saeed

In *Ahmed Saeed Flugreisen v Zentrale zur Bekämpfung Unlauteren Wettbewerbs eV*[26] the Court of Justice held that the approval by aeronautical authorities of air tariffs fixed by agreement by airlines involved a breach by Member States of their obligations under Article 4(3) TEU and Articles 101 and 102 TFEU. The material distinction between this case and *Ministère Public v Asjes*[27] was that by the time of the litigation in *Ahmed Saeed* the implementing regulation in the air transport sector had come into effect[28], so that there was no longer the problem that existed at the time of the earlier case[29].

(D) Consorzio Industrie Fiammiferi

In *Consorzio Industrie Fiammiferi*[30] the Court of Justice held that the Italian competition authority was required by Article 4(3) TEU to disapply an Italian law of 1923 which regulated

---

[22] OJ [1976] L 231/24, [1976] 2 CMLR D63.   [23] OJ [1982] L 379/1, [1983] 2 CMLR 240.

[24] Case 136/86 [1987] ECR 4789, [1988] 4 CMLR 331.

[25] Case 311/85 [1987] ECR 3801, [1989] 4 CMLR 213.

[26] Case 66/86 [1989] ECR 803, [1990] 4 CMLR 102.

[27] Cases 229/84 etc [1986] ECR 1425, [1986] 3 CMLR 173.   [28] See ch 6 n 20 above.

[29] See 'The INNO doctrine', pp 218–219 above.

[30] Case C-198/01 [2003] ECR I-8055, [2003] 5 CMLR 829; for comment see Nebbia (2004) 41 CML Rev 839; Kaczorowska 'The Power of a National Competition Authority to Disapply National Law Incompatible

the manufacture and sale of matches in Italy in so far as that law required or facilitated price fixing and market sharing contrary to Article 101; it added that penalties could be imposed on the undertakings involved in the unlawful period, except to the extent that the behaviour in question was required as opposed to merely being permitted by the legislation.

In each of these cases an infringement of Article 4(3) was found where the legislation of a Member State strengthened or encouraged anti-competitive agreements that were already in existence; in *Yves Aubert* and *Ahmed Saeed* the Member States had delegated the power to fix prices to private operators, subsequently reinforcing the effect of their decisions. In *P Van Eycke v ASPA*[31] a claimant, disappointed at the interest rate payable on a deposit of his savings, claimed that the rate had been reduced below his expectations because of tax legislation which contravened Article 101. The Court of Justice held that the *INNO* doctrine was inapplicable as there was no suggestion that the legislation in question encouraged or extended a prior anti-competitive private agreement. In its judgment the Court said that the case law showed that a Member State would be in breach of Article 4(3) TEU in conjunction with Article 101 TFEU if it were:

> to require or favour the adoption of agreements, decisions or concerted practices contrary to Article [101] or to reinforce their effects, or to deprive its own legislation of its official character by delegating to private traders responsibility for taking decisions affecting the economic sphere[32].

This is a formulation that the Court of Justice has repeated on subsequent occasions[33]. A particularly clear application of the doctrine is to be found in *Commission v Italy*[34], an action brought by the Commission under Article 258 TFEU, challenging – successfully – Italian legislation which required the National Council of Customs Agents to set compulsory tariffs for customs agents. The Court of Justice concluded that the National Council had itself infringed Article 101(1) by adopting the tariff[35]. However it held further that Italy had also infringed the Treaty by requiring the Council to compile a compulsory, uniform tariff[36]: by wholly relinquishing to private economic operators the powers of the public authorities to set tariffs[37]; by prohibiting, in the primary legislation, any derogation from the tariff[38]; and by adopting a Decree having the appearance of approving the tariff by public regulation[39].

(iii) No liability where there is no agreement between undertakings

Several challenges to national legislation have failed where the final determination of prices remained with a Member State: Article 4(3) TEU in conjunction with Article 101 is infringed only where a Member State requires, favours or reinforces an anti-competitive agreement or abandons its own price-setting powers and delegates them to private operators. Thus in *Meng*[40] the Court of Justice declined to strike down a German regulation which prohibited

---

with EC Law – and its Practical Consequences' (2004) 25 ECLR 591; for discussion of the *CIF* judgment in the UK see Case No 1027/2/3/04 *VIP Communications Ltd (in administration) v OFCOM* [2009] CAT 28, [2010] CompAR 13 paras 20–27.

[31] Case 267/86 [1988] ECR 4769, [1990] 4 CMLR 330.   [32] Ibid, para 16.

[33] See eg Case C-185/91 *Reiff* [1993] ECR I-5801, [1995] 5 CMLR 145, para 14; Case C-153/93 *Delta Schiffahrts- und Speditionsgesellschaft* [1994] ECR I-2517, [1996] 4 CMLR 21, para 14; Case C-38/97 *Autotrasporti Librandi v Cuttica Spedizioni e Servizi Internazionali* [1998] ECR I-5955, [1998] 5 CMLR 966, para 26.

[34] Case C-35/96 [1998] ECR I-3851, [1998] 5 CMLR 889; the Commission's decision finding that the National Council itself had infringed Article 101(1), OJ [1993] L 203/27, [1995] 5 CMLR 495, was upheld on appeal by the General Court in Case T-513/93 *CNSD v Commission* [2000] ECR II-1807, [2000] 5 CMLR 614.

[35] [1998] ECR I-3851, [1998] 5 CMLR 889, para 51.   [36] Ibid, para 56.

[37] Ibid, para 57.   [38] Ibid, para 58.   [39] Ibid, para 59.

[40] Case C-2/91 [1993] ECR I-5751; note that *Meng* was decided at about the same time as Case C-267/91 *Keck and Mithouard* [1993] ECR I-6097, [1995] 1 CMLR 101, in which the Court of Justice declined to apply

insurance companies from passing on commissions to their customers: unlike the position in *Vlaamse*, where Belgium had acted to reinforce prior agreements between travel agents, there was no agreement in *Meng*[41]; similar conclusions were reached in *Ohra*[42], *Reiff*[43] and in a number of later judgments[44]. In *Arduino*[45] the Court of Justice held that the involvement of the Italian National Bar Council in the production of a draft tariff for legal fees did not divest the tariff adopted by the Minister of the character of legislation[46]. The insistence that there must be an agreement contrary to Article 101 before a Member State can be found to have infringed Article 4(3) places an obvious limit on the extent to which it is possible to use the *INNO* doctrine to challenge state measures; in particular it is clear that Article 4(3) cannot be used simply because a state measure produces effects similar to those of a cartel. The other requirements for the application of Article 101 TFEU, such as the concepts of undertaking[47] and effect on trade between Member States[48], also limit the application of the *INNO* doctrine. Furthermore it can apply only where any agreement that is entered into is one that infringes Article 101. This was not the case in *AG2R Prévoyance v Beaudort Père et Fils SARL*[49]: there the agreement was the result of collective bargaining between employers' and employees' organisations within the French traditional bakery and pastry-making sector, a type of agreement that the Court of Justice has held to fall outside Article 101[50].

(D) Application of the case law to lawyers' fees

Having analysed the case law under the *INNO* doctrine we should return briefly to the alternative situations set out above in relation to legal fees[51]:

- in the case of Member State A lawyers agreed to comply with the recommendations of a privately-established bar association: this could clearly amount to an infringement of Article 101(1) TFEU, assuming an appreciable effect on competition and inter-state

Article 34 TFEU to national marketing rules forbidding the use of loss-leaders (selling below cost) in retail outlets: see Reich 'The "November Revolution" of the European Court of Justice: *Keck, Meng* and *Audi* Revisited' (1994) 31 CML Rev 459.

[41] Case C-2/91 [1993] ECR I-5751, para 14; Case C-245/91 [1993] ECR I-5851.
[43] Case C-185/91 [1993] ECR 5801, [1995] 5 CMLR 145.
[44] See eg Case C-153/93 *Delta Schiffahrts- und Speditionsegesellschaft* [1994] ECR I-2517, [1996] 4 CMLR 21; Case C-412/93 *Société d'Importaton Edouard Leclerc-Siplec v TFI and M6* [1995] ECR I-179, [1995] 3 CMLR 422; Case C-96/94 *Centro Servizi Spediporto v Spedizioni Marittima del Golfo* [1995] ECR I-2883, [1996] 4 CMLR 613; Cases C-140/94 etc *DIP SpA v Commune di Bassano del Grappa* [1995] ECR I-3257, [1996] 4 CMLR 157; Case C-38/97 *Autotrasporti Librandi v Cuttica Spedizioni e Servizi Internazionali* [1998] ECR I-5955, [1998] 5 CMLR 966; Case C-266/96 *Corsica Ferries* [1998] ECR I-3949, [1998] 5 CMLR 402; Case C-446/05 *Ioannis Doulamis* [2008] ECR I-1377, [2008] 5 CMLR 376.
[45] Case C-35/99 [2002] ECR I-1529, [2002] 4 CMLR 866; for discussion of this case see Thunstrom, Carle and Lindeborg 'State Liability Under the EC Treaty Arising from Anti-competitive State Measures' (2002) 25 World Competition 515.
[46] Case C-35/99 [2002] ECR I-1529, [2002] 4 CMLR 866, paras 40–44; see to similar effect Case C-250/03 *Mauri*, order of 17 February 2005 [2005] ECR I-1267, [2005] 4 CMLR 723, paras 31–38; Cases C-94/04 etc *Cipolla* [2006] ECR I-11421, [2007] 4 CMLR 286, paras 48–54; Case C-386/07 *Hospital Consulting Srl & Ors v Estate SpA & Ors*, order of 5 May 2008; Opinion of Advocate General Mengozzi given on 11 November 2010 in Case C-437/09 *AG2R Prévoyance* [2011] ECR I-000, [2011] 4 CMLR 1029, paras 36–47.
[47] See Case C-350/07 *Kattner Stahlbau GmbH v Maschinenbau- und Metall- Berufsgenossenschaft* [2009] ECR I-1513, [2009] 2 CMLR 1339, para 70.
[48] See Case C-393/08 *Emanuela Sbarigia v Azienda USL RM/A* [2010] ECR I-000, para 32.
[49] Case C-437/09 [2011] ECR I-000, CMLR, paras 37–39.
[50] See ch 3, 'Employees and trades unions', pp 90–91 on the *Albany* judgment.
[51] See 'The case law predominantly concerns Article 4(3) TEU in conjunction with Article 101 TFEU', pp 217–218 above.

trade; however there is no involvement on the part of the state, so the application of Article 4(3) TEU does not arise[52]

- in the second situation Member State B itself fixed the fees: however in this case there is no suggestion of an agreement, and so there can be no infringement of Article 101(1); this situation may be suitable for 'competition advocacy' by the competition authority of Member State B[53]

- in the third case Member State C established a regulatory mechanism, but left it to the bar association to decide whether to recommend fees and, if so, to determine what their level should be: the association in doing so would be infringing Article 101(1), but it is not clear whether the Member State has acted unlawfully; it has given freedom to the bar association to decide how to act, rather than requiring it to act

- in the case of Member State D, however, it has delegated its regulatory role to the bar association and required it to fix fees, so that it would be held responsible for the price fixing that ensues

- Member State E could be considered to be strengthening the effect of an agreement contrary to Article 101 by issuing a decree compelling compliance with the bar association's recommendations. However the Court of Justice has held that if the Minister is free to vary the tariff, acting on the advice of other public bodies, there would be no infringement; the decree retains the character of legislation rather than amounting to the encouragement or reinforcement of an agreement[54].

3. **Article 106 TFEU – Compliance with the Treaties**[55]

Article 106 provides that:

1. In the case of public undertakings and undertakings to which Member States grant special or exclusive rights, Member States shall neither enact nor maintain in force any measure contrary to the rules contained in the Treaties, in particular to those rules provided for in Article 18 and Articles 101 to 109.

2. Undertakings entrusted with the operation of services of general economic interest or having the character of a revenue-producing monopoly shall be subject to the rules contained in the Treaties, in particular to the rules on competition, in so far as the application of such rules does not obstruct the performance, in law or in fact, of the particular tasks assigned to them. The development of trade must not be affected to such an extent as would be contrary to the interests of the Union.

3. The Commission shall ensure the application of the provisions of this Article and shall, where necessary, address appropriate directives or decisions to Member States.

---

[52] On the application of the competition rules to the professions see ch 3, 'The professions', p 90.
[53] On competition advocacy see ch 1, 'Competition advocacy and public restrictions of competition', p 25.
[54] Case C-35/99 *Arduino* [2002] ECR I-1529, [2002] 4 CMLR 866; Cases C-94/04 etc *Cipolla* [2006] ECR I-11421, [2007] 4 CMLR 286.
[55] For further reading on Article 106 see Buendia Sierra *Exclusive Rights and State Monopolies under EC Law* (Oxford University Press, 1999): this book contains an extensive bibliography of literature on Article 106 at pp 431–451; Faull and Nikpay *The EC Law of Competition* (Oxford University Press, 2nd ed, 2007), ch 6; Bellamy and Child *European Community Law of Competition* (Oxford University Press, 6th ed, 2008, eds Roth and Rose), paras 11.009–11.028; see also Blum and Logue *State Monopolies under EC Law* (Wiley, 1998); Edwards and Hoskins 'Article 90: Deregulation and EC Law: Reflections Arising from the XVI FIDE Conference' (1995) 32 CML Rev 157; Holmes 'Fixing the Limits of EC Competition Law: State Action and the Accommodation of the Public Services' (2004) 57 Current Legal Problems 149.

Article 106(1) is a prohibition addressed to Member States themselves; Article 106(2) provides a limited exception for certain undertakings from the application of the competition rules; Article 106(3) provides the Commission with important powers to ensure
compliance with the provisions of Article 106. The law of Article 106 is complex and still
developing. After a long period when it was little used it has proved to be a formidable provision in the process of liberalising numerous markets in Europe, in particular in 'utility'
sectors such as telecommunications, energy and post and related services. The Court of
Justice has said in *Spain v Commission* that:

> [P]aragraph 2 of Article [106 TFEU], read with paragraph (1) thereof, seeks to reconcile the
> Member States' interest in using certain undertakings, in particular in the public sector, as
> an instrument of economic or social policy with the [EU's] interest in ensuring compliance
> with the rules on competition and the preservation of the unity of the [internal] market.[56]

(A) **Article 106(1)**

Article 106(1) is closely related to Article 4(3): each seeks to ensure effective adherence to
the Treaty on the part of Member States. However Article 106 goes beyond Article 4(3)
in that it has its own sphere of application and is not limited to compliance with general
principles of law. Article 106(1) imposes an obligation on Member States not to enact nor
to maintain in force measures *'contrary to those rules contained in the Treaties, in particular to those rules provided for in Article 18 and Articles 101 to 109'*. Two important features
of Article 106(1) should be noted at the outset. The first is that Article 106(1) is a 'renvoi'
provision or a 'reference rule', that is to say it does not have an independent application
but applies only in conjunction with another Article or other Articles of the Treaties. The
second point is that Article 106(1) is not limited in its scope only to infringements of the
competition rules; although the competition rules (and the rule of non-discrimination
in Article 18) are specifically mentioned, measures that infringe, for example, Article 34
on the free movement of goods[57], Article 45 on the free movement of workers[58], Article
49 on the freedom of establishment[59] and Article 56 on the free movement of services[60],
could all result in an infringement of Article 106(1). It follows that Article 106(1) did not
need to have been placed in the chapter of the Treaty on competition law; however the fact
that it is there indicates that the Treaty's authors were aware of the potential for Member
States to distort competition through the legislative and other measures that they adopt.
The importance of Article 106(1) in relation to the competition rules is that, in certain
circumstances, a Member State can be liable for the abuses that have been, or would be,
carried out by undertakings.

(i) **Undertakings**

Article 106(1) applies to measures concerning 'public undertakings and undertakings to
which Member States grant special or exclusive rights'. The term 'undertaking' has been
considered in the context of Articles 101 and 102 in earlier chapters[61]. In particular it

---

[56] Case C-463/00 [2003] ECR I-4581, [2003] 2 CMLR 557, para 82.
[57] See eg Case C-18/88 *RTT* [1991] ECR I-5941.
[58] See eg Case C-179/90 *Merci* [1991] ECR I-5889, [1994] 4 CMLR 422.
[59] See eg *Greek Insurance* OJ [1985] L 152/25.
[60] See eg Case C-260/89 *ERT v Dimotiki* [1991] ECR I-2925, [1994] 4 CMLR 540.
[61] See ch 3, 'Undertaking and Associations of Undertakings', pp 83–99 and ch 5, 'Undertakings', pp 177–178.

should be noted that state-owned bodies can be acting as undertakings, but that organs of the state that are not involved in any economic activity fall outside the definition[62].

(ii) Public undertakings[63]

The term 'public undertaking' appears only in Article 106(1) TFEU, and is not defined. There is no uniform notion of this expression among the Member States, and state intervention in and control of economic behaviour takes many different forms. For this reason Advocate General Reischl has stated that the term must be a concept of EU law which should be given a uniform interpretation for all Member States[64]. In Article 2(1)(b) of the Transparency Directive[65] the Commission said that a public undertaking means:

> any undertaking over which the public authorities may exercise, directly or indirectly, a dominant influence by virtue of their ownership of it, their financial participation therein, or the rules which govern it.

On appeal the Court of Justice upheld the legality of the Directive and approved the above definition, without elaborating further[66]. The crucial question in each case should be whether the state does have such influence, not the legal form of the undertaking in question.

(iii) Undertakings with 'special or exclusive rights'

Article 106(1) applies to measures in the case both of public undertakings and of undertakings having 'special or exclusive rights': sometimes the latter are referred to as 'privileged undertakings' to distinguish them from public undertakings. It is important to understand what each of the expressions 'special' and 'exclusive' means. The Treaty does not define them, but definitions can be found in Article 2(f) and (g) of the Transparency Directive[67]. Often special or exclusive rights will have been given to a public undertaking, in which case it is unnecessary to give separate consideration to this head of Article 106(1); however many undertakings may have exclusive or special rights without being 'public'. In *FIFA v Commission*[68] FIFA failed to persuade the General Court that the Secretary of State for Culture, Media and Sport had conferred exclusive or special rights on the BBC and ITV, two free-to-air television stations, by placing World Cup football matches on a list that they would then be able to broadcast on a non-exclusive basis. FIFA's complaint was that this led to a distortion of competition in which pay-TV companies could not bid for the very valuable right to show such games on an exclusive basis. The Court observed that the pay-TV companies could still broadcast on a non-exclusive basis[69].

(A) Exclusive rights[70]

A company established by insurance undertakings to perform a specific statutory task[71], an agricultural marketing board[72], an entity granted a monopoly over the provision of recruitment services[73], a dock-work undertaking entrusted with the exclusive right to

---

[62] See in particular ch 3, 'Regardless of the legal status of the entity and the way in which it is financed', pp 85–88.

[63] For detailed discussion of this concept see *Buendia Sierra*, paras 1.113–1.139.

[64] Cases 188/80 etc *France v Commission* [1982] ECR 2545, p 2596.

[65] Commission Directive 80/723/EEC, OJ [1980] L 195/35; this has now been repealed and replaced by Commission Directive 2006/111/EC, OJ [2006] L 318/17.

[66] Cases 188/80 etc *France v Commission* [1982] ECR 2545, [1982] 3 CMLR 144, para 25.

[67] See ch 6 n 65, above.   [68] Case T-68/08 [2011] ECR II-000.   [69] Ibid, paras 174–180.

[70] On the concept of exclusive rights see *Buendia Sierra*, paras 1.01–1.214.

[71] Case 90/76 *Van Ameyde v UCI* [1977] ECR 1091.

[72] Case 83/78 *Pigs Marketing Board v Redmond* [1978] ECR 2347, [1979] 1 CMLR 177.

[73] Case C-41/90 *Höfner & Elser v Macrotron GmbH* [1991] ECR I-1979, [1993] 4 CMLR 306, para 34.

organise dock work for third parties[74], a limited partnership between a Member State, a district authority and eight industrial undertakings responsible for waste management[75] and a state-owned post office granted a monopoly over postal services which do not form part of a universal service obligation[76] are examples of bodies that were considered to have been granted exclusive rights. It would appear that an 'exclusive' right can be granted to more than one undertaking: in *Entreprenørforeningens Affalds v Københavns Kommune*[77] the Court of Justice held that three undertakings authorised to receive building waste in Copenhagen had been granted an exclusive right, but it did not explain why these rights were exclusive rather than special, which would have been a more natural finding.

In principle it seems appropriate that a functional rather than a formalistic approach should be taken to the meaning of 'exclusive rights'. Rights may be exclusive in substance, even though they are not described as such (or as monopolies) in the measure in question. For example in *La Crespelle*[78] the Court of Justice concluded that a scheme for the artificial insemination of cattle in France involved exclusive rights because of the way the national legislation was operated in practice[79]. Furthermore the exclusive rights may derive from a series of different legislative and administrative measures rather than just one[80]. On the other hand the Court has held that the mere fact that a body exercises powers conferred upon it by the state and that it has a dominant position in the market is not sufficient in itself to establish that it has exclusive rights[81]. This is consistent with an early Commission decision that a copyright collecting society that could derive benefits from national copyright legislation did not have exclusive rights where there was no impediment to other such societies claiming the same benefit[82]; nevertheless the Commission did conclude that the society in question had a dominant position for the purpose of Article 102. The concepts of 'exclusive rights' and 'dominant position' are independent of one another.

(B) Special rights[83]

The Court of Justice's judgment in *France v Commission*[84] indicates that there is a distinction between exclusive and special rights. The Court held that the provisions in the Commission's Directive on Telecommunications Equipment[85] were void in so far as they required Member States to remove special rights from national telecommunications services providers, since it had failed to specify which rights were special or why they were incompatible with the Treaty. In the subsequent Directive on Telecommunications

---

[74] Case C-179/90 *Merci* [1991] ECR I-5889, [1994] 4 CMLR 422.

[75] Case C-203/96 *Dusseldorp* [1998] ECR I-4075, [1998] 3 CMLR 873, para 58.

[76] Case C-340/99 *TNT Traco SpA v Poste Italiane SpA* [2001] ECR I-4109, [2003] 4 CMLR 663.

[77] Case C-209/98 [2000] ECR I-3743, [2001] 2 CMLR 936.

[78] Case C-323/93 [1994] ECR I-5077.

[79] Although the Court of Justice did not address the point directly, the Opinion of Advocate General Gulmann indicates that the parties agreed that exclusive rights existed.

[80] See *Exclusive Rights to Broadcast Television Advertising in Flanders* OJ [1997] L 244/18, [1997] 5 CMLR 718, paras 1 and 2, upheld on appeal Case T-266/97 *Vlaamse Televisie Maatschappij NV v Commission* [1999] ECR II-2329, [2000] 4 CMLR 1171.

[81] Case C-387/93 *Banchero* [1995] ECR I-4663.

[82] *GEMA* OJ [1971] L 134/15, [1971] CMLR D35.

[83] On the concept of special rights see *Buendia Sierra* (ch 6 n 55, p 222 above), paras 2.01–2.22.

[84] Case C-202/88 [1991] ECR I-1223, [1992] 5 CMLR 552, paras 31–47; see similarly Cases C-271/90 etc *Spain v Commission* [1992] ECR I-5833, paras 32 and 34.

[85] Commission Directive 88/301/EEC, OJ [1988] L 131/73, [1991] 4 CMLR 922.

Liberalisation[86] the Commission states at Article 1(4) that, in the telecommunications sector, special rights include:

> rights that are granted by a Member State to a limited number of undertakings, through any legislative, regulatory or administrative instrument which, within a given geographical area, limits to two or more the number of undertakings, otherwise than according to objective, proportional and non-discriminatory criteria[87].

This definition can presumably be carried over to other sectors of the economy, unless there is specific legislation containing a different one. In *Second Operator of GSM Radiotelephony Services in Italy*[88] the Commission decided that the grant to Telecom Italia of the right to operate a GSM radiotelephony network qualified as a special right, since the operator had been designated otherwise than according to objective and non-discriminatory criteria. In *French savings accounts* the Commission concluded that the grant to three banks of the right to distribute tax-free savings products was a special right[89]. In *MOTOE* the power of the Greek Motorcycling Federation, ELPA, to authorise motorcycling events was held to be a special right within the meaning of Article 106(1)[90].

(iv) 'Measures'

For a Member State to be in breach of Article 106(1) it must have adopted a 'measure'. This expression has been given a wide meaning by the Commission, and its approach has been endorsed by the Court of Justice. In an early Directive under Article 34[91] the Commission said that measures in that Article included 'laws, regulations, administrative provisions, administrative practices, and all instruments issued from a public authority, including recommendations'; there is no reason to suppose that the expression should have a different meaning under Article 106(1). In another case under Article 34, *Commission v Ireland*[92], the Court of Justice said that a measure did not have to be legally binding, provided that it might be capable of exerting an influence and of frustrating the aims of the Union[93]. The measure does not have to have been adopted by central government or by a national Parliament: a measure of any body that is a manifestation of the state could fall within Article 106(1), such as the local communes in *Corinne Bodson v Pompes Funèbres*[94].

Numerous examples can be given to support the view that the expression 'measures' has a wide meaning under Article 106(1): for example in *Second Operator of GSM Radiotelephony in Italy*[95] and *Second Operator of GSM Radiotelephony in Spain*[96] the grant of a second mobile licence subject to a substantial licence fee which had not been levied on the incumbent operator amounted to a measure; in *Port of Rødby*[97] the refusal to grant a

---

[86] Commission Directive 2008/63/EC, OJ [2008] L 162/20; for discussion of this definition see the Opinion of Advocate General Jacobs in Case C-475/99 *Ambulanz Glöckner v Landkreis Südwestpfalz* [2001] ECR I-8089, [2002] 4 CMLR 726, paras 83–89.

[87] See similarly Article 2(g) of the Commission's Transparency Directive, ch 6 n 65, p 224 above.

[88] OJ [1995] L 280/49, para 6; see similarly *Second Operator of GSM Radio Telephony Services in Spain* OJ [1997] L 76/19, para 10.

[89] Commission decision of 10 May 2007.

[90] Case C-49/07 *Motosykletistiki Omospondia Ellados NPID (MOTOE) v Elliniko Dimosio* [2008] ECR I-4863, [2008] 5 CMLR 790, para 43.

[91] Commission Directive 70/50/EEC based on the provisions of Article 33(7) on the abolition of measures which have an effect equivalent to quantitative restrictions on imports and are not covered by other provisions adopted in pursuance of the EEC Treaty, JO [1970] L 13/29.

[92] Case 249/81 [1982] ECR 4005 (the *'Buy Irish'* case).   [93] Ibid, para 28.

[94] Case 30/87 [1988] ECR 2479, [1989] 4 CMLR 984.   [95] OJ [1995] L 280/49.

[96] OJ [1997] L 76/19.   [97] OJ [1994] L 55/52.

ferry company access to a state-run Danish port was a measure; and in *Brussels National Airport (Zaventem)*[98], *Portuguese Airports*[99] and *Spanish Airports*[100] systems of stepped landing fee discounts at various national airports were measures.

In each of the above cases the Member State had adopted specific measures which affected the conduct of the public undertaking or the undertaking given special or exclusive rights. In some cases a public authority enters into an agreement with an undertaking granting the latter an exclusive right to perform a particular task: for example to provide funeral services[101]. The question here is whether this amounts to a measure granting exclusive rights, in which case Article 106(1) may apply, or an agreement between undertakings that restricts competition, in which case Article 101(1) may apply. In *Bodson* the Court of Justice considered that Article 101(1) would not be applicable where a local authority was acting pursuant to its public law powers, since it would not be acting as an undertaking[102].

(v) The obligations on Member States under Article 106(1)

Article 106(1) requires Member States to refrain from enacting or maintaining in force any measure contrary to the Treaties, and in particular one which would contravene Article 18, Article 101 or Article 102. The relationship of Article 106(1) with Articles 101 and 102 is one of the most difficult areas of competition law. Articles 101 and 102 are addressed to undertakings, but Article 106 to Member States: as in the case of Article 4(3)[103] the conceptual issue is to determine how, and in what circumstances, these provisions can operate in such a way as to lead to an infringement of the Treaties by a Member State. As has been seen, under Article 4(3) TEU the liability of Member States in relation to Article 101 is quite limited; however the jurisprudence of the Court of Justice has been more dramatic in cases dealing with Article 106(1) in conjunction with Article 102. For many years this issue was barely addressed at all; however the position began to change as a result of a remarkable series of cases in 1991 in which the Court of Justice delivered four judgments on the relationship between Article 106(1) and other Treaty Articles, including in particular Article 102. A further landmark judgment, in the *Corbeau* case, followed in 1993[104].

(vi) The judgments of 1991

(A) *Höfner & Elser v Macrotron*

In April 1991 the Court of Justice held in *Höfner & Elser v Macrotron GmbH*[105] that a Member State which had conferred exclusive rights on a public employment agency could be in breach of Article 106(1) where the exercise by that agency of its rights would inevitably involve an infringement of Article 102. In Germany the Federal Employment Office ('the FEO') had a legal monopoly as an intermediary in the employment market, though in practice it was unable to satisfy demand and tolerated 'head-hunting' agencies which, strictly, were acting illegally. An agency seeking payment of its fee for having successfully recruited on behalf of a client was met with the defence that, as the agency was acting

---

[98] OJ [1995] L 216/8, [1996] 4 CMLR 232.

[99] OJ [1999] L 69/31, [1999] 5 CMLR 103, upheld on appeal Case C-163/99 *Portugal v Commission* [2001] ECR I-2613, [2002] 2 CMLR 1319.

[100] OJ [2000] L 208/36, [2000] 5 CMLR 967.

[101] Case 30/87 *Corinne Bodson v Pompes Funèbres* [1988] ECR 2479, [1989] 4 CMLR 984.

[102] See ch 3, 'Activities connected with the exercise of the powers of a public authority are not economic', p 89.

[103] See 'Article 4(3) TEU – duty of sincere cooperation', pp 216–222 above.

[104] Case C-320/91 [1993] ECR I-2533, [1995] 4 CMLR 621.

[105] Case C-41/90 [1991] ECR I-1979, [1993] 4 CMLR 306.

unlawfully, it could not enforce the contract; thus the alleged infringement by Germany of EU law was raised as a defence to a contract action between two private undertakings. The matter was referred to the Court of Justice pursuant to Article 267. The Court held that the fact that Germany had granted a legal monopoly to the FEO did not in itself entail a breach of Articles 102 and 106(1)[106]; however there would be a breach if the mere exercise of its right would inevitably lead to an abuse under Article 102. This could be the case if the undertaking was manifestly unable to satisfy demand, as was the case here by the admission of the FEO, and if the legal monopoly prevented a competitor from trying to satisfy that demand[107].

(B) *ERT v Dimotiki*

In June 1991 the Court of Justice considered in *ERT v Dimotiki*[108] the compatibility with the Treaty of the Greek television and radio station's monopoly over broadcasting. The Court held that the existence of the monopoly in itself was not contrary to the Treaty, but that the manner in which it was exercised could be so[109]. Specifically on Article 102 the Court of Justice held that, if a Member State which had granted the exclusive right to transmit television broadcasts then granted the same undertaking the right to retransmit broadcasts, it would infringe Article 106(1) if this created a situation in which the broadcaster would be led to infringe Article 102 by virtue of a discriminatory policy which favours its own broadcasts. In contrast to *Höfner* there do not appear to have been any national rules that obliged ERT to pursue a discriminatory broadcasting policy; it was sufficient that the exclusive rights bestowed on ERT placed it in a position where it might practise discrimination.

(C) *Merci Convenzionali Porto di Genova v Siderurgica Gabrielli*

In December 1991 the Court of Justice gave its judgment in *Merci Convenzionali Porto di Genova v Siderurgica Gabrielli*[110]. Merci was a private undertaking given an exclusive concession for the handling of loading operations in the harbour of Genoa. As a result of a strike at Merci, Siderurgica was unable to unload goods imported in a ship from Germany. Siderurgica sued for damages. The Court stated that the simple fact of creating a dominant position by granting exclusive rights is not as such incompatible with Article 106(1)[111]; however the Court repeated the ideas in *Höfner* and *ERT* that there could be an infringement by a Member State if the undertaking in question, merely by exercising the exclusive rights granted to it, cannot avoid abusing its dominant position (*Höfner*), or when such rights are liable to create a situation in which that undertaking is induced to commit such abuses (*ERT*)[112]. In this case the Court observed that Merci appeared to have been induced to demand payment for services which had not been requested, to charge disproportionate prices, to refuse to have recourse to modern technology and to treat customers in a discriminatory manner: matters which are specifically mentioned as possible abuses in Article 102(2)(a), (b) and (c)[113].

(D) *RTT v GB-Inno-BM*

The Court of Justice delivered a further judgment in December 1991, three days after the judgment in *Merci*, in *RTT v GB-Inno-BM*[114]. RTT had exclusive rights in Belgium

---

[106] Ibid, para 29.
[107] Ibid, paras 30–31.   [108] Case C-260/89 [1991] ECR I-2925, [1994] 4 CMLR 540.
[109] Ibid, paras 12 and 32.
[110] Case C-179/90 [1991] ECR I-5889, [1994] 4 CMLR 422; see Gyselen (1992) 29 CML Rev 1229.
[111] [1991] ECR I-5889, [1994] 4 CMLR 422, para 16.   [112] Ibid, para 17.
[113] Ibid, paras 18 and 19.   [114] Case C-18/88 [1991] ECR I-5941; see *Gyselen*, ch 6 n 110 above.

for the operation of telephone services and for the approval of telecommunications terminal equipment such as telephones; it was also a supplier of telephones itself. GB-Inno sold telephones in Belgium which had been imported from the Far East. RTT asked for an injunction to prevent such sales, since this encouraged people to connect equipment which had not been approved according to Belgian law. The Court referred to earlier case law, that an abuse is committed where an undertaking holding a dominant position on a particular market reserves to itself an ancillary activity which might be carried out by another undertaking as part of its activities on a neighbouring but separate market, with the possibility of eliminating all competition from such an undertaking[115]. The Court went on to say that, where a state measure brings about such a reservation of an ancillary activity, the measure in question infringes Article 106(1)[116]. RTT argued that there would be an infringement of Article 106(1) only where the Member State favoured an abuse, for example by acting in a discriminatory manner[117], but the Court rejected this, stating that the extension of RTT's monopoly was itself a state measure contrary to Article 106(1)[118]. The establishment of a regulatory system which gave RTT the power to determine at will which telephone equipment could be connected to the public telephone network, thereby placing itself at an obvious advantage over its competitors, was unlawful[119].

(vii) The *Corbeau* judgment

A further judgment of great significance was *Corbeau* in 1993[120]. Criminal proceedings had been brought against Corbeau, a businessman from Liège, for infringing the Belgian legal monopoly for postal services. Corbeau was operating a door-to-door express delivery service in the Liège area: he was not conducting the service of delivering letters on a daily-delivery basis. The Court of Justice, after referring to the requirement in Article 106(1) not to enact nor to maintain in force measures contrary to the competition rules[121], spent the rest of its judgment considering, under Article 106(2), whether the breadth of the monopoly given to the Belgian Post Office was greater than was necessary to enable it to carry out the task of general economic interest entrusted to it[122]. The significance of the judgment for Article 106(1) was that the Court of Justice, in effect, was ruling that the breadth of the monopoly granted to the Belgian Post Office was, to the extent that it could not be justified under Article 106(2), unlawful under the Treaty. In other words the Court was challenging the exclusive rights themselves, despite its numerous statements that the creation of dominance is not in itself incompatible with the Treaty.

(viii) Making sense of the case law on Article 102 in conjunction with Article 106(1)

The difficulty with these cases, and with the Court of Justice's subsequent judgments[123], is to determine the circumstances in which a Member State can be liable under Article 106(1)

---

[115] Ibid, para 18, referring to Case 311/84 *CBEM* (the *Télémarketing* judgment) [1985] ECR 3261, [1986] 2 CMLR 558.

[116] Ibid, para 21.   [117] Ibid, para 22.   [118] Ibid, para 23.

[119] In reaching this finding the Court of Justice relied on another of its judgments in 1991, the *Telecommunications Directive* case, ch 6 n 84, p 225 above, at para 51.

[120] Case C-320/91 [1993] ECR I-2533, [1995] 4 CMLR 621; see Hancher (1994) 31 CML Rev 105.

[121] [1993] ECR I-2533, [1995] 4 CMLR 621, para 12.

[122] For discussion of Article 106(2), and of the *Corbeau* judgment on this issue, see 'Article 106(2)', pp 235–241 below.

[123] There have been several subsequent judgments on the relationship between Article 102 and Article 106(1): see in particular Case C-393/92 *Almelo* [1994] ECR I-1477; Case C-18/93 *Corsica Ferries Italia srl v Corpo del Piloti del Porto di Genoa* [1994] ECR I-1783; Case C-323/93 *Centre d'Insémination de la Crespelle v Coopérative de la Mayenne* [1994] ECR I-5077; Case C-111/94 *Job Centre (I)* [1995] ECR I-3361; Case C-242/95 *GT-Link*

for an infringement of Article 102. Two points can be made at the outset. First, as Advocate General Jacobs explained at paragraph 388 of his Opinion in *Albany*[124], a Member State cannot be held responsible for independent anti-competitive behaviour on the part of an undertaking simply because it takes place within its jurisdiction. Article 106(1) can be infringed 'only where there is a causal link between a Member State's legislative or administrative intervention on the one hand and anti-competitive behaviour of undertakings on the other hand'. Secondly, the mere creation of a dominant position by the grant of exclusive rights does not infringe Article 106(1); this has been stressed by the Court of Justice on many occasions[125]: the point is exemplified by the judgment in *Crespelle*[126], where the Court concluded that French legislation conferring legal monopolies on insemination centres for the provision of certain services to cattle breeders did not lead to an abuse for which France was responsible.

Helpful though these two points are, they do not shed any light on the circumstances in which a Member State will be found to have infringed Article 106(1) as a result of an abuse that infringes Article 102. Furthermore, the frequently-repeated statement that the mere creation (or reinforcement) of dominance does not in itself infringe Article 106(1) does not sit easily with judgments such as *ERT*, *RTT* and *Corbeau* which do seem, in effect, to have concluded that the monopoly rights in question were incompatible with the Treaty. The judgments of the Court of Justice on the necessary causal link between the measure under Article 106(1) and the abuse under Article 102 are neither clear nor consistent: in *Höfner* the Court considered that a measure would be unlawful where it led to an 'inevitable' abuse; in *ERT* if it would induce an infringement; in *Banchero*[127] the Court of Justice considered that there would be an infringement only if the Member State created a situation in which the undertaking in question 'cannot avoid abusing its dominant position'[128]. In *Dusseldorp*[129] the Court was much less guarded: a Member State infringes Article 106(1) in conjunction with Article 102 'if it adopts any law, regulation or administrative provision which enables an undertaking on which it has conferred rights to abuse its dominant position'[130]. Some formulations of the necessary causal link impose quite a high threshold before a Member State will be found liable; others, such as the one in *Dusseldorp*, suggest a lower threshold. What seems clear is that the causal link must

---

A/S v De Danske Statsbaner [1997] ECR I-4349, [1997] 5 CMLR 601; Case C-387/93 *Banchero* [1995] ECR I-4663; Case C-55/96 *Job Centre (II)* [1997] ECR I-7119, [1998] 4 CMLR 708; Case C-70/95 *Sodemare v Regione Lombardia* [1997] ECR I-3395, [1998] 4 CMLR 667; Case C-163/96 *Silvano Raso* [1998] ECR I-533, [1998] 4 CMLR 737; Case C-266/96 *Corsica Ferries France SA v Gruppo Antichi Ormeggiatori del Porto di Genova* [1998] ECR I-3949, [1998] 5 CMLR 402; Case C-203/96 *Dusseldorp* [1998] ECR I-4075, [1998] 3 CMLR 873; Cases C-67/96 etc *Albany International BV v SBT* [1999] ECR I-5751, [2000] 4 CMLR 446; Cases C-147/97 and C-148/97 *Deutsche Post AG v GZS* [2000] ECR I-825, [2000] 4 CMLR 838; Case C-258/98 *Giovanni Carra* [2000] ECR I-4217, [2002] 4 CMLR 285; Case C-209/98 *Entreprenørforeningens Affalds/Miljøsektion v Københavns Kommune* [2000] ECR I-3743, [2001] 2 CMLR 936, on which see van Calster 'Exclusive Rights Ruling No Safe Harbour for Export Restrictions' (2001) 26 CML Rev 502; Case C-340/99 *TNT Traco SpA v Poste Italiane SpA* [2001] ECR I-4109, [2003] 4 CMLR 663; Case C-475/99 *Ambulanz Glöckner v Landkreis Südwestpfalz* [2001] ECR I-8089, [2002] 4 CMLR 726; Case C-49/07 *Motosykletistiki Omospondia Ellados NPID (MOTOE) v Elliniko Dimosio* [2008] ECR I-4863, [2008] 5 CMLR 790.

124 Cases C-67/96 etc *Albany International BV v SBT* [1999] ECR I-5751, [2000] 4 CMLR 446.

125 Specific paras in which the Court has said this were cited above in relation to the 1991 judgments in *Höfner, ERT* and *Merci*: see 'The judgments of 1991', pp 227–229 above.

126 Case C-323/93 *Centre d'Insémination de la Crespelle v Coopérative de la Mayenne* [1994] ECR I-5077; see also Cases C-180/98 etc *Pavel Pavlov v Stichting Pensioenfonds Medische Specialisten* [2000] ECR I-6451, [2001] 4 CMLR 30, para 127.

127 Case C-387/93 [1995] ECR I-4663.   128 Ibid, para 51.

129 Case C-203/96 [1998] ECR I-4075, [1998] 3 CMLR 873.

130 Ibid, para 61, citing the *RTT* judgment (see ch 6 n 114, p 228 above).

be stronger in some kinds of cases than others, depending on how likely it is that abusive behaviour will follow from the measure in question.

Many attempts have been made to make sense of the cases, in particular by identifying specific categories[131]; this is a natural response to the case law, but it is noticeable that different commentators have devised different categories, or have assigned the cases differently. This is not surprising: the cases can be explained in different, and sometimes in overlapping, ways, and the jurisprudence is still evolving. As Advocate General Fennelly stated in his Opinion in *Silvano Raso*[132]:

> I do not think that any general test can be enunciated for determining in advance the existence of such a [causal] link. Instead, in each individual case, it will be necessary to assess the impact of impugned national rules in the economic and factual circumstances in which they operate[133].

The text that follows attempts a categorisation, but must be read subject to the caveat that it is simply one way, among several others, of trying to make sense of the jurisprudence of the Court of Justice and the decisional practice of the Commission.

(A) *Manifest inability to meet demand*

In *Höfner & Elser v Macrotron GmbH*[134] the Court of Justice held that there would be an infringement of Article 106(1) where Germany had created a situation in which the FEO was 'manifestly not in a position to satisfy demand' for recruitment services, and its legal monopoly prevented a competitor from satisfying that demand. The idea that inability to meet demand can be abusive can be traced back to Article 102(2)(b), which gives as an example of abuse 'limiting production, markets or technical development to the prejudice of consumers'. On similar facts to *Höfner*, in *Job Centre (II)*[135] the Court concluded that the enforcement of an employment procurement monopoly enforced in Italy through criminal proceedings was a measure contrary to Article 106(1). In the *Albany* judgment[136] the Court seems to have considered that the exclusive right given to the operator of a sectoral pension fund amounted to a limitation of demand[137], although it went on to decide that this could be justified under Article 106(2)[138]. The judgment in *Merci*[139] can be explained, in part, on the basis that the entrusted undertaking had refused to have recourse to modern technology, which resulted in a failure to satisfy the demand of customers. In *Dusseldorp*[140] a requirement that waste for recovery could be supplied only to the entrusted undertaking, and could not be exported to a third undertaking, was held to restrict outlets and to contravene Article 106(1) in conjunction with Article 102[141].

---

[131] See eg *Buendia Sierra* (ch 6 n 55, p 222 above), paras 5.68–5–109; see also Buendia Sierra in Faull and Nikpay *The EC Law of Competition* (Oxford University Press, 2nd ed, 2007), paras 5.52–5.79; Edward and Hoskins 'Article 90: Deregulation and EC Law: Reflections arising from the XVI FIDE Conference' (1995) 32 CML Rev 157; Advocate General Jacobs in his Opinion in *Albany* (ch 6 n 124 above), paras 396–440; Ritter, Braun and Rawlinson *European Competition Law: a Practitioner's Guide* (Kluwer Law International, 3rd ed, 2005), pp 764–767; see also, on the issue of causation, the Opinion of Advocate General Fennelly in Case C-163/96 *Silvano Raso* [1998] ECR I-533, [1998] 4 CMLR 737, paras 57–66.

[132] Case C-163/96 [1998] ECR I-533, [1998] 4 CMLR 737.   [133] Ibid, para 65.

[134] Case C-41/90 [1991] ECR I-1979, [1993] 4 CMLR 306.

[135] Case C-55/96 [1997] ECR I-7119, [1998] 4 CMLR 708; see also Case C-258/98 *Giovanni Carra* [2000] ECR I-4217, [2002] 4 CMLR 285.

[136] Cases C-67/96 etc [1999] ECR I-5751, [2000] 4 CMLR 446.

[137] Ibid, para 97.

[138] See 'Article 106(2)', pp 235–242 below.

[139] Case C-179/90 [1991] ECR I-5889, [1994] 4 CMLR 422.

[140] Case C-203/96 [1998] ECR I-4075, [1998] 3 CMLR 873.

[141] Ibid, para 63.

However in *Ambulanz Glöckner v Landkreis Südwestpfalz*[142] Advocate General Jacobs suggested that a Member State would be liable under Article 106(1) only where there is a systemic failure to meet demand and not where there is a failure merely due to inefficient management[143]. The Commission's decisions on courier services, *Dutch Express Delivery Services*[144] and *Spanish International Courier Services*[145], on licences for mobile telephony operators, *Second Operator of GSM Radiotelephony Services in Italy*[146] and *Second Operator of GSM Radiotelephony Services in Spain*[147] and on *Slovakian postal legislation relating to hybrid mail services*[148] can be included, in part, in this category of cases[149].

(B) Conflict of interest

In *ERT v Dimotiki*[150] the Court of Justice held that there would be an infringement of Article 106(1) where Greece had created a situation in which the broadcaster ERT would be led to infringe Article 102 by virtue of a discriminatory policy in favour of its own broadcasts. A notable feature of this case was that it was not necessary for ERT to have actually abused its dominant position in the manner suggested: the granting of the exclusive right made this sufficiently likely that the measure in question infringed Article 106(1). The Court seems to have considered it to be inevitable that an undertaking in the position of ERT, because of its conflict of interest, would act abusively. The same idea was presumably present in *RTT v GB-Inno-BM*[151], since the regulatory function of RTT inevitably gave rise to a conflict of interest, although the Court specifically relied there on the extension of monopoly rights to neighbouring markets[152]. In *Silvano Raso*[153], a dock-work scheme granted an undertaking the exclusive right to supply temporary labour to terminal concessionaires, but also enabled it to compete with them on the market for the provision of dock services: merely by exercising its monopoly rights the entrusted undertaking would be able to distort competition in its favour, for example by imposing on its competitors unduly high costs or by supplying them with labour less suited to the work to be done[154]; the Court of Justice specifically mentioned the conflict of interest of the entrusted undertaking in this judgment[155]. A further example of a conflict of interest case is *MOTOE*[155a] in which a provision of the Greek Road Traffic Code infringed Articles 102 and 106(1) by granting ELPA, a body which organised motorcycling events, the exclusive and unfettered power to authorise competing motorcycling events in Greece, thereby placing ELPA at an obvious advantage over its competitors. The Court would be less likely to find

---

[142] Case C-475/99 [2001] ECR I-8089, [2002] 4 CMLR 726.

[143] Ibid, para 148 of his Opinion; the Court of Justice did not deal with this point explicitly, though the tone of its comments at paras 62–65 appear to be consistent with the views of the Advocate General.

[144] OJ [1990] L 10/47, [1990] 4 CMLR 947 quashed on appeal Cases C-48/90 and C-66/90 *Netherlands and Koninklijke PTT Nederland v Commission* [1992] ECR I-565, [1993] 5 CMLR 316.

[145] OJ [1990] L 233/19, [1991] 4 CMLR 560, para 11.

[146] OJ [1995] L 280/49, [1996] 4 CMLR 700, para 17(ii).

[147] OJ [1997] L 76/19, para 21(ii).

[148] Decision of 7 October 2008, paras 149–155, on appeal Case T-556/08 *Slovenská Pošta v commission*, not yet decided.

[149] The same decisions can also be included in the 'reservation of an ancillary activity' category: see below.

[150] Case C-260/89 [1991] ECR I-2925, [1994] 4 CMLR 540.

[151] Case C-18/88 [1991] ECR I-5941.   [152] See below.

[153] Case C-163/96 [1998] ECR I-533, [1998] 4 CMLR 737; the Commission condemned various aspects of the same dock-work legislation in *Provisions of Italian Ports Legislation Relating to Employment* OJ [1997] L 301/17; it noted the conflict of interest created by the legislation at para 30(b) and (c) of its decision, referring to this as 'inherently an abuse'.

[154] Case C-163/96 [1998] ECR I-533, [1998] 4 CMLR 737, paras 28–31.

[155] Ibid, para 28.   [155a] See n 90 above.

an infringement of Article 106(1) where provision exists for judicial review of the decisions made by an apparently conflicted undertaking[156].

(C) *Reservation of an ancillary activity*

In *RTT v GB-Inno-BM*[157] the Court of Justice held that a measure that resulted in the extension of RTT's monopoly to an ancillary activity on a neighbouring but separate market infringed Article 106(1). As noted in the preceding paragraph, the Court of Justice could have reached the same conclusion on the basis of a conflict of interest, but it decided the case specifically on the basis of its earlier judgment in the *Télémarketing* case[158]. In *Ambulanz Glöckner v Landkreis Südwestpfalz*[159] the Court of Justice held that a law adopted by Länder in Germany concerning the provision of ambulance services infringed Article 106(1) because medical aid organisations that had an exclusive right to provide emergency ambulance services were enabled to also offer non-emergency patient transport services, which could have been carried out by independent operators[160]. The Commission considered that there were abuses under this head in *Dutch Express Delivery Services*[161] and *Spanish International Courier Services*[162]. In each of *Second Operator of GSM Radiotelephony Services in Italy*[163] and *Second Operator of GSM Radiotelephony Services in Spain*[164] the Commission decided that, in requiring a second mobile operator to make a substantial payment for a mobile telephony licence that had not been paid by the incumbent telecommunications companies, there had been state measures capable of extending the monopoly rights of the latter. The judgment of the Court of Justice in *Connect Austria Gesellschaft für Telekommunications GmbH v Telekom-Control-Kommission*[165], an Article 267 reference from an Austrian court, points to the same conclusion. The Commission also considered that there was an abuse under this head in *Port of Rødby*[166] where the refusal by a port operator, DSD, to allow Euro-Port A/S access to the port of Rødby eliminated competition in the downstream market for ferry services from Rødby to Puttgarden, in which it was collectively dominant with Deutsche Bahn. Similarly, the Commission objected to Italy[167] and Slovakia[168] respectively extending the statutory monopoly of the incumbent postal operators to the delivery of hybrid mail services, which had previously been open to competition. In the case of *Greek Lignite*[169] the Commission found that Greece had reinforced the dominant position of PPC, a state-owned electricity company, in the wholesale electricity market by granting it quasi-monopolistic rights for access to lignite, a cheap fuel used to produce electricity. Greece subsequently took steps to ensure fair access to Greek lignite deposits[170].

---

[156] Case C-67/96 *Albany International BV v SBT* [1999] ECR I-5751, [2000] 4 CMLR 446, paras 116–121.

[157] Case C-18/88 [1991] ECR I-5941.

[158] Case 311/84 [1985] ECR 3261, [1986] 2 CMLR 558; see also Cases C-271/90 etc *Spain v Commission* [1992] ECR I-5833, para 36.

[159] Case C-475/99 [2001] ECR I-8089, [2002] 4 CMLR 726.

[160] Ibid, para 43.

[161] OJ [1990] L 10/47, annulled on appeal Cases C-48/90 and C-66/90 *Netherlands and Koninklijke PTT Nederland v Commission* [1992] ECR I-565, [1993] 5 CMLR 316.

[162] OJ [1990] L 233/19, [1991] 4 CMLR 560, para 10.

[163] OJ [1995] L 280/49, [1996] 4 CMLR 700, para 17(i).   [164] OJ [1997] L 76/19, para 21(i).

[165] Case C-462/99 [2003] ECR I-5147, [2005] 5 CMLR 302.   [166] OJ [1994] L 55/52.

[167] *New Postal Services in Italy* OJ [2001] L 63/59.

[168] *Slovakian postal legislation relating to hybrid mail services*, Commission decision of 7 October 2008, paras 116–148, on appeal Case T-556/08 *Slovenská Pošta v Commission*, not yet decided.

[169] Decision of 5 March 2008, paras 180–238, on appeal Case T-169/08 *DEI v Commission*, not yet decided.

[170] Decision of 4 August 2009, on appeal Case T-421/09 *DEI v Commission*, not yet decided; the decision is under review by the Commission: see Commission Press Release IP/11/34, 14 January 2011.

(D) Corbeau

In Corbeau[171] the Court of Justice did not discuss Article 106(1) in any detail, but instead considered the extent to which the postal monopoly of the Belgian Post Office could be justified under Article 106(2)[172]. However the interest of the case under Article 106(1) is that, to the extent that the monopoly was not justifiable under Article 106(2), the Court of Justice seems to have considered that it would amount to a measure contrary to Article 106(1). This could be seen as an example of the unlawful extension of a monopoly right to an ancillary activity, as in the cases just discussed. More radically, however, the case seems to suggest that it is possible to strike down monopolies that are too broad: in RTT, for example, that company would be able to use its monopoly right to extend its activities into the neighbouring market; in Corbeau the Court seems simply to have regarded the monopoly of the Belgian Post Office as too broad in itself. To the extent that this is a correct interpretation of Corbeau the judgment is very radical, and seems to go beyond the often-repeated assertion that the grant of an exclusive right is not, in itself, unlawful. Since Corbeau a specific Directive has been adopted in the postal sector determining the permitted extent of the 'reserved area' (that is to say the monopoly) in the postal sector[173]. As for the judgment itself, it is possible that this was the 'high tide' of intervention under Article 106(1), and that the Court of Justice has since taken a more cautious approach, as the judgments in Crespelle[174] and Banchero[175] seem to suggest[176].

(E) Discrimination

In Merci[177] the Court of Justice referred to the discriminatory treatment of customers as an abuse for which a Member State could be responsible under Article 106(1). In GT-Link A/S v De Danske Statsbaner[178] the Court stated that, where a public undertaking which owns and operates a commercial port waives the port duties on its own ferry services and some of its trading partners whilst charging the full duties to other customers, there could be an infringement of Article 102(2)(c), which refers to the application of dissimilar conditions to equivalent transactions placing other trading parties at a competitive disadvantage[179]. Appropriately transparent accounting would be needed to show that this was not the case[180]. In a series of decisions in relation to charges levied for the use both of airports[181] and ports[182] the Commission has expressly condemned price discrimination contrary to Article 102(2)(c), and found the Member State in question to have adopted a measure contrary to Article 106(1). In these cases the airport or port was a natural monopoly[183], which would result in a particularly strict responsibility not to act in an

---

[171] Case C-320/91 [1993] ECR I-2533, [1995] 4 CMLR 621.

[172] See 'Successful claims based on Article 106(2)', pp 240–241 below.

[173] See ch 23, 'Legislation', pp 984–985.

[174] Case C-323/93 Centre d'Insémination de la Crespelle v Coopérative de la Mayenne [1994] ECR I-5077.

[175] Case C-387/93 [1995] ECR I-4663.

[176] On these two judgments see Buendia Sierra Exclusive Rights and State Monopolies under EC Law, paras 5.110–5.128.

[177] Case C-179/90 [1991] ECR I-5889, [1994] 4 CMLR 422.

[178] Case C-242/95 [1997] ECR I-4349, [1997] 5 CMLR 601.

[179] Ibid, para 41; on Article 102(2)(c) generally, see ch 18, 'Price Discrimination', pp 759–764.

[180] [1997] ECR I-4349, [1997] 5 CMLR 601, para 42.

[181] See Brussels National Airport (Zaventem) OJ [1995] L 216/8, [1996] 4 CMLR 232, paras 12–18; Portuguese Airports OJ [1999] L 69/31, [1999] 5 CMLR 103, paras 24–40; Spanish Airports OJ [2000] L 208/36, [2000] 5 CMLR 967, paras 45–56.

[182] See Tariffs for Piloting in the Port of Genoa OJ [1997] L 301/27, paras 11–21.

[183] For discussion of the meaning of natural monopoly see ch 1, 'Economies of scale and scope and natural monopolies', p 10.

abusive manner[184]; and it may be necessary, under the so-called 'essential facilities doctrine'[185], for the owner of such infrastructure to grant access to third parties on non-discriminatory terms[186].

(ix) Remedies and direct effect

Article 106(1) has direct effect when applied in conjunction with another directly applicable provision of EU law, with the consequence that individuals can bring an action in a national court against a Member State which has infringed it[187]. Furthermore, the direct effect of Article 106(1) means that, as in the case of *Höfner & Elser v Macrotron GmbH*[188], one undertaking may be able to invoke it against another before a national court. An interesting question is whether an individual or a third party can bring an action for damages against a Member State which has acted in breach of Article 106(1). After the *Factortame* litigation in 1996[189], in which the Court of Justice held that in certain circumstances a Member State may have to compensate individuals who suffer loss or damage as a result of infringing EU law, this must at least be arguable.

(B) Article 106(2)

Article 106(2) is a somewhat awkwardly drafted provision[190]. It is in three parts. To begin with, it states that undertakings entrusted with the operation of services of general economic interest or having the character of a revenue-producing monopoly shall be subject to the rules in the Treaty, and in particular to the competition rules. It then states, however, that this subjection to the rules applies only 'in so far as the application of such rules does not obstruct the performance, in law or in fact, of the particular tasks assigned to them'. Perhaps an easier way to think of Article 106(2) is to ask whether it provides a way of justifying what would otherwise amount to an infringement of the competition rules[191]. Since Article 106(2) results in the non-application of Articles 101 and 102, it must be interpreted strictly[192]. Article 106(2) requires that any restriction of competition should satisfy the principle of proportionality[193]. The burden of proof is on the undertaking

---

[184] See ch 5, 'Dominant Position', pp 179–189 on the responsibilities of dominant, and 'super-dominant', undertakings.

[185] See ch 18, 'Refusal to Supply', pp 697–711.

[186] See eg *Port of Rødby* OJ [1994] L 55/52, where the Commission decided that a refusal to allow access to the port was an unlawful extension of the monopoly right enjoyed by the port operator: see 'Reservation of an ancillary activity', p 233 above.

[187] See for example Case 155/73 *Sacchi* [1974] ECR 409, [1974] 2 CMLR 177, para 18; Case C-179/90 *Merci Convenzionale Porto di Genova SpA v Siderurgica Gabrielli SpA* [1991] ECR I-5889, [1994] 4 CMLR 422, para 23; for a more recent statement to the same effect, and citing other judgments of the Court of Justice on the point see Case C-258/98 *Giovanni Carra* [2000] ECR I-4217, [2002] 4 CMLR 285, para 11.

[188] See ch 6 n 105, above.

[189] Cases C-46/93 and C-48/93 *Brasserie du Pêcheur SA and Factortame* [1996] ECR I-6297, [1996] 1 CMLR 889, paras 31 and 51.

[190] Its counterpart in UK law will be found in the Competition Act 1998, Sch 3, para 4, although that provision is drafted rather more elegantly; for detailed discussion of Article 106(2) see *Buendia Sierra* (ch 6 n 55, above) paras 8.01–8.324; see also Buendia Sierra in *Faull and Nikpay* (ch 6 n 66, above) paras 6.131–6.216; Auricchio 'Services of General Economic Interest and the Application of EC Competition Law' (2001) 24 World Competition 65.

[191] See Case C-475/99 *Ambulanz Glöckner v Landkreis Südwestpfalz* [2001] ECR I-8089, [2002] 4 CMLR 726.

[192] See Cases C-157/94 etc *Commission v Netherlands* [1997] ECR I-5699, [1998] 2 CMLR 373, para 37; see also *Reims II* OJ [1999] L 275/17, [2000] 4 CMLR 704, para 92.

[193] See *Buendia Sierra* (ch 6 n 55, above) paras 8.115–8.261; also Buendia Sierra in *Faull and Nikpay* (ch 6 n 55, above) paras 6.162–6.204.

seeking to rely on this provision[194]. However to succeed under Article 106(2) it is not necessary to show that an undertaking's survival would be threatened if it were to be subjected to the competition rules[195]; nor to prove that there is no other conceivable measure that could secure that the task in question could be performed[196]. A third limb to Article 106(2) adds that the development of trade must not be affected to such an extent as would be contrary to the interests of the EU; the burden is on the Commission or third party complainants to prove this[197].

The effect of Article 106(2) is that some undertakings can successfully claim that Articles 101 and 102 do not apply where their application would prevent them from carrying on the tasks assigned to them by a Member State; however a Member State's interest in doing this must be balanced against the EU's interest in ensuring free competition and a single market. A good example of circumstances in which Article 106(2) may be applicable is afforded by postal services: all Member States must ensure that users enjoy the right to a universal service involving the permanent provision of a postal service of specified quality at all points in their territory at affordable prices for all users[198]. The postal operator will charge the same price for the delivery of letters to all parts of the country. In effect, this means that the inhabitants of urban areas subsidise the postal services of those living in rural ones: delivering a letter from one part of London to another is cheaper than from the south-west of England to the north-east of Scotland. In a sense, therefore, the uniform tariff is discriminatory and could be attacked as such under Article 102. However, in so far as the uniform tariff provides an income to the postal operator that enables it to maintain the universal service, Article 106(2) is applicable and the undertaking is not subject to the competition rules.

A number of points require consideration.

(i) Services of general economic interest

An undertaking can claim to be excluded from the rules in the Treaties only if it has been entrusted with services of general economic interest or if it has the character of a revenue-producing monopoly. It is not enough in itself that the undertaking performs that service; it must have been entrusted with that performance, which will mean that it is under certain obligations[199]. It is not necessary that the undertaking has been entrusted with the performance of the service by a legislative measure; this could have come about, for example, as a result of the terms and conditions of a concession agreement[200]. The fact that an undertaking is entrusted at its own request does not mean that Article 106(2) is inapplicable as long as its position derives from an act of public authority[201].

The expression 'services of general economic interest' is not defined in the TFEU. Advocate General Colomer has suggested that to be of general economic interest a service should be uninterrupted, for the benefit of all consumers in the relevant territory and be available at a uniform tariff: put more succinctly there should be continuity, universality

---

[194] See Cases 157/94 etc *Commission v Netherlands* [1997] ECR I-5699, [1998] 2 CMLR 373, para 51.
[195] Ibid, para 43.   [196] Ibid, para 58.
[197] See 'Adverse development of trade', p 241 below.
[198] See Article 3 of Directive 97/67/EC, OJ [1998] L 15/14, as amended by Directive 2008/6/EC, OJ [2008] L 52/3.
[199] See the Opinion of Advocate General Jacobs in Case C-203/96 *Dusseldorp* [1998] ECR I-4075, [1998] 3 CMLR 873, para 103.
[200] Case 30/87 *Corinne Bodson v Pompes Funèbres* [1988] ECR 2479, [1989] 4 CMLR 984.
[201] Case T-17/02 *Fred Olsen SA v Commission* [2005] ECR II-2031, paras 187–190.

and equality, with perhaps transparency and affordability added to this trinity[202]. Obvious examples of such services are the operation of the basic postal service[203] and the provision of services, for example in the transport sector, which are not economically viable in their own right[204]. However it is noticeable that, in recent judgments, the Court of Justice has recognised that the 'protection' of Article 106(2) can extend beyond the conventional utilities: for example it has been found to be capable of application to pension schemes[205], ambulance services[206], the treatment of waste material[207] and the provision of private medical insurance[208]. The General Court has held that Member States enjoy a wide discretion to define what they regard as services of general economic interest[209].

The protection afforded to services of general economic interest is a sensitive political issue and was addressed at the 1997 Inter-Governmental Conference. Proposals to amend Article 106(2) itself were rejected in favour of the insertion of Article 16 EC by the Treaty of Amsterdam (now Article 14 TFEU). This expressly preserves the application of Article 106 because of:

> the place occupied by services of general economic interest in the shared values of the Union as well as their role in promoting social and territorial cohesion[210].

Article 14 TFEU reinforces the commitment of the EU and Member States to support undertakings required to provide services of general economic interest. The Commission has issued numerous publications clarifying the application of internal market and competition rules to services of general interest[211]. A *Green Paper on services of general interest* was published in May 2003[212]. This was followed in 2004 by the publication of a *White Paper on services of general interest*[213] which recognised the importance of well-functioning, accessible, affordable and high-quality services of general interest for the quality of life of European citizens, the environment and the competitiveness

---

[202] See his Opinion on Case C-265/08 *Federutility v Autorità per l'energia elettrica e il gas* [2010] ECR I-000, paras 54–55; on the concept of universality see Case T-289/03 *BUPA v Commission* [2008] ECR II-81, [2009] 2 CMLR 1043, paras 186, 187 and 203.

[203] Case C-320/91 *Corbeau* [1993] ECR I-2533, [1995] 4 CMLR 621, para 15: 'it cannot be disputed that Régie des Postes is entrusted with a service of general economic interest consisting in its obligation to collect, carry and distribute mail on behalf of all users throughout the territory of the Member State concerned, at uniform tariffs…'.

[204] See eg Case 66/88 *Ahmed Saeed* [1989] ECR 803, [1990] 4 CMLR 102, para 55.

[205] Cases C-67/96 etc *Albany International BV v Stichting Bedrijfspensioenfonds Textielindustrie* [1999] ECR I-5751, [2000] 4 CMLR 446.

[206] Case C-475/99 *Ambulanz Glöckner v Landkreis Südwestpfalz* [2001] ECR I-8089, [2002] 4 CMLR 726.

[207] Case C-203/96 *Dusseldorp* [1998] ECR I-4075, [1998] 3 CMLR 873; Case C-209/98 *Entreprenørforeningens Affalds/Miljøsektion v Københavns Kommune* [2000] ECR I-3743, [2001] 2 CMLR 936, para 75.

[208] Case T-289/03 *BUPA v Commission* [2008] ECR II-81, [2009] 2 CMLR 1043; further examples are contained in the Opinion of Advocate General Colomer in Case C-265/08 *Federutility v Autorità per l'energia elettrica e il gas* [2010] ECR I-000, para 53.

[209] See Case T-106/95 *FFSA v Commission* [1997] ECR II-229, para 99 and Case T-17/02 *Fred Olsen SA v Commission* [2005] ECR II-2031, paras 215–228.

[210] Article 14 TFEU; see further the Commission's XXVIIth *Report on Competition Policy* (1997), points 96–98; Ross 'Article 16 EC and Services of General Economic Interest: from Derogation to Obligation' (2000) 25 EL Rev 22; Szyszczak 'Public Services in Competition Markets' [2001] Yearbook of European Law (Oxford University Press, eds Eeckhout and Tridimas), ch 2; Ross 'Promoting solidarity: From public services to a European model of competition?' (2007) 44 CML Rev 1057; Boeger 'Solidarity and EC competition law' (2007) ELRev 319; Szyszczak *The Regulation of the State in Competitive Markets in the EU* (Hart Publishing, 2007).

[211] Available at www.ec.europa.eu/services_general_interest/index_en.htm; the concept of 'services of general interest' covers services of general economic interest and non-economic services of general interest, which are not subject to the rules in the TFEU.

[212] COM(2003)270 final, available at www.ec.europa.eu/services_general_interest/index_en.htm.

[213] COM(2004)374, available at www.ec.europa.eu/services_general_interest/index_en.htm.

of European enterprises. In December 2009 the Lisbon Treaty entered into force: this reformulated Article 16 EC as Article 14 TFEU and annexed Protocol 26 on services of general interest to the Treaties[214]. Protocol 26 emphasises 'the essential role and the wide discretion of national, regional and local authorities' in the provision of services of general economic interest[215] and confirms that EU law does not affect the competence of Member States to control the provision of non-economic services of general interest. In May 2010 Commissioner Alumnia indicated that the Commission intends to reflect further on the relationship between competition policy and services of general economic interest[216].

(ii) Undertakings having the character of a revenue-producing monopoly

This expression is not defined in the TFEU. It would apply to a monopoly created in order to raise revenue for the state; usually this monopoly would be conferred upon a public undertaking which would contribute its profits to the state, but it could also be conferred upon a private undertaking in exchange for revenue. Undertakings that have the character of a revenue-earning monopoly may also be subject to Article 37, and the Court of Justice has established that Article 106(2) may be invoked as a defence in an action under that provision[217].

(iii) Scope of the exception: obstruction of the performance of the tasks assigned

In a number of cases undertakings have argued that they were shielded from the competition rules by virtue of Article 106(2); in *BRT v SABAM*[218] the Court of Justice ruled that, as Article 106(2) involves a derogation from the application of the competition rules, it should be construed narrowly, and the Commission and the EU Courts have consistently done so, thereby maximising the application of Articles 101 and 102. In particular they have been sceptical of the assertion that anti-competitive behaviour is *necessary* to enable undertakings to carry out the tasks assigned to them.

(A) Unsuccessful claims based on Article 106(2)

Claims based on Article 106(2) have often been rejected[219]. For example, in *ANSEAU-NAVEWA*[220] the Commission held that an agreement requiring purchasers in Belgium to

---

[214] Protocols to the Treaties form an integral part thereof: Article 51 TEU.

[215] This point is reiterated by Article 36 of the Charter of Fundamental Rights which, in accordance with Article 6(1) TEU, has the same legal value as the other Treaties.

[216] SPEECH/10/276, 31 May 2010; see also SPEECH/11/96, 11 February 2011.

[217] See 'Article 37 TFEU – state monopolies of a commercial character', pp 245–246 below.

[218] Case 127/73 [1974] ECR 313, [1974] 2 CMLR 238.

[219] As well as the cases mentioned in the text see Case 172/80 *Züchner v Bayerische Vereinsbank* [1981] ECR 2021, [1982] 1 CMLR 313 and *Uniform Eurocheques* OJ [1985] L 35/43, [1985] 3 CMLR 434, paras 29 and 30 (both cases on banking); *Decca Navigator System* OJ [1989] L 43/27, [1990] 4 CMLR 627, para 128; *Magill TV Guide/ITP, BBC and RTE* OJ [1989] L 78/43, [1989] 4 CMLR 757, para 25; *Dutch Express Delivery Services* OJ [1990] L 10/47, paras 16–18; *Spanish International Courier Services* OJ [1990] L 233/19, [1991] 4 CMLR 560, paras 13–14; Case C-179/90 *Merci Convenzionale Porto di Genova v Siderurgica Gabrielli* [1991] ECR I-5889, [1994] 4 CMLR 540, paras 25–28; Case C-18/88 *RTT v GB-Inno-BM* [1991] ECR I-5941, paras 14–28; *IJsselcentrale* OJ [1991] L 28/32, [1992] 5 CMLR 154, paras 39–42; Case C-242/95 *GT-Link A/S v De Danske Statsbaner* [1997] ECR I-4349, [1997] 5 CMLR 601, paras 47–55; Case C-393/92 *Almelo* [1994] ECR I-1477, paras 46–51; when this case returned to the Dutch court the claim based on Article 106(2) was unsuccessful: see Hancher (1997) 34 CML Rev 1509; Case T-271/03 *Deutsche Telekom v Commission* [2008] ECR II-477, [2008] 5 CMLR 631, para 314; *CISAC*, Commission decision of 16 July 2008, paras 256–259, on appeal on this point in Case T-411/08 *Artisjus Magyar Szerzői Jogvédő Iroda Egyesület v Commission*, not yet decided.

[220] OJ [1982] L 167/39 as amended at L 325/20, [1982] 2 CMLR 193; upheld on appeal, Cases 96/82 etc *IAZ International Belgium Nv v Commission* [1983] ECR 3369, [1984] 3 CMLR 276.

acquire 'conformity labels' before washing machines and dishwashers could be plumbed in infringed Article 101(1) because it had the effect of discriminating against imports from other Member States. The association of Belgian water authorities involved in running the scheme claimed the benefit of Article 106(2). The Commission accepted that they qualified as a body to whom services of a general economic interest had been entrusted, but went on to hold that the scheme in question was much more restrictive than necessary, saying that:

> a possible limitation of the application of the rules on competition can only be envisaged in the event that the undertaking concerned has no other technically and economically feasible means of performing its particular task[221].

Similarly in *British Telecommunications*[222] the Commission rejected BT's defence based on Article 106(2); when the Italian Government challenged this decision before the Court of Justice the Commission's decision was upheld[223]. The Court held that Italy had failed to show that the Commission's censure of BT, for prohibiting private message-forwarding agencies from using its network to forward messages from other Member States, put the performance of its tasks in jeopardy. Article 106(2) also failed in *Air Inter v Commission*[224], where the General Court rejected TAT's appeal against a Commission decision requiring the termination of exclusive rights on French air routes. The General Court accepted that the airline was entrusted with a public task of maintaining unprofitable domestic air routes. However it held that subjection to the competition rules would merely hinder or make more difficult the performance of this task; for Article 106(2) to apply it was necessary to show that this would obstruct it, in fact or in law[225]. The General Court reached a similar conclusion in respect of a recycling scheme in *Duales System Deutschland v Commission*[226].

A particularly important judgment on Article 106(2) is *Corbeau*[227]. As we have seen, the case concerned the operation of an express delivery service in Liège, in contravention of the Belgian Post Office's postal monopoly[228]. The core of the Court of Justice's judgment dealt with the extent to which the postal monopoly could be justified under Article 106(2)[229]. The Court acknowledged that the Post Office was entrusted with a service of general economic interest[230], and that it might be necessary for it to benefit from a restriction of competition in order to be able to offset less profitable activities against profitable ones[231]: put more colloquially, it may be legitimate to prevent an entrant into the market from 'cream-skimming' or 'cherry-picking', leaving the incumbent postal operator to carry out unprofitable services pursuant to its universal service obligation. However the Court continued that:

> the exclusion of competition is not justified as regards specific services dissociable from the service of general interest which meet special needs of economic operators and which call for certain additional services not offered by the traditional postal service, such as collection from the senders' address, greater speed or reliability of distribution or the possibility of changing the destination in the course of transit, in so far as such services, by their nature and the conditions in which they are offered, such as the geographical area in

---

[221] OJ [1982] L 167/39, [1982] 2 CMLR 193, para 66.
[222] OJ [1982] L 360/36, [1983] 1 CMLR 457.
[223] Case 41/83 *Italy v Commission* [1985] ECR 873, [1985] 2 CMLR 368.
[224] Case T-260/94 [1997] ECR II-997, [1997] 5 CMLR 851.
[225] Ibid, paras 134–141.
[226] Case T-151/01 [2007] ECR II-1607, [2007] 5 CMLR 300, paras 207–210.
[227] Case C-320/91 [1993] ECR I-2533, [1995] 4 CMLR 621.
[228] See 'The *Corbeau* judgment', p 229 above.
[229] Case C-320/91 [1993] ECR I-2533, [1995] 4 CMLR 621, paras 13–21.   [230] Ibid, para 15.
[231] Ibid, paras 17–18.

which they are provided, do not compromise the economic equilibrium of the service of general economic interest performed by the holder of the exclusive right[232].

Since this was a reference under Article 267, the Court then stated that it would be for the national court to make a decision under Article 106(2) on the particular facts of the case[233], but it is clear that it was giving a strong indication that it should not be possible to maintain a monopoly over express courier services in order to sustain the basic service of the daily delivery of letters[234].

(B) Successful claims based on Article 106(2)

It would be wrong to suppose from the foregoing that claims based on Article 106(2) are always unsuccessful. In particular, as the competition rules have come to be applied with greater regularity to the utilities (gas, electricity, water and similar sectors) and to areas of activity for which the state has historically taken responsibility, so too Article 106(2) has been invoked more often with successful effect. This point can be demonstrated by reference to five judgments of the Court of Justice from 1998 to 2001. In *Corsica Ferries France SA v Gruppo Antichi Ormeggiatori del Porto di Genova*[235] the Court was concerned with Italian legislation requiring ships from other Member States using the ports of Genoa and La Spezia in Italy to use the services of local mooring companies. It considered that mooring operations were of general economic interest: mooring groups are obliged to provide at any time and to any user a universal mooring service, for reasons of safety in port waters[236]. As a result it was not incompatible with Article 106(1) in conjunction with Article 102 to include in the price of the service a component designed to cover the cost of maintaining the universal mooring service, and Article 106(2) was applicable[237].

In the *Albany* judgment[238] the Court of Justice held that the exclusive right of a pension fund to manage supplementary pensions in a particular sector could be justified under Article 106(2), since otherwise 'young employees in good health engaged in non-dangerous activities' would leave the scheme, leaving behind members who would be bad insurance risks, thereby undermining the success of the system[239]. In *Deutsche Post AG v Gesellschaft für Zahlungssysteme mbH and Citicorp Kartenservice GmbH*[240] the Court considered that Article 106(2) justified the grant by a Member State to its postal operators of a statutory right to charge internal postage on items of so-called 'remail'[241]. Environmental considerations led to the successful application of Article 106(2) in *Entreprenørforeningens Affalds/Miljøsektion v Københavns Kommune*[242]. In *Ambulanz Glöckner v Landkreis Südwestpfalz*[243] the Court considered that a national law which protected the providers of emergency ambulance services against competition from independent operators, even on a related non-emergency transport market, could be justified under Article 106(2) if this was necessary for them to perform their tasks in economically

---

[232] Ibid, para 19.   [233] Ibid, para 20.

[234] See to similar effect Case C-220/06 *Asociación Profesional de Empresas de Reparto y Manipulado de Correspondencia v Administración del Estado*, [2007] ECR I-12175, paras 79–83, a case concerned with the Postal Services Directive; similarly Case C-162/06 *International Mail Spain* [2007] ECR I-9991, [2008] 4 CMLR 18, para 38.

[235] Case C-266/96 [1998] ECR I-3949, [1998] 5 CMLR 402.   [236] Ibid, para 45.

[237] Ibid, paras 46–47.

[238] Cases C-67/96 etc *Albany International BV v SBT* [1999] ECR I-5751, [2000] 4 CMLR 446.

[239] Ibid, paras 98–111.   [240] Cases C-147/97 etc [2000] ECR I-825, [2000] 4 CMLR 838.

[241] Ibid, paras 41–54.

[242] Case C-209/98 [2000] ECR I-3743, [2001] 2 CMLR 936, paras 74–83.

[243] Case C-475/99 [2001] ECR I-8089, [2002] 4 CMLR 726.

acceptable conditions[244]. In *AG2R Prévoyance v Beaudort Père et Fils SARL*[245] the Court considered that Article 106(2) could apply to an exclusive right granted to a provident society to manage a scheme for the supplementary reimbursement of healthcare costs[246].

Although Article 106(2) is drafted in terms of the position of undertakings, it has become clear that Member States themselves can rely on it. For example in *Dusseldorp*[247] the Court of Justice, following the Opinion of Advocate General Jacobs, confirmed that the Netherlands could rely on Article 106(2) in relation to its 'Long Term Plan' relating to waste disposal. The same point arose in *Commission v Netherlands*[248]. The Court of Justice has also held that Article 106(2) may be invoked by a Member State in defence of state aid that might otherwise be incompatible with the internal market[249]. The implications of this judgment are considered in a Commission decision[250].

(iv) Adverse development of trade

It is not possible to rely on Article 106(2) if the development of trade would be affected to such an extent as would be contrary to the interest of the EU. This must mean something more than an effect on inter-state trade in the sense of Articles 101 and 102, since without such an effect the EU competition rules would not be applicable anyway. The Court of Justice has held in *Commission v Netherlands* that the Commission must prove whether the exclusive right has affected and continued to affect the development of intra-EU trade 'to an extent which is contrary to the interests of the [EU]'[251]. An application will be dismissed where it fails to do so[252]. If the matter were to arise in domestic litigation, not involving the Commission, it would presumably fall upon the claimant to demonstrate an adverse effect on the development of trade.

(v) Direct effect

In *Belgische Radio en Televisie (BRT) v SABAM*[253] the Court of Justice established that Articles 101(1) and 102 are directly applicable to the undertakings described in Article 106(2) so that an action may be brought against them in domestic proceedings, whether the Commission has acted under Article 106(3) or not. A national court should investigate whether the undertaking falls within Article 106(2); if it does not, the court may go ahead and apply the competition rules[254]. In cases of doubt the national court can stay the action whilst the opinion of the Commission is sought[255].

---

[244] Ibid, paras 51–65.

[245] Case C-437/09 [2011] ECR I-000, [2011] 4 CMLR 1029.

[246] Ibid, paras 66–81.

[247] Case C-203/96 [1998] ECR I-4075, [1998] 3 CMLR 873, para 67.

[248] Cases C-157/94 etc [1997] ECR I-5699, [1998] 2 CMLR 373, paras 51–64.

[249] See eg Case T-289/03 *BUPA v Commission* [2008] ECR II-81, [2009] 2 CMLR 1043.

[250] Commission decision of 28 November 2005 on the application of Article [106(2) TFEU] to State aid, OJ [2005] L 312/67; see also the Commission Staff Working Document *Frequently asked questions on the application of Article [106(2) TFEU] to state aid*, available at www.ec.europa.eu/services_general_interest; the Commission has launched a consultation on its approach: see Commission Press Release IP/10/715, 10 June 2010.

[251] Cases C-157/94 etc [1997] ECR I-5699, [1998] 2 CMLR 373, paras 65–68; Advocate General Cosmas considered that there should be evidence that the measure has in fact had a *substantial* effect on intra-EU trade: ibid, para 126; see similarly the Opinion of Advocate General Léger in Case C-309/99 *Wouters* [2002] ECR I-1577, [2002] 4 CMLR 913, para 166.

[252] See Case C-159/94 *Commission v France* [1997] ECR I-5815, [1998] 2 CMLR 373, paras 109–116.

[253] Case 127/73 [1974] ECR 313, [1974] 2 CMLR 238.

[254] Case 155/73 *Italy v Sacchi* [1974] ECR 409, [1974] 2 CMLR 177.

[255] Case C-260/89 *ERT v Dimotiki* [1991] ECR I-2925, [1994] 4 CMLR 540, para 34 and Case C-393/92 *Almelo* [1994] ECR I-1477, para 50.

It remains uncertain whether the final sentence of Article 106(2), which requires that trade must not be affected contrary to the interests of the EU, has direct effect. It is arguable that only the Commission should be entitled to carry out the task of assessing the interests of the EU.

(C) **Article 106(3)**[256]

Article 106(3) provides that the Commission shall ensure the application of Article 106(1) and (2) and that, where necessary, it shall address appropriate decisions or directives to Member States. The Commission began to employ it in the 1980s, most notably in the context of the telecommunications sector[257], and it is now an important part of its armoury. The advantage of Article 106(3) from the Commission's perspective is that it can adopt a decision or directive itself; in doing so, it is not subject to any particular procedural framework, although it must of course comply with the general principles of EU law, and must provide adequate reasons for its action, in accordance with Article 296 TFEU[258]. The Commission liaises with other interested parties, including the Parliament, when exercising its powers under Article 106(3), and particularly when adopting a directive[259]. If the Commission did not have its Article 106(3) powers, it would be able to proceed against measures that offend Article 106(1) only by taking proceedings before the Court of Justice under Article 258 or by persuading the Council to adopt the measures it favours.

Article 106(3) enables the Commission to adopt both decisions and directives: a decision can be adopted establishing that a Member State is in breach of an EU obligation; but a directive can go further and legislate for the elimination of existing violations of the Treaty and the prevention of future ones.

(i) Decisions

In *Greek Public Property Insurance*[260] the Commission required Greece, by decision under Article 106(3), to alter its domestic legislation requiring that all public property in Greece be insured by Greek public-sector insurance companies and that staff of Greek state-owned banks recommend to their customers insurance with companies affiliated to the public banking sector and controlled by it. When Greece failed to take the necessary measures to do this within the prescribed period the Commission brought an action under Article 258 for failure to fulfil its Treaty obligations. The Court of Justice made the declaration[261], holding in the course of its judgment that a decision by the Commission under Article 106(3) is 'binding in its entirety' on the person to whom it is addressed so that the addressee must comply with it until it obtains from the Court a suspension of its operation or a declaration that it is void. In *Spanish Transport Fares*[262] the Commission addressed a decision to Spain condemning its discriminatory fares for passengers from mainland Spain to the Balearic and Canary Islands. The Commission also adopted decisions under Article 106(3) in:

---

[256] On Article 106(3) generally, see Buendia Sierra *Exclusive Rights and State Monopolies under EC Law*, paras 10.01–10.184 and Buendia Sierra in *Faull and Nikpay* (ch 6 n 55, p 222 above) paras 6.217–6.257.

[257] See 'Directives', pp 243–244 below.

[258] The Commission's decision in *Dutch Express Delivery Services* was quashed for various procedural improprieties: see ch 6, n 263 below.

[259] See XXVth *Report on Competition Policy* (1995), point 100.   [260] OJ [1985] L 152/25.

[261] Case 226/87 *Commission v Greece* [1988] ECR 3611, [1989] 3 CMLR 569.

[262] OJ [1987] L 194/28.

- *Dutch Express Delivery Services*[263]
- *Spanish International Courier Services*[264]
- *Port of Rødby*[265]
- *Second Operator of GSM Radiotelephony Services in Italy*[266]
- *Second Operator of GSM Radiotelephony Services in Spain*[267]
- *Brussels National Airport (Zaventem)*[268]
- *Exclusive Right to Broadcast Television Advertising in Flanders*[269]
- *Italian Ports Legislation Relating to Employment*[270]
- *Tariffs for Piloting in the Port of Genoa*[271]
- *Portuguese Airports*[272]
- *Spanish Airports*[273]
- *New Postal Services in Italy*[274]
- *La Poste*[275]
- *German postal legislation*[276]
- *French savings accounts*[277]
- *Greek lignite*[278]
- *Slovakian postal legislation*[279].

(ii) Directives

The competence of the Commission to adopt directives under Article 106(3) has been considered by the Court of Justice on three occasions. The Transparency Directive[280] was challenged in *France v Commission*[281] on the basis that, since it concerned the surveillance of state aids, it should have been adopted under Article 109 rather than Article 106(3). The Court ruled that the fact that the Commission could have proceeded under Article 109 did not mean that it could not also do so under Article 106(3). Towards the end of the

---

[263] OJ [1990] L 10/47, annulled on appeal Cases C-48/90 and C-66/90 *Netherlands and Koninklijke PTT Nederland v Commission* [1992] ECR I-565, [1993] 5 CMLR 316 as the Commission had failed to give the Dutch Government a fair hearing.

[264] OJ [1990] L 233/19, [1991] 4 CMLR 560.   [265] OJ [1994] L 55/52.

[266] OJ [1995] L 280/49, [1996] 4 CMLR 700.   [267] OJ [1997] L 76/19.

[268] OJ [1995] L 216/8, [1996] 4 CMLR 232.

[269] OJ [1997] L 244/18, [1997] 5 CMLR 718, upheld on appeal Case T-266/97 *Vlaamse Televisie Maatschappij NV v Commission* [1999] ECR II-2329, [2000] 4 CMLR 1171.

[270] OJ [1997] L 301/17.   [271] OJ [1997] L 301/27.

[272] OJ [1999] L 69/31, [1999] 5 CMLR 103, upheld on appeal Case C-163/99 *Portugal v Commission* [2001] ECR I-2613, [2002] 4 CMLR 1319.

[273] OJ [2000] L 208/36, [2000] 5 CMLR 967.   [274] OJ [2001] L 63/59.

[275] OJ [2002] L 120/19.   [276] Commission decision of 20 October 2004.

[277] Commission decision of 10 May 2007.

[278] Commission decision of 5 March 2008, on appeal Case T-169/08 *DEI v Commission*, not yet decided.

[279] Commission decision of 7 October 2008, on appeal Case T-556/08 *Slovenská Pošta v Commission*, not yet decided.

[280] Commission Directive 80/723/EEC, OJ [1980] L 195/35, repealed and replaced by Commission Directive 2006/111/EC, OJ [2006] L 318/17.

[281] Cases 188/80 etc [1982] ECR 2545, [1982] 3 CMLR 144; for a later challenge related to this Directive, see Case C-325/91 *France v Commission* [1993] ECR I-3283.

1980s the Commission's concern about the fragmented nature of the telecommunications market in the EU and the consequent lack of competition led to the adoption of two directives, the first on the telecommunications terminal equipment market[282] and the second on telecommunications themselves[283]. Opposition from Member States to these Directives was considerable and both were challenged before the Court of Justice. In each case the Court upheld the competence of the Commission to have proceeded under Article 106(3)[284]. In *France v Commission*[285] three Member States complained that the Commission should have proceeded under Article 258 rather than Article 106(3). The Court held that there had been no misuse of powers: the Commission may use the powers conferred upon it by Article 106(3) to specify in general terms the obligations that arise under Article 106(1); however the Commission may not use a directive under Article 106(3) to rule upon specific infringements of the TFEU, for which the Article 258 procedure must be used[286]. The Court also held that the fact that the Council had competence to adopt legislation relating to telecommunications did not mean that the Commission had no competence[287]. The Court annulled Articles 2, 7 and 9 of the Directive on terminal equipment since the Commission had failed to explain which rights were 'special' and why they were contrary to EU law[288]. It is not possible to use Article 106(3) for the purpose of achieving harmonisation, the legislative base for which is provided by Articles 114 and 115 TFEU: this explains why in the telecommunications sector there are Article 106(3) Directives, dealing with the conditions of competition, and a raft of separate measures under Articles 114 and 115 on harmonisation[289].

(iii) Judicial review of the Commission's powers under Article 106(3)

The Commission enjoys a wide discretion in the field covered by Article 106(1) and (3)[290]. The Court will not annul a decision or directive unless it is reasonably likely that an error on the part of the Commission may have affected it in a material respect. Third parties cannot, except in an exceptional situation, bring an action against a Commission decision not to use its powers under Article 106(3)[291].

---

[282] Commission Directive 88/301/EEC, OJ [1988] L 131/73, [1991] 4 CMLR 922; this Directive was replaced by Commission Directive 2008/63/EC, OJ [2008] L 162/20.

[283] Commission Directive 90/388/EEC, OJ [1990] L 192/10, [1991] 4 CMLR 932; this Directive was replaced by Commission Directive 2002/77/EC, OJ [2002] L 249/21.

[284] See Case C-202/88 *France v Commission* [1991] ECR I-1223, [1992] 5 CMLR 552 (terminal equipment); Cases C-271/90 etc *Spain, Belgium and Italy v Commission* (telecommunications) [1992] ECR I-5833, [1993] 4 CMLR 100.

[285] See ch 6 n 281 above.   [286] [1991] ECR I-1223, [1992] 5 CMLR 552, paras 16–18.

[287] Ibid, paras 19–27; see similarly Cases 188/80 etc *France v Commission* [1982] ECR 2545, [1982] 3 CMLR 144, para 14.

[288] Case C-202/88 (n 266 above), paras 45–47 and 53–58.

[289] See ch 23, 'Legislation', pp 980–981.

[290] Case C-107/95 P *Bundesverband der Bilanzbuchhalter v Commission* [1997] ECR I-947, [1997] 5 CMLR 432, para 27; see also Case T-266/97 *Vlaamse Televisie Maatschappij NV v Commission* [1999] ECR II-2329, [2000] 4 CMLR 1171, para 75 and Case T-52/00 *Coe Clerici Logistics SpA v Commission* [2003] ECR II-2123, [2003] 5 CMLR 539, paras 106–189.

[291] Case C-107/95 P *Bundesverband der Bilanzbuchhalter v Commission* [1997] ECR I-947, [1997] 5 CMLR 432, para 28; see also Case C-141/02 P *Commission v T-Mobile Austria GmbH, formerly max.mobil Telecommunications service GmbH* [2005] ECR I-1283, [2005] 4 CMLR 735, paras 69–73 where the Court of Justice annulled a judgment of the General Court which had suggested greater rights for third parties to challenge the Commission's decision not to act; for comment see Hocepied 'The *Max.mobil* Judgment: the Court of Justice clarifies the role of complainants in Article 86 procedures' (2005) (Summer) *Competition Policy Newsletter* 53: 'the judgment...clarifies a question which had been debated nearly 15 years'.

4. Article 37 TFEU – State Monopolies of a Commercial Character [292]

Article 37(1) of the Treaty provides that:

> Member States shall adjust any State monopolies of a commercial character so as to ensure that no discrimination regarding the conditions under which goods are procured and marketed exists between nationals of Member States[293].

Article 37(1) goes on to state that it applies to any body through which a Member State supervises, determines or appreciably influences imports or exports between Member States, and also that it applies to monopolies delegated by the state to others. Article 37(2) obliges Member States not to introduce any new measure contrary to the principles in Article 37(1) or which restricts the scope of the Treaty Articles dealing with the prohibition of customs duties and quantitative restrictions between Member States. However Article 37 does not require the abolition of existing monopolies; only that they should be adjusted to prevent discrimination.

Article 37 is designed to prevent state monopolies of a commercial character discriminating against nationals of other Member States. One way of ensuring that Member States do not discriminate in this way is to alter their public procurement policies, in which area the Council has been active[294]. The Commission continues to monitor the conduct of Member States under Article 37; details of its application of Article 37 will be found in its annual reports on competition policy[295]. In *Commission v Greece*[296] the Court of Justice held that Greece was obliged to terminate exclusive rights to import and sell petroleum derivatives since those rights discriminated against exporters of such products in other Member States and since they upset the normal conditions of competition between Member States. Where the Commission suspects infringement of Article 37 it may take proceedings against the Member State under Article 258 or it could make use of the powers available to it under Article 106(3)[297]. Where the Commission brings Article 258 proceedings it must prove that a Member State has failed to fulfil its obligations and it must place before the Court of Justice the information needed to enable it to decide whether this is the case[298]. An injured undertaking could bring an action in a national court, as Article 37 is directly effective[299].

In *Commission v Netherlands* the Court of Justice found that import and export monopolies for gas and electricity in the Netherlands, Italy and France amounted to an infringement of Article 37(1)[300]. However the Court considered that Article 106(2) could be invoked by Member States in proceedings brought under Article 37 to justify such monopolies. Justification was possible, provided that the maintenance of monopoly rights was necessary to enable the undertaking in question to perform the tasks of general economic interest entrusted to it under economically acceptable conditions; it was not

---

[292] See generally Buendia Sierra *Exclusive Rights and State Monopolies under EC Law* (Oxford University Press, 1999) paras 3.01–3.201; also Buendia Sierra in *Faull and Nikpay*, paras 6.106–6.121.

[293] Note that Article 37 TFEU is not identical to the original Article 37 EEC, which contained transitional rules that had become redundant.

[294] See ch 2 n 7, p 50 above.

[295] See eg the Commission's XXVIth *Report on Competition Policy* (1996), points 132–135; XXVIIth *Report on Competition Policy* (1997), points 137–144; XXXIInd *Report on Competition Policy* (2002), point 636; XXXIIIrd Report on Competition Policy (2003), point 659.

[296] Case C-347/88 [1990] ECR I-4747.   [297] See 'Article 106(3)', pp 242–244 above.

[298] See eg Cases C-157/94 etc *Commission v Netherlands* [1997] ECR I-5699, [1998] 2 CMLR 373, para 59.

[299] Case 91/78 *Hansen v Hauptzollamt Flensberg* [1979] ECR 935.

[300] See Cases C-157/94 etc *Commission v Netherlands* [1997] ECR I-5699, [1998] 2 CMLR 373: the nature of the monopolies varied from state to state.

necessary to demonstrate that the survival of the undertaking itself would be threatened in the absence of such a monopoly. On the facts the Commission failed to satisfy the Court that the monopolies could not be justified under Article 106(2). In *Krister Hanner*[301] the Court of Justice considered, in an Article 267 reference from a Swedish court, that Article 37(1) precluded a sales regime that conferred a legal monopoly at the retail level of trade in medicinal preparations on Apoteket, an entity in which the Swedish state had a majority shareholding and the management of which was predominantly in the hands of politicians and civil servants. The Court's concern was that Apoteket's procurement arrangements were liable to discriminate against medicinal preparations from outside Sweden[302]. In October 2007 the Commission announced that it would bring proceedings under Article 37 against Malta unless it adjusted a monopoly for the importation, storage and wholesale of petroleum products[303]; the case was closed after Malta took steps to open the market to third parties[304].

5. Articles 107 to 109 TFEU – State Aids[305]

The Treaty provides the Commission with power under Articles 107 to 109 TFEU to deal with state aids that could distort competition in the internal market. A considerable amount of DG COMP's energies go into this issue[306], but lack of space prevents a detailed discussion of the topic here.

Article 107(1) provides that:

> Save as otherwise provided in the Treaties, any aid granted by a Member State or through State resources in any form whatsoever which distorts or threatens to distort competition by favouring certain undertakings or the production of certain goods shall, in so far as it affects trade between Member States, be incompatible with the internal market.

Article 107(2) provides that aids having a social character granted to individual consumers, aids to make good the damage caused by national disasters or exceptional occurrences and aids granted to the economy of certain areas of Germany affected by the division of that country after the Second World War[307] shall be compatible with the internal market. Article 107(3) gives the Commission discretion to permit other aids, for example to promote the economic development of areas where the standard of living is abnormally low or where there is serious unemployment, or to promote the execution of an important project of common European interest or to remedy a serious disturbance in the economy of a Member State. The Commission has proactively applied these provisions since

---

[301] Case C-438/02 [2005] ECR I-4551, [2005] 2 CMLR 1010.

[302] Ibid, paras 32–49.   [303] Commission Press Release IP/07/1544, 18 October 2007.

[304] Commission Press release IP/07/1952, 18 December 2007.

[305] For further reading on state aids see Hancher, Ottervanger and Slot *EC State Aids* (Sweet & Maxwell, 3rd ed, 2006); Wyatt and Dashwood *European Union Law* (Sweet & Maxwell, 5th ed, 2006), ch 24; Faull and Nikpay *The EC Law of Competition* (Oxford University Press, 2nd ed, 2007), ch 16; Bellamy and Child *European Community Law of Competition* (Oxford University Press, 6th ed, 2008, ed Roth and Rose), ch 15; Quigley *European State Aid Law* (Hart Publishing, 2nd ed, 2009); Bacon *European Community Law of State Aid* (Oxford University Press, 2009); the Commission's *Annual Report on Competition Policy* contains a detailed account of its activities under the state aids provisions.

[306] DG AGRI and DG MARE deal with state aids in agriculture and fisheries respectively.

[307] Article 107(2) provides that the Council, acting on a proposal from the Commission, may adopt a decision repealing this point after 1 December 2014.

autumn 2008 so that Member States could adopt measures to safeguard the stability of their financial systems without unduly distorting competition[308]. DG COMP has established an Economic Crisis Team to handle the state aid implications of national measures designed to promote economic recovery[309].

Article 108 deals with procedure. The Commission may, by Article 108(2)(i), adopt a decision that a state aid which is incompatible with the internal market shall be abolished or altered. If the Member State does not comply with this decision within the stated time, the Commission or another Member State may take the matter to the Court of Justice under Article 108(2)(ii) without having to resort to the procedure under Articles 258 and 259 TFEU[310]. Repayment of state aids will usually be demanded. Article 108(3) requires plans to grant or alter aids to be notified to the Commission in sufficient time to enable it to submit its comments. The procedural powers of the Commission in relation to state aids are set out in Council Regulation 659/1999[311] and Commission Regulation 794/2004[312]. The aid may not be implemented until the Commission has reached a decision. Article 108(3) is directly effective[313] and an individual may seek relief in a domestic court where aid is granted without notification under Article 108(3) or put into effect before the Commission's decision[314].

It can be difficult to tell, in the absence of relevant information, whether competition is being distorted where a Member State controls part of the economy directly or grants financial aids to certain firms. To overcome this problem the Commission issued a Directive in 1980 to increase the transparency of the relationship between Member States and public undertakings[315], which was unsuccessfully challenged in *France v Commission*[316]; the Directive has been amended a number of times and was codified in November 2006[317]. The Commission uses the data that it receives through this Directive to monitor the compatibility of state aids with Article 107.

Article 109 TFEU authorises the Council to adopt regulations on state aid, in particular exempting aid from notification. The Council has adopted Regulation 994/98[318] which confers powers on the Commission to adopt 'group exemptions' for certain categories of state aid, and to adopt a regulation on *de minimis* aids. Several regulations have been adopted by the Commission under Regulation 994/98: they can be accessed on the website of DG COMP[319]. That website provides a considerable amount of other information about state aid policy, including details of current developments, a register of cases, reports on state aid matters and discussion of the measures introduced as a result of the Commission's *State Aid Action Plan*[320].

---

[308] See eg Commission Communication *The application of state aid rules to measures taken in relation to financial institutions in the context of the current global financial crisis* OJ [2008] C 270/8 and MEMO/11/68, 3 February 2011.

[309] See www.ec.europa.eu/competition/recovery/real_economy.html.

[310] It cannot proceed under Article 108(2)(ii) in respect of a later state aid which was not within the scope of an earlier decision: Case C-294/90 *British Aerospace plc v Commission* [1992] ECR I-493, [1992] 1 CMLR 853.

[311] OJ [1999] L 83/1.   [312] OJ [2004] L 140/1.

[313] Case 120/73 *Lorenz v Germany* [1973] ECR 1471.

[314] See eg *R v A-G, ex p ICI* [1987] 1 CMLR 72, CA.   [315] OJ [1980] L 195/35.

[316] See ch 6 n 66, p 224 above.   [317] Commission Directive 2006/111/EC OJ [2006] L 318/17.

[318] OJ [1998] L 142/1.

[319] See www.ec.europa.eu/comm/competition/index_en.html.

[320] *State Aid action plan: Less and better targeted state aid: a roadmap for state aid reform 2005-2009* COM(2005)107, 7 June 2005.

7

Articles 101 and 102: public enforcement by the European Commission and national competition authorities under Regulation 1/2003

Infringement of Articles 101 and 102 has serious consequences for guilty undertakings. Such is the importance of competition law that undertakings are well advised to put in place effective compliance programmes to ensure that the competition rules are not infringed and that employees understand what types of behaviour must be avoided; the Commission and the EU Courts are unimpressed by arguments sometimes put forward by undertakings that they intended to comply with competition law, but that their employees disobeyed instructions and wrongly entered into price-fixing or similar agreements[1]. The powers of the Commission to enforce Articles 101 and 102 were originally contained in Regulation 17 of 1962[2]. Major changes in the enforcement of Articles 101 and 102 were effected by Regulation 1/2003[3], which became applicable on 1 May 2004[4]. This chapter will explain the main features of the public enforcement system: there are numerous practitioners' books that provide a more detailed analysis of the position[5]. The chapter will begin with a brief overview of Regulation 1/2003. Section 2 provides a

---

[1] See eg Case T-53/03 *BPB v Commission* [2008] ECR II-1333, [2008] 5 CMLR 1201, para 360; *Candle Waxes*, Commission decision of 1 October 2008, paras 642–643: the decision is on appeal Cases T-543 etc *RWE and RWE Dea v Commission*, not yet decided.

[2] JO 204/62, OJ (Special Edition 1959–62), p 57.

[3] OJ [2003] L 1/1, as amended by Regulation 411/2004, OJ [2004] L 68/1 and Regulation 1419/2006, OJ [2006] L 269/1.

[4] The temporal effect of Regulation 1/2003 is under examination in Case C-17/10 *Toshiba Corpn v Úřad pro ochranu hospodářské soutěže*, not yet decided; for discussion of the issues see the Opinion of AG Kobott of 8 September 2011.

[5] See in particular Kerse and Khan *EC Antitrust Procedure* (Sweet & Maxwell, 5th ed, 2005); Ortiz Blanco *European Community Competition Procedure* (Oxford University Press, 2nd ed, 2006); Faull and Nikpay *The EC Law of Competition* (Oxford University Press, 2nd ed, 2007), ch 2; Bellamy and Child *European Community Law of Competition* (Oxford University Press, 6th ed, 2008, eds Roth and Rose), ch 13; for a series of seminal essays on all aspects of public enforcement see Wils *The Optimal Enforcement of EC Antitrust Law* (Kluwer Law International, 2002); Wils 'Principles of European Antitrust Enforcement'

detailed examination of the Commission's enforcement powers; it also describes the procedure introduced by the Commission in 2008 whereby it sometimes settles cartel cases. Section 3 discusses the operation of the European Competition Network ('the ECN') that brings together the Commission and the national competition authorities of the Member States ('the NCAs'). The final section of the chapter will provide a brief account of judicial review of the Commission's decisions. Articles 101 and 102 are directly applicable and may be invoked in proceedings in the domestic courts of the Member States: the private enforcement of the competition rules will be considered in chapter 8.

In understanding the extent of – or rather the limits to – the Commission's powers, it is important to have reference to the general principles of EU law some of which, such as respect for the rights of the defence and the principles of proportionality, equal treatment, the protection of legitimate interests, legal certainty and non-retroactivity, have obvious significance for the enforcement of the competition rules[6]. Two further important issues are the relationship between the Commission's procedures and the standards required by the European Convention on Human Rights[7] and by the Charter of Fundamental Rights of the European Union[8]; recital 37 of Regulation 1/2003 states that it should be interpreted in accordance with the rights and principles recognised in the Charter, and Article 6(1) TEU provides that the Charter has the same force as the other Treaties[9]. In *Knauf Gips KG v Commission* the Court of Justice specifically relied on the Charter when allowing an appeal by Knauf which claimed that its rights of defence had been infringed[10]. However whilst it is important to ensure that the rights of the defence are properly respected, it is also important to avoid them being so elevated that it becomes disproportionately difficult for the Commission to enforce the law: a balance has to be struck between the private interest of undertakings not to be found guilty of behaviour of which they are innocent and the public interest of punishing serious infringements of the law. A related point is that the law of 'human' rights was developed with the laudable goal of protecting natural persons from arbitrary and oppressive behaviour, including physical maltreatment. It would not be surprising if the EU Courts were to develop different standards of human rights for natural persons on the one hand and for well-resourced multinational corporations on the other with access to sophisticated legal advice in the context of administrative proceedings based on Articles 101 and 102 TFEU[11].

(Hart Publishing, 2005); Wils *Efficiency and Justice in European Antitrust Enforcement* (Hart Publishing, 2008): these essays are also available at www.ssrn.com.

  [6] On general principles of EU law see the books cited in ch 7 n 5 above and Usher *General Principles of EC Law* (Addison Wesley Longman, 1998); Wyatt and Dashwood's *European Union Law* (Hart Publishing, 6th ed, 2011), ch 10; Tridimas *The General Principles of EU Law* (Oxford University Press, 2nd ed, 2007); Hartley *The Foundations of European Union Law* (Oxford University Press, 7th ed, 2010), ch 5.

  [7] Available at www.echr.coe.int/ECHR.   [8] OJ [2010] C 83/389.

  [9] For full discussion of this topic see Wils 'EU Antitrust Enforcement Powers and Procedural Rights and Guarantees: The Interplay between EU Law, National Law, the Charter of Fundamental Rights of the EU and the European Convention of Human Rights' (2011) 34(2) World Competition 189.

  [10] Case C-407/08 P [2010] ECR I-000, [2010] 5 CMLR 708, paras 91–93.

  [11] See eg the Opinion of Advocate General Geelhoed in Case C-301/04 P *Commission v SGL Carton* [2006] ECR I-5915, [2006] 5 CMLR 877, paras 62–69 and the judgment of the Court of Justice in Case C-411/04 P *Salzgitter v Commission* [2007] ECR I-965, [2007] 4 CMLR 682, paras 40–50; note however the judgment of the European Court of Human Rights in *Jussila v Finland* (2007) 45 EHRR 892, categorising infringements of competition law as criminal for the purpose of Article 6 of the European Convention on Human Rights, but noting the distinction between the 'hard-core' of criminal cases and cases not belonging to the traditional categories of criminal law: see Wils 'The Increased Level of EU Antitrust Fines, Judicial Review and the ECHR' (2010) 33(1) World Competition 5; see also the same Court's judgment in *Menarini Diagnostics Srl v Italy*, judgment of 27 September 2011.

1. Overview of Regulation 1/2003

Regulation 1/2003 abolished the notification of agreements to the Commission for individual exemption and the Commission's exclusive power to make decisions on the application of Article 101(3) in individual cases: that provision is now directly applicable in the same way that Articles 101(1), 101(2) and 102 have always been[12]. One of the reasons for this fundamental change in the procedural regime was to enable the Commission to use its resources for investigating serious infringements of the competition rules, such as price-fixing and market-sharing cartels, rather than having to devote a large amount of time to examining agreements and practices notified to it which, for the most part, did not raise serious competition problems[13]. However Regulation 1/2003 did not deal only with these matters: the opportunity was taken to refresh the enforcement powers of the Commission generally, and the Regulation adopted a number of new provisions including, for example, the possibility of the Commission adopting decisions on the basis of legally binding commitments as to undertakings' future behaviour (Article 9) and the power to conduct inspections at people's homes (Article 21).

(A) The content of Regulation 1/2003

Regulation 1/2003 consists of 11 chapters:

- Chapter I is entitled 'Principles': Article 1 provides for the direct applicability of Articles 101 and 102, Article 2 explains who bears the burden of proof in cases under Articles 101 and 102 and Article 3 deals with the relationship between those provisions and national competition law[14]
- Chapter II of the Regulation sets out the powers of the Commission, the NCAs and national courts
- Chapter III provides for various types of Commission decision: findings of infringement, interim measures, the acceptance of commitments and findings of inapplicability
- Chapter IV is concerned with cooperation between the Commission, NCAs and national courts
- Chapter V deals with the Commission's powers of investigation
- Chapter VI deals with penalties
- Chapter VII is concerned with limitation periods for the imposition and enforcement of penalties
- Chapter VIII deals with hearings and professional secrecy
- Chapter IX provides for the withdrawal of the benefit of block exemption regulations in certain circumstances
- Chapter X contains general provisions
- Chapter XI contains transitional, amending and final provisions.

---

[12] See ch 4, 'Regulation 1/2003', pp 166–168.

[13] For a discussion of the background to the adoption of Regulation 1/2003, including the Commission's *White Paper on Modernisation*, see the fifth edition of this book, ch 7, pp 245–251 and the extensive list of literature cited there.

[14] The relationship between EU and domestic competition law is discussed in ch 2, 'The Relationship Between EU Competition Law and National Competition Laws', pp 75–79.

(B) **Supporting measures**

The Commission has adopted a number of supporting measures necessary for the successful application of Regulation 1/2003. These measures consist of one Commission Regulation and a number of Notices, as follows:

- Commission Regulation 773/2004 relating to the conduct of proceedings under Articles 101 and 102, the 'Implementing Regulation'[15]
- *Notice on cooperation within the network of competition authorities*[16]
- *Notice on the cooperation between the Commission and courts of the EU Member States in the application of Articles [101 and 102 TFEU]*[17]
- *Notice on the handling of complaints by the Commission under Articles [101 and 102 TFEU]*[18]
- *Notice on informal guidance relating to novel questions concerning Articles [101 and 102 TFEU] that arise in individual cases (Guidance letters)*[19]
- *Notice on the effect on trade concept contained in Articles [101 and 102 TFEU]*[20]
- *Guidelines on the application of Article [101(3) TFEU]*[21]
- *Notice on the conduct of settlement procedures in view of the adoption of Decisions pursuant to Article 7 and Article 23 of Council Regulation No 1/2003 in cartel cases*[22]
- *Explanatory note to an authorisation to conduct an inspection*[23]

The Commission also published three documents in October 2011 that provide details of its procedure in competition cases[24]:

- *Best Practices on the conduct of proceedings concerning Articles 101 and 102 TFEU*
- *Best Practices for the submission of economic evidence and data collection in cases concerning the application of Articles 101 and 102 TFEU and in merger cases*
- *Decision of the President of the Commission on the function and terms of reference of the hearing officer in certain competition proceedings*[25].

2. **The Commission's Enforcement Powers under Regulation 1/2003**

(A) **Burden of proof**

Article 2 of Regulation 1/2003 provides that the burden of proving an infringement of Article 101(1) or Article 102 is on the person or competition authority alleging the infringement and that the burden of showing that Article 101(3) is satisfied is on the person making that claim. There may be circumstances where the party bearing the burden of proof produces evidence that requires the other party to provide an explanation or justification,

---

[15] OJ [2004] L 123/18, as amended by Regulation 622/2008, OJ [2008] L 171/3.
[16] OJ [2004] C 101/43. [17] OJ [2004] C 101/54. [18] OJ [2004] C 101/65.
[19] OJ [2004] C 101/78. [20] OJ [2004] C 101/81. [21] OJ [2004] C 101/97.
[22] OJ [2008] C 167/1.
[23] Available at www.ec.europa.eu/competition/antitrust/legislation/legislation.html. [24] Ibid.
[25] All three documents are available at www.ec.europa.eu.

failing which it is permissible to conclude that the burden of proof has been satisfied[26]. The Commission's *Guidelines on the application of Article [101(3) TFEU][27]* explain the kind of evidence that undertakings should provide when defending an agreement under Article 101(3).

The Regulation does not discuss the burden of proof where an undertaking raises objective justification as a defence under Article 102. The position is that the evidential burden in such a situation rests with the undertaking asserting the justification, and that it is then incumbent on the Commission to show why that justification is inapplicable[28]. Similarly it would seem that an undertaking that asserts that a contractual restriction is ancillary bears the evidential burden of showing that this is so, and that the Commission should then have to show why this is not so[29].

(B) Chapter II: powers

Articles 4 to 6 deal with the powers of the Commission, the NCAs and national courts respectively.

(i) Article 4: powers of the Commission

Article 4 states that the Commission shall have the powers provided for by Regulation 1/2003: of particular importance are the decision-making powers in Chapter III; the powers of investigation contained in Chapter V; and the powers to impose penalties provided by Chapter VI; these are described below.

(ii) Article 5: powers of the NCAs

Recital 6 of the Regulation states that, to ensure the effective application of the competition rules, NCAs should be associated more closely with their application. Article 5 therefore provides that NCAs shall have the power to apply Articles 101 and 102 in individual cases. For this purpose the NCAs may make decisions requiring the termination of an infringement, ordering interim measures, accepting commitments and imposing fines and periodic penalty payments; they may also decide that there are no grounds for action on their part, but not that the EU competition rules are not infringed[30]. Article 35 of the Regulation requires Member States to designate the competition authority or authorities responsible for the application of Articles 101 and 102 in such a way that its provisions are effectively complied with; the designated authorities can include courts. Designated national authorities must have the right to participate, as a defendant or respondent, in judicial proceedings against a decision that the authority has taken in relation to Articles 101 and/or 102[31]. The Commission works with the NCAs through the medium of the ECN, the work of which is discussed in section 3 below.

---

[26] Cases C-204/00 P etc *Aalborg Portland A/S v Commission* [2004] ECR I-123, [2005] 4 CMLR 251, para 79.

[27] OJ [2004] C 101/97.

[28] See eg Case T-201/04 *Microsoft Corpn v Commission* [2007] ECR II-3601, [2007] 5 CMLR 846, para 688.

[29] On this point see a case under the UK Competition Act 1998, Case Nos 1035/1/1/04 etc *Racecourse Association v OFT* [2005] CAT 29, [2006] CompAR 99, paras 130–134.

[30] Case C-375/09 *Prezes Urzędu Ochrony Konkurencji I Konsumentów v Tele2 Polska sp. Z o.o., now Netia SA* [2011] ECR I-000, [2011] 5 CMLR 48.

[31] Case C-439/08 *Vlaamse deferatie van verenigingen van Brood- en Banketbakkers, Ijsbereiders en Chocoladebewerkers (VEBIC) VZW* [2010] ECR I-000, [2011] 4 CMLR 635.

(iii) Article 6: powers of the national courts

Article 6 provides specifically that national courts shall have the power to apply Article 101, in its entirety, and Article 102: the role of national courts is discussed in chapter 8.

(C) Chapter III: Commission decisions

Articles 7 to 10 deal with Commission decisions. The Commission has also issued a *Notice on informal guidance relating to novel questions concerning Articles [101 and 102 TFEU] of the EC Treaty that arise in individual cases (Guidance letters)*[32] explaining the (rare) circumstances in which it might be prepared to give undertakings informal guidance on the application of the competition rules. In 2008 the Commission introduced a system whereby some cartel cases can be settled. Informal guidance and settlements will be discussed after the powers conferred by Articles 7 to 10 have been described.

(i) Article 7: finding and termination of an infringement

Article 7(1) provides that where the Commission, acting on a complaint or on its own initiative, finds an infringement of Article 101 or 102, it may by decision require an end to it. Article 7(1) continues by stating that the Commission may impose on undertakings behavioural or structural remedies which are proportionate to the infringement and necessary to bring the infringement effectively to an end.

(A) Behavioural remedies

A behavioural remedy may be negative, for example to stop a certain kind of conduct, or positive, to order an undertaking to do something. In a typical cartel case the Commission will require the participants in the cartel to stop the illegal behaviour, in so far as they have not already done so, and to refrain from any act or conduct having the same or a similar object or effect in the future[33].

The ability of the Commission to make a positive order under Regulation 17 was confirmed by the Court of Justice in *Commercial Solvents Co v Commission*[34]; there is no reason to suppose that its powers would be any different under Regulation 1/2003. In *Commercial Solvents* that firm was found guilty of an unlawful refusal to supply contrary to Article 102 and was ordered to resume supplies to a former customer. In *Microsoft*[35] the General Court upheld the Commission's infringement decision, but held that the Commission did not have the right to appoint an independent monitoring trustee to enforce the remedy: this went 'far beyond' retaining an expert to advise it on implementation of the remedies[36].

Whereas an undertaking can be ordered to supply a distributor or customer where it has infringed Article 102, this cannot be done following an infringement of Article 101[37]. Articles 101 and 102 have a different logic: Article 101 prohibits agreements, and the Commission may make an order to terminate them; Article 102 prohibits abuse, and again the Commission can make an order to terminate an abuse. However a refusal to

---

[32] OJ [2004] C 101/78.

[33] See eg Article 3 of the Commission's decision in *Gas Insulated Switchgear* of 24 January 2007; see however Case T-395/94 *Atlantic Container Line AB v Commission* [2002] ECR II-875, [2002] 4 CMLR 1008, paras 410–420.

[34] Cases 6/73 and 7/73 [1974] ECR 223, [1974] 1 CMLR 309.

[35] Commission decision of 24 March 2004, substantially upheld on appeal Case T-201/04 *Microsoft Corpn v Commission* [2007] ECR II-3601, [2007] 5 CMLR 846.

[36] Ibid, paras 1251–1279.

[37] Case T-24/90 *Automec v Commission (No 2)* [1992] ECR II-2223, [1992] 5 CMLR 431.

supply cannot in itself be unlawful under Article 101. The Commission could order an undertaking to terminate an agreement not to supply, but it does not follow that it can also make an order to supply. Any further civil law consequences of an infringement of Article 101 should be determined in the domestic courts of Member States[38].

(B) Structural remedies

Regulation 17 did not specifically provide for a structural remedy, and the explicit inclusion of this possibility in Regulation 1/2003 was controversial. Article 7(1) states that structural remedies can be imposed only where there is no equally effective behavioural remedy or where a behavioural remedy would be more burdensome for the undertaking concerned than the structural remedy. Recital 12 adds that changes to the structure of an undertaking as it existed before the infringement was committed would be proportionate only where there is a substantial risk of a lasting or repeated infringement that derives from the very structure of the undertaking. A possible example of this could arise where a vertically-integrated undertaking consistently denies access to an essential facility or discriminates against downstream competitors in relation to a vital input; another example could be where an undertaking repeatedly indulges in margin-squeezing[39]. The Commission has not yet imposed a structural remedy under Article 7; however in several cases, particularly in the energy sector, structural commitments were offered to, and accepted by, the Commission under Article 9 of the Regulation[40].

(C) Past infringements

Article 7(1) of Regulation 1/2003 ends by providing that the Commission, where it has a legitimate interest in doing so, may adopt a decision that an infringement has been committed in the past[41]. There might be an interest in doing so, for example in order to clarify an important point of principle or as a way of facilitating a follow-on action for damages[42]. However the Commission must explain why there is an EU interest in the adoption of a decision relating to past behaviour, and a failure to do so could lead to the decision being annulled on appeal[43]; an example of such an explanation can be found in *Morgan Stanley/Visa International and Visa Europe*, where the Commission gave, among its reasons, that Visa continued to deny that its behaviour was contrary to Article 101 and that it wished to impose a fine[44]. The Commission cannot state in the narrative of its decision that an undertaking has committed an infringement of the competition rules unless it also reaches a conclusion to that effect in the operative part of its decision: the undertaking has a right of appeal only in relation to the operative part of the decision and

---

[38] Ibid, para 50; see also Cases C-377/05 and C-376/05 *A Brünsteiner GmbH v Bayerische Motorenwerke AG* [2006] ECR I-11383, [2007] 4 CMLR 259, paras 48–51.

[39] See ch 17, 'Refusal to Supply a new customer', pp 697–711 and ch 18, 'Margin Squeezing', pp 754–759 on these practices.

[40] See 'Article 9: commitments', pp 255–261 below.

[41] This was possible under Regulation 17: see Case 7/82 *GVL v Commission* [1983] ECR 483, [1983] 3 CMLR 645; *Bloemenveilingen Aalsmeer* OJ [1988] L 262/27, [1989] 4 CMLR 500, paras 164–168; *Distribution of Package Tours During the 1990 World Cup* OJ [1992] L 326/31; *Zera/Montedison* OJ [1993] L 272/28, [1995] 5 CMLR 320, para 132; *Europe Asia Trades Agreement* OJ [1999] L 193/23, [1999] 5 CMLR 1380, paras 182–185.

[42] See ch 8, 'Article 16: uniform application of EU competition law', pp 304–305.

[43] See Joined Cases T-22/02 and 23/02 *Sumitomo Chemical Co Ltd v Commission* [2005] ECR II-4065, [2006] 4 CMLR 42, paras 129–140.

[44] Commission decision of 3 October 2007, upheld on appeal Case T-461/07 *Visa Europe v Commission* [2011] ECR II-000, [2011] 5 CMLR 74.

should not be exposed to the risk, for example, of a damages claim in relation to asser-tions of fact which it has no ability to challenge[45].

(D) *Complainants*

Article 7(2) of the Regulation provides that those entitled to lodge a complaint for the purpose of Article 7(1) are natural or legal persons who can show a legitimate interest and Member States. The position of complainants is considered below[46].

(ii) Article 8: interim measures

Article 8(1) of the Regulation provides that, in cases of urgency due to the risk of seri-ous and irreparable damage to competition, the Commission, acting on its own initia-tive[47], may, on the basis of a prima facie finding of infringement, order interim measures. Article 8(2) states that an order shall be for a specified period of time, and may be renewed in so far as this is necessary and appropriate. Regulation 17 was silent on the issue of interim measures, but the Court of Justice established in *Camera Care v Commission*[48] that the Commission did have power under Article 3 of that Regulation to grant interim relief. Recital 11 of Regulation 1/2003 says that explicit provision should be made for interim measures. In practice the Commission did not often adopt interim measures under the *Camera Care* judgment: it preferred third parties to seek interim relief in their domestic courts[49] or from NCAs[50]. The Commission has yet to impose interim measures under Article 8[51]. On a few occasions the Commission has negotiated an interim settle-ment with undertakings without formally adopting an interim decision. This happened for example in *Hilti*[52]; the terms of the undertaking were subsequently broken and the Commission took this into account in its final decision.

(iii) Article 9: commitments

Article 9 provides for the adoption of decisions by the Commission whereby undertak-ings under investigation make legally-binding commitments as to their future behaviour;

---

[45] Case T-474/04 *Pergan Hilfsstoffe für Industrielle Prozesse GmbH v Commission* [2007] ECR II-4225, [2008] 4 CMLR 148.

[46] See 'The position of complainants', p 286 below.

[47] Note that interim measures are adopted, if at all, at the initiative of the Commission and not pursuant to any 'right' of complainants to ask the Commission to act: see Nordsjo 'Regulation 1/2003: Power of the Commission to Adopt Interim Measures' (2006) 27 ECLR 299.

[48] Case 792/79 R [1980] ECR 119, [1980] 1 CMLR 334.

[49] On applications for interim measures in the UK courts see ch 8, 'Interim relief', p 310.

[50] On the powers of the OFT in the UK to adopt interim measures see ch 10, 'Interim measures', p 398.

[51] The decisions that the Commission adopted prior to Regulation 1/2003 will be relevant if and when it makes any decisions under Article 8: see eg *Ford Werke AG-Interim Measure* OJ [1982] L 256/20, [1982] 3 CMLR 263: this decision was annulled on appeal to the Court of Justice Cases 228/82 and 229/82 *Ford Werke AG v Commission* [1984] ECR 1129, [1984] 1 CMLR 649; *ECS/AKZO* OJ [1983] L 252/13, [1983] 3 CMLR 694; *BBI/Boosey and Hawkes: Interim Measures* OJ [1987] L 286/36, [1988] 4 CMLR 67; *Ecosystem SA v Peugeot SA* [1990] 4 CMLR 449, upheld on appeal Case T-23/90 *Peugeot v Commission* [1991] ECR II-653, [1993] 5 CMLR 540; *Langnese-Iglo/Mars* unreported decision of 25 March 1992; see XXIInd *Report on Competition Policy* (1992), point 195: this decision was suspended in part in Cases T-24/92 and 28/92 R *Langnese-Iglo GmbH v Commission* [1992] ECR II-1839; *Sealink/B & I – Holyhead: Interim Measures* [1992] 5 CMLR 255; *Sea Containers v Stena Sealink – Interim Measures* OJ [1994] L 15/8, [1995] 4 CMLR 84; *Irish Continental Group v CCI Morlaix* [1995] 5 CMLR 177; and *NDC Health/IMS Health: Interim Measures* OJ [2002] L 59/18: this decision was subsequently withdrawn: Commission Press Release 1P/03/1159, 13 August 2003.

[52] The undertakings given by Hilti were attached as an Annex to the Commission's final decision: *Eurofix-Bauco v Hilti* OJ [1988] L 65/19, [1989] 4 CMLR 677; other examples of interim undertakings include *Ford Motor Co* XVth *Report on Competition Policy* (1985), point 49; *British Sugar/Napier Brown* XVIth *Report on Competition Policy* (1986), point 74; *Irish Distillers Group v G C & C Brands Ltd* [1988] 4 CMLR 840.

the Commission then closes its file without making a finding as to whether there has been or continues to be an infringement of Articles 101 and/or 102. As the Court of Justice explained in *Commission v Alrosa*[53] the Article 9 procedure enables the rapid solution of some cases and is based on considerations of procedural economy. Article 9 was influenced by the practice in the US of settling cases on the basis of 'consent decrees'[54]. Article 9 was an innovatory provision in Regulation 1/2003: there were no provisions in Regulation 17 whereby a case could be settled on the basis of legally-binding commitments. Despite this there were several cases in which the Commission did close its file on the basis of commitments, some of which were clearly of great significance: among the best known were *IBM*[55], *Microsoft (licensing agreements)*[56], *Interbrew*[57], *IRI/Nielsen*[58] and *Digital*[59]. Article 9 of Regulation 1/2003 for the first time provided a legal basis for commitments; it has generated quite a lot of literature[60]. By 20 June 2011 commitments had been accepted in 23 cases, as shown in Table 7.1 below ('Table of Article 9 commitment decisions', p 259).

(A) Article 9: substantive rules

Article 9(1) of Regulation 1/2003 provides that, where the Commission intends to adopt a decision requiring that an infringement of Articles 101 and/or 102 be brought to an end and the undertakings concerned offer commitments to meet the concerns expressed by the Commission in its preliminary assessment, the Commission may adopt a decision that makes those commitments binding on the undertakings. The final sentence of Article 9(1) provides that the decision may be for a specified period (though this is not a requirement[61]) and shall conclude that there are no longer grounds for action by the Commission. Article 9(2) provides that the Commission may reopen the proceedings in certain specified circumstances, for example where the undertakings concerned act contrary to their commitments. Recital 13 of the Regulation states that the Article 9 procedure is not appropriate in cases where the Commission intends to impose a fine: commitment decisions are therefore excluded in the case of hard-core cartels. Furthermore the Commission is never obliged to accept commitments under Article 9 rather than

---

[53] Case C-441/07 P [2010] ECR I-000, [2010] 5 CMLR 643, para 35.

[54] See Sullivan, Hovenkamp and Shelanski *Antitrust Law, Policy and Procedure: Cases, Materials, Problems* (LexisNexis, 6th ed, 2009).

[55] See the Commission's XIVth *Report on Competition Policy* (1984), pp 77–79.

[56] See the Commission's XXIVth *Report on Competition Policy* (1994), pp 364–365.

[57] See the Commission's XXVIth *Report on Competition Policy* (1996), pp 139–140.

[58] Ibid, pp 144–148.

[59] See the Commission's XXVIIth *Report on Competition Policy* (1997), pp 153–154.

[60] See eg Temple Lang 'Commitment Decisions under Regulation 1/2003: Legal Aspects of a New Kind of Competition Decision' (2003) 24 ECLR 347; Furse 'The Decision to Commit: Some pointers from the US' (2004) 25 ECLR 5; Temple Lang 'Commitment Decisions and Settlements with Antitrust Authorities and Private Parties under European Antitrust Law' [2005] Fordham Corporate Law Institute (ed Hawk, 2006), 265; Kerse and Khan *EC Antitrust Procedure* (Sweet & Maxwell, 5th ed, 2005), pp 357–360; Davies and Das 'Private Enforcement of Commission Commitment Decisions: a Steep Climb not a Gentle Stroll' [2005] Fordham Corp L Inst (ed Hawk, 2006), 199, also published in (2006) 29 Fordham International Law Journal 917; Wils 'Settlements of EU Antitrust Investigations: Commitment Decisions under Article 9 of Regulation 1/2003' (2006) 29(3) World Competition, 345; Whish 'Commitment Decisions under Article 9 of the EC Modernisation Regulation: Some Unanswered Questions' in *Liber Amicorum in Honour of Sven Norberg* (Bruylant, 2006), pp 555–572; Wils 'The Use of Settlements in Public Antitrust Enforcement: Objectives and Principles' (2008) 31(3) World Competition 335; Falconi 'Commitment Decisions in the EU and UK – Developments, Open Issues and Considerations for Companies and Competition Authorities' (2011) 10(1) Competition Law Journal 41.

[61] See Case T-170/06 *Alrosa Company Ltd v Commission* [2007] ECR II-2601, [2007] 5 CMLR 494, para 91.

proceeding under Article 7 to a finding of infringement[62]. In a memorandum of 17 September 2004 the Commission said that commitments may be behavioural or structural and may be limited in time[63]; structural commitments have been accepted in several cases in the energy and transport sectors[64].

The Court of Justice has held that a decision under Article 9 is conceptually distinct from an infringement decision under Article 7: the purpose of Article 7 is to bring an infringement to an end, whereas a decision under Article 9 is intended to address any concerns that the Commission might have following its preliminary assessment[65]. It follows that the Commission is not obliged, when agreeing to accept a commitment under Article 9, to equate the remedy offered with a measure that it could have imposed under Article 7[66]; an undertaking might offer a change of behaviour under Article 9 that the Commission could not have demanded under Article 7[67].

Article 23(2)(c) of Regulation 1/2003 provides that fines can be imposed on an undertaking that fails to comply with a commitment of up to 10 per cent of its total turnover in the preceding business year. Article 24(1)(c) provides for the imposition of periodic penalty payments of up to 5 per cent of average daily turnover in the previous business year for a continuing infringement of a commitment decision.

(B) *Article 9: procedure*

The Article 9 procedure is a formal one and entails the initiation of proceedings by the Commission. The Commission does not have to issue a statement of objections: it would suffice that it sends the undertakings concerned a 'preliminary assessment' of its case which may be shorter and less formal than a statement of objections. The preliminary assessment may be contained in a letter or may be sent as an independent document. The preliminary assessment or statement of objections gives the undertakings concerned a period of time within which to respond to the Commission's concerns and to offer draft commitments.

The Court of Justice has held that a third party is not a 'party concerned' in the sense of Article 27(2) of Regulation 1/2003[68] which means that it does not have a right of access to the Commission's file in a case being conducted under the commitments procedure[69].

Article 27(4) of the Implementing Regulation provides that where the Commission intends to adopt an Article 9 decision it must publish a concise summary of the case and the main content of the commitments; third parties are then given an opportunity to comment within a fixed time limit of not less than one month. The Commission has said that it will publish the full text of the draft commitments in their original language on the Internet[70]. It adds that the process of 'market testing' the draft commitments may reveal weaknesses in them that could lead the Commission to renegotiate them or abandon the Article 9 procedure and revert to the possibility of proceeding to an infringement decision under Article 7: this happened in the case of *CISAC*[71]. Article 30 of Regulation 1/2003 provides that the Commission must publish its Article 9 decisions.

---

[62] Ibid, para 130.   [63] Commission MEMO/04/217, available at www.europa.eu/rapid.

[64] See 'Comment', pp 258–261 below.

[65] Case C-441/07 P *Commission v Alrosa* [2010] ECR I-000, [2010] 5 CMLR 643, para 46.

[66] Ibid, para 47.   [67] Ibid, paras 48–50.

[68] Ibid, para 90, annulling the judgment of the General Court in Case T-170/06 *Alrosa Company Ltd v Commission* [2007] ECR II-2601, [2007] 5 CMLR 494, paras 197–204.

[69] See also the decision of the Ombudsman in Complaint 2953/2008/FOR against the European Commission, 27 July 2010, rejecting third party access to the Commission's preliminary assessment in *E.ON*; the decision is available at www.ombudsman.europa.eu/home.faces.

[70] See Commission MEMO/04/217, 17 September 2004.   [71] See Table 7.1 below.

(C) *Article 9: practical considerations*

Various practical points should be noted about Article 9 commitments. First, recital 13 of Regulation 1/2003 says that commitment decisions will not conclude whether or not there has been or still is an infringement of the competition rules, and adds that commitment decisions are without prejudice to the powers of NCAs and national courts to decide upon the case, a point repeated in the final sentence of recital 22. It follows that the fact that the Commission accepts commitments from undertakings as to their future behaviour in no way immunises them from the possibility of a challenge as to their past behaviour; in particular they remain vulnerable to a standalone action for damages in a national court.

Where undertakings give commitments to the Commission as to their future behaviour the question arises of whether third parties could challenge conduct that is consistent with the commitments as being unlawful under Articles 101 and/or 102. Article 9 of the Regulation simply states that the Commission's decision 'shall conclude that there are no longer grounds for action by the Commission'. However this does not in itself mean that the Commission has concluded that there is no longer an infringement: it could mean that it has decided, having been offered suitable commitments, that the case is no longer one that, as a matter of administrative priority, it wishes to pursue. It would seem to follow that a commitment decision does not provide immunity as to future behaviour either.

Given that the Article 9 procedure is voluntary on the part of the parties that offer commitments it is unlikely that they would appeal against the substance of an Article 9 decision, and this has never happened; however they may wish to challenge aspects of the Commission's procedure, such as their right of access to the file. Undertakings that offer commitments could appeal against the Commission's refusal to accept them; however, the General Court having said that the Commission is never obliged to accept commitments, it seems unlikely that such appeals will succeed[72]. Third parties may wish to bring Article 9 cases to the General Court. This might happen where they have complained to the Commission of anti-competitive behaviour, but where they believe that a commitment has been accepted which is inadequate to bring an end to the infringement: this happened in the case of *Hynix Semiconductor v Commission*[73], an appeal against the Commission's decision in *Rambus*.

Table 7.1 provides details of cases in which the Commission had accepted commitments by 20 June 2011.

(D) *Comment*

A few observations may be made about the Article 9 decisions adopted since Regulation 1/2003 entered into force. The first is that it is probably true to say that there have been more Article 9 decisions than was anticipated when the Regulation was adopted. In particular nine decisions were adopted in 2009 and 2010; this may, in part, be explained by a desire on the part of Commissioner Kroes to bring an end to a number of high-profile and complex cases, such as *Microsoft (tying)*, before the end of her term as Commissioner for Competition. A second point is that more than half of the Article 9 decisions arose from investigations concerning possible infringements of Article 102 rather than Article 101. This is not surprising: as noted, the Article 9 procedure is not used in the case of hardcore cartels, and the Commission adopts several infringement decisions each year under

---

[72] Note the pending appeals in Case T-421/08 *Performing Right Society v Commission* and Case T-433/08 *Societá Italiana degli Autori ed Editori v Commission*, not yet decided.

[73] Cases T-148 and 149/10, not yet decided; see ch 19, 'Vexatious behaviour and abase of process', p 806.

7.1 Table of Article 9 commitment decisions

Case name	Date of publication of proposed commitments	Date when commitments were made legally binding	Date until which commitments to remain in force
DFB	14.9.2004	19.1.2005	30.6.2009
Coca-Cola	19.10.2004	22.6.2005	31.10.2010
Repsol CPP SA[74]	20.10.2004	12.4.2006	31.12.2011
Alrosa[75]	3.6.2005	22.2.2006	Infinite duration
BUMA/SABAM (Santiago Agreement)	17.8.2005	No decision taken	
Austrian Airlines/ SAS cooperation agreement	22.9.2005	No decision taken	
The Football Association Premier League Limited	30.4.2004	22.3.2006	30.6.2013
Cannes Agreement	23.5.2006	4.10.2006	Infinite duration
Carmakers (DaimlerChrysler, Opel, Toyota and Fiat)	22.3.2007	14.9.2007	May 2010
Distrigaz	5.4.2007	11.10.2007	31.10.2010
CISAC	9.6.2007	The Commission abandoned the Article 9 procedure and adopted an infringement decision[76]	
Sky Team	19.10.2007	No decision taken	

(continued)

[74] On appeal Case T-274/06 *Estaser El Mareny v Commission*, order of 25 October 2007 dismissing the action as inadmissible; see also Case T-45/08 *Transportes Evaristo Molina v Commission*, order of 14 November 2008 dismissing the action as inadmissible; appeal dismissed, Case C-36/09 P, order of 11 November 2010.

[75] Decision annulled on appeal to the General Court, Case T-170/06 *Alrosa Co Ltd v Commission*, [2007] ECR II-2601, [2007] 5 CMLR 494; on appeal the Court of Justice set aside the judgment of the General Court, Case C-441/07 P *Commission v Alrosa Co* [2010] ECR I-000, [2010] 5 CMLR 643.

[76] *CISAC* Commission decision of 16 July 2008, on appeal Cases T-442/08 etc *CISAC v Commission*, not yet decided.

7.1 *(continued)*

Case name	Date of publication of proposed commitments	Date when commitments were made legally binding	Date until which commitments to remain in force
German electricity wholesale market and German electricity balancing market	12.6.2008	26.11.2008	Infinite duration
RWE gas foreclosure	26.11.2008	18.3.2009	Infinite duration
Ship classification	10.6.2009	14.10.2009	14.10.2014
Rambus[76a]	12.6.2009	9.12.2009	9.12.2014
GDF foreclosure	26.6.2009	3.12.2009	Various
Swedish interconnectors	6.10.2009	14.4.2010	24.4.2020
Microsoft (tying)	7.10.2009	16.12.2009	16.12.2014
Long term electricity contracts in France	14.10.2009	17.3.2010	Various
British Airways, American Airlines and Iberia	10.3.2010	14.7.2010	14.7.2020
ENI	5.3.2010	29.9.2010	Infinite duration
Visa MIF	28.5.2010	8.12.2010	8.12.2014

Article 7 in relation to them. Article 102 cases tend to be more complex than cartels, and a negotiated outcome that involves a change of behaviour to the satisfaction of the Commission but no finding of an infringement on the part of the undertaking concerned clearly can have benefits for both parties.

A third point is that a significant number of the Article 9 decisions – *Distrigaz, German electricity, RWE gas foreclosure, GDF foreclosure, Swedish interconnectors, Long term electricity contracts in France* and *ENI* – involved gas or electricity markets: the Commission's sectoral investigation of these markets had identified a series of concerns[77], many of which have been allayed as a result of these decisions. A final point to note is that in three out of seven of these energy cases the Commission accepted structural rather than, or in addition

---

[76a] On appeal Case T-148/10 *Hynix Semiconductor v Commission*, not yet decided.

[77] See 'Article 17: investigations into sectors of the economy and into types of agreements', pp 267–268 below.

to, behavioural commitments: an obvious example being ENI's commitment to divest itself of its interests in three cross-border gas pipelines, thereby terminating the conflict of interest that arose from its vertical integration as both a supplier and transporter of gas[78]. The Commission has never imposed a structural remedy under Article 7, and yet it obtained structural remedies in these cases.

(iv) Article 10: finding of inapplicability

Article 10 provides that, where the EU public interest requires, the Commission may adopt a 'finding of inapplicability' that Article 101 and/or Article 102 do not apply to an agreement or practice. Firms do not have a right to ask for such a decision, but the Commission might decide to adopt one (in 'exceptional cases', as recital 14 says) where this would clarify the law and ensure its consistent application throughout the EU; the same recital adds that this might be particularly useful where new types of agreements or practices occur in relation to which there is no case law or administrative practice. The Commission had not adopted any Article 10 decisions by 20 June 2011[79]. Article 10 (or informal guidance, discussed below) might be a useful tool with which the Commission could illustrate the circumstances in which vertical agreements imposing resale price maintenance might be permitted[80] or apparently abusive behaviour might be objectively justified or economically efficient[81].

(v) Informal guidance

The need for undertakings to have legal certainty in order to promote innovation and investment is acknowledged in recital 38 of Regulation 1/2003: it says that where there is genuine uncertainty because of novel or unresolved questions of competition law undertakings may seek informal guidance from the Commission. Both Article 10 and recital 38 address the anxieties of those who were concerned that the procedure of notifying agreements for individual exemptions under Article 101(3) was to be abolished. The Commission has issued a *Notice on informal guidance relating to novel questions arising under Articles [101 and 102 TFEU] (Guidance letters)*[82]. The *Notice* points out that undertakings have access to a substantial body of case law, decisional practice, block exemptions, guidelines and notices enabling them to undertake a self-assessment of the legality of their commercial plans[83]; however it also notes that there might be cases in which a guidance letter would be appropriate[84]. The Commission says that issuing a guidance letter would be considered only where the following cumulative criteria are satisfied:

- there is no current case law, guidance or precedent in relation to a particular type of agreement or practice
- guidance would be useful taking into account the economic importance from the point of view of the consumer of the goods or services to which the agreement or practice relates and/or
- the extent to which the agreement or practice corresponds to more widely spread economic usage in the marketplace and/or

---

[78] Structural commitments (the divestiture of airport slots) were also accepted by the Commission in *British Airways, American Airlines and Iberia*, decision of 14 July 2010.

[79] See Commission Staff Working Paper accompanying the *Report on the functioning of Regulation 1/2003* SEC(2009) 574 final, para 114, available at www.ec.europa.eu.

[80] See ch 16, 'Resale price restrictions', pp 647–649.

[81] See ch 5, 'Defences', pp 210–212.   [82] OJ [2004] C 101/78.

[83] Ibid, para 3.   [84] Ibid, para 5.

- the scope of the investments linked to the transaction in relation to the size of the undertakings concerned and the extent to which the transaction relates to a structural operation such as the creation of a non-full-function joint venture

- guidance can be given on the basis of information already provided to the Commission and no further fact-finding is required[85].

The Commission will not issue guidance letters in relation to purely hypothetical questions[86]. A memorandum should be submitted with a request for a guidance letter containing information specified by the Commission[87]. A guidance letter will set out a summary of the facts on which it is based and the principle legal reasoning underlying the Commission's understanding of the novel questions raised by the request[88]. Guidance letters will be published on the Commission's website, subject to the deletion of business secrets[89]. Guidance letters are not Commission decisions and do not bind NCAs or national courts[90]. No such letters had been issued by 20 June 2011.

(vi) Settlements of cartel cases[91]

(A) Introduction

In July 2008 the Commission introduced a system for settling cartel cases: the package consisted of Regulation 622/2008 that amends Regulation 773/2004, in particular by inserting a new Article 10a into that Regulation, entitled 'Settlement procedure in cartel cases'[92] and a *Settlements Notice*[93]. The procedure is available for any case that was pending at the time of publication of the *Settlements Notice* in the Official Journal (2 July 2008) and any subsequent case[94]. The essence of the settlement system is that at a certain point in a cartel investigation the parties, having seen the evidence in the Commission's file, acknowledge their involvement in the cartel and their liability for it; in return for this the Commission reduces the fine that it would otherwise have imposed on them by 10 per cent[95]. The reduction of a fine is a reward for cooperation: settlements are *not* a negotiation between the Commission and the cartelists as to the existence of the infringement or the level of the penalty[96]. The advantages to the Commission of the settlements procedure are that cases can be concluded more quickly than would otherwise have been the case, and that it is unlikely that there will be any appeals to the EU Courts: this frees up resources that can be deployed on other cartel investigations. The advantages to the parties, apart from the reduced fine, are that less time and money are

---

[85] Ibid, para 8.   [86] Ibid, para 10.
[87] Ibid, para 14.   [88] Ibid, para 19.   [89] Ibid, para 21.   [90] Ibid, para 25.
[91] Note that the competition authorities in the UK have also made use of settlements procedures: see ch 10, 'Settlements and early resolution of cases', p 418; for discussion of settlements see Whish 'Settlements – the Future of Competition Litigation?' in *Current Developments in European and International Competition Law* (14th st Gallen International Competition Law Forum, ed Baudenbacher, Helbing Lichtenhahn, 2008); Lawrence and Sansom 'The Increasing Use of Administrative Settlement Procedures in UK and EC Competition Investigations' (2007) 3 Competition Law Journal 163; some papers on settlements will be found in *European Competition Law Annual 2006: Enforcement of Prohibition of Cartels* (Hart Publishing, 2007, eds Ehlermann and Atansiu), 597ff; Wils 'The Use of Settlements in Public Antitrust Enforcement: Objectives and Principles' (2008) 31(3) World Competition. The OECD held a roundtable discussion on *Plea Bargaining/Settlement of Cases* in 2006, available at www.oecd.org; see also the settlement agreed between the South African Competition Commission and Pioneer Foods, Media Release of 2 November 2010, available at www.compcom.co.za, where Pioneer agreed not only to pay a fine and to adjust its prices of flour and bread, but also to create a fund to make finance available on favourable terms that would enable small and medium-sized enterprises to enter the market.
[92] OJ [2008] L 171/3.
[93] *Notice on the conduct of settlement procedures in view of the adoption of Decisions pursuant to Article 7 and Article 23 of Council Regulation No 1/2003 in cartel cases* OJ [2008] C 167/1.
[94] *Settlements Notice*, para 34.   [95] Ibid, para 32.   [96] Ibid, para 2.

spent on the investigation; and there may also be reputational benefits where investigations are speedily concluded rather than lasting for many years.

Reduced fines under the *Settlements Notice* are conceptually distinct from reductions granted for voluntarily providing information under the Commission's *Leniency Notice*[97]: it follows that an undertaking may be able to obtain cumulative reductions[98].

(B) Settlements procedure

The settlements procedure, as provided for by the amendments to Regulation 773/2004, is described in Part 2 of the Commission's *Settlements Notice*: an overview of the procedure will be found at the end of the *Notice*. Paragraph 5 makes clear that the Commission retains a broad margin of discretion to determine which cases may be suitable for settlement; the Commission cannot impose a settlement on the parties[99], but nor do the parties have a right to settle[100]. The Commission has the right at any time during the procedure to discontinue settlement discussions, in relation to a case generally or to one or more of the parties involved, where it considers that procedural efficiencies are unlikely to be achieved[101].

Where undertakings indicate a willingness to participate in settlement discussions, the Commission may decide to pursue the settlement procedure on the basis of bilateral contacts[102]; it will control their order and sequence[103]. Article 10a(2) of Regulation 773/2004 provides that the parties to settlement discussions may be informed by the Commission of:

- its objections to their behaviour
- the evidence used to determine those objections
- non-confidential versions of relevant documents; and
- the range of potential fines.

Article 15(1a) of the Implementing Regulation provides that, once proceedings have been initiated, the Commission will disclose that information to the parties: the idea of this 'early disclosure' is that it should enable the parties to make an informed decision on whether or not to settle[104]. In appropriate cases the Commission will set a time limit of at least 15 working days for an undertaking to produce a 'settlement submission'[105]; undertakings can call upon the Hearing Officer at any point during the procedure, whose duty is to ensure that the effective exercise of the rights of defence is respected[106]. If the parties fail to introduce a settlement submission the case will continue under the standard investigative procedure[107].

Parties opting for the settlement procedure must make a formal request in the form of a settlement submission[108]. After receipt of a settlement submission the Commission will send the parties a statement of objections; this will be able to take into account the views of the parties, as contained in their submission[109]. The Commission would expect

---

[97] See 'The Commission's Leniency Notice', pp 280–282 below.

[98] This happened to three of the undertakings concerned, Infineon, Hynix and Samsung, in the Commission's first settlement decision, *DRAM*, Commission decision of 19 May 2010.

[99] *Settlements Notice*, para 4; see also Recital 4 of Regulation 622/2008.

[100] *Settlements Notice*, para 6.   [101] Article 10a(4) of Regulation 773/2004.

[102] *Settlements Notice*, para 14.

[103] Ibid, para 15.   [104] Ibid, para 16.

[105] Article 10a(2), final subparagraph, of Regulation 773/2004 and para 17 of the *Settlements Notice*.

[106] *Settlements Notice*, para 18.

[107] Ibid, para 19; on the standard procedure see 'A typical case', pp 285–286 below.

[108] See para 20 of the *Settlements Notice* which specifies the content of a settlement submission.

[109] Ibid, para 25.

them then to reply, within a period of not less than two weeks, simply confirming that the statement of objections corresponds to their submissions and that they remain committed to the settlement procedure[110]. The Commission may decide not to accept the parties' settlement submission, in which case it could issue a statement of objections in accordance with the standard procedure[111].

Assuming that the case does proceed to a settlement, the parties will not seek an oral hearing; nor will they request access to the file after receiving the statement of objections: these are examples of the procedural efficiencies that lead to quicker decisions[112]. As already noted, paragraph 32 of the *Settlements Notice* states that the fine imposed by the Commission will be reduced by 10 per cent from what it would otherwise have been; the 10 per cent reduction will be made to the amount of the fine after the 10 per cent cap on the maximum fine payable has been applied[113], and any increase for deterrence will not exceed a multiplication of two[114].

Paragraphs 35 to 40 of the *Settlements Notice* deal with the disclosure of settlement submissions to other parties to the alleged cartel, complainants, NCAs and national courts, and adopt a predominantly cautious approach[115]. Paragraph 41 of the *Settlements Notice* acknowledges the fact that all final decisions taken by the Commission under Regulation 1/2003 can be appealed to the General Court and, on a point of law, to the Court of Justice. However this is unlikely to happen often in practice. None of the parties in the *DRAM* case appealed. The only undertaking to do so in the second settlement case, *Animal Feed Phosphates*[116], was Timab[117], which had originally participated in the settlement discussions but then decided to withdraw and to contest the case.

(D) Chapter IV: cooperation

Recital 15 of Regulation 1/2003 states that the Commission and the NCAs should form a 'network of public authorities'. The network is known as the European Competition Network; its composition and operation in practice are described in section 3 below[118]. The members of the ECN are linked by a secure Intranet. Recital 21 adds that cooperation between the Commission and the national courts is also necessary, and recital 22 stresses the need for uniform application of the competition rules on the part of the Commission, NCAs and national courts. Articles 11 to 16 of the Regulation contain provisions to promote cooperation between the Commission, NCAs and national courts. The Commission has issued two important notices on cooperation, the *Notice on cooperation within the network of competition authorities* ('the *Notice on NCA cooperation*')[119] and the *Notice*

---

[110] Article 10a(3) of Regulation 773/2004 and paragraph 26 of the *Settlements Notice*.
[111] *Settlements Notice*, para 27.　　[112] Ibid, para 28.
[113] On this cap see 'Article 23: fines', pp 275–276 below.
[114] On the uplift of fines for deterrence see 'Basic amount of the fine', p 277 below.
[115] See also Article 6(1) of Regulation 773/2004 which provides that a complainant does *not* have a right to receive a non-confidential version of the statement of objections in a settlement case, but only written information about the nature and subject-matter of the procedure. There is an appeal against the Commission's decision to refuse access to decisions fixing the probable ranges of fines imposed following the settlement procedure in *Animal Feed Phosphates*, Cases T-14/11 and T-211/11 *Timab Industries and CFPR v Commission*, not yet decided.
[116] See Commission Press Release IP/10/985, 20 July 2010.
[117] Case T-456/10 *Timab Industries SA v Commission*, not yet decided.
[118] See 'Case allocation under Regulation 1/2003', p 289.
[119] OJ [2004] C 101/43; note that this *Notice* is subject to periodic review by the Commission and the NCAs: ibid, para 70.

on the co-operation between the Commission and courts of the EU Member States in the application of Articles [101 and 102 TFEU][120].

(i) Article 11: cooperation between the Commission and the NCAs[121]

Article 11(1) of the Regulation provides that the Commission and the NCAs are to apply the competition rules in close cooperation. Article 11(2) requires the Commission to transmit to NCAs the most important documents it has collected with a view to the adoption of decisions under Articles 7 to 10 (above) or Article 29(1) (below). Article 11(3) requires NCAs to inform the Commission in writing before or without delay after commencing proceedings under Article 101 or Article 102; this information may also be made available to the NCAs via the Intranet. The *Notice on NCA cooperation* explains that the purpose of Article 11(2) and (3) is to ensure that cases can be allocated to a 'well placed' authority[122]. The *Notice* sets out the principles by reference to which a well-placed authority is to be identified[123]. The Commission is particularly well placed where an agreement or practice has effects in more than three Member States[124].

Article 11(4) and Article 11(6) are of particular importance. Article 11(4) provides that, not later than 30 days before adopting an infringement decision, accepting commitments or withdrawing the benefit of a block exemption, NCAs must inform the Commission: guidance on the application of Article 11(4) will be found in the *Notice on NCA cooperation*[125]. Article 11(6) provides that the initiation by the Commission of proceedings shall relieve NCAs of their competence to apply Articles 101 and 102[126]; the *Notice* provides guidance on how this provision is to be applied in practice[127]. Article 11(4) and (6) are central to the functioning of Regulation 1/2003 and mean that the Commission can halt the proceedings of an NCA and take a case over itself. The *Notice on NCA cooperation* explains the limited range of circumstances in which the Commission is likely to make use of Article 11(6)[128]. The power to terminate the proceedings of an NCA had not been exercised in any case as at 20 June 2011.

Article 11(5) provides that NCAs may consult with the Commission on any case involving the application of EU competition law.

(ii) Article 12: exchange of information

(A) *Free movement of information*

Article 12 of the Regulation provides for the exchange of information between the Commission and NCAs. It must be read in conjunction with Article 28 which contains provisions restricting the use or disclosure of information covered by an obligation of professional secrecy[129]. The Commission's view is that Article 12 is a key element in the

---

[120] OJ [2004] C 101/54; this *Notice* is discussed in ch 8, 'Private enforcement and Regulation 1/2003', pp 302–304.

[121] See Wils 'The EU Network of Competition Authorities, the European Convention on Human Rights and the Charter of Fundamental Rights of the EU' in *European Competition Law Annual 2002: Constructing the EU Network of Competition Authorities* (Hart Publishing, 2003, eds Ehlermann and Atanasiu), pp 433–464; Brammer 'Concurrent jurisdiction under Regulation 1/2003 and the issue of case allocation' (2005) 42 CML Rev 1383; Andreangeli 'The impact of the Modernisation Regulation on the guarantees of due process in competition proceedings' (2006) 31 EL Rev 342; Brammer *Co-operation Between National Competition Agencies in the Enforcement of EC Competition Law* (Hart Publishing, 2009).

[122] OJ [2004] C 101/43, paras 16 and 17.   [123] Ibid, paras 5–15.   [124] Ibid, para 14.

[125] Ibid, paras 43–49.

[126] Article 11(6) of the Regulation requires that, if an NCA is already acting on a case, the Commission shall initiate proceedings only following consultation.

[127] OJ [2004] C 101/43, paras 50–57.   [128] Ibid, para 54.

[129] See 'Article 28: professional secrecy', p 286 below.

proper functioning of the ECN and a precondition to the efficient and effective allocation of cases[130]. Article 12(1) provides that the Commission and NCAs have the power
to provide one another with and use in evidence any matter of fact or law, including
confidential information: the exchange of information can take place both between the
Commission and the NCAs and also between NCAs[131]. Article 12(2), however, states that
information exchanged can be used only for the purpose of applying Articles 101 and 102
and in respect of the subject-matter for which it was collected; an exception to this is that
an NCA can use information received in order to apply its domestic law, where the same
case involves the parallel application of Article 101 or Article 102 and the outcome would
be the same under both systems of law[132].

(B) Restrictions on the use of information

In some Member States natural persons can be the subject of fines, or even terms of
imprisonment: this is true, for example, where the 'cartel offence' is committed under
the Enterprise Act 2002 in the UK[133]. There are restrictions on the use of information
exchanged between competition authorities in these circumstances[134]. The first indent
of Article 12(3) provides that information exchanged pursuant to Article 12(1) can be
used in evidence to impose sanctions on natural persons only where the law of the transmitting authority foresees sanctions of a similar kind in relation to an infringement of
Article 101 or Article 102; this means, for example, that if the law of both the transmitting
and the receiving authority were to provide for terms of imprisonment to be imposed, the
information exchanged could be used as evidence in a criminal case leading to imprisonment. The second indent of Article 12(3) provides that, where it is not the case that the law
of the transmitting authority foresees sanctions of the same kind as the law of the receiving authority, the information can be used by the latter only where it has been collected
by the former in a way which respects the same level of protection of the rights of defence
of natural persons as provided for under the national rules of the receiving authority;
however in this case the information cannot be used to impose custodial sentences at all,
but only for other sanctions such as fines.

(C) The exchange of information with third countries

Article 12 does not discuss the issue of information exchange between the European
Commission and institutions outside the EU. To some extent this is dealt with in
cooperation agreements entered into, for example, with the US, Canada and Japan[135]. An
attempt by AMD, a plaintiff in proceedings brought in the US, to obtain an order from a
court there against Intel requiring it to produce information about alleged violations of
EU competition law being investigated by the European Commission failed in *AMD Inc v
Intel Corporation*[136]; the Commission indicated in an *amicus curiae* brief to the US court
that it did not want it to make such an order.

---

[130] *Notice on NCA cooperation*, para 26.

[131] Ibid, para 27.

[132] Note that it follows from this wording that information could not be exchanged for the purpose
of applying stricter national law on unilateral behaviour, as to which see ch 2, 'Conflicts: Article 102',
pp 77–78.

[133] See ch 10, 'The cartel offence', pp 425–434.

[134] See the *Notice on NCA cooperation*, para 28(c).

[135] See ch 12, 'The EU's dedicated cooperation agreements on competition policy', pp 509–511.

[136] Order of 4 October 2004, Case No C 01–7033 MISC JW: see also the earlier judgment of the US Supreme
Court in *Intel Corporation v Advanced Micro Devices* 542 US 241 (2004); an attempt to obtain the statement
of objections and a transcript of the oral hearing in the *Visa International* case, Commission decision of

(iii) Article 13: suspension or termination of proceedings

Article 13 contains provisions to avoid the duplication of investigations; the *Notice on NCA cooperation* provides additional guidance[137]. Article 13(1) provides that, where an NCA is dealing with a case, this is a sufficient ground for another NCA or the Commission to suspend proceedings or to reject a complaint; however there is no obligation to do so, thereby leaving the NCAs with some discretion as to whether to proceed or not[138]. Article 13(2) states that an NCA or the Commission may reject a complaint which has already been dealt with by another competition authority. Recital 18 of the Regulation adds that the provisions of Article 13 are without prejudice to the right of the Commission to reject a complaint due to lack of EU interest[139].

(iv) Article 14: Advisory Committee[140]

Article 14(1) of the Regulation requires the Commission to consult with the Advisory Committee on Restrictive Practices and Dominant Positions when taking key decisions, such as findings of an infringement or the imposition of a fine. Article 14(2) deals with the constitution of the Advisory Committee. Article 14(3) and (4) explain the consultation procedure, which may take place at a meeting or (an innovation introduced by the Regulation) in writing. Article 14(5) requires the Commission to take the 'utmost account' of the Advisory Committee's opinion. Article 14(7) provides that cases being decided by an NCA may be discussed at the Advisory Committee, and that an NCA may request that the Advisory Committee should be consulted when the Commission is contemplating the initiation of proceedings under Article 11(6).

(v) Article 15: cooperation with national courts

Article 15 deals with cooperation with national courts: this is discussed in chapter 8[141].

(vi) Article 16: uniform application of EU competition law

Article 16 of the Regulation deals with the effect of Commission decisions on national courts (Article 16(1)) and NCAs (Article 16(2)). The position of national courts is discussed in chapter 8[142]. Article 16(2) provides that NCAs cannot take decisions which would run counter to a decision adopted by the Commission.

(E) Chapter V: powers of investigation

Chapter V of the Regulation gives the Commission various powers of investigation: of particular importance are Article 18, which enables it to request information, and Articles 20 and 21, which enable it to conduct inspections, even of an individual's home.

(i) Article 17: investigations into sectors of the economy and into types of agreements

Article 17(1) enables the Commission to conduct an investigation into a sector of the economy or a type of agreement where it appears that there may be a restriction or distortion of competition, for example because of the lack of new entrants into a market or the

---

9 August 2001, failed in *In Re Payment Card Interchange Fee and Merchant Discount Antitrust Litigation*, judgment of the Eastern New York District Court of 27 August 2010.

[137] OJ [2004] C 101/43, paras 20–25.   [138] Ibid, para 22.

[139] See 'The position of complainants', p 286 below.

[140] See *Notice on NCA cooperation*, paras 58–68.

[141] See ch 8, 'Private enforcement and Regulation 1/2003', pp 302–304.   [142] Ibid.

rigidity of prices[143]. Article 17(2) gives the Commission the power to request information and to conduct inspections of business (not residential) premises for the purpose of conducting a sectoral investigation. The third indent of Article 17(1) states that the Commission may publish a report on the results of its inquiry and invite comments from interested parties. The Commission does not have any remedial powers following such a sectoral investigation[144]. The European Commission conducts a sectoral investigation under Article 17 in order to obtain a better understanding of the competition conditions within a sector, and decides at the end of the process what should happen next.

In recent years the Commission has conducted three investigations under Article 17, into financial services, energy markets and pharmaceuticals; each took about 18 months. Full information about these investigations, including the reports themselves, can be obtained from DG COMP's website[145]. Commissioners for Competition[146] have spoken of the important role that sectoral investigations play in EU competition policy.

(ii) Article 18: requests for information

(A) The Commission's powers

Article 18 of Regulation 1/2003 enables the Commission, in order to carry out its duties under the Regulation, to require 'all necessary information'[147]; Article 18(1) of Regulation 1/2003 provides that the Commission may simply request information, or may require it by decision.

Article 18(2) deals with simple requests: the Commission must state the legal basis and the purpose of the request, specify what information is required and fix the time limit within which it is to be provided; it must also explain the penalties in Article 23 of the Regulation for supplying incorrect or misleading information[148]. There is no obligation to comply with a simple request. However, undertakings must respond to a Commission decision requiring information: Article 18(3) says that, where the Commission requires information by decision, it must also explain that a penalty can be imposed under Article 23 for not supplying the information at all, and that the undertaking required to provide the information may seek a judicial review of the decision by the General Court. The fact that an undertaking considers that the Commission has no grounds for action

---

[143] A similar power had existed in Article 12 of Regulation 17, although it was not used on many occasions; the last investigation under Article 12 was of *Sports content over third generation mobile networks*, Commission Report of 21 September 2005, available at www.ec.europa.eu/comm/competition/antitrust/others/sector_inquiries/new_media/3g/index.html.

[144] In this respect sectoral inquiries are like an OFT market study in the UK, on which see ch 11, 'OFT Market Studies', pp 458–466; but not like a market investigation by the Competition Commission under the Enterprise Act 2002, where that institution does have remedial powers: on market investigations see ch 11, 'Market Investigation References', pp 466–473.

[145] See www.ec.europa.eu/comm/competition/antitrust/sector_inquiries.html.

[146] See Kroes 'Five years of sector and antitrust inquiries', speech of 3 December 2009; Almunia 'Competition v Regulation: where do the roles of sector specific and competition regulators begin and end?', speech of 23 March 2010.

[147] Information for this purpose includes documents: Case 374/87 *Orkem v Commission* [1989] ECR 3283, [1991] 4 CMLR 502, paras 13–14; Case 27/88 *Solvay & Cie v Commission* [1989] ECR 3355, [1991] 4 CMLR 502, paras 13–14; on the meaning of 'necessary information' see Case C-36/92 P *SEP v Commission* [1994] ECR I-1911; see also Case T-46/92 *Scottish Football Association v Commission* [1994] ECR II-1039.

[148] Penalties were imposed on a number of occasions for the provision of misleading information under Article 11 of Regulation 17: see eg *Telos* OJ [1982] L 58/19, [1982] 1 CMLR 267; *National Panasonic (Belgium) NV* OJ [1982] L 113/18, [1982] 2 CMLR 410; *National Panasonic (France) SA* OJ [1982] L 211/32, [1982] 3 CMLR 623; *Comptoir Commercial d'Importation* OJ [1982] L 27/31, [1982] 1 CMLR 440; *Peugeot* OJ [1986] L 295/19, [1989] 4 CMLR 371; *Anheuser-Busch Incorporated/Scottish & Newcastle* OJ [2000] L 49/37, [2000] 5 CMLR 75.

under Article 101 does not entitle it to resist a request for information[149]. However the Commission would not be entitled to request information for a purpose other than the enforcement of the competition rules, and in exercising its discretion under Article 18 it must have regard to the principle of proportionality[150].

Article 18(4) explains who should provide the information: authorised lawyers can supply information on behalf of a client, although the client remains responsible for incomplete, incorrect or misleading information. Article 18(5) requires the Commission to inform NCAs in the relevant Member State of information required of undertakings by decision, and Article 18(6) provides that the Commission can request information from governments and NCAs.

Quite often the Commission will request information under Article 18 *after* it has carried out an on-the-spot investigation under Article 20 or 21[151], for example because it needs to check particular points that have arisen out of the inspection or to pursue certain matters further.

The issue arises under Article 18 (and also where the Commission conducts an inspection under Article 20 or Article 21) of whether it is possible to resist answering questions or providing information on the basis that this would be self-incriminating, or that the information sought is protected by legal professional privilege. Recital 23 of Regulation 1/2003 (in acknowledgement of the case law discussed below) states that undertakings, when complying with a decision requesting information, cannot be forced to admit that they have committed an infringement; however it adds that they are obliged to answer factual questions and to provide documents, even if this information may be used to establish an infringement against them or another undertaking. The Regulation is silent on the issue of legal professional privilege. There was case law of the EU Courts on both types of privilege under Regulation 17, and it will continue to apply under Regulation 1/2003.

(B) Privilege against self-incrimination

In the *Orkem* and *Solvay* cases[152] the Court of Justice considered whether undertakings could refuse to answer certain questions in a Commission request for information on the basis that to do so would be self-incriminating. The Court of Justice's conclusion was that there is a limited privilege against self-incrimination in EU law, which entitles undertakings to refuse to answer questions that would require them to admit to the very infringement the Commission is seeking to establish; however this privilege does not entitle them to refuse to hand over documents to the Commission which might serve to establish

---

[149] See eg *Fire Insurance* OJ [1982] L 80/36, [1982] 2 CMLR 159 and *Deutsche Castrol* OJ [1983] L 114/26, [1983] 3 CMLR 165.

[150] Case C-36/92 P *SEP v Commission* [1994] ECR I-1911.

[151] See 'Article 21: the Commission's powers of inspection', pp 272–274 below.

[152] Case 374/87 *Orkem v Commission* [1989] ECR 3283, [1991] 4 CMLR 502: for comment see Lasok 'The Privilege against Self-incrimination in Competition Cases' (1990) 11 ECLR 90; Case 27/88 *Solvay & Cie v Commission* [1989] ECR 3355, [1991] 4 CMLR 502; see also Case T-34/93 *Société Générale v Commission* [1995] ECR II-545, [1996] 4 CMLR 665, paras 72–74; as to privilege against self-incrimination in domestic courts see Case C-60/92 *Otto v Postbank* [1993] ECR I-5683: for comment on this case see Kerse (1994) 31 CML Rev 1375; Cumming '*Otto v Postbank* and the Privilege Against Self-Incrimination in Enforcement Proceedings of Articles [81] and [82] before the English Courts' (1995) 16 ECLR 401; on self-incrimination generally see Wils 'Self-incrimination in EC antitrust enforcement: A legal and economic analysis' (2003) 26 World Competition, p 566; Vesterdorf 'Legal Professional Privilege and the Privilege against Self-incrimination in EC Law: Recent Developments and Current Issues' in [2004] Fordham Corporate Law Institute (ed Hawk), 701; MacCulloch 'The privilege against self-incrimination in competition investigations: theoretical foundations and practical implications' (2006) 26(2) Legal Studies 211.

an infringement by the undertaking concerned or by another one. It is presumably the case that the same doctrine applies in the case of inspections under Articles 20 and 21. The Court of Justice has held that privilege against self-incrimination can be claimed only where the Commission requires information under compulsion, that is to say in an Article 18(3) case; privilege does not attach to information provided in response to a mere request under Article 18(2)[153].

In *Mannesmann-Röhrenwerke AG v Commission*[154] the General Court held that there is no absolute right to silence in competition proceedings[155], except in so far as a compulsion to provide answers would involve an admission of the existence of an infringement[156]; in the Court's view certain questions asked by the Commission did go beyond what it was entitled to ask[157]. Judgments of the European Court of Human Rights in *Funke v France*[158] and *Saunders v United Kingdom*[159] have recognised a right to remain silent in criminal cases involving natural persons, but it seems after the *Mannesmann* judgment that EU law will not extend privilege this far in relation to cases under Articles 101 and 102.

In *Commission v SGL Carbon AG*[160] the Court of Justice held that undertakings are required to produce documents in their possession, even if those documents can be used to establish the existence of an infringement: privilege against self-incrimination applies only where the Commission requires answers to questions addressed to undertakings under investigation[161].

(C) Legal professional privilege[162]

That some documents are covered by legal professional privilege under EU law was established by the Court of Justice in *AM & S Europe Ltd v Commission*[163], where certain papers had been withheld from Commission officials during an inspection; the same principle must surely apply to a request for information under Article 18. The *AM & S* case dealt with two issues: first, whether there is a doctrine of privilege in EU law; secondly, if there is one, what mechanism should be adopted to ascertain whether any particular document is privileged. On the first question the Court held that some, but not all, correspondence between a client and an independent lawyer based in the EU (and now the EEA) was privileged, but that dealings with an in-house lawyer or with a lawyer in a third country were not. The limitation of privilege to correspondence with EU and EEA lawyers is overtly discriminatory; at one point the Commission intended to try to persuade the Council to rectify this[164], but it is understood that it subsequently dropped the idea. Privilege mainly extends to correspondence relating to the defence of a client after the initiation of proceedings by the Commission, although it also applies to correspondence before the initiation of proceedings though intimately linked with their subject-matter. The privilege belongs to the client, not the lawyer. Correspondence between an undertaking's external lawyer and a lawyer acting for a third party does not enjoy privilege[165].

---

[153] Case C-407/04 P *Dalmine v Commission* [2007] ECR I-835, paras 33–36.

[154] Case T-112/98 [2001] ECR II-729, [2001] 5 CMLR 54.   [155] Ibid, para 66.

[156] Ibid, para 67.   [157] Ibid, paras 69–74.

[158] [1993] 1 CMLR 897; for comment on *Funke* see van Overbeek 'The Right to Remain Silent in Competition Investigations' (1994) 15 ECLR 127.

[159] (1996) 23 EHRR 313.   [160] Case C-301/04 P [2006] ECR I-5915, [2006] 5 CMLR 877.

[161] Ibid, paras 33–51.

[162] See Gippini Fournier 'Legal Professional Privilege in Competition Proceedings Before the European Commission: Beyond the Cursory Glance' (2005) 28 Fordham International Law Journal 967.

[163] Case 155/79 [1982] ECR 1575, [1982] 2 CMLR 264.

[164] See the XIIIth *Report on Competition Policy* (1983), point 78 and Faull 'Legal Professional Privilege (*AM and S*): the Commission Proposes International Negotiations' (1985) 10 EL Rev 119.

[165] *Perindopril (Servier)*, Commission decision of 23 July 2010.

The Court of Justice limited privilege to dealings with independent lawyers because in many Member States employed lawyers are not subject to professional codes of discipline. In some Member States, for example the UK, Ireland and the Netherlands, in-house lawyers may remain subject to the rules of the Bar Council or the Law Society, so that it is arguable that this reason for excluding privilege ought not to apply; however the Court of Justice's judgment in *AM & S* was quite clear that there was no privilege in these circumstances[166]. In *John Deere*[167] the Commission relied on written advice by an in-house lawyer to show that an undertaking knew that it was infringing Article 101. However the position was slightly relaxed in *Hilti v Commission*[168], where the General Court held that privilege does extend to an internal memorandum prepared by an in-house lawyer which simply reports what an independent lawyer has said.

The issue of legal professional privilege for advice given by in-house lawyers was litigated again in a case involving Akzo Nobel Chemicals and its subsidiary, Akros Chemicals, which were under investigation for participation in an alleged cartel in heat stabilisers[169]. In *Akzo Nobel Chemicals Ltd v Commission*[170] the General Court was invited to reconsider the Court of Justice's ruling in *AM & S*, but it very clearly declined to do so[171]. Akzo appealed against the General Court's judgment to the Court of Justice, in particular on the basis that the in-house lawyer in the *Akzo* case was subject to the legal professional rules of the Dutch Bar Council; however the Court still considered that, as an employee of Akzo, the lawyer lacked independence from his employer and therefore saw no reason to depart from the position that it had taken in the *AM & S* case[172]. The Court rejected a number of other arguments for departing from *AM & S*, including that the status of privilege in the laws of the Member States had evolved to a point that the law should be revised[173].

On the question of how claims to privilege should be adjudicated the Court of Justice in *AM & S* held, in effect, that it (or, now, the General Court) should fulfil this task. This seems cumbersome, but is better than allowing the Commission itself to see the documents: even if a Commission official were to accept that they were privileged, an undertaking would be bound to suspect that he or she had been influenced by what had been seen. It follows that, as a matter of law, what has to happen in the case of a dispute as to privilege is that the Commission must make a formal decision, requiring the documents in question; this decision may then be appealed to the General Court, which will resolve the issue: indeed this is what happened in the *Akzo* case. In October 2011 the Mandate of the Hearing Officer was amended to give the holder of that office a role in settling disputes as to privilege[174].

---

[166] See however the strong argument of Advocate General Slynn to the contrary in the *AM & S* case; note that under s 30 UK Competition Act 1998 communications with in-house lawyers do enjoy privilege: see ch 10, 'Legal professional privilege', p 399.

[167] OJ [1985] L 35/58, [1985] 2 CMLR 554; see similarly *London European-Sabena* OJ [1988] L 317/47, [1989] 4 CMLR 662; privilege was unsuccessfully claimed in *VW* OJ [1998] L 124/60, [1998] 5 CMLR 55, para 199.

[168] Case T-30/89 [1990] ECR II-163, [1990] 4 CMLR 16.

[169] The Commission adopted an infringement decision in relation to this cartel on 11 November 2009; the decision is on appeal to the General Court Cases T-23/10 etc *Arkema v Commission*, not yet decided.

[170] Cases T-125/03 etc [2007] ECR II-3523, [2008] 4 CMLR 97.   [171] Ibid, paras 165–179.

[172] Case C-550/07 P *Akzo Nobel Chemicals Ltd v Commission* [2010] ECR I-000, [2010] 5 CMLR 1143, paras 40–51; see also, for detailed discussion of the issues, paras 87–192 of the Opinion of Advocate General Kokott in this case.

[173] Case C-550/07 [2010] ECR I-000, [2010] 5 CMLR 1143, paras 69–77.

[174] See the Decision of the President of the European Commission of 13 October 2011 on the function and terms of reference of the hearing officer in certain competition proceedings, Article 4(2)(a).

(iii) Article 19: power to take statements

Regulation 1/2003 confers power on the Commission by Article 19 to interview natural or legal persons, with their consent, for the purpose of collecting information relating to the subject-matter of an investigation. Article 3 of the Implementing Regulation sets out the procedure for conducting voluntary interviews. NCAs must be informed of interviews within their territory, and they have a right to be present. There are no penalties for providing incorrect or misleading information at an interview. The Commission has used the Article 19 procedure regularly in recent years, and is reflecting on the absence of penalties under this provision[175].

(iv) Article 20: the Commission's powers of inspection[176]

An important part of a competition authority's armoury is the ability to conduct a 'dawn raid' – better described as a 'surprise inspection' – on undertakings: those responsible for hard-core cartels, for example, are perfectly aware that what they are doing is illegal, and they may go to great lengths to suppress evidence of their activities. Article 20 of Regulation 1/2003 enables the Commission to conduct inspections of business premises, either by agreement or by surprise; Article 21 allows an inspection of 'other premises', including an individual's home: this had no counterpart in Regulation 17.

Article 20(1) enables the Commission, in order to be able to carry out its duties under the Regulation, to conduct 'all necessary inspections'. Article 20(2) empowers those conducting the inspection:

- to enter premises
- to examine books and other records, including data stored in electronic form, for example on a hard disk, a CD-ROM or a memory stick
- to take or obtain copies or extracts from them: it is sensible to make photocopying facilities available to the inspectors and to make a duplicate set of all items copied for retention by the undertaking that is being investigated
- to seal premises, books or records to the extent necessary for the inspection: this can be important, for example, where an inspection will go into a second day (or longer, as sometimes happens) and the inspectors wish to ensure that evidence will not be interfered with overnight[177]. In January 2008 the Commission imposed a fine of €38 million on E.ON Energie AG for breaching a seal that had been affixed to documents during an inspection in May 2006[178]; a fine of €8 million was imposed for the same reason in 2011 on Suez Environnement[179]
- to ask for explanations of facts or documents and to record the answers.

---

[175] See the Commission *Staff Working Paper accompanying the Report on the functioning of Regulation 1/2003* SEC(2009) 574 final, para 84.

[176] On the position of dawn raids under the European Convention on Human Rights see Case 37971/97 *Société Colas Est v France* (2004) 39 EHRR 17, European Court of Human Rights, finding France to have infringed the applicants' fundamental rights and awarding damages as the inspectors had entered without prior judicial warrant and Case 41604/98 *Buck v Germany* (2006) 42 EHRR 440, stating that it must be clearly established that the proportionality principle has been adhered to in order for a home search to be justified.

[177] Recital 25 of Regulation 1/2003 states that seals should not normally be affixed for more than 72 hours.

[178] See Commission Press Release IP/08/108, 30 January 2008: the Commission's decision was upheld on appeal to the General Court, Case T-141/08 *E.ON Energie v Commission* [2010] ECR II-000; this case is now on appeal to the Court of Justice, Case C-89/11 P, not yet decided.

[179] See Commission Press Release IP/11/632, 24 May 2011; in the Netherlands the Dutch Competition Authority imposed a fine of €269,000 on Sara Lee for breaching seals affixed to a door during an inspection: decision of 20 October 2008 available at www.nmanet.nl/engels/home/index.asp.

The rules on self-incrimination and legal professional privilege, discussed above, would apply to inspections. Undertakings may submit to an inspection voluntarily; however they must submit to an inspection ordered by decision under Article 20(4), which may be conducted without prior announcement: the so-called 'dawn raid'. The Commission does not have an obligation to attempt a voluntary inspection prior to a dawn raid[180].

(A) Voluntary investigations

In the case of a voluntary investigation Article 20(3) requires the Commission's officials and other accompanying persons authorised by the Commission (for example a forensic IT specialist, whose function is to search computer records, emails and other electronic media) to produce an authorisation in writing; it must specify the subject-matter and purpose of the investigation and the penalties which may be imposed for incomplete production of the required books and business records or the provision of incorrect or misleading information. NCAs must be informed of inspections in their territory. The Commission held (in decisions under Regulation 17) that a firm being investigated is under a positive duty to assist the Commission's officials in finding the information they want: it is not sufficient simply to grant them unlimited access to all the filing cabinets or the IT system[181]; this has been confirmed in the case law of the EU Courts[182].

(B) Mandatory investigations

The Commission may adopt a decision under Article 20(4) requiring an undertaking to submit to an inspection[183]. The Commission must consult with the local NCA before carrying out such an inspection in its territory, but this can be done in an informal manner, by telephone if necessary[184]. The Commission has said that, although there is no entitlement to the presence of a lawyer at an inspection, the undertaking may consult a lawyer; however the Commission will accept only a short delay for consultation with the lawyer before beginning the inspection[185]. The Commission's decision must explain the penalties for non-compliance with the decision ordering the inspection, and that the decision can be reviewed by the General Court[186]. The Commission imposed fines on several occasions for non-compliance under Regulation 17[187]. Surprise inspections may take place in a number of jurisdictions – not just within the EU – as a result of coordination between different competition authorities[188].

Quite apart from these penalties the Commission's recent practice has been to regard a lack of cooperation during an inspection as an aggravating factor when it comes to determining the level of the fine for the substantive infringement of Article 101 and/or 102.

---

[180] Case 136/79 *National Panasonic (UK) Ltd v Commission* [1980] ECR 2033, [1980] 3 CMLR 169, paras 8–16.

[181] See *Fabbrica Pisana* OJ [1980] L 75/30, [1980] 2 CMLR 354 and *Pietro Sciarra* OJ [1980] L 75/35, [1980] 2 CMLR 362; the same would be true of an investigation under Article 20(4).

[182] See eg Case C-301/04 P *Commission v SGL Carbon* [2006] ECR I-5915, [2006] 5 CMLR 877, para 40.

[183] See *Explanatory note to an authorisation to conduct an inspection in execution of a Commission decision under Article 20(4) of Council Regulation No 1/2003*, as well as a sample *Authorisation to conduct an inspection*, both available at www.ec.europa.eu/competition/antitrust/legislation.html.

[184] Case 5/85 *AKZO Chemie BV v Commission* [1986] ECR 2585, [1987] 3 CMLR 716, para 24.

[185] *Explanatory note*, para 6.

[186] Such an appeal was dismissed in Case T-23/09 *CNOP and CCG v Commission* [2010] ECR II-000.

[187] See eg *CSM NV* (€3,000); *Ukwal* OJ [1992] L 121/45, [1993] 5 CMLR 632 (€5,000); *Mewac* OJ [1993] L 20/6, [1994] 5 CMLR 275 (€4,000); *AKZO* OJ [1994] L 294/31 (€5,000).

[188] See Commission MEMO/03/33 of 13 February 2003 noting simultaneous inspections in the EU, US, Japan and Canada in relation to the *Heat Stabilisers* cartel; this decision is on appeal Cases T-23/10 etc *Arkema v Commission*, not yet decided.

For example in *Dutch Bitumen*[189] the fine on KWS was increased by 10 per cent because it refused to allow the Commission officials access to the premises and in *Professional video-tapes* the fine on Sony was increased by 30 per cent because one of its employees refused to answer questions during an inspection and another shredded documents during it[190].

(C) The involvement of Member States

Article 20(5) of Regulation 1/2003 provides that officials of NCAs shall, at the request of the Commission, actively assist its officials with their inspections[191]. Where an undertaking refuses to submit to an inspection, Article 20(6) requires the Member State concerned to afford the Commission the necessary assistance to enable the inspection to take place: this may require the involvement of the police or an equivalent enforcement authority. The Commission itself is not entitled to use force to enter premises[192]. Article 20(7) states that, if judicial authorisation is required, for example to obtain entry to premises, this must be applied for. Article 20(8), which gives expression to the judgment of the Court of Justice in *Roquette Frères SA v Commission*[193], sets out the role of the judicial authority in circumstances where it is asked, for example, to issue a warrant ordering entry into premises. The court should ensure that the Commission's decision is authentic and that the coercive measures sought are neither arbitrary nor excessive; for this purpose the court may address questions to the Commission. However the court may not call into question the necessity for the inspection, nor demand that it be provided with all the information in the Commission's file.

(v) Article 21: inspection of other premises

Recital 26 of Regulation 1/2003 states that experience has shown that there are cases where business records are kept in people's homes, and that therefore it should be possible, subject to judicial authorisation, to conduct inspections there. The *SAS/Maersk Air*[194] decision provides an example of this, where important documents relating to a market-sharing agreement were kept in individuals' homes. Article 21 therefore confers a power on the Commission to inspect 'other premises', which can include homes; Article 21(3) requires prior authorisation by a court. It is reasonable to predict that this power will be exercised rarely, but in principle it seems correct that the Commission should be able to conduct such inspections where it has reason to believe that the individuals responsible for cartels (or, less likely, abusive practices) are keeping relevant information at home. The Commission is known to have exercised this power on two occasions between 1 May 2004 and 1 May 2009[195].

(vi) Article 22: investigations by NCAs

Article 22(1) of Regulation 1/2003 enables an NCA to conduct an inspection in its territory on behalf of an NCA in another Member State[196]. Article 22(2) provides that NCAs

---

[189] Commission decision of 13 September 2006, paras 340–341, on appeal Cases T-357/06 etc *Koninklijke Wegenbouw Stevin v Commission*, not yet decided.

[190] Commission Press Release IP/07/1724, 20 November 2007.

[191] On the position in the UK see ch 10, 'EU investigations', p 402.

[192] See para 82 of Advocate General Kokott's Opinion in Case C-550/07 P *Akzo Nobel Chemicals and Akcros Chemicals v Commission* [2010] ECR I-000, [2010] 5 CMLR 1143.

[193] Case C-94/00 [2002] ECR I-9011, [2003] 4 CMLR 46.

[194] OJ [2001] L 265/15, [2001] 5 CMLR 1119, paras 7, 89 and 123.

[195] See para 75 of the Commission Staff Working Paper accompanying the *Report on the functioning of Regulation 1/2003*.

[196] A striking example of this occurred when the OFT conducted an inspection in the UK on behalf of the French Competition Authority investigating a complaint about behaviour in Réunion in the Indian Ocean: see www.ec.europa.eu/competition/ecn/brief/01_2010/brief_01_2010_short.pdf, p2.

shall carry out inspections which the Commission considers to be necessary under Article 20(1) or Article 20(4)[197].

(F) **Chapter VI: penalties**

Articles 23 and 24 provide for fines and periodic penalty payments. The Commission cannot impose fines on individuals, except in so far as an individual acts as an undertaking[198], nor can it sentence them to terms of imprisonment. Some Member States, including the UK, do have powers to impose sanctions on individuals[199].

(i) **Article 23: fines**[200]

Article 23 enables fines to be imposed on undertakings both for procedural and for substantive infringements. Procedural fines can be imposed under Article 23(1) on undertakings that commit offences in relation to requests for information or inspections under Article 17, 18 or 20 of the Regulation (fines cannot be imposed on individuals whose homes are inspected under Article 21). A typical infringement would be the supply of incorrect or misleading information, or the refusal by an undertaking to submit to an inspection.

Article 23(2) provides for very substantial fines to be imposed where undertakings infringe Articles 101 and 102 TFEU, where they contravene an interim measures decision made under Article 8 of the Regulation, or where they fail to comply with a commitment made binding by a decision under Article 9. In these cases the maximum fine that can be imposed is 10 per cent of an undertaking's worldwide turnover in the preceding business year[201]: clearly this can be an enormous amount, in particular since it is not limited to turnover in the market affected by the infringement, nor to turnover within the EU. Decisions can be found where the Commission has had to limit fines because the 10 per cent worldwide turnover limit had been attained[202]; Figure 1.11 of the Commission's Cartel Statistics shows that from 2006 to 2010 the fines on 22 of the 150 undertakings punished for infringing Article 101 represented 9 to 10 per cent of their worldwide turnover[203].

---

[197] On the position in the UK see ch 10, 'EU investigations', p 402.

[198] See ch 3, 'Regardless of the legal status of the entity and the way in which it is financed', pp 86–87; the Commission has never imposed a fine on an individual, although in *French beef* it imposed fines on trade unions representing individual farmers: OJ [2003] L 209/12, upheld on appeal to the General Court, Cases T-217/03 and T-245/03 *FNCBV v Commission* [2006] ECR II-4987, [2008] 5 CMLR 406 and on appeal to the Court of Justice, Cases C-101/07 P and C-110/07 P *Coop de France bétail and viande v Commission* [2008] ECR I-10193, [2009] 4 CMLR 743.

[199] See ch 10, 'The cartel offence', pp 425–434.

[200] See Wils 'The European Commission's 2006 Guidelines on Antitrust Fines: A Legal and Economic Analysis' (2007) 30(2) World Competition 197; Motta 'On Cartel Deterrence and Fines in the European Union' (2008) 29 ECLR 209; Manzini 'European Antitrust in Search of the Perfect Fine' (2008) 31(1) World Competition 3; Vesterdorf 'The Court of Justice and Unlimited Jurisdiction: What Does It Mean in Practice?' (2009) 6(2) CPI Antitrust Chronicle, Spring 2009; Wils 'The Increased Level of EU Antitrust Fines, Judicial Review, and the ECHR' (2010) 33(1) World Competition 5; Castillo de la Torre 'The 2006 Guidelines on Fines: Reflections on the Commission's Practice' (2010) 33 World Competition 359; Barbier de La Serre and Winckler 'Legal Issues Regarding Fines Imposed in EU Competition Proceedings' (2010) 1(4) Journal of European Competition Law & Practice 327.

[201] Where an undertaking had no turnover in the preceding year an earlier year can be used: Case C-76/06 *Britannia Alloys v Commission* [2007] ECR I-4405, [2007] 5 CMLR 251, paras 10–33.

[202] See eg Case T-71/03 *Tokai Carbon v Commission* [2005] ECR II-10, [2005] 5 CMLR 489, paras 388–390; *Sodium Chlorate*, Commission decision of 11 June 2008, in the case of Finnish Chemicals; *Car Glass*, Commission decision of 12 November 2008, in the case of Soliver.

[203] Available at www.ec.europa.eu/competition/cartels/statistics.

In fixing the level of a fine, the Commission is required by Article 23(3) to have regard to the gravity and to the duration of the infringement. Where a fine is imposed on a trade association Article 23(4) provides that, if the association is insolvent, the association must call for contributions from its members to cover the fine; in case of default the Commission can impose the fine on the members themselves.

It is noticeable that the cartel cases in recent years that have been appealed to the General Court contain at least as much, if not more, analysis of the level of fines than on the finding of the substantive infringement. A detailed study of the 'science' of setting the right level of a fine is beyond the scope of this book: the practitioners' works cited earlier contain extensive commentary on the subject[204].

The General Court has an unlimited jurisdiction on appeal to determine the level of fines; this includes the power to increase as well as to decrease the fines imposed by the Commission[205].

In 2006 the Commission adopted two important Notices (replacing earlier ones) on its fining policy. The first concerned its method of calculating the level of a fine and the second its policy of allowing leniency towards whistleblowers.

(ii) The Commission's guidelines on the method of setting fines

The Commission enjoys a wide margin of appreciation when determining the level of fines[206]. However, in the interests of transparency and impartiality, it decided in 1998 to publish guidelines on its methodology when setting fines[207]; they were replaced in 2006 by new guidelines building on the Commission's subsequent experience[208]. The *Fining Guidelines* apply in relation to cases in which the Commission issued a statement of objections after 1 September 2006, the date on which they were published in the Official Journal[209]. The *Fining Guidelines* respond to the criticism that, even if the Commission has a wide margin of appreciation, it is not an unfettered one; in the US, for example, there are sentencing guidelines that enable the level of a fine (and the duration of a prison sentence) to be predicted with a fairly high degree of accuracy[210]. The Commission points out in the *Guidelines* that fines should have a sufficiently deterrent effect both on the undertakings involved in a particular infringement of the competition rules ('specific deterrence') and also on other undertakings that might be inclined to act unlawfully ('general deterrence')[211]. The Court of Justice has repeatedly held that the need to deter infringements of the competition rules is one of the factors to be taken into account when determining the level of fines[212] and has established that the Commission is entitled to change its methodology for the setting of fines, including introducing higher fines, where

---

[204] See ch 7 n 5 above.

[205] See 'Article 261: penalties', pp 293–294 below.

[206] See eg Cases C-189/02 P etc *Dansk Rørindustri A/S and others v Commission* [2005] ECR I-5425, [2005] 5 CMLR 796, para 172.

[207] *Guidelines on the method of setting fines imposed pursuant to Article 15(2) of Regulation No 17 and Article 65(3) of the ECSC Treaty* OJ [1998] C 9/3.

[208] *Guidelines on the method of setting fines imposed pursuant to Article 23(2)(a) of Regulation 1/2003* OJ [2006] C 210/2, available at www.ec.europa.eu/comm/competition/antitrust/legislation/fines.html.

[209] Ibid, para 38.

[210] See the Sentencing Reform Act 1984 and the US Sentencing Commission *Guidelines Manual*, available at www.ussc.gov.

[211] *Fining Guidelines* OJ [2006] C 210/2, para 4.

[212] See eg Cases 100/80 etc *Musique Diffusion Française SA v Commission* [1983] ECR 1825, [1983] 3 CMLR 221, paras 105–106; Case C-289/04 P *Showa Denko KK v Commission* [2006] ECR I-5859, [2006] 5 CMLR 840, para 16.

this is necessary for the effective enforcement of the competition rules[213]. The Court of Justice has held that an undertaking cannot deduct fines when assessing its taxable profits[214].

The *Guidelines* of 2006 propose a two-step methodology when setting fines.

(A) Basic amount of the fine

The Commission begins by setting a 'basic amount' for the fine, which is determined by reference to the value of the sales of the goods or services to which the infringement relates[215]. It is not necessary for the Commission to conduct a full definition of the relevant market for these purposes[216]. The basic amount will be related to a proportion of the value of such sales, depending on the degree of gravity of the infringement, multiplied by the number of years of infringement[217]. The gravity of the infringement is determined on a case-by-case basis[218]; as a general rule it will be set at a level of up to 30 per cent of the value of sales[219]. Hard-core cartel infringements are likely to be at the top end of the scale[220]. The amount determined as a result of the rules just mentioned will then be multiplied by the number of years of participation in the cartel[221]. Furthermore an amount of between 15 and 25 per cent of the basic amount will be imposed as a sanction for participating in the infringement in the first place, a so-called 'entry fee' intended to act as an additional deterrent[222]. Clearly these rules can lead to enormous fines, in particular where a cartel has lasted for a long time: the Commission's Press Release in relation to the *Organic Peroxides* cartel suggested that it had lasted for 29 years, a very significant 'multiplier'[223]; the *Animal Feed Phosphates* cartel lasted for almost 35 years, although not all the cartelists were involved throughout[224]. However it should be recalled that Article 23(2) of the Regulation provides that a fine cannot exceed 10 per cent of an undertaking's worldwide turnover.

(B) Adjustments to the basic amount

Having determined the basic amount of the fine, the Commission then takes into account various aggravating and mitigating circumstances[225]. Aggravating circumstances are set out in paragraph 28 of the *Guidelines* and include:

- the fact that an undertaking is a recidivist: the basic amount will be increased by up to 100 per cent for each past finding of an infringement of Article 101 or 102, whether by the Commission or an NCA[226]

---

[213] See eg Case C-189/02 P *Dansk Rørindustri Als v Commission* [2005] ECR I-5425, [2005] 5 CMLR 796, paras 227–228; Case C-397/03 P *Archer Daniels Midland Co v Commission* [2006] ECR I-4429, [2006] 5 CMLR 230, paras 21–22.

[214] Case C-429/07 *Inspecteur van de Belastingdienst v X BV* [2009] ECR I-4833, [2009] 5 CMLR 1745, para 39.

[215] *Fining Guidelines* OJ [2006] C 210/2, paras 12–26.

[216] Case T-48/02 *Brouwerij Haacht NV v Commission* [2005] ECR II-5259, [2006] 4 CMLR 621, para 59.

[217] Ibid, para 19.   [218] Ibid, para 20.

[219] Ibid, para 21; the Commission adds that the particularities of a given case might mean that it would depart from the methodology in the *Guidelines*, including the 30 per cent figure: ibid, para 37.

[220] Ibid, para 23.   [221] Ibid, para 24.   [222] Ibid, para 25; see also para 7.

[223] Commission Press Release IP/03/1700, 10 December 2003.

[224] Commission Press Release IP/10/985, 10 July 2010.

[225] *Fining Guidelines* OJ [2006] C 210/2, paras 27–29.

[226] The largest uplifts for recidivism to date for one previous infringement have been of 50 per cent, in *Calcium Carbide* Commission decision of 22 July 2009: uplift on Evonik Degussa of 50 per cent; in *Power Transformers* Commission decision of 7 October 2009: uplift on ABB of 50 per cent; and in *Air Cargo*, Commission decision of 9 November 2010: uplift on SAS of 50 per cent; in *Heat Stabilisers* Commission

- refusal to cooperate with or obstruction of the Commission in its investigation[227]
- acting as leader or instigator of the infringement[228].

Increases for recidivism have become common; appeals to the EU Courts against uplifts for recidivism generally fail[228a]. The Court of Justice confirmed in *Groupe Danone v Commission*[229] that the Commission is entitled to treat recidivism as an aggravating circumstance where past infringers need to be induced to change their behaviour[230]. There is no limitation period for considering past infringements[231]: the test is whether an undertaking shows a tendency to infringe the competition rules and not to draw appropriate conclusions from a finding of infringement on the part of the Commission[232]. An uplift can be applied for recidivism even if no fine was imposed on a previous occasion[233]; it would appear to be the case that the fine could be increased for a past infringement even where a firm had blown the whistle on that occasion. The previous infringements do not have to have been in the same product market[234], and may have been committed by different legal entities within the same economic unit[235]. However a previous violation of Article 101 would not provide a pretext for a recidivist uplift of a fine in a subsequent finding of an infringement of Article 102[236].

Mitigating circumstances are set out in paragraph 29 and include:

- early termination of infringing behaviour as soon as the Commission began its investigation (this does not apply to secret agreements or concerted practices, in particular cartels[237])
- negligent, as opposed to intentional, infringements
- having a limited role in the infringement
- cooperating with the Commission outside the scope of the *Leniency Notice*[238]
- authorisation or encouragement of the infringement by public authorities or by legislation.

decision of 11 November 2009 the uplift on Arkema for three previous infringements was 90 per cent (upheld on appeal in Case T-343/08 *Arkema France v Commission* [2011] ECR II-000) and in *Calcium Carbide* the uplift on Akzo for four previous infringements was 100 per cent.

[227] See the *Dutch Bitumen* and *Professional Videotapes* decisions discussed at 'Mandatory investigations', pp 273–274 above.

[228] See eg *Candle Waxes*, Commission decision of 1 October 2008, paras 681–686, where the fine on Sasol was increased by 50 per cent as it was the leader of the cartel; this decision is on appeal to the General Court, Cases T-541/08 etc *Sasol v Commission*, not yet decided.

[228a] Note however two judgments in 2011 in which appeals against recidivist uplifts succeeded: Case T-39/07 *ENI v Commission* [2011] ECR II-000 and Case T-144/07 *Thyssenkrupp Liften v Commission* [2011] ECR II-000.

[229] Case C-3/06 P [2007] ECR I-1331, [2007] 4 CMLR 701　　　[230] Ibid, paras 26–29.

[231] Ibid, para 38; see also Case C-413/08 P *Lafarge SA v Commission* [2010] ECR I-000, [2010] 5 CMLR 586, para 72; Cases T-101/05 and T-111/05 *BASF AG v Commission* [2007] ECR II-4949, [2008] 4 CMLR 347, para 67.

[232] Case C-413/08 P *Lafarge SA v Commission* [2010] ECR I-000, [2010] 5 CMLR 586, paras 69–71; the test includes previous cartel infringements committed under the European Coal and Steel Community Treaty: Case T-20/05 *Outokumpu Oyj v Commission* [2010] ECR II-000, [2010] 5 CMLR 1276, para 63.

[233] Ibid, para 41.

[234] Cases T-101/05 and T-111/05 *BASF AG v Commission* [2007] ECR II-4949, [2008] 4 CMLR 347, para 64.

[235] See *Candle Waxes*, Commission decision of 1 October 2008, paras 672–678; the decision is on appeal Cases T-543/08 etc *RWE and RWE Dea v Commission*, not yet decided.

[236] Case T-57/01 *Solvay v Commission* [2009] ECR II-4621, paras 506–511 and Case T-66/01 *ICI v Commission* [2010] ECR II-000, paras 376–387.

[237] See eg Case T-329/01 *Archer Daniels Martin Co v Commission* [2006] ECR II-3255, [2006] 5 CMLR 230, paras 272–287 in which the General Court upheld the Commission's refusal to recognise termination of participation in a secret cartel as an attenuating circumstance.

[238] See eg *Power transformers*, Commission decision of 7 October 2009, paras 262–274.

In exceptional cases the inability of an undertaking to pay a fine, to the point that its economic viability would be jeopardised, may be taken into account by the Commission[239]. In assessing whether a fine may result in a firm going into liquidation and exiting the market the Commission will typically consider a firm's financial statements, its liquidity, solvency and other financial ratios and its relations with banks and shareholders[240]. In 2010 the Commission accepted claims of inability to pay in three of its six new cartel decisions, *Bathroom Fittings*[241], *Prestressing Steel*[242] and *Animal Feed Phosphates*[243]; the maximum reduction to date is 95 per cent for one of the undertakings in the *Heat Stabilisers* cartel[244].

The fact that an undertaking adopts a competition law compliance programme is not a factor that the Commission is obliged to take into account as an attenuating factor[245], nor that it has taken disciplinary action against employees involved in the infringement[246]. The Commission is not required to reduce a fine on the basis that a defendant has paid damages to the victims of its anti-competitive behaviour[247].

The principle of *ne bis in idem* prevents the same person from being fined more than once for the same unlawful conduct. The principle is subject to three cumulative conditions: the facts must be identical; the offender must be the same undertaking; and the legal interest protected must be the same[248]. It follows that the principle does not apply where a fine has been imposed, for example, in the US, since it does not relate to the same interest as that protected by EU law[249]. Furthermore the Commission is permitted to cure a procedural irregularity – for example by reopening a case against a defendant whose rights of the defence have been violated[250] – without infringing the principle of *ne bis in idem*[251]. By readopting decisions in this way the Commission seeks to make the point that, although it may be possible to win procedural points on appeal to the EU Courts,

---

[239] *Fining Guidelines* OJ [2006] C 210/2, para 35; see eg *Electrical and mechanical carbon and graphite products*, Commission decision of 3 December 2003, paras 340–363, upheld on appeal Case T-68/04 *SGL Carbon AG v Commission* [2008] ECR II-2511, [2009] 4 CMLR 7; further upheld on appeal to the Court of Justice, Case C-564/08 P *SGL Carbon AG v Commission* [2009] ECR I-191.

[240] See Commission MEMO/10/290, 30 June 2010.   [241] Commission decision of 23 June 2010.

[242] Commission decision of 6 October 2010.   [243] Commission decision of 20 July 2010.

[244] For discussion see Kienapfel and Wils 'Inability to Pay – First Cases and Practical Experiences', (2010) 3 *Competition Policy Newsletter* 3.

[245] Case T-329/01 *Archer Daniels Midland Co v Commission* [2006] ECR II-3255, [2007] 4 CMLR 43, paras 299–302; Case T-59/02 *Archer Daniels Midland Co v Commission* [2006] ECR II-3627, [2006] 5 CMLR 1528, para 359; Case T-13/03 *Nintendo v Commission* [2009] ECR II-947, [2009] 5 CMLR 1421, para 74.

[246] *Choline Chloride* Commission decision of 9 December 2004, para 217.

[247] Case T-59/02 *Archer Daniels Midland Co v Commission* [2006] ECR II-3627, [2006] 5 CMLR 1528, para 354; Case T-13/03 *Nintendo v Commission* [2009] ECR II-947, [2009] 5 CMLR 1421, para 74.

[248] Cases C-204/00 P etc *Aalborg Portland v Commission* [2004] ECR I-123, [2005] 4 CMLR 251, para 338; see generally Wils 'The Principle of "Ne Bis in Idem" in EC Antitrust Enforcement: A Legal and Economic Analysis' (2003) 26(2) World Competition 131.

[249] See eg Case C-308/04 P *SGL Carbon AG v Commission* [2006] ECR I-5977, [2006] 5 CMLR 922, paras 26–39; Case C-289/04 P *Showa Denko KK v Commission* [2006] ECR I-5858, [2006] 5 CMLR 840, paras 50–63; Case T-329/01 *Archer Daniels Midland Co v Commission* [2006] ECR II-3255, [2007] 4 CMLR 43 (the *Sodium Gluconate* case), paras 290–295; Case T-59/02 *Archer Daniels Midland Co v Commission* [2006] ECR II-3627, [2006] 5 CMLR 1528 (the *Citric Acid* case), paras 61–73.

[250] See eg *Carbonless Paper* Commission decision of 23 June 2010 reimposing a fine of €21 million on Bolloré following annulment of its earlier decision in Case C-322/07 P *Papierfabrik August Koehler v Commission* [2009] ECR I-7191, [2009] 5 CMLR 2301; the Commission's second decision is on appeal Case T-372/10 *Bolloré v Commission*, not yet decided; see similarly *Concrete reinforcing bars* Commission decision of 30 September 2009 reimposing fines of €83 million following annulment of its earlier decision in Case T-27/03 *SP SpA v Commission* [2007] ECR II-4331, [2008] 4 CMLR 176.

[251] Case T-24/07 *ThyssenKrupp Stainless AG v Commission* [2009] ECR II-2309, [2009] 5 CMLR 1773, paras 178–192.

ultimately this will be to no avail if it is possible to cure the procedural deficiency by reopening the case.

(iii) The Commission's Leniency Notice[252]

Undertakings that participate in cartels are usually fully aware that their behaviour is unlawful and go to great lengths to maintain secrecy and to avoid detection. Competition authorities therefore face considerable difficulties in detecting cartels. A crucial tool in practice is to incentivise participants in cartels to 'blow the whistle' to the relevant competition authority or authorities. The Commission's policy is to allow total immunity – a fine of zero – to the first undertaking in a cartel to blow the whistle, and to impose lower fines than would otherwise be the case on undertakings that provide it with further evidence that enables it to proceed more effectively with the investigation of a case. The encouragement of whistleblowing has proved to be immensely successful in the US in prosecuting cartels[253]; the US policy can be accessed on the home page of the Department of Justice[254]. Nearly all of the cartel cases brought by the Commission in recent years began with a whistleblower[255]. However it should be noted that some major cases are brought on the Commission's own initiative: it is not dependent on whistleblowers[256]; for example the Commission's decision in *Car Glass* originated in a 'tip-off' from an anonymous source[257]. It is important to point out that whistleblowing does not affect the liability of a whistleblower to pay damages to victims of a cartel as a matter of civil law[258].

The Commission first adopted a Notice on leniency in 1996[259] which was replaced in 2002[260]. A new Notice was published in December 2006 setting out the Commission's current policy; the 2006 *Notice* is intended to provide greater transparency as to what is expected of undertakings when they apply for leniency; it also introduced some procedural innovations[261]. The *Notice* is in line with the principles of the ECN's *Model Leniency Programme* which was adopted by the heads of the NCAs in September 2006[262]. After some introductory comments, Section II of the *Leniency Notice* explains the circumstances in which an undertaking may qualify for immunity from fines; Section III deals with the possibility of reduced fines; Section IV discusses ways of making 'corporate statements',

---

[252] See Wils 'Leniency in Antitrust Enforcement: Theory and Practice' (2007) 30(1) World Competition 25; for a global review see *Leniency Regimes: Jurisdictional Comparisons* (eds Arquit, Buhart and Antoine) European Lawyer Reference 2007; Global Antitrust Leniency Manual (Oxford University Press, 2008, ed Mobley (Baker & McKenzie)); see also Botana 'Antitrust Enforcement and Deterrence of Collusive Behaviour: The Role of Leniency Programs' (2006/2007) 13(1) Columbia Journal of Law 47.

[253] Major cases in the US such as *Vitamins*, *Citric Acid* and *Sotheby's/Christies* all came to light as a result of whistleblowing.

[254] See www.justice.gov/atr/public/guidelines.

[255] Between 2007 and 2010 19 out of 26 decisions of the Commission started with a whistleblower; in the period 2009–2010 this was true of 10 out of 11 decisions.

[256] See eg *Flat Glass* Commission decision of 28 November 2007, para 80, discussed at 'Case allocation under Regulation 1/2003', p 289 below; *Professional Videotapes* Commission decision of 20 November 2007, para 44; *Elevators and Escalators* Commission decision of 21 February 2007, para 91.

[257] See *Car Glass* Commission decision of 12 November 2008, para 38; the decision is on appeal to the General Court, Cases T-56/09 etc *Saint Gobain Glass France v Commission*, not yet decided.

[258] See Commission's *Leniency Notice* OJ [2006] C 298/17, para 39.

[259] OJ [1996] C 207/4.

[260] OJ [2002] C 45/3.

[261] *Notice on Immunity from fines and reduction of fines in cartel cases* OJ [2006] C 298/17, available at www.ec.europa.eu/comm/competition/cartels/legislation/leniency_legislation.html; for discussion of the 2006 Notice see Suurnäkki and Tierno Centella 'Commission adopts revised Leniency Notice to reward companies that report hard-core cartels' (2007) (Spring) *Competition Policy Newsletter* 7.

[262] See 'Leniency', p 289 below.

including the possibility of doing so orally in order to avoid problems that might arise in civil litigation. It should be noted that there is no 'one-stop shop' for leniency applications, either within the EU or internationally: it follows that a potential leniency applicant may have to blow the whistle in a number of different jurisdictions in order fully to protect its position[263]. However, within the EU, there has been fairly substantial convergence of national systems of leniency[264].

(A) Section I: introduction

The *Notice* sets out the framework for the Commission to reward undertakings that are or have been members of secret cartels that cooperate with it in its investigation[265]. The *Notice* recognises two types of leniency: immunity from fines and a reduction of fines. It states that immunity from fines may be justified where an undertaking makes a decisive contribution to the opening of an investigation or to the finding of an infringement[266]; a reduction of a fine may be justified where an undertaking provides the Commission with evidence that adds 'significant value' to that already in its possession[267]. The Court of Justice has held that a reduction under the leniency programme can be justified only where the conduct of the undertaking concerned demonstrates a genuine spirit of cooperation on its part[268]. The Commission acknowledges in the introduction to the *Leniency Notice* that the making of corporate statements ought not to expose undertakings to risks in civil litigation not experienced by undertakings that do not cooperate with it[269].

(B) Section II: immunity from fines

Immunity from a fine will be granted to the first undertaking in a cartel to submit information to the Commission that will enable it to carry out an inspection or to find an infringement of Article 101 in connection with the cartel[270]; immunity will not be granted if the Commission already had sufficient evidence to proceed to an inspection or to a final decision[271]. The whistleblower must make a corporate statement to the Commission containing specified information such as a description of the cartel, the names, positions, office locations and, where necessary, home addresses of the individuals involved in the cartel and details of any other competition authorities that have been contacted as well as any other relevant evidence in the whistleblower's possession[272]. The whistleblower must comply with a series of conditions in order to qualify for immunity:

- genuine, continuous and expeditious cooperation[273]
- termination of any involvement in the cartel, unless the Commission considers that continuing involvement might be useful for the preparation of inspections: if the

---

[263] On this point see Schwab and Steinle 'Pitfalls of the European Competition Network – Why Better Protection of Leniency Applicants and Legal Regulation of Case Allocation is Needed' (2008) 29 ECLR 523.

[264] See the ECN's *ECN Model Leniency Programme: Report on Assessment of the State of Convergence*, available at www.ec.europa.eu/competition/ecn/documents.html.

[265] Note that the *Notice* does not apply to cooperation in relation to vertical agreements, for example involving resale price maintenance; however para 29 of the *Fining Guidelines* (ch 7 n 211 above) provides for reductions in fines for cooperation with the Commission 'outside the scope of the Leniency Notice'.

[266] *Leniency Notice* OJ [2006] C 298/17, para 4.   [267] Ibid, para 5.

[268] Case C-301/04 P *Commission v SGL Carbon AG* [2006] ECR I-5915, [2006] 5 CMLR 877, paras 66–70.

[269] *Leniency Notice*, para 6.   [270] Ibid, para 8.   [271] Ibid, paras 10 and 11.

[272] Ibid, para 9.

[273] For a case in which the Commission denied an undertaking immunity on the ground that it had failed in its duty of cooperation see *Italian Raw Tobacco* Commission decision of 20 October 2005, paras 430–485, on appeal Case T-12/06 *Deltafina v Commission*, upheld, [2011] ECR II-000, paras 102–182.

whistleblower were to be absent from cartel meetings, for example, the other participants might guess what has happened and realise that inspections are imminent

- it must not have destroyed, falsified or concealed any relevant evidence when contemplating its application for immunity[274].

The *Leniency Notice* explains the procedure for making an application for immunity[275], including the so-called 'marker system' whereby an undertaking can contact the
Commission and agree with it a date by when it will provide the evidence needed to pass
the threshold for leniency. If the undertaking 'perfects' the marker by the agreed date its
application will be deemed to have been made at the time of the original approach to the
Commission, and will therefore rank higher in the queue of leniency applicants than an
undertaking that made an application before the marker was perfected[276].

(C) Section III: reduction of fines

An undertaking that does not qualify for immunity, for example because it was not the
first to blow the whistle, may nevertheless qualify for a reduced fine where it provides
evidence to the Commission 'which represents significant added value'[277]. Reductions in
the range of 20 to 50 per cent are available for such an undertaking[278]. The *Leniency Notice*
explains the procedure for such cases[279].

(D) Section IV: corporate statements

The *Leniency Notice* discusses how corporate statements may be made[280], and makes specific provision for such statements to be oral rather than written[281]. The reason for this is
the fear that, if an undertaking were to prepare a written corporate statement, this might
be discoverable in the event of a treble damages action in the US: this might deter the
undertaking from blowing the whistle at all, in which case the cartel might go undetec-
ted. An oral statement is rendered into writing by the Commission. As it is not a document of the whistleblower it cannot be discovered from it; and any attempt by a US court
to demand that the Commission should hand its own document over would probably fail
on public interest grounds[282].

(iv) Article 24: periodic penalty payments

Article 24 provides for the imposition of periodic penalty payments on undertakings, for
example where they persist in an infringement of Article 101 or Article 102 even after a
decision requiring it to end, or where they continue to fail to supply complete and accurate information in response to a Commission request. The fines are up to 5 per cent of an
undertaking's average daily turnover in the preceding business year. In July of 2006 the
Commission adopted a decision that Microsoft had failed to comply with its obligation
to supply full interoperability information in accordance with its decision of March 2004
and imposed a fine of €280.5 million, €1.5 million per day from 16 December 2005 to 20
June 2006[283]. This was followed by a second fine, of €899 million, in February 2008 for
charging unreasonable prices for access to interface documentation[284].

---

[274] *Leniency Notice*, para 12.   [275] Ibid, paras 14–22.   [276] Ibid, para 15.
[277] Ibid, paras 24 and 25.   [278] Ibid, para 26.   [279] Ibid, paras 27–30.
[280] Ibid, paras 31–35.   [281] Ibid, para 32.
[282] See *In Re Rubber Chemicals Antitrust Litigation* 486 F Supp 2d 1078 (ND Cal 2007) in which the
District Court refused a discovery request for certain communications between an EU leniency applicant
and the Commission; see further 'The exchange of information with third countries', p 266 above.
[283] Commission decision of 12 July 2006.
[284] Commission decision of 27 February 2008, on appeal Case T-167/08 *Microsoft v Commission*, not yet
decided.

(G) Chapter VII: limitation periods

(i) Article 25: limitation periods for the imposition of penalties

Article 25 of Regulation 1/2003, which replaces the rules formerly contained in Regulation 2988/74[285], establishes limitation periods for action on the part of the Commission against competition law infringements: the period is three years in the case of provisions concerning requests for information or the conduct of inspections, and five years in the case of all other infringements; provision is made for the interruption of the limitation period in the event of certain action taken by the Commission or an NCA[286]. The burden of proving the duration of an infringement of the competition rules – and therefore of demonstrating that the limitation period has not expired – rests with the Commission[287]. A finding by the Commission that there has been a single continuous agreement or abuse may mean that the Commission is able to impose fines, provided that it brings proceedings within three or five years of when the infringement ceases[288]; if the correct analysis were to be that there had been a series of separate agreements or abuses, it might transpire that some of them had ended so long ago that a fine could no longer be imposed[289].

The Commission sometimes addresses a decision to an undertaking stating that it has been in a cartel, but does not impose a fine because of the limitation rule. The Commission's interest in doing so includes that the undertaking might be sued for damages on a follow-on basis in the courts of a Member State. However the Commission must explain its reason for addressing the decision to the undertaking[290].

(ii) Article 26: limitation period for the enforcement of penalties

Article 26 provides that the limitation period for enforcing fines and periodic penalty payments is five years[291].

(H) Chapter VIII: hearings and professional secrecy

Articles 26 and 27 deal respectively with hearings and with professional secrecy.

(i) Article 27: hearing of the parties, complainants and others

(A) The provisions of Article 27

Article 27(1) provides that, before decisions are taken under Articles 7 and 8 (infringement and interim measures decisions) or under Articles 23 and 24 (fines and periodic penalty payments), the undertakings that are the subject of the proceedings have a right to be heard. The Commission may base its decisions only on objections on which the par-

---

[285] OJ [1974] L 319/1.

[286] Regulation 1/2003, Article 25(3)–(6); for discussion of the rules on interruption under Regulation 2988/74 see Case T-276/04 *Compagnie maritime belge SA v Commission* [2008] ECR II-1277, [2009] 4 CMLR 968, paras 22–38.

[287] Case T-120/04 *Peróxidos Orgánicos SA v Commission* [2006] ECR II-4441, [2007] 4 CMLR 153, para 52; Case T-58/01 *Solvay SA v Commission* [2009] ECR II-4781, paras 294–295.

[288] Regulation 1/2003, Article 25(2).

[289] See the cases discussed in ch 3, 'The concept of a "single, overall agreement"', pp 103–104 under Article 101 where this is precisely the point that was under consideration.

[290] See 'Past infringements', pp 254–255 above.

[291] For litigation under the predecessor of Article 26 in Regulation 2988/74 see Case T-153/04 *Ferrière Nord SpA v Commission* [2006] ECR II-3889, [2006] 5 CMLR 1416, reversed on appeal to the Court of Justice, Case C-516/06 P *Commission v Ferrière Nord SpA* [2007] ECR I-10685, [2008] 4 CMLR 267, paras 27–34; this case traces back to the Commission's decision in *Welded Steel Mesh* as long ago as 1989, OJ [1989] L 260/1, [1991] 4 CMLR 13.

ties have had an opportunity to comment. Complainants 'shall be closely associated with the proceedings'.

Article 27(2) provides that the rights of the defence shall be fully respected during the Commission's proceedings, including the right to have access to the Commission's file. Article 27(2) of the Regulation makes clear that there is no right of access to confidential information, nor to internal documents of the Commission and the NCAs and correspondence within the ECN. Article 27(3) provides that the Commission may hear third parties with a sufficient interest, and Article 27(4) provides that, where the Commission intends to adopt a decision under Article 9 or 10, it must publish the fact of its intention and allow third parties an opportunity to be heard.

(B) The conduct of proceedings

Commission Regulation 773/2004[292] ('the Implementing Regulation') explains how and when the Commission may initiate proceedings, and how the right to be heard is exercised, in competition cases. Specifically it sets out the rules in relation to the statement of objections that must be sent to the parties and the right to be heard, and confers upon the parties a right to an oral hearing; third parties with a sufficient interest may also be heard[293]. The Regulation sets out the rules for the oral hearing, which is conducted by a Hearing Officer. A Commission decision of October 2011 sets out the terms of reference of the Hearing Officers in competition cases[294]; also of significance is the Commission's *Best practices for the conduct of proceedings concerning Articles 101 and 102 TFEU*[295]. Regulation 1/2003 also explains how confidential information is to be dealt with during proceedings, and how disputes should be resolved.

The Commission's *Notice on the rules for access to the Commission's file*[296] explains its current policy on access to the file in the context of the relevant legislation, including Regulation 1/2003 and the Implementing Regulation and the jurisprudence of the EU Courts. Access to the file for competition law purposes is subject to different criteria and exceptions from the right of access to EU documents under Regulation 1049/2001[297]. The *Notice on access to the file* explains who is entitled to access to the file; which documents can be accessed; and when access may be granted. Complaints about denial of access may be taken to the Hearing Officer; another possibility, if the approach to the Hearing Officer does not provide a satisfactory outcome, would be to approach the European Ombudsman[298].

Where the Commission is in possession of documents that might provide exculpatory evidence for a defendant undertaking, it must make them available, although a failure to do so would lead to the annulment of the Commission's decision only if their availability

---

[292] OJ [2004] L 123/18; note that the Implementing Regulation was amended by Regulation 622/2008, OJ [2008] L 171/3, as a result of the introduction by the Commission of the procedure for settling cartel cases: see 'Settlements of cartel cases', pp 262–264 above.

[293] They are also entitled to receive a non-confidential version of the statement of objections: Cases T-213/01 and T-214/01 *Österreichische Postsparkasse AG v Commission* [2006] ECR II-1601, [2007] 4 CMLR 506.

[294] Available at www.europa.eu/competition/hearing-officers; on the role of the Hearing Officer see Durande and Williams 'The practical impact of the exercise of the right to be heard: A special focus on the effect of Oral Hearings and the role of the Hearing Officers' (2005) (Summer) *Competition Policy Newsletter* 22; Commissioner Almunia has announced that the Mandate of the Hearing Officer will be amended: 'Fair process in EU competition enforcement', SPEECH/11/396, 30 May 2011.

[295] Available at www.ec.europa.eu/.

[296] OJ [2005] C 325/7; this *Notice* replaces an earlier one, OJ [1997] C 27/3.

[297] OJ [2001] L 145/43; see the *Notice on access to the file*, para 2.   [298] See below.

would have led to a different outcome[299]. In *Salzgitter v Commission*[300] the Court of Justice confirmed that the Commission may attach probative value to evidence provided by a source that insists on anonymity.

The Court of Justice has established that undertakings are entitled to expect that competition law proceedings will be concluded within a reasonable period[301].

Apart from recourse to the Hearing Officer, in recent years a practice has arisen, in some cases, of complaints about maladministration on the part of the Commission being taken to the European Ombudsman[302]. This occurred with some success in the case of *Intel*[303] and *Ryanair*[304], though was unsuccessful in the case of *X, E.ON*[305]. A complaint may be made to the Ombudsman only after appropriate approaches have been made to the institutions concerned; and the Ombudsman's decisions are not binding.

(C) A typical case

In a typical cartel case[306] the Commission's procedure would be as follows:

- a whistleblower applies to the Commission for immunity from fines, or the Commission decides to start an investigation on its own initiative
- the Commission conducts surprise inspections
- the Commission considers the evidence it has obtained and sends requests for or requires further information
- the Commission issues statements of objections to the undertakings it considers to be in the cartel
- the undertakings submit written replies to the statements of objections
- an oral hearing is held[307]
- DG COMP prepares a draft decision
- the draft decision goes to the Commissioner for Competition
- the Advisory Committee is consulted on the draft decision
- the draft decision is seen by the College of Commissioners
- the College adopts the final decision.

---

[299] See eg Case T-314/01 *Coöperatieve Verkoop- en Productievereniging van Aardappelmeel en Derivaten Avebe BA v Commission* [2006] ECR II-3085, [2007] 4 CMLR 9, paras 66–67 and the case law cited therein.

[300] Case C-411/04 P [2007] ECR I-965, [2007] 4 CMLR 682, paras 40–50.

[301] Case C-185/95 P *Baustahlgewebe v Commission* [1998] ECR I-8417, [1999] 4 CMLR 1203, paras 28–49; see similarly Cases C-105/04 and C-113/04 P *Nederlandse Federatieve Vereniging voor de Groothandel op Elektrontechnisch Gebied v Technische Unie BV v Commission* [2006] ECR I-8725, [2006] 5 CMLR 1257, paras 35–52; Case C-385/07 *Duales System Deutschland GmbH v Commission* [2009] ECR I-6155, [2009] 5 CMLR 2215, paras 176–196.

[302] For further information about the Ombudsman see www.ombudsman.europa.eu; for discussion see Amory and Desmedt 'The European Ombudsman's First Scrutiny of the EC Commission in Antitrust matters' (2009) 30 ECLR 205.

[303] See Decision of the European Ombudsman closing his inquiry into complaint 1935/2008/FOR against the European Commission, 14 July 2009.

[304] See Decision of the European Ombudsman closing his inquiry into complaint 1342/2007/FOR against the European Commission, 27 April 2009.

[305] See Decision of the European Ombudsman closing his inquiry into complaint 2953/2008/FOR against the European Commission, 27 July 2010.

[306] An Article 102 case would be very similar but, for obvious reasons, would not involve a whistleblower; where the parties decide to settle a cartel case, and the Commission considers this to be an appropriate way to proceed, the procedure may be shorter than the one outlined in the text: see 'Settlements of cartel cases', pp 262–264 above.

[307] In some cases undertakings waive their right to an oral hearing.

(D) The position of complainants

Various provisions in Regulation 1/2003, including Article 27(3), acknowledge that third parties with a sufficient interest have a right to participate in proceedings, although these rights are less than those of the undertakings accused of an infringement. Chapter IV of the Implementing Regulation[308] also deals with the handling of complaints, and the Commission has published a *Notice on the handling of complaints by the Commission under Articles [101 and 102 TFEU]*[309]. Part II of the *Notice on Complaints* discusses the complementary roles of public and private enforcement of the competition rules, pointing out the benefits for complainants, in some circumstances, of going to a court rather than a competition authority: for example only a court can award damages or determine the effect on a contract of the voidness provided for by Article 101(2)[310]. It also explains the provisions on case allocation within the ECN, which should assist a complainant in deciding which public authority it would be sensible to approach if that is preferred to private litigation[311]. Part III of the *Notice on Complaints* explains in detail how the Commission goes about handling complaints, and specifies the information that must be supplied on Form C, the form that must be used when making a complaint[312]. The *Notice* discusses the Commission's right to prioritise its enforcement efforts and to concentrate on cases that have a 'Community interest'[313]; the right of the Commission to do so was clearly restated by the General Court in 2008 in *Scippecercola v Commission*[314], and in 2010 the same Court repeated earlier case law that complainants do not have a right to a final decision as to the existence or non-existence of an infringement of Articles 101 and/or 102[315]. The final part of the *Notice* explains the Commission's procedure when dealing with complaints, including the procedural rights of complainants and Commission decisions to reject complaints[316].

The Commission is entitled to make use of evidence provided by third parties on condition of their anonymity being maintained, although such evidence would not be sufficient in itself to sustain a finding of infringement but would have to be part of a body of evidence[317].

(ii) Article 28: professional secrecy

Article 28 contains two provisions: first, information collected under the Regulation may be used only for the purpose for which it was acquired; secondly, the Commission and the NCAs must not disclose information acquired or exchanged by them under the Regulation if that information is covered by an obligation of professional secrecy. Quite apart from the provisions of Article 28 of the Regulation, Article 339 TFEU itself imposes restrictions on the transmission of such information: paragraph 28(a) of the Commission's *Notice on NCA cooperation* provides guidance on the practical application of Article 28.

---

[308] OJ [2004] L 123/18.   [309] OJ [2004] C 101/65.   [310] Ibid, para 16.
[311] Ibid, paras 19–25.   [312] Ibid, paras 29–32.
[313] Ibid, paras 41–45; see Wils 'Discretion and Prioritisation in Public Antitrust Enforcement' (2011) 34(3) World Competition 353.
[314] Case T-306/05 [2008] ECR II-4, [2008] 4 CMLR 1418, paras 91–93.
[315] Case T-432/05 *EMC Development AB v Commission* [2010] ECR II-000, [2010] 5 CMLR 757, upheld on appeal Case C-367/10 P *EMC Development AB v Commission*, order of 31 March 2011.
[316] Ibid, paras 53–81.
[317] Case C-411/04 P *Salzgitter Mannesmann GmbH v Commission* [2007] ECR I-965, [2007] 4 CMLR 682, paras 47 and 50.

(I) Chapter IX: exemption regulations

Article 29 of Regulation 1/2003 provides power for the Commission and the NCAs to withdraw the benefit of block exemptions in individual cases[318].

(J) Chapter X: general provisions

(i) Article 30: publication of decisions

Article 30(1) requires the Commission to publish its decisions under Articles 7 to 10, 23 and 24, having regard to the legitimate interests of the parties in the protection of their business secrets.

(ii) Article 31: review by the Court of Justice

Article 31 provides that the EU Courts have unlimited jurisdiction to review decisions in which the Commission has imposed a fine or a periodic penalty payment.

(K) Chapter XI: transitional, amending and final provisions

Articles 35 to 42 contain transitional and final provisions.

(i) Article 34: transitional provisions

Article 34(1) provides that all existing notifications for an individual exemption to the Commission lapsed on 1 May 2004. Individual exemptions granted under Regulation 17 continue in force[319].

(ii) Article 35: designation of competition authorities of Member States

Article 35 requires Member States to designate the competition authority or authorities responsible for the application of Articles 101 and 102[320].

(iii) Articles 36–42: miscellaneous amendments

The provisions on the transport Regulations in Articles 36, 38, 39 and 41 have been overtaken by subsequent events[321]. Article 37 repeals the provisions of Regulation 2988/74 on limitation periods, since they are now dealt with by Articles 25 and 26. Article 40 repeals the powers in earlier Regulations to enable the withdrawal of the benefit of block exemptions; since the power to do this is now conferred by Article 29[322], Article 42 is no longer significant.

(iv) Article 43: repeal of Regulations 17 and 141

Article 43(1) repeals Regulation 17, except in relation to conditions and obligations attached to individual exemptions already granted by the Commission[323]. Article 43(2) repeals Regulation 141, which had exempted the transport sector from Regulation 17[324].

---

[318] For discussion of the possibility of withdrawing the benefit of Regulation 330/2010 from vertical agreements see ch 16, 'Withdrawal of the block exemption by the Commission or by a Member State', p 671.

[319] See ch 4, 'Regulation 1/2003', pp 166–167.

[320] See 'Article 5: powers of the NCAs', p 250 above.   [321] See ch 23, 'Transport', pp 967–977.

[322] See 'Chapter IX: exemption regulations', see above.

[323] See ch 4, 'Regulation 1/2003', pp 166–167.

[324] See ch 23, 'Transport', pp 961–970.

(v) Article 44: Report on the application of Regulation 1/2003

The Commission was required to report to the Parliament and the Council in 2009 on the functioning of the Regulation, in particular on Article 11(6) and Article 17, and assess whether it is appropriate to propose any revisions. In its *Report on the functioning of Regulation 1/2003*[325] the Commission reported that the Regulation had worked well in practice, significantly improving its enforcement of Articles 101 and 102 and bringing about coherence in their application throughout the EU. However the Commission also noted certain issues – for example the fact that different Member States have different procedures for the enforcement of Articles 101 and 102 and the divergence of national laws in the area of unilateral conduct – where further evaluation is called for, but left open the question of whether amendments to existing rules or practice are required.

3. Regulation 1/2003 in Practice[326]

Since 2004 the European Commission shares the task of enforcing the competition rules in the TFEU with the NCAs of the 27 Member States and with the national courts. The Commission and the NCAs together operate within the framework of the ECN, a manifestation of the general duty of sincere cooperation required by Article 4(3) TEU. Articles 101 and 102 are now applied with far greater frequency by the NCAs than by the Commission.

(A) The European Competition Network

The ECN does not have legal identity nor is it an international organisation as such. Rather it provides a framework within which the Commission and the NCAs discuss the sharing of work: for example which authority is best placed to handle a particular investigation. Information is exchanged between competition authorities within the framework of the ECN, as is experience gathered both in relation to actual cases and the development of policy. Members of the ECN are linked by a secure Intranet. The Commission takes the lead role in ensuring coherence in the application of the competition rules, in particular as a result of its examination of draft decisions of the NCAs in conjunction with its power to initiate its own proceedings, and thereby to suspend those of an NCA, under Article 11(6) of the Regulation. Information about the work of the ECN is obtainable from the website of DG COMP including, for example, the number of investigations under Articles 101 and 102 reported to the ECN and the proportion of them that had been started by an NCA on the one hand or the Commission on the other[327]. The Directors General of the NCAs meet once a year to discuss major policy issues within the ECN: this is the top

---

[325] SEC(2009) 574: see also the Commission's *Staff Working Paper accompanying the Report on the functioning of Regulation 1/2003*, COM(2009) 206 final, which contains detailed analysis of the operation of Regulation 1/2003 between 2004 and 2009; both documents are available at www.ec.europa.eu/competition/antitrust/legislation.html.

[326] See DeKeyser and Gauer 'The new enforcement system for Articles 81 and 82 EC and the rights of defence' in *2004 Annual Proceedings of the Fordham Corporate Law Institute* (Juris Publishing 2005, ed Hawk), 549; DeKeyser and Jaspers 'A New Era of ECN Cooperation' (2007) 30(1) World Competition 3; Commission's *Report on Competition Policy 2006*, COM(2007) 358 final, pp 86–89; Reichelt 'To what extent does the cooperation within the European Competition Network protect the rights of undertakings?' (2005) 42 CML Rev 745; the Commission's *Annual Report on Competition Policy* also provides helpful detail on the operation of the ECN.

[327] See www.ec.europa.eu/comm/competition/ecn/index_en.html.

level of the ECN framework. The so-called 'ECN Plenary' consisting of officials in the NCAs and the Commission meets four times a year. It has a number of working groups, for example on issues of cooperation, leniency and sanctions, and it also has a number of sectoral sub-groups, for example on the liberal professions, energy and financial services. The ECN, since January 2010, has published a periodical *Brief* in which it provides information about its activities and those of its members[328].

(B) Case allocation under Regulation 1/2003

The *Notice on NCA cooperation*[329] sets out the jurisdictional principles according to which cases should be allocated within the ECN[330]. An example of a case being reallocated from an NCA to the Commission is *iTunes*, where the OFT in the UK considered that the Commission was in a better position to consider a complaint by Which? (formerly the Consumers' Association) that Apple's iTunes service discriminated on price according to the user's country of residence, in particular since this gave rise to issues concerning the wider single market in Europe[331]. The Commission announced that Apple had agreed to equalise the prices of its downloads across Europe in January 2008[332]. Another interesting case is *Flat Glass*, where several NCAs cooperated with the Commission within the ECN, leading to the imposition by the Commission of fines totalling €488 million[333]. The fact that an NCA has started to investigate a matter does not mean that the Commission cannot carry out a surprise inspection in relation to the same behaviour[334].

(C) 'Soft' convergence

An interesting by-product of Regulation 1/2003 and the establishment of the ECN has been the considerable amount of soft convergence that has taken place in relation to national competition laws and procedures. Although the Regulation did not explicitly require there to be convergence, the reality is that in many respects – for example the abolition of national systems of notification and individual exemption, the alignment of investigative procedures, the introduction of leniency programmes and of commitments procedures similar to those in Article 9 – national laws have been brought into alignment with those of the EU. Information about the reform of the competition laws of the Member States since Regulation 1/2003 came into force is available on the website of the ECN[335] and in the *Staff Working Paper accompanying the Report on the functioning of Regulation 1/2003*.

(D) Leniency

The work of the ECN in the area of leniency has been of particular importance. Under the aegis of the ECN, 26 of the 27 NCAs now have a leniency programme[336], and the ECN has produced a *Model Leniency Programme* aimed at achieving soft harmonisation through

---

[328] Available at www.ec.europa.eu/competition/ecn/brief.pdf.   [329] OJ [2004] C 101/43.

[330] Ibid, paras 5–15.

[331] OFT Press Release, 3 December 2004, available at www.oft.gov.uk/news/press/2004/itunes.

[332] Commission Press Release IP/08/22, 9 January 2008; see also the Commission's *Statement on Apple's iPhone policy changes*, Commission Press Release IP/10/1175, 25 September 2010.

[333] Commission decision of 28 November 2007; see Commission Press Release IP/07/1781.

[334] Case T-339/04 *France Télécom v Commission* [2007] ECR II-521, [2008] 5 CMLR 502, para 80.

[335] See www.ec.europa.eu/comm/competition/ecn/index_en.html.

[336] The only Member State not to do so is Malta.

convergence. The *Model Leniency Programme* has been endorsed by the heads of all the NCAs and is available on the ECN's website[337]. The ECN published a *Report on Assessment of the State of Convergence* in October 2009[338] which noted that most Member States have aligned their leniency programmes with the key features of the Model Programme.

4. Judicial Review[339]

It is possible to bring an action before the General Court (and ultimately the Court of Justice on points of law) in respect of Commission decisions on competition matters; Article 265 TFEU of the Treaty deals with failures to act, Article 263 with actions for annulment and Article 261 with penalties. The EU Courts have exclusive competence to consider whether acts of the Commission are lawful or not[340]. Proceedings before the General Court must be completed within a reasonable time; reasonableness is tested by reference to the importance of the case for the person concerned, its complexity and the conduct of the applicant and the competent authorities[341].

(A) Article 265: failure to act

Under Article 265 it is possible to bring an action against the Commission where, in infringement of the Treaty, it has failed to act. The Commission must have been under a specific duty to carry out the act in question. An action may be brought only where the Commission has been required to act and has failed to do so within two months; the action itself must be brought within the following two months[342]. Article 265 is sometimes invoked by complainants wishing to force the Commission to investigate complaints against undertakings suspected of infringing the competition rules[343].

---

[337] See www.ec.europa.eu/comm/competition/ecn/index_en.html; for discussion see Gauer and Jaspers 'ECN Model Leniency Programme – a first step towards a harmonised leniency policy in the EU' (2007) (Spring) *Competition Policy Newsletter* 35.

[338] See MEMO/09/456, 15 October 2009; the Report is available at www.ec.europa.eu/competition/ecn/documents.htm.

[339] See Kerse and Khan *EC Antitrust Procedure* (Sweet & Maxwell, 5th ed, 2005), ch 8; Craig *EU Administrative Law* (Oxford University Press, 2006), Part 2; Bailey 'Scope of Judicial Review Under Article 81 EC' (2004) 41 CML Rev 1328; Vesterdorf 'Judicial Review in EC Competition Law: Reflections on the Role of the Community Courts in the EC System of Competition Law Enforcement' (2005) 1(2) Competition Policy International 3; Forrester 'A Bush in Need of Pruning: The Luxuriant Growth of Light Judicial Review' in *European Competition Law Annual 2009: Evaluation of Evidence and its Judicial Review in Competition Cases* (Hart Publishing, 2010, eds Ehlermann and Marquis); Castillo de la Torre 'Evidence, Proof and Judicial Review in Cartel Cases', ibid; Jaeger 'The standard of Review in Competition Cases Involving Complex Economic Assessments: Towards the Marginalisation of the Marginal Review?' (2011) 2(4) Journal of European Competition Law and Practice 295.

[340] See Case C-344/98 *Masterfoods* [2000] ECR I-11369, [2001] 4 CMLR 449; the EU Courts have no jurisdiction to review decisions by NCAs or judgments of national courts: see Case T-386/09 *Grúas Abril Asistencia, SL v Commission*, order of the General Court of 24 August 2010.

[341] Case C-185/95 P *Baustahlgewebe GmbH v Commission* [1998] ECR I-8417, [1999] 4 CMLR 1203; the fine was reduced by €50,000 in this case because of the delay in the proceedings; see also Case C-385/07 *Duales System Deutschland GmbH v Commission* [2009] ECR I-6155, [2009] 5 CMLR 2215, paras 176–196.

[342] Article 265(2); time limits are applied strictly by the General Court: see Case T-12/90 *Bayer v Commission* [1991] ECR II-219, [1993] 4 CMLR 30, paras 14, 16 and 46.

[343] See 'The position of complainants', p 286 above.

Where the Commission is guilty of a failure to act, an undertaking that suffers damage in consequence may bring an action against the Commission for compensation under Article 268 and Article 340 TFEU[344].

(B) Article 263: action for annulment

Under Article 263 it is possible to bring an action to have various 'acts' of the Commission annulled. Proceedings must be commenced within two months of the applicant hearing of the act in question[345]. Where an action succeeds in part only, Article 264 enables the unlawful parts of a decision to be severed and annulled, leaving the remainder intact. Four issues in particular need consideration: who may sue; what 'acts' may be challenged; on what grounds an action may be brought; and whether damages are available once a decision has been annulled.

(i) Standing

Apart from Member States and the Council, Article 263(4) provides that any undertaking may challenge a decision addressed to it or to another person if it is of 'direct and individual concern' to it. This clearly entitles third parties in some situations to sue. In *Metro v Commission*[346] the Court of Justice confirmed that a complainant under Article 3(2) of Regulation 17 (Article 7(2) of Regulation 1/2003) could proceed under Article 263[347]; if one applicant has standing, it is not necessary for other applicants concerned in the same application do so[348]. In some cases the applicant's interest may be altogether too vague to give standing[349]. The recipients of adverse decisions may themselves bring an action under Article 263, and their right to do so is not limited to cases in which fines have been imposed.

(ii) Acts

It is not only decisions, but other 'acts' which may be challenged under Article 263. Formal decisions of the Commission applying Articles 101 and 102 of course can be challenged. In *Coca-Cola Co v Commission*[350] the General Court held that it is settled law that any measure which produces binding legal effects such as to affect the interest of an applicant by bringing about a distinct change in its legal position is an act or decision which may be the subject of an action under Article 263[351]. In *IBM v Commission*[352] the Court of Justice held that a statement of objections could not normally be challenged, because it was

---

[344] To date such actions in the context of the competition rules have failed: see eg Case T-64/89 *Automec Srl v Commission* [1990] ECR II-367, [1991] 4 CMLR 177; Case T-28/90 *Asia Motor France v Commission* [1992] ECR I-2285, [1992] 5 CMLR 431, paras 48–51.

[345] Article 230(5); see ch 7 n 342 above on the General Court's approach to time limits.

[346] Case 26/76 [1977] ECR 1875, [1978] 2 CMLR 1.

[347] See also Case 43/85 *ANCIDES v Commission* [1987] ECR 3131, [1988] 4 CMLR 821; a third party successfully challenged the grant of an individual exemption in Cases T-528/93 etc *Métropole v Commission* [1996] ECR II-649, [1996] 5 CMLR 386.

[348] Case T-306/05 *Scippacercola v Commission* [2008] ECR II-4, [2008] 4 CMLR 1418, para 71.

[349] See eg Case 246/81 *Bethell v Commission* [1982] ECR 2277, [1982] 3 CMLR 300; Case C-70/97 P *Kruidvat BVBA v Commission* [1998] ECR I-7183, [1999] 4 CMLR 68.

[350] Cases T-125/97 and T-127/97 [2000] ECR II-1733, [2000] 5 CMLR 467.

[351] The General Court cited for this proposition the judgments in Case 60/81 *IBM v Commission* [1981] ECR 2639, [1981] 3 CMLR 635, para 9; Cases C-68/94 and C-30/95 *France v Commission* [1998] ECR I-1375, [1998] 4 CMLR 829, para 62; and Case T-87/95 *Assuriazioni Generali v Commission* [1999] ECR II-203, [2000] 4 CMLR 312, para 37.

[352] Case 60/81 [1981] ECR 2639, [1981] 3 CMLR 635.

simply a preliminary step in the formal procedure[353]. In *BAT v Commission*[354] the Court of Justice held that letters from the Commission to two complainants, finally rejecting their complaints, were acts capable of challenge under Article 263. The General Court held in the *Omni-Partijen Akkoord* judgments[355] that a letter from the Commissioner for Competition to a Member State that was purely factual in nature produced no legal effects and could not be challenged under Article 263. Mere silence on the part of an EU institution cannot produce binding legal effects unless express provision to this effect is made for it in EU law[356].

(iii) Grounds of review

The EU Courts must assess the legality of the Commission's decision according to the grounds of review specified in Article 263(2). The Commission may be challenged on grounds of:

> lack of competence, infringement of an essential procedural requirement, infringement of the Treaties or of any rule of law relating to their application, or misuse of powers.

To some extent these grounds overlap. Of particular significance will be a failure by the Commission to give a fair hearing[357]; a failure to articulate properly the reasoning behind its decision[358]; and a failure to base a decision on adequate evidence[359]. The Commission is not required to set out in its decision exhaustively all the evidence available; it is sufficient if it refers to the conclusive evidence[360].

The EU Courts have tended to review the decisions of the Commission with a degree of self-restraint, having due regard to the margin of appreciation enjoyed by the Commission when making complex technical and economic assessments[361]. However, within the limits of the review that it may carry out under Article 263, the General Court has been prepared to exercise its power of review of the substance of Commission decisions in a

---

[353] See similarly Cases T-10/92 etc *SA Cimenteries CBR v Commission* [1992] ECR II-2667, [1993] 4 CMLR 259; Cases T-377/00 etc *Philip Morris International Inc v Commission* [2003] 1 CMLR 676; Case T-48/03 *Schneider Electric v Commission*, order of 31 January 2006 [2006] ECR II-111, which held that a Commission decision under the EU Merger Regulation to take a case into Phase II is not susceptible to judicial review: an appeal to the Court of Justice was dismissed in Case C-188/06 P [2007] ECR I-35; see also Case C-516/06 P *Commission v Ferriere Nord SpA* [2007] ECR I-10685, [2008] 4 CMLR 267: no Commission act capable of judicial review; Case T-457/08 R *Intel Corp v Commission*, order of the President of the General Court of 27 January 2009: decisions of the Commissioner and of the Hearing Officer in that case not capable of judicial review.

[354] Cases 142 and 156/84 [1987] ECR 4487, [1988] 4 CMLR 24; see also Case 210/81 *Demo-Studio Schmidt v Commission* [1983] ECR 3045, [1984] 1 CMLR 63.

[355] Cases T-113/89 etc *Nefarma v Commission* [1990] ECR II-797.

[356] Cases T-189/95 etc *Service pour le Groupement d'Acquisitions v Commission* [1999] ECR II-3587, [2001] 4 CMLR 215, paras 26–29.

[357] See eg Case 17/74 *Transocean Marine Paint Association v Commission* [1974] ECR 1063, [1974] 2 CMLR 459 where the members of the association were not given an opportunity to be heard on the conditions which the Commission intended to attach to an individual exemption.

[358] See eg Case 73/74 *Groupement des Fabricants des Papiers Peints de Belgique v Commission* [1975] ECR 1491, [1976] 1 CMLR 589 where the Commission failed to explain the mechanism whereby the agreement in question could affect inter-state trade.

[359] See eg Case 41/69 *ACF Chemiefarma v Commission* [1970] ECR 661, [1970] CMLR 43 where the Commission's decision was partially annulled for lack of evidence.

[360] Case T-2/89 *Petrofina SA v Commission* [1991] ECR II-1087.

[361] See eg Case 42/84 *Remia BV and Verenigde Bedrijven and Nutricia v Commission* [1985] ECR 2545, [1987] 1 CMLR 1, para 34; Cases 142/84 and 156/84 *BAT and Reynolds v Commission* [1987] ECR 4487, [1988] 4 CMLR 24, para 62; Case T-201/04 *Microsoft Corp v Commission* [2007] ECR II-3601, [2007] 5 CMLR 846, paras 87–88.

comprehensive and exacting manner. This is exemplified by a series of judgments rendered by the General Court on the application of the EU Merger Regulation: *Airtours v Commission*[362], *Schneider Electric v Commission*[363] and *Tetra Laval v Commission*[364] at a time when considerable disquiet was being expressed about the fact that the Commission had the combined powers to investigate and prohibit mergers. In each case the General Court engaged in an exhaustive review of the substantive as well as the procedural propriety of the Commission's decision and, again in each case, annulled the decision. These cases, as well as the later judgment in *General Electric v Commission*[365], demonstrate that the Commission must provide adequate reasoning in its decisions, based on accurate and persuasive evidence.

(iv) Actions for damages

In the event that the General Court annuls a decision of the Commission under Article 340 TFEU it may be possible for the successful applicants to bring an action for damages for any losses they have suffered as a result of the unlawful decision. The General Court considered that the Commission's erroneous prohibition of the *Schneider/Legrande* merger did give rise to a right to damages in *Schneider Electric v Commission*[366]; however on appeal the Court of Justice held that the Commission's decision was not the cause of the economic loss suffered by Schneider, other than the costs involved in the second investigation that followed from the prohibition[367]. A claim for damages was rejected in *SELEX v Commission*[368].

(C) Article 261: penalties

Under Article 261 the General Court has unlimited jurisdiction in respect of penalties imposed by the Commission. Article 31 of Regulation 1/2003 provides that the EU Courts may cancel, reduce or increase fines or periodic penalties imposed. In the exercise of its unlimited jurisdiction the Courts may review a decision in its entirety – on factual as well as legal grounds – and many of its judgments have dealt exhaustively with the facts of the case. When the General Court finds that there is a factual error in the Commission's assessment it will not hesitate to adjust the fine. This can occur, for example, where the General Court considers that the Commission has exaggerated the duration of an undertaking's participation in a cartel[369] or has wrongly attributed to an undertaking the role of instigator or ringleader of a cartel[370]. The General Court will also make adjustments to fines where it feels that an undertaking has been the victim of unequal treatment

---

[362] Case T-342/99 [2002] ECR II-2585, [2002] 5 CMLR 317.

[363] Case T-310/01 [2002] ECR II-4071, [2003] 4 CMLR 768.

[364] Case T-5/02 [2002] ECR II-4381, [2002] 5 CMLR 1182.

[365] Case T-210/01 [2005] ECR II-5575, [2006] 4 CMLR 686.

[366] Case T-351/03 [2007] ECR II-2237, [2008] 4 CMLR 1533.

[367] Case C-440/07 P *Commission v Schneider Electric SA* [2009] ECR I-6413, [2009] 5 CMLR 2051; this case, and the General Court's judgment in Case T-212/03 *MyTravel v Commission* [2008] ECR II-1967, [2008] 5 CMLR 1429, are discussed in ch 21, 'Damages claims against the Commission', p 897.

[368] Case T-86/05, order of 29 August 2007; an appeal was rejected, Case C-481/07 P *SELEX Sistemi Integrati SpA v Commission* [2009] ECR-I 127.

[369] See eg Cases T-44/00 etc *Mannesmannröhren-Werke AG v Commission* [2004] ECR II-2223; Case T-58/01 *Solvay SA v Commission* [2009] ECR II-4781, paras 292–306; Case T-18/05 *IMI plc v Commission* [2010] ECR II-000, [2010] 5 CMLR 1215, paras 79–97.

[370] Case T-15/02 *BASF v Commission* [2006] ECR II-497, [2006] 5 CMLR 27, paras 280–464; Case T-29/05 *Deltafina SpA v Commission*, [2010] ECR II-000, [2011] 4 CMLR 467, paras 319–336.

compared with other members of the same cartel[371]. The General Court has not actively sought to substitute its own opinion on the level of the fine for that of the Commission, where the Commission has a margin of appreciation[372]. However it is important to understand that the General Court has the power to increase, as well as to decrease the level of a fine, and that it has on a few occasions done so[373].

(D) Accelerated procedure

An important development for the way in which cases are handled by the General Court is the introduction of the so-called 'accelerated procedure' which entered into force on 1 February 2001[374]. This procedure enables the General Court to expedite the hearing and determination of appeals and has been used in several cases[375].

(E) Interim measures

It is possible to apply to the General Court for interim measures suspending the operation of a Commission decision pending an appeal. Three conditions must be fulfilled in order for interim relief to be granted: first, the applicant must establish a prima facie case that the Commission's assessment is unlawful; secondly, it must demonstrate the urgency of interim measures to prevent it from suffering serious and irreparable damage; and thirdly it must explain why the balance of interests favours the adoption of such measures[376]. In cases where there is an imminent risk of severe and lasting harm to one or more of the parties, the General Court may suspend the operation of a Commission decision *ex parte*, pending the outcome of the proceedings for interim relief; this happened, for example, in *NDC Health/IMS Health: Interim Measures*[377].

---

[371] See eg Cases T-109/02 etc *Bolloré SA v Commission* [2007] ECR II-947, [2007] 5 CMLR 66, where the fine on Arjo Wiggins Appleton was reduced by €33 million as a result of unequal treatment; Case T-13/03 *Nintendo Co Ltd v Commission* [2009] ECR II-947, [2009] 5 CMLR 1421, paras 169–189, where Nintendo's fine was reduced from €149 million to €119 million because the Court considered that Nintendo should have received the same reduction of its fine for cooperation as had been awarded to John Menzies; Case T-18/03 *CD-Contact Data GmbH v Commission* [2009] ECR II-1021, [2009] 5 CMLR 1469, paras 91–121, where CD-Contact Data's fine was reduced as its passive role in the infringement had not been taken into account as an attenuating circumstance in determining the fine, whereas another undertaking, Concentra, had benefited from a reduction on this basis; Case T-18/05 *IMI v Commission* [2010] ECR II-000, [2010] 5 CMLR 1215, paras 152–174 and Case T-21/05 *Chalkor v Commission*, [2010] ECR II-000, [2010] 5 CMLR 1295, paras 90–113.

[372] See ch 13, 'Appeals to the General Court', pp 520–521 and Vesterdorf 'The Court of Justice and Unlimited Jurisdiction: What Does It Mean in Practice?' (2009) CPI Antitrust Chronicle, Spring 2009, Vol 6 No 2.

[373] See eg Cases T-101/05 and T-111/05 *BASF AG v Commission* [2007] ECR II-4949, [2008] 4 CMLR 347, paras 212–223 where the fine on BASF was marginally increased.

[374] OJ [2000] L 322/4; see further ch 21, 'Examples of third party appeals', pp 895–897.

[375] See eg Case T-310/01 *Schneider Electric v Commission* [2002] ECR II-4071, [2003] 4 CMLR 768; Case T-5/02 *Tetra Laval v Commission* [2002] ECR II-4381, [2002] 5 CMLR 1182.

[376] Examples of cases in which interim measures have been granted are Cases 76/89 R etc *Radio Telefís Eireann v Commission* [1989] ECR 1141, [1989] 4 CMLR 749; Case T-395/94 R *Atlantic Container Line AB v Commission* [1995] ECR II-595; Case T-41/98 R *Bayer AG v Commission* [1997] ECR II-381; Case T-65/98 R *Van den Bergh Foods Ltd v Commission* [1998] ECR II-2641, [1998] 5 CMLR 475.

[377] Case T-184/01 R *IMS Health v Commission* [2001] ECR II-3193, [2002] 4 CMLR 58, upheld on appeal Case C-481/01 P(R) [2002] ECR I-3401, [2002] 5 CMLR 44.

8

Articles 101 and 102: private enforcement in the courts of Member States

1. Introduction[1]

Chapter 7 was concerned with the public enforcement of Articles 101 and 102 by the European Commission and the national competition authorities ('the NCAs'). This chapter discusses the private enforcement of the competition rules, that is to say the situation where litigants take their disputes to a domestic court or, quite often, to arbitration.

Historically within the EU, public enforcement of competition law has been much more important than private enforcement[2]. However the competition authorities in the EU have limited resources and they are unable to investigate every alleged infringement of the competition rules. Private enforcement can therefore be an important complement to their activities[3]. The Commission has for a long time been eager that Articles 101 and 102 should be applied more frequently in national courts, thereby relieving it of some of

[1] See generally Jones *Private Enforcement of Antitrust Law in the EU, UK and USA* (Oxford University Press, 1999); *European Competition Law Annual 2001: Effective Private Enforcement of EC Antitrust Law* (Hart Publishing, 2003, eds Ehlermann and Atanasiu); Kerse and Khan *EC Antitrust Procedure* (Sweet & Maxwell, 5th ed, 2005), ch 5, paras 5–054–5–068; Komninos *EC Private Antitrust Enforcement: Decentralised Application of EC Competition Law by National Courts* (Hart Publishing, 2007); Bellamy and Child *European Community Law of Competition* (Oxford University Press, 6th ed, 2008, eds Roth and Rose), paras 14.042–14.142; *Competition Litigation: UK Practice and Procedure* (Oxford University Press, 2010, eds Brealey and Green); *Private Antitrust Litigation* (Global Competition Review, 2011, ed Mobley); OECD *Private remedies* 2008; note also the legal periodical Global Competition Litigation Review, established in 2008, which is exclusively concerned with the issues under consideration in this chapter.

[2] See Jones *Private Enforcement of Antitrust Law in the EU, UK and USA* (Oxford University Press, 1999) who estimates that approximately 90 per cent of all antitrust cases in the US involve private rather than public action, and that as many as 2,000 cases have been brought in a single year (ibid, p 79); however this figure includes a large number of follow-on actions pursuant to earlier public enforcement, so that the contrast is not as great as these figures may suggest. Official statistics on the number of private antitrust actions in the US are available at www.albany.edu/sourcebook.

[3] For a study of the complementary role of damages actions in the US see Lande and Davis *Report of the American Institute's Private Enforcement Project: Benefits From Private Antitrust Enforcement: An Analysis of Forty Cases* (American Antitrust Institute, 2007).

the burden of enforcement. Statements to this effect can be found more than 20 years ago[4]. Commissioner Monti reaffirmed the Commission's desire for more private enforcement in a speech to the Sixth EU Competition Law and Policy Workshop in Florence in June 2001[5]. One of the driving forces behind Regulation 1/2003 was the Commission's desire that national courts and NCAs should share with it the task of enforcing the competition rules, thereby enabling the Commission to concentrate its resources on pursuing the most serious infringements of the law[6]. Articles 6, 15 and 16 of Regulation 1/2003 contain important provisions dealing respectively with the powers of national courts, cooperation between national courts and the Commission and the uniform application of EU competition law. These provisions, and the accompanying Commission *Notice on the co-operation between the Commission and the courts of the EU Member States in the application of Articles [101 and 102 TFEU]*[7] ('the *Co-operation Notice*'), are incorporated into the text that follows. Regulation 1/2003 and the *Co-operation Notice* are silent on the subject of arbitration[8].

A study published in August 2004, usually referred to as the *Ashurst Report*[9], was carried out for the Commission to identify and analyse the obstacles to successful damages actions in the Member States based on infringements of competition law. The Report concluded that the picture was one of 'astonishing diversity and total underdevelopment'; on the latter point the Report found only 60 or so cases leading to a judgment on damages, 28 of which had actually led to an award of damages[10]. These figures to some extent misrepresent the number of damages actions that have been brought, since it is well known that many cases are settled out of court on the basis of confidentiality[11]; nevertheless the *Ashurst Report* did highlight numerous obstacles to private enforcement of the competition rules. This led the Commission to publish a Green Paper in December 2005, *Damages actions for breach of the EC antitrust rules*[12], the purpose of which was to identify the main obstacles to a more efficient system of damages claims and to set out different options to promote more such claims; this was followed in April 2008 by a White Paper bearing the

---

[4]　See eg the Commission's XIIIth *Report on Competition Policy* (1983), point 217.

[5]　The speech is available at www.ec.europa.eu.int/comm/competition/speeches; see further *European Competition Law Annual 2001: Effective Private Enforcement of EC Antitrust Law* (Hart Publishing, 2003, eds Ehlermann and Atanasiu); for a contrary view, arguing that 'public antitrust enforcement is inherently superior to private enforcement', see Wils 'Should Private Antitrust Enforcement Be Encouraged in Europe?' (2003) 26(3) World Competition 473 and Wils 'Should Private Antitrust Enforcement be Encouraged' in ch 4 of his book *Principles of European Antitrust Enforcement* (Hart Publishing, 2005).

[6]　See recitals 3 and 7 of Regulation 1/2003.　　　[7]　OJ [2004] C 101/4.

[8]　On arbitration see 'Arbitration', pp 325–326 below.

[9]　*Study on the conditions of claims for damages in case of infringement of EC competition rules*, August 2004, available at www.ec.europa.eu/comm/competition/antitrust/others/actions_for_damages/study.html.

[10]　Ibid, p 1; there has undoubtedly been an increase in the award of damages in competition law cases since the *Ashurst Report*: see eg judgment of the District Court of Dortmund of April 2004 (13 O 55/02) awarding damages of €1.6 million to August Storck KG against Hoffmann-la Roche following the Commission's decision in the *Vitamins* case; Case 85/2005 *Conduit Europe v Telefónica*, judgment of the Commercial Court of Madrid of 11 November 2005, awarding damages of €639,000 for refusal to supply contrary to Article 102; *Europe Investor Direct v VPC*, judgment of the Stockholm District Court of 20 November 2008, awarding damages of approximately €384,000 against VPC for abusing its dominant position; judgment of the Valladolid Provincial Court of 9 October 2009 awarding damages of €1.1 million to nine producers of biscuits and confectionery who had to pay higher prices for sugar due to the existence of a cartel in that market.

[11]　See eg Rodger 'Private Enforcement of Competition Law, the Hidden Story: Competition Law Litigation Settlements 2000–2005' (2008) 29 ECLR 96.

[12]　COM(2005) 672 final, 19 December 2005, available at www.ec.europa.eu/comm/competition/antitrust/actionsdamages; see also the accompanying Staff Working Paper which contains a rich source of research material.

same title[13]. It is noticeable that, whereas the Green Paper seemed to regard the availability of damages for infringements of Articles 101 and 102 as having an important deterrent effect, the White Paper is much more concerned with damages as a method of compensating the victims of breaches of the law. It is important that policy in this area should be clear-sighted as to its aims: the Commission's current position would appear to be that deterrence is best achieved through effective public enforcement of the law, and compensation through private actions[14].

The Green and White Papers are discussed in the final section of this chapter; so too is the Commission's consultation document, *Towards a Coherent European Approach to Collective Redress*. The final section will also mention proposals for possible reform in the UK[15].

Section 2 of this chapter will deal with actions for an injunction and/or damages based on infringements of Articles 101 and/or 102 TFEU as a matter of EU law. Section 3 deals with damages actions in the UK courts including, specifically, so-called 'follow-on' actions for damages in the UK Competition Appeal Tribunal under section 47A of the Competition Act 1998. Section 4 deals with the use of competition law not as a 'sword', where the claimant's cause of action is based on an infringement of competition law, but rather as a 'shield', that is to say as a defence, for example to an action for breach of contract or infringement of an intellectual property right. Section 5 contains a brief discussion of issues that can arise where competition law disputes are referred to arbitration rather than to a court for resolution. Section 6 discusses the options for reform that are currently under consideration in the EU and the UK.

2. Actions for an Injunction and/or Damages

(A) Is there a right to damages under Articles 101 and 102?

Articles 101 and 102 are directly applicable and produce direct effects: they give rise to rights and obligations which national courts have a duty to safeguard and enforce[16]. However until 2001 there had not been a judgment of the Court of Justice dealing specifically with the question of whether Member States have an obligation, as a matter of EU law, to provide a remedy in damages where harm has been inflicted as a result of an infringement of the competition rules. The issue is particularly important given that the Commission has no power to award damages, although it may be able to encourage a defendant to compensate its victims in return for a reduction in its fine[17]. The principles of non-discrimination and full effectiveness ('*effet utile*')[18], the judgment of the Court

---

[13] COM(2008) 154 final, 2 April 2008.

[14] For discussion see Wils 'The Relationship between Public Antitrust Enforcement and Private Actions for Damages' (2009) 31 (1) World Competition 3.

[15] See 'Proposals for Reform' pp 327–329.

[16] Case 127/73 *BRT v SABAM* [1974] ECR 51, [1974] 2 CMLR 238, para 16; Case C-453/99 *Courage Ltd v Crehan* [2001] ECR I-6297, [2001] 5 CMLR 1058, para 23.

[17] See eg *Pre-Insulated Pipe Cartel* OJ [1999] L 24/1, para 172; *Nintendo* Commission decision of 30 October 2002, OJ [2003] L 255/33, paras 440–441.

[18] See Case 106/77 *Simmenthal* [1978] ECR 629, [1978] 3 CMLR 263, para 16; Case 158/80 *REWE v Hauptzollamt Kiel* [1981] ECR 1805, [1982] 1 CMLR 449, para 44; Case 199/82 *Amministrazione delle Finanze dello Stato v San Giorgio* [1983] ECR 3595, [1985] 2 CMLR 658; Case C-213/89 *Factortame* [1990] ECR I-2433, [1990] 3 CMLR 1, para 19.

of Justice in *Francovich v Italy*[19] and the opinion of Advocate General van Gerven in *HJ Banks v British Coal Corpn*[20] all pointed towards the possibility of an action for damages; and the courts in the UK had assumed, in several cases, that such an action was available[21]. In 2001 the Court of Justice's judgment in *Courage Ltd v Crehan*[22] clarified the position, emphatically establishing a right to damages. A subsequent judgment of the Court of Justice in 2006, *Manfredi*[23], was equally emphatic.

(B) *Courage Ltd v Crehan*

In *Courage Ltd v Crehan* the Court of Justice held that:

> The full effectiveness of Article [101 TFEU] and, in particular, the practical effect of the prohibition laid down in Article [101(1)] would be put at risk if it were not open to any individual to claim damages for loss caused to him by a contract or by conduct liable to restrict or distort competition.
>
> Indeed the existence of such a right strengthens the working of the [EU] competition rules and discourages agreements or practices, which are frequently covert, which are liable to restrict or distort competition. From that point of view, actions for damages before the national courts can make a significant contribution to the maintenance of effective competition in the [EU][24].

The judgment in *Courage Ltd v Crehan* was a landmark in the private enforcement of Articles 101 and 102. It was a particularly striking case in that the claimant, Crehan, was not, for example, a customer of a cartel seeking damages for harm inflicted by a horizontal agreement the object of which was to restrict competition. Rather Crehan was himself party to a vertical agreement for the supply of beer by a brewer to him. At most the agreement was one that restricted competition by effect rather than by object, and, as a co-contractor, it was arguable that Crehan should not be able to recover damages as a result of losses caused by an unlawful agreement for which he was himself partly responsible. In English law there is a rule that one party to an agreement cannot recover damages from another party if they are both equally responsible for it ('*in pari delicto*')[25]. The Court of Justice's view was that there should not be an absolute bar to a person in the position of

---

[19] Cases C-6/90 and 9/90 [1991] ECR I-5357, [1993] 2 CMLR 66; see also Case C-5/94 *R v Ministry of Agriculture, Fisheries and Food, ex p Hedley Lomas* [1996] ECR I-2553, [1992] 2 CMLR 391; Cases C-178/94 etc *Dillenkofer v Germany* [1996] ECR I-4845, [1996] 3 CMLR 469.

[20] Case C-128/92 [1994] ECR I-1209, [1994] 5 CMLR 30; for comment on this case see Friend 'Enforcing the ECSC Treaty in National Courts' (1995) 20 EL Rev 59.

[21] See 'Damages Actions in the UK Courts', pp 306–307 below.

[22] Case C-453/99 [2001] ECR I-6297, [2001] 5 CMLR 1058; see Komninos 'New prospects for private enforcement of EC competition law: Courage v Crehan and the Community right to damages' (2002) 39 CML Rev 447; Reich 'The "Courage" doctrine encouraging or discouraging compensation for antitrust injuries' (2005) 42 CML Rev 35; Drake 'Scope of Courage and the principle of "individual liability" for damages: further development of the principle of effective judicial protection by the Court of Justice' (2006) 31 EL Rev 841; Odudu 'Effective Remedies and Effective Incentives in Community Competition Law' (2006) 5(2) Competition Law Journal 134.

[23] Cases C-295/04 etc *Vincenzo Manfredi v Lloyd Adriatico Assicurazioni SpA* [2006] ECR I-6619, [2006] 5 CMLR 17.

[24] Case C-453/99 [2001] ECR I-6297, [2001] 5 CMLR 1058, paras 26–27.

[25] See Monti 'Anticompetitive Agreements: the Innocent Party's Right to Damages' (2002) 27 EL Rev 282 (critical of the judgment); Odudu and Edelman, ibid, 327; Cumming 'Courage Ltd v Crehan' (2002) 27 ECLR 199; Jones and Beard 'Co-contractors, Damages and Article 81: The ECJ Finally Speaks' (2002) 23 ECLR 246; on the position in the US, see *Perma Life Mufflers Inc v International Parts Corpn* 392 US 134 (1968).

Crehan bringing an action[26]: the national court should take into account matters such as the economic and legal context in which the parties find themselves and the respective bargaining power and conduct of the two parties to the contract[27]. Of particular importance would be whether a person in the position of Crehan found himself in a markedly weaker position than a brewer such as Courage, so as seriously to compromise or even eliminate his freedom to negotiate the terms of the contract and his capacity to avoid the loss or reduce its extent[28]. A further point was that, in a situation such as that in *Crehan*, the restrictive effect of Courage's agreement with Crehan arose from the fact that it was one of many similar agreements having a cumulative effect on competition[29]: in those circumstances Crehan could not be considered to bear significant responsibility for the infringement of the competition rules[30].

Unfortunately for Crehan when the case reverted to the English High Court in the UK Park J held that the agreement did not infringe Article 101 anyway and dismissed his claim[31]; this finding was ultimately upheld on appeal to the House of Lords (now the Supreme Court)[32]. After 13 years of litigation Crehan recovered no damages whatsoever; however he made a crucial contribution to the important issue of the private enforcement of competition law.

(C) *Manfredi*

In *Manfredi* the Italian Competition Authority had found that various insurance companies had violated Italian competition law through the unlawful exchange of information; the decision was upheld on appeal to the Council of State. Customers of the insurance companies sued for damages for breaches of both Italian and EU competition law. Various questions were submitted to the Court of Justice under Article 267 TFEU, partly as to the right to damages under Article 101 and partly as to specific Italian provisions concerning damages claims under internal Italian law. On the right to damages the Court of Justice repeated what it had said in *Crehan*. The full effectiveness of Article 101(1) required that:

> any individual can claim compensation for the harm suffered where there is a causal relationship between that harm and an agreement or practice prohibited under Article [101 TFEU][33].

In *Manfredi* there were some specific points about Italian procedural law that seemed to complicate the claimants' actions: for example there were rules that allocated jurisdiction in actions for damages based on competition law to a different court from the one that would deal with 'normal' damages claims, thereby increasing the cost and length of the litigation; there were limitation periods that could be harmful to their cause; and there were rules that might prevent them from recovering the full amount of their losses. The Article 267 reference asked the Court of Justice whether these domestic rules were compatible with EU law. The Court of Justice's answer, in essence, was that these were matters of domestic law, provided that they did not offend the EU principles of equivalence and effectiveness. What the *Manfredi* judgment did was to reveal that, despite the Court of

---

[26] Case C-453/99 [2001] ECR I-6297, [2001] 5 CMLR 1058, para 28.   [27] Ibid, para 32.

[28] Ibid, para 33.

[29] On this point see ch 16, 'Factors to be considered in determining whether single branding agreements infringe Article 101(1)', p 638.

[30] Case C-453/99 [2001] ECR I-6297, [2001] 5 CMLR 1058, para 34; it is interesting to speculate as to what would have happened if a third party had sued Courage and Crehan for harm suffered as a result of the agreement: the Court of Justice's reasoning would suggest that Courage, but not Crehan, should be liable.

[31] *Crehan v Inntrepreneur Pub Co* [2003] EWHC 1510.

[32] [2006] UKHL 38, [2006] UKCLR 1232.

[33] Cases C-295/04 etc *Vincenzo Manfredi v Lloyd Adriatico Assicurazioni SpA* [2006] ECR I-6619, [2006] 5 CMLR 17, para 61.

Justice's enthusiasm for damages actions, there remains the 'problem' that Member States retain autonomy in relation to the procedural rules of their domestic judicial systems, as well as the substantive rules of recovery in tort, delict, restitutionary and other actions, and that these rules might inhibit successful damages claims[34]. This is precisely why the European Commission set out to identify the 'obstacles' that lie in the way of damages actions and to consider ways of reducing or eliminating them. This issue will be returned to in the final section of this chapter.

(D) The 'passing-on' defence and the position of indirect purchasers

Crehan and *Manfredi* leave no doubt that damages are available where Articles 101 and/ or 102 are infringed. However the judgments do not deal specifically with two interrelated conundra that arise in this context, namely the possible existence of a passing-on defence, and the right of sub-purchasers from the immediate victim(s) of anti-competitive behaviour to bring an action for damages for any loss that they may have suffered.

Suppose that members of a widget cartel have been fixing prices for the last five years. Their immediate customers, who purchase widgets in order to produce widget dioxide, will have paid more for the widgets than they would have done in the absence of the cartel. However it may be the case that some – or even all – of the increased price will be 'passed on' to their own customers, the purchasers of widget dioxide. Indeed those purchasers may themselves be able to pass all or some of the increased price further down the distribution chain. Two questions arise in this situation: first, if the producers of widget dioxide sue the members of the widget cartel for damages, can the latter raise as a defence that the widget dioxide producers have passed on their loss to their customers? And if the answer to the latter question is 'yes', does it follow that sub-purchasers (also referred to as indirect purchasers) can bring an action for damages for the increased price that has been passed on to them? These are far from simple questions. To *refuse* a passing-on defence could mean that the widget dioxide producers will be allowed to recover damages for a loss that they have not actually incurred; however to *allow* a passing-on defence suggests that firms, or even end-consumers, further down the distribution chain should be able to recover. As one descends through the distribution chain, however, it becomes more difficult to calculate the actual harm suffered, and a danger exists that the harm suffered by individual firms or natural persons is so small that no one would bother to sue for damages at all: that would leave an ill-gotten gain in the hands of the cartelists, the least desirable outcome. Various economic and econometric techniques have been suggested to facilitate the calculation of damages in competition cases[35], and the European Commission has published a draft guidance paper on the subject[35a].

---

[34] When the case returned to Italy Mr Manfredi was awarded €889.10 in damages and €500 for legal costs by the small claims court: see Nebbia 'So What Happened to Mr Manfredi? The Italian Decision Following the Ruling of the European Court of Justice' (2007) 28 ECLR 591.

[35] See Oxera study on *Quantifying antitrust damages: Towards non-binding guidance for courts*, December 2009; Noble 'How to Quantify Damages? A Brief Overview of Economic Concepts and Techniques' (2008) 7(1) Competition Law Journal 57; for more general discussion of the issues under consideration see Hoseinian 'Passing-on Damages and Community Antitrust Policy – An Economic Background' (2005) 28(1) World Competition 3–23; Petrucci 'The Issues of the Passing-on Defence and Indirect Purchasers' Standing in European Competition Law' (2008) 29 ECLR 33; van Dijk and Verboven 'Implementing the passing-on defence in cartel damages actions' (2010) 3 Global Competition Litigation Review 98; De Coninck 'Estimating private antitrust damages' Concurrences No 1–2010, 39; Commission Staff Working Paper accompanying the White Paper on *Damages actions for breach of the EC antitrust rules* COM(2008) 404, paras 201–225.

[35a] Quantifying harm in actions for damages based on Articles 101 and 102 of the Treaty on the Functioning of the European Union, June 2011, available at www.ec.europa.eu.

In the US the Supreme Court rejected the passing-on defence in *Hanover Shoe Inc v United Shoe Machinery Corp*[36], because there damages do play an important role in the deterrence of cartels[37]. As to indirect purchasers, the Supreme Court held in *Illinois Brick Co v Illinois*[38] that in general claims by indirect purchasers should not be allowed, a natural corollary of the judgment in *Hanover Shoe*. However several individual states have amended their own laws to provide for indirect purchasers to sue[39], and the US Antitrust Modernisation Commission recommended legislative action to improve the law on indirect purchasers[40]. This thorny topic will be returned to below, both in the context of the enforcement of Articles 101 and 102 in the UK[41] and in the discussion of possible reform of the law at EU and/or UK level[42]. The Court of Justice's judgments in *Crehan* and *Manfredi* did not deal with this topic specifically[43], although the Court's statement in paragraph 26 of *Crehan* and paragraph 56 of *Manfredi* that it should be open to 'any' individual for claim damages for loss caused by anti-competitive conduct would lend support to the proposition that indirect as well as direct purchasers should be able to sue; this point was repeated in paragraph 28 of the Court's judgment in *Pfleiderer AG v Bundeskartellamt*[44].

(E) Interim relief

Crehan and *Manfredi* establish that there is a right to damages for harm caused by an infringement of the competition rules. Quite often a claimant is as interested in obtaining an injunction to bring anti-competitive behaviour to an end as in receiving damages; more specifically the claimant may seek interim relief pending the outcome of a competition investigation by a competition authority.

The Commission has power under Article 8 of Regulation 1/2003 to adopt interim measures[45]; NCAs have similar powers[46]. However the competition authorities, acting in the public interest, are sparing in their adoption of interim measures; a claimant in need of interim relief may find that an application to a national court is a more effective way to proceed, the function of the court being to achieve justice between the parties. In his Opinion in *AOK Bundersverband*[47] Advocate General Jacobs considered that the *Crehan* principle that damages should be available to protect the *effet utile* of Article 101

---

[36] 392 US 481 (1968).

[37] This is further exemplified by the award of treble damages to successful plaintiffs rather than single (compensatory) damages.

[38] 431 US 720 (1977); the English High Court has described the judgment in *Hanover Shoe* 'as a policy decision not open to the English courts, damage being a necessary ingredient of the cause of action': *Emerald Supplies Ltd v British Airways plc* [2009] EWHC 741, [2009] UKCLR 801, para 37; see also Brealey 'Adopt Perma Life, but Follow Hanover Shoe to Illinois? – Who Can Sue for Damages for Breach of EC Competition Law?' (2002) 1 Competition Law Journal 127.

[39] See *California v ARC America Corp* 490 US 93 at 105–106 (1989).

[40] See Chapter IIIB of the Report, available at www.amc.gov; these recommendations had not been implemented as at 20 June 2011.

[41] See 'Can an indirect purchaser sue?', p 311 below.

[42] See 'Proposals for Reform', pp 327–329 below.

[43] The Court of Justice has dealt with this topic in the context of non-contractual liability of the EU under Article 340(2) TFEU: see eg Case 238/78 *Ireks-Arkady v Council and Commission* [1979] ECR 2955.

[44] Case C-360/09 [2011] ECR I-000, [2011] 5 CMLR 219.

[45] See ch 7, 'Article 8: interim measures', p 255.

[46] On the OFT's powers under UK law to adopt interim measures see ch 10, 'Interim measures', p 407.

[47] Case C-264/01 [2004] ECR I-2493.

applied equally to applications for interim relief[48]. Applications for interim relief in the UK courts, which have sometimes been successful, are discussed below[49].

(F) Private enforcement and Regulation 1/2003

Recital 7 of Regulation 1/2003 states that national courts have an 'essential part' to play in applying the competition rules. Article 6 of the Regulation states simply that:

> National courts shall have the power to apply Articles [101 and 102 TFEU].

There are two further provisions in Regulation 1/2003 of considerable importance to private enforcement: Article 15 on cooperation with national courts and Article 16 on the uniform application of EU competition law. They should be read in conjunction with the Commission's *Co-operation Notice*.

(i) Article 15: cooperation with national courts

Recital 21 of Regulation 1/2003 refers to the importance of consistency in the application of the competition rules across the EU, and to the consequent need to establish arrangements for cooperation between the Commission and national courts, whether those courts are dealing with litigation between private parties, are acting as enforcers of the law or are sitting as courts of appeal or judicial review. Article 15 provides for various types of cooperation with national courts, as set out below. The cooperation envisaged under Article 15 is between the Commission and the national courts, not between the Commission and the litigants themselves: when asked to assist a national court the Commission will not have any direct dealings with the parties to the litigation and, if approached by them, it will inform the national court of the fact[50].

Regulation 1/2003 does not provide for a 'network of national courts' in the way that it establishes a 'network of national competition authorities'[51]; however, an 'Association of European Competition Law Judges' was established in 2002 in order to bring together judges of the national courts to discuss and debate points of common interest[52].

(A) Requests by national courts for information or an opinion

Article 15(1) of Regulation 1/2003 provides that a national court may request the Commission to transmit to it information in the Commission's possession or to provide it with an opinion concerning the procedural or substantive application of the EU competition rules. The Commission will endeavour to reply to a request for information within one month[53]. An important point is that Article 339 TFEU provides that the Commission is not allowed to transmit information covered by the obligation of professional secrecy, which may be both confidential information and business secrets: the Commission will not provide such information to a national court unless the latter can guarantee that it will protect it[54]. The Commission will not transmit to a national court information voluntarily submitted to it by a leniency applicant without its consent[55]. The Commission will endeavour to reply to a request for an opinion within four months[56]. When giving its opinion the Commission will limit itself to providing the national court with the factual information

---

[48] See para 104 of the Opinion.
[49] See 'Interim relief', p 310 below.   [50] *Co-operation Notice*, para 19.
[51] See ch 7, 'Case allocation under Regulation 1/2003', p 289.
[52] The website of the AECLJ is www.aeclj.com.
[53] *Co-operation Notice*, para 22.   [54] Ibid, paras 23–25.   [55] Ibid, para 26.
[56] Ibid, para 28.

or the economic or legal clarification asked for without considering the merits of the case[57]. The Article 15(1) procedure has been used on a number of occasions: for example in the course of 2006 the Commission provided two opinions to national courts[58]; three opinions were provided during 2007[59]; several during 2008[60] and five during 2009[61]. Of course a national court requiring advice on a point of law could also, should it prefer to do so, make a preliminary reference under Article 267 TFEU to the Court of Justice[62].

A national court wishing to approach the Commission for assistance may do so by post, but may also do so by sending an email to a bespoke address: comp-amicus@ec.europa.eu.

(B) Submission of judgments to the Commission

Article 15(2) of Regulation 1/2003 requires Member States to submit any written judgment deciding on the application of Articles 101 and 102 to the Commission, without delay after the full written judgment is notified to the parties. The Commission has created a database of all such judgments which is accessible on its website; it contains non-confidential versions of judgments in their original language, classified according to the Member State of origin[63]. Unfortunately it does not appear to be up to date.

(C) Observations by national competition authorities and the Commission

Article 15(3) of Regulation 1/2003 makes provision for NCAs and the Commission to make observations to national courts. Each may make written observations acting on their own initiative; oral observations may be made with the permission of the court. In order to enable them to make such observations NCAs and the Commission may request the relevant court to transmit or ensure the transmission to them of documents necessary for an assessment of the case. This provision is similar to the practice in some Member States that enables an NCA to intervene in cases before the national courts; in France, for example, the French Competition Authority may give expert testimony in civil proceedings[64]. Regulation 1/2003 does not provide a procedural framework for the submission of observations; this is therefore a matter for the rules and practices of the court of the Member State to which they are made[65].

In 2006 the Commission made its first intervention under Article 15(3) to the Paris Court of Appeal in relation to the interpretation of the motor vehicle block exemption regulation[66]; in 2007 the Commission intervened in a case in the Netherlands concerning the deductibility of Commission competition fines[67]; and in 2009 the Commission submitted observations in front of the Paris Court of Appeal in a case about restrictions of online sales in selective distribution agreements[68]. The Commission also intervened under Article 15(3) in the *Beef Industry Development Society* case[69]. In the UK the Office

---

[57] Ibid, para 29.

[58] See Commission's XXXVIth *Report on Competition Policy* (2006), para 70.

[59] See Commission's XXXVIIth *Report on Competition Policy* (2007), para 90.

[60] See Commission's XXXVIIIth *Report on Competition Policy* (2008), para 115.

[61] See Commission's XXXIXth *Report on Competition Policy* (2009), para 162.

[62] On Article 267 references see ch 10, 'Which courts or tribunals in the UK can make an Article 267 reference in a case under the Competition Act 1998?', p 450.

[63] See www.ec.europa.eu/comm/competition/antitrust/national_courts/index_en.html.

[64] Commission's White Paper on modernisation of the rules implementing [Articles 101 and 102 TFEU] OJ [1999] C 132/1, [1999] 5 CMLR 208, para 107.

[65] *Co-operation Notice*, paras 34–35.

[66] See Commission's XXXVIth *Report on Competition Policy* (2006), para 72.

[67] See Commission's XXXVIIth *Report on Competition Policy* (2007), para 92.

[68] See Commission's XXXIXth *Report on Competition Policy* (2009), para 162; this case was subsequently referred to the Court of Justice: see Case C-439/09 *Pierre Fabre Dermo–Cosmétique* [2011] ECR I-000.

[69] See ch 4, '*Matra Hachette v Commission*', pp 153–155.

of Rail Regulation, relying on Article 15(3) of Regulation 1/2003, made observations to the court in the case of *English Welsh & Scottish Railway Ltd v E.ON*[70].

(D) Wider national powers

Article 15(1) to (3) of Regulation 1/2003 establishes EU rules on cooperation; Article 15(4) states that the rules therein are without prejudice to any wider powers that might exist under national law in a particular Member State allowing competition authorities to make observations.

(ii) Article 16: uniform application of EU competition law

Article 16(1) of Regulation 1/2003, which is concerned with the uniform application of the EU competition rules, explains the effect of Commission decisions on national courts. As recital 22 of the Regulation points out, it is important that the competition rules should be applied uniformly throughout the EU and that conflicting decisions should be avoided. The Regulation therefore clarifies, in accordance with the case law of the Court of Justice[71], the effect of Commission decisions on national courts (and NCAs). The Regulation also addresses the position of a national court dealing with a case which the Commission is investigating at the same time, without having yet reached a decision.

(A) The effect of Commission decisions

The first sentence of Article 16(1) gives expression to Article 288 TFEU and the Court of Justice's judgment in *Masterfoods*[72]. It states that, where national courts rule on a matter which has already been the subject of a Commission decision under Article 101 or Article 102, they cannot reach conclusions running counter to that of the Commission. The Regulation does not state specifically that an appellate court in a Member State would be bound by a Commission decision even where a lower court had reached a contrary conclusion prior to the Commission's decision; however this point was established by the Court of Justice in *Masterfoods*[73]. If the Commission's decision is on appeal to the General Court or the Court of Justice the national court should stay its proceedings pending a definitive decision on the matter by the EU Courts[74]. If a national court considers that a Commission decision is wrong, and if it has not been the subject of an appeal to the EU Courts, the only option available to the national court would be to make an Article 267 reference to the Court of Justice[75].

Sometimes the Commission states that an undertaking has participated in a cartel, but does not impose a fine because this has become time-barred: the undertaking may challenge the reference to it in the decision because the fact renders it vulnerable to a damages claim[76].

(B) Parallel proceedings

The second sentence of Article 16(1) states that, where a national court is hearing an action, it must avoid giving a decision which would conflict with a decision contemplated by the Commission in proceedings that it has initiated. Article 16(1) adds that the national

---

[70] [2007] EWHC 599, [2007] UKCLR 1653.

[71] Of particular importance is the judgment of the Court of Justice in Case C-344/98 *Masterfoods Ltd v HB Ice Cream Ltd* [2000] ECR I-11369, [2001] 4 CMLR 449; see generally Nazzini *Concurrent Proceedings in Competition Law* (Oxford University Press, 2004), esp ch 7 and Komninos 'Effect of Commission decisions on private antitrust litigation: Setting the story straight' (2007) 44 CML Rev 1387.

[72] See ch 8 n 71 above.   [73] *Masterfoods*, para 60.

[74] Ibid, paras 52 and 57; *Co-operation Notice*, para 13.

[75] Ibid, para 13.   [76] See ch 7, 'Past infringements', pp 254–255.

court in this situation should consider whether to stay its proceedings; if it were to do so, it is likely that the Commission would expedite its own proceedings in order to enable the outcome of the civil dispute to be decided. The national court could order interim measures to protect the interests of the parties while awaiting the Commission's decision[77].

Where a national court has reason to believe that the Commission is conducting a parallel investigation of a possible infringement of Article 101 or 102 it could seek information from the Commission under the provisions of Article 15 of Regulation 1/2003 discussed above about any proceedings it may have in motion, what it is likely to decide in that case and when. The Commission has a duty under Article 4(3) TEU to cooperate with the judicial authorities in Member States in matters of this kind[78].

(G) The relationship between private and public enforcement of Articles 101 and 102

A complex issue is the relationship between the private and public enforcement of Articles 101 and 102. As a general proposition the Commission is in a much better position than a private plaintiff to discover infringements of the competition rules, in particular given the wide-ranging investigative powers that it can deploy throughout the EU. The Commission has resources and experience that enable it to identify infringements that many plaintiffs lack; and it is probably better able to quantify the harm caused by infringements of Articles 101 and 102. The Commission also is able to incentivise undertakings to inform it of infringements of Article 101 as a result of its leniency programme[79].

Given the Commission's desire to see more private enforcement of the competition rules, one might suppose that it would facilitate follow-on actions by (a) inserting as much information in its decisions as possible about any infringement; (b) allowing access to the file to third parties that wish to obtain more information than can be found in the Commission's decision; and (c) allowing third parties access to leniency applications made by members of cartels where this might facilitate a follow-on action. However, from the Commission's point of view there is a danger that, in acceding to claimants' wishes in this respect, it may (a) infringe the EU rules on protecting confidentiality and business secrets; and (b) undermine the leniency programme, if the fear of leniency applications being disclosed were to deter undertakings from whistleblowing and cooperating with the Commission in other ways. This is not an easy balance to strike, and there are a number of current cases in which claimants are seeking to obtain access to information in the Commission's possession in order to progress their private litigation[80].

The Court of Justice considered this issue in *Pfleiderer AG v Bundeskartellamt*[81]. In that case the Bundeskartellamt had imposed a fine on members of a décor paper cartel. Pfleiderer brought an action for damages and sought access to the BKA's file, including the leniency applications that had been made. The Court of Justice recognised, on the one

---

[77] *Masterfoods*, para 58; *Co-operation Notice*, para 14.

[78] See Case C-234/89 *Delimitis v Henninger Bräu* [1991] ECR I-935, [1992] 5 CMLR 210, para 53; see also Cases C-319/93 etc *Hendrik Evert Dijkstra v Friesland (FRICO Domo) Coöperatie BA* [1995] ECR I-4471, [1996] 5 CMLR 178, para 34; on the Commission's duty of sincere cooperation see the order of the Court of Justice in Case C-2/88 R *Zwartveld* [1990] ECR I-3365, [1990] 3 CMLR 457, para 18 and Case C-275/00 *Commission v First NV and Franex NV* [2002] ECR I-10943, [2005] 2 CMLR 257, para 49.

[79] See ch 7, 'The Commission's *Leniency Notice*', pp 280–282.

[80] See eg Case T-173/09 *Z v Commission (Marine Hoses)*, not yet decided; Case T-437/08 *CDC Hydrogene Peroxide v Commission (Bleaching Chemicals)*, not yet decided; Case T-380/08 *Kingdom of Netherlands v Commission (Dutch Bitumen)*, not yet decided; Case T-344/08 *EnBW Energie Baden-Württemberg v Commission (Gas Insulated Switchgear)*, not yet decided.

[81] Case C-360/09 [2011] ECR I-000, [2011] 5 CMLR 219.

hand, the important role of leniency programmes in uncovering and bringing an end to cartels[82], and that disclosure of leniency applications could compromise the success of such programmes[83]. However it also recognised the important principle that claimants should be able to recover compensation for harm suffered[84]. The Court's conclusion was that it should be left to national courts to weigh these different considerations on a case-by-case basis, according to national law, taking into account all the relevant factors in the case[85].

A claimant in a damages action in the US might also seek discovery of documents in the European Commission's possession, including leniency applications; such claims will be denied where the Court considers that it is appropriate in order to maintain the confidentiality of the materials sought[86].

(H) The duty of national courts

An important issue is whether a national court has a duty, of its own motion, to raise issues of competition law irrespective of whether one or more of the litigants do so. This matter was considered by the Court of Justice in *van Schijndel*[87] and is summarised in paragraph 3 of the Commission's *Co-operation Notice*. Where domestic law requires a national court to raise points of law based on binding domestic rules which have not been raised by the parties the same obligation also exists where binding EU rules, such as those on competition, exist; the same is the case where the national court has a discretion to raise such points of law. However EU law does not require national courts to raise a point of EU law where this would require them to abandon the passive role assigned to them by going beyond the ambit of the dispute defined by the parties.

3. Damages Actions in the UK Courts[88]

(A) The availability of damages in the UK courts

The UK courts established nearly 30 years ago (long before *Crehan*) that damages could be available for harm caused by infringements of Articles 101 and 102[89]. The Competition Act 1998 does not explicitly confer a right to damages where the Chapter I and Chapter II prohibitions are infringed. However there is no doubt that damages are available[90]: this follows

---

[82] Ibid, para 25.   [83] Ibid, paras 26 and 27.

[84] Ibid, paras 28 and 29.   [85] Ibid, para 31.

[86] See eg the order of 26 April 2011 of the Special Master in Case No M:070cv001827-si, US District Court, Northern District of California.

[87] Cases C-430/93 etc [1995] ECR-4705; on this case see Prechal 'Community Law in National Courts: The Lessons from Van Schijndel' (1998) 35 CML Rev 681.

[88] See Rodger 'Competition Law Litigation in the UK Courts: A Study of All Cases to 2004' [2006] 27 ECLR 241, 279 and 341 and Rodger 'UK Competition Law and Private Litigation' in Rodger (ed) *Ten Years of UK Competition Law Reform* (Dundee University Press, 2010), ch 3.

[89] See eg *Garden Cottage Foods v Milk Marketing Board* [1984] AC 130, [1983] 3 CMLR 43; *An Bord Bainne Co-operative Ltd v Milk Marketing Board* [1984] 1 CMLR 519, affd [1984] 2 CMLR 584; *Bourgoin SA v Minister of Agriculture Fisheries and Food* [1985] 1 CMLR 528, on appeal [1986] 1 CMLR 267.

[90] See generally Yeung 'Privatizing Competition Regulation' (1998) 18 OJLS 581; Kon and Maxwell 'Enforcement in National Courts of the EC and New UK Competition Rules: Obstacles to Effective Enforcement' (1998) 19 ECLR 443; Turner 'The UK Competition Act 1998 and Private Rights' (1999) 20 ECLR 62; MacCulloch 'Private Enforcement of the Competition Act Prohibitions' in *The Competition Act: A New Era for UK Competition Law* (Hart Publishing, 2000, eds Rodger and MacCulloch); Roth 'The New UK Competition Act – The Private Perspective' in [2000] Fordham Corporate Law Institute (ed Hawk),

from the *Crehan* and *Manfredi* judgments, read in conjunction with section 60(2) of the Act, requiring consistency with the jurisprudence of the EU Courts[91]; from sections 47A and 58A of the Act, which provide for follow-on actions pursuant to findings of an infringement of EU or UK competition law by the competition authorities; and from the debate in Parliament on the Competition Bill[92].

(B) The OFT's Discussion Paper and Recommendations on private enforcement of the competition rules

Public policy in the UK has moved in favour of more private enforcement of the competition rules: in particular various provisions in the Enterprise Act 2002 were designed to facilitate damages claims, as will be seen in the text that follows. In April 2007 the OFT published a Discussion Paper, *Private actions in competition law: effective redress for consumers and business*[93]; this was followed in November of the same year by *Private actions in competition law: effective redress for consumers and business: Recommendations from the Office of Fair Trading*[94]: both documents will be briefly considered at the end of this chapter[95]. The UK Government is considering the case for reforming the law relating to private actions[96].

(C) Which court to sue in: the jurisdiction of the High Court and the Competition Appeal Tribunal

A claimant seeking damages in the UK has two options: to bring a 'standalone' action in the Chancery Division of the High Court[97] and prove an infringement of the competition rules without the benefit of a prior decision to that effect by a public authority, or, where the Office of Fair Trading ('the OFT'), a sectoral regulator or the European Commission has adopted a decision finding an infringement of EU or UK competition law, to bring a 'follow-on' action in the High Court or the Competition Appeal Tribunal ('the CAT'). Section 16 of the Enterprise Act 2002 makes provision for the Lord Chancellor to make regulations for the transfer of standalone cases to the CAT[98]; to date no such regulations have been made[99]. The following sections will discuss the issues that have arisen, or may arise, in the context of damages actions before the UK courts.

---

ch 7; Rodger 'Private Enforcement and the Enterprise Act: An Exemplary System of Awarding Damages?' (2003) 24 ECLR 103; see also the Government's White Paper *Productivity and Enterprise – A World Class Competition Régime* Cm 5233 (2001), ch 8.

[91] See ch 9, '"Governing Principles Clause": Section 60 of the Competition Act 1998', pp 369–374.

[92] See eg Lord Simon, HL 2R, 30 October 1997, col 1148; Margaret Beckett, HC 2R, 11 May 1998, col 35; see also DTI Press Release P/98/552, 9 July 1998.

[93] OFT 916, available at www.oft.gov.uk.   [94] OFT 916resp, available at www.oft.gov.uk.

[95] See 'The Office of Fair Trading's Discussion Paper', pp 328–329 below.

[96] BIS *A Competition Regime for Growth: A Consultation on Options for Reform*, March 2011, paras 5.49–5.52, available at www.bis.gov.uk.

[97] Civil Procedure Rules, r 30.8(1) and (3); in some cases proceedings may be commenced in the Commercial Court of the Queen's Bench Division: r 30.8(4); see also the CPR Practice Direction – Competition Law – Claims relating to the application of Articles [101 and 102 TFEU] and Chapters I and II or Part I of the Competition Act 1998, which deals, among other matters, with Articles 15 and 16 of Regulation 1/2003; it is available at www.justice.gov.uk.

[98] See Lever 'Restructuring Courts and Tribunals Hearing UK and EC Competition Law Cases' (2002) 1 Competition Law Journal 47; Brown 'Section 16 Enterprise Act 2002 – Time for Activation?' (2007) 28 ECLR 488.

[99] Note however that there is provision for the transfer between the High Court and the CAT of follow-on actions that satisfy the terms of s 47A of the Competition Act: see 'Monetary claims before the CAT', pp 317–318 below.

(D) Private international law

The issue of which Member States' courts have jurisdiction in relation to a competition law case are determined by reference to the *Brussels Regulation on Jurisdiction and the Recognition and Enforcement of Judgments in Civil and Commercial Matters*[100]. The basic rule under Article 2 of the Regulation is that the defendant should be sued where it is domiciled, although there are a number of exceptions to this: for example under Article 5 it is also possible to bring an action where the harmful act occurred or where the harm was suffered. The issue of which substantive law should be applied in a case of non-contractual obligations arising out of a restriction of competition is determined by reference to the *Regulation on the Law Applicable to Non-contractual Obligations ('Rome II')*[101]: the basic rule is that the law of the place where the market is affected or likely to be affected should be applied.

Numerous actions have been commenced in the High Court in recent years, and there have been several in the CAT as well under section 47A of the Competition Act 1998[102]; this suggests that litigants see certain advantages to litigating in England and Wales as opposed to suing in other Member States. There are various explanations for this: for example the helpful rules for discovery of evidence, effective case management procedures and considerable experience of handling complex international litigation. The judgment of the High Court in *Roche Products Ltd v Provimi Ltd*[103] revealed an interesting jurisdictional possibility. The claimant sought damages as a result of harm alleged to have been inflicted upon it by the *Vitamins* cartels[104]. Proceedings were commenced against Roche Products Ltd of the UK ('Roche UK') on the basis of Article 2 of the Brussels Regulation, as it was domiciled there. Provimi persuaded the High Court that it had 'an arguable case' that Roche UK had infringed Article 101(1) by (even unknowingly) implementing the cartels entered into by its Swiss parent company, Roche Vitamine Europa AG. The High Court also acceded to Provimi's request to join the Swiss company on the basis of Article 6 of the Regulation, which says that other entities can be joined where the claims against them are 'so closely connected that it is expedient to hear and determine them together to avoid the risk of irreconcilable judgments resulting from separate proceedings'. This meant that the presence of a subsidiary in the UK (or, more precisely, in England and Wales) could be used to establish jurisdiction over a non-UK parent. The judgment has been criticised[105], and in *Cooper Tire & Rubber Company v Shell Chemicals UK Ltd*[106] the Court of Appeal cast doubt on its correctness; however it did not actually overrule it since the point was not germane to the actual appeal in that case.

An attempt to claim jurisdiction on the basis of Article 5(3) of the Regulation, which allows a claimant to sue in the courts of the country in which it suffered harm, failed

---

[100] Council Regulation 44/2001, OJ [2001] L 12/1; for commentary on the Brussels Regulation see Dicey, Morris and Collins *The Conflict of Laws* (Sweet & Maxwell, 15th ed, 2006), ch 11 and the European Commission's *Report on the application of Regulation 44/2001* COM(2009) 174 final, 21 April 2009.

[101] Regulation 864/2007, OJ [2007] L 199/40; for discussion see Segan 'Applicable Law 'Shopping'? Rome II and Private Antitrust Enforcement in the EU' (2008) 7(3) Competition Law Journal 251; Holzmueller and von Koeckritz 'Private Enforcement of Competition Law Under the Rome II Regulation' (2010) 3(3) Global Competition Litigation Review 91; *Competition Litigation: UK Practice and Procedure* (Oxford University Press, 2010, eds Brealey and Green), ch 6.

[102] See 'Monetary claims before the CAT', pp 317–318 below.

[103] [2003] EWHC 961, [2003] UKCLR 493.   [104] OJ [2003] L 6/1, [2003] 4 CMLR 1030.

[105] See Bulst 'The Provimi Decision of the High Court: Beginnings of Private Antitrust Litigation in Europe' (2003) European Business Organisation Law Review 623 and Kennelly 'Antitrust Forum-Shopping in England: Is Provimi Ltd v Aventis Correct?' May 10(2) CPI Antitrust Chronicle, available at www.competitionpolicyinternational.com.

[106] [2010] EWCA Civ 864, [2010] UKCLR 1277, paras 45–47.

in *Sandisk Corporation v Koninklijke Philip Electronics NV*[107] where the claimant failed to demonstrate a 'good arguable case' and where other Member States indisputably had jurisdiction[108].

Under the Brussels Regulation, if litigation between two or more parties is commenced in one Member State, the courts of the other Member States are required by Article 27 of the Regulation to refrain from taking jurisdiction in relation to the same matter. In *National Grid Electricity Transmission plc v ABB Ltd*[109] the claimant commenced proceedings in the High Court in England and Wales in order to pre-empt the possibility of any of the other litigants initiating proceedings in another jurisdiction.

In some circumstances a claimant may be able to sue in the US, where it may obtain the benefit of treble damages[110]; however this may not be possible if no antitrust harm has been suffered within the US[111].

(E) **The cause of action**

The claimant's cause of action is generally considered to be for breach of statutory duty, the statute in question being the European Communities Act 1972 or the Competition Act 1998[112]. The point is not free from doubt. In *Courage Ltd v Crehan*[113] the Court of Appeal noted that Crehan would not have been able to recover damages according to the rules of that tort, since the harm he had suffered was not of the kind that Article 101 intended to prevent. However the Court of Appeal recognised that Crehan should be able to recover damages because of the direction to that effect from the Court of Justice: the EU principle of *effet utile* overrode the position at common law[114]. In *Devenish Nutrition v Sanofi-Aventis*[115] the Court of Appeal held that it is not possible to make a restitutionary award in competition cases; an 'account of profits' was precluded in particular where compensatory damages are an adequate remedy[116].

(F) **Standard of proof**

The standard of proof has been considered in a number of cases[117]: the burden of proof is on the claimant and it is incumbent on it to prove its allegations on the balance of probabilities. A similar approach has been adopted by the CAT[118]. The seriousness of what

---

[107] [2007] EWHC 332, [2007] UKCLR 1539.   [108] Ibid, para 41.

[109] [2009] EWHC 1326, [2009] UKCLR 838.

[110] On the treble damages action in US law see Jones *Private Enforcement of Antitrust Law in the EU, UK and USA* (Oxford University Press, 1999), pp 79–84.

[111] See *Hoffmann-la Roche v Empagran* 542 US 155 (2004).

[112] This was the approach taken by the House of Lords (now the Supreme Court) as regards the European Communities Act 1972 in *Garden Cottage Foods v Milk Marketing Board* [1984] AC 130, [1983] 3 CMLR 43 and in most cases since.

[113] [2004] EWCA 637, [2004] UKCLR 1500.

[114] Ibid, paras 154–168.

[115] [2008] EWCA Civ 1086, [2008] UKCLR 783, paras 104–111 (per Arden LJ) and 142–149 (per Longmore LJ); for discussion see Bailey and Brown 'Devenish Nutrition Ltd v Sanofi-Aventis SA (France): A Case Note' (2009) 8 Competition Law Journal 271.

[116] [2008] EWCA Civ 1086, [2008] UKCLR 783, para 108.

[117] *Shearson Lehman Hutton Inc v Watson Co Ltd* [1989] 3 CMLR 429 at 570; see also *Application by Anley Maritime Agencies Ltd for Judicial Review* [1999] Eu LR 97; *Arkin v Borchard Lines Ltd* [2001] Eu LR 232 and [2003] EWHC 687; *Chester City Council v Arriva plc* [2007] EWHC 1373, para 10. For discussion of this issue in the Irish High Court see *Masterfoods Ltd v HB Ice Cream Ltd* [1992] 3 CMLR 830 at 873.

[118] See eg Case No 1001/1/1/01 *Napp Pharmaceutical Holdings Ltd v Director General of Fair Trading* [2002] CAT 1, paras 98–109; Case No 1021/1/1/03 *JJB Sports Plc v OFT* [2004] CAT 17, [2005] CompAR 29,

is alleged is taken into account when considering the probabilities of an infringement having occurred; the more unlikely the allegation, the stronger the evidence must be to establish it[119]. A claim will be struck out where it does not adequately plead the facts and matters relied on to establish an alleged infringement to the requisite standard[120].

(G) Interim relief

The test for the grant of interim relief in competition cases is to decide which course (that is to say the grant or the refusal of the injunction) would involve less risk of injustice if it turns out to be wrong[121]. Applications for interim relief have sometimes been rejected on the ground that an award of damages at the trial of the action would be an adequate remedy[122]. However some applications have been successful, particularly where individuals' livelihoods were at stake[123], but also sometimes between more substantial litigants[124]. An interim injunction was granted to the claimant in *Jobserve Ltd v Network Multimedia Television*[125], where the judge was of the view that there was an arguable case that it was an abuse of a dominant position for Jobserve to refuse to accept job vacancy advertisements on its website: pending trial the balance of justice lay in the claimant's favour. A particularly striking example of a successful application for interim relief is the case of *Adidas-Salomon AG v Roger Draper and Paul Howorth*[126] in which Adidas was granted an interim injunction against the International Tennis Federation and the 'Grand Slam' tennis tournaments in relation to the dress rules for tennis players; a settlement was subsequently reached so that the case did not go to trial[127]. Interim orders were also successfully obtained in relation to a dispute in the mobile telephony sector in *Software Cellular Network Ltd v T-Mobile (UK) Ltd*[128].

An application for an interim injunction was unsuccessful in *AAH Pharmaceuticals Ltd v Pfizer Ltd*[129] where the claimants were considered to have unduly delayed their application to the court, having earlier sought (and failed to obtain) interim measures from the OFT.

(H) Is there a passing-on defence?

It has not yet been decided in the UK courts whether a purchaser that purchases goods or services from a cartel at an inflated price, but which then passes that price on to its own

---

paras 187–208.

[119] See *Ineos Vinyls Ltd v Huntsman Petrochemicals (UK) Ltd* [2006] EWHC 1241, para 211; *Chester City Council v Arriva plc* [2007] EWHC 1373, [2007] UKCLR 1582, para 10.

[120] See eg *Sel-Imperial Ltd v British Standards Institution* [2010] EWHC 854, [2010] UKCLR 493, paras 17–18; *Humber Oil Terminals Trustee Ltd v Associated British Ports* [2011] EWHC 352, paras 34 and 45.

[121] See *AAH Pharmaceuticals Ltd v Pfizer Ltd* [2007] EWHC 565, [2007] UKCLR 1561, paras 49–57; see to similar effect an earlier judgment of the Court of Appeal in *Zockoll Group Ltd v Mercury Communications Ltd* [1997] EWCA Civ 2317.

[122] See eg *Garden Cottage Foods v Milk Marketing Board* [1984] AC 130, [1983] 3 CMLR 43; *Argyll Group plc v Distillers Co plc* [1986] 1 CMLR 764; *Plessey Co plc v General Electric Co* [1990] ECC 384; *Megaphone v British Telecom* 28 February 1989, unreported, QBD; *Macarthy v UniChem* [1991] ECC 41.

[123] *Cutsforth v Mansfield Inns* [1986] 1 CMLR 1; *Holleran and Evans v Thwaites plc* [1989] 2 CMLR 917.

[124] For example ECS succeeded in obtaining an interim injunction against AKZO in the High Court as well as persuading the Commission to proceed under Article 102 in *ECS/AKZO* OJ [1983] L 252/13, [1983] 3 CMLR 694; see also *Sockel GmbH v Body Shop International plc* [1999] Eu LR 276.

[125] [2001] UKCLR 814, upheld on appeal [2002] UKCLR 184.

[126] [2006] EWHC 1318, [2006] UKCLR 823.

[127] See press release by International Tennis Federation of 4 October 2006, available at www.itftennis.com.

[128] [2007] EWHC 1790, [2007] UKCLR 1663.   [129] [2007] EWHC 565, [2007] UKCLR 1561.

customers, has a right to damages: arguably, since it has suffered no harm, the defendants should be able to rely on a 'passing-on' defence[130].

(I) Can an indirect purchaser sue?

A related issue is whether an 'indirect purchaser' – for example the customer that purchased from the immediate victim of the cartel and to whom the higher price was passed – should be able to sue for damages[131]. The policy issues around these interrelated issues are complex, and a ruling on them is eagerly awaited. In two cases pending before the CAT indirect purchasers are claiming damages against participants in the *Methionine* cartel[132].

(J) Causation

A claimant must be able to demonstrate that the anti-competitive behaviour of which it complains caused the loss it suffered[133]. In *Enron Coal Services Ltd v English Welsh & Scottish Railway Ltd*[134] the Court of Appeal agreed with the CAT that there was insufficient evidence that Enron would have won a contract but for the infringement by EW&S[135]. The fact that the Office of Rail Regulation ('the ORR') had found that EW&S had put Enron at a competitive disadvantage did not mean that Enron would have been awarded the contract; a competition authority does not necessarily find facts about causation in an infringement decision[136].

(K) Quantum

The question of quantum, that is to say the calculation of the amount of damages to be paid, remains to be decided in a competition law case. The claimant should be able to recover the difference between the price it actually paid and the price that would have prevailed in the absence of an infringement[137]: a simple principle to state, but something that can be very hard to establish in practice. The European Commission has published draft guidance on the methods that can be used to quantify damages[138].

The date at which damages are to be calculated can have an important effect on the outcome of a case. In *Courage Ltd v Crehan*[139] the High Court assessed damages at the time of the trial of the action[140]; however on appeal the Court of Appeal determined damages

---

[130] On the passing-on defence and the related issue of the right of indirect purchasers to sue see 'The "passing-on" defence and the position of indirect purchasers', pp 300–301 above; see also Kennelly 'Damages Actions before the CAT and the Passing On Defence' (2004) 3 Competition Law Journal 238; Beard 'Damages in Competition Law Litigation' in *Competition Litigation in the UK* (Sweet & Maxwell, 2005, eds Ward and Smith), paras 7–049–7–061.

[131] See 'The "passing-on" defence and the position of indirect purchasers', pp 300–301 above.

[132] Case No 1147/5/7/09 *Moy Park Ltd v Evonik Degussa GmbH*, not yet decided and Case No 1153/5/7/10 *Marshall Food Group Ltd v Evonik Degussa GmbH*, not yet decided.

[133] See eg the judgment of the Queen's Bench Division of the High Court in *Arkin v Bochard Lines Ltd* [2003] EWHC 687, paras 489–570, where the court found that there was no causation between the conduct complained of and the harm suffered by the claimant.

[134] [2009] CAT 36, [2010] CompAR 108.   [135] [2011] EWCA Civ 2.   [136] Ibid, para 150.

[137] See *Devenish Nutrition Ltd v Sanofi-Aventis SA* [2007] EWHC 2394, [2008] UKCLR 28, para 19.

[138] See also the Commission's White Paper on *Damages actions for breach of the EC antitrust rules* COM(2008) 165 final, para 2.5 and the Oxera study, ch 8 n 35 above; DG COMP's website is a valuable source of material on quantification of harm: www.ec.europa.eu/competition.

[139] See [2003] EWHC 1510, [2003] UKCLR 834.   [140] Ibid, paras 267–268.

at the time of the loss[141]. According to the High Court's formulation, Crehan would have been entitled to damages of £1,311,500: but that Court determined that, in fact, there had been no infringement of Article 101, and that therefore Crehan was not entitled to damages at all; the House of Lords agreed with the High Court[142]. The Court of Appeal did consider that Article 101 was infringed, but, by taking a different date at which to assess the harm, would have awarded only £131,336.

(L) Interest

The Court of Justice has said that interest is an essential component of compensation[143]. The High Court[144] and the CAT[145] have power to award pre-judgment interest on any damages payable; this could lead to a substantial increase in the amount that a claimant can recover.

(M) Exemplary damages?

A further issue in relation to damages actions is whether a claimant is able to recover 'punitive' or 'exemplary', as well as compensatory, damages. English law does provide for exemplary damages[146]. Where a defendant has already been ordered to pay a substantial penalty, for example by the OFT or the European Commission, for infringing competition law the High Court has held that exemplary damages are not available as this would violate the principle of *ne bis in idem*[147]; the Court was of the view that Article 16 of Regulation 1/2003 also precludes an award of exemplary damages[148]. On the other hand the CAT has acknowledged that such an award may be possible where a claimant is harmed by particularly serious anti-competitive behaviour, such as targeted and sustained predatory pricing, and where there has been no fine imposed by a competition authority[149].

(N) Sections 58 and 58A of the Competition Act 1998: findings of fact and findings of infringements

(i) Section 58: findings of fact

Section 58(1) of the Competition Act provides that, unless the court directs otherwise, findings of fact by the OFT[150] in proceedings based on UK or EU competition law are binding on the parties in proceedings before the High Court and before the CAT[151], pro-

---

[141] [2004] EWCA 637, [2004] UKCLR 1500, paras 173–180.   [142] [2007] 1 AC 333.

[143] See eg Case C-271/91 *Marshall v Southampton and South-West Hampshire Area Health Authority* [1993] ECR I-4367, para 31.

[144] Senior Courts Act 1981, s 35A.

[145] Competition Appeal Tribunal Rules 2003, SI 2003/1372, r 56(2).

[146] *Rookes v Barnard* [1964] AC 1129; *Kuddus v Chief Constable of Leicestershire* [2002] 2 AC 122; see also Clerk & Lindsell *Torts* (Sweet & Maxwell, 20th ed, 2010), paras 28.137–28.151.

[147] *Devenish Nutrition Ltd v Sanofi-Aventis SA* [2007] EWHC 2394, [2008] UKCLR 28, para 52.

[148] Ibid, para 55.

[149] Case No 1166/5/7/10 *Albion Water Ltd v Dŵr Cymru Cyfyngedig* [2010] CAT 30, paras 27–38.

[150] Or a sectoral regulator with concurrent powers to enforce Articles 101 and 102 and the Chapter I and Chapter II prohibitions: see s 371 of the Communications Act 2003 in relation to the Office of Communications (OFCOM) and s 54 of and Sch 10 to the Competition Act 1998 in relation to the other regulators.

[151] On the application of s 58 to section 47A proceedings before the CAT see *Enron Coal Services Ltd (in liquidation) v English Welsh & Scottish Railway Ltd* [2011] EWCA Civ 2, [2011] UKCLR 303, paras 33–56.

vided that the time for appeal against the finding has expired, or that the OFT's findings are confirmed on appeal. This means that parties that initiate such proceedings will not have to go through the process of producing all the evidence once again, but can proceed on the 'coat-tail' of the OFT's findings. The wording of the OFT's decision is obviously very important for the purposes of section 58. There is a significant distinction between a statement that 'A and B agreed to fix prices' and one that says 'it appears to the OFT that A and B may have fixed prices': only the former involves a finding of fact. The Court of Appeal has emphasised that section 58(1) applies only to a clearly identifiable finding of fact, and not to passages in a decision from which a finding of fact might arguably be inferred[152].

Section 58(3) of the Act enables rules of court to be made for the OFT to provide assistance to the court in private actions; no such rules have been made.

(ii) Section 58A: findings of infringement

Section 58A of the Competition Act provides that findings by the OFT[153] or the CAT of infringements of UK or EU competition law are binding on courts in which damages or other sums of money are claimed once any appeal periods have elapsed. Section 58A goes beyond section 58 of the Act, which simply relates to findings of fact; section 58A means that the substantive assessment of the OFT and the CAT binds the court hearing the claim[154].

(O) Article 16(1) of Regulation 1/2003

Section 58A of the Competition Act does not say anything about the effect of findings of infringement by the European Commission. However this matter is dealt with by Article 16(1) of Regulation 1/2003, which states that a national court cannot reach a conclusion different from that of the Commission[155]. The *Crehan* litigation shed interesting light on the operation of this provision. In that case the Commission had reached the conclusion, in relation to beer supply agreements entered into by, for example, Whitbread[156], Bass[157] and Scottish & Newcastle[158], that access to the retail level of the beer market in the UK market was foreclosed. However Crehan's agreement was not with any of those brewers, but with Courage, and the Commission had not made any findings in relation to Courage's agreements. An issue in the litigation, therefore, was whether the court was 'bound' by the Commission's findings in the *Whitbread* case. The answer given by Park J[159] and the House of Lords on appeal[160] (disagreeing with the Court of Appeal[161]) was that, since those decisions did not deal with the same facts and the same parties, they were not binding on the court, although they were admissible as evidence[162]. Park J conducted his

---

[152] Ibid, paras 56 and 148. [153] Or a sectoral regulator: see ch 8 n 150 above.

[154] Section 58A is equivalent to s 47A(9) in relation to proceedings under s 47A in the CAT; on monetary claims under s 47A see 'Section 47A: monetary claims before the CAT', pp 317–318 below.

[155] See 'Article 16: uniform application of EU competition law', pp 304–305 above.

[156] OJ [1999] L 88/26, [1999] CMLR 118, upheld on appeal in Case T-131/99 *Shaw v Commission* [2002] ECR II-2023, [2002] 5 CMLR 81.

[157] OJ [1999] L 186/1, [1999] 5 CMLR 782, upheld on appeal in Case T-231/99 *Joynson v Commission* [2002] ECR II-2085, [2002] 5 CMLR 123.

[158] OJ [1999] L 186/28, [1999] 5 CMLR 831.   [159] [2003] EWHC 1510, [2004] ECC 78.

[160] [2007] 1 AC 333, [2006] UKCLR 1232; for comment see Beal 'Crehan and Post-modern Malaise' (2007) 6(1) Competition Law Journal 17; Hanley (2007) 44 CML Rev 817.

[161] [2004] EWCA 637, [2004] ECC 407.

[162] On this point see *Iberian UK Ltd v BPB Industries and British Gypsum* [1996] 2 CMLR 601, [1997] Eu LR 1 (per Laddie J).

own assessment of the market and reached the conclusion that there was no foreclosure of the UK beer market, and that therefore the agreements in question did not infringe Article 101(1); the House of Lords upheld this finding.

(P) Group litigation orders and representative actions

Actions for damages may be facilitated by a 'group litigation order'[163] or 'representative actions'[164] under the English civil procedure rules. Group litigation orders provide for the case management of claims that give rise to common or related issues of fact or law[165]. Representative actions may provide a convenient means by which to avoid a large number of substantially similar actions; in *Emerald Supplies Ltd v British Airways plc*[166] the Court of Appeal, upholding the decision of the Chancellor of the High Court[167], concluded that the procedure could not be used in that case where the claimants wished to represent both direct and indirect purchasers from undertakings in the *Air Cargo* cartel[168]. The Court held that these two groups did not have the same interest as required by the relevant rule: an indirect purchaser would presumably agree with the defendant(s) that there is a passing-on defence, so that it (the indirect purchaser) can recover rather than the direct purchaser.

(Q) Costs and funding arrangements

The costs of litigation can be substantial. The general rule in proceedings before the High Court is that costs follow the event[169]. The CAT has a discretion in relation to costs[170], but its starting point in private actions has been to award costs against the unsuccessful party[171]. The level of costs and the likelihood that the 'loser pays' may inhibit private enforcement to an extent, although it may also guard against unmeritorious cases. In November 2010 the Ministry of Justice began a consultation exercise on reform of civil litigation funding and costs[172]. The fact that lawyers are entitled to work on a conditional fee basis may be of assistance to would-be claimants[173].

---

[163] Civil Procedure Rules, rr 19.10–19.15; a register of group litigation orders is available at www.justice.gov.uk.

[164] Civil Procedure Rules, r 19.6.

[165] The group litigation order procedure has been used in a competition case: 2001 Folio 398 *Prentice Ltd v DaimlerChrysler UK Ltd* (the case was settled before trial).

[166] [2010] EWCA Civ 1284.

[167] [2009] EWHC 741, [2009] UKCLR 801; for comment see Mulheron 'Emerald Supplies Ltd v British Airways plc; A Century Later, the Ghost of *Markt* Lives on' (2009) 8(3) Competition Law Journal 159.

[168] [2010] EWCA Civ 1284, para 62.

[169] Senior Courts Act 1981, s 51 and Civil Procedure Rules, r 44.3.

[170] Competition Appeal Tribunal Rules 2003, SI 2003/1372, r 55(2).

[171] See eg Case No 1098/5/7/08 *BCL Old Co Ltd v BASF SE* [2010] CAT 6, [2010] CompAR 214, paras 5–7.

[172] *Proposals for Reform of Civil Litigation Funding and Costs in England and Wales: Implementation of Lord Justice Jackson's Recommendations*, Cm 7947, November 2010, available at www.justice.gov.uk.

[173] Courts and Legal Services Act 1990, s 58, as amended by Access to Justice Act 1999, s 27; agreements entered into before 1 November 2005 had in addition to comply with the Conditional Fee Agreements Regulations 2000, SI 2000/692 and Conditional Fee Agreements Order 2000, SI 2000/823; after 1 November 2005 agreements must comply with the Courts and Legal Services Act 1990 and the Solicitors' Code of Conduct, 2007, r 2.03.

(R) **Limitation rules**

The limitation period for bringing actions in the High Court is generally six years from the date on which the loss was suffered[174]. The limitation period is postponed if material facts are deliberately concealed by the defendant[175], as in the case of secret cartels; time starts to run from when the claimant knew or ought to have known of those facts, which will often be when a competition authority publishes an infringement decision. A different time limit applies to follow-on actions before the CAT: proceedings must be commenced within two years of the 'relevant date'[176], which will usually be the date of the decision plus any appeal period[177]. In *BCL Old Co Ltd v BASF SE*[178] the Court of Appeal, reversing the judgment of the CAT[179], held that, where defendants appeal against the level of fines imposed by the Commission in an Article 101 case, but not against its substantive finding of an infringement, the relevant date is that of the Commission decision and not the later date of any judgment on the fines of the EU Courts. The CAT rejected a subsequent application by the claimants to be allowed to file a damages claim out of time[180]. On appeal the Court of Appeal held that the CAT has no power to extend time for a claim under section 47A[181]; likewise the High Court has no power to extend time.

(S) **Mediation**

It is understood that in some cases the High Court and the CAT encourage the parties to consider the possibility of mediation of their dispute, and that this process has led to several settlements out of court[182].

(T) **Duty of disclosure**

The High Court suggested in *Ineos Vinyls Ltd v Hunstman Petrochemicals (UK) Ltd* that a claimant before the court has a duty to inform it of any contact that it may have had with the OFT (or presumably the European Commission)[183].

(U) **Standalone actions in the High Court**

(i) **Successful claims**

Successful claims under UK and EU competition law have been fairly rare in the UK[184], although it is well known that many cases have been settled out of court in which the

---

[174] Limitation Act 1980, s 2; see generally McGee *Limitation Periods* (Sweet & Maxwell, 6th ed, 2010) and *Competition Litigation: UK Practice and Procedure* (Oxford University Press, 2010, eds Brealey and Green), ch 4.

[175] Limitation Act 1980, s 32(1)(b).   [176] Competition Appeal Tribunal Rules 2003, SI 2003/1372, r 31.

[177] For an interpretation of r 31 of the CAT's Rules see Case No 1077/4/7/07 *Emerson Electric Co v Morgan Crucible Company plc* [2007] CAT 28, [2008] CompAR 9; the CAT gave Emerson permission to make a claim for damages against Morgan Crucible on 16 November 2007: [2007] CAT 30, [2008] CompAR 37. However the CAT subsequently adopted a different interpretation of r 31 in Case No 1173/5/7/10 *Deutsche Bahn AG v Morgan Crucible Company plc* [2011] CAT 16; this conflict of authority led the CAT to grant permission to the Court of Appeal, [2011] CAT 22.

[178] *BCL Old Co Ltd v BASF SE* [2009] EWCA Civ 434, [2009] UKCLR 789.

[179] [2008] CAT 24, [2008] CompAR 210.

[180] Case 1098/5/7/08 *BCL Old Co Ltd v BASF SE* [2009] CAT 29, [2010] CompAR 1.

[181] *BCL Old Co Ltd v BASF SE* [2010] EWCA Civ 1258; BCL has appealed to the Supreme Court, not yet decided.

[182] See eg in the CAT Case No 1088/3/7/07 *ME Burgess v W Austin & Sons Ltd*, transcript of case management conference of 20 November 2007.

[183] [2006] EWCA 1241, paras 262–265.

[184] Successful applications for interim relief were discussed in 'Interim relief', p 310 above.

claimant has received substantial damages[185]. There are no final judgments in which damages have been awarded. A partially successful action was *Hendry v World Professional Billiards and Snooker Association*[186] in which Lloyd J held that, for the most part, the rules of the association did not infringe competition law; however one rule, which restricted the tournaments in which players could participate in certain circumstances, was found to infringe both the Chapter I and Chapter II prohibitions[187], as well, probably, as Articles 101 and 102 TFEU[188]. An important case was *Attheraces v British Horse Racing Board*[189] in which the High Court concluded that the British Horseracing Board had abused its dominant position under Article 102 by charging excessive and/or discriminatory prices for the supply of information to Attheraces about horseracing events conducted under its auspices; however this judgment was reversed on appeal[190]. In the case of *Purple Parking Ltd v Heathrow Airport Ltd*[191] Mann J found Heathrow Airport guilty of discrimination under Article 102(2)(c) in relation to the provision of valet parking services.

(ii) Unsuccessful claims

In *Claritas (UK) Ltd v Post Office* an application by Claritas Ltd for an interim injunction against the Post Office under the Chapter II prohibition was rejected[192]; subsequently the OFT also rejected the Claritas complaint, albeit on different grounds from those of the High Court[193]. An action for a declaration, injunction and damages under the Chapter II prohibition failed in *Chester City Council v Arriva plc*[194] where the court held that the claimant had failed to adduce any evidence demonstrating that Arriva held a dominant position. In *Bookmakers Afternoon Greyhound Services Ltd v Amalgamated Racing Ltd*[195] the High Court dismissed a claim that arrangements between a number of British racecourses for distributing their rights to broadcast horseracing infringed Article 101 and the Chapter I prohibition; the judgment was affirmed by the Court of Appeal[196]. Several other attempts to invoke the Competition Act in litigation have failed[197].

---

[185] For example some damages claims have been settled between pharmaceutical producers and the Department of Health: see eg Department of Health Press Notice of 1 April 2005, announcing the payment by Ranbaxy (UK) Ltd of £4.5 million, and the Press Releases of 4 April 2006, 22 June 2007 and 26 February 2010; see similarly Scottish Government Press Release of 4 March 2008, announcing that the Goldshield Group had agreed to pay damages of £750,000. In a different case it was announced in February 2008 that British Airways and Virgin Atlantic had made £73.5 million available to settle cases in the UK arising out of the air fuel surcharge cartel: see www.airpassengerrefund.co.uk. See further Rodger 'Private Enforcement of Competition Law, the Hidden Story: Competition Litigation Settlements in the United Kingdom, 2000–2005' (2008) 29 ECLR 96.

[186] [2002] UKCLR 5, [2002] ECC 96; for (critical) comment see Harris 'Abusive Sports Governing Bodies: Hendry v WPBSA' (2002) 1 Competition Law Journal 101; on the market definition in this case see Veljanovski 'Markets in Professional Sports: Hendry v WPSBA and the Importance of Functional Markets' (2002) 23 ECLR 273.

[187] [2002] UKCLR 5, [2002] ECC 96, para 112.

[188] Ibid, para 113.   [189] [2005] EWHC 3015, [2006] UKCLR 167.

[190] [2007] EWCA Civ 38, [2007] UKCLR 309; for further discussion of this case see ch 18, 'Cases on excessive prices', pp 725–727.

[191] [2011] EWHC 987.

[192] [2001] UKCLR 2, [2001] ECC 117.

[193] *Consignia plc/Postal Preference Service Ltd* OFT decision of 15 June 2001, available at www.oft.gov.uk.

[194] [2007] EWHC 1373, [2007] UKCLR 1582.

[195] [2010] EWHC 1743, [2010] UKCLR 1335; the High Court also dismissed, by a separate judgment, counterclaims alleging unlawful collusion between the bookmakers [2008] EWHC 2688, [2009] UKCLR 1.

[196] [2009] EWCA Civ 750, [2009] UKCLR 853; for comment see Vajda and Woolfe 'The Chapter I prohibition: Is it a Safe Bet?' (2010) 9(2) Competition Law Journal 198.

[197] *Synstar Computer Services (UK) Ltd v ICL (Sorbus) Ltd* [2001] UKCLR 585; *Land Rover Group Ltd v UPF (UK) Ltd (in receivership)* [2002] All ER (D) 323; *Getmapping plc v Ordnance Survey* [2002] EWHC 1089,

(V) **Follow-on actions in the CAT and the High Court**

The Enterprise Act 2002 amended the Competition Act 1998 in order to facilitate 'follow-on' damages actions that can be brought in the CAT and the High Court. Each of these possibilities will now be considered.

(i) **Section 47A: monetary claims before the CAT**

Section 47A of the Competition Act provides for follow-on actions for damages or any other sum of money to be brought before the CAT where there has been a finding of an infringement of UK or EU competition law by the OFT[198], the CAT or the European Commission; proceedings can be brought only with permission before any relevant appeal periods have elapsed[199]. The two-year limitation period for section 47A proceedings was discussed above[200]. The Act does not provide for a follow-on action where an NCA of another Member State has found an infringement of Articles 101 and/or 102. The right to bring a follow-on action before the CAT is without prejudice to the right to bring proceedings before the High Court[201]. Part IV of the *Competition Appeal Tribunal Rules 2003*[202] contains provisions on claims for damages under section 47A; in the CAT's view these rules are a coherent and self-standing set of procedural rules and are more general and flexible than the Civil Procedure Rules[203]. Provision is made for the transfer of claims for damages from the CAT to the High Court or County Court[204] and of follow-on actions from the High Court to the CAT[205]. Section 49 of the Act provides for an appeal on a point of law, with permission, to the Court of Appeal from a decision of the CAT on damages[206].

Four follow-on actions in the CAT arose from the European Commission's decision in the *Vitamins* case[207], of which two settled[208] and two were brought out of time[209]. In *BCL Old Co Ltd v Aventis SA*[210] the CAT declined the defendants' request that the claimants should be required to give security for costs; the CAT was concerned not to place undue obstacles in the way of the claimants. Two claims followed the European Commission's decision in *Electrical and Mechanical Carbon and Graphite Products*[211];

[2002] UKCLR 410; *Intel Corpn v VIA Technologies* [2002] EWHC 1159, reversed on appeal [2002] EWCA Civ 1905; *Suretrack Rail Services Ltd v Infraco JNP Ltd* [2002] EWHC 1316, [2002] All ER (D) 261 (Jun); *Sel-Imperial Ltd v British Standards Institution* [2010] EWHC 854, [2010] UKCLR 493 (striking out two parts of a claim alleging an infringement of Article 101); *Humber Oil Terminals Trustee Ltd v Associated British Ports* [2011] EWHC 352.

198 Or a sectoral regulator: see ch 8 n 150 above.

199 Competition Act 1998, s 47A(5), (7) and (8).

200 See 'Limitation rules', p 315 above.

201 Competition Act 1998, s 47A(10).

202 SI 2003/1372.

203 Case No 1028/5/7/04 *BCL Old Co Ltd v Aventis SA* [2005] CAT 1, [2005] CompAR 470, para 41.

204 SI 2003/1372, r 48.   205 Ibid, r 49.

206 On the scope of s 49 of the Competition Act see *English Welsh & Scottish Railway Ltd v Enron Coal Services Ltd* [2009] EWCA Civ 647, [2009] UKCLR 816, paras 22–24.

207 OJ [2003] L 6/1, [2003] 4 CMLR 1030.

208 Case Nos 1028 and 1029/5/7/04, Consent Orders of the CAT of 7 April 2005 and 24 November 2005; the CAT gave two judgments in these proceedings, one dealing with limitation [2005] CAT 1, [2005] CompAR 470 and one dealing with security for costs [2005] CAT 2, [2005] CompAR 485.

209 Case Nos 1098 and 1101/5/7/08 *BCL Old Co Ltd v BASF SE* [2008] CAT 24, on appeal [2009] EWCA Civ 434; an application for an extension of time was rejected in Case No 1098/5/7/08 *BCL Old Co Ltd v BASF SE* [2009] CAT 29, [2010] CompAR 1, upheld on appeal *BCL Old Co Ltd v BASF SE* [2010] EWCA Civ 1258; BCL has appealed to the Supreme Court, not yet decided.

210 Case No 1028/5/7/04 [2005] CAT 2, [2005] CompAR 485.

211 Case No 1077/5/7/07 *Emerson Electric Co v Morgan Crucible Co plc*, not yet decided and Case No 1173/5/7/10 *Deutsche Bahn AG v Morgan Crucible Co plc* [2011] CAT 16, [2011] CAT 22.

they have given rise to various procedural and jurisdictional issues[212]. Two actions relied on the European Commission's decision in *Methionine*[213]. Nine follow-on actions have arisen from decisions finding infringements of the Chapter II prohibition. An award of interim damages was made in one of these cases, *Healthcare at Home v Genzyme Ltd*[214], the first (and only) time that this has happened in a competition law case in the UK. The actions for damages in *ME Burgess v W Austin & Sons Ltd*[215] and *Albion Water v Dŵr Cymru* arose out of the CAT's own decisions in *Burgess v OFT*[216] *and Albion Water v Water Services Regulation Authority*[217] respectively; the *Burgess* case was settled. Two claims arose from the ORR's decision that EW&S had abused its dominant position: one was withdrawn[218], and the other was partly struck out[219] and partly dismissed at trial[220]. Four damages claims have been made in reliance on the OFT's infringement decision in *Cardiff Bus*: one by the liquidator of the alleged victim of the predatory conduct and three by its former directors[221].

(ii) Section 47B: claims brought on behalf of consumers

Section 47B of the Competition Act 1998 provides for a specified consumer body to bring a 'representative' or 'collective' follow-on action before the CAT on behalf of two or more consumers[222]; it is for the Secretary of State to specify consumer bodies for this purpose[223]. The Rules of the CAT contain provisions on claims under this section[224]. The *Specified Body (Consumer Claims) Order 2005*[225] names the Consumers' Association (now known as Which?) for the purpose of section 47B. An advantage of representative claims is that, in some cases, the economic loss suffered by individual consumers may be so small as to make litigation uneconomic. However if enough individual claims can be aggregated litigation may become viable; the representative claimant then apportions any damages recovered between the consumers that consented to the action[226]. An important limitation of section 47B is that it provides for the recovery of damages only on behalf of consumers that give their consent: this is often referred to as the 'opt-in' model. This differs from a possible alternative, the so-called 'opt-out' model, where the action is brought on behalf of a defined category of consumers; in this system consumers can opt out of

---

[212] For an overview of the *Emerson* litigation see Case No 1077/5/7/07 *Emerson Electric Co v Mersen UK Portslade Ltd* [2011] CAT 4, para 5.

[213] Case No 1147/5/7/09 *Moy Park Ltd v Evonik Degussa GmbH*, not yet decided and Case No 1153/5/7/10 *Marshall Food Group Ltd v Evonik Degussa GmbH*, not yet decided.

[214] Case No 1060/5/7/06 [2006] CAT 29, [2007] CompAR 474; note that the CAT held that the claimant could claim damages not only for the period that the OFT and the CAT itself had held that the Chapter II prohibition had been infringed, but also for the subsequent period in which the infringement continued: ibid, para 59.

[215] Case No 1087/2/3/07, order of the CAT of 25 February 2008.

[216] Case No 1044/2/1/04 [2005] CAT 25, [2005] CompAR 1151.

[217] Case No 1046/2/4/04 [2006] CAT 23, [2007] CompAR 22; [2006] CAT 36, [2007] CompAR 328 and [2008] CAT 31, [2009] CompAR 28.

[218] Case No 1105/5/7/08 *Freightliner Limited v English Welsh & Scottish Railway Ltd*, order of the CAT of 28 January 2009.

[219] Case No 1106/5/7/08 *Enron Coal Services Ltd (in liquidation) v English Welsh & Scottish Railway* [2009] CAT 7, upheld on appeal [2009] EWCA Civ 647, [2009] UKCLR 816.

[220] Case No 1106/5/7/08 *Enron Coal Services Ltd (in liquidation) v English Welsh & Scottish Railway* [2009] CAT 36, [2010] CompAR 108, partly upheld on appeal [2011] EWCA Civ 2.

[221] Case Nos 1175 to 1178/5/7/10 *DH Francis v Cardiff City Transport Services Ltd*, not yet decided.

[222] There are no provisions for representative actions to be brought on behalf of businesses as opposed to consumers.

[223] Competition Act 1998, s 47B(9).   [224] SI 2003/1372, r 33.   [225] SI 2005/2365.

[226] See s 47B(3) of the Competition Act 1998.

the litigation and, should they so wish, bring their own claims[227]. Just one representative action has been brought under section 47B, *The Consumers' Association v JJB Sports*[228]; this case arose out of the OFT's *Football Shirts* decision[229]. It was settled by agreement early in 2008 and the action was withdrawn[230].

(iii) Follow-on actions in the High Court

A number of follow-on actions for damages have been commenced in the High Court rather than in the CAT[231]. Many have relied on infringement decisions of the European Commission pursuant to Article 16 of Regulation 1/2003[232], but some have arisen from decisions of the OFT under section 58A of the Competition Act[233]. Given that the CAT is a specialist competition body, and that it has jurisdiction to deal with follow-on actions, it is interesting that some claimants nevertheless prefer to litigate in the High Court. There are various explanations for this. First, proceedings can be commenced automatically in the High Court, even when there are pending appeals against the infringement decision relied on; however claimants in the CAT must seek permission before an action can be commenced, and there is a danger that, while such permission is being sought, a litigant might bring an action in another Member State, in which case Article 27 of the Brussels Regulation would deprive the CAT of jurisdiction[234].

A second reason for selecting the High Court rather than the CAT, as already noted, is that different limitation periods apply, and in some cases the rules that apply in the High Court may be preferable to the CAT's[235]. The Court of Appeal has said that the interrelationship between the jurisdiction of the High Court and that of the CAT in this area 'may merit reassessment in the light of experience to date'[236].

4. Competition Law as a Defence

(A) Article 101(2)

(i) The sanction of voidness

Many systems of competition law deploy an important sanction, in addition to the imposition of fines and damages actions, in order to persuade undertakings to obey the law: the sanction of voidness. Article 101(2) TFEU and section 2(4) of the Competition Act 1998

---

[227] See generally Wells 'Collective Actions in the UK' (2008) 7(1) Competition Law Journal 57; Mulheron 'The Case for an Opt-out Class Action for European Member States: a Legal and Empirical Analysis' (2009) 15(3) Columbia Journal of European Law 409.

[228] Case No 1078/7/9/07.   [229] OFT decision of 1 August 2003 [2004] UKCLR 6.

[230] Case No 1078/7/9/07, order of the CAT of 14 January 2008.

[231] See for example HC08C03243 *National Grid Electricity Transmission plc v ABB Ltd* (*Gas Insulated Switchgear*); A3/2009/2487 *Cooper Tire & Rubber Company v Shell Chemicals UK Ltd* (*Butadiene Rubber*); HC10C04218 *Waha Oil v Dunlop Oil & Marine* (*Marine Hoses*); *X v Exxon Oil* (*Candle Waxes*); HC11C00383 *Honda of the UK Manufacturing Ltd v Asahi Glass Co Ltd* (*Car Glass*); there are also a number of damages claims arising out of the OFT's infringement decision of 12 April 2011 in *Reckitt Benckiser*, HC11C00319 *Secretary of State for Health v Reckitt Benckiser*.

[232] See 'Article 16: uniform application of EU competition law', pp 304–305 above.

[233] See 'Section 58A: findings of infringement', p 313 above.

[234] Competition Act 1998, s 47(5)(a) and Competition Appeal Tribunal Rules 2003, SI 2003/1372, r 31(3), on which see ch 8 n 177 above.

[235] See 'Limitation rules', p 315 above.

[236] *Enron Coal Services Ltd (In Liquidation) v English Welsh & Scottish Railway Ltd* [2011] EWCA Civ 2, para 143.

provide that an agreement that restricts competition in the sense of Article 101(1) and that does not satisfy the terms of Article 101(3) is void. In some cases the sanction of voidness may not be a very real one: the members of a price-fixing or a market-sharing cartel would not normally think of trying to enforce their agreement in a court. Their main concern will be to conceal the cartel from the competition authorities, although the latter have considerable powers to unearth this type of practice[237] and to penalise the recalcitrant firms[238]. In other cases, however, the sanction of voidness may be much more significant. If a patentee grants a licence of a patent it will calculate carefully what rate of royalties the licensee should pay and protracted negotiations may take place to settle the other terms of the bargain, for example on the quantities to be produced, the areas in which the products are to be sold and the treatment and ownership of any improvements made by the licensee. For its part the licensee will often have been granted an exclusive territory in which to manufacture and sell. If it transpires that certain aspects of the licence are void and unenforceable this will undermine the deal struck between the parties. The same would be true of an exclusive purchasing term imposed by a supplier on a distributor, as typically occurs in agreements for the sale and purchase of beer and petrol; and of non-competition covenants imposed, for example, when a vendor sells a business as a going concern to a purchaser. In these cases the threat that competition law poses is not that the Commission or some other competition authority will impose a fine, but that a key term of a contract will be unenforceable in commercial litigation. It will be noted from this that the sanction of voidness, as a general proposition, impacts not on serious infringements of the competition rules, such as the operation of cartels, but on more innocuous agreements where the harm to competition is much less obvious; this is a powerful reason for urging competition authorities to adopt a 'realistic' approach to the application of Article 101(1) and its progeny in the Member States to agreements[239].

(ii) *Eco Swiss China Time Ltd v Benetton*

Judges tend to be hostile by instinct to what may be seen as technical – even scurrilous – attempts to avoid contractual obligations by invoking points of competition law. However the Court of Justice's judgment in *Eco Swiss China Time Ltd v Benetton*[240] has confirmed how significant the sanction of voidness is in the legal system of the EU: where an agreement infringes Article 101(1), voidness is an important consequence. At the risk of oversimplification, the Court of Justice was asked by the Dutch Supreme Court to determine whether the EU competition rules could be considered to be rules of public policy: on this question turned the possibility of an appeal being brought against an arbitral award. The Court of Justice was quite clear[241]:

> Article [101 TFEU] constitutes a fundamental provision which is essential for the accomplishment of the tasks entrusted to the [EU] and, in particular, for the functioning of the internal market. The importance of such a provision led the framers of the Treaty to provide expressly, in Article [101(2) TFEU], that any agreements or decisions prohibited pursuant to that Article are to be automatically void.

---

[237] For the Commission's powers of investigation see ch 7, 'Chapter V: powers of investigation', pp 267–275.

[238] See ch 7, 'Chapter VI: penalties', pp 275–282.

[239] See ch 3, 'The "object of effect" of preventing, restricting or distorting competition', pp 115–140, in particular on what is meant by an agreement having as its 'effect' the restriction of competition.

[240] Case C-126/97 [1999] ECR I-3055, [2000] 5 CMLR 816; see also Case C-453/99 *Courage Ltd v Crehan* [2001] ECR I-6297, [2001] 5 CMLR 1058, paras 20–22.

[241] Case C-126/97 [1999] ECR I-3055, [2000] 5 CMLR 816, paras 36–37; this case is discussed further at 'Arbitration', pp 325–326 below.

It follows that where its domestic rules of procedure require a national court to grant an application for annulment of an arbitration award where such an application is founded on failure to observe national rules of public policy, it must also grant such an application where it is founded on failure to comply with the prohibition laid down in Article [101(1) TFEU].

(B) The 'problem' of Article 101(3) and the Commission's role in relation to individual exemptions

Previous editions of this book, at this point, dealt at length with the fact that only the Commission could apply Article 101(3) to individual agreements, and that this threw up numerous problems as to the enforceability of agreements between the parties; these problems concerned the rules on notification, the retrospectivity of individual exemptions, the concept of provisional validity and parallel Commission and national court proceedings. However the entry into force of Regulation 1/2003 on 1 May 2004 abolished the process of notifying agreements to the Commission for an individual exemption[242], and the Regulation itself contains several provisions on the role of national courts in the new regime[243]. For this reason the text on the 'problem' of applying Article 101(3) has been dropped from more recent editions of this book. Of course, the enforceability of an unnotified restrictive agreement prior to 1 May 2004 could still arise in domestic litigation, and readers should consult practitioners' textbooks should this problem arise in practice[244].

(C) The classic 'Euro-defence'

As suggested above there seems little doubt that the judicial mind is unsympathetic to an Article 101(2) defence where one party to an agreement freely entered into, attempts to walk away from it on the ground that it is void under competition law. The maxim 'pacta sunt servanda' – contracts should be honoured – has a powerful influence where an undertaking purports, on the basis of a 'technicality' of competition law, to avoid a contractual obligation. There are many cases in which Euro-defences have failed, including the *George Michael* case where the singer was attempting to extricate himself from a recording contract that he had entered into with Sony[245]; *Society of Lloyd's v Clementson*[246] and *Higgins v Marchant & Eliot Underwriting Ltd*[247] which concerned the plight of individuals – known as 'names' – called upon by Lloyds of London to contribute substantial sums of money as a result of insurance losses; *Oakdale (Richmond) Ltd v National Westminster Bank plc*[248] concerning the restrictive terms of an all-moneys debenture arrangement; and *Leeds City Council v Watkins*[249] where the judge was highly critical of both parties' economics experts[250].

---

[242] See in particular ch 4, 'Regulation 1/2003', pp 166–167.

[243] See 'Private enforcement and Regulation 1/2003', pp 302–305 above.

[244] See eg Bellamy and Child *European Community Law of Competition* (Oxford University Press, 6th ed, 2008, eds Roth and Rose), paras 13–004–13–007.

[245] *Panayiotou v Sony Music Entertainment (UK) Ltd* [1994] ECC 395, [1994] EMLR 229.

[246] [1995] 1 CMLR 693, [1995] ECC 390.   [247] [1996] 1 Lloyd's Rep 313, [1996] 3 CMLR 314.

[248] [1997] ECC 130, [1997] Eu LR 27, upheld on appeal [1997] 3 CMLR 815.

[249] [2003] EWHC 598, [2003] UKCLR 467.

[250] Ibid, paras 88–117; Euro-defences also failed in *LauritzenCool AB v Lady Navigation Inc* [2004] EWHC 2607; in *Days Medical Aids v Pihsiang* [2004] Eu LR 477, [2004] ECC 297; in *The Qualifying Insurers Subscribing to the ARP v Ross* [2006] ECC 33; in *Pirtek (UK) Ltd v Joinplace Ltd* [2010] EWHC 1641, [2010] UKCLR 1297; and in *A Nelson & Co Ltd v Guna SpA* [2011] EWHC 1202 (Comm).

However, the fact that many Euro-defences have failed does not mean that the invocation of Article 101(2) is always doomed to failure. Two cases demonstrate how powerful the provision can be. In *Calor Gas Ltd v Express Fuels (Scotland) Ltd*[251] the Scottish Court of Session held that an exclusive dealing agreement was unenforceable by the supplier, Calor Gas, as it infringed Article 101(1); and in *Jones v Ricoh UK Ltd*[252] the High Court held that a clause in a confidentiality agreement infringed Article 101(1) because it went much further than could reasonably be required to protect the information of the claimant.

(D) Severance

The preceding section reveals that judges may view with distaste technical invocations of the competition rules in order to avoid contractual obligations. However there will be occasions when voidness does follow from an infringement of Article 101(1): the facts of *Eco Swiss China Time v Benetton*[253] reveal how this might happen.

Where Article 101(1) is successfully invoked in litigation a problem can arise over the effect of the voidness upon the remainder of the agreement. The Court of Justice has held that, provided that it is possible to sever the offending provisions of the contract from the rest of its terms, the latter remain valid and enforceable[254]. However the Court did not lay down an EU-wide principle of severance, so that the mechanism whereby this is to be effected is a matter to be decided according to the domestic law of each Member State[255]. This in turn gives rise to issues under the Brussels Regulation[256] and Rome II[257]; the former determines where litigation may take place in civil and commercial cases, while the latter determines the law that should be applied in contractual disputes. Assuming that severability is regarded as a matter of substance rather than procedure the Brussels Regulation ought not to affect the outcome of litigation, since in principle Rome II should lead to the same finding of the applicable law, wherever the litigation takes place; however the determination of the applicable law may be crucial to the outcome of the litigation, since different Member States have different methods of severing unlawful restrictions from contracts.

As a matter of English contract law severance is possible in certain circumstances, although the rules on this subject are complex[258]. The Court of Appeal was called upon to examine severability in a competition law context in *Chemidus Wavin Ltd v Société pour la Transformation*[259]. A patentee was suing for royalties payable under an agreement that arguably infringed Article 101(1). The court held that the minimum royalties

---

[251] [2007] CSOH 170.   [252] [2010] EWHC 1743, [2010] UKCLR 1335.

[253] See Case C-126/97 [1999] ECR I-3055, [2000] 5 CMLR 816; the facts of the case are discussed at 'Arbitration', pp 325–326 below.

[254] Case 56/65 *Société Technique Minière v Maschinenbau Ulm* [1966] ECR 235, [1966] CMLR 357; Case 319/82 *Société de Vente de Ciments et Bétons de l'Est v Kerpen and Kerpen GmbH* [1983] ECR 4173, [1983] ECR 4173, [1985] 1 CMLR 511.

[255] Case 319/82 *Ciments et Bétons* (ch 8 n 254 above); Case 10/86 *VAG France SA v Etablissements Magne SA* [1986] ECR 4071, [1988] 4 CMLR 98.

[256] Council Regulation 44/2001 on Jurisdiction and the recognition and enforcement of judgments in civil and commercial matters, OJ [2001] L 12/1.

[257] Regulation 864/2007 of the European Parliament and of the Council on the law applicable to non-contractual obligations, OJ [2007] L 199/40.

[258] See *Chitty on Contracts* (Sweet & Maxwell, 30th ed, 2008), ch 16, paras 16.194–16.203; for discussion of the obligations of a national court to comply with EU law when determining whether to sever clauses in an agreement that infringes Article 101(1) see also *Re The Nullity of a Beer Agreement* [2002] ECC 26 (Austrian Supreme Court).

[259] [1977] FSR 181, [1978] 3 CMLR 514, CA.

provision was enforceable, irrespective of whether other parts of the agreement might infringe Article 101(1). Buckley LJ said:

> It seems to me that, in applying Article [101] to an English contract, one may well have to consider whether, after the excisions required by the Article of the Treaty have been made from the contract, the contract could be said to fail for lack of consideration or on any other ground, or whether the contract would be so changed in its character as not to be the sort of contract that the parties intended to enter into at all.

The test in *Chemidus Wavin* has been applied in several subsequent cases[260]. If the effect of severing certain clauses from an agreement would be that its scope and intention would be entirely altered, bringing about a fundamental change in the bargain between the parties, the entire agreement would become unenforceable[261]. This was the conclusion in *English Welsh & Scottish Railway Ltd v E.ON UK plc*[262] where Field J held that the directions of the ORR, that various terms of a coal carriage agreement between the parties were unlawful under the Chapter II prohibition and Article 102 and should be removed or modified, altered the contract so fundamentally that it became void and unenforceable in its entirety.

(E) Void or illegal?

Agreements which infringe Article 101(1) are stated by Article 101(2) to be void; however an important question is whether they are 'merely' void or whether they are also illegal. On this classification turn the important issues of whether any money paid under the contract by one party to the other would be irrecoverable, applying the principle *in pari delicto potior est conditio defendentis* (which roughly translates as 'where both parties are to blame the defendant's position is more powerful')[263], and whether one party to the agreement could bring an action against the other for damages for harm suffered as a result of the operation of the agreement. This issue was discussed above in relation to the judgment in *Courage Ltd v Crehan*[264].

(F) Transient voidness

One issue to have come before the Court of Appeal is whether the statutory prohibition in Article 101(2) may be 'turned on and off' depending on the surrounding facts[265]. In *Passmore v Morland plc*[266] the Court of Appeal upheld the Chancery Division's judgment that an agreement could move from voidness to validity (and back again) according to the effect that it might be having on the market at any particular point in time.

---

[260] *Inntrepreneur Estates Ltd v Mason* [1994] 68 P & CR 53, [1993] 2 CMLR 293; *Inntrepreneur Estates (GL) Ltd v Boyes* [1995] ECC 16, [1993] 2 EGLR 112; *Trent Taverns Ltd v Sykes* [1998] Eu LR 571, upheld on appeal [1999] Eu LR 492.

[261] See *Richard Cound Ltd v BMW (GB) Ltd* [1997] Eu LR 277; *Benford Ltd v Cameron Equipment Ltd* [1997] Eu LR 334 (Mercantile Court); *Clover Leaf Cars Ltd v BMW (GB) Ltd* [1997] Eu LR 535; *First County Garages Ltd v Fiat Auto (UK) Ltd* [1997] Eu LR 712; *Fulton Motors Ltd v Toyota (GB) Ltd* [1998] Eu LR 327.

[262] [2007] EWHC 599, [2007] UKCLR 1653.

[263] See Goff and Jones *The Law of Restitution* (Sweet & Maxwell, 7th ed, 2006), ch 24.

[264] See '*Courage Ltd v Crehan*', pp 298–299 above.

[265] See the Commission's *Guidelines on the application of Article [101(3) TFEU]* OJ [2004] C 101/97, para 44; see also the judgment of the Court of Justice in Case C-279/06 *CEPSA Estaciones de Servicio SA v LV Tobar e Hijos SL* [2008] ECR I-6681, [2008] 5 CMLR 1327, para 75.

[266] [1998] 4 All ER 468, [1998] Eu LR 580; affd [1999] Eu LR 501, [1999] 1 CMLR 1129.

(G) **Article 102**

It may be that a contractual term infringes Article 102, because it amounts to an abuse of a dominant position, as well as infringing Article 101. For example an agreement to purchase one's entire requirements of a particular product from a dominant firm is quite likely to infringe both Article 101 and Article 102[267], because it might foreclose access to the market on the part of competitors; it is irrelevant for this purpose whether the undertaking that accepts the obligation is willing or unwilling to accept it[268]. Similarly a system of loyalty rebates, which falls short of a contractual requirement not to buy from competitors but which may have the same effect, may amount to an abuse[269]. In this situation it has been assumed that the prohibition of Article 102 means that the offending provisions are void, although there is nothing on the face of Article 102, as there is in the case of Article 101(2), to say so. It would follow that a customer tied by an exclusive purchasing commitment which infringes Article 102 could safely ignore it and purchase supplies elsewhere. The impact of any such invalidity on the remainder of the agreement would raise the same question of severability discussed above[270]. In *English Welsh & Scottish Railway Ltd v E.ON UK plc*[271] the High Court concluded that abusive terms in coal carriage agreements rendered them void and unenforceable[272].

(H) **Third party as defendant**

The discussion so far has concerned contractual actions where a defendant raises UK or EU competition law as a defence. However on some occasions the competition rules (usually Article 102) are raised as a defence by a third party. In several cases the owner of an intellectual property right such as a patent, registered design or copyright has brought an action against a defendant for infringement; the defendant has then claimed that it has a defence under Article 102 on the basis that the claimant is guilty of abusing its dominant position. In particular, the defendant may claim that, by refusing to grant a licence of the intellectual property right in question, it (the claimant) is guilty of an abuse under Article 102. Whether or not a refusal to license can be abusive is itself a controversial question; it is considered in chapter 19[273]. However even if the claimant is abusing its dominant position, this will not in itself confer on the defendant a valid defence. The courts have established that there must be a sufficient nexus between the claimant's abusive behaviour and the defendant to entitle it to rely on Article 102. In *Chiron Corpn v Organon Teknika Ltd*[274] Aldous J said that:

> The fact that a person is abusing a dominant position does not mean that all wrongdoers have a defence in respect of all actions brought by that person. It is only in those cases where the exercise or existence of that right creates or buttresses the abuse will the court refuse to give effect to the exercise of the right[275].

---

[267] See eg Case 85/76 *Hoffmann-La Roche v Commission* [1979] ECR 461, [1979] 3 CMLR 211.
[268] On agreements of this kind see ch 17, 'Tying', pp 688–696.
[269] On practices of this kind see ch 18, 'Rebates that have effects similar to exclusive dealing agreements', pp 728–736.
[270] See 'Severance', pp 322–323 above.
[271] [2007] EWHC 599, [2007] UKCLR 1653.   [272] See 'Void or illegal?', p 323 above.
[273] See ch 19, 'Article 102 and Intellectual Property Rights', pp 796–806.
[274] [1993] FSR 324, [1992] 3 CMLR 813, upheld on appeal [1993] FSR 567.
[275] [1993] FSR 324, [1992] 3 CMLR 813, para 44.

In several cases the necessary nexus has been lacking[276] and the defence therefore struck out. Where there is a sufficient nexus between the parties, for example where the dominant undertaking is abusing its market power specifically in order to harm the defendant, a defence based on Articles 101 and/or 102 may be pleaded[277].

5. Arbitration

Commercial agreements very often provide for the arbitration of disputes, and it is not uncommon for competition law issues – for example the enforceability of a non-compete clause or of an exclusive purchasing obligation – to be referred to arbitration. The subject is complex; there is a growing body of literature on it[278]. The European Commission is conscious of the amount of arbitration (and of other forms of alternative dispute resolution) that takes place; indeed in its own remedies it quite often provides mechanisms for the settlement of disputes[279]. The Commission has been known to investigate cases *after* parties have settled a dispute in arbitration proceedings[280].

---

[276] See eg *ICI v Berk Pharmaceuticals* [1981] 2 CMLR 91, [1981] FSR 1; *British Leyland Motor Corpn v Armstrong Patents Co Ltd* [1984] 3 CMLR 102 (this decision was overturned in the House of Lords (now Supreme Court) on the issue of copyright protection for functional objects: [1986] AC 577); *Ransburg-GEMA AG v Electrostatic Plant Systems* [1989] 2 CMLR 712; *Philips Electronics v Ingman Ltd* [1998] Eu LR 666, ChD; *Sandvik Aktiebolag v KR Pfiffner (UK) Ltd* [1999] Eu LR 755; *HMSO v Automobile Association Ltd* [2001] Eu LR 80, [2001] ECC 273; *P&S Amusements Ltd v Valley House Leisure Ltd* [2006] EWHC 99, [2006] UKCLR 855.

[277] See eg *British Leyland v TI Silencers* [1981] 2 CMLR 75; *Lansing Bagnall v Buccaneer Lift Parts* [1984] 1 CMLR 224, [1984] FSR 241; *Pitney Bowes Inc v Francoyp-Postalia GmbH* [1990] 3 CMLR 466, [1991] FSR 72; *Intel Corpn v Via Technologies* [2002] EWCA Civ 1905, [2002] All ER (D) 346 (Dec): see Curley 'Eurodefences and Chips: "A Somewhat Indigestible Dish"' (2003) 25 EIPR 282; *Intergraph Corpn v Solid Systems* [1998] Eu LR 221; see also *Sportswear SpA v Stonestyle Ltd* [2006] EWCA 380, [2006] UKCLR 893; *Oracle America Inc v M-Tech Data Ltd* [2010] EWCA Civ 997, [2011] ECC 4, paras 36–39 (both cases under Article 101 rather than Article 102).

[278] See *Competition and Arbitration Law* (International Chamber of Commerce, 1993); Atwood 'The Arbitration of International Antitrust Disputes: A Status Report and Suggestions' [1994] Fordham Corporate Law Institute (ed Hawk), ch 15; von Mehren 'Some Reflections on the International Arbitration of Antitrust Issues' ibid, ch 16; Atwood, von Mehren and Temple Lang 'International Arbitration' ibid, ch 17; Schmitthoff 'The Enforcement of EC Competition Law in Arbitral Proceedings' [1996] Legal Issues in European Integration 101; Lugard 'EC Competition Law and Arbitration: Opposing Principles?' (1998) 19 ECLR 295 (written prior to the judgment in *Eco Swiss*); Komninos 'Arbitration and the Modernisation of European Competition Law Enforcement' (2001) 24 World Competition 211; Baudenbacher and Higgins 'Decentralization of EC Competition Law Enforcement and Arbitration' [2002] Columbia Journal of Community Law 1; Baudenbacher 'Enforcement of EC and EEA Competition Rules by Arbitration Tribunals Inside and Outside the EU' in *European Competition Law Annual 2001: Effective Enforcement of EC Antitrust Law* (Hart Publishing, 2003, eds Ehlermann and Atansiu); Dolmans and Grierson 'Arbitration and the Modernisation of EC Antitrust Law: New Opportunities and New Responsibilities' (2003) 14 ICC International Court of Arbitration Bulletin, p 37; Blessing *Arbitrating Antitrust and Merger Control Issues* (Helbing & Lichtenhahn, 2003); Nazzini 'International Arbitration and Public Enforcement of Competition Law' (2004) 25 ECLR 153; Nazzini *Concurrent Proceedings in Competition Law: Procedure, Evidence and Remedies* (Oxford University Press, 2004), chs 10 and 11; Bowsher 'Arbitration and Competition' in *Competition Litigation in the UK* (Sweet & Maxwell, 2005, eds Ward and Smith), ch 11; Landolt *Modernised EC Competition Law in International Arbitration* (Kluwer Law International, 2006); Stylopoulos 'Powers and Duties of Arbitrators in the Application of Competition Law: An EC Approach in the Light of Recent Developments' (2009) 30 ECLR 118; Blanke and Landolt *EU and US Antitrust Arbitration* (Kluwer Law International, 2011); on arbitration and the antitrust rules in the US see *Mitsubishi Motors v Soler Chrysler-Plymouth Inc* 473 US 614 (1985) and *In re Cotton Yarn Antitrust Litigation* 505 F3d 274 (4th Cir 2007).

[279] See Bowsher, ch 8 n 278 above, paras 11–036–11–042.

[280] See eg the discussion of the *Marathon* case in (2004) (Summer) *Competition Policy Newsletter* 41–43.

In *Eco Swiss China Time Ltd v Benetton International NV*[281] the Court of Justice was asked to consider the impact of the competition rules on arbitration proceedings. Benetton had granted a trade mark licence to Eco Swiss to market watches under the Benetton name. Benetton subsequently terminated the licence and Eco Swiss referred the matter to an arbitrator, under Dutch law, in accordance with the agreement. The arbitrator awarded Eco Swiss substantial damages. No competition law point was taken by the parties, and the arbitrator did not raise one. In fact the trade mark licence infringed Article 101(1) and was ineligible for block exemption under Regulation 240/96 on technology transfer agreements[282]. Benetton subsequently decided to argue that the award of damages to Eco Swiss amounted to enforcing an agreement that was contrary to EU competition law. Under Dutch law an arbitration award can be challenged before the courts, in the absence of agreement between the parties, only on grounds of public policy. The Dutch Supreme Court held that the enforcement of competition rules did not amount to public policy in Dutch law, so that if the matter were purely domestic Benetton would be unsuccessful. However, since Benetton's case rested on the EU competition rules, the matter was referred to the Court of Justice under Article 267.

As noted above the Court of Justice stressed the fundamental importance of the competition rules in the Treaty, and the importance of the sanction of voidness in ensuring compliance with them[283]. A consequence of this was that, if domestic law allowed an appeal against an arbitration award on grounds of public policy, the possibility that there might be a breach of the EU competition rules should be investigated. On a separate point the Court of Justice recognised that domestic procedural rules which prescribe time limits for the challenging of arbitral awards could have the effect of preventing an appeal based on the competition rules; provided that the time limits were not so fierce as to infringe the requirement of effective application of the competition rules they would themselves be valid.

The Court of Justice did not say anything specifically about the obligations of arbitrators themselves, but the case is of obvious importance to their role. Arbitration is intended to enable parties to disputes to reach a reasonably rapid and cheap settlement of disputes. If an arbitrator ignores points of competition law, but these can subsequently be raised on appeal as, subject to the time limit point, in *Eco Swiss*, the speedy and cheap conclusion of cases would be undermined. It seems sensible therefore that the arbitrator should apply his or her mind to the issue; however the Court of Justice's judgment in *Van Schijndel*[284] established that there is no obligation upon a national court (nor therefore upon an arbitral panel) proactively to root out infringements of the competition rules[285].

It would appear to be the case that an arbitrator could not refer an issue of competition law to the Court of Justice under Article 267; the establishment of an arbitration panel is a consensual process, with the result that it is not a 'court or tribunal of a Member State'[286].

---

[281] Case C-126/87 [1999] ECR I-3055, [2000] 5 CMLR 816; see Komninos (2000) 37 CML Rev 459.

[282] This Regulation has since been replaced by Regulation 772/2004, OJ [2004] L 123/11; it is discussed in ch 19, 'Technology Transfer Agreements: Regulation 772/2004', pp 781–791.

[283] See 'The sanction of voidness', pp 319–320 above.

[284] Cases C-430/93 etc [1995] ECR I-4705, [1996] 1 CMLR 801: see 'The duty of national courts', p 306 above; on the point in the text see *Thalès Air Defense v Euromissile*, judgment of the Paris Court of Appeal of 18 November 2004 [2006] ECC 6, where an appeal against an award of damages by an arbitral panel was dismissed since the Article 101 point had not been raised during the course of the arbitration but was only raised after the event.

[285] An interesting question is whether an arbitrator in a non-EU country would apply the competition rules, as a matter of public policy, where an agreement infringes Article 101 (or Article 102); on this point see Bowsher, n 278 above, paras 11–063–11–069.

[286] Case 102/81 *Nordsee Deutsche Hochseefischerei GmbH v Reederei Mond* [1982] ECR 1095; see further the Opinion of Advocate General Colomer in Case C-17/00 *de Coster v Collège des Bourgmestres* [2001] ECR I-9445, [2002] 1 CMLR 285.

6. Proposals for Reform

(A) The European Commission's Green and White Papers

In December 2005 the European Commission published a Green Paper, *Damages actions for breach of the EC antitrust rules*[287], which identified a number of obstacles to a more efficient system of damages claims and set out various options as to how they might be addressed. The Staff Working Paper that accompanied the Green Paper provides very useful additional information about the matters raised. These included the issue of access to evidence; the question of whether liability to damages should depend on a finding of fault; the nature and level of damages; the position of indirect purchasers and the 'passing-on' defence; representative actions on behalf of consumers; costs; the relationship between public and private enforcement; and jurisdiction and the applicable law. The Commission received a large number of responses to the Green Paper[288].

In April 2008 the Commission published a White Paper, *Damages actions for breach of the EC Antitrust Rules*[289]. At the same time it also published a Staff Working Paper[290] and an *Impact Assessment*[291] which suggested that the victims of competition infringements may be foregoing anything between €5.7 to €23.3 billion in damages per annum as a result of obstacles to private enforcement.

The key recommendations of the White Paper were that:

- victims of anti-competitive behaviour should be able to claim **single damages** for their harm, but not multiple damages; indirect purchasers should be able to claim as well as purchasers that have direct dealings with those responsible for the infringement

- **collective redress** should be available to consumers and small and medium-sized businesses through representative actions by qualified bodies such as consumer associations, state bodies and trade associations and opt-in collective actions in which victims expressly decide to combine their individual claims into a single action

- there should be a **minimum level of disclosure of evidence** across the EU between parties involved in litigation, subject to strict judicial control; adequate protection should be given to corporate statements by leniency applicants and to the investigations of competition authorities

- decisions of NCAs should have a **binding effect** on courts in the same way that Commission decisions are binding by virtue of Article 16(1) of Regulation 1/2003

- where a Member State's national law requires a finding of fault before damages can be awarded, there should be a rule that, once the victim has shown a breach of Article 101 or 102, the infringer should be liable in damages unless it can show that the infringement was the result of **excusable error.**

---

[287] COM(2005) 672 final, 19 December 2005; see also the accompanying Staff Working Paper which contains a rich source of research material; see Diemer 'The Green Paper on Damages Actions for Breach of the EC Antitrust Rules' (2006) 27 ECLR 309; Pheasant 'Damages Actions for Breach of the EC Antitrust Rules: The European Commission's Green Paper' (2006) 27 ECLR 365; Homes and Doig 'Views on the Commission's Green Paper on Damages Actions for Breach of EC Antitrust Rules: Causation and Passing-on Defence' (2006) 5 Competition Law Journal 123; Eilmansberger 'The Green Paper on damages actions for breach of the EC antitrust rules and beyond: Reflections on the utility and feasibility of stimulating private enforcement through legislative action' (2007) 44 CML Rev 431; Nebbia 'Damages actions for the infringement of EC competition law: compensation or deterrence?' (2007) 33 EL Rev 23.

[288] Available at www.ec.europa.eu.   [289] COM(2008) 154 final, 2 April 2008.
[290] SEC(2008) 404.   [291] SEC(2008) 405.

Following a period of consultation, no legislation was forthcoming; opinions differed substantially between Member States as to the nature and extent to which domestic civil procedures should be reformed.

When the new Commission took office in February 2010 it promised to consider ways in which to strengthen the private enforcement of EU law generally, not just competition law. In October 2010 Commissioner Alumnia announced that improving procedures for collective redress, such as representative actions, would be a priority[292]. In February 2011 the Commission published a consultation document *Towards a Coherent European Approach on Collective Redress*[293] in which it seeks to identify common legal principles relating to collective redress in order to develop a coherent European approach. The Commission identified six 'common core principles' to guide possible future EU initiatives on collective redress:

- a system of collective redress should deliver legally certain and fair outcomes within a reasonable time frame, while respecting the rights of all parties involved

- victims of infringements of EU law should be aware of the possibilities of bringing a collective claim and the role of representative bodies

- parties should have the option to resolve their dispute out of court through mechanisms of collective consensual dispute resolution

- there should be strong safeguards to avoid abusive litigation and the excesses of US 'class actions'

- there should be appropriate mechanisms for financing collective redress in particular for individuals and small businesses

- the rules on European civil procedural law and on applicable law should work efficiently in practice for collective actions.

The Commission invited comments on these principles by 30 April 2011. It remains to be seen how the Commission will take this agenda forward. It is possible that it will propose a directive on collective redress generally and that it will subsequently make specific proposals on facilitating damages actions in competition law cases.

(B) The Office of Fair Trading's Discussion Paper

In April 2007 the OFT published a Discussion Paper, *Private actions in competition law: effective redress for consumers and business*[294]. The Discussion Paper first discussed the principles that should inform any proposals designed to make private competition law actions more effective. It proceeded to discuss representative actions, including the possibility that representative bodies should be allowed to bring standalone actions on behalf of consumers as well as follow-on ones, and that they should be able to bring both standalone and follow-on actions on behalf of businesses. It also discussed costs and funding arrangements. The Discussion Paper then addressed evidential issues, including the suggestion that the burden of proving that a claimant has 'passed on' any higher prices to its customers should lie with the defendant. Other matters covered included the

---

[292] 'Common standards for group claims across the EU', Speech of 15 October 2010, available at www.ec.europea.eu.

[293] SEC(2011) 173, 4 February 2011, available at www.ec.europa.eu/competition/index_en.html.

[294] OFT 916, available at www.oft.gov.uk.

applicable law, effective claims resolution, and the interface with public enforcement and consistency of policy.

The OFT received a large number of responses to its Discussion Paper: these can be accessed on its website[295]. Most of the responses were favourable to steps being taken to facilitate more private actions, although there was a general recognition that care should be taken to ensure that vexatious and frivolous cases should be avoided: establishing a 'competition culture' in which victims of anti-competitive behaviour can sue for compensation should not lead to a 'litigation culture' in which unmeritorious claims are made. The responses were also clear that private actions should be a complement to, but not a replacement for, effective public enforcement by the OFT and sectoral regulators.

In November 2007 the OFT published its recommendations to the Government[296]. These were that the Government should consult on the following measures, to be designed and implemented is such a way as to comply with the principles outlined above:

- modify existing or introduce new procedures to allow representative bodies to bring standalone and follow-on actions for damages and injunctions on behalf of consumers[297]

- modify existing or introduce new procedures to allow representative bodies to bring standalone and follow-on actions for damages and injunctions on behalf of businesses

- introduce conditional fee arrangements in representative actions which allow for an increase of greater than 100 per cent on lawyers' fees

- codify courts' discretion to cap parties' costs liabilities and to provide for the courts' discretion to give the claimant cost-protection in appropriate cases

- establish a merits-based litigation fund

- require UK courts and tribunals to 'have regard' to decisions and guidance of the OFT and the sectoral regulators

- confer power on the Secretary of State to exclude leniency documents from use in litigation without the consent of the leniency applicant

- confer power on the Secretary of State to remove joint and several liability for immunity recipients in private actions for damages in competition law cases.

In March 2011 the Government announced that it will consider the OFT's recommendations following the outcome of the European Commission's consultation on collective redress[298].

---

[295] Available at www.oft.gov.uk.

[296] *Private actions in competition law: effective redress for consumers and business*, OFT 916resp, available at www.oft.gov.uk.

[297] See also the Civil Justice Council Report *Improving Access to Justice through Collective Actions*, December 2008, available at www.civiljusticecouncil.gov.uk, and the Government's response, July 2009, available at www.justice.gov.uk.

[298] *A Competition Regime for Growth: A Consultation on Options for Reform*, March 2011, paras 5.49–5.52, available at www.bis.gov.uk.

9

Competition Act 1998 – substantive provisions

1. Introduction

The Competition Act 1998, the main provisions of which entered into force on 1 March 2000, radically reformed the domestic law of the UK on restrictive agreements and anti-competitive practices. The Competition Act swept away much of the system that had been established over the preceding 50 years: the Restrictive Trade Practices Acts 1976 and 1977, the Resale Prices Act 1976 and the provisions on anti-competitive practices in the Competition Act 1980 were all repealed[1]. The Enterprise Act 2002 implemented further changes to UK competition law including the creation of a new system of market investigations[2] and merger control[3], the introduction of criminal sanctions for individuals involved in 'hard-core' cartels[4] and the disqualification of directors of companies that infringe competition law[5]. Further changes, in particular to the Competition Act 1998, were effected by the Competition Act 1998 and Other Enactments (Amendment) Regulations 2004[6] ('the Amendment Regulations') in order to bring domestic law into alignment with the principles of Regulation 1/2003[7]; these changes are incorporated in the text that follows.

Section 2 of this chapter will provide an overview of the Competition Act. Sections 3 and 4 will consider in turn the so-called Chapter I and Chapter II prohibitions in the Competition Act which are modelled upon Articles 101 and 102 TFEU respectively. Section 5 discusses the relationship between EU and domestic competition law, including the important 'governing principles' clause in section 60 of the Competition Act, which is intended to achieve consistency with EU law. Section 6 contains a table of all the decisions under the Competition Act to have been published on the website of the Office of Fair Trading ('the OFT') by 20 June 2011 and discussion of the application of the Competition Act in practice.

---

[1] On the background to the reform of domestic competition law see the fifth edition of this book, pp 306–308; Wilks 'The Prolonged Reform of UK Competition Policy' in Comparative Competition Policy (Clarendon Press, 1996, eds Doern and Wilks); Wilks *In the Public Interest* (Manchester University Press, 1999), pp 296–305; Whish 'The Competition Act 1998 and the Prior Debate on Reform' in *The Competition Act: A New Era for UK Competition Law* (Hart Publishing, 2000, eds Rodger and MacCulloch).

[2] See ch 11.   [3] See ch 22.

[4] See ch 10, 'The cartel offence', pp 425–434.

[5] See ch 10, 'Company director disqualification', pp 435–436.   [6] SI 2004/1261.

[7] OJ [2003] L 1/1.

Many of the decisions of the OFT and the sectoral regulators under the Competition Act, and Articles 101 and 102, will be discussed further in the contextual chapters in the second half of this book[8]. Private enforcement of the Act is discussed in chapter 8; public enforcement by the OFT and the sectoral regulators is considered in chapter 10.

2. The Competition Act 1998 – Overview

(A) Outline of the Act

The Competition Act 1998 is a complex piece of legislation; a number of amendments to it were made by the Enterprise Act 2002, and more by the Amendment Regulations of 2004. The Competition Act is divided into four parts, consisting of 76 sections. It contains numerous schedules which contain important detail, for example on exclusions, commitments and the role of the sectoral regulators.

(i) Part I: the Chapter I and Chapter II prohibitions

The most important provisions are found in Part I of the Act, which is divided into five chapters. In particular it introduces prohibitions that are modelled upon Article 101 TFEU ('the Chapter I prohibition') and Article 102 TFEU ('the Chapter II prohibition'). The Act confers substantial powers of investigation and enforcement on the OFT and the sectoral regulators[9]. The Act established the Competition Commission ('the CC') as the successor to the former Monopolies and Mergers Commission[10]; the CC is responsible for carrying out in-depth merger and market investigations. The Competition Appeal Tribunal ('the CAT') hears appeals against decisions of the OFT and the regulators under the Competition Act; it also has various other functions under the Enterprise Act 2002.

(ii) Part II: European investigations

Part II of the Competition Act is concerned with investigations in relation to Articles 101 and 102 TFEU, giving specific powers to a High Court judge to issue a warrant authorising the OFT to enter premises in connection with an investigation ordered or requested by the European Commission[11]. Part 2A of the Act is concerned with investigations conducted by the OFT on behalf of a competition authority of another EU Member State pursuant to Article 22 of Regulation 1/2003[12].

(iii) Part III: amendments to the Fair Trading Act 1973

Part III of the Act made some amendments to the monopoly provisions of the Fair Trading Act 1973; these, however, have been repealed and replaced by the market investigation provisions in the Enterprise Act 2002: they are described in chapter 11.

(iv) Part IV: miscellaneous amendments

Part IV of the Competition Act 1998 contains supplemental and transitional provisions, including the repeal of sections 44 and 45 of the Patents Act 1977, and provisions on Crown application.

---

[8] See eg ch 13, 'UK Law', pp 552–558 on cartels cases and see ch 18 generally.
[9] See ch 10, 'Concurrency', pp 437–439 on the concurrent powers of the OFT and the sectoral regulators.
[10] Competition Act 1998, s 45.
[11] See ch 10, 'EU investigations', p 402.
[12] Ibid.

(B) **OFT guidance**

The Competition Act 1998 requires the OFT to publish general advice and information as to how it will apply the law in practice[13]. The sectoral regulators may issue similar advice and information in relation to their respective sectors and have done so in conjunction with the OFT. A number of guidelines were published in 2000, when the Act first entered into force; most of these were revised to take into account changes introduced as a result of the adoption of Regulation 1/2003 and experience acquired under the Act. On 20 June 2011 the following guidelines had been published under the Competition Act[14]:

- *Agreements and concerted practices*[15]
- *Abuse of a dominant position*[16]
- *Market definition*[17]
- *Powers of investigation*[18]
- *Concurrent application to regulated industries*[19]
- *Enforcement*[20]
- *Trade associations, professional and self-regulatory bodies*[21]
- *Assessment of market power*[22]
- *The application of the Competition Act in the telecommunications sector*[23]
- *Vertical agreements*[24]
- *Land agreements*[25]
- *Services of general economic interest*[26]
- *The application of the Competition Act in the water and sewerage sectors*[27]
- *OFT's Guidance as to the appropriate amount of a penalty*[28]
- *Application in the energy sector*[29]
- *Application to services relating to railways*[30]
- *Application to the Northern Ireland energy sectors*[31]
- *Public transport ticketing schemes block exemption*[32]
- *Modernisation*[33]
- *Involving third parties in Competition Act investigations*[34]
- *Leniency and no-action*[35], which deals with leniency applications under both the Competition Act 1998 and the Enterprise Act 2002
- *A guide to the OFT's investigation procedures in competition cases*[36].

The following guidelines explain the application of the cartel offence and company director disqualification introduced by the Enterprise Act 2002:

- *Competition disqualification orders*[37]
- *The cartel offence*[38]
- *Powers for investigating criminal cartels*[39].

---

[13] Competition Act, s 52.   [14] The guidelines are available at www.oft.gov.uk.
[15] OFT 401, December 2004.   [16] OFT 402, December 2004.   [17] OFT 403, December 2004.
[18] OFT 404, December 2004.   [19] OFT 405, December 2004.   [20] OFT 407, December 2004.
[21] OFT 408, December 2004.   [22] OFT 415, December 2004.   [23] OFT 417, February 2000.
[24] OFT 419, December 2004.   [25] OFT 1280a, March 2011.   [26] OFT 421, December 2004.
[27] OFT 422, March 2010.   [28] OFT 423, December 2004.   [29] OFT 428, January 2005.
[30] OFT 430, October 2005.   [31] OFT 437, July 2001.   [32] OFT 439, November 2006.
[33] OFT 442, December 2004.   [34] OFT 451, April 2006.   [35] OFT 803, January 2008.
[36] OFT 1263, March 2011.   [37] OFT 510, June 2010.   [38] OFT 513, April 2003.
[39] OFT 515, January 2004.

Further guidance documents were published by the OFT on 27 June 2011.

- *Company directors and competition law*[40]
- *How your business can achieve compliance with competition law*[41].

(C) **Other information about the Competition Act**

The OFT's website[42] contains a large amount of information about the Competition Act 1998. The guidelines listed above will be found there, as will a series of 'quick guides' on particular aspects of the Act and a video on *Understanding Competition Law*. It is also possible to follow OFT investigations and consultations on the website. The OFT maintains a public register of decisions under the Competition Act, accessible on its website.

(D) **Delegated legislation under the Act**

The Secretary of State has made a number of Orders, Rules and Regulations pursuant to his powers under the Competition Act 1998, including in particular:

- The Competition Act 1998 (Small Agreements and Conduct of Minor Significance) Regulations[43]
- The Competition Act 1998 (Determination of Turnover for Penalties) Order[44]
- The Competition Act 1998 (Concurrency) Regulations 2004[45]
- The Competition Act 1998 (Appealable Decisions and Revocation of Notification of Excluded Agreements) Regulations 2004[46]
- The Competition Act 1998 (Land Agreements Exclusion and Revocation) Order 2004[47]
- The Competition Act 1998 and Other Enactments (Amendment) Regulations 2004[48]
- The Competition Act 1998 (Office of Fair Trading's Rules) Order 2004[49]
- The Competition Act 1998 (Land Agreements Exclusion Revocation) Order 2010[50]

(E) **Literature**

A large number of books and articles have been written on the Competition Act[51].

3. **The Chapter I Prohibition**

The provisions on the Chapter I prohibition are contained in sections 1 to 11 of the Act. Section 50 provides for the exclusion, by order, of vertical agreements and agreements

---

[40] OFT 1340, June 2011.   [41] OFT 1341, June 2011.   [42] www.oft.gov.uk.
[43] SI 2000/262.   [44] SI 2000/309, as amended by SI 2004/1259.   [45] SI 2004/1077.
[46] SI 2004/1078.   [47] SI 2004/1260.   [48] SI 2004/1261.   [49] SI 2004/2751.
[50] SI 2010/1709.
[51] Many of the books published in the immediate aftermath of the passage of the Act are now of little more than historical interest: a full list of them can be found on p 327 of the 6th edition of this book; of current interest see Ward and Smith (eds) *Competition Litigation in the UK* (Sweet & Maxwell, 2003); O'Neill and Sanders *UK Competition Procedure* (Oxford University Press, 2007); Green and Brealey (eds) *Competition Litigation: UK Practice and Procedure* (Oxford University Press, 2010); Roger (ed) *Ten Years of UK Competition Law Reform* (Dundee University Press, 2010); and the series of essays in (2010) 9 Competition Law Journal 141–294.

relating to land: this was effected by SI 2000/310 but was repealed for vertical agreements with effect from May 2005 by SI 2004/1260 and for land agreements with effect from April 2011 by SI 2010/1709[52]. Section 1 repealed the Acts referred to at the start of this chapter with effect from 1 March 2000. The OFT's Guidelines *Agreements and concerted practices*[53] and *Modernisation*[54] provide a useful overview of the Chapter I prohibition[55].

Section 2 contains the actual Chapter I prohibition. Section 3 provides for excluded agreements. Sections 4 and 6 provide for the making of block exemptions. Section 9 reflects Article 101(3) TFEU, setting out the criteria that an agreement must satisfy to be exempt from the Chapter I prohibition. Section 10 provides for so-called 'parallel exemption' and section 11 provided exemption for certain other agreements, but this provision is now otiose. Sections 4, 5 and 12 to 16, which dealt with the notification of agreements to the OFT for individual exemption, have been repealed by the Amendment Regulations: given that Regulation 1/2003 abolished the notification of agreements to the European Commission as a matter of EU law, it was thought appropriate to do the same as a matter of domestic law. The Chapter I prohibition is closely modelled upon Article 101 TFEU, although it is not identical in every respect[56]. Where an agreement has an effect on trade between Member States the OFT is obliged, if it decides to proceed under domestic competition law, also to apply EU law as a result of Article 3(1) of Regulation 1/2003, and Article 3(2) prevents it from reaching a stricter conclusion under domestic than under EU law[57].

The OFT has imposed penalties in several Chapter I prohibition decisions, including some in which it also found an infringement of Article 101 TFEU[58].

(A) **Section 2(1): the prohibition**

Section 2(1) provides that:

> Subject to section 3, agreements between undertakings, decisions by associations of undertakings or concerted practices which—
> (a) may affect trade within the UK, and
> (b) have as their object or effect the prevention, restriction or distortion of competition within the UK,
> are prohibited unless they are exempt in accordance with the provisions of this Part.

Section 2(2) provides an illustrative list of the kinds of agreements that might be caught by section 2(1)[59].

(i) 'Subject to section 3'

Section 3 provides for various agreements to be excluded from the Chapter I prohibition. These exclusions are considered below[60].

---

[52] See 'Section 50: land agreements', p 356 below.   [53] OFT 401, December 2004.
[54] OFT 442, December 2004.
[55] See also *Trade associations, professional bodies and self-regulatory organisations*, OFT 408; *Vertical agreements*, OFT 419; and *The application of competition law following the revocation of the Land Agreements Exclusion Order*, OFT 1280a.
[56] For detailed discussion of Article 101 TFEU see chs 3 and 4.
[57] See ch 2, 'Regulation 1/2003', pp 76–78.
[58] See the 'Table of decisions', p 374 below.
[59] See 'Section 2(2): illustrative list', p 346 below.
[60] See 'The Chapter I prohibition: excluded agreements', pp 348–356 below.

(ii) Agreements between undertakings, decisions by associations of undertakings or concerted practices

These words are identical to those in Article 101(1). These expressions are ones that have been considered in numerous judgments of the EU Courts which, as a general proposition, the OFT and sectoral regulators, the CAT and the domestic courts in the UK are obliged to follow as a result of section 60(2) of the Act[61].

(iii) 'Undertakings'

(A) General comments

As in the case of EU law[62], the term 'undertaking' is interpreted by the OFT to include any natural or legal person capable of carrying on commercial or economic activities relating to goods or services; an entity may engage in economic activity in relation to some of its functions but not others[63]. The OFT has issued a policy note on *The Competition Act 1998 and public bodies*[64]. In *Institute of Independent Insurance Brokers v Director General of Fair Trading*[65] the CAT considered that the General Insurance Standards Council (GISC), established upon the private initiative of its members rather than pursuant to a statutory requirement, was probably an undertaking for the purposes of the Chapter I prohibition, although this was not a necessary finding for the judgment[66].

A parent company and its subsidiaries will be treated as one undertaking where the subsidiaries lack economic independence with the result that agreements between them would not be subject to the Chapter I prohibition; the same would be true of agreements between two companies under the control of a third[67]. Similarly an agreement between entities which form a single economic entity are not subject to the Chapter I prohibition; this was one of the OFT's conclusions in *Anaesthetists' groups*[68], where the OFT said that a group of individuals would be treated as a single entity only if they operate and present themselves as a single entity on the market. Individuals acting under a contract of employment do not do so as undertakings[69]. In *Bid rigging in the construction industry in England* the OFT considered that firms within the same corporate group that formed a single undertaking were jointly and severally liable for the infringements[70].

The Chapter I prohibition applies to agreements 'between undertakings', but certain provisions of the Act refer to 'persons' rather than undertakings. The reason for this is that in some contexts the word 'person' is a more appropriate expression; however, in order to prevent undertakings arguing to the contrary, section 59 provides that the expression 'persons' includes 'undertakings'[71].

---

[61] For discussion of s 60 see '"Governing Principles Clause": Section 60 of the Competition Act 1998', pp 369–374 below.

[62] On the meaning of undertakings in EU law see ch 3, 'Undertakings and Associations of Undertakings', pp 83–91 and ch 5, 'Undertakings', pp 177–178.

[63] *Agreements and concerted practices*, OFT 401, para 2.5.

[64] OFT 443, August 2004 and *FENIN: Appeals and judgments*, OFT 939, January 2007.

[65] Case No 1002/2/1/01 [2001] CAT 4, [2001] CompAR 62.   [66] Ibid, paras 252–258.

[67] *Agreements and concerted practices*, OFT 401, para 2.6.

[68] OFT decision of 15 April 2003 [2003] UKCLR 695.

[69] See *ET Plus SA v Welter* [2005] EWHC 2115, [2006] 1 Lloyd's Rep 251, para 84.

[70] OFT decision of 21 September 2009 [2010] UKCLR 322, paras III.13–III.24, upheld on appeal Case No 1121/1/1/09 *Durkan Holdings Ltd v OFT* [2011] CAT 6, paras 13–92; see similarly *Construction Recruitment Forum*, OFT decision of 29 September 2009 [2010] UKCLR 14, paras 2.2–2.11.

[71] See HL Report Stage, 23 February 1998, cols 511–512.

An unusual finding in *Exchange of information on future fees by certain independent fee-paying schools*[72] was that the Secretary of State for Defence, in his capacity as the person responsible for the governance of the Royal Hospital School, was acting as an undertaking but that, as he constituted the Crown for this purpose, no penalty could be imposed as a result of section 73(1)(b) of the Competition Act[73]. The OFT held that the other schools involved in this case were undertakings, their charitable status notwithstanding[74].

(B) The Bettercare case

The scope of application of the competition rules to public-sector organisations, both as purchasers and as providers of goods and services, is clearly a matter of major significance. The issue arose in *BetterCare Group v Director General of Fair Trading*[75]. The OFT had received a complaint from BetterCare that the North & West Belfast Health and Social Services Trust had abused a dominant position by offering unfairly low prices and unfair terms in its purchases of social care from BetterCare. The Trust had a statutory duty to provide nursing and residential care to elderly people: it had nursing homes of its own, but also 'contracted out' to the private sector. The OFT considered, for a variety of reasons[76], that the Trust was not an undertaking for the purpose of the Competition Act when it purchased residential and nursing care, and therefore closed its file[77]. When upholding BetterCare's appeal[78] the CAT concluded that the Trust was, indeed, acting as an undertaking when purchasing care from private providers, and remitted the matter to the OFT to address the question of whether the Trust had acted in an abusive manner. In reaching its decision the CAT, after a thorough review of the case law of the EU Courts, concluded that no precedent addressed the factual circumstances of the case in hand[79]. In the CAT's view the contracting-out activities of the Trust amounted to an economic activity[80]: the fact that it was a purchaser rather than a provider did not affect the analysis[81]; and the Trust was active on 'a market', namely for the supply of residential and nursing care services in Northern Ireland[82]. Furthermore the Trust did not provide its services gratuitously, but sought to recover as much as possible as it could of the cost of providing care[83]. The CAT stressed that its finding that the Trust was an undertaking was quite separate from the question of whether it was guilty of abusive behaviour[84].

The subsequent judgments of the EU Courts in *FENIN v Commission*[85] cast doubt on the correctness of *BetterCare*, in that the Courts took a rather robust view that, where a public-sector body purchases goods or services in order to provide a social service, it

---

[72] OFT decision of 20 November 2006 [2007] UKCLR 361.   [73] Ibid, para 174.

[74] Ibid, paras 1311–1320.

[75] Case No 1006/2/1/01 [2002] CAT 7, [2002] CompAR 299; for comment see Skilbeck '*BetterCare*; The Conflict Between Social Policy and Economic Efficiency' [2002] 1 Comp Law 260.

[76] The OFT's arguments as to why the Trust was not an undertaking are set out at paras 221–276 of the CAT's judgment.

[77] *North & West Belfast Health and Social Services Trust* 30 April 2002 [2002] UKCLR 428.

[78] Case No 1006/2/1/01 *BetterCare Group Ltd v Director General of Fair Trading* [2002] CAT 7, [2002] CompAR 299; in an earlier judgment the CAT had found that it had jurisdiction to hear the appeal, Case No 1006/2/1/01 [2002] CAT 6, [2002] CompAR 226; on appealable decisions under the Competition Act see ch 10, 'Appealable decisions', pp 440–443.

[79] Case No 1006/2/1/01 *BetterCare Group Ltd v Director General of Fair Trading* [2002] CAT 7, [2002] CompAR 299, para 176.

[80] Ibid, paras 191–192.   [81] Ibid, paras 193–194.   [82] Ibid, paras 195–200.

[83] Ibid, para 201.   [84] Ibid, paras 210–217.

[85] Case T-319/99 *FENIN v Commission* [2003] ECR II-357, [2003] 5 CMLR 34, upheld on appeal Case C-205/03 P [2006] ECR I-6295, [2006] 5 CMLR 559: see ch 3, 'Procurement that is ancillary to a non-economic activity is not economic', pp 89–90 for discussion of this case, and the comments on it in relation to the *BetterCare* judgment.

does not do so as an undertaking. There are factual differences between the two cases: in particular the Trust had a role as a supplier as well as a purchaser of services and charged for its services, albeit not at a full market rate; this was not the case in *FENIN*. However, at a policy level, there seems to be an unwillingness in the *FENIN* judgments to extend the application of the competition rules to the procurement activities of the Spanish Health Service[86], but less of an unwillingness on the CAT's part in *BetterCare* in relation to the Health Trust. When the matter in *BetterCare* was remitted to the OFT for further consideration it reached the conclusion that the Health Trust was not abusing a dominant position anyway; it therefore did not need to decide whether the Trust was acting as an undertaking[87].

(C) The OFT's subsequent decisional practice

The OFT has not refrained from considering the application of the competition rules to other public-sector entities. For example it investigated Companies House, an executive agency of the former Department of Trade and Industry, which is required by statute to maintain a register of information about companies; it also acts commercially in markets for the provision of information[88]. In the OFT's view Companies House was acting as an undertaking when operating on these commercial markets[89]; however it found no evidence that it was cross-subsidising from its statutory operations in order to predate or to impose a margin squeeze in the commercial markets[90]. In *Cardiff Bus*[91] the OFT held that a bus company owned by Cardiff Council was acting as an undertaking when providing commercial bus services; it concluded that Cardiff Bus had abused its dominant position by predatory pricing[92].

(iv) 'Agreements'

This term is to be determined in a manner consistent with the jurisprudence of the EU Courts under Article 101(1) TFEU[93], the wording of which is followed in section 2(1). The Chapter I prohibition is capable of applying both to agreements between undertakings operating at the same level of trade (horizontal agreements) and to agreements between undertakings at different levels (vertical agreements). Agreements may be written or spoken and do not need to be legally binding[94]; a reluctant participant in an agreement can still be liable, although such reluctance may be relevant to the level of any penalty[95]. It is not legally necessary to distinguish between agreements and concerted practices. In some cases the European Commission has found a 'single overall agreement' to which a number of undertakings are party[96]. The OFT has taken the same approach in some of

---

[86] The principles in *FENIN* have since been applied by the Commission and the EU Courts in the air traffic management systems sector: Case T-155/04 *SELEX Sistemi Integrati SpA v Commission* [2006] ECR II-4797, [2007] 4 CMLR 372, paras 59–69, on appeal Case C-113/07 P [2009] ECR I-2207, [2008] 4 CMLR 1083, paras 65–123.

[87] *BetterCare Group Ltd/North & West Belfast Health & Social Services Trust*, OFT decision of 18 December 2003 [2004] UKCLR 455.

[88] OFT decision of 25 October 2002 [2003] UKCLR 24.   [89] Ibid, para 12.

[90] On predatory pricing see ch 18, 'Predatory Pricing', pp 739–754 and on vertical margin squeezes see ch 18, 'Margin Squeezing', pp 754–759.

[91] OFT decision of 18 November 2008 [2009] UKCLR 332.   [92] See Chapter 7 of the decision.

[93] See ch 3, 'Agreements', pp 99–110.

[94] *Agreements and concerted practices*, OFT 401, para 2.7, and see *Arriva/First Group*, OFT decision of 5 February 2002 [2002] UKCLR 322, paras 29–33.

[95] *Agreements and concerted practices*, OFT 401, para 2.8, and see *Construction Recruitment Forum*, OFT decision of 29 September 2009 [2010] UKCLR 14, paras 4.49, 4.81, 4.171 and 4.330.

[96] See ch 3, 'The concept of a "single, overall agreement"', pp 103–104.

its cartel decisions[97]; however the 'single overall agreement' analysis does not always apply in bid-rigging, where there may be a series of discrete agreements in relation to particular contracts, each one requiring individual analysis rather than an overall plan[98].

Two cases, best referred to as *Football Shirts* and *Toys and Games*, are of considerable interest to the meaning of agreement and/or concerted practice under the Act. In each case the OFT had found there to be agreements and/or concerted practices as to the retail prices at which these consumer goods were sold to the public[99]. The interesting feature of the cases is that the OFT decided not only that there were bilateral vertical agreements between the suppliers and their dealers, but also that there were horizontal agreements between the dealers themselves, and that these agreements had come about not, or not only, from direct contact between the dealers but also through the role played by the supplier in each case.

This can be presented in diagrammatic form:

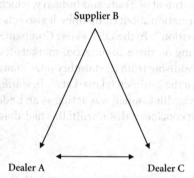

The OFT's case was that not only were there bilateral agreements between B and A and between B and C. It also found that there were trilateral agreements in each case between A, B and C which, as between A and C, were horizontal rather than vertical. At no time was there any direct communication between A and C. These horizontal agreements had come about as a result of indirect contact between A and C through the medium of B. This phenomenon is sometimes referred to as one of 'hub and spokes', where B represents the 'hub' and each of A and C is on the end of a 'spoke'.

---

[97] See eg *Construction Recruitment Forum*, OFT decision of 29 September 2009 [2010] UKCLR 14, paras 4.332–4.343 (finding that a collective boycott and price fixing formed a single overall agreement).

[98] See eg *West Midland Roofing Contractors*, OFT decision of 17 March 2004 [2004] UKCLR 1119, upheld on appeal in Case Nos 1032/1/1/04 etc *Apex Asphalt & Paving Co Ltd v OFT* [2005] CAT 4, [2005] CompAR 507; *Bid rigging in the construction industry in England*, OFT decision of 21 September 2009 [2010] UKCLR 332, paras VI.14–VI.20 (pp 1631–1632); see ch 13, 'Collusive Tendering', pp 555–557 for discussion of the OFT's decisions on bid-rigging.

[99] *Football Kit price-fixing*, OFT decision of 1 August 2003 [2004] UKCLR 6 and *Hasbro UK Ltd/Argos Ltd/Littlewoods Ltd*, OFT decision of 2 December 2003 [2004] UKCLR 717; note that, in the case of *Football Shirts*, the Consumers' Association, trading as Which?, brought a follow-on action for damages in the CAT on behalf of consumers that were overcharged: see ch 8, 'Section 47B: claims brought on behalf of consumers', pp 318–319.

The CAT agreed with the OFT's findings of a trilateral agreement in each of the cases[100]. Further appeals were taken to the Court of Appeal; the two cases were heard together and a single judgment was given[101]. The Court of Appeal agreed that there had been trilateral agreements[102]. However it suggested that the CAT's formulation of how a trilateral agreement could come about in these circumstances 'may have gone too far'[103]. The CAT had suggested that, if A were to disclose its future pricing intentions to B in circumstances in which it was 'reasonably foreseeable' that B might make use of that information and pass it on to C, there would be a concerted practice between A, B and C[104]. The Court of Appeal preferred a slightly narrower formulation, omitting the reference to reasonable foreseeability:

> If (i) retailer A discloses to supplier B its future pricing intentions in circumstances where A may be taken to intend that B will make use of that information to influence market conditions by passing that information to other retailers (of whom C is one or may be one), (ii) B does, in fact, pass that information to C in circumstances where C may be taken to know the circumstances in which the information was disclosed by A to B and (iii) C does, in fact, use the information in determining its own future pricing intentions, then A, B and C are all to be regarded as parties to a concerted practice having as its object the restriction or distortion of competition. The case is all the stronger where there is reciprocity: in the sense that C discloses to supplier B its future pricing intentions in circumstances where C may be taken to intend that B will make use of that information to influence market conditions by passing that information to (amongst others) A, and B does so.

Clearly these cases mean that an undertaking in the position of B must take care to ensure that it does not, consciously or unconsciously, act as the agent of a horizontal agreement between A and C. The point was put to the Court of Appeal that the formulation of an agreement and/or concerted practice in these cases could jeopardise normal commercial dealings between suppliers and dealers. The Court of Appeal rejected this: bilateral discussions between a supplier and a dealer of a purely vertical nature about matters such as likely retail prices, profit margins and wholesale prices and terms of sale would not give rise to problems of unlawfulness: what would be problematic would be discussions which clearly have 'a horizontal element'[105]. Permission to appeal to the House of Lords (now the Supreme Court) was rejected[106].

Where there is direct contact between two undertakings – between A and C in the example above – involving the disclosure of pricing information it is much easier to establish an agreement and/or concerted practice[107]. In the case of *Loan Pricing* Royal Bank of Scotland agreed to pay a penalty of £28.59 million after admitting direct

---

[100] Some of the OFT's findings of fact were annulled in *Football Shirts*, Case Nos 1021/1/1/03 and 1022/1/1/03 *JJB Sports plc v OFT* [2004] CAT 17, [2005] CompAR 29; the decision in *Toys and Games* was upheld in its entirely on substance, although the CAT adjusted the level of the penalties, Case Nos 1014 and 1015/1/1/03 *Argos Ltd v OFT* [2004] CAT 24, [2005] CompAR 588 (judgment on liability) and Case Nos 1014 and 1015/1/1/03 *Argos Ltd v OFT* [2005] CAT 13, [2005] CompAR 834 (judgment on penalty).

[101] *Argos Ltd v OFT* (the *Toys and Games* appeal) and *JJB Sports plc v OFT* (the *Football Shirts* appeal) [2006] EWCA Civ 1318, [2006] UKCLR 1135; see Bailey 'Contours of Collusion: Football Shirts and Toys and Games' [2006] 4 Competition Law Journal 236 and Odudu 'Indirect information Exchange: The Consistent Elements of Hud and Spoke Conclusion' (2011) 7(2) European Competition Journal 205.

[102] See paras 92–106 of the judgment in the case of *JJB Sports* and paras 138–145 in the case of *Argos Ltd*.

[103] Ibid, paras 91 and 140.

[104] See para 659 of the CAT's judgment in the *Football Shirts* appeal.

[105] See para 106 of the Court of Appeal judgment.

[106] See OFT Press Release 17/07, 7 February 2007.

[107] Case No 1061/1/1/06 *Makers UK Ltd v OFT* [2007] CAT 11, [2007] CompAR 699, paras 99–100, distinguishing such a situation from the ones in *Football Shirts* and *Toys and Games*.

collusion over the price of loan products to professional services firms; the other party to this agreement, Barclays, blew the whistle and therefore was not fined[108].

(v) 'Decisions by associations of undertakings'

This expression has been broadly interpreted in EU law[109]. A body can be classified as an association of undertakings irrespective of whether it carries on any commercial or economic activity of its own[110], and the fact that it is a 'loose knit association' does not prevent it from being an association of undertakings[111]. However a body must be 'a self-standing entity with ongoing existence', usually with members, in order to be an association of undertakings[112]. Trade associations, agricultural cooperatives and associations of sporting bodies are typical examples of associations of undertakings.

The term 'decision' has a broad meaning, including the rules of trade associations, recommendations, resolutions of the management committee and rulings of the chief executive; the crucial issue is whether the object or effect of the decision is to influence the conduct or coordinate the activity of the members[113]. The Guideline on *Trade associations, professions and self-regulating bodies*[114] provides additional guidance on the meaning of decisions[115]; it also discusses the extent to which typical activities of a trade association, such as the promulgation of codes of conduct, can infringe Article 101 TFEU and the Chapter I prohibition[116]. This Guideline also has a specific section on the position of the professions[117] and of self-regulating bodies[118].

In *Northern Ireland Livestock and Auctioneers' Association*[119] the OFT concluded that a non-binding recommendation by the Association as to the commission that its members should charge for the purchase of livestock in Northern Ireland cattle marts amounted to a decision within the Chapter I prohibition[120]. The Standard Conditions of the Film Distributors' Association were found to be a decision of an association of undertakings; certain clauses to which the OFT objected, including those that limited the ability of cinemas to determine their own prices and promotional activities, were dropped[121].

Standard conditions drawn up by a trade association will be less likely to have an appreciable effect on competition where its members have the freedom to adopt different conditions if they so wish[122].

The effect that a decision of an association might have on the UK market will depend to a certain extent on the size of the membership of the association concerned: the broader the membership of an association, the greater the influence of the association is likely to be[123].

---

[108] OFT Press Releases 34/10, 30 March 2010 and 102/10, 29 September 2010.

[109] See ch 3, 'Decisions by associations of undertakings', pp 110–112.

[110] See *GISC*, n 65 above, paras 248–250.

[111] *Northern Ireland Livestock and Auctioneer's Association* OFT decision of 3 February 2003 [2003] UKCLR 433, para 35.

[112] *Sel-Imperial Ltd v The British Standards Institution* [2010] EWHC 854, [2010] UKCLR 493, paras 36–46.

[113] *Agreements and concerted practices*, OFT 401, para 2.9.   [114] OFT 408.

[115] Ibid, paras 2.1–2.5.   [116] Ibid, paras 3.1–3.20.   [117] Ibid, paras 6.10–6.7.

[118] Ibid, paras 7.1–7.3.   [119] OFT decision of 3 February 2003 [2003] UKCLR 433.

[120] Ibid, paras 37–49.

[121] *Notification by the Film Distributors' Association of its Standard Conditions for Licensing the Commercial Exhibition of Films* OFT decision of 1 February 2002 [2002] UKCLR 343, paras 43–45.

[122] *Trade associations, professionals and self-regulating bodies*, OFT 408, para 3.18: see OFT Press Release PN 02/03, 9 January 2003, for details of amendment to three trade associations' rules to provide such freedom; see also *Royal Institute of British Architects*, Competition case closure summaries (2003), pp 5–6, available at www.oft.gov.uk/OFTwork/competition-act-and-cartels/ca98/closure/.

[123] *Trade associations, professions and self-regulating bodies*, OFT 408, para 5.3.

(vi) 'Concerted practices'

This expression will be interpreted in line with the jurisprudence of the EU Courts[124] which identifies the main elements of a concerted practice as a form of practical cooperation, knowingly entered into by the parties, which is intended to amount to a substitution for competition in the market[125]. The Court of Appeal has pointed out that concerted practices can take many different forms, and the courts have always been careful not to define or limit what may amount to a concerted practice for this purpose[126]. Contacts or communications which influence market behaviour, depending on the nature of the contact or the effect, or even potential effect, on competition, may be caught if the conduct leads to, or would have led to, a different result had the undertakings not embarked on this conduct[127].

The OFT's Guideline *Agreements and concerted practices* discusses the factors that it will take into account in establishing whether a concerted practice exists, such as whether behaviour in the market is influenced as a result of direct or indirect contact between undertakings[128]. In *Bookmakers' Afternoon Greyhound Services Ltd v Amalgamated Racing Ltd (No 2)*[129] the High Court held that, although there was some parallel behaviour on the part of a number of bookmakers, there was insufficient evidence of an alleged collective boycott by them of a new horseracing television service or of a concerted withdrawal of sponsorship from certain racecourses.

In *Apex Asphalt and Paving Co Ltd v OFT*[130] the CAT considered the meaning of a concerted practice in a case where the OFT had imposed fines on undertakings for participating in collusive tendering in relation to roofing contracts in the West Midlands[131]. Having analysed the case law of the EU Courts[132] the CAT distilled a number of principles, including that a concerted practice can arise where there are reciprocal contacts between undertakings which remove or reduce uncertainty as to their future conduct. The CAT continued that:

> reciprocal contacts are established where one competitor discloses its future intentions or conduct on the market to another when the latter requests it or, at the very least, accepts it.

The CAT proceeded to uphold the finding of the OFT that there had been an infringement in this case[133]. The OFT has applied these principles in many subsequent decisions on collusive tendering[134] and notably, in one decision, imposed fines totalling £129.2 million on 103 undertakings for *Bid rigging in the construction industry in England*[135]. On appeal the CAT annulled this decision in relation to four undertakings because the OFT had erred in its findings of fact[136].

---

[124] See ch 3, 'Meaning of concerted practice', pp 112–115.

[125] Case 48/69 *ICI v Commission* [1972] ECR 619, [1972] CMLR 557.

[126] *Argos Ltd v OFT* [2006] EWCA Civ 1318, [2006] UKCLR 1135, para 22.

[127] Cases 40/73 etc *Suiker Unie v Commission* [1975] ECR 1663, [1976] 1 CMLR 295.

[128] OFT 401, para 2.13.   [129] [2008] EWHC 2688, [2009] UKCLR 1.

[130] Case No 1032/1/1/04 [2005] CAT 4, [2005] CompAR 507.

[131] OFT decision of 17 March 2004 [2004] UKCLR 1119.

[132] Case No 1032/1/1/04 [2005] CAT 4, [2005] CompAR 507, paras 195–205.

[133] For further discussion of this case see ch 13, 'Collusive Tendering', pp 555–557 and Kar and Bailey 'The Apex Judgment: When does a Practice become Concerted?' [2005] 4 Competition Law Journal 17; on concerted practices see also Case No 1061/1/1/06 *Makers UK Ltd v OFT* [2007] CAT 11, [2007] CompAR 699, paras 99–110.

[134] See ch 13, 'Collusive Tendering', pp 555–557.

[135] OFT decision of 21 September 2009 [2010] UKCLR 322.

[136] Case No 1118/1/1/09 *GMI Construction Holdings plc v OFT* [2011] CAT 12; Case No 1121/1/1/09 *Durkan Holdings Ltd v OFT* [2011] CAT 6, paras 93–125; Case No 1122/1/1/09 *AH Willis & Sons Limited v*

(vii) 'Object or effect the prevention, restriction or distortion of competition within the UK'

(A) General comments

This concept is understood and applied in the same way as Article 101(1)[137]. In the *GISC* case[138] the CAT said that the first step is normally to determine the object of an agreement; if it is not plain that the object is to restrict competition one should then move on to consider the effects[139]. Useful guidance on the distinction between agreements that restrict by object rather than by effect can be found in the European Commission's *Guidelines on the application of [Article 101(3)]*, to which the High Court specifically had regard in *Bookmakers' Afternoon Greyhound Services v Amalgamated Racing*[140].

(B) Restriction of competition by object

The concept of a restriction of competition by object has been considered by the OFT, the CAT and the ordinary courts in several cases. The first case of note is *GISC*[141] in which the CAT held that the rules of GISC, which prevented its insurer members from dealing with insurance intermediaries unless they were themselves members of GISC, 'clearly' fell within section 2(1)(b) of the Competition Act[142]. The Tribunal's view appears to have been that the rules had the object of restricting competition[143]. The CAT annulled the OFT's decision that there was no infringement, and remitted the matter to the OFT[144] which adopted a second non-infringement decision when the offending rule had been dropped[145].

In *Exchange of information on future fees by certain independent fee-paying schools*[146] the OFT found that the exchange of future price information between 50 independent schools about the level of their intended fees had as its object the restriction of competition and made no finding on effects[147]; this case was settled by agreement between the OFT and the schools, and it actually benefited the schools that the OFT did not find anti-competitive effects – that is to say higher school fees – since that might have encouraged follow-on damages actions against them.

In *Cityhook v OFT* the High Court considered that classifying an alleged collective boycott by purchasers of a supplier offering a new technology as a restriction of competition by object had 'the attraction of simplicity'[148], but recognised that the contrary view was not unreasonable[149]: existing case law established only that a boycott of a purchaser by suppliers was restrictive by object. The judge in *Cityhook* was reluctant to add a 'new'

OFT [2011] CAT 3; Case No 1124/1/1/09 *North Midland Construction plc v OFT* [2011] CAT 14, paras 14–34; the CAT dismissed two appeals on liability see Case No 1126/1/1/09 *ISG Pearce Ltd v OFT* [2011] CAT 10, paras 24–36; Case No 1120/1/1/09 *Quarmby Construction Company Ltd v OFT* [2011] CAT 11, paras 8–140.

[137] See ch 3, 'The "object or effect" of preventing, restricting or distorting competition', p 117ff.
[138] Case No 1003/2/1/01 [2001] CAT 4, [2001] CompAR 62.
[139] [2001] CAT 4, [2001] CompAR 62, paras 169–170.
[140] [2008] EWHC 1978, [2009] UKCLR 547.
[141] Case No 1003/2/1/01 [2001] CAT 4, [2001] CompAR 62. [142] Ibid, para 192.
[143] Ibid, paras 179–192; see also paras 214–215.
[144] It is interesting to compare the approach taken by the CAT in the *GISC* case with the Court of Justice's subsequent judgment in Case C-309/99 *Wouters v Algemene Raad van de Nederlandse Orde van Advocaten* [2002] ECR I-1577, [2002] 4 CMLR 913; after *Wouters* might the CAT have asked whether the GISC rule fell outside the Chapter I prohibition, subject to a test of proportionality: see ch 3, 'Regulatory ancillarity: the judgment of the Court of Justice in *Wouters*', pp 130–133.
[145] *General Insurance Standards Council* OFT decision of 22 November 2002, [2003] UKCLR 39.
[146] OFT decision of 20 November 2006 [2007] UKCLR 361. [147] Ibid, paras 1348–1358.
[148] *R (Cityhook Ltd) v OFT* [2009] EWHC 57, [2009] UKCLR 255, para 131.
[149] Ibid, paras 132–135.

restriction by object to the existing category of such cases. The discovery of 'new' restrictions by object cannot be ruled out, but it is reasonable to suppose that this will be a rare occurrence[150]. In *Jones v Ricoh (UK) Ltd*[151] Roth J considered that a confidentiality agreement does not normally have the object of restricting competition, but held that the agreement in that case did have such an object because it went much further than could reasonably be required to protect the information of the claimant.

In *Bookmakers' Afternoon Greyhound Services v Amalgamated Racing* the High Court, upheld by the Court of Appeal, dismissed a claim by several British bookmakers that arrangements by a number of British racecourses for the collective negotiation and exclusive licensing of media rights to their own broadcasting joint venture infringed the Chapter I prohibition and Article 101(1) TFEU. The Court of Appeal endorsed the judge's conclusion that the purpose of the arrangements was to introduce competition into the previously monopsonistic market for the purchasing of horseracing media rights and that any increase in price was the consequence of that increase in competition[152]. It followed that the arrangements did not have as their object the restriction of competition[153].

The OFT and the CAT have characterised various types of collusive tendering as restrictive of competition by object[154].

In *Tobacco*[155] the OFT concluded that two tobacco manufacturers and ten retailers had entered into a number of bilateral, vertical agreements whereby the prices of various tobacco brands were linked to those of competitors' brands; the OFT did not find any multilateral or horizontal agreements. The OFT concluded that these 'price-matching' arrangements restricted each retailer's ability independently to set resale prices for cigarettes and considered that they restricted competition by object[156]. The OFT does not consider that the subjective intentions of the parties to an agreement are relevant to determining whether an agreement has as its object the restriction of competition[157].

(C) Restriction of competition by effect

Where an agreement does not have the object of restricting competition there remains the possibility that its effect, considered within its market and economic context, might be to do so[158]. Two judgments, of the CAT in *Racecourse Association v OFT*[159] and the Court of Appeal in *Bookmakers' Afternoon Greyhound Services v Amalgamated Racing*[160], were concerned with this issue. In *Racecourse Association* the CAT reached the conclu-

---

[150] See further ch 3, 'Refinement of the range of agreements within the object box', pp 124–125.

[151] [2010] EWHC 1743, [2009] UKCLR 1335.

[152] [2009] EWCA Civ 750, [2009] UKCLR 863, paras 73–94; the Court also pointed out that, in the absence of the racecourses' collaboration, there was only one buyer for the media rights and consequently no competition to be restricted: ibid, para 92.

[153] Ibid, para 94; in reaching its conclusion the Court of Appeal referred to the Court of Justice's judgment in Case C-209/07 *Competition Authority v Beef Industry Development Society Ltd* [2008] ECR I-8637, [2009] 4 CMLR 310: see ch 3, 'Market sharing, quotas, collective exclusive dealing', pp 122–123.

[154] See eg OFT decision of 21 September 2009 [2010] UKCLR 322, paras III.97–III.114 (cover bidding) and III.143–III.154 (compensation payments).

[155] OFT decision of 15 April 2010.

[156] The decision is under appeal to the CAT, Case Nos 1160–1165/1/1/10 *Imperial Tobacco Group plc & Ors v OFT*, not yet decided.

[157] *Memorandum of Understanding on the Supply of Oil Fuels in an Emergency*, OFT decision of 25 October 2001, paras 39–40.

[158] OFT 401, para 7.2; see also Case No 1003/2/1/01 *Institute of Independent Insurance Brokers v Director General of Fair Trading* [2001] CAT 4, [2001] CompAR 62, para 170.

[159] Cases Nos 1035/1/1/04 and 1041/2/1/04 [2005] CAT 29, [2005] CompAR 99.

[160] [2008] EWHC 1978, [2009] UKCLR 547, upheld on appeal [2009] EWCA Civ 750, [2009] UKCLR 863.

sion that the OFT had failed to demonstrate that the collective selling of broadcasting rights to horseracing events by racecourse owners had an anti-competitive effect: in particular the Tribunal considered that the OFT had proceeded on the basis of a 'somewhat shifting, hypothetical counterfactual situation'[161].

In *Bookmakers* the Court of Appeal considered that there was a 'strong analogy' with the *Racecourse Association* case: in each there was a need for the purchaser of rights granted by racecourses to acquire a 'critical mass' of them and, in practice, it would be very difficult to acquire those rights on the basis of individual negotiation with each racecourse owner. In particular in *Bookmakers* the Court held that the racecourses' collaboration, which meant that they could not sell their rights to licensed betting offices individually, did not have an anti-competitive effect because they arose in the context of a desire by them to create a second distributor of media rights in a market in which there had previously been only one undertaking, which was itself owned by the bookmakers. The Court of Appeal also accepted that the restrictions on the racecourses should be treated as ancillary restraints within the concept of 'objective necessity' articulated by the General Court in *Métropole télévision v Commission*[162] as they were necessary to enable the creation of a second distributor in the market. In *Pirtek (UK) Ltd v Joinplace Ltd*[163] the High Court reached a similar conclusion, that a post-term non-compete obligation in a franchise agreement was necessary and objectively justified to protect know-how.

(viii) Appreciability

The Chapter I prohibition (and Article 101 TFEU) applies only where an agreement brings about an *appreciable* restriction of competition. In determining whether an agreement has an appreciable effect the OFT has said[164] that it will have regard to the European Commission's approach as set out in the *Notice on Agreements of Minor Importance*[165]. Essentially that *Notice* states that agreements between actual or potential competitors do not appreciably restrict competition where the parties' market shares are below 10 per cent and that agreements between undertakings that are not actual or potential competitors do not do so where both parties' market share is below 15 per cent: however the *Notice* does not apply in the case of 'hard-core' restrictions of competition such as horizontal price fixing, market sharing and output restriction, nor to vertical agreements, for example to fix minimum prices or to restrict passive sales[166]. The OFT would not impose financial penalties on undertakings that have relied in good faith on the Commission's *Notice*[167]. The fact that an agreement exceeds the thresholds of the Commission's *Notice* does not mean, in itself, that any restriction of competition is appreciable: such a finding would require further analysis, in particular to determine how much market power the parties to the agreement possess[168].

---

[161] [2008] EWHC 1978, [2009] UKCLR 547, paras 177–202.
[162] Case T-112/99 [2001] ECR II-2459, [2001] 5 CMLR 1236: ancillarity is discussed at paras 469–474 and 496 of the High Court's judgment and paras 111–123 of the Court of Appeal's judgment.
[163] [2010] EWHC 1641, [2010] UKCLR 1297.
[164] *Agreements and concerted practices*, OFT 401, para 2.18.
[165] OJ [2001] C 368/13; see ch 3, 'The Commission's *Notice on Agreements of Minor Importance*', pp 140–143.
[166] See para 11 of the *Notice*.
[167] *Agreements and concerted practices*, OFT 401, para 2.19.   [168] Ibid, para 2.20.

In *GISC*[169] the CAT held that the rule of GISC prohibiting insurer members from dealing with intermediaries who were not themselves members of GISC resulted in an appreciable restriction of competition[170]. In *Construction Recruitment Forum* the OFT considered that the 'single overall agreement', comprising price fixing and a collective boycott, was capable of appreciably restricting competition, but also noted that the parties' market shares exceeded the thresholds in the Commission's *de minimis* Notice[171]. In *P&S Amusements Ltd v Valley House Leisure Ltd*[172] the High Court concluded that there was no prospect of it being found that a beer tie in a lease of a public house in Blackpool would be found to have as its effect an appreciable restriction of competition[173]. In *North Midland Construction plc v OFT*[174] the CAT confirmed the OFT's finding that an instance of cover pricing had an appreciable impact on competition[175].

(ix) Applicable law and territorial scope

Where the OFT intends to take action in relation to an agreement that it considers may be anti-competitive it must decide whether to do so on the basis of the Chapter I prohibition alone or whether it should also proceed under Article 101 TFEU. Where an agreement may affect trade between Member States Article 3(1) of Regulation 1/2003 requires it to apply Article 101[176]. The OFT will have regard to the European Commission's *Guidelines on the Effect on Trade Concept contained in Articles [101 and 102 TFEU]*[177] when considering whether an agreement might infringe Article 101 TFEU.

As far as the Chapter I prohibition is concerned, this applies only where trade *within the UK* is affected. The OFT has said that its focus will be on whether an agreement appreciably restricts competition within the UK since, if it does so, it will also affect trade there[178]. The CAT has held that the requirement that there should be an effect on trade within the UK does not require that that effect should be appreciable[179]. Its reasoning was that in EU law the requirement of an appreciable effect on trade was a jurisdictional rule to demarcate the respective spheres of application of EU and domestic competition law, and that there was no need to transcribe that reasoning to a purely domestic context. However the Chancellor of the High Court felt 'considerable misgivings' as to whether the CAT was correct on this point in *P&S Amusements Ltd v Valley House Leisure Ltd*[180]; Briggs J shared the Chancellor's reservations in *Pirtek (UK) Ltd v Joinplace Ltd*[181].

---

[169] Case No 1003/2/1/01 [2001] CAT 4, [2001] CompAR 62; for discussion of appreciability in a vertical case see *Independent Media Support Ltd/BBC Broadcast* OFCOM decision of 30 May 2007 [2007] UKCLR 1357, paras 8.1–8.25, upheld on appeal [2008] CAT 13, [2008] CompAR 161; permission to appeal was refused [2008] EWCA Civ 1402.

[170] Case No 1003/2/1/01 [2001] CAT 4, [2001] CompAR 62, paras 185–189.

[171] OFT decision of 29 September 2009 [2010] UKCLR 14, paras 4.407–4.408.

[172] [2006] EWHC 1510, [2006] UKCLR 867.

[173] Ibid, paras 23–26.   [174] Case No 1124/1/1/09 [2011] CAT 14.   [175] Ibid, paras 35–63.

[176] See ch 2, 'Obligation to apply Articles 101 and 102', pp 76–77.

[177] *Agreements and concerted practices*, OFT 401, para 2.23.   [178] Ibid, para 2.25.

[179] Case No 1009/1/1/02 *Aberdeen Journals Ltd v OFT* [2003] CAT 11, [2003] CompAR 67, paras 459–462; this was a case on the Chapter II prohibition, but in Case No 1124/1/1/09 *North Midland Construction plc v OFT* [2011] CAT 14, para 49 the CAT held that its reasoning applies equally to the Chapter I prohibition and that it would be 'irrational' to distinguish between the two; for comment see Bailey '(Appreciable) effect on trade within the United Kingdom' (2009) 30 ECLR 353.

[180] [2006] EWHC 1510, [2006] UKCLR 867, paras 21, 22 and 34.

[181] [2010] EWHC 1641, paras 61–67, in particular at para 62.

(B) **Section 2(2): illustrative list**

Section 2(2) provides that:

> Subsection (1) applies, in particular, to agreements, decisions or practices which—
>
> (a) directly or indirectly fix purchase or selling prices or any other trading conditions;
>
> (b) limit or control production, markets, technical development or investment;
>
> (c) share markets or sources of supply;
>
> (d) apply dissimilar conditions to equivalent transactions with other trading parties, thereby placing them at a competitive disadvantage;
>
> (e) make the conclusion of contracts subject to acceptance by the other parties of supplementary obligations which, by their nature or according to commercial usage, have no connection with the subject of such contracts.

This list, which exemplifies the sorts of agreement which would infringe section 2(1), is identical to the list in Article 101(1) TFEU. However it is important to stress that Article 101(1) has been applied to many other agreements that are *not* explicitly mentioned in the list, and that the same is true in the case of the Chapter I prohibition. For example an exchange of information between competitors in relation to future prices falls within Article 101(1)[182], although there is no specific reference to information exchanges in the Article itself[183]. This is because the list is merely illustrative and in each case the critical issue is whether the agreement has as its object or effect the restriction of competition. The OFT's Guideline *Agreements and concerted practices* sets out numerous examples of agreements that could infringe the Chapter I prohibition at paragraphs 3.3 to 3.27; these will be examined further in chapter 13 on cartels and hard-core restrictions of competition[184].

Section 2(2)(d) and (e) suggest that agreements to discriminate and tie-ins may amount to infringements of Article 101 or the Chapter I prohibition. It is fair to point out, however, that in the history of the application of Article 101 by the Commission there have been few cases under Article 101(1)(d) and (e). Discrimination and tie-ins are matters which usually give rise to concern in competition law only where there is significant market power on the part of the party which is practising discrimination or which is imposing the tie. For this reason these phenomena are usually investigated, if at all, under Article 102 rather than under Article 101[185].

(C) **Section 2(3): extraterritorial application**

The extraterritorial scope of the Act is considered in chapter 12[186].

(D) **Section 2(4): voidness**

Section 2(4) provides that:

> Any agreement or decision which is prohibited by subsection (1) is void.

This mirrors Article 101(2) TFEU. The possibility that agreements may be void is of considerable significance: for many firms it is the possibility that their agreements may turn

---

[182] Case C-8/08 [2009] ECR I-4529, [2009] 5 CMLR 1701, para 93.

[183] Another example would be restrictions imposed on advertising: see *Lladró Comercial*, OFT decision of 31 March 2003 [2003] UKCLR 652, paras 68–71.

[184] See ch 13, 'UK Law', pp 552–558.

[185] See ch 18, 'Price Discrimination', pp 759–764 and ch 17, 'Tying', pp 688–696.

[186] See ch 12, 'Competition Act 1998', pp 501–502.

out to be unenforceable that has as much, and in many cases more, significance than the possibility of being fined. A considerable compliance effort has to be maintained in order to ensure that important commercial transactions will not be undermined by one or more parties to an agreement subsequently reneging on it and claiming it to be unenforceable. These issues are considered in chapter 8[187]. A couple of points are worthy of mention here.

(i) Severance[188]

Section 2(4) provides that 'any agreement' which violates section 2(1) is void. It does not say that the voidness might relate only to the provisions in the agreement that violate the Chapter I prohibition, nor does it say anything about the consequence of such voidness on the remaining provisions of the agreement. However, despite the clear wording of both section 2(4) and Article 101(2) TFEU that the agreement is void, it has been established by the Court of Justice that it may be possible to sever the offending clauses, leaving the remainder of the agreement enforceable[189]. The intention is that the courts in the UK should interpret section 2(4) in the same way as the Court of Justice has interpreted Article 101(2)[190], and this will be possible by virtue of section 60 of the Act.

English contract law provides that severance is possible in certain circumstances, although the rules on this subject are complex[191]. It is a matter for the applicable law of the contract, rather than the *lex fori* of the court in which the action is brought, to determine whether, and, if so, by what criteria, severance is to be effected[192].

(ii) Void or illegal?

In *Gibbs Mew plc v Gemmell*[193] the Court of Appeal concluded that an agreement that infringes Article 101(1) is not only void and unenforceable, but is also illegal. This has serious consequences: for example a party who has paid money to another under an illegal agreement cannot recover that money unless it can be shown that the parties were not *in pari delicto*[194]. In *Crehan v Courage Ltd*[195], a case concerning Article 101 TFEU referred to the Court of Justice by the Court of Appeal under Article 267 TFEU, the Court held that it would be contrary to the effective application of Article 101 for national law to impose an absolute bar on an action by one party to an agreement that restricts competition against another party to it[196]; however, EU law does not prevent national law from denying a party who has significant responsibility for the restriction of competition the right to obtain damages from the other contracting party[197]. The principles in *Courage Ltd v Crehan* would presumably be applied in a case concerning section 2(4) of the Competition Act, pursuant to the governing principles clause in section 60 of the Competition Act[198].

---

[187] See also Whish 'The Enforceability of Agreements under EC and UK Competition Law' in *Lex Mercatoria: Essays on International Commercial Law in Honour of Francis Reynolds* (LLP, 2000, ed Rose).

[188] See generally ch 8, 'Severance', pp 322–323.

[189] Ibid.   [190] HL Report Stage, 9 February 1998, col 890.

[191] See *Chitty on Contracts* (Sweet & Maxwell, 30th ed, 2008, ed Beale), paras 16.194–16.203.

[192] See Regulation 593/2008 of the European Parliament and of the Council on the law applicable to contractual obligations OJ [2008] L 177/6; *Dicey Morris & Collins on the Conflict of Laws* (Sweet & Maxwell, 14th ed, 2006), chs 32 and 33.

[193] [1998] Eu LR 588; see also *Trent Taverns Ltd v Sykes* [1999] Eu LR 492, CA.

[194] See Goff and Jones *Law of Restitution* (Sweet & Maxwell, 7th ed, 2009), ch 24.

[195] Case C-453/99 [2001] ECR I-6297, [2001] 5 CMLR 1058; for discussion of *Crehan* see ch 8, 'Courage Ltd v Crehan', pp 298–299.

[196] [2001] ECR I-6297, [2001] 5 CMLR 1058, para 28.   [197] Ibid, paras 31–33.

[198] On s 60 of the Act, see '"Governing Principles Clauses": Section 60 of the Competition Act 1998', pp 369–374 below.

(iii) Transient voidness

In *Passmore v Morland plc*[199] the Court of Appeal held that an agreement may, in its life-time, drift into and out of unlawfulness under Article 101(1), and therefore be void and unenforceable at some times but not at others. The same presumably will be true of section 2(4) of the Competition Act.

(E) Sections 2(5) and 2(6): interpretation

These provisions explain that, except where the context otherwise requires, any reference in the Act to an agreement includes a reference to a concerted practice and a decision by an association of undertakings.

(F) Section 2(7): the UK

Section 2(7) provides that '"the UK" means, in relation to an agreement which operates or is intended to operate only in a part of the UK, that part'[200]. The UK for this purpose includes England, Wales, Scotland plus the subsidiary islands (excluding the Isle of Man and the Channel Islands) and Northern Ireland.

(G) Section 2(8): the 'Chapter I prohibition'

Section 2(8) provides that:

> The prohibition imposed by subsection (1) is referred to in this Act as 'the Chapter I prohibition'.

The expression 'the Chapter I prohibition' is therefore a legislative one, and is mirrored by section 18(4) which recognises the companion 'Chapter II prohibition'.

(H) The Chapter I prohibition: excluded agreements

Section 3 provides for a number of exclusions from the Chapter I prohibition. Some, but not all, of these exclusions apply also in the case of the Chapter II prohibition[201]. Section 50 provides for the possibility of vertical and land agreements to be excluded. Vertical and land agreements were excluded from 1 March 2000 to 1 May 2005 in the case of vertical agreements and 6 April 2011 in the case of land agreements, after which they must be assessed under the Chapter I prohibition in the same way as any other type of agreement[202]. Section 59(2) provides that if the effect of one or more exclusions is that the Chapter I prohibition is inapplicable to one or more provisions of an agreement, those provisions do not have to be disregarded when considering whether the agreement itself infringes the prohibition for other reasons. In other words, the effect of the agreement as a whole can be considered.

Section 3(1) provides that the Chapter I prohibition does not apply in any of the cases in which it is excluded by or as a result of Schedule 1 on mergers and concentrations; Schedule 2 on competition scrutiny under other enactments; and Schedule 3 on

---

[199] [1999] 3 All ER 1005, [1999] 1 CMLR 1129; see ch 8, 'Transient voidness', p 323.
[200] See eg *Arriva/First Group* OFT decision of 5 February 2002, [2002] UKCLR 322, paras 44–45.
[201] See 'Exclusions', p 369 below.
[202] See 'Section 50: vertical agreements' and 'Section 50: land agreements', p 356 below and ch 16, 'Vertical agreements under the Competition Act 1998', pp 678–680.

planning obligations and other general exclusions. Schedule 4, which excluded from the Competition Act 1998 the regulatory rules of various professions, was repealed by section 207 of the Enterprise Act 2002. The regulatory rules of the legal profession are subject to competition scrutiny under sections 57 to 61 of the Legal Services Act 2007. Section 3(2) to (5) of the Competition Act makes provision for the Secretary of State to amend Schedules 1 and 3 in certain circumstances, whether by adding additional exclusions or by amending or removing existing ones[203]. Section 3(6) notes that Schedule 3 itself enables the Secretary of State in certain circumstances to exclude agreements from the Chapter I prohibition[204].

(i) Schedule 1: mergers and concentrations

Schedule 1 to the Competition Act deals with the application of the Chapter I and Chapter II prohibitions to mergers and concentrations. The basic policy of the Schedule is that the prohibitions will not apply to mergers under the Enterprise Act nor to concentrations in respect of which the European Commission has exclusive jurisdiction under the EU Merger Regulation ('the EUMR')[205]. The exclusion in Schedule 1 is automatic and does not require an application to the OFT.

(A) Relationship of the Chapter I and Chapter II prohibitions with UK merger control[206]

Schedule 1, paragraph 1(1) provides that the Chapter I prohibition does not apply to an agreement or combination of agreements which results or would result in any two enterprises 'ceasing to be distinct enterprises' for the purposes of Part 3 of the Enterprise Act[207]. The exclusion applies to any transaction whereby enterprises cease to be distinct, irrespective of whether there is a 'relevant merger situation' capable of being investigated under the Enterprise Act[208]. If this were otherwise the Competition Act would have revolutionised the control of mergers in the UK by bringing all those transactions that are not subject to the Enterprise Act, because they fall below the relevant thresholds, within the scope of the 1998 Act, which would be an absurdity.

Schedule 1, paragraph 1(2) provides in addition that the exclusion of the Chapter I prohibition extends to 'any provision directly related and necessary to the implementation of the merger provisions': this means that 'ancillary restrictions' also fall outside the Chapter I prohibition. To be ancillary the restriction must be both 'directly related [to]' and 'necessary to the implementation of' the merger provisions. The OFT has said that it will generally follow the European Commission's approach as set out in the *Notice on restrictions directly related and necessary to concentrations*[209]. Ancillary restrictions include, for example, appropriately limited non-compete clauses, licences of intellectual property rights and know-how and purchase and supply agreements. The OFT will

---

[203] This order-making power is subject to s 71 of the Act, which requires an affirmative resolution of each House of Parliament.

[204] See 'Public policy', p 354 below on Sch 3, para 7.

[205] Council Regulation 139/2004, OJ [2004] L 24/1.

[206] See *Mergers – Jurisdictional and procedural guidance*, OFT 527, June 2009, paras 4.79–4.82.

[207] For the meaning of 'ceasing to be distinct' see s 26 Enterprise Act 2002 and ch 22, 'Enterprises ceasing to be distinct', pp 919–927; the UK exclusion is wider than the disapplication of Article 101 to concentrations in the EU, effected by Article 21(1) of the EUMR, since 'ceasing to be distinct' is a broader concept than that of a concentration under Article 3(2) of the EUMR: see ch 22, 'Enterprises ceasing to be distinct', pp 919–921; see also HL Third Reading, 5 March 1998, col 1365 (Lord Simon of Highbury).

[208] See ch 22, 'Relevant merger situations', pp 918–923.

[209] OJ [2005] C 56/24; see ch 21, 'Contractual restrictions directly related and necessary to a merger: "ancillary restraints"', pp 882–884.

not normally state in a clearance decision which restrictions are ancillary[210]: it will provide guidance only in the case of a novel or unresolved questions giving rise to genuine uncertainty[211].

(B) Newspaper mergers

Schedule 1, paragraph 3 to the Competition Act as originally drafted provided the same exclusion from the Chapter I prohibition for newspaper mergers as defined in section 57 of the Fair Trading Act 1973, and any ancillary restraints; however section 57 was repealed by the Communications Act 2003[212].

(C) Clawback

Schedule 1, paragraph 4 provides for the possibility of 'withdrawal of the paragraph 1 exclusion' by the OFT. The 'clawback' provision applies only to the Chapter I prohibition[213]; it does not apply to the Chapter II prohibition. Paragraph 4(5) therefore provides that the OFT may, by a direction in writing[214], remove the benefit of the exclusion where it considers that (a) an agreement would, if not excluded, infringe the Chapter I prohibition; and (b) the agreement is not a protected agreement[215]. These provisions will be exercised only rarely.

(D) Protected agreements

The OFT cannot exercise the right of clawback in relation to a 'protected agreement'. The Act defines four categories of protected agreement. First, an agreement in relation to which the OFT or Secretary of State, as the case may be, has published its or his decision not to make a reference to the CC; the OFT cannot override the decision not to refer a merger under the Enterprise Act by seeking to apply the Competition Act 1998. Secondly, an agreement in relation to which the CC has found there to be a relevant merger situation. Thirdly, an agreement that would result in enterprises ceasing to be distinct in the sense of section 26 of the Enterprise Act, other than as a result of subsections (3) and (4)(b) of that section[216]. Fourthly, an agreement which the CC has found gives rise to a merger in the sense of section 32 of the Water Industry Act 1991.

(E) Relationship of the Chapter I and Chapter II prohibitions with EU merger control[217]

Paragraph 6 of Schedule 1 provides that the Chapter I prohibition does not apply to concentrations which have a Community dimension. This provision is necessary in order to comply with Article 21(3) of the EUMR[218]; it provides that no Member State may apply its national legislation on competition to any concentration that has a Community dimension, since the European Commission has exclusive jurisdiction in such cases. Paragraph 6 does not mention ancillary restraints specifically, but since they are deemed to be cleared

---

[210] *Mergers – Jurisdictional and procedural guidance*, OFT 527, June 2009, para 4.81.

[211] Ibid, para 4.82.

[212] See ch 22, 'Public interest cases', pp 956–958.

[213] See the statement of Lord Simon before the HL Committee, 13 November 1997, col 328.

[214] Competition Act 1998, Sch 3, para 4(7)(a); the direction cannot be retrospective: see para 4(7)(b).

[215] Ibid, Sch 3, para 5; on protected agreements see below.

[216] See above.

[217] See the joint OFT and CC *Merger Assessment Guidelines* CC2 (Revised) OFT 1254, September 2010, paras 1.13–1.18; on the EUMR generally see ch 21.

[218] For an interpretation of Article 21(3) of the EUMR see Case No 1174/4/1/11 *Ryanair Holdings plc v OFT* [2011] CAT 23, paras 68–130; see further ch 21, 'The benefits of one-stop merger control', pp 844–845.

by a Commission decision permitting a concentration it presumably follows that Member States cannot take action in relation to them[219].

(F) *No clawback*

Since Schedule 1, paragraph 6 deals with matters that are within the exclusive jurisdiction of the European Commission, it follows that the OFT does not in this situation enjoy a right of clawback as it does under paragraph 4 in relation to mergers that are subject to the Enterprise Act 2002.

(ii) Schedule 2: competition scrutiny under other enactments[220]

Schedule 2 excludes agreements which are subject to 'competition scrutiny' under some other piece of legislation: the Government explained during the passage of the Competition Bill that, in so far as particular agreements are subject to competition scrutiny under regimes constructed to deal with the circumstances of specific sectors, it is inappropriate to subject them to the Chapter I prohibition as well, as 'that would just create an unwelcome and unjustified double jeopardy'[221].

(A) *Communications Act 2003*

Section 293 of the Communications Act 2003 requires that the Office of Communications ('OFCOM') periodically should review the 'networking arrangements' between Independent Television Ltd and the 13 regional Channel 3 licensees, including an assessment of their effect on competition. OFCOM has conducted annual reviews of these arrangements since 2005[222].

(B) *Financial Services and Markets Act 2000*[223]

This Act established the Financial Services Authority ('the FSA') with the regulatory objectives of achieving market confidence, public awareness, the protection of consumers and the reduction of financial crime[224]. Section 95 makes provision for the Treasury, by order, to establish competition scrutiny of the FSA in relation to the official listing of securities. Sections 159 to 163 provide for competition scrutiny in relation to regulating provisions and practices adopted by the FSA. The OFT must keep them under review and may report on provisions and practices having a significant adverse effect on competition[225]. Where the OFT makes a report to this effect, the CC will investigate the matter further[226]. Where the CC's report is adverse, the Treasury is given power to give directions, although it is not always bound to do so[227]. Section 164 provides for exclusion from both the Chapter I and Chapter II prohibitions for agreements, practices or conduct that are encouraged by any of the FSA's regulating provisions. Similar provisions are to be found in sections 302 to 312 in relation to recognised investment exchanges and clearing houses. The OFT published a report under section 304(3) of the Financial Services and

---

[219] See ch 21, 'Contractual restrictions directly related and necessary to a merger: "ancillary restraints"', pp 882–884.

[220] Note that the provisions in the Competition Act, as originally enacted, excluding the supervision and qualification of auditors (Sch 2, paras 2 and 3) and of certain environmental matters (Sch 2, para 6) from the Chapter I prohibition, were repealed by the Competition Act 1998 and Other Enactments (Amendment) Regulations 2004, SI 2004/1261.

[221] HL Committee, 13 November 1997, col 342.

[222] The reviews can be found at www.ofcom.org.uk.

[223] See the OFT's market study of March 2004 into the competitive effects of the Financial Services and Markets Act 2000, OFT 757, available at www.oft.gov.uk.

[224] Financial Services and Markets Act 2000, ss 1 and 2.   [225] Ibid, ss 159 and 160.

[226] Ibid, s 162 and Sch 14.   [227] Ibid, s 163.

Markets Act 2000 in July 2004 into the issuer fees of the London Stock Exchange; this investigation led to a significant reduction of earlier fee increases[228]. The OFT has agreed a *Memorandum of Understanding* with the FSA which records the basis on which they will cooperate on financial services matters[229].

(C) *Legal Services Act 2007*

Sections 57 to 61 of this legislation make provision for competition scrutiny of the regulatory rules of the legal profession by the OFT and the CC.

(D) *No power to amend Schedule 2*

There is no power to amend Schedule 2. Section 3 of the Competition Act provides the power to amend only in relation to Schedule 1 and Schedule 3.

(iii) Schedule 3: planning obligations and other general exclusions

Schedule 3 is entitled 'General Exclusions' and sets out various matters that are excluded, some of which are of considerable importance.

(A) *Planning obligations*

Paragraph 1 of Schedule 3 provides that the Chapter I prohibition does not apply to agreements involving planning obligations, for example where planning permission is given subject to the developer agreeing to provide certain services or access to facilities[230].

(B) *Section 21(2) Restrictive Trade Practices Act 1976*

Paragraph 2 of Schedule 3 provided that agreements that were the subject of directions under section 21(2) of the Restrictive Trade Practices Act 1976 were excluded from the Chapter I prohibition; however this provision was repealed with effect from 1 May 2007[231].

(C) *EEA regulated markets*

Paragraph 3 of Schedule 3 provides that the Chapter I prohibition does not apply to various matters concerning 'EEA regulated [financial services] markets'. This expression is defined in paragraph 3(5) as meaning a market which is listed by another EEA State[232] and which does not require a dealer on the market to have a presence where trading facilities are provided or on any other trading floor of that market.

(D) *Services of general economic interest*

Paragraph 4 of Schedule 3 provides that neither the Chapter I nor the Chapter II prohibition shall apply to an undertaking:

> entrusted with the operation of services of general economic interest or having the character of a revenue-earning monopoly in so far as the prohibition would obstruct the performance, in law or in fact, of the particular tasks assigned to it.

This important provision is modelled upon Article 106(2) TFEU[233], although the language of the Schedule is somewhat less tortuous than that to be found in the Treaty.

---

[228] Available at www.oft.gov.uk.
[229] Available at www.oft.gov.uk.   [230] See Town and Country Planning Act 1990, s 106.
[231] Competition Act 1998 and Other Enactments (Amendment) Regulations 2004, SI 2004/1261, reg 4, Sch 1, para 50a; for a discussion of s 21(2) of the Restrictive Trade Practices Act see vol 47 of *Halsbury's Laws of England*, para 269.
[232] Pursuant to Article 16 of Council Directive 93/22/EEC, OJ [1993] L 141/27.
[233] See ch 6, 'Article 106(2)', pp 235–242.

The OFT has published *Services of general economic interest exclusion*[234] containing important guidance on this provision. The OFT will interpret the exclusion strictly[235]. The guidance notes that, as various public-sector activities become exposed to competition or economic regulation, it is possible that certain functions that once might have been considered to be administrative or social become regarded as economic; this can have the result that an entity engaged in those activities might come to be regarded as an undertaking, and therefore fall within the purview of competition law[236]. The guidance discusses what is meant by the notion of 'entrusting' an undertaking with performance of services[237]; it also considers the meaning both of 'services'[238] and of 'general economic interest'[239]. In *Pool Reinsurance Co Ltd* the OFT was not satisfied that the scheme of terrorism reinsurance for commercial property related to services of general economic interest[240].

The OFT's guidance notes that in a number of EU cases Article 106(2) has been held to be applicable where an undertaking was subject to a universal service obligation and needed to be protected from 'cream-skimming' or 'cherry-picking'[241]. However it also notes that in the UK the combined effect of privatisation, liberalisation and EU initiatives has been that the number of exclusive rights held by undertakings has been significantly reduced[242]. The OFT's view is that, in general, effective competition will best serve the interests of consumers over time, which is why it will interpret the exclusion narrowly. The OFT's guidance concludes by saying that it is unlikely that there are any 'revenue-earning monopolies' of the kind referred to in Schedule 3, paragraph 4 in the UK[243].

The OFT has published specific guidance on the exclusion of services of general economic interest within the energy and railway sectors[244].

(E) Compliance with legal requirements

Paragraph 5 of Schedule 3 provides that neither the Chapter I nor the Chapter II prohibition applies to an agreement or to conduct that is required to comply with a legal requirement. For this purpose a legal requirement is one imposed by or under any enactment in force in the UK, by or under the TFEU or the EEA Agreement and having legal effect in the UK without further enactment, or under the law in force in another Member State having legal effect in the UK. An example of the operation of this exclusion occurred in the case of *Vodafone*[245], in which OFCOM accepted that Vodafone had printed prices on its 'pre-pay mobile phone vouchers' in order to comply with a licence condition; it followed that Vodafone could not be found guilty of infringing the Chapter I prohibition[246]. OFCOM subsequently removed the price publication requirement from Vodafone's licence, so that the exclusion no longer applied. Similarly an undertaking could not be found liable under the Act where it had done something required, for example, by a Commission Directive adopted under Article 106(3) TFEU[247].

The exclusion in paragraph 5 of Schedule 3 applies only where the regulated undertaking is required to act in a certain way; it does not apply to the discretionary behaviour of that undertaking. In *Re-investigation of a complaint from VIP Communications Ltd*[248]

---

[234] OFT 421, December 2004.

[235] Ibid, para 1.9.   [236] Ibid, para 2.7.   [237] Ibid, paras 2.9–2.15.   [238] Ibid, paras 2.16–2.18.

[239] Ibid, paras 2.19–2.22.   [240] OFT decision of 15 April 2004 [2004] UKCLR 893, paras 71–74.

[241] *Services of general economic interest* OFT 421, para 3.4.

[242] Ibid, para 3.5.   [243] Ibid, paras 4.1–4.4.

[244] *Application in the energy sector*, OFT 428, January 2005, paras 3.34–3.38 and *Application to services relating to railways*, OFT 430, October 2005, paras 3.18–3.21.

[245] OFTEL decision of 5 April 2002.   [246] Ibid, para 47.

[247] See ch 6, 'Article 106(3)', pp 242–244.

[248] OFCOM decision of 28 June 2005 [2005] UKCLR 914, appeal rejected in Case No 1027/2/3/04 *VIP Communications Ltd (in administration) v OFCOM* [2009] CAT 28, [2010] UKCLR 13.

OFCOM considered that T-Mobile was able to rely on Schedule 3, paragraph 5 in refusing to supply certain services to VIP Communications in circumstances where it knew that VIP would use those services in order to act unlawfully in violation of the Wireless Telegraphy Act 1949: OFCOM considered that T-Mobile was required by law to desist from conduct that would result in illegal behaviour[249].

In *Albion Water Ltd* the CAT disagreed with the view of the Regulation Authority Water Services[250] that the new provisions of the Water Industry Act 1991 constituted a legal requirement for the purposes of Schedule 3, paragraph 5(3)[251].

(F) *Avoidance of conflict with international obligations*

Paragraph 6(1) of Schedule 3 gives to the Secretary of State the power to make an order to exclude the application of the Chapter I prohibition from an agreement or a category of agreements where this would be appropriate in order to avoid a conflict between the provisions of the Competition Act and an international obligation of the UK. The order can provide that the exclusion shall apply only in specified circumstances[252] and may be retrospective[253]. Similar provisions are contained in Schedule 3, paragraph 6(4) and (5) for exclusion from the Chapter II prohibition. Schedule 3 paragraph 6(6) was introduced in the House of Lords as a Government amendment to extend the meaning of the term 'international obligation' to include inter-governmental arrangements relating to civil aviation: the reason for this is that such arrangements, permitting flights between the UK and other countries, are often not made as treaties[254] and so do not give rise to international 'obligations' as such.

(G) *Public policy*

Paragraph 7 of Schedule 3 gives power to the Secretary of State to make an order to exclude the application of the Chapter I prohibition from an agreement or a category of agreements where there are 'exceptional and compelling reasons of public policy' for doing so. The order can provide that the exclusion shall apply only in specified circumstances[255], and may be retrospective[256]. Similar provisions are contained in paragraph 7(4) and (5) of Schedule 3 for exclusion from the Chapter II prohibition. Three orders have been made under paragraph 7 in relation to the defence industry[257]. The TFEU provides a specific exclusion from the competition rules for certain matters related to defence in Article 346 TFEU, but there are no specific exclusions for this area from the Competition Act.

(H) *Coal and steel*

Paragraph 8 of Schedule 3 provides that the Chapter I and Chapter II prohibitions do not apply to agreements and conduct within the exclusive jurisdiction of the European Commission under the European Coal and Steel Treaty. These exclusions ceased to have effect when the ECSC Treaty expired on 23 July 2002[258].

---

[249] Ibid, para 205.   [250] Decision of 26 May 2004 [2004] UKCLR 1973, paras 23–24.
[251] Case No 1046/2/4/04 *Albion Water Ltd v Water Services Regulation Authority* [2006] CAT 23, [2007] CompAR 22, paras 931 and 978.
[252] Competition Act, Sch 3, para 6(2).   [253] Ibid, Sch 3, para 6(3).
[254] HL Deb 9 February 1998, cols 972–973.   [255] Competition Act, Sch 3 para 7(2).
[256] Ibid, Sch 3, para 7(3).
[257] Competition Act 1998 (Public Policy Exclusion) Order 2006, SI 2006/605 (maintenance and repair of warships); Competition Act 1998 (Public Policy Exclusion) Order 2007, SI 2007/1896 (strategic and tactical weapons and their supporting technology); Competition Act 1998 (Public Policy Exclusion) Order 2008, SI 2008/1820 (design, construction, maintenance and disposal of nuclear submarines).
[258] Competition Act, Sch 3, para 8(2) and (4); see ch 23, 'Coal and Steel', p 967.

(l) Agricultural products

Paragraph 9 of Schedule 3 provides exclusion from the Chapter I prohibition for agreements that fall outside Article 101 TFEU by virtue of Regulation 1184/2006[259]. If the European Commission decides that an agreement is not excluded from Article 101 by Regulation 1184/2006, the exclusion from paragraph 9 of Schedule 3 ceases on the same date[260]. Provision is made for clawback[261].

(iv) Professional rules

When the Competition Act 1998 was passed, paragraph 1(1) of Schedule 4 provided that the Chapter I prohibition did not apply to designated professional rules. The Government felt that professional rules which served to protect the public, which contained disciplinary arrangements and which were liable to judicial review should be excluded[262]. Following a detailed review of the level of competition in the professions[263] the OFT concluded that there was a strong case for repealing Schedule 4 to the Competition Act 1998, a view with which the Secretary of State agreed[264]. Section 207 of the Enterprise Act 2002 repealed Schedule 4 with effect from 1 April 2003. The application of the Chapter I prohibition to professional rules must now be considered in the light of the judgment of the Court of Justice in *Wouters*[265], where it held that certain restrictions of competition might fall outside Article 101 TFEU in so far as they are necessary for the proper practice of a profession.

The OFT has established a dedicated team for reviewing the conditions of competition in the markets for professional services[266]. The OFT's work in this area was usefully reviewed in a speech by its chairman in September 2006[267]. Following a super-complaint from the consumer organisation Which? in May 2007 the OFT made recommendations to the Scottish executive in July 2007 that various restrictions imposed on the providers of legal services in Scotland should be lifted[268]. The Scottish executive accepted some of the OFT's recommendations, and in November 2010 the Scottish Parliament enacted the Legal Services (Scotland) Act with a view to liberalising the legal services market in Scotland. In England and Wales the Legal Services Act 2007 provides for competition scrutiny of the regulatory rules of the legal profession[269]. In January 2011 the OFT announced that the Bar Council of Northern Ireland had agreed to amend its Code of Conduct to remove restrictions of access to justice[270].

---

[259] OJ [2006] L 214/7, as amended by Regulation 1234/2007, OJ [2007] L 299/1; see ch 23, 'Agriculture', pp 963–967.

[260] Competition Act, Sch 3, para 9(2).   [261] Ibid, para 9(6) and (7).

[262] HL Committee, 13 November 1997, col 292; see also HL Deb 9 February 1998, cols 896–898.

[263] See *Competition in the professions*, OFT 328, March 2001 and *Competition in professions (progress statement)*, OFT 385, April 2002.

[264] DTI Press Release P/2001/141, 9 March 2001; see also White Paper *Productivity and Enterprise: A World Class Competition Regime* Cm 5233, (DTI, 31 July 2001), para 9.4.

[265] Case C-309/99 *Wouters v Algemene Raad van de Nederlandsche Orde van Advocaten* [2002] ECR I-1577, [2002] 4 CMLR 913; on this judgment see further ch 3, 'Regulatory ancillarity: the judgment of the Court of Justice in *Wouters*', pp 130–133.

[266] See www.oft.gov.uk/OFTwork/financial-and-professional/professional-services/.

[267] See Collins 'Promoting competition in professions: Development in the UK', available at www.oft. gov.uk.

[268] See *Restrictions on business structures and direct access in the Scottish legal profession*, OFT 946, July 2007.

[269] See also three OFT reports on the likely competition effects of modifications to codes of conduct and other professional rules under the Courts and Legal Services Act 1990, June 2009, available at www.oft.gov.uk.

[270] OFT Press Release 02/11, 5 January 2011.

(v) Section 50: vertical agreements[271]

Section 50 of the Act makes provision for the exclusion or exemption of vertical agreements from the Chapter I, but not the Chapter II, prohibition. This was effected, except in relation to vertical price fixing, by the Competition Act 1998 (Land and Vertical Agreements Exclusion) Order 2000[272]. However the adoption of Regulation 1/2003 meant that it was desirable that the treatment of vertical agreements in domestic and EU law should be brought into alignment with one another. As a result of this the exclusion of vertical agreements from the Chapter I prohibition was repealed[273]; however they may enjoy the benefit of the EU block exemption for vertical agreements[274].

(vi) Section 50: land agreements

As the Competition Bill passed through Parliament the Government recognised that there was a compelling case for excluding certain agreements relating to land from the Chapter I, though not the Chapter II[275], prohibition: an obvious case would be commercial leases containing covenants and conditions imposed for the sake of good estate management[276]. In particular it would be undesirable if there was widespread uncertainty as to whether such covenants and conditions might be rendered void and unenforceable as a result of section 2(4) of the Act. Pursuant to the power in section 50 of the Act the Competition Act 1998 (Land and Vertical Agreements Exclusion) Order 2000 excluded land agreements from the Chapter I prohibition from 1 March 2000 until 30 April 2005[277]; from 1 May 2005 until 5 April 2011 exclusion was effected by the Competition Act 1998 (Land Agreements Exclusion and Revocation) Order 2004[278]. However, following a consultation in 2009[279], the exclusion was revoked with effect from 6 April 2011 by the Competition Act 1998 (Land Agreements Exclusion Revocation) Order 2010[280]. Anyone concerned with determining whether a land agreement was excluded from the Chapter I prohibition between 1 March 2000 and 5 April 2011 should refer to the 2000 and 2004 statutory instruments, which should be read in conjunction with the OFT's Guideline *Land agreements*[281].

(I) The Chapter I prohibition: exemptions

(i) Introduction

As in the case of Article 101(3) TFEU the Competition Act provides a 'legal exception' to the Chapter I prohibition. The provisions in sections 4 and 5 of the Act whereby the OFT could grant an 'individual exemption' to an agreement notified to it were repealed by the Amendment Regulations of 2004: as in the case of EU law undertakings must conduct a

---

[271] On vertical agreements generally see ch 16.

[272] SI 2000/310; the application of this exclusion order to the arrangements in *Tobacco* has been raised on appeal to the CAT in Case Nos 1160–1164/1/1/10 etc *Imperial Tobacco Group plc v OFT*, not yet decided.

[273] This was effected by the Competition Act 1998 (Land Agreements Exclusion and Revocation) Order 2004, SI 2004/1260, which repealed SI 2000/310 that had created the exclusion for vertical agreements in the first place.

[274] See ch 16, 'Repeal of the exclusion for vertical agreements', p 678.

[275] On the application of the Chapter II prohibition and Article 102 TFEU to land agreements see *Land agreements*, OFT 12802, March 2011, paras 6.1–6.15.

[276] The registrability of restrictive covenants in commercial leases under the Restrictive Trade Practices Act 1976 was the subject of a test case in *Re Ravenseft Property Ltd's Application* [1978] QB 52, [1977] 1 All ER 47, RPC; on the position of shopping centre leases in Ireland see Maher *Competition Law: Alignment and Reform* (Round Hall Sweet & Maxwell, 1999) pp 430–431.

[277] SI 2000/310.   [278] SI 2004/1260.

[279] See the *Government Response to the Consultation on the Competition Act 1998 Land Agreements Exclusion and Revocation Order 2004*, January 2010, available at www.bis.gov.uk.

[280] SI 2010/1709.   [281] OFT 1280a, March 2011; see also the 6th edition of this book, pp 348–350.

self-assessment of whether an agreement that infringes the Chapter I prohibition satisfies the criteria of section 9 of the Act, which mirrors Article 101(3)[282]. Sections 6 and 8 of the Competition Act make provision for the adoption of block exemptions, while section 10 provides for so-called 'parallel exemption' where an agreement satisfies one of the EU block exemptions, or would do if it were to affect trade between Member States[283]. Section 11 of the Act, which provided 'exemptions for other agreements', and which was primarily concerned with certain agreements in the air transport sector, is now obsolete[284].

The operation of these provisions will be explained below, after a consideration of the criteria according to which exemption may be available.

(ii) Exemption criteria

The exemption criteria are set out in section 9(1) of the Competition Act. Exemption is available for any agreement which:

(a) contributes to—
  (i) improving production or distribution, or
  (ii) promoting technical or economic progress, while allowing consumers a fair share of the resulting benefit; but
(b) does not—
  (i) impose on the undertakings concerned restrictions which are not indispensable to the attainment of those objectives; or
  (ii) afford the undertakings concerned the possibility of eliminating competition in respect of a substantial part of the products in question.

The wording of section 9 is very similar to, but not quite identical with, Article 101(3) TFEU. The latter refers to 'improving the production or distribution *of goods*' (emphasis added), but the domestic provision is not so limited, and can therefore be applied to services as well. Section 9(2) of the Act provides that undertakings claiming the benefit of section 9(1) bear the burden of proving that the conditions it contains are satisfied[285]. In applying section 9(1) the OFT has said[286] that it will have regard to the European Commission's *Guidelines on the application of Article [101(3) TFEU]*[287]. The OFT's own guidance on *Agreements and concerted practices* does not provide a commentary on the constituent parts of section 9(1)[288], presumably since this would be likely simply to duplicate what is in the Commission's *Guidelines*.

There have been only a few applications of section 9(1) by the OFT and the courts in the years since it has been in force. In *LINK Interchange Network Ltd*[289] the OFT granted an 'individual exemption' to arrangements that provided for a centrally-set multilateral interchange fee for the operation of the LINK network of automated teller machines, in which the major banks and building societies in the UK participate. The OFT recognised

---

[282] On self-assessment under Article 101(3) TFEU see ch 4, 'Self-assessment', pp 167–168.

[283] On the EU block exemptions see ch 4 'Block exemptions', pp 168–172.

[284] See ch 23, 'Air transport', pp 974–977.

[285] This mirrors Article 2 of Regulation 1/2003, OJ [2003] L 1/1: see ch 4, 'The burden of proving that the conditions of Article 101(3) are satisfied', pp 152–153.

[286] *Agreements and concerted practices*, OFT 401, December 2004, para 5.5.

[287] OJ [2004] C 101/97; these *Guidelines* are discussed in ch 4, 'The Commission's approach in the *Article 101(3) Guidelines*', pp 160–162.

[288] On the application of the criteria in section 9 to land agreement see the OFT's Guideline *The application of competition law following the revocation of the Land Agreements Exclusion Order*, OFT 1280a, March 2011, ch 5.

[289] OFT decision of 16 October 2001 [2002] UKCLR 59.

that charging such a fee could lead to an improvement in distribution by preventing one bank from taking a free ride on the investment of others[290]. The OFT considered whether the level of the multilateral interchange fee exceeded the cost of operating the network of cash machines but found that it did not[291]. The OFT granted an individual exemption to the arrangements in question until 16 October 2006; today the parties to such an agreement would have to self-assess the application of section 9(1).

In *MasterCard UK Members Forum Ltd*[292] the OFT concluded that the collective fixing of the interchange fee did not satisfy the requirement in section 9 (and Article 101(3)) of indispensability since it extended to services that were not within the scope of the payment system[293].

In *Memorandum of Understanding on the supply of oil fuels in an emergency*[294] the OFT granted an individual exemption to an agreement which would improve distribution by enabling the Government to direct supplies of fuel to 'essential users' such as providers of emergency services in the event of a fuel shortage[295]. In *Lucite International UK Ltd and BASF plc*[296] the OFT concluded that the restrictions inherent in a long-term agreement for the supply of hydrogen cyanide were indispensable because they helped solve the 'hold-up problem' that may occur when one party is required to invest in client-specific investment[297]. In *Pool Reinsurance Co Ltd*[298] the OFT concluded that rules designed to provide reinsurance against acts of terrorism in the UK restricted competition but satisfied the conditions of section 9. In *Association of British Insurers' General Terms of Agreement*[299] the OFT considered that, if certain provisions of the General Terms of Agreement were amended, it might satisfy section 9. The decision was set aside on appeal to the CAT[300]. The OFT subsequently decided to close the file since the case did not constitute an administrative priority[301].

In *Newspapers and magazine distribution* the OFT published in October 2008 an Opinion on the application of the Chapter I prohibition and section 9(1) to agreements between newspaper and magazine publishers and their respective wholesalers[302]. An interesting feature of the Opinion is that it explains the OFT's thinking on the treatment of sub-national exclusive agreements which confer absolute territorial protection upon the wholesaler; the OFT indicated such agreements could satisfy the criteria of section 9(1) if evidence could be adduced to demonstrate that they would lead to economic efficiency[303].

In *Pirtek (UK) Ltd v Joinplace Ltd*[304] the High Court held that a franchise agreement plainly contributed to improving the production or distribution of replacement hydraulic hoses due, in particular, to the provision of know-how and assistance to franchisees;

---

[290] Ibid, paras 42–45.

[291] OFT decision of 16 October 2001 [2002] UKCLR 59, paras 47–49.

[292] OFT decision of 6 September 2005 [2006] UKCLR 236; for discussion see Vickers 'Public Policy and the Invisible Price: Competition Law, Regulation and the Interchange Fee' [2005] 4 Competition Law Journal 5.

[293] OFT decision of 6 September 2005 [2006] UKCLR 236, para 519 and paras 533–649.

[294] OFT decision of 25 October 2001 [2002] UKCLR 74.   [295] Ibid, paras 62–63.

[296] OFT decision of 29 November 2002 [2003] UKCLR 176, paras 45–46; see ch 16.

[297] See ch 16, 'The hold-up problem', p 627.

[298] OFT decision of 15 April 2004 [2004] UKCLR 893.

[299] OFT decision of 22 April 2004 [2004] UKCLR 917.

[300] Case No 1036/1/1/04 *Association of British Insurers v OFT*, order of 30 July 2004.

[301] Case closure notice of 29 January 2007, available at www.oft.gov.uk/advice_and_resources/resource_base/ca98/closure.

[302] OFT 1025, October 2008.   [303] Ibid, paras 4.29–4.144.

[304] [2010] EWHC 1641, [2010] UKCLR 1297.

it also concluded that the restrictive covenant at issue satisfied the other criteria in section 9(1)[305].

During the parliamentary debates on section 9 Lord Simon stated twice in the House of Lords that he expected the criteria in section 9 to be interpreted in the same broad way as Article 101(3) TFEU. The OFT gave an indication of the breadth of the exemption criteria in *Lucite International UK Ltd and BASF plc*[306], where it considered that the agreement under consideration would have beneficial environmental effects. In May 2010 the OFT published a discussion paper, *Article 101(3) – A Discussion of a Narrow Versus Broad Definition of Benefits*, which notes the debate about whether Article 101(3), and as a corollary section 9(1), should be interpreted in a broad manner having regard to non-economic benefits or more narrowly according to an economic efficiency standard. The European Commission considers that, since Article 101(3) is directly applicable[307], it should be applied according to the narrower approach, and, as already noted, the OFT's duty is to have regard to the Commission's position. The breadth of the criteria in Article 101(3) is discussed in chapter 4, to which reference should be made[308].

(iii) Block exemptions

Section 6 of the Competition Act allows the Secretary of State, acting upon a recommendation from the OFT, to adopt block exemptions. A block exemption may contain conditions and obligations and may be of limited duration, by virtue of sections 6(5) and 6(7) respectively. The procedure for adopting block exemptions is set out in section 8. There are a number of EU block exemptions, and these are applicable to agreements caught by the Chapter I prohibition by virtue of the parallel exemption provisions in section 10[309]. One block exemption has been adopted under the Competition Act, for public transport ticketing schemes that allow passengers to purchase tickets that can be used on the services of the participating travel operators. The block exemption entered into force on 1 March 2001[310] and will expire on 29 February 2016[311]. The OFT produced an updated guideline on 30 November 2006[312]; Annex A of the guideline contains a consolidated text of the block exemption as amended.

(iv) Parallel exemptions

Section 10 of the Competition Act 1998 makes provision for 'parallel exemptions'. Many agreements are block exempted by an EU block exemption[313]; there are others that would be exempt but for the fact that they do not produce an effect on trade between Member States: since such agreements would not infringe Article 101(1) they would not require or benefit from block exemption under Article 101(3). Section 10(1) and (2) of the Act provides that any agreement that benefits from a block exemption under EU law, or that would do if it were to affect trade between Member States, will also be exempted from the Chapter I prohibition.

---

[305] Ibid, paras 68–71.

[306] OFT decision, 29 November 2002 [2003] UKCLR 176, paras 39–41.

[307] See Council Regulation 1/2003, OJ [2003] L 1/1, Article 51(1)–(2).

[308] See ch 4, 'First condition of Article 101(3): an improvement in the production or distribution of goods or in technical or economic progress', pp 155–162.

[309] See below.

[310] Competition Act 1998 (Public Transport Ticketing Schemes Block Exemption) Order 2001, SI 2001/319, as amended by the Competition Act 1998 (Public Transport Ticketing Schemes Block Exemption) (Amendment) Order 2005, SI 2005/3347.

[311] Competition Act 1998 (Public Transport Ticketing Schemes Block Exemption) (Amendment) Order 2011, SI 2011/227.

[312] *Public transport ticketing schemes block exemption*, OFT 439.

[313] For discussion of the EU block exemptions see ch 4, 'Block Exemptions', pp 168–172.

A consequence of the availability of parallel exemption is that the parties to such agreements do not need a block exemption under domestic law. Section 10(4) ensures that the duration of any parallel exemption is in line with the position in EU law. The most important effect of section 10 is that vertical agreements may benefit from Regulation 330/2010[314] and that licences of intellectual property rights may benefit from Regulation 772/2004[315]. Research and development agreements and specialisation agreements could benefit from Regulation 1217/2010[316] and Regulation 1218/2010[317] respectively.

Section 10(5) makes provision for the OFT, in accordance with rules made under section 51 of the Act, to impose, vary or remove conditions and obligations subject to which a parallel exemption is to have effect, or even to cancel a parallel exemption. Section 10(6) enables this cancellation to be retrospective from before the date of the OFT's notice. However Article 3(2) of Regulation 1/2003 makes clear that, as a matter of EU law, it is not open to the OFT to impose stricter standards to an agreement that fulfils the conditions under Article 101(3) TFEU[318]. A different point is that Article 29(2) of Regulation 1/2003[319] specifically authorises a Member State to withdraw the benefit of an EU block exemption in certain, specified, circumstances.

4. The Chapter II Prohibition

The Chapter II prohibition is contained in section 18(1) of the Competition Act 1998. The OFT's Guidelines *Abuse of a dominant position*[320], *Assessment of market power*[321] and *Modernisation*[322] provide a useful overview of the Chapter II prohibition. The domestic competition authorities and courts will also have regard to the European Commission's 2008 Communication *Guidance on the Commission's enforcement priorities in applying Article [102 TFEU] to abusive exclusionary conduct by dominant undertakings*[323]. The *Guidance* does not purport to state the law of exclusionary abuse under Article 102[324]. However it is not unreasonable to suppose that competition authorities and courts, faced with competing arguments as to the proper scope of the law, will, at the least, be aware of the Commission's approach to certain business behaviour and that, over a period of time, the *Guidance* will have an influence on the future orientation of the Chapter II prohibition and Article 102 in its application to exclusionary behaviour[325].

The OFT and sectoral regulators have found infringements of the Chapter II prohibition in seven cases. The OFT has imposed fines in four cases: it imposed a penalty of £3.21

---

[314] See ch 16, 'Vertical Agreements: Regulation 330/2010', pp 649–672.

[315] See ch 19, 'Technology Transfer Agreements: Regulation 772/2004', pp 781–791.

[316] See ch 15, 'The block exemption for research and development agreements: Regulation 1217/2010', pp 595–599.

[317] See ch 15, 'The block exemption for specialisation agreements: Regulation 1218/2010', pp 601–603.

[318] See ch 2, 'Article 102: conflicts', pp 77–78; the OFT would presumably be under no constraint in a s 10(2) case, where there is, *ex hypothesi*, no EU jurisdiction.

[319] Council Regulation 1/2003, OJ [2003] L 1/1; see also the European Commission's *Guidelines on Vertical Restraints* OJ [2010] C 130/1, paras 74–78, on which see ch 16, 'Article 29(1) of Regulation 1/2003: withdrawal by the Commission', p 671.

[320] OFT 402, December 2004.   [321] OFT 415, December 2004.   [322] OFT 442, December 2004.

[323] OJ [2009] C 45/7; for a general discussion see ch 5, 'The Commission's *Guidance on Article 102 Enforcement Priorities*', pp 174–177.

[324] Ibid, para 3.

[325] The *Guidance* was referred to by the ORR in its decision in *DB Schenker Rail (UK) Ltd*, decision of 2 August 2010, para 82 and by the OFT in its decision in *Flybe Ltd*, decision of 5 November 2010, paras 6.36–6.39; both decisions are available at www.oft.gov.uk.

million for abusive pricing in *Napp*[326], reduced to £2.2 million on appeal[327]; in *Aberdeen Journals*[328] it imposed a fine of £1.32 million for predatory pricing, reduced to £1 million on appeal[329]; in *Genzyme*[330] it fined Genzyme £6.8 million for engaging in various exclusionary practices, reduced to £3 million on appeal[331]; and in *Reckitt/Benckiser* that undertaking agreed to pay a fine of £10.2 million for withdrawing and de-listing a drug from the NHS prescription channel[332]. The Office of Rail Regulation ('the ORR') imposed a fine of £4.1 million in the case of *English Welsh & Scottish Railway Ltd*[333], and the Gas and Electricity Markets Authority ('GEMA') imposed a fine of £41.6 million in *National Grid*[334], reduced to £15 million on appeal[335]. In *Cardiff Bus*[336] the OFT concluded that Cardiff Bus had abused its dominant position by engaging in predatory conduct aimed at eliminating a competitor; no fine could be imposed in that case since Cardiff Bus's turnover was below £50 million[337]. On two occasions the CAT has found an abuse of a dominant position in circumstances where the OFT or sectoral regulator had decided that there was not one[338]. The OFT has published research into the costs of inappropriate intervention and non-intervention under the law of abuse of dominance[339].

(A) The prohibition

(i) Section 18

The prohibition of the abuse of a dominant position is contained in section 18(1) of the Competition Act. Section 18 draws heavily on the text of Article 102[340]:

(1) Subject to section 19, any conduct on the part of one or more undertakings which amounts to the abuse of a dominant position in a market is prohibited if it may affect trade within the UK.

(2) Conduct may, in particular, constitute such an abuse if it consists in—

(a) directly or indirectly imposing unfair purchase or selling prices or other unfair trading conditions;

(b) limiting production, markets or technical development to the prejudice of consumers;

(c) applying dissimilar conditions to equivalent transactions with other trading parties, thereby placing them at a competitive disadvantage;

---

[326] OFT decision of 30 March 2001 [2001] UKCLR 597.

[327] Case No 1000/1/1/01 *Napp Pharmaceutical Holdings Ltd v Director General of Fair Trading* [2002] CAT 1, [2002] CompAR 13.

[328] *Aberdeen Journals Ltd – remitted case*, OFT decision of 16 September 2002 [2002] UKCLR 740.

[329] Case No 1009/1/1/02 *Aberdeen Journals Ltd v OFT* [2003] CAT 11, [2003] CompAR 67.

[330] OFT decision of 27 March 2003 [2003] UKCLR 950.

[331] Case No 1016/1/1/03 *Genzyme Ltd v OFT* [2004] CAT 4, [2004] CompAR 358; interim relief was granted against the directions imposed by the OFT: Case No 1013/1/03 (IR) *Genzyme Ltd v OFT* [2003] CAT 8, [2003] CompAR 290.

[332] OFT decision of 13 April 2011.   [333] ORR decision of 17 November 2006 [2007] UKCLR 937.

[334] GEMA decision of 21 February 2008 [2008] UKCLR 171.

[335] Case No 1099/1/2/08 *National Grid plc v Gas and Electricity Markets Authority* [2009] CAT 14, [2009] CompAR 282, on appeal *National Grid plc v Gas and Electricity Markets Authority* [2010] EWCA Civ 114, [2010] UKCLR 386; permission to appeal to the Supreme Court was refused by order of 5 August 2010.

[336] OFT decision of 18 November 2008 [2009] UKCLR 332.

[337] See ch 10, 'Immunity for small agreements and conduct of minor significance', pp 413–414.

[338] Case No 1044/2/1/04 *ME Burgess, JJ Burgess and SJ Burgess v OFT* [2005] CAT 25, [2005] CompAR 1151 and Case No 1046/2/4/04 *Albion Water Ltd v Water Services Regulation Authority* [2006] CAT 36, [2007] CompAR 328.

[339] OFT 864, September 2006, available at www.oft.gov.uk.

[340] For detailed discussion of EU law on the abuse of a dominant position see chs 5, 17 and 18.

(d) making the conclusion of contracts subject to acceptance by the other parties of supplementary obligations which, by their nature or according to commercial usage, have no connection with the subject of the contracts.

(3) In this section—

'dominant position' means a dominant position within the UK; and 'the UK' means the UK or any part of it.

(4) The prohibition imposed by subsection (1) is referred to in this Act as 'the Chapter II prohibition'.

(ii) 'The Chapter II prohibition'

Section 18(4) of the Act establishes the term 'the Chapter II prohibition' to refer to the prohibition set out in section 18.

(iii) 'Undertakings'

This term has the same meaning as in the Chapter I prohibition and in Articles 101 and 102 TFEU[341]. The *BetterCare*[342] case, in which the CAT ruled that the North & West Belfast Health and Social Services Trust was an undertaking for the purpose of the Competition Act, was a case on the Chapter II prohibition[343].

(iv) Affecting trade within the UK

As with the Chapter I prohibition there is a requirement that trade within the UK be affected; most conduct that is an abuse of a dominant position within the UK will also affect trade there. The CAT has held that there is no need to show an *appreciable* effect on trade within the UK[344], although the High Court has questioned the correctness of this[345]. The requirement of an effect on trade within the UK could exclude from the scope of the prohibition an abuse of a dominant position within the UK that has its effects entirely outside the UK[346].

(v) Voidness

The Competition Act does not refer explicitly to voidness in the case of the Chapter II prohibition. Prohibited conduct can nevertheless include agreements. In *English Welsh & Scottish Railway Ltd v E.ON UK plc*[347] the High Court held that coal carriage agreements that infringed the Chapter II prohibition (and Article 102 TFEU) were void and unenforceable.

(vi) Market size

Section 18(3) provides that a dominant position means a dominant position in the UK, and that the UK means the UK 'or any part of it'. Unlike Article 102[348], which refers to a dominant position '…within the internal market *or in a substantial part of it*', there is no need for the dominant position to be in the whole or a 'substantial' part of the UK,

[341] See 'Undertakings', pp 335–337 above.
[342] Case No 1006/2/1/01 *BetterCare Group Ltd v Director General of Fair Trading* [2002] CAT 7, [2002] CompAR 299.
[343] The case is discussed at 'The *BetterCare* case', pp 336–337 above.
[344] Case No 1009/1/1/02 *Aberdeen Journals Ltd v OFT* [2003] CAT 11, [2003] CompAR 67, paras 459–462.
[345] See 'Applicable law and territorial scope', p 345 above.
[346] See ch 12, 'Chapter II prohibition', p 502.   [347] [2007] EWHC 599, [2007] UKCLR 1653.
[348] See ch 5, 'A substantial part of the internal market', pp 189–190.

and a relatively small part of the UK could constitute a 'market' within the meaning of section 18. The Chapter II prohibition is therefore a potentially far-reaching instrument for competition authorities and litigants alike. Firms that have market power which is on only a local scale and which therefore run little risk of infringing Article 102 for lack of any appreciable effect on inter-state trade, or are dominant only in an insubstantial part of the common market, might find that they are infringing the Chapter II prohibition. Local dominance can be expected to be found in some sectors, such as the operation of bus services[349]: there were numerous investigations of bus services under the old Competition Act 1980[350] and there is an ongoing market investigation of local bus services under the Enterprise Act 2002[351]. In *First Edinburgh*[352] the OFT concluded that that company had not infringed the Chapter II prohibition by charging predatory prices or by increasing the frequency of bus services in order to foreclose access to the market to a rival bus operator, Lothian Buses plc. In November 2008 the OFT decided that Cardiff Bus was guilty of predatory conduct by running a 'no-frills' service to eliminate 2 Travel, its only competitor, from the market[353]. In *Burgess v OFT*[354] the CAT concluded that W Austin & Sons had abused a dominant position by refusing access to a crematorium in the Stevenage/Knebworth area of Hertfordshire.

(vii) The relevant market

As in the case of EU law a finding of dominance requires an assessment of the relevant market. Market definition has been discussed in detail in chapter 1[355]. In the UK guidance on market definition can be found in the first judgment of the CAT in the *Aberdeen Journals* case[356] and in its judgment of December 2006 in *Albion Water v Water Services Regulation Authority*[357]; the OFT has also issued a Guideline on *Market definition*[358]. In general the OFT's Guideline on *Market definition* follows the approach of the European Commission's *Notice on the definition of the relevant market for the purposes of [EU] competition law*[359].

Where the OFT concludes that an allegation of abusive behaviour cannot be substantiated, it may refrain from reaching a conclusion as to the relevant product and geographic

---

[349] On the application of the competition rules to the bus industry see OFT information leaflets *Frequently asked questions on competition law and the bus industry*, OFT 448, updated July 2006, and *A brief guide to the role of the OFT in the bus industry* and *The OFT and the bus industry*, OFT 397, February 2003.

[350] See eg *Thamesway Ltd*, OFT, August 1993; *Fife Scottish Omnibuses Ltd*, OFT, March 1994; *United Automobile Services Ltd*, OFT, March 1995.

[351] See ch 11, 'The Market Investigation Provisions in Practice', pp 479–485; there were several inquiries under the now-repealed monopoly provisions of the Fair Trading Act 1973: see eg *The supply of bus services in the north-east of England* Cm 2933 (1995).

[352] OFT decision of 29 April 2004 [2004] UKCLR 1554.

[353] OFT decision of 18 November 2008 [2009] UKCLR 332; three individuals and the liquidator of 2 Travel Group, a bus company, have brought follow-on actions for damages following the *Cardiff Bus* decision: see ch 8, 'Section 47A: monetary claims before the CAT', p 318.

[354] Case No 1044/2/1/04, [2005] CAT 25, [2005] CompAR 1151.

[355] See ch 1, 'Market definition', pp 27–42.

[356] Case No 1005/1/1/01 *Aberdeen Journals Ltd v Director General of Fair Trading* [2002] CAT 4, [2002] CompAR 167.

[357] Cases No 1046/2/4/04 and 1032/2/4/04 (IR) [2006] CAT 36, [2007] CompAR 328, paras 90–117; see also Case No 1099/1/2/08 *National Grid plc v Gas and Electricity Markets Authority* [2009] CAT 14, [2009] CompAR 282, paras 34–46.

[358] OFT 403, December 2004; the OFT's Guideline *Abuse of a dominant position*, OFT 402, December 2004, contains a briefer discussion of market definition at paras 4.4–4.9.

[359] OJ [1997] C 372/5, [1998] 4 CMLR 177.

markets[360]. However in *Freeserve* the CAT emphasised that it will often be appropriate, for clarity of analysis, for the OFT or sectoral regulator to indicate which markets seem to be potentially relevant in a particular case[361].

(viii) Assessing dominance

The OFT has issued a Guideline *Assessment of market power*[362]. As paragraph 1.2 of the *Guideline* points out the concept of market power is not part of the Competition Act; however market power is a useful tool in assessing potentially anti-competitive behaviour. The *Guideline* states that market power arises where an undertaking does not face effective competitive pressure[363] and can be thought of as the ability profitably to sustain prices above competitive levels or to restrict output or quality below competitive levels[364]. The *Guideline* quotes the well-known definition of a dominant position from *United Brands v Commission*[365], the ability to 'prevent effective competition being maintained on the relevant market'[366]. In *Napp Pharmaceutical Holdings Ltd v Director General of Fair Trading* (and in subsequent cases) the CAT has adopted the same definition[367]. In *Cardiff Bus* the OFT noted that market power is a question of degree and that it is not necessary for a finding of dominance that an undertaking has eliminated all opportunity for competition in the market[368]. In *Albion Water v Water Services Regulation Authority*[369] the CAT, perhaps concerned at the lack of findings of infringement of the Chapter II prohibition by the OFT and the sectoral regulators, said that:

> when assessing dominance under the Competition Act, it is unnecessary for the competition authority to investigate distant or theoretical possibilities with a view to dotting every 'i' or crossing every 't' that could conceivably be imagined. While a sensible analysis is required, there is no need to make the issue of dominance more complicated than it really is[370].

The OFT's Guideline on the *Assessment of market power* says that an undertaking will not be dominant unless it enjoys 'substantial market power'[371]: the European Commission's *Guidance on Article 102 Enforcement Priorities*[372] makes the same point[373]. The *Guideline* adds that assessing market power requires an examination of the competitive constraints that an undertaking faces, and it proceeds to discuss market shares (Part 4), entry barriers (Part 5) and other factors relevant to an assessment of market power (Part 6).

(A) Market shares

Paragraph 2.11 of the *Guideline* makes the point that there is no fixed market share threshold for the determination of market power: market power depends on a variety of factors of which market share is one; paragraph 2.12 notes that there is a presumption in EU law of dominance at 50 per cent or above[374], and adds that the OFT considers it unlikely that

[360] See eg OFT decision of 11 December 2002, *Association of British Travel Agents and British Airways plc* [2003] UKCLR 136, paras 10–19.

[361] Case No 1007/2/3/02 *Freeserve.com plc v Director of Telecommunications* [2003] CAT 5, [2003] CompAR 202, para 131.

[362] OFT 415, December 2004; the OFT's Guideline *Abuse of a dominant position*, OFT 402, December 2004, contains a briefer discussion of market definition at paras 4.10–4.22.

[363] *Assessment of market power*, para 1.3.   [364] Ibid, para 1.4.

[365] Case 27/76 [1978] ECR 207, [1978] 1 CMLR 429.

[366] See ch 5, 'Dominant Position', pp 179–189.

[367] Case No 1000/1/1/01 [2002] CAT 1, [2002] CompAR 13, para 164.

[368] Decision of 18 November 2008 [2009] UKCLR 332, paras 5.6–5.7.

[369] Cases No 1046/2/4/04 and 1032/2/4/04 (IR) [2006] CAT 36, CompAR 328.

[370] Ibid, para 185.   [371] *Assessment of market power*, para 2.9.

[372] See ch 5, 'The Commission's *Guidance on Article 102 Enforcement Priorities*', pp 174–177.

[373] OJ [2009] C 45/7, para 10.

[374] See ch 5, 'The *AKZO* presumption of dominance where an undertaking has a market share of 50 per cent or more', pp 182–183.

an undertaking would be dominant with a market share below 40 per cent[375]. However in *NCNN 500* OFCOM concluded that BT, with a market share below 31 per cent, was dominant as there were sufficient additional factors indicating dominance[376].

Paragraph 3.3 points out that one of the competitive constraints upon an undertaking comes from existing competitors within the relevant market, and market shares help[377] to assess the extent of this constraint. Part 4 of the *Guideline* discusses market shares in more detail. Market power is more likely to exist where an undertaking has a persistently high market share[378]. It is the development of market shares over a period of time that is important, not their calculation at a single point in time[379]. The *Guideline* explains various reasons why market shares might not be a reliable guide to market power, for example because barriers to entry are low or because the market is a 'bidding market'[380]. In the circumstances of the recently liberalised market for the provision of domestic gas meters in *National Grid* the CAT treated market shares as high as 89 per cent as one indicator of market power but as not raising a presumption of dominance[381]. Paragraphs 4.6 to 4.8 provide insights into methods of calculating market shares.

(B) Entry barriers

Paragraph 3.3 of the *Guideline* points out that one of the competitive constraints upon an undertaking comes from potential competition, and entry barriers are relevant to an examination of this issue. Part 5 of the *Guideline* discusses barriers to entry; paragraph 5.1 explains that firms already in the market may experience barriers to expansion, and that such barriers can be analysed in the same way as barriers to entry. Entry barriers are important to the assessment of potential competition: the lower they are, the more likely it is that potential competition will prevent undertakings already in the market from profitably sustaining prices above competitive levels[382].

The *Guideline* acknowledges that there are various ways of classifying barriers to entry; it examines the issue under six heads[383]:

- **sunk costs**: that is to say costs that must be incurred to enter a market, but which are not recoverable on exiting the market, may give incumbent firms an advantage over potential entrants[384]

- **poor access to key inputs and distribution outlets**: there can be a barrier to entry where an incumbent has privileged access to a scarce input or distribution outlet, for example to essential facilities or intellectual property rights[385]

- **regulation**: for example a limitation of the numbers of undertakings licensed to operate in a market or standards that an incumbent can satisfy but that new entrants find it difficult to, can amount to a barrier to entry[386]

- **economies of scale**: the fact that an undertaking may need to enter the market on a large scale can constitute a barrier to entry[387]

---

[375] The European Commission makes the same point in its *Guidance on Article 102 Enforcement Priorities*, para 14.

[376] Decision of 1 August 2008 [2008] UKCLR 501, paras 5.1–5.166.

[377] Market share figures do not yield any information about the competitive constraint that arises from the ability of existing firms within the market to expand.

[378] *Assessment of market power*, para 4.2.　　[379] Ibid, para 4.2.

[380] See ch 1, 'Market shares', p 43.

[381] Case No 1099/1/2/08 [2009] CAT 14, CompAR 282, para 51.

[382] *Assessment of market power*, para 5.2.　　[383] Ibid, para 5.6.　　[384] Ibid, paras 5.8–5.11.

[385] Ibid, paras 5.12–5.15.　　[386] Ibid, paras 5.16–5.17.　　[387] Ibid, paras 5.18–5.20.

- **network effects**: as in the case of economies of scale, network effects can make it hard for a new firm to enter the market where the minimum viable scale of the network is large in relation to the size of the market[388]
- **exclusionary behaviour**: behaviour such as predation, margin squeezes and refusals to supply may act as barriers to entry[389].

The *Guideline* discusses ways of assessing the effects of barriers to entry and the type of evidence that a firm should adduce where it wishes to argue that potential competition (that is to say an absence of barriers to entry) amounts to an effective competition constraint upon its behaviour[390].

(C) *Other factors in the assessment of market power*

Part 6 of the *Guideline* considers other matters that are relevant to an assessment of market power. These include:

- **buyer power**: buyer power may act as a constraint on an undertaking's market power; however that buyer power does not come from size alone: the buyer must have a choice of supplier[391], a point emphasised by the CAT in the *Genzyme*[392] and *National Grid*[393] cases
- **behaviour and performance**: the behaviour and performance of the undertaking under investigation may provide evidence of market power, for example where it can set prices consistently above an appropriate measure of cost or where it can persistently earn excessive profits[394]
- **economic regulation**: economic regulation may prevent an undertaking from raising prices above a competitive level, although this does not in itself mean that that undertaking does not have market power[395]. In the *Napp* case[396] the CAT rejected the argument that the Pharmaceutical Price Regulation Scheme, which limits the rate of return on a company's total sales of all its branded prescription medicines to the National Health Service, meant that Napp did not enjoy a dominant position[397].

(D) *Super-dominance*

In the *Napp* case[398] the CAT recognised that certain firms may be 'super-dominant', with the result that the 'special responsibility' not to impair undistorted competition that they bear may be particularly onerous[399]. In *BT Broadband*[400] the Office of Telecommunications (OFTEL, the predecessor of OFCOM) concluded that BT, with a market share in the relevant market of 65–70 per cent, was not in a super-dominant position[401]. In *English Welsh & Scottish*

---

[388] Ibid, paras 5.21–5.22.   [389] Ibid, paras 5.23–5.28.   [390] Ibid, paras 5.29–5.36.

[391] Ibid, paras 6.1–6.4.

[392] Case No 1016/1/1/03 *Genzyme Ltd v OFT* [2004] CAT 4, [2004] CompAR 358, paras 241–289.

[393] Case No 1099/1/2/08 *National Grid plc v Gas and Electricity Markets Authority* [2009] CAT 14, CompAR 282, paras 60–78.

[394] Ibid, paras 6.5–6.6.

[395] Ibid, para 6.7.

[396] Case No 1000/1/1/01 *Napp Pharmaceutical Holdings Ltd v Director General of Fair Trading* [2002] CAT 1, [2002] CompAR 13.

[397] Ibid, paras 161–168.

[398] Case No 1000/1/1/01 *Napp Pharmaceutical Holdings Ltd v Director General of Fair Trading* [2002] CAT 1, [2002] CompAR 13, para 219.

[399] Ibid, para 219; see further ch 5, 'The emergence of super-dominance', pp 187–189.

[400] Decision of 11 July 2003 [2003] UKCLR 1141.   [401] Ibid, para 2.23.

Railway Ltd[402] the ORR noted that EW&S had a 'very high degree of market power' which should be taken into account when determining the scope of its 'special responsibility'.

(ix) **Abuse**

(A) *Examples of abuse*

Section 18(2) sets out a non-exhaustive list of abuses, in identical terms to those in Article 102 TFEU. Unlike Article 102, sections 18(1) and 18(2) refer to 'conduct' which amounts to an abuse, rather than merely an abuse. It is hard to see how the use of the term 'conduct' improves on the EU version, and indeed it is not entirely apt: there is no doubt, for example, that a refusal to supply could, in certain circumstances, amount to an abuse of a dominant position; semantically it is somewhat strange to characterise inaction as conduct.

The CAT has pointed out that the primary interest to be protected under the Chapter II prohibition is the process of competition, and ultimately the interest of the consumer, rather than the private interest of a particular competitor; but that in some cases protecting the competitive process necessarily involves having regard to the situation of competitors[403].

In *National Grid plc v Gas and Electricity Markets Authority*[404] the Court of Appeal held that, in an abuse case, it is not necessary to ask, in isolation, whether a dominant undertaking has departed from 'normal competition' or 'competition on the merits': these are not sufficiently hard-edged concepts that they can be determined as a matter of law; rather it is necessary to look at conduct 'in the round' and to decide whether it is abusive as a matter of expert appreciation. The court added that, although there are benchmarks against which to consider whether particular conduct (for example predatory pricing or a refusal to supply) amount to an abuse, it does not follow that there must be a benchmark for all allegations of abuse, let alone a benchmark that can tell one precisely where the line between lawful and unlawful conduct is to be drawn. Abuse cases are 'highly fact sensitive and dependent upon an evaluation of a wide range of factors'[405]. In *Purple Parking Ltd v Heathrow Airport Ltd*[406] Mann J said that it is not necessary to bring abuse of dominance cases within any particular 'pigeon-hole' of established cases of abuse[407].

The OFT's Guideline *Abuse of a dominant position*[408] contains a brief discussion of the meaning of abuse, but does little more than to repeat what is contained in Article 102 TFEU and section 18. The OFT published a draft Guideline *Assessment of conduct* in April 2004 which, if adopted, would have provided much more detailed discussion of the concept of abuse; although the draft Guideline is still available on its website[409] it is understood that the OFT will not be issuing a final guideline on this topic. The European Commission has since published its *Guidance on Article 102 Enforcement Priorities* in respect of exclusionary behaviour: as already noted the OFT must have regard to the Commission's position[410], and it is likely to be influenced by what the Commission has had to say in that document. The guidelines for particular sectors such as the energy sector and railways contain discussion of the concept of abuse in the circumstances of those

---

[402] ORR decision of 17 November 2006 [2007] UKCLR 937.

[403] Case No 1046/2/4/04 *Albion Water Ltd v Director General of Water Services* [2005] CAT 40, [2006] CompAR 269, para 262.

[404] [2010] EWCA Civ 114, [2010] UKCLR 386.

[405] Ibid, para 54; see, to similar effect, para 102 of Mann J's judgment in *Purple Parking Ltd v Heathrow Airport Ltd* [2011] EWHC 987 (Ch), [2011] UKCLR 492.

[406] [2011] EWHC 987 (Ch).   [407] Ibid, paras 75–108.

[408] OFT Guideline 402, December 2004.   [409] OFT 414a, available at www.oft.gov.uk.

[410] On s 60(3) of the Competition Act see 'Having regard to decisions or statements of the Commission', p 373 below.

markets[411]. The OFT will also apply its *OFT Prioritisation Principles*[412] when selecting cases for investigation.

The jurisprudence of the EU Courts on the meaning of abuse is highly influential in the application of the Chapter II prohibition, not least because of the 'general principles' clause in section 60 of the Act[413]: as a result the reader is referred to chapter 5 for a general discussion of the meaning of abuse under Article 102[414]. Abusive practices themselves are considered in detail in chapter 17, which deals with non-pricing abuses, and chapter 18, which deals with pricing abuses. In each chapter specific attention is given to the application of the Chapter II prohibition[415].

(B) *Objective justification*

A dominant undertaking can raise a defence to an accusation of abuse where it can show that it had an objective justification for its behaviour[416]. In *Floe Telecom Ltd (in administration) v OFCOM*[417] the CAT held that OFCOM should have conducted a much more extensive inquiry before concluding that Vodafone's refusal to supply was objectively justified[418]. When OFCOM re-examined the matter, in the light of the CAT's comments, it continued to believe that Vodafone's behaviour was objectively justified[419]. In *Re-investigation of a complaint from VIP Communications Ltd*[420] OFCOM considered that T-Mobile's refusal to supply VIP was objectively justified for the same reason that applied in *Floe*[421]. The ORR accepted a defence of objective justification in *Complaint from NTM Sales and Marketing Ltd against Portec Rail Products (UK) Ltd*[422]. In *Cardiff Bus* the OFT was not convinced by Cardiff Bus's explanation for launching its new bus services since it was not able to produce any contemporaneous evidence to show that the services were introduced to test market demand for 'no frills' services rather than merely to weaken its principal competitor[423]. In *Flybe Ltd*[424] the OFT said that it would have been prepared in that case to have decided that Flybe had an objective justification for incurring losses on an aviation route that it had newly entered, and therefore that it had not abused a dominant position[425]; however the OFT decided anyway that there were no grounds for action. Mann J rejected objective justification as a defence in *Purple Parking Ltd v Heathrow Airport Ltd*[426].

(C) *Conduct of minor significance*

Conduct of minor significance cannot be the subject of a financial penalty[427]: this was the reason that Cardiff Bus was not fined, even though the OFT found it guilty of abuse[428]; this does not apply to transgressions of Article 102 TFEU.

---

[411] These guidelines are listed at 'OFT guidance', pp 332–333 above.

[412] OFT 953, October 2008: see ch 10, 'Inquiries and Investigations', p 395.

[413] See 'Questions arising…in relation to competition', p 372 below.

[414] See ch 5, 'Abuse', pp 192–210.   [415] See chs 17 and 18 generally.

[416] Case No 1016/1/1/03 *Genzyme Ltd v OFT* [2004] CAT 4, [2004] CompAR 358, paras 577–578; see ch 5, 'Objective justification', pp 211–212.

[417] Case No 1024/2/3/04 [2004] CAT 18, [2005] CompAR 290.   [418] Ibid, paras 334–339.

[419] Decision of 28 June 2005 [2005] UKCLR 1112, paras 246–312, upheld on appeal to the CAT Case No 1024/2/3/04 [2006] CAT 17, [2006] CompAR 637, and on appeal to the Court of Appeal *Office of Communications v Floe Telecom Ltd* [2009] EWCA Civ 47, [2009] UKCLR 659.

[420] OFCOM decision of 28 June 2005 [2005] UKCLR 1112; an appeal to the CAT was rejected in Case No 1027/2/3/04 *VIP Communications Ltd (in administration) v OFCOM* [2009] CAT 29, [2010] CompAR 1.

[421] Ibid, paras 239–254.   [422] ORR decision of 19 August 2005 [2006] UKCLR 12, paras 168–185.

[423] OFT decision of 18 November 2008 [2009] UKCLR 332, paras 1.13 and 7.27.

[424] OFT decision of 5 November 2010.   [425] Ibid, paras 6.97–6.108.

[426] [2011] EWHC 987 (Ch), [2011] UKCLR 492, paras 179–238.

[427] See ch 10, 'Immunity for small agreements and conduct of minor significance', pp 413–414.

[428] See 'The Chapter II Prohibition', p 360 above.

(D) *Article 3(2) Regulation 1/2003*

Unilateral conduct that is not abusive may, nevertheless, be subject to a stricter rule of national law[429].

(B) **Exclusions**[430]

(i) **Exclusions for mergers subject to UK or EU merger control**

The Chapter II prohibition does not apply to conduct resulting in a relevant merger situation[431] or in a concentration having a Community dimension[432]. This exclusion is closely related to the exclusion of mergers from the Chapter I prohibition, which was described above[433].

(ii) **Financial Services and Markets Act 2000**

The Chapter II prohibition will not apply to certain conduct pursuant to the regulatory provisions of the Financial Services and Markets Act 2000[434].

(iii) **Other exclusions**

Section 19(1) provides that the Chapter II prohibition does not apply to cases excluded by Schedule 3[435]. Some of the exclusions in Schedule 3 apply only to the Chapter I prohibition; however paragraph 4 of Schedule 3 (services of general economic interest), paragraph 5 (compliance with legal requirements), paragraph 6 (avoidance of conflict with international obligations) and paragraph 7 (exceptional and compelling reasons of public policy) also exclude the application of the Chapter II prohibition.

5. 'Governing Principles Clause': Section 60 of the Competition Act 1998

Regulation 1/2003 requires that, where a competition authority or a court apply domestic competition law they must, in so far as an agreement or conduct has an effect on trade between Member States, also apply Articles 101 and/or 102 TFEU. The relationship between EU and national competition law, and in particular the scope for applying stricter rules than those of the EU, has already been considered in the final section of chapter 2[436]. In the years since Regulation 1/2003 entered into force there has been no difficulty in applying the EU and domestic rules in a harmonious fashion[437], although the European Commission has indicated that the apparent divergence of standards regarding unilateral conduct is an area which merits further evaluation[438].

---

[429] See ch 2, 'Article 102: conflicts', pp 77–78.

[430] See the detailed discussion of exclusions in the context of the Chapter I prohibition at 'The Chapter I prohibition: excluded agreements', pp 348–356 above.

[431] CA 1998, s 19 and Sch 1, para 2 ('normal' mergers).   [432] Ibid, s 19 and Sch 1, para 6.

[433] See 'Schedule 1: mergers and concentrations', pp 349–351 above.

[434] See 'Financial Services and Markets Act 2000', pp 351–352 above.

[435] For a discussion of Sch 3 see 'Schedule 3: planning obligations and other general exclusions', p 352 above.

[436] See ch 2, 'The Relationship Between EU Competition Law and National Competition Laws', pp 75–79.

[437] See Communication from the Commission to the European Parliament and the Council, *Report on the functioning of Regulation 1/2003*, COM(2009) 206 final, paras 12, 28 and 39.

[438] Ibid, para 27.

This section of this chapter deals with a different point which is that UK law itself, as a result of the 'governing principles clause' found in section 60 of the Competition Act, requires that there should be consistency, where possible, in the application of domestic and EU competition law. Section 60 has been extremely important in practice and will continue to be so in cases where there is no effect on trade between Member States with the result that domestic law alone is applicable.

Section 60 of the Competition Act sets out the governing principles to be applied in determining questions which arise in relation to competition within the UK; essentially, the principle is that there should be close conformity between the Act and the EU regime; section 60 is also applicable in relation to questions arising under the provisions for the disqualification of company directors[439]. Section 60 enables the UK competition authorities and courts to apply EU competition law when making decisions under the Act.

(i) Section 60(1)

Section 60(1) sets out the purpose of the governing principles clause: the duties to which it gives rise are imposed by section 60(2) and (3). Section 60(1) provides that:

> The purpose of this section is to ensure that so far as is possible (having regard to any relevant differences between the provisions concerned), questions arising under this Part in relation to competition within the UK are dealt with in a manner which is consistent with the treatment of corresponding questions arising in [EU] law in relation to competition within the [EU].

The objective of consistency is not absolute: consistency is envisaged only 'so far as is possible', having regard to 'relevant differences' and is required as to 'corresponding questions' that arise 'in relation to competition'. The Government stated that 'we are satisfied that the drafting of [section] 60 accurately expresses the concept that [EU] jurisprudence is to be followed unless the court is driven to some different interpretation by some provision in that part of the [Act]'[440]. Where the factual circumstances of the case law of the EU Courts differ from those in a UK case, the CAT in *BetterCare* nevertheless observed that its duty under section 60 was to approach an issue of competition law 'in the manner in which we think the European Court would approach it, as regards the principles and reasoning likely to be followed by that Court'[441].

(A) 'So far as is possible'

The purpose of the Act is to achieve consistency 'so far as is possible'. Clearly this is not possible where the Act explicitly differs from EU law: examples of this are given in the next section. Where there is some doubt in a particular case, these words indicate that there is a policy preference towards maintaining consistency with EU law.

(B) 'Having regard to any relevant differences'

A critical issue is the identification of any 'relevant differences' between EU law and the Act. Some examples appear on the face of the Act itself: for example it contains a few exclusions

---

[439] See s 9A(11) of the Company Directors Disqualification Act 1986, inserted by s 204 Enterprise Act 2002.

[440] HL Consideration of Commons' Amendments, 20 October 1998, col 1383 (Lord Simon of Highbury).

[441] Case No 1006/2/1/01 *BetterCare Group v Director General of Fair Trading* [2002] CAT 7, [2002] CompAR 299, para 32.

which are not available under EU law[442]; the Act provides a wider privilege for correspond-ence with lawyers than in the EU[443]; the exclusion under the Competition Act for mergers is wider than that provided for under EU law; and the Act makes specific provision for par-ticular agreements to be excluded[444]. Secondly, the procedural and enforcement rules under the Act are not identical to those in EU law. For example there is an appeal on the merits to the CAT against decisions of the OFT and the CAT has a power to remit a case to the OFT[445] and the sectoral regulators; in the EU, judicial review may provide a less effective remedy to an applicant. Another procedural difference is that the provisions on leniency in the UK are different from those in the EU[446]. The same is true of the limitation period for imposing and the method of calculating the level of a fine; the CAT has said that there is a relevant diffe-rence between domestic and EU law and practice to the setting of penalties[447].

A further example of a relevant difference, but one that is not apparent on the face of the Act, is that the EU competition rules are applied, in part, with the objective of single mar-ket integration in mind. The Competition Act, presumably, does not have to be applied for this purpose, since the goal of market integration is 'relevantly different' from one arising in relation to competition within the UK: this could lead to some divergence in the way in which the Chapter I and Chapter II prohibitions and Articles 101 and 102 are applied. In *Newspapers and magazine distribution* the OFT's opinion was that a court would be unlikely to import the single market objective into an analysis of vertical agreements under the Competition Act[448].

A further area in which relevant differences might exist will arise in the substantive analysis of particular cases; for example it is provided by the OFT/OFCOM Guidelines that a different measure of costs will be used to assess alleged predatory pricing[449], due to the specific features of the telecommunications sector, from the one suggested by the Court of Justice in the *AKZO* judgment[450].

In *Aberdeen Journals Ltd v OFT*[451] the CAT concluded that there was no need to import a rule of 'appreciability' into the expression 'affect trade' in section 18(1) of the Competition Act, and that this was a 'relevant difference' from the test of 'effect on trade' in Article 102 TFEU[452].

---

[442] On the exclusions from the Chapter I and Chapter II prohibitions see 'The Chapter I prohibition: excluded agreements', pp 348–356 and 'Exclusions', p 369 above.

[443] See ch 10, 'Legal professional privilege', p 379.

[444] See 'Section 50: vertical agreements', p 356 above and 'Section 50: land agreements', p 356 above on s 50 of the Competition Act 1998; in Case No 1006/2/1/01 *BetterCare Group v Director General of Fair Trading* [2002] CAT 7, [2002] CompAR 299, para 288, the CAT left open the question of whether para 5 of Sch 3 was relevantly different from EU law.

[445] See eg Case No 1005/1/1/01 *Aberdeen Journals v Director General of Fair Trading* [2002] CAT 4, [2002] CompAR 167, para 190; similarly the CAT has held that its power to adopt its own decision on appeal is a relevant difference: see Case No 1027/2/3/04 *VIP Communications v OFCOM* [2007] CAT 3, [2007] CompAR 666, para 51.

[446] See ch 10, 'Whistleblowing: the leniency programme', pp 414–418.

[447] See eg Case No 1120/1/1/09 *Quarmby Construction Company Ltd v OFT* [2011] CAT 11, paras 43–48 (on the limitation period) and Case Nos 1117/1/1/09 etc *GF Tomlinson Building Ltd v OFT* [2011] CAT 7, paras 100–102 (on the method for setting fines).

[448] OFT 1025, October 2008, para 4.13.

[449] OFT 417, February 2000, paras 7.6–7.19 where instead of the EU assessment of predation using average variable costs and average total costs, the OFT and OFCOM will consider long run incremental cost; see also Case No 1007/2/3/02 *Freeserve.com plc v Director General of Telecommunications* [2003] CAT 5, [2003] CompAR 202, paras 212–225.

[450] See also *Guidance on the Application of the Competition Act 1998 in the Water and Sewerage Sectors* OFT 422, March 2010, paras 4.39–4.40; on Case C-62/86 *AKZO v Commission* [1991] ECR I-3359, [1993] 5 CMLR 215, see ch 18, 'AKZO v Commission', pp 742–743.

[451] Case No 1009/1/1/02 [2003] CAT 11, [2003] CompAR 67.   [452] Ibid, paras 459–460.

(C) 'Corresponding questions'

In *MasterCard UK Members Forum Ltd*[453] the OFT considered that the questions under consideration in that case did not 'correspond with' those in the European Commission's decision in *Visa International – Multilateral Interchange Fee*[454] since the latter was explicitly concerned with a cross-border payment system whereas the OFT's decision was dealing with a payment system within the UK[455].

(D) 'Questions arising…in relation to competition'

The duty to maintain consistency arises only where there are 'questions arising in relation to competition'. The view of the UK Government when the Bill was proceeding through Parliament was that it was not necessary for the OFT (or sectoral regulators) to follow the same detailed procedures as the European Commission: indeed that might be undesirable, given that it is a very different institution from the OFT; it can reasonably be argued that the procedural rules do not themselves raise questions 'in relation to competition'. However it was accepted in the House of Lords by Lord Simon of Highbury that section 60 does import the general principles of EU law as well as the specific jurisprudence on Articles 101 and 102 themselves, save where there is a relevant difference[456]. Examples of what have come to be termed in discussion of the Act as 'high level principles' are equality, legal certainty, legitimate expectation, proportionality and privilege against self-incrimination: each of these is well established in EU law[457]. Other general principles noted by the EU Courts include the duty to state reasons for a decision with sufficient precision[458], the principle of good administration[459], the right of access to the file[460] and equality of arms[461]. In *Pernod-Ricard v OFT*[462] the CAT considered that the rights of a third party complainant in competition proceedings raised a question which indirectly arose 'in relation to competition' for the purposes of section 60(2) of the Act[463]. The Tribunal also referred extensively to the jurisprudence of the EU Courts in *Apex v OFT*[464] when considering whether there were procedural defects in a statement of objections issued by the OFT[465].

(ii) Section 60(2) and (3)

Section 60(2) and (3) provide that:

> (2) At any time when the court[466] determines a question arising under this Part, it must act (so far as is compatible with the provisions of this Part[467] and whether or not it would

---

[453] OFT decision of 6 September 2005 [2006] UKCLR 236.

[454] OJ [2002] L 318/17, [2003] 4 283 CMLR 283.

[455] Ibid, paras 97–106.   [456] HL Committee, 25 November 1997, cols 960–963.

[457] See Wyatt and Dashwood's *European Union Law* (Sweet & Maxwell, 5th ed, 2006, eds Arnull, Dashwood, Dougan, Ross, Spaventa and Wyatt), ch 7.

[458] Case T-241/97 *Stork Amsterdam BV v Commission* [2000] ECR II-309, [2000] 5 CMLR 31, para 74; the duty to give reasons is also contained in Article 296 TFEU.

[459] Case T-127/98 *UPS Europe SA v Commission* [1999] ECR II-2633, [2000] 4 CMLR 94, para 37.

[460] Cases T-25/95 etc *Cimenteries CBR SA v Commission* [2000] ECR II-491, [2000] 5 CMLR 204, para 142.

[461] Ibid, para 143; the OFT has since adopted a Guideline on *Involving third parties in Competition Act investigations*, OFT 451, April 2006, which substantially brings domestic law into alignment with EU law.

[462] Case No 1017/2/1/03 [2004] CAT 10, [2004] CompAR 707.

[463] Ibid, paras 228–234; note that the CAT distinguished *Pernod* in concluding that the power to impose penalties in s 36 of the Act is not limited by any limitation period: Case No 1120/1/1/09 *Quarmby Construction Company Ltd v OFT* [2011] CAT 11, para 43.

[464] Case No 1032/1/1/04 [2005] CAT 4, [2005] CompAR 507.   [465] Ibid, paras 92–100.

[466] 'Court' in this context, rather unusually, includes the Competition Commission, the OFT and the sectoral regulators: Competition Act 1998, s 60(5).

[467] 'This Part' of the Act deals with all matters to do with the prohibitions and their enforcement of them, but not investigations under the Enterprise Act 2002.

otherwise be required to do so) with a view to securing that there is no inconsistency[468] between—

(a) the principles applied, and decision reached, by the court in determining that question; and

(b) the principles laid down by the Treaty[469] and the European Court[470], and any relevant decision of that Court, as applicable at that time in determining any corresponding question arising in [EU] law.

(3) The court must, in addition, have regard to any relevant decision or statement of the Commission.

(A) *The duty of consistency*

Consistency must be maintained between the principles applied and the decision reached by the domestic authority or court and the principles laid down by the Treaty and the EU Courts and any decisions of those Courts in determining corresponding questions that may be applicable at that time. As already noted, 'high level' principles such as equality and proportionality will be imported by virtue of section 60(2).

(B) *Having regard to decisions or statements of the Commission*

The competition authorities and courts under section 60(3) must 'have regard to' any relevant decision[471] or statement of the Commission; this is a lesser obligation than the obligation to ensure that there is no inconsistency under section 60(2). Decisions and statements of other bodies such as the Council of Ministers[472] or the European Parliament are not included. The Act itself does not explain what is meant by Commission statements. However the OFT's view is that the statements must carry the authority of the Commission as a whole such as, for example, decisions in individual cases under Articles 101 and/or 102, Commission Notices and clear statements about its policy approach as published in its Annual Report on Competition Policy[473]. In *Albion Water Ltd*[474] the Court of Appeal held that the CAT was correct to direct itself by reference to the test of margin squeeze as expressly formulated in the European Commission's guidance[475] and the case law[476].

In *MasterCard UK Members Forum Ltd*[477] the OFT said that the duty to 'have regard' to Commission decisions and statements did not mean that it was bound to comply with them, but only to give serious consideration to them[478].

---

[468] Section 60(1) puts the objective positively and is preferable to this double negative.

[469] 'Treaty' in this context refers to the EC Treaty (now the Treaty on the Functioning of the European Union): CA 1998, s 59(1); it would not apply to jurisprudence or decisions under the ECSC Treaty, nor under the EEA Agreement.

[470] 'European Court' refers to both the Court of Justice and the General Court: ibid; it does not refer to the opinions of the Advocates General, as to which see Buxton LJ in *Napp Pharmaceutical Holdings Ltd v Director General of Fair Trading* [2002] EWCA Civ 796, [2002] 4 All ER 376, who nevertheless characterised such opinions as 'important and authoritative'; nor to the EFTA Court.

[471] On the meaning of decision see CA 1998, s 60(6).

[472] Documents such as the Minutes of the Council's deliberations about the EUMR or Regulation 1/2003 would therefore not need to be considered, although they could be relevant in a particular case.

[473] *Modernisation*, OFT 442, para 4.11.

[474] *Dŵr Cymru Cyfyngedig v Albion Water Ltd* [2008] EWCA Civ 536, [2008] UKCLR 457.

[475] *Notice on the application of the competition rules to access agreements in the telecommunications sector* OJ [1988] C 265/2.

[476] *Dŵr Cymru Cyfyngedig v Albion Water Ltd* [2008] EWCA Civ 536, [2008] UKCLR 457, para 105, referring in particular to the judgment of the General Court in Case T-271/03 *Deutsche Telekom v Commission* [2008] ECR II-477, [2008] 5 CMLR 631, upheld on appeal Case C-280/08 P *Deutsche Telekom v Commission* [2010] ECR I-000, [2010] 5 CMLR 1495.

[477] OFT decision of 6 September 2005 [2006] UKCLR 236.   [478] Ibid, paras 107–116.

(C) References to the Court of Justice

The UK CAT, the Court of Appeal of England and Wales, the Court of Session in Scotland, the Court of Appeal in Northern Ireland and the UK Supreme Court can make references to the Court of Justice for a preliminary ruling under Article 267 TFEU. This is considered further in chapter 10[479].

6. The Competition Act 1998 in Practice

The OFT maintains a register of decisions adopted by itself and by the sectoral regulators under the Competition Act. The following table sets out the decisions that have been adopted by 20 June 2011.

Table 9.1   Table of published decisions of the OFT and sectoral regulators and appeals to the CAT[1] under the Competition Act 1998 and/or Articles 101 and 102 TFEU

Case name	Date of decision	Outcome	On appeal to the CAT
General Insurance Standards Council **NB: second decision adopted 13.11.2002 – see below**	26.1.2001 and 11.5.2001	No infringement of Chapter I prohibition	Decision annulled[2]
Napp Pharmaceutical Holdings Ltd	5.4.2001	Infringement of Chapter II prohibition **Fine of £3.21m**	Finding of infringement upheld **Fine reduced to £2.2 million**[3]
Swan Solutions Ltd/ Avaya ECS Ltd **(OFTEL)**	6.4.2001	No infringement of Chapter I and II prohibitions	
DSG Retail Ltd ('Dixons')/ Compaq Computer Ltd/ Packard Bell NEC Ltd	18.4.2001	No infringement of Chapter I and II prohibitions	
BT Surf Together and BT Talk & Surf Together pricing packages **(OFTEL)**	4.5.2001	No infringement of Chapter II prohibition	
Consignia and Postal Preference Service Limited	15.6.2001[4]	No infringement of Chapter II prohibition	

---

[479] See ch 10, 'Article 267 References', pp 449–450.

Case name	Date of decision	Outcome	On appeal to the CAT
Aberdeen Journals Ltd NB: **second decision adopted 16.09.2002 – see below**	16.7.2001	Infringement of Chapter II prohibition **Fine of £1.3 million**	Decision annulled and remitted to the OFT for re-definition of relevant product market[5]
ICL/Synstar	24.7.2001	No infringement of Chapter II prohibition	
LINK Interchange Network Ltd	16.10.2001	Infringement of Chapter I prohibition Granted an individual exemption	
Memorandum of Understanding on the Supply of Oil Fuels	25.10.2001	Infringement of Chapter I prohibition Granted an individual exemption No infringement of Chapter II prohibition	
Virgin Trains **(ORR)**	30.11.2001	No infringement of Chapter II prohibition	
XDSL Wholesale Products of BT **(OFTEL)**	24.1.2002	No infringement of Chapter II prohibition	
Market sharing by Arriva plc and FirstGroup plc	30.1.2002	Infringement of Chapter I prohibition **Fines of £848,027** (before leniency) **Fines of £203,632** (after leniency)	
Notification by the Film Distributors' Association	1.2.2002	No infringement of Chapter I prohibition	
BT's Wholesale DSL Products: alleged anti-competitive pricing **(OFTEL)**	28.3.2002	No infringement of Chapter II prohibition	
Vodafone's distribution agreements for pre-pay mobile phone vouchers **(OFTEL)**	05.4.2002	No infringement of Chapter I prohibition	

(continued)

Table 9.1 (*continued*)

Case name	Date of decision	Outcome	On appeal to the CAT
The North & West Belfast Health and Social Services Trust **NB: second decision adopted 23.12.03 – see below**	30.4.2002	No infringement of Chapter II prohibition	(i) Judgment holding that the OFT had made an appealable decision when rejecting BetterCare's complaint[6] (ii) Judgment holding that the Health Trust was an undertaking and remitting the matter to the OFT[7]
John Bruce (UK) Ltd, Fleet Parts Ltd and Truck and Trailer Components	17.5.2002	Infringement of Chapter I prohibition **Fines of £33,737**	
Agreement refusing to supply interconnection services for BT Ignite's Multimedia Voice over Internet Protocol service **(OFTEL)**	12.7.2002	Parties renounced agreement so case was closed	
Harwood Park Crematorium Ltd **NB: decision withdrawn, 9.4.2003; second decision adopted 12.8.2004 – see below**	6.8.2002	No infringement of Chapter II prohibition	
Aberdeen Journals Ltd II **NB: second decision**	16.9.2002	Infringement of Chapter II prohibition **Fine of £1.3 million**	Finding of infringement upheld on appeal **Fine reduced to £1 million**[8]
Companies House	25.10.2002	No infringement of Chapter II prohibition	
General Insurance Standards Council **NB: second decision**	13.11.2002	No infringement of Chapter I prohibition following amendment of the GISC rules	

Case name	Date of decision	Outcome	On appeal to the CAT
Lucite International UK Ltd	29.11.2002	No infringement of Chapter I prohibition as the agreement was vertical and therefore covered by the Exclusion Order for vertical agreements; no reason to 'clawback' exclusion	
Hasbro I	6.12.2002	Infringement of Chapter I prohibition **Fine of £4.95 million**	Appeal withdrawn following grant of 100% leniency to Hasbro in *Hasbro II* – see below[9]
ABTA and British Airways plc	11.12.2002	No infringement of Chapter II prohibition	
BT Group plc **NB: second decision adopted 19.12.2003 – see below** (OFTEL)	9.1.2003	No infringement of Chapter II prohibition	(i) Judgment holding that OFTEL (the predecessor of OFCOM) had made an appealable decision[10] (ii) Judgment partially annulling OFTEL's decision but otherwise dismissing the appeal[11]
BSkyB investigation **NB: refusal to vary or withdraw decision 12.8.2003 – see below**	17.12.2002	No infringement of Chapter II prohibition	
Northern Ireland Livestock and Auctioneers's Association	4.2.2003	Infringement of Chapter I prohibition **No fine**	
Elite Greenhouses Ltd	14.2.2003	No infringement of Chapter I prohibition	

(continued)

Table 9.1 (*continued*)

Case name	Date of decision	Outcome	On appeal to the CAT
Hasbro II **NB: fresh decision adopted 2.12.2003 – see below**	19.2.2003	Infringement of Chapter I prohibition	Remitted to the OFT so that key witness statements may be put to the parties[12]
Lladró Comercial SA	31.3.2003	Infringement of Chapter I prohibition **No fine**	
Thames Water Utilities Ltd/Bath House Albion Yard **(OFWAT)**	31.3.2003	No infringement of Chapter II prohibition	
Anaesthetists Group	15.4.2003	No infringement of Chapter I prohibition	
Genzyme Ltd	27.4.2003	Infringement of Chapter II prohibition **Fine of £6.8 million**	(i) One finding of infringement annulled on appeal; second finding upheld **Fine reduced to £3 million**[13] (ii) Judgment on remedy given on 29 September 2005[14]
BT/BSkyB broadband promotion **(OFTEL)**	19.5.2003	No infringement of Chapter I and II prohibitions	
BT UK-SPN calls service alleged anti-competitive pricing **(OFTEL)**	23.5.2003	No infringement of Chapter II prohibition	
Alleged cross-subsidy of BT's discounts **(OFTEL)**	28.5.2003	No infringement of Chapter II prohibition	
BT TotalCare **(OFTEL)**	10.6.2003	No infringement of Chapter II prohibition	
BT Broadband **(OFTEL)**	11.7.2003	No infringement of Chapter II prohibition	

Case name	Date of decision	Outcome	On appeal to the CAT
Replica football kits	01.8.2003	Infringement of Chapter I prohibition **Fines of £18.668 million** (before leniency) **Fines of £18.627 million** (after leniency)	(i) Finding of infringement substantially upheld[15] (ii) **Fine reduced to £15.49 million**[16] (iii) Judgment of Court of Appeal of 19 October 2006 upholding the CAT[17] (iv) House of Lords (now the Supreme Court) refused permission to appeal on 7 February 2007
BSkyB decision dated 17 December 2002: rejection of applications under section 47 Competition Act **NB: second decision**	12.8.2003	No infringement of Chapter II prohibition	
London Electricity plc **(OFGEM)**	17.9.2003	No infringement of Chapter II prohibition	
E.I. du Pont de Nemours & Co	22.9.2003	No infringement of Chapter II prohibition	
Disconnection of Floe Telecom Ltd's Services by Vodafone Limited **NB: fresh decision adopted 30.6.2005 – see below** **(OFTEL)**	3.11.2003	No infringement of Chapter II prohibition	(i) Judgment of 19 November 2004 requiring OFCOM to reconsider the matter[18] (ii) Ruling of 20 July 2005 refusing permission to appeal to the Court of Appeal[19] (iii) The Court of Appeal gave permission to appeal, including intervener status to the OFT, leading to a judgment providing guidance on the CAT's jurisdiction on 15 June 2006[20]

(*continued*)

Table 9.1 (*continued*)

Case name	Date of decision	Outcome	On appeal to the CAT
Hasbro II **NB: second decision**	2.12.2003	Infringement of Chapter I prohibition **Fines of £38.25 million** (before leniency) **Fines of £22.66 million** (after leniency)	(i) Finding of infringement upheld[21] **(ii) Fine reduced to £19.50 million**[22] (iii) Ruling of 29 April 2005 refusing permission to appeal to the Court of Appeal[23] (iv) Judgment of Court of Appeal of 19 October upholding the CAT[24] (v) House of Lords (now the Supreme Court) refused permission to appeal on 7 February 2007
Alleged predatory pricing by English Welsh and Scottish Railway (ORR)	3.12.2003	No infringement of Chapter II prohibition	
BT/Openworld **NB: second decision** (OFTEL)	19.12.2003	No infringement of Chapter II prohibition **NB: non-infringement decision 2 November 2010**	Appeal withdrawn, 16 December 2010[25]
BetterCare Group Ltd/ North & West Belfast Health & Social Services Trust **NB: second decision**	23.12.2003	No infringement of Chapter II prohibition	
Disconnection of VIP Communications Limited's services by T-Mobile Limited **NB: fresh decision adopted 30.6.2005 – see below (OFTEL)**	31.12.2003	No infringement of Chapter II prohibition	Decision set aside by Order of the CAT[26] and matter remitted to OFCOM
BT Publishing its 118500 directory enquiries number on the front of the BT phonebook (OFTEL)	31.12.2003	No infringement of Chapter II prohibition	

Case name	Date of decision	Outcome	On appeal to the CAT
United Utilities Electricity plc (OFGEM)	10.2.2004	No infringement of Chapter II prohibition	
West Midlands roofing contractors	17.3.2004	Infringement of Chapter I prohibition **Fines of £971,186** (before leniency) **Fines of £297,625** (after leniency)	Finding of infringement fully upheld on appeal[27] **Fines reduced to £288,625**[28]
Pool Reinsurance Company Limited	15.4.2004	Infringement of Chapter I prohibition Granted an individual exemption	
Association of British Insurers	22.4.2004	Infringement of Chapter I prohibition Conditionally granted an individual exemption	Decision on exemption suspended; the OFT subsequently closed the case[29]
Attheraces	10.5.2004	Infringement of Chapter I prohibition	Judgment of 2 August 2005 annulling the OFT's decision[30]
Albion Water/Dŵr Cymru (OFWAT)	27.5.2004	No infringement of Chapter II prohibition	(i) Judgment finding infringement of the Chapter II prohibition on 18 December 2006[31] (ii) Permission to appeal refused on 2 February 2007[32] (iii) Order of the Court of Appeal on 26 July 2007 granting permission to appeal[33] (iv) Judgment of the Court of Appeal on 22 May 2008, dismissing the appeal[34] (v) Judgment of the CAT on 7 November 2008 finding that the price charged by Dŵr Cymru was both excessive and unfair[35]

(*continued*)

Table 9.1 (*continued*)

Case name	Date of decision	Outcome	On appeal to the CAT
			(vi) Judgment of the CAT on 9 April 2009 on remedy and costs[36]
Suspected margin squeeze by Vodafone, O2, Orange and T-Mobile (OFCOM)	27.5.2004	No infringement of Chapter II prohibition	
Complaint against Network Rail by the Sub Contractors Welding Federation (ORR)	4.6.2004	No infringement of Chapter II prohibition	
First Edinburgh/Lothian	9.6.2004	No infringement of Chapter II prohibition	
NPower (OFGEM)	9.6.2004	No infringement of Chapter II prohibition	
Suretrack Rail Services Ltd and P Way Services Ltd/London Underground Group (ORR)	5.7.2004	No infringement of Chapter II prohibition	
Investigation against BT about potential anti-competitive exclusionary behaviour (OFCOM)	12.7.2004	No infringement of Chapter II prohibition	
Southern Water Services Ltd/Provision of new infrastrstructure in East Kent (OFWAT)	3.8.2004	No infringement of Chapter II prohibition	
Refusal to supply JJ Burgess Ltd with access to Harwood Park Crematorium **NB: second decision**	12.8.2004	No infringement of Chapter II prohibition	Judgment of 6 July 2005 setting aside the OFT's decision and concluding that W. Austin and Sons had abused a dominant position in relation to access to Harwood Park[37]

Case name	Date of decision	Outcome	On appeal to the CAT
BT 0845 and 0870 retail price change (**OFCOM**)	12.8.2004	No infringement of Chapter II prohibition	
TM Property Services Ltd/MacDonald Ltd	29.9.2004	No infringement of Chapter II prohibition (NB: OFT market study launched, December 2004)	
Pricing of BT Analyst (**OFCOM**)	28.10.2004	No infringement of Chapter II prohibition	
UOP Ltd/Ukae Ltd Etc (*Desiccants*)	9.11.2004	Infringement of Chapter I Prohibition **Fines of £2.433 million** (before leniency) **Fines of £1.707 million** (after leniency)	**Fines reduced to £1.635 million** by Consent Order of 19 May 2005[38]
United Utitilies Electricity plc (**OFGEM**)	21.12.2004	No infringement of Chapter II prohibition	
Collusive tendering for mastic asphalt flat-roofing contracts in Scotland	8.4.2005	Infringement of Chapter I Prohibition **Fines of £231,445** (before leniency) **Fines of £87,353** (after leniency)	
Collusive tendering for felt and single ply flat-roofing contracts in the North East of England	8.4.2005	Infringement of Chapter I Prohibition **Fines of £598,223** (before leniency) **Fines of £471,029** (after leniency)	
Treatement of tankered landfill leachate (**OFWAT**)	20.5.2005	No infringement of Chapter II prohibition	
Complaint from Gamma Telecom Ltd against BT Wholesale (**OFCOM**)	16.6.2005	No infringement of Chapter II prohibition	

(*continued*)

Table 9.1 (*continued*)

Case name	Date of decision	Outcome	On appeal to the CAT
Re-investigation of Floe Telecom **NB: second decision** (OFCOM)	30.6.2005	No infringement of Chapter II prohibition	(i) Judgment of 31 August 2006 rejecting Floe's appeal[39] (ii) Judgment of 15 March 2007 refusing application by T-Mobile for permission to appeal[40] (iii) Judgment of 15 March 2007 refusing application by OFCOM for permission to appeal[41] (iv) Order of the Court of Appeal on 19 June 2007 granting OFCOM and T-Mobile permission to appeal[42] (v) Judgment of the Court of Appeal on 10 February 2009 setting aside parts of CAT's judgment[43]
Re-investigation of VIP Communications **NB: second decision** (OFCOM)	30.6.2005	No infringement of Chapter II prohibition	(i) Ruling of 19 November 2009 that the application to amend the notice of appeal be dismissed and that the notice of appeal should be rejected[44]. (ii) Ruling on costs 3 February 2010[45]
Collusive tendering for felt and single ply roofing contracts in Western Central Scotland	12.7.2005	Infringement of Chapter I prohibition **Fines of £258,576** (before leniency) **Fines of £138,515** (after leniency)	
Complaint from NTM Sales and Marketing Against Portec Rail Products (UK) Ltd (ORR)	19.8.2005	No infringement of Chapter I or Chapter II prohibitions	

Case name	Date of decision	Outcome	On appeal to the CAT
Investigation of the multilateral interchange fees – MasterCard	6.9.2005	Infringement of Chapter I prohibition	Judgment of 10 July 2006 setting aside OFT's decision[46]
Collusive tendering for flat roof and car park surfacing contracts in England and Scotland	23.2.2006	Infringement of Chapter I prohibition **Fines of £1.852 million** (before leniency) **Fines of £1.557 million** (after leniency)	Decision upheld on appeal[47]
London Metal Exchange – interim measures direction	27.2.2006	Interim measures direction issued to the London Metal Exchange: suspected infringement of Chapter II prohibition; decision subsequently withdrawn by OFT	Judgment of 8 September 2006 on costs[48]
Stock check pads	4.4.2006	Infringement of Chapter I prohibition **Fines of £2,184,767** (before leniency) **Fines of £168,318** (after leniency)	Decision upheld on appeal[49]
Aluminium spacer bars	29.6.2006	Infringement of Chapter I prohibition **Fines of £1,384,050** (before leniency) **Fines of £898,470** (after leniency)	Judgment of 9 March 2007 rejecting DQS's appeal[50]
BT's pricing of digital and cordless phones **(OFCOM)**	7.8.2006	No infringement of Chapter II prohibition	
English Welsh and Scottish Railway Ltd **(ORR)**	17.11.2006	Infringement of Chapter II prohibition **Fine of £4.1 million**	

(*continued*)

Table 9.1 (*continued*)

Case name	Date of decision	Outcome	On appeal to the CAT
Schools: exchange of information on future fees	20.11.2006	Infringement of Chapter I prohibition **Fines of £10,000 for each school that participated in the infringement**	
EDF's electricity metering and related services (OFGEM)	24.1.2007	No infringement of Chapter II prohibition	
BBC Broadcast access services (OFCOM)	5.6.2007	No infringement of Chapter I or Chapter II prohibitions	(i) Judgment of 20 May 2008 rejecting IMS's appeal[51] (ii) Order of the CAT on 24 July 2008 refusing application by IMS for permission to appeal (iii) Judgment of the Court of Appeal of 24 November 2008 refusing application by IMS for permission to appeal[52]
British Airways[53]	1.8.2007	Infringement of the Chapter I prohibition **Fine of £121.5 million**	
National Grid (OFGEM)	25.2.2008	Infringement of Chapter II prohibition and Article 102 **Fine of £41.6 million**	(i) Substance of GEMA's decision upheld on appeal; **fine reduced to £30 million**[54] (ii) Ruling on costs on 23 July 2009[55] (iii) CAT on finding of abuse upheld, **but fine further reduced to £15 million**, on appeal to the Court of Appeal[56] (iv) Supreme Court refused permission to appeal, 5 August 2010

Case name	Date of decision	Outcome	On appeal to the CAT
BT's charges for NTS call termination (OFCOM)	1.8.2008	No infringement of Chapter II prohibition	
Cardiff Bus	18.11.2008	Infringement of Chapter II prohibition **No fine imposed**	
Construction bid rigging	22.09.2009	Infringement of Chapter I prohibition **Fines of £129.5 million**	After appeals to the CAT **fines reduced to £63.9 million**[57]
Recruitment Agencies	30.09.2009	Infringement of Chapter I prohibition **Fines of £39.27 million**	After appeals to the CAT **fines reduced to £8.14 million**[58]
Loan Pricing	30.3.2010	Infringement of Chapter I prohibition and Article 101 TFEU **RBS has agreed to pay a fine of £28.59 million**	
Tobacco	16.4.2010	Infringement of Chapter I prohibition; two manufacturers and ten retailers **fined a total of £225 million**	On appeal to the CAT[59]
DB Schenker Rail (UK) Ltd (ORR)	2.8.2010	No infringement of Chapter II prohibition or of Article 102	
Reckitt Benckiser	15.10.2010	Infringement of Chapter II prohibition **Reckitt Benckiser has agreed to pay a fine of £10.2 million**	
Flybe Limited	5.11.2010	'No grounds for action' decision (alleged infringement of Chapter II prohibition and/or of Article 102 TFEU)	

(*continued*)

Table 9.1 (*continued*)

Case name	Date of decision	Outcome	On appeal to the CAT
Dairy products[60]	10.8.11	Infringement of Chapter I prohibition **Fines of £49.51 million**	On appeal to CAT, Case No 1118/1/1/11 *Tesco Stores Ltd v OFT* not yet decided

[1] Note: in the course of an appeal the CAT may hand down a number of rulings and judgments on various matters: these will all be found on its website, www.catribunal.org.uk; this Table refers only to the key phases in any particular case.

[2] Cases 1002–1004/2/1/01 *Institute of Independent Insurance Brokers v Director General of Fair Trading* [2001] CAT 4, [2001] CompAR 62.

[3] Cases 1000–1/1/1/01 *Napp Pharmaceutical Holdings Ltd v Director General of Fair Trading* [2002] CAT 1, [2002] CompAR 13.

[4] Cf also the judgment of the Chancery Division of 2 November 2000, rejecting Claritas's application for interim measures.

[5] Case 1005/1/1/01 *Aberdeen Journals Ltd v Director General of Fair Trading* [2002] CAT 4, [2002] CompAR 167.

[6] Case 1006/2/1/01 *BetterCare Group v Director General of Fair Trading* [2002] CAT 6, [2002] CompAR 226.

[7] Case 1006/2/1/01 *BetterCare Group Ltd v Director General of Fair Trading* [2002] CAT 7, [2002] CompAR 299.

[8] Case 1009/1/1/02 *Aberdeen Journals v Director General of Fair Trading* [2003] CAT 11, [2003] CompAR 67.

[9] Case 1010/1/1/03 *Hasbro UK Limited v The Director General of Fair Trading*.

[10] Case 1007/2/3/02 *Freeserve v Director General of Telecommunications* [2002] CAT 8, [2003] CompAR 1.

[11] Case 1007/2/3/02 *Freeserve v Director General of Telecommunications* [2003] CAT 5, [2003] CompAR 202.

[12] Case 1014 and 1015/1/1/03 *Argos Ltd and Littlewoods Ltd v Office of Fair Trading* [2003] CAT 16, [2004] CompAR 80.

[13] Case 1016/1/1/03 *Genzyme v Office of Fair Trading* [2004] CAT 4, [2004] CompAR 358.

[14] Case 1016/1/1/03 *Genzyme v Office of Fair Trading* [2005] CAT 32, [2005] CompAR 195.

[15] Cases 1021/1/1/03 etc. *JJB v OFT* [2004] CAT 17, [2005] CompAR 29.

[16] Case 1019/1/1/03 etc *Umbro Holdings Ltd v OFT* [2005] CAT 22, [2005] CompAR 106.

[17] [2006] EWCA Civ 1318.

[18] Case 1024/2/3/04 *Floe Telecom Ltd (in administration) v OFCOM* [2004] CAT 18, [2005] CompAR 290.

[19] Case 1024/2/3/04 *Floe Telecom Ltd (in administration) v OFCOM* [2005] CAT 28, [2006] CompAR 1132.

[20] [2006] EWCA Civ 768.

[21] Cases 1014/1/1/03 and 1015/1/1/03 *Argos Ltd and Littlewoods Ltd v OFT* [2004] CAT 24, [2005] CompAR 588.

[22] Cases 1014/1/1/03 and 1015/1/1/03 *Argos Ltd and Littlewoods Ltd v OFT* [2005] CAT 13, [2005] CompAR 834.

[23] Cases 1014/1/1/03 and 1015/1/1/03 *Argos Ltd and Littlewoods Ltd v OFT* [2005] CAT 16, [2005] CompAR 1000.

[24] [2006] EWCA Civ 768.

[25] Case 1026/2/3/04 *Wanadoo (UK) plc (formerly Freeserve.com plc) v OFCOM*, order of the CAT of 16 December 2010.

[26] Case 1027/2/3/04 *VIP Communications Ltd (in administration) v OFCOM*, order of the CAT of 1 December 2004.

[27] Cases 1032/1/1/04 etc *Apex Asphalt v OFT* [2005] CAT 4 [2005] CompAR 507 and [2005] CAT 5, [2005] CompAR 801.

[28] Cases 1032/1/1/04 etc *Apex Asphalt v OFT* [2005] CAT 11 [2005] CompAR 825 and [2005] CAT 12.

[29] Case 1036/1/1/04 *Association of British Insurers v OFT*.

[30] Case 1035/1/1/04 *The Racecourse Association v OFT* and Case No. 1041/2/1/04 *British Horseracing Board v OFT* [2005] CAT 29, [2006] CompAR 99.

[31] Case 1046/2/4/04 *Albion Water Limited v Director General of Water Services (Dŵr/Shotton Paper)* [2006] CAT 36, [2007] CompAR 328.

[32] [2007] CAT 8, [2007] CompAR 567.

[33] Cases C1/2007/0373 and C1/2007/0374.

[34] [2008] EWCA Civ 538.

[35] Case 1046/2/4/04 *Albion Water Limited v Director General of Water Services (Dŵr/Shotton Paper)* [2008] CAT 31, [2009] CompAR 28.

[36] [2009] CAT 12, [2009] CompAR 223.

[37] Case 1044/2/1/04 *Burgess v OFT* [2005] CAT 25, [2005] CompAR 1151.

[38] Case 1048/1/1/05 *Double Quick Supplyline Ltd v OFT.*

[39] Case 1024/2/3/04 *Floe Telecom Ltd (in administration) v OFCOM* [2006] CAT 17, [2006] CompAR 637.

[40] Case 1024/2/3/04 *Floe Telecom Ltd (in administration) v OFCOM* [2007] CAT 16, [2007] CompAR 688.

[41] Case 1024/2/3/04 *Floe Telecom Ltd (in administration) v OFCOM* [2007] CAT 15, [2007] CompAR 679.

[42] Cases C3/2007/0658 *OFCOM v Floe Telecom Ltd* and C3/2007/0665 *T-Mobile Ltd v Floe Telecom Ltd*

[43] [2009] EWCA Civ 47.

[44] Case 1027/2/3/04 *VDP Communications Ltd (in administration) v OFCOM* [2009] CAT 28.

[45] Case 1027/2/3/04 *VDP Communications Ltd (in administration) v OFCOM* [2010] CAT 3.

[46] Cases 1054–1056/1/1/05 *MasterCard UK Members Forum Limited v OFT* [2006] CAT 14, [2006] CompAR 595.

[47] Case 1061/1/1/06 *Makers UK Ltd v OFT* and Case No. 1065/1/1/06 *Prater Ltd v OFT* [2007] CAT 11.

[48] Case 1062/1/1/06 *London Metal Exchange v OFT* [2006] CAT 19, [2006] CompAR 781.

[49] Case 1067/1/1/06 *Achilles Group Ltd v OFT* [2006] CAT 24.

[50] Case 1072/1/1/06 *Sepia Logistics Ltd v OFT* [2007] CAT 13, [2007] CompAR 747.

[51] Case 1087/2/3/07 *Independent Media Support Ltd v OFCOM* [2008] CAT 13, [2008] CompAR 161.

[52] [2008] EWCA Civ 1402.

[53] Note: formal decision to be adopted and published in due course.

[54] Case No 1099/1/2/08 *National Grid plc v GEMA* [2009] CAT 14.

[55] [2009] CAT 24.

[56] [2010] EWCA Civ 114.

[57] Case Nos etc 1114/1/1/09 *Kier Group plc v OFT* [2011] CAT 3.

[58] Case Nos etc 1140/1/1/09 *Eden Brown Ltd v OFT* [2011] CAT 8.

[59] Cases 1160/1/1/10 *Imperial Tobacco Group plc v OFT*, not yet decided.

[60] Case No 1188/1/1/11 *Tesco Stores Ltd v OFT*, not yet decided.

A number of points can be made about the public enforcement of the Competition Act since March 2000.

(A) Total number of infringement decisions

The OFT has found infringements of the Chapter I prohibition and Article 101 TFEU on 28 occasions; one of these decisions was set aside entirely on appeal to the CAT. The OFT will adopt formal decisions in the case of *British Airways* in due course. The OFT has found infringements of the Chapter II prohibition on five occasions. The ORR has found an infringement of Chapter II and Article 102 TFEU on one occasion, as has GEMA. The fines imposed, after allowing for reductions as a result of leniency, settlement negotiations and appeals to the CAT and the Court of Appeal, amount to £608.1 million.

(B) Findings of infringement by the CAT

In addition to the findings of infringement by the OFT, the ORR and GEMA, on two occasions the CAT has made its own finding of an infringement of the Chapter II prohibition; this happened in appeals from non-infringement decisions of the OFT and Water Services Regulation Authority respectively. In *JJ Burgess & Sons v OFT*[480] the CAT concluded that W. Austin & Sons had abused a dominant position by refusing to grant access to Burgess, a competing firm of funeral directors, to its crematorium facilities at Harwood Park in Hertfordshire. In *Albion Water Ltd v Water Services Regulation Authority*[481] the CAT concluded that Dŵr Cymru had abused its dominant position by applying a margin squeeze to Albion Water, thereby preventing the latter from supplying water to a paper factory in Wales[482].

(C) Appeals against infringement decisions

Several of the OFT's infringement decisions have been appealed to the CAT. Most of them were upheld on substance. Some of the findings of infringements were set aside in the *Football Shirts* case[483] and in the *Construction bid-rigging* appeals[484]. The only infringement decision to have been overturned in its entirety was *Attheraces*[485]. The OFT had concluded that the collective selling by the Racecourse Association of the non-licensed betting office ('non-LBO') media rights to horseracing at 59 racecourses in Great Britain infringed the Chapter I prohibition; and that it did not satisfy the criteria of section 9(1) of the Competition Act, which provides a defence for restrictive agreements that produce economic efficiencies. The Racecourse Association (and the British Horseracing Board) appealed to the CAT, which disagreed with the OFT's analysis[486]. In the CAT's view the OFT had failed to define the relevant market correctly. The OFT had defined a market for non-LBO media rights, but the CAT considered that this was too narrow: the CAT concluded that this was a sufficient reason in itself to set the decision aside[487]. However the CAT also went on to consider whether, assuming the OFT had correctly defined the relevant market, the collective selling amounted to an infringement of the Chapter I prohibition[488]. In the CAT's opinion, the collective selling of the media rights in question was objectively necessary:

> an acquisition via a central negotiation was the only realistic way forward both from the viewpoint of both bidder and sellers (*sic*) and we regard is as probable that any initial attempt at a self-assembly exercise via individual negotiations would have led quickly to a centrally negotiated one[489].

---

[480] Case No 1044/2/1/04 [2005] CAT 25, [2005] CompAR 1151.

[481] Case No 1046/2/4/04 [2006] CAT 36, [2007] CompAR 328.

[482] *Dŵr Cymru Cyfyngedig v Albion Water Ltd* [2008] EWCA Civ 536, [2008] UKCLR 457; note that Albion subsequently brought a follow-on action for damages in the CAT: see ch 8, 'Section 47A: monetary claims before the CAT', p 318.

[483] Case Nos 1021/1/1/03 etc *JJB Sports plc v OFT* [2004] CAT 17, [2005] CompAR 29.

[484] Case No 1118/1/1/09 *GMI Construction Holdings plc v OFT* [2011] CAT 12; Case No 1121/1/1/09 *Durkan Holdings Ltd v OFT* [2011] CAT 6, paras 93–125; Case No 1122/1/1/09 *AH Willis & Sons Ltd v OFT* [2011] CAT 3; Case No 1124/1/1/09 *North Midland Construction plc v OFT* [2011] CAT 14, paras 14–34.

[485] OFT decision of 10 May 2004 [2004] UKCLR 995.

[486] Case Nos 1035/1/1/04 etc *Racecourse Association v OFT* [2005] CAT 29, [2006] CompAR 99.

[487] Ibid, paras 135–150.   [488] Ibid, paras 160–176.   [489] Ibid, para 171.

The CAT also concluded that the OFT had failed to demonstrate that collective selling led to an appreciable increase in price[490]; nor that it resulted in a loss of non-price competition[491]. The CAT's judgment in this case is a most interesting one, in which it takes a robust, 'commonsense' approach to the question of whether competition was restricted on the facts of the case. The discussion of the necessity of collective selling acknowledges that the *evidential* burden of proving such necessity lay with the parties to the agreement rather than with the OFT, even though the overall burden of showing an infringement of Chapter I was on the OFT[492]. The CAT noted the difficulty of reconciling the judgments of the Court of Justice in *Wouters*[493] and *Gøttrup-Klim*[494] with the General Court's judgment in *Métropole v Commission*[495], concluding, in relation to the Court of Justice's judgments, that:

> What these cases show is that ostensibly restrictive arrangements which are *necessary* to achieve a proper commercial objective will not, or may not, constitute an anti-competitive infringement at all. Whether or not they will do so requires an objective analysis of the particular arrangement entered into by the parties, assessed by reference to their subjective 'wants' and against the evidence of the particular market in which they made their arrangement. The task then is to consider whether the restrictive arrangement of which complaint is made is 'necessary' to achieve the objective[496].

(D) Total number of non-infringement decisions

The OFT and sectoral regulators have adopted 57 non-infringement decisions under the Chapter I and Chapter II prohibitions and/or Articles 101 and 102 TFEU. Four individual exemptions were granted before the abolition of notification and exemption, one of which was suspended on appeal.

(E) Appeals against non-infringement and case-closure decisions

The first decision of the OFT under the Competition Act, *General Insurance Standards Council*[497], was a finding of non-infringement of the Chapter I prohibition, which was annulled on appeal to the CAT[498]. On several occasions third party complainants have challenged decisions by the OFT or one of the sectoral regulators to close the file before the CAT. The CAT has sometimes held that the authority had decided that the prohibitions in the Act had not been infringed and had made an implicit non-infringement decision; in several cases the CAT found that the authority had simply closed their file on administrative grounds, without expressing a view on the substance. These cases are discussed in chapter 10[499].

---

[490] Ibid, paras 177–202.   [491] Ibid, paras 207–211.   [492] Ibid, paras 130–134.

[493] Case C-309/99 *Wouters v Algemene Raad van de Nederlandse Orde van Advocaten* [2002] ECR I-5777, [2002] 4 CMLR 913.

[494] Case C-250/92 *Gøttrup-Klim Grovvareforreininger v DanskLandburgs Grovvareselskab AmbA* [1994] ECR-5641, [1996] CMLR 191.

[495] Case T-112/99 [2001] ECR II-2459, [2001] 5 CMLR 1236.   [496] See para 167 of the judgment.

[497] OFT decision of 26 January 2001.

[498] Case Nos 1002–1004/2/1/01 *Institute of Independent Insurance Brokers v Director General of Fair Trading* [2001] CompAR 62; on the GISC case see above 'General comments', p 335.

[499] See ch 10, 'Successful appeals against implicit non-infringement decisions', p 442.

(F) **Sectoral regulators**

There have been only two findings of an infringement by a sectoral regulator. The first was the case of *English Welsh & Scottish Railway Ltd*[500] and the second was the fine imposed on *National Grid* by GEMA[501]. In another case GEMA accepted commitments from SP Manweb, which had been accused by independent connection providers in the electricity sector of discriminatory behaviour in favour of its own affiliated connections business, that it would provide connection services in a non-discriminatory manner within recommended timescales[502].

[500]   ORR decision of 17 November 2006 [2007] UKCLR 937.
[501]   GEMA decision of 21 February 2008, on appeal Case No 1099/1/2/08 *National Grid plc v Gas and Electricity Markets Authority* [2009] CAT 14, [2009] CompAR 282, on appeal [2010] EWCA Civ 114, [2010] UKCLR 386; permission to appeal to the Supreme Court was refused by order of 5 August 2010.
[502]   See OFGEM press release R/42 of 27 October 2005, available at www.ofgem.gov.uk.

10

Competition Act 1998 and the cartel offence: public enforcement and procedure

1. Introduction

The Competition Act 1998 gives wide powers of enforcement to the Office of Fair Trading ('the OFT') and to the sectoral regulators. The exercise of these powers must satisfy the Human Rights Act 1998, which received the Royal Assent on the same day as the Competition Act 1998 (9 November 1998) and which entered into force on 2 October 2000[1]. The Enterprise Act 2002 amended and reinforced the Competition Act 1998 in significant ways: for example it simplified third party appeals[2] and made provision for monetary claims pursuant to findings of an infringement of UK or EU competition law by the competition authorities[3]; it provided for so-called 'super-complaints'[4]; it introduced a criminal 'cartel offence' which can result in the imprisonment of individuals for up to five years[5]; and it provided for company director disqualification where a director knew, or ought to have known, of an infringement of EU or UK competition law[6]. Significant changes were made to the Competition Act by the Competition Act 1998 and Other Enactments (Amendment) Regulations 2004[7] (the 'Amendment Regulations') in order to bring domestic law into alignment with the principles of Regulation 1/2003[8]; these changes are incorporated into the text that follows.

---

[1] On the Human Rights Act 1998 see 'Human Rights Act 1998 and Police and Criminal Evidence Act 1984', pp 400–401 below and, more generally, Lester, Pannick and Herberg *Human Rights Law and Practice* (LexisNexis, 3rd ed, 2009); for further discussion of procedural issues in the UK see Ward and Smith (eds) *Competition Litigation in the UK* (Sweet & Maxwell, 2003); O'Neill and Sanders *UK Competition Procedure* (Oxford University Press, 2007); Green and Brealey (eds) *Competition Litigation: UK Practice and Procedure* (Oxford University Press, 2010).

[2] See 'Appealable decisions', pp 440–443 below.

[3] See ch 8, 'Follow-on actions in the CAT and the High Court', pp 317–319.

[4] See ch 11, 'Super-Complaints', pp 454–455.   [5] See 'The cartel offence', pp 425–434 below.

[6] See 'Company director disqualification', pp 435–436 below.   [7] SI 2004/1261.

[8] OJ [2003] L 1/1; see ch 7, 'Overview of Regulation 1/2003', pp 250–251.

This chapter will begin with a consideration of the way in which inquiries and investigations are carried out under the Competition Act. After a section on complaints and super-complaints it will consider the extent to which it may be possible to receive guidance from the OFT on the application of the Act. Section 4 deals with enforcement and section 5 with the cartel offence and company director disqualification. Section 6 considers the issue of concurrency. Section 7 contains a discussion of the appeal mechanism under the Competition Act and section 8 examines the possibility of Article 267 references to the Court of Justice. The private enforcement of the Competition Act (and of Articles 101 and 102 TFEU) in the UK was discussed in chapter 8 of this book[9].

2. Inquiries and Investigations

The purpose of the 1998 Act is to eradicate cartels and abusive behaviour and it provides the OFT and the sectoral regulators with wide powers to conduct inquiries and investigations. These powers are set out in sections 25 to 29 of the Act as modified by the Amendment Regulations. Pursuant to Articles 20 to 22 of Regulation 1/2003 the OFT also has powers to conduct investigations on behalf of the European Commission or at the request of a national competition authority ('NCA') of another Member State of the EU: these powers are set out in sections 61 to 65 of the Competition Act, again as modified by the Amendment Regulations[10]. The OFT's powers to conduct inquiries and investigations are explained in some detail in the OFT's Guideline *Powers of investigation*[11]. The OFT has introduced a pilot project whereby rewards may be given to informants that provide it with intelligence about cartel behaviour[12]. These, and all the other guidance documents referred to in this chapter, are available on the OFT's website[13].

In March 2011 the OFT published *A guide to the OFT's investigation procedures in competition cases*[14]: this guide does not replace earlier Guidelines, but it does contain detailed guidance on a number of aspects of both the law and practice on investigations under the Competition Act[15].

Section 25 of the Competition Act provides that the OFT may conduct an investigation if there are 'reasonable grounds for suspecting' that either of the prohibitions in the Competition Act or that Article 101 or 102 TFEU have been infringed; this is often referred to as the 'section 25 threshold'[16], and requires less evidence than an infringement decision[17]. Section 25 gives the OFT a discretion whether or not to conduct an investigation: it is not under a duty to conduct one. The manner in which the OFT conducts investigations, and the priority it gives to different phases of an investigation, are matters that

---

[9] See ch 8, 'Damages Actions in the UK Courts', pp 306–319.

[10] See 'EU investigations', p 402 below for a brief discussion of investigations under these provisions.

[11] OFT 404, December 2004.

[12] See OFT Press Release of 29 February 2008; more information is available at www.oft.gov.uk/advice_and_resources/resource_base/cartels/rewards.

[13] www.oft.gov.uk.   [14] OFT 1263, March 2011, available at www.oft.gov.uk.

[15] The *Guide* does not apply to investigations undertaken by sectoral regulators: ibid, para 1.4.

[16] On the circumstances in which the OFT's powers can be used see *Powers of investigation*, para 2; the OFT's powers are equally available to the sectoral regulators listed in s 54 of the Competition Act and it should be assumed throughout this chapter that anything that applies to the OFT applies equally to them unless otherwise stated.

[17] On the section 25 threshold see further 'Written inquiries', pp 395–396 below; on the sources of the OFT's investigations see *A guide to the OFT's on investigation procedures*, ch 3.

fall within its discretion[18]. In *R (Cityhook Ltd) v OFT*[19] the Administrative Court held that the scope of the discretion conferred by section 25 does not become more circumscribed once a decision to investigate has been taken and an investigation commenced[20].

A 2005 report by the National Audit Office ('NAO'), *The Office of Fair Trading: Enforcing competition in markets*[21], suggested that the OFT should do more to improve the resourcing and prioritisation of its casework and the transparency and speed of its case management. The OFT accepted the NAO's conclusions[22], and in October 2008 it published its *OFT Prioritisation Principles*[23] which explain the principles that the OFT takes into account when selecting a new project or case for investigation. In 2009 the NAO published a further report which recognised the progress that the OFT had made in this respect[24]. In *Cityhook*[25] the Administrative Court upheld the right of the OFT to prioritise its enforcement efforts. It is entitled, for example, to take into account consumer interests and the nature of an alleged infringement when selecting cases for investigation[26]. In *Tobacco* the OFT applied its *OFT Prioritisation Principles* when deciding to reduce the number of parties to its investigation in order to progress the case effectively and deliver a high impact outcome[27].

The Act gives the OFT power to make written inquiries (section 26) and to enter business and domestic premises (sections 27 to 29)[28]. These powers are also available to enable the OFT to decide whether to apply for a company director disqualification order[29].

(A) **Written inquiries**[30]

Where the section 25 threshold has been reached, a written request for information may be made by a notice under section 26 requiring a person to produce to the OFT a specified document[31] or specified information which the OFT considers relevant to the investigation[32]. Where it is practical and appropriate to do so, the OFT will send the notice to the proposed addressee in draft[33]. The notice must indicate the subject-matter and purpose of the investigation[34] and the offences involved in the event of non-compliance[35]. Specification can be by reference to a particular item or by category and the notice may state when and where the document or information is to be provided as well as how and in what form[36].

---

[18] *Crest Nicholson Plc v OFT* [2009] EWHC 1875, [2009] UKCLR 895, paras 45 and 77.

[19] [2009] EWHC 57, [2009] UKCLR 255.   [20] Ibid, para 97.

[21] HC 593, Session 2005–06, available at www.nao.org.uk.

[22] See the OFT's evidence before the House of Commons Public Accounts Committee, available at www.publications.parliament.uk/pa/cm200506/cmselect/cmpubacc/841/841.pdf.

[23] OFT 953, October 2008, available at www.oft.gov.uk.

[24] *Progress Report on Maintaining Competition in Markets*, HC 127, Session 2008–09, available at www.nao.org.uk.

[25] [2009] EWHC 57, [2009] UKCLR 255; similarly the European Commission is entitled to assign different degrees of priority to cases: see Case T-24/90 *Automec Srl v Commission (No 2)* [1992] ECR II-2223, [1992] 5 CMLR 431, paras 76–77; see ch 7, 'The position of complainants', p 286.

[26] *R (Cityhook Ltd) v OFT*, paras 102–107 and 110–112.

[27] OFT decision of 15 April 2010, para 2.99.

[28] Details of the inspections conducted by the OFT under the Act can be found in Annex C to the OFT's Annual Report and Resource Accounts 2008–09 (HC 475) and 2009–10 (HC 301). Note that ss 61–64 deal with investigations under Articles 101 and 102 TFEU.

[29] Company Directors Disqualification Act 1986, s 9C, inserted by Enterprise Act 2002, s 204.

[30] See *Powers of investigation*, para 3.

[31] Documents include 'information recorded in any form': for example records held on computers, mobile phones, mobile email and other electronic devices: Competition Act, s 59(1); see *Powers of investigation*, para 3.6.

[32] Competition Act 1998, s 26(1), (2).   [33] *A guide to the OFT's investigation procedures*, para 6.8.

[34] Competition Act 1998, s 26(3)(a).   [35] Ibid, s 26(3)(b).

[36] Ibid, s 26(4) and (5); s 59(3) provides that, if information is not in legible form, the OFT may require a copy in legible form.

The OFT has the further power to take copies or extracts from a document produced in response to the notice and to ask for an explanation of it, or, if the document is not produced, to ask where it is believed to be[37]. Notices can be addressed to any person, which is defined to include an undertaking[38]; they may be sent not only to the undertakings suspected of infringement, but also to third parties such as complainants, suppliers, customers, competitors, liquidators or administrators of companies[39]. It should be noted that while section 26 applies equally to documents and to information, the Guideline on *Powers of investigation* makes clear that the power to obtain information means that the OFT can require a person to create a document incorporating that information: for example a person may be asked to provide market share information or to describe a particular market on the basis of their knowledge or experience or that of their staff[40]. Some section 26 notices are sent after on-site investigations in order to seek clarification of documents obtained[41].

(B) **Power to enter premises without a warrant**[42]

Section 27(1) of the Act provides that any officer of the OFT who is authorised in writing by the OFT to do so ('an investigating officer') may enter any business premises[43] in connection with an investigation under section 25[44].

The operation of the power of entry varies depending on whether the premises are occupied by a 'third party', that is to say someone who is not suspected of an offence, or by a party under investigation for a possible infringement. In the case of a third party at least two working days' notice of the inspection must be given, together with a document explaining the subject-matter and the purpose of the investigation[45]. If, however, the officer has taken all reasonable steps to give notice but has been unable to do so he may dispense with the notice requirement[46]. In the case of a party under investigation there is no requirement to give prior warning or notice[47], but the subject-matter and purpose of the investigation must be explained. It is not necessary for the OFT first to have attempted to obtain information under the powers conferred by section 26[48].

When entering the premises the officer may:

- take with him any necessary equipment: this could be a laptop computer or tape-recording equipment[49]

- require 'any person'[50] to produce any documents which the officer considers relevant, to say where a document may be found, and, in relation to any document produced, may require an explanation of it

---

[37] Ibid, s 26(6); see 'Self-incrimination', pp 399–400 below for discussion of the scope of the power to request explanations and the law on self-incrimination.

[38] Ibid, which refers to the Interpretation Act 1978 ('person' includes a body of persons corporate or unincorporate).

[39] *Powers of investigation*, para 3.4.   [40] Ibid, para 3.7.   [41] Ibid, para 3.2.

[42] Ibid, para 4.

[43] Competition Act 1998, s 27(6); premises includes any land or means of transport: ibid, s 59(1).

[44] As to investigations under s 27 on Crown land see the Competition Act 1998, s 73(4)(a) and the Competition Act 1998 (Definition of Appropriate Person) Regulations 1999, SI 1999/2282; the Secretary of State may certify in the interests of national security that specified Crown premises may not be entered under this section (see s 73(8)).

[45] Competition Act 1998, s 27(2).   [46] Ibid, s 27(3)(b).   [47] Ibid, s 27(3)(a).

[48] *Powers of investigation*, para 3.2.   [49] Ibid, para 4.6.

[50] In this instance this term presumably (although not necessarily) refers to an individual rather than to an undertaking, but there is no restriction as to who the person needs to be; it could include secretaries, IT personnel and messengers as well as directors; see HL Committee, 17 November 1997, col 391 (Lord Simon of Highbury).

- take copies of or extracts from any document produced (but not the originals)
- require the production in visible, legible and portable form of any relevant information that is held on computer
- take any steps necessary to preserve or prevent interference with any document relevant to the investigation[51].

The procedure when conducting an inspection without a warrant is explained in the OFT's Guideline[52].

It is not permissible under section 27 to use force to enter or once on the premises; it follows that permitted equipment would not include crowbars or other tools. Section 27 entry may therefore be described as a 'right of peaceful entry'. Where force might be required to gain entry, as would be the case for example when the premises are unoccupied, the powers in section 28 must be used. Section 27 does not give a power of search: again this is available only under section 28.

(C) Power to enter premises with a warrant[53]

The OFT may apply for a warrant giving power to enter and search business[54] or domestic premises[55] to named officers of the OFT[56] and to non-employees, such as IT experts, who may be able to assist with the investigation[57]. Where the OFT wishes to enter domestic premises it can be anticipated that the Human Rights Act 1998 might be invoked, since one of the 'Convention Rights' protected by that Act is the right to respect for private and family life, the home and correspondence[58]. A section 28 investigation cannot be conducted on Crown land[59]. The OFT also has powers to conduct inspections under the Enterprise Act 2002 where it has reasonable grounds for suspecting that the cartel offence established by section 188 of that Act has been committed[60].

A warrant may be issued in specified circumstances by the High Court[61] and in this case reasonable force may be used to obtain entry[62]. The circumstances are that:[63]

- there are reasonable grounds for suspecting that a document sought by written notice, or by an investigation without a warrant, but not produced, is on the premises
- there are reasonable grounds for suspecting that a document that the OFT could obtain by written notice or by peaceful entry is on the premises but would be interfered with if it were required to be produced
- (in the case of business premises) entry without a warrant for the purpose of investigation has been impossible and there are reasonable grounds for suspecting that documents are on the premises that could have been required if entry had been obtained.

---

[51] Competition Act 1998, s 27(5); see also s 59(3).

[52] *Powers of investigation*, paras 4.7–4.11; see also *A guide to the OFT's investigation procedures*, paras 6.21–6.24.

[53] *Powers of investigation*, para 5; see also Peretz 'Warrants under Section 28 of the CA 1998: *OFT v D*' [2003] 2 Competition Law Journal 129.

[54] Competition Act 1998, s 28.   [55] Ibid, s 28A.

[56] Ibid, s 28(2) (business premises) and s 28A(2) (domestic premises).

[57] Ibid, s 28(3A) (business premises) and s 28A(4) (domestic premises).

[58] Human Rights Act, Sch 1, Art 8; case law of the EU Courts and the ECHR is discussed in the opening section of ch 7, p 249.

[59] Competition Act 1998, s 73(4)(b).

[60] See 'Powers of investigation and search', pp 427–428 below.

[61] Or the Court of Session in Scotland.

[62] Competition Act 1998, s 28(2)(a) (business premises) and s 28A(2)(a) (domestic premises).

[63] Ibid, s 28(1) (business premises) and s 28A(1) (domestic premises).

The section 28 powers therefore confer a 'right of forcible entry'.

Investigation by warrant is a serious matter and the investigator's powers are more extensive than under section 26 or 27. The subject-matter and purpose of the investigation, and the offences for non-compliance, must be indicated in the warrant itself[64]. It follows that the party being investigated should inspect this document carefully.

The investigators may use reasonable force to gain entry, but must lock the premises up in as secure a manner as they found them before leaving[65]. They may take 'equipment' to exercise such force but may not use force against any person[66]. As with investigations without a warrant the authorised officer may require documents to be produced, but the scope of this power depends on the situation in which the warrant was issued. The warrant will accordingly specify documents of 'the relevant kind'[67], that is to say those subject to a specific request under section 26 or 27, or those of the kind that could have been required on investigation under section 27 but were not provided. In addition to all the powers investigators would have on entry without a warrant, including the power to require information to be accessed from computers[68], they can also take away *originals* of documents and retain them for three months if copying them on the premises is not practicable or if taking them away appears necessary to prevent their disappearance[69]. When acting under section 28, but not section 28A, investigating officers have the additional powers contained in section 50 of the Criminal Justice and Police Act 2001[70]. The investigators can also take any other necessary steps to preserve the existence of documents[71]. The procedure when conducting an inspection with a warrant is explained in the OFT's Guideline[72].

(D) Powers of surveillance

The OFT also has powers of directed surveillance and to make use of covert human intelligence sources in order to investigate infringements of the Competition Act[73].

(E) Access to lawyers

There is no statutory right to obtain outside legal help in the case of an investigation with or without a warrant, and certainly none to delay the start of an investigation until an undertaking's external lawyer arrives on the scene[74]. The OFT's Rules provide expressly for this right 'if the officer considers it reasonable in the circumstances to do so and if he is satisfied that such conditions as he considers…appropriate…will be complied

---

[64] Ibid, s 29(1).

[65] Ibid, s 28(5) (business premises), s 28A(6) (domestic premises).

[66] *Powers of investigation*, para 5.5.

[67] Competition Act 1998, s 28(2)(b) (business premises) and s 28A(2)(b) (domestic premises).

[68] Ibid, s 28(3).

[69] Ibid, s 28(2)(c), (7) (business premises) and s 28A(2)(c), (8) (domestic premises).

[70] See 'Power to enter premises under a warrant', p 428 below.

[71] Competition Act 1998, s 28(2)(d) (business premises) and s 28A(2)(d) (domestic premises).

[72] *Powers of investigation*, paras 5.10–5.14; *A guide to the OFT's investigation procedures*, paras 6.25–6.36.

[73] See 'Powers of surveillance', pp 429–430 below.

[74] During the passage of the Competition Bill through Parliament Lord Simon of Highbury stated that the OFT would follow European Commission practice in this regard by giving a firm without internal legal assistance a reasonable period to obtain external help: HL Committee, 17 November 1997, col 404.

with'[75]. The Guideline *Powers of investigation* provides further guidance on this issue[76]. The investigating officer will not wait for an external lawyer to arrive if the firm being investigated has an internal legal adviser[77], apparently irrespective of whether he or she is specialised in competition law.

(F) Limitation on the use of the powers of investigation[78]

(i) Legal professional privilege

The OFT's power to obtain documents, whether by written notice or during an inspection, does not extend to privileged communications[79]. The privilege belongs to the client. Privileged communications are defined as communications either between a professional legal adviser and his client or those made in connection with, or in contemplation of, legal proceedings and which, for the purposes of those proceedings, would be protected from disclosure in High Court proceedings[80]. 'Professional legal adviser' includes professionally qualified lawyers employed by firms (in-house counsel) as well as those practising in their own right, and in this respect privilege under the 1998 Act is more extensive than under EU competition law[81]. Not only does EU law not extend to correspondence with 'in-house' (that is to say employed) lawyers; nor does it apply to dealings with independent professional lawyers not qualified in a Member State[82]. It follows that some communications can legitimately be withheld where the inspection is one that the OFT conducts on its own behalf but not where it is assisting the European Commission's own inspections under Articles 20 and 21 of Regulation 1/2003. The more generous domestic rules on privilege do apply where the OFT conducts an inspection on behalf of the European Commission[83] or on behalf of a competition authority of another Member State[84].

In the case of a dispute as to privilege during an inspection the communication(s) in question may be sealed in an envelope[85]. If the OFT decides to require the disclosure of the communication(s), this decision is subject to judicial review.

(ii) Self-incrimination

The OFT accepts that the privilege against self-incrimination means that it may not ask for explanations that might involve admissions of an infringement and will instead seek explanations of matters of fact, such as whether a particular employee was at a particular meeting[86]; however the distinction between these two will not always be clear-cut[87]. A statement made by a person in response to a requirement arising from sections 26 to 28A of the

---

[75] SI 2004/2751, r 3(1).

[76] *Powers of investigation*, paras 4.10–4.11; see also *A guide to the OFT's investigation procedures*, paras 6.33–6.34.

[77] *Powers of investigation*, para 4.11.   [78] Ibid, para 6.1.   [79] Competition Act 1998, s 30.

[80] On the English law of litigation privilege see Green and Brealey (eds) *Competition Litigation: UK Practice and Procedure* (Oxford University Press, 2010), chs 10 and 13; *Halsbury's Laws* (4th ed), paras 71–85; in Scotland the privilege is known as 'confidentiality of communications'.

[81] See *Powers of investigation*, paras 6.1–6.2, 9.7–9.9 and 10.5.

[82] For a discussion of privilege in EU competition law see ch 7, 'The Commission' powers', pp 268–269.

[83] Competition Act 1998, s 65A.   [84] Ibid, s 65J.

[85] *A guide to the OFT's investigation procedures*, para 7.3.   [86] *Powers of investigation*, para 6.6.

[87] The power of the OFT to obtain documents already in existence does not offend the right against self-incrimination: see Case C-301/04 P *Commission v SGL Carbon AG* [2006] ECR I-5915, [2006] 5 CMLR 877, paras 33–51; this judgment of the Court of Justice will apply to the OFT's actions by virtue of s 60(2) of the Competition Act, on which see ch 9, '"Governing Principles Clause": Section 60 of the Competition Act 1998', pp 369–374.

Act cannot be used against him for the purposes of a prosecution under the cartel offence unless he makes statements inconsistent with it or adduces evidence in relation to it[88].

The OFT's power to demand an 'explanation' of a document is expressly linked to and limited to documents that are produced[89]. However, in the case of an investigation with a warrant, an explanation can be sought in relation to 'any document appearing to be of the relevant kind'[90] without any specific reference to the document having been produced: this is because, in the case of a search, documents may be found as well as produced. The investigator could in theory require explanation of a document that appears to exist but which he has been unable to find, but the OFT's guidelines do not indicate any intention to act in this way.

(iii) Confidentiality

There are detailed provisions in Part 9 of the Enterprise Act 2002 about restrictions on the disclosure of information obtained during the course of an investigation (and as a result of the operation of Part I of the Act generally) and these provide a degree of reassurance to disclosing parties. However parties subject to an investigation or to a request for information should identify any confidential information that is supplied to the OFT in order to support any subsequent claim that it should not be published or disclosed to anyone else; indeed the OFT will usually ask them to do this, particularly where significant amounts of information or numbers of documents are sought. There is no right to withhold information from the OFT's investigators on grounds of confidentiality[91]. The OFT's Guidelines explain the OFT's rights and obligations as regards publication[92].

(iv) Human Rights Act 1998 and Police and Criminal Evidence Act 1984 ('PACE')

In *Napp Pharmaceutical Holdings Ltd v Director General of Fair Trading*[93] the question arose whether penalty proceedings under the Competition Act were 'criminal' for the purpose of Article 6 of the European Convention on Human Rights, which is given effect in domestic law by the Human Rights Act 1998. The Competition Appeal Tribunal ('the CAT') held that proceedings under the Competition Act 1998 are 'criminal'[94] and that it followed from this that the undertaking concerned is entitled, amongst other things, to a fair and public hearing by an independent and impartial tribunal and to be presumed innocent: it is for the OFT to prove the infringements alleged[95]. However the CAT also concluded that this did not mean that they should be subject to the same rules of evidence or procedures as ordinary criminal proceedings[96]. In particular the CAT held that the Human Rights Act 1998 does not require that the criminal standard of proof 'beyond all reasonable doubt' should be applied; instead it concluded that the civil standard 'balance of probabilities' was the appropriate standard although, where a fine is imposed, this would require the OFT to provide 'strong and compelling evidence'[97]. The CAT added that that approach did not preclude the OFT from relying on presumptions, for example that a firm with a very high market share is dominant;

---

[88] Competition Act 1998, s 30A.   [89] Ibid, ss 26(6)(a)(ii), 27(5)(b)(ii).

[90] Ibid, s 28(2)(e) (business premises) and s 28A(2)(b) (domestic premises).

[91] See r 6 of the OFT's Rules in relation to information provided by third parties; confidential information is defined in r 1(1).

[92] *Powers of investigation*, paras 6.8–6.13 and *A guide to the OFT's investigation procedures*, paras 7.6–7.11.

[93] Case No 1000/1/1/01 [2002] CAT 1, [2002] CompAR 13.

[94] Ibid, paras 93 and 98; the European Court of Human Rights came to the same conclusion in *Menarini Diagnostics Srl v Italy*, judgment of 27 September 2011. See also the interim judgment, Case No 1001/1/1/01 [2001] CAT 3, [2001] CompAR 33, paras 69–70.

[95] Case No 1000/1/1/01 [2002] CAT 1, [2002] CompAR 13, para 99.   [96] Ibid, para 101.

[97] Ibid, paras 105 and 109.

such presumptions do not reverse the burden of proof or set aside the presumption of innocence[98]. In subsequent judgments the CAT has stressed that the standard of proof is the balance of probabilities, laying less emphasis on the requirement that evidence should be 'strong and compelling'[99]. The CAT may have felt that the latter standard was having a chilling effect on findings of infringements by the OFT and the sectoral regulators. The High Court adopts the same approach to the burden and standard of proof as the CAT[100].

On a separate point, in *Toys and Games*[101] the OFT rejected an argument that it should, when conducting interviews with employees of Hasbro Ltd as to the possibility of an infringement of the Chapter I prohibition, have complied with the procedures required by PACE[102]. The OFT has indicated that it would act in accordance with PACE when investigating a possible commission of the cartel offence[103].

(G) Offences[104]

There are criminal sanctions for non-compliance with the powers of investigation. These offences must be indicated in section 26 notices and in warrants issued under sections 28 and 28A and must also be mentioned at the outset of voluntary interviews. Individuals as well as legal persons may commit offences; the penalties in some cases include imprisonment[105]. The relevant offences are set out in sections 42 to 44 of the Competition Act and fall into five main categories:

- failing to comply with a requirement imposed under sections 26, 27, 28 or 28A[106]
- intentionally obstructing an officer investigating without a warrant[107]
- intentionally obstructing an officer investigating with a warrant[108]
- intentionally or recklessly destroying, disposing of, falsifying or concealing documents, or causing or permitting those things to happen[109]
- knowingly or recklessly supplying information which is false or misleading in a material particular either directly to the OFT, or to anyone else, knowing it is for the purpose of providing information to the OFT[110].

The Act allows various defences to these penal provisions. If a person is charged with not producing a document it is a defence to show that he did not have it in his possession or control and it was not reasonably practical for him to get it[111]. A similar statutory defence applies to failure to provide information. In relation to all requirements under sections 26 and 27 (written notice and investigation without a warrant) there is a general defence if the investigator failed to act in accordance with the section[112]. This shows the importance of ensuring that all the procedural steps are properly taken. There is no statutory defence in relation to investigations with a warrant, presumably because the judge asked to issue the warrant would effectively consider them anyway; furthermore it is possible to challenge

---

[98] Ibid, paras 110–111.
[99] See eg Case Nos 1021 and 1022/1/1/03 *JJB Sports plc and Allsports Ltd v OFT* [2004] CAT 17, [2005] CompAR 29, paras 195–208; also Case No 1061/1/1/06 *Makers UK Ltd v OFT* [2007] CAT 11, paras 45–52.
[100] See eg *Chester City Council v Arriva* [2007] EWHC 1373, [2007] UKCLR 1582, para 10; *Bookmakers' Afternoon Greyhound Services v Amalgamated Racing* [2008] EWHC 1978, [2009] UKCLR 547, para 392.
[101] *Hasbro UK Ltd, Argos Ltd and Littlewoods Ltd* OFT decision of 19 February 2003, [2003] UKCLR 553.
[102] Ibid, para 186.   [103] *Powers for investigating criminal cartels*, OFT 515, January 2004, para 4.1.
[104] *Powers of investigation*, para 7.   [105] See below.
[106] Competition Act 1998, s 42(1).   [107] Ibid, s 42(5).   [108] Ibid, s 42(7).
[109] Ibid, s 43(1).   [110] Ibid, s 44(1), (2).   [111] Ibid, s 42(2), (3).
[112] Ibid, s 42(4).

the issue of the warrant itself. There are no statutory defences to the charges of knowingly or recklessly destroying documents or providing false or misleading information.

The penalties can be substantial and depend on whether the offence is tried summarily or is serious enough to be taken on indictment to the Crown Court[113]. Usually the penalties are financial but in the case of any obstruction of investigators with a warrant, destruction of documents or provision of false or misleading information imprisonment for up to two years is possible (as well as a fine in some cases)[114].

As already described the powers of investigation, and the offences, are applicable to 'persons', which can include an undertaking[115]. In addition, under section 72, officers of bodies corporate are liable to punishment if they have consented to or connived at an offence or it is due to neglect on their part[116]. Officer means a director, manager, secretary or other similar officer, or anyone purporting to act as such[117]. There are similar provisions applicable to companies managed by their members (who can be liable) and, in Scotland, to partners and partnerships[118]. The fact that individuals themselves can be personally liable under these provisions of the Competition Act, and that there is even a possibility of imprisonment, will no doubt concentrate the minds of those responsible for ensuring compliance with the legislation[119].

(H) EU investigations

The European Commission has power, under Articles 20 and 21 of Regulation 1/2003, to conduct on-site investigations in relation to possible infringements of Articles 101 and 102 TFEU, and may seek the assistance of an NCA when doing so. Article 22(1) of the Regulation enables the Commission to ask an NCA to conduct an investigation on its behalf, and Article 22(2) gives the same power to the competition authorities of the other Member States of the EU[120]. Sections 61 to 65 of the Competition Act 1998 set out, in considerable detail, the rules that govern inspections by the OFT under Regulation 1/2003, and the OFT has provided guidance on their application in practice[121].

3. Complaints and Super-Complaints

(A) Complaints

Although the Competition Act 1998 does not establish a procedure for complaining to the OFT, complaints are an important source of information about possible infringements.

---

[113] *Powers of investigation*, para 7.5; the offence would be tried in the High Court of Justiciary in Scotland.

[114] Competition Act 1998, ss 42(6), (7), 43(2), 44(3); *Powers of investigation*, para 7.7 describes the penalties in detail.

[115] Competition Act 1998, s 59(1); see *Powers of investigation*, para 4.3.

[116] Competition Act 1998, s 72(2); see *Powers of investigation*, para 7.4.

[117] Competition Act 1998, s 72(3).

[118] Ibid, s 72(4)–(6).

[119] This point is even more significant given the existence of the criminal cartel offence ('The cartel offence', pp 425–434) and company director disqualification ('Company director disqualification', pp 435–436).

[120] The OFT conducted an investigation on behalf of the French Competition Authority in a case that resulted in fines for four oil companies that distorted competition in a tender process organised by Air France: see Press Release of 4 December 2008, available at www.autoritedelaconcurrence.fr/.

[121] *Powers of investigation*, paras 9 and 10.

Provision is made in the OFT's *A guide to the OFT's investigation procedures*[122] for a 'pre-complaint discussion' as to whether a matter would be likely to be investigated if a formal complaint were to be made.

The OFT has issued a Guideline on *Involving third parties in Competition Act investigations*[123] which sets out the mandatory[124] and optional[125] information that should be included in a written, reasoned complaint; this may lead to the establishment of 'Formal Complainant' status. A Formal Complainant enjoys defined rights in relation to file closures[126], statements of objections[127] and interim measures applications[128]. The OFT aims to inform a complainant whether it will conduct an investigation under the Act within four months of the complaint[129].

Complaints raise questions of confidentiality which can be difficult. Where a complainant provides confidential information to the OFT[130] the OFT requires a non-confidential version of such information that can be disclosed to the complainee[131]. Some complainants wish to remain anonymous and this can make it difficult for the OFT to pursue the complaint. The complainant should explain to the OFT why its identity should not be disclosed; if the OFT is satisfied that this is the case it will seek to maintain the anonymity 'to the extent that this is consistent with the OFT's statutory obligations'[132]; this may not be sustainable once the OFT proposes to adopt an infringement decision[133]. Part 9 of the Enterprise Act 2002 contains rules against the disclosure of certain information about individuals or undertakings unless disclosure is permitted by one of the so-called 'gateways' set out in sections 239 to 242 of the Act. These provisions are explained in the OFT's guidelines[134]. The OFT's Procedural Adjudicator may resolve disputes as to confidentiality[135].

The right of a complainant to challenge a rejection of a complaint is considered in section 7 below[136].

(B) **Super-complaints**

The Enterprise Act 2002 provides a procedure whereby nominated bodies may make a 'super-complaint' to the OFT or to a sectoral regulator: this possibility is dealt with in the chapter on market investigations under that Act[137].

4. **Opinions and Informal Advice**

The Competition Act as originally enacted provided a system of notification to the OFT for guidance or a decision as to whether the Chapter I or Chapter II prohibitions were

---

[122] OFT 1263, March 2011, paras 3.17–3.21; see also *OFT's Prioritisation Principles*, OFT 953, October 2008.
[123] OFT 451, April 2006.
[124] Ibid, Annexe, Part B (setting out the mandatory information to be included).
[125] Ibid, Annexe, Part C (setting out the optional information to be included).
[126] Ibid, para 2.   [127] Ibid, para 3.   [128] Ibid, para 4.
[129] *A guide to the OFT's investigation procedures*, para 4.6.
[130] Confidential information for this purpose is defined in r 1(1) of the OFT's Rules, SI 2004/2751.
[131] *Involving third parties*, para 2.14.
[132] Ibid, para 2.15; see also *A guide to the OFT's investigation procedures*, para 3.22.
[133] *Guide on investigation procedures*, para 3.23.
[134] OFT 442, December 2004, para 9 and *A guide to the OFT's investigation procedures*, paras 7.6–7.11.
[135] On the Procedural Adjudicator see 'Procedure', p 405 below.
[136] See 'Appeals', pp 439–449 below.   [137] See ch 11, 'Super-Complaints', pp 454–455.

being infringed[138]. The abolition of notification under EU law[139] has been mirrored in domestic law: the Amendment Regulations repealed the provisions on notification with effect from 1 May 2004. This led the OFT, in its Guideline *Modernisation*[140], to set out in Part 7 the circumstances in which it might provide an Opinion[141] or give informal advice[142].

(i) Opinions

The OFT will consider a request for an Opinion only where the following three conditions are fulfilled:

- there is no sufficient precedent in EU or UK case law
- there is a need for a published Opinion, for example because of the economic importance for consumers of the goods or services affected by the agreement or conduct in question or because of the scope of the investment related to the agreement or conduct
- it is possible to provide an Opinion without the need for substantial further fact-finding[143].

Undertakings that request an Opinion may withdraw their request[144]. Any Opinion given by the OFT will be published on its website[145]. One Opinion had been issued by 20 June 2011: in October 2008 the OFT issued an Opinion providing detailed guidance to facilitate 'self-assessment' of agreements for the distribution of newspapers and magazines under the Competition Act[146].

As part of the procedure on giving Opinions the OFT has introduced a trial process whereby it may give a 'Short-form Opinion' on how EU and/or UK competition law applies to a prospective collaboration between competitors that raises novel or unresolved questions[147]. Short-form Opinions are subject to both the criteria that apply to Opinions and the *OFT's Prioritisation Principles*. One Short-form Opinion had been issued by 20 June 2011; it concerned a joint purchasing agreement[148].

(ii) Informal advice

The OFT may provide confidential informal advice to undertakings on the application of EU and/or UK competition law on an *ad hoc* basis, but such advice is not binding[149], and would not be given in a case that does not satisfy the *OFT's Prioritisation Principles*.

5. Enforcement

This section will explain the various possibilities that exist where the OFT or a sectoral regulator[150] intends to take enforcement action under the Competition Act.

---

[138] The relevant provisions were the Competition Act, ss 12–16 and Schs 5 and 6; they are described at pp 371–376 of the fifth edition of this book.

[139] See ch 4, 'Regulation 1/2003', pp 166–168.   [140] OFT 442, December 2004.

[141] *Modernisation*, paras 7.5–7.19.   [142] Ibid, para 7.20.

[143] Ibid, para 7.5.   [144] Ibid, para 7.14.   [145] Ibid, para 7.15.

[146] OFT 1025, October 2008; see Muysert and Dobson 'Split Opinion: The Office of Fair Trading Opinion on Newspaper and Magazine Distribution' [2010] Competition Law Journal 262.

[147] See OFT Press Release 44/10, 27 April 2010; an explanation of the short-form opinion process is available at www.oft.gov.uk.

[148] *P&H/Makro joint purchasing agreement*, available at www.oft.gov.uk.

[149] *Modernisation*, para 7.20.   [150] As defined in the Competition Act 1998, s 54 (as amended).

(A) **Procedure**

Where the OFT has 'reasonable grounds for suspecting' an infringement of the Act or of Article 101 or 102 TFEU it will first carry out an investigation pursuant to section 25. The OFT has introduced a trial process whereby parties may ask the Procedural Adjudicator to review decisions by the case team on certain procedural matters such as confidentiality[151]. If, as a result of that investigation, the OFT proposes to adopt a decision that there is or has been an infringement of the Chapter I and/or Chapter II prohibition or of Articles 101 and/or 102 TFEU section 31 of the Act requires it to give 'written notice' – better known as a 'statement of objections' – to the person or persons 'likely to be affected'[152] and to give that person (or persons) an opportunity to make representations[153]. The form of the statement of objections is set out in rules 4 and 5 of the OFT's Rules[154]; rule 5 also deals with access to the file[155] and the right to make oral representations[156]. The CAT summarised the principles applicable to the statement of objections in *Apex v OFT*[157]; in that case it concluded that a defect in the statement of objections should not lead to the annulment of the decision since the defect had not caused Apex any prejudice[158]. Chapter 9 of *A guide to the OFT's investigation procedures* explains how it goes about its assessment of evidence and arguments received in response to a statement of objections.

Various possibilities exist following the issue of a statement of objections. One is that the OFT might decide not to proceed with the case or to state that it has no grounds for action[159]. A different possibility is that the OFT may close a case, without a finding of infringement, by accepting legally binding 'commitments' that the undertaking(s) will modify their behaviour in order to resolve the competition problems that led to the initiation of the investigation (see section B below). Provision is made for the OFT to adopt interim measures during an investigation (section C). Where the OFT finds an infringement it may give directions to bring the infringement to an end (section D) and may require an infringing undertaking to pay a penalty (section E). Undertakings that 'blow the whistle' on infringements of the Chapter I prohibition or Article 101 may be able to claim immunity from penalties, or at least substantial reductions (section F). Some infringement decisions are adopted following discussions between the OFT and the undertakings concerned that are sometimes referred to as 'early resolution' or settlements (section G). Section H will consider how the provisions on penalties have been applied in practice.

(B) **Commitments**

Just as Article 9 of Regulation 1/2003 introduced a procedure enabling the European Commission to adopt a decision whereby undertakings under investigation make legally-binding commitments as to their future behaviour in order to address its competition concerns, so too the Amendment Regulations introduced sections 31A to 31E into the Competition Act 1998. The OFT has published guidance on the commitments procedure in Part 4 of *Enforcement*[160]. Section 31(2) enables the OFT to accept commitments from

---

[151] See *A guide to the OFT's investigation procedures*, paras 6.14, 7.11, 9.17, 12.4 and 14.2; see also *Trial of Procedural Adjudicator in Competition Act 1998 Cases: Briefing Note*, March 2011, available at www.oft.gov.uk.

[152] Competition Act 1998, s 31(1)(a).   [153] Ibid, s 31(1)(b).   [154] SI 2004/2751.

[155] Ibid, r 5(3).   [156] Ibid, r 5(4).

[157] Case No 1032/1/1/04 [2005] CAT 4, [2005] CompAR 507, para 100.

[158] Ibid, paras 109–110, relying on the General Court's judgment in Case T-48/00 *Corus UK v Commission* [2004] ECR II-2325, paras 154–158.

[159] On challenges to such decisions before the CAT see 'Appealable decisions', pp 440–443 below.

[160] *Enforcement*, OFT 407, December 2004; on the advantages of the commitments regime over accepting voluntary assurances see the judgments of the CAT in Case No 1017/2/1/03 *Pernod-Ricard SA v OFT* [2005]

undertakings to take such action or to refrain from taking such action as the OFT considers appropriate; provision is made for the variation[161], substitution[162] and release[163] of commitments. Schedule 6A to the Act sets out the procedural requirements that are to be followed in commitments cases. Where the OFT accepts commitments it will discontinue its investigation and it cannot make a decision finding an infringement under section 31 or issue a direction under section 35[164]. Where an undertaking fails to adhere to its commitments the OFT may apply to the court for an order to enforce compliance[165].

It is for the undertakings concerned to approach the OFT to discuss the possibility of commitments. The OFT has said that it is likely to consider accepting commitments only in limited cases where the competition concerns are readily identifiable and are fully addressed by the commitments offered and where the commitments are capable of being implemented effectively and, if necessary, within a short period of time[166]. The OFT would not, other than in very exceptional cases, accept commitments in the case of hard-core cartels or serious abuses of dominance[167]; however such cases might culminate in a settlement whereby the undertakings concerned are fined a lesser sum than they would have been in return for enabling the OFT to reach an infringement decision more quickly than would otherwise have been the case[168]. Commitments may be both structural and behavioural[169]. There is a consultation process under the commitments procedure in which third parties are given an opportunity to comment[170]. If accepted the OFT will publish the full text of the commitments on its website. Decisions by the OFT not to release commitments when requested by the parties that offered them to do so can be appealed to the CAT[171], as can decisions where there are no longer grounds for competition concerns[172]; third parties can appeal to the CAT against decisions to accept or release commitments or to accept a material variation[173].

By 20 June 2011 commitments had been accepted in three cases. In *TV Eye* the OFT accepted commitments from TV Eye, a company owned by four broadcasters, to modify some of the terms and conditions on which it sold airtime to media agencies, thereby placing them in a stronger bargaining position[174]. The OFT also accepted commitments in *Associated Newspapers* where that company agreed to modify the exclusive contracts that it had entered into with London Underground, Network Rail and several train operating companies, in order to provide for the distribution at their railway stations of competing newspapers[175]. In *Manweb*[176] the Gas and Electricity Markets Authority accepted commitments that Manweb would provide connection services to independent providers in a non-discriminatory manner and within recommended timescales[177]. In January 2011 the OFT announced that it may accept commitments to address concerns arising out of

---

CAT 9, [2005] CompAR 894, para 7 and Case No 1026/2/3/04 *Wanadoo (UK) Plc v OFCOM* [2004] CAT 20, [2005] CompAR 430, para 124.

[161] Competition Act 1998, s 31A(3)(a).   [162] Ibid, s 31A(3)(b).   [163] Ibid, s 31A(4).
[164] Ibid, s 31B.   [165] Ibid, s 31E; 'court' for this purpose is defined in s 59 of the Act.
[166] *Enforcement*, para 4.3.
[167] Ibid, para 4.4.   [168] See 'Settlements and early resolution of cases', p 418 below.
[169] *Enforcement*, para 4.6.
[170] Competition Act 1998, Sch 6A and *Enforcement*, paras 4.21–4.22.
[171] Competition Act 1998, s 46(3)(g).   [172] Ibid, s 46(3)(h).   [173] Ibid, s 47(1)(c).
[174] See OFT Press Release 93/05, 24 May 2005; some of the commitments were released in March 2006: see OFT Press Release 58/06; the Press Releases are available, along with the OFT decision and the text of the commitments, at www.oft.gov.uk.
[175] See OFT Press Release 44/06, 2 March 2006, available at www.oft.gov.uk/.
[176] See OFGEM Information Note R/42 of 27 October 2005, available at www.ofgem.gov.uk.
[177] The commitments were subsequently varied by OFGEM decision letter of 17 December 2007, available at www.ofgem.gov.uk.

the exchange of pricing information between motor car insurers using a market analysis tool[178].

(C) Interim measures

If the OFT has begun an investigation under section 25 and has not completed it, it may adopt interim measures if this is necessary as a matter of urgency to prevent serious, irreparable damage to a particular person or category of persons or to protect the public interest[179]; however it cannot adopt interim measures if undertakings are able to show on the balance of probabilities that the criteria in section 9 of the Competition Act or Article 101(3) TFEU are satisfied[180]. The OFT must give notice to the affected persons before giving directions, thus giving them an opportunity to make representations[181]. Such notice must indicate the nature of the proposed direction and the OFT's reasons[182]. The OFT has indicated that it may be willing, in some cases, to accept informal interim assurances in lieu of adopting formal interim measures decisions[183]; it has accepted informal assurances on a few occasions[184]. Decisions by the OFT to grant or refuse interim measures can be appealed to the CAT[185].

The only occasion on which the OFT adopted an interim measures decision was in the case of *London Metal Exchange*[186] where the OFT was concerned that the LME might have been about to abuse its dominant position by extending the hours of trading on its electronic trading platform, LME Select: it was possible that this might amount to predatory conduct. The LME appealed to the CAT against this decision; subsequently the OFT, having received substantial new evidence, withdrew the decision. In a judgment awarding the LME the costs of the work done on the appeal the CAT likened the process in interim measures cases to the procedure before the High Court when a party seeks an interim injunction[187]. The OFT should be circumspect about relying solely on uncorroborated information not contained in response to a section 26 notice[188].

(D) Directions

Section 32(1) of the Competition Act provides that, when the OFT has made a decision that an agreement infringes the Chapter I prohibition or Article 101 TFEU, it may give to such person or persons as it considers appropriate directions to bring the infringement to an end. Section 32(3) expands on the content of these directions which may require the parties to an agreement to modify it or require them to terminate it. There are corresponding provisions in section 33 for directions in the case of infringements of

---

[178] See OFT Press Release 04/11, 13 January 2011; in September 2011 the OFT consulted on modified commitments: see OFT Press Release 108/11; the Press Releases are available, along with the consultation document and proposed commitments, at www.oft.gov.uk.

[179] Competition Act 1998, s 35(1) and (2); the OFT Guideline *Enforcement*, OFT 407, December 2004, explains the OFT's approach to the interim measures procedure.

[180] Competition Act 1998, s 35(8) and (9).

[181] Ibid, s 35(3); see also the OFT's Rules, r 9.   [182] Competition Act 1998, s 35(4).

[183] *Enforcement*, paras 3.17–3.20.

[184] See eg *Robert Wiseman Dairies* OFT Press Release PN 39/01, 14 September 2001; *Oakley (UK) Ltd*, case closure of February 2007; *Nationwide Independent Bodyshop Suppliers Ltd*, case closure of February 2009, available at www.oft.gov.uk.

[185] Competition Act 1998, ss 46(3) and 47(1)(d)–(e).   [186] OFT decision of 27 February 2006.

[187] Case No 1062/1/1/06 *London Metal Exchange v OFT* [2006] CAT 19, [2006] CompAR 781, paras 139–140, citing the *Practice Direction – Interim Injunctions* (CPR Part 25); the OFT subsequently closed the file in this case on 20 April 2007, available at www.oft.gov.uk.

[188] Case No 1062/1/1/06 [2006] CAT 19, [2006] CompAR 781, paras 141–142.

the Chapter II prohibition or Article 102 TFEU; in this case section 33(3) provides that the direction may require the person concerned to modify the conduct in question, or require him to cease that conduct. In either case directions may also include other provisions such as positive action and reporting obligations[189]. Recipients of directions must be informed in writing of the facts on which the directions are based and the reasons for them[190]; directions under sections 32 and 33 must be published[191].

(i) Can directions be structural?

It is not clear whether the power to give directions includes the right to impose structural remedies such as the right to require the divestiture of assets or the break-up of an undertaking; Article 7 of Regulation 1/2003 explicitly provides that the European Commission can impose structural and behavioural remedies[192]. Where an infringement of the Chapter I or II prohibitions or of Article 101 or 102 is itself the consequence of a structural change in the market it would seem, in principle, that a structural remedy to bring the infringement to an end would be justified: for example if undertakings were to establish, contrary to the Chapter I prohibition or Article 101, a joint venture company to act as a joint sales agency the most effective remedy would probably be a structural one, requiring the dissolution of the company. It is less obvious, however, that it is possible to impose a structural remedy, for example, to break up a dominant firm guilty of serial abusive behaviour; such a situation would appear to be more suitable for a market investigation reference under the Enterprise Act 2002, under which legislation a structural remedy is, explicitly, available[193].

(ii) The directions provisions in practice

In some cases the OFT refrains from giving directions since the infringement of the Act has ended by the time of its decision[194]. However in other cases the OFT has issued directions: for example in *Napp*[195] that company was ordered to amend its prices for certain morphine medicines to bring its abusive pricing to an end, while in *Lladró Comercial* the OFT required the porcelain producer to modify its distribution agreements to make clear that the practice of resale price maintenance would not continue[196]. Similarly in *Genzyme*[197] the OFT obliged that company to charge separately for Cerezyme, a drug that it produced, and for the various homecare services it provided; and to offer Cerezyme to competing homecare operators at a price no higher than that charged to the National Health Service[198]. There were protracted proceedings in the CAT as to the correct price to be charged by Genzyme[199], during which the CAT stated that the primary responsibility

---

[189] See *Enforcement*, para 2.3.   [190] OFT Rules, SI 2004/2751, r 8(1).
[191] Ibid, r 8(3).   [192] See ch 7, 'Structural remedies', p 254.
[193] See ch 11, 'Final powers', pp 476–477 and in particular the discussion of the investigation of BAA Ltd.
[194] See eg *Price fixing and market sharing in stock check pads*, OFT decision of 31 March 2006 [2007] UKCLR 211, para 235; *Agreement to fix prices and share the market for aluminium double glazing bars*, OFT decision of 28 June 2006 [2006] UKCLR 921, para 535.
[195] *Directions given by the Director General of Fair Trading under section 33 of the Competition Act 1998 to Napp Pharmaceutical Holdings Ltd and its subsidiaries*, 4 May 2001, upheld on appeal Case No 1000/1/1/01 *Napp Pharmaceutical Holdings Ltd v Director General of Fair Trading* [2002] CAT 1, [2002] CompAR 13, [2002] ECC 177, paras 553–562.
[196] OFT decision of 31 March 2003, [2003] UKCLR 652, paras 117–118.
[197] OFT decision of 27 March 2003, substantially upheld on appeal Case No 1016/1/1/03 *Genzyme Ltd v OFT* [2004] CAT 4, [2004] CompAR 358.
[198] Case No 1016/1/1/03 *Genzyme Ltd v OFT* [2005] CAT 32, [2006] CompAR 195.
[199] Case No 1013/1/1/03 (IR) *Genzyme Ltd v OFT* [2003] CAT 8, [2003] CompAR 290.

for bringing the abuse to an end in that case rested with Genzyme, rather than with the OFT or the CAT[200].

In the case of *English Welsh & Scottish Railway*[201] the Office of Rail Regulation ('ORR') found that EW&S was guilty of abusing a dominant position in the market for the carriage by rail of industrial coal to power stations; it gave directions to EW&S requiring it to remove or modify various terms in the coal carriage agreements it had entered into with some of its customers, including the power company E.ON[202]. E.ON appealed against these directions to the CAT, arguing that they were excessive in scope and too uncertain to be valid[203]. In the meantime the High Court held in *English Welsh & Scottish Railway v E.ON UK* that the directions of the ORR meant that the offending clauses had been void from their inception and that, since they could not be severed, the entire coal carriage agreement was void and unenforceable[204]. E.ON appealed against this judgment to the Court of Appeal, but the case was settled out of court; the CAT subsequently granted E.ON permission to withdraw its appeal.

In *National Grid v GEMA*[205] the CAT did not accept the criticism that the regulator's direction that National Grid 'refrain from engaging in conduct having the same or equivalent exclusionary effect' to its abusive contracts was unacceptably vague or inappropriate[206].

(iii) Persons who may be the subject of directions

Directions may be given to 'appropriate' persons, who will not necessarily be the parties to the agreement or perpetrators of the unlawful conduct. The purpose of this is to enable the OFT to give directions to parent companies, affiliates or private individuals with the ability to influence or procure actions by the infringing persons[207]. Section 34 of the Act allows the court to order an undertaking or its officers to obey a direction relating to the management of that undertaking if the person subject to the direction has failed to comply.

(iv) Enforcement of compliance with directions

If a person subject to directions (whether interim or final) fails to comply without reasonable excuse the OFT may apply to the court[208] for an order requiring compliance within a specified time or, if the direction concerns the management of an undertaking, ordering another officer to carry it out[209]. Breach of such an order would be contempt of court, punishable by fines or imprisonment, at the court's discretion[210]. There is nothing in section 34 that limits the court's order-making powers to persons within the UK[211].

---

[200] See the transcript of the hearing of 13 October 2004, available at www.catribunal.org.uk.

[201] ORR decision of 17 November 2006 [2007] UKCLR 937.   [202] Ibid, paras D2–D5.

[203] Case No 1076/2/5/07 *E.ON UK Plc v Office of Rail Regulation*.

[204] [2007] EWHC 599, [2007] UKCLR 1653; on the doctrine of severance in the English law of contract see *Chitty on Contracts* (Sweet & Maxwell, 30th ed, 2008), paras 16-194–16-203.

[205] Case No 1099/1/2/08 [2009] CAT 14, [2009] CompAR 282.

[206] Ibid, para 222: however the CAT accepted that the time limit set for compliance with the directions was unrealistic: ibid, para 226; see also Case No 1046/2/4/04 *Albion Water Ltd v Water Services Regulation Authority* (remedy) [2009] CAT 12, paras 37–39.

[207] See *Enforcement*, para 2.2.

[208] 'Court' for this purpose is defined in Competition Act 1998, s 59(1).   [209] Ibid, s 34.

[210] *Enforcement*, para 2.9.

[211] On the territorial scope of the Act see ch 12, 'The Extraterritorial Application of UK Competition Law', pp 501–504.

(E) **Penalties**

Section 36(1) of the Competition Act provides that a penalty may be imposed for an infringement of the Chapter I prohibition or Article 101 TFEU; section 36(2) provides correspondingly for an infringement of the Chapter II prohibition or Article 102 TFEU. As a prerequisite for the imposition of a penalty section 36(3) requires that the OFT must be satisfied that the infringement has been committed intentionally or negligently[212]; it is sufficient to decide that the infringement was *either* intentional *or* negligent, without deciding which[213], and the distinction between intention and negligence goes, at most, to mitigation of the fine[214]. Intention may be deduced from internal documents or from deliberate concealment of the agreement or conduct in question[215]. The Competition Act does not specify a limitation period for the imposition or recovery of penalties. In *Quarmby v OFT*[216] the Tribunal held that neither the limitation period in Article 25 of Regulation 1/2003[217] nor the Limitation Act 1980[218] applies to the imposition of penalties under the Competition Act[219]. Penalties received by the OFT are paid into the Consolidated Fund[220]: that is to say they go to the Government and not, for example, to the victims of the anti-competitive behaviour. The latter may be able to obtain compensation through recourse to the courts[221]. Where a penalty has not been paid by the date required by the OFT it may be recovered through the courts as a civil debt[222]. An appeal to the CAT postpones the obligation to pay any penalty until the appeal is determined[223]; however the CAT normally adds interest to any penalty imposed[224].

(i) **Maximum amount of a penalty**

Section 36(8) provides that penalties may not exceed 10 per cent of an undertaking's worldwide turnover in the business year preceding the OFT's decision[225].

---

[212] See *Enforcement*, paras 5.4–5.13.

[213] Case No 1000/1/1/01 *Napp Pharmaceutical Holdings Ltd v Director General of Fair Trading* [2002] CAT 1, [2002] CompAR 13, para 453; on the meaning of 'intentional' and 'negligent' see paras 456 and 457 of that judgment.

[214] Case No 1009/1/1/02 *Aberdeen Journals Ltd v OFT* [2003] CAT 11, [2003] CompAR 67, para 484.

[215] *Enforcement*, para 5.11.

[216] Case No 1120/1/1/09 [2011] CAT 11.

[217] Ibid, paras 43–48 (finding that there is a 'relevant difference' for the purposes of s 60 of the Competition Act), on which see ch 9, '"Governing Principles Clause": Section 60 of the Competition Act 1998', pp 369–374.

[218] Case No 1120/1/1/09 [2011] CAT 11, paras 54–56.

[219] Note however that the Limitation Act 1980 does apply to the recovery of penalties as a civil debt under s 37 of the Competition Act.

[220] Competition Act 1998, s 36(9).

[221] See ch 8, 'Actions for an Injunction and/or Damages', pp 297–306.

[222] Competition Act 1998, s 37.

[223] Ibid, s 46(4); there is no provision for the OFT to ask for security for the penalty (or for the costs of the appeal): it follows that, if an undertaking goes out of business in the meantime, the penalty may be irrecoverable.

[224] See the Competition Appeal Tribunal Rules 2003, SI 2003/1372, r 56; see eg Case No 1000/1/1/01 *Napp Pharmaceutical Holdings Ltd v Director General of Fair Trading* [2002] CAT 1, [2002] CompAR 13, paras 542–543; Case No 1099/1/2/08 *National Grid Plc v Gas and Electricity Markets Authority* [2009] CAT 14, [2009] CompAR 282, para 229(c); Case Nos 1114/1/1/09 etc *Kier Group plc & Ors v OFT* [2011] CAT 3, para 343.

[225] See the Competition Act 1998 (Determination of Turnover for Penalties) Order 2000, SI 2000/309, as amended with effect from 1 May 2004 by SI 2004/1259.

(ii) The OFT's Guidance as to the appropriate amount of a penalty

The OFT has published *Guidance as to the appropriate amount of a penalty*[226] ('the *Guidance on penalties*') pursuant to section 38 of the Act; the *Guidance* has been approved by the Secretary of State, as required by that provision[227]. Section 3 of the *Guidance on penalties* dealing with 'whistleblowing' must be read in light of the new guidance the OFT has published on this subject (see section F below).

The Court of Appeal has explained that the *Guidance on penalties* is not binding on the OFT, but that it must give reasons for any significant departure from it[228]. The CAT is not bound by the OFT's *Guidance on penalties*[229]. Paragraph 1.4 of the *Guidance* sets out the OFT's policy objectives in setting the level of penalties: to reflect the seriousness of the infringement and to deter the infringing undertakings and other undertakings from engaging or continuing to engage in anti-competitive practices. In *Kier Group plc & Ors v OFT*, its first *Construction bid-rigging* judgment, the CAT held that it will consider whether the final penalty is reasonable and proportionate having regard to those policy objectives[230].

Paragraph 1.15 explains that undertakings found to have infringed both UK and EU competition law will not be fined twice for the same anti-competitive effects; however paragraph 1.16 adds that there might be different levels of penalties for the EU and the domestic infringements, for example if the infringement of EU law pre-dated the entry into force of the Competition Act in March 2000.

(iii) The OFT's five-step approach

In determining the level of the penalty the OFT adopts a five-step approach[231]; the OFT must give reasons for its decision, including setting out the methodology whereby it reaches its conclusion[232]:

- **Step 1—starting point**[233]: the starting point is to apply a percentage of the 'relevant turnover' of the undertaking to be fined according to the seriousness of the infringement[234]; this reflects not only the seriousness of the infringement but also, by applying the percentage to turnover, the scale of the undertaking in the relevant market. In determining the seriousness of an infringement the OFT will take a number of factors into consideration including the nature of the infringement and the effect of the anti-competitive behaviour on competitors, third parties and, most importantly, consumers[235]. In cases based on Articles 101 and/or 102 TFEU, effects in another Member State may be taken into account if that Member State expressly gives its consent[236]. Relevant turnover for this purpose means the turnover in the relevant product and geographic markets affected by the infringement in the

---

[226] OFT 423, December 2004; this replaced the earlier *Guidance* of March 2000.

[227] *Guidance on penalties*, para 1.8.

[228] *Argos Ltd and Littlewoods Ltd v OFT* and *JJB Sports plc v OFT* [2006] EWCA Civ 1318, [2006] UKCLR 1135, para 161; the OFT gave reasons for departing from its *Guidance on penalties* in *Independent fee-paying schools*, OFT decision of 20 November 2006 [2007] UKCLR 361, paras 1424–1432.

[229] *Argos Ltd and Littlewoods Ltd v OFT* and *JJB Sports plc v OFT* [2006] EWCA Civ 1318, [2006] UKCLR 1135, para 160; the CAT considered its role in penalty appeals in Case Nos 1114/1/1/09 etc *Keir Group plc v OFT* [2011] CAT 3, paras 74–77.

[230] See Case Nos 1114/1/1/09 etc [2011] CAT 3, para 175.   [231] *Guidance on penalties*, para 2.1.

[232] Case No 1061/1/1/06 *Makers UK Ltd v OFT* [2007] CAT 11, [2007] CompAR 699, para 134.

[233] *Guidance on penalties*, paras 2.3–2.9.   [234] Ibid, para 2.3.

[235] Ibid, paras 2.4–2.5.   [236] Ibid, para 2.6.

undertaking's last business year[237]; the starting point cannot exceed 10 per cent of an undertaking's relevant turnover[238]. Where several undertakings are involved in the same infringement the starting point will be worked out for each of them individually in order to take account of each undertaking's impact on the market[239]. In *Kier Group plc & Ors v OFT*[240] the CAT indicated that 'some modification of the Step 1 range may be worthy of consideration' when the *Guidance* is reviewed[241]

- **Step 2—adjustment for duration**[242]: having established the starting point the OFT, at Step 2, may increase or, exceptionally, decrease[243] the penalty to take into account the duration of the infringement. Where the infringement lasts longer than one year the penalty may be increased by not more than the number of years of the infringement; the OFT may treat part of a year as a whole year, although in some cases it has decided to apply a smaller multiplier[244]

- **Step 3—adjustment for other factors**[245]: at Step 3 the OFT will take into account 'adjustments for other factors' in order to achieve the policy objectives set out in paragraph 1.4 of the *Guidance*, in particular the need for deterrence, not only of the undertakings involved in the infringement but of others that might be contemplating anti-competitive behaviour[246]. At this stage the OFT may take into account the gains made by the infringing undertaking from its behaviour[247]

- **Step 4—adjustment for aggravating and mitigating factors**[248]: at Step 4 the OFT will consider whether there are any aggravating and mitigating factors
  Aggravating factors include[249]:

  - an undertaking was a leader in, or the instigator of, the infringement

  - directors or senior managers were involved

  - retaliatory or coercive action was taken against other undertakings in order to continue the infringement

  - the infringement was continued after the commencement of an investigation

  - repeated infringements by the same undertaking or undertakings in the same group (recidivism)

  - intentional rather than negligent infringement

  - retaliation against a leniency applicant

---

[237] Ibid, para 2.7; in Case Nos 1114/1/1/09 etc *Kier Group plc v OFT* [2011] CAT 3 the CAT held that the last business year prior to the infringement was the appropriate year for determining relevant turnover: ibid, paras 130–139; see similarly Case Nos 1117/1/1/10 etc *GF Tomlinson Building Ltd v OFT* [2011] CAT 7, paras 82–113 and Case Nos 1125/1/1/09 etc *Barrett Estate Services Ltd v OFT* [2011] CAT 9, paras 19–25.

[238] *Guidance on penalties*, para 2.8.   [239] Ibid, para 2.9.   [240] See n 237 above.

[241] Ibid, para 109.   [242] *Guidance on penalties*, para 2.10.

[243] Note Case No 1032/1/1/04 *Apex Asphalt Paving Co v OFT* [2005] CAT 4, [2005] CompAR 507, para 278: in the case of collusive tendering, the fact that a particular tendering process might take place over a short period does not necessarily mean that there should be a reduction of the penalty.

[244] See eg para 323 of the OFT decision in *Hasbro UK Ltd, Argos Ltd and Littlewoods Ltd* of 19 February 2003 [2003] UKCLR 553, where the OFT applied a multiplier of 1.2, as opposed to 2, where the duration of the infringement was in the region of 14½ months.

[245] *Guidance on penalties*, paras 2.11–2.13.

[246] Ibid, para 2.11; on the application of Step 3 in the *Construction bid-rigging* decision see eg Case Nos 1114/1/1/09 etc *Kier Group plc v OFT* [2011] CAT 3, paras 164–186.

[247] *Guidance on penalties*, para 2.11.   [248] Ibid, paras 2.14–2.16.   [249] Ibid, para 2.15.

Mitigating factors include[250]:

- an undertaking acted under severe duress or pressure
- genuine uncertainty on the part of an undertaking as to whether its agreement or conduct constituted an infringement
- adequate steps having been taken with a view to ensuring compliance with competition law
- termination of the infringement as soon as the OFT intervenes
- cooperation which enables the OFT's enforcement process to be concluded more effectively and/or speedily

- **Step 5—adjustment to prevent the maximum penalty being exceeded and to avoid double jeopardy**[251]: at Step 5 the OFT will make any necessary adjustments to ensure that the statutory maximum penalty of 10 per cent of worldwide turnover is not exceeded[252]. If a fine has been imposed by the European Commission or by a court or competition authority in another Member State this must also be taken into account at Step 5 in order to avoid double jeopardy[253].

(iv) Immunity for small agreements and conduct of minor significance

Section 39, in conjunction with section 36(4), of the Competition Act confers immunity from penalties for infringing the Chapter I prohibition in the case of 'small agreements', other than price-fixing agreements[254], where the OFT is satisfied that an undertaking acted on the reasonable assumption that section 39 gave it immunity. A small agreement is one where the combined turnover of the parties in the preceding calendar year was £20 million or less[255]. Provision is made by section 39(3)–(8) for the OFT to withdraw this immunity, subject to the observation of some basic procedures[256]. There is no immunity from penalties for agreements that infringe Article 101 TFEU, which is why section 39 refers only to 'partial' immunity in its heading.

Section 40 provides similar partial immunity for 'conduct of minor significance'. Conduct is of minor significance where the perpetrator's worldwide turnover in the preceding calendar year was £50 million or less[257]. Section 40(3)–(8) provides power for withdrawal of the immunity. There is no immunity from penalties for infringements of Article 102 TFEU.

As the OFT points out in its guidance on *Enforcement* the immunity provided by sections 39 and 40 does not prevent it from taking other enforcement action, and the immunity does not prevent third parties from bringing damages actions[258]. This point

---

[250] Ibid, para 2.16.

[251] Ibid, paras 2.17–2.20.

[252] See 'Maximum amount of a penalty', p 410 above; note that, prior to 1 May 2004, the maximum penalty under s 36(8) was calculated by reference to UK turnover rather than worldwide turnover, and that this may, in some cases, require a further adjustment of the penalty: see *Guidance on penalties*, para 2.18 and *Bid-rigging in the construction industry in England*, OFT decision of 21 September 2009, para VI.370 (p 1711).

[253] *Guidance on penalties*, para 2.20.

[254] A price-fixing agreement for this purpose is defined in s 39(9) of the Act.

[255] See the Competition Act 1998 (Small Agreements and Conduct of Minor Significance) Regulations 2000, SI 2000/262, reg 3.

[256] The OFT must give the parties or persons in respect of which the immunity is withdrawn written notice of its decision and must specify a date which gives them time to adjust (ss 39(5), (8), 40(5), (8) Competition Act 1998).

[257] See the Competition Act 1998 (Small Agreements and Conduct of Minor Significance) Regulations 2000, SI 2000/262, reg 4.

[258] *Enforcement*, para 5.20.

is nicely illustrated by the case of *Burgess v OFT*. In its judgment in this case the CAT found that Austin had abused a dominant position by refusing one of its competitors, Burgess, access to its crematorium[259]. The CAT noted that Austin would not be subject to a penalty since its conduct was of minor significance under section 40 of the Act[260]. Subsequently, however, Burgess brought a 'follow-on' action for damages before the CAT[261]; the case was settled out of court[262]. Similarly in *Cardiff Bus* the OFT concluded that Cardiff Bus was guilty of abusive predatory conduct but, due to its turnover, it benefited from immunity under section 40[263]; subsequently four damages claims were brought before the CAT[264].

(F) Whistleblowing: the leniency programme

The OFT encourages whistleblowing. Decisions establishing an infringement of the Chapter I prohibition (and Article 101 TFEU) very often originate from an application for leniency[265]. A parent company may make a leniency application on behalf of a subsidiary[266]. The OFT has published three sets of guidance on its leniency policy: the OFT's *Guidance as to the appropriate amount of a penalty*[267] deals with civil cases under the Competition Act 1998; *The cartel offence – Guidance on the issue of no-action letters for individuals*[268] deals with criminal cases under the Enterprise Act 2002 and *Leniency and no-action guidance*[269] deals with both civil and criminal cases. The *Leniency and no-action guidance* supplements, but does not replace, the earlier guidelines; it provides a comprehensive view of the current position and is the suggested starting point for anyone needing guidance on the subject. A pro-forma corporate leniency agreement and pro-forma no-action letters as well as a helpful 'leniency flow-chart' are included in the Annexes to the *Leniency and no-action guidance*. The aim of the *Leniency and no-action guidance* is to make those policies more attractive and more transparent to undertakings or individuals considering whether to blow the whistle.

(i) Terminology

Paragraph 1.6 of the *Leniency and no-action guidance* sets out the terminology of the subject, including the following:

- 'leniency': this is a 'catch all' term that refers to all the types of immunity and reduced fines that are available under the *Guidance*

- 'civil immunity': this refers to immunity granted to undertakings from penalties for infringing the Chapter I prohibition or Article 101 TFEU

- 'criminal immunity': this refers to immunity granted to individuals from prosecution for the cartel offence in the Enterprise Act 2002

- 'Type A immunity': this refers to a situation where an undertaking is granted *automatic* civil immunity and all of its current and former employees and directors who cooperate with the OFT are granted automatic criminal immunity for cartel activity;

---

[259] Case No 1044/2/1/04 *JJ Burgess & Sons v OFT* [2005] CAT 25, [2005] CompAR 1151.
[260] Ibid, paras 117–118.   [261] Case No 1088/5/7/07.
[262] See the CAT's order of 18 February 2008.
[263] *Abuse of a dominant position by Cardiff Bus*, OFT decision of 18 November 2008 [2009] UKCLR 332.
[264] Case Nos 1175–1178/5/7/11 etc *DH Francis v Cardiff City Transport Services Ltd*, not yet decided.
[265] See below.
[266] *Collusive tendering for mastic asphalt flat-roofing contracts in Scotland*, OFT decision of 15 March 2005 [2005] UKCLR 638, para 396.
[267] OFT 423, December 2004.
[268] OFT 513, April 2003.   [269] OFT 803, December 2008.

Type A immunity is available where the undertaking was the first to apply and there was no pre-existing civil and/or criminal investigation into such activity

- **'Type B immunity'**: this refers to a situation where the type of immunity available under Type A is granted on a *discretionary* rather than an automatic basis. Type B immunity is available where the undertaking was the first to apply but there was already a pre-existing civil and/or criminal investigation into the cartel activity

- **'Type B leniency'**: this refers to a situation where an undertaking is granted any level of reduction of, but not immunity from, a financial penalty in a cartel case. As in the case of Type B immunity, Type B leniency arises where the undertaking was the first to apply but there was already an investigation under way into the cartel in question

- **'Type C leniency'**: this refers to a situation in which a reduction in the penalty of up to 50 per cent is granted where the undertaking was not the first to apply whether or not there was already a pre-existing civil and/or criminal investigation into the cartel.

(ii) Key features of the UK leniency system

Paragraph 1.7 of the *Leniency and no-action guidance* sets out the key features of the UK leniency system, including:

- **informal guidance:** the OFT will provide informal guidance on a no-names basis about 'hypothetical' cases when asked

- **the 'marker system':** markers will be available while the application is perfected (a marker system is also available under the EU leniency system)[270], thereby enabling an undertaking to preserve its position in a queue of leniency applicants

- **oral applications:** applications do not always have to be in writing (oral applications are also available under the EU system)[271]

- **guarantees of criminal immunity:** criminal immunity is available for all cooperating current and former employees and directors in Type A or Type B immunity cases

- **ready availability of Type B immunity:** Type B immunity will be common, rather than exceptional, where an undertaking is the first to approach the OFT, even if there is a pre-existing investigation into the cartel in question

- **a 'high bar for coercion':** the OFT will impose a high bar, both as to the circumstances and standard of proof, in which an undertaking will be found to be a coercer and therefore ineligible for civil and/or criminal immunity.

(iii) Confidential guidance

Part 2 of the *Leniency and no-action guidance* explains that, at the outset, individuals or undertakings may approach the OFT for confidential guidance on any aspect of the OFT's leniency and no-action programmes. An important feature of this procedure is that the OFT will consider itself to be bound by confidential guidance provided that it is followed by an application in a reasonable time, the information given was not misleading and there has not been a material change in circumstances.

---

[270] See ch 7, 'Section II: immunity from fines', pp 281–282.
[271] See ch 7, 'Section IV: corporate statements', p 282.

(iv) Type A immunity

The *Leniency and no-action guidance* explains the procedure when applying for Type A immunity. To qualify, the undertaking must be the first to provide the OFT with all information available to it regarding the cartel[272]; this information should enable the OFT to use its powers of investigation[273]. The OFT must also be satisfied that the other conditions for the grant of immunity are, and continue to be, met[274]: the applicant must:

- maintain continuous and complete cooperation throughout the OFT's investigation
- refrain from partaking any further in the cartel once it has blown the whistle (unless the OFT directs otherwise) and
- not have 'coerced' another undertaking to participate in the cartel.

There is a 'marker' system whereby an undertaking can fix its position as the first applicant for Type A immunity pending the submission of all the information, documents and evidence of the activities of a cartel available to it[275]. Generally the OFT will not accept joint approaches made simultaneously by, or on behalf of, two or more undertakings; in other words it is not possible to share Type A immunity[276]. Where an undertaking is also making a leniency application to the European Commission a marker will be allowed on a 'no-names' basis while the Commission is considering its position[277].

(v) Type B immunity

The *Leniency and no-action guidance* also sets out the position in relation to Type B immunity. Although Type B immunity is discretionary, it is expected to be common rather than exceptional in cases where an undertaking satisfies the conditions set out above on eligibility for Type A immunity[278]. The sooner an undertaking approaches the OFT for Type B immunity, the more likely it is to be available and to be granted. Type B applications often arise as a result of the OFT conducting an inspection at an undertaking's premises: markers can be granted only by the OFT's Senior Director of Cartels and his deputies, not by the officials present at the inspection[279]. Paragraphs 4.10 to 4.13 explain how an applicant for Type B immunity should go about perfecting its marker.

(vi) Type B and Type C leniency

The *Leniency and no-action guidance* discusses Type B and Type C leniency. In determining the amount of any discount available to the applicant the OFT will take into account the overall added value of the material provided by the applicant[280], the time at which the undertaking came forward, the evidence the OFT already has, the probative value of the evidence provided and the overall level of cooperation. The applicant must also comply with the other conditions set out in paragraph 3.15 of the *Guidance*. The OFT has insufficient experience in granting Type B leniency to give guidance about the percentage reductions that might be available, but it expects reductions in the range of 25 to 50 per cent in Type C cases[281].

---

[272] *Leniency and no-action guidance*, para 3.11.   [273] Ibid, para 3.14.
[274] Ibid, para 3.15; see also *Guidance on penalties*, OFT 423, para 3.9 and *Guidance on issue of no-action letters*, OFT 513, April 2003, para 3.3; see further 'No-action letters', pp 422–423 below.
[275] *Leniency and no-action guidance*, paras 3.11–3.17.   [276] Ibid, para 3.19.
[277] Ibid, paras 3.20–3.22.
[278] Ibid, paras 4.1 and 4.9–4.11.   [279] Ibid, para 4.8.   [280] Ibid, para 5.5.
[281] Ibid, para 5.6.

(vii) **The coercer test**

Type A and Type B immunity are not available to an undertaking that has coerced another firm or firms into taking part in cartel activity. Part 6 of *Leniency and no-action guidance* does not provide a definition of coercion, but indicates that there must be clear evidence of an undertaking taking steps to force another to join the cartel. Physical violence or threats of physical violence and strong economic pressure such as the organisation of a collective trade boycott of a small firm that might cause it to exit the market might be examples of coercion[282].

(viii) **The grant of criminal immunity: no-action letters**

This part of the OFT's guidance will be discussed below in the context of the cartel offence under the Enterprise Act 2002[283].

(ix) **Other issues in relation to civil leniency and no-action letters**

A leniency applicant is expected to maintain continuous and complete cooperation throughout the OFT's investigation. This duty implies that an applicant must genuinely assist the OFT and not, for example, seek to deny involvement in the cartel[284]. Normally a whistleblower must terminate its involvement in the cartel. In rare cases, however, it is possible that the OFT might direct an applicant to continue to participate, for example so that the other members of the cartel will not suspect that it has been in contact with the OFT[285]. Paragraphs 8.7 to 8.10 explain the circumstances in which a leniency application might fail due to a failure to cooperate with the OFT, and paragraphs 8.11 to 8.17 discuss the idea of bad faith – that is to say an applicant taking positive steps to hinder an investigation going beyond non-cooperation – which can even lead to prosecution of individuals under sections 43 and 44 of the Competition Act and section 201 of the Enterprise Act. The *Guidance* also discusses the way in which undertakings and their advisers conduct their internal investigations both prior to and following an approach to the OFT for leniency[286]; and the use and transfer to third parties, the Serious Fraud Office and to the European Commission and the NCAs of the Member States of information received by the OFT as a result of a leniency application[287].

(x) **Leniency plus**

Paragraphs 3.16 and 3.17 of the OFT's *Guidance on penalties*[288] provide for an 'amnesty-plus' or 'two for one' policy: if a firm is already cooperating with an investigation in respect of one cartel, and comes forward with information that entitles it to total immunity in relation to a second cartel, it may receive an additional reduction in the penalty to be applied in relation to the first cartel[289]. The *Leniency and no-action guidance* indicates that reductions under this policy are not likely to be high and will depend on factors such as the effort by the applicant to uncover the second cartel[290].

---

[282] Ibid, para 6.5.   [283] See 'No-action letters', pp 432–433 below.

[284] *Leniency and no-action guidance*, paras 8.2–8.3; the OFT does not exclude the making of certain limited representations commenting on specific elements of its case.

[285] Ibid, para 8.4.

[286] Ibid, paras 8.19–8.31.   [287] Ibid, paras 8.32–8.53.   [288] OFT 423, December 2004.

[289] Leniency was provided on this basis in *Collusive tendering for mastic asphalt flat-roofing contracts in Scotland*, OFT decision of 15 March 2005 [2005] UKCLR 638, para 410.

[290] *Leniency and no-action guidance*, para 9.9.

(xi) Resale price maintenance

The OFT's *Guidance as to the appropriate amount of a penalty*[291] allows for leniency in respect of resale price maintenance[292]. The *Leniency and no-action guidance* adds that leniency might be available where vertical behaviour might be said to facilitate horizontal cartel activity[293].

(G) Settlements and early resolution of cases[294]

One of the mitigating factors mentioned in Step 3 of the OFT's *Guidance on penalties* is co-operation which enables the OFT's enforcement process to be concluded more effectively and/or speedily. On seven occasions the OFT (in *Independent fee paying schools, British Airways, Dairy products, Tobacco, Professional Loans* and *Reckitt Benckiser*) and the ORR (in *English Welsh & Scottish Railway*) have adopted, or are in the process of adopting, decisions in which all or some of the parties to the investigation entered into a settlement agreement in which they admitted the infringement and agreed to pay a reduced penalty, with the discount reflecting the time and administrative resource savings as a result of the agreement not to contest the case[295]. This process is sometimes referred to as one of 'settlement' or 'early resolution'; it should be distinguished from applications for leniency whereby full immunity or a reduced penalty are allowed in return for the provision of information to the OFT that enables it to investigate a case[296]. The OFT intends to publish a statement on its experience of the early resolution process[297].

(H) The penalty provisions in practice

By 20 June 2011 penalties had been imposed in 26 cases under the Chapter I and Chapter II prohibitions and Articles 101 and 102 TFEU.

(i) Statistical analysis

The total amount of the penalties imposed under the Competition Act (and Articles 101 and 102) by 20 June 2011 was £956.6 million before reductions for leniency and £733.3 million after leniency. On appeal to the CAT (and the Court of Appeal) some of the penalties were reduced: after making allowance for those reductions the figure should be reduced to £598.5 million. Clearly the penalty in the case of *Tobacco*, of £225 million, represents a major landmark in the competition policy in the UK since it is considerably higher than in any previous case. The *British Airways* case is also of interest as BA agreed to pay a fine of £121.5 million, which will be the largest ever fine imposed by the OFT for a single infringement of the Chapter I prohibition and Article 101(1) TFEU[298].

---

[291] OFT 423, December 2004.

[292] Ibid, fn 8; note that the European Commission's *Leniency Notice* does not apply in the case of vertical price fixing: see ch 7 n 265, p 281.

[293] *Leniency and no-action guidance*, para 9.13.

[294] On settlements under EU law see ch 7, 'Settlements of cartel cases?', pp 262–264; see also Lawrence and Sansom 'The Increasing Use of Administrative Settlement Procedures in UK and EC Competition Investigations' [2007] Competition Law Journal 163 and Burrows and Gilbert 'OFT Competition Act Enforcement: Key Developments over the First Decade' [2010] Competition Law Journal 178.

[295] See the 'Table of penalties' below.

[296] See 'Whistleblowing: the leniency programme', pp 414–418 above.

[297] See Collins 'CA98: Shaping the future of Competition Act cases', Speech of 2 March 2011, available at www.oft.gov.uk.

[298] OFT Press Release 113/07, 1 August 2007.

Table 10.1 Table of penalties

Decision	Date of the Decision	Amount of the penalty (before and after leniency)	Amount of the penalty after appeal to the CAT
Napp Pharmaceutical Holding Ltd	5.4.2001	£3.21 million Infringement of Chapter II prohibition	Reduced to £2.2million[1]
Market sharing by Arriva plc and First Group plc	5.2.2002	£848,027 (before leniency) £203,632 (after leniency) Infringement of Chapter I prohibition	No appeal
John Bruce Ltd, Fleet Parts Ltd and Truck and Trailer Components	17.5.2002	£33,737 Infringement of Chapter I prohibition	No appeal
Aberdeen Journals Ltd	16.9.2002	£1.328 million Infringement of Chapter II prohibition	Reduced to £1 million[2]
Hasbro I	6.12.2002	£9 million (before leniency) £4.95 million (after leniency) Infringement of Chapter I prohibition	No reduction as appeal was withdrawn[3]
Genzyme Ltd	27.3.2003	£6.8 million Infringement of Chapter II prohibition	Reduced to £3 million[4]
Replica Football Kits	1.8.2003	£18.668 million (before leniency) £18.627 million (after leniency) Infringement of Chapter I prohibition	Reduced to £15.49 million[5]
Hasbro II	2.12.2003	£38.25 million (before leniency) £22.66 million (after leniency) Infringement of Chapter I prohibition	Reduced to £19.50 million[6]
West Midlands roofing contractors	17.3.2004	£971,186 (before leniency) £297,625 (after leniency) Infringement of Chapter I prohibition	Reduced to £288,625[7]

(continued)

Table 10.1 (*Continued*)

Decision	Date of the Decision	Amount of the penalty (before and after leniency)	Amount of the penalty after appeal to the CAT
UOP Ltd/Ukae Ltd etc (Desiccants)	9.11.2004	**£2.433 million** (before leniency) **£1.707 million** (after leniency)	Reduced to £1.635 million[8]
Collusive tendering for felt and single ply flat-roofing contracts in the North East of England	8.4.2005	**£598,223** (before leniency) **£471,029** (after leniency) Infringement of Chapter I prohibition	No appeal
Collusive tendering for mastic asphalt flat-roofing contracts in Scotland	8.4.2005	**£231,445** (before leniency) **£87,353** (after leniency) Infringement of Chapter I prohibition	No appeal
Collusive tendering for felt and single ply roofing contracts in Western Central Scotland	12.7.2005	**£238,576** (before leniency) **£138,515** (after leniency) Infringement of Chapter I prohibition	No appeal
Collusive tendering for flat roof and car park surfacing contracts in England and Scotland	23.2.2006	**£1.852 million** (before leniency) **£1.557 million** (after leniency) Infringement of Chapter I prohibition	No reduction[9]
Stock check pads	4.4.2006	**£2.184 million** (before leniency) **£168,318** (after leniency) Infringement of Chapter I prohibition	No reduction[10]
Aluminium spacer bars	29.6.2006	**£1.384 million** (before leniency) **£898,470** (after leniency) Infringement of Chapter I prohibition	No reduction[11]

Decision	Date of the Decision	Amount of the penalty (before and after leniency)	Amount of the penalty after appeal to the CAT
English Welsh & Scottish Railway Ltd (ORR)	17.11.2006	£4.1 million Infringement of Chapter II prohibition	No appeal as to penalty (appeal by a third party against the directions given by ORR, subsequently withdrawn)[12]
Schools: exchange of information on future fees	21.11.2006	£489,000 (before leniency) £467,500 (after leniency) Infringement of Chapter I prohibition	No appeal
British Airways	1.8.2007	£121.5 million Infringement of Chapter I prohibition	No appeal
National Grid (OFGEM)	25.2.2008	Fine of £41.6 million Infringement of Chapter II prohibition and Article 102 TFEU	Reduced to £30 million[13] Further reduced to £15 million on appeal to the Court of Appeal[14]
Construction bid rigging	22.9.2009	£194.1 million (before leniency) £129.5 million (after leniency) Infringement of Chapter I prohibition	Reduced to £63.9 million[15]
Recruitment Agencies	30.09.2009	£173 million (before leniency) £39.27 million (after leniency) Infringement of Chapter I prohibition	Reduced to £8.14 million[16]
Loan pricing	30.3.2010	£28.59 million Infringement of Chapter I prohibition and Article 101 TFEU	
Tobacco	16.4.2010	£225 million Infringement of Chapter I prohibition	On appeal to the CAT[17], not yet decided

(continued)

Table 10.1 (*Continued*)

Decision	Date of the Decision	Amount of the penalty (before and after leniency)	Amount of the penalty after appeal to the CAT
Reckitt Benckiser	13.4.2011	**£10.2 million** Infringement of Chapter II prohibition	
Dairy products	10.8.11	Infringement of Chapter I prohibition **Fine of £49.51 million**	On appeal to CAT, not yet decided[18]

[1] Case No 1001/1/1/01 *Napp Pharmaceutical Holding Ltd v Director General of Fair Trading* [2002] CAT 1, [2002] CompAR 13.

[2] Case No 1009/1/1/02 *Aberdeen Journals Ltd v OFT* [2003] CAT 11, [2003] CompAR 67.

[3] Case No 1010/1/1/03 *Hasbro UK Ltd v The Director General of Fair Trading* [2003] CAT 1, [2003] CompAR 47.

[4] Case No 1016/1/1/03 *Genzyme Ltd v OFT* [2004] CAT 4, [2004] CompAR 358.

[5] Case Nos 1019/1/1/03 etc *Umbro Holdings Ltd v OFT*, [2005] CAT 22, [2005] CompAR 1060.

[6] Case Nos 1014/1/1/03 and 1015/1/1/03 *Argos Ltd and Littlewoods Ltd v OFT* [2005] CAT 13, [2005] CompAR 834.

[7] Case No 1032/1/1/04 *Apex Asphalt and Paving Co Ltd v OFT* [2005] CAT 4, [2005] CompAR 507, and Case No 1033/1/1/04 *Richard W Price Ltd v OFT* [2005] CAT 5, [2005] CompAR 801.

[8] Case No 1048/1/1/05 *Double Quick Supplyline Ltd v OFT*, consent order of 19 May 2005.

[9] Case No 1061/1/1/06 *Makers UK Ltd v OFT* and Case No 1065/1/1/06 *Prater Ltd v OFT* [2006] CAT 11, [2006] CompAR 624.

[10] Case No 1067/1/1/06 *Achilles Paper Group Ltd v OFT* [2006] CAT 24, [2007] CompAR 1.

[11] Case No 1072/1/1/06 *Sepia Logistics Ltd v OFT* [2007] CAT 13, [2007] CompAR 747.

[12] Case No 1076/2/5/07 *E.ON UK plc v Office of Rail Regulation*.

[13] Case No 1099/1/2/08 *National Grid plc v GEMA* [2009] CAT 14.

[14] [2010] EWCA Civ 114.

[15] Case Nos 1114/1/1/09 etc *Kier Group plc v OFT* [2011] CAT 3.

[16] Case Nos 1140/1/1/09 etc *Eden Brown Ltd v OFT* [2011] CAT 8.

[17] Case Nos 1160/1/1/10 etc *Imperial Tobacco Group plc v OFT*.

[18] Case No 118/1/1/11 *Tesco Stores Ltd v OFT*, not yet decided.

(ii) Appeals against decisions imposing penalties

There have been numerous appeals to the CAT in relation to the penalties imposed by the OFT for infringements of the Competition Act. On appeal the CAT may impose, revoke or vary the fines imposed[299]. The CAT's practice has been to review the OFT's application of the *Guidance on penalties* and then to set out its own views on the seriousness of the infringement and to make its own assessment of the level of the penalty on the basis of a 'broad brush' approach, taking the case as a whole. The Court of Appeal has said that it thinks that this is an appropriate approach for the CAT to take. The CAT has emphasised that, other than in matters of legal principle, there is limited precedent value in decisions relating to penalties[300].

---

[299] Competition Act 1998, Sch 8, para 3(2)(b).

[300] Case Nos 1114/1/1/09 etc *Kier Group plc & Ors v OFT* [2011] CAT 3, para 116; Case Nos 1140/1/1/09 etc *Eden Brown Ltd v OFT* [2011] CAT 8, paras 78 and 97.

In some cases the CAT decided not to interfere with the OFT's determination[301]; however the CAT has amended the OFT's decisions on penalties on several occasions, usually downwards[302] but on one occasion upwards[303]. The CAT's approach can be seen, for example, in *Construction Bid-rigging*[304] in which the penalty of £129.2 million imposed by the OFT was reduced by the CAT to £63.9 million. The CAT held that the penalties imposed by the OFT for 'simple' cover pricing were excessive given, in particular, the nature of the infringement and the harm it was likely to cause, and the general mitigation resulting from the perceptions of legitimacy in the construction industry[305]. The CAT further held that the OFT had used the wrong financial year to arrive at the starting figure for the penalties[306]. The CAT also disagreed with the method the OFT had used to secure deterrence[307].

In *National Grid* the CAT reduced the penalty from £41.6 million to £30 million to reflect the fact that the Gas and Electricity Markets Authority had been closely involved in discussions with National Grid that had led to the infringing agreements[308]; the Court of Appeal further reduced the fine to £15 million for the same reason[309]. The reduced fine is still the highest imposed in the UK for an abuse of a dominant position.

(iii) Aggravating factors

In *Genzyme Ltd* the OFT considered that the fact that Genzyme had committed a further infringement after the OFT had begun its investigation into Genzyme's pricing practices was an aggravating factor[310]. In the first *Hasbro* case[311] the OFT increased Hasbro's fine by 10 per cent at Step 4 because senior management were aware of the infringement and because the resale price maintenance took place on Hasbro's initiative[312]. In *Construction Bid-rigging*[313] and *Construction Recruitment Forum*[314] the OFT increased the fines by between 5 and 15 per cent on undertakings whose directors had been involved in the infringements; and in *Construction Bid-rigging* the OFT increased Wildgoose Construction's fine by 15 per cent because it had paid an individual to engage in cover pricing[315].

---

[301] See eg Case Nos 1032 and 1033/1/1/04 *Apex Asphalt and Paving Co Ltd v OFT* [2005] CAT 4, [2005] CompAR 507 and Case No 1067/1/1/06 *Achilles Paper Group Ltd v OFT* [2006] CAT 24.

[302] Case No 1000/1/1/01 *Napp Pharmaceutical Holdings Ltd v Director General of Fair Trading* [2002] CAT 1, [2002] CompAR 13, paras 533–534; Case No 1009/1/1/02 *Aberdeen Journals Ltd v OFT* [2003] CAT 11, [2003] CompAR 67, paras 491–499; Case No 1016/1/1/03 *Genzyme Ltd v OFT* [2005] CAT 32, [2006] CompAR 195, paras 700–708; Case Nos 1014 and 1015/1/1/03 *Argos Ltd v OFT* [2005] CAT 13, [2005] CompAR 834; Case Nos 1019–1022/1/1/03 *JJB Sports Plc v OFT* [2005] CAT 22, [2005] CompAR 1060

[303] See 'The CAT can increase penalties', p 424 below.

[304] Case Nos 1114/1/1/09 etc *Kier Group plc v OFT* [2011] CAT 3.

[305] Ibid, paras 92–118.

[306] Ibid, paras 130–139.

[307] Ibid, paras 164–185; see similarly the *Construction Recruitment Forum* appeals in Case Nos 1140/1/1/09 etc *Eden Brown Ltd v OFT* [2011] CAT 8, paras 81–102.

[308] Case No 1099/1/2/08 *National Grid plc v Gas and Electricity Markets Authority* [2009] CAT 14, paras 201–220.

[309] *National Grid plc v Gas and Electricity Markets Authority* [2010] EWCA Civ 114, [2010] UKCLR 386, paras 90–115.

[310] OFT decision of 27 March 2003 [2003] UKCLR 950, para 436.

[311] OFT decision of 28 November 2002 [2003] UKCLR 150.   [312] Ibid, paras 89–92.

[313] OFT decision of 21 September 2009 [2010] UKCLR 322, paras VI.301–VI.314 (pp 1696–1698).

[314] OFT decision of 29 September 2009 [2010] UKCLR 14, paras 5.311–5.334.

[315] OFT decision of 21 September 2009 [2010] UKCLR 322, paras VI.295–VI.299 (p 1695); see similarly para IV.4424 (p 1197).

(iv) The CAT can increase penalties

The CAT has power to increase as well as to decrease a penalty[316]. In *Football Shirts* the CAT increased the penalty on one of the appellants, Allsports, by £170,000[317]. The OFT had allowed a 5 per cent decrease of the penalty that would otherwise have been imposed on Allsports in recognition of its cooperation. In the proceedings before the CAT it became clear, when witnesses were subjected to cross-examination, that Allsports had been less co-operative than the OFT had thought, and the reduction was therefore revoked.

(v) Decisions in which no penalty was imposed

There have been occasions when the OFT has found an infringement but decided not to impose a penalty. In *Northern Ireland Livestock and Auctioneers' Association*[318] the OFT decided not to impose a penalty on the Association which had recommended to its members a standard commission that should be paid by purchasers of livestock at Northern Ireland cattle marts, since the recommendation was publicised, there was no attempt to conceal it and since the beef industry in Northern Ireland had been badly hit by the unfortunate combination of 'mad cow' disease and foot and mouth disease[319]. In *Lladró Comercial*[320] no penalty was imposed on Lladró, despite a finding that it had fixed the retail selling price of its merchandise, since the European Commission had sent a comfort letter to Lladró which it could reasonably have interpreted as suggesting that its agreements did not infringe the Competition Act[321].

6. The Cartel Offence and Company Director Disqualification

The Enterprise Act 2002 introduced two provisions designed to encourage individuals to ensure compliance with competition law. First, Part 6 of the Act established the 'cartel offence', the commission of which can lead, on indictment, to a term of imprisonment of up to five years and/or an unlimited fine[322]. Secondly, the Act introduced the possibility of company directors being disbarred from office for a period of up to 15 years where they knew, or ought to have known, that their company was guilty of an infringement of EU or UK competition law[323]. These important provisions attempt to address the problem that the imposition of fines – even very substantial ones – on undertakings may not have a sufficiently deterrent effect, especially where the cost of the fines is simply transferred to customers through higher prices; and that if a fine is so large that it results in the insolvency and liquidation of an undertaking, this will result in the loss of a competitor from the market, a somewhat perverse achievement for a system of competition law[324]. The

---

[316] Competition Act 1998, Sch 8, para 3(2)(b).

[317] Case Nos 1019–1022/1/1/03 *JJB Sports Plc & Allsports Ltd v OFT* [2005] CAT 22, [2005] CompAR 1060, paras 208–235.

[318] OFT decision of 3 February 2003 [2003] UKCLR 433.

[319] Ibid, para 72; see similarly Case T-86/95 *Compagnie Générale Maritime v Commission* [2002] ECR II-1011, [2002] 4 CMLR 1115, para 481, where the General Court decided that no fine should be imposed on a cartel, among other reasons, because it was not secret but was widely known to exist.

[320] OFT decision of 31 March 2003 [2003] UKCLR 652.   [321] Ibid, para 124.

[322] Enterprise Act 2002, s 190(1).

[323] Ibid, s 204.

[324] For discussion of criminalisation, both generally and as a matter of UK law, see Hammond and Penrose 'Proposed criminalisation of cartels in the UK' OFT 365, November 2001; Pickford 'The Introduction of a New Economic Crime' (2002) 1 Competition Law Journal 35; Harding 'Business Cartels as a Criminal Activity: Reconciling North American and European Models of Regulation' (2002) 9 Maastricht Journal of European and Comparative Law 393; Harding and Joshua 'Breaking up the Hard Core: Prospects for

criminal sanction is a very important feature of US law on cartels: there have been many high-profile cases in recent years in which senior executives of major companies have had to serve terms of imprisonment[325]. At least 13 Member States of the EU, including the UK, have some form of criminal sanction against individuals for infringements of substantive competition law[326]. Other countries have also been active in recent times in this area: in 2009 Australia adopted the Trade Practices Amendment (Cartel Conduct and Other Measures) Act and South Africa passed the Competition Amendment Act, each introducing criminal sanctions for the first time, while Canada adopted the Budget Implementation Act, amending the Competition Act, to provide for more effective criminal enforcement.

As a separate matter the House of Lords has held, in *Ian Norris v Government of the USA*[327], that 'mere' price fixing, without aggravating features, does not amount to conspiracy to defraud, a criminal offence at common law; this matter is discussed in section C below[328]. It is at least arguable that some types of cartel activity might infringe section 4 of the Fraud Act 2006[329].

(A) The cartel offence

(i) Definition of the cartel offence

Section 188 of the Enterprise Act 2002 established the criminal 'cartel offence'. The cartel offence is quite distinct from Article 101 TFEU and the Chapter I prohibition in the Competition Act: this means that where a price-fixing agreement is detected the possibility exists that the undertakings involved may be the subject of proceedings under Article 101 or the Chapter I prohibition, leading to the imposition of fines, and that the individuals responsible for setting up the agreement may be prosecuted criminally under the cartel offence. An example of this occurred in the *Marine Hoses* case, where

the New Cartel Offence' (2002) Criminal Law Review (December) 933; Joshua 'A Sherman Act Bridgehead in Europe or a Ghost Ship in Mid-Atlantic?' (2002) 23 ECLR 231; Green 'The Road to Conviction – the Criminalisation of Cartel Law' [2003] Fordham Corporate Law Review (ed Hawk), ch 2; Macdonald and Thompson 'Dishonest agreements' (2003) 2 Competition Law Journal 94; Beard 'The Cartel Criminal Offence' (2003) 2 Competition Law Journal 156; MacNeil 'Criminal Investigations in Competition Law' (2003) 24 ECLR 151; Joshua 'The UK's new cartel offence and its implications for EC competition law: a tangled web' (2003) 28 EL Rev 620; Dobbin and Peretz 'The Cartel Offence' in Ward and Smith (eds) *Competition Litigation in the UK* (Sweet & Maxwell, 2003), ch 5; Furse and Nash *The Cartel Offence* (Hart Publishing, 2004); Rosochowicz 'The Appropriateness of Criminal Sanctions in the Enforcement of Competition Law' (2004) 25 ECLR 752; Perrin 'Challenges facing the EU Network of Competition Authorities: insights from a comparative criminal law perspective' (2006) 31 EL Rev 540; MacCulloch 'Honesty, Morality and the Cartel Offence' (2007) 28 ECLR 355; Whelan 'A Principled Argument for Personal Criminal Sanctions as Punishment under EC Cartel Law' (2007) 4(1) Competition Law Review 7, available online at www.clasf. org; Stephan 'The UK Cartel Offence: Lame Duck or Black Mamba', Centre for Competition Policy Working Paper No 08-19 (November 2008); Kane *The Law of Criminal Cartels: Practice and Procedure* (Oxford University Press, 2009); Riley 'Outgrowing the European Administrative Model? Ten Years of British Anti-cartel Enforcement' and MacCulloch 'The Cartel Offence: is Honesty the Best Policy?' both in *Ten Years of UK Competition Law Reform* (Dundee University Press, 2010, ed Rodger); *Criminalising Cartels* (Hart Publishing, 2011, eds Beaton-Wells and Ezrachi).

[325] See ch 13, 'Recent cartel cases outside the EU', pp 516–517.

[326] See Bellamy and Child *European Community Law of Competition* (Oxford University Press, 6th ed, 2008, eds Roth and Rose), para 14.171.

[327] [2008] UKHL 16, [2008] 1 AC 920, reversing the judgment of the High Court on this point, *Ian Norris v Government of the USA* [2007] EWHC 71, [2007] UKCLR 1487.

[328] See 'Conspiracy to defraud at common law', pp 436–437 below.

[329] See Corker and Smith, arguing against the application of the Fraud Act to price fixing, in 'Cartels: who's liable?' (2007) 157 New Law Journal 1593.

the European Commission imposed fines of €131 million on various undertakings engaged in allocating tenders, market sharing and price fixing[330], while three individuals were imprisoned in the UK for infringing section 188[331]. The criminal prosecution of individuals is likely to precede the proceedings against the undertakings, as happened in the *Marine Hoses* case[332], to ensure that the more rigorous evidential standards in criminal cases affecting individuals whose personal liberty is at stake are observed.

The Court of Appeal has held in *IB v The Queen* that the cartel offence is not a 'national competition law' in the sense of Article 3 of Regulation 1/2003; had it decided to the contrary it was arguable that the Crown Court, which is not a designated competition authority for the purposes of that Regulation, would have had no jurisdiction to impose a penalty under section 188 of the Enterprise Act[333].

Section 188 of the Enterprise Act provides (in formalistic, indeed tortuous, terms) that an individual is guilty of an offence if he or she dishonestly agrees with one or more other persons that undertakings[334] will engage in one or more of the following cartel activities, namely direct and indirect price fixing[335]; limitation of supply[336] or production[337]; market sharing[338]; or bid-rigging[339]. The Act specifically provides that, in relation to price fixing and the limitation of supply or production, the parties must have entered into a reciprocal agreement[340]; this is not specified in relation to market sharing and bid-rigging, since these actions are, by their nature, reciprocal. The fact that there must be a reciprocal agreement does not mean that there must be mutual dishonesty: it is sufficient that one individual acted dishonestly, without having to show that other individuals also did so[341].

A key feature of the criminal offence is that there must have been dishonesty on the part of the individuals concerned. In *R v Ghosh*[342] the Court of Appeal established a two-part test for determining dishonesty: the first part asks, as an objective matter, whether the defendant was acting dishonestly according to the standards of reasonable and honest people; the second asks, as a subjective matter, whether the defendant must have realised that what he was doing was dishonest by those standards. To be found guilty the jury must decide beyond reasonable doubt that the answer to both of these questions is yes. The trial judge in the case against four employees of British Airways[343] said that the test in *Ghosh* is the correct one to apply to the meaning of dishonesty in section 188 of the Enterprise Act, a view that was accepted by the Court of Appeal[344]. The Court of Appeal has said that the question of whether the conduct of an individual is dishonest is a matter of fact to be decided in each case[345]. The offence applies

---

[330] Commission decision of 28 January 2009.

[331] See 'The cartel offence in practice', p 434 below.   [332] Ibid.

[333] [2009] EWCA Crim 2575, [2009] UKCLR 1, paras 21–39.

[334] The term 'undertaking' has the same meaning for this purpose as it has in the Competition Act 1998: Enterprise Act 2002, s 188(7).

[335] Enterprise Act 2002, s 188(2)(a); indirect price fixing would include, for example, agreements about relative price levels or price ranges, rebates and discounts: see the DTI's *Enterprise Bill: Explanatory Notes*, para 391.

[336] Enterprise Act, s 188(2)(b).   [337] Ibid, s 188(2)(c).   [338] Ibid, s 188(2)(d) and (e).

[339] Ibid, s 188(2)(f): a definition of bid-rigging is provided by s 188(5) of the Act; there is no offence where the person requesting the bids is aware of the bid-rigging arrangements: ibid, s 188(6).

[340] Ibid, s 188(3).

[341] *R v George & Ors* [2010] EWCA Crim 1148, [2010] UKCLR 1383, paras 8–18.

[342] [1982] QB 1053, [1982] 2 All ER 689.

[343] See 'The cartel offence in practice', p 434 below.

[344] *R v George & Ors* [2010] EWCA Crim 1148, [2010] UKCLR 1383, para 6.

[345] *IB v The Queen* [2009] EWCA Crim 2575, [2009] UKCLR 1, para 27.

only in respect of horizontal agreements[346]: vertical agreements, including resale price maintenance, are not covered by the cartel offence. The cartel offence will have been committed irrespective of whether the agreement reached between the individuals is implemented by the undertakings, and irrespective of whether or not they have authority to act on behalf of the undertaking at the time of the agreement[347]. Individuals could also be prosecuted for the inchoate offences of attempting to commit the criminal offence[348] and conspiracy to do so[349]. If the agreement is entered into outside the UK, proceedings may be brought only where the agreement has been implemented in whole or in part in the UK[350].

(ii) Powers of investigation and search

The OFT may conduct an investigation if there are reasonable grounds for suspecting that the cartel offence has been committed[351], and the Enterprise Act gives it powers to require information and documents[352] and to enter and search premises under a warrant[353]. The OFT has published guidance on how it intends to exercise the powers conferred upon it for this purpose[354]. There are criminal sanctions for non-compliance with the powers of investigation: for example the intentional destruction of documents could lead to a maximum prison sentence of five years[355]. The OFT may also obtain information about the cartel offence through informal inquiries: it will make clear to individuals and undertakings that there is no compulsion to respond to informal inquiries[356].

(A) Powers to require information and documents

The OFT can, by written notice, require a person to answer questions, provide information or produce documents for the purposes of a criminal investigation[357]; the term 'document' includes information recorded in any form and includes information that may be held electronically[358]. The OFT can exercise this power against any person it has reason to believe has relevant information[359], who must provide the information or documents required other than communications protected by professional privilege[360] or confidential information between a bank and its client[361]. In urgent cases the OFT may require immediate compliance with a notice[362]. The OFT can also require, in writing, a person to attend a 'compulsory interview' to answer questions on any matter relevant to the investigation[363]. Section 197 of the Act imposes restrictions on the use of statements (but not of documents) obtained under section 193 (and section 194, dealt with below)[364] in order to protect against self-incrimination[365]. There are also restrictions on the disclosure of confidential information[366]. The OFT issued 14 notices under section 193 in the period to which the 2006–2007 Annual Report relates, one to a business and 13 to individuals

---

[346] Enterprise Act 2002, ss 188(4) and 189.

[347] *The cartel offence: Guidance on the issue of no-action letters for individuals*, OFT 513, April 2003, para 2.3 and *Powers for investigating criminal cartels*, OFT 515, January 2004, para 1.1.

[348] Criminal Attempts Act 1981, s 1.   [349] Criminal Law Act 1977, s 1.

[350] Enterprise Act 2002, s 190(3).   [351] Ibid, s 192(1).

[352] Ibid, s 192(2).   [353] Ibid, s 194.

[354] *Powers for investigating criminal cartels*, OFT 515, January 2004, available at www.oft.gov.uk.

[355] Enterprise Act 2002, s 201; see also *Powers for investigating criminal cartels*, paras 7.1–7.4 and Table 7.1.

[356] Ibid, para 2.3.

[357] Enterprise Act 2002, s 193; *Powers for investigating criminal cartels*, paras 3.2–3.5.

[358] Enterprise Act 2002, s 202.

[359] Ibid, s 193(1).   [360] Ibid, s 196(1).

[361] Ibid, s 196(2).   [362] *Powers for investigating criminal cartels*, para 3.4.

[363] Ibid, para 3.2.   [364] Enterprise Act 2002, s 197.

[365] See *Powers for investigating criminal cartels*, paras 6.3–6.5.

[366] Enterprise Act 2002, ss 237–246 and *Powers for investigating criminal cartels*, paras 6.6–6.8.

relating to two separate cases[367]; the corresponding figures for the next three years (not broken down as to businesses and individuals) were 99, 14 and just two in 2009–2010[368].

(B) *Power to enter premises under a warrant*

The OFT may apply to the High Court (or in Scotland the procurator fiscal may apply to the sheriff) for a warrant authorising a named officer of the OFT, or any other authorised person such as a forensic IT expert, to enter premises[369]. This power permits forcible entry into and a search of the premises[370]; explanations of documents can be required[371] and the OFT can require that information stored in an electronic form can be taken away in a visible and legible form[372]. The OFT's officers may take away original documents[373]; a copy of documents removed will be provided as soon as is reasonably practicable after the execution of the warrant[374]. Privileged information cannot be insisted upon[375]. A warrant may be issued, first, if there are reasonable grounds for believing that there are documents on any premises that the OFT could require by written notice[376] and, secondly, if a person has failed to comply with a written notice[377]; or if it is not practicable to serve such a notice[378]; or if the service of such a notice might seriously prejudice the investigation[379].

Entry under a warrant will be conducted in accordance with the requirements of Code B of the PACE Codes of Practice[380]. Although PACE does not apply in Scotland, the OFT may follow its procedures there[381].

The investigating officer will not wait for a legal adviser to be present before commencing a search, though he will normally ensure that the search is witnessed by a third party[382]. A person under investigation will, however, be entitled to seek legal advice in the event that he or she is required to attend an interview or if the OFT intends to exercise its 'seize and sift' powers[383]. The OFT may exercise seize and sift powers that enable its officers pre-emptively to seize material when it is not reasonably practicable to determine on the premises whether the material is seizeable or not[384]. It is an offence to obstruct a search[385].

The exercise of these powers is subject to strict safeguards such as a requirement to give a written notice of what material has been seized[386], and an obligation to return any material which is subject to legal privilege[387]. The OFT visited four business premises under the authority of section 194 criminal search warrants in the period covered by the 2006–2007 Annual Report, relating to two separate cases[388]; there were four inspections in relation to three different cases (two of them of domestic premises) in 2007–2008[389], none in 2008–2009 and one in 2009–2010[390].

---

[367] 2006–2007 Annual Report and Resource Accounts of the Office of Fair Trading Annex C, p 1.
[368] 2009–2010 Annual Report and Resource Accounts of the Office of Fair Trading Annex C, p 3.
[369] Enterprise Act 2002, ss 194 and 195; *Powers for investigating criminal cartels*, paras 3.6–3.14.
[370] Enterprise Act 2002, s 194(2)(a) and (b).   [371] Ibid, s 194(2)(c).
[372] Ibid, s 194(2)(d).   [373] Ibid, s 194(2)(b)(i).
[374] *Powers for investigating criminal cartels*, para 3.8.   [375] Enterprise Act 2002, s 196.
[376] Ibid, s 194(1)(a).
[377] Ibid, s 194(1)(b)(i).
[378] Ibid, s 194(1)(b)(ii).   [379] Ibid, s 194(1)(b)(iii).
[380] *Powers for investigating criminal cartels*, paras 3.10–3.16.   [381] Ibid, para 3.17.
[382] Ibid, para 3.15.   [383] Ibid, para 3.16.
[384] Enterprise Act 2002, s 194(5) incorporating the statutory powers of seizure under the Criminal Justice and Police Act 2001, s 50; see also *Powers for investigating criminal cartels*, paras 3.13–3.14.
[385] Enterprise Act 2002, s 201(6).   [386] Criminal Justice and Police Act 2001, s 52.
[387] Ibid, s 55.
[388] 2006–2007 Annual Report and Resource Accounts of the Office of Fair Trading Annex C, p 1.
[389] 2007–2008 Annual Report and Resource Accounts of the Office of Fair Trading Annex C, p 2.
[390] 2009–2010 Annual Report and Resource Accounts of the Office of Fair Trading Annex C, p 3.

(iii) Powers of surveillance

(A) Enterprise Act: intrusive surveillance and property interference

The Enterprise Act gives powers of 'intrusive surveillance' and 'property interference' to the OFT for the purpose of investigating the commission of the cartel offence: these powers are not available for investigations under the Competition Act[391]. In certain circumstances the Chairman of the OFT, with prior approval from the Office of the Surveillance Commissioners[392], may issue an authorisation for the presence of an individual or the planting of surveillance devices in residential premises, including hotels, and in private vehicles in order to hear or see what is happening there ('intrusive surveillance')[393]. The criteria for the grant of an authorisation are contained in section 32(3) of the Regulation of Investigatory Powers Act 2000 and include situations in which the use of intrusive surveillance is necessary for the prevention or detection of a serious crime, such as the cartel offence, and where it is necessary to act in the interests of the economic well-being of the UK. The OFT could use these powers, for example, to obtain a recording of a meeting of cartel members in a hotel room following a 'tip-off' from one of their employees or a disaffected member of the cartel. An authorisation by the Chairman of the OFT under section 93 of the Police Act 1997, as amended by section 200 of the Enterprise Act, allows for the covert installation of a surveillance device: if it were not for this section the installation would involve some element of trespass.

(B) Further powers: directed surveillance, covert human intelligence sources and access to communications data[394]

The OFT has been given further powers that are regulated by the Regulation of Investigatory Powers Act 2000. The Regulation of Investigatory Powers (Directed Surveillance and Covert Human Intelligence Sources) Order 2003[395] adds the OFT to the list of public authorities that are able to authorise 'directed surveillance': this would allow it, for example, to carry out covert surveillance of a person's office[396]; the OFT may also use 'covert human intelligence sources', for example by asking informants to attend cartel meetings and to report back to it[397]. The Regulation of Investigatory Powers (Communications Data) Order 2003[398] provides that the OFT may be given access to communications data such as the times, duration and recipients of telephone calls, though not their content. The first two of these powers are available in both civil and criminal investigations: the last only for a criminal case.

(C) OFT Codes of Practice

The OFT has published two Codes of Practice explaining how it will exercise the additional powers described in the preceding paragraph, *Covert surveillance in cartel*

---

[391] Enterprise Act 2002, s 199 amending Regulation of Investigatory Powers Act 2000, ss 32ff and Enterprise Act 2002, s 200 amending Police Act 1997, ss 93–94.

[392] Note that the Office of Surveillance Commissioners has a website, www.surveillancecommissioners. gov.uk, containing relevant information and links to recent judgments.

[393] *Powers for investigating criminal cartels*, paras 5.2–5.3; in situations of urgency, the Chairman of the OFT may authorise the use of intrusive surveillance and give notice to the Surveillance Commissioner, who will be the ultimate arbiter in such cases: ibid, para 5.3.

[394] See *Powers for investigating criminal cartels*, paras 5.4–5.5.

[395] SI 2003/3171; since 1 February 2010 written authorisations to use a covert human intelligences source have effect for only three months: Regulation of Investigatory Powers (Covert Human Intelligence Sources: Matters Subject to Legal Privilege) Order 2010, SI 2010/123.

[396] See Regulation of Investigatory Powers Act 2000, s 28.

[397] Ibid, s 29.

[398] SI 2003/3171.

investigations[399] and *Covert human intelligence sources in cartel investigations*[400]. The codes follow closely best practice guidelines issued by the Home Office.

(iv) Prosecution and penalty

The cartel offence is triable on indictment before a jury in the Crown Court, where a term of imprisonment of up to five years may be imposed[401] or an unlimited fine[402], or in a magistrates' court, where the maximum prison sentence would be six months and where a fine may also be imposed[403]. The two cases to have been brought so far under the Act were both dealt with by Southwark Crown Court in London[404]. Prosecutions may be brought by the Serious Fraud Office (SFO) or the OFT[405]; the SFO may undertake this function in England, Wales and Northern Ireland where serious or complex fraud is involved[406]. The factors that the SFO will take into account in defining a serious or complex fraud case include whether the value of the alleged fraud exceeds £1 million[407]; whether the case is likely to give rise to national publicity and widespread public concern; and whether legal, accounting and investigative skills need to be brought together[408]. If the SFO agrees to accept a case it may carry out additional inquiries using its powers under section 2 of the Criminal Justice Act 1987, which are broadly the same as the powers of the OFT under the Enterprise Act[409]. The SFO is bound by the Code for Crown Prosecutors[410]. Prosecutions in Scotland are brought by the Lord Advocate[411]. The OFT can decide to prosecute a case itself where it unearths a hard-core cartel that does not amount to a serious fraud for the SFO's purposes; it conducted the prosecutions in *Marine Hoses* and *British Airways*, discussed below.

The OFT has agreed a *Memorandum of Understanding* with the SFO which records the basis on which they will cooperate to investigate and/or prosecute individuals in respect of the cartel offence where 'serious or complex fraud' is suspected; a similar *Memorandum of June 2009*, revising an earlier one of 2003, has been agreed with the National Casework Division of the Crown Office in Scotland: both *Memoranda* are available on the OFT's website[412]. Initial inquiries into possible cartel activity will be undertaken by the OFT; if it considers that the SFO's 'acceptance' criteria are satisfied – that is to say that serious or complex fraud may be involved – the OFT will refer the matter to the SFO, the Director of which will endeavour to decide whether to accept the case, or to require the OFT to make

---

[399] OFT 738, August 2004, available at www.oft.gov.uk.

[400] OFT 739, August 2004, available at www.oft.gov.uk.

[401] A custodial sentence can be imposed only where the court is of the opinion that the offence is so serious that only such a sentence can be justified: Powers of Criminal Courts (Sentencing) Act 2000, s 79.

[402] Enterprise Act 2002, s 190(1)(a).

[403] Ibid, s 190(1)(b); the maximum fine in the magistrates' court would be £5,000: Magistrates Courts' Act 1980, s 32(9).

[404] See 'The cartel offence in practice', p 434 below.

[405] Enterprise Act 2002, s 190(2)(a).

[406] *The cartel offence: Guidance on the issue of no-action letters for individuals*, OFT 513, para 2.7.

[407] See the *Background note to the Memorandum of Understanding*, available at www.oft.gov.uk; the value of the fraud presumably relates to the loss caused to the victims or to the profit made by the fraudsters.

[408] *Powers for investigating criminal cartels*, para 3.18.   [409] Ibid, paras 3.20–3.23.

[410] Available on the website of the Crown Prosecution Service: www.cps.gov.uk/Home/CodeForCrownProsecutors.

[411] In Scotland the Lord Advocate exercises the same powers as the SFO under the Criminal Law (Consolidation) (Scotland) Act 1995.

[412] See OFT 547, October 2003 (SFO) and OFT 546, June 2009 (NCD), available at www.oft.gov.uk.

further inquiries, within 28 days[413]. Where the SFO accepts an OFT referral the case team will consist of both SFO and OFT staff, under the direction of an SFO case controller[414].

Both the OFT and the SFO are bound by the disclosure provisions of the Criminal Procedure and Investigations Act 1996 which require them to disclose to the defendant any prosecution material which, in the prosecutor's opinion, might undermine the case for the prosecution against the accused.

The OFT is responsible for the grant of leniency and the issue of no-action letters, but where this could affect the outcome of an SFO investigation the OFT will consult with it[415]. The SFO would not prosecute a cartel as a conspiracy to defraud or under the Fraud Act 2006 where the OFT has granted immunity under the Enterprise Act. There is no system in the UK of 'plea bargaining' of the kind that operates under the criminal provisions in US law[416].

(v) Parallel OFT criminal and administrative investigations

When the OFT first receives information about alleged cartel activity it may not immediately be clear whether the case will involve a criminal prosecution of individuals, or whether it will 'merely' lead to an administrative procedure against the undertakings concerned under the Competition Act. In order not to compromise any criminal prosecution the OFT will, where appropriate, follow the procedures required by PACE and its associated Codes of Practice from the outset; this will include giving individuals the standard criminal caution before being questioned, and allowing the presence of a legal adviser[417]. If the OFT decides to conduct a 'compulsory' interview, the difference between this and a 'voluntary' interview must be explained, as well as the restrictions on the use of information obtained in a voluntary interview[418].

Where there is a possibility of both criminal and administrative proceedings, and where the SFO is conducting the criminal case, the OFT and the SFO will consult on timing; the OFT will not institute an administrative procedure without prior consultation with the SFO[419]. Where the OFT and SFO are proceeding simultaneously the two investigating teams will maintain an 'on-going dialogue' in order to ensure that the administrative procedure does not prejudice the parallel criminal investigation[420]. If the OFT conducts both the criminal and administrative proceedings, different case teams are established for each investigation.

Statements obtained under the Competition Act will usually not be available for the purpose of a criminal prosecution if they have not been obtained according to criminal law standards; it may therefore be necessary to conduct a further interview in accordance with PACE procedures[421]. It is possible that a civil claim for damages might be stayed until a criminal trial has been held[422].

---

[413] *Memorandum of Understanding*, paras 3 and 4.　　　[414] Ibid, para 6.

[415] Ibid, para 13; leniency and no-action letters are discussed below.

[416] For discussion of the possible benefits of introducing plea bargaining for criminal cartel cases in the UK see Lawrence, O'Kane, Rab and Nakhwal 'Hardcore Bargains: What Could Plea Bargaining Offer in UK Criminal Cartel Cases?' (2008) 7 Competition Law Journal 17.

[417] *Powers for investigating criminal cartels*, paras 4.1–4.2.

[418] Ibid, para 4.3.

[419] Ibid, para 4.6.

[420] Ibid, para 4.7.

[421] Ibid, para 4.8.

[422] See *Secretary of State for Health v Norton Healthcare Ltd* [2004] Eu LR 12, para 40.

(vi) No-action letters

Section 190(4) of the Enterprise Act provides for the issue by the OFT of so-called 'no-action letters' whereby individuals who provide information about cartels to the OFT will be granted immunity from prosecution. This is a further example of encouraging whistle-blowers to provide information about cartels in return for leniency[423]. The OFT has published two sets of guidance on the issue of no-action letters, *The cartel offence: Guidance on the issue of no-action letters for individuals*[424] and *Leniency and no-action guidance*[425], in particular Part 7 thereof. The latter document does not replace the former one, but it does make some significant amendments to it; it is therefore the suggested starting point for anyone needing guidance on the subject: a pro-forma no-action letter for individuals is set out at Annex B of the *Leniency and no-action guidance*. The OFT cannot offer leniency from prosecution in Scotland since that is a matter for the Lord Advocate; however the Lord Advocate will accord serious weight to any recommendation from the OFT as to leniency in a case falling to be prosecuted in Scotland when deciding whether to prosecute[426].

The OFT will not reach a final decision on whether an individual will be required to admit participation in the criminal offence until the investigation is at or near its conclusion and until specialist criminal counsel has had the opportunity to advise the OFT on this issue[427]. If the OFT decides that it is appropriate that an individual who qualifies for criminal immunity should make an admission of participation in it, including dishonesty, that individual will be offered immunity only on condition that such an admission is made[428]; if such an admission is deemed not to be appropriate, the individual will be offered a 'comfort letter' stating that the OFT does not consider that there is sufficient evidence for it to prosecute[429]. If an individual works for an undertaking that is not itself a coercer[430], the individual will not be refused criminal immunity unless he or she enjoyed a position of power independent of their position within the undertaking and used that power for the purpose of coercion[431].

Where an undertaking is granted Type A immunity[432] all current and former employees and directors will gain automatic criminal immunity[433]; the same is true where Type B immunity is granted[434]: the *Leniency and no-action guidance* refers to this as 'blanket' immunity. Blanket immunity is not available in Type B leniency and Type C leniency cases: in those cases immunity is considered by the OFT on an individual-by-individual basis[435]. Immunity may also be granted to individuals on their own account, that is to say irrespective of any approach to the OFT by an undertaking[436]. There will be automatic criminal immunity where an individual tells the OFT about cartel activity before any other individual or undertaking and where there is no pre-existing criminal or civil investigation[437]. In other cases criminal immunity may be available on a discretionary basis[438]. Guidance is provided on the process of interviewing individuals who apply for criminal immunity[439]. The *Leniency and no-action guidance* also examines the relationship between the cartel

---

[423] On leniency for undertakings see 'Whistleblowing: the leniency programme', pp 414–418 above.
[424] OFT 513, April 2003.
[425] OFT 803, December 2008.
[426] See paras 13–16 of the *Memorandum of Understanding between the Office of Fair Trading and the National Casework Division, Crown Office, Scotland*, OFT 546, June 2009.
[427] *Leniency and no-action guidance*, para 7.3.   [428] Ibid, para 7.4.   [429] Ibid.
[430] See 'The coercer test', p 417 above on the position of undertakings that are coercers seeking immunity.
[431] *Leniency and no-action guidance*, para 7.10.
[432] See 'Terminology', pp 414–415 above on the terminology used in this section.
[433] *Leniency and no-action guidance*, para 7.13.   [434] Ibid, para 7.15.
[435] Ibid, paras 7.19–7.21.   [436] Ibid, para 7.22.   [437] Ibid, para 7.24.
[438] Ibid, paras 7.25–7.29.   [439] Ibid, paras 7.30–7.33.

offence and leniency applications to the European Commission[440], in particular in light of the concern that exposure to criminal action in the UK might deter undertakings from applying for leniency to the Commission. One way of addressing this is to allow an undertaking that applies to the Commission also to put down a 'marker' for Type A blanket immunity on a no-names basis with the OFT[441].

(vii) Extradition

The Extradition Act 2003 makes provision for the extradition of individuals who commit the cartel offence or who conspire to or attempt to commit it. This means that, in so far as another country, such as the US, has a criminal offence that corresponds with the cartel offence under the Enterprise Act, it can apply to the UK for the extradition of an individual or individuals and vice versa. This provision, of course, is not retrospective, so that there is no possibility of anyone being extradited under the Extradition Act in respect of conduct occurring before section 188 of the Enterprise Act entered into force on 20 June 2003.

The process of extradition as between the UK and 'designated territories'[442] is governed by the Extradition Act 2003. The extradition arrangements differ according to whether the partner country is a 'Category 1' or a 'Category 2' country. The US falls into Category 2. The Act provides that where a Category 2 country seeks extradition it does not have to prove a prima facie case that extradition should be allowed: indeed section 84(7) of the Act forbids a court from considering the sufficiency of the evidence of the requesting State[443]. Instead the requesting State simply has to prove 'double criminality', that is to say it must show that:

- the conduct complained of occurred in the territory of the requesting State

- the conduct would constitute a criminal offence under UK law punishable by a term of imprisonment of at least 12 months if it had occurred in the UK

- the conduct is subject to the same punishment under the law of the requesting State[444].

The House of Lords (now the Supreme Court) has said that it is not necessary to show that the US offence of price fixing includes a dishonesty element as in the case of section 188 of the Enterprise Act[445]. Extradition may be denied where it would be unjust or oppressive by reason of passage of time since the extradition offence occurred[446].

(viii) Relationship between the cartel offence and proceedings against cartels under EU competition law

Where a European Commission cartel investigation involves a potential criminal cartel offence under the Enterprise Act the OFT will cooperate with the Commission to coordinate the progress of the two investigations[447].

---

[440] Ibid, paras 7.34–7.46.

[441] Ibid, paras 3.15–3.16 and 7.38.

[442] See the Extradition Act 2003 (Designation of Part 1 Territories) Order 2003, SI 2003/3333 and the Extradition Act 2003 (Designation of Part 2 Territories) Order 2003, SI 2003/3334.

[443] On this point, and on the controversy over a lack of reciprocity over extradition between the US and the UK, see the related case of *R (Norris) v Secretary of State for the Home Department*, High Court [2006] EWHC 280 (Admin).

[444] Extradition Act 2003, s 64(2) (for part 1 territories) and Extradition Act 2003, s 137(2) (for part 2 territories).

[445] *Norris v Government of the United States of America* [2008] UKHL 16, [2008] 1 AC 920, para 91.

[446] Extradition Act 2003, s 82.

[447] *Powers for investigating criminal cartels*, para 4.10.

(ix) The cartel offence in practice

The first case under section 188 of the Enterprise Act arose from a cartel in the supply of marine hoses, and resulted in terms of imprisonment on three individuals between two and a half and three years[448], reduced slightly on appeal to the Court of Appeal[449]; it declined, because of the circumstances of that case[450], to lay down any general guidance as to the terms of imprisonment to be imposed in other cases. The OFT's investigation in the *Marine Hoses* case was closely coordinated with those of the competition authorities in other jurisdictions, including the European Commission, which imposed fines of €131 million on the undertakings involved in this case[451], and the US Department of Justice, where the same individuals pleaded guilty to illegal price fixing and agreed to terms of imprisonment there[452].

The OFT commenced proceedings in August 2008 against four employees of British Airways under section 188 of the Enterprise Act in connection with the fixing of prices of fuel surcharges for long-haul passenger flights; each of them pleaded not guilty[453]. At their trial in the spring of 2010 at Southwark Crown Court the OFT decided to withdraw the proceedings, and the defendants were formally acquitted. This was because, at a very late stage in the proceedings, after the commencement of the trial, a substantial volume of electronic material was discovered which neither the OFT nor the defence had been able to review; the OFT's opinion was that it would not have been fair to seek an adjournment of the trial while the fresh evidence was analysed[454]. Three non-executive directors of the OFT conducted a review of what had occurred in this case, and made a number of recommendations to the Board as to steps to be taken to ensure that appropriate lessons were learned from the experience[455].

As at 17 October 2011 there was one pending criminal case, in the commercial vehicle sector[456].

(x) Reform of the cartel offence

In March 2011 the Government published a consultation document, *A Competition Regime for Growth: a consultation on options for reform*[457]. One of the proposals in this document is the removal of the requirement of 'dishonesty' in the cartel offence[458]; another is that the offence would not apply to agreements made openly.

---

[448] See OFT Press Release 72/08, 11 June 2008.

[449] See *R v Whittle and others* [2008] EWCA Crim 2560.

[450] See ch 10 n 452 below.

[451] See ch 10 n 330 above.

[452] See the US Department of Justice Press Release of 12 December 2007, available at www.justice.gov; as part of the US plea agreement in this case the defendants had agreed not to seek from the UK court a shorter term of imprisonment than the one agreed to in the US proceedings: the Court of Appeal expressed its 'doubts' as to the propriety of the US prosecutor seeking to inhibit the way in which the proceedings in the UK could be conducted: ibid, para 28.

[453] OFT Press Release 93/08, 7 August 2008; British Airways agreed to pay a penalty of £121.5 million for its admitted participation in this cartel: see 'Statistical analysis', p 418 above.

[454] OFT Press Release 47/10, 10 May 2010; for critical comment see Purnell, Bellamy, Kar, Piccinin and Sahathevan 'Criminal Cartel Enforcement – More Turbulence Ahead? The Implications of the *BA/Virgin* Case' [2010] Competition Law Journal 313.

[455] See the 'Project Condor Board Review', available at www.oft.gov.uk.

[456] See www.oft.gov.uk/OFTwork/competition-act-and-cartels.   [457] Available at www.bis.gov.uk.

[458] For discussion of the requirement of dishonesty see Stephan 'How Dishonesty Killed the Cartel Offence' [2011] Criminal Law Review 446; Bailin 'Doing Away with Dishonesty' (2011) 10(3) Competition Law Journal 169.

(B) **Company director disqualification**

The Enterprise Act 2002 introduced a second provision designed to encourage individuals to ensure compliance with competition law: under section 204, which inserted new sections into the Company Directors Disqualification Act 1986 (the 'CDDA 1986'), company directors can be disqualified for up to 15 years where their companies are guilty of a competition law infringement: it is important to understand that disqualification of individuals is *not* limited to circumstances in which the cartel offence has been committed, but applies to any infringement of Articles 101 and 102 TFEU and of the Chapter I and Chapter II prohibitions[459]. It is for the High Court (or the Court of Session in Scotland) to make a competition disqualification order ('a CDO'), not the OFT or the sectoral regulators[460]: their function is to determine whether to seek such an order, which the CDDA 1986 gives them power to do[461], and whether to accept an undertaking in lieu of an order, for which provision is also made[462]. The OFT originally published guidance on these powers in May 2003, but that document was replaced in June 2010 by a revised one indicating a greater preparedness on its part to make use of them[463].

Three company directors were disqualified for periods of between five and seven years as a result of their participation in the *Marine Hose* cartel[464]; as a matter of technical law, however, these disqualifications were based on the fact that they had committed the criminal cartel offence, and were disqualified under the CDDA 1986: the court did not need to invoke the additional power conferred by section 204 of the Enterprise Act. To put the point another way, the power in section 204 has yet to be used to disqualify a director.

(i) **Grounds for disqualification**

Under section 9A of the CDDA 1986 the court must make a CDO against a person if a company of which he is a director commits an infringement of EU and/or UK competition law[465] and the court considers that his conduct as a director makes him unfit to be concerned in the management of a company[466]; the OFT considers that the term 'director', for this purpose, includes a *de facto* director[467]. In deciding whether the conduct of a director makes him unfit, the court must have regard to whether his conduct contributed to the breach of competition law; or, where this is not the case, whether he had reasonable grounds to suspect a breach and took no steps to prevent it; or, if he did not know of the breach, he ought to have done[468]. Furthermore the court may have regard to his conduct as a director of a company in connection with any other breach of competition law[469]. The maximum period of disqualification is 15 years[470], and during that time it is a criminal offence to be a director of a company, to act as a receiver of a company's property, to promote, form or manage a company or to act as an insolvency practitioner[471]. Any person involved in the management of a company in contravention of a CDO is personally liable for the debts of the company[472] and may be placed on a public register maintained by the Secretary of State for Business, Innovation and Skills[473].

---

[459] CDDA 1986, s 9A(4).   [460] Ibid, s 9E(3).

[461] Ibid, s 9A(10): s 9D provides that the Secretary of State may make regulations as to the concurrent functions of the OFT and the sectoral regulators in relation to CDOs; in the text that follows the term OFT is used to include the powers of the sectoral regulators.

[462] CDDA 1986, s 9B.

[463] *Director disqualification orders in competition cases*, OFT 510, June 2010; see also *Company directors and competition law*, OFT 1340, June 2011.

[464] OFT Press Release 72/08, 11 June 2008.   [465] CDDA 1986, s 9A(2).

[466] Ibid, s 9A(3).   [467] *Director disqualification orders*, para 2.3; see also para 4.5.

[468] CDDA 1986, s 9A(5)(a) and (6).   [469] Ibid, s 9A(5)(b).   [470] Ibid, s 9A(9).

[471] Ibid, ss 1(1) and 13.   [472] Ibid, s 15(1)(a).   [473] Ibid, s 18.

(ii) **Procedure**

The OFT has power to make inquiries and investigations under sections 26 to 30 of the Competition Act for the purpose of deciding whether to apply for a disqualification order[474]. The OFT may accept undertakings in lieu of seeking a CDO[475]. When deciding whether to apply for an order the OFT will take into account the factors set out in its guidance[476]. It will follow a five-step process in which it will consider:

- whether there has been a breach of competition law
- the nature of the breach and whether a financial penalty has been imposed
- whether the company in question benefited from leniency
- the extent of the director's responsibility for the breach of competition law and
- whether there are any aggravating and mitigating factors[477].

The OFT guidance then provides more detail on each of these five factors. The OFT will not seek a CDO in respect of any current director whose company has benefited from leniency in relation to the activities to which the leniency relates[478]; this largesse would not extend to a director who has been removed as a director as a result of his role in the breach of competition law or for opposing the relevant application for leniency, nor to a director who fails to cooperate with the leniency process[479]. The extent of the director's responsibility for the breach of competition law will be relevant to the decision whether to apply to the court, and the 2010 guidance adopts a stricter approach in this respect than its 2003 predecessor: in particular the OFT will ask whether the director's conduct contributed to the breach[480]; whether he had reasonable grounds to suspect breach but took no steps to prevent it[481]; and whether he ought to have known of the breach[482]. The guidance sets out various aggravating and mitigating factors[483]. The OFT would not seek a CDO if an individual is being prosecuted under the cartel offence, since the court dealing with that matter would have the right to make a CDO anyway[484]; nor would it proceed against anyone who is the beneficiary of a no-action letter[485]. The OFT must send a notice to anyone in relation to whom it applies for a CDO: the information that will be contained in this notice is set out in the OFT's guidance[486].

(C) **Conspiracy to defraud at common law**[487]

In *Norris v Government of the United States of America*[488] the US Government was seeking extradition of Mr Norris under the terms of the Extradition Act 2003. The conduct complained of by the US authorities was price fixing contrary to section 1 of the Sherman Act 1890. Under the Extradition Act the US had to demonstrate 'double criminality', that is to say that price fixing was illegal under US law and that the same conduct, if it

---

[474] Ibid, s 9C, inserted by Enterprise Act 2002, s 204.
[475] CDDA 1986, s 9B; *Director disqualification orders*, paras 3.1–3.5.   [476] Ibid, paras 4.1–4.29.
[477] Ibid, para 4.2.   [478] Ibid, para 4.13.   [479] Ibid, para 4.14.
[480] Ibid, paras 4.19–4.20.   [481] Ibid, para 4.21.   [482] Ibid, paras 4.22–4.23.
[483] Ibid, paras 4.25–4.26.   [484] Ibid, paras 4.27–4.28.
[485] Ibid, para 4.29; on no-action letters see 'No-action letters', pp 432–433 above.
[486] *Director disqualification orders*, paras 5.1–5.2.
[487] See Lever and Pike 'Cartel Agreements, Criminal Conspiracy and the Statutory "Cartel Offence"' (2005) 26 ECLR 90 and (2005) 26 ECLR 164; Lester 'Prosecuting Cartels for Conspiracy to Defraud' [2008] 7 Competition Law Journal 134.
[488] [2008] UKHL 16, [2008] 1 AC 920, reversing the judgment of the High Court on this point in *Ian Norris v The Government of the USA* [2007] EWHC 71 (Admin), [2007] UKCLR 1487.

had occurred in the UK, would have been punishable there by a term of imprisonment of at least 12 months. At the relevant time the cartel offence under the Enterprise Act 2002 did not exist. The Administrative Court had held that price fixing could amount to conspiracy to defraud, a criminal offence at common law pre-dating the Enterprise Act, where there is an agreement 'between two or more persons dishonestly to prejudice or to risk prejudicing another's right, knowing that they have no right to do so'[489]. On appeal the House of Lords held that 'mere' price fixing did not amount to conspiracy to defraud: it followed that there was no double criminality and that Norris could not be extradited on this ground[490]. A price-fixing agreement could be conspiracy to defraud only where there were aggravating features: fraud, misrepresentation, violence and intimidation were referred to as examples[491]. *Norris* was subsequently followed by the Court of Final Appeal in Hong Kong[492].

7. Concurrency

An interesting feature of the 1998 Act is that concurrent powers are given to the OFT and the sectoral regulators to enforce the Chapter I and Chapter II prohibitions and Articles 101 and 102 TFEU. In their respective spheres of activity the Office of Communications, the Gas and Electricity Markets Authority, the Water Services Regulation Authority, the Civil Aviation Authority[493], the Office for the Regulation of Gas and Electricity (Northern Ireland) and the Office of Rail Regulation enjoy concurrent powers. The Government is proposing to give Monitor concurrent powers in respect of providers of health or adult social care[494]. The availability of these competition law powers raises the interesting dilemma for the sectoral regulators of whether they should use competition law when they suspect there to be anti-competitive behaviour or whether they should use the sector-specific regulatory powers available to them under their governing legislation[495].

(i) The Concurrency Regulations and the Concurrency Guideline

As far as the Competition Act itself is concerned provisions have been put in place in order to ensure that concurrency operates in a satisfactory manner; the Act deals with this issue in section 54 and Schedule 10. Acting under section 54 of the Competition Act the Secretary of State has adopted the Competition Act (Concurrency) Regulations 2004[496]. The OFT, in conjunction with the regulators, has published a Guideline on

---

[489] Ibid, para 56.

[490] Mr Norris was subsequently extradited to the US on the different ground of perverting the course of justice; he was convicted and sentenced to 18 months imprisonment: see US Department of Justice Press Release, 10 December 2010, available at www.justice.gov/otr.

[491] [2008] UKHL 16, para 17; see also *R v GG plc* [2008] UKHL 17, a case arising out of the SFO's prosecution of a number of pharmaceutical companies for price fixing prior to the entry into force of the cartel offence in the Enterprise Act 2002: the SFO subsequently sought leave to amend the indictment in this case, but this was refused: see *R v GG plc (No 2)* [2008] EWCA Crim 3061.

[492] *HKSAP v Yip* FACC No 4 of 2010, judgment of 13 December 2010.

[493] The Government intends to extend the CAA's concurrent powers beyond the supply of air traffic services to include services provided by airport operators and third party airport service providers: see Department for Transport, *Consultation Responses and Decision on Concurrent Powers*, July 2010, available at www.dft.gov.uk.

[494] Department of Health, *Liberating the NHS: regulating healthcare providers*, July 2010, available at www.dh.gov.uk.

[495] See 'Regulated Industries', ch 23, pp 977–980.   [496] SI 2004/1077.

Concurrent application to regulated industries[497]. The *Guideline* provides the best picture of the operation of the concurrency provisions. It explains that the regulators have the same powers as the OFT[498], save that only the latter can issue guidance on penalties and make and amend the OFT's Rules[499]. The *Guideline* describes the purpose of the Concurrency Regulations[500] and explains the role of the Concurrency Working Party ('the CWP'), which is chaired by a representative of the OFT and brings together officials from all the regulators[501]. The CWP discusses, among other things, general principles and information sharing, the guidelines and disagreements over who should exercise jurisdiction in a particular case[502]. The proceedings of the CWP are confidential, and no minutes of its meetings are made publicly available. The *Guideline* considers how cases will be allocated: in the event of a dispute on jurisdiction the matter will be referred to the Secretary of State[503]: this has never occurred, and it can reasonably be assumed that it will happen only exceptionally. Complaints may be made to the OFT or the relevant regulator[504]; the same is true for applications for interim measures[505]. The *Guideline* also discusses the relationship between the regulators' powers under competition law and their sector-specific powers[506] and explains the law on confidentiality and disclosure of information[507]. In *R (Cityhook Ltd) v OFT*[508] the Administrative Court considered the Concurrency Regulations in detail and concluded that the OFT had failed to consider whether a long-running case should be transferred to the Office of Communications ('OFCOM') before closing its file[509].

(ii) The concurrency arrangements in practice

The only infringement decisions to have been adopted by a sectoral regulator by 20 June 2011 were taken by the ORR in the case of *English Welsh & Scottish Railway Ltd* in November 2006[510] and by the Gas and Electricity Markets Authority in the case of *National Grid plc* in February 2008[511]. There is public debate in the UK as to why it has not been possible, after ten years of the Competition Act, for the regulators to have found more infringements[512]. There have been a number of non-infringement decisions[513]; several of the non-infringement decisions of OFCOM and the Water Services Regulation Authority were appealed to the CAT which, in some of its judgments, has shown frustration with both the slowness of the procedure and the substantive outcome[514]. In the case of *Albion Water* the

---

[497] OFT 405, December 2004; note that all of the concurrent regulators, with the exception of the CAA, have published guidelines on the application of competition law to their respective sectors: see ch 9, 'OFT guidance', pp 332–333 for a list of all the available guidelines.

[498] OFT 405, paras 2.2–2.3.

[499] Ibid, para 2.4; note also that only the OFT can proceed under Part 6 of the Enterprise Act in relation to the cartel offence.

[500] Ibid, paras 3.1–3.3.

[501] Ibid, para 3.9–3.11.   [502] Ibid, para 3.10.   [503] Ibid, paras 3.12–3.19.

[504] Ibid, para 3.20.   [505] Ibid, para 3.23.   [506] Ibid, paras 4.1–4.3.

[507] Ibid, paras 5.1–5.6.   [508] [2009] EWHC 57, [2009] UKCLR 255.

[509] Ibid, paras 166–187.   [510] ORR decision of 16 November 2006 [2007] UKCLR 937.

[511] GEMA decision of 21 February 2008 [2008] UKCLR 171, on appeal Case No 1099/1/2/08 *National Grid Plc v Gas and Electricity Markets Authority* [2009] CAT 14, [2009] CompAR 282 and, on appeal to the Court of Appeal [2010] EWCA Civ 114, [2010] UKCLR 386.

[512] See eg Bloom 'The Competition Act at 10 Years Old: Enforcement by the OFT and the Sector Regulators' (2010) 9(2) Competition Law Journal 141 and Pimlott 'Concurrency and the Role of the Competition Appeal Tribunal as Supervisor of the Sectoral Regulators' (2010) 9(2) Competition Law Journal 162.

[513] See the 'Table of published decisions, in ch 9, pp 374–388.

[514] See, in particular, the history of the litigation of the *Freeserve, Floe, VIP* and *Albion Water* cases contained in the 'Table of published decisions', ch 9, pp 374–388.

CAT set aside the non-infringement decision of the Water Services Regulation Authority and substituted its own finding that there had been an abusive margin squeeze[515].

(iii) Reviews of concurrency arrangements

The functioning of the concurrency arrangements was considered by the Government in 2006, a House of Lords Select Committee in 2007 and the National Audit Office in 2010[516]. Each of these bodies concluded that the concurrency arrangements should be retained, but that it might be possible to enhance the existing cooperation between the OFT and the sectoral regulators. The National Audit Office, in particular, noted that the regulators have made limited use of their concurrent powers to enforce competition law, and recommended that the Government should evaluate whether the incentives within the regime for regulators to use their concurrent powers are appropriate to establish the body of case law required for an effective system of competition law. In March 2011 the Government confirmed the retention of the regulator's concurrent competition enforcement powers, but is consulting on measures that encourage the use of competition law rather than regulation where this is possible and appropriate[516a].

8. Appeals

The Competition Act deals with appeals in sections 46 to 49 and in Schedule 8, as amended by the Enterprise Act 2002. The powers available to the OFT and the sectoral regulators under the Act are considerable. To balance this, and to ensure compliance with the Human Rights Act 1998 which requires that decisions should be made by an independent and impartial tribunal, it was felt that a right of appeal – not merely the possibility of judicial review – should be available; furthermore that the appellate body should be one with appropriate expertise in matters of competition law. For this reason appeals are taken to the CAT[517]. The Court of Appeal has acknowledged that the CAT, as a specialist tribunal, is better placed to determine complex matters of competition law and economics than the 'ordinary' courts[518]. Once an appeal has been lodged with the CAT it can be withdrawn only with the Tribunal's permission unless the authority itself withdraws the decision under challenge: the CAT deals with cases in the public interest, and improper pressure should not be applied by one litigant upon another to withdraw an appeal[519]. In so far as the Act does not provide for an appeal there remains the possibility that a claim for judicial review may be brought before the Administrative Court of the Queen's Bench Division of the

[515] Case No 1046/2/4/04 *Albion Water Ltd v Water Services Regulation Authority* [2006] CAT 36, [2007] CompAR 420, upheld on appeal [2008] EWCA Civ 536, [2008] UKCLR 457.

[516] See HM Treasury/Department of Trade and Industry, *Concurrent competition powers in sectoral regulation*, URN 06/1244, May 2006, available at www.bis.gov.uk; the responses of the OFT and the CWP are available on the OFT's website: www.oft.gov.uk; House of Lords Select Committee on Regulators *UK Economic Regulators*, November 2007, available at www.parliament.uk; National Audit Office *Review of the UK's Competition Landscape*, March 2010, available at www.nao.org.uk.

[516a] *A Competition Regime for Growth: a consultation on options for reform*, ch 7, available at www.bis.gov.uk.

[517] The establishment and the functions of the CAT are described in ch 2, 'Functions of the CAT', pp 72–73; appeals to the CAT are governed by Part II of the Competition Appeal Tribunal Rules 2003, SI 2003/1372 as amended by the Competition Appeal Tribunal (Amendment and Communications Act Appeals) Rules 2004, SI 2004/2068.

[518] *Napp Pharmaceutical Holdings Ltd v Director General of Fair Trading* [2002] EWCA Civ 796, [2002] 4 All ER 376, paras 31 and 34 and *National Grid Plc v Gas and Electricity Markets Authority* [2010] EWCA Civ 114, [2010] UKCLR 386, paras 24–26.

[519] SI 2003/1372, r 11; see Case No 1008/2/1/02 *Claymore Dairies Ltd v OFT* [2006] CAT 3, [2006] CompAR 360, paras 82–89.

High Court[520] in relation to perceived procedural irregularities[521] or the improper exercise of administrative discretion[522]. It may be that permission to apply for judicial review would be refused if the Administrative Court were to consider that a particular issue can be addressed within the statutory appeal procedure[523].

(A) 'Appealable decisions'

Section 46[524] of the Competition Act sets out a list of 'appealable decisions' and states that the recipients of such decisions may appeal them to the CAT; appealable decisions include, for example, decisions as to whether the Chapter I and Chapter II prohibitions or Articles 101 and 102 TFEU have been infringed[525], interim measures decisions and decisions as to the imposition of, or the amount of, a penalty[526]. As can be seen from the Table of Competition Act decisions in chapter 9 many of the OFT's infringement decisions have been appealed to the CAT[527], both as to substance and as to the level of the penalty. For the most part the OFT's infringement decisions have been upheld by the CAT: only one such decision has been annulled in its entirety[528]. The penalties imposed by the OFT have been reduced in some cases, as shown in the Table of penalties earlier in this chapter[529].

Section 47 of the Competition Act, as substituted by section 17 of the Enterprise Act 2002[530], gives third parties with a sufficient interest a right to appeal to the CAT in relation to appealable decisions. The CAT has said that there is no difference in principle between its treatment of an appeal against an infringement decision and an appeal by a third party against a non-infringement decision[531]. In practice, however, the CAT's role in third party appeals has been to control the adequacy of the authority's reasons and their correctness in law. There have been several appeals to the CAT by third parties disappointed that either the OFT or a sectoral regulator had failed to find an infringement of the Competition Act or of Article 101 or 102 TFEU. In some cases the OFT or regulator had explicitly decided that there was no infringement, so that there was no doubt that an appealable decision had been adopted; in some other cases, however, the OFT or regulator closed the file without explicitly or consciously deciding that there was no infringement: in these cases the CAT has had to decide whether, at least implicitly, a find-

---

[520] On the judicial review procedure, see Part 54 of the Civil Procedure Rules 1998, available at www.justice.gov.uk.

[521] See eg *Crest Nicholson Plc v OFT* [2009] EWHC 1875, [2009] UKCLR 895 and *OFCOM v Floe Telecom Ltd (in administration)* [2006] EWCA Civ 768, [2006] ECC 445, para 45.

[522] See eg *R (Cityhook Ltd) v OFT* [2009] EWHC 57, [2009] UKCLR 255.

[523] See *R (Sivasubramaniam) v Wandsworth County Court* [2002] EWCA Civ 1738, [2003] 2 All ER 160, paras 46–47 and the case law there cited; on judicial review where an appeal system is in place see Craig *Administrative Law* (Sweet & Maxwell, 6th ed, 2008), pp 912–913.

[524] As amended by art 10 of the Competition Act 1998 (Notification of Excluded Agreements and Appealable Decisions) Order 2000, SI 2000/263.

[525] Competition Act 1998, s 46(3)(a) and (b).

[526] Ibid, s 46(3)(i).

[527] See ch 9, 'The Competition Act 1998 in Practice', pp 374–392.

[528] Case No 1035/1/1/04 *The Racecourse Association and Others v OFT* [2005] CAT 29, [2006] CompAR 99.

[529] See 'Table of penalties', pp 419–422 above.

[530] The amended 47 avoids the cumbersome procedure for third parties in the Competition Act 1998 as originally drafted, of which the CAT was critical in Case No 1006/2/1/01 *BetterCare Group v Director General of Fair Trading* [2002] CAT 6, [2002] CompAR 226, paras 115–125.

[531] Case No 1046/2/4/04 *Albion Water Ltd v Director General of Water Services* [2005] CAT 40, [2006] CompAR 269, para 243, citing earlier judgments in Case No 1007/2/3/02 *Freeserve.com plc v Director General of Telecommunications* [2003] CAT 5, [2003] CompAR 202 and *JJ Burgess & Sons v OFT* [2005] CAT 25, [2005] CompAR 1151.

ing of non-infringement had been reached, in which case an appealable decision could be brought before the CAT. If a decision is not appealable to the CAT, at most a third party can seek a judicial review in the Administrative Court[532].

(i) Successful appeals against explicit non-infringement decisions

There have been several successful appeals[533] by third parties against explicit non-infringement decisions of the OFT or a sectoral regulator. The first decision of the OFT under the Competition Act, *General Insurance Standards Council*[534], was taken on appeal by third parties to the CAT[535]. The CAT disagreed with the OFT's finding that the rules of GISC, which prevented its insurer members from dealing with insurance intermediaries unless they were themselves members of GISC, did not infringe the Chapter I prohibition and remitted the case to the OFT for further consideration. As the rule to which the appellants had taken objection was then dropped the OFT was able to adopt a second non-infringement decision[536].

An appeal was brought by a third party against a decision by the OFT that there had been no infringement of the Chapter II prohibition in *Refusal to supply JJ Burgess Ltd with access to Harwood Park Crematorium*[537]. The case concerned a refusal on the part of W Austin, a funeral director, to provide access to a crematorium to a competitor, JJ Burgess. In *JJ Burgess & Sons v OFT*[538] the CAT set aside the OFT's non-infringement decision and substituted its own finding of infringement. The CAT was frustrated at the amount of time that the administrative proceedings had taken, and was concerned that a small operator such as JJ Burgess had failed to get redress from the OFT. It is of interest to note that the Consumers' Association (now known as Which?) intervened in this case in support of JJ Burgess, and that the CAT welcomed the intervention. It remains to be seen how the CAT's apparent concern that small operators should have access to justice can be reconciled with the *OFT's Prioritisation Principles*, according to which the OFT will select cases that will have the highest impact and greatest effect[539].

In *Floe Telecom Ltd v Director General of Telecommunications*[540] the CAT annulled a non-infringement decision of the Director General of Telecommunications (now OFCOM), *Disconnection of Floe Telecom Ltd's Services by Vodafone Ltd*[541]. OFCOM subsequently adopted a second non-infringement decision which was upheld on appeal to the CAT, albeit on different grounds from those given by OFCOM[542]; the CAT's judgment was set aside on appeal to the Court of Appeal[543]. The CAT set aside a non-infringement decision of the Office of Water Services ('OFWAT') in *Albion Water/Thames Water*[544].

---

[532] In Case No 1071/2/1/06 *Cityhook v OFT* Cityhook not only appealed to the CAT but also sought judicial review in the Administrative Court.

[533] For an example of an unsuccessful appeal against an explicit non-infringement decision see Case No 1073/2/1/06 *Terry Brannigan v OFT* [2007] CAT 23, [2007] CompAR 956.

[534] OFT decision of 26 January 2001 [2001] UKCLR 331.

[535] Case Nos 1002–1004/2/1/01 *Institute of Independent Insurance Brokers v Director General of Fair Trading* [2001] CAT 4, [2001] CompAR 62.

[536] *General Insurance Standards Council*, 13 November 2002 [2003] UKCLR 39.

[537] OFT decision of 12 August 2004 [2004] UKCLR 1586; there had been an earlier decision to the same effect in *Harwood Park Crematorium*, OFT decision of 6 August 2002; this decision was withdrawn by the OFT by decision of 9 April 2003 pursuant to s 47(5) of the Competition Act.

[538] Case No 1044/2/1/04 [2005] CAT 25, [2005] CompAR 1151.

[539] OFT 939, October 2008, available at www.oft.gov.uk.

[540] Case No 1024/2/3/04 [2004] CAT 18, [2005] CompAR 290.

[541] OFTEL decision of 3 November 2003 [2004] UKCLR 313.

[542] OFCOM decision of 28 June 2005 [2005] UKCLR 1112, upheld on appeal Case No 1024/2/3/04 *Floe Telecom Ltd v OFCOM* [2006] CAT 17, [2006] CompAR 637.

[543] *OFCOM v Floe Telecom Ltd* [2009] EWCA Civ 47, [2009] UKCLR 659.

[544] [2006] CAT 7, [2006] CompAR 451.

It also annulled OFWAT's finding of non-infringement in *Albion Water/Dŵr Cymru*[545] and adopted a decision that Dŵr Cymru had abused its dominant position by imposing a margin squeeze on Albion Water[546] and by charging unfairly high prices[547].

(ii) Successful appeals against implicit non-infringement decisions[548]

On four occasions the OFT or a regulator, having received a complaint that the Competition Act or that Article 101 or 102 TFEU had been infringed, decided to close the file and to inform the complainant accordingly; the complainant then successfully appealed to the CAT that the decision was in fact one of non-infringement. In three of the cases, *BetterCare Group v Director General of Fair Trading*[549], *Freeserve.com plc v Director General of Telecommunications*[550] and *Claymore Dairies Ltd and Express Dairies plc v Director General of Fair Trading*[551], the CAT concluded that the OFT or regulator had adopted an appealable decision that there was no infringement of the Chapter II prohibition, and rejected the argument that the closure of the file was simply an administrative decision not to proceed with the matter: as a consequence the CAT had jurisdiction to deal with the substance of the appeal. In *Pernod-Ricard SA v OFT*[552] the CAT held that the OFT had adopted a non-infringement decision when it closed its file against voluntary assurances offered by Bacardi that it would change its distribution practices in relation to light rum.

In the *Claymore* judgment the CAT summarised the law on the meaning of an appealable decision as follows[553]. First, the question of whether an appealable decision has been taken is primarily a question of fact, to be decided in accordance with the particular circumstances of the case. Secondly, whether such a decision has been taken is a question of substance, not form, to be determined objectively, taking into account all the circumstances of the case: the test to be applied is whether a decision has been taken on an appealable matter, 'either expressly or by necessary implication'. Thirdly, there is a distinction between the mere exercise of an administrative discretion not to proceed to the adoption of a decision, and the actual adoption of an appealable decision. At paragraph 151 of *Claymore* the CAT gave examples of various reasons for the closure of a case file that would not amount to an appealable decision: for example, where the OFT concludes that, as a matter of priority, other cases have a higher importance[554]. An example not mentioned by the CAT would presumably arise where the matter complained of was the subject of private litigation in the 'ordinary' courts[555].

---

[545] OFWAT decision of 26 May 2004 [2004] UKCRL 1317.

[546] Case No 1046/2/4/04 *Albion Water Ltd v Water Services Regulation Authority* [2006] CAT 36, [2007] CompAR 420, upheld on appeal to the Court of Appeal [2008] EWCA Civ 536, [2008] UKCLR 457.

[547] Case No 1046/2/4/04 [2008] CAT 31, [2009] CompAR 28.

[548] For comment on the issue of appealable decisions see Bailey 'When are decisions appealable under the Competition Act 1998?' [2003] 2 Competition Law Journal 41; Alese 'The Office Burden: Making a Decision Without Making a Decision for a Third Party' (2003) 24 ECLR 616; Rayment 'What is an Appealable Decision under the Competition Act 1998?' [2004] 3 Competition Law Journal 132.

[549] Case No 1006/2/1/01 [2002] CAT 6, [2002] CompAR 226.

[550] Case No 1007/2/3/02 [2002] CAT 8, [2003] CompAR 1.

[551] Case No 1008/2/1/02 [2003] CAT 3, [2004] CompAR 1.

[552] [2004] CAT 10, [2004] CompAR 707.

[553] [2003] CAT 3, [2004] CompAR 1, para 122.

[554] On this point the CAT specifically referred to the judgment of the General Court in Case T-24/90 *Automec v Commission (No 2)* [1992] ECR II-2223, [1992] 5 CMLR 431.

[555] Note that this was a reason for the Commission's closure of the file in the *Automec* case, ch 10 n 554 above.

(iii) Unsuccessful appeals by third party complainants

In five cases, *Aquavitae (UK) Ltd v Director General of Water Services*[556], *Independent Water Company v Director General of Water Services*[557], *Casting Book Ltd v OFT*[558], *Cityhook Ltd v OFT*[559] and *Independent Media Support Ltd v OFCOM*[560], the CAT reached the conclusion that the OFT or the sectoral regulator had not adopted an appealable decision, with the consequence that the appeals were outside the jurisdiction of the CAT and inadmissible. In *Aquavitae* the CAT accepted that the regulator had not made an appealable decision that the Chapter II prohibition had not been infringed: rather he had chosen to deal with the problems raised by Aquavitae by introducing a scheme for retail licensing under new regulatory rules to be established by the Water Act 2003. In *Independent Water Company* the CAT concluded that the Water Services Regulation Authority had not adopted an appealable decision under the Competition Act but had instead decided to deal with the terms and prices on which Bristol Water was to supply bulk water under the regulatory provisions of the Water Industry Act 1991. In *Casting Book Ltd v OFT* the CAT was satisfied that the OFT had closed its investigation into an alleged collective boycott for reasons genuinely independent of the merits of the case and without having reached any conclusion on those merits. In *Cityhook Ltd v OFT* the CAT concluded that the OFT, when closing its file, had not adopted an appealable decision, but said that it had not found the case an easy one to decide[561]; the CAT also noted the 'incongruous' result that this meant that Cityhook did not have a right to appeal on the merits to the CAT[562]. The former President of the CAT drew attention to the position in the CAT's Annual Report for 2006–2007, saying that the 'invidious' position of complainant's having to choose whether to apply to the CAT or to the Administrative Court for a judicial review, depending on whether a decision was appealable or not, 'should have no place in a modern legal system'[563]. In *Independent Media Support Ltd v OFCOM* the CAT drew attention to the same problem. In that case the CAT was satisfied that, when OFCOM decided to close its file, it had 'genuinely abstained from expressing a firm view, one way or the other, on the question of infringement'[564]; however it considered that the position of the complainant was therefore an unsatisfactory one, but one that could be remedied only by legislation[565].

(B) The Competition Appeal Tribunal Rules 2003

Following a Department of Trade and Industry consultation document[566] the Secretary of State adopted the Competition Appeal Tribunal Rules 2003[567]. The CAT has published

---

[556] Case No 1012/2/3/03 [2003] CAT 17, [2004] CompAR 117.

[557] Case No 1058/2/4/06 [2007] CAT 6, [2007] CompAR 614.

[558] Case No 1068/2/1/06 [2006] CAT 35, [2007] CompAR 446.

[559] Case No 1071/2/1/06 [2007] CAT 18, [2007] CompAR 813.

[560] Case No 1087/2/3/07 [2007] CAT 29, [2007] CompAR 48.

[561] Ibid, para 296.

[562] Ibid, para 299; Cityhook subsequently (unsuccessfully) challenged the OFT's case closure decision by way of judicial review: *R (Cityhook Ltd) v OFT* [2009] EWHC 57, [2009] UKCLR 255.

[563] See the CAT's Annual Review and Accounts 2006/2007, p 4.

[564] Ibid, para 42.

[565] Ibid, para 56.

[566] URN 99/1154, October 1999.

[567] SI 2003/1372, repealing and replacing, for cases commenced on or after 20 June 2003, the earlier Competition Commission Appeal Tribunal Rules 2000, SI 2000/261; the 2003 Rules were amended by the Competition Appeal Tribunal (Amendment and Communications Act Appeals) Rules 2004, SI 2004/2068.

A Guide to Proceedings[568]. The CAT has also created a User Group to discuss points relating to the practical operation of the Tribunal; the minutes of the meetings are available on its website[569]. The CAT has pointed out that, when a case reaches it, the matter ceases to be an administrative procedure, as it is when the OFT acts as investigator, prosecutor and decision-maker, and becomes, instead, a judicial proceeding[570]. The rules of the CAT are based on five main principles[571]:

- first, early disclosure of each party's case, and of the evidence relied on
- second, active case management by the CAT to identify the main issues early on and avoid delays
- third, strict timetables, with straightforward cases to be completed within nine months: for example when rejecting an application for an extension of time in which to lodge an appeal in the *Hasbro* case the CAT said that respect for the deadline in commencing proceedings is, in many ways, the 'keystone' of the whole procedure[572]
- fourth, effective procedures to establish contested facts
- fifth, the conduct of oral hearings within defined time limits.

(C) **Procedure before the CAT**[573]

The rules of the CAT give the CAT broad case-management powers[574]; a brief perusal of the CAT's website reveals a substantial number of rulings on procedural issues which have arisen during the course of proceedings, often at case management conferences[575]. The procedure before the CAT is predominantly written; submissions should be kept as short as possible. Where an expert is asked to produce a report, that expert's duty is to assist the Tribunal, and this overrides its obligation to the person from whom the instructions were received and from whom payment was received[576]. The oral hearing should be regarded as an opportunity to debate contentious issues rather than to state a case which has already been made in writing. In cases where facts are in dispute between the OFT (or

---

[568] October 2005, available at www.catribunal.org.uk; see also Rayment 'Practice and Procedure in the Competition Commission Appeal Tribunal' (2002) 1 Competition Law Journal 23.

[569] See www.catribunal.org.uk/5300/User-Group.html.

[570] Case No 1000/1/1/01 *Napp Pharmaceutical Holdings Ltd v Director General of Fair Trading* [2002] CAT 1, [2001] CompAR 13, para 117.

[571] See *Guide to Proceedings*, para 3.4.

[572] Case No 1010/1/1/03 *Hasbro UK Ltd v Director General of Fair Trading* [2003] CAT 1, [2003] CompAR 47: this point was reiterated by the President in Case No 1143/1/1/09 *Fish Holdings Ltd v OFT* [2009] CAT 34, [2010] CompAR 169, para 16; in practice some cases before the CAT have been quite protracted: for example OFWAT's decision in the case of *Albion Water/Dŵr Cymru* of 26 May 2004 [2004] UKCLR 1317 was annulled by the CAT on 18 December 2006, Case No 1046/2/4/04 *Albion Water Ltd v Water Services Regulation Authority* [2006] CAT 36, [2007] CompAR 328.

[573] See further Rayment 'Practice and Procedure before the Competition Appeal Tribunal' in Ward and Smith eds *Competition Litigation in the UK* (Sweet & Maxwell, 2003), ch 4 and Green and Brealey (eds) *Competition Litigation: UK Practice and Procedure* (Oxford University Press, 2010).

[574] SI 2003/1372, rr 19–24.

[575] www.catribunal.org.uk.

[576] *Guide to Proceedings*, October 2005, para 12.9 and CPR 35.3(1); see Case No 1009/1/1/02 *Aberdeen Journals Ltd v OFT* [2003] CAT 11, [2003] CompAR 67, para 288; see also Case No 1000/1/1/01 *Napp Pharmaceutical Holdings Ltd v Director General of Fair Trading* [2002] CAT 1, [2001] CompAR 13, para 254; see also (in proceedings in the High Court) *Leeds City Council v Watkins* [2003] UKCLR 467, para 88.

a regulator) and the appellants, such as *Toys and Games*[577], *Football Shirts*[578] and *National Grid*[579], the CAT's ability to probe the evidence and to provide for the cross-examination of witnesses has been an important feature of the procedure. To some extent the CAT can act in an inquisitorial capacity where complex issues of fact are involved, and this may provide a better way of discovering the true facts of a case than occurs in purely adversarial proceedings.

As a general proposition an appellant is not limited to placing before the CAT the evidence it has placed before the OFT[580]; however the fact an appellant did not put forward a positive case during the administrative procedure may cast doubt on the veracity of the evidence put forward during an appeal[581]. The OFT or regulator is normally expected to defend its decision on the basis of the material before it when it took its decision, although it may be permitted to adduce new evidence to ensure the fairness of the appeal process[582]. The CAT has held that the strict rules of evidence do not apply in proceedings before it, and has held that it will be guided by overall considerations of fairness, rather than technical rules[583].

Where third parties appeal against a decision of the OFT or a sectoral regulator the CAT considers that the onus is on the appellant to show why the decision should be set aside on the basis of the material before the OFT[584].

The CAT has been extremely meticulous in its work, producing lengthy and very detailed judgments, although the Court of Appeal in the *Toys and Games* and *Football Shirts* judgment[585] did wonder whether, in the future, the CAT might be able 'to express its findings of facts and its reasoning in more succinct form'[586]. In *Floe II* the Court of Appeal indicated that the CAT should take care to confine its judgments to 'deciding what is necessary for the adjudication of the actual disputes between the parties'[587].

(D) **The powers of the CAT**

The Competition Act provides for an appeal 'on the merits' and the powers of the CAT are extensive: considerably wider than those of a court exercising judicial review in the UK or the General Court when dealing with cases under Article 263 TFEU[588]. The CAT has held that an appeal on the merits requires it to consider whether a decision was the

---

[577] Case Nos 1014 and 1015/1/1/03 *Argos Ltd and Littlewoods Ltd v OFT* [2004] CAT 24, [2005] CompAR 588.

[578] Case Nos 1021 and 1022/1/1/03 *JJB Sports plc and Allsports Ltd v OFT* [2004] CAT 17, [2005] CompAR 1145.

[579] Case No 1099/1/2/08 *National Grid Plc v Gas and Electricity Markets Authority* [2009] CAT 14, [2009] CompAR 282.

[580] See Case No 1000/1/1/01 *Napp Pharmaceutical Holdings Ltd v Director General of Fair Trading* [2001] CAT 3, [2001] CompAR 33, para 76.

[581] See Case No 1061/1/1/06 *Makers UK Ltd v OFT* [2007] CAT 11, [2007] CompAR 699, paras 42 and 79.

[582] See Case Nos 1014 and 1015/1/1/03 *Argos Ltd and Littlewoods Ltd v OFT* [2003] CAT 16, para 66 (summarising the principles to be distilled from the CAT's earlier case law).

[583] Ibid, para 105.

[584] See Case No 1007/2/3/02 *Freeserve.com plc v Director General of Telecommunications* [2003] CAT 5, [2003] CAT 202, paras 114–115.

[585] *Argos Ltd and Littlewoods Ltd v OFT* and *JJB Sports plc v OFT* [2006] EWCA Civ 1318, [2006] UKCLR 1135, para 161.

[586] Ibid, paras 5 and 6, a point which it repeated in *Dŵr Cymru Cyfyngedig v Albion Water Ltd* [2008] EWCA Civ 53, [2008] UKCLR 457, paras 130–131.

[587] *OFCOM v Floe Telecom Ltd* [2009] EWCA Civ 47, [2009] UKCLR 659, para 20.

[588] See Case No 1007/2/3/02 *Freeserve.com plc v Director of Telecommunications* [2003] CAT 5, [2003] CompAR 202, para 106.

right one rather than whether a decision was within the range of reasonable responses[589]. The appeals process does not envisage a re-run of the administrative procedure; rather the CAT reviews a decision through the prism of the specific errors that are alleged by an appellant[590]. The CAT's powers are set out in paragraph 3 of Schedule 8 to the Competition Act, and include the power to adopt interim measures[591], to confirm or set aside the decision that is the subject of the appeal, to remit the matter to the OFT or sectoral regulator, to impose or revoke or vary the amount of a penalty[592], to give directions, for example to bring an end to an abuse of a dominant position[593] or to make a decision, for example finding an infringement of the Competition Act or the EU competition rules[594].

The way in which the CAT exercises its jurisdiction will depend on the particular circumstances of the case. In the *Aberdeen Journals* case[595] the CAT was dissatisfied with the OFT's treatment of market definition in a Chapter II case but remitted the matter to the OFT for further consideration rather than substituting its finding which, as a matter of law, it was at liberty to do. Similarly in the *Freeserve* case[596] the CAT remitted the issue of whether BT was guilty of abusive pricing practices to OFCOM. In each of these cases the CAT was mindful of the need to avoid the risk of converting itself from an appellate tribunal into a court of first instance. However there have been some occasions when the CAT has made its own decisions on substance, as in the *JJ Burgess v OFT* and the *Albion Water Ltd v OFWAT* cases that were discussed above[597]. In *VIP Communications Ltd v OFCOM*[598] the CAT rejected an argument of T-Mobile that it should not make a decision that T-Mobile had abused a dominant position since this would be to confuse the roles of OFCOM as the administrative body charged to make decisions and the CAT as an appellate body: in the CAT's view this would fail to take into account the fact

---

[589] Case No 1083/3/3/07 *Hutchison 3G UK Ltd v OFCOM* [2008] CAT 11, para 164; this was an appeal under the Communications Act 2003, but there is no reason in principle to suppose that the CAT would have reached a different conclusion under the Competition Act 1998.

[590] Case No 1151/3/3/10 *British Telecommunications Plc v OFCOM* [2010] CAT 17, para 78, upheld on appeal to the Court of Appeal [2011] EWCA Civ 245.

[591] Competition Act 1998, Sch 8, para 3(2)(d) and SI 2003/1372, r 61; see Case No 1000/1/1/01 (IR) *Napp Pharmaceuticals Holdings Ltd v Director General of Fair Trading* [2001] CAT 1, [2001] CompAR 1, where the President of the CAT followed judgments of the EU Courts, pursuant to s 60 of the Competition Act 1998, in determining the appropriate test for the adoption of interim measures; the CAT also ordered interim measures in Case No 1013/1/1/03 (IR) *Genzyme Ltd v OFT* [2003] CAT 8, [2003] CompAR 290; Case Nos 1034/2/4/04 (IR) and 1046/2/4/04 *Albion Water Ltd v Director General of Water Services* [2005] CAT 19, [2005] CompAR 993 as varied by [2006] CAT 33, [2007] CompAR 325; the CAT rejected an application for interim measures in Case No 1074/2/3/06 (IR) *VIP Communications Ltd (in administration) v OFCOM* [2007] CAT 12, [2007] CompAR 781, which it considered to be 'manifestly unfounded': ibid, paras 100–103.

[592] The penalty is automatically suspended pending the appeal (Competition Act 1998, s 46(4)), but the CAT may order that interest is payable (ibid, Sch 8, para 10 and SI 2003/1372, r 56): see Case No 1099/1/2/08 *National Grid Plc v Gas and Electricity Markets Authority* [2009] CAT 14, [2009] CompAR 282, para 229(c)).

[593] See eg Case No 1016/1/1/03 *Genzyme Ltd v OFT* [2005] CAT 32, [2006] CompAR 195 and Case Nos 1034/2/4/04 (IR) and 1046/2/4/04 *Albion Water Ltd v Water Services Regulation Authority* [2009] CAT 12, [2009] CompAR 223.

[594] The Court of Appeal confirmed that the CAT had such jurisdiction in *Dŵr Cymru Cyfyngedig v Albion Water Ltd* [2008] EWCA Civ 536, [2008] UKCLR 457, paras 112–128.

[595] Case No 1005/1/1/01 *Aberdeen Journals v Director General of Fair Trading* [2002] CAT 4, [2002] CompAR 167.

[596] Case No 1007/2/3/02 *Freeserve.com plc v Director General of Telecommunications* [2003] CAT 5, [2003] CompAR 202; OFCOM subsequently adopted a second non-infringement decision on 2 November 2010.

[597] See 'Successful appeals against explicit non-infringement decisions', p 442 above.

[598] Case 1027/2/3/04 [2007] CAT 3, [2007] CompAR 666.

that an appeal to the CAT is a 'full merits' jurisdiction[599]. The CAT has on a number of occasions substituted its own finding on the level of penalties[600].

In *Floe Telecom Ltd v Director General of Telecommunications*[601] the CAT annulled a non-infringement decision of OFTEL, *Disconnection of Floe Telecom Ltd's Services by Vodafone Ltd*[602]. The CAT was concerned at the amount of time that the proceedings had taken in this case and it imposed a timetable on OFCOM for its reconsideration of the matter. OFCOM and the OFT appealed to the Court of Appeal on the question of whether the CAT had the power to set a time limit in this way and the Court of Appeal held that the CAT did not have the power to do so[603]. In the opinion of Lloyd LJ:

> The Tribunal, as a statutory body, has the task of deciding such appeals as are brought to it in accordance with the provisions of the 1998 Act and the rules, but it does not have a more general statutory function, of supervising regulators. On that basis it seems to me that the CAT's reasoning is based on a misconception of the relationship between the Tribunal and the regulators. When a decision is set aside and remitted to the relevant regulator, that particular matter is then to be dealt with by that regulator in accordance with its own statutory duties and functions[604].

While the CAT's concern as to the apparent slowness of proceedings may be understandable, equally the OFT and the sectoral regulators have a real problem in determining how to deploy the limited resources at their disposal. As Lloyd LJ said in the *Floe* case:

> The Tribunal cannot know what are the competing demands on the resources of the particular regulator at the given time. It may well be that it cannot properly be told of this by the regulator because of issues of confidentiality as to current investigations. It cannot, therefore, form any proper view as to the relative priority of one case as compared with others[605].

(E) Costs[606]

The Competition Appeal Tribunal Rules 2003[607] enable the CAT to make such order as it thinks fit in relation to costs[608].

The CAT rules do not apply the conventional rule in civil litigation that 'costs follow the event': the CAT has a wide discretion in relation to costs and has repeatedly said that 'the only rule is that there are no rules'[609]. In the *Merger Action Group* judgment (dealing with a merger under the Enterprise Act rather than an enforcement decision under the Competition Act) the CAT gave the following guidance on its approach to costs (expenses in Scotland):

---

[599] Ibid, para 45.

[600] See 'Table of penalties' at pp 419–422 above.

[601] Case No 1024/2/3/04 [2004] CAT 18, [2005] CompAR 290.

[602] OFTEL decision of 3 November 2003 [2004] UKCLR 313.

[603] *OFCOM and OFT v Floe Telecom Ltd* [2006] EWCA Civ 768, [2006] ECC 30.

[604] Ibid, para 34.

[605] Ibid, para 37; see similarly *Crest Nicholson Plc v OFT* [2009] EWHC 1875, [2009] UKCLR 895, para 45.

[606] See *Guide to Proceedings*, October 2005, paras 17.1–17.9.

[607] SI 2003/1372.

[608] Ibid, r 55(2); even if the parties reach an agreement on costs, the CAT considers it has the power to make an alternative costs order: see Case Nos 1014 and 1015/1/1/03 *Argos Ltd v OFT* [2005] CAT 15, [2005] CompAR 996, paras 4–5.

[609] See eg Case No 1062/1/1/06 *The London Metal Exchange v OFT* [2006] CAT 19, [2006] CompAR 781, para 108 and Case Nos 1054/1/1/05 etc *MasterCard UK Members Forum Ltd v OFT* [2006] CAT 15, [2006] CompAR 607, para 46.

- the CAT must always exercise its discretion so as to deal with a case justly[610]
- the factors relevant to the award of costs are too many and too varied to be identified exhaustively, but the CAT will normally consider:
  - the success or failure overall or on particular issues
  - the parties' conduct in relation to the proceedings
  - the nature, purpose and subject-matter of the proceedings[611]
- the CAT considers that there is no inconsistency between the CAT's wide discretion, and an approach to its exercise which adopts a specific starting point[612]; for example the starting point in appeals under the Competition Act is that a successful party would normally (but not always) obtain a costs award in its favour[613]
- the CAT will take note where appropriate of the approach adopted in analogous proceedings by courts and tribunals in the various jurisdictions of the UK[614].

In addition to this general guidance some more specific trends can be discerned.

First, the CAT has not wanted to deter small or medium-sized firms from appealing against cartel decisions of the OFT for fear of having to pay the OFT's costs if unsuccessful: this can be seen in *Apex Asphalt and Paving Co v OFT*[615], although the CAT also noted other factors in that case that contributed to its decision to make no order for costs against the unsuccessful appellant[616]. However in *Sepia Logistics Ltd v OFT*[617] the CAT did award costs to the OFT in a case where the unsuccessful appellant was not a substantial undertaking, but where the appeal did not involve novel points of law. The CAT noted that the appellant had raised a number of points that lacked merit and that this had added significantly to the length and complexity of the case. Similarly in *National Grid* the CAT decided that the regulator 'should not have to pick up the tab' for the costs of rebutting points, in particular on market definition, which the CAT considered were 'bound to fail'[618].

A second point is that the CAT does not have the same anxiety in the case of more substantial firms. In *Aberdeen Journals v OFT*[619] the CAT expressed concern at the significant costs to the public purse involved in competition law appeals, a point repeated in *Genzyme v OFT*[620] and in *Football Shirts*[621]. In *National Grid* the CAT specifically pointed out that the appellant was a large and well-resourced company and that an award of costs against it would be unlikely to dissuade such a company from bringing an appeal[622].

---

[610] Case No 1107/4/10/08 *Merger Action Group v Secretary of State for Business, Enterprise and Regulatory Reform* [2009] CAT 19, [2009] CompAR 269, para 16.

[611] Ibid, para 19.

[612] Ibid, para 21.

[613] See eg Case Nos 1035/1/1/04 etc *Racecourse Association v OFT* [2006] CAT 1, [2006] CompAR 438, para 8; Case Nos 1140/1/1/09 etc *Eden Brown Ltd v OFT* [2011] CAT 29, para 18.

[614] Case No 1107/4/10/08 [2009] CAT 19, [2009] CompAR 269, para 22.

[615] Case No 1032/1/1/04 *Apex Asphalt and Paving Co Ltd v OFT* [2005] CAT 11, [2005] CompAR 825; see similarly in the context of a follow-on action for damages in Case No 1028/5/7/04 *BCL Old Co Ltd v Aventis SA* [2005] CAT 2, [2005] CompAR 485.

[616] Ibid, para 26.

[617] Case 1072/1/1/06 [2007] CAT 14, [2007] CompAR 779.

[618] Case No 1099/1/2/08 *National Grid Plc v Gas and Electricity Markets Authority* [2009] CAT 14, [2009] CompAR 282.

[619] [2002] CAT 21.

[620] Case No 1013/1/1/03 (IR) and Case No 1016/1/1/03 consent order of 14 November 2005 and Case No 1016/1/1/03 consent order of 29 November 2005.

[621] Case Nos 1019/1/1/03 etc *Umbro Holdings Ltd v OFT* [2005] CAT 26, [2005] CompAR 1232.

[622] Case No 1099/1/2/08 [2009] CAT 24, [2009] CompAR 375, para 16.

Thirdly, it is clear that the CAT has, on some occasions, felt disquiet at the level of the fees charged by City law firms for their advice; and in particular at the number of hours charged by partners as opposed to associates[623].

(F) Appeals from the CAT to the Court of Appeal

Appeals on points of law lie, with permission, from the CAT to the Court of Appeal[624]. The CAT has indicated that permission to appeal should be granted sparingly[625]; permission will usually be granted where there is a real prospect of success or there is some other compelling reason why the appeal should be heard[626]. A request for permission to appeal was rejected both by the CAT[627] and by the Court of Appeal in *Napp Pharmaceutical Holdings Ltd v Director General of Fair Trading*[628]. There have been several occasions on which the CAT has refused permission to appeal, but the Court of Appeal has subsequently granted it[629].

9. Article 267 References

An important aid to the consistency of application of EU law in Member States is the preliminary ruling procedure of Article 267 TFEU, which enables the Court of Justice to rule on questions referred by national courts or tribunals[630]. Two questions arise: first, can an Article 267 reference be made by a court or tribunal when applying the Competition Act, as opposed to Articles 101 and/or 102 TFEU; and second, which courts or tribunals in the UK are able to make an Article 267 reference.

(A) Can an Article 267 reference be made where a court or tribunal is applying the Competition Act 1998?

Since Regulation 1/2003 the competition authorities and courts in the UK apply Articles 101 and 102 TFEU themselves when they apply the Competition Act to agreements or conduct has an effect on trade between Member States. However there will be some cases where the effect on trade is purely within the UK and where only the Competition Act is applicable. The question then arises of whether an Article 267 reference can be made where a court or tribunal is considering corresponding issues under Chapters I and II.

---

[623] See eg Case Nos 1035/1/1/04 etc *The Racecourse Association v OFT* [2006] CAT 1, [2006] CompAR 438, paras 30–35; Case No 1049/4/1/05 *UniChem Ltd v OFT* [2005] CAT 31, [2006] CompAR 172, paras 27–31; and Case No 1104/6/8/08 *Tesco Plc v Competition Commission* [2009] CAT 26, [2009] CompAR 429, paras 42–46.

[624] Competition Act 1998, s 49.

[625] Case No 1151/3/3/10 *British Telecommunications Plc v OFCOM* [2010] CAT 22, para 7(c).

[626] See eg Case No 1023/4/1/03 *IBA Health Ltd v OFT* [2003] CAT 28, paras 4–5.

[627] Case No 1000/1/1/01 *Napp Pharmaceutical Holdings Ltd v Director General of Fair Trading* [2002] CAT 5.

[628] Case No C/2002/0705 *Napp Pharmaceutical Holdings Ltd v Director General of Fair Trading* [2002] EWCA Civ 796, [2002] 4 All ER 376.

[629] See eg *Argos Ltd and Littlewoods Ltd v OFT* and *JJB Sports plc v OFT* [2006] EWCA Civ 1318, [2006] UKCLR 1135; *OFCOM v Floe Telecom Ltd* [2006] EWCA Civ 768, [2006] ECC 30; *Dŵr Cymru v Albion Water Ltd* [2008] EWCA Civ 536, [2008] UKCLR 457; *OFCOM v Floe Telecom Ltd* and *T-Mobile Ltd v Floe Telecom Ltd* [2009] EWCA Civ 47, [2009] UKCLR 659; *National Grid plc v Gas and Electricity Markets Authority* [2010] EWCA Civ 114, [2010] UKCLR 386.

[630] See generally Green and Brealey (eds) *Competition Litigation: UK Practice and Procedure* (Oxford University Press, 2010), ch 21; it is for the referring court or tribunal to determine the content of the questions to be put to the Court of Justice, which will not opine on questions raised by the parties to the litigation unless the referring court asks it to: Cases C-376/05 etc *A Brünsteiner GmbH v Bayerische Motorenwerke AG* [2006] ECR I-11383, [2007] 4 CMLR 259, paras 25–29.

The jurisprudence of the Court of Justice strongly suggests that references under Article 267 will be possible in such cases[631]. This approach helpfully avoids national laws based upon Articles 101 and 102 being interpreted in a substantially different way from the meaning given to them by EU institutions.

(B) Which courts or tribunals in the UK can make an Article 267 reference in a case under the Competition Act 1998?

It is obvious that the Supreme Court, the Court of Appeal and the High Court can make Article 267 references. It is also assumed that the CAT can do so: provision is made for this in its Rules[632]. What is less clear is whether the OFT or the sectoral regulators could make a reference. It is a matter of EU law to determine who qualifies as courts or tribunals[633]. Lord Simon, in the House of Lords debate on the third reading of the Bill, thought that it would be possible for the OFT and/or the sectoral regulators to make a reference[634], although he subsequently resiled from this position[635]. It may be that the point will not arise, since the OFT and the regulators may determine of their own volition not to attempt to make such a reference. In this connection it is of interest to note that, in the *Syfait* case, the Court of Justice reached the conclusion that the Greek Competition Authority was not a court or tribunal for the purposes of Article 267 TFEU[636].

---

[631] See eg Case C-7/97 *Oscar Brönner GmbH v Mediaprint* [1998] ECR I-7791, [1999] 4 CMLR 112, paras 17–20; Case C-238/05 *Asnef-Equifax, Servicios de Informaci sobre Solvencia y Crédito, SL v Asociación de Usuarios de Servicios Bancarios (Ausbanc)* [2006] ECR I-11125, [2007] 4 CMLR 224, paras 12–25; Case C-217/05 *Confederación Española de Empresarios de Estaciones de Servicio v Compañía Española de Petróleos SA* [2006] ECR I-11987, [2007] 4 CMLR 181, paras 13–24; Case C-280/06 *Autorità Garante della Concurrenza e del Mercato v Ente tabacchi italiani – ETI SpA* [2007] ECR I-10893, [2008] 4 CMLR 277, paras 19–29.

[632] Competition Appeal Tribunal Rules 2003, SI 2003/1372, r 60; the CAT considered whether to make an Article 267 reference, but declined to do so in Case No 1100/3/3/08 *Number (UK) Ltd v OFCOM* [2008] CAT 33, paras 159–173: the Court of Appeal subsequently made a reference on 15 December 2009 and the Court of Justice gave its preliminary ruling in Case C-16/10 *The Number Ltd, Conduit Enterprises Ltd v Office of Communications, British Telecommunications plc* [2011] ECR I-000.

[633] See eg Case C-54/96 *Dorsch Consult Ingenieurgesellschaft mbH v Bundesbaugessellschaft Berlin mbH* [1997] ECR I-4961, [1998] 2 CMLR 237; Case C-178/99 *Re Salzman* [2001] ECR I-4421, [2003] 1 CMLR 918; on this point see Brown and Jacobs *The Court of Justice of the European Communities* (Sweet & Maxwell, 5th ed, 2000), pp 223–227; Dashwood, Dougan, Rodger, Spaventa and Wyatt (eds) *European Union Law* (Hart Publishing, 6th ed, 2011), pp 214–216.

[634] HL Committee, 25 November 1997, col 963.

[635] Ibid, col 975.

[636] Case C-53/03 *Synetairismos Farmakopoion Aitolias & Akarnanias and Others v GlaxoSmithKline Plc* [2005] ECR I-4609, [2005] 5 CMLR 7, paras 29–38.

11

Enterprise Act 2002: market studies and market investigations

I. Introduction

This chapter is concerned with two, to some extent related, ways in which the domestic law of the UK addresses a problem of market failure in circumstances where Articles 101 and 102 TFEU or the Chapter I and Chapter II prohibitions in the Competition Act 1998 are inapplicable for want of evidence of an agreement or abuse. First, the Office of Fair Trading ('the OFT')[1] may itself conduct a 'market study'[2] to understand as well as possible how markets are working and whether the needs of consumers are being met; and secondly the OFT (and sectoral regulators such as the Office of Communications ('OFCOM'))[3] may make a 'market investigation reference' to the Competition Commission ('the CC')[4]. If the CC concludes that any 'feature' of the market 'prevents, restricts or distorts competition', various powers are available to rectify the situation.

Section 2 of this chapter will provide an overview of market investigations. Sections 3 and 4 discuss the ways in which the OFT obtains and analyses information about markets, in particular through the receipt and investigation of 'super-complaints' and by conducting market studies. Section 5 describes the market investigation provisions in the Enterprise Act and considers the relationship between that Act, the Competition Act 1998 and EU Regulation 1/2003[5]. 'Public interest cases' are briefly referred to in section

---

[1] See ch 2, 'The OFT', pp 63–68.

[2] In March 2010 it was estimated that 40 competition authorities that are members of the International Competition Network have the power to carry out market studies: see Draft Market Studies Good Practice Handbook (April 2010), available at www.internationalcompetitionnetwork.org.

[3] See ch 2, 'Sectoral regulators', pp 68–69.

[4] See ch 2, 'Competition Commission', pp 69–72.

[5] See 'Relationship between the Competition Act and market investigation', pp 469–470.

6, while sections 7 and 8 deal with the issue of enforcement and other supplementary matters. Section 9 of the chapter considers how the market investigation provisions have been working in practice since the Enterprise Act entered into force. The final section of the chapter briefly refers to the enforcement and review of undertakings and orders still in force under the monopoly provisions in the Fair Trading Act 1973.

2. Overview of the Provisions on Market Investigation References

(A) Part 4 of the Enterprise Act 2002

Part 4 of the Enterprise Act 2002 entered into force on 20 June 2003. It consists of four chapters; the Government's *Explanatory Notes* to the Bill as introduced into Parliament on 26 March 2002 are a helpful adjunct to the Act itself[6]. Chapter 1 of Part 4 of the Act is entitled 'Market investigation references': it deals both with the making of references and their determination. Chapter 2 of Part 4 of the Act deals with 'public interest cases', which are rare in practice and are described below in brief outline. Chapter 3 contains rules on enforcement which set out the various undertakings that can be accepted by the OFT and the CC in the course of market investigations and the orders that may be made to remedy any adverse effects on competition and detrimental effects on consumers. Chapter 4 deals with supplementary matters such as investigatory powers and review by the Competition Appeal Tribunal ('the CAT').

(B) Brief description of the system of market investigation references

The OFT (concurrently with the sectoral regulators such as the Gas and Electricity Markets Authority and OFCOM) has power to make a reference to the CC where it has reasonable grounds for suspecting that any 'feature or combination of features' of a market prevent, restrict or distort competition in the UK or a part of it; the possibility also exists for the Secretary of State, in limited circumstances, to make a reference. Provision is made for the OFT or a sectoral regulator to accept legally binding undertakings in lieu of a reference. The CC must determine whether there is an adverse effect on competition; if so it must decide on suitable remedies, bearing in mind the need to achieve as comprehensive a solution as is reasonable and practicable to any adverse effects identified. In taking remedial action the CC may also take into account any 'relevant customer benefits', as defined by the Act. A wide array of powers to change markets prospectively is available to the CC following its investigation including, where appropriate, the power to impose a structural remedy. However the market investigation system does not involve any sanctions for past behaviour, nor does it confer or impose any enforceable rights or obligations upon anyone who was harmed by or who indulged in anti-competitive behaviour. References by the OFT and reports of the CC are required to be published.

(C) Institutional arrangements

As explained above, market investigation references can be made by the OFT and the sectoral regulators; in exceptional cases the Secretary of State can make a reference. Within

---

[6] The *Explanatory Notes* are available at www.legislation.gov.uk; on their legal significance see *Westminster City Council v National Asylum Support Service* [2002] UKHL 38, [2002] 1 WLR 2956, para 5.

the OFT the Markets and Projects division is responsible for assessing markets that might be appropriate for reference; the actual decision to refer is taken by the Board of the OFT[7]. The CC decides whether competition is being restricted in the cases referred to it and, if so, what remedies should be adopted; the CC makes the final determination in market investigation references. The OFT has a duty to monitor remedies and to advise on whether they should be varied or revoked. Decisions of the OFT, the Secretary of State and the CC are subject to review by the CAT. Appeals on points of law lie, with permission, from the CAT to the Court of Appeal.

(D) **Guidelines, rules of procedure and other relevant publications**

In addition to Part 4 of the Enterprise Act, various guidelines, rules and other publications seek to explain the operation of the UK system of market investigations.

(i) **OFT publications**

The OFT has published *Market investigation references: Guidance about the making of references under Part 4 of the Enterprise Act*[8], replacing earlier *Guidance* published in 2003, which explains how it intends to apply the Act.

(ii) **CC publications**

Acting under Schedule 7A to the Competition Act, inserted by Schedule 12 to the Enterprise Act 2002, the CC has adopted the *Competition Commission Rules of Procedure 2006*, which superseded the earlier rules of June 2003; they are available on its website[9]. The CC has also published three sets of guidelines of relevance to market investigations and one document setting out best practice:

- *Market Investigation References: Competition Commission Guidelines*[10]
- *General Advice and Information*[11]
- *Statement of Policy on Penalties*[12]
- *Suggested best practice for submissions of technical economic analysis from parties to the CC*[13]

The Chairman of the CC has published three further documents of relevance to market investigations:

- *Guidance to Groups*[14]
- *Disclosure of Information in Merger and Market Inquiries*[15]
- *Disclosure of Information by the Competition Commission to Other Public Authorities*[16].

---

[7] See the OFT Board's Rules of Procedure, available at www.oft.gov.uk.

[8] OFT 511, March 2006, available at www.oft.gov.uk.

[9] CC1, March 2006, available at www.competition-commission.org.uk.

[10] CC3, June 2003; in March 2010 the CC launched a public consultation on its *Guidelines*: details of the consultation and responses to it can be found at www.competition-commission.org.uk.

[11] CC4, March 2006.   [12] CC5, June 2003.

[13] 24 February 2009, available at www.competition-commission.org.uk.

[14] CC6, March 2006.   [15] CC7, July 2003.   [16] CC12, April 2006.

(iii) Department for Business, Innovation and Skills

The Secretary of State has adopted the Competition Appeal Tribunal Rules 2003[17] which govern the way in which the CAT deals with applications for review of decisions of the OFT, the Secretary of State and the CC in relation to market investigations. Statutory instruments have also been adopted in relation to the making of 'super-complaints'[18].

(iv) CAT

The CAT has published a *Guide to Proceedings*, section 6B of which deals specifically with applications for review under the Enterprise Act 2002[19].

3. Super-Complaints

Section 11 of the Enterprise Act provides for so-called 'super-complaints' to be made to the OFT. Super-complaints are handled within the OFT by the Markets and Projects division. The OFT has published *Super-complaints: Guidance for designated consumer bodies*[20] to assist those wishing to make a super-complaint. The *Guidance* describes the information that should be contained in a super-complaint, how cases will be handled and possible outcomes. Section 205 of the Act enables the Secretary of State to extend the system so that super-complaints can be made to the sectoral regulators; this was effected by statutory instrument in 2003[21]. The *Guidance* explains how these concurrency arrangements will work[22]; the terms of reference of the Concurrency Working Party in relation to super-complaint concurrent duties can be found on the OFT's website[23].

The idea of a super-complaint is that a designated consumer body can make a complaint to the OFT about features of a market for goods or services in the UK which appear to be significantly harming the interests of consumers[24]. This is a way of making the consumer's voice more powerful: individual consumers often lack the knowledge, motivation or experience to complain effectively, but a designated consumer body should have the resources and ability to do so. In such a case the OFT must publish a 'fast-track' report on what action, if any, it intends to take within 90 days[25]; the Secretary of State has power to amend the 90-day period[26]. The OFT, when dealing with a super-complaint, can request information under section 5(1) of the Enterprise Act 2002; however it has formal powers to demand information under section 174 of the Act only where it believes it has power to make a market investigation reference.

In practice the requirement to investigate and report within 90 days imposes a considerable burden on the OFT to gather evidence, synthesise it and form a view, which in turn results in a corresponding burden on the parties that are the subject of the super-

---

[17] SI 2003/1372.　　[18] See section 3 below.

[19] Available at www.catribunal.org.uk.

[20] OFT 514, July 2003, available at www.oft.gov.uk.

[21] The Enterprise Act 2002 (Super-complaints to Regulators) Order 2003, SI 2003/1368, as amended by the Enterprise Act 2002 (Water Services Regulation Authority) Order 2006, SI 2006/522.

[22] *Super-complaints: Guidance for designated consumer bodies*, paras 3.1–3.4.

[23] OFT 548, November 2003, available at www.oft.gov.uk; the operation of the Concurrency Working Party is explained in ch 10, 'The Concurrency Regulations and the Concurrency Guideline', pp 437–438.

[24] Enterprise Act 2002, s 11(1).　　[25] Ibid, s 11(2).　　[26] Ibid, s 11(4).

complaint; the 90-day period leaves little time for the OFT and the parties concerned to consider possible remedies to any problems identified. As will be seen from the Table of super-complaints below, it is quite likely that a super-complaint will lead to an OFT market study or even to a market investigation reference to the CC: in other words a super-complaint may lead to a lengthy period of scrutiny of the market, and the firms that operate on the market, to which the complaint relates. The super-complaint on *Payment Protection Insurance* of September 2005 led to a lengthy market study by the OFT which was followed by a market investigation reference to the CC in February 2007, which published its final report in January 2009; following litigation the CC reconsidered one of its remedies and made an order in April 2011.

Consumer bodies are designated by the Secretary of State[27], and the Department of Trade and Industry (now the Department for Business, Innovation and Skills) has issued *Guidance for bodies seeking designation as super-complainants* on the designation criteria and on how to apply for designated status[28]. Designations are made once yearly, in October; application must be submitted by 30 April of that year at the latest[29]. In 2007 the Secretary of State rejected an application by What Car? to become a super-complainant as it did not satisfy the criteria in the *Guidance*[30]. As of 20 June 2011 the Secretary of State has designated the following bodies as super-complainants:

- The Campaign for Real Ale (CAMRA)
- The Consumer Council for Water (formerly known as the WaterVoice Council)
- Which? (formerly known as the Consumers' Association)
- The General Consumer Council for Northern Ireland
- Citizens Advice (formerly known as the National Association of Citizens Advice Bureaux)
- The National Consumer Council (which subsumed Energywatch, the former National Consumer Council (including the Scottish and Welsh Consumer Councils) and Postwatch)
- The Scottish Association of Citizens Advice Bureaux[31].

A super-complaint can lead to a number of responses, including, though not limited to, competition or consumer law enforcement, referral to a sectoral regulator, the launch of a market study by the OFT or a market investigation reference to the CC[32].

By 20 June 2011, 13 super-complaints had been received by the OFT, as set out in Table 11.1 below. The first three of these were received on a non-statutory basis prior to the entry into force of section 11 of the Act, but were dealt with as though section 11 was in force.

---

[27] Ibid, s 11(5) and (6); see also the Electricity Act 2002 (Part 8 Designated Enforcers: Criteria for Designation, Designation of Public Bodies as Designated Enforcers and Transitional Provisions) Order 2003, SI 2003/1399, as amended by SI 2006/522.

[28] March 2009, available at www.bis.gov.uk.

[29] Ibid, para 1.3. The applications are available at www.bis.gov.uk.

[30] See www.bis.gov.uk/policies/consumer-issues/enforcement-of-consumer-law/super-complaints.

[31] See the Enterprise Act 2002 (Bodies Designated to make Super-complaints) (Amendment) Order 2009, SI 2009/2079, which came into force on 1 October 2009.

[32] *Super-complaints: Guidance for designated consumer bodies*, para 2.25.

Table 11.1 Table of super-complaints

Title	Date of super-complaint	Super-complainant	Date of announcement of result by OFT	Outcome
Private dentistry	25 October 2001	Which? (known at the time as the Consumers' Association)	23 January 2002	OFT market study
Doorstep selling	3 September 2002	National Association of Citizens Advice Bureaux	12 November 2002	OFT market study
Mail consolidation	17 March 2003	Postwatch	16 April 2003	Following discussions with the Postal Services Commission as to the regulatory position the OFT decided that no further action was necessary
Care homes	5 December 2003	Which? (known at the time as the Consumers' Association)	3 March 2004	OFT market study
Home credit	14 June 2004	National Consumer Council	10 September 2004	Market investigation reference to the CC
Northern Ireland banking	15 November 2004	Which? in conjunction with the General Consumer Council for Northern Ireland	11 February 2005	Market investigation reference to the CC
Payment Protection insurance	13 September 2005	Citizens Advice	8 December 2005	OFT market study followed by market investigation reference to the CC

Title	Date of super-complaint	Super-complainant	Date of announcement of result by OFT	Outcome
Credit card interest rate	2 April 2007	Which?	26 June 2007	OFT to carry out a programme of work with the credit card industry and consumer bodies to make the cost of credit cards easier for consumers to understand
Scottish legal profession	9 May 2007	Which?	31 July 2007	OFT made recommendations to the Scottish Government and the legal profession to lift restrictions that could be causing harm to consumers
Supply of beer in UK pubs	24 July 2009	The Campaign for Real Ale	22 October 2009	No further action needed **Appeal by CAMRA to the CAT challenging OFT's decision not to make an MIR; appeal was subsequently withdrawn**[1]
Cash ISAs	31 March 2010	Consumer Focus	29 June 2010	OFT made various recommendations to Cash ISA providers; also ISA providers voluntarily agreed to alter their behaviour so as to improve the performance of the market
Sub-prime credit brokerage and debt management	3 March 2011	Citizens Advice	1 June 2011	Series of measures including asking the Government to consider the introduction of new legislation in the relevant market
Credit and debit card surcharges	30 March 2011	Which?		Not yet concluded

[1] Case 1148/6/1/09 *CAMRA v OFT*, order of 7 February 2011.

4. OFT Market Studies

Section 5 of the Enterprise Act provides that one of the general functions of the OFT is to obtain, compile and keep under review information about matters relating to the carrying out of its functions. One of the ways in which the OFT carries out this general function is by conducting 'market studies' of markets which appear not to be working well for consumers but where enforcement action under competition or consumer law does not, at first sight, appear to be the most appropriate response[33]. The general function contained in section 5 is the only legal basis for OFT market studies; there are no further provisions, and therefore no specific legal framework. There is an obvious similarity between the OFT's market studies and the sectoral investigations that the European Commission conducts under Article 17 of Regulation 1/2003[34]. As when dealing with super-complaints, the OFT can *request* information under section 5(1) of the Enterprise Act 2002; however it has formal powers to *demand* information under section 174 of the Act only where it believes it has power to make a market investigation reference[35]. It follows that firms, should they so wish, could decide not to cooperate with an OFT market study if they were satisfied that the conditions for a market investigation reference are not met.

The OFT sometimes publishes reports on significant matters without designating them as market studies; these tend to be investigations that involve information gathering without any expectation that one of the outcomes usually expected of market studies is anticipated[36].

(A) OFT guidance

The OFT has published *Market Studies: Guidance on the OFT approach*[37] on the procedure that it normally follows when selecting a market for study and when carrying out such a study. The *Guidance* explains why the OFT conducts market studies; how it chooses and manages them; what their possible outcomes might be; and its evaluation of previous studies.

(B) Purpose of market studies

Market studies are usually carried out by the Markets and Projects division of the OFT; they are intended to enable the OFT to understand as well as possible how markets are working and whether the needs of consumers are being met. A market study is not limited to a relevant market in an economic sense; it may deal with practices across a range of goods and services[38]. An important feature of the OFT's market studies is that they are a way of scrutinising the extent to which governmental behaviour and legislation

---

[33] The sectoral regulators also conduct market studies: see eg Office of Rail Regulation's *Approach to reviewing markets* (October 2009) and *The Leasing of Rolling Stock for Franchised Passenger Services* (November 2006), both available at www.rail-reg.gov.uk; OFGEM's review of energy supply markets in February 2008, available at www.ofgem.gov.uk; and OFCOM's review of *Pay TV* (March 2010), available at www.ofcom.org.uk.

[34] See ch 7, Article 17: investigations into sectors of the economy and into types of agreements', pp 267–268.

[35] See 'powers of investigation', p 477 below.

[36] See eg *Review of barriers to entry, expansion and exit in retail banking*, November 2010, OFT 1282; *Stock-take of infrastructure ownership and control*, December 2010, OFT 1290.

[37] OFT 519, June 2010.

[38] *Market studies: Guidance on the OFT approach*, OFT 519, June 2010, para 2.3.

might have a harmful effect on the way in which markets work[39]. The market studies into, for example, *Pharmacies, Taxi Services, Public Procurement, European State Aid Control* and *Public Subsidies* were all concerned with what might be termed 'public' as opposed to private distortions of competition[40]: several cases ended with the OFT providing advice to the Government, as the Table of market studies below shows. The Government has indicated that it will respond to OFT reports on public restrictions within 90 days[41].

Market studies are distinct from market investigation references under Part 4 of the Enterprise Act, although it is possible that a market study might lead to a market investigation reference. This occurred, for example, in the cases of *Store Card Credit Services, Payment Protection Insurance, Airports* and *Local Buses*: the possibility that an OFT market study might be followed by a market investigation can lead to a somewhat prolonged scrutiny of some markets[42]. The OFT will try to consult within six months or less of the launch of a study when a market investigation reference is an outcome that is being considered at the time of the launch[43]. The desirability of avoiding unnecessary duplication of work is a factor that the OFT takes into account when deciding whether to launch a market study.

(C) **Procedure before the OFT**

Market studies may be triggered in various ways: for example the OFT might commence one on its own initiative, trading standards officers might bring problems to the OFT's attention, or a market study might be prompted by a super-complaint from a designated consumer body[44]; any other interested stakeholders may request the OFT to conduct a market study. The OFT welcomes reasoned suggestions of domestic markets to be considered for market studies, and has produced an electronic suggestions form which is available on its website[45].

Chapter 4 of the OFT's *Guidance* explains how it goes about market studies. The major stages of a study include selection of a market; applying the *OFT's Prioritisation Principles*[46]; pre-launch work; the decision to launch a market study; gathering and analysis of evidence[47]; informal consultation on the OFT's findings; publication of a report on the OFT's website[48]; and follow-up work. The duration of a market study depends on various factors including the scale and complexity of the market; the average length of a market study from launch to publication of a report has been around 12 months, but some studies have been as short as five months[49].

---

[39] Ibid, paras 2.8–2.10.

[40] On this point see the UK Contribution to the OECD Roundtable on *Market Studies* (2008), available at www.oecd.org.

[41] See the Government's White Paper *Productivity and Enterprise – A World Class Competition Regime* Cm 5233 (2001), paras 4.15 and 6.37.

[42] On this point see Pickering 'UK Market Investigations: An Economic Perspective' (2006) 5 Competition Law Journal 215.

[43] OFT 519, June 2010, para 5.13.

[44] See 'Super-Complaints', pp 454–455 above.

[45] See www.oft.gov.uk/shared_oft/investigations/marketstudiesideas.doc.

[46] OFT 939, October 2008.

[47] Enterprise Act, s 5(3) provides a statutory basis for the OFT to outsource the market study or part of it to an external consultancy; see *Market Studies: Guidance on the OFT approach*, para 4.16 and *Financial Services and Markets Act 2000*, December 2004, available at www.oft.gov.uk.

[48] www.oft.gov.uk; the website also contains any Government response to a market study.

[49] *Market Studies: Guidance on the OFT approach*, para 4.4.

Table 11.2 Table of market studies

Completed market studies	Date of OFT report	Outcome of study
Extended Warranties for Electrical Goods	July 2002	Complex monopoly reference made to the Competition Commission under the (now-repealed) Fair Trading Act 1973
Consumer IT Goods and Services	December 2002	Generally the consumer IT market works well for consumers; OFT will continue to monitor the market
Pharmacies	January 2003	Recommendation that the Government should take action to liberalise entry to the community pharmacy market No action was taken to implement this recommendation
Private Dentistry (note that this followed a super-complaint by Which? (formerly the Consumers' Association))	March 2003	Better information on prices and treatments should be given to consumers, and there should be improvements to the self-regulation of the market The Department of Trade and Industry published an action plan in June 2003 to implement the OFT's proposals[1]
Payment Systems	May 2003	OFT to examine the effectiveness of the commitment within the Banking Code to inform consumers about the length of clearing cycles; to complete the investigation of the *MasterCard* notification; to consider whether action is required on access to merchant acquiring and on debit card networks; and to monitor undertakings following the CC's report under the Fair Trading Act 1973 on banking services
Liability Insurance Market	June 2003	Changes recommended to certain practices and the OFT to keep the market under review
Taxi Services	November 2003	Recommendation that elements of the regulatory framework for taxi services should be improved: in particular the removal of *quantity* restrictions, and the encouragement of proportionate *quality* restrictions In November 2006 the Department for Transport issued guidance on quantity restrictions
New Car Warranties	December 2003	Manufacturers and dealers should improve their advice to consumers on their servicing options; also they should remove servicing restrictions from their new car warranties: failure to do so could lead to a formal investigation by the OFT under Article 101 TFEU. Subsequently servicing ties were removed from new car warranties and a voluntary code of conduct was adopted

Completed market studies	Date of OFT report	Outcome of study
Debt Consolidation	March 2004	Better financial awareness among consumers and provision of clear, accurate and relevant information by credit providers needed to make the use of debt consolidation fairer and clearer
Store Cards	March 2004	Market investigation reference to the CC
Estate Agents	March 2004	Recommendation that the Estate Agent Act 1979 should be amended to improve enforcement, that self-regulation should be improved, and that consumers should take further action to protect their own position; key recommendations have been implemented by the Consumers, Estate Agents and Redress Act 2007
Doorstep Selling (note that this followed a super-complaint by the NACAB)	May 2004	Consumers require better information as to their rights in relation to doorstep selling, and existing legislation requires amendment to extend cooling-off periods to all forms of doorstep selling; key recommendations have been implemented by the Consumers, Estate Agents and Redress Act 2007
Financial Services and Markets Act 2000	December 2004	No adverse effects on competition found to flow from the Act
Ticket Agents	January 2005	Society of Ticket Agents and Retailers to develop model terms for its members to use in consumer contracts
Classified Directory Advertising Services	April 2005	Market investigation reference to the CC
Care Homes (note that this followed a super-complaint by Which? (formerly the Consumers' Association)	May 2005	The OFT recommended that the Government should establish a central information point or 'one-stop shop' where people can get clear information about care for older people; better access to complaints procedures should be achieved; there is a need for fairer contracts The Government announced in August 2005 that it broadly accepted the OFT recommendations[2]
Public Sector Procurement	May 2005	Preliminary research published; further research to be conducted in relation to procurement in the waste management and construction sectors; discussions to take place with the Office of Government Commerce with a view to the OFT publishing guidelines for public sector procurers on how to make the most of competition when procuring construction services

(continued)

Table 11.2 (*continued*)

Completed market studies	Date of OFT report	Outcome of study
Liability Insurance Market Follow-up Review	June 2005	The OFT identified lower increases in premiums, better communication between insurers and policyholders and a reduction in the number of businesses denied cover as key improvements in this follow-up review to its earlier market study
Property Searches	September 2005	Recommendation that central Government should provide clearer guidance to local authorities on how they should set prices for providing property information; also that there should be an agreement as to revised targets with local authorities to ensure that this information is made available quickly and on the same time-scale that they apply to themselves The Government announced in December 2005 that it accepted all but one of the report's recommendations[3]
European State Aid Control	November 2005	Recommendation that the European Commission should adopt an effects-based approach to the assessment of state aid in its guidelines; most cases would be assessed in a 'Phase I' investigation; cases that do not fall within the Commission's guidelines would be subject to a 'Phase II' assessment. National competition authorities should be allowed to give formal advice as to whether a proposed aid meets the criteria of the Commission's guidelines
Public Subsidies	January 2006	Recommendations by OFT that guidance should be given to providers of subsidies on whether the subsidies are likely to have a significant impact on competition. The OFT recommended that the guidance should be issued as a supplement to the HM Treasury 'Green Book', which requires that all costs and benefits should be taken into account when appraising any Government programme or project
School Uniforms	September 2006	The OFT found that exclusive contracts between schools and retailers have an adverse effect on the prices paid by parents. The OFT passed its findings to the Department of Education and also called on school governors to eliminate exclusive agreements

Completed market studies	Date of OFT report	Outcome of study
Commercial Use of Public Information	December 2006	Recommendation that public sector information holders, such as the Met Office, the National Archives and the Ordnance Survey, should make as much public sector information available for public use as possible, ensure that businesses have access to such information at the earliest point that it is useful to them, provide such information on a non-discriminatory basis and at a reasonable price and enable better regulation by the Office of Public Sector Information The Government announced in June 2007 that it accepted all but two of OFT's recommendations[4]
Payment Protection Insurance (note that this followed a super-complaint by Citizens Advice)	October 2006	Market investigation reference to the CC
UK Airports	December 2006	Market investigation reference to the CC Recommendations also made to the Government in relation to airports in the north of England
Pharmaceutical Price Regulation Scheme	February 2007	Recommendation that the Pharmaceutical Price Regulation Scheme, whereby the Government seeks to control the prices of branded medicines through a mix of profit and price controls, should be reformed in order to make the prices paid by the National Health Service reflect the therapeutic value to patients of the drug in question The Government responded in June 2009[5]
Internet Shopping	June 2007	The rapid growth of internet selling has been successful for both consumers and businesses; OFT to conduct further work to improve aspects of internet selling
Medicines Distribution	December 2007	Recommendations by the OFT that the Government should make further amendments to the Pharmaceutical Price Regulation Scheme and seek the agreement of manufacturers to adopt minimum service standards for the benefit of pharmacies. The OFT will continue monitoring the situation in the market Government responded to the OFT's recommendations in May 2008[6]

(*continued*)

Table 11.2 (*continued*)

Completed market studies	Date of OFT report	Outcome of study
Personal Current Accounts in the UK	July 2008	OFT came to the conclusion that the market is not working well for consumers. The OFT liaised with relevant stakeholders in order to adopt appropriate measures in order to correct the problems identified In March 2011 the OFT published a short update on progress in the PCA market[7]
Homebuilding in the UK	September 2008	Market broadly competitive; housebuilding industry to develop a code of conduct to provide redress scheme for customers who experience faults or delays Homebuilding Industry to establish a voluntary code of conduct to address issues in the report
Sale and Rent Back	October 2008	There should be statutory regulation of the sector by the FSA
Scottish Property Managers	February 2009	Market not working well for consumers; recommendation for a self-regulatory scheme promoted by the Scottish Government and for the development of an advice and mediation service The Scottish Government responded to the OFT's recommendations in May 2009[8]
Northern Rock	March 2009	The study found that public-sector support for Northern Rock had no significant adverse impact on competition during the period February 2008 to February 2009
Isle of Wight Ferry Services	October 2009	OFT decided not to make an MIR
Second-hand Cars	December 2009	Initial research published
	June 2010	OFT published guidance for second-hand car dealers
Local Bus Services	January 2010	Market investigation reference to the CC
Home Buying and Selling	February 2010	Some updating of legislation in this sector would be beneficial

Completed market studies	Date of OFT report	Outcome of study
Online Targeting of Advertising	May 2010	Appropriate self-regulation is needed so that better information is provided to consumers about how personal data are collected and used; if industry fails to deliver, enforcement action by either the OFT, ICO or OFCOM is to address the problem
Insolvency Practitioners	June 2010	Fundamental changes to the regulatory system recommended
Advertising of Prices	December 2010	Some pricing practices have the potential to mislead customers; advice on traders to review their promotional advertising so as to stay compliant with the law
Outdoor Advertising	February 2011	Market broadly competitive; there is a possibility that anti-competitive agreements entered into by Clear Channel and JCDecaux with local authorities may be having an adverse effect on entry into the market, and they will therefore be investigated under Article 101 TFEU/the Chapter I prohibition: the OFT refers to their long duration and some 'potentially restrictive terms'
Consumer Contracts	February 2011	Study provided OFT with a better understanding of the kinds of contract terms that are most likely to harm consumers
Equity Underwriting	February 2011	Market lacks effective competition; fees to investment banks have been increasing. Companies and institutional investors should do more to protect themselves

[1] See www.dti.gov.uk/files/file25886.pdf.
[2] See www.dti.gov.uk/files/file17611.pdf.
[3] See www.dti.gov.uk/files/file25861.pdf.
[4] See www.bis.gov.uk/files/file39966.pdf.
[5] See www.berr.gov.uk/files/file51657.pdf.
[6] See www.bis.gov.uk/files/file45998.pdf.
[7] See *Personal current accounts in the UK*, March 2011, OFT 1319.
[8] See www.scotland.gov.uk/Topics/Built-Environment/Housing/quality/16193/PolicyandLegislation/oftresponse.

(D) **Outcomes of market studies**

Various outcomes may follow a market study by the OFT. The following possibilities are set out in the OFT's *Guidance*:

- a clean bill of health for the market in question
- consumer-focused action, for example to raise their awareness in such a way that they make better purchasing decisions
- making recommendations to business to change their behaviour, for example on matters such as information about after-sales services, standard terms and conditions and improving consumer redress
- making recommendations to the Government or regulators
- investigation or enforcement action under consumer or competition law
- a market investigation reference to the CC under Part 4 of the Enterprise Act[50].

The OFT publishes performance monitoring arrangements for market studies and reports on success against the targets in its Annual Report[51]. The OFT has estimated that consumer savings as a result of its market studies and reviews from 2007 to 2010 amounted to £107 million every year[52].

(E) **Examples of market studies**

An account of the OFT's work in studying markets can be found in its Annual Report and Resource Accounts[53], and a section of the OFT's website provides details of its completed and current market studies[54]. Table 11.2 above contains a list of market studies which were completed by 20 June 2011.

5. **Market Investigation References**[55]

Chapter 1 of Part 4 of the Enterprise Act establishes the system of market investigation references. Sections 131 to 133 deal with the making of references and sections 134 to 138 with their determination. The OFT's *Market investigation references: Guidance about the making of references under Part 4 of the Enterprise Act* ('the *OFT Guidance*')[56] and the CC's *Market Investigation References: Competition Commission Guidelines*[57] provide

---

[50] Ibid, paras 5.1–5.13.
[51] See eg OFT's *Annual Plan for 2011/12*, OFT 1294, p 16, available at www.oft.gov.uk.
[52] See the OFT's *Annual Report and Resource Accounts 2009–10*, HC 301, p 30, available at www.oft.gov.uk.
[53] See eg the *Annual Report 2008–09*, pp 31–36; the *Annual Report 2009–10*, pp 29–32.
[54] See www.oft.gov.uk.
[55] See Geroski 'The UK Market Inquiry Regime' [2004] Fordham Corporate Law Institute (ed Hawk), 1, also available at www.competition-commission.org.uk; see also Geroski 'Market Inquiries and Market Studies: The View from the Clapham Omnibus' and Freeman 'Investigating Markets and Promoting Competition: The Competition Commission's role in UK Competition Enforcement', Beesley Lecture of 18 October 2007, both available at the same website; see further Freeman 'Market Investigations in the United Kingdom: The Story So Far' in *Economic Law and Justice in Times of Globalisation* (Nomos, 2007, eds Monti et al); Jenkins and Casanova 'The UK Market Investigations Regime: Taking Stock after 5 Years (2008) 7(4) Competition Law Journal 346; Cartlidge 'The UK Market Investigation Regime: A Review' (2009) 8(4) Competition Law Journal 312; Ahlborn and Piccinin 'Between Scylla and Charybdis: Market Investigations and the Consumer Interest' in *Ten Years of UK Competition Law Reform* (Dundee University Press, 2010, ed Rodger).
[56] OFT 511, March 2006, available at www.oft.gov.uk.
[57] CC3, June 2003.

helpful direction on market investigation references. The market investigation regime is a notable feature of the UK system of competition law, and recognises that not every market failure can be cured through the application of the 'conventional' tools of competition law, Articles 101 and 102 and their domestic analogues. The market investigation regime focuses on markets rather than on the behaviour of individual firms, and enables the CC to investigate whether features of the market have an adverse effect on competition. A wide range of remedies is available to eliminate, as far as possible, such adverse effects and any detrimental effects on customers that the CC identifies.

(A) The making of references

(i) The power of the OFT to make a reference

The OFT (concurrently with the sectoral regulators)[58] may make a market investigation reference to the CC when it has 'reasonable grounds for suspecting'[59] that one or more 'features' of a market prevent, restrict or distort competition in the supply or acquisition of goods or services in the UK or in a part thereof[60]. A decision to make a market investigation reference is made by the Board of the OFT. The CAT has made clear that the 'reasonable grounds for suspecting' test does not impose a particularly high burden on the OFT: the scheme of the Act is that the full investigation of a market is to be carried out by the CC, not the OFT[61]. At the same time the CAT stressed that the first-stage investigation by the OFT should not be unduly protracted[62]. Features of a market include the structure of the market concerned or any aspect thereof[63]; the conduct of persons supplying or acquiring goods or services who operate on that market, whether that conduct occurs in the same market or not[64]; and conduct relating to the market concerned of customers of any person who supplies or acquires goods or services[65]. Conduct for these purposes includes a failure to act and need not be intentional[66]. The OFT, when making a reference, is not required to specify whether particular features of a market are a matter of structure on the one hand or of conduct on the other[67].

Section 132 of the Act allows the Secretary of State to make a reference when he is not satisfied with a decision of the OFT not to make a reference under section 131, or when he considers that the OFT will not make such a reference within a reasonable period. Section 132 sits a little oddly with Parliament's intention that the Secretary of State should be removed from cases except where exceptional public issues arise, for which special provision is made[68]. The section 132 power had not been exercised by 20 June 2011. In June 2010 the Government created the Independent Commission on Banking ('ICB') to consider ways in which the UK banking sector could be reformed to promote financial stability and competition[69]; the ICB was not established under the Enterprise Act, and is not subject to any specific legal framework. Its recommendations to the Government were published on 12 September 2011.

---

[58] On the powers of the sectoral regulators in relation to market investigation references see the Enterprise Act 2002, Sch 9, Part 2.

[59] Note that the Government resisted a proposed amendment to the Enterprise Bill that would have required the OFT to have reasonable grounds for *believing* rather than for *suspecting* there to be a problem: see Lord Sainsbury of Turville, Hansard, 18 July 2002, col 1511, available at www.parliament.uk.

[60] Enterprise Act 2002, s 131(1).

[61] Case No 1054/6/1/05 *Association of Convenience Stores v OFT* [2005] CAT 36, [2006] CompAR 183, para 7.

[62] Ibid, para 8.   [63] Enterprise Act 2002, s 131(2)(a).   [64] Ibid, s 131(2)(b).

[65] Ibid, s 131(2)(c).   [66] Ibid, s 131(3).   [67] *OFT Guidance*, para 1.9.

[68] See 'Public Interest Cases', p 474 below.

[69] See bankingcommission.independent.gov.uk; the ICB published an Interim Report: Consultation on Reform Options on 11 April 2011.

Section 133 specifies what the OFT must include in a market investigation reference; in particular it must provide a description of the goods or services to which the feature or combination of features that are restrictive of competition relate[70]. A reference may be framed so as to require the CC to confine its investigation to goods or services supplied or acquired in a particular place or to or from particular persons[71]. Provision is made for the variation of references[72]. This occurred, for example, in the case of *Store Card Credit Services* so that network cards and insurance services such as payment protection insurance could be included in the investigation; the variation was made as a result of a request from the CC[73]. In the case of *Classified Directory Advertising Services* the CC issued a notice clarifying the scope of the reference, although the reference itself was not varied[74].

Section 169 of the Act requires the OFT to consult before making a reference and section 172 requires it to give reasons for its decision; these may be given after the date of the reference[75]. The Act leaves open the form and extent of the consultation process: the consultation may be a public one, though not necessarily so. The consultation provisions are important, and the OFT takes great care to ensure that it complies with them. An example of these provisions operating in practice is afforded by the reference of *Airports*: the OFT published its market study and its proposal to send the matter to the CC on 12 December 2006, and called for comments by 8 February 2007: the actual reference to the CC was made on 30 March 2007.

The OFT maintains a close relationship with the CC so that the latter body is aware of cases that might be referred to it[76]; this means that the process of transferring a case from the OFT to the CC can be managed as efficiently as possible.

(ii) The discretion of the OFT whether to make a reference

The OFT has a discretion to make a market investigation reference when the statutory criteria appear to be met. The OFT rejected a submission by CAMRA that the OFT is under a duty to refer a market where it has reasonable grounds to suspect that features of a market restrict competition[77]. Paragraph 2.1 of the *OFT Guidance* says that it will make a reference only when the following criteria, in addition to the statutory ones, are met:

- it would not be more appropriate to deal with any competition issues under the Competition Act 1998 or by other means, for example the powers of the sectoral regulators

- it would not be more appropriate to accept undertakings in lieu of a reference[78]

- the scale of the suspected problem, in terms of the adverse effect on competition, is such that a reference would be appropriate

- there is a reasonable chance that appropriate remedies will be available.

The *OFT Guidance* provides further insights into each of these criteria.

---

[70] Enterprise Act 2002, s 133(1)(c).

[71] Ibid, s 133(2) and (3); this power was exercised in the case of *Airports*.   [72] Ibid, s 135.

[73] See www.competition-commission.org.uk and OFT Press Release 41/05, 3 March 2005; a variation was also made in the case of *Domestic Bulk Liquefied Petroleum Gas*: see www.competition-commission.org.uk and OFT Press Release of 20 October 2004.

[74] See www.competition-commission.org.uk.   [75] Enterprise Act 2002, s 172(6).

[76] To this end the OFT and CC have created a joint working group: OFT Press Release 41/09, 8 April 2009.

[77] OFT 1279, October 2010, para 9.15 and fn 215; in *Newspaper and magazine distribution*, OFT 1121, September 2009, the OFT decided that, although the criteria for making a reference to the CC were met, it should exercise its discretion not to make a reference: ibid, ch 5.

[78] See 'Undertakings in lieu of a reference to the CC', pp 475–476 below.

(A) Relationship between the Competition Act and market investigations

The OFT's policy is to consider first whether a suspected problem can be addressed under the Competition Act 1998; it would consider a market investigation reference only where it has reasonable grounds to believe that market features restrict competition, but not to establish a breach of the Chapter I and/or Chapter II prohibitions (or of Articles 101 and/or 102 TFEU), or when action under the Competition Act has been or is likely to be ineffective for dealing with any adverse effect on competition identified[79]. The OFT Guidance goes on to explain that a market investigation reference might be appropriate for dealing with tacit coordination in oligopolistic markets[80] or with problems arising from parallel networks of similar vertical agreements[81]. It adds that the majority of references are likely to involve industry-wide market features or multi-firm conduct, of which tacit coordination and parallel vertical agreements are examples[82]. The OFT will review these criteria in the light of emerging case law on the Chapter II prohibition should it appear that it is inadequate to deal with conduct by a single dominant firm which has an adverse effect on competition[83]; also it may make a reference where there has been an infringement of the Chapter II prohibition and it seems that a structural remedy going beyond what could be imposed under the Competition Act is necessary[84].

(B) Relationship with Regulation 1/2003

The OFT Guidance discusses the relationship between Regulation 1/2003 and the market investigation provisions[85]. That Regulation requires national competition authorities to apply Articles 101 and 102 where agreements or abusive conduct have an effect on inter-state trade; as a general proposition it is not possible to apply stricter national law than Article 101, but this is possible in the case of Article 102[86]. The OFT Guidance points out that this does not prevent investigations of agreements and conduct that infringe Articles 101 and 102, but that it does affect the remedies that can be imposed[87]. Where Article 101 is applicable to an agreement or agreements, it is unlikely that the OFT would make a reference[88]. However the OFT notes the possibility that in certain circumstances the benefit of a block exemption can be withdrawn from vertical agreements, and that this could be a recommendation of the CC[89]. The OFT Guidance also notes that the CC could impose remedies in relation to behaviour which amounted to an infringement of Article 102, in which case the OFT would take those remedies into account in the event of it carrying out its own investigation of the infringement of that provision[90]. In the event that the CC were, during the course of a market investigation reference, to discover an infringement of Article 101 or 102, it would not itself have the power to apply those provisions to the behaviour in question, since it has not been designated as a national competition authority for the purpose of applying the EU competition rules: only the OFT and

---

[79] OFT Guidance, para 2.3.

[80] Ibid, para 2.5; on this point see the OFT's decision in Local bus services OFT 1158, January 2010, para 5.28, available at www.oft.gov.uk.

[81] OFT Guidance, para 2.6.   [82] Ibid, para 2.7.   [83] Ibid, para 2.8, second indent.

[84] Ibid, para 2.8, third indent; on structural remedies under the Competition Act, see ch 10, 'Can directions be structural?', p 408.

[85] OFT Guidance, paras 2.9–2.18.

[86] See generally ch 2, 'The Relationship Between EU Competition Law and National Competition Laws', pp 75–79.

[87] OFT Guidance, para 2.12.

[88] Ibid, para 2.14; the OFT noted this point in reaching its decision not to make a reference of the UK beer and pub market: CAMRA's super-complaint, OFT 1279, October 2010, para 9.41 and fn 227.

[89] OFT Guidance, paras 2.17–2.18.

[90] Ibid, para 2.15.

the sectoral regulators have been so designated.[91] In *Store Card Credit Services* the CC was satisfied that its proposed remedies were not in conflict with the provisions of EU law[92]. In *Payment Protection Insurance* the CC rejected an argument that its remedies package infringed the EU freedom of establishment[93].

(C) *Scale of the problem*

The *OFT Guidance* discusses the proposition that a reference would be made only where the scale of a suspected problem, in terms of its effect on competition, is such that a reference would be an appropriate response. It will consider whether the adverse effects on competition of features of a market are likely to have a significant detrimental effect on customers through higher prices, lower quality, less choice or less innovation; where the effect is insignificant the OFT would consider that the burden on business and the cost of a reference to the CC would be disproportionate[94]. The limited evidence of consumer detriment was an important factor in the OFT's decision not to refer *Isle of Wight Ferry Services*[95].

The *OFT Guidance* also says that, generally speaking, the OFT would not refer a very small market; a market only a small proportion of which is affected by the features having an adverse effect on competition; or a market where the adverse effects are expected to be short-lived[96]. In *Newspaper and magazine distribution* the OFT decided not to make a reference where any adverse effect on competition appeared to be offset by customer benefits in the form of lower prices and wider circulation[97].

(D) *Availability of remedies*

The OFT would not refer a market if it appeared that there were unlikely to be any available remedies to deal with an adverse effect on competition, for example where a market is global and a remedy under UK law would be unlikely to have any discernible effect[98].

(iii) Restrictions on the OFT's ability to make a reference

The OFT cannot make a reference if it has accepted undertakings in lieu of a reference within the preceding 12 months[99]. This limitation does not apply where an undertaking has been breached[100]; nor where it was accepted on the basis of false or misleading information[101].

(iv) The OFT's application of the reference test

Part II of the *OFT Guidance* contains a helpful discussion of the OFT's interpretation of the reference test set out in section 131 of the Act. In chapter 4 it discusses the meaning of 'prevention, restriction or distortion of competition'. In chapter 5 it considers structural features of markets, including the concentration level within a market, vertical integration, conditions of entry, exit and expansion, regulations and government policies, informational asymmetries, switching costs and countervailing power. Chapter 6 deals with firms' conduct, in particular the conduct of oligopolies, facilitating practices, custom and

[91] See ch 7, 'Article 5: powers of the NCAs', p 252.

[92] See www.competition-commission.org.uk, para 10.9.

[93] Final Report, para 10.66; the right to freedom of establishment is contained in Article 49 TFEU.

[94] *OFT Guidance*, para 2.27, on whether the cost of making a reference would be disproportionate see *CAMRA super-complaint – OFT final decision*, OFT 1279, October 2010, para 9.37.

[95] OFT 1135, October 2009, paras 7.24 and 7.33.   [96] *OFT Guidance*, para 2.28.

[97] OFT 1121, September 2009, paras 5.16–5.25; see also *OFT Guidance*, para 2.29.

[98] *OFT Guidance*, paras 2.30–2.32.

[99] Enterprise Act 2002, s 156(1); on undertakings in lieu see 'Undertakings in lieu of a reference to the CC', pp 475–476 below.

[100] Ibid, s 156(2)(a).   [101] Ibid, s 156(2)(b).

practice and networks of vertical agreements. Chapter 7 considers the conduct of customers, which section 131(2)(c) of the Act considers to be a feature of a market, and specifically considers the issue of search costs, that is to say the cost that customers may have to incur in order to make an informed choice. By 20 June 2011 the OFT had made nine market investigation references to the CC, and the Office of Rail Regulation and OFCOM had each made one: they are set out in the Table of market investigation references towards the end of this chapter with some accompanying commentary[102].

(B) **The determination of references**

(i) **Questions to be decided**

Once a reference has been made to the CC it must decide whether any feature, or combination of features, prevents, restricts or distorts competition in the referred market(s)[103]. If the CC considers that there is an adverse effect on competition, it must decide three additional questions: first, whether it should take action to remedy, mitigate or prevent the adverse effect on competition or any detrimental effect on customers it has identified[104]: detrimental effects are defined as higher prices, lower quality, less choice of goods or services and less innovation[105]; secondly, whether it should recommend that anyone else should take remedial action[106]; and thirdly, if remedial action should be taken, what that action should be[107]. The CAT has stated that it is likely to be a relatively rare case in which the CC, having identified an adverse effect on competition and detrimental effects, will exercise its discretion to take no remedial action under the Act[108]. When considering remedial action, the CC must have regard to the need to achieve as comprehensive a solution as is reasonable and practical to the adverse effect on competition and any detrimental effects on customers[109], and may in particular have regard to the effect of any action on any relevant customer benefits[110]. If the CC finds that there is no anti-competitive outcome, the question of remedial action does not arise.

(ii) **Investigations and reports**

Section 136(1) of the Act requires the CC to prepare and publish a report; this must be done within two years[111]. The report must contain the decisions of the CC on the questions to be decided under section 134, its reasons for those decisions and such information as the CC considers appropriate for facilitating a proper understanding of those questions and the reasons for its decisions[112]. The CC's report on *Store Card Credit Services* sets out, at paragraphs 24 to 37, a summary of the features of that market that prevent, restrict or distort competition, the detrimental effects on customers, the need for remedial action and the decisions on remedies; these matters are then dealt with in more detail in sections 9 and 10 of the report[113]. The time limit of two years may not be extended[114], but the Secretary State may reduce it by order[115]. In the *Tesco* case the CAT rejected a submis-

---

[102] See 'Table of market investigation references', pp 480–483 below.

[103] Enterprise Act 2002, s 134(1)–(3).

[104] Ibid, s 134(4)(a); the phrase 'remedy, mitigate or prevent' in sections 134 and 138 of the Act recognises that there may be cases where an AEC cannot, because of the constraints of reasonableness or practicability, be fully remedied or prevented, but only mitigated.

[105] Enterprise Act 2002, s 134.   [106] Ibid, s 134(4)(b).   [107] Ibid, s 134(4)(c).

[108] *Tesco Plc v Competition Commission* [2009] CAT 6, [2009] CompAR 168, para 57.

[109] Enterprise Act 2002, s 134(6).

[110] Ibid, s 134(7); on the meaning of relevant customer benefits, see s 134(8).   [111] Ibid, s 137(1).

[112] Ibid, s 136(2).   [113] Available at www.competition-commission.org.uk.

[114] Enterprise Act 2002, s 137(4).   [115] Ibid, s 137(3).

sion that the time limit applied to its power to refer a matter back to the CC following a successful review[116].

Experience of the first few years of the market investigation regime shows that the CC is likely to need the full two years to complete its investigation, although it has stated that it will attempt to do so in the future in a shorter period[117]; and that a further period of time thereafter may be needed to implement any necessary remedies (the *implementation* phase of the CC's procedure falls outside the statutory period within which the investigation must be conducted). It is probably correct to suggest that many parties under investigation will not be in a great hurry to facilitate a quicker conclusion to cases than this, since, in the event of a finding of an adverse effect on competition, it is likely that they will be called upon to alter their behaviour in some way at the end of the process.

(iii) Duty to remedy adverse effects

When the CC has prepared and published a report under section 136 and concluded that there is an adverse effect on competition, section 138(2) requires it to take such action as it considers to be reasonable and practicable to remedy, mitigate or prevent the adverse effect on competition and any detrimental effects on customers that have resulted from, or may result from, the adverse effect on competition[118]. The CC would, where it is possible to do so, prefer to address the root cause of the problem – that is to say the adverse effect on competition – than the consequences of it[119]. When deciding what action to take the CC must be consistent with the decisions in its report on the questions it is required to answer, unless there has been a material change of circumstances since the preparation of the report or the CC has a special reason for deciding differently[120]. In making its decision under section 138(2) the CC shall have regard to the need to achieve as comprehensive a solution as is reasonable and practicable to any adverse effects on competition or detrimental effects on customers[121], having regard to any relevant customer benefits of the market features concerned[122]. The remedies phase of a market investigation reference can be quite protracted[123].

(iv) Procedure before the CC

The procedures of the CC during market investigation references are set out in the CC's *Rules of Procedure*[124] and the *Chairman's Guidance to Groups*[125]. Rule 6 of the *Rules of Procedure* requires the CC to draw up an administrative timetable for its investigation. The major stages of an investigation include the gathering and verification of evidence; providing a statement of issues; hearings; notifying provisional findings; notifying and considering possible remedies; the publication of the final report; and deciding on remedies. Each investigation has its own home page on the CC's website, and it is a simple matter to follow the progress of the investigation in this way. This accords with the CC's aim to be open and transparent in its working[126]. The home page sets out the core documents

---

[116] *Tesco Plc v Competition Commission* [2009] CAT 9, [2009] CompAR 359, paras 20–29.

[117] See the CC's *Corporate Plan 2009/10*, Table 4, point 1.1 and the CC's Note for the CBI Competition Committee, 7 July 2009, available at www.competition-commission.org.uk.

[118] Enterprise Act 2002, s 138(2).   [119] *CC Guidance*, para 4.6.

[120] Enterprise Act, s 138(3); see eg the CC's Final Report of 19 July 2011 concluding that there were no material changes in circumstances that would justify amending its original decision in *Airports*; the Report of 2011 is the subject of an appeal to the CAT in Case No 1185/6/8/11 *BAA Ltd v Competition Commission*, not yet decided.

[121] Enterprise Act 2002, s 138(4).   [122] Ibid, s 138(5).

[123] See 'The Market Investigation Provisions in Practice', pp 479, 483–485 below.

[124] CC1, March 2006.

[125] CC6, March 2006.

[126] See *Chairman's Guidance on Disclosure of Information in Merger and Market Inquiries* (CC7, July 2003), paras 1.5 and 1.6, available at www.competition-commission.org.uk.

of the inquiry; contains the CC's announcements, for example on its 'emerging thinking', provisional findings and final report; and makes available the submissions and the evidence provided to the CC. The home page may also contain surveys and working papers of relevance to the investigation and an account of roundtable discussions, for example with academic economists, held on particular topics: for example in *Groceries* economic roundtables were held on local competition and on buyer power and in *Local Buses* the CC appointed researchers for a study on distinguishing exclusionary conduct, tacit co-ordination and competition[127].

The first completed market investigation was *Store Card Credit Services*, and the home page sets out the core documents which provide a helpful insight into the progress of that case:

- terms of reference (**18 March 2004**)
- members of the inquiry
- administrative timetable
- 'issues statement' (**22 September 2004**)
- the CC's 'emerging thinking' (**11 January 2005**)
- variation of terms of reference
- notice of provisional findings (**14 September 2005**)
- notice of possible remedies
- statement of provisional decisions on remedies
- final report (**7 March 2006**)
- administrative timetable for making of Order
- notice of intention to make an Order
- draft Order
- notice of making Order
- *Store Cards Market Investigation Order* (**27 July 2006**).

In July 2009 the CC announced that it intends to streamline its procedures so that it might be able to complete some investigations within 18 months[128]; subsequently the Goverment consulted on a proposal to reduce the time limit by statute.[128a]

(v) The CC's Guidance

The CC has published *Market Investigation References: Competition Commission Guidelines*[129] which explain its approach to market investigation references. They deal in turn with issues of market definition, the assessment of competition and remedial action, and contain an extremely useful guide to the competitive process and various factors that adversely affect competition.

---

[127] See. www.competition-commission.org.uk.

[128] See www.competition-commission.org.uk; for criticism of the length of market investigation references see Callaghan 'What Every In-house Lawyers Needs to Know About a UK Competition Commission Inquiry Before it Starts – 10 Suggestions to Help You Manage the Process' (2009) 3(9) International In-house Counsel Journal 1365.

[128a] See *A Competition Regime for Growth: a consultation on options for reform*, para 3.18–3.20, available at www.bis.org.uk.

[129] CC3, June 2003.

6. Public Interest Cases

Chapter 2 of Part 4 of the Act provides for 'public interest cases'. These are rare and are discussed here in outline only[130]. The Secretary of State may give an 'intervention notice' to the CC within the first four months of a market investigation reference[131], provided that the reference has yet to be determined[132] and that he believes that one or more public interest considerations are relevant to a market investigation[133]. The Secretary of State may also give an intervention notice to the OFT when it is considering undertakings in lieu of a reference[134]. Section 140(1) specifies the information that an intervention notice must contain. The Enterprise Act specifies national security as a public interest consideration[135]; the Secretary of State can add a new public interest consideration by statutory instrument, but this would require the approval of Parliament[136].

When an intervention notice has been given to the CC it will investigate whether features of the market are having an adverse effect on competition and, if so, consider the question of remedies; however it must prepare one set of remedies on the basis that the Secretary of State might decide the case, and a separate set of remedies in case the matter reverts to it[137]. The CC will then publish its report[138]. The Secretary of State must then decide, within 90 days of receipt of the report, whether any public interest considerations raised by the intervention notice are relevant to the remedial action proposed by the CC[139]; if so, the Secretary of State may take such action as he considers to be reasonable and practicable to remedy the adverse effects on competition identified by the CC in the light of the relevant public interest considerations[140]. If, however, the Secretary of State does not make and publish his decision within 90 days of receipt of the report, the matter reverts to the CC which will proceed on the basis of the remedies that it proposed in the eventuality of the matter reverting back to it[141].

Section 150 of the Act gives the Secretary of State power to veto the acceptance by the OFT of an undertaking in lieu of a market investigation reference where any public interest considerations outweigh the considerations that led the OFT to propose accepting the undertaking[142].

The OFT has a function of informing the Secretary of State of cases that might raise public interest considerations[143], and the OFT and CC must bring to his attention any representations about the exercise of his powers as to what constitutes a public interest consideration[144].

7. Enforcement

Chapter 3 of Part 4 of the Enterprise Act deals with the powers of the OFT and the CC to accept undertakings or to impose orders to ensure compliance with the Act and to monitor and enforce them. It begins with the powers of the OFT to accept undertakings in lieu of a reference to the CC; it then sets out the interim and final powers of the CC.

---

[130] The procedure in public interest cases is described in the *CC Guidance*, paras 5.1–5.11.
[131] Enterprise Act 2002, s 139(1)(a)–(b).
[132] Ibid, s 139(1)(c).   [133] Ibid, s 139(1)(d).
[134] Ibid, s 139(2).   [135] Ibid, s 153(1).   [136] Ibid, s 143(3) and (4).   [137] Ibid, s 141.
[138] Ibid, s 142.   [139] Ibid, s 146.   [140] Ibid, s 147.   [141] Ibid, s 148.   [142] Ibid, s 150.
[143] Ibid, s 152.   [144] Ibid, s 152.

Undertakings and orders are legally binding and enforceable in the courts[145]. The OFT is required to maintain a register of undertakings and orders made under the market investigation provisions in the Enterprise Act; it is accessible on the OFT's website[146].

(A) Undertakings and orders

(i) Undertakings in lieu of a reference to the CC[147]

Section 154(2) of the Act gives power to the OFT to accept an undertaking in lieu of a reference to the CC. It can do this only where it considers that it has the power to make a reference to the CC and otherwise intends to make such a reference[148]. In proceeding under section 154(2) the OFT must have regard to the need to achieve as comprehensive a solution as is reasonable and practicable to the adverse effect on competition concerned and any detrimental effects on customers[149], taking into account any relevant customer benefits[150]. The OFT has said that it considers that undertakings in lieu are unlikely to be common[151]; given that the OFT does not conduct a full investigation of the market – that is the function of the CC – it may not be in possession of sufficient information to know whether undertakings in lieu would be adequate to remedy any perceived detriments to competition. This having been said, it may be that, as the system develops, more use will be made of them: some firms may decide that it would be preferable to offer undertakings in lieu than to bear the intrusion and cost of a two-year investigation; others, however, may prefer a delay of two years (or more) before potentially having to abandon the behaviour in question. If firms were to offer undertakings in lieu but the OFT were to proceed nevertheless to make a market investigation reference, they could apply to the CAT for a review of the decision. It is likely that the OFT (or a sectoral regulator) will find it easier to make use of the undertaking in lieu provisions when there are only a few firms involved (or even just one) than when a large number of firms are under investigation.

Before accepting undertakings in lieu the OFT is obliged to publish details of the proposed undertaking, to allow a period of consultation and to consider any representations received[152]; a further period of consultation is required should the OFT intend to modify the undertakings[153]. If an undertaking in lieu has been accepted it is not possible to make a market investigation reference to the CC within the following 12 months[154], unless there is a breach of the undertaking or unless it was accepted on the basis of false or misleading information[155].

Undertakings in lieu of a reference had been accepted in two cases by 20 June 2011, *Postal Franking Machines*[156], an OFT case, and *BT*[157], a case involving OFCOM. In the case of *Postal Franking Machines* the OFT accepted undertakings from the two leading suppliers of franking machines, Pitney Bowes and Neopost, together with Royal Mail; the undertakings were intended to facilitate greater customer choice and more competition in the market, for example by making better price information available and encouraging the provision of third-party maintenance services. This market had been the subject of an investigation under the now-repealed Fair Trading Act 1973 in 1988; the OFT decided

---

[145] Ibid, s 167; as to whether a person injured by breach of an undertaking or order could bring an action for damages, see *MidKent Holdings v General Utilities plc* [1996] 3 All ER 132, [1997] 1 WLR 14, brought under s 93 of the (now-repealed) Fair Trading Act 1973.

[146] Enterprise Act 2002, s 166; the OFT's website is www.oft.gov.uk.

[147] See generally *OFT Guidance*, paras 2.20–2.26.   [148] Enterprise Act 2002, s 154(1).

[149] Ibid, s 154(3).   [150] Ibid, s 154(4).   [151] *OFT Guidance*, paras 2.21 and 2.25.

[152] Enterprise Act 2002, s 155(1)–(3).   [153] Ibid, s 155(4)–(5).   [154] Ibid, s 156(1).

[155] Ibid, s 156(2).   [156] OFT, 17 June 2005, available at www.oft.gov.uk.

[157] OFCOM, 22 September 2005, available at www.ofcom.org.uk.

to review the market since the undertakings given in 1988 appeared not to have been effective. In *BT* OFCOM accepted more than 230 separate undertakings from the Board of BT designed to achieve operational separation between BT's infrastructure, where it benefits from a 'bottleneck monopoly', and those parts of its business where it is subject to competition; the monopoly part of the BT business is now operated by 'Openreach', and 'Chinese walls' are established between it and the rest of the BT business. Openreach is required to provide wholesale services to communications providers on an equivalent basis. The intention is that this will prevent BT from discriminating in favour of its own vertically-integrated business units. OFCOM publishes a quarterly report setting out BT's progress in implementing the undertakings, and an annual report looking at their overall impact[158].

(ii) Interim undertakings and orders to prevent pre-emptive action

The CC, after a report has been published, can accept interim undertakings and make interim orders to prevent pre-emptive action which might prejudice any final remedy adopted by the CC[159]. The Secretary of State may exercise these powers in public interest cases[160].

(iii) Final powers

Sections 159 to 161 of the Enterprise Act deal with the final undertakings and orders that are available to the CC after it has completed its investigation and reached its conclusion on the questions contained in section 134. Section 159 provides for the acceptance of undertakings and section 160 for the making of an order where an undertaking is not being fulfilled or where false or misleading information was given to the OFT or CC prior to the acceptance of the undertaking. Section 161 empowers the CC to make a final order. The orders that can be made are set out in Schedule 8 to the Act; they include orders to restrict certain conduct on the part of firms, and also to prohibit acquisitions or even to provide for the division of a business[161]. The provisions that may be contained in an undertaking are not limited to those permitted by Schedule 8 in the case of orders[162]. The CC has a choice of whether to seek undertakings or to make an order, and will proceed on the basis of practicality such as the number of parties concerned and their willingness to negotiate and agree undertakings in the light of the CC's report[163].

The first order to be made by the CC under these powers was the *Store Cards Market Investigation Order* of 27 July 2006. It made provision for full information to be made available to consumers on store card statements, including a warning as to the annual percentage rate of the interest payable; for a direct debit facility to be made available to users of store cards; and for the provision of payment protection insurance as a separate product from the store card itself[164]. In the case of *Classified Directory Advertising Services* the CC decided that it would accept undertakings from Yell, the publisher of Yellow Pages, rather

---

[158] Details of OFCOM's ongoing work in relation to BT's undertakings can be found at www.ofcom.org.uk.

[159] Enterprise Act 2002, ss 157 and 158.   [160] Ibid, s 157(6)(a).

[161] On structural remedies under the Act and its predecessors see Speech of Peter Freeman of 7 October 2010, available at www.competition-commission.org.uk.

[162] Enterprise Act 2002, s 164(1).   [163] *CC Guidance*, paras 4.42–4.44.

[164] Available at www.competition-commission.org.uk; the Order was slightly amended in 2011 by the *Store Cards market Investigation Order Variation Order 2011* to take into account the coming into force of the Directive 2008/48/EC of the European Parliament and of the Council on credit agreements for consumers, OJ [2008] L 133/66.

than make an order; the final undertakings were accepted on 3 April 2007[165]. As will be seen from the Table of market investigation references below, the CC had made final orders in seven cases by 28 June 2011.

(B) Enforcement functions of the OFT

Section 162 of the Act requires the OFT to keep enforcement undertakings and enforcement orders under review[166] and to ensure that they are complied with[167]; it is also required to consider whether, by reason of a change of circumstances, there is a case for release, variation, supersession or revocation[168]. The CC may ask the OFT to assist in the negotiation of undertakings[169]. Section 167 provides that there is a duty to comply with orders and undertakings; this duty is owed to anyone who may be affected by a breach of that duty[170]. Any breach of the duty is actionable if such a person sustains loss or damage[171], unless the subject of the undertaking or order took all reasonable steps and exercised all due diligence to avoid a breach of the order or undertaking[172]. Compliance with an order or undertaking is also enforceable by civil proceedings brought by the OFT[173] or the CC[174] for an injunction.

8. Supplementary Provisions

Chapter 4 of Part 4 of the Enterprise Act contains a number of supplementary provisions.

(A) Regulated markets

Section 168 provides that, where the CC or the Secretary of State consider remedies in relation to regulated markets such as telecommunications, gas and electricity, they should take into account the various sector-specific regulatory objectives that the sectoral regulators such as the Gas and Electricity Markets Authority and OFCOM have. These may go beyond preventing adverse effects on competition: for example there is a legal obligation to ensure the maintenance of a universal postal service.

(B) Consultation, information and publicity

Sections 169 to 172 of the Act impose various consultation, information and publication obligations on the OFT, the CC and the Secretary of State.

(C) Powers of investigation

Section 174 gives the OFT powers to require information for the purpose of market investigation references; section 175 creates criminal offences where, for example, a person intentionally and without reasonable excuse fails to comply with a notice under section 174; the

---

[165] See www.competition-commission.org.uk.
[166] Enterprise Act 2002, s 162(1).   [167] Ibid, s 162(2)(a).
[168] Ibid, s 162(2)(b)–(c).
[169] Ibid, s 162.   [170] Ibid, s 167(2)–(3).
[171] Ibid, s 167(4); as to whether such a person could bring an action for damages, see ch 11 n 145 above.
[172] Ibid, s 167(5).   [173] Ibid, s 167(6).   [174] Ibid, s 167(7).

level of financial penalties depends on whether the offence is tried summarily or is serious enough to be taken on indictment to the Crown Court.

Section 176 of the Act gives the CC the same powers to require the attendance of witnesses, the production of documents and the supply of information as it has under the provisions in Part 3 of the Act on merger control. These provisions are described in chapter 22 of this book[175].

(D) **Reports**

Section 177 of the Act makes provision for excisions of inappropriate matter from reports made under the provisions on public interest cases[176], and section 178 allows a dissenting member of the Commission to publish his reasons for disagreeing with the majority. Dissenting opinions are possible: the only two times that this had occurred by 20 June 2011 were in the case of *Rolling Stock Leasing* where one member of the CC dissented on the comprehensiveness of the remedies package[177] and in *Groceries* where there was a split decision in relation to the competition test to be inserted in the planning regime[178].

(E) **Review of decisions under Part 4 of the Enterprise Act**

Section 179 of the Act makes provision for review of decisions under Part 4 of the Act. Section 179(1) provides that any person aggrieved by a decision of the OFT, the Secretary of State or the CC may apply to the CAT for review of that decision: the aggrieved person could be a third party with sufficient interest. The application must be made within two months of the date on which the applicant was notified of the disputed decision or of its date of publication, whichever is earlier[179]. When dealing with applications under section 179(1) the CAT must apply the same principles as would be applied by a court on an application for judicial review[180]. The CAT's concern is therefore not with the correctness of the decision, but with the lawfulness of the decision-making process which it adopted[181]. The CAT may dismiss the application or quash the whole or part of the decision to which it relates[182]; and, in the latter situation, it may refer the matter back to the

---

[175] See ch 22, 'Investigation Powers and Penalties', p 949.

[176] See 'Public Interest Cases', p 474 above on public interest cases.

[177] See Final Report, para 9.272 and Note of dissent accompanying the report; both documents are available at www.competition-commission.org.uk.

[178] See Final Report, paras 11.100–11.104, available at www.competition-commission.org.uk.

[179] Competition Appeal Tribunal Rules 2003, SI 2003/1372, as amended by SI 2004/2068, r 27.

[180] Enterprise Act 2002, s 179(4); the fact that the CAT is a specialist tribunal does not mean that it should apply judicial review principles in a different way to the ordinary courts: see Lloyd LJ in *British Sky Broadcasting Group Plc v Competition Commission* [2010] EWCA Civ 2, [2010] UKCLR 351, paras 28–41, dealing with the merger control provisions in Part 3 of the Act, but which would apply in the same way to the market investigation provisions.

[181] Case No 1109/6/8/09 *Barclays Bank Plc v Competition Commission* [2007] CAT 27, [2009] CompAR 381, para 22.

[182] Enterprise Act 2002, s 179(5)(a).

original decision-maker for further consideration[183]. An appeal may be brought before the Court of Appeal, with permission, against the CAT's decision on a point of law[184]. Part 3 of the Competition Appeal Tribunal Rules 2003 makes provision for applications under section 179 of the Act[185].

Five applications for review under the market investigation provisions of the Enterprise Act had been made by 20 June 2011. In the case of *Association of Convenience Stores v OFT*, the Association was dissatisfied with a decision of the OFT not to refer the groceries market to the CC; however the OFT subsequently decided that it would reconsider the matter, with the consequence that the CAT handed down a ruling quashing the OFT's decision not to refer and referring the matter back to the OFT[186]. The OFT subsequently referred the groceries market to the CC in May 2006. The challenges to the CC's decisions to impose certain remedies in its *Groceries* and *Payment Protection Insurance* investigations are discussed in the section on the market investigation provisions in practice[187]. In *BAA v Competition Commission*[188] the CAT upheld a claim by BAA that the *Airports* market investigation had been tainted by apparent bias of one of the CC's members, but rejected its argument that the CC's chosen remedies were disproportionate. On appeal the Court of Appeal held the CC's final report was not tainted by apparent bias, and restored the CC's decision that BAA should divest itself of three UK airports[189]. One further case, *Campaign for Real Ale v OFT*, was adjourned while the OFT re-consulted on its original decision not to refer the pub industry to the CC. In October 2010 the OFT took a new decision reaching the same conclusion; the proceedings in the CAT were subsequently withdrawn with permission[190].

9. The Market Investigation Provisions in Practice

By 20 June 2011 the OFT had made nine market investigation references to the CC, six of which had been completed; two of which were at the order-making stage and one was pending; there had also been one reference from each of the Office of Rail Regulation and OFCOM. The references to date are set out in the following Table of market investigation references.

---

[183] Ibid, s 179(5)(b); on which see the ruling on relief in Case No 1104/6/8/08 *Tesco Plc v Competition Commission* [2009] CAT 9, [2009] CompAR 359.

[184] Enterprise Act 2002, s 179(6) and (7).

[185] SI 2003/1372, as amended by SI 2004/2068.

[186] Case 1052/6/1/05 [2005] CAT 36, [2006] CompAR 183 and order of the Tribunal of 7 November 2005.

[187] See 'The Market Investigation Provisions in Practice', pp 479–485 below.

[188] Case No 1110/6/8/09 [2009] CAT 35, [2010] CompAR 23.

[189] *Competition Commission v BAA Ltd* [2010] EWCA Civ 1097; the Supreme Court subsequently refused BAA permission to appeal: see CC News Release 05/11, 18 February 2011.

[190] Case No 1148/6/1/09, order of 7 February 2011.

Table 11.3 Table of market investigation references

Title of report	Date of reference	Date of report	Outcome
Store card credit services	18 March 2004	7 March 2006	Adverse effect on competition in relation to the supply of consumer credit through store cards and associated insurance in the UK; in particular most store card holders pay higher prices for their credit than would be expected in a competitive market. The CC estimated the customer detriment to be in the region of £55 million a year since 1999, and possibly significantly more The *Store Cards Market Investigation Order* of 27 July 2006 requires full information to be made available to store card users, including as to the annual percentage rate of interest; direct debit facilities to be made available to users; and the provision of payment protection insurance as a separate product Slight variation to the *Store Cards Order* on 11 February 2011 to take into account the entry into force of the EU Consumer Credit Directive
Domestic bulk liquefied petroleum gas (LPG)	5 July 2004	29 June 2006	Adverse effect on competition in relation to the supply of domestic bulk liquefied petroleum gas in the UK; in particular there was very little switching by customers between suppliers for a variety of reasons leading to higher prices for the large majority of customers The *Domestic Bulk Liquefied Petroleum Gas Market Investigation Order* of 13 October 2008 and the *Domestic Bulk Liquefied Petroleum Market Investigation (Metered Estates) Order* of 6 May 2009
Home credit (note that this reference followed a super-complaint from the National Consumer Council)	20 December 2004	30 November 2006	Adverse effect on competition in relation to the supply of home credit; in particular the weakness of price competition led to higher prices than could be expected in a competitive market The *Home Credit Market Investigation Order* of 13 September 2007 requires home credit

Title of report	Date of reference	Date of report	Outcome
			lenders to share customer repayment data with other potential lenders; to publish information, in particular price information, about the loans they offer to customers; and to provide, at most every three months, an account statement, free of charge, when any of their borrowers ask for one. The Order was slightly varied on 24 February 2011 to take into account the entry into force of the EU Consumer Credit Directive
Classified directory advertising services	5 April 2005	21 December 2006	Adverse effect on competition in relation to classified directory advertising services; Yell's prices for advertising in Yellow Pages would be higher than in a well-functioning market if it were not for the fact that it was already subject to price control as a result of an earlier monopoly investigation under the Fair Trading Act 1973 On 3 April 2007 the CC accepted final undertakings from Yell Group plc capping its advertising prices; undertakings were also given in relation to other matters such as tying and bundling and the provision of accounts
Northern Ireland personal banking (note that this followed a super-complaint from Which? in conjunction with the General Consumer Council for Northern Ireland)	26 May 2005	15 May 2007	Adverse effect on competition in relation to personal current accounts in Northern Ireland; competition limited by banks' unduly complex charging structures and practices, their failure adequately to explain them and customers' reluctance to switch to another bank The *Northern Ireland PCA Banking Market Investigation Order* of 19 February 2008 requires Northern Irish banks to ensure that certain types of communications with customers are easy to understand and to inform customers that they can switch; the Order also deals with the provision of information to the OFT Slight variation to the *Northern Ireland PCA Banking Market Investigation Order* of 28 February 2011 to take into account the entry into force of the EU Consumer Credit Directive and Payment Services Directive

(continued)

Title of report	Date of reference	Date of report	Outcome
Groceries Market **On appeal the CAT found that the CC's report contained errors in relation to remedies**[1]**; in a further judgment the CAT quashed part of CC's decision and remitted the matter back to it**[2]	9 May 2006	30 April 2008	Grocery markets in many respects provide a good deal for consumers; however action is needed to improve competition in local markets and to address relationships between retailers and their suppliers On remittal, following the appeal, the CC came to substantially the same conclusion again on 2 October 2009 The *Groceries Supply Code of Practice* came into force on 4 February 2010; legislation is proposed to create a Groceries Code Adjudicator who will enforce the *Code* The CC adopted the *Controlled Land Order* on 10 August 2010 which addresses the issue of exclusivity agreements and restrictive covenants that could restrict entry to the groceries market
Payment Protection Insurance (note that this followed a super-complaint from Citizens Advice) **On appeal the CAT quashed the CC's decision to impose a 'point of sale prohibition' for PPI and remitted the matter to the CC**[3]	7 February 2007	29 January 2009	Serious competition problems in the PPI market; various measures proposed, including a ban on the sale of PPI during the sale of the credit product and for seven days afterwards; also informational remedies On remittal, following the appeal, the CC came to substantially the same conclusion again on the point of sale prohibition on 14 October 2010. This led to the *Payment Protection Insurance Market Investigation Order* of 24 March 2011
BAA Airports **On appeal the CAT found apparent bias**[4]**; the CC's report for the most part was quashed and the matter was remitted back to it**[5] **The Court of Appeal upheld some of the CC's appeal and restored its original report**[6]	29 March 2007	19 March 2009	BAA ordered to sell three airports, including Gatwick and Stansted and one of Glasgow or Edinburgh; BAA sold Gatwick Airport in November 2009 to Global Infrastructure Partners On 19 April 2011 the CC accepted final undertakings from BAA in relation to Aberdeen airport On 19 July 2011 the CC decided that there were no material changes of circumstances that would justify amending its decision to require BAA to sell Stansted Airport and one of Glasgow or Edinburgh[7]

Title of report	Date of reference	Date of report	Outcome
Rolling stock leasing market investigation	26 April 2007	7 April 2009	Competition in the market for rolling stock is restricted by the limited number of alternative fleets available to TOCs. Various recommendations made *Rolling Stock Leasing Market Investigation Order* of 22 December 2009
Local bus services	7 January 2010	Ongoing	
Movies on Pay-TV	4 August 2010	Ongoing	

[1] Case No 1104/6/8/08 *Tesco plc v CC* [2009] CAT 6, [2009] CompAR 168.
[2] [2009] CAT 9, [2009] CompAR 359.
[3] Case No 1109/6/8/09 *Barclays plc v CC* [2009] CAT 27, [2009] CompAR 381.
[4] Case No 1110/6/8/09 *BAA Ltd v CC* [2009] CAT 35.
[5] [2010] CAT 9, [2010] CompAR 201.
[6] *CC v BAA* [2010] EWCA Civ 1097, [2011] UKCLR 1.
[7] The Report of July 2011 is new the subject of an appeal to the CAT, Case No 1185/6/8/11, *BAA v Competition Commission*, not yet decided.

As stated at the outset of the chapter the market investigation provisions (as well as the OFT's market studies) are an important supplement to the 'conventional' competition law tools of Articles 101 and 102 TFEU and the Chapter I and Chapter II prohibitions. Not all market failures are caused by cartels and abusive behaviour by dominant firms. It is important that competition authorities should have other tools at their disposal such as the powers afforded by the Enterprise Act.

A number of points can be made about the investigations that the CC has so far completed.

(A) Meaning of 'adverse effect on competition'

The CC has had to grapple with the meaning of the terms 'features of the market' and 'adverse effect on competition' ('AEC'), which appeared in UK law for the first time in the Enterprise Act 2002. In doing so the CC has typically used economic thinking to facilitate its understanding and analysis of competition in the market under investigation. The CC has not laid down a definitive test of what constitutes an AEC, but it is possible to tell from its reports that it often sees the issue in terms of a realistic comparison between 'a well-functioning market' and the competitive conditions observed in practice[191]. The text that follows will briefly examine the approach that has been taken to identifying an AEC by the CC.

[191] See eg the Final Reports in *Home Credit*, para 8.4; *Groceries*, para 10.7; and *Rolling Stock Leasing*, paras 8.4–8.6 and 8.20.

(i) Market definition

In its reports the CC has frequently defined the relevant market and, by doing so, identified those products or services that currently constrain the prices of those under investigation[192]. Market definition provides a helpful framework for the CC's evidence gathering and economic analysis. The goods or services specified in the reference may or may not correspond to the relevant market. The CC undertook considerable econometric analysis and modelling to inform its market definition in *Groceries*[193].

(ii) Counterfactual

In several reports the CC has tried to identify the appropriate 'counterfactual' against which to determine whether any feature of the market restricts competition[194]. A well-functioning market does not require perfect competition[195], but is likely to be a market in which competition is as effective as possible given the nature of the product[196].

(iii) Theories of harm

The CC typically uses economics to frame its analysis of a particular market and consider various 'theories of competitive harm' which may arise from one or more 'features' of the market. The CC seeks to identify a plausible case that the market under scrutiny could lead to significant harmful effects on competition. The CC's *Market Investigation References Guidelines* provide detailed guidance on its assessment of competition, and include consideration of issues such as switching costs and barriers to entry, or market imperfections, such as informational asymmetries. For example in *Northern Ireland Banking*[197] the CC concluded that the features of the market harming competition were that banks had unduly complex charging structures and practices; that they did not fully or sufficiently explain them; and that customers generally did not actively search for alternative suppliers[198]. In *BAA* the CC's theory of harm was different: it was concerned that the common ownership of many airports in the UK meant that there was a lack of competition between them, resulting in problems such as a lack of responsiveness to the interests of airlines and passengers. This feature of the airports market could have an AEC in more than one market: for example if there were inadequate investment at an airport caused by lack of competition between airports, that lack of investment may adversely affect competition between airlines[199]. In the case of *Local Buses* the CC explicitly identified four theories of harm which it proposed to examine[200].

(iv) Performance and prices

In some cases the CC has considered the level of prices and profitability as factors indicating the lack of competitive pressure in a market[201]. In *Home Credit* the CC concluded that the fact that excessive profits were being earned was not in itself an adverse effect on competition, although it was indicative of features of the market, such as an incumbency

---

[192] This is consistent with the CC's *Market Investigation References Guidelines*, part 2.

[193] See the Final Report, paras 4.13–4.14.

[194] See eg the Final Report in *Home Credit*, para 8.4, available at www.competition-commission.org.uk.

[195] See the Final Report in *Rolling Stock Leasing*, para 4.28.

[196] Final Reports in *Home Credit*, para 8.4, *Groceries*, para 10.7 and *Rolling Stock Leasing*, para 8.20.

[197] See the Final Report, available at www.competition-commission.org.uk; for criticism of this investigation see Ridyard 'The Competition Commission's Northern Ireland Banking Market Investigation – Some Unanswered Questions on the Role of Market Investigations' (2008) 29 ECLR 173.

[198] Final Report, para 5.9.   [199] Final Report, para 8.2.   [200] Issues Statement, 4 February 2010.

[201] See the Final Reports in *Store Cards*, paras 8.11 and 8.82, *Groceries*, para 6.76 and *Classified Directory Advertising Services*, section 7.

advantage and a lack of customer switching, that did have an adverse effect on competition. On other occasions the CC has noted that a number of conceptual and practical difficulties have constrained its ability to conduct informative profitability analysis[202].

(B) Findings of adverse effects on competition

The CC has found an adverse effect on competition in each of the investigations so far completed. It is noticeable that in several of these cases the CC was concerned about the lack of information, or the complexity of the information, available to customers: this was true, for example, in *Store Card Credit Services*, *Home Credit* and *Northern Ireland Banking*. Another recurrent theme is problems for consumers in switching between suppliers of goods and services: this was a key feature of the investigation into *Liquefied Petroleum Gas* and was a concern of the CC in *Northern Ireland Banking* and *Payment Protection Insurance*. The impact of government policy and economic regulation has also been a concern in several investigations. An example of this is *Classified Directory Advertising Services* in which Yell's prices were already subject to a system of regulation, following an earlier investigation in 1996; nevertheless the CC concluded that features of the market did have an adverse effect on competition in that Yell's prices would be higher than in a well-functioning market but for the price regulation[203]. The CC was also critical of aspects of government policy in *Rolling Stock Leasing* and *BAA*.

(C) Remedies

One of the important changes introduced by the Act was that it gave the CC responsibility for determining and implementing as full and effective a remedy for any adverse effects on competition as possible. Aspects of the remedies imposed in two investigations – *Groceries*[204] and *Payment Protection Insurance*[205] – were successfully challenged before the CAT. In both cases the CAT was critical of the CC's approach to evaluating the likely costs and benefits of its remedies. On reconsideration of the matters the CC adopted essentially the same remedies[206]. In February 2010 the CC published the outcome of an internal review of its remedies procedures[207]; the CC intends to publish more detailed guidance in due course[208].

(D) Evaluation of the system

The OFT and the CC regularly evaluate the effectiveness of market studies and market investigations[209]. The CC has estimated that action taken following market studies and market investigations saved consumers £317 million between April 2009 and March

---

[202] See for example the Final Reports in *Liquefied Petroleum Gas*, para 5.16 (profitability analysis was inconclusive) and *Rolling Stock Leasing market investigation*, para 8.18 (profitability analysis was not practicable).

[203] See the Final Report, paras 8.25–8,26, available at www.competition-commission.org.uk.

[204] Case No 1104/6/8/09 *Tesco plc v Competition Commission* [2009] CAT 6, [2009] CompAR 168.

[205] Case No 1109/6/8/09 *Barclays Bank Plc v Competition Commission* [2009] CAT 27, [2009] CompAR 381.

[206] See also Case No 1110/6/8/09 *BAA Ltd v Competition Commission* [2009] CAT 35, [2010] CompAR 23, paras 205–283.

[207] CC News Release 12/10, 24 February 2010.   [208] See www.competition-commission.org.uk.

[209] See eg *Evaluation strategy for market studies*, OFT 862, September 2006; OFT's *Positive Impact 2009/2010 – Consumer benefits of the OFT's work*, OFT 1251, July 2010; and *Understanding past market investigation remedies: Store Cards*, available at www.competition-commission.org.uk.

2010[210]. The OFT and CC are working together to speed up market investigation references[211] and share information more effectively[212].

10. Orders and Undertakings Under the Fair Trading Act 1973

The monopoly provisions in the Fair Trading Act 1973[213] were superseded by the market investigation provisions in the Enterprise Act 2002. Over the years the CC (or its predecessors) published a large number of reports dealing with many sectors of the economy and numerous practices. Many of these reports led to the Secretary of State accepting undertakings or, in some cases, making orders designed to remedy any competition problems identified. Despite the repeal of the substantive provisions of the Fair Trading Act some of these undertakings and orders remain in force[214].

The OFT maintains a *Register of orders and undertakings – market investigations and monopolies* containing details of orders and undertakings made under the Fair Trading Act (and the Enterprise Act): the register is accessible on the OFT's website[215]. The OFT has a continuing obligation to keep these orders and undertakings under review and may give advice to the Secretary of State and the CC as to whether their release, revocation, variation or termination is appropriate. The OFT has agreed a *Memorandum of Understanding* with the CC on undertakings and orders under the Fair Trading Act and Enterprise Act[216].

The 'undertakings in lieu' under section 159 of the Enterprise Act 2002 in the case of *Postal Franking Machines*[217] followed a review by the OFT of undertakings originally given under the Fair Trading Act. The market investigation references of *Classified Directory Advertising Services* and of *Groceries* followed the review of undertakings that had been given following Fair Trading Act investigations.

---

[210] *Quantification of CC Actions 2009/10*, para 22, available at www.competition-commission.org.uk.

[211] OFT Press Release 41/09, 8 April 2009.

[212] CC Corporate Plan 2009/10, work stream strategic objective 1.

[213] For an account of these provisions see *Halsbury's Laws of England*, vol 47 (Butterworths, 4th ed reissue, 2001), paras 116–125.

[214] Enterprise Act 2002, Sch 24, paras 14–18.

[215] The contents of the register are available to the public between 10.00 am and 4.00 pm on working days: see the OFT Register of Undertakings and Orders (Available Hours) Order 2003, SI 2003/1373.

[216] The *Memorandum* is available on the OFT's website: www.oft.gov.uk; see also OFT Press Release 15/09, 17 February 2009.

[217] See 'Undertakings in lieu of a reference to the CC', pp 475–476 above.

12

The international dimension of competition law

1. Introduction

This book so far has described the main provisions, other than those dealing with mergers[1], of EU and UK competition law, and the way in which those provisions are enforced. This chapter is concerned with an issue of growing importance: the international dimension of competition law.

Dramatic changes have taken place in the world's economies in a remarkably short period of time. State-controlled economies have been exposed to the principles of the market; legal monopolies have been reduced or entirely eliminated; and domestic markets have been increasingly opened up to foreign trade and investment. The World Trade Organization ('the WTO') performs a central role in promoting international trade. These developments present significant challenges for systems of competition law. The economic effects of cartels and anti-competitive behaviour on the part of firms with market power and of mergers are not constrained by national boundaries. It is perfectly possible for a few producers to operate a cartel that has significant effects throughout the world: the OPEC oil cartel is an obvious example of this, although there are both legal and political constraints that prevent competition authorities from tackling this particular organisation[2]. Many of the cartels investigated in recent years by the Department of Justice in the US and the European Commission in Brussels have had a wide geographical

---

[1] On mergers see chs 20–22.

[2] To the extent that the actors in this cartel are sovereign States as opposed to undertakings, the doctrine of sovereign immunity prevents the application of the EU competition rules: see ch 3, 'Undertakings and Associations of undertakings', pp 83–99 on the meaning of 'undertakings' in Articles 101 and 102; on sovereign immunity in US law see the Foreign Sovereign Immunity Act 1976, 28 USC §§1602–1611 (1988) and the joint Department of Justice and Federal Trade Commission *Antitrust Enforcement Guidelines for International Operations* (April 1995), para 3.31: these *Guidelines* can be accessed on the Department of Justice's website at www.justice.gov/atr/public/international/index.html; note also the position in the US on foreign sovereign compulsion, ibid, para 3.32, and the Act of State doctrine, ibid, para 3.33.

reach, the *Vitamins* and *Air Cargo* cartels being good examples of this[3]; non-US citizens responsible for unlawful cartels face the possibility of extradition to and imprisonment in the US. Undertakings such as Microsoft produce products, such as its computer operating system, that are truly global: Microsoft has been the subject of competition law investigations in several jurisdictions, including the US and the EU. International mergers, for example between car manufacturers, aluminium producers or telecommunications companies, may produce effects in a multitude of countries, and may be subject to notification to a large number of different competition authorities[4]. It is now common practice for competition authorities to cooperate closely with one another when they are conducting investigations that have an international dimension[5].

Until relatively recently the international component of competition law was predominantly concerned with the question of whether one country could apply its competition rules extraterritorially against an undertaking or undertakings in another country, where the latter behave in an anti-competitive manner having adverse effects in the territory of the former; and whether there should be laws (so-called 'blocking statutes') to prevent the 'excessive' assertion of extraterritorial jurisdiction. These issues are considered in sections 2 to 6 of this chapter. However the international dimension of competition law has undoubtedly evolved beyond these somewhat parochial concerns: the challenge today is to find ways in which to encourage cooperation between competition authorities and, so far as possible, foster convergence between competition policies, procedures and substantive analysis. The International Competition Network ('the ICN') was established in 2001 as an international forum for competition authorities to address these issues. The work of the ICN and other international organisations will be discussed briefly in section 7 of this chapter.

2. Extraterritoriality: Theory

The limits upon a State's jurisdictional competence – and therefore upon its ability to apply its competition laws to overseas undertakings – are matters of public international law[6]. There are two elements to a State's jurisdictional competence. First, a State has jurisdiction to make laws, that is to say to 'lay down general or individual rules through its legislative, executive or judicial bodies'[7]: this is known variously as a State's legislative, prescriptive or subject-matter jurisdiction. Secondly, a State has jurisdiction to enforce its laws, that is 'the power of a State to give effect to a general rule or an individual decision by means of substantive implementing measures which may include even coercion by the authorities'[8]: this is known as a State's enforcement jurisdiction. It is not necessarily the case that the limits of subject-matter and enforcement jurisdiction should be the same: they do not have to be coextensive. An assertion of subject-matter jurisdiction by one State over natural or legal

---

[3] See ch 13, 'The European Commission's Approach to Cartels', pp 517–521.

[4] See ch 20, 'The Proliferation of Systems of Merger Control', pp 812–813.

[5] On international cooperation see 'The Internationalisation of Competition Law', pp 506–511 below.

[6] For a general account of the relevant principles of public international law see Brownlie *Principles of Public International Law* (Clarendon Press, 7th ed, 2008), ch XV; see also Mann 'The Doctrine of Jurisdiction in International Law' (1964) 111 RDC 9; Akehurst 'Jurisdiction in International Law' (1972–73) 46 British Yearbook of International Law 145; Mann 'The Doctrine of International Jurisdiction Revisited' (1984) 186 RDC 18; Rosenthal and Knighton *National Laws and International Commerce: the Problem of Extraterritoriality* (1982); Lowe *Extraterritorial Jurisdiction* (1983); Olmstead *Extraterritorial Application of Laws and Responses Thereto* (1984).

[7] Per Advocate General Darmon in Cases 114/85 etc *A Ahlström Oy v Commission* (*Wood Pulp I*) [1988] ECR 5193, p 5217, [1988] 4 CMLR 901, p 923.

[8] Ibid.

persons in another may not lead to a conflict at all, provided that the former does not seek to enforce its law in the territory of another State. However when a State goes further and seeks enforcement – for example by serving a claim on a person located in another State or demanding the production of evidence there – the possibility of conflict is obvious. Most of the controversial conflicts between States in these matters have concerned enforcement rather than subject-matter jurisdiction, and it is essentially against enforcement measures that States have adopted blocking statutes[9]. An issue that has arisen in the US is whether it is possible to apply its competition law extraterritorially as a way of gaining access to foreign markets[10].

(A) Subject-matter jurisdiction

As far as subject-matter jurisdiction is concerned, it is generally accepted in public international law that a State has power to make laws affecting conduct within its territory (the 'territoriality principle') and to regulate the behaviour of its citizens abroad, citizens for this purpose including companies incorporated under its law (the 'nationality principle'). The territoriality principle has been extended in a logical way so that a State is recognised as having jurisdiction not only where acts originate in its territory (known as 'subjective territoriality'), but also where the objectionable conduct originates abroad but is completed within its territory ('objective territoriality'). The classic textbook illustration is of a shot being fired across a national boundary: although part of the conduct happened outside the State, it will have jurisdiction as the harmful event occurred within it. A consequence of this is that more than one State may assert jurisdiction in the same matter where the conduct in question straddles national borders. What is controversial is whether, in the area of economic law, it is legitimate to apply the idea of objective territoriality to the *effects* of an agreement entered into, or an anti-competitive act committed in, another State.

For the purpose of subject-matter jurisdiction the territoriality and nationality principles are sufficient to comprehend a great number of infringements of competition law, either because the overseas undertaking will have committed some act – for example taking over a competitor or charging predatory prices – within the territory of the State concerned to apply its law, or because an agreement will have been made between a foreign undertaking and a firm established within the State in question. Alternatively it may be that an act has been committed within that State by a subsidiary company of an overseas parent. In this case the question arises whether it is legitimate to treat the two companies as being in reality one economic entity, so that the conduct of the subsidiary can be considered to be that of the parent. If so the territoriality principle will suffice to establish jurisdiction over the parent company. The single economic entity doctrine is a significant feature of EU law[11].

However even the objective territoriality principle and the economic entity theory may not be sufficient to account for all cases in which a State may wish to assume jurisdiction over foreign undertakings. For example if all the producers of widgets in Japan were to agree not to export widgets to the UK, their agreement could obviously produce commercial effects in the UK; however it is hard to see how it can be meaningfully said

---

[9] See 'Resistance to Extraterritorial Application of Competition Law', pp 504–506 below.

[10] See 'The extraterritorial application of US competition law to gain access to foreign markets', pp 494–495 below.

[11] See ch 3, 'The "single economic entity" doctrine', pp 92–97 and 'The economic entity doctrine', pp 495–496 below.

that there is any conduct there. The controversial public international law question is whether a State may assert subject-matter jurisdiction simply on the basis that foreign undertakings produce commercial effects within its territory, even though they are not present there and have not committed any act there. The traditional principles of public international law are inadequate to deal with these issues, since they were developed with physical rather than economic conduct in mind. As a matter of logic, it does not seem absurd to suggest that harmful economic effects as well as physical ones emanating from another State ought in some cases to establish jurisdiction: it is not difficult to see the analogy between a shot being fired across the border of one State into a neighbouring one and a conspiracy by firms in one State to charge fixed and excessive prices or to boycott customers in another one. However some commentators reject the notion of jurisdiction based on effects alone, and the Government of the UK has consistently objected to the idea[12].

(B) Enforcement jurisdiction

Enforcement jurisdiction tends to give rise to the most acute conflicts between States[13]. It is generally recognised that even if subject-matter jurisdiction exists in relation to the conduct of someone in another State, it is improper to attempt to enforce the law in question within that State's territory without its permission. For these purposes enforcement does not mean only the exaction of penalties and the making of final orders such as perpetual injunctions, but refers to all authoritative acts such as the service of a summons, a demand for information or carrying out an investigation. Gathering information can be a particular problem for competition authorities: as business becomes increasingly global, the likelihood of a national authority requiring information which is located outside its jurisdiction increases correspondingly. A problem is that jurisdictional rules developed in the nineteenth century are not particularly well suited to the business context or the information technology of the twenty-first century.

Many legal systems contain provisions whereby States assist one another in relation to these matters. For example the Hague Convention on the Taking of Evidence Abroad in Civil or Commercial Matters[14] provides for one State to assist another in the gathering of evidence: this Convention is given effect in UK law by the Evidence (Proceedings in Other Jurisdictions) Act 1975. The recognition and enforcement of foreign judgments is an important part of private international law: most foreign judgments can be enforced in the UK[15], though not where they are penal[16]. However cooperation on evidence and the enforcement of judgments is often not provided by one State to another where the former takes exception to an attempt by the latter to assert its law extraterritorially, and most legal systems contain restrictions on the divulging by competition authorities of confidential information. Negotiations took place between the UK and the US for relaxation of these rules in so far as this might assist the pursuit of cartels; this led to an extension

---

[12] See Jennings 'Extraterritorial Jurisdiction and the United States Antitrust Laws' (1957) 33 British Yearbook of International Law 146; Higgins 'The Legal Bases of Jurisdiction' in Olmstead *Extraterritorial Application of Laws and Responses Thereto* (1984); Lowe pp 138–186; on the UK's position, see further 'The Extraterritorial Application of UK Competition Law', pp 501–504 below.

[13] See *Brownlie*, pp 310–312.   [14] Cmnd 3991 (1968).

[15] See Dicey, Morris and Collins *The Conflict of Laws* (Sweet & Maxwell, 14th ed, 2010), ch 15 and Cheshire, North and Fawcett *Private International Law* (Oxford University Press, 14th ed, 2008), ch 15.

[16] Treble damage awards in the US are probably penal: *British Airways Board v Laker Airways Ltd* [1984] QB 142 at 163 and, in the Court of Appeal, at 201 see also the Protection of Trading Interests Act 1980, s 5, which introduced a statutory prohibition on the enforcement of awards of multiple damages: 'Resistance to Extraterritorial Application of Competition Law', pp 504–506 below.

of the scope of the UK/US Mutual Assistance Treaty to criminal infringements of competition law[17]; requests for mutual assistance in criminal matters are the responsibility of the Home Office[18].

Part 9 of the Enterprise Act 2002 consolidates and codifies the powers of the Office of Fair Trading ('the OFT') to disclose information to overseas public authorities for the purpose (among other matters) of civil and criminal competition law investigations. Section 237 of the Act imposes a general restriction on the disclosure of information; however section 243 sets out circumstances in which, subject to conditions[19], information can be disclosed to an overseas competition authority. Information gathered by the OFT during a merger or market investigation cannot be disclosed[20], and the Secretary of State has power in certain circumstances to direct that information should not be disclosed[21].

3. The Extraterritorial Application of US Competition Law[22]

(A) The *Alcoa* and *Hartford Fire Insurance* cases

As has been mentioned, it is not clear that public international law permits jurisdiction to be taken on the basis of effects alone. However US law has undoubtedly embraced the 'effects doctrine'. In *United States v Aluminum Co of America*[23] (*Alcoa*) Judge Learned Hand said that:

> it is settled law…that any State may impose liabilities, even upon persons not within its allegiance, for conduct outside its borders which has consequences within its borders which the State reprehends; and these liabilities other States will ordinarily recognise[24].

The US courts had not always accepted this view[25]; the statement may not have been necessary to the case[26]; and as formulated the doctrine was extremely wide. However *Alcoa* was of seminal importance and triggered off much controversy between the US and other countries. There was some disagreement between US courts as to whether the effects on US commerce had to be substantial[27]; this was resolved by the Foreign Trade Antitrust Amendment Act 1982, which provides that the Sherman Act 1890[28] does not apply to conduct involving trade or commerce with foreign nations unless such conduct

---

[17] See *UK/US Mutual Legal Assistance Treaty* Cm 5375 (2001), accessible at www.fco.gov.uk; the UK is in negotiation with Australia, Canada and New Zealand with a view to signing memoranda of mutual assistance in respect of competition and consumer protection enforcement: see *The overseas disclosure of information*, OFT consultation paper 507, April 2003, para 4.26.

[18] For further information see the *Mutual Legal Assistance Guidelines: Obtaining assistance in the UK and Overseas* (8th ed, 2010), available at www.homeoffice.gov.uk.

[19] See in particular ss 243(6) and 244 of the Enterprise Act 2002.   [20] Ibid, s 243(3)(d).

[21] Ibid, s 243(4).

[22] See Waller *Competition Policy in the Global Economy* (Institute for Consumer Antitrust Studies: Online Case Book, 2007), ch 1, available at www.luc.edu/law/academics/special/center/antitrust/online_case_book.

[23] 148 F 2d 416 (2nd Cir 1945).   [24] Ibid at 444.

[25] See eg *American Banana Co v United Fruit Co* 213 US 347 (1909) in which the Supreme Court held that the Sherman Act did not apply to activities outside the US.

[26] It is arguable that there was conduct within the US since one of the firms involved in the alleged conspiracy, Aluminum Ltd of Canada, had its effective business headquarters in New York and was in the same group as the Aluminum Company of America.

[27] See eg *Industrie Siciliana Asfalti, Bitumi, SpA v Exxon Research & Engineering Co* 1977-1 Trade Case (CCH) (SDNY 1977) (no substantial effect required) and *Todhunter-Mitchell & Co Ltd v Anheuser-Busch* 383 F Supp 586 (ED Pa 1974) (requiring proof of a substantial effect).

[28] 15 USC §§ 1–7.

has a 'direct, substantial and foreseeable effect' on trade or commerce in the US[29]. The most recent Supreme Court judgment on extraterritoriality is *Hartford Fire Insurance Co v California*[30], where the Court repeated that jurisdiction could be taken over 'foreign conduct that was meant to produce and did in fact produce some substantial effect in the United States'. The joint Department of Justice/Federal Trade Commission *Antitrust Enforcement Guidelines for International Operations* ('the DoJ/FTC *International Guidelines*') of 1995[31] explain, by reference to a series of illustrative examples, how those enforcement agencies interpret the jurisdictional scope of US antitrust law in the light of these, and other, judgments.

An issue that has recently been litigated is whether a foreign plaintiff can sue for damages in a US court, even though the harm it suffered occurred outside the US. For plaintiffs this is an attractive prospect, given that damages actions are well established in the US, where damages can be trebled, contingency fees can be negotiated with legal advisers and unsuccessful plaintiffs do not have to pay the costs of successful defendants[32]. The question of access to US courts reached the Supreme Court in a case arising from the *Vitamins* cartel, *Hoffmann-la Roche v Empagran SA*[33]. The Court had to consider the application of the Foreign Trade Antitrust Amendment Act 1982, and concluded that, if the plaintiffs had suffered harm not in the US but in Ukraine, Panama, Australia and Ecuador, they could not sue in the US; the Court of Appeals for the District of Columbia subsequently concluded that the foreign plaintiffs could not recover damages in the US[34]. The Court was sensitive to the argument that over-exposure to treble damages claims in the US on the part of non-US plaintiffs might amount to a serious deterrent to members of cartels, for example in Europe or East Asia, making a whistleblowing application to local competition authorities: Germany, Canada and the US enforcement authorities had all submitted *amicus curiae* briefs, pointing out this danger to the Court. However an important feature of the Supreme Court judgment in *Empagran* is that it left open the question of whether the foreign plaintiffs could sue in the US if the foreign injury that they had suffered was inseparable from the domestic harm caused by the cartel to customers in the US[35]. In 2007 the Antitrust Modernization Commission recommended that purchases made outside the US from firms outside the US should not be deemed to give rise to the

---

[29]   15 USC § 6a.

[30]   509 US 764 (1993); for comment on this case see Roth 'Jurisdiction, British Public Policy and the US Supreme Court' (1994) 110 LQR 194; Robertson and Demetriou 'The Extraterritorial Application of US Antitrust Laws in the US Supreme Court' (1994) 43 ICLQ 417; also, by the same authors, 'US Extraterritorial Jurisdiction in Antitrust Matters: Recent Developments' (1995) 16 ECLR 461; Trenor 'Jurisdiction and the Extraterritorial Application of Antitrust Laws after *Hartford Fire*' (1995) 62 University of Chicago Law Review 1582; Waller 'From the Ashes of *Hartford Fire*: The Unanswered Questions of Comity' [1998] Fordham Corporate Law Institute (ed Hawk), ch 3; see also *United States v Nippon Paper* 109 F 3d 1 (1st Cir 1997), for comment on which see Reynolds, Sicilian and Wellman 'The Extraterritorial Application of the US Antitrust Laws to Criminal Conspiracies' (1998) 19 ECLR 151.

[31]   See ch 12 n 2, p 470 above; for commentary on the Guidelines see Griffin *US International Antitrust Enforcement: A Practical Guide to the Agencies' Guidelines* (Bureau of National Affairs, 1996).

[32]   On private enforcement of US antitrust law see Hovenkamp *Antitrust Enterprise: Principle and Execution* (Harvard University Press, 2006), ch 4; on private enforcement of competition law generally see ch 8 of this book.

[33]   544 US 155 (2004); for comment see Wurmnest 'Foreign Private Plaintiffs, Global Conspiracies, and the Extraterritorial Application of US Antitrust Law' (2005) 28(2) Hastings International and Comparative Law Review 205.

[34]   *Empagran SA v Hoffmann-la Roche Ltd* 417 F 3d 1267 (DC Cir 2005); see similarly *In re Monosodium Glutamate Antitrust Litigation* 477 F 3d 535 (8th Cir 2007) and *In re Dynamic Random Access Memory (DRAM) Antitrust Litigation* 538 F 3d 1107, 1109 (9th Cir 2008).

[35]   For an account of the case law after *Empagran* see Suhr 'Keeping the Door Ajar for Foreign Plaintiffs in Global Cartel Cases After Empagran' (2007) 105 Michigan Law Review 779.

requisite effects under the Foreign Trade Antitrust Amendment Act. This proposal had not been enacted as at 20 June 2011[36].

(B) Comity

Some US courts, drawing on the principle of judicial comity, have attempted to apply the effects doctrine in a relatively restrictive way, requiring not only that there should be a direct and substantial effect within the US, but also that the respective interests of the United States in asserting jurisdiction and of other States which might be offended by such assertion should be weighed against one another[37]. The origins of this approach can be traced back to Brewster's *Antitrust and American Business Abroad* in 1958 in which he called for a 'jurisdictional rule of reason'. The DoJ/FTC *International Guidelines* set out various factors relevant to comity analysis, including the relative significance to the alleged violation of conduct within the US, as compared to conduct abroad; the nationality of the persons involved or affected by the conduct; the presence or absence of an intention to affect US consumers, markets or exporters; and the relative significance and foreseeability of the effects on the US compared to the effects abroad[38]. Dealing with the problem of conflicts of jurisdiction by resort to the criterion of reasonableness has its critics, not least because a court hardly seems an appropriate forum in which to carry out such a delicate balancing process[39]. The principle of comity, however, is an important one which has been recognised in the EU by the General Court in *Gencor v Commission*[40] and in the dedicated cooperation agreements that the EU has entered into with the US, Canada, Japan and South Korea[41].

(C) Extraterritorial application of US antitrust law

The competition authorities in the US have had little compunction about enforcing their antitrust laws against overseas companies and have sometimes demanded, for example, that commercial documents located abroad should be handed over; the courts have even issued final orders requiring that foreign companies should change their commercial practices or restructure their industry[42]. An example of extraterritorial action in the US in relation to a foreign merger arose in the case of *Institut Mérieux*[43], where the Federal Trade Commission took action in respect of the acquisition by Institut Mérieux, a

---

[36] See Recommendation 42 of the Antitrust Modernisation Commission *Report and Recommendations* (April 2007), available at govinfo.library.unt.edu/amc; on international antitrust enforcement more generally see chapter II.D of the Report.

[37] See *Timberlane Lumber Co v Bank of America* 549 F 2d 597 (9th Cir 1976) and *Mannington Mills v Congoleum Corpn* 595 F 2d 1287 (3rd Cir 1979); for an account of this development see Fox 'Reasonableness and Extraterritoriality' [1986] Fordham Corporate Law Institute (ed Hawk), p 49.

[38] See the DoJ/FTC *International Guidelines*, para 3.2.

[39] See Judge Wilkey in *Laker Airways Ltd v Sabena* 731 F 2d 909 at 945–952 (DC Cir 1984), [1984] ECC 485; Rosenthal and Knighton *National Laws and International Commerce: the Problem of Extraterritoriality* (1982); Mann 'The Doctrine of International Jurisdiction Revisited After Twenty Years' (1984) 186 RDC 19.

[40] Case T-102/96 [1999] ECR II-753, [1999] 4 CMLR 971: see '*Gencor v Commission*', p 500 below.

[41] See 'The EU's dedicated cooperation agreements on competition policy', pp 493–495 below.

[42] See eg *United States v Imperial Chemical Industries Ltd* 105 F Supp 215 (SDNY 1952, p 509) where the US court ordered ICI to refrain from relying upon its patent rights under UK law: for the response, and other examples of the extraterritorial assertion of US law, see 'Resistance to Extraterritorial Application of Competition Law', pp 504–506 below.

[43] 55 Fed Reg 1614 (1990).

French company, of Connaught BioSciences, a Canadian company, because of perceived detriments to competition in the US in the market for anti-rabies vaccines[44].

The International Antitrust Enforcement Assistance Act 1994[45] is intended to improve the ability of the US enforcement agencies to obtain evidence located abroad by providing for reciprocal agreements to be entered between the US and other countries to facilitate the exchange of information, including confidential information. The US entered into an 'Antitrust Mutual Assistance Agreement' with Australia in 1999[46]. It is relevant also to note that certain violations of US antitrust law are criminal offences, and that it is possible for individuals to be sentenced to terms of imprisonment. There have been recent examples of foreign executives being required to serve terms of imprisonment in the US for violations of the antitrust rules[47].

(D) The extraterritorial application of US competition law to gain access to foreign markets

The antitrust laws in the US are applied not only to extraterritorial behaviour that affects imports into the US. Jurisdiction may also be asserted where US companies are obstructed by anti-competitive behaviour in their attempts to gain access to foreign markets. The so-called 'Structural Impediments Initiative'[48] in the US identified the lax enforcement of the Japanese Anti-Monopoly Act against Japanese undertakings as a contributing factor to the difficulties of US firms in expanding into Japanese markets; the Japanese Large Scale Retail Stores Act was considered to be an additional obstacle to would-be import-ers. The Department of Justice threatened to apply the US antitrust rules against Japanese restrictive practices having the effect of excluding US exporters from Japanese markets[49]. Subsequently the Japanese Government substantially increased the penalties that can be imposed for infringement of the Japanese legislation[50]. The first case in which the US challenged conduct abroad that denied foreign access was *US v Pilkington*[51]: the case was settled through a consent decree whereby Pilkington agreed not to enforce certain

---

[44] See Owen and Parisi 'International Mergers and Joint Ventures: a Federal Trade Commission Perspective' [1990] Fordham Corporate Law Institute (ed Hawk), ch 1 at pp 5–14.

[45] 15 USC §§ 6201–6212 (Supp 1995).

[46] See www.justice.gov/atr/public/international/int_arrangements.htm.

[47] See ch 13 n 21, p 516.

[48] See Lipsky 'Current Developments in Japanese Competition Law: Antimonopoly Act Enforcement Guidelines resulting from the Structural Impediments Initiative' (1991) 60 Antitrust LJ 279 and Anwar 'The Impact of the Structural Impediments Initiative on US–Japan Trade' (1992–93) 16(2) World Competition 53; see also the dispute between Eastman-Kodak and Fuji, which ended up as a complaint by the US to the disputes settlement body of the WTO, noted by Furse 'Competition Law and the WTO Report: "Japan – Measures Affecting Consumer Photographic Film and Paper"' (1999) 20 ECLR 9.

[49] See the Department of Justice's *Antitrust Enforcement Policy Regarding Anticompetitive Conduct that Restricts US Exports* 3 April 1992; see also Rill 'International Antitrust Policy – A Justice Department Perspective' [1991] Fordham Corporate Law Institute (ed Hawk), pp 29–43; Coppel 'A Question of Keiretsu: Extending the Long Arm of US Antitrust' (1992) 13 ECLR 192; Ohara 'The New US Policy on the Extraterritorial Application of Antitrust Laws, and Japan's Response' (1993–94) 17(3) World Competition 49; Davidow 'Application of US Antitrust Laws to *Keiretsu* Practices' (1994–95) 18(1) World Competition 5; Yamane and Seryo 'Restrictive Practices and Market Access in Japan – Has the JFTC been Effective in Eliminating Barriers in Distribution?' (1999) 22(2) World Competition 1.

[50] See Yamada 'Recent Developments of Competition Law and Policy in Japan' [1997] Fordham Corporate Law Institute (ed Hawk), ch 5; also by the same author 'Japanese antitrust law; recent developments and an agenda for the years ahead' (2011) 2(2) Journal of European Competition Law & Practice 165.

[51] (1994–2) Trade Cases (CCH) para 70,482 (1994); for comment see Byowitz 'The Unilateral Use of US Antitrust Laws to Achieve Foreign Market Access: A Pragmatic Assessment' [1996] Fordham Corporate Law Institute (ed Hawk), ch 3.

provisions in technology licences against US firms. The competition authorities in the US may also take action against foreign cartels that have no effect within the US, but that raise prices in relation to transactions where the US Government contributes more than half the funding[52].

4. The Extraterritorial Application of EU Competition Law[53]

Many non-EU undertakings have been held to have infringed the EU competition rules. The Court of Justice has not yet ruled specifically whether there is an effects doctrine under EU law, since it has always been possible in cases under Articles 101 and 102 to base jurisdiction on some other ground, such as the economic entity doctrine or the fact that an agreement entered into outside the European Union was implemented within it. In both the *Dyestuffs*[54] and *Wood Pulp*[55] cases the question of whether EU law should recognise the effects doctrine was argued at length, but the Court of Justice was able to avoid a pronouncement upon the issue since jurisdiction could be taken on other bases. The EU Merger Regulation ('the EUMR') has often been applied to mergers outside the EU; the General Court has given an important judgment on the territorial application of the EUMR in *Gencor v Commission*[56], but again without explicitly adopting the effects doctrine[57]. This section will deal with subject-matter and enforcement jurisdiction under Articles 101 and 102, and will then discuss the position under the EUMR.

(A) Subject-matter jurisdiction

Articles 101 and 102 apply only to the extent that an agreement or abuse has an appreciable effect upon inter-state trade. However there is no reason in principle why, for example, conduct by a US firm might not satisfy this test, particularly given the liberal way in which it has been applied[58]. In *Javico v Yves St Laurent*[59] the Court of Justice held that it was possible that an export ban imposed upon distributors in the Ukraine and Russia could infringe Article 101(1).

(i) The economic entity doctrine

In the *Dyestuffs* case[60] the Court of Justice developed the single economic entity doctrine. The Court came to the conclusion that Geigy, Sandoz and ICI, three non-EU undertakings, had participated in illegal price fixing within the EU through the medium of subsidiary companies located in the EU but under the control of non-EU parents. The Court was willing to go beyond the legal façade of the separate legal personalities of the parent and subsidiary companies, and to say that in reality each parent and subsidiary

---

[52] See the DoJ's Press Release of 18 August 2000 in relation to a construction cartel in Egypt.
[53] See Allen 'The Development of EC Antitrust Jurisdiction over Alien Undertakings' [1974] 2 LIEI 35; Kuyper 'European Community Law and Extraterritoriality: Some Trends and Recent Developments' (1984) 33 ICLQ 1013; Slot and Grabandt 'Extraterritoriality and Jurisdiction' (1986) 23 CML Rev 544; Brittan 'Jurisdictional Issues in EC Competition Policy' in *Merger Control in the Single European Market* (Grotius Publications, 1991).
[54] Cases 48/69 etc *ICI v Commission* [1972] ECR 619, [1972] CMLR 557.
[55] Cases 114/85 etc *A Ahlström Oy v Commission* [1988] ECR 5193, [1988] 4 CMLR 901.
[56] Case T-102/96 [1999] ECR II-753, [1999] 4 CMLR 971.
[57] See 'EU Merger Regulation', pp 499–500 below.
[58] See ch 3, 'The Effect on Trade between Member States', pp 144–149.
[59] Case C-306/96 [1998] ECR I-1983, [1998] 5 CMLR 172.   [60] See ch 12 n 54 above.

formed one economic entity. This approach was criticised, not only because of the refusal to respect the independent legal personalities of the companies concerned, but also because the Court seemed prepared to hold that a parent controlled its subsidiary on limited evidence[61]; however the single economic entity doctrine is now undoubtedly a part of EU competition law. The EU Courts and the Commission have relied on the economic entity approach on a number of subsequent occasions, both in the subject-matter and enforcement jurisdiction contexts[62]. The crucial issue is whether the parent exercises decisive influence over the conduct of its subsidiary, for which purpose the size of the shareholding, the representation on the board of directors of the subsidiary, the ability to influence the latter's affairs and actual evidence of attempts to do so will all be relevant[63]. A consequence of the economic entity doctrine is that a claimant may be able to bring an action in the English courts against a UK subsidiary of a foreign parent that participated in an agreement contrary to Article 101 TFEU[64].

(ii) Does EU law recognise the effects doctrine?

Many of the Commission's decisions have involved and been addressed to non-EU undertakings[65], but in every case the non-EU firm, either itself or through a subsidiary company[66], entered into an agreement with an EU undertaking[67] or committed some act within the EU. In other words jurisdiction in these cases did not depend upon the existence in EU law of an effects doctrine, since it could be explained in more orthodox ways. The Commission has quite often asserted that EU law does indeed recognise the effects doctrine[68], and this belief was supported by Advocate General Mayras in the *Dyestuffs* case[69] and by Advocate General Darmon in *Wood Pulp*[70]; other Advocates General have also appeared to support this view[71]. However there has been no definitive statement from the Court of Justice on this issue.

(iii) The Court of Justice's judgment in *Wood Pulp*

Against this background the appeal to the Court of Justice against the Commission's decision in *Wood Pulp*[72] was eagerly awaited. The Commission, in finding that there was a concerted practice between undertakings in several non-EU countries, had held that

---

[61] On *Dyestuffs* see Mann 'The Dyestuffs Case in the Court of Justice of the European Communities' (1973) 22 ICLQ 35; Acevedo 'The EC Dyestuffs Case: Territorial Jurisdiction' (1973) 36 MLR 317.

[62] The doctrine may be used to overcome any perceived difficulty in sending a decision to a company in a non-EU State by serving it instead on the EU subsidiary.

[63] See ch 3, 'Parent and subsidiary', pp 93–97.

[64] See *Provimi Ltd v Aventis Animal Nutrition SA* [2003] EWHC 961, [2003] UKCLR 493; the *Provimi* case, which may have been incorrectly decided, is discussed in ch 8, 'Private international law', pp 308–309.

[65] See eg *Genuine Vegetable Parchments Association* OJ [1978] L 70/54, [1978] 1 CMLR 534; *Zinc Producer Group* OJ [1984] L 220/27, [1985] 2 CMLR 108; *Associated Lead Manufacturers* OJ [1979] L 21/16, [1979] 1 CMLR 464; *Cast Iron and Steel Rolls* OJ [1983] L 317/1, [1984] 1 CMLR 694; in each of these cases a non-EU firm was fined.

[66] See eg *Johnson and Johnson* OJ [1980] L 377/16, [1981] 2 CMLR 287.

[67] See eg *French-Japanese Ballbearings* OJ [1974] L 343/19, [1975] 1 CMLR D8; *Franco-Taiwanese Mushroom Packers* OJ [1975] L 29/26, [1975] 1 CMLR D83.

[68] See eg the Commission's XIth *Report on Competition Policy* (1981), points 34–42; the Commission's decisions in *Wood Pulp* OJ [1985] L 85/1, [1985] 3 CMLR 474 and *Aluminum Products* OJ [1985] L 92/1, [1987] 3 CMLR 813 were explicitly adopted on the basis of the effects doctrine.

[69] Cases 48/69 etc [1972] ECR 619, pp 687–694, [1972] CMLR 557, pp 593–609.

[70] Cases 114/85 etc *A Ahlström Oy v Commission* [1988] ECR 5193, p 5227, [1988] 4 CMLR 901, p 932.

[71] See eg Advocate General Roemer in Case 6/72 *Continental Can v Commission* [1973] ECR 215, [1972] CMLR 690; Advocate General Warner in Cases 6 and 7/73 *Commercial Solvents v Commission* [1974] ECR 223, [1974] 1 CMLR 309.

[72] OJ [1985] L 85/1, [1985] 3 CMLR 474.

jurisdiction could be based on the effects of the concerted practice in the EU. However the Court of Justice, no doubt keen to avoid the adoption of this controversial doctrine if possible, concluded that the case could be settled by reference to conventional public international law criteria. It held[73] that, on the facts of the case, the agreement had been *implemented* within the EU; it was immaterial for this purpose whether this implementation was effected by subsidiaries, agents, sub-agents or branches within the EU. Since the agreement was implemented within the EU, it was unnecessary to have recourse to the effects doctrine: the universally recognised territoriality principle was sufficient to deal with the matter. The Commission expressly cited the *Wood Pulp* judgment in *Amino Acids*, where it imposed fines on a cartel including US, Japanese and Korean companies[74]. The Court of Justice in *Wood Pulp* did not comment on what the position would have been if the agreement had been formed *and implemented* outside the EU, but had produced economic effects within it; an example would be a collective boycott by members of a non-EU cartel, whereby they refuse to supply customers within the EU: could one argue in such circumstances that this agreement is 'implemented' within the EU by the refusal to supply there? Linguistically this seems hard to sustain; however there is no doubt in this situation that the *effects* of the agreement would be felt within the EU. This issue is unresolved[75]. However there will be relatively few cases in which the pure effects doctrine is crucial in jurisdictional terms: in most cases the economic entity doctrine or the reasoning of the Court of Justice in *Wood Pulp* will be sufficient to establish jurisdiction. In its decision on *Gas Insulated Switchgear*[76] the Commission imposed fines of €750 million on a number of European and Japanese undertakings for bid-rigging and related practices in relation to switchgear: in essence, the European undertakings would stay out of the Asian market and the Japanese undertakings would not operate in Europe. The Commission reached the conclusion that Article 101(1) was infringed without resorting to the effects doctrine.

(B) Enforcement jurisdiction

(i) Initiating proceedings

Where proceedings are started by the Commission under Article 101 or 102, Article 2(2) of Regulation 773/2004[77] requires that the undertakings concerned must be informed. If the undertaking cannot be served within the EU, the question arises whether a statement of objections may be sent to it abroad. As suggested above this could be considered to contravene public international law, since it amounts to an enforcement of one State's law in the territory of another[78]. However the Court of Justice has rejected the notion

---

[73] Cases 114/85 etc *A Ahlström Oy v Commission* [1988] ECR 5193, [1988] 4 CMLR 901, paras 11–23; for comment see Ferry 'Towards Completing the Charm: the *Wood Pulp* Judgment' (1989) 11 EIPR 19; Mann 'The Public International Law of Restrictive Trade Practices in the European Court of Justice' (1989) 38 ICLQ 375; Lowe 'International Law and the Effects Doctrine in the European Court of Justice' (1989) 48 CLJ 9; Christoforou and Rockwell 'EC Law: the Territorial Scope of Application of EC Antitrust Law – the *Wood Pulp* Judgment' (1989) 30 Harvard International Law Journal 195; Lange and Sandage 'The *Wood Pulp* Decision and its Implications for the Scope of EC Competition Law' (1989) 26 CML Rev 137; Van Gerven 'EC Jurisdiction in Antitrust Matters: the *Wood Pulp* Judgment' [1989] Fordham Corporate Law Institute (ed Hawk), ch 21.

[74] OJ [2001] L 152/24, [2001] 5 CMLR 322, para 182.

[75] The Commission's *Guidelines on the effect on trade concept contained in Articles [101 and 102 TFEU]* OJ [2004] C 101/81, cite the *Gencor* case, discussed under the EUMR below, as authority for the effects doctrine, but this is a questionable interpretation of that judgment.

[76] Commission decision of 24 January 2007.

[77] OJ [2004] L 123/18.

[78] The *initiation* of proceedings is unlikely to be an issue of enforcement, as it is not in itself a coercive act.

that service without the consent of the foreign State is invalid and vitiates the proceedings. Provided that the non-EU undertaking has received the statement of objections in circumstances which enabled it to take cognisance of the case against it, the service is valid. In *Geigy v Commission*[79] the Commission sent its statement of objections to Geigy's Swiss offices. Geigy returned it, acting on instructions from the Swiss authorities, claiming that the service was unlawful both under internal and public international law. The Court of Justice rejected this. It is sufficient for EU law purposes, therefore, for the Commission to send a registered letter to the non-EU undertaking concerned.

(ii) Information and investigations

The Court of Justice has not been called upon to consider the extent to which the Commission may require information from or conduct investigations of undertakings abroad under Articles 18 and 20 respectively of Regulation 1/2003[80]. There would seem to be little objection to the Commission simply asking for information under Article 18(2), there being no compulsion to comply with such a request; in practice the Commission does send Article 18(2) requests to non-EU undertakings. It is less certain whether the Commission can make a demand for information under Article 18(3) of the Regulation, and the better view is that this is not possible.

It is inconceivable that Article 20 entitles the Commission to carry out an investigation abroad unless it has the authority of the State concerned. However the fact that the Commission intends to investigate a trade association within the EU which represents non-EU undertakings does not entitle that association to refuse to submit to the investigation[81]; and if the Commission carries out an investigation in a new Member State of the EU and discovers information relating to infringements carried out by undertakings prior to that State's accession to the EU, the Commission is entitled to take that information into account[82]. The Commission will not be sympathetic to the argument that a non-EU undertaking is unable to provide it with information because of some constraint imposed upon it by its domestic law[83].

(iii) Final decisions

Two problems arise in relation to the adoption of final decisions. First, there is the problem of whether a final decision, for example finding an infringement of the competition rules and imposing penalties, may be served on non-EU undertakings. This is more an act of enforcement than merely serving a statement of objections, and so is more open to objection in terms of public international law. For this reason the Commission will often look to serve the decision on a subsidiary within the EU, as it did in the *Dyestuffs* cases, or seek the assistance of the foreign State concerned[84]. However the Court of Justice has held

---

[79] See Case 52/69 [1972] ECR 787, [1972] CMLR 557 (one of the *Dyestuffs* cases).

[80] OJ [2003] L 1/1, [2003] 4 CMLR 551: on the conduct of Commission investigations see ch 7, 'Chapter V: powers of investigation', pp 267–275; in Case 27/76 *United Brands Continental BV v Commission* [1978] ECR 207, [1978] 1 CMLR 429 the Court of Justice suggested at one point that the Commission might have obtained some information which it needed from United Brands; however United Brands had subsidiaries within the EU, so that it cannot be deduced from this remark that the Court was advocating extraterritorial requests for information under Article 11(3) of Regulation 17, the predecessor of Regulation 1/2003.

[81] *Ukwal* OJ [1992] L 121/45 [1993] 5 CMLR 632.

[82] Cases 97–99/87 *Dow Chemical Ibérica SA v Commission* [1989] ECR 3165, [1991] 4 CMLR 410, paras 61–65; this has been an issue in the course of a Commission investigation of Slovak Telekom's behaviour under Article 102: Case T-458/09 and Case T-171/10 *Slovak Telekom v Commission*, not yet decided.

[83] See *Centraal Stikstof Verkoopkantoor (CSV)* OJ [1976] L 192/27.

[84] In the *Dyestuffs* cases the Commission tried in the first place to serve the final decision on the non-EU undertakings by using diplomatic channels; only when this failed did it serve the EU subsidiaries.

that service direct upon the non-EU undertaking is valid provided that, as in the case of a statement of objections, it reaches the undertaking and enables it to take cognisance of it; it is no defence that the undertaking received the decision and sent it back without reading it[85].

The second problem is whether it is possible for the final decision to include orders against and impose penalties upon a non-EU undertaking. It is clear that the Court of Justice does not object to orders being made against foreign undertakings[86], although it is recognised by both the Commission and the EU Courts that it would not be possible actually to enforce the order in the territory of a foreign State. It would, however, be possible to seize any assets that were present within the EU.

(C) **EU Merger Regulation**

(i) **The jurisdictional criteria in the EUMR**

Under Article 1(2) of the EUMR[87] concentrations that have a Community dimension must be pre-notified to the Commission in Brussels. Concentrations have a Community dimension where the combined turnover of the undertakings involved exceeds €5,000 million worldwide, provided that at least two of the undertakings have a turnover within the EU of at least €250 million and that their business is not primarily within one and the same Member State[88]; Article 1(3) of the EUMR contains an alternative set of jurisdictional criteria in an attempt to deal with the problem of multiple notification to Member States. The jurisdictional criteria in the EUMR clearly mean that concentrations involving undertakings which conduct a substantial proportion of their business outside the EU, or which involve transactions far removed physically from the EU, may, nevertheless, have a Community dimension. Countless numbers of concentrations that have little or no effect within the EU have to be notified because of the way in which the thresholds in the EUMR operate. For example a joint venture between two substantial undertakings that brings about a merger of their widget businesses in Thailand could be notifiable under the EUMR, even though the joint venture will have no presence or effect on the EU market, if the parents exceed the turnover thresholds in Article 1. Cases such as this may, however, benefit from the simplified procedure used for the speedy disposal of some notifications under the EUMR[89].

---

[85] See Case 6/72 *Europemballage and Continental Can v Commission* [1973] ECR 215, [1973] CMLR 199.

[86] See eg Cases 6 and 7/73 *Istituto Chemioterapico Italiano Spa and Commercial Solvents Corp v Commission* [1974] ECR 223, [1974] 1 CMLR 309 where the Court of Justice upheld the Commission's order that supplies to Zoja be resumed; this would clearly affect CSC in the US; see also *Warner-Lambert/Gillette* OJ [1993] L 116/21, [1993] 5 CMLR 559, where the Commission ordered Gillette, a US company, to reassign trade marks in third countries to Eemland Holdings NV in order to remove distortions of competition within the EU; the decision was not appealed.

[87] See ch 21 for a general discussion of this Regulation.

[88] The thresholds are considered in detail in ch 21, 'Article 1: concentrations having a Community dimension', pp 839–844.

[89] See the Commission's *Notice on a simplified procedure for treatment of certain concentrations under Council Regulation (EC) No 139/2004* OJ [2005] C 56/04; this procedure is explained briefly in ch 21, 'Notifications', p 857; for discussion generally of the application of the EUMR to non-EU concentrations see Ezrachi 'Limitations on the Extraterritorial Reach of the European Merger Regulation' (2001) 22 ECLR 137.

(ii) *Gencor v Commission*

In *Gencor/Lonrho*[90] the Commission prohibited a merger between two South African undertakings on the basis that it would have created a dominant duopoly (collective dominance) in the platinum and rhodium markets, as a result of which effective competition would be significantly impeded in the common market. Gencor appealed to the General Court, *inter alia* on the ground that the Commission did not have jurisdiction under the EUMR to prohibit activities in South Africa which, furthermore, the Government there had approved. In *Gencor v Commission*[91] the General Court upheld the Commission's decision, and reviewed at some length the jurisdictional position[92]. The Court's findings on jurisdiction were divided into two parts, first an assessment of the territorial scope of the EUMR[93] and second a consideration of the compatibility of the Commission's decision with public international law[94]. As to the former, the General Court noted that the parties to the merger exceeded the turnover thresholds in Article 1(2) of the EUMR. It acknowledged that recital 11 of the Regulation required that the parties should have substantial operations in the EU, but stated that these operations could as well consist of sales as production. The Court added that the *Wood Pulp* judgment, requiring 'implementation' within the EU, did not contradict the Commission's assertion of jurisdiction in this case: indeed the requirement in Article 1(2) of the EUMR, that the parties should have turnover in excess of €250 million within the Community, was consistent with the *Wood Pulp* judgment, since it meant that they must have acted in some way on the EU market.

On the issue of public international law, the General Court said that application of the EUMR is justified under public international law where it is foreseeable that a proposed concentration will have an immediate and substantial effect in the EU[95]. The Court's view was that these criteria were satisfied, but went on to consider whether the exercise of jurisdiction in this case 'violated a principle of non-interference or the principle of proportionality'[96]: in other words it acknowledged that comity analysis should be undertaken when applying the EUMR. The Court's view was that neither principle was violated, so that there was no jurisdictional objection to the Commission's decision.

Clearly this judgment is of considerable significance. It will be noted that the General Court did not adopt an effects doctrine as a matter of EU law, since it determined the Commission's subject-matter jurisdiction on the basis of the turnover thresholds in the EUMR and equated them to the 'implementation doctrine' in *Wood Pulp*; rather the General Court considered the effects of the merger, and the possible comity objections to jurisdiction, as a matter of public international law. As in the case of the Court of Justice's judgments in *Dyestuffs* and *Wood Pulp*, the General Court avoided the adoption of the effects doctrine. In practice, of course, the Commission could have great problems in enforcing a prohibition decision against non-EU undertakings which are unwilling to cooperate and which are protected by their national Governments. However the Commission works very closely with the competition authorities in other jurisdictions, and in particular with the Department of Justice and the Federal Trade Commission in the US, in order to try to prevent serious conflicts breaking out[97].

---

[90] OJ [1997] L 11/30, [1999] 4 CMLR 1076.
[91] Case T-102/96 [1999] ECR II-753, [1999] 4 CMLR 971; for comment see Fox 'The Merger Regulation and Its Territorial Reach: *Gencor Ltd v Commission*' (1999) 20 ECLR 334.
[92] Case T-102/96 [1999] ECR II-753, [1999] 4 CMLR 971, paras 48–111.   [93] Ibid, paras 78–88.
[94] Ibid, paras 89–111.   [95] Ibid, para 90.   [96] Ibid, para 102.
[97] See further 'The EU's dedicated cooperation agreements on competition policy', p 509 below.

5. The Extraterritorial Application of UK Competition Law

The view has always been taken in the UK that jurisdiction cannot be based simply upon commercial effects, but that the territoriality and nationality principles alone are applicable in this area. This is clearly stated in the Aide-Memoire which the UK Government submitted to the Court of Justice following the Commission's decision in *Dyestuffs*[98], and is further illustrated by the Protection of Trading Interests Act 1980 which is considered later in this chapter. The submissions of the UK Government in the *Wood Pulp* case maintained its traditional hostility to the effects doctrine. The domestic competition statutes do not always deal explicitly with jurisdictional issues, but, even where they do not do so, in practice they are not applied extraterritorially on the basis of effects.

(A) **Competition Act 1998**

(i) **Chapter I prohibition**

The Chapter I prohibition in the Competition Act 1998 has been discussed in chapter 9[99]. On the issue of jurisdiction section 2(1), which contains the Chapter I prohibition, provides that an agreement will be caught only where it may affect trade and competition within the UK. This in itself does not answer the jurisdictional issue of whether the Act is applicable to undertakings that are located outside the UK. The answer to this question is given by section 2(3), which provides that:

> Subsection (1) applies only if the agreement, decision or practice is, or is intended to be, implemented in the UK.

Section 2(3) is specifically intended to give legislative effect in the UK to the 'implementation doctrine' espoused by the Court of Justice in the *Wood Pulp* case[100]. This is a sensible resolution on the part of the Government: as already mentioned, the *Wood Pulp* doctrine falls short of being an 'effects doctrine', with the result that section 2(3) does not amount to a reversal of the traditional attitude of the UK described above. At the same time, the Competition Act is able to adopt a position in relation to jurisdiction which is consistent with EU law as set out in *Wood Pulp*. It follows that agreements implemented in the UK by non-UK undertakings would be caught by the Chapter I prohibition, provided that they meet all the other requirements of that prohibition. What would be interesting in the future would be a situation in which the Court of Justice extends the jurisdictional reach of the EU competition rules to include an effects doctrine. In such a situation the basic rule in section 60(2) of the Competition Act, that there should be no inconsistency between interpretation of the UK legislation and the principles laid down in the Treaty and by the EU Courts, would suggest that the UK should adopt the effects doctrine. However section 60(1) specifically provides that consistency must be achieved, 'having regard to any relevant differences between the provisions concerned'[101]. Presumably this would be a situation in which the explicit wording of section 2(3) would indicate a 'relevant differ-

---

[98] Cases 48/69 etc *ICI Ltd v Commission* [1972] ECR 619, [1972] CMLR 557. The Aide-Memoire is produced in full in *Lowe* pp 144–147; details are given there of various diplomatic exchanges between the US and UK Governments on jurisdictional conflicts and other expressions of the UK's views at pp 147–186; see also the UK Government's Amicus Curiae brief in *Washington Public Power Supply System v Western Nuclear Inc* [1983] ECC 261.

[99] See ch 9, 'The Chapter I Prohibition', pp 333–360.

[100] HL Committee, 13 November 1997, col 261 (Lord Simon of Highbury).

[101] See ch 9, '"Governing Principles Clause": Section 60 of the Competition Act 1998', pp 369–374.

ence' between the Competition Act and the new case law of the EU Courts, with the consequence that the UK competition authorities and courts would not be required under the Act to adopt the effects doctrine. An intriguing twist, following Regulation 1/2003, would arise if the OFT was investigating a case in which Article 101 (or Article 102) was involved: presumably then it would be required to apply EU law, including any newly-embraced effects doctrine.

The OFT's guidelines on the Competition Act are silent on the issue of extraterritoriality, which perhaps is itself indicative of the delicate and complex nature of this issue.

(ii) Chapter II prohibition

The Chapter II prohibition has also been discussed in chapter 9[102]. There is no mention of extraterritorial application in section 18, which sets out the Chapter II prohibition, and in particular there is no equivalent of section 2(3) which limits the ambit of the Chapter I prohibition to agreements that are implemented in the UK. Section 18(3) does require that the dominant position must be within the UK. In the debate during the passage of the Bill Lord Simon explained that this would not be the case if the market in which the dominant position is held was entirely outside the UK; however there could be a case in which the dominant position extends beyond the UK, provided that it includes some part of the UK territory[103].

An interesting question is whether the Chapter II prohibition would apply in a case where the dominant position is (wholly or partly) within the UK but the abuse occurs in a related market outside the UK, or its effects are felt entirely outside the UK (for example a refusal by a UK company to supply an overseas customer). Here the requirement that trade must be affected within the UK would come into play and determine whether the prohibition applies.

In *Aberdeen Journals v OFT*[104] the CAT held that the requirement of an effect on trade within the UK is not subject to a requirement of appreciability[105], although the correctness of this conclusion has been doubted in subsequent cases[106].

(B) Enterprise Act 2002

(i) Market investigations[107]

As far as subject-matter jurisdiction is concerned, the OFT (or sectoral regulator) may make a market investigation reference to the Competition Commission ('the CC') where it has reasonable grounds for suspecting that one or more features of a market in the United Kingdom for goods or services prevent, restrict or distort competition there or in a part of it. Section 131(6) provides that a 'market in the United Kingdom' includes a market which operates there and in another country or territory or in a part of another country or territory ('supra-national markets')[108] and any market which operates only in a part of the United Kingdom ('sub-national markets')[109]. Where the geographical market is wider than the UK, the reference to the CC would be concerned only with the UK part

---

[102] See ch 9, 'The Chapter II Prohibition', pp 360–369.
[103] HL Third Reading, 5 March 1998, col 1336 (Lord Simon of Highbury).
[104] Case No 1009/1/1/02 [2003] CAT 11, [2003] CompAR 67.
[105] Ibid, paras 459–461: see ch 9, 'Applicable law and territorial scope', p 345.
[106] See ch 9, 'Having regard to any relevant differences', pp 370–371.
[107] The market investigation provisions of the Enterprise Act 2002 are described in ch 11.
[108] Enterprise Act 2002, s 131(6)(a).   [109] Ibid, s 131(6)(b).

of it[110]. In determining whether to exercise its discretion to make a reference, the OFT will consider whether an effective remedy might be available to cure any competition problems: where the relevant market is global, or at least much wider than the UK, it may be that a remedy that applied only to the UK would have little discernible impact on the competition problem there, in which case a reference would not be made[111].

As far as enforcement jurisdiction is concerned, the OFT has power to obtain information under section 174 of the Enterprise Act 2002, and the CC has power to do so under section 176[112]. The Act is silent on the territorial scope of these provisions, as is the guidance issued by each of these bodies on market investigations[113]. It is thought to be unlikely that either the OFT or the CC would seek to exercise these powers against persons or undertakings with no presence in the UK. As far as remedies are concerned, sections 154 to 161 set out a number of possibilities, ranging from the acceptance by the OFT of undertakings in lieu of a reference to the making by the CC of final orders, using the powers provided by Schedule 8 to the Act. Again, the Act is silent as to the territorial scope of these powers, but it is assumed that they are not available extraterritorially[114].

(ii) Mergers[115]

As far as subject-matter jurisdiction is concerned, sections 22(1) and 33(1) of the Enterprise Act provide that merger references may be made to the CC where a relevant merger situation has been or would be created, and where that situation has resulted or would result in 'a substantial lessening of competition within any market or markets in the United Kingdom for goods or services'. As in the case of market investigations, section 22(6) provides that a 'market in the United Kingdom' includes supra-national[116] and sub-national markets[117]. Further jurisdictional requirements for the application of domestic merger control are that the value of the turnover of the enterprise being acquired amounts to more than £70 million in the UK[118] or that the 25 per cent 'share of supply' test is satisfied in the UK or in a substantial part of it[119]. The OFT's *Jurisdictional and procedural guidance* states that these requirements apply equally to non-UK companies that sell to (or acquire from) UK customers or suppliers[120].

As far as enforcement jurisdiction is concerned, section 31 of the Enterprise Act gives the OFT the power to obtain information in relation to completed mergers and the CC has investigatory powers under section 109. The Act is silent on the extraterritorial application of these provisions and, as in the case of market investigations, it is thought that they would not be used against persons or undertakings with no presence in the UK. The remedies available in merger cases are set out in sections 71 to 95 of the Act. Section 86(1) of the Act provides that an enforcement order may extend to a person's conduct outside the United Kingdom if (and only if) he is a UK national, a body incorporated under UK law or a person carrying on business within the UK; a similar limitation is found in relation to restrictions on share dealings[121].

---

[110] *Market investigation references: Guidance about the making of references under Part 4 of the Enterprise Act*, OFT 511, March 2006, para 4.11.

[111] Ibid, para 2.30.   [112] See ch 11, 'Powers of investigation', p 477.

[113] *Market investigation references: Guidance about the making of references under Part 4 of the Enterprise Act*, OFT 511, March 2006; *Market Investigation References: Competition Commission Guidelines*, CC 3, June 2003.

[114] OFT 511, March 2006, para 2.30, seems to make this assumption.

[115] The merger provisions of the Enterprise Act 2002 are described in ch 22.

[116] Enterprise Act 2002, s 22(6)(a).   [117] Ibid, s 22(6)(b).   [118] Ibid, s 23(1).

[119] Ibid, s 23(2)–(4).

[120] OFT 527, June 2009, para 3.4.   [121] Enterprise Act 2002, ss 77(7) and 78(5).

(iii) The cartel offence

The cartel offence in section 188 of the Enterprise Act is committed only where the agreement is implemented in whole or in part in the UK[122]. Subject to that, individuals guilty of the cartel offence would be liable to a fine and/or imprisonment, irrespective of their domicile or place of residence. An important additional point is that the Extradition Act 2003 makes provision for the possibility of extradition from or to the UK[123].

6. Resistance to Extraterritorial Application of Competition Law

(A) Introduction

The *Alcoa*[124] case triggered off a number of battles between the US and other States which objected to the extraterritorial application of US antitrust laws[125]. Apart from diplomatic protests, several countries have passed 'blocking statutes', whereby they attempt to thwart excessive assumptions of jurisdiction[126]. There are no provisions in EU law which have this effect: instead this is essentially a matter for the Governments of individual Member States. The UK has taken a consistently hostile view of US practice, which culminated in the Protection of Trading Interests Act 1980[127].

The earliest attempt made by the UK Government to prevent the extraterritorial application of US law came in 1952[128]; thereafter it secured the passage of the Shipping Contracts and Commercial Documents Act 1964, the provisions of which were used on several occasions to prevent disclosure of information to US authorities[129]. The courts in the UK have also objected to US practice. In *British Nylon Spinners v ICI*[130] the Court of Appeal ordered ICI not to comply with a court order in the US, requiring it to reassign certain patents to Du Pont; the US court considered that the parties were dividing the market horizontally. In *Rio Tinto Zinc v Westinghouse Electric Corpn*[131] the House of Lords declined to assist in the process of discovery in a US court, investigating an alleged uranium cartel, where it considered that the information so acquired would subsequently be used for an improper assertion of extraterritorial jurisdiction. The UK courts are obliged by the Evidence (Proceedings in Other Jurisdictions) Act 1975 to assist

---

[122] (Enterprise Act 2002, s 190(3); see ch 10, 'The cartel offence', pp 425–434.

[123] See ch 10, 'Extradition', p 433; note that in *Norris v Government of the USA* [2008] UKHL 16, [2008] 1 AC 920, the House of Lords concluded that 'mere' price fixing did not amount to criminal conspiracy to defraud at common law, with the result that he could not be extradited on that basis (his alleged infringement predated the entry into force of the provisions of the Enterprise Act); note also that Mr Norris was extradited for a different reason – that he had obstructed the course of justice – and that for this he was sentenced in the US to a term of 18 months in jail: see Department of Justice Press Release of 10 December 2010, available at www.justice.gov/atr/index.html.

[124] See 'The *Alcoa* and *Hartford Fire Insurance* cases', pp 491–493 above.

[125] See Griffin 'Foreign Governmental Reactions to US Assertions of Extraterritorial Jurisdiction' (1998) 19 ECLR 64, and the references in n 1 thereof.

[126] See *Lowe*, pp 79ff where he lists the many blocking statutes that have been passed; further blocking statutes have been passed since then.

[127] For similar statutes in Australia and Canada see respectively the Foreign Antitrust Judgment (Restriction of Enforcement) Act 1979 and the Foreign Extraterritorial Measures Act 1985.

[128] See *Lowe*, pp 138–139.   [129] Ibid, pp 139–143.

[130] [1955] Ch 37, [1954] 3 All ER 88 and [1953] Ch 19, [1952] 2 All ER 780.

[131] [1978] AC 547, [1978] 1 All ER 434.

in requests for discovery by foreign courts[132]. However the Act provides exceptions to this obligation, and the House of Lords (now the Supreme Court) considered that this case fell within these exceptions for two reasons: first, because the request for information was in reality a 'fishing expedition' without merit; and secondly, because Rio Tinto might incriminate itself under EU competition law by divulging the documents sought.

The 1975 Act did not allow a court to resist a request for information simply because the foreign court was making a claim to extraterritorial jurisdiction; this is now dealt with by section 4 of the Protection of Trading Interests Act 1980 (below). At common law a UK court has discretion to order a litigant to restrain foreign proceedings which are oppressive: in *Midland Bank plc v Laker Airways plc*[133] the Court of Appeal ordered Laker to discontinue proceedings against Midland Bank in the US which would have involved the extraterritorial application of US antitrust law. In *British Airways Board v Laker Airlines Ltd*[134], however, the House of Lords refused British Airway's application for a stay; in this case there was no doubt that BA was carrying on business in the US, so that it was subject to US law on conventional jurisdictional principles. If Laker were deprived of the opportunity to litigate in the US, it would have been unable to sue in the UK since it had no cause of action under UK law. In those circumstances the House of Lords was prepared to allow the US litigation to go ahead.

(B) **Protection of Trading Interests Act 1980**

The Protection of Trading Interests Act 1980 contains wide-ranging provisions[135]. It is not limited to blocking US enforcement of antitrust laws, but may be invoked in any case in which US law is being applied in a way which could harm the commercial interests of the UK[136]. Section 1 enables the Secretary of State to make orders requiring UK firms to notify him of, and forbidding them to comply with, measures taken under the law of a foreign country affecting international trade and which threaten to damage the trading interests of the UK. This power has been exercised on three occasions[137]. The first order was not concerned with antitrust laws, but with the saga of the Siberian pipeline[138]. The second was concerned with competition law, but not with the specific issue of extraterritoriality; the objection to the US action in question was that it involved a breach of Treaty obligations concerning air travel between the US and the UK[139]. The third was adopted in response to regulations adopted by the US Government on trade with Cuba.

---

[132] The 1975 Act implements the Hague Convention in the UK, on which see 'Enforcement jurisdiction', pp 490–491 above.

[133] [1986] QB 689, [1986] 1 All ER 526.   [134] [1985] AC 58, [1984] 3 All ER 39.

[135] See generally on this Act Huntley 'The Protection of Trading Interests Act – Some Jurisdictional Aspects of Enforcement of Antitrust Laws' (1981) 30 ICLQ 213; Lowe 'Blocking Extraterritorial Jurisdiction – The British Protection of Trading Interests Act 1980' (1981) 75 American Journal of International Law 257; Jones 'Protection of Trading Interests Act 1980' (1981) 40 Cambridge Law Journal 41; Collins 'Blocking and Clawback Statutes: the UK Approach' [1986] JBL 372 and 452.

[136] The Shipping Contracts and Commercial Documents Act 1964 could be invoked only where there was an infringement of UK *jurisdiction*; the 1980 Act is wider, as it applies where there is harm to UK commercial interests, whether there is an infringement of jurisdiction or not.

[137] See the Protection of Trading Interests (US Re-export Control) Order 1982, SI 1982/885; the Protection of Trading Interests (US Antitrust Measures) Order 1983, SI 1983/900; and the Protection of Trading Interests (US Cuban Assets Control Regulations) Order 1992, SI 1992/2449.

[138] See *Lowe*, pp 197–219.

[139] The vires of the Order in this case were challenged, unsuccessfully, by the plaintiff in the US antitrust action: see *British Airways Board v Laker Airways Ltd* [1984] QB 142, [1983] 3 All ER 375; on appeal [1985] AC 58, [1984] 3 All ER 39; the House of Lords also reversed the Court of Appeal's decision that Laker should

Section 2 of the Act gives the Secretary of State power to prohibit compliance with a requirement by an overseas authority to submit commercial information to it which is not within its territorial jurisdiction. This provision replaces the Shipping and Commercial Documents Act 1964. Section 3 provides for the imposition of penalties upon anyone who fails to comply with orders under the foregoing provisions, but, consistently with the UK approach to these issues, these may be imposed only in accordance with the UK's conventional interpretation of the international law principles of territoriality and nationality. Section 4 provides that a UK court should not comply with a foreign tribunal's request for assistance in the discovery process where this would infringe UK sovereignty. This is statutory reinforcement of the House of Lords' judgment in *Rio Tinto Zinc v Westinghouse Electric Corpn*[140].

Section 5 provides that foreign multiple damages awards shall not be enforceable in the UK. This means that a claimant in the UK could not enforce a treble damages award obtained in the US[141]. Section 6 goes even further and provides that, where a UK defendant has actually paid US multiple damages, he may bring an action in the UK to 'claw back' the excess of such damages over the amount actually required to compensate the claimant. This provision symbolises the degree of antipathy in the UK towards various aspects of US antitrust practice.

7. The Internationalisation of Competition Law[142]

It is clearly unsatisfactory that there should be acrimonious disputes between States over the extraterritorial application of competition law. Principles of public international law do not provide an adequate answer to the problems that arise when true conflicts occur between competition authorities, and yet the scope for such conflicts could increase as more States adopt their own codes of competition law and as business becomes increasingly international. Transnational mergers pose a particular problem where several competition authorities investigate the same transaction and have different perceptions of whether it should be permitted or not. A different, and more positive, point is that competition authorities have become increasingly aware that, since national systems of competition law are not always adequate to deal with cartels, anti-competitive practices and mergers that transcend national boundaries, international cooperation between them may increase the chances of achieving a successful solution. Many steps have been taken towards greater international cooperation between competition authorities, some of which are considered below.

---

discontinue its US action against British Airways as this would mean there was no forum in which it could sue: see ch 12 n 134 above.

   140 [1978] AC 547, [1978] 1 All ER 434; see 'Introduction', pp 487–488 above.

   141 At common law foreign judgments can normally be enforced in the UK but 'penal' judgments cannot be; note that under s 5 of the Act the whole sum is unenforceable, not just the penal element; one order has been made under s 5, the Protection of Trading Interests (Australian Trade Practices) Order 1988, SI 1988/569; s 5 of the Act was considered by the Court of Appeal in *Lewis v Eliades* [2003] EWCA Civ 1758, [2004] 1 All ER 1196, paras 40–53; leave to appeal was refused [2004] 1 WLR 1393.

   142 See Dabbah *The Internationalisation of Antitrust Policy* (Cambridge University Press, 2003); Gerber *Global Competition: Law, Markets and Globalization* (Oxford University Press, 2010); Papadopoulos *The International Dimension of EU Competition Law and Policy* (Cambridge University Press, 2010).

(A) **UNCTAD**[143]

The United Nations Conference on Trade and Development ('UNCTAD') has taken an interest in the development of competition policy for many years. In 1980 the General Assembly of the UN adopted a voluntary, non-binding code, *The Set of Multilaterally Agreed Equitable Principles and Rules for the Control of Restrictive Business Practices*[144], setting out suggested core principles to be adopted in systems of competition law. UNCTAD fulfils an important role in providing technical assistance to developing countries: for example, in 2004 UNCTAD adopted a *Model Law on Competition*[145] which is used by countries that intend to adopt (or reform) a domestic system of competition law.

(B) **OECD**

The Organisation for Economic Co-Operation and Development ('the OECD') is active in matters of competition policy. In 1995 it published a *Revised Recommendation Concerning Cooperation between Member Countries on Restrictive Business Practices Affecting International Trade*[146] which provides for voluntary notification, consultation and cooperation in competition law cases involving the legitimate interests of foreign Governments; this Recommendation replaced an earlier one of 1986. The OECD has published a number of documents which are of particular interest to the issue of cartel enforcement as well as studies on aspects of competition policy, details of which can be found on its website[147].

(C) **WTO**

Chapter 5 of the post-war Havana Charter for an International Trade Organization contained an antitrust code[148]; however this was not incorporated into the General Agreement on Tariffs and Trade of 1947, the organisation from which the WTO developed. The WTO was established on 1 January 1995, and is predominantly concerned with issues of trade, rather than with competition policy. The relationship between trade and competition policy is a major subject in its own right, as is the debate as to the institutional mechanisms needed to deal with the new economic order[149]. The rules of the WTO do

---

[143] See Brusick 'UNCTAD's Role in Promoting Multilateral Cooperation on Competition Law and Policy' (2001) 24 World Competition 23; Lianos 'The Contribution of the United Nations to the Emergence of Global Antitrust Law' (2007) 15(2) Tulane Journal of International and Comparative Law 145.

[144] Resolution 35/63 of 5 December 1980; the UN reaffirmed the code by resolution of 4 October 2000.

[145] Available at www.unctad.org.   [146] OECD Doc C(95) 130 (final), 27 July 1995.

[147] Available at www.oecd.org/competition.

[148] The Charter is set out in Wilcox *A Charter for World Trade* (The Macmillan Company, 1949), pp 231–327; see also speech by Wood 'The Internationalisation of Antitrust Law: Options for the Future', 3 February 1995, available at www.justice.gov/atr/public/speeches/0099.htm.

[149] The literature on these matters is vast, and the subject merits a separate book. Many of the issues are captured in an interesting series of essays in the Journal of International Economic Law for 1999, for example by Pitofsky 'Competition Policy in a Global Economy' (1999) 3 JIEL 403 and Roessler 'Should Principles of Competition Policy be Incorporated into WTO Law Through Non-Violation Complaints?' ibid, 413; see also Matsushita 'Reflections on Competition Policy/Law in the Framework of the WTO' [1997] Fordham Corporate Law Institute (ed Hawk), ch 4; *New Dimensions of Market Access in a Globalising World Economy* (OECD, 1995), in particular the chapters in Part III on Trade and Competition Policies in the Global Market Place; a series of essays on the relationship between competition and trade policy will be found in [1998] Fordham Corporate Law Institute (ed Hawk), chs 13–19; see also Iacobucci 'The Interdependence of Trade and Competition Policies' (1997–98) 21(2) World Competition 5; Rodgers 'Competition Policy, Liberalism and Globalisation: A European Perspective' (2000) 6 Columbia Journal of European Law 289; Guzman

not impose obligations on undertakings in relation to competition. A working group has been established to examine the interaction between trade and competition policy; a helpful summary of its work can be found in the European Commission's *Annual Report on Competition Policy* for 2002[150]. It seems unlikely at the current stage of its development that the WTO will metamorphose into a global competition authority[151], although it is possible that its system of dispute settlement could be extended to competition law matters[152].

(D) ICN

An important contribution to the debate on the future of international competition policy was the *Final Report of the International Competition Policy Advisory Committee to the US Attorney General and Assistant Attorney General for Antitrust* (the so-called 'ICPAC Report'), published in February 2000[153]. The ICPAC Report led, in October 2001, to the establishment of the ICN as an international forum for competition law and policy. The ICN is an informal, virtual network that seeks to facilitate cooperation between competition authorities and to promote procedural and substantive convergence of competition laws; a Steering Group oversees the conduct of its business. The ICN's work is complementary to that of other international organisations such as UNCTAD and the OECD. Membership is open to national and multinational organisations responsible for the enforcement of competition law. The ICN seeks advice and contributions from the private sector and from non-governmental organisations involved in the application of competition law.

The first annual conference of the ICN was held in September 2002 and brought together representatives from 59 competition authorities and various non-governmental agencies; that number has grown since then and now exceeds 100: a list of members is available on the ICN website[154]. The ICN has established various working groups over the years of its existence: there are currently five, on mergers, cartels, unilateral conduct, advocacy, and agency effectiveness. The work plans of these groups and their output can be accessed on the ICN's website. These working groups have published a series of recommended practices, toolkits, workbooks and various other working documents, all of which provide an invaluable source of learning and guidance. In 2010 the ICN published a *Statement of Achievements* recording (*inter alia*) a remarkable degree of voluntary convergence in the handling of international mergers and the 'fight against cartels', in particular through the refinement of practical enforcement techniques. A further achievement has been the number of ICN recommendations that have led to 'soft harmonisation' in the form of legislative changes in numerous jurisdictions. In 2011 the ICN is expected to review its mission and adopt a strategy for its second decade.

'Antitrust and International Regulatory Federalism' (2001) 76 NYULR 1142; Davidow and Shapiro 'The Feasibility and Worth of a WTO Competition Agreement' (2003) 37 Journal of World Trade 49.

[150] See points 669–672 of the Report.

[151] In July 2004 the General Council of the WTO decided that the interaction between trade and competition policy would no longer form part of its work during the 'Doha Round'; further information can be found on the WTO's website, www.wto.org.

[152] See Ehlermann and Ehring 'WTO Dispute Settlement and Competition Law' (2003) 26 Fordham International Law Journal 1505.

[153] Copies are available from the US Government Printing Office; see also Janow and Lewis 'International Antitrust and the Global Economy' (2001) 24 World Competition 3.

[154] www.internationalcompetitionnetwork.org.

(E) International cooperation agreements[155]

International cooperation between competition authorities has been advanced by the adoption of several bilateral and multilateral agreements. For example the US has negotiated agreements in relation to competition law enforcement with Germany, Australia, Canada and Russia[156]. US–Canadian cooperation is also facilitated by the Mutual Legal Assistance Treaty which applies to criminal law enforcement generally, but which can be used in relation to criminal law prosecutions in competition law cases[157]. The Closer Economic Relations Agreement, which entered into force between Australia and New Zealand on 1 January 1983[158], provides for close cooperation between those two countries, even allowing for one country to apply the other's law where it is appropriate to do so. Denmark, Iceland, Norway and Sweden entered into an Agreement on cooperation in competition law matters in April 2003[159]. Regional agreements have an important role to play in developing a cooperative approach to competition issues; the EU itself is an example of regional cooperation, and Chapter 15 of the North American Free Trade Agreement contains provisions for consultation, cooperation and coordination between the US, Canada and Mexico in matters of competition policy.

(F) The EU's dedicated cooperation agreements on competition policy[160]

The EU has entered into dedicated cooperation agreements with the US, Canada, Japan and South Korea[161]; the principles of the agreements with Canada, Japan and South Korea are the same as those with the US. The text that follows will examine the agreements with the US; it will then discuss cooperation in practice. The Commission has also agreed to a structured dialogue with China[162] and with India[163]. A Memorandum of Understanding was signed between DG COMP and the Brazilian competition authorities in October 2009[164] and with the Russian Anti-Monopoly Service in March 2011[165].

(i) The EU/US Cooperation Agreement of 23 September 1991[166]

The first Cooperation Agreement was entered into on 23 September 1991[167]. The French Government successfully challenged the legal basis on which the Commission had proceeded, since the Council of Ministers should have been involved in the adoption of the

---

[155] A useful summary of such agreements will be found in Parisi 'Enforcement Cooperation Among Antitrust Authorities' (1999) 20 ECLR 133; Zanetti *Cooperation Between Antitrust Agencies at the International Level* (Hart Publishing, 2002).

[156] Antitrust Cooperation Agreements are available at www.justice.gov/atr/public/international/int_arrangements.htm.

[157] See Goldman and Kissack 'Current Issues in Cross-Border Criminal Investigations: A Canadian Perspective' [1995] Fordham Corporate Law Institute (ed Hawk), ch 4.

[158] See Brunt 'Australian and New Zealand Competition Law and Policy' [1992] Fordham Corporate Law Institute (ed Hawk), ch 7.

[159] Available at www.kkv.se.

[160] See Papadopoulos *The International dimension of EU competition law and policy* (Cambridge University Press, 2010).

[161] Available at www.ec.europa.eu/comm/competition/international/bilateral/index.html.

[162] See the *Commission Staff Working Document Accompanying the Report from the Commission on Competition Policy 2009*, SEC(2010)666 final, para 529.

[163] Ibid, para 530.   [164] See Commission Press Release IP/09/1500, 9 October 2009.

[165] See Commission Press Release IP/11/278, 10 March 2011.

[166] See Ham 'International Cooperation in the Antitrust Field and in particular the Agreement between the United States and the Commission of the European Communities' (1993) 30 CML Rev 571; Torremans 'Extraterritorial Application of EC and US Competition Law' (1996) 21 EL Rev 280.

[167] [1991] 4 CMLR 823.

Agreement[168]. The position was rectified by the adoption of a joint decision of the Council and the Commission of 10 April 1995[169].

The Agreement sets out detailed rules for cooperation on various aspects of the enforcement of EU and US competition law. Article II requires the competent authorities in each jurisdiction to notify each other whenever they become aware that their enforcement activities may affect important interests of the other party. Article II(3) contains special provisions on the timing of notifications in the case of mergers. Article III deals with the exchange of information between the authorities in each jurisdiction, and provides for regular meetings between officials of the EU and the US to discuss matters of mutual interest. Article IV deals with cooperation and coordination in enforcement activities, in relation to which each agency will assist the other. Article V is a novel provision going beyond Article IV, as it embodies the idea of 'positive comity': one agency may ask the other to take action in order to remedy anti-competitive behaviour in the *former's* territory[170]. The idea of positive comity is taken further in the second Cooperation Agreement, discussed below.

Article VI requires the parties to avoid conflicts in enforcement activities, and lays down criteria that should be taken into account when an agency is deciding whether to proceed. These criteria reflect the principle of (negative) comity discussed in the context of the US 'jurisdictional rule of reason'[171]. Article VII of the Agreement requires the parties to consult with one another in relation to the matters dealt with by it. Article VIII provides that neither party to the Agreement can be required to provide information to the other where this is prohibited by the law of the party possessing it or where to do so would be incompatible with important interests of the party possessing it; furthermore each party agrees to keep the information it receives from the other confidential to the fullest extent possible. Article IX provides that neither party can be required to do anything under the Agreement that would be inconsistent with existing laws. The Agreement is terminable on 60 days' notice by either party.

(ii) The Positive Comity Agreement of 4 June 1998

A second EU/US Cooperation Agreement was entered into on 4 June 1998, and develops the principle of positive comity in Article V of the first Agreement. The Council and the Commission gave their approval to the Positive Comity Agreement in a joint Decision of 29 May 1998[172]. Article I provides that the Agreement is to apply where one party can demonstrate to the other that anti-competitive activities are occurring within the latter's territory which are adversely affecting the interests of the former. Article II contains definitions; it is important to note that mergers do not fall within the scope of this Agreement as a result of the definition of 'competition law(s)' in Article II(4). Article III contains the principle of positive comity: the competition authorities of a 'Requesting Party' may request the authorities in the Requested Party to investigate and, if warranted, to remedy anti-competitive activities in accordance with the latter's competition laws. Article IV provides that the Requesting Party may defer or suspend the application of its law while

---

[168] Case C-327/91 *France v Commission* [1994] ECR I-3641, [1994] 5 CMLR 517: see Riley 'Nailing the Jellyfish: the Illegality of the EC/US Government Competition Agreement' (1992) 13 ECLR 101 and again in (1995) 16 ECLR 185.

[169] OJ [1995] L 95/45, corrected by OJ [1995] L 131/38.

[170] See Atwood 'Positive Comity – is it a Positive Step?' [1992] Fordham Corporate Law Institute (ed Hawk), ch 4.

[171] See 'Comity', p 493 above.

[172] OJ [1998] L 173/26, [1999] 4 CMLR 502; the first case to be initiated on the basis of positive comity was *Sabre*: see the Commission's XXXth *Report on Competition Policy* (2000), point 453.

the Requested Party is applying its. Article V deals with confidentiality and the use of information. Article VI provides that the Positive Comity Agreement shall be interpreted consistently with the 1991 Agreement. The Positive Comity Agreement is terminable on 60 days' notice by either party.

(iii) The cooperation agreements in practice

The cooperation agreements have been highly successful in practice. Cooperation between the Commission and the competition authorities in the US, Canada, Japan and South Korea is now a fact of daily life: if anything the degree of cooperation has been greater than could have been imagined in the early 1990s. The Commission's annual *Report on Competition Policy* (and the Staff Working Paper that accompanies it) provide a helpful account of the cooperation agreements in practice; in particular details are given of specific cases in which the authorities worked together[173]: obvious examples include *Thomson Corporation/Reuters Group*[174], where DG COMP's and the DoJ's investigations and negotiations of remedies were conducted in parallel and included joint meetings and discussions with the parties, and *Panasonic/Sanyo*[175], where DG COMP worked closely with the FTC in the US and the Fair Trade Commission in Japan. An EU–US merger working group has been established, which led to the adoption in 2002 of guidelines on 'best practices' to be followed where the same transaction is being investigated on both sides of the Atlantic; it was revised in October 2011[176].

A great deal of attention, including press coverage, is given to the few cases where there is friction between the EU and the US, as in the cases of *Boeing/McDonnell Douglas*[177] and *GE/Honeywell*[178]. In the *Boeing* case the FTC in the US reached a majority decision not to oppose the merger, while the European Commission seemed likely, at one point, to prohibit it in its entirety; in the event commitments to modify the transaction were offered to the Commission with the result that it was given conditional clearance. In *GE/Honeywell* a merger had been permitted in the US but was prohibited by the European Commission. However exceptional cases such as *Boeing/McDonnell Douglas* and *GE/Honeywell* ought not to obscure the fact that a large number of cases, particularly mergers, are successfully completed without any friction between the two jurisdictions. No matter how sophisticated the machinery for cooperation between the EU and the US, there will always be some cases in which there is disagreement as to the appropriate outcome. The success of the Cooperation Agreements should be assessed on the basis of how rare these cases are, and on this basis they have been very successful.

---

[173] See eg the *Report on Competition Policy for 2005*, SEC(2006)761 final, pp 187–191.

[174] Case M 4726, decision of 3 September 2007.

[175] Case M 5421, decision of 29 September 2009; for discussion of this case see Devai, Maass, Magos and Thomas 'Merger Case M.5421 Panasonic/Sanyo – Batteries Included or "Lost in Translation"' (2010) 1 *Competition Policy Newsletter* 60.

[176] Available at www.ec.europa.eu/competition/international/legislation/agreements.html.

[177] Case M 877 OJ [1997] L 336/16; for comment, see Bavasso '*Boeing/McDonnell Douglas*: Did the Commission Fly Too High?' (1998) 19 ECLR 243; Banks 'The Development of the Concept of Extraterritoriality under European Merger Law Following the *Boeing/McDonnell Douglas* Decision' (1998) 19 ECLR 306; Fiebig 'International Law Limits on the Extraterritorial Application of the European Merger Control Regulation and Suggestions for Reform' (1998) 19 ECLR 323.

[178] Case COMP/M.2220, upheld on appeal Cases T-209/01 *Honeywell v Commission* [2005] ECR II-5527, [2006] 4 CMLR 652 and T-210/01 *General Electric v Commission* [2005] ECR II-5575, [2006] 4 CMLR 686.

13

Horizontal agreements (1) – cartels

The previous chapters have described the main principles of EU and UK competition law. The focus of attention in this and the following chapters is different. Instead of looking at the individual provisions of competition law, such as Articles 101 and 102 TFEU and the Chapter I and Chapter II prohibitions in the UK Competition Act 1998, a contextual approach will be adopted and the application of the law to various types of agreements and business practices will be analysed.

There are 11 'contextual' chapters. The first three consider horizontal issues: first, cartels; then the 'problem' of tacit collusion and oligopoly; and lastly horizontal cooperation agreements that competition authorities might be willing to countenance. Chapter 16 deals with vertical agreements. Chapters 17 and 18 analyse practices that might be found to be abusive under Article 102 TFEU and/or the Chapter II prohibition in the Competition Act 1998; the possible application of the UK Enterprise Act 2002 to such practices will also be considered. Chapter 19 considers the relationship between intellectual property rights and competition law, including technology transfer agreements. Chapters 20 to 22 deal with merger control, and the book concludes with a brief discussion of how competition law impacts upon specific sectors of the economy, in particular so-called utilities such as electronic communications and energy markets.

The scheme of this chapter is as follows. Section 1 discusses the hardening attitude of competition authorities worldwide towards hard-core cartels, and gives examples of recent decisions in a variety of non-EU jurisdictions in which significant fines and sentences of imprisonment have been imposed. Section 2 looks at the European Commission's enforcement activity in relation to cartels in recent years. The chapter then considers the application of Article 101 to particular types of cartels: price fixing, market sharing, production quotas and analogous practices. The final section of this chapter reviews the record in the UK in enforcing the prohibition on cartels.

1. The Hardening Attitude of Competition Authorities Worldwide Towards Cartels

(A) Introduction

The mysteries of some aspects of competition policy should never be allowed to obscure the most simple fact of all: that competitors are meant to compete with one another for the business of their customers, and not to cooperate with one another to distort the process of competition. Horizontal agreements between independent undertakings to fix prices, divide markets, to restrict output and to fix the outcome of supposedly competitive tenders are the most obvious target for any system of competition law. Hard-core cartels are prohibited by virtually all systems of competition law and are the subject of ever more draconian penalties[1].

Writing in 1776 Adam Smith famously remarked in *The Wealth of Nations* that:

> People of the same trade seldom meet together, even for merriment and diversion, but the conversation ends in a conspiracy against the public, or in some contrivance to raise prices.

Evidence suggests that the tendency of competitors to meet in smoke-filled rooms – or perhaps now in smoke-free Internet chat rooms – is just as strong today as it was in the eighteenth century: cartels appear to be alive and kicking throughout the world. The phenomenon described by Smith was not a new discovery in 1776: cartels were recognised – and prohibited – in the days of the Eastern Roman Empire (Byzantium). The Constitution of Zeno of 483 AD punished price fixing in relation to clothes, fishes, sea urchins and other goods with perpetual exile, usually to Britain[2]. Adam Smith's comment was prescient: cartels have thrived through the subsequent centuries, often with implicit or even explicit support from Governments. Even the adoption of competition laws with tough sanctions has not been sufficient to suppress cartel activity.

The members of cartels go to great lengths to suppress evidence of their illegal activity: for example the Commission's decision in *Gas Insulated Switchgear*[3] says that participants in the cartel used codes to conceal their companies' names and encryption software to protect the secrecy of emails and telephone conversations; made use of free email providers and the anonymous mailboxes made available by them; sent messages as password-protected documents: the passwords were regularly changed; systematically destroyed emails; downloaded attachments on to memory sticks rather than on to their computers; and made use of mobile telephones provided by a member of the cartel that contained

---

[1] For detailed texts on cartels and competition law see Jephcott and Lübigg *Law of Cartels* (Jordans, 2003); Sakkers and Ysewyn *European Cartel Digest* (Wolters Kluwer, 2005); Arbaut and Sakkers in Faull and Nikpay *The EC Law of Competition* (Oxford University Press, 2nd ed, 2007), ch 8; Gerard et al *Cartel Law*, vol III of *EU Competition Law* (Claeys and Casteels, 2007, eds Siragusa and Rizza); *European Competition Law Annual 2006: Enforcement of Prohibition of Cartels* (Hart Publishing, 2007, eds Ehlermann and Atanasiu); Bellamy and Child *European Community Law of Competition* (Oxford University Press, 6th ed, 2008, eds Roth and Rose), ch 5; *Anti-Cartel Enforcement Worldwide* (Cambridge University Press, 2009, eds Dabbah and Hawk); Harding and Joshua *Regulating Cartels in Europe* (Oxford University Press, 2nd ed, 2010); see also the series of contributions on the topic in [2006] Fordham Corporate Law Institute (ed Hawk), chs 1–7.

[2] See Codex Iustinianus, c 4, 59, 2, p 186 (Weidmann, 1954); exile to Rome for commission of the UK criminal cartel offence under the Enterprise Act 2002 is thought unlikely to have a sufficiently deterrent effect and is therefore not an available option.

[3] Commission decision of 24 January 2007, substantially upheld on appeal Cases T-117/07 etc *Areva v Commission* [2011] ECR II-000, [2011] 4 CMLR 1421.

encryption options[4]. The cartels in *Organic peroxides*[5] and *Heat stabilisers*[6] went further and used a consultancy firm to oversee and conceal their illicit arrangements. Courts have recognised that competition authorities are at a disadvantage where members of cartels resort to these secretive practices, and that therefore they may have to prove the existence of a cartel by relying on inferences from circumstantial evidence[7].

(B) **The global agenda**

There is a very real sense today among the world's competition authorities that, if competition law is about one thing above all, it is the detection and punishment of hard-core cartels. In the European Union Mario Monti, the former Commissioner for Competition, once described cartels as 'cancers on the open market economy'[8], and the Supreme Court in the US has referred to cartels as 'the supreme evil of antitrust'[9]. At both a moral and a practical level there is not a great deal of difference between price fixing and theft. US law has for many decades treated hard-core cartels as *per se* infringements of the Sherman Act and as criminal offences, punishable not only by fines but also by the imprisonment of individuals. In 2008 the House of Lords, the highest appeal court in the UK (now known as the Supreme Court) reached the conclusion that some forms of price fixing amount to the crime of conspiracy to defraud at common law: in other words some cartels could lead to the imprisonment of individuals even without the criminal cartel offence established by section 188 of the Enterprise Act 2002[10].

As a separate matter, many developed and developing countries around the world are experiencing, or are expected to experience, an economic downturn. It is easy to understand that, during such a recession, firms that face uncertainty, and even the danger of bankruptcy, may find the idea of collusion to be attractive. The question arises whether such an economic crisis justifies a more lenient approach towards cartels[11]. It seems that competition authorities continue to root out and punish cartels with the same determination[12] at a time of crisis as in more prosperous times; the danger is actually in allowing them.

(C) **The position of the OECD in relation to cartels**[13]

The Organisation for Economic Co-Operation and Development ('the OECD') has been at the forefront of policy in relation to cartels. This in itself reflects an obvious but important point, that cartels are often international in nature, whereas for the most part systems of competition law are purely national in scope. The rules of the European Union

---

[4] Commission decision of 24 January 2007, paras 170–176.

[5] Commission decision of 10 December 2003, upheld on appeal Case T-99/04 *AC-Treuhand AG v Commission* [2008] ECR II-1501, [2008] 5 CMLR 962; for comment see Harding 'Capturing the cartel's friends: cartel facilitation and the idea of joint criminal enterprise' (2009) 34(2) EL Rev 298.

[6] Commission decision of 11 November 2009, on appeal Cases T-23/10 etc *Arkema France v Commission*, not yet decided.

[7] See eg Cases C-204/00 P etc *Aalborg Portland A/S v Commission* [2004] ECR I-123, [2005] 4 CMLR 241, paras 55–57; Case T-113/07 *Toshida v Commission* [2011] II–000, paras 78–84.

[8] Speech of 11 September 2000, available at www.ec.europa.eu.

[9] See *Verizon Communications Inc v Law Offices of Curtis V Trinko* 540 US 398 (2004).

[10] See ch 10, 'Conspiracy to defraud at common law', pp 436–437.

[11] See eg speech by John Fingleton of 20 January 2009, available at www.oft.gov.uk and speech by Christine Varney of 12 May 2009, available at www.justice.gov.

[12] See 'Recent cartel cases outside the EU, pp 561–517 and 'The European Commission's approach to cartels', pp 517–521 below.

[13] The OECD documents referred to in this section can all be found at www.oecd.org.

are an important exception, since they apply throughout the 27 Member States as well as the three Contracting States of the European Economic Area. International business phenomena such as cartels necessitate an international response, and the OECD is in an important position to give a lead in this respect.

In 1998 the OECD adopted a *Recommendation of the Council concerning Effective Action Against Hard Core Cartels* in which it called upon its member countries to ensure that their laws 'effectively halt and deter hard-core cartels', and invited non-member countries to associate themselves with the *Recommendation* and to implement it. In particular the *Recommendation* said that countries should provide for effective sanctions of a kind and at a level to deter firms and individuals from participating in such cartels as well as effective enforcement procedures to detect and remedy hard-core cartels. The *Recommendation* defined a hard-core cartel as:

> an anti-competitive agreement, anti-competitive concerted practice, or anti-competitive arrangement by competitors to fix prices, make rigged bids (collusive tenders), establish output restrictions or quotas, or share or divide markets by allocating customers, suppliers, territories, or lines of commerce.

Subsequently the OECD has published a number of further documents which are of particular interest to the issue of cartel enforcement[14]. The OECD has examined the harm that arises from cartels: whilst acknowledging how difficult it is to quantify such harm, it found that it amounted to billions of dollars worldwide each year. The OECD has also discussed the need to penetrate the cloak of secrecy that surrounds hard-core cartels, and the contribution that the encouragement of whistleblowers can make to this need. Whistleblowing and leniency applications were discussed in chapters 7 and 10 of this book, and are an important feature of competition authorities' pursuit of cartels[15]. Strong sanctions against firms and individuals increase the effectiveness of leniency programmes. The OECD has advocated the imposition of larger penalties in cartel cases; in its view sanctions have yet to reach the optimal level for deterrence. A separate matter is whether competition authorities might decide to introduce rewards or financial incentives for informants: this has been done, for example, in South Korea[16] and the UK[17].

The OECD has stressed the need for greater international cooperation in combating cartels which, as noted earlier, often transcend national boundaries. The increasing levels of cooperation between competition authorities is discussed in chapter 12 of this book[18].

(D) The International Competition Network

The International Competition Network ('the ICN') has a cartels working group: it is composed of two sub-groups, one of which looks at the general framework and principles for the fight against cartels and the other at enforcement techniques. The work plan and output of the cartels working group are available on the ICN's website[19]. The

---

[14] See eg *Report on Leniency Programmes to Fight Hard Core Cartels* (2001); *Report on the Nature and Impact of Hard Core Cartels and Sanctions against Cartels under National Competition Laws* (2002); *Hard Core Cartels: Recent Progress and Challenges Ahead* (2003); *Third Report on the Implementation of the 1998 Recommendation* (2005); *Guidelines for Fighting Bid Rigging in Public Procurement* (2009), all available at www.oecd.org.

[15] See ch 7, 'The Commission's *Leniency Notice*', pp 280–282 and ch 10, 'Whistleblowing: the leniency programme', pp 414–418.

[16] See www.ftc.go.kr/data/hwp/rewardsystem.doc.

[17] OFT Press Release 31/08, 29 February 2008.

[18] See ch 12, 'The Internationalisation of Competition Law', pp 506–511.

[19] www.internationalcompetitionetwork.org.

ICN produced, in 2005, a helpful series of *Anti-Cartel Enforcement Templates* which summarise anti-cartel laws in over 40 jurisdictions. The ICN has also published an *Anti-Cartel Enforcement Manual*, each chapter of which discusses enforcement techniques and identifies approaches that have proven effective and successful. The ICN holds an annual (anti-)Cartel Workshop to share learning and experience on how to address the problems raised by international cartels.

(E) Recent cartel cases outside the EU

The commitment of competition authorities around the world to the detection and prohibition of cartels is demonstrated by the number of cases that have been decided in recent years, both in 'mature' systems of competition law and in new jurisdictions, and in all types of economy. A few examples of major cartel cases in recent years illustrate how active competition authorities throughout the world have been:

- in the US to date more than $1.7 billion in criminal fines were imposed as a result of the Department of Justice's investigation into price fixing in the air transportation industry[20]. In 2007 34 individuals were sentenced to imprisonment, and the total number of actual days of incarceration imposed by the courts was 31,391, the highest number in history[21]

- in Japan the Japanese Fair Trade Commission imposed fines in May 2011 of approximately €124 million on four manufacturers of air separation gases for price fixing[22]

- in South Korea the Korean Fair Trade Commission imposed fines in May 2011 of approximately €282 million on four refineries for allocating amongst themselves the gas stations to which they would sell their products[23]

- in Australia the Federal Court of Australia imposed fines in April 2010 of approximately €8 million on four suppliers of marine hoses for engaging in cartel conduct[24]

- in South Africa the South African Competition Tribunal confirmed a settlement reached between the South African Competition Commission and with one undertaking involved in a price-fixing cartel in the maize milling industry. The settlement involved, amongst other things, the payment of an administrative fine of approximately €26 million[25].

Several countries have also been active in the introduction of criminal sanctions in cartel cases: in 2009 Australia adopted the Trade Practices Amendment (Cartel Conduct and Other Measures) Act and South Africa passed the Competition Amendment Act, while

---

[20] See Department of Justice's Press Release of 30 November 2010 available at www.justice.gov/atr/index.html.
[21] Useful statistics on the enforcement activities of the Antitrust Division of the US Department of Justice in relation to cartels (and to other types of case) are available at www.justice.gov/atr/public/workload-statistics.html. The Department of Justice in the US has adopted a policy of placing indicted individuals, accused of violating the Sherman Act, on a 'Red Notice' list maintained by Interpol, with the result that they might be arrested when attempting to cross a national boundary and extradited to the US for prosecution: see speech by Scott Hammond, Deputy Assistant Attorney General for Criminal Enforcement at the Department of Justice, 16 November 2005, www.usdoj.justice/atr.
[22] See JFTC's press release of 26 May 2011, available at www.jftc.go.jp/en/pressreleases/index.html.
[23] See KFTC's press release of 26 May 2011, available at www.eng.ftc.go.kr.
[24] See ACCC's press release of 14 April 2010, available at www.accc.gov.au.
[25] See Consent Order of 30 November 2010 by the South African Competition Tribunal, available at www.comptrib.co.za/cases/consent-order.

Canada amended its competition legislation to provide for more effective criminal enforcement. New Zealand is in the process of introducing criminal sanctions.

2. The European Commission's Approach to Cartels

The Commission now attaches a higher priority to cartels than at any time in its history[26]. The most obvious expression of this was the creation in June 2005 within DG COMP of a Cartel Directorate with responsibility for prosecuting cartel cases and, in conjunction with the Directorate for Policy and Strategy, for developing policy and coordinating the Commission's contributions to international fora such as the OECD and ICN. A second manifestation of the Commission's continuing determination to combat cartels is the *Leniency Notice*, the most recent of which appeared in 2006 and is discussed in chapter 7[27]. The immunity or reduction of the fine for whistleblowers has been very successful in bringing cartels to light, as can be seen from the statistics below. Thirdly, the Commission revised its *Fining Guidelines* in 2006 and the level of penalties being imposed on firms is now substantial, and it can be anticipated that this trend will continue[28]. Fourthly, the introduction of a settlement system in 2008 is expected to lead to more decisions than has been possible to date[29]: by 20 June 2011 the Commission had settled three cartel cases[30]. Fifthly, actual evidence of the Commission's keenness to punish and eradicate cartels has been its enforcement activity in recent years.

Bearing in mind that undertakings that cartelise markets can also be sued for damages[31], and that individuals in some jurisdictions also face the possibility of imprisonment[32], it is hard to believe that the deterrent effect of the law on cartels in the EU is insubstantial[33]; and yet the Commission (and the national competition authorities) continue to discover them in significant numbers and in all kinds of markets[34]. In numerous cases the Commission increases the fine that would otherwise have been paid because an undertaking is a recidivist, that is to say a repeat offender[35]; and it often discovers a series of cartels in the same industry[36]. Some of these cartels were of very long duration: for example 35 years in the case of *Animal Feed Phosphates*[37] and 29 years in each of the car-

---

[26] See the Commission's *Report on Competition Policy* (2008), paras 5–14, available at www.ec.europa.eu.

[27] See ch 7, 'The Commission's *Leniency Notice*', pp 280–282.

[28] See ch 7, 'The Commission's guidelines on the method of setting fines', pp 276–280; see also Castillo de la Torre 'The 2006 Guidelines on Fines: Reflections on the Commission's Practice' (2010) 33(3) World Competition 359.

[29] See ch 7, 'A system of settlements for cartel cases?', pp 263–264

[30] See 'Appeals to the General Court', pp 520–521 below.   [31] See ch 8 generally.

[32] See eg ch 10, 'The cartel offence', pp 425–434 on the position in the UK.

[33] On the issue of deterrence and cartels generally see Wils *The Optimal Enforcement of EC Antitrust Law Essays in Law and Economics* (Kluwer Law International, 2002), ch 2 and Wils *Efficiency and Justice in European Antitrust Enforcement* (Hart Publishing, 2008), ch 3.

[34] DG COMP's website includes a drop-down menu on cartels which includes a 'What's new' section: it provides details of new cases in which inspections have been carried out or a statement of objections sent.

[35] See eg *Nitrine Butadiene Rubber*, Commission decision of 23 January 2008, where Bayer's fine was increased by 50 per cent for recidivism; see further ch 7, 'Adjustments to the basic amount', p 278.

[36] See eg *Nitrine Butadiene Rubber*, Commission decision of 23 January 2008; this was the fourth decision in the synthetic rubber industry in just over three years.

[37] Commission decision of 20 July 2010; not all of the producers were involved for the entire period.

tels in *Sorbates*[38] and *Organic Peroxides*[39]. It is also noticeable in the Commission's decisions how often cartel meetings were held during or just after trade association meetings, as for example in the cases of *Industrial bags*[40], *Synthetic rubber*[41] and *Copper Fittings*[42].

(A) Statistics

In the years from 2001 onwards the European Commission has been particularly active in enforcing the prohibition on cartels: there have been numerous decisions and the fines have, in many cases, been enormous. 2001 was a particularly striking year, in which the fines imposed in ten decisions totalled €1,836 billion: by far the largest amount in any one year up until that point. The Commission's statistics on its enforcement activity in relation to cartels are available on its website and are regularly updated[43]. These statistics speak eloquently of the Commission's continuing determination to search for and eradicate cartels. Between 2006 and 2010 the total amount of penalties imposed by the Commission in 35 decisions was €12,110 billion. On appeal to the EU Courts some of the penalties were slightly reduced: after making allowance for those reductions the figure was €11,999 billion. In the calendar year 2010 the Commission adopted six decisions in which the fines totalled €2,598 billion, *DRAM*, *Prestressing Steel*, *Bathroom Equipment*, *Animal Feed Phosphates*, *Air Cargo* and *LCD Panels*. The fines are paid into the European Union budget: to that extent they benefit the treasuries of the Member States, whose contributions are proportionally reduced. A separate point is that the Commission has estimated that it saved consumers €7 billion in 2010 as a result of its anti-cartel enforcement[44].

This picture of rigorous enforcement is a very clear one. Some commentators have expressed concerns about the high level of fines imposed by the Commission and, in particular, about the combination of powers vested in it and the lack of a 'fresh pair of eyes' within the system[45]. Others, however, note the need for severe penalties to be imposed for serious infringements and argue that the EU enforcement system satisfies the requirements of the European Convention on Human Rights[46], Article 6 of which recognises the right to a fair and public hearing in matters of criminal law. It remains to be seen whether the EU Courts will respond to this debate, in particular since the Lisbon Treaty brought the Charter of Fundamental Rights into effect, by changing their practice when conducting appeals in cartel (and abuse) cases[47].

---

[38] Commission decision of 1 October 2003, substantially upheld on appeal Case T-410/03 *Hoechst v Commission* [2008] ECR II-881, [2008] 5 CMLR 839.

[39] Commission decision of 10 December 2003, upheld on appeal Case T-99/04 *AC-Treuhand AG v Commission* [2008] ECR II-1501, [2008] 5 CMLR 962.

[40] Commission decision of 20 November 2005.

[41] Commission decision of 29 November 2006.

[42] Commission decision of 20 September 2006, substantially upheld on appeal Cases T-375/06 etc *Viega v Commission* [2011] ECR II-000.

[43] www.ec.europa.eu/comm/competition/cartels/statistics/statistics/pdf.

[44] Speech by Alexander Italianer of 25 March 2011, available at www.ec.europa.eu/competition/index_en.html.

[45] See eg Forrester 'Due Process in EC competition cases: a distinguished institution with flawed procedures' (2009) 6 EL Rev 817 and the essays in *Evaluation of Evidence and its Judicial Review in Competition Cases* (Hart Publishing, 2010, eds Ehlermann and Marquis).

[46] See eg Wils 'The Increased Level of EU Antitrust Fines, Judicial Review, and the European Convention on Human Rights' (2010) 33(1) World Competition 5.

[47] The compatibility of the Commission's procedures and the standards required by the European Convention of Human Rights has been raised before the General Court, see eg Cases T-56/09 etc *Saint-Gobain Glass France v Commission*, not yet decided.

The Commission remains committed to an extremely tough stance on cartels. However it has become more receptive to claims that too high a fine may mean that an offending firm is put out of business[48]: not an attractive proposition for a competition authority, since this would mean that there would be fewer competitors on the market than there were before. The Commission reduced some of the fines in *Prestressing Steel*[49], *Bathroom Equipment*[50] and *Animal Feed Phosphates*[51] for this reason.

(B) Some landmark decisions

Some of the cartel cases in recent years are of particular interest. In *Vitamins*[52] the Commission imposed fines on eight undertakings totalling €855.23 million (reduced to €790.50 million on appeal): of this amount, Roche was fined €462 million for its participation in each of the 12 different vitamin cartels; the next largest fine was on BASF, of €296.16 million[53]; Aventis would have been fined €114.4 million, but it paid only €5.04 million as it had blown the whistle on most of the cartels. This cartel was investigated not only under EU law: the Commission's decision followed fines in the US on the major participants of US$862 million and in Canada of Canadian $84.5 million[54]; fines of Australian $26 million were imposed on Roche, BASF and Aventis Animal Nutrition under the Australian Trade Practices Act 1974 on 28 February 2001[55]. Senior executives of Roche and BASF also served terms of imprisonment in the US for their roles in this cartel[56]. Fines were also imposed in South Korea[57]. There have also been a series of actions for damages arising from the vitamins cartel[58].

Other notable decisions in recent years include, in 2007, *Elevators and escalators*[59] and *Gas Insulated Switchgear*[60] for the sheer size of the fines, €992.31 million in the case of the former and €750.71 in the latter. In 2008 fines of €676 million were imposed in the case

---

[48] See the Commission's *Guidelines on the method of setting fines* OJ [2006] C 210/2, para 35; see Kienapfel and Wils 'Inability to Pay – First cases and practical experiences' (2010) *Competition Policy Newsletter*.

[49] Commission Press Release IP/10/970, 23 June 2010, p 3.

[50] Commission Press Release IP/10/683, 30 June 2010.

[51] Commission Press Release IP/10/985, 20 July 2010.   [52] OJ [2003] L 6/1, [2003] 4 CMLR 1030.

[53] BASF's fine was reduced on appeal to €236.84 million, Case T-15/02 *BASF AG v Commission* [2006] ECR II-497, [2006] 5 CMLR 27.

[54] OJ [2003] L 6/1, [2003] 4 CMLR 1030, paras 155–157 and see Canadian Competition Bureau News Release, 22 September 1999.

[55] *Australian Competition & Consumer Commission v Roche Vitamins Australia Pty Ltd* [2001] FCA 150; see also ACCC Media Release MR 37/01, 1 March 2001.

[56] Department of Justice Press Release, 5 May 2000, available at www.justice.gov/atr/public.

[57] Press Release of 25 April 2003, available at www.ftc.go.kr.

[58] See eg in the US *Empagran SA v Hoffmann-La Roche Ltd* 315 F 3d 338 (DC Cir 2003) (see ch 12, 'The *Alcoa* and *Hartford Fire Insurance* cases', pp 491–493); in the UK see *Provimi Ltd v Aventis Animal Nutrition SA* [2003] EWHC 961; Case No 1028/5/7/04 *BCL Old Co Ltd v Aventis* (which was settled out of court), order of the CAT of 7 April 2005; *Devenish v Sanofi-Aventis* [2007] EWHC 2394, [2008] UKCLR 28, upheld on appeal *Devenish Nutrition Ltd v Sanofi-Aventis SA (France)* [2008] EWCA Civ 1086, [2008] UKCLR 783; Case Nos 1098/5/7/08 etc *BCL Old Co Ltd v BASF SE* [2008] CAT 24, [2008] CompAR 210, reversed on appeal *BCL Old Co Ltd v BASF SE* [2009] EWCA Civ 434, [2009] UKCLR 789 (the claims were found to have been brought out of time); the CAT refused to extend time: [2009] CAT 29, [2010] CompAR 1, upheld on appeal [2010] EWCA Civ 1258; the case is on appeal to the Supreme Court, and is due to be heard in June 2012.

[59] Commission decision of 21 February 2007, substantially on appeal Cases T-145/07 etc *OTIS v Commission*, [2011] ECR II-000.

[60] Commission decision of 24 January 2007, substantially upheld on appeal Cases T-110/07 etc *Siemens v Commission* [2011] ECR II-000, [2011] 4 CMLR 1421.

of *Paraffin Wax*[61], and of €1.383 billion in the case of *Car Glass*[62]; a point of particular interest about this decision is that the fine imposed on Saint-Gobain, of €896 million, was the largest ever to have been imposed on one undertaking in an Article 101 decision. In 2009 the Commission fined E.ON and GDF a total of €1,106 billion for sharing the German and French gas markets[63]. In 2010 fines of €799 million were imposed on 11 air cargo carriers for fixing fuel and security surcharges[64]; this case involved extensive cooperation with competition authorities in other jurisdictions such as the US. It is also of interest to note that, whereas a few years ago several of the Commission's decisions followed earlier enforcement by the Department of Justice in the US in relation to the same cartel[65], in recent years the Commission has prosecuted a number of cases where the cartels were purely European: examples are a series of decisions imposing fines on cartels in the beer sector[66], haberdashery products[67], flat glass[68] and bathroom equipment[69].

(C) **Appeals to the General Court**

Undertakings found to have infringed Article 101 have a right of appeal to the General Court, which has an unlimited jurisdiction in relation to the level of fines[70]; this includes the right to increase as well as to decrease them, which may act as a disincentive to appeal in some cases[71]. Some of these cases have run for a very long time; in particular, the litigation

---

[61] Commission decision of 1 October 2008, on appeal Cases T-543/08 etc *RWE and RWE Dea v Commission*, not yet decided.

[62] Commission decision of 12 November 2008, on appeal Cases T-56/09 etc *Saint-Gobain Glass France and others v Commission*, not yet decided.

[63] Commission decision of 8 July 2009, on appeal Cases T-360/09 etc *E.ON Ruhrgas and E.ON v Commission*, not yet decided.

[64] Commission decision of 9 November 2010, on appeal Cases T-9/11 etc *Air Canada v Commission*, not yet decided.

[65] See eg *Vitamins*, ch 13 n 52 above; see also *Graphite Electrodes* Commission decision of 18 July 2001, OJ [2002] L 100/1, [2002] 5 CMLR 829, on appeal Cases T-236/01 etc *Tokai Carbon v Commission* [2004] ECR II-1181, [2004] 5 CMLR 1465, on further appeal Cases C-289/04 P *Showa Denko v Commission* [2006] ECR I-5859, [2006] 5 CMLR 840; Case C-301/04 P *Commission v SGL Carbon AG* [2006] ECR I-5915, [2006] 5 CMLR 877 and Case C-308/04 P *SGL Carbon AG v Commission* [2006] ECR I-5977, [2006] 5 CMLR 922.

[66] *Belgian Beer* Commission decision of 5 December 2001, upheld on appeal to the General Court, Case T-38/02 *Group Danone v Commission* [2005] ECR II-4407, [2006] 4 CMLR 1428, on further appeal Case C-3/06 P *Group Danone v Commission* [2007] ECR I-1331, [2007] 4 CMLR 701; *Luxembourg Beer* Commission decision of 5 December 2001, upheld on appeal to the General Court, Cases T-49/02 etc *Brasserie Nationale SA and others v Commission* [2005] ECR II-3033, [2006] 4 CMLR 222; *French Beer* Commission decision of 29 September 2004; *Dutch Beer* Commission decision of 18 April 2007, substantially upheld on appeal Cases T-240/07 etc *Heineken Netherland and Heineken v Commission* [2011] ECR II-000.

[67] *PO/Needles* Commission decision of 26 October 2004 [2005] 4 CMLR 792, substantially upheld on appeal to the General Court, Case T-30/05 *Prym and Prym Consumer v Commission* [2007] ECR II-107, [2007] 4 CMLR 919, and to the Court of Justice, Case C-534/07 P *William Prym GmbH & Co KG v Commission* [2009] ECR I-7415, [2009] 5 CMLR 2377 and Case T-36/05 *Coats Holdings Ltd v Commission* [2007] ECR II-110, [2008] 4 CMLR 45, on further appeal Case C-468/07 P *Coats Holdings Ltd & J & P Coats Ltd v Commission* [2008] ECR I-127, [2009] 4 CMLR 301; *Fasteners* Commission decision of 19 September 2007, on appeal Cases T-454/07 etc *Prym and others v Commission*, not yet decided.

[68] Commission decision of 28 November 2007, on appeal Case T-82/03 *Guardian Industries and Guardian Europe v Commission*, not yet decided.

[69] Commission decision of 23 June 2010, on appeal Cases T-364/10 etc *Duravit v Commission*, not yet decided.

[70] Article 261 TFEU; see ch 7, 'Judicial Review', pp 290–294 on appeals to the General Court.

[71] See eg Cases T-101/05 etc *BASF v Commission* [2007] ECR II-4949, [2008] 4 CMLR 347.

arising from the *PVC* decision of 1988 did not end until the Court of Justice's judgment in 2002[72].

Where the Commission is guilty of factual errors the General Court will, of course, reduce the level of fines; it will also do so, for example, where it considers that one member of a cartel has been treated unequally compared with others in the same cartel. However the Court is fairly reluctant to interfere with the Commission's margin of appreciation in relation to the level of fines, and, as already noted, the Commission's statistics show that, overall, the level of reductions by the Court is not great[73]. No doubt many undertakings that are fined substantial sums will feel that it is worthwhile appealing in the hope of some reduction; and clearly law firms have an interest in their doing so, since this is lucrative work. However appeals consume public resources – of both the Commission and the Courts themselves. This is one of the reasons why a settlements procedure is attractive: not only can quicker decisions be expected under such a regime, but there should be considerably fewer appeals in the future, if the settlement procedure is frequently used, than is currently the case. There were no appeals in the first case to be settled under the Commission's settlements procedure[74], *DRAM*[75]; the only appeal in the second case, *Animal Feed Phosphates*[76] was made by the one undertaking that did not participate in the settlement procedure.

In some cases points have been won on appeal where the Commission had made a procedural error in its administrative procedure, for example failing to address a statement of objections to the legal entity that was subsequently fined. On two occasions in 2006 the Commission, having lost on appeal before the EU Courts on procedural grounds such as these, decided to reopen its administrative procedure in order to correct the error: this happened both in *Alloy Surcharge*[77] and in *Steel Beams*[78]. The General Court mostly affirmed the readopted decisions in both cases[79]; the General Court's judgments were upheld by the Court of Justice[80]. Clearly the Commission intends, by adopting decisions such as these[81], to suggest to the legal and business communities that appeals of a technical nature are unlikely to be successful in the end, since the technicality is something that can, in the long run, be corrected.

---

[72] Cases C-238/99 P etc *Limburgse Vinyl Maatschappij (LVM) v Commission and Others* [2002] ECR I-8375, [2003] 4 CMLR 397.

[73] See Vesterdorf 'The Court of Justice and Unlimited Jurisdiction: What Does it Mean in Practice?' Global Competition Policy (June 2009, Release 2), available at www.competitionpolicyinternational.com.

[74] See ch 7, 'A system of settlements for cartel cases?', pp 263–264 for discussion of the Commission's settlements procedure.

[75] Commission decision of 19 May 2010.

[76] Commission decision of 20 July 2010; one of the six firms under investigation refused to settle and has appealed to the General Court: Case T-456/10 *Timab Industries and CFPR v Commission*, not yet decided; it is also challenging the Commission's refusal to disclose settlement case documents to it: Case T-14/11, not yet decided.

[77] Commission Press Release of 20 December 2006.

[78] Commission Press Release of 8 November 2006.

[79] Case T-24/07 *ThyssenKrupp Stainless v Commission* [2009] ECR II-2309, [2009] 5 CMLR 1773 (*Alloy Surcharge*) and Cases T-405/06 etc *ArcelorMittal Luxembourg v Commission* [2009] ECR II-771, [2010] 4 CMLR 787 (*Steel Beams*).

[80] Case C-352/09 P *ThyssenKrupp Nirosta GmbH v Commission* [2011] ECR I-000 (*Alloy Surcharge*) and Cases C-201/09 P etc *ArcelorMittal SA Luxembourg v Commission* [2011] ECR I-000 [2011] 4 CMLR 1097 (*Steel Beams*).

[81] See also the Commission's readoption of a decision in the *PVC* case which was upheld on appeal: Cases C-238/99 P etc *Limburgse Vinyl Maatschappij v Commission* [2002] ECR I-8375, [2003] 4 CMLR 397.

3. Horizontal Price Fixing

Horizontal price fixing would be regarded by most people as the most blatant and un-desirable of restrictive trade practices.

It is interesting in passing to note that price fixing has not always attracted the oppro-brium that it does today. In the UK, for example, it was characteristic of most industries during the first half of the twentieth century that prices were set at an agreed level; this was thought to provide stability, to protect firms against cyclical recession and overseas competition, and to facilitate orderly and rational marketing from which purchasers too would benefit[82]. The introduction of power to inhibit price fixing in the Monopolies and Restrictive Practices (Inquiry and Control) Act 1948 was resented and even now resist-ance to price competition remains deep-rooted in some parts of the economy.

It might be assumed that in the absence of competition laws – or at any rate in the ab-sence of any significant prospect of being detected and punished for breaking them – all competitors would find the urge to cartelise and to maximise profits an irresistible one. However participation in a cartel itself has its price and membership will be more prof-itable to some firms than others[83]. Costs will be incurred in negotiating to fix the price at which the product is to be sold and these costs will inevitably increase as more firms are brought into the agreement and the range of products to be comprehended by it is extended. Firms may find it difficult both to agree a price and to remain faithful to the level set. It will be to the advantage of more efficient firms to fix a lower price, since output (and so their revenue) will then be greater; the producer of strongly differentiated goods will want a higher price, which will cover the cost of promoting its brand image. Having fixed prices, further expense will have to be incurred in monitoring the agreement. Meetings will be necessary to reappraise matters from time to time, resources will need to be expended in policing it to ensure that individual firms are not cheating by cutting prices secretly, offering discounts and bonuses or altering the quality of the product[84]. To prevent cheating, the agreement may fix quotas and provide for the imposition of fines upon firms that exceed them. Further resources may have to be devoted to arrangements such as collective boycotts, patent pooling and the offer of aggregated rebates in order to prevent new entrants coming on to the market with a view to sharing in any supra-competitive profits that are being earned. A system of collective resale price maintenance may have to be established to buttress the stability of the cartel. A trade association may have to be established to reinforce the cartel.

The problems inherent in the cartelisation process itself explain why in some indus-tries price fixing has a tendency to break down in the long term and why the parties may attempt to limit competition in other ways than by direct limitations on pricing strategy. For example, it may be easier to prevent 'cheating' where each firm is given an exclusive geographical market or a particular class of customers with which to deal. Furthermore the fact that price fixing becomes more difficult as the number of participants involved in the agreement increases may be considered to signify that competition authorities ought to expend their enforcement resources on those markets where collusion is most likely to

---

[82] See eg Allen *Monopoly and Restrictive Practices* (George Allen & Unwin, 1968), ch 14.

[83] See Scherer and Ross *Industrial Market Structure and Economic Performance* (Houghton Mifflin, 3rd ed, 1990), chs 7 and 8; Neven, Papandropoulos and Seabright *Trawling for Minnows* (CEPR, 1998), ch 3; Bishop and Walker *The Economics of EC Competition Law* (Sweet & Maxwell, 3rd ed, 2010), paras 5.007–5.033.

[84] It is not uncommon for a cartel agreement to break down, or to run the risk of doing so, because of the ex-tent of cheating indulged in by members: see eg *Zinc Producer Group* OJ [1984] L 220/27, [1985] 2 CMLR 108, paras 23–63.

be privately profitable because of the high level of concentration that exists or the homo-geneity of the products sold[85].

It should not be assumed from the foregoing comments that price fixing is rare. Even the existence of antitrust laws backed up by severe penalties has not dissuaded some firms from attempts to control the market. Experience shows that some industries are particu-larly prone to cartelisation: any review of enforcement activity in this area will quickly reveal, for example, that this is true of the cement, chemical and construction sectors. It is also important to appreciate that prices can be fixed in numerous different ways, and that a fully effective competition law must be able to comprehend not only the most bla-tant forms of the practice but also a whole range of more subtle collusive behaviour whose object is to limit price competition. For example, where firms agree to restrict credit to customers, to abstain from offering discounts and rebates, to refrain from advertising prices, to notify one another of the prices they charge to customers or intend to recom-mend their distributors to charge, or to adopt identical cost accounting methods, the object or effect of the agreement may be to diminish or totally prevent price competition. Indeed, agreements to divide markets or fix production quotas can in a sense be seen as covert price-fixing agreements, in that they limit the extent to which firms can compete with one another on price. These and other similar agreements will be dealt with separ-ately later in this chapter.

(A) Article 101(1)

Article 101(1) specifically provides that agreements, decisions and concerted practices which 'directly or indirectly fix purchase or selling prices or any other trading condi-tions' may be caught. Many aspects of Article 101(1) have been discussed earlier in this book. The expressions 'agreement' and 'concerted practice' are given a wide meaning[86]: specifically, the Commission may find a 'single, overall agreement'[87], may adopt a dual classification of an agreement 'and/or' a concerted practice[88]; and attendance at meet-ings at which prices are discussed between competitors is highly incriminating[89]. The EU Courts and the Commission regard price-fixing agreements as having as their *object* the restriction of competition for the purposes of Article 101(1), so that there is no need also to show that they have the effect of doing so[90]. The Commission has said that it is not obliged to engage in market definition[91] nor to consider the issue of countervailing buyer power[92] in cartel cases. However, it is necessary to show that an agreement will have an appreciable effect on competition[93] and on trade between Member States[94] for there to be an infringement of Article 101(1). Furthermore Article 101(1) is capable of being

---

[85] See Posner *Antitrust Law* (University of Chicago Press, 2nd ed, 2002), ch 4.

[86] See ch 3, 'Agreements, Decisions and Concerted Practices', pp 99ff.

[87] See ch 3, 'The concept of a "single, overall agreement"', pp 103–104.

[88] Ch 3, 'Agreement "and/or" concerted practice', pp 102–103.

[89] Ch 3, 'The concept of a "single, overall agreement"', pp 103–104.

[90] Ch 3, 'Market sharing, quotas, collective exclusive dealing', pp 122–123; note that there are some excep-tional circumstances in which price fixing has been found not to restrict competition by object, but to do so by effect: ibid, 'Refinement of the range of agreements within the object box', pp 124–125.

[91] See eg *Candle Waxes*, Commission decision of 1 October 2008, para 279, on appeal Cases T-540/08 etc *Esso ea v Commission*, not yet decided; see however the General Court's judgement in Case T-199/08 *Ziegler v Commission* [2011] ECR II-000, [2011] 5 CMLR 261, paras 41–45.

[92] *Candle Waxes*, para 322; see also *Bananas*, Commission decision of 15 October 2008, para 282, on appeal Cases T-587/08 etc *Fresh Del Monte Produce v Commission*, not yet decided.

[93] Ch 3, 'The *De Minimis* Doctrine', pp 140–144.

[94] Ch 3, 'The Effect on Trade between Member States', pp 144–149.

applied extraterritorially to agreements entered into outside but implemented within the EU[95]. This section examines more closely the application of Article 101(1) to price-fixing agreements.

(i) Price fixing in any form is caught

It is clear from the decisions of the Commission and the judgments of the EU Courts that it is not just blatant price fixing that is caught, but that Article 101(1) will catch any agreement that might directly or indirectly suppress price competition. In *IFTRA Rules on Glass Containers*[96] the Commission condemned rules of a glass manufacturers' association which might reduce price competition by including an obligation not to offer discounts, an open information scheme, the adoption of a common accounting procedure and a term providing for the charging of uniform delivered prices. In this decision the Commission pointed out that in the particular product market the potential for non-price competition was weak, the corollary being that maintenance of price competition was particularly important. An agreement not to discount off published prices was held to infringe Article 101(1) in *FETTCSA*[97], even though the parties had not expressly agreed on the level of their published prices. In *Vimpoltu*[98] an agreement to observe maximum discounts and to offer the same credit terms was caught. In *Italian Flat Glass*[99] the participants in the cartel had agreed not only to fix prices, but also to offer identical discounts and to ensure that these were applied downstream in the market.

Many other decisions have condemned agreements which might directly or indirectly facilitate level pricing. Prior consultation on price lists, with a commitment not to submit quotations before such consultation, is prohibited[100]. A substantial body of material on information agreements now exists[101], restrictions upon advertising may be caught[102], as are agreements on terms and conditions which limit price competition[103], agreements on recommended prices[104], maximum pricing[105] and collective resale price maintenance[106]. Objection has been taken to a scheme whereby members of a cartel at times refused to sell and at others themselves purchased zinc on the London Metal Exchange in order to

---

[95] This jurisdictional issue has been raised by some of the appeals to the General Court in *Air Cargo*: see eg Case T-38/11 *Cathay Pacific Airways v Commission*, not yet decided; see further ch 12, 'The Extraterritorial Application of EU Competition Law', pp 495–499.

[96] OJ [1974] L 160/1, [1974] 2 CMLR D50; see similarly *IFTRA Rules for Producers of Aluminium Containers* OJ [1975] L 228/10, [1975] 2 CMLR D20.

[97] OJ [2000] L 268/1, [2000] 5 CMLR 1011, paras 132–139 (citing *IFTRA Rules on Glass Containers* and *IFTRA Rules for Producers of Aluminium Containers*), upheld on appeal Case T-213/00 *CMA CGM v Commission* [2003] ECR II-913, [2003] 5 CMLR 2573, para 184.

[98] OJ [1983] L 200/44, [1983] 3 CMLR 619.

[99] OJ [1989] L 33/44, [1990] 4 CMLR 535, annulled on appeal Cases T-68/89 etc *Società Italiano Vetro SpA v Commission* [1992] ECR II-1403, [1992] 5 CMLR 302.

[100] *Re Cast Iron Steel Rolls* OJ [1983] L 317/1, [1984] 1 CMLR 694: the parties here had established an 'alarm system' in the event that competition authorities should become aware of their cartel, upheld on appeal Cases 29 and 30/83 *Compagnie Royale Asturienne des Mines SA and Rheinzink GmbH v Commission* [1984] ECR 1679, [1985] 1 CMLR 688.

[101] See 'Exchanges of Information', pp 539–547 below.

[102] See 'Advertising Restrictions', pp 547–550 below.

[103] See 'Agreements Relating to Terms and Conditions', pp 538–539 below.

[104] Case 8/72 *Cementhandelaren v Commission* [1972] ECR 977, [1973] CMLR 7; see also *Ferry Operators Currency Surcharges* OJ [1996] L 26/23, [1997] 4 CMLR 798.

[105] *European Glass Manufacturers* OJ [1974] L 160/1, [1974] 2 CMLR D50.

[106] Cases 43 and 63/82 *VBVB & VBBB v Commission* [1984] ECR 19, [1985] 1 CMLR 27.

maintain its price[107]. Where an industry considers that cooperation is necessary because of the depressed state of the market, this is a matter which should be weighed at the stage of considering whether the terms of Article 101(3) are met.

Price fixing as part of a strategy to isolate national markets is caught[108], and agreements between distributors are caught as well as between producers[109]. An agreement the effect of which is to maintain a traditional price differential between two geographical markets will infringe Article 101(1)[110]. Fixing the price of imports into the EU has been caught[111], as has manipulating the price of exports within the EU[112].

In the case of *British Sugar*[113] the Commission did not find that the prices for sugar had actually been fixed, but that the parties to the agreement/concerted practice could rely on the other participants to pursue a collaborative strategy of higher pricing in 'an atmosphere of mutual certainty'[114]. In *Fenex*[115] the Commission considered that the regular and consistent practice of drawing up and circulating recommended tariffs to members of a trade association infringed Article 101(1)[116]. In *Bananas*[117] the Commission imposed a fine of €60.3 million on three producers of bananas for holding bilateral phone calls to discuss or disclose their pricing intentions. The Commission's view was that these discussions reduced uncertainty as to the quotation prices set by the producers and concerned the fixing of prices[118]. Where undertakings agree to increase prices, and announce to their customers what those increases will be, it is irrelevant to a finding of infringement of Article 101 that prices are subsequently negotiated with individual customers that differ from what was agreed: the General Court has stated that price announcements always have an impact on the final outcome even if the final price is negotiated with the customer[119].

The fact that an undertaking is not active on the cartelised market does not preclude a finding that it participated in the cartel[120]. It is no defence that a participant in a cartel sometimes does not respect the agreed price increases[121]. Likewise undertakings cannot justify price fixing by claiming that it did not have a direct effect on the prices paid by

[107] *Zinc Producer Group* OJ [1984] L 220/27, [1985] 2 CMLR 108.

[108] Case 41/69 *ACF Chemiefarma NV v Commission* [1970] ECR 661, [1970] CMLR 43.

[109] Cases 100/80 etc *Musique Diffusion Française SA v Commission* [1983] ECR 1825, [1983] 3 CMLR 221.

[110] *Scottish Salmon Board* OJ [1992] L 246/37, [1993] 5 CMLR 602.

[111] *Re Franco-Japanese Ballbearings Agreement* OJ [1974] L 343/19, [1975] 1 CMLR D8; *Re French and Taiwanese Mushroom Packers* OJ [1975] L 29/26, [1975] 1 CMLR D83; *Wood Pulp* OJ [1985] L 85/1, [1985] 3 CMLR 474; *Aluminum Imports* OJ [1985] L 92/1, [1987] 3 CMLR 813.

[112] *Milchförderungsfonds* OJ [1985] L 35/35, [1985] 3 CMLR 101.

[113] OJ [1999] L 76/1, [1999] 4 CMLR 1316, substantially upheld on appeal Cases T-202/98 etc *Tate & Lyle v Commission* [2001] ECR II-2035, [2001] 5 CMLR 859.

[114] See the Commission's XXVIIIth *Report on Competition Policy* (1998), pp 138–140.

[115] OJ [1996] L 181/28, [1996] 5 CMLR 332.

[116] Ibid, paras 45–74.

[117] Commission decision of 15 October 2008, on appeal Cases T-587/08 etc *Fresh Del Monte Produce v Commission*, not yet decided. The Commission also found that the bananas importers exchanged quotation prices which enabled them to monitor prices: ibid, paras 273–277.

[118] Commission decision of 15 October 2008, paras 263–328 on appeal Cases T-587/08 etc *Fresh Del Monte Produce v Commission*, not yet decided.

[119] See eg Cases T-109/02 etc *Bolloré v Commission* [2007] ECR II-947, [2007] 5 CMLR 66, paras 450–453.

[120] Case T-99/04 *AC-Treuhand AG v Commission* [2008] ECR II-1501, [2008] 5 CMLR 962, paras 112–158, and in particular para 122; see also Case T-29/05 *Deltafina SpA v Commission* [2010] ECR II-000, [2011] 4 CMLR 467, paras 45–64.

[121] Case T-308/94 *Cascades v Commission* [1998] ECR II-925, para 230; see also Case T-377/06 *Comap SA v Commission* [2011] ECR II-000, [2011] 4 CMLR 1576, para 99.

consumers[122]. The Commission may reduce the fine where an undertaking's involvement in a cartel is limited, as happened in the cases of *DRAM*[123] and *Prestressing Steel*[124].

(ii) Joint selling agencies

The Commission is wary of joint selling agencies, which it regards as horizontal cartels and generally unlikely to benefit from Article 101(3)[125], unless they are established pursuant to some other permissible form of cooperation, such as a research and development agreement or a specialisation agreement[126].

Joint selling by sporting associations such as UEFA (a European association of national football associations) may infringe Article 101(1): the Commission will consider both the horizontal effects of joint selling, for example in so far as it prevents the individual sale of broadcasting rights by particular football clubs, as well as any vertical foreclosure effects[127].

(iii) Horizontal price fixing in conjunction with other infringements of Article 101(1)

In many cases undertakings have been found guilty of price fixing in conjunction with other types of horizontal collusion. In *Polypropylene*[128] the Commission found price fixing and market sharing; in *Belgian Roofing Felt*[129] the parties were found guilty of price fixing, establishing production quotas and taking collective action to prevent imports into Belgium; in *Italian Flat Glass*[130] the Commission condemned firms for the apportionment of quotas and agreements to exchange products as well as for fixing prices. In *Pre-Insulated Pipes*[131] the Commission identified infringements of virtually every kind, including market sharing, systematic price fixing, collective tendering, exchanging sensitive sales information and attempts to eliminate the only substantial non-member of the cartel. As Karel Van Miert, the former Commissioner for Competition, said: 'it is difficult to imagine a worse cartel'[132]. In *Amino Acids*[133] the Commission found agreements to fix prices, to determine quotas and to exchange information. In *Methylglucamine*[134] the Commission imposed a fine on Aventis and Rhône-Poulenc for both price fixing and

---

[122] Case C-8/08 *T-Mobile Netherlands v Raad van bestuur van de Nederlanse Medeingingsautoriteit* [2009] ECR I-4529, [2009] 5 CMLR 1701, para 39.

[123] Commission decision of 19 May 2010; the fines imposed on Hynix, Toshiba and Mitsubishi were reduced on this basis.

[124] Commission decision of 6 October 2010; the fines imposed on Proderac and Emme Holding were reduced for this reason.

[125] *Re Cimbel* OJ [1972] L 303/24, [1973] CMLR D167; *Re Centraal Stikstof Verkoopkantoor* OJ [1978] L 242/15, [1979] 1 CMLR 11; *Re Floral* OJ [1980] L 39/51, [1980] 2 CMLR 285; *Re Italian Flat Glass* OJ [1981] L 326/32, [1982] 3 CMLR 366; *Ansac* OJ [1991] L 152/54; *Astra* OJ [1993] L 20/23, [1994] 5 CMLR 226; *HOV SVZ/MCN* OJ [1994] L 104/34, upheld on appeal Case T-229/94 *Deutsche Bahn AG v Commission* [1997] ECR II-1689, [1998] 4 CMLR 220 and further on appeal Case C-436/97 P [1999] ECR I-2387, [1999] 5 CMLR 776; see also the Commission's *Guidelines on Horizontal Cooperation Agreements* OJ [2011] C 11/1, paras 234–235 and 246.

[126] On horizontal cooperation agreements generally see ch 15.

[127] *Joint selling of the media rights of the UEFA Champions League on an exclusive basis* OJ [2002] C 196/3, [2002] 5 CMLR 1153; see also Commission Press Release IP/03/1105, 24 July 2003 on the individual exemption given to UEFA's sale of the media rights to the Champions League.

[128] OJ [1986] L 230/1, [1988] 4 CMLR 347.   [129] OJ [1986] L 232/15, [1991] 4 CMLR 130.

[130] OJ [1989] L 33/44, [1990] 4 CMLR 535.

[131] OJ [1999] L 24/1, [1999] 4 CMLR 402, substantially upheld on appeal Cases T-9/99 etc *HFB Holding v Commission* [2002] ECR II-1487, [2001] 4 CMLR 1066.

[132] Commission Press Release IP/98/917, 21 October 1998.

[133] OJ [2001] L 154/24, [2001] 5 CMLR 322, substantially upheld on appeal Cases T-220/00 etc *Cheil Jedang v Commission* [2003] ECR II-2473.

[134] OJ [2004] L 38/18, [2004] 4 CMLR 1062.

market sharing. In *Plasterboard*[135] the Commission found market sharing combined with the exchange of information on future prices and sales volumes; the decision on this point was affirmed by the General Court[136]. In *Industrial Bags*[137] the Commission imposed fines of €290.71 million on 16 firms for agreeing on prices and sales quotas by geographical area, sharing the orders of large customers, organised collusive bidding and the exchange of information on sales volumes. In *Candle Waxes* the Commission condemned the division of markets and exchange of information by certain firms to support fixing prices in that industry[138].

(iv) Price fixing in the services sector

Price fixing in the services sector is also subject to Article 101(1)[139]. In *Eurocheque: Helsinki Agreement*[140] the Commission imposed a fine of €6 million where French banks had agreed between themselves on the commissions they would charge to customers and on their amount[141]; the decision was partially annulled and the fines reduced on appeal[142]. In *Bank charges for exchanging euro-zone currencies – Germany* the Commission fined five banks a total of €120.8 million for fixing the charges for exchanging currencies in the euro zone[143]; however the decision was annulled on appeal for lack of evidence[144]. In *Austrian Banks – 'Lombard Club'* the Commission imposed fines of €124.26 million on eight Austrian banks for their participation in a wide-ranging price cartel[145]; the substance of this decision was upheld on appeal but one of the fines was slightly reduced[146]. A fine of €1 million was imposed in *Distribution of Railway Tickets by Travel Agents*[147] where the Commission found that the International Union of Railways was responsible for price fixing in the sale of railway tickets; the decision was annulled on appeal, as the Commission had proceeded under the wrong procedural regulation[148]. In 1999, in the *Greek Ferries* decision, fines were imposed in the case of price fixing in ferry services between Italy and Greece[149]. The *Air Cargo* case in 2010 has already been referred to above.

---

[135] OJ [2005] L 166/8.

[136] Case T-53/03 *BPB v Commission* [2008] ECR II-1333, [2008] 5 CMLR 1201.

[137] Commission Press Release IP/05/1508, 30 November 2005.

[138] Commission decision of 1 October 2008, paras 2, 276 and 328(2), on appeal Cases T-540/08 etc *Esso ea v Commission*, not yet decided.

[139] See eg *Re Nuovo CEGAM* OJ [1984] L 99/29, [1984] 2 CMLR 484 (common tariff system infringed Article 101(1)); *Re Fire Insurance* OJ [1985] L 35/20, [1985] 3 CMLR 246, upheld on appeal Case 45/85 *VdS v Commission* [1987] ECR 405, [1988] 4 CMLR 264 (recommendations on tariffs infringed Article 101(1)).

[140] OJ [1992] L 95/50, [1993] 5 CMLR 323.

[141] Ibid, paras 46–55.

[142] Cases T-39/92 etc *Groupement des Cartes Bancaires v Commission* [1994] ECR II-49, [1995] 5 CMLR 410.

[143] OJ [2003] L 15/1, [2003] 4 CMLR 842; see also Commission Press Release IP/01/1796, 11 December 2001 and Commission's XXXIst *Report on Competition Policy*, p 20.

[144] Cases T-44/02 etc *Dresdner Bank and others v Commission* [2006] ECR II-3567, [2007] 4 CMLR 467; note that in this case the Commission failed to lodge a defence to the appeals, and the General Court therefore ruled on the merits of the case purely on the basis of the applications received from the banks: a subsequent application by the Commission to have the Court's judgments set aside was rejected in September 2006, Cases T-44/02 P etc *Dresdner Bank v Commission* [2006] ECR II-3567, [2007] 4 CMLR 467.

[145] Commission Press Release IP/02/844, 11 June 2002.

[146] Cases T-259/02 etc *Raiffeisen Zentralbank Österreich AG v Commission* [2006] ECR II-5169, [2007] 5 CMLR 1142, upheld on appeal Cases C-125/07 P etc *Erste Bank der österreichischen Sparkassen AG v Commission* [2009] ECR I-8681, [2010] 5 CMLR 443.

[147] OJ [1992] L 366/47.

[148] Case T-14/93 *Union Internationale des Chemin de Fer* [1995] ECR II-1503, [1996] 5 CMLR 40.

[149] OJ [1999] L 109/24, [1999] 5 CMLR 47, upheld on appeal Cases T-56/99 etc *Marlines v Commission* [2003] ECR II-5225, [2005] 5 CMLR 28.

The Commission is concerned about restrictions of competition in the professional services sector[150]. In *Belgian Architects*[151] it imposed a fine of €100,000 on the Belgian Architects' Association for adopting a minimum fee scale for the provision of architectural services in Belgium. In *ONP*[152] the Commission imposed a fine of €5 million on the National Pharmaceutical Society for stipulating minimum prices for clinical laboratory tests in France.

(v) Price fixing in regulated markets

The Commission will examine particularly carefully markets in which price competition is already limited by extraneous factors, in order to ensure that the parties themselves do nothing further to limit competition[153], and its decision will not be affected by the fact that the state itself sanctioned or extended the effect of a price-fixing agreement[154].

(vi) Buyers' cartels

In some cases buyers, rather than sellers, are accused of cartel activity. In *Spanish raw tobacco*[155] and *Italian Raw Tobacco*[156] the Commission found tobacco processors had colluded on the prices and other trading conditions that they would offer to tobacco growers and other intermediaries; on the allocation of suppliers and quantities; on the exchange of information in order to coordinate their purchasing behaviour; and on the coordination of bids for public auctions. The Commission considered that competition was restricted by object rather than effect[157], even though an agreement to pay *lower* prices than might have been paid in the absence of the agreement might have been expected to lead to lower prices for consumers. In the Commission's view an agreement on purchasing eliminates the autonomy of strategic decision-making and competitive conduct, preventing the undertakings concerned from competing on the merits and enhancing their position vis-à-vis less efficient firms[158].

---

[150] See *European Competition Law Annual: The Relationship Between Competition Law and the Liberal Professions* (Hart Publishing, 2006, eds Ehlermann and Atanasiu); *Overview of National Competition Authorities' Advocacy and Enforcement Activities in the Area of Professional Services* (October 2006), available at www.ec.europa.eu/competition/sectors/professional_services/overview_en.html.

[151] Commission decision of 24 June 2004; see de Waele 'Liberal professions and recommended prices: the Belgian architects case' (2004) (Autumn) *Competition Policy Newsletter* 44.

[152] Commission decision of 8 December 2010, on appeal Case T-90/11 *ONP v Commission*, not yet decided; the General Court dismissed an appeal by the associations against an inspection in this case: Case T-23/09 *CNOP and CCG v Commission* [2010] ECR II-000.

[153] Cases 209/78 etc *Van Landewyck v Commission* [1980] ECR 3125, [1981] 3 CMLR 134; similarly see Case 85/76 *Hoffmann-La Roche v Commission* [1979] ECR 461, [1979] 3 CMLR 211, para 123; *British Sugar plc* OJ [1999] L 76/1, [1999] 4 CMLR 1316, para 87, upheld on appeal Case T-202/98 *Tate & Lyle v Commission* [2001] ECR II-2035, [2001] 5 CMLR 859.

[154] *AROW v BNIC* OJ [1982] L 379/1, [1983] 2 CMLR 240; *Zinc Producer Group* OJ [1984] L 220/27, [1985] 2 CMLR 108; *Benelux Flat Glass* OJ [1984] L 212/13, [1985] 2 CMLR 350 (where competition was also limited by the similar costs faced by glass producers and the structure of the market); see ch 3, 'State compulsion in highly regulated markets', pp 137–138 and ch 6 generally on the relationship of the competition rules with state regulation of economic activity.

[155] OJ [2007] L 102/14, [2006] 4 CMLR 866, substantially upheld on appeal Case T-24/05 *Alliance One International v Commission* [2010] ECR II-000, [2011] 4 CMLR 545; Case T-29/05 *Deltafina SpA v Commission* [2010] ECR II-000, [2011] 4 CMLR 467, and Case T-37/05 *World Wide Tobacco España v Commission* [2011] ECR II-000; on appeal Cases C-537/10 P etc, not yet decided.

[156] OJ [2006] L 353/45, [2006] 4 CMLR 1766, upheld on appeal Case T-12/06 *Deltafina SpA v Commission*, [2011] ECR II-000.

[157] See ch 3, 'The "object or effect" of preventing, restricting or distorting competition', pp 117ff on the 'object or effect' distinction in Article 101(1).

[158] See *Italian Raw Tobacco*, para 285.

(B) **Article 101(3)**

As would be expected the Commission has stated that price-fixing agreements are unlikely to satisfy Article 101(3)[159]. This attitude is manifested in Regulation 1217/2010[160] on research and development agreements and Regulation 1218/2010[161] on specialisation agreements: neither block exemption is available to agreements containing obvious restrictions of competition, such as the fixing of prices, the limitation of output or the allocation of markets or customers.

However it should be recalled that, as a matter of law, it is always open to the parties to an agreement to argue that the terms of Article 101(3) are satisfied[162]. On a few occasions the Commission has permitted arrangements which could limit price competition. For example in *Uniform Eurocheques*[163] the Commission considered that the criteria of Article 101(3) were satisfied in the case of an agreement whereby commissions for the cashing of Eurocheques were fixed: this meant that consumers using such cheques knew that they would be charged a common amount throughout the EU. In *Insurance Intermediaries*[164] the Commission indicated its intention to authorise agreements between non-life insurers to fix maximum discounts. These and other[165] decisions suggest that the Commission might take a slightly more indulgent approach towards agreements that limit price competition in the services sector than in the goods sector.

The Commission's decision in *Reims II*[166], which authorised an agreement fixing the level of cross-border mail charges between 17 postal operators, was discussed in chapter 4[167]. In *Visa International – Multilateral Interchange Fee*[168] the Commission stated that it is not the case that an agreement concerning prices is always to be classified as a restriction by object or incapable of satisfying Article 101(3)[169]: in that decision it authorised the multilateral interchange fee ('MIF') agreed upon between 'acquiring' and 'issuing' banks within the Visa system until the end of 2007. In 2010 the Commission accepted commitments from Visa Europe under Article 9 of Regulation 1/2003[170] in respect of the MIF for its debit cards[171]. In *MasterCard*[172] the Commission decided in December 2007 that the

---

[159] See eg Commission's *Guidelines on the application of [Article 101(3)]* OJ [2004] C 101/97, paras 46 and 79 and *Guidelines on Horizontal Cooperation Agreements* OJ [2011] C 11/1, para 246.

[160] OJ [2010] L 335/36; for commentary on this Regulation see ch 15, 'The block exemption for research and development agreements: Regulation 1217/2010', pp 595–599.

[161] OJ [2010] L 335/43; for commentary on this Regulation see ch 15, 'The block exemption for specialisation agreements: Regulation 1218/2010', pp 601–603

[162] Case T-17/93 *Matra Hachette SA v Commission* [1994] ECR II-595, para 85; see ch 4, '*Matra Hachette v Commission*', pp 153–155.

[163] OJ [1985] L 35/43, [1985] 3 CMLR 434.   [164] OJ [1987] C 120/5.

[165] See also *Nuovo CEGAM* OJ [1984] L 99/29, [1984] 2 CMLR 484; *P and I Clubs* OJ [1985] L 376/2, [1989] CMLR 178; *Associazione Bancaria Italiana* OJ [1987] L 43/51, [1989] 4 CMLR 238; *Tariff Structures in the Combined Transport of Goods* OJ [1993] L 73/38.

[166] OJ [1999] L 275/17, [2000] 4 CMLR 704; the Commission extended the application of Article 101(3) to this agreement until 2006: OJ [2004] L 56/76; see also Commission Press Release IP/03/1438, 23 October 2003.

[167] See ch 4, '*Matra Hachette v Commission*', pp 153–155.

[168] OJ [2002] L 318/17, [2003] 4 CMLR 283; for comment see Gyselen 'Multilateral Interchange Fees under EU Antitrust Law: A One-Sided View on a Two-Sided Market' (2005) Columbia Business Law Review 703.

[169] Ibid, para 79.

[170] See ch 7, 'Article 9: commitments', pp 255–261 on Article 9 of Regulation 1/2003.

[171] Commission decision of 8 December 2010; the commitments do not cover Visa Europe's MIFs for consumer credit and deferred debit card transactions, which remain under investigation by the Commission.

[172] Commission decision of 19 December 2007; see Repa, Malczewska, Teixeira and Martinez Rivero 'Commission prohibits MasterCard's multilateral interchange fees for cross-border card payments in the EEA' (2008) 1 *Competition Policy Newsletter* 1.

MIF imposed in that card system infringed Article 101 because its level raised the cost of accepting payments with MasterCard without increasing efficiencies. The decision has been appealed[173]. In the meantime the level of the MIFs of both Visa and MasterCard are under scrutiny under many other systems of competition law, including in the UK[174].

In *AuA/LH*[175] the Commission considered that a 'lasting alliance' between Austrian Airlines and Lufthansa which entailed joint pricing and market sharing[176] satisfied the criteria of Article 101(3) as the alliance would result in 'important synergistic effects and attractive connections for consumers': the Commission could foresee cost savings, improved network connection, better planning of frequencies, a higher load factor, improved organisation of sales systems and groundhandling services, potential for new sales channels such as e-ticketing and access, on Austrian Airlines's part, to a superior airmiles scheme[177]. In *IFPI 'Simulcasting'*[178] the Commission concluded that an agreement that facilitated the grant of international licences of copyright to 'simulcast' music on the Internet involved price restrictions[179] but that the terms of Article 101(3) were satisfied since it led to efficiencies in the field of collective management of copyright and neighbouring rights[180].

(C) **Collective dominance**

The extent to which parallel pricing might amount to an infringement of Article 102 is considered in chapter 14[181].

4. **Horizontal Market Sharing**

Competition may be eliminated between independent undertakings in other ways than through direct or indirect price fixing. One way of doing so is for firms to agree to apportion particular markets between themselves. For example, three firms in the UK might agree that each will have exclusivity in a particular geographical area and that none will poach on the others' territories; a similar device is division of the market according to classes of customers, for example that one firm will supply trade customers only, another retailers and another public institutions. Geographical market-sharing agreements may be more effective than price fixing from the cartel's point of view, because the expense and difficulties of fixing common prices are avoided: the agreement means that there will be no price competition anyway. Policing the agreement is also relatively simple, because the mere presence of a competitor's goods on one's own 'patch' reveals cheating. Geographical market sharing is particularly restrictive from the consumer's point of view since it diminishes choice: at least where the parties fix prices a choice of product remains and it is possible that the restriction of price competition will force the parties to compete in other ways. Market-sharing agreements in the EU context may be viewed particularly seriously because, apart from the obviously anti-competitive effects already

---

[173] Case T-111/08 *MasterCard v Commission*, not yet decided.

[174] See 'Horizontal Price Fixing', pp 554–555 below.

[175] OJ [2002] L 242/25, [2002] 4 CMLR 487; for legal and regulatory reasons these undertakings were unable to merge in the sense of the EU Merger Regulation which is why this case was conducted under Article 101.

[176] OJ [2002] L 242/25. [2002] 4 CMLR 487, para 76.

[177] Ibid, paras 87–88.   [178] OJ [2003] L 107/58.   [179] Ibid, paras 61–80.

[180] Ibid, paras 84–123.

[181] See ch 14, 'Abuse of collective dominance under Article 102', pp 579–582.

described, they serve to perpetuate the isolation of geographical markets and to retard the process of single market integration which is a prime aim of the EU.

It is sometimes argued in favour of geographical market-sharing agreements that they should be permitted since they reduce the distribution costs of producers, who are relieved of the need to supply outside their exclusive geographical territories or to categories of customers other than those allotted to them. This is unconvincing, as it does not explain why the benefit claimed is dependent upon the horizontal agreement. If a producer found it profitable to do so, it would want to sell outside its allotted territory or class of customer and in determining the profitability of doing so it would take distribution costs into account. All the agreement does is to foreclose this possibility. Potential competition is removed with the same adverse effect upon consumer welfare that other hard-core restrictions may produce: a reduction in output and an increase in price.

It is not inconceivable that in some cases market sharing might be beneficial: in other words that restrictions accepted might enhance efficiency, in particular by enabling firms to compete more effectively with large undertakings. For example, a number of small retailers may decide to combine to promote their own 'house-label' in order to try to match other multiple chains[182]. Individually they may be weak and unable to undertake the enormous costs involved in advertising and promotion, but in combination they may be able to do so. It could be argued that each retailer should be able to claim an exclusive sales territory so that it will be encouraged to take its full part in the campaign in the knowledge that it will reap the benefit in its area. The corollary is that without this incentive it will not promote the brand label so actively and enthusiastically. The argument is similar to that applicable to many vertical restraints[183]. The conclusion ought therefore to be that in some exceptional cases horizontal market sharing should be permitted.

(A) **Article 101(1)**

There have been many decisions under Article 101 on market sharing, which is specifically mentioned in Article 101(1)(c)[184]. There are two obvious reasons for this. First, geographical market sharing can be achieved relatively easily in the EU context, since there are many ways of segregating national markets from one another. Until a truly internal market is established, the factual, legal and economic disparities between national markets will continue to act as an obstacle to inter-state trade. Secondly, one of the priorities of the Commission is to take action to prevent anything which might inhibit market penetration. It can be anticipated that horizontal market sharing will be punished severely. In *Peroxygen Products*[185] fines totalling €9 million were imposed on five producers which, from 1961 until at least 1980, operated a 'home market' agreement which covered most of the EU. A consequence of this was that prices for consumers varied widely between different geographical markets. In *Soda-ash – Solvay/ICI*[186] the Commission imposed fines on Solvay and ICI for geographical market sharing.

---

[182] See eg Commission's *Guidelines on Horizontal Cooperation Agreements* OJ [2011] C 11/1, para 252.

[183] See ch 16, 'Vertical agreements: possible benefits to competition', pp 626–628.

[184] See ch 3, 'Market sharing, quotas, collective exclusive dealing', pp 122–123.

[185] OJ [1985] L 35/1, [1985] 1 CMLR 481.

[186] OJ [1991] L 152/1, [1994] 4 CMLR 454: this investigation resulted in three other decisions imposing fines on ICI and Solvay for breaches of Article 102: *Soda-ash – Solvay* OJ [1991] L 152/21, *Soda-ash – ICI* OJ [1991] L 152/40, both reported at [1994] 4 CMLR 645 and on Solvay and CFK for market sharing: *Soda ash – Solvay, CFK* OJ [1991] L 152/16, [1994] 4 CMLR 482; the decisions were annulled for procedural reasons in Cases T-30/91 etc *Solvay v Commission* [1995] ECR II-1775, [1996] 5 CMLR 57, and the General Court's judgment was upheld in Cases C-286/95 P etc *Commission v ICI* [2000] ECR I-2341, [2000] 5 CMLR 413 and 454; the Commission readopted the decisions against Solvay and ICI in December 2000: OJ [2003] L 10/1,

In *Quinine*[187] the Court of Justice upheld the Commission's decision[188] to fine the members of the quinine cartel who had indulged in price fixing, the allocation of quotas and market division, and there have been many other similar cases since[189]. The infringements in the *Pre-Insulated Pipes*[190] decision were wide-ranging. The Commission accused the parties of dividing national markets and, ultimately, the whole European market amongst themselves; of price fixing; and of taking measures to hinder the one substantial competitor outside the cartel and to drive it out of the market. The fines amounted to €92 million. In some cases there have been elements both of vertical and horizontal market division; distributors must refrain from market division as well as producers[191]. In *Cement*[192] the Commission found that cement producers had agreed on the 'non-transshipment of cement to home markets', which prohibited any export of cement within Europe which could threaten neighbouring markets. In *Seamless Steel Tubes*[193] the Commission found that eight producers of stainless steel tubes had colluded to protect their respective domestic markets; the fines imposed totalled €99 million[194], reduced on appeal to the General Court to €86 million because the Commission had failed to establish the entire duration of the infringement[195].

In *Gas Insulated Switchgear*[196] fines of €750 million were imposed on a cartel which, amongst other things, divided the world market for switchgear apparatus with the result that Japanese undertakings did not compete for contracts in Europe and vice versa[197]; there was also an agreement among the European participants to respect each other's home market rights[198]. In *PO/Needles*[199] the Commission imposed fines of €60 million on a 'pure' product and geographic market-sharing agreement between Coats and Prym; on appeal the fines were reduced from €60 million to €47 million[200].

An unusual feature of the cartel in *Luxembourg Brewers* is that this case concerned a written cooperation agreement between five brewers, which sought to defend the

upheld on appeal Case T-58/01 *Solvay v Commission* [2009] ECR II-4781, [2011] 4 CMLR 101 the case is now on appeal to the Court of Justice Case C-110/10 P, not yet decided.

[187]　Cases 41/69 etc *ACF Chemiefarma NV v Commission* [1970] ECR 661.

[188]　*Re Quinine Cartel* JO [1969] L 192/5, [1969] CMLR D41.

[189]　Cases 40/73 etc *Coöperatieve Vereniging Suiker Unie UA v Commission* [1975] ECR 1663, [1976] 1 CMLR 295; *Re Van Katwijk NTs Agreement* JO [1970] L 242/18, [1970] CMLR D43; Cases 29 and 30/83 *Compagnie Royale Asturienne des Mines SA etc v Commission* [1984] ECR 1679, [1985] 1 CMLR 688; *Zinc Producer Group* OJ [1984] L 220/27, [1985] 2 CMLR 108.

[190]　OJ [1999] L 24/1, [1999] 4 CMLR 402, substantially upheld on appeal Cases T-9/99 etc *HFB Holding v Commission* [2002] ECR II-1487, [2001] 4 CMLR 1066.

[191]　See eg Cases 100–103/80 *Musique Diffusion Française SA v Commission* [1983] ECR 1825, [1983] 3 CMLR 221 in which the Court of Justice upheld the Commission's decision (OJ [1980] L 60/21, [1980] 1 CMLR 457) that distributors had engaged in concerted practices *amongst themselves* to isolate the French market.

[192]　OJ [1994] L 343/1, [1994] 4 CMLR 327, para 45.

[193]　OJ [2003] L 14/1, on appeal Cases T-67/00 etc *JFE Engineering and others v Commission* [2004] ECR II-2501, [2005] 4 CMLR 27 and on further appeal Cases C-403 and 405/04 P *Sumitomo Metal Industries v Commission* [2007] ECR I-729, [2007] 4 CMLR 650.

[194]　Commission Press Release IP/99/957, 8 December 1999; see also *SAS/Maersk* OJ [2001] L 265/15, [2001] 5 CMLR 1119: fines of €52.5 million for market sharing in the aviation sector, upheld an appeal Case T–241/01 *SAS v Commission* [2005] ECR II-2917, [2005] 5 CMLR 922.

[195]　Cases T-44/00 etc *Mannesmannröhren-Werke v Commission* [2004] ECR II-2223; the General Court's judgment was upheld on appeal to the Court of Justice, Cases C-411/04 P etc *Salzgitter Mannesmann GmbH v Commission* [2007] ECR I-959, [2007] 4 CMLR 682.

[196]　Commission decision of 24 January 2007, substantially upheld on appeal Cases T-117/07 etc *Areva v Commission* [2011] ECR II-000, [2011] 4 CMLR 1421.

[197]　Commission decision of 24 January 2007, para 114.　　　[198]　Ibid, para 115.

[199]　Commission decision of 26 October 2004.　　　[200]　Cases T-30/05 etc [2007] ECR II-107.

Luxembourg market against imports from other Member States. The Commission considered that the agreement had as its object the restriction of competition. The Commission concluded that the parties could not avail themselves of the *de minimis* Notice[201], since 'hard-core' restrictions can infringe Article 101(1) even below the thresholds in that Notice[202], and even where a participant is a small or medium-sized undertaking[203].

In the *Gas*[204] case the Commission condemned an agreement between E.ON and GDF to refrain from selling gas transported from Russia over a jointly-owned pipeline into each other's home markets. The Commission found that the agreement helped E.ON and GDF to maintain strong positions at a time of market liberalisation; each firm was fined €533 million. In *Power Transformers* fines totalling €67.6 million were imposed on seven producers which operated a 'gentleman's agreement' to share the Japanese and European markets[205].

Article 101(1) has also been applied to horizontal agreements involving customer restrictions[206].

(B) **Article 101(3)**

A horizontal geographical market-sharing agreement is unlikely to satisfy the criteria of Article 101(3), in view of the overriding goal of achieving single market integration. However in exceptional circumstances Article 101(3) may be applicable to market sharing that is indispensable for improvements in efficiency[207].

5. **Quotas and Other Restrictions on Production**

A further way in which a cartel might be able to earn supra-competitive profits is by agreeing to restrict its members' output. If output is reduced, price will rise; the oil cartel operated by OPEC does not fix prices as such, but instead determines how much oil each member country will export. Horizontal agreements to limit production need to be carefully monitored, because over-production by some members of the cartel would result in the market price falling, unless the scheme is run in conjunction with a price-fixing system, as often happens. In the absence of price fixing, the cartel members will often agree on a quota system whereby they will each supply a specified proportion of the entire industry output within any given period. As in the case of price fixing there will be costs involved in negotiating these quotas, because some firms will be larger or more efficient or expanding more rapidly than others so that there may have to be hard and protracted bargaining. The quotas having been fixed, some mechanism will have to be established to

---

[201] OJ [1997] C 372/13, [1998] 4 CMLR 192.

[202] Ibid, para 11; the same conclusion would be reached under the current Notice: see OJ [2001] C 368/13, [2002] 4 CMLR 699, para 11(1)(c); on the current Notice see ch 3, 'the Commission's *Notice on Agreements of Minor Importance*', pp 140–144.

[203] *Notice on Agreements of Minor Importance* OJ [2001] C 368/13, [2002] 4 CMLR 699, para 3.

[204] Commission decision of 8 July 2009, on appeal Cases T-360/09 etc *E.ON Ruhrgas and E.ON v Commission*, not yet decided.

[205] Commission decision of 7 October 2009, on appeal Cases T-517/09 etc *Alstom v Commission*, not yet decided.

[206] See eg *Re William Prym-Werke and Beka Agreement* OJ [1973] L 296/24, [1973] CMLR D250 where the Commission required the deletion of a customer restriction clause; *Atka A/S v BP Kemi A/S* OJ [1979] L 286/32, [1979] 3 CMLR 684 where BP was to supply customers with consumption of at least 100,000 gallons; *Belgian Roofing Felt* OJ [1986] L 232/15, [1991] 4 CMLR 130.

[207] See *Transocean Marine Paint Association* JO [1967] L 163/10, [1967] CMLR D9.

prevent cheating. This may be done, for example, by requiring detailed information about production and sales to be supplied to a trade association or 'cartel consultancy'. The agreement will also commonly provide a system whereby those that exceed their allocated quotas have to make compensating payments to those who, as a necessary corollary, fail to dispose of theirs. Complicated rules may have to be settled on how such payments are to be made. A firm which 'over-produces' will have to sell its products on the market at a higher price than it would wish if it is to make a profit and make a payment to the other cartel members; the loss to the consumer of such schemes is clear.

Some agreements which involve restrictions of production may be beneficial: specialisation agreements, joint production, research and development agreements, restructuring cartels and standardisation agreements may in some circumstances be considered desirable. This chapter is concerned with hard-core restrictions on production which limit output without producing any compensating benefits; agreements involving restrictions of production which may be ancillary to some legitimate objective will be discussed in chapter 15.

(A) **Article 101(1)**

Article 101(1)(b) specifically applies to agreements to 'limit or control production, markets, technical development, or investment' and has been applied to agreements to limit production on many occasions. Straightforward quota systems have often been condemned[208].

In *Peroxygen Products*[209] the Commission found that, as well as sharing markets geographically, members of the cartel had entered into a series of detailed national agreements dividing markets in agreed percentages. In *MELDOC*[210] a quota and compensation scheme in the dairy sector in the Netherlands was held to infringe Article 101, and the Commission imposed fines totalling €6,565,000. An exacerbating fact in this decision was the fact that the Dutch milk producers also agreed to a coordinated response to the threat posed to their market position by imports from other Member States. An agreement not to expand production without the approval of rival firms infringes Article 101(1)[211] and the Commission will not easily be persuaded that a quota scheme will bring about beneficial specialisation[212]. It is not permissible to establish a joint venture to apportion orders between competitors[213], nor will the Commission allow joint production which simply limits competition without producing any compensating benefits[214]. Not infrequently quota agreements confer on particular undertakings exclusive or priority rights in supplying their own domestic markets: they will certainly not be tolerated[215].

An interesting example of a quota scheme condemned by the Commission is *Associated Lead Manufacturers Ltd (White Lead)*[216]. Firms producing white lead in the UK, Germany and the Netherlands agreed that each would supply one-third of the white lead to be

---

[208] See eg *Zinc Producer Group* OJ [1984] L 220/27, [1985] 2 CMLR 108; *Benelux Flat Glass* OJ [1984] L 212/13, [1985] 2 CMLR 350; also the various cement cases decided by the Commission involving quota arrangements: see *Re Cementregeling voor Nederland* JO [1972] L 303/7, [1973] CMLR D149; *Re Cimbel* JO [1972] L 303/24, [1973] CMLR D167; *Re Nederlandse Cement-Handelmaatschappij NV* JO [1972] L 22/16, [1973] CMLR D257; see also *Belgian Roofing Felt* OJ [1986] L 232/15, [1991] 4 CMLR 130; *Welded Steel Mesh* OJ [1989] L 260/1, [1991] 4 CMLR 13.

[209] OJ [1985] L 35/1, [1985] 1 CMLR 481.   [210] OJ [1986] L 348/50, [1989] 4 CMLR 853.

[211] *Re Cimbel* JO [1972] L 303/24, [1973] CMLR D167.

[212] *Re Italian Cast Glass* OJ [1980] L 383/19, [1982] 2 CMLR 61.

[213] *Air Forge* Commission's XIIth *Report on Competition Policy* (1982), point 85.

[214] *Re WANO Schwarzpulver GmbH* OJ [1978] L 322/26, [1979] 1 CMLR 403.

[215] Case 41/69 *ACF Chemiefarma NV v Commission* [1970] ECR 661.

[216] OJ [1979] L 21/16, [1979] 1 CMLR 464.

exported to non-EU countries. A central office was established which gathered information from them on their deliveries of white lead. The producers supplied this office with details of *all* deliveries, including exports to other EU countries. The Commission held that in practice the quota scheme related to all exports, that is to say to intra-EU as well as extra-EU trade, and that it clearly amounted to an attempt to limit and control markets within the terms of Article 101(1)(b). Furthermore the Commission held that it was irrelevant that the quotas were not always meticulously observed: an agreement did not cease to be anti-competitive because it was temporarily or even repeatedly circumvented by one of the parties to it[217].

In *Compagnie Royale Asturienne des Mines SA and Rheinzink GmbH v Commission*[218] the Court of Justice held that it was an infringement of Article 101(1) for competitors to supply products to each other on a continuing basis. Whereas this might be acceptable to deal with certain emergencies, it was not permissible for competitors to enter into agreements of indeterminate length and for considerable quantities. The effect of doing so was to institutionalise mutual aid in lieu of competition, producing conditions on the market analogous to those brought about by quota arrangements. In *Soda-ash – Solvay/CFK*[219] the Commission condemned an agreement whereby Solvay agreed to allow CFK a guaranteed minimum sales tonnage and to purchase from it any shortfall in order to compensate it. In *Italian Flat Glass*[220] the Commission condemned an agreement between manufacturers to exchange products and agree quantities sold to particular customers. The General Court overturned this aspect of the decision for lack of evidence[221], but it did not question the principle that such an agreement restricts competition. The first fine for a substantive infringement of Article 101 in the maritime transport sector was imposed in *French-West African Shipowners' Committees*[222] upon shipowners which had agreed to a cargo-sharing system in respect of traffic between France and various west African countries.

An elaborate 'price before tonnage scheme' was found to be anti-competitive by the Commission in *Cartonboard*[223] which involved the 'freezing' of market shares, the constant monitoring and analysis of them, and the coordination of 'machine downtime' in an effort to sustain prices and control supply. In *Europe Asia Trades Agreement*[224] the Commission concluded that an agreement for 'capacity non-utilisation' coupled with the exchange of information in relation to maritime transport infringed Article 101(1); in its view the agreement artificially limited liner shipping capacity, thereby reducing price competition[225]. In *Danish Association of Pharmaceutical Producers and the Danish Ministry for Health*[226] the Commission investigated a quota arrangement aimed at controlling public spending on price subsidies for pharmaceuticals, but closed the file after the parties agreed not to renew the arrangement. In *Zinc Phosphate*[227] the Commission considered that the 'cornerstone' of the cartel was the allocation of sales quotas, although

---

[217] Similarly see *Re Cast Iron and Steel Rolls* OJ [1983] L 317/1, [1984] 1 CMLR 694 where the Commission fined various French undertakings which operated a quota scheme in respect of deliveries to the Saarland in Germany.

[218] Cases 29 and 30/83 [1984] ECR 1679, [1985] 1 CMLR 688.

[219] OJ [1991] L 152/16, [1994] 4 CMLR 482.   [220] OJ [1989] L 33/44, [1990] 4 CMLR 535.

[221] Cases T-68/89 etc *Società Italiana Vetro SpA v Commission* [1992] ECR II-1403, [1992] 5 CMLR 302.

[222] OJ [1992] L 134/1, [1993] 5 CMLR 446.

[223] OJ [1994] L 243/1, [1994] 5 CMLR 547, paras 129–132, on appeal Cases T-311/94 etc *BPB de Eendracht v Commission* [1998] ECR II-1129.

[224] OJ [1999] L 193/23, [1999] 5 CMLR 1380.   [225] Ibid, paras 148–156.

[226] Commission Press Release IP/99/633, 17 August 1999; Commission's XXIXth *Report on Competition Policy* (1999), p 170.

[227] OJ [2003] L 153/1.

it also found that there was an agreement on the fixing of 'bottom' or recommended prices and some allocation of customers[228].

In *Gas Insulated Switchgear*[229] the Commission found that not only were the members of the cartel dividing the global market along geographical lines, but that they had also agreed worldwide quotas; and that the agreed European quota had itself been divided between the European undertakings in the cartel[230]. In *Heat Stabilisers* the Commission found agreements to establish quotas, to fix prices and to exchange information which had been supervised by a consultancy firm[231].

(B) Article 101(3)

It is unlikely that the type of agreements discussed in this section would satisfy the criteria of Article 101(3), although agreements on capacity and production volume may be permitted when indispensable to efficiencies brought about by a specialisation agreement[232].

6. Collusive Tendering

Collusive tendering is a practice whereby firms agree amongst themselves to collaborate over their response to invitations to tender. It is particularly likely to be encountered in the engineering and construction industries where firms compete for very large contracts; often the tenderee will have a powerful bargaining position and the contractors feel the need to concert their bargaining power. From a contractor's point of view collusion over tendering has other benefits apart from the fact that it can lead to higher prices: it may mean that fewer contractors actually bother to price any particular deal (tendering itself can be a costly business) so that overheads are kept lower; it may mean that a contractor can make a tender which it knows will not be accepted (because it has been agreed that another firm will tender at a lower price) and yet which indicates that it is still interested in doing business, so that it will not be crossed off the tenderee's list; and it may mean that a contractor can retain the business of its established, favoured customers without worrying that they will be poached by its competitors.

Collusive tendering takes many forms. At its simplest, the firms in question simply agree to quote identical prices, the hope being that in the end each will receive its fair share of orders. Level tendering, however, is extremely suspicious and is likely to attract the attention of the competition authorities, so that more subtle arrangements are normally made. The more complicated these are, the greater will be the cost to the tenderers themselves. One system is to notify intended quotes to each other, or more likely to a central secretariat, which will then cost the order and eliminate those quotes which it considers would result in a loss to some or all of the association's members. Another system is to rotate orders, in which case the firm whose turn it is to receive an order will ensure

---

[228] Ibid, paras 64–72.

[229] Commission decision of 24 January 2007, substantially upheld on appeal Cases T-117/07 *Areva v Commission* [2011] ECR II-000, [2011] 4 CMLR 1421.

[230] Commission decision of 24 January 2007, paras 116–120.

[231] Commission decision of 11 November 2009, paras 380–387, on appeal Cases T-27/10 etc *Arkema v Commission*, not yet decided.

[232] See the Commission's *Guidelines on Horizontal Cooperation Agreements* OJ [2011] C 11/1, paras 183–186; on specialisation agreements, see ch 15, 'The block exemption for specialisation agreements: Regulation 1218/2010', pp 601–603.

that its quote is lower than everyone else's. Again it may be that orders are allocated by the relevant trade association which will advise each member how it should proceed.

There is no doubt that collusive tendering is caught by Article 101(1)[233]. The Commission condemned the practice in *Re European Sugar Cartel*[234]. In *Building and Construction Industry in the Netherlands*[235] the Commission imposed a fine of €22.5 million for regulating prices and tendering in the Dutch building and construction industry. Twenty-eight associations of firms had established an organisation, the SPO, which established a system of uniform price-regulating rules which were binding on all members. The rules restricted competition, as members exchanged information with one another prior to tendering, concerted their behaviour in relation to the prices for tenders and operated a system whereby the 'entitled' undertaking could be certain of winning a particular contract. The fact that the Dutch Government approved of the system did not provide a defence under Article 101(1): rather it led to the Commission threatening proceedings against the Netherlands under Article 258 for having encouraged this anti-competitive behaviour. The Commission rejected arguments in favour of application of Article 101(3) in this decision[236]. In *Pre-Insulated Pipes*[237] the Commission concluded that the allocation of contracts on the basis of 'respect for existing "traditional" customer relationships', as well as various measures to support the bid-rigging, infringed Article 101(1)[238].

The Commission found undertakings guilty of bid-rigging in *Gas Insulated Switchgear*[239] and *Elevators and Escalators*[240]. In the former the Commission imposed fines of €750 million for bid-rigging, price fixing, allocation of projects, market sharing and the exchange of information. In *Elevators and Escalators* the Commission imposed fines of €992 million on a series of undertakings for bid-rigging, price fixing, allocation of projects, market sharing and the exchange of information in relation to the installation and maintenance of lifts and escalators in Belgium, Germany, Luxembourg and the Netherlands[241]. The Commission said that the undertakings concerned informed each other of calls for tender and coordinated their bids according to pre-agreed cartel quotas. In *Car Glass*[242] the Commission imposed fines of €1.3 billion – the largest set of fines for one decision in the history of Article 101. The Commission objected to, amongst other illicit practices, cover pricing: that is to say bids that gave the pretence of competition, but that were deliberately set at a higher price than that of the member of the cartel whose turn it was to be awarded a contract[243]. Updated project lists were circulated among the members of the cartel, and there was an understanding that, where a member of the cartel

[233] Note that collusive tendering is also illegal in some countries, for example under a specific law in Germany and under the cartel offence in the UK where the agreement involves dishonesty: on the latter offence see ch 10, 'The cartel offence', pp 425–434.

[234] OJ [1973] L 140/17, [1973] CMLR D65.

[235] OJ [1992] L 92/1, [1993] 5 CMLR 135, upheld on appeal Case T-29/92 *SPO v Commission* [1995] ECR 11-289.

[236] OJ [1992] L 92/1, [1993] 5 CMLR 135, paras 115–131.

[237] OJ [1999] L 24/1, [1999] 4 CMLR 402, substantially upheld on appeal Cases T-9/99 etc *HFB Holding v Commission* [2002] ECR II-1487, [2001] 4 CMLR 1066.

[238] OJ [1999] L 24/1, [1999] 4 CMLR 402, para 147.

[239] Commission decision of 24 January 2007, upheld on appeal Cases T-110/07 etc *Siemens v Commission* [2011] ECR II-000, [2011] 4 CMLR 1335.

[240] Commission decision of 21 February 2007, substantially upheld on appeal Cases T-145/07 etc *General Technic–Otis v Commission*, [2011] ECR II-000.

[241] Note that fines of €75.4 million have also been imposed by the Austrian competition authority in this sector: the press release can be found at www.bwb.gv.at.

[242] Commission decision of 12 November 2008, on appeal Cases T-56/09 etc *Saint-Gobain Glass France and others v Commission*, not yet decided.

[243] Commission decision of 12 November 2008, para 103.

had a long-standing or good relationship with a particular customer, it would get most of its business. In *Marine Hoses*[244] the parties were found guilty of allocating tenders, as well as price fixing, determining quotas, market sharing and exchanging sensitive information; and one of the infringements in *International Removal Services*[245] was cover pricing.

7. Agreements Relating to Terms and Conditions

We have seen above that apart from agreements directly fixing prices, supra-competitive profits can also be earned in other ways, for example by limiting production, fixing quotas and dividing markets geographically. Similarly restrictive agreements which limit competition in the terms and conditions offered to customers can have this effect. An agreement not to offer discounts is in effect a price restriction, as would be an agreement not to offer credit; it may well exist to buttress a price-fixing agreement. In some market conditions it might be that non-price competition is particularly significant because of the limited opportunities that exist for price cutting; for example, in an oligopolistic market one oligopolist might be able to attract custom because it can offer a better after-sales service or guarantees or a free delivery service[246].

Although competition in terms and conditions is an important part of the competitive process, it is also true to say that in some circumstances standardisation of terms and conditions can be beneficial. This might have the effect of enhancing price transparency: that is to say a customer might be able more easily to compare the 'real' cost of goods or services on offer if he or she does not have to make some (possibly intuitive) allowances for the disparity in two sets of terms and conditions on offer. Again a trade association may have the knowledge and expertise (and legal resources) to draft appropriate standard form contracts which suit the needs of individual members whereas, acting individually, they would be unable to negotiate and conclude a set of terms and conditions suitable for their purpose. Competition law monitors the activities of trade associations carefully in order to ensure that they do not act as a medium for the restriction of competition, but will usually tolerate this function. Industry-based codes of practice may fall within the ambit of competition legislation, although they may be desirable and may be encouraged or even required by consumer legislation[247].

Article 101 is capable of catching agreements which limit competition on terms and conditions, and to the extent that this is effected through the medium of trade associations the application of that Article to 'decisions by associations of undertakings' will be particularly apposite. The Commission has condemned agreements only to supply on prescribed general conditions of sale[248] and it has also objected to them where they formed part of wider reciprocal exclusive dealing arrangements[249]. In *Vimpoltu*[250] the Commission condemned an agreement on terms and conditions which limited important 'secondary aspects of competition'. In *Publishers' Association: Net Book Agreements*[251]

---

[244] Commission decision of 28 November 2009, on appeal Cases T-146/09 etc *Parker ITR and Parker Hannifin v Commission*, not yet decided.

[245] Commission decision of 11 March 2008, substantially upheld on appeal Cases T-204/08 etc *Team Relocations NV v Commission* [2011] ECR II-000.

[246] On oligopoly generally see ch 14, 'The theory of oligopolistic interdependence', pp 560–567.

[247] See eg s 8 of the Enterprise Act 2002.

[248] See *European Glass Manufacturers* OJ [1974] L 160/1, [1974] 2 CMLR D50; see similarly *FEDETAB* OJ [1978] L 224/29, [1978] 3 CMLR 524.

[249] See eg *Donck v Central Bureau voor de Rijwielhandel* OJ [1978] L 20/18, [1978] 2 CMLR 194.

[250] OJ [1983] L 200/44, [1983] 3 CMLR 619.   [251] OJ [1989] L 22/12, [1989] 4 CMLR 825.

agreements to impose on resellers standard conditions of sale and measures taken to implement this were condemned, as they deprived retailers of the ability to deviate from fixed retail prices. In *TACA*[252] the Commission concluded that an agreement that prohibited members of a liner conference from entering into individual service contracts at rates negotiated between a shipper and an individual line infringed Article 101(1); under the agreement members were permitted to offer standard service contracts only on the terms negotiated by the TACA secretariat, which constituted a serious fetter on their ability to compete with one another. In *Marine Hoses*[253] the parties agreed sales conditions as part of a plan to control rival bids for marine hoses tenders.

The Commission has recognised the advantages for undertakings in having accessible and non-binding standard terms and conditions for the sale of consumer goods or services and has indicated that their use will not infringe Article 101(1) unless their application in practice seriously limits customer choice[254]. Also the Commission applied Article 101(3) in the fire insurance sector to an agreement whereby insurance companies would be likely (though not obliged) to adopt the standard terms and conditions of Concordato, a non-profit-making trade association[255].

8. Exchanges of Information[256]

(A) Introduction

An important competition law issue is whether undertakings run the risk of infringing Article 101 when they exchange information with one another. This is an issue that the Commission has given consideration to over many years, from as early as 1968 in its *Notice on Cooperation Agreements*[257] and in numerous decisions from the 1970s onwards. At the end of 2010 the Commission adopted new *Guidelines on the applicability of Article 101 [TFEU] to horizontal co-operation agreements* ('*Guidelines on Horizontal Cooperation Agreements*' or '*the Guidelines*')[258]. The *Guidelines* provide helpful guidance on exchanges of information and draw substantially on the case law of the EU Courts[259], in particular *John Deere v Commission*[260], *Asnef-Equifax v Ausbanc*[261] and *T-Mobile v NMa*[262]. Reference

---

[252] OJ [1999] L 95/1, [1999] 4 CMLR 1415, paras 379–380, upheld on this point on appeal in Cases T-191/98 etc *Atlantic Container Line AB v Commission* [2003] ECR II-3275, [2005] 4 CMLR 1283; the Commission subsequently authorised a revised version of *TACA* OJ [2003] L 26/53, [2003] 4 CMLR 1001.

[253] Commission decision of 28 November 2009, on appeal Cases T-146/09 etc *Parker ITR and Parker Hannifin v Commission*, not yet decided.

[254] See the Commission's *Guidelines on Horizontal Cooperation Agreements* OJ [2011] C 11/1, paras 302–305.

[255] *Concordato Incendio* OJ [1990] L 15/25, [1991] 4 CMLR 199.

[256] See generally *The Pros and Cons of Information Sharing* (Swedish Competition Authority, 2006) for a series of essays on the law and economics of information sharing; see also Capobianco 'Information exchange under EC competition law' (2004) 41 CML Rev 1247 and Bennett and Collins 'The Law and Economics of Information Sharing: The Good, the Bad and the Ugly' (2010) 6(2) European Competition Journal 311.

[257] JO [1968] C 75/3, [1968] CMLR D5; this Notice was repealed by the Commission's *Guidelines on the applicability of Article [101] to Horizontal Cooperation Agreements* OJ [2001] C 3/2, which in turn have been replaced by the Commission's *Guidelines on Horizontal Cooperation Agreements* OJ [2011] C 11/1: ibid, para 18.

[258] OJ [2011] C 11/1; for comment see the series of essays in Antitrust Chronicle, February 2011(1), available at www.competitionpolicyinternational.com.

[259] A judgment which the *Guidelines* do not mention but is relevant to this issue is that of the Court of Justice in *Steel Beams*, Case C-194/99 *Thyssen Stahl v Commission* [2003] ECR I-10821.

[260] Cases C-7/95 and C-8/95 [1998] ECR I-3111 and 3175, [1998] 5 CMLR 311; see Lenares 'Economic Foundations of EU Legislation Sharing Among Firms' (1997) 18 ECLR 66.

[261] Case C-238/05 [2006] ECR I-11125, [2007] 4 CMLR 224.

[262] Case C-8/08 [2009] ECR I-4529, [2009] 5 CMLR 1701.

will be made to the *Guidelines on Horizontal Cooperation Agreements* below, although the reader is reminded that this document is not legally binding; however it explains in a helpful way the Commission's thinking on how Article 101 should apply to the exchange of information. The *Guidelines* do not apply to the extent that sector-specific rules, for example on agreements in the transport sector and insurance sectors, are in place[263]. The *Horizontal Cooperation Guidelines* begin by describing the arguments in favour of and against exchanges of information; they then explain the different types of exchange of information; thereafter the concept of a concerted practice and exchanges of information that have as their object or effect the restriction of competition are dealt with. This is followed by a short discussion of the criteria in Article 101(3). This sequence will broadly be retained in the text that follows.

(B) Arguments in favour of and against exchanges of information

It is important to understand that information – including, therefore, the exchange of information – may be highly beneficial, to competitors, consumers and to the competitive process. The *Guidelines on Horizontal Cooperation Agreements* acknowledge that exchanging information is a common feature of many competitive markets[264]. Competitors cannot compete in a statistical vacuum: the more information they have about market conditions, the volume of demand, the level of capacity that exists in an industry and the investment plans of rivals, the easier it is for them to make rational and effective decisions on their production and marketing strategies. Competitors may benefit, without harming their customers, by exchanging information on matters such as methods of accounting, stock control, book-keeping or the draftsmanship of standard-form contracts.

However there are, of course, dangers to the competitive process if certain types of information are exchanged in certain market conditions. In most cases the question is whether the exchange of information is likely to have significant anti-competitive effects, although some types of information agreement may have the object of restricting competition. The *Guidelines on Horizontal Cooperation Agreements* identify two main competition concerns arising from an exchange of information: first, it may enable undertakings to predict each other's future behaviour and to coordinate their behaviour on the market; and secondly, it may result in anti-competitive foreclosure of access to the market in which the exchange of information takes place or to a related market. The Commission says that it does not claim that these concerns are exclusive or exhaustive[265].

(C) Types of exchange of information

Information is exchanged in various contexts. It is therefore necessary to characterise the exchange of information in order to ascertain whether competition is likely to be harmed. Two situations should be noted.

(i) Information exchange in support of a horizontal cooperation agreement

Where an exchange of information forms part of another type of horizontal cooperation agreement its assessment should be carried out in combination with the assessment of that agreement; an obvious example would be the parties to a production agreement sharing information about costs. Exchanges of information which are necessary for the

---

[263] *Guidelines on Horizontal Cooperation Agreements*, para 18; on information exchange in the maritime transport sector see ch 23, 'Transport', p 971; see also ch 15, 'Insurance sector', pp 613–614.

[264] *Guidelines on Horizontal Cooperation Agreements*, para 57.   [265] Ibid, section 2.2.1, fn 1.

implementation of research and development or specialisation agreements may benefit from the block exemption available for those agreements[266].

(ii) Information exchange in support of a cartel

There have been many cases in which the Commission has held that the exchange of information was unlawful where it was part of a mechanism for monitoring and/or enforcing compliance with some other agreement that was itself unlawful. For example where undertakings establish a cartel they will invariably put in place mechanisms that enable them to be sure that each participant is complying with the agreed rules, and the exchange of information is an important part of this policing function. Sometimes there will be a simple exchange of information between the members of the cartel; in other situations the collection, processing and dissemination of the information may be achieved through a trade association or cartel consultancy. If one looks at almost any of the Commission's decisions on hard-core cartels in the last few years, it will be seen that the unlawful agreement(s) in question – for example to fix prices, share out geographical markets, allocate quotas or to restrict competition in some other way – included the exchange of commercially sensitive business information.

In the case of *Gas Insulated Switchgear*[267] the Commission imposed fines of €750.7 million on a cartel involving European and Japanese firms that divided the market geographically and allocated quotas. A feature of this case was that cartel secretaries were appointed in Europe and Japan whose function was to receive and disseminate among the members information about forthcoming projects in the sector; this led to discussions about who was interested in winning the contract, whether some members of the cartel would make cover bids to give the (false) impression of competition, and to a final report as to who had actually won the contest[268]. The illegality of information exchanges of this kind is established by virtue of the fact that it is a mechanism for supporting behaviour that is illegal anyway[269]. Just as ancillary restrictions supportive of a legitimate agreement are legal[270], the exchange of information pursuant to an illegal agreement is itself illegal.

(D) Agreement and/or concerted practice to exchange information

Information exchange can take various forms: data can be directly shared between competitors or indirectly exchanged through a trade association or a third party, such as a common supplier. To infringe Article 101(1) there must be an agreement and/or concerted practice between undertakings to exchange information or a decision by an association of undertakings to the same effect. In *Asnef-Equifax v Ausbanc*[271] the Court of Justice held that, where credit institutions participated in the creation of a register of information about the solvency of customers, it was not important to decide whether this happened as a result of an agreement, a concerted practice or a decision of an association of undertakings[272]. Paragraphs 60 to 63 of the *Guidelines on Horizontal Cooperation Agreements*

---

[266] See *Guidelines on Horizontal Cooperation Agreements*, para 88, fn 1; see generally ch 15 on block exemption Regulations 1217/2010 and 1218/2010.

[267] Commission decision of 24 January 2007, substantially upheld on appeal Cases T-117/07 etc *Areva v Commission* [2011] ECR II-000, [2011] 4 CMLR 1421.

[268] Commission decision of 24 January 2007, paras 121–123.

[269] *Guidelines on Horizontal Cooperation Agreements*, para 59.

[270] See ch 3, 'Cases in which agreements containing contractual restrictions were found not to have anticompetitive effects', pp 128–129.

[271] Case C-238/05 [2006] ECR I-11125, [2007] 4 CMLR 224.   [272] Ibid, paras 30–32.

provide useful guidance on the concept of concerted practice in the context of exchange of information. The case law on this concept is discussed in chapter 3 of this book[273]. The *Guidelines* say that Article 101(1) applies to sharing of 'strategic data', that is to say data that reduces strategic uncertainty in the market[274], between competitors. The *Guidelines* also explain that a unilateral disclosure of strategic information can give rise to a concerted practice[275]; there is a presumption that, by receiving such information from a competitor, a firm accepts it and adapts its future conduct on the market[276]. Where a firm makes a unilateral announcement that is genuinely public, for example in the press, a concerted practice is unlikely[277]. In *Wood Pulp*[278] the Court of Justice ruled that the fact that pulp producers publicly announced price rises to users before those rises came into effect was not, in itself, sufficient to constitute an infringement of Article 101(1)[279].

(E) Assessment under Article 101(1)

The *Guidelines* recognise that the exchange of information can have positive effects, in particular when they enable firms to become more efficient. However, there are also situations where the exchange of information can be harmful to competition. The problem for competition law is to distinguish those exchanges of information which have a neutral or beneficial effect upon efficiency from those which seriously threaten the competitive process by facilitating collusive behaviour. This section will consider the application of Article 101(1) to exchanges of information[280].

(i) Restrictions of competition by object

The case law of the EU Courts has established that any discussion among competitors about their prices is likely to be regarded as giving rise to an anti-competitive price-fixing agreement. Paragraph 74 of the *Guidelines* suggests that the exchange of information between competitors which identify the future intended prices or quantities of individual firms has as its object the restriction of competition and is unlikely to satisfy the criteria of Article 101(3). The *Guidelines* do not say, but it is the case, that there does not need to be a direct effect on prices paid by end-consumers[281]. Nor is it necessary for A and B to have explicitly *agreed* that they will increase their prices: the mere fact of providing information to one another about future pricing behaviour – or even for one to provide such information to the other – is likely to be sufficient for a finding of an agreement on prices. In *Bananas*[282] the Commission considered that three producers of bananas were party to a concerted practice that restricted competition by object where they regularly

---

[273] See ch 3, 'Concerted practices', pp 112–115.

[274] *Guidelines on Horizontal Cooperation Agreements*, para 86, which explains that 'strategic data' includes information relating to prices, customer lists, production costs, quantities, turnovers, sales, capacities, qualities, marketing plans, risks, investments, technologies, research and development programmes and their results.

[275] *Guidelines on Horizontal Cooperation Agreements*, para 62.

[276] Ibid, para 62; for discussion of the case law establishing this presumption see ch 3, 'Concerted practices', pp 113–114.

[277] *Guidelines on Horizontal Cooperation Agreements*, para 63; the possibility cannot be entirely ruled out in cases where competitors make public announcements to signal future strategic behaviour to one another.

[278] Cases C-89/85 etc *A Ahlström Oy v Commission* [1993] ECR I-1307, [1993] 4 CMLR 407.

[279] Ibid, paras 59–65.

[280] See *Guidelines on Horizontal Cooperation Agreements*, paras 105–110 for helpful examples of the Commission's thinking on a number of hypothetical situations.

[281] See eg Case C-8/08 *T-Mobile Netherlands BV v Raad van Bestuur van de Nederlandse Mededingingsautoriteit* [2009] ECR I-4529, [2009] 5 CMLR 1701, paras 36–39.

[282] Commission decision of 15 October 2008, on appeal Cases T-587/08 etc *Fresh Del Monte Produce v Commission*, not yet decided.

communicated with one another, before setting the prices that they quoted to their customers on a weekly basis, as to the factors that they considered were relevant for setting quotation prices for the week ahead, including their views on prices trends: in the Commission's view this enabled them to coordinate the setting of quotation prices instead of deciding on them independently[283].

It is not a defence for an undertaking to argue that it attended a meeting at which prices were discussed, but that it maintained silence throughout the meeting, and gave no indication of its own intentions. Attendance is sufficient to implicate the undertaking in the price fixing unless it left the meeting and took positive action to 'publicly distance' itself from any unlawful behaviour[284]. In *T-Mobile v NMa*[285] the Court of Justice confirmed that an exchange of price information between competitors at a single meeting could give rise to a concerted practice that has as its object the restriction of competition[286]. The message could hardly be clearer: do not remain at a meeting at which competitors discuss prices or quantities.

(ii) Restrictions of competition by effect[287]

Exchanges of information that do not support an agreement that is itself anti-competitive, and that do not concern future prices or quantities, do not restrict competition by object, but may do so by effect. This section will consider when such 'pure' exchanges of information can infringe Article 101(1) in their own right. The analysis of information agreements of the kind under discussion in this section requires effects analysis – that is to say a full review of the context in which the exchange of information is taking place is required[288]. The point is made clearly in the Court of Justice's judgment in *Asnef-Equifax*[289]:

[t]he compatibility of an information exchange system ... with the [EU] competition rules cannot be assessed in the abstract. It depends on the economic conditions on the relevant markets and on the specific characteristics of the system concerned, such as, in particular, its purpose and the conditions of access to it and participation in it, as well as the type of information exchanged – be that, for example, public or confidential, aggregated or detailed, historical or current – the periodicity of such information and its importance for the fixing of prices, volumes or conditions of service[290].

In the *T-Mobile* case the Court of Justice explained that the purpose of this analysis is to determine whether the exchange could 'reduce or remove' uncertainty between undertakings so that competition is restricted[291]. The Commission's *Guidelines on Horizontal Cooperation Agreements* explain how it approaches 'pure' exchanges of information; the crucial question always is whether it could enable undertakings to achieve and/or sustain coordination. The *Guidelines* examine two issues, each of which accords with economic theory: the economic conditions on the relevant markets and the characteristics of information exchanged.

---

[283] Ibid, para 263.

[284] See ch 3, 'The concept of a "single, overall agreement"', pp 103–104.

[285] Case C-8/08 [2009] ECR I-4529, [2009] 5 CMLR 1701, paras 58–61.   [286] Ibid, paras 58–61.

[287] See Grassani 'Oligopolies and "Pure" Information Exchanges in the EU: New Crops are Growing on the Soils Plowed by "UK Tractors"' [2007] Fordham Corporate Law Institute (ed Hawk); this article helpfully reviews – and expresses some concerns about – recent decisions by the national competition authorities of France, Italy, Spain and the UK, where it perceives possible inconsistencies in enforcement activities.

[288] See ch 3, '"The "object or effect" of preventing, restricting or distorting competition', p 117, for a discussion of the distinction between object and effect analysis under Article 101.

[289] Case C-238/05 [2006] ECR I-11125, [2007] 4 CMLR 224.   [290] Ibid, para 54.

[291] Case C-8/08 *T-Mobile Netherlands BV v Raad van Bestuur van de Nederlandse Mededingingsautoriteit* [2009] ECR I-4529, [2009] 5 CMLR 1701; para 35 and the case law cited therein.

(iii) **The economic conditions on the relevant markets**

In the first place it is important to consider the characteristics of the market. Paragraph 76 of the *Guidelines* explains that exchanges of information are more likely to have anti-competitive effects in markets where conditions for coordination are propitious. The *Guidelines* say that coordination is more likely on markets which are sufficiently transparent, concentrated, non-complex, stable and symmetric. Each of these factors is explored further in succeeding paragraphs of the *Guidelines*. They point out that exchanges of information are not likely to be anti-competitive in very fragmented markets, unless the information exchanged increases transparency or changes the market situation in another way that is conducive for coordination[292]. This illustrates a more general point made by the *Guidelines*: whether an exchange of information facilitates collusive behaviour depends on not only the initial market conditions but also how the exchange of information may change those conditions. In deciding whether coordination will be sustainable the Commission will consider whether there is a credible threat of retaliation to prevent other firms from cheating[293].

The Commission's concern with the economic conditions of the market when considering whether an exchange of information could be caught by Article 101(1) can be seen in its practice over many years[294]. In *UK Agricultural Tractor Registration Exchange*[295] the Commission condemned an information-exchange system, placing considerable emphasis on the fact that the UK tractor market was oligopolistic: in particular it took into account that four firms on the UK market had a combined market share of approximately 80 per cent and that in some geographical areas the concentration was higher; that barriers to entry were high, especially as extensive distribution and servicing networks were necessary; that the market was stagnant or in decline and there was considerable brand loyalty; and that there was an absence of significant imports[296]. The Commission published a Press Release after this decision in which it said that the same result would not necessarily arise in the car market, which is much more competitive[297]. In *Eudim*[298] the Commission was more relaxed about the exchange of information between wholesalers of plumbing, heating and sanitary materials since the affected markets were sufficiently competitive.

In *Asnef-Equifax*[299] the question arose of whether agreements between credit institutions in Spain for the exchange of information about the creditworthiness of borrowers were restrictive of competition. As this was an Article 267 TFEU reference the Court of Justice did not make a finding on the facts of the case. However it did set out the criteria that would be relevant to an assessment of whether the exchange of such information restricted competition by effect[300]. The Court specifically noted that the market in question was a fragmented one: that is to say that it was not concentrated, which would have

---

[292] *Guidelines on Horizontal Cooperation Agreements*, para 79; on this point see the judgment of the Court of Justice in *Steel Beams*, Case C-194/99 P *Thyssen Stahl AG v Commission* [2003] ECR I-10821, para 86.

[293] Ibid, para 85.

[294] See eg *International Energy Program* OJ [1983] L 376/30, [1984] 2 CMLR 186; see also *Non-ferrous Semi-manufacturers* Commission's Vth *Report on Competition Policy* (1975), point 39.

[295] OJ [1992] L 68/19, [1993] 4 CMLR 358.

[296] Ibid, para 35; see similarly *Wirtschaftsvereinigung Stahl* OJ [1998] L 1/10, [1998] 4 CMLR 450, paras 39 and 44–46; this decision was annulled on appeal Case T-16/98 *Wirtschaftsvereinigung Stahl v Commission* [2000] ECR II-1217, [2001] 5 CMLR 310.

[297] Commission Press Release IP/92/148, 4 March 1992.

[298] OJ [1996] C 111/8, [1996] 4 CMLR 871.

[299] Case C-238/05 [2006] ECR I-11125, [2007] 4 CMLR 224.

[300] The Court held that the exchange of such information did not restrict competition by object: ibid, para 48.

been a factor conducive to coordinated behaviour[301]. The Court's judgment in this case is a most interesting one, in which it took an economic approach to the question of whether competition was likely to be restricted. It seems fairly clear that its view was that the exchange in question did not infringe Article 101(1).

(iv) Characteristics of the information exchanged

A very important consideration is the type or quality of information which is exchanged. The Commission's *Guidelines on Horizontal Cooperation Agreements* explain that the exchange between competitors of strategic data is more likely to fall within the mischief of Article 101[302]. The *Guidelines* point out that information on prices and quantities is the most strategic in nature, followed by information about costs and demand[303]. The exchange of investment plans may also be strategic[304]. The *Guidelines* explain that the strategic usefulness of data also depends on its market coverage, aggregation, age and frequency of exchange. The exchange must affect a sufficiently large part of the relevant market in order for it to be capable of having a restrictive effect on competition[305]. The exchange of individual data about particular undertakings is more problematic than aggregated data[306]. The age of the data is relevant[307]: the question is whether the information facilitates collusive behaviour, so that historic data are less significant than future ones[308]. The Commission tends to regard information that is more than one year old as historic[309]. The frequency of any information exchange is also a relevant factor[310].

The *Guidelines* point out that the exchange of 'genuinely public information' is unlikely to infringe Article 101(1)[311]; information is genuinely public in nature if the costs of obtaining it are the same for all competitors and customers. If the information exchanged is in the public domain, but is not equally accessible to competitors and customers, the Commission considers that Article 101(1) may apply as it would do to any other agreement. A further consideration is whether the information exchanged is shared with customers or not: the Commission states in the *Guidelines on Horizontal Cooperation Agreements* that the more the information is shared with customers, the less likely it is to be problematic[312].

Some Commission decisions illustrate its past decisional practice in relation to the type of information exchanged. For obvious reasons it has always been concerned about price information, but other concerns can be seen. In *Re Cimbel*[313] it condemned the obligation upon members of a trade association that they should inform each other of projected increases in industrial capacity: such an obligation could prevent one firm from gaining an advantage over competitors by expanding in time to meet an increase in demand. In *Steel Beams*[314] the Commission found an information exchange on orders and deliveries of beams by individual companies in each Member State to go 'beyond what is admissible'[315], since the figures exchanged showed the deliveries and orders received by each individual

---

[301] Ibid, para 58.
[302] OJ [2011] C 11/1, para 86.   [303] Ibid, para 86.
[304] See eg *Zinc Producer Group* OJ [1984] L 220/27, [1985] 2 CMLR 108.
[305] *Guidelines on Horizontal Cooperation Agreements*, paras 87–88.   [306] Ibid, para 89.
[307] Ibid, para 90.   [308] Ibid, para 90.   [309] Ibid, para 90, fn 2.
[310] Ibid, para 91.   [311] Ibid, para 92.
[312] Ibid, para 94; see similarly *UK Agricultural Tractor Registration Exchange* OJ [1992] L 68/19, [1993] 4 CMLR 358; *Re VNP and COBELPA* OJ [1977] L 242/10, [1977] 2 CMLR D28; *Genuine Vegetable Parchment Association* OJ [1978] L 70/54, [1978] 1 CMLR 534.
[313] OJ [1972] L 303/24, [1973] CMLR D167.
[314] OJ [1994] L 116/1, [1994] 5 CMLR 353, paras 263–272, upheld on appeal to the General Court, Cases T-141/94 etc *Thyssen Stahl AG v Commission* [1999] ECR II-347, [1999] 4 CMLR 810, paras 385–412 and further upheld on appeal to the Court of Justice, Case C-194/99 P [2003] ECR I-10821.
[315] OJ [1994] L 116/1, [1994] 5 CMLR 353, para 267.

company for delivery to their respective markets; this information was updated every week and circulated rapidly among the participants. The Commission added that the exchange was not limited to figures 'of a merely historical value with no possible impact on competition'[316]. The General Court confirmed the Commission's assessment, since the exchange of confidential information undermined the principle that every trader must determine its market strategy independently. In *Wirtschaftsvereinigung Stahl* the Commission decided that an exchange of information on deliveries and market shares in relation to various steel products infringed Article 65(1) ECSC; on appeal the General Court annulled this decision because the Commission had erred in its findings of fact[317].

(F) Assessment under Article 101(3)

This provision has been discussed at length in chapter 4, and the Commission discusses its application to exchanges of information in paragraphs 95 to 104 of its *Guidelines*. They should be read in conjunction with the Commission's *Article 101(3) Guidelines*[318]. The Commission explains in paragraph 95 that benchmarking, whereby undertakings measure their performance against 'best practice' in their industry, may enable them to improve their efficiency[319]. In certain situations information may be exchanged to ensure an optimal allocation of resources, thereby reducing any mismatch between supply and demand. By spreading technological know-how, information agreements can help to increase the number of firms capable of operating on the market[320]. The exchange of consumer data in markets characterised by asymmetric information about consumers may bring about efficiencies; an example would be the exchange of information between credit institutions about the solvency and default record of their customers[321].

Consumers too can benefit from an increase in public information: the more they know about the products available and their prices, the easier it will be for them to make satisfactory choices. Indeed perfect competition is dependent on consumers having perfect information about the market[322]: market transparency is, in general, to be encouraged. Quite often the reason why a market does not work well for consumers is that the information available to them is too sparse or confusing; in some markets there may actually be too much information for consumers to be able to digest. The Commission says that consumers are less likely to benefit from exchanges of future pricing intentions than exchanges of present and past data[323]. Further, the parties must show that the subject-matter, aggregation, age, confidentiality, frequency and coverage of their exchange of information carries the lowest risks of facilitating collusion indispensable for creating the claimed efficiencies[324].

---

[316] Ibid, para 268.

[317] OJ [1998] L 1/10, [1998] 4 CMLR 450, annulled on appeal Case T-16/98 *Wirtschaftsvereinigung Stahl v Commission* [2001] ECR II-1217 (see fn 296, above), [2001] 5 CMLR 310.

[318] OJ [2004] C 101/97; see ch 4, 'The Commission's approach in the *Article 101(3) Guidelines*', pp 160–162.

[319] *Guidelines on Horizontal Cooperation Agreements*, para 95; see Henry 'Benchmarking and Antitrust' (1993) 62 Antitrust LJ 483; on benchmarking and EC law see Carle and Johnsson 'Benchmarking and EC Competition Law' (1998) 19 ECLR 74; Boulter 'Competition Risks in Benchmarking' (1999) 20 ECLR 434.

[320] See Teece 'Information Sharing, Innovation and Antitrust' (1993) 62 Antitrust LJ 465.

[321] In *Asnef-Equifax*, ch 13 n 261 above, the Court of Justice suggested that such an exchange of information might satisfy the criteria of Article 101(3).

[322] See ch 1, 'The model of perfect competition is based on assumptions unlikely to be observed in practice', pp 7–8.

[323] *Guidelines on Horizontal Cooperation Agreements*, paras 99–100.   [324] Ibid, para 101.

The Commission rejected arguments that the exchange of information in *UK Agricultural Tractor Registration Exchange*[325] would generate efficiencies in terse terms.

Some exchanges of information in the insurance sector are given block exemption by Articles 2(a) and 3 of Regulation 267/2010[326].

(G) Fines

On one occasion, in *Fatty Acids*[327], the Commission imposed a fine of €50,000 on undertakings which entered into an agreement to exchange information which enabled each to identify the individual business of its two main rivals on a quarterly basis, thereby removing an important element of uncertainty on the part of each as to the activities of the others. It is not clear whether the Commission would today impose a fine in a case such as this: certainly this would be unusual in the case of a restriction by effect rather than object.

(H) B2B markets[328]

A specific issue in relation to the exchange of information is whether the establishment of 'B2B' electronic markets may give rise to competition law problems, in particular by facilitating collusion and/or foreclosing access to the market. Clearly competition authorities would not be happy if Internet chat rooms were to become the twenty-first century equivalent of the 'smoke-filled rooms' of the nineteenth and twentieth centuries. In a B2B market undertakings establish an electronic marketplace where it is possible, for example, to sell and purchase goods and services. Typically electronic marketplaces result in a considerable exchange of information, both between sellers and purchasers but also between competitors themselves, on both the selling and purchasing side of the market. Universal access to the Internet means that this information is instantly accessible to everyone involved in the electronic market. The Commission has not adopted any formal decisions on B2B markets under Article 101; however it has settled several cases informally[329]. The Commission does not discuss B2Bs markets in the *Guidelines*. However, it is not unreasonable to suppose that it will analyse the exchange of information by analogy to the principles contained in the *Guidelines*.

9. Advertising Restrictions

The function of advertising in competition policy raises important and controversial issues which can be dealt with only briefly here[330]. Advertising is an essential part of the

---

[325] OJ [1992] L 68/19, [1993] 4 CMLR 358.   [326] OJ [2010] 83/1.

[327] OJ [1985] L 3/17, [1989] 4 CMLR 445.

[328] See Vollebregt 'E-Hubs, Syndication and Competition Concerns' (2000) 21 ECLR 437; Lancefield 'The Regulatory Hurdles Ahead in B2B' (2001) 22 ECLR 9; Lucking 'B2B e-marketplaces and EC competition law: where do we stand?' (2001) (October) *Competition Policy Newsletter* 14.

[329] See *Covisint* Commission Press Release IP/01/1155, 31 July 2001; *Eutilia and Endorsia* Commission Press Release IP/01/1775, 10 December 2001; *Eurex* Commission Press Release IP/02/4, 3 January 2002; *Inreon* Commission Press Release IP/02/ 761, 24 May 2002; *Multi-bank trading platform* Commission Press Release IP/02/943, 27 June 2002; *Ondeo and Thames Water* Commission Press Release IP/02/956, 28 June 2002.

[330] See eg Cowling *Advertising and Economic Behaviour* (Macmillan, 1975); Telser 'Advertising and Competition' 72 J Pol Ec 536 (1964); Brozen 'Entry Barriers: Advertising and Product Differentiation' in *Industrial Concentration: The New Learning* (Little Brown, 1974); Scherer and Ross *Industrial Market Structure and Economic Performance* (Houghton Mifflin, 3rd ed, 1990), pp 436ff.

competitive process. Unless the consumer knows what goods and services are on offer and what their price is he or she will be unable to choose what to buy and competition between suppliers will be diminished.

Competition is about attracting business and a vital part of the process is to advertise one's products. Therefore competition policy should ensure that advertising is not restricted[331]. Indeed it may be thought appropriate to impose upon businesses a duty to advertise prices, terms and conditions or details of quality in order to provide the consumer with the information needed to enable him or her to make a rational choice; however it should be noted that a perverse consequence of forcing undertakings to publicise their prices could be to facilitate tacit collusion between them. A separate point is that the significance of advertising means that steps should be taken to ensure the truth of advertisements and, perhaps, to prevent the appropriation of innovative advertising ideas by competitive rivals; comparative advertising, whereby a competitor's products are unfavourably compared with one's own, might also be objected to[332].

In some circumstances collaboration between undertakings in their advertising activities may not be harmful. For example, a group of small producers may decide to sell a product under a common label and agree on the specifications and publicity of the product in question; they will all contribute to the advertising costs of this product. By doing this they may be able to present a strong brand image which will enhance their ability to compete with other firms on the market. Such schemes may be pro-competitive, although it will be necessary to ensure that nothing in the agreement limits competition unnecessarily, such as direct price fixing or market sharing. Again there may be a case for some collaboration on advertising – for example by agreeing to limit the number of industrial exhibitions visited in a year – if this will have the effect of rationalising advertising efforts and reducing advertising costs.

The importance of advertising in competition policy has an important side effect: namely that the advertising media themselves should function efficiently and be free from restrictive trade practices which might reduce the availability of advertising space. Various cases in the US have endeavoured to maintain an open advertising market[333].

Against the above line of reasoning there runs a quite different argument. This is that advertising costs are a serious barrier to entry to new firms wishing to enter a market as well as being a wasteful use of resources[334]. In some markets, such as lager, detergents and breakfast cereals, enormous amounts of money are spent in building up a brand image and it is argued that new entrants would be unable to expend the money on advertising necessary to match this. The problem, it is said, is accentuated by the fact that established firms have the accumulated advantage of past advertising and also that they have the capacity to indulge in 'predatory' advertising, that is short-term expensive campaigns designed to prevent the new entrant establishing a toe-hold in the market. Opinion on the barrier-raising effect of advertising is divided. Bork and other commentators have argued forcefully that it should not be treated as a barrier and there is empirical evidence which sheds doubt on the argument[335].

A separate objection to advertising comes from a quite different quarter, namely the liberal professions. They have argued that advertising is inimical to their ethical

---

[331] Restrictions on advertising in the US are regarded as an indirect form of price fixing and are accordingly *per se* illegal; cf *California Dental Association v Federal Trade Commission* 526 US 756 (1999).

[332] Note that there is an EU directive on misleading, including comparative, advertising: Directive 97/55/EC, OJ [1997] L 290/18.

[333] See eg *Lorain Journal Co v United States* 342 US 143 (1951).

[334] See eg Turner 'Conglomerate Mergers and s 7 of the Clayton Act' (1965) 78 Harv L Rev 1313.

[335] See eg Bork *The Antitrust Paradox* (The Free Press, 1993), pp 314–320.

standards and that consumer protection in their spheres of activity is best served by maintaining professional standards through self-regulation, codes of practice and professional ethics.

(A) **Article 101(1)**

Article 101(1) applies to agreements to restrict advertising which have anti-competitive effects. In several decisions the Commission has stated that it considers that such restrictions limit an important aspect of competitive behaviour[336]. In the case of trade fairs, it has often held that the rules for participation infringe Article 101(1), although it has gone on to permit exemption subject to conditions (see below). Trade fair rules may affect competition in various ways: participants may be required not to take part in other fairs, thus limiting their competitive opportunities; other organisers of such fairs will lose business as a result of such exclusivity rules; and potential participants might be excluded from a trade fair by its rules, thus limiting their impact on the market. In 1988 the Commission, for the first time in a trade fair case, imposed a fine of €100,000 on the *British Dental Trade Association*[337] for anti-competitive exclusion of would-be exhibitors.

In a number of decisions[338] the Commission has revealed a benevolence towards advertising restrictions which might promote a particular brand image without seriously impairing competition in other ways. However in *Belgian Roofing Felt*[339] the Commission condemned joint advertising of roofing felt under the Belasco trade mark where this led to the uniform image of products in a sector in which individual advertising may facilitate differentiation and therefore competition. The Commission's *Guidelines on Horizontal Cooperation Agreements* provide guidance on the application of Article 101 to so-called 'commercialisation agreements'[340], which may involve joint advertising. The *Guidelines* state that joint advertising might lead to anti-competitive effects if it entails a significant commonality of costs which might increase the risk of collusive behaviour[341].

Restrictions on comparative advertising by patent agents practising at the European Patent Office in Munich were held to infringe Article 101(1) in *EPI Code of Conduct*[342] but to benefit from Article 101(3) for a short period whilst new rules were adopted[343].

(B) **Article 101(3)**

The Commission has accepted that in appropriate circumstances it can be advantageous to rationalise and coordinate advertising efforts. In a series of cases on trade fairs the Commission has authorised agreements which contain rules requiring participants to limit the number of occasions on which they exhibit elsewhere and restricting the extent

---

[336] See eg *Re Vimpoltu* OJ [1983] L 200/44, [1983] 3 CMLR 619.

[337] OJ [1988] L 233/15, [1989] 4 CMLR 1021; the Commission decided that, for a period of ten years, Article 101(3) applied to the Association's rules as modified to satisfy the Commission.

[338] *Re VVVF* OJ [1969] L 168/22, [1970] CMLR D1; *Re Association pour la Promotion du Tube d'Acier Soude Electriquement* JO [1970] L 153/14, [1970] CMLR D31; *Re Industrieverband Solnhofener Natursteinplatten* OJ [1980] L 318/32.

[339] OJ [1986] L 232/15, [1991] 4 CMLR 130, upheld on appeal Case 246/86 *Belasco v Commission* [1989] ECR 2117, [1991] 4 CMLR 96.

[340] OJ [2011] C 11/1.   [341] Ibid, para 243; see ch 15, 'Purchasing Agreements', pp 603–605.

[342] OJ [1999] L 106/14, [1999] 5 CMLR 540, paras 39–45, partially annulled on appeal to the General Court, Case T-144/99 *Institut des Mandataires Agréés v Commission* [2001] ECR II-1087, [2001] 5 CMLR 77; see the Commission's XXIXth *Report on Competition Policy* (1999), pp 53 and 159–160.

[343] OJ [1999] L 106/14, [1999] 5 CMLR 540, paras 46–48.

to which they are allowed to advertise in other ways[344]. The Commission has often applied conditions to such authorisations. For example in *UNIDI*[345] the Commission required the introduction of an arbitration procedure to deal with complaints by exhibitors excluded from an exhibition. In *VIFKA*[346] it required the removal of a provision requiring exhibitors of office equipment not to exhibit elsewhere for a period of two years, as this was too long.

10. Anti-Competitive Horizontal Restraints

The agreements so far considered have been concerned with cartels limiting competition and raising prices to earn supra-competitive profits. It is likely however that, in the absence of barriers to entry, this in itself will attract new entrants into the market. It is because of this that the members of a cartel will frequently take further action designed to fend off the possibility of new competition in just the same way that a monopolist might. For example, a collective reciprocal exclusive dealing arrangement might be negotiated whereby a group of suppliers agree with a group of dealers to deal only with one another. The effect may be to exclude other producers from the market if they cannot find retail outlets for their products. This is not an inevitable result however: to have an anti-competitive foreclosing effect there would have to be a lack of alternative retail outlets, for example due to barriers to entry at the retail level. A common pricing system may be supported by an aggregated rebates cartel, whereby purchasers are offered rebates calculated according to their purchases from all the members of the cartel; the disincentive to buy elsewhere is obvious[347]. Again it may be decided to boycott any dealer who handles the products of producers outside the cartel. As one would expect, exclusionary devices such as these which can cause serious harm to the competitive process are *per se* illegal in the US[348], although it has been argued that the breadth of the rule against collective boycotts is inappropriate[349]. The pejorative label given to group boycotts conceals the fact that in some cases independent firms will inevitably decide to refuse to deal with certain people, for example by refusing inadequately trained people entrance to a profession or inefficient dealers access to a branded product. A distinction should be made between naked restraints which are clearly intended to be exclusionary on the one hand and agreements which promote efficiency and which therefore may be permitted.

The Commission and the EU Courts have had to deal with a great number of collective exclusive dealing arrangements and other potentially exclusionary practices. Often such

---

[344] *Re CECIMO* OJ [1969] L 69/13, [1969] CMLR D1, renewed OJ [1979] L 11/16, [1979] 1 CMLR 419 and again OJ [1989] L 37/11; *Re BPICA* OJ [1977] L 299/18, [1977] 2 CMLR D43, renewed OJ [1982] L 156/16, [1983] 2 CMLR 40; *Re Cematex* JO [1971] L 227/26, [1973] CMLR D135, renewed OJ [1983] L 140/27, [1984] 3 CMLR 69; *Re UNIDI* OJ [1975] L 228/14, [1975] 2 CMLR D51, renewed OJ [1984] L 322/10, [1985] 2 CMLR 38; *Re Society of Motor Manufacturers and Traders Ltd* OJ [1983] L 376/1, [1984] 1 CMLR 611; *VIFKA* OJ [1986] L 291/46; *Internationale Dentalschau* OJ [1987] L 293/58; *Sippa* OJ [1991] L 60/19, [1992] 5 CMLR 529.

[345] OJ [1984] L 322/10, [1985] 2 CMLR 38, upheld on appeal Case 43/85 *ANCIDES v Commission* [1987] ECR 3131, [1988] 4 CMLR 821.

[346] OJ [1986] L 291/46.

[347] Aggregated rebates cartels are unlikely where prices are *not* fixed, because they would discriminate against those offering lower prices.

[348] See eg *Klor's Inc v Broadway-Hale Stores Inc* 359 US 207 at 212 (1959): for a review of US case law see Glazer 'Concerted Refusals to Deal under Section 1 of the Sherman Act' (2002) 70 Antitrust LJ 1; see also the UK Competition Appeal Tribunal in Case No 1003/2/1/01 *Institute of Independent Insurance Brokers v Director General of Fair Trading* [2001] CAT 4, [2001] CompAR 62, para 189.

[349] See eg Bork *The Antitrust Paradox* (The Free Press, 1993), ch 17.

agreements are entered into by a national association which is keen to keep imports out of the domestic market. A more obvious target for the Commission it is hard to imagine and the EU Courts have usually upheld its findings. A scheme designed to keep washing machines out of the Belgian market was found by the Court of Justice to infringe Article 101(1)[350], as was a marketing system which could prevent imports of fruit into Holland[351]. The Court agreed with the Commission that an exclusive purchasing agreement which obliged members of an association to acquire rennet solely from a Dutch cooperative was unlawful[352]. The Court also held that practices designed to buttress the collective resale price maintenance of Dutch and Belgian books infringed Article 101[353].

The Court of Justice upheld the Commission's decision to condemn rigid collective exclusive dealing systems in two cigarette cases, affecting the Belgian and Dutch markets respectively[354]. The Commission has dealt with many other similar situations, always striking such agreements down[355]. In *Hudson's Bay – Dansk Pelsdyravlerforening*[356] the Commission imposed a fine of €500,000 on a Danish trade association for imposing an obligation on its members that they should sell their entire production to a subsidiary of the association, thereby preventing them from selling their products to other Member States. In *Dutch Mobile Cranes*[357] the Commission imposed fines on a trade association found to have operated a price-fixing system whereby its members were obliged to charge 'recommended' rates for the hiring of mobile cranes; it also condemned the rules of a second association that effectively prohibited members from hiring cranes from firms not affiliated to it.

In *Dutch Electrotechnical Equipment*[358] the Commission imposed fines of €4.4 million on FEG and €2.15 million on TU for entering into collective exclusive dealing arrangements intended to prevent supplies to non-members of the associations by directly and indirectly restricting the freedom of members to determine their selling prices independently. The facts of this case resemble many of the decisions of the Commission on collective exclusive dealing from the 1970s and 1980s[359]: the fact that there are still arrangements like this in existence is perhaps a vindication of the Commission's desire to focus its resources on the elimination of practices that one might have assumed had long since been discontinued. In this decision, the Commission reduced the fine it would otherwise

---

[350] Cases 96/82 etc *NV IAZ International Belgium v Commission* [1983] ECR 3369, [1984] 3 CMLR 276; note the additional fine subsequently imposed by the Commission in this case: *Re IPTC Belgium SA* OJ [1983] L 376/7, [1984] 2 CMLR 131.

[351] Case 71/74 *FRUBO v Commission* [1975] ECR 563, [1975] 2 CMLR 123; see similarly *Irish Timber Importers Association* XXth *Report on Competition Policy* (1990), point 98.

[352] Case 61/80 *Cooperatieve Stremsel-en Kleurselfabriek v Commission* [1981] ECR 851, [1982] 1 CMLR 240.

[353] Cases 43 and 63/82 *VBVB & VBBB v Commission* [1984] ECR 19, [1985] 1 CMLR 27.

[354] Cases 209/78 etc *Van Landewyck v Commission* [1980] ECR 3125, [1981] 3 CMLR 134; Cases 240/82 etc *SSI v Commission* [1985] ECR 3831, [1987] 3 CMLR 661 and Case 260/82 *NSO v Commission* [1988] 4 CMLR 755.

[355] *Re Gas Water-Heaters* OJ [1973] L 217/34, [1973] CMLR D231; *Re Stoves and Heaters* OJ [1975] L 159/22, [1975] 2 CMLR D1; *Re Bomée Stichting* OJ [1975] L 329/30, [1976] 1 CMLR D1; *Groupement d'Exportation du Leon v Société d'Investissements et de Cooperation Agricoles (Cauliflowers)* OJ [1978] L 21/23, [1978] 1 CMLR D66; *Donck v Centraal Bureau voor de Rijweilbandel* OJ [1978] L 20/18, [1978] 2 CMLR 194; *Re IMA Rules* OJ [1980] L 318/1, [1981] 2 CMLR 498; *Re Italian Flat Glass* OJ [1981] L 326/32, [1982] 3 CMLR 366.

[356] OJ [1988] L 316/43, [1989] 4 CMLR 340, upheld on appeal Case T-61/89 *Dansk Pelsdyravlerforening v Commission* [1992] ECR II-1931.

[357] OJ [1995] L 312/79, [1996] 4 CMLR 565, upheld on appeal Cases T-213/95 etc *SCK and FNK v Commission* [1997] ECR II-1739, [1997] 4 CMLR 259.

[358] OJ [2000] L 39/1, [2000] 4 CMLR 1208, on appeal Cases T-5/00 etc *NAVEG v Commission* [2003] ECR II-5761, [2004] 5 CMLR 969, on further appeal Cases C-105/04 P etc [2006] ECR I-8725, [2006] 5 CMLR 1257; see also the Commission's XXIXth *Report on Competition Policy* (1999), p 135.

[359] See ch 13 n 355 above.

have imposed due to the prolonged period of the proceedings, which had begun in 1991, for which it was partly to blame[360].

In *Road Bitumen*[361] the Commission imposed fines of €266.71 million for price fixing on the part of eight suppliers and six purchasers of road bitumen in the Netherlands. An interesting feature of the case is that the large construction companies that were in the cartel were not particularly concerned that the suppliers were fixing prices: road building in the Netherlands is paid for, ultimately, by the taxpayer. The large construction companies were simply concerned to win as many orders as possible, and there were price rebates on offer from the suppliers that discriminated in favour of them, and against smaller competitors: in other words the pricing system in this case operated to exclude third parties from the market.

In *Morgan Stanley/Visa*[362] the Commission imposed a fine of €10.2 million on Visa for refusing to admit Morgan Stanley to the Visa system without objective justification. This is an example of an anti-competitive horizontal restraint in that Visa consists of a number of undertakings that determine who may become a Visa member. There was a rule that said that membership was not available to a bank that issued a card that would compete with the Visa card. The rule did not restrict competition by object; however the Commission considered that the way it had been applied in relation to Morgan Stanley had an appreciable anti-competitive effect: first, it did not issue a card that competed with Visa *within the EU*: Morgan Stanley's Discover Card had a presence only in the US; and, secondly, Visa had, in practice, allowed other banks to join that did have cards in Europe, so that the rules had been applied in a discriminatory manner. The Commission's decision was upheld on appeal[363]. In another decision on payment systems, *Groupement des Cartes Bancaires*[364], the Commission decided that the way in which the rules of the 'Cartes Bancaires' systems were applied in France infringed Article 101 because they operated in favour of the major banks in France and to the detriment, for example, of banks established by retailers such as Carrefour and Auchan and Internet banks.

In *ONP*[365] the Commission found that, as well as prescribing minimum prices, the National Pharmaceutical Society had taken decisions to hinder the development of certain groups of laboratories in France.

11. UK Law[366]

The UK competition authorities share the European Commission's determination to eliminate cartels. The Competition Act 1998 gives to the Office of Fair Trading ('the OFT') and sectoral regulators substantial powers of investigation and enforcement[367], resembling those of the Commission, to enforce Article 101 TFEU and the Chapter I

---

[360] See paras 151–153 of the decision: the Commission was applying the judgment of the Court of Justice in Case C-185/95 P *Baustahlgewebe v Commission* [1998] ECR I-8417, [1999] 4 CMLR 1203, reducing (very slightly) a fine due to the protracted hearing of the appeal to the General Court.

[361] Commission decision of 13 September 2006, on appeal Cases T-343/06 etc *Shell Petroleum v Commission*, not yet decided.

[362] Commission decision of 3 October 2007.

[363] Case T-461/07 *Visa Europe v Commission* [2011] ECR II-000.

[364] Commission decision of 17 October 2007, on appeal Case T-491/07 *CB v Commission*, not yet decided.

[365] Commission decision of 8 December 2010, on appeal Case T-90/11 *ONP v Commission*, not yet decided.

[366] See generally chs 9 and 10 on the substantive and procedural rules of the Competition Act 1998.

[367] See ch 10, 'Inquiries and Investigations', pp 394–402 and 'Enforcement', 404–424.

prohibition. Some introductory points can be made in respect of the OFT's approach to the eradication of cartels in the UK. First, the OFT has published a number of Guidelines on the Competition Act[368]; paragraphs 3.3 to 3.27 of the Guideline on *Agreements and Concerted Practices*[369] provide guidance on a number of types of agreement that might infringe Article 101 or the Chapter I prohibition. A second introductory point is that the OFT has published a booklet designed to enable purchasers to identify cartel activity and to encourage them to bring their suspicions to the attention of the OFT[370]; it has also published an empirical study into the economic and structural factors that contribute to the formation, maintenance and detection of cartels[371]. Thirdly, the OFT has a dedicated cartels and criminal enforcement group[372]. Fourthly, the OFT's policy is to encourage whistleblowers, and it has received a large number of applications for immunity and leniency from fines since the Act entered into force[373]. Finally, the Enterprise Act 2002 establishes a criminal 'cartel offence' which can result in the fining or imprisonment of individuals responsible for dishonest cartel activity[374].

The OFT's enforcement activity in relation to cartels was somewhat limited in the early years of the Competition Act. The position began to change from 2004 onwards, as the OFT began to adopt a series of decisions imposing fines for collusive tendering in the construction sector[375]. However a significant change occurred in 2007 when, in the case of *British Airways*[376], the OFT announced that British Airways had admitted colluding with Virgin Atlantic over the price of long-haul passenger fuel surcharges between August 2004 and January 2006; BA agreed to pay a fine of £121.5 million. A formal decision against BA recording the decision will be taken in due course. There was no fine on Virgin Atlantic as it had blown the whistle. The criminal proceedings brought against individuals involved in the cases of *British Airways* and *Marine Hoses* were discussed in chapter 10 of this book[377].

Other notable decisions in recent years include, in 2009, *Construction bid-rigging*[378] and *Construction Recruitment Forum*[379]. In the former the OFT imposed fines of £129.2 million on 103 undertakings involved in unlawful cover pricing and other bid-rigging activities. In the latter the OFT condemned a collective boycott and price fixing and imposed fines totalling £39.27 million. *Construction bid-rigging* is of interest as it was the largest investigation ever undertaken by the OFT and one in which the OFT made a 'fast-track offer', whereby it reduced fines for 45 undertakings implicated in bid-rigging (that had not already applied for leniency) in return for cooperation. In both *Construction bid-rigging*[380] and *Construction Recruitment Forum*[381] the Competition Appeal Tribunal ('the CAT') reduced the penalties imposed by the OFT, which, in its view, were excessive and insufficiently tailored to the circumstances of individual firms.

---

[368] See ch 9, 'OFT guidance', pp 332–333.

[369] OFT 401, December 2004; see also *Trade Associations, professions and self-regulating bodies*, OFT 408, December 2004.

[370] *Cartels and the Competition Act 1998: a Guide for Purchasers*, OFT 435, March 2005.

[371] *Predicting cartels*, OFT 773, March 2005.   [372] See ch 2, 'The staff of the OFT', p 64.

[373] See ch 10, 'Whistleblowing: the leniency programme', pp 414–418.

[374] See ch 10, 'The cartel offence', pp 425–454.

[375] See 'Collusive Tendering', pp 555–557 below.

[376] OFT Press Release 113/07, 1 August 2007.

[377] See ch 10, 'The cartel offence in practice', p 434.

[378] See OFT decision of 21 September 2009 [2010] UKCLR 322.

[379] See OFT decision of 29 September 2009 [2010] UKCLR 14.

[380] See Case Nos 1114/1/1/09 etc *Kier Group plc v OFT* [2011] CAT 3; Case Nos 1117/1/1/10 etc *GF; Tomlinson Building Ltd v OFT* [2011] CAT 7; and Case Nos 1125/1/1/09 etc *Barrett Estate Services Ltd v OFT* [2011] CAT 9.

[381] Case Nos 1140/1/1/09 etc *Eden Brown Ltd v OFT* [2011] CAT 8.

In the case *Dairy Products* the OFT imposed fines of £49.51 million[382] for price-fixing practices, of both a horizontal and a vertical nature; Arla was given 100 percent immunity as it had blown the whistle. The fines on all other firms, except Tesoo, were reduced for ageering to early resolution of the case[383].

It is known that the OFT is investigating suspected cartel activity in a number of sectors, including outdoor advertising, the supply of e-books and hotel online booking[384].

(A) **Horizontal price fixing**[385]

The *British Airways*, *Dairy Products* and *Construction Recruitment Forum* cases have already been referred to above. The OFT's decisions to date in relation to collusive tendering are discussed further in section D below. The OFT's decisions in *Football Shirts* and *Toys and Games*, which involved horizontal and vertical price fixing, were discussed in detail in chapter 9[386].

The OFT has dealt with price fixing in a few other cases, some of which were settled informally in the early years of the legislation. In a Press Release in January 2001 the OFT warned that allegations of price fixing, even between small businesses such as private cab firms, would be investigated under the Competition Act 1998[387]. In *Northern Ireland Livestock and Auctioneers' Association*[388] the OFT concluded that a recommendation by the Association as to the commission that its members should charge for the purchase of livestock in Northern Ireland cattle marts infringed the Chapter I prohibition, but it decided not to impose a fine, not least because the infringement occurred at a time when the beef sector was suffering as a result of so-called 'mad cow' disease[389]. The OFT closed its investigation into the fee guidance provided by the Royal Institute of British Architects to its members after RIBA varied the guidance so that it could no longer facilitate collusion on prices[390]. In *Stock Check Pads*[391] the OFT imposed fines of £2,184,767, reduced to £168,318 for leniency, on undertakings found to have fixed prices (and shared markets) for stock check pads, used by staff in cafes and restaurants to record customers' orders. In *Aluminium Spacer Bars*[392] fines of £1,384,050, reduced to £898,470 for leniency, were imposed for price fixing, customer allocation and market sharing for aluminium spacer bars used in double glazing. The OFT closed its file on joint selling arrangements between suppliers of car paint and ancillary equipment, against assurances that its members would be free to set prices[393].

In *LINK Interchange Network Ltd*[394] the OFT granted individual exemption to the multilateral interchange fee collectively agreed between banks whose customers withdraw cash from cash points. The OFT's decision that MasterCard's interchange fees infringed the

---

[382] OFT Press Release 89/11, 10 August 2011; for the background on the case see OFT Press Releases 170/07, 7 December 2007 and 22/08, 15 February 2008 30 April 30 2010 and OFT Press Release 45/10 and 46/10.

[383] The decision is on appeal to the CAT, Case No 1188/1/1/11 *Tesco stores ltd v OFT*, not yet decided.

[383] 384 See www.oft.gov.uk.

[385] See *Agreements and Concerted Practices*, OFT 401, December 2004, paras 3.4–3.8.

[386] See ch 9, 'Agreements', pp 337–340.   [387] OFT Press Release PN 01/01, 10 January 2001.

[388] OFT decision of 3 February 2003 [2003] UKCLR 433.   [389] Ibid, paras 37–49.

[390] See *Royal Institute of British Architects* Weekly Gazette of the OFT, Competition case closure summaries, 17–23 May 2003; see similarly the case closures in the case of *The Notaries Society*, 30 April 2004 and in the case of *British Chemical Distributors and Traders Association*, 11 May 2004.

[391] OFT decision of 4 April 2006 [2007] UKCLR 211, upheld on appeal in Case No 1067/1/1/06 *Achilles Group Ltd v OFT* [2006] CAT 24, [2007] CompAR 1.

[392] OFT decision of 29 June 2006 [2006] UKCLR 921, upheld on appeal in Case No 1072/1/1/06 *Sepia Logistics Ltd v OFT* [2007] CAT 13, [2007] CompAR 747.

[393] Case closure of February 2009, available at www.oft.gov.uk.

[394] OFT decision of 16 October 2001.

Chapter I prohibition was subsequently withdrawn[395]; the OFT continues to investigate MasterCard's current fees.

(B) Agreements relating to terms and conditions[396]

Agreements on terms and conditions and codes of practice may be caught by the Chapter I prohibition.

(C) Horizontal market sharing[397]

The first fine to be imposed under the Competition Act in a cartel case occurred in *Market Sharing by Arriva plc and FirstGroup plc*[398], where those two companies were found to have shared bus routes in the Leeds area. The *Stock Check Pads*[399] decision involved market sharing as well as price fixing, and the *Aluminium Spacer Bars*[400] decision included findings of customer allocation and market sharing.

A market-sharing agreement was terminated following investigation by the OFT in the case of *Suppliers of Laboratory Materials*[401].

(D) Quotas and other restriction on production[402]

The OFT decided to permit an agreement in *Memorandum of Understanding on the supply of oil fuels in an emergency*[403] which would enable the Government to direct supplies of fuel to 'essential users' such as providers of emergency services in the event of a fuel shortage: the OFT's view was that the agreement satisfied the criteria of section 9 of the Competition Act for a period of ten years[404].

(E) Collusive tendering[405]

Beginning with *West Midland Roofing Contractors* in 2004 the OFT has adopted a number of decisions involving collusive tendering. The fines imposed (before and after allowances for leniency and appeals) in these cases were as follows:

- *West Midland Roofing Contractors*[406]: £971,186, reduced to £297,625 after leniency and to £288,625 after appeal[407]
- *Mastic Asphalt Flat-roofing Contracts in Scotland*[408]: £231,445, reduced to £87,353 after leniency

---

[395] OFT decision of 5 September 2005 [2006] UKCLR 236.

[396] See *Agreements and Concerted Practices*, OFT 401, December 2004, para 3.9.

[397] Ibid, paras 3.10–3.11   [398] OFT decision of 30 January 2002, [2002] UKCLR 322.

[399] OFT decision of 4 April 2006 [2007] UKCLR 211, upheld on appeal in Case No 1067/1/1/06 *Achilles Group Ltd v OFT* [2006] CAT 24, [2007] CompAR 1.

[400] OFT decision of 29 June 2006 [2006] UKCLR 921, upheld on appeal in Case No 1072/1/1/06 *Sepia Logistics Ltd v OFT* [2007] CAT 13, [2007] CompAR 747.

[401] OFT Press Release 26/04, 12 February 2004.

[402] See *Agreements and Concerted Practices*, OFT 401, December 2004, paras 3.12–3.13.

[403] OFT decision, 25 October 2001, [2002] UKCLR 74   [404] Ibid, paras 62–63.

[405] See *Agreements and Concerted Practices*, OFT 401, December 2004, para 3.14.

[406] OFT decision of 17 March 2004 [2004] UKCLR 1119.

[407] Case No 1032/1/1/04 *Apex Asphalt and Paving Co Ltd v OFT* [2005] CAT 4, [2005] CompAR 507 and Case No 1033/1/1/04 *Richard W Price Ltd v OFT* [2005] CAT 5, [2005] CompAR 801.

[408] OFT decision of 7 April 2005 [2005] UKCLR 638.

- *Felt and Single Ply Roofing Contracts in Western-Central Scotland*[409]: £238,576, reduced to £138,515 after leniency
- *Flat Roof and Car Park Surfacing Contracts in England and Scotland*[410]: £1.852 million, reduced to £1.557 million after leniency
- *Bid rigging in the construction industry in England*[411]: £194.1 million, reduced to £129.2 million after leniency and the 'fast-track offer' and to £63.992 million after appeals.

In January 2007 the OFT, in conjunction with the Office of Government Commerce, published a joint guide for public-sector procurers of construction services on achieving value through the competitive process; it also highlights practical steps to avoid falling victim to collusive tendering[412].

The judgment of the Competition Appeal Tribunal in *Apex Asphalt and Paving Co Ltd v OFT*[413] is particularly useful on the legal analysis of collusive tendering. The OFT had concluded that various roofing contractors, including Apex, were guilty of colluding in relation to the making of tender bids for flat roofing contracts in the West Midlands. Having set out the principles of relevance to determining whether undertakings are party to a concerted practice[414], the CAT proceeded to apply them to a tendering process in which some of the participating undertakings make 'cover bids', that is to say that they submit a price for a contract that is not intended to win the contract (the reason for doing this is that it maintains the appearance of competition, and indicates that the person offering the cover bid wishes to continue participating in future invitations to tender). In the CAT's view:

- a tendering process is designed to produce competition in a very structured way
- bidders are sometimes required to certify that they have not had contact with competitors in the preparation of their bids
- where the tendering is selective rather than open to all potential bidders the loss of independence through knowledge of the intentions of other selected bidders is particularly likely to distort competition[415].

The CAT was satisfied on the facts of the case that Apex was party to a concerted practice. The CAT applied the same reasoning in *Makers UK Ltd v OFT*[416], an unsuccessful appeal against the OFT's decision in *Flat Roof and Car Park Surfacing Contracts in England and Scotland*. The OFT's decision in *Construction bid-rigging* was discussed above. A report in June 2010 found that there had been significant improvements in awareness of competition law and changes in behaviour since the OFT's decision[417]. On appeal the CAT

---

[409] OFT decision of 11 July 2005 [2005] UKCLR 1015.
[410] OFT decision of 23 February 2006 [2006] UKCLR 579.
[411] OFT decision of 21 September 2009 [2010] UKCLR 322.
[412] *Making competition work for you*, available at www.ogc.gov.uk; see similarly OECD *Guidelines for Fighting Bid-Rigging in Public Procurement* (2009), available at www.oecd.org.
[413] Case No 1032/1/1/04 [2005] CAT 4, [2005] CompAR 507.   [414] Ibid, para 206.
[415] Ibid, paras 208–212.
[416] Case No 1061/1/1/06 [2007] CAT 11, [2007] CompAR 699, paras 103–110.
[417] *Evaluation of the impact of the OFT's investigation into bid rigging in the construction industry*, OFT 1240, see also OFT Press Release 60/10, 4 June 2010.

upheld the decision in four cases[418], partially annulled the decision in four cases[419], and reduced the fines in 20 cases[420].

(F) **Information agreements**[421]

In *Exchange of Information on Future Fees by Certain Independent Fee-Paying Schools*[422] the participant schools submitted details of their current fee levels, proposed fee increases (expressed as a percentage) and the resulting intended fee levels to the bursar of one of the schools, who then circulated the information to all the other participants in a tabular form. The OFT concluded that this agreement restricted competition by object; it made no finding as to the effect of the agreement[423]. The OFT declined to accept commitments from the schools under section 31A of the Competition Act since the infringement was a serious one[424]. Each school agreed to pay a nominal fine of £10,000, and they agreed to make *ex gratia* payments of £3 million into a trust fund to benefit pupils who attended the schools during the period of the information exchange[425]. In *Loan pricing*[426] the OFT found that Royal Bank of Scotland had unlawfully disclosed generic and specific confidential future pricing information for loan products to Barclays; RBS admitted the infringement and agreed to pay a fine of £28.59 million. There was no fine on Barclays as it had blown the whistle.

In *Motor Car Insurers* the OFT was concerned that private motor insurers were exchanging price information through an IT product, possibly with the object of restricting competition. In January 2011 the OFT announced that it intends to accept commitments under section 31A of the Act, whereby the parties would agree only to exchange pricing information that is anonymous and averaged across at least five insurers; in the OFT's view this should prevent the possibility of coordination from arising[427].

(G) **Advertising restrictions**[428]

The OFT accepts that the restriction of advertising may diminish competition; however, attempts to curb misleading advertising, or to ensure that advertising is legal, truthful and decent, are unlikely to have an appreciable effect on competition[429].

---

[418] Case No 1121/1/1/09 *Durkan Holdings Ltd v OFT* [2011] CAT 6, paras 13–92; Case No 1126/1/1/09 *ISG Pearce Ltd v OFT* [2011] CAT 10, paras 11–36; Case No 1120/1/1/09 *Quarmby Construction Co Ltd v OFT* [2011] CAT 11, paras 8–140; Case No 1124/1/1/09 *North Midland Construction plc v OFT* [2011] CAT 14, paras 35–63.

[419] See Case No 1121/1/1/09 *Durkan Holdings Ltd v OFT* [2011] CAT 6, paras 93–125; Case No 1118/1/1/09 *GMI Construction Holdings plc v OFT* [2011] CAT 12; Case No 1122/1/1/09 *AH Willis & Sons Ltd v OFT* [2011] CAT 13; Case No 1124/1/1/09 *North Midland Construction plc v OFT* [2011] CAT 14, paras 14–34.

[420] See Case Nos 1114/1/1/09 etc *Kier Group plc v OFT* [2011] CAT 3 and Case Nos 1117/1/1/09 etc *GF Tomlinson Building Ltd v OFT* [2011] CAT 7 and Case Nos 1125/1/1/09 etc *Barrett Estate Services Ltd v OFT* [2011] CAT 9; Case No 1121/1/1/09 *Durkan Holdings Ltd v OFT* [2011] CAT 6, paras 126–180; Case No 1124/1/1/09 *North Midland Construction plc v OFT* [2011] CAT 14, paras 64–111.

[421] See *Agreements and Concerted Practices*, OFT 401, December 2004, paras 3.17–3.23.

[422] OFT decision of 20 November 2006, [2007] UKCLR 361.   [423] Ibid, paras 1348–1358.

[424] Ibid, paras 31–32; on the section 31A commitments procedure see ch 10, 'Commitments', pp 405–407.

[425] OFT Press Releases 165/06, 22 November 2006 and 182/06, 21 December 2006 provide details of the trustees appointed to administer the fund.

[426] OFT decision of 20 January 2011.

[427] OFT *Notice of intention to accept binding commitments to modify a data exchange tool used by Motor Insurers*, OFT 1301, see also OFT Press Release 04/11, 13 January 2011; in September 2011, the OFT issued a *Notice of intention to modify proposed binding commitments on a data exchange tool used by Motor Insurers*, OTF 1377, see also OFT Press Release 108/11, 30 September 2011.

[428] See *Agreements and Concerted Practices*, OFT 401, December 2004, para 3.24.

[429] See also *Trade Associations, Professions and Self-Regulating Bodies*, OFT 408, December 2004, para 3.14.

(H) Anti-competitive horizontal restraints

Other anti-competitive agreements may also be subject to the Chapter I prohibition. In the *General Insurance Standards Council* decision[430] the OFT concluded that the rules of that association did not appreciably restrict competition. On appeal the CAT held that a rule that meant that intermediaries could not sell the general insurance products of GISC's members unless they (the intermediaries) were also members of GISC amounted to a collective boycott and therefore a restriction of competition contrary to the Chapter I prohibition; in the Tribunal's view, the rules could be upheld, if at all, only by recourse to the criteria in section 9 of the Act[431]. In the event the offending rule was dropped, so that the OFT was able to adopt a fresh non-infringement decision[432]. The OFT has closed its files on several other cases concerning allegedly exclusionary rules of sports and professional associations, often following amendments to ensure open, non-discriminatory access to those associations[433].

In the case of *Construction Recruitment Forum*[434] the OFT considered a collective boycott of a new entrant was among the most serious kind of infringement; the OFT's decision on this point was affirmed by the CAT[435].

[430] OFT decision of 26 January 2001 [2001] UKCLR 331.

[431] Case No 1003/2/1/01 *Institute of Independent Insurance Brokers v Director General of Fair Trading* [2001] CAT 4, [2001] CompAR 62, para 261.

[432] OFT decision of 22 November 2002, [2003] UKCLR 39.

[433] *English Rugby Ltd*, Case closure of 6 August 2003; *Glasgow Solicitors Property Centre*, OFT Press Release 154/03, 1 December 2003; *Bar Council of Northern Ireland*, OFT Press Release 02/11, 5 January 2011, all available at www.oft.gov.uk.

[434] OFT decision of 29 September 2009 [2010] UKCLR 14.

[435] Case Nos 1140/1/1/09 etc *Eden Brown Ltd v OFT* [2011] CAT 8, para 75.

14

Horizontal agreements (2) – oligopoly, tacit collusion and collective dominance

1. Introduction

This chapter is concerned with the related topics of oligopoly, tacit collusion and collective dominance. Put at its simplest, a problem for competition policy arises in markets in which there are only a few operators who are able, by virtue of the characteristics of the market, to behave in a parallel manner and to derive benefits from their collective market power, without, or without necessarily, entering into an agreement or concerted practice to do so in the sense of Article 101 TFEU or the Chapter I prohibition of the Competition Act 1998. This phenomenon is known in economics as 'tacit collusion', an expression which jars with lawyers, who associate the notion of collusion with actively conspiratorial behaviour of the kind captured by the expressions 'agreement' and 'concerted practice' in Article 101 and the Chapter I prohibition. The terms 'tacit coordination' and 'coordinated effects' may be preferable to tacit collusion, in that they connote the idea of parallel behaviour without attaching the opprobrious term 'collusion'[1]. Nevertheless 'tacit collusion' is included in the title of this chapter in deference to the weight of the economics literature which uses it.

The issue for competition policy is to determine, assuming that the problem just described does indeed exist, how to deal with it: is the 'oligopoly problem' one of behaviour, in which case is it possible to deal with it through the application of Articles 101 and 102 and their domestic equivalents; or is it one that arises from the structure of the industry in question, in which case structural solutions, most obviously through the system of merger control but also, in the UK, through the market investigation provisions of the Enterprise Act 2002, may be needed to address it?

This chapter will begin with discussion of oligopolistic interdependence. Sections 3 and 4 will consider the extent to which Articles 101 and 102 can be used to address it. Section 5 of the chapter discusses UK law and, in particular, the possible use of the market investigation provisions of the Enterprise Act or the system of merger control established

---

[1] See 'Terminology: "tacit collusion"; "conscious parallelism"; "tacit coordination"; "coordinated effects"', p 562 below.

by it. The extent to which the problem of coordinated behaviour on the part of oligopolists can be addressed in the investigation of mergers is discussed further in chapters 20 to 22 of this book.

2. The Theory of Oligopolistic Interdependence

(A) Outline of the theory

The basic objection to monopoly is that a monopolist is able to restrict output and thereby increase the price of its goods or services. As a result it earns supra-competitive profits and society is deprived of the output it has suppressed. In perfect competition no firm has sufficient power over the market to affect prices by an alteration in its output; each firm 'takes' the price from the market and that price will coincide with the cost of producing the product in question[2]. Competition law typically seeks to prevent independent under-takings from coordinating their marketing behaviour and appreciably restricting competition: horizontal price-fixing agreements and analogous cartels are subject to Article 101 TFEU and the Chapter I prohibition[3].

(i) The meaning of oligopoly and a warning about the term

In reality few markets are perfectly competitive and many are oligopolistic; the general trend in recent years has undoubtedly been towards an increase in industrial concentration. There is a vast literature on the 'problem' of oligopoly[4]. Oligopoly is a phenomenon that exists somewhere on the continuum that begins at monopoly and ends at perfect competition, or 'polypoly', where 'mono' means one, 'oligo' a few and the first 'poly' in polypoly means many.

The expression oligopoly is not entirely helpful in describing the situation of concern for competition policy, since there are many markets in which there are only a few sellers and yet which are highly competitive; and there are others in which there may be many firms and yet a failure of the competitive process. Economic models of oligopolists competing on price or output are supportive of this point[5]: some oligopolies are 'benign' in

---

[2] See ch 1, 'The benefits of perfect competition', pp 4–6.   [3] See ch 13 generally.

[4] See eg Turner 'The Definition of Agreement under the Sherman Act: Conscious Parallelism and Refusals to Deal' (1962) 75 Harvard Law Review 655; Posner 'Oligopoly and the Antitrust Laws: A Suggested Approach' (1969) 21 Stanford Law Review 1562; Tirole *The Theory of Industrial Organisation* (MIT Press, 1988), ch 6; Scherer and Ross *Industrial Market Structure and Economic Performance* (Houghton Mifflin, 3rd ed, 1990), chs 6–8; Stevens 'Covert Collusion and Conscious Parallelism in Oligopolistic Markets: A Comparison of EC and US Competition Law' (1995) Yearbook of European Law 47; Monti 'Oligopoly: Conspiracy? Joint Monopoly? Or Enforceable Competition?' (1996) 19(3) World Competition 59; Lopatka 'Solving the Oligopoly Problem: Turner's Try' (1996) 41 Antitrust Bulletin 843; National Economic Research Associates *Merger Appraisal in Oligopolistic Markets* (OFT Research Paper 19, 1999); Europe Economics *Study on Assessment Criteria for Distinguishing between Competitive and Dominant Oligopolies in Merger Control* (DG Enterprise, May 2001); Bishop and Walker *The Economics of EC Competition Law* (Sweet & Maxwell, 3rd ed, 2010), paras 7.049–7.075; Ivaldi, Jullien, Rey, Seabright and Tirole 'The Economics of Tacit Collusion' Final Report for DG Competition, March 2003; Stroux *US and EC Oligopoly Control* (Kluwer, 2004); Werden 'Economic Evidence on the Existence of Collusion: Reconciling Antitrust Law with Oligopoly' (2004) 71 Antitrust Law Journal 719; Brock 'Antitrust Policy and the Oligopoly Problem' (2006) 51 Antitrust Bulletin 227; Lipsey and Chrystal *Principles of Economics* (Oxford University Press, 11th ed, 2007), pp 185–199; see also some of the earlier economics literature, eg Hall and Hitch 'Price Theory and Business Behaviour' (1939) 2 Oxford Economic Papers 12–45; Sweezy 'Demand under Conditions of Oligopoly' (1937) 47 J Pol Ec 568–575; Stigler 'The Kinky Oligopoly Demand Curve' (1947) 55 J Pol Ec 431.

[5] For a general discussion of these models see Carlton and Perloff *Modern Industrial Organisation* (Longman, 4th ed, 2004), ch 6; Church and Ware *Industrial Organisation: A Strategic Approach*

terms of competition; others may be malign where they are particularly conducive to uncompetitive outcomes. For this reason it is increasingly recognised that to address the problem of 'oligopoly', as if the problem were purely numerical, is to miss the correct target. The expression oligopoly means 'sale by a few sellers', but it is not the fact of 'few-ness', in itself, that is the problem. To depict the problem as a matter of numbers does not do full justice to economists' concept of 'market power'; it is market power, whether individual or collective, that confers the ability to suppress output and to raise price to the detriment of consumers. It is true that the fewer the number of players in a market, the more likely it is that market power will exist; however, the identification of market power is not simply a matter of counting heads. There is, nevertheless, a certain catchiness in talking of 'the oligopoly problem', and there is no harm in using the expression provided that the caveat just entered is kept in mind.

(ii) The oligopoly problem

The main argument against oligopoly is that the characteristics of the market in which oligopolists operate are such that they will not compete with one another on price and will have little incentive to compete in other ways; furthermore they will be able to earn supra-competitive profits without entering into an agreement or concerted practice generally proscribed by competition law. In a perfectly competitive market a firm which cuts its price will have an imperceptible effect on its competitors, so that they will not need to respond. In an oligopoly a reduction in price would swiftly attract the custom-ers of the other two or three rivals, the effect upon whom would be so devastating that they would have to react by matching the cut. Similarly an oligopolist could not increase its price unilaterally, because it would be deserted by its customers if it did so. Thus the theory runs that in an oligopolistic market rivals are interdependent: they are acutely aware of each other's presence and are bound to match one another's marketing strategy. The result is that price competition between them will be minimal or non-existent; oli-gopoly produces non-competitive stability. The literature on so-called 'game theory' and 'the Prisoner's Dilemma', which recognises that firms take into account the likely actions (and reactions) of competitors when deciding how to behave, is supportive of this view of oligopoly[6].

The argument can be taken further. All firms have a will to maximise profits: profits are greater in monopolistic markets in which output is suppressed. Oligopolists recog-nise their interdependence as well as their own self-interest. By matching each other's conduct they will be able to achieve and charge a profit-maximising price which will be set at a supra-competitive level, without actually communicating with one another. There does not need to be any communication: the structure of the market is such that, through interdependence and mutual self-awareness, prices will rise towards the monopolistic level. Also the non-competitive environment in which oligopolists function will enable them to act in an inefficient and wasteful manner.

(McGraw-Hill/Irwin, 2000), ch 8; Bishop and Walker *The Economics of EC Competition Law* (Sweet & Maxwell, 3rd ed, 2010), paras 2.020–2.033.

[6] See *Tirole* pp 205–208; *Scherer and Ross* pp 208–215; *Bishop and Walker* paras 2.28–2.30; *Lipsey and Chrystal* pp 188–192; Franzosi 'Oligopoly and the Prisoner's Dilemma: Concerted Practices and "As If" Behaviour' (1988) 9 ECLR 385; *Carlton and Perloff* ch 6; *Church and Ware* chs 3 and 4; Cabral *Introduction to Industrial Organization* (MIT Press, 2000); Van den Bergh and Camesasca *European Competition Law and Economics: A Comparative Perspective* (Sweet & Maxwell, 2nd ed, 2006), pp 156–159; Motta *Competition Policy: Theory and Practice* (Cambridge University Press, 2004), ch 8; see generally Philips *Competition Policy: A Game Theoretic Perspective* (Cambridge University Press, 1995).

These theoretical arguments have been buttressed by empirical research which purports to show that there is a direct correlation between industrial structure and profit levels, which are said to increase in line with the concentration ratio of the industry in question[7], although the soundness of much of this evidence has been called into question[8]. The logical conclusion of the case against oligopoly is that, since it is the market structure itself which produces the problem, structural measures should be taken to remedy it by deconcentrating the market. Unless this is done, there will be an area of consciously parallel action in pricing strategies which is beyond the reach of laws against cartels and yet which has serious implications for consumer welfare.

(iii) Terminology: 'tacit collusion'; 'conscious parallelism'; 'tacit coordination'; 'coordinated effects'

There is little doubt that there are markets in which it is possible for firms to coordinate their behaviour without entering into an agreement or being party to a concerted practice in the sense of Article 101(1) or the Chapter I prohibition; such behaviour will be to their own self-advantage and to the disadvantage of customers and ultimately consumers. This situation is often described by economists as 'tacit collusion': enjoying the benefits of a particular market structure without actually entering into an agreement to do so. If the firms in question had achieved the same end through explicit collusion, economists would have the same objection – that prices would be higher than they would be without coordination. Economists have no particular interest in whether collusion is 'tacit' or 'explicit': it is the effects of the collusion that matter.

Lawyers, however, are considerably less comfortable with the expression tacit collusion. 'Collusion' is the evil at which Article 101 and the Chapter I prohibition are directed ('any *agreement* or *concerted practice* which has as its object or effect the prevention, restriction or distortion of competition'); in the same way section 1 of the US Sherman Act forbids 'every *contract* or *conspiracy* in restraint of trade', where the notion of collusiveness is inherent in the ideas of contract and conspiracy. For many lawyers, to ask whether tacit collusion could be caught, for example, by the concept of collective dominance under Article 102 or the Chapter II prohibition in the UK is bizarre, since any behaviour that could be called collusive in a legal sense would be caught by Article 101 or the Chapter I prohibition anyway. If behaviour is not collusive under Article 101, lawyers not unnaturally feel uncomfortable at characterising the same behaviour as tacitly collusive and abusive under Article 102. An alternative expression for the conduct in question, 'conscious parallelism', may cause lawyers slightly less discomfort, the opprobrious word 'collusive' being avoided; but even 'consciousness' seems to move the inquiry back to a search for something sufficiently conspiratorial that it should really be investigated, if at all, under Article 101. In the interests of finding terminology which is meaningful and tolerable both to economists and to lawyers when considering the application of Article 102 it might be better to use the expression 'tacit coordination', since this at least eliminates the pejorative word 'collusion' whilst retaining the notion of parallel behaviour which is beneficial to the collectively dominant operators on the market and disadvantageous to customers and consumers. In the context of merger control, competition authorities often ask whether a merger would make it more likely that there would be 'coordinated effects' on the market, which again has the benefit of avoiding reference to the idea of collusion.

---

[7] See eg Bain 'Relation of Profit Rate to Industry Concentration' (1951) 65 Qu J Ec 293–324.

[8] See eg Weiss 'The Concentration and Profits Issue' in *Industrial Concentration: The New Learning* (Little Brown, 1974); Brozen 'The Concentration-Collusion Doctrine' (1977) 46 Antitrust Law Journal 826.

(iv) 'Non-collusive oligopoly'

An additional complication is the recognition that certain mergers might give rise to competition problems where they would result in 'non-collusive oligopoly', that is to say a situation in which one or more members of an oligopoly, without being individually dominant, would be able to derive benefits from their market power without being dependent on the coordinated response of the other oligopolists. The existence of this possibility is now broadly accepted, albeit that it is fairly rare, and is something that can be addressed under the EU Merger Regulation ('the EUMR')[9].

(v) The conditions needed for the successful exercise of collective market power

For tacit coordination to occur it is necessary for firms to indulge in a common form of behaviour[10]. Typically this would involve the charging of similar prices; however it might also involve parallel decisions to reduce production or not to expand capacity: such decisions would, through the suppression of output, in themselves have an impact on prices in the industry in question. Tacit coordination also requires that each firm will be able to monitor quickly and easily how the others are behaving on the market: successful parallel behaviour requires that no one should deviate from the common conduct; transparency is therefore vital to each economic operator to enable it to know what the others are doing, both in terms of their prices and their output. Finally it is important that discipline among the firms with collective market power can be maintained. The benefits to the few of tacit coordination will be lost if one or more firms depart from the appropriate behavioural standard; in order to prevent this from happening, it is necessary that some retaliatory mechanism should be in place to impose sanctions on deviant firms. The most obvious sanction would be a sharp price war which would be harmful to everyone, and would send a severe warning that abandonment of tacit coordination will be to everyone's disadvantage. Finally, the reactions of competitors, customers and consumers should not be such as to jeopardise the results expected from the tacit coordination[11].

(B) Criticisms of the theory

The theory of oligopolistic interdependence has attracted criticism[12]. Four particular problems have been pointed out.

The first is that the theory tends to overstate the interdependence of oligopolists. Even in a symmetrical three-firm oligopoly one firm might be able to steal a march on its rivals by cutting its price if, for example, there would be a delay before the others discovered what it had done: in the meantime the price-cutter may make sufficient profit to offset the cost of any subsequent retaliation. It may also be that the rivals will be unable to expand their capacity in order to meet the increased demand that could be expected to follow a price cut. Anyway, an expansion in output may simply mean that the price-cutter attracts new customers, not that existing ones switch from its rivals.

A second problem is that the theory of oligopoly presents too simplistic a picture of real-life markets. In a symmetrical, stable oligopoly where producers produce identical

---

[9] See ch 21, 'The non-collusive oligopoly gap', pp 864–866.

[10] The indicia of tacit coordination have been particularly well explained in the European Commission's *Guidelines on the assessment of horizontal mergers* OJ [2004] C 31/3; they are discussed in ch 21, 'Coordinated effects', pp 871–873.

[11] As will be seen, the Court of Justice's judgment in *Sony/BMG* (see ch 14 n 119 below) defines collective dominance under the EUMR consistently with the conditions set out in this paragraph: see 'The judgments of the Court of Justice in *Compagnie Maritime Belge Transports v Commission*', p 578 below.

[12] See eg Bork *The Antitrust Paradox* (Free Press, 1993), ch 8.

goods at the same costs interdependence may be strong, but in reality market conditions are usually more complex. The oligopolists themselves will almost inevitably have different cost levels; they may be producing differentiated goods and will usually benefit from at least some consumer loyalty; and their market shares will often not be equal. Furthermore there may be a fringe of smaller sellers which may be a competitive constraint on the oligopolists and, depending on barriers to entry, other firms not operating on the market may enter if and when it becomes clear that supra-competitive profits are available. Many other factors affect the competitive environment in which oligopolists operate. The concentration of the market on the buying side is also important: the more concentrated it is, the less the oligopolists might compete with one another since it will be relatively easy to detect attempts to attract the custom of particular customers. The transparency of price information is significant: the easier it is to conceal the price of goods from competitors, the less will be the interdependence or mutual awareness of the oligopolists. Similarly oligopolists may be able, through secret rebates, to charge prices lower than those in their published price lists. These and many other factors mean that oligopolistic markets differ considerably from one another and this in turn makes it difficult to provide a convincing theoretical explanation of how such markets function and how they should be dealt with.

A third problem with the theory of interdependence is that it fails to explain why in some oligopolistic markets competition is intense. Firms quite clearly do compete with one another in some oligopolies. Such competition may take various forms. Open price competition may be limited, although price wars do break out periodically in some oligopolistic markets, for example between supermarkets or petrol companies. Where open price competition is restricted, this does not mean that secret price cutting does not occur. Non-price competition may be particularly strong in oligopolistic markets. This may manifest itself in various ways: offering better quality products and after-sales service; striving for a lead in technical innovation and research and development (sometimes described as the 'grass-roots' of competition in oligopoly); by introducing loyalty schemes of the kinds offered by airlines and supermarkets; and by making large investments in advertising to promote brand image[13]. Whilst expenditure on advertising has been objected to because it is wasteful of resources and amounts to a barrier to entry to new entrants, it is inconsistent with the theory that oligopolists do not compete with one another[14].

A fourth objection to the theory of oligopolistic interdependence is that it does not explain satisfactorily its central proposition, which is that oligopolists can earn supra-competitive profits without explicitly colluding. The interdependence theory says they cannot increase price unilaterally because they will lose custom to their rivals and yet, to earn supra-competitive profits, prices must have been increased from time to time: how could this have been achieved without explicit collusion? A possible answer to this is that a pattern of price leadership develops whereby one firm raises its price and this acts as a signal to the others to follow suit. Prices therefore remain parallel without conspiracy amongst the oligopolists, although this is not particularly convincing[15]. Economists have suggested that price leadership may take three forms[16]. Dominant price leadership exists

---

[13] This is a particular feature of certain retail markets such as breakfast cereals, household detergents and alcoholic drinks such as lagers.

[14] See *Scherer and Ross* pp 592–610.

[15] See Posner *Antitrust Law* (University of Chicago Press, 1976), p 59.

[16] See Markham 'The Nature and Significance of Price Leadership' (1951) 41 Am Ec Rev 891–905; the classification suggested there was adopted in the former Monopolies and Mergers Commission's report *Parallel Pricing* Cmnd 5330 (1973).

where a dominant firm raises its price and other firms in the industry follow suit because it is in their best interests to do so. This is not what happens in an oligopoly, where no firm is dominant. Secondly, barometric price leadership occurs where one firm raises its price because increased costs (for example, in wages or raw materials) force it to do so: other firms faced with the same increase in costs then follow suit. It would be unreasonable to condemn parallel increases in price if they are explicable on an objective basis in this way. The third type of price leadership is termed collusive: here there is an understanding that firms in an industry will follow the signal emitted from time to time by the price leader. However in this case it would seem to be perfectly reasonable to brand their action as an agreement or a concerted practice under competition law.

Besides these criticisms, there are other objections to the theory of interdependence. One is that it concentrates solely on the tendency to non-collusive price fixing without asking other questions such as why a market is oligopolistic in the first place: this might be because of the superior efficiency associated with economies of scale. In this case, it is necessary to consider at what point the advantages arising from these economies are offset by the adverse effects of a loss of price competition. Others would argue that, even if oligopolists earn supra-competitive profits over a short period, that would attract new entrants to the market and increase competition in the long run unless there are significant barriers to entry to the market. In this case the 'problem' of oligopoly is ephemeral: the market could be left to self-correct the problem.

(C) Possible ways of dealing with oligopoly

Having considered this theoretical debate, the pertinent question is what, if anything, should be done about oligopoly in competition law, assuming that a problem exists.

(i) A structural approach

If economic theory were to demonstrate convincingly that oligopoly inevitably leads to non-collusive parallelism of price and an absence of non-price competition, and also that there are no redeeming features of oligopolistic markets, this would suggest that the problem should be seen as a structural one and dealt with as such. In this case it would be necessary to establish a system capable of preventing the structure of the market from becoming conducive to tacit coordination in the first place. As will be seen in chapters 20 to 22, this is a key consideration in merger control. An important question however is whether further structural powers are needed to deconcentrate industries that become oligopolistic other than through the process of mergers: should competition law include powers to dismantle oligopolistic markets, or at least to inject competitiveness into a sleepy, uncompetitive, market? Where an infringement of Article 101 or 102 is the consequence of the structural conditions of the market and there is no effective behavioural remedy, Article 7 of Regulation 1/2003 provides for the possibility of structural remedies to bring that infringement to an end[17]. UK competition law does not explicitly provide such a power under the Competition Act. However a structural solution to the problem of oligopolistic markets is possible under the market investigation regime of the Enterprise Act[18]. It goes without saying that it would require an exceptional case for these draconian remedies to be used, but it is important to be aware of the fact that the possibility does exist.

---

[17] See ch 7, 'Structural remedies', p 254.
[18] See 'Market investigations under the Enterprise Act 2002', pp 568–569 below and ch 11, 'Final powers', pp 476–477.

(ii) A behavioural approach

An alternative approach is to see the problem as essentially behavioural in nature, in which case control is necessary to prevent oligopolists behaving in a way that is uncompetitive. Some would favour making any parallelism in price between oligopolists illegal. This however would be quite inappropriate: it would be absurd to forbid firms from behaving in a parallel manner if this is a rational response to the structure of the market. To put the point another way, it would be strange indeed if competition law were to mandate that firms should behave irrationally, by not acting in parallel, in order to avoid being found to have infringed competition law.

Where oligopolists really do collude, for example to fix prices or to share markets, there is no reason why they – like firms in less concentrated markets – should not be subject to the provisions of Article 101 and the Chapter I prohibition of the Competition Act 1998. The term 'concerted practice' catches any situation in which firms knowingly substitute practical cooperation for the risks of competition. However when this concept is applied to oligopolists a different problem arises: it can be difficult to distinguish conduct which is collusive in the sense of Article 101 and the Chapter I prohibition from parallel conduct which is attributable to the oligopolistic structure of a market. This problem is compounded by the fact that in many cases there is little or no evidence of unlawful contact between firms, such as the minutes of a meeting: firms that really do intend to rig the market are wise enough usually to destroy incriminating evidence. The danger is that a competition authority or court will too readily reach the conclusion that parallel conduct means that there is collusion; this can be avoided only by considering the alternative explanations for such conduct, including an economic analysis of the market in question. An understanding of the economics of oligopoly is vital when trying to decide whether parallel conduct is collusive (in the legal sense) or not[19].

As a separate matter, it may be appropriate in oligopolistic markets to prohibit 'facilitating practices' that encourage parallel behaviour: an obvious example is the exchange of information between oligopolists that makes it easier for them to behave in the same way. As we have seen, the structure of the market is one of the factors taken into account when analysing information agreements under Article 101 and the Chapter I prohibition[20]. The possibility that an agreement might facilitate parallel behaviour may also be taken into account when considering whether an agreement satisfies the criteria of Article 101(3)[21]. Finally, it may be sensible to prevent exclusionary abuses of a collective dominant position which have the effect of eliminating actual or potential competitors from oligopolistic markets; as will be seen, there have been a few cases in which Article 102 has been used to deal with behaviour of this sort.

(iii) A regulatory approach

A different possibility would be to regulate the prices of undertakings that operate in an oligopolistic environment. This, however, would be a counsel of despair. As a matter of policy direct regulation should be a remedy of last resort. Competition authorities should not be price regulators; they should be the guardians of the competitive process. Where markets are oligopolistic and entry is limited, competition authorities should be concerned with the question of whether there are barriers to entry and whether the

---

[19] See further the discussion in ch 3, 'Concerted practices' pp 112–115.

[20] See ch 13, 'Exchanges of Information', pp 539–547 and 'Article 101(1), the exchange of information and other facilitating practices', pp 569–570 below.

[21] See 'Article 101(3)', p 571 below.

state itself, for example through restrictive licensing rules, regulation or legislation, is responsible for a lack of competition.

(iv) An investigatory approach

A problem of market failure of the kind described above may be tackled by conducting an investigation; this may enable the competition authority to understand better why a market is not functioning well, and what steps should be taken to improve the situation. Sectoral inquiries in the EU[22] and market investigations in the UK[23] are examples of this approach.

3. Article 101

(A) Does parallel behaviour amount to a concerted practice under Article 101?

Both the Commission and the EU Courts appreciate that price competition in an oligopoly may be muted and that oligopolists react to one another's conduct, so that parallel behaviour does not, in itself, amount to a concerted practice under Article 101(1)[24]. In *Dyestuffs*[25] the Court of Justice said at paragraphs 65 and 66 that:

> By its very nature, then, the concerted practice does not have all the elements of a contract but may *inter alia* arise out of coordination which becomes apparent from the behaviour of the participants. *Although parallel behaviour may not itself be identified with a concerted practice,* it may however amount to strong evidence of such a practice if it leads to conditions of competition which do not respond to the normal conditions of the market, having regard to the nature of the products, the size and number of the undertakings, and the volume of the said market. Such is the case especially where the parallel behaviour is such as to permit the parties to seek price equilibrium at a different level from that which would have resulted from competition, and to crystallise the status quo to the detriment of effective freedom of movement of the products in the [internal] market and free choice by consumers of their suppliers (emphasis added).

The Court added at paragraph 68 that the existence of a concerted practice could be appraised correctly only:

> if the evidence upon which the contested decision is based is considered, not in isolation, but as a whole, account being taken of the specific features of the products in question.

In *Dyestuffs* the parties argued that they had acted in a similar manner only because of the oligopolistic market structure. The Court rejected this assertion since the market was not a pure oligopoly: rather it was one in which firms could realistically be expected to adopt their own pricing strategies, particularly in view of the compartmentalisation of the markets along national boundaries. The Court recognised that there might be situations in which a firm must take into account a rival's likely responses, but said that this did not entitle them actually to coordinate their behaviour:

---

[22] On sectoral inquiries see ch 7, 'Article 17: investigations into sectors of the economy and into types of agreements', pp 267–268.

[23] On market investigations see ch 11, 'Overview of the Provisions on Market Investigation References', pp 452–454.

[24] On concerted practices generally see ch 3, 'Concerted practices' pp 112–115.

[25] Cases 48/69 etc [1972] ECR 619, [1972] CMLR 557.

Although every producer is free to change his prices, taking into account in so doing the present or foreseeable conduct of his competitors, nevertheless it is contrary to the rules on competition contained in the Treaty for a producer to cooperate with his competitors, in any way whatsoever, in order to determine a coordinated course of action relating to a price increase and to ensure its success by prior elimination of all uncertainty as to each other's conduct regarding the essential elements of that action, such as the amount, subject-matter, date and place of the increases[26].

In *Züchner v Bayerische Vereinsbank AG*[27] the Court of Justice repeated that intelligent responses to a competitor's behaviour would not bring firms within the scope of Article 101(1). In *Zinc Producer Group*[28] the Commission said that it did not intend to condemn parallel action between 1977 and 1979 which might be explicable in terms of 'barometric price leadership'[29], saying that in such circumstances 'parallel pricing behaviour in an oligopoly producing homogeneous goods will not in itself be sufficient evidence of a concerted practice'[30]. In *Peroxygen Products*,[31] however, the Commission rejected an argument that an agreement between oligopolists fell outside Article 101(1) since, even without the agreement, the structure of the market would have meant that they would have behaved in the same way. In the Commission's view, the very fact that the firms had entered into an agreement at all indicated that the risks of competition might have led to different market behaviour.

In *Wood Pulp*[32] the Commission held that producers of wood pulp were guilty of a concerted practice to fix prices in the EU. There had been parallel conduct on the market from 1975 until 1981, but there was no evidence of explicit agreements to fix prices. However the Commission concluded that there was a concerted practice, basing its finding on two factors. The first was that there had been direct and indirect exchanges of price information which had created an artificial transparency on the market. The second was that, in the Commission's view, an economic analysis of the market demonstrated that it was not a narrow oligopoly in which parallel pricing might be expected. On appeal, the Court of Justice substantially annulled the Commission's findings[33]. The fact that pulp producers announced price rises to users in advance on a quarterly basis did not in itself involve an infringement of Article 101(1): making information available to third parties did not eliminate the producers' uncertainty as to what each other would do[34]. Furthermore, there were alternative explanations for the system of and simultaneity of price announcements, and the parallelism of prices could be explained other than by the existence of a concerted practice. Information was widely available on the market as buyers informed each other of the prices available, some agents acted for several producers and so were well informed about prices and the trade press was dynamic. As to parallelism, the evidence of experts appointed by the Court was that the market was more oligopolistic (on both sides of the market) than the Commission had supposed, and that economic problems had discouraged producers from engaging in price cutting which their competitors would inevitably follow; the experts also considered that there was evidence to suggest that there could not have been concertation: for example, market shares had varied from

---

[26] [1972] ECR 619, [1972] CMLR 557, para 118.
[27] Case 172/80 [1981] ECR 2021, [1982] 1 CMLR 313, para 14.
[28] OJ [1984] L 220/27, [1985] 2 CMLR 108.   [29] See 'Criticisms of the theory', pp 563–565 above.
[30] OJ [1984] L 220/27, [1985] 2 CMLR 108, paras 75–76.
[31] OJ [1985] L 35/1, [1985] 1 CMLR 481, para 50.   [32] OJ [1985] L 85/1, [1985] 3 CMLR 474.
[33] Cases C-89/85 etc *A Ahlström Oy v Commission* [1993] ECR I-1307, [1993] 4 CMLR 407; see Jones '*Wood Pulp*: Concerted Practice and/or Conscious Parallelism?' (1993) 14 ECLR 273; Van Gerven and Varano 'The *Wood Pulp* Case and the Future of Concerted Practices' (1994) 31 CML Rev 575.
[34] [1993] ECR I-1307, [1993] 4 CMLR 407, paras 59–65.

time to time, which would be unlikely if there had been a concerted practice; and the alleged cartel members had not tried to establish production quotas, which they could be expected to have done if they wished to control the market[35].

This important judgment demonstrates that the burden is on the Commission to prove the existence of a concerted practice and, when it relies solely on the conduct of the firms in question[36], to deal with any alternative explanations advanced by the parties of parallel behaviour on the market. The judgment does acknowledge, however, that, in an appropriate case, parallelism could be evidence of a concerted practice where there is no plausible alternative explanation[37].

In *British Sugar*[38] British Sugar deployed the argument that the oligopolistic nature of the market meant that price competition was limited, and that its price leadership should not be regarded as evidence of a concerted practice. The Commission's reply to this was that, where competition in a market is already restricted, it should be particularly vigilant to ensure that the competition which does exist is not restricted[39]; the General Court upheld this finding on appeal[40]. This is consistent with the judgment in *Steel Beams*[41].

In *CISAC* the Commission prohibited a number of collecting societies from restricting competition by limiting their ability to offer services outside their domestic territory; the Commission found that the only possible explanation for the societies' parallel behaviour was a concerted practice[42].

(B) Article 101(1), the exchange of information and other facilitating practices

The previous section has discussed the difficulties in determining whether parallel behaviour may be attributable to a concerted practice. A competition authority must avoid reaching a conclusion that a concerted practice exists if there is an alternative explanation of any parallel behaviour. However this is not to say that Article 101(1) cannot be deployed in other ways to deal with the problem of parallel behaviour: in particular it can be applied to what are often referred to as 'facilitating practices', that is to say practices that make it easier for firms to achieve the benefits of tacit coordination. The most obvious of these is the exchange of information which increases the transparency of the market and so makes parallel behaviour easier. It is for this reason that the application of Article 101(1) to information agreements focuses, amongst other things, on the structure of the market[43]: it was the oligopolistic structure of the market in *UK Agricultural Tractor*

---

[35] Ibid, paras 66–127.

[36] See eg Cases T-67/00 etc *JFE Engineering Corp v Commission* [2004] ECR II-2501, [2005] 4 CMLR 27, para 186.

[37] Cases C-89/85 etc [1993] ECR I-1307, [1993] 4 CMLR 407, para 71; for an interesting judgment in the US dealing with the relevance of parallel behaviour under the Sherman Act see *Re High Fructose Corn Syrup Antitrust Litigation* 295 F 3d 651 (7th Cir 2002); cert denied 123 S Ct 1251 (2003).

[38] OJ [1999] L 76/1, [1999] 4 CMLR 1316; see also *Cartonboard* OJ [1994] L 243/1, [1994] 5 CMLR 547, para 73.

[39] OJ [1999] L 76/1, [1999] 4 CMLR 1316, para 87.

[40] Cases T-202/98 etc *Tate & Lyle v Commission* [2001] ECR II-2035, [2001] 5 CMLR 859, para 46.

[41] Case T-141/94 *Thyssen Stahl AG v Commission* [1999] ECR II-347, [1999] 4 CMLR 810, para 302.

[42] Commission decision of 16 July 2008 [2009] 4 CMLR 577, paras 156–223, on appeal in Cases T-398/08 etc *Stowarzyszenie Autorów v Commission*, not yet decided; an application for interim measures was dismissed in Case T-411/08 R *Artisjus v Commission*, order of 14 November 2008, upheld on appeal in Case C-32/09 R, order of 31 August 2010.

[43] See ch 13, 'Exchanges of Information', pp 539–547.

Registration Exchange[44] that led the Commission to conclude that Article 101(1) had been infringed; and the more competitive nature of the cars' market that led it to the opposite conclusion in relation to it[45]. In *Thyssen Stahl v Commission*[46] the General Court held that, where the structure of a market is oligopolistic, it is all the more important to ensure the decision-making independence of undertakings and residual competition, and that therefore the exchange of recent data on market shares could infringe Article 101(1)[47]. The Commission applied this principle in *Bananas* when condemning three banana producers for coordinating their quotation prices[48].

The Commission will look for other facilitating practices. For example at paragraph 20 of its *Guidelines on Vertical Restraints*[49] it says that it will examine agency agreements, even where the principal bears all the financial and commercial risks, if they could facilitate collusion[50]. This could happen, in the Commission's view, if a number of principals use the same agents whilst collectively preventing others from doing so, or where they use agents to collude on marketing strategy or to exchange sensitive information between themselves. Similar concerns are expressed throughout the *Guidelines* as to the possibility of vertical agreements facilitating collusion[51].

The Commission's *Guidelines on Horizontal Cooperation Agreements*[52] state that, in assessing horizontal cooperation agreements other than 'hard-core' cartels of the kind that almost always fall within Article 101(1)[53], the characteristics of the market will be taken into account[54]: some agreements may be found not to be anti-competitive where the market is reasonably competitive, but to be problematic where it is oligopolistic. The application of these *Guidelines* is considered in some detail in chapter 15[55].

The Commission has applied the *de minimis* doctrine narrowly in the case of an oligopoly[56] and has more readily found an appreciable effect on inter-state trade of an agreement where the market was oligopolistic[57].

---

[44] OJ [1992] L 68/19, [1993] 4 CMLR 358, para 16, upheld on appeal to the General Court in Cases T-34/92 and T-35/92 *Fiatagri UK Ltd v Commission* [1994] ECR II-905 and 957 and on appeal to the Court of Justice in Cases C-7/95 and C-8/95 P *John Deere v Commission* [1998] ECR I-3111, and 3175, [1998] 5 CMLR 311.

[45] See ch 13, 'The economic conditions on the relevant markets', pp 544–545; para 79 of the Commission's *Guidelines an Horizontal Cooperation Agreements* is specifically concerned with information agreements in oligopolistic markets.

[46] See ch 14 n 41 above.

[47] [1993] ECR I-1307, [1993] 4 CMLR 407, paras 393–412; see similarly Case T-53/03 *BPB v Commission* [2008] ECR II-1333, [2008] 5 CMLR 1201, paras 108–109.

[48] Decision of 15 October 2008, para 280, on appeal Cases T-587/08 and T-588/08 *Del Monte v Commission*, not yet decided.

[49] OJ [2010] C 130/1.

[50] As a general principle agency agreements fall outside Article 101(1): see ch 16, 'Commercial Agents', pp 621–623.

[51] See eg the following paragraphs in the *Guidelines on Vertical Restraints*, all of which refer to the possibility of the facilitation of collusion: paras 100(b)–(c), 101, 115, 121, 130, 134, 151, 154, 157, 166 (specifically on exclusive dealerships in an oligopolistic market), 168, 175, 178, 181, 182, 206, 211, 212, 224 and 227.

[52] OJ [2011] C 11/1.

[53] That is to say those agreements that have as their object the restriction of competition: see ch 3, 'The "object or effect" of preventing, restricting or distorting competition', pp 117–121 and ch 13 generally.

[54] OJ [2011] C 11/1, paras 39–47.   [55] See ch 15 generally.

[56] *Floral* OJ [1980] L 39/51, [1980] 2 CMLR 285, on the *de minimis* doctrine see ch 3, 'The *De Minimis* Doctrine', pp 140–144.

[57] *Cast Iron and Steel Rolls* OJ [1983] L 317/1, [1984] 1 CMLR 694, upheld on appeal Cases 29 and 30/83 *Compagnie Royale Asturienne des Mines SA and Rheinzink GmbH v Commission* [1984] ECR 1679, [1985] 1 CMLR 688.

(C) **Article 101(3)**

The structure of the market will be relevant to the analysis of agreements under Article 101(3), in particular since that provision requires that there should be no substantial elimination of competition[58]. The fact that the Commission's block exemptions contain market share caps in itself means that firms in an oligopoly will often not be able to avail themselves of these legal instruments[59]. In *P&O Stena Line*[60] the Commission decided that the criteria of Article 101(3) were satisfied in the case of a joint venture for cross-channel ferry services for a limited period of three years; the decision considered at length whether there was a risk that the joint venture would create a duopoly on the 'short sea tourist market', but concluded that the joint venture and Eurotunnel, the operator of the Channel Tunnel, could be expected to compete with each other rather than to act in parallel to raise prices[61].

An agreement might be found to satisfy Article 101(3) where it would have the effect of introducing more competition into an oligopolistic market[62].

4. **Article 102 and Collective Dominance**[63]

One of the most complex and controversial issues in EU competition law has been the application – or non-application – of Article 102 TFEU (and the EUMR) to so-called 'collective dominance'[64]. Discussion of this question in relation to Article 102 can be traced back at least to the early 1970s[65]; an enormous body of literature has developed[66]. The law

---

[58] See ch 4, 'Determining whether competition will be substantially eliminated', pp 164–165.

[59] On the market share caps in the block exemptions see ch 4, 'The format of block exemptions', pp 171–172.

[60] OJ [1999] L 163/61, [2000] 5 CMLR 682.   [61] Ibid, para 127.

[62] See eg *Carlsberg* OJ [1984] L 207/26, [1985] 1 CMLR 735.

[63] The text that follows is based, in part, on 'Collective Dominance', in the Liber Amicorum in Honour of Lord Slynn of Hadley *Judicial Review in European Union Law* (Kluwer Law International, 2000, eds O'Keeffe and Bavasso), ch 37.

[64] At various times the expressions 'collective dominance', 'joint dominance' and 'oligopolistic dominance' have been used interchangeably. In Cases C-395/96 P etc *Compagnie Maritime Belge Transports SA v Commission* [2000] ECR I-1365, [2000] 4 CMLR 1076 Advocate General Fennelly indicated that he saw no meaningful distinction between these terms, but used the expression 'collective dominance' as this was the one that the Court itself usually employed; in its judgment in the same case the Court of Justice used the expression 'collective dominance' throughout: see in particular para 36; it also did so in Case C-413/06 P *Bertelsmann AG v Impala* [2008] ECR I-4951, [2008] 5 CMLR 1073, a case under the EUMR.

[65] See ch 14 n 79 below.

[66] See eg Whish and Sufrin 'Oligopolistic Markets and EC Competition Law' (1992) 12 Oxford Yearbook of European Law 59; Winkler and Hansen 'Collective Dominance under the EC Merger Control Regulation' (1993) 30 CML Rev 787; Ridyard 'Economic Analysis of Single Firm and Oligopolistic Dominance under the European Merger Regulation' (1994) 15 ECLR 255; Rodger 'Market Integration and the Development of European Competition Policy to Meet New Demands: A Study of Oligopolistic Markets and the Concept of a Collective Dominant Position under Article 86 of the Treaty' [1994(2)] Legal Issues of European Integration 1; Rodger 'Oligopolistic Market Failure: Collective Dominance versus Complex Monopoly' (1995) 16 ECLR 21; Briones 'Oligopolistic Dominance: is there a Common Approach in Different Jurisdictions?' (1995) 16 ECLR 334; Soames 'An Analysis of the Principles of Concerted Practice and Collective Dominance: a Distinction without a Difference' (1996) 17 ECLR 24; Morgan 'The Treatment of Oligopoly under the European Merger Control Regulation' (1996) 41 Antitrust Bulletin 203; Tillotson and MacCulloch 'EC Competition Rules, Collective Dominance and Maritime Transport' (1997) 21(1) World Competition 51; Venit 'Two Steps Forward and No Steps Back: Economic Analysis and Oligopolistic Dominance after *Kali und Salz*' (1998) 35 CML Rev 1101; Elliott 'The Gencor Judgment: Collective Dominance, Remedies and Extraterritoriality under the Merger Regulation' (1999) 24 EL Rev 638; Korah '*Gencor v Commission*: Collective Dominance' (1999) 20 ECLR 337; Stroux 'Is EC Oligopoly Control Outgrowing Its Infancy?' (2000) 23(1) World Competition 3; Fernandez 'Increasing Powers and Increasing Uncertainty: Collective Dominance and Pricing Abuses' (2000)

and decisional practice on collective dominance, under both legal instruments, developed considerably in the years from 1998 to 2002; of particular importance are the Court of Justice's judgments in *France v Commission* (the so-called *Kali und Salz* case)[67], a case decided under the EUMR, and *Compagnie Maritime Belge Transports v Commission*[68] and two judgments under the EUMR of the General Court, *Gencor v Commission*[69] and *Airtours v Commission*[70]. A further judgment of the Court of Justice, in the *Sony/BMG* case[71], followed in 2008. This section will consider in particular the development of the law under Article 102; it would appear to be the case that the expression 'collective dominance' has the same meaning under Article 102 as it has under the EUMR.

(A) **The linguistic background**

There is a linguistic background to the issue of collective dominance. Article 102 applies to '[a]ny abuse *by one or more undertakings* of a dominant position within the common market' (emphasis added). The same wording has been adopted in numerous domestic systems of competition law[72]. The fact that Article 102 is capable of application to dominance held on the part of more than one undertaking clearly envisages the possibility, though not the inevitability, of 'collective' dominance being enjoyed by legally and economically separate undertakings; a narrow reading would be that the reference to more than one undertaking refers to different legal entities within the same corporate group[73]. In contradistinction to Article 102, Article 2(3) of the EUMR as it was originally drafted in 1989[74] provided that a concentration that creates or strengthens a dominant position as a result of which competition would be significantly impeded in the common market or a substantial part of it may be declared incompatible with the common market; however this provision does not refer specifically to a dominant position *enjoyed by one or more undertakings*. Linguistically, therefore, it could be argued – as indeed it was by France (among others) in the *Kali und Salz* case[75] – that the EUMR applies only to single firm dominance, even if Article 102 is capable of application to collective dominance. It took many years for the EU Courts to determine the proper scope of Article 102 and the EUMR: in each case in favour of the application of the measure in question to collective dominance.

25 EL Rev 645; Stroux, commenting on *CMBT v Commission* (2000) 37 CML Rev 1249; Etter 'The Assessment of Mergers in the EC under the Concept of Collective Dominance' (2000) 23(3) World Competition 103; Kloosterhuis 'Joint Dominance and the Interaction Between Firms' (2000) ECLR 79; Monti 'The Scope of Collective Dominance under Article 82' (2001) 38 CML Rev 131; Niels 'Collective Dominance – More than Just Oligopolistic Interdependence' (2001) 22 ECLR 168; Temple Lang 'Oligopolies and Joint Dominance in Community Antitrust Law' [2002] Fordham Corporate Law Institute (ed Hawk), ch 12.

  [67] Cases C-68/94 and 30/95 [1998] ECR I-1375, [1998] 4 CMLR 829.
  [68] Cases C-395 and 396/96 P [2000] ECR I-1365, [2000] 4 CMLR 1076.
  [69] Case T-102/96 [1999] ECR II-753, [1999] 4 CMLR 971.
  [70] Case T-342/99 [2002] ECR II-2585, [2002] 5 CMLR 317 annulling the Commission's prohibition decision in Case IV/M.1524 *Airtours/First Choice* OJ [2000] L 93/1, [2000] 5 CMLR 494.
  [71] Case C-413/06 P *Bertelsmann AG v Commission* [2008] ECR I-4951, [2008] 5 CMLR 1073 setting aside the General Court's judgment in Case T-464/04 *Impala v Commission* [2006] ECR II-2289, [2006] 5 CMLR 1049 annulling the Commission's clearance decision in Case COMP/M.3333 *Sony/BMG* OJ [2005] L 62/30.
  [72] See eg s 18 of the UK Competition Act 1998.
  [73] See 'The definition of collective dominance under Article 102', p 573 below.
  [74] Note that Article 2(3) of Regulation 139/2004, OJ [2004] L 24/1, places emphasis on the question of whether a merger would significantly impede effective competition in the common market, 'in particular as a result of the creation or strengthening of a dominant position'.
  [75] See ch 14 n 67 above.

(B) **The definition of collective dominance under Article 102**

(i) 'One or more undertakings': the narrow view of Article 102

Article 102 prohibits the abuse of a dominant position 'by one or more undertakings'. The 'narrow' view of the reference to more than one undertaking was that it meant that the market power and behaviour of undertakings within the same corporate group could be aggregated and dealt with under Article 102. In several of the cases on Article 102 a dominant position was found to exist among the members of a group forming a single economic entity. For example in *Continental Can*[76] three different companies in the same group were involved in the Commission's analysis: Continental Can (a US company), SLW (its German subsidiary) which held a dominant position in Germany and Europemballage (also its subsidiary) which acquired a competitor, TDV. It was the overall effect of these companies' position and behaviour which led to a finding of abuse of dominance. Similarly in *Commercial Solvents v Commission*[77] there were two legal entities within the same corporate group, the US parent, Commercial Solvents, and its Italian subsidiary, ICI. It is easy enough to see that the reference in Article 102 to an abuse *by one or more undertakings* might be thought to refer to an abuse that could be attributed to separate legal entities within the same corporate group; it should be added, however, that if those entities are to be regarded as *one* undertaking – as they should be – the approach set out above fails to explain what is meant by an abuse by more than one undertaking[78].

(ii) 'One or more undertakings': the wide view of Article 102

An alternative approach to the reference in Article 102 to one or more undertakings is that it has a wider meaning, so that legally and economically independent firms might be considered to hold a 'collective dominant position'. It would follow that abusive market behaviour on the part of collectively dominant firms could be controlled under Article 102 (and, after the adoption of the EUMR, that the Commission would have control over a larger number of concentrations if the same approach could be taken in relation to that legal instrument). The Commission dabbled with the idea of collective dominance under Article 102 in the early 1970s[79], but the Court of Justice appeared to have rejected it in *Hoffmann-La Roche v Commission*[80]. There the Court seemed to suggest that problems of tacit coordination could not be controlled under Article 102:

> A dominant position must also be distinguished from parallel courses of conduct which are peculiar to oligopolies in that in an oligopoly the courses of conduct interact, whilst in the case of an undertaking occupying a dominant position the conduct of the undertaking which derives profits from that position is to a great extent determined unilaterally[81].

---

[76] JO [1972] L 7/25, [1972] CMLR D11, the decision was annulled on appeal due to the Commission's failure to define the relevant product market in Case 6/72 *Europemballage Corpn and Continental Can Co Inc v Commission* [1973] ECR 215, [1973] CMLR 199.

[77] JO [1972] L 299/51, [1973] CMLR D50, upheld on appeal Cases 6/73 etc [1974] ECR 223, [1974] 1 CMLR 309.

[78] See ch 3, 'The "single economic entity" doctrine', pp 92–97.

[79] See eg the *Report on the Behaviour of the Oil Companies during the period from October 1973 to March 1974*: COM(75) 675, 10 December 1975; *Sugar Cartel* OJ [1973] L 140/17, [1973] CMLR D65 where the Commission held that two Dutch producers held a collective dominant position: the Court of Justice said nothing about this because it considered there was no abuse by the companies anyway, Cases 40/73 etc *Suiker Unie v Commission* [1975] ECR 1663, [1976] 1 CMLR 295.

[80] Case 85/76 [1979] ECR 461, [1979] 3 CMLR 211.

[81] Ibid, para 39; similarly see Case 172/80 *Gerhard Züchner v Bayerische Vereinsbank* [1981] ECR 2021, [1982] 1 CMLR 313, para 10.

This apparent rejection of Article 102 as a tool for controlling oligopolistic behaviour was understandable. Oligopolists that participate in agreements or concerted practices would be caught by Article 101(1) anyway. The Court of Justice appears to have taken the view that where oligopolists behave in an identical fashion because of the structure of the market on which they operate, rather than because of participation in an agreement or concerted practice, they should not be condemned for abusing their position if their conduct is rational – even inevitable – behaviour. An approach to the 'oligopoly problem' which is based on the concept of abuse in Article 102 seemed inappropriate: or to put it another way, where there was no explicit collusion contrary to Article 101, the Court was not prepared to characterise the economist's notion of tacit collusion as abusive under Article 102. After *Hoffmann-La Roche* a period of relative inactivity followed. For example in *Alcatel v NOVASAM*[82] the Commission invited the Court of Justice to adopt a theory of collective dominance in an Article 267 reference, but the Court declined to comment on the point in its judgment. In *Magill*[83] the Commission took objection to the refusal of three television companies to grant licences of copyright in their TV schedules to a third party wishing to produce a TV listings magazine. The Commission could have tried a collective dominance approach to the case, holding that the companies had collectively abused a collective dominant position in the TV schedules market; instead it found three individual dominant positions on the part of each company, and three individual abuses.

(iii) Confirmation of the wide view

Any suggestion that the concept of collective dominance had been laid to rest was subsequently shown to be wrong. In *Italian Flat Glass*[84] the Commission held that three Italian producers of flat glass had a collective dominant position and that they had abused it. As participants in a tight oligopolistic market they enjoyed a degree of independence from competitive pressures that enabled them to impede the maintenance of effective competition, notably by not having to take into account the behaviour of other market participants. The conduct held to fall within Article 102 had already been condemned earlier in the decision as a concerted practice under Article 101. However the decision opened up the possibility that in other situations the conduct of oligopolists, *though not within Article 101*, might be attacked under Article 102. On appeal the General Court overturned the Commission's decision on collective dominance on the ground that the Commission had simply 'recycled' the facts relied on as constituting an infringement of Article 101, instead of properly defining the relevant product and geographic markets in order to weigh up the undertakings' economic power, as is necessary in Article 102 cases.

Nevertheless, the General Court confirmed the principle of collective dominance at paragraph 358 of its judgment:

> There is nothing, in principle, to prevent two or more independent economic entities from being, on a specific market, united by such economic links that, by virtue of that fact, together they hold a dominant position vis-à-vis the other operators on the same market. This could be the case, for example, where two or more independent undertakings jointly have, through agreements or licences, a technological lead affording them the power to behave to an appreciable extent independently of their competitors, their customers and

[82] Case 247/86 [1988] ECR 5987.

[83] *Magill TV Guide* OJ [1989] L 78/43, [1989] 4 CMLR 757, upheld on appeal Cases T-69/89 etc *RTE v Commission* [1991] ECR II-485, [1991] 4 CMLR 586 and on appeal to the Court of Justice, Case C-241/91 P [1995] ECR I-743, [1995] 4 CMLR 718.

[84] OJ [1989] L 33/44, [1990] 4 CMLR 535.

ultimately of their consumers (judgment of the Court in *Hoffmann-La Roche,* cited above, paragraphs 38 and 48)[85].

The judgment in *Italian Flat Glass* was exciting and frustrating in equal measure. Collective dominance on the part of 'two or more independent entities' could exist under Article 102, although the Commission had failed to demonstrate that it existed in this particular case. Clearly, the General Court considered that infringements of Articles 101 and 102 were conceptually independent of one another: this is why the Commission was not permitted simply to 'recycle the facts' used to find an infringement of Article 101 in order to determine an abuse of collective dominance[86]. Each Article must be applied according to its own terms. Behaviour that amounts to a concerted practice is not automatically also abusive; and vice versa[87]. However, what is frustrating about the judgment is that it did not advance our understanding of what collective dominance or abuse of collective dominance consists of. Given that we now have the benefit of the judgments in *Compagnie Maritime Belge Transports v Commission* under Article 102 and *France v Commission, Gencor v Commission, Airtours v Commission* and *Impala v Commission* under the EUMR it is not necessary to spend time in trying to understand what was meant by paragraph 358 of *Italian Flat Glass.* It is sufficient to say that an important landmark had been reached in this judgment, but that later case law has shed much more light on the concept of collective dominance.

(iv) Further judgments and decisions on collective dominance under Article 102

In the years after *Italian Flat Glass* there were several more judgments and decisions in which collective dominance was referred to, but not until *France v Commission* and *Gencor v Commission* under the EUMR and *Compagnie Maritime Belge Transports v Commission* under Article 102 did a true picture begin to emerge of what was meant by the concept. In *Almelo*[88] the Court of Justice said that:

42 However, in order for such a collective dominant position to exist, the undertakings in the group must be linked in such a way that they adopt the same conduct on the market.

43 It is for the national court to consider whether there exist between the regional electricity distributors in the Netherlands links which are sufficiently strong for there to be a collective dominant position in a substantial part of the common market.

This formulation suggested that the Court of Justice was looking at what economists would look at: the adoption of the same conduct on the market or, in other words, tacit coordination. This was an improvement on *Italian Flat Glass,* in that it provided an economic rationale for collective dominance, but it still failed to explain what could amount to collective dominance.

---

[85] Cases T-68/89 etc *Società Italiano Vetro SpA v Commission* [1992] ECR II-1403, [1992] 5 CMLR 302; note that the reference to *Hoffmann-La Roche* in this paragraph is a reference to the meaning of market power as defined in that judgment, *not* to the meaning of collective dominance which, as mentioned earlier, the Court appeared to reject.

[86] The differences between Articles 101 and 102 are very clearly stated in the judgment of the General Court in Case T-41/96 *Bayer v Commission* [2000] ECR II-3383, [2001] 4 CMLR 126, paras 174–180 and by the Court of Justice in the appeal to it from that judgment, Cases C-2 and 3/01 P *Commission v Bayer* [2004] ECR I-23, [2004] 4 CMLR 653, para 70.

[87] This point is specifically confirmed at paras 43 and 44 of the Court of Justice's judgment in Cases C-395/96 and C-396/96 P *Compagnie Maritime Belge Transports v Commission* [2000] ECR I-1365, [2000] 4 CMLR 1076: see 'The judgment of the Court of Justice in *Compagnie Maritime Belge Transports v Commission*', pp 577–579 below.

[88] Case C-393/92 *Almelo v NV Energiebedrijf Ijsselmij* [1994] ECR I-1477.

In *Spediporto*[89], *DIP*[90] and *Sodemare*[91] the Court of Justice repeated the *Almelo* formulation, but did not advance its notion of collective dominance. In the *Bosman case*[92] Advocate General Lenz assumed that football clubs in a professional football league could be 'united by such economic links' as to be regarded as collectively dominant; the Court did not address the issue. In the meantime the Commission began to reach findings of collective dominance in a number of decisions, both under Article 102 and under the EUMR. The decisions under Article 102 did not greatly add to the notion of collective dominance, since they involved undertakings which unmistakably were linked in some way. For example in three decisions in the maritime transport sector the undertakings were members of liner conferences. In *French-West African Shipowners' Committees*[93] the Commission concluded that members of the shipowners' committees had abused a collective dominant position by taking action designed to prevent other shipping lines establishing themselves as competitors on routes between France and 11 west African states[94]. This decision was adopted after the General Court's judgment in the *Italian Flat Glass* case, and the Commission specifically imposed a fine for the infringement of Article 102 as well as the agreements that were caught by Article 101. In its decision on *Cewal*[95] the Commission found collective dominance between shipping lines that were members of a liner conference. The Commission's finding of collective dominance was upheld on appeal to the General Court[96] and to the Court of Justice: the latter judgment is of major importance on collective dominance under Article 102 and is considered in some detail below[97].

In *TACA*[98] the Commission imposed fines totalling €273 million on the members of a liner conference for abuses of collective dominance. On appeal to the General Court the Commission's finding of collective dominance was upheld[99]; the Court stated specifically that, although competition between undertakings in a collectively dominant position was necessarily restricted, this did not imply that competition between them should be entirely eliminated[100]. The Commission's finding that members of TACA had abused their collective dominant position by inducing competitors to join their shipping conference, thereby harming the competitive structure of the market, was annulled, as were the fines[101].

The Commission also reached a finding of collective dominance in *Port of Rødby*[102], where it considered that two ferry undertakings that fixed common rates, coordinated timetables and marketed their services jointly were collectively dominant. In *Irish*

---

[89] Case C-96/94 *Centro Servizi Spediporto Sri v Spedizioni Marittime del Golfo Sri* [1995] ECR I-2883, [1996] 4 CMLR 613, para 33.

[90] Cases C-140/94 etc *DIP SpA v Commune di Bassano del Grappa* [1995] ECR I-3257, [1996] 4 CMLR 157, para 26.

[91] Case C-70/95 *Sodemare SA, Anni Azzurri Holding SpA and Anni Azzurri Rezzato Sri v Regione Lombardia* [1997] ECR I-3395, [1998] 4 CMLR 667, para 46.

[92] Case C-415/93 *Union Royale Belge des Societes de Football Association v Bosman* [1995] ECR I-4921, [1996] 1 CMLR 645.

[93] OJ [1992] L 134/1, [1993] 5 CMLR 446.   [94] Ibid, paras 52–69.

[95] OJ [1993] L 34/20, [1995] 5 CMLR 198.

[96] Cases T-24/93 etc *Compagnie Maritime Belge Transports SA v Commission* [1996] ECR II-1201, [1997] 4 CMLR 273.

[97] See 'The judgment of the Court of Justice in *Compagnie Maritime Belge Transports v Commission*', pp 577–579 below.

[98] OJ [1999] L 95/1, [1999] 4 CMLR 1415.

[99] Cases T-191/98 etc *Atlantic Container Line v Commission* [2003] ECR II-3275, [2005] 4 CMLR 1283, paras 649–657.

[100] Ibid, paras 653–655.   [101] Ibid, paras 1192–1369 and paras 1597–1634.

[102] OJ [1994] L 55/52, [1994] 5 CMLR 457.

Sugar[103] the Commission found 'vertical' collective dominance between Irish Sugar and a distributor of sugar, Sugar Distributors Ltd (SDL). Without finding legal or *de facto* control of SDL, the Commission concluded that the combination of Irish Sugar's equity holding, the structure of policy-making of the two companies and the communication process established to facilitate it, led to direct economic ties between them which created a clear parallelism of interest which amounted to collective dominance of the markets for industrial and retail sugar in Ireland[104]. On appeal the General Court upheld this finding of vertical collective dominance, without shedding any particular light on what this concept consists of[105].

These judgments and decisions under Article 102 after the General Court's judgment in *Italian Flat Glass* see the concept of collective dominance being quite regularly applied, and thereby becoming more familiar to officials, courts and practitioners. However, they did relatively little to answer any of the questions raised by that judgment, other than to affirm the idea of the adoption of common conduct on the market as a significant feature of collective dominance. An interesting glimpse of the way in which the Commission's view of collective dominance was developing was provided by its *Notice on Access Agreements in the Telecommunications Sector*[106]. At paragraph 79 it said that:

> In addition, for two or more companies to be jointly dominant it is necessary, though not sufficient, for there to be no effective competition between the companies on the relevant market. This lack of competition may in practice be due to the fact that the companies have links such as agreements for cooperation, or interconnection agreements. *The Commission does not, however, consider that either economic theory or [EU] law implies that such links are legally necessary for a joint dominant position to exist.* It is a sufficient economic link if there is the kind of interdependence which often comes about in oligopolistic situations. *There does not seem to be any reason in law or in economic theory to require any other economic link between jointly dominant companies.* This having been said, in practice such links will often exist in the telecommunications sector where national [Telecommunications Operators] nearly inevitably have links of various kinds with one another (emphasis added).

(v) The judgment of the Court of Justice in *Compagnie Maritime Belge Transports v Commission*

Important light was shed on the meaning of collective dominance by the judgment of the Court of Justice in *Compagnie Maritime Belge Transports v Commission*[107], an appeal from the General Court's judgment[108] upholding the Commission's decision in *Cewal*[109] that there had been an infringement of Article 102. The Court deals with collective dominance at paragraphs 28 to 59 of its judgment. At paragraph 36 it states that collective dominance implies that a dominant position may be held by two or more economic entities legally independent of each other provided that from an economic point of view 'they present themselves or act together on a particular market as a collective entity'. The Court says that this is how the expression 'collective dominant position' should be

---

[103] OJ [1997] L 258/1, [1997] 5 CMLR 666.

[104] Ibid, paras 111–113.

[105] Case T-228/97 [1999] ECR II-2969, [1999] 5 CMLR 1300, paras 61–64; the Commission applied this judgment in *Coca-Cola*, decision of 22 June 2005, paras 23–25, a decision under Article 9 of Regulation 1/2003, on which see ch 7, 'Acts', pp 291–292.

[106] OJ [1998] C 265/2, [1998] 5 CMLR 521.

[107] Case C-396/96 P [2000] ECR I-1365, [2000] 4 CMLR 1076; for commentary on this judgment, see Stroux (2000) 37 CML Rev 1249.

[108] Case T-24/93 [1996] ECR II-1201, [1997] 4 CMLR 273.

[109] OJ [1993] L 34/20, [1995] 5 CMLR 198.

understood in the judgment. It will be noted that this definition of collective dominance focuses on the notion of a collective entity, and not on the links between the undertakings in question. The Court then states that, in order to establish collective dominance, it is necessary to examine 'the economic links or factors which give rise to a connection between the undertakings concerned'[110], citing its earlier judgments in *Almelo*[111] under Article 102 and *France v Commission*[112] under the EUMR: the Court does not appear to consider that collective dominance has a different meaning under these two provisions. It continues that 'in particular' it must be asked whether economic links exist which enable them to act independently of their competitors[113]. However it then says that the fact that undertakings have entered into agreements does not in itself mean that they are collectively dominant[114]; but they might be if it caused them to appear as a collective entity[115]. Importantly, the Court of Justice then says that:

> the existence of an agreement or of other links in law is not indispensable to a finding of a collective dominant position; such a finding may be based on other connecting factors and would depend on an economic assessment and, in particular, on an assessment of the structure of the market in question[116].

This passage is consistent with the Court of Justice's judgment in *France v Commission* on collective dominance under the EUMR, where it had placed emphasis on 'connecting factors' rather than on economic links in determining whether there was collective dominance[117], and it is explicit that the existence of an agreement or concerted practice is not a pre-requisite to a finding of collective dominance. On the actual facts of the case the Court was satisfied that the members of the liner conference in question were collectively dominant[118].

This is clearly a very important judgment on collective dominance under Article 102: specifically, it would appear that the Court of Justice considers that the test of collective dominance is the same under Article 102 and the EUMR; and the Court specifically states that there is no legal requirement of an agreement or other links in law for there to be a finding of collective dominance. It is therefore possible that firms could be held to be collectively dominant where the oligopolistic nature of the market is such that they behave in a parallel manner, thereby appearing to the market as a collective entity. The judgment of the Court of Justice in *Impala v Commission*[119] is consistent with this interpretation: the essence of collective dominance is parallel behaviour within an oligopoly, that is to say tacit collusion or tacit coordination, depending on linguistic preference, as described earlier in this chapter[120]. The General Court's judgment in *Laurent Piau v Commission*[121] states that legally independent economic entities may be collectively dominant where

---

[110] Ibid, para 41.   [111] Case C-393/92 P [1994] ECR I-1477.

[112] Cases C-68/94 etc [1998] ECR I-1375, [1998] 4 CMLR 829.

[113] Case C-396/96 P [2000] ECR I-1365, [2000] 4 CMLR 1076, para 42.   [114] Ibid, para 43.

[115] Ibid, para 44.   [116] Ibid, para 45.

[117] Cases C-68/94 and 30/95 [1998] ECR I-1375, [1998] 4 CMLR 1029.

[118] Case C-396/96 P [2000] ECR I-1365, [2000] 4 CMLR 1076.

[119] Case C-413/06 P *Bertelsmann and Sony Corporation of America v Commission* [2008] ECR I-4951, [2008] 5 CMLR 1073; see similarly Case T-342/99 *Airtours v Commission* [2002] ECR II-2585, [2002] 5 CMLR 317.

[120] See 'Terminology: "tacit collusion"; "conscious parallelism"; "tacit coordination"; "coordinated effects"', p 562 above.

[121] Case T-193/02 [2005] ECR II-209, [2005] 5 CMLR 42; note that paras 43–50 of the DG COMP's *Discussion Paper on the application of Article [102 TFEU] to exclusionary abuses* summarises the concept of collective dominance in the same terms.

'they present themselves or act together on a particular market as a collective entity'[122]. The General Court went on to say that there were three cumulative conditions for a finding of collective dominance:

- each member of the dominant oligopoly must have the ability to know how the other members are behaving in order to monitor whether or not they are adopting the common policy
- the situation of tacit coordination must be sustainable over time, meaning that there must be an incentive not to depart from the common policy on the market
- the foreseeable reaction of current and future competitors, as well as of consumers, must not jeopardise the results expected from the common policy[123].

In *Laurent Piau* the General Court concluded that FIFA, national football associations and the football clubs forming them were collectively dominant on the market for the provision of players' agents' services, but that there was no abusive behaviour on their part[124].

One final point is that the Court of Justice has said that, where a market is highly heterogeneous and characterised by a high degree of internal competition, such as the market for legal services in the Netherlands, collective dominance would not be found in the absence of structural links[125].

(C) **Abuse of collective dominance under Article 102**

Having established that Article 102 is applicable to collective as well as single firm dominance, it is necessary to consider what kind of conduct would constitute an abuse of a collective dominant position under that provision: it is important to recall that it is not unlawful, in itself, under Article 102 to have a dominant position (whether individual or collective); for there to be an infringement of Article 102 there must be conduct which amounts to an abuse[126]. What qualifies as an abuse of collective dominance is underdeveloped in the case law[127]. The economic theory around which the doctrine of collective dominance has developed under the EUMR is that in certain market conditions firms may be able to derive benefits from tacit coordination; and the very reason why the Commission might prohibit under the EUMR a concentration that would create or strengthen a collective dominant position is that it would make it easier for firms to benefit from this phenomenon[128]. Does it follow from this that tacit coordination, when actually practised, should be condemned as an abuse of a collective dominant position under Article 102? Is price parallelism in itself an abuse? To put the point another way, does symmetry require that, since predicted tacit coordination can be prevented through the prohibition of a concentration under the EUMR, actual coordination should be

---

[122] Case T-193/02 [2005] ECR II-209, [2005] 5 CMLR 42, para 110.   [123] Ibid, para 111.

[124] Ibid, paras 117–121.

[125] Case C-309/99 *Wouters v Algemene Raad van de Nederlandsche Orde van Advocaten* [2002] ECR I-1577, [2002] 4 CMLR 913, para 114.

[126] See ch 5, 'The "special responsibility" of dominant firms', pp 192–193; the point is made specifically in relation to collective dominance by the Court of Justice in its judgment in *CMBT v Commission* at paras 37–38.

[127] Paragraphs 74–76 of the DG COMP's *Discussion Paper on the application of Article [102 TFEU] to exclusionary abuses* had virtually nothing to say about the idea of the abuse of a collective dominant position, and paragraph 4 of the Commission's subsequent *Guidance on the Commission's Enforcement Priorities in Applying Article [102 TFEU] to Abusive Exclusionary Conduct by Dominant Undertakings* OJ [2009] C45/7 is explicitly limited to single dominant firms; both documents are available at www.europa.eu.

[128] See ch 21, 'Coordinated effects', pp 871–873.

condemned under Article 102? If the answer to this question is no, what types of behaviour ought to be condemned under Article 102?

(i) Exploitative abuse of a collective dominant position

Commentators on Article 102 habitually make a distinction between those abuses that are 'exploitative' and those that are 'exclusionary', whilst recognising that this is not a watertight distinction[129]. It could be argued that tacit coordination by collectively dominant undertakings is exploitative, since prices are charged which are higher than they would be in a competitive market, albeit without the need to enter into an explicit agreement. However the Commission has not attempted to condemn tacit coordination itself under Article 102, and it is submitted that, as a matter of law, it should not be able to do so. As explained earlier in this chapter[130], parallel behaviour *per se* is not caught by Article 101(1) if it does not arise from an agreement or a concerted practice in the sense of that provision. Tacit coordination comes about in certain market conditions, not because of an agreement or concerted practice between the collectively dominant firms in the legal sense of those terms, but because they react rationally according to the conditions of the market on which they operate. To condemn their parallel behaviour as abusive in itself would be a nonsense: if Article 102 were to mandate that firms must behave *irrationally* in order to comply with the law, it would be a very odd provision. This explains the position taken by the Court of Justice as long ago as *Hoffmann-La Roche*: parallel behaviour should be condemned where it is attributable to an agreement or concerted practice contrary to Article 101(1); it is not, in itself, abusive under Article 102[131]. It might seem that this shows an inconsistency between the law under Article 102 and the EUMR: how can it be that the prospect of tacit coordination can be avoided under the Merger Regulation and yet the actuality of the same behaviour cannot be condemned under Article 102? The truth is that the difference makes perfect sense: it is precisely because of the difficulty that competition law has in addressing the problem of tacit coordination when it does occur that systems of merger control seek to prevent a market structure that will be conducive to this phenomenon from arising in the first place.

A distinct issue is whether collectively dominant firms could be held to have abused their position by charging *excessively high* prices: here the abuse would lie not in the *parallelism* of the prices, but in their level. Article 102(2)(a) explicitly condemns unfairly high prices, and it is not obvious that collectively dominant firms should enjoy an immunity from this offence which an individually dominant firm would not enjoy. In principle, therefore, it would seem that action could be taken against excessive and unfair pricing in an oligopoly. Such actions are likely to be rare, however, since the Commission does not want to establish itself as a price regulator: there have been very few investigations of high prices under Article 102, and those that have been conducted were often motivated by different considerations, for example that the excessive prices amounted to an obstacle to parallel imports[132]. The Commission contemplated a finding of an exploitative abuse of a collective dominant position of a different nature in its *P&I* decision[133]. The P & I clubs were members of the International Group, and were found to be collectively dominant. They had limited the level of insurance cover available to customers: this was considered

---

[129] See ch 5, 'Exploitative, exclusionary and single market abuses', pp 201–202; the Commission itself made this distinction in its decision on *P&I Clubs* OJ [1999] L 125/12, [1999] 5 CMLR 646, paras 127–136.

[130] See 'Does parallel behaviour amount to a concerted practice under Article 101?', pp 567–569 above.

[131] See 'The definition of collective dominance under Article 102', pp 573–579 above.

[132] See ch 18, 'Exploitative Pricing Practices' pp 718–728 and 'Pricing Practices That are Harmful to the Single Market', pp 764–766.

[133] OJ [1999] L 125/12, [1999] 5 CMLR 646.

by the Commission to be contrary to Article 102(2)(b), since it 'left a very substantial share of the demand unsatisfied'; however an alteration in the rules of the Group meant that the Commission did not reach a formal finding to this effect[134].

(ii) Anti-competitive abuse of a collective dominant position

Article 102 has been applied by the Commission to anti-competitive abuses of collective dominance on several occasions. Exclusionary abuses are considered in some detail in chapters 17 and 18. It seems reasonable in principle that Article 102 should be applicable to the exclusionary behaviour not only of individually but also of collectively dominant undertakings. Given that tacit coordination is likely to arise where a few firms, without explicit collusion, are able to set prices above the competitive level, the 'subversive' effect of new entrants into markets conducive to this phenomenon is likely to be welcomed by competition authorities: their entry may make tacit coordination less easy to achieve. In *Cewal*[135] the Commission held that Article 102 had been infringed where collectively-dominant members of a liner conference were found to have engaged in various practices with the intention of eliminating competitors from the market, such as selective price cutting and the grant of loyalty rebates. The findings of abuse were upheld on appeal to the General Court[136] and the Court of Justice[137], although the fines were annulled by the Court of Justice since the Commission had not referred to the possibility that they might be imposed in the statements of objections sent to the individual members of the conference[138]. The Commission's findings of abuse in *TACA*[139] – refusal by members of a liner conference to offer individual service contracts to customers and the abusive alteration of the competitive structure of the market by acting to eliminate potential competition – were annulled on appeal to the General Court for lack of evidence[140].

It can be anticipated that the Commission will investigate closely allegations of abusive behaviour by collectively dominant firms where the complainants are actual or potential competitors which might be able to subvert tacit coordination on the market.

(iii) Individual abuse of a collective dominant position

The final question under Article 102 is whether a collective dominant position can be abused only by all of the undertakings which hold that position, or whether it is possible for one or some of them to commit an abuse. To put the matter another way, must there be 'collective' abuse of collective dominance; or can there also be 'individual' abuse? This has been clearly answered by the General Court in the *Irish Sugar* appeal[141]: 'undertakings occupying a joint dominant position may engage in joint or individual abusive conduct', although that was a case on vertical, as opposed to horizontal, collective dominance, and it would have been helpful if the judgment had explained in more detail how the Court arrived at its conclusion: it does not fit well with the idea that collectively

---

[134] OJ [1999] L 125/12, [1999] 5 CMLR 646, paras 128–132.

[135] OJ [1993] L 34/2, [1995] 5 CMLR 198; exclusionary abuse was also found in the earlier *French-West African Shipowners' Committees* decision: OJ [1992] L 134/1, [1993] 5 CMLR 446; see also *P&I Clubs* (ch 14 n 129 above) paras 134–136.

[136] Cases T-24/93 etc *Compagnie Maritime Belge Transports SA v Commission* [1996] ECR II-1201, [1997] 4 CMLR 273.

[137] See ch 14 n 107, p 577 above.

[138] See Case C-395/96 P, [2000] ECR I-1365, [2000] 4 CMLR 1076, paras 140–150; the Commission subsequently re-adopted its infringement decision: OJ [2005] L 171/28, upheld on appeal in Case T-276/04 *Compagnie Maritime Belge SA v Commission* [2008] ECR II-1277, [2009] 4 CMLR 968.

[139] OJ [1999] L 95/1, [1999] 4 CMLR 1415.

[140] Cases T-191/98 etc *Atlantic Container Line v Commission* [2003] ECR II-3275, [2005] 4 CMLR 1283.

[141] Case T-228/97 [1999] ECR II-2969, [1999] 5 CMLR 1300, para 66.

dominant undertakings should present themselves to the market as a single entity, which implies that they are bound to behave collectively rather than individually. However, if one of several collectively dominant undertakings resorts to anti-competitive behaviour in order to foreclose competitors, it could be argued that this is done to protect the oligopoly generally, and not just that one firm; perhaps this could explain why, at least in some cases, it may be possible for there to be an individual abuse of a collective dominant position.

5. UK Law

(A) **Competition Act 1998**

The Chapter I and Chapter II prohibitions in the Competition Act 1998 are based on Articles 101 and 102 TFEU, and section 60 of that Act requires that consistency should be maintained with the jurisprudence of the EU Courts and that account should be taken of the decisional practice of the Commission[142]. It follows that the discussion in the earlier part of this chapter of the application of Articles 101 and 102 to tacit coordination and oligopolistic markets is directly relevant under the Competition Act. However two additional points should be made about the domestic law of the UK in relation to this issue. First, the market investigation provisions of the Enterprise Act 2002 provide an alternative mechanism whereby oligopolistic markets may be investigated[143]. Secondly, the domestic system of merger control requires the Competition Commission ('the CC') to determine whether a merger may be expected to result in a substantial lessening of competition. The following two sections will briefly examine the extent to which these provisions could be deployed to deal with the problem of tacit coordination.

(B) **Market investigations under the Enterprise Act 2002**

The market investigation provisions of the Enterprise Act 2002 have been described in chapter 11. The Office of Fair Trading ('the OFT') has said that it would not make a reference to the CC if it was more appropriate to proceed under the Competition Act; other factors, such as the scale of any competition problem and the likelihood of appropriate remedies being available, would also influence the exercise of its discretion[144]. However the OFT specifically notes that there could be problems associated with oligopolistic markets that are not capable of being addressed under the Competition Act, not least because of the uncertainty as to what constitutes an abuse of a collective dominant position under Article 102 TFEU and therefore, by extension, under the Chapter II prohibition[145]. The possibility exists, therefore, of market investigation references, in particular where problems arise that are industry-wide or that involve multi-firm conduct[146].

The OFT's guidance goes on to refer to the possibility that firms in an oligopoly may be able to coordinate their behaviour for mutual advantage or, at least, lack an incentive to compete, and sets out various factors of a market, such as high barriers to entry, the homogeneity of products and the symmetry of firms' market shares that might be con-

---

[142] On s 60 of the Act see ch 9, '"Governing Principles Clause": Section 60 of the Competition Act 1998', pp 369–374.

[143] An OFT market study, which may or may not lead to a market investigation reference, may also fulfil this function: see ch 11, 'OFT Market Studies', pp 455–466.

[144] *Market investigation references*, OFT 511, March 2006, para 2.1, available at www.oft.gov.uk.

[145] OFT 511, para 2.5.   [146] Ibid, para 2.7.

ducive to parallel behaviour[147]. It says that many of the markets that the OFT is likely to be interested in will be oligopolistic[148]; in such markets, price competition may be limited, and firms instead may compete through advertising, loyalty-inducing schemes and similar practices: though these practices may be pro-competitive, they could also be harmful to competition where they raise barriers to entry to new competitors[149]. The OFT also notes that tacit coordination can have a severe effect on competition[150]. In such a case the OFT would look at the pattern of price changes over time, price inertia and the oligopolists' rates of return compared to returns in comparable markets or to the cost of capital[151]. Switching costs and informational inadequacies may be relevant to the state of competition in a market[152], and the OFT will consider whether there are any facilitating practices that make it easier for firms to act in a coordinated manner[153]. The CC's Guidelines also note the same characteristics of oligopolistic markets[154].

The market investigation provisions are an important part of the overall structure of UK competition law. Many competition law problems will be addressed under the Competition Act 1998. However, as the discussion in the early part of this chapter has shown, the 'problem' of oligopoly is a complex one, and the tools provided by Articles 101 and 102 and their domestic analogues are not always suitable for this purpose. The possibility of a market investigation by the CC, as a 'safety net' for those situations in which there is a failure of the competitive market mechanism that cannot be dealt with under the Competition Act, is in principle desirable; this is not to deny, however, that there are some people in business and legal circles who view these powers with a certain scepticism, since a market investigation can be time-consuming, expensive and intrusive.

The operation of the market investigation provisions in practice was discussed in chapter 11, in several of which the CC was concerned with switching costs and imperfect information for consumers in concentrated markets[155].

A separate point is that there may be some circumstances in which the OFT might find that the lack of competition in an oligopolistic market may be attributable to a 'public' restriction of competition – for example legislation or regulatory rules – in which case it could play an advocacy role in trying to remove the problem[156].

(C) **Merger investigations under the Enterprise Act 2002**

The Enterprise Act 2002 subjects 'relevant merger situations' to a 'substantial lessening of competition' test[157]. Prior to the entry into force of the Enterprise Act mergers were subject to a public interest test which, for many years, had been applied according to the

---

[147] Ibid, paras 5.5–5.7; the OFT has investigated whether market conditions were conducive to parallel behaviour on several occasions: see eg *CAMRA super-complaint*, OFT 1279, October 2010, paras 5.42–5.67.

[148] Ibid, para 6.4.   [149] Ibid, para 6.5.   [150] Ibid, para 6.6.   [151] Ibid, para 6.7.

[152] Ibid, para 6.8; on switching costs see OFT Economic Discussion Paper 5 (OFT 655) *Switching Costs* (National Economic Research Associates, April 2003), available at www.oft.gov.uk.

[153] OFT 511, paras 6.9–6.11.

[154] *Market Investigation References: Competition Commission Guidelines* (CC 3, June 2003), paras 3.58–3.71, available at www.competition-commission.org.uk; note that the Commission published various reports on oligopolistic markets under the now-repealed provisions of the Fair Trading Act 1973, including *Parallel Pricing* Cmnd 5330 (1973); *Credit Card Services* Cm 718 (1989); *White Salt* Cmnd 9778 (1986); *The Supply of Petrol* Cm 972 (1990); *Supermarkets* Cm 4842 (2000); *The Supply of banking services by clearing banks to small and medium-sized enterprises* Cm 5319 (2002); and (under the Enterprise Act 2002) *Groceries*, Final Report of 30 April 2008, section 8.

[155] See ch 11, 'Findings of adverse effects on competition', p 485.

[156] See ch 11, 'OFT Market Studies', pp 455–466.

[157] See ch 22 generally, and on the SLC test specifically 'The "substantial lessening of competition" test', pp 932–940 thereof.

'substantial lessening of competition' standard anyway. UK merger law, therefore, has not had to suffer the growing pains of the concept of collective dominance, examined at length earlier in this chapter in the context of EU law. The competition authorities in the UK have for many years been concerned with the possibility of tacit coordination in merger cases[158].

Under the Enterprise Act the OFT and the CC have given clear guidance as to the way in which they will approach this issue in merger investigations: the economic considerations are, of course, the same as for market investigation references, although a prospective analysis must be carried out in the case of mergers. The OFT/CC *Merger Assessment Guidelines* discuss the ways in which a merger may adversely affect competition in an oligopoly: either through 'unilateral effects'[159], through 'coordinated effects'[160] or through a combination thereof[161]. The *Guidelines* explains that a merger giving rise to unilateral effects may lead to a market being less competitive than it was, either through a loss of existing competition or the elimination of potential competition, irrespective of the way other competitors behave; the authorities will examine high market concentration and weak competitive constraints in a market where products are undifferentiated and the closeness of substitution between the parties' products in mergers with differentiated products[162]. On the problem of coordinated effects the OFT and the CC adopt essentially the same approach as that taken by the Court of Justice in *Sony/BMG*[163].

The 'SLC' test is well suited to the 'problem' of oligopoly, since it asks a straightforward question: will there be substantially less competition in the market after a merger than there was before: a merger that makes a market more conducive to tacit coordination will clearly be less competitive. There have not been a large number of cases on coordinated effects under the Enterprise Act: those that have arisen are discussed in chapter 22[164].

---

[158] See eg *Interbrew SA/Bass plc* Cm 5014 (2001) and *Lloyds TSB Group plc/Abbey National plc* Cm 5208 (2001).

[159] CC2 (Revised), OFT 1254, September 2010, section 5.4, available at www.oft.gov.uk; on the problem of unilateral effects see ch 21, 'The non-collusive oligopoly gap', pp 864–866.

[160] CC2 (Revised), OFT 1254, section 5.5.   [161] Ibid, para 4.2.4.

[162] Ibid, paras 5.4.4–5.4.12.   [163] Ibid, para 5.5.9.

[164] See ch 22, 'Coordinated effects', pp 936–937.

15

Horizontal agreements (3) – cooperation agreements

1. Introduction

The previous two chapters have considered the law on hard-core cartels and the phenomenon of tacit collusion in oligopolistic markets. However it is important to appreciate that there may be circumstances in which horizontal competitors enter into cooperation agreements with one another that produce economic benefits for consumers: the Commission acknowledges this in paragraph 2 of its *Guidelines on the Applicability of Article 101 of the Treaty on the Functioning of the European Union to Horizontal Cooperation Agreements*[1] ('the *Guidelines on Horizontal Cooperation Agreements*' or 'the *Guidelines*'), noting that horizontal cooperation 'can be a means to share risk, save costs, increase investments, pool know-how, enhance product quality and variety, and launch innovation faster'. It follows that competition law cannot simply prohibit all horizontal agreements: efficiency gains may follow from cooperation that are sufficient to outweigh any restriction of competition that it might entail. This chapter is concerned with horizontal cooperation agreements which the competition authorities in the EU and the UK may be prepared to countenance.

2. Full-Function Joint Ventures

Where firms decide to cooperate, the medium for their collaboration can vary widely from one case to another. For example firms that cooperate in research and development

---

[1] OJ [2011] C 11/1.

('R&D') may simply meet on a periodic basis to discuss matters of common interest; they may share out research work and pool the results; they may establish a committee to oversee the R&D programme; or they may go further and establish a joint venture company to conduct their R&D, while maintaining their independence as producers and suppliers to the market. The same range of possibilities exists in relation to other types of cooperation, for example on production and commercialisation. As a matter of competition law the medium chosen for the horizontal cooperation will not normally affect the legal analysis of an agreement, with one very important exception: where the parties to an agreement establish a joint venture to carry out their objectives, this may amount to a concentration (to use the language of the EU Merger Regulation ('the EUMR')) or a merger (the term used in the UK Enterprise Act 2002); if so, the joint venture will be considered not under Article 101 or the Chapter I prohibition of the Competition Act 1998, but under the EUMR or the relevant domestic merger control provisions of the Member States[2]. It follows that it is necessary in any particular case to begin by considering whether parties intend to create a full-function joint venture amounting to a concentration or a merger: the meaning of a concentration under the EUMR is dealt with in chapter 21[3]; and chapter 22 considers what is meant by a merger in UK law[4]. It may even be the case that contractual integration, without the establishment of a joint venture company, will amount to a full-function joint venture under the EUMR[5]. Only where it is clear that there is no concentration or merger will it be relevant to consider the possible application of Article 101 and the Chapter I prohibition to horizontal cooperation agreements. Paragraph 21 of the *Guidelines on Horizontal Cooperation Agreements* notes that cooperation that falls to be analysed under Article 101 may have similar effects to those of a horizontal merger, suggesting, without actually saying so, that a similar approach ought to be taken to both phenomena.

3. The Application of Article 101 to Horizontal Cooperation Agreements and the Commission's *Guidelines on Horizontal Cooperation Agreements*[6]

(A) **Introduction**

The general principles involved in the application of Article 101(1) and Article 101(3) have been described in chapters 3 and 4 of this book; this chapter assumes a knowledge of those principles and focuses specifically on the jurisprudence of the EU Courts and the decisional practice and the *Guidelines* of the Commission in relation to horizontal cooperation agreements under Article 101[7].

---

[2] The European Commission explicitly makes this point at para 6 of its *Guidelines on Horizontal Cooperation Agreements*.

[3] See ch 21, 'Article 3: meaning of a concentration', pp 834–839.

[4] See ch 22, 'Enterprises ceasing to be distinct', pp 919–921.

[5] See ch 21, 'Joint ventures - the concept of full functionality', pp 837–838.

[6] For a helpful analysis of the Commission's approach to the application of Article 101 to horizontal cooperation agreements see González Díaz in Faull and Nikpay *The EC Law of Competition* (Oxford University Press, 2nd ed, 2007), ch 7.

[7] For discussion of the position in the US see the Department of Justice and Federal Trade Commission *Antitrust Guidelines for Collaborations Among Competitors*, April 2000, available at www.justice.gov/atr/public/guidelines/jointindex.html; see also Brodley 'Joint Ventures and Antitrust Policy' (1982) 95 Harvard Law Review 1523; McFalls 'The Role and Assessment of Classical Market Power in Joint Venture Analysis' (1997–98)

(B) The EU Courts and horizontal cooperation agreements

There is very little case law of the EU Courts specifically on the application of Article 101 to horizontal cooperation agreements. A few cases have reached the Court of Justice from national courts under the procedure in Article 267 TFEU[8], such as *Gøttrup-Klim Grovvareforeninger v Dansk Landburgs Grovvareselskab AmbA*[9]. As for Commission decisions, since the entry into force of Regulation 1/2003 in May 2004 the Commission could formally decide that the criteria of Article 101(3) were satisfied in relation to a particular agreement only by adopting a declaration of inapplicability under Article 10 of that Regulation, something which, to date, it has declined to do[10]; nor has it provided informal guidance on any such agreement[11]. Prior to Regulation 1/2003 the Commission could grant an 'individual exemption' stating that the criteria of Article 101(3) were satisfied in the case of a horizontal cooperation agreement[12]; where it did so there was usually little incentive for the parties to appeal against the finding that the agreement infringed Article 101(1) in the first place. A notable exception to this was the judgment of the General Court in *European Night Services v Commission*[13] where an appeal was successfully launched against the Commission's decision, in which it had attached conditions and obligations to an individual exemption which the parties considered to be unduly onerous. The Court concluded that the Commission had failed to demonstrate that the agreement would appreciably restrict competition, as a result of which the decision was annulled. Another exception to the proposition that undertakings authorised by the Commission to go ahead with a horizontal cooperation agreement under Article 101(3) would be unlikely to appeal was *O2 (Germany) GmbH & Co OHG v Commission*[14], where O2 was successful in persuading the General Court that national roaming agreements in the mobile telephony sector did not restrict competition in the sense of Article 101(1), and therefore did not need authorisation under Article 101(3)[15].

There have been some other cases in which a third party has challenged the Commission's decision that Article 101(3) was satisfied, but these have usually been unsuccessful[16]. Significant exceptions to this include *Métropole télévision SA v Commission*[17] and *M6 v Commission*[18], where the General Court upheld two consecutive appeals by a third

---

66 Antitrust Law Journal 651; Werden 'Antitrust Analysis of Joint Ventures: An Overview' ibid, 701; Correia 'Joint Ventures: Issues in Enforcement Policy' ibid, 737; Gutterman *Innovation and Competition Policy: A Comparative Study of the Regulation of Patent Licensing and Collaborative Research & Development in the United States and the European Community* (Kluwer Law International, 1997).

[8] See ch 2, 'Court of Justice', p 55 on the Article 267 procedure.

[9] Case 250/92 [1994] ECR I-5641, [1996] 4 CMLR 191; see also Cases C-399/93 etc *HG Oude Luttikhuis v Coberco* [1995] ECR I-4515, [1996] 5 CMLR 178.

[10] See ch 7, 'Article 10: finding of inapplicability', p 261.

[11] See ch 4, 'Self-assessment', pp 167–168 on informal guidance.

[12] See ch 4, 'The Commission's former monopoly over the grant of individual exemptions', pp 166–167.

[13] Cases T-374/94 etc [1998] ECR II-3141, [1998] 5 CMLR 718: see ch 3, 'Actual and potential competition', pp 127–128; see similarly Cases T-79/85 and 80/95 *SNCF v Commission* [1996] ECR II-1491, [1997] 4 CMLR 334; the recipients of an individual exemption in *TPS* OJ [1999] L 90/6, [1999] 5 CMLR 168 appealed unsuccessfully to the General Court in Case T-112/99 *Métropole v Commission* [2001] ECR II-2459, [2001] 5 CMLR 1236; on the *TPS* decision see Nikolinakos 'Strategic Alliances in the Pay TV Market: The *TPS* case' (2000) 21 ECLR 334.

[14] Case T-328/03 [2006] ECR II-1231, [2006] 5 CMLR 258.

[15] The case is discussed in ch 3, 'The need to establish a "counter-factual"', p 127.

[16] See eg Case 43/85 *ANCIDES v Commission* [1987] ECR 3131, [1988] 4 CMLR 821; Case T-17/93 *Matra Hachette SA v Commission* [1994] ECR II-595.

[17] Cases T-528/93 etc [1996] ECR II-649, [1996] 5 CMLR 386.

[18] Cases T-185/00 etc [2002] ECR II-3805, [2003] 4 CMLR 707.

party that the Commission had erred in law in concluding that the rules of the European Broadcasting Union satisfied Article 101(3)[19].

(C) **The Commission's** *Guidelines on Horizontal Cooperation Agreements*

The Commission published its latest *Guidelines on Horizontal Cooperation Agreements* early in 2011[20]; they replaced earlier guidelines of 2001[21]. The 2011 *Guidelines* are less formalistic and adopt a more dynamic view of markets than their predecessor of 2001; in particular the 2011 *Guidelines* make no use of the Herfindahl-Hirschmann Index, which the 2001 version did, and de-emphasise market shares as a way of identifying agreements that might produce anti-competitive effects. The *Guidelines* consist of seven chapters. In the first, the Commission explains the purpose and scope of the *Guidelines* and sets out basic principles for the assessment of horizontal cooperation agreements under Article 101. Chapters then follow on agreements relating to each of the following matters: information exchange; R&D; production; purchasing; commercialisation; and standardisation[22]. This chapter will follow the pattern of the *Guidelines*, with the exception that the exchange of information, which in some circumstances may be tantamount to a cartel, has already been discussed in chapter 13[23]; the chapter will conclude with a discussion of various other types of agreement that are not discussed in the *Guidelines* but which may be permissible and with a brief review of the position under UK law.

Paragraph 19 of the *Guidelines* says that they should be read in conjunction with the Commission's *Guidelines on the application of Article [101(3)] of the Treaty*[24] which provide important insights into its approach generally to the application of both Article 101(1) and Article 101(3) and, in particular, to the evidence needed to mount a successful argument based on the latter provision[25].

(i) **Purpose and scope of the** *Guidelines on Horizontal Cooperation Agreements*

Paragraph 1 of the *Guidelines* explains that they are concerned with cooperation agreements between actual or potential competitors. Undertakings are actual competitors if they are active on the same market[26]; potential competitors are those that, in response to a small but significant non-transitory increase in price ('SSNIP')[27], would undertake the necessary investments to enter the market 'within a short period of time'[28]. What constitutes a short period of time depends on the particular facts of any case[29]; paragraph 10 of the *Guidelines* concludes by saying that the assessment of potential competition must

---

[19] See ch 4, 'Judicial review by the General Court', pp 165–166.

[20] For a helpful discussion of the Commission's intentions when adopting the new *Guidelines* see the speech of the Director General of DG COMP, Alexander Italianer, 'Doing Business in Europe: the Review of the Rules on Co-operation Agreements Between Competitors', 1 March 2011, available at www.ec.europa. eu; see also a series of articles in the February 2011 edition of Competition Policy International, available at www.competitionpolicyinternational.com.

[21] OJ [2001] C 3/2.

[22] Note that, whereas the 2001 *Guidelines* contained a separate chapter on environmental agreements, this is not true of the 2011 *Guidelines*; however agreements setting out standards on environmental performance are covered by ch 7: see 'Standardisation Agreements', pp 607–611 below.

[23] See ch 13, 'Exchanges of Information', pp 539–547.   [24] OJ [2004] C 101/8.

[25] The *Article [101(3)] Guidelines* are discussed in ch 4, 'The Article 101(3) Criteria', pp 155 ff.

[26] *Guidelines on Horizontal Cooperation Agreements*, para 10.

[27] See ch 1, 'Demand-side substitutability', pp 31–32.

[28] *Guidelines on Horizontal Cooperation Agreements*, para 10.

[29] The Commission says in fn 3 to para 10 that a longer period might be considered to be 'short' in the case of a party to the agreement than when asking whether a third party might be a competitive constraint on the parties to the agreement.

be based on realistic grounds, and that a theoretical possibility is not sufficient[30]. In this formulation of potential competition the Commission refers to a policy statement that it made at point 55 of its XIIIth *Report on Competition Policy* in 1983[31], and to its decision in *Elopak/Metal Box-Odin*[32], where it concluded that a joint venture between those two undertakings to design a new kind of carton did not infringe Article 101(1) since they were not actual or potential competitors[33]. Paragraph 1 of the *Guidelines* says that they also apply to agreements between undertakings that are active in the same product market but in different geographic markets but without being potential competitors. The *Guidelines* are a complement to the block exemptions for R&D agreements[34] and for specialisation agreements[35]. They do not purport to provide guidance on cartels (although they do contain some discussion of the meaning of a 'concerted practice' in the context of information exchange)[36]. The *Guidelines* do not apply to 'pure' vertical agreements, which are the subject of the *Guidelines on Vertical Restraints* and which may benefit from Regulation 330/2010 on vertical agreements[37]; however the *Guidelines on Horizontal Cooperation Agreements* do apply to vertical agreements entered into between competitors[38].

As mentioned above, the *Guidelines* apply to six types of agreements: information exchange, R&D, production, purchasing, commercialisation and standardisation. In any particular case it is therefore necessary to characterise the agreement in order to be able to determine whether it falls into any of these six categories and, if so, which one. Not surprisingly, agreements in commercial practice do not divide themselves neatly in this way: for example undertakings that agree to conduct R&D together will often decide to produce and commercialise the product if the R&D is successful, while the parties to a joint production agreement might agree to some joint R&D as a by-product of their cooperation. Paragraphs 13 and 14 of the *Guidelines* attempt to provide a basis for allocating agreements to the appropriate category by introducing the notion of an agreement's 'centre of gravity'.

The Commission states that account should be taken of two factors: the first is the starting point of the cooperation and the second is the degree of integration of the different functions that are being combined. Two examples are given. In the first, the parties enter into an R&D agreement and envisage the possibility of proceeding, if successful, to joint production: here, the cooperation originates as an R&D agreement and is characterised as such. In the second, the parties agree to integrate their production facilities, but

---

[30] One of the criticisms of the Commission by the General Court in *European Night Services v Commission* (ch 15 n 13, p 587 above) was that it had failed convincingly to demonstrate that the agreement was entered into between potential competitors: see ch 3, 'Actual and potential competition', pp 127–128.

[31] See also Faull 'Joint Ventures under the EEC Competition Rules' (1984) 9 EL Rev 358.

[32] OJ [1990] L 209/15, [1991] 4 CMLR 832.

[33] Other decisions in which the Commission reached a similar conclusion include *Optical Fibres* OJ [1986] L 236/30; *Mitchell Cotts/Sofiltra* OJ [1987] L 41/31, [1988] 4 CMLR 111; *Konsortium ECR 900* OJ [1990] L 228/31, [1992] 4 CMLR 54; *Iridium* OJ [1997] L 16/87, [1997] 4 CMLR 1065; *Cégétel+4* OJ [1999] L 218/14, [2000] 4 CMLR 106; see also a related decision, *Télécom Développement* OJ [1999] L 218/24, [2000] 4 CMLR 124; *P&I Clubs* OJ [1999] L 125/12, [1999] 5 CMLR 646; *Société Air France/Alitalia Linee Aeree Italiane SpA* OJ [2004] L 362/17, paras 110–126.

[34] See 'The block exemption for research and development agreements: Regulation 1217/2010', pp 595–599 below.

[35] See 'The block exemption for specialisation agreements: Regulation 1218/2010', pp 601–603 below.

[36] See ch 3, 'Agreement "and/or" concerted practice', pp 102–103 and ch 13, 'Agreement and/or concerted practice to exchange information', pp 541–542.

[37] See ch 16, 'Vertical Agreements: Regulation 330/2010', pp 649–672.

[38] *Guidelines on Horizontal Cooperation Agreements*, para 12.

only partially to integrate their R&D: here, the agreement is essentially concerned with production and should be analysed as such.

Paragraph 18 of the *Guidelines* says that they do not apply to the extent that sector-specific rules apply, as in the case of certain agreements in the agriculture[39], transport[40] and insurance sectors[41].

(ii) Basic principles for the assessment of horizontal cooperation agreements under Article 101

Chapter 1.2 of the *Guidelines* begins, at paragraph 20, by explaining that agreements are analysed under Article 101 in two stages: the first is to determine whether the agreement has as its object or effect a restriction of competition in the sense of Article 101(1); if so any pro-competitive effects are then analysed in the context of Article 101(3)[42]. Paragraph 20 also points out that, in the event that the pro-competitive effects do not outweigh any restriction of competition, Article 101(2) stipulates that the agreement is automatically void.

(A) *Article 101(1)*

Paragraphs 23 to 31 discuss agreements that restrict competition by object and those that may restrict by effect: these ideas were explored in detail in chapter 3 of this book[43]. In relation to anti-competitive effects, paragraph 28 says that they are likely to occur where it can be expected that, due to the agreement, the parties would be able to profitably raise prices or reduce output, product quality, product variety or innovation; and that this depends on various factors such as the nature and content of the agreement, the parties' individual or joint market power and the extent to which the agreement contributes to the creation, maintenance, strengthening or exploitation of that market power. Without using the term, paragraph 29 says that, when determining whether an agreement has or could have anti-competitive effects, it is necessary to consider the 'counter-factual', that is to say the competitive position in the absence of the agreement[44].

The *Guidelines* then discuss, in turn, the *nature and content of the agreement* and *market power and other market characteristics*. These paragraphs are not among the finest to be found in the various guidance documents of the Commission: however, in essence, what they purport to do is to set out various theories of harm – the expression actually used in paragraph 32 is 'types of possible competition concerns' – in the section on the nature and content of the agreement, and to explain aspects of market power in the following section.

Paragraph 32 says that the *nature and content of the agreement* relate to factors such as the area and objective of the cooperation, the competitive relationship between the parties and the extent to which they combine their activities. These determine the types of competition concerns that can arise from horizontal cooperation agreements. Paragraph 33 notes that such agreements may result in exclusivity, because the parties cease to compete with one another or with third parties; or in reduced independence of decision-making, because the parties contribute assets to the cooperation or alter their

---

[39] See ch 23, 'Agriculture', pp 963–967.

[40] See ch 23, 'Transport', pp 967–977.

[41] See 'Insurance sector', pp 613–614 below.

[42] See ch 4, 'The Article 101[3] Criteria', pp 115ff, for discussion of the nature and scope of the provisions of Article 101(3).

[43] See ch 3, 'The object or effect of preventing, restricting or distorting competition', pp 117ff.

[44] For discussion of the counter-factual see ch 3, 'The need to establish a "counter-factual"', p 127.

financial interests as a result of it. The following paragraphs set out competition concerns that may follow as a result:

- **higher prices**: paragraph 34 discusses the possibility that the loss of competition between the parties may lead to them – and potentially to their competitors – raising prices: in the parlance of the *Horizontal Merger Guidelines*, the concern is about non-coordinated effects[45]

- **coordination**: paragraphs 35 to 37 discuss the possibility that horizontal cooperation agreements may facilitate coordination between the parties, within or outside the field of cooperation, for example as a result of the disclosure of strategic information to each other or the achievement of a significant commonality of costs (for example where they jointly produce an input that represents a high proportion of the value of a product that they sell in competition with one another)

- **foreclosure**: agreements such as production and standardisation agreements might give rise to concerns about anti-competitive foreclosure of third parties from the market.

Paragraphs 39 to 47 discuss market power, a topic that has been considered in some detail in chapter 1 of this book[46]. Paragraph 43 refers to the need to define the relevant market(s) according to the Commission's *Notice on Market Definition*[46a]: it adds that the *Guidelines* provide additional guidance, where needed, on matters such as purchasing markets and technology markets. Paragraph 44 makes the obvious point that, where the parties have a low combined market share, their agreement is unlikely to give rise to restrictive effects on competition. It adds that what amounts to a 'low' market share is sometimes discussed in specific chapters of the *Guidelines* which sometimes provide 'safe harbour' thresholds[47]; and that the Commission's *De Minimis* Notice also provides guidance on this[48]. Paragraph 44 adds an important point, that if one of just two parties has only an insignificant market share and if it does not possess important resources, even a high combined market share normally cannot be seen as indicating a likely restrictive effect on competition.

(B) *Article 101(3)*

Paragraph 48 of the *Guidelines* refers to Article 2 of Regulation 1/2003, which states that the burden of proving that an agreement will result in economic efficiencies in accordance with Article 101(3) rests on the undertaking(s) seeking to defend the agreement[49]. Paragraph 50 explains that, just as the block exemptions for R&D and specialisation agreements are premised upon the idea that the combination of complementary skills can be a source of substantial efficiencies, so too the analysis of agreements on an individual basis under Article 101(3) will to a large extent focus on identifying complementary skills and assets. Paragraph 52 says that agreements that do not involve the combination of complementary skills are less likely to lead to efficiency gains that benefit consumers. Paragraph 53 of the *Guidelines* cross-refers the reader to the Commission's *Article [101(3)] Guidelines*.

---

[45] See ch 21, 'Non-coordinated effects', pp 870–871.

[46] See ch 1, 'Market power', pp 42–45.

[46a] OJ [1997] C 372/5.

[47] See eg para 208 which provides a safe harbour for joint purchasing agreements where the parties have a market share not exceeding 15 per cent of their purchasing or selling markets: see 'Restrictions by effect', p 604.

[48] See ch 3, 'The *De Minimis* Doctrine', pp 140–144.

[49] See on this point ch 4, 'The burden of proving that the conditions of Article 101(3) are satisfied', pp 152–153.

4. Information Agreements

Chapter 4 of the *Guidelines on Horizontal Cooperation Agreements* discusses the exchange of information. Paragraph 57 points out that information exchange may generate efficiency gains; whereas paragraph 58 notes that it can also lead to restrictions of competition. The subject is complex, and careful analysis is required. We have chosen to deal with this subject in the chapter on cartels[50], but this is not intended to suggest that the exchange of information is by its nature cartel-like behaviour. There is a long and complicated continuum: at one end can be found exchanges of information which are, in truth, pure cartels, or mechanisms for monitoring and enforcing cartels; at the other are exchanges that make markets more efficient. We do not wish to pretend that a clear line can be drawn that separates 'bad' from 'good' exchanges of information, by allocating some to the chapter on cartels and others to this chapter; this is why they are dealt with in one place only.

5. Research and Development Agreements[51]

Chapter 3 of the *Guidelines on Horizontal Cooperation Agreements* deals with agreements that have as their centre of gravity R&D. Chapter 3.2 deals with market definition in R&D cases, first in relation to existing product and technology markets and then in relation to markets for innovation, also referred to as 'R&D efforts'; chapter 3.3 considers the assessment of R&D agreements under Article 101(1) and chapter 3.4 discusses the application of Article 101(3). Chapter 3.5 provides five examples of how Article 101 would apply to various types of agreement. Block exemption is conferred on some R&D agreements by Regulation 1217/2010[52].

(A) Market definition

Paragraph 112 of the *Guidelines* states that the key to defining markets in R&D cases is to identify those products, technologies or R&D efforts that act as a constraint on the parties to the agreement. In some cases innovation leads to the creation of a new product which is merely a slight improvement on an existing one; at the other end of the spectrum an entirely new product may be created that forms a new market. Some innovation falls between these two extremes.

(i) Existing product and technology markets

Where an agreement concerns improvements to existing products, they and their close substitutes form the relevant market[53]. Where R&D is aimed at a significant change of existing products, or even the creation of a new one to replace them, the old and the potentially new products do not belong to the same market; however in this situation the possibility exists that cooperation in the new market could lead to coordination

---

[50] See ch 13, 'Exchanges of information', pp 539–547.

[51] For a useful discussion of research and development agreements see *Faull and Nikpay*, paras 7.107–7.212.

[52] OJ [2010] L 335/36; see 'The block exemption for research and development agreements: Regulation 1217/2010', pp 595–599 below.

[53] *Guidelines*, para 113.

in the old one[54]. Where the R&D concerns an important component in a final product the market for the component may be relevant to the competition assessment, but the existing market for the final product may also be relevant if the component is technically or economically a key element in the final product and if the parties have market power with respect to that product[55]. In some cases the market may be one for technology rather than products, and paragraphs 116 to 118 explain how the market should be defined and market share calculated in those circumstances; paragraph 117 cross-refers to the Commission's *Technology Transfer Guidelines* which also discuss this topic[56].

(ii) Competition in innovation (R&D efforts)

Where the parties conduct R&D in relation to innovation and the creation of entirely new products the position is more complex, and the *Guidelines* say at paragraph 119 that it may not be sufficient in such cases to look only at existing product and/or technology markets[57]. Paragraph 120 says that it may be possible to identify competing 'poles' of R&D, in which case it is necessary to consider whether, if two competing undertakings were to enter into an R&D agreement, there would be a 'sufficient number of remaining R&D poles'. The remaining poles must be 'credible': the credibility of an R&D pole is assessed according to the nature, scope and size of other R&D efforts, their access to financial and human resources, know-how, patents and other special- ised assets and their capability to exploit the results. Where it is not possible to identify R&D poles, the Commission would limit its assessment to related product and/or tech- nology markets[58].

(iii) Market shares

Paragraphs 123 to 126 of the *Guidelines* discuss how market shares should be calculated in the case of R&D agreements, and in particular the different approaches to be taken when dealing with innovation and entirely new products as opposed to the improvement of existing ones. Since market shares are particularly important when considering the application of the R&D block exemption, this issue will be discussed in section D below on Regulation 1217/2010[59].

(B) The application of Article 101(1) to R&D agreements

(i) Main competition concerns

Paragraphs 127 to 140 of the *Guidelines* discuss the assessment of R&D agreements under Article 101(1). Three possible anti-competitive effects are noted: a reduction or slowing down of innovation; a restriction of competition or the facilitation of coordin- ation between the parties in markets outside the scope of the agreement; and foreclosure, although this would be a problem only if at least one of the parties to the agreement has significant market power (though not necessarily dominance)[60].

---

[54] Ibid, para 114.   [55] Ibid, para 115.
[56] See ch 19, 'Technology markets', p 785.
[57] For discussion on competition in innovation see OFT Economic Discussion Paper 3 (OFT 377) *Innovation and Competition Policy* (Charles River Associates, 2002), available at www.oft.gov.uk.
[58] *Guidelines*, para 122.
[59] See 'The block exemption for research and development agreements: Regulation 1217/2010', pp 595–599 below.
[60] *Guidelines*, para 127.

(ii) Restrictions by object

Paragraph 128 says that an R&D agreement would restrict competition by object if it is in reality a tool to engage in a disguised cartel; however it adds that an R&D agreement which includes the joint exploitation of future results is not necessarily restrictive of competition[61].

(iii) Restrictions by effect

Paragraphs 129 to 140 consider when R&D agreements might infringe Article 101(1) because of their anti-competitive effects. R&D agreements that relate to cooperation 'at an early stage, far removed from the exploitation of possible results', fall outside Article 101(1)[62]. So too would agreements between non-competitors[63], unless there is a possibility of a foreclosure effect and one of the parties has significant market power with respect to key technology[64]. The outsourcing of R&D to research institutes and academic bodies which are not active in the exploitation of the results would normally not be caught by Article 101(1)[65]; and 'pure' R&D agreements, that do not extend to joint exploitation of the results, would rarely do so: they would do so only where they appreciably reduce effective competition in innovation[66].

Paragraph 133 states that an R&D agreement is likely to infringe Article 101(1) only where the parties have market power on the existing markets or where competition with respect to innovation is appreciably reduced; no market share figure is given for the application of Article 101(1) to R&D agreements[67], although the Commission points out that a safe haven is provided by Article 4 of Regulation 1217/2010, the block exemption for R&D agreements, where the parties' market share is below 25 per cent[68]. The *Guidelines* say that where the parties have a market share of more than 25 per cent it does not necessarily follow that Article 101(1) is infringed, but they continue by saying that an infringement becomes more likely as the parties' position on the market becomes stronger[69]. Paragraph 137 explains that an R&D agreement that extends to joint production and/or marketing would need to be scrutinised for competition concerns more carefully than one that relates purely to R&D. The *Guidelines* then provide guidance on R&D agreements in relation to entirely new products or technologies[70] and on agreements that lie between the improvement of existing products or technologies and the development of entirely new ones[71].

(C) The application of Article 101(3) to R&D agreements[72]

Paragraphs 141 to 146 discuss the assessment of R&D agreements under Article 101(3). Paragraph 142 states that the hard-core restrictions that are listed in Article 5 of Regulation 1217/2010, and which prevent the application of the block exemption, would be unlikely to be regarded as indispensable in the case of the individual assessment of an agreement under Article 101(3). Paragraphs 145 and 146 deal with the date for assessing the application of Article 101(3): they explain that it is necessary to take into account any sunk costs that the parties incur when investing in the R&D project and the time that they may need to be able to recoup their investment[73]; and also that different aspects of an agreement

---

[61] Ibid, para 128.   [62] Ibid, para 129.

[63] Ibid, para 130.   [64] Ibid, fn 1 to para 130.   [65] Ibid, para 131.

[66] Ibid, para 132.   [67] Ibid, para 133.   [68] Ibid, para 134; on the block exemption see below.

[69] *Guidelines*, para 135.

[70] Ibid, para 138.   [71] Ibid, para 139.

[72] For examples of R&D agreements that the Commission considered satisfied the criteria of Article 101(3) see *Asahi/St Gobain* OJ [1994] L 354/87; *Philips/Osram* OJ [1994] L 378/34, [1996] 4 CMLR 48.

[73] *Guidelines*, para 145.

may need to be assessed at different times: for example the effects of cooperation in R&D should be considered at the date of the original agreement, but joint production may give rise to issues at a later date, if and when the agreement leads to the development of successful products[74].

(D) **The block exemption for R&D agreements: Regulation 1217/2010**

Acting under powers conferred upon it by Council Regulation 2821/71[75] the Commission adopted a block exemption for R&D agreements on 14 December 2010[76]. Regulation 1217/2010, which replaced Regulation 2659/2000[77], entered into force on 1 January 2011 and will expire on 31 December 2022[78]. Article 8 provides transitional relief until 31 December 2012 for agreements which were in force on 31 December 2010 and which satisfied the conditions for exemption in the old Regulation.

The Regulation consists of 22 recitals and 9 Articles. Recital 2 refers specifically to Article 179(2) TFEU, which calls upon the Union to encourage undertakings, including small and medium-sized ones, in their R&D activities and to support efforts on their part to cooperate with one another. Article 1 defines key terms such as 'research and development agreement', 'exploitation of the results', 'actual competitor' and 'potential competitor'. Article 2 confers block exemption on R&D agreements subject to the provisions of the Regulation. Article 3 sets out conditions for application of the block exemption. Article 4 imposes a market share cap and deals with the duration of the exemption. Article 5 sets out a list of 'hard-core' restrictions the inclusion of which prevents an agreement from benefiting from block exemption. Article 6 provides that certain 'excluded restrictions' do not benefit from block exemption, although their inclusion in an agreement does not prevent application of the Regulation to the rest of it. Article 7 contains provisions on the application of the market share threshold. Withdrawal of the block exemption by the Commission or by the national competition authorities of a Member State is possible by virtue of Article 29 of Regulation 1/2003.

(i) **Article 1: definitions**

Article 1 contains definitions of expressions used in Regulation 1217/2010. Of particular importance is Article 1(1)(a) which defines an R&D[79] agreement as one between two or more parties relating to the conditions under which they pursue:

(a) joint research and development of contract products or contract technologies and joint exploitation of the results of that research and development;

(b) joint exploitation of the results of research and development of contract products or contract technologies jointly carried out pursuant to a prior agreement between the same parties; or

(c) joint research and development of contract products or contract technologies.

Article 1(1) also includes within the definition of an R&D agreement those where one party merely finances the R&D activities of another party[80].

Recital 9 of the Regulation states that joint exploitation can be considered as the natural consequence of joint R&D: exploitation is defined in Article 1(1)(g) to include:

---

[74] Ibid, para 146.   [75] OJ [1971] L 285/46.

[76] Regulation 1217/2010, OJ [2010] L 335/36.   [77] OJ [2000] L 304/7.

[78] Regulation 1217/2010, Article 9; note also recital 22.

[79] The term R&D itself is defined in Article 1(1)(c) of the Regulation.

[80] Regulation 1217/2010, recital 8 and Article 1(1)(a)(iv)–(vi).

the production or distribution of the contract products or the application of the contract technologies or the assignment or licensing of intellectual property rights or the communication of know-how required for such manufacture or application.

R&D and exploitation are 'joint' where the work is carried out by a joint team, organisation or undertaking, is jointly entrusted to a third party or is allocated between the parties by way of specialisation in research and development or exploitation[81].

(ii) Article 2: exemption

Article 2(1) confers block exemption on R&D agreements, subject to the provisions of the Regulation. Article 2(2) provides that the block exemption also applies to provisions in R&D agreements which relate to the assignment or licensing of intellectual property rights:

provided that those provisions do not constitute the primary object of such agreements, but are directly related to and necessary for their implementation.

(iii) Article 3: conditions for exemption

Article 3(1) provides that block exemption is available subject to the conditions set out in paragraphs 2 to 5 thereof; Article 3 should be read in conjunction with recitals 11 and 12. It should be stressed that these conditions are applicable only where an agreement infringes Article 101(1) so that the parties wish to avail themselves of the block exemption; if an agreement is not restrictive in the sense of Article 101(1), there is no need to comply with Article 3 of the Regulation.

Article 3(2) provides that all the parties must have full access to the final results of the joint R&D for the purposes of further research or exploitation; however if they limit their rights of exploitation in accordance with the Regulation, for example by agreeing to specialise in the context of exploitation, access to the rights may be limited accordingly. The third sentence of Article 3(2) specifically provides that research institutes, academic bodies or undertakings which supply R&D as a commercial service but are not normally active in exploitation of the results may agree to confine their use of the results to conducting further research. This means, for example, that a pharmaceutical company that enters into an R&D agreement with a research institute or a university can require its partner not to exploit the results commercially but to limit itself only to further research; if this restriction were not possible, the pharmaceutical company might refrain from beneficial joint R&D with the undertaking in question for fear that it would extend its activities beyond research into commercialisation.

Article 3(3) provides that, subject to Article 3(2), where an agreement provides only for joint R&D, each party must be granted access to pre-existing know-how of the other parties if it is indispensable for the purposes of its exploitation of the results; the agreement can provide for compensation to be paid for such access, but the rate must not be so high as to impede such access.

Article 3(4) provides that joint exploitation is permissible only where it relates to results of cooperation in R&D which are protected by intellectual property rights or constitute know-how and which are indispensable for the manufacture of the contract products or the application of the contract technologies. The reason for this condition is that cooperation at the level of exploitation should be limited to those cases in which joint R&D has led to economic benefits; where this is not the case, the rationale for granting block exemption to joint exploitation is not satisfied.

---

[81] Ibid, Article 1(1)(m).

Article 3(5) provides that undertakings charged with manufacture by way of special-isation in production must be required to fulfil orders for supplies from all the parties, except where the R&D also provides for joint distribution or where the parties have agreed that only the party manufacturing the contract products may distribute them. The explanation for this is that where, for example, one party agrees to produce widgets and the other blodgets, each should have access to the products produced by the other and be able to compete in the relevant market; this is not necessary, however, where the parties carry out their distribution jointly.

(iv) Article 4: duration of exemption and the market share threshold

Article 4 deals with the duration of the exemption and the market share threshold; Article 4 should be read in conjunction with recitals 13 to 16. A distinction is made between the treatment of agreements between non-competing undertakings and an agreement between competing ones. Paragraphs 123 and 124 of the *Guidelines on Horizontal Cooperation Agreements* explain that, where existing products or technologies are being improved or replaced, market shares can be based on the existing ones; paragraph 125 specifically discusses the calculation of market shares for technology markets. Paragraph 126 says that, where the agreement relates to innovation, market shares cannot be calculated, in which case the agreement is treated as one between non-competing undertakings and Articles 4(1) and 4(3) of the Regulation apply.

Article 4(1) provides that, where the parties are not competing undertakings[82], the exemption shall apply for the duration of the R&D; where the results are jointly exploited the exemption shall continue to apply for seven years from the time the contract products or contract technologies are first put on the market within the internal market. These rules apply irrespective of the parties' market share; in case, in exceptional circumstances, it proves necessary to take action in relation to an agreement between non-competing undertakings, this would be done by withdrawal of the block exemption[83]. Article 4(3) provides that, at the end of the seven-year period, the exemption will continue as long as the parties' combined market share does not exceed 25 per cent.

Article 4(2) deals with the position where the parties are competing undertakings. In that case the block exemption applies only if, at the time the parties entered into the agreement, their share of the market for the contract products or contract technologies did not exceed 25 per cent; in the case of paid-for R&D the financing party's market share is also to be taken into account for the purposes of this rule[84]. Article 7 contains rules on how to apply the market share threshold; it contains specific rules to deal with the situation where the undertakings outgrow the market share cap[85].

(v) Article 5: hard-core restrictions

Article 5(1), which is shorter and less restrictive than its predecessor, prevents the block exemption from applying where agreements contain 'severe restrictions of competition'[86]

---

[82] For the definition of this term see Regulation 1217/2010, Article 1(1)(r)–(t); note in particular that a potential competitor is an undertaking that might enter within *three* years in response to a SSNIP (as to which see ch 1, 'Demand-side substitutability', pp 31–32), rather than a period of *one* year that is the usual test when determining whether a potential competitor produces an effective competitive constraint on undertakings already in the market, a different question from the one under consideration here.

[83] Regulation 1217/2010, recital 18; on withdrawal of the block exemption see 'Withdrawal of the block exemption by the Commission and national competition authorities', p 599 below.

[84] Regulation 1217/2010, Article 4(2)(b).

[85] Ibid, Article 7(d)–(f).   [86] Ibid, recital 15.

which 'directly or indirectly, in isolation or in combination with other factors under the control of the parties, have as their object' any of the following:

- a restriction of the freedom of the parties to carry out R&D in a field unconnected to the agreement
- a limitation on output or sales. There are exceptions to this: the setting of production or sales targets in the event of joint exploitation or joint distribution; specialisation in the context of exploitation[87]; and a non-competition clause during the period of joint exploitation. Recital 15 of Regulation 1217/2010 also states that field-of-use restrictions will not be regarded as constituting limitations of output or sales (nor as restrictions on territories or customers)
- the fixing of prices when selling the contract products or licensing the contract technologies to third parties, with the exception of fixing the prices or royalties charged to immediate customers in the event of joint exploitation or distribution
- a restriction of the territories to which or the customers to whom the parties may passively sell the contract products or license the contract technologies, with the exception of the requirement exclusively to license the results to another party
- a requirement not to make any, or to limit, active sales in territories or to customers which have not been exclusively allocated to one of the parties by way of specialisation in the context of exploitation
- a requirement to refuse to meet demand from customers in the parties' respective territories or from customers otherwise allocated between the parties by way of specialisation in the context of exploitation, who would market them in other territories within the internal market
- a requirement to make it difficult for users or resellers to obtain the contract products from other resellers within the internal market.

The inclusion of any of these provisions excludes the entire agreement, not just the offensive provisions, from the block exemption. Where such provisions fall within Article 101(1), which is likely to be the case[88], paragraph 142 of the *Guidelines* states that they are less likely to satisfy the terms of Article 101(3) on an individual basis, but continues that undertakings may be able to demonstrate that such restrictions are indispensable to an R&D agreement.

(vi) Article 6: excluded restrictions

Article 6 lists two 'excluded restrictions' which are not block exempted, but the inclusion of which does not prevent the application of the Regulation to the remaining parts of the agreement if they are severable from the excluded restrictions. The first is an obligation not to challenge the validity of intellectual property rights relevant to, or arising from, the R&D, without prejudice to the right to terminate the agreement in the event of such a challenge. No-challenge clauses were treated as hard-core restrictions in Regulation 2659/2000, the predecessor to Regulation 1217/2010. The second excluded restriction is an obligation not to grant licences to third parties to manufacture the contract products or to apply the contract technologies unless the agreement provides for exploitation of the results of the R&D by at least one of the parties to the agreement. Again, such an obligation was regarded as hard-core by Regulation 2659/2000.

---

[87] Note that Regulation 2659/2000 did *not* apply to specialisation in exploitation.

[88] Note that even hard-core restrictions might, as a matter of law, fall outside Article 101(1) where they could not have an appreciable effect on competition or on inter-state trade: see ch 3, 'The *De Minimis* Doctrine', pp 140–144 and 'The concept of appreciability', p 147.

(vii) Article 7: application of the market share threshold

Article 7 was referred to above in the context of the market share cap in Article 4[89].

(viii) Article 8: transitional period

The transitional relief for agreements that benefited from the exemption provided for in Regulation 2659/2000 was explained above[90].

(ix) Article 9: period of validity

The Regulation entered into force on 1 January 2011 and will expire on 31 December 2022.

(x) Withdrawal of the block exemption by the Commission and national competition authorities

As explained in chapter 4 of this book, Article 29 of Regulation 1/2003 enables the Commission and the national competition authorities of the Member States to withdraw the benefit of a block exemption from agreements which have effects which are incompatible with Article 101(3). As noted above, recital 18 of Regulation 1217/2010 says that this might be done in the exceptional circumstance that an agreement between non-competing undertakings is harmful to competition. Recital 21 gives some further examples of when this might happen, for example where the R&D agreement substantially restricts the scope for third parties to carry out R&D or where the contract products or technologies do not face effective competition in the internal market.

6. Production Agreements[91]

Chapter 4 of the *Guidelines on Horizontal Cooperation Agreements* deals with production agreements. Paragraph 150 notes that such agreements vary in form and scope, from production carried out by a jointly-controlled company to sub-contracting agreements. The *Guidelines* apply to all forms of joint production agreements, including horizontal sub-contracting agreements, that is to say agreements between undertakings operating in the same market irrespective of whether they are actual or potential competitors[92]. Vertical sub-contracting agreements between undertakings operating at different levels of the market are not covered by the *Guidelines on Horizontal Cooperation Agreements*; however they may be covered by the Commission's *Guidelines on Vertical Restraints*, by the block exemption for vertical agreements, Regulation 330/2010, or by the Commission's *Notice on Sub-contracting Agreements*[93].

In determining whether Article 101(1) applies to production agreements, the relevant product and geographic markets must be defined; it may also be necessary to consider the possibility that there may be a 'spillover effect' in an upstream, downstream or neighbouring market[94].

---

[89] See 'Article 4: the market share threshold and duration of exemption', p 597 above.

[90] See 'Article 6: excluded restrictions', p 598 above.

[91] See further *Faull and Nikpay*, paras 7.213–7.251.

[92] *Guidelines on Horizontal Cooperation Agreements*, para 151.

[93] Ibid, para 154; see ch 16, 'Sub-Contracting Agreements', pp 676–677.

[94] *Guidelines on Horizontal Cooperation Agreements*, para 156; note that spillover effects must also be considered in the case of a joint venture that amounts to a concentration under the EUMR: see ch 21, 'Articles 2(4) and 2(5) of the EUMR: full-function joint ventures and "spillover effects"', pp 880–882.

(A) The application of Article 101(1) to production agreements

(i) Main competition concerns

The Commission expresses three main concerns about production agreements. First, that they may lead to a direct restriction of competition between the parties, even if they market the products independently[95]. Secondly that they may lead to a coordination of the parties' competitive behaviour, in particular when the production agreement leads to a high commonality of their variable costs[96]. The Commission's third concern is that production agreements may lead to third parties being foreclosed from a related market; however it notes that a foreclosure effect is likely only if at least one of the parties has a 'strong market position' in the market where the risks of foreclosure are assessed[97].

(ii) Restrictions by object

Paragraph 160 of the *Guidelines* notes that agreements to fix prices, limit output or to share markets or customers restrict competition by object. However it goes on to explain that in two situations restrictions concerning output and prices in the context of joint production would not amount to restrictions by object. The first is where the parties agree on the level of output that is the subject-matter of the production agreement; the second is an agreement on the prices at which the jointly-produced products (and only those products) will be sold, provided that this is necessary for joint production.

(iii) Restrictions by effect

Paragraphs 162 to 182 deal with production agreements that may have the effect of restricting competition. Paragraph 163 explains that it is necessary to consider what the situation would have been in the absence of the agreement – that is to say to identify the 'counter-factual'; if the production agreement enables the parties to enter a market that they would otherwise have been unable to, the agreement will not be found to have as its effect the restriction of competition. Paragraph 165 says that none of the competition concerns discussed in paragraphs 157 to 159 would arise where the parties to a production agreement lack market power. Market power is discussed in paragraphs 168 to 173: the *Guidelines* do not provide a 'safe harbour' for agreements below a specific threshold[98], although the Commission draws attention to the 20 per cent threshold below which agreements may benefit from the block exemption for specialisation agreements[99]. Even where the parties have high market shares, a production agreement may not have the effect of restricting competition where the market is dynamic, that is to say it is one in which entry occurs and market positions change frequently[100]. The *Guidelines* make the point that a production agreement is more likely to restrict competition by effect where it extends to commercialisation of the products rather than being limited purely to production: the nearer the parties' agreement brings them to the consumer, the higher the risk to competition[101].

---

[95] *Guidelines on Horizontal Cooperation Agreements*, para 157; see also para 174.

[96] Ibid, para 158; see also paras 175–182.   [97] Ibid, para 159.

[98] It should be recalled, however, that the Commission's *De Minimis* Notice provides a safe harbour for agreements between competitors that do not contain hard-core restrictions where the parties' combined market share is below 10 per cent: see ch 3, 'The *De Minimis* Doctrine', pp 140–144.

[99] See 'Article 3: the market share threshold', p 602 below; the Commission also provides a 'safe harbour' for horizontal sub-contracting agreements with a view to expanding production, where the parties' market share is below 20 per cent: *Guidelines on Horizontal Cooperation Agreements*, para 169.

[100] *Guidelines on Horizontal Cooperation Agreements*, para 171.   [101] Ibid, para 167.

(B) **The application of Article 101(3) to production agreements**

Paragraphs 183 to 186 discuss the criteria in Article 101(3) and their application to production agreements[102].

(C) **The block exemption for specialisation agreements: Regulation 1218/2010**

Acting under powers conferred upon it by Council Regulation 2821/71[103] the Commission adopted a new block exemption for specialisation agreements on 14 December 2010[104]. The Regulation entered into force on 1 January 2011 and will expire on 31 December 2022[105]. The new Regulation replaces Regulation 2658/2000[106]. Article 6 provides transitional relief for agreements which were in force on 31 December 2010 and which satisfied the conditions for exemption in the old Regulation: they are exempt until 31 December 2012.

The Regulation consists of 16 recitals and 7 Articles. Article 1 contains definitions. Article 2 confers block exemption on specialisation agreements subject to the provisions of the Regulation. Article 3 imposes a market share cap of 20 per cent. Article 4 sets out a list of 'hardcore' restrictions the inclusion of which prevents an agreement from benefiting from block exemption. Article 5 contains provisions on the application of the market share threshold.

(i) **Article 1: definitions**

Article 1 of Regulation 1218/2010 contains definitions of expressions used in the Regulation. Of particular importance is Article 1(2)(a) which defines 'specialisation agreement'[107]: this term covers unilateral specialisation agreements, reciprocal specialisation agreements and joint production agreements. Each of these terms is then defined.

A unilateral specialisation agreement means an agreement between two parties:

which are active on the same product market by virtue of which one party agrees to fully or partly[108] cease production of certain products or to refrain from producing those products and to purchase them from the other party, who agrees to produce and supply those products[109].

A reciprocal specialisation agreement means an agreement between two or more parties:

which are active on the same product market, by virtue of which two or more parties on a reciprocal basis agree fully or partly[110] to cease or refrain from producing certain but different products and to purchase these products from the other parties, who agree to produce and supply them[111].

A joint production agreement means an agreement between two or more parties:

by virtue of which two or more parties agree to produce certain products jointly[112].

---

[102] For examples of 'individual exemptions' granted by the Commission under Regulation 17 of 1962 to production agreements that satisfied the terms of Article 101(3) see eg *Fiat/Hitachi* OJ [1993] L 20/10, [1994] 4 CMLR 571; *Ford/Volkswagen* OJ [1993] L 20/14, [1993] 5 CMLR 617; *Exxon/Mobil* OJ [1994] L 144/20: see Commission's XXIVth *Report on Competition Policy* (1994), pp 169–171; *Fujitsu/AMD* OJ [1994] L 341/66.

[103] OJ [1971] L 285/46. [104] OJ [2010] L 335/43. [105] Regulation 1218/2010, Article 7.

[106] OJ [2000] L 304/3. [107] See also recitals 7 and 8 of the Regulation.

[108] An important change in Regulation 1218/2010 is that it can apply to partial cessation of production; its predecessor applied only in the case of a total cessation.

[109] Regulation 1218/2010, Article 1(1)(b). [110] See ch 15 n 108 above.

[111] Regulation 1218/2010, Article 1(1)(c). [112] Ibid, Article 1(1)(d).

(ii) Article 2: exemption

Article 2(1) of Regulation 1218/2010 confers block exemption on specialisation agreements as defined in Article 1. Article 2 adds that block exemption extends to specialisation agreements:

> containing provisions which relate to the assignment or licensing of intellectual property rights to one or more of the parties, provided that those provisions do not constitute the primary object of such agreements, but are directly related to and necessary for their implementation.

Article 2(3) provides that the exemption also applies to specialisation agreements whereby the parties accept an exclusive purchase or supply obligation, each of which expression is defined in Article 1; and to agreements whereby the parties jointly distribute the products that are the subject of the agreement, rather than selling them independently. Recital 9 of the Regulation explains that, in order to ensure that the benefits of specialisation materialise without one party leaving the market downstream of production entirely, unilateral and reciprocal specialisation agreements must provide for supply and purchase obligations between the parties or for joint distribution; the supply and purchase obligations do not have to be exclusive, but if they are, they are block exempted by virtue of Article 2(3).

(iii) Article 3: the market share threshold

Article 3 provides that the block exemption applies on condition that the combined market share of the participating undertakings does not exceed 20 per cent. The expression 'parties' includes 'connected undertakings', as defined in Article 2(2). Article 5 contains rules on how to apply the market share threshold; it contains specific rules to deal with the situation where the undertakings outgrow the market share cap[113]. Recital 10 of the Regulation says that, where the 20 per cent market share threshold is exceeded, there is no presumption that an agreement infringes Article 101(1) or that it fails to satisfy Article 101(3): rather an individual assessment of the agreement would have to be conducted.

(iv) Article 4: hard-core restrictions

Article 4(1) prevents the block exemption from applying where agreements contain the following 'severe restrictions of competition'[114], that is to say agreements which:

> directly or indirectly, in isolation or in combination with other factors under the control of the parties, have as their object any of the following:
>
> (a) the fixing of prices when selling the products to third parties with the exception of the fixing of prices charged to immediate customers in the context of joint distribution;
> (b) the limitation of output or sales with the exception of:
>   (i) provisions on the agreed amount of products in the context of unilateral or reciprocal specialisation agreements or the setting of the capacity and production volume in the context of a joint production agreement; and
>   (ii) the setting of sales targets in the context of joint distribution;
> (c) the allocation of markets or customers.

The inclusion of any of these provisions excludes the entire agreement, not just the offensive provisions, from the block exemption[115].

---

[113] Ibid, Article 5(d) and (e).
[114] Ibid, recital 11.   [115] *Guidelines*, para 37.

(v) Article 5: application of the market share threshold

Article 5 was referred to above in the context of the market share cap in Article 4[116].

(vi) Article 6: transitional period

The transitional relief for agreements that benefit from the exemption provided for in Regulation 2658/2000 was explained above[117].

(vii) Article 7: period of validity

The Regulation entered into force on 1 January 2011 and will expire on 31 December 2022.

(viii) Withdrawal of the block exemption by the Commission and national competition authorities

As noted in chapter 4 of this book, Article 29 of Regulation 1/2003 enables the Commission and the national competition authorities of the Member States to withdraw the benefit of a block exemption from agreements which have effects which are incompatible with Article 101(3). Recital 15 of Regulation 1218/2010 says that this might happen, for example, where the relevant market is very concentrated and competition is already weak, in particular because of the individual market positions of other market participants or links between other market participants created by parallel specialisation agreements.

7. Purchasing Agreements[118]

Chapter 5 of the *Guidelines on Horizontal Cooperation Agreements* deals with joint purchasing agreements. Surprisingly the *Guidelines* do not refer to the judgment of the Court of Justice on joint purchasing organisations in *Gøttrup-Klim Grovvareforeninger v Dansk Landburgs Grovvareselskab AmbA*[119]. The *Guidelines* point out that joint purchasing usually aims at the creation of buyer power: for example an alliance of retailers who group together to negotiate lower prices with their suppliers; it may be that this enables them in turn to offer lower prices to consumers[120]. The *Guidelines* consider the horizontal relationship between the members of the group purchasing organisation; the vertical relationships, between it and its suppliers and between it and its members, fall to be considered under the rules on vertical agreements[121].

Joint purchasing must be considered in the context of the relevant procurement market[122]; in some cases it may also be necessary to look at the selling market, if the parties to the joint purchasing agreement also actively compete in that market[123].

---

[116] See above.

[117] See 'The block exemption for specialisation agreements: Regulation 1218/2010', p 601 above.

[118] See further *Faull and Nikpay*, paras 7.301–7.354; see also OFT Economic Discussion Paper (OFT 863) *The competitive effect of buyer groups* (RBB Economics, January 2007), available at www.oft.gov.uk.

[119] Case C-250/92 [1994] ECR I-5641, [1996] 4 CMLR 191; see also Cases C-399/93 etc *HG Oude Luttikhuis v Coberco* [1995] ECR I-4515, [1996] 5 CMLR 178; on the position in the US see eg *US v Topco Associates Inc* 405 US 596 (1972) and the *Antitrust Guidelines for Collaborations Among Competitors* of the Department of Justice and Federal Trade Commission of April 2000, available at www.ftc.gov.

[120] *Guidelines on Horizontal Cooperation Agreements*, paras 194 and 196.

[121] Ibid, para 194; see ch 16, 'Article 2(2): associations of retailers', pp 655–656, on the application of Article 2(2) of Regulation 330/2010, the block exemption for vertical agreements, to agreements between associations of retailers and their suppliers and their members.

[122] *Guidelines on Horizontal Cooperation Agreements*, para 198; see also ch 1, 'Procurement markets', p 38.

[123] *Guidelines on Horizontal Cooperation Agreements*, para 199.

(A) Application of Article 101(1) to joint purchasing agreements

(i) Main competition concerns

The *Guidelines* set out three possible concerns raised by joint purchasing agreements. The first arises in the purchasers' *selling* market: if they have a significant degree of market power (not necessarily amounting to dominance) in that market, it may be that they will have no incentive to pass on to consumers any lower prices that they extract from their suppliers[124]; the possibility of a collusive outcome in the selling market is discussed further in paragraphs 213 to 216 of the *Guidelines*. The second concern is that, if the parties have significant market power in their *purchasing* market, they may force their suppliers to reduce the range or quality of the products they produce[125]. The third concern is that purchasers with buyer power may be able to foreclose competing purchasers by limiting their access to efficient suppliers[126].

(ii) Restrictions by object

Joint purchasing agreements restrict competition by object if they do not truly concern joint purchasing, but serve instead as a disguised cartel[127]; however where the parties agree the price to be paid for the products that are the subject of the joint purchasing agreement, this would not amount to a restriction by object: rather an effects analysis would have to be conducted to determine whether any of the concerns expressed above might arise[128].

(iii) Restrictions by effect

In determining whether joint purchasing could have the effect of restricting competition it is necessary to look both at the purchasing and the selling markets[129]. The extent of the parties' market power is obviously relevant to any assessment of possible restrictive effects. There is no threshold *above* which such effects can be presumed; however 'in most cases it is unlikely' that Article 101(1) would be infringed where the market shares in both the purchasing and selling markets are below 15 per cent, and anyway the conditions of Article 101(3) would be likely to be fulfilled[130]. Where these market share thresholds are exceeded a detailed assessment of the effects of an agreement would be required involving, but not limited to, factors such as market concentration and any possible countervailing power of strong suppliers[131].

The application of Article 101 to 'B2B' joint purchasing, that is to say joint procurement through an electronic marketplace, was considered by the Commission in the case of *Covisint*, leading to the closure of the file by comfort letter[132].

(B) Application of Article 101(3) to joint purchasing agreements[133]

Paragraphs 217 to 220 of the *Guidelines* discuss Article 101(3) and joint purchasing agreements. Paragraph 217 notes that joint purchasing can give rise to significant efficiency

---

[124] Ibid, para 201.
[125] Ibid, para 202.   [126] Ibid, para 203.   [127] Ibid, para 205.
[128] Ibid, para 206.   [129] Ibid, para 207.   [130] Ibid, para 208.   [131] Ibid, para 209.
[132] Commission Press Release IP/01/1155, 31 July 2001; see further Vollebregt 'E-Hubs, Syndication and Competition Concerns' (2000) 10 ECLR 437; ch 13, 'B2B markets', p 547; Commission's XXXIst *Report on Competition Policy* (2001), pp 58–60.
[133] For examples of joint purchasing agreements that the Commission authorised under Article 101(3) see *National Sulphuric Acid Association* OJ [1980] L 260/24, [1980] 3 CMLR 429; *National Sulphuric Acid Association (No 2)* OJ [1989] L 190/22, [1991] 4 CMLR 612; *ARD/MGM* OJ [1989] L 284/36, [1991] 4 CMLR 841; *European Broadcasting Union* OJ [1993] L 179/23, [1995] 4 CMLR 56, annulled on appeal Cases T-528/93 etc *Métropole télévision SA v Commission* [1996] ECR II-649, [1996] 5 CMLR 386 and readopted

gains, leading to lower prices, reduced transaction, transportation and storage costs, and innovation on the part of suppliers. Paragraph 218 notes that an obligation to purchase exclusively through the joint purchasing organisation may be regarded as indispensable to achieve the necessary volume for the realisation of economies of scale, but says that this must be assessed in the context of each case. In *Rennet*[134] the Commission considered that an exclusive purchasing requirement that members of a cooperative should purchase all their rennet from the cooperative was a restriction of competition and that it did not satisfy the criteria of Article 101(3).

Paragraph 219 stresses that, for Article 101(3) to apply to a joint purchasing agreement, there must be a passing-on of a fair share of the benefit to consumers: savings or efficiencies that benefit only the parties to the agreement would not be permitted; a critical issue is whether the parties to the joint purchasing agreement have market power in their selling market(s).

8. Commercialisation Agreements[135]

Chapter 6 of the *Guidelines on Horizontal Cooperation Agreements* deals with commercialisation agreements, that is to say cooperation between competitors in the selling, distribution or promotion of their products[136]. Distribution agreements generally are covered by the regime for vertical agreements, including some non-reciprocal agreements entered into between competitors[137]. Where competitors agree on a reciprocal basis to distribute one another's products, horizontal issues arise as well, and they should be analysed in accordance with the *Guidelines*; the same may be true of non-reciprocal agreements[138]. Where joint commercialisation is agreed upon pursuant to some other cooperation, for example on R&D or joint production, the agreement should be analysed under the corresponding chapter of the *Guidelines*[139].

(A) The application of Article 101(1) to commercialisation agreements

(i) Main competition concerns

The *Guidelines* concern about commercialisation agreements is that they may lead to cartel behaviour: price fixing[140], output limitation[141], market division[142] and parallel behaviour through the exchange of strategic information[143]. Further concerns about collusive outcomes are expressed in paragraphs 242 to 245 of the *Guidelines*.

---

as *Eurovision* OJ [2000] L 151/18, [2000] 5 CMLR 650, annulled on appeal Cases T-185/00 etc *Métropole télévision SA v Commission* [2002] ECR II-3805, [2003] 4 CMLR 707; the Commission decided that Article 101(3) did not apply in the case of *Rennet* OJ [1980] L 51/19, [1980] 2 CMLR 402, upheld on appeal Case 61/80 *Coöperatieve Stremsel-en Kleurselfabriek v Commission* [1981] ECR 851, [1982] 1 CMLR 240, and *Screensport/EBU Members* OJ [1991] L 63/32, [1992] 5 CMLR 273.

[134] See ch 15 n 133 above.
[135] See further *Faull and Nikpay*, paras 7.252–7.300.
[136] *Guidelines on Horizontal Cooperation Agreements*, para 225.
[137] Ibid, para 226; see ch 16, 'Article 2(4): agreements between competing undertakings', pp 658–659 on Article 2(4) of Regulation 330/2010.
[138] *Guidelines*, para 227.   [139] Ibid, para 228.   [140] Ibid, para 230.
[141] Ibid, para 231.   [142] Ibid, para 232.   [143] Ibid, para 233.

(ii) Restrictions by object

The commercialisation agreements most likely to give rise to concern under Article 101(1) are those that give rise to price fixing. The *Guidelines* say that joint selling is likely to have as its object the restriction of competition, since it eliminates price competition between the parties on substitute products and may also restrict the total volume of products to be delivered by the parties within the framework of a system for allocating orders[144]. There have been several examples of the Commission finding that joint sales agencies infringed Article 101(1)[145]; in some of these cases the Commission found the conditions of Article 101(3) were fulfilled[146].

The *Guidelines* also express the concern that reciprocal distribution agreements between undertakings that are active in different geographical markets may be an instrument for market partitioning if they do so in order to eliminate competition between them: such agreements restrict competition by object; while it would be necessary to consider whether a non-reciprocal agreement constitutes the basis for a mutual understanding to avoid entering each other's territory[147].

(iii) Restrictions by effect

Paragraph 237 of the *Guidelines* says that a commercialisation agreement would not normally restrict competition if it is objectively necessary to allow one party to enter a market it could not have entered individually; it gives an example of consortia projects in which a number of parties participate, where no one firm could compete for the project individually[148]. Paragraph 240 provides a safe harbour for commercialisation agreements where the parties' market share is below 15 per cent; above that figure an individual assessment would be required.

(B) The application of Article 101(3) to commercialisation agreements

Paragraphs 246 to 251 discuss Article 101(3). Paragraph 246 says that commercialisation agreements can give rise to significant efficiencies; however price fixing can generally not be justified 'unless it is indispensable for the integration of other marketing functions, and this integration will generate substantial efficiencies'. Any efficiencies must result from the integration of economic activities[149], and must be clearly demonstrated[150]. Paragraph 250 stresses the need to show that any efficiencies will be passed on to consumers, and says that the greater the parties' market power, the less likely this is to be the case; the paragraph suggests that a pass-on is likely where the parties' market share is less than 15 per cent (although it is questionable in that case whether the agreement would infringe Article 101(1) in the first place).

The Commission has, on a few occasions, concluded that joint selling arrangements satisfied the criteria of Article 101(3). In *Cekanan*[151] the Commission authorised a joint venture that would enable the parties, based in Sweden and Germany, to enter new markets in the EU with new types of packaging. In the case of *UIP*[152] the Commission decided that a joint venture for the distribution and licensing of the films of Paramount,

---

[144] Ibid, paras 234–235; on joint selling see *Faull and Nikpay*, paras 6.259–6.292.

[145] See eg *Floral* OJ [1980] L 39/51, [1980] 2 CMLR 285; *UIP* OJ [1989] L 226/25, [1990] 4 CMLR 749; *Cekanan* OJ [1990] L 299/64, [1992] 4 CMLR 406; *Ansac* OJ [1991] L 152/54.

[146] See below.   [147] *Guidelines on Horizontal Cooperation Agreements*, para 236.

[148] See similarly ibid, para 30.   [149] Ibid, para 247.   [150] Ibid, para 248.

[151] OJ [1990] L 299/64, [1992] 4 CMLR 406.

[152] OJ [1989] L 226/25, [1990] 4 CMLR 749, renewed by comfort letter OJ [1999] C 205/6, [1999] 5 CMLR 732; see the Commission's XXIXth *Report on Competition Policy* (1999), pp 148–149.

Universal Studios and MGM satisfied Article 101(3). An issue of particular interest in recent years has been the collective selling of broadcasting rights to sporting events[153]. The Commission authorised the rules of UEFA for selling such rights[154]; and it accepted commitments under Article 9 of Regulation 1/2003 in the case of the German Bundesliga and the English Premier League[155].

9. Standardisation Agreements

Chapter 7 of the *Guidelines on Horizontal Cooperation Agreements* deals with standardisation agreements and standard terms. Standardisation agreements have as their primary objective the definition of technical or quality requirements with which current or future products, production processes or methods may comply[156], including agreements setting out standards on environmental performance[157]. Standard terms are covered by the *Guidelines* to the extent that they establish standard conditions of sale or purchase between competitors and consumers for competing products[158]. The *Guidelines* do not apply to standards set as part of the execution of public powers[159]; nor to professional rules[160]. The *Guidelines* take into account the Commission's practice and case law since the earlier guidelines of 2001[161], in particular as regards the use of intellectual property rights in standardisation[162]. They also incorporate insights from the best practice of standard-setting organisations and the body of literature that has developed[163]. The

---

[153] See eg Brinckman and Vollebregt 'The Marketing of Sport and its Relation to EC Competition Law' (1998) 19 ECLR 281; Fleming 'Exclusive Rights to Broadcast Sporting Events in Europe' (1999) 20 ECLR 143; Bishop and Oldale 'Sports Rights: the UK Premier League Football Case' (2000) 21 ECLR 185; Nitsche 'Collective Marketing of Broadcasting by Sports Associations in Europe' (2000) 21 ECLR 208; Commission's XXXIst *Report on Competition Policy* (2001), point 166.

[154] OJ [2003] L 291/25.

[155] See ch 7, 'Article 9: commitments', pp 255–261 discussing the Article 9 commitments procedure and providing details of these two cases.

[156] *Guidelines on Horizontal Cooperation Agreements*, para 257.

[157] For discussion of agreements specifically concerned with environmental matters see *Faull and Nikpay*, paras 7.403–7.413; see further the Commission's XXVIIIth *Report on Competition Policy* (1998), points 129–134 and pp 150–153 on *EUCAR, ACEA, EACEM and Valpak*; XXIXth *Report on Competition Policy* (1999), p 160 on *JAMA*; *CECED* OJ [2000] L 187/47, [2000] 5 CMLR 635; *CEMEP*, Commission Press Release IP/ 00/58, 23 May 2000; *Dishwashers and Water Heaters*, Commission Press Release IP/01/1659, 26 November 2001; *DSD* OJ [2001] L 319/1, [2002] 4 CMLR 405, upheld on appeal by the General Court Case T-289/01 *Duales System Deutschland v Commission* [2007] ECR II-1691, [2007] 5 CMLR 356 and by the Court of Justice Case C-385/07 P ECR I-6155, [2009] 5 CMLR 2215; *Eco-Emballages* OJ [2001] L 233/37, [2001] 5 CMLR 1096; *ARA, ARGEV, ARO* OJ [2004] L 75/59, upheld on appeal Case T-419/03 *Altstoff Recycling Austria v Commission* [2011] ECR II-000.

[158] Note that the sector-specific block exemption for cooperation on standards terms in the insurance sector has expired; the *Guidelines* provide guidance on standard terms in all industries.

[159] *Guidelines on Horizontal Cooperation Agreements*, para 258; on this subject see Case C-113/07 *SELEX Sistemi Integrati v Commission* [2009] ECR I-2207, [2009] 4 CMLR 1083, para 92.

[160] *Guidelines on Horizontal Cooperation Agreements*, para 258; on this subject see *Belgian Architects Association*, Commission decision of 24 June 2004, OJ [2005] L 4/10, paras 39–44.

[161] See eg *Ship Classification* Commission decision of 14 October 2009; Case T-432/05 *EMC Development v Commission* [2010] ECR II-000, [2010] 5 CMLR 757, upheld on appeal to the Court of Justice Case C-367/10 P, order of the Court of Justice of 31 March 2011.

[162] See eg *Rambus* Commission decision of 9 December 2009, on appeal Case T-148/10 *Hynix Semiconductor v Commission*, not yet decided; *Qualcomm* Commission MEMO/09/516, 24 November 2009.

[163] See eg Anton and Yao 'Standard-Setting Consortia, Antitrust, and High-Technology Industries' (1995) 64 Antitrust Law Journal 247; Shapiro 'Setting Compatibility Standards: Cooperation or Collusion?' in Dreyfuss, Zimmerman and First (eds) *Expanding the Boundaries of Intellectual Property* (Oxford University

Guidelines are considerably more sophisticated than their predecessor. This section will consider the application of Articles 101(1) and 101(3) to standardisation agreements; it will then briefly discuss the position in relation to standard terms.

(A) The application of Article 101(1) to standardisation agreements[164]

(i) Main competition concerns

Standardisation agreements may have effects in four markets:

- in the market for the product itself
- in the technology market where the standard involves the selection of technology
- in the service market for the setting of standards, and
- in the market for testing and certification[165].

Paragraph 263 of the *Guidelines* acknowledges that standardisation agreements 'usually produce significant positive economic effects'[166], in particular by promoting innovation and ensuring interoperability. However paragraph 264 notes that standard-setting may harm competition in three ways: a reduction in price competition following anticompetitive discussions; foreclosure of innovative technologies; and the prevention of effective access to the standard. Standards that involve intellectual property rights may in particular lead to foreclosure effects[167]. Each of these negative effects is discussed in the subsequent paragraphs of the *Guidelines*[168].

(ii) Restrictions by object

Agreements that use a standard as part of a broader restrictive agreement aimed at excluding actual or potential competitors restrict competition by object[169]. The Commission gives as an example of this its decision in *Pre-insulated Pipe Cartel*[170], where part of the infringement of Article 101(1) was the use of norms and standards to prevent or delay the introduction of new technology to the market that would have led to price reductions. Agreements to reduce competition by using the disclosure of most restrictive licensing terms prior to the adoption of a standard as a cover for jointly fixing prices are also treated as restrictions by object[171]. Agreements requiring members of a standard-setting

---

Press, 2001); Ohana, Hansen and Shah 'Disclosure and Negotiation of Licensing Terms Prior to Adoption of Industry Standards: Preventing Another Patent Ambush?' (2003) 24(12) ECLR 644; Farrell, Hayes, Shapiro and Sullivan 'Standard Setting, Patents, and Hold-up' (2007) 74 Antitrust Law Journal 603; Geradin and Rato 'Can Standard-Setting Lead to Exploitative Abuse? A Dissonant View on Patent Hold-up, Royalty Stacking and the Meaning of FRAND' (2007) 3 European Competition Journal 101; Madero and Banasevic 'Standards and Market Power' May-08 Antitrust Chronicle, available at www.competitionpolicyinternational.com; OECD Best Practices Roundtable *Standard Setting* (2010), available at www.oecd.org; Koenig and Spiekermann 'EC Competition Law Issues of Standard Setting by Officially-entrusted Versus Private Organisations' (2010) 31(11) ECLR 449; Layne-Farrar 'Nondiscriminatory Pricing: Is Standard Setting Different?' (2010) 6(4) Journal of Competition Law & Economics 811.

[164] See *Guidelines on Horizontal Cooperation Agreements*, paras 325–332 for examples of the Commission's approach to the application of Article 101 to standardisation agreements.

[165] Ibid, para 261.   [166] Ibid, paras 263 and 308.

[167] Ibid, paras 267–269; see also *European Telecommunications Standards Institute* OJ [1995] C 76/6, [1995] 5 CMLR 352; Commission's XXVth *Report on Competition Policy* (1995), pp 131–132 and the cases cited in ch 15 n 161 above.

[168] *Guidelines on Horizontal Cooperation Agreements*, paras 265–268.   [169] Ibid, para 273.

[170] OJ [1999] L 24/1, para 147.

[171] *Guidelines on Horizontal Cooperation Agreements*, para 274; note that this does not prevent *ex ante* unilateral disclosure of most restrictive licensing terms, as described in para 299 of the *Guidelines*; nor does it

organisation to sell products only that comply with a standard may, in certain circumstances, restrict competition by object[172]: this is consistent with the Commission's past practice[173].

(iii) A (fairly) safe harbour

Paragraphs 277 to 291 of the *Guidelines* are headed 'Agreements normally not restrictive of competition': in other words they produce a safe harbour, although the use of the word 'normally' means that this harbour is fairly safe rather than entirely so. To begin with the *Guidelines* say that standardisation agreements may have the effect of restricting competition only where the parties have market power[174]: however they do not provide a market share threshold for this purpose. The *Guidelines* say that there is no presumption that an undertaking holding or exercising intellectual property rights essential to a standard has market power[175]. Where there is effective competition between several voluntary standards, standardisation agreements do not restrict competition[176].

Paragraphs 280 to 286 of the *Guidelines* set out four principles, and state that standard-setting agreements that comply with them normally fall outside Article 101(1). The principles are that[177]:

- participation in the standard-setting is unrestricted
- the procedure for adopting the standard is transparent
- there is no obligation to comply with the standard
- there is effective access to the standard on fair, reasonable and non-discriminatory ('FRAND') terms.

These four principles are consistent with the General Court's judgment in *EMC v Commission*[178] where it held that the adoption of a non-binding standard following an open, non-discriminatory and transparent procedure does not restrict competition[179]. In cases involving intellectual property rights, effective access to the standard involves good faith disclosure of rights that might be essential for its implementation and a commitment to license on FRAND terms[180]. The *Guidelines* provide guidance on methods to assess the level of FRAND in the event of a dispute[181], but there is clearly a limit to how far one can define inherently imprecise words. This may explain why agreements may instead provide for disclosure of the most restrictive terms that firms would charge if their technology were incorporated in a standard: the *Guidelines* say that 'unilateral ex ante disclosures' of this kind do not restrict competition[182].

---

prevent the creation of patent pools that comply with the principles in the Commission's *Technology Transfer Guidelines* OJ [2004] C 101/2; for discussion of patent pools see ch 19, 'Technology pools', pp 791–794.

[172] *Guidelines on Horizontal Cooperation Agreements* , para 293.

[173] See eg *Video Cassette Recorders* OJ [1977] L 47/42, para 23.

[174] *Guidelines on Horizontal Cooperation Agreements*, para 277.   [175] Ibid, para 277.

[176] Ibid, para 277.

[177] Ibid, paras 280–283.

[178] Case T-432/05 *EMC Development v Commission* [2010] ECR II-000, [2010] 5 CMLR 757, upheld on appeal to the Court of Justice Case C-367/10 P, order of 31 March 2011.

[179] Ibid, paras 79–104 and 113–130.

[180] *Guidelines on Horizontal Cooperation Agreements*, paras 284–286; see also Commission MEMO/09/549, 10 December 2009 on IPCom agreeing to take over Robert Bosch GmbH's commitment to grant irrevocable patent licences on FRAND terms following its acquisition of Bosch's mobile telephony patent portfolio.

[181] *Guidelines on Horizontal Cooperation Agreements*, para 299.   [182] Ibid, para 299.

(iv) Restrictions by effect

Paragraph 279 of the *Guidelines* says that there is no presumption that, where the four principles are not satisfied, an agreement infringes Article 101(1) or that it will fail to satisfy Article 101(3). Rather an effects-based assessment will be required, as set out in paragraphs 292 to 299. A standardisation agreement that departs from the principles may be caught by Article 101(1) where the members of a standard-setting organisation are not free to develop alternative standards or products[183], or where access to a standard or to the standard-setting process is limited[184]. In *Ship Classification*[185] the Commission was concerned that the rules of the International Association of Classification Societies foreclosed third parties; the case was closed on the parties giving commitments under Article 9 of Regulation 1/2003[186] that ensured access to a standard-setting body and its information.

The market shares of the goods or services based on the standard are also relevant to the application of Article 101(1), although the *Guidelines* acknowledge that a high market share will not necessarily lead to a competition problem[187]. A standard-setting agreement that clearly discriminates against any of the participating or potential members could lead to a restriction of competition[188].

(B) The application of Article 101(3) to standardisation agreements

The Commission states at paragraph 308 that standardisation agreements frequently give rise to significant efficiency gains. Different standards have different beneficial effects: EU-wide standards facilitate market integration; compatibility standards promote technical interoperability between complementary products; while standards on quality, safety and environmental aspects of a product facilitate customer choice. Standards may also reduce transaction costs and promote innovation. For the benefits of standardisation agreements to be realised, the necessary information to apply the standard must be available to those wishing to enter the market[189]. All competitors in the markets affected should have the possibility of being involved in discussions on the standards, unless it can be shown that this would give rise to significant inefficiencies or unless there are recognised procedures for the collective representation of interests, as happens in the case of standards bodies[190]. Standards that are binding on an industry are in principle not indispensable[191]. Standards that facilitate interoperability or encourage competition between new and existing products are presumed to benefit consumers[192]. Where the result of a standardisation agreement is the establishment of a *de facto* industry standard, foreclosure of third parties must be avoided[193].

---

[183] Ibid, para 293.   [184] Ibid, paras 294 and 295.

[185] Commission decision of 14 October 2009; see Dohms and Rieder 'Commitment Decision in the Ship Classification Case: Paving the way for more competition' (2010) 1 *Competition Policy Newsletter*, p 41.

[186] On commitments decisions under Article 9 see ch 7, 'Article 9: commitments', pp 255–261.

[187] *Guidelines on Horizontal Cooperation Agreements*, para 296.   [188] Ibid, para 297.

[189] Ibid, para 309.

[190] Ibid, para 316.

[191] Ibid, para 318.

[192] Ibid, para 321.

[193] Ibid, para 324; see eg *Canon/Kodak* Commission's XXVIIIth *Report on Competition Policy* (1998), p 147.

(C) **The application of Article 101(1) to standard terms**[194]

Standard terms may have three negative effects on the downstream market where the undertakings using the terms compete by selling their products to consumers[195]: a limitation of choice and innovation in cases where the standard terms define the scope of the product sold; a distortion in the conditions of sale; and, where standard terms become industry practice, foreclosure of access to the market[196].

(i) **Restrictions by object**

Standard terms may have the object of restricting competition where they are really a disguised cartel or contain provisions that directly affect price[197].

(ii) **Restrictions by effect**

Effectively accessible and non-binding standard terms for the sale of consumer goods or services generally do not restrict competition[198]. Paragraphs 303 to 305 of the *Guidelines* describe two situations in which a more detailed assessment of such terms is required. The first is where the widespread use of standard terms that define the scope of the product limits product variety and innovation. The second is where the standard terms are a decisive part of the transaction with the customer. Individual assessment is most likely to be necessary where the standard terms are binding[199].

(D) **The application of Article 101(3) to standard terms**

Possible improvements in efficiency attributable to standard terms are considered at paragraphs 312 to 313: in particular standard terms can facilitate switching by making it easier to compare products. However, the use of binding standard terms is unlikely to be indispensable[200]. Paragraphs 322 to 323 consider the extent to which standard terms yield a fair share of any benefits to consumers.

(E) **Article 102 and standards**

The Commission may proceed under Article 102 where it believes that a dominant firm may be guilty of abusing a standard-setting procedure, for example through 'patent ambushing'[201].

10. **Other Cases of Permissible Horizontal Cooperation**

As the General Court stated in *Matra Hachette v Commission*[202], there is no type of agreement which, by its nature, is incapable of satisfying the criteria of Article 101(3). For

---

[194] See *Guidelines on Horizontal Cooperation Agreements*, paras 333–335 for examples of the Commission's approach to the application of Article 101 to standard terms.

[195] Ibid, para 262.

[196] Ibid, paras 270–272.

[197] Ibid, paras 275–276; for examples of agreements relating to terms and conditions condemned by the European Commission under Article 101(1) see ch 13, 'Agreements Relating to Terms and Conditions', pp 538–539.

[198] *Guidelines on Horizontal Cooperation Agreements*, paras 301–302.

[199] Ibid, para 306.   [200] Ibid, para 320.

[201] See ch 19, 'Vexatious behaviour and abuse of process', pp 805–806.

[202] Case T-17/93 [1994] ECR II-595.

example in the case of *REIMS II*[203] the Commission considered that Article 101(3) was applicable to a price-fixing agreement 'with unusual characteristics' in the postal services sector. The fact that a horizontal cooperation agreement does not fit into one of the categories discussed in the *Guidelines* does not mean that it falls within Article 101(1) or cannot satisfy the terms of Article 101(3). In each case, the question is whether the parties can demonstrate either that there is no restriction of competition or that the agreement will bring about efficiencies of the type envisaged in Article 101(3).

(A) Restructuring agreements

There may be circumstances in which an industry faces severe problems – perhaps because of recession or because of over-capacity within it – where the competition authorities may be prepared to countenance some degree of cooperation to overcome this. As a general proposition, each operator on the market should make its own independent decision as to what and how much to produce. However making rational decisions about how to 'slim down' production in some economic sectors, perhaps where capital investment is high or where there is extensive vertical integration, may be difficult in the absence of an intelligent understanding of what competitors are going to do. There is a danger that each competitor may slim down so much that the market goes from a position of over-capacity to under-capacity; it may be difficult to put the process into reverse. A different consideration is that the restructuring of industry has a social cost involving loss of employment and harm to the fabric of local communities; there is therefore a political component as well as an economic one to this issue[204].

Restructuring agreements, whereby undertakings agree on their respective levels of output, are likely to infringe Article 101(1): output limitation has as its object the restriction of competition[205]. In *The Competition Authority v Beef Industry Development Society Ltd*[206] the Court of Justice had no doubt that an agreement between processors of beef in Ireland to reduce their beef-processing capacity there – those that would remain in the market would pay those that would leave it to do so – had as its object the restriction of competition: any arguments that the agreement would lead to economic efficiencies were required to be raised under Article 101(3)[207]. The matter was referred back to the Irish High Court, but no decision was ever reached on the application of Article 101(3) as the BIDS withdrew its defence[208]; it is known that the Commission wrote an amicus curiae brief in this case under Article 15(3) of Regulation 1/2003, but unfortunately it has not entered the public domain. Insights into the Commission's thinking can be found in its contribution to the OECD's Global Forum on Competition in February 2011, available at www.oecd.org.

The fact that an industry faces a crisis does not mean that undertakings can enter into agreements that restrict competition and claim immunity from Article 101(1); the fact that an industry is in crisis may help to mitigate a fine[209]. However where a restructuring agreement is entered into pursuant to state aid authorised by the Commission, it may not

---

[203] OJ [1999] L 275/17, [2000] 4 CMLR 704; the Commission extended the application of Article 101(3) to this agreement until 2006: OJ [2003] C 94/3, [2003] 4 CMLR 1176; see also Commission Press Release IP/03/557, 23 April 2003.

[204] See ch 4, 'The Article 101(3) Criteria', pp 155–166 for a discussion of the issues which can legitimately be taken into account under Article 101(3).

[205] See ch 3, 'Market sharing, quotas, collective exclusive dealing', pp 122–123.

[206] Case C-209/07 [2008] ECR I-8637, [2009] 4 CMLR 310.   [207] Ibid, paras 39–40.

[208] See Press Release by the Irish Competition Authority of 25 January 2011, available at www.tca.ie.

[209] See eg Case T-145/89 *Baustahlgewebe v Commission* [1995] ECR II-987, para 122.

infringe Article 101(1) where it is so indissolubly linked to the purpose of the aid that it cannot be separately evaluated[210].

The Commission has on a few occasions allowed restructuring agreements under Article 101(3). It first did so in 1984, having indicated in its Annual Reports that it might be inclined to do so[211]. In *Synthetic Fibres*[212] the Commission permitted an agreement which was to last for three years and which would involve the closure of 18 per cent of production capacity. The parties agreed to supply information to each other about their reductions of capacity, to consult one another in the event of important changes in the market, not to increase capacity and to compensate each other if they failed to implement the reductions. The Commission held that this agreement would lead to improved production which would be slimmed down in a socially acceptable way; consumers would get a fair share of the resulting benefit as in due course they would be able to purchase from a healthier industry.

The Commission has permitted several restructuring agreements in the petrochemical and thermoplastics sectors. In *BPCL/ICI*[213] it allowed an agreement achieved by specialisation and the reciprocal sale of plant, assets and goodwill. A similar 'swap' deal was granted exemption in *ENI/Montedison*[214] and again in *Enichem/ICI*[215]. The decision in *BPCL/ICI* was followed by *Bayer/BP Chemicals*[216] in the same sector. Formal comfort letters were sent by the Commission in *Shell/AKZO*[217] and *EMC/DSM (LVM)*[218]. In *Stichting Baksteen*[219] the Commission granted individual exemption to plans for restructuring the Dutch brick industry, which involved agreed action to close plants and to cut capacity.

(B) **Insurance sector**[220]

In the insurance sector the Commission has authorised a number of horizontal cooperation agreements, for example in *Nuovo* CEGAM[221], *Concordato Incendio*[222], *Teko*[223], *P & I Clubs*[224], *Assurpool*[225] and again in *P & I Clubs*[226].

Council Regulation 1534/91 granted to the Commission the power to adopt a block exemption in the insurance sector[227]; in March 2010 the Commission adopted Regulation 267/2010[228], which replaced Regulation 358/2003 and which is narrower in scope[229]. The new block exemption should be read in conjunction with the Commission's *Communication on the application of Article 101(3) of the TFEU to certain categories of agreements, decisions*

---

[210] Case T-197/97 *Weyl Beef Products v Commission* [2001] ECR II-303, [2001] 2 CMLR 459, para 83.

[211] See eg the Commission's XIIth *Report on Competition Policy* (1982), points 38–41; XIIIth *Report on Competition Policy* (1983), points 56–61; see also XXIIIth *Report on Competition Policy* (1993), points 82–89.

[212] OJ [1984] L 207/17, [1985] 1 CMLR 787.   [213] OJ [1984] L 212/1, [1985] 2 CMLR 330.

[214] OJ [1987] L 5/13, [1988] 4 CMLR 444.   [215] OJ [1988] L 50/18, [1989] 4 CMLR 54.

[216] OJ [1988] L 150/35, [1989] 4 CMLR 24; see subsequently *Bayer/BP Chemicals* OJ [1994] L 174/34.

[217] Commission's XIVth *Report on Competition Policy* (1984), point 85.   [218] OJ [1988] C 18/3.

[219] OJ [1994] L 131/15, [1995] 4 CMLR 646; see XXIVth *Report on Competition Policy* (1994), pp 178–180.

[220] See further *Faull and Nikpay*, paras 11.92–11.133; Bellamy and Child *European Community Law of Competition* (Oxford University Press, 6th ed, 2008, eds Roth and Rose), paras 12.169–12.179.

[221] OJ [1984] L 99/29, [1984] 2 CMLR 484.   [222] OJ [1990] L 15/25, [1991] 4 CMLR 199.

[223] OJ [1990] L 13/34, [1990] 4 CMLR 957.   [224] OJ [1985] L 376/2, [1989] 4 CMLR 178.

[225] OJ [1992] L 37/16, [1993] 4 CMLR 338.

[226] OJ [1999] L 125/12, [1999] 4 CMLR 646; some other cases have been settled informally: see eg Commission's XXVIth *Report on Competition Policy* (1996), pp 131–132; XXVIIIth *Report on Competition Policy* (1998), points 111–115.

[227] OJ [1991] L 143/1.

[228] OJ [2010] L 83/1; see McCarthy and Stefanescu 'The New Block Exemption for the Insurance Sector' (2010) 2 *Competition Policy Newsletter* 6.

[229] OJ [2003] L 53/8.

and concerted practices in the insurance sector[230]. The *Communication* explains that some types of agreement – on standard policy conditions and security devices – that were block exempted under the previous Regulation are not covered by the new one since they are not specific to the insurance sector, and so should be the subject of self-assessment[231]; however the *Communication* specifically points out that agreements on standards would be addressed in the Commission's *Guidelines on Horizontal Cooperation Agreements*, which it subsequently adopted[232].

Regulation 267/2010 grants block exemption to two categories of agreements.

(i) Joint compilations, tables and studies

Article 2 of Regulation 267/2010, which entered into force on 1 April 2010, grants block exemption to agreements in the insurance sector with respect to:

- the joint compilation and distribution of information necessary for the following purposes:
  - calculation of the average cost of covering a specified risk in the past
  - construction of mortality tables, and tables showing the frequency of illness, accident and invalidity in connection with insurance involving an element of capitalisation

- the joint carrying-out of studies on the probable impact of general circumstances external to the interested undertakings, either on the frequency or scale of future claims for a given risk or risk category or on the profitability of different types of investment, and the distribution of the results of such studies.

Article 3 of Regulation 267/2010 sets out a series of conditions that must be satisfied for the block exemption in Article 2 to apply. Article 4 of the Regulation deals with agreements that are not covered by the block exemption.

(ii) Common coverage of certain types of risks

Article 5 of Regulation 267/2010 grants block exemption to agreements in the insurance sector with respect to the setting-up and operation of pools of insurance undertakings or reinsurance undertakings for the common coverage of a specific category of risks in the form of co-insurance or co-reinsurance. Article 6 of the Regulation contains market share thresholds for its application.

Regulation 267/2010 will expire on 31 March 2017[233].

(C) Banking sector[234]

The Commission has dealt with many horizontal cooperation agreements in the banking sector. Such agreements might be found not to affect trade between Member States, as the Court of Justice concluded in *Bagnasco*[235] and the Commission in *Dutch Banks*[236]. The Commission has published a *Notice on Cross-border Credit Transfers*[237] on the extent

---

[230] OJ [2010] C 82/20.   [231] *Communication*, paras 19–28.

[232] See 'The Commission's *Guidelines on Horizontal Cooperation Agreements*', pp 588–591 above.

[233] Regulation 267/2010, Article 9.

[234] Commission Press Release IP/08/596, 17 April 2008. See *Faull and Nikpay*, paras 11.09–11.64.

[235] Cases C-215 and 216/96 [1999] ECR I-135, [1999] 4 CMLR 624.

[236] OJ [1999] L 271/28, [2000] 4 CMLR 137.

[237] OJ [1995] C 251/3; see Commission's XXVth *Report on Competition Policy* (1995), points 45–48; XXVIth *Report on Competition Policy* (1996), point 109 and pp 128–130.

to which cooperation between banks is permissible under the competition rules in order to improve cross-border credit transfers. In its decision in *Uniform Eurocheques*[238] the Commission permitted an agreement which fixed standard terms and conditions in relation to the cashing of Eurocheques. The Commission also permitted a second agreement relating to the production and finishing of the actual Eurocheques and cheque cards[239]. A cooperation agreement was authorised for ten years in *Banque Nationale de Paris/Dresdner Bank*[240] between two major banks operating in neighbouring Member States.

The Commission decided in *Visa International – Multilateral Interchange Fee* that Visa International's 'multilateral interchange fee' ('MIF') agreed upon between banks participating within the Visa system satisfied the criteria of Article 101(3)[241]; subsequently the Commission accepted commitments from Visa under Article 9 of Regulation 1/2003 as to the future level of the MIF for its debit cards[242]. In *MasterCard*[243], a decision taken in December 2007, the Commission concluded that the MasterCard's MIF infringed Article 10(1) and did not satisfy Article 101(3): that decision is on appeal to the General Court[244]; it is possible that the Commission will accept Article 9 commitments from MasterCard as to the future level of its MIF[245].

(D) Transport

Several horizontal cooperation agreements have been allowed in the transport sector. Some of these are discussed in chapter 23[246].

11. The Application of the Chapter I Prohibition in the UK Competition Act 1998 to Horizontal Cooperation Agreements

(A) Introduction

The general principles involved in the application of the Chapter I prohibition in the Competition Act 1998 have been described in chapter 9[247]; the procedural aspects of Chapter I were dealt with in chapter 10[248]. Agreements that benefit from block exemption under EU law, or that would do so if they were to affect trade between Member States, enjoy parallel exemption under UK law; it follows, for example, that research and development agreements, horizontal technology transfer agreements, and specialisation agreements might benefit from this facility[249].

---

[238] OJ [1985] L 35/43, [1985] 3 CMLR 434.

[239] OJ [1989] L 36/16; most of this agreement was cleared under Article 101(1) rather than exempted under Article 101(3); for other exemptions on banking see *Belgian Banks* OJ [1986] L 7/27, [1989] 4 CMLR 141; *Associazione Bancaria Italiana* OJ [1986] L 43/51, [1989] 4 CMLR 238.

[240] OJ [1996] L 188/37, [1996] 5 CMLR 582; Commission's XXVIth *Report on Competition Policy* (1996), point 108.

[241] OJ [2002] L 318/17.

[242] Commission decision of 8 December 2010; the commitments do not cover Visa Europe's MIFs for consumer credit and deferred debit card transactions, which remain under investigation by the Commission; on commitments decisions under Article 9 see ch 7, 'Article 9: Commitments', pp 255–261.

[243] Commission decision of 19 December 2007.

[244] Case T-111/08 *MasterCard Inc v Commission*, not yet decided.

[245] For the latest position in this case see Commission Press Release IP/09/515, 1 April 2009 and Commission MEMO/09/143, 1 April 2009.

[246] See ch 23, 'Transport', pp 967–977.

[247] See ch 9, 'The Chapter I Prohibition', pp 333–360.

[248] See ch 10 generally.

[249] Competition Act 1998, s 10; on parallel exemptions see ch 9, 'Parallel exemptions', pp 359–360.

(B) **Decisions under the Competition Act**

There have been few decisions and little case law on horizontal cooperation agreements in the UK since the Competition Act entered into force. The Office of Fair Trading ('the OFT') has examined – and in some cases authorised – horizontal cooperation agreements in a few cases, such as *LINK Interchange Network Ltd*[250], *Memorandum of Understanding on the Supply of Oil Fuels in an Emergency*[251] and *Pool Reinsurance Company Ltd*[252]. They have already been discussed in chapter 9, in the context of the exemption criteria in section 9 of the Competition Act, and the reader is referred to those pages[253]. The OFT issued its first 'Short-form Opinion' in the case of *Makro-Self Service/Palmer & Harvey* on a joint purchasing agreement indicating that, following some modifications to prevent inappropriate exchanges of information, the agreement would be unlikely to raise competition concerns[254]. In *Sel-Imperial v British Standards Institution*[255] an application to strike out a claim alleging breach of EU and UK competition law in relation to the application of a standard for car parts was partially rejected[256].

(C) **Block exemption for ticketing agreements**

The Secretary of State has adopted a block exemption for public transport ticketing schemes: it is discussed in chapter 9[257].

[250] OFT decision of 16 October 2001 [2002] UKCLR 59.
[251] OFT decision of 25 October 2001 [2002] UKCLR 74.
[252] OFT decision of 15 April 2004 [2004] UKCLR 893.
[253] See ch 9, 'Exemption criteria', pp 357–359.
[254] Opinion of 27 April 2010, available at www.oft.gov.uk.
[255] [2010] EWHC 854, [2010] UKCLR 493.
[256] Ibid, paras 23–35 and 42–46 (referring in para 33 to the Commission's 2001 *Guidelines*); a settlement was subsequently reached so that case did not go to trial.
[257] See ch 9, 'Block exemptions', p 359.

16

Vertical agreements[1]

1. Introduction

The previous three chapters have been concerned with horizontal relationships between undertakings. This chapter deals with the application of Article 101 TFEU and Chapter I of the Competition Act 1998 to vertical agreements, and assumes a knowledge of the contents of chapters 3, 4 and 9. The chapter begins with a brief description of the distribution chain, and then contains sections on how the law applies to vertical integration and to agency agreements. Section 5 discusses the competition policy considerations raised by vertical agreements. Section 6 explains the application of Article 101 to various vertical agreements in the light of the case law of the EU Courts and the position of the Commission in its *Guidelines on Vertical Restraints*[2] ('the *Vertical guidelines*' or 'the *Guidelines*'). This will be followed by a section on the provisions of Regulation 330/2010, the block exemption for vertical agreements. Section 8 deals with the application of Article 101(3) to vertical agreements. The chapter then contains sections on Regulation 461/2010 on motor vehicle distribution and on sub-contracting agreements. Section 11 will look at the position in UK law. To the extent that vertical agreements might result in the abuse of a dominant position, contrary to Article 102 TFEU and the Chapter II prohibition in the Competition Act 1998, they are dealt with in chapters 17 and 18.

---

[1] For further reading on Article 101 and vertical agreements see Faull and Nikpay *The EC Law of Competition* (Oxford University Press, 2nd ed, 2007), ch 9; Bellamy and Child *European Community Law of Competition* (Oxford University Press, 6th ed, 2008, eds Roth and Rose), ch 6; Wijckmans and Tuytschaever *Vertical Agreements in EU Competition Law* (Oxford University Press, 2nd ed, 2011); Goyder *EU Distribution Law* (Hart Publishing, 5th ed, 2011).

[2] OJ [2010] C 130/1, replacing earlier guidelines of 2000, OJ [2000] C 291/1; the *Guidelines* are without prejudice to the case law of the EU Courts: ibid, para 4.

2. The Distribution Chain

A producer of goods or a supplier of services will either require them for its own consumption or will want to supply them to the market. A firm wishing to sell its products must decide how to do so. There are various possibilities: it may carry out both the production and the sales and distribution functions itself: this is often referred to as vertical integration; it may use the services of a commercial agent to find customers; or it may supply its products to an independent distributor whose function is to resell them to other persons, who may or may not be the final consumer.

For many products it is possible to depict a fairly simple distribution chain: for example a producer may sell goods to a retailer, who deals with the final consumer:

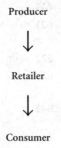

Producer

↓

Retailer

↓

Consumer

Fig.16.1

In other markets a wholesaler may carry out an important intermediate function, standing between the producer and the retailer:

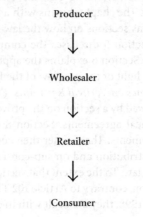

Producer

↓

Wholesaler

↓

Retailer

↓

Consumer

Fig.16.2

A vertically-integrated producer might deal directly with the consumer, for example by mail order, by establishing its own retail outlets or by selling through the Internet. An example of vertical integration is Apple supplying music from its 'iTunes' music website direct to the consumer[3]:

---

[3] See 'Vertical Integration', pp 619–620 below.

Apple/iTunes

↓

Consumer

Fig.16.3

There can, of course, be many other configurations, in which quite different relationships are involved in the delivery of goods or services to their final consumer. For example a brand owner in the food industry might sub-contract manufacture to a sub-contractor; the brand owner may then negotiate sales directly with supermarkets, and engage a transport company to arrange for the physical distribution of the products from the sub-contractor to the supermarket, in which case the diagram would look quite different:

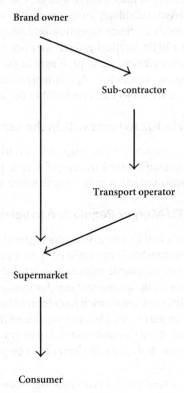

Brand owner

Sub-contractor

Transport operator

Supermarket

Consumer

Fig.16.4

It will be appreciated that many other vertical relationships are possible in the manufacture and supply of goods and services. The following sections of this chapter will provide some guidance on how competition law impacts upon each of these vertical relationships.

3. **Vertical Integration**

One option available for firms is vertical integration. This can be achieved internally by setting up retail outlets or by establishing subsidiary companies to which the task of distribution is entrusted. Some firms may be able to sell their products through the Internet, thereby eliminating the need to appoint distributors: this process is known as disintermediation. Alternatively vertical integration may be achieved through external growth, by taking over distribution networks downstream in the market. Various considerations will influence a producer in its decision whether or not to integrate vertically[4]. On the one hand it may be costly to set up or take over one's own distribution channels; also it may be more efficient to appoint another undertaking with knowledge of and expertise in the distributive trade than to attempt to break into this area oneself. On the other hand vertical integration may mean that a high degree of efficiency and coordination can be achieved in a way that would not occur where products are distributed by third parties.

(A) Non-application of Article 101 to agreements within a single economic entity

One reason for achieving vertical integration might be that this will result in some immunity from Article 101. The Court of Justice confirmed in *Viho v Commission*[5] that Article 101(1) does not apply to parent–subsidiary agreements: this means that an intra-group agreement forbidding a subsidiary from exporting or selling below a minimum price would not infringe Article 101(1)[6]. Vertical growth may not be the most efficient use of resources in terms of allocative efficiency and yet it may be the logical defensive response of firms fearful of transgressing Article 101[7]. Agreements entered into between members of the group and third parties are subject to Article 101 in the same way as any other.

(B) Application of Article 102 to firms within the same corporate group

Vertical integration may be relevant for the purpose of deciding whether an undertaking holds a dominant position within the meaning of Article 102[8], and the group may be guilty of an abuse of a dominant position in the way in which it behaves on the market[9].

(C) Application of the EU Merger Regulation to vertical integration

Vertical mergers are notifiable to the Commission under the EU Merger Regulation where the Community dimension thresholds are satisfied[10]. As a general proposition vertical integration is likely to increase economic efficiency, a fact that is explicitly recognised in the Commission's *Guidelines on the assessment non-horizontal mergers*[11]. However there have been occasions on which the Commission has required modifications to, or even the abandonment of, vertical mergers[12]. An obvious example of this is *Time-Warner/AOL*[13], which required the approval of the Commission: this was granted subject to a severance of the structural links between AOL and Bertelsmann, a competitor of Time-Warner.

---

[4] See Coase 'The Nature of the Firm' (1937) 4 Economica 386; Williamson 'The Vertical Integration of Production; Market Failure Considerations' (1971) 61 Am Ec Rev 112; Lever and Neubauer 'Vertical Restraints, Their Motivation and Justification' (2000) 21 ECLR 7.

[5] Case C-73/95 P [1996] ECR I-5457, [1997] 4 CMLR 419.

[6] See ch 3, 'The "single economic entity" doctrine', pp 92–97.

[7] Advocate General Warner's Opinion warned of this danger in Case 30/78 *Distillers v Commission* [1980] ECR 2229, [1980] 3 CMLR 121.

[8] See ch 5, 'Economic advantages', pp 184–185.

[9] See *Interbrew* Commission's XXVIth *Report on Competition Policy* (1996), point 53 and pp 139–140 and *GVG/FS* Commission decision of 27 August 2003, paras 72–81.

[10] See ch 21, 'Article 1: concentrations having a Community dimension', pp 839–844 on these turnover thresholds.

[11] See ch 21, 'Non-horizontal mergers', pp 876–880.

[12] See ch 21, 'Recent cases on non-horizontal mergers', pp 879–880.

[13] Case COMP/M 1845 OJ [2001] L 268/28, [2002] 4 CMLR 454.

4. Commercial Agents

Some producers choose to sell through commercial agents. The function of a sales agent is to negotiate business and to enter into contracts on the producer's behalf[14]. In this case the agent may be paid a commission for the business it transacts or it may be paid a salary. The essential point about its position is that it does not bear any risk itself; no property passes to it under the agreement; and it does not directly share in the profits (or losses) of its principal's business. The agent's position is analogous to that of an employee.

(A) Non-application of Article 101 to agency agreements

Where an agent is appointed which simply negotiates on behalf of a principal it is treated by EU competition law as forming part of the business organisation of the principal, so that the agreement between the parties is an internal matter of that economic entity rather than an agreement between undertakings. The consequence is that the agreement will normally fall outside Article 101(1). Commercial agency is a more common feature of distribution in continental Europe than in the UK. The Council of the European Union has adopted a Directive on the treatment of commercial agents[15], which provides them with protection against wrongful dismissal and with compensation where this occurs.

(B) The application of the Commission's *Vertical guidelines* to agency agreements

As early as 1962 the Commission published a Notice on agency agreements[16] stating that they were not subject to Article 101(1). It became necessary to amend this Notice, in particular since subsequent case law of the Court of Justice, for example in *Suiker Unie v Commission*[17] and *Vlaamse Reisbureaus*[18], made clear that it was not entirely reliable. The successor to the 1962 Notice is now Section II (paragraphs 12 to 21) of the Commission's *Vertical guidelines*[19]. The *Vertical guidelines* draw on the decisional practice of the Commission and the jurisprudence of the EU Courts, in particular *DaimlerChrysler v Commission*[20] and *Confederación Española de Empresarios de Staciones de Servicio v Compañía de Petróleos*[21].

Paragraph 12 of the *Vertical guidelines* defines agency agreements as those that cover a situation where one person negotiates and/or concludes contracts on behalf of another for the purchase or sale of goods or services, by or from the principal[22]. Paragraph 13 provides that the determining factor in assessing whether Article 101(1) is applicable is 'the financial or

---

[14] Agents are sometimes appointed simply to canvass potential customers or to introduce them to the producer rather than to negotiate contracts.

[15] Council Directive on the Coordination of the Laws of Member States relating to Self-Employed Commercial Agents 86/653, OJ [1986] L 382/17; the Directive was implemented in the UK by the Commercial Agents (Council Directive) Regulations 1993, SI 1993/3053, as amended by SI 1993/3173.

[16] *Notice on exclusive dealing contracts with commercial agents* [1962] OJ 139/2921.

[17] Cases 40/73 etc [1975] ECR 1663, [1976] 1 CMLR 295.

[18] Case 311/85 *Vereniging van Vlaamse Reisbureaus v Sociale Dienst van de Plaatselijke en Gewestelijke Overheidsdiensten* [1987] ECR 3801, [1989] 4 CMLR 213.

[19] OJ [2010] C 130/1, replacing the previous Guidelines OJ [2000] C 291/1, paras 12–20.

[20] Case T-325/01 [2005] ECR II-3319, [2007] 4 CMLR 559; the General Court upheld a finding of agency in Case T-66/99 *Minoan Lines v Commission* [2003] ECR II-5515, [2005] 5 CMLR 1597, paras 121–130.

[21] Case C-217/05 [2006] ECR I-11997, [2007] 4 CMLR 181.

[22] The *Vertical guidelines* do not use the language of 'genuine agency agreements' and 'non genuine agent agreements' which had been used in their predecessor: see OJ [2000] C 291/1, para 13.

commercial risk borne by the agent in relation to the activities for which it has been appointed as an agent by the principal'; paragraph 13 states that it is immaterial whether the agent acts for one or several principals, a view that is difficult to reconcile with the judgment of the Court of Justice in *Vlaamse Reisbureaus*[23]; the parties' views and the position under domestic commercial law are similarly irrelevant. Paragraphs 14 to 17 examine the meaning of risk for this purpose. Paragraphs 18 to 21 consider the application of Article 101(1) to agency agreements.

(i) The criterion of risk

(A) *Paragraphs 14 to 17 of the* Vertical guidelines

Paragraph 14 states that there are three types of financial or commercial risk that are material to the definition of an agency agreement: first, 'contract-specific risks' that are directly related to the contracts concluded and/or negotiated by the agent on behalf of the principal, such as the financing of stocks; secondly, those risks that are related to 'market-specific investments', meaning risks that the agent undertakes in order to be appointed; thirdly, those risks that are related to other activities that the principal requires the agent to perform on the same product market, such as risks relating to after-sales or repair services[24]. Paragraph 15 states that, where the agent bears no or only insignificant risks in relation to these matters, the agency agreement falls outside Article 101(1): in such a case the selling or purchasing function forms an integral part of the principal's activities, despite the fact that the agent is a separate legal entity. Paragraph 15 states that it is immaterial whether the agent bears risks that are related to the activity of providing agency services in general, such as the risk of the agent's income being dependent upon its success as an agent.

Paragraph 16 provides that an agency agreement exists and Article 101(1) would not normally be applicable where the title to the goods does not vest in the agent; nor where the agent does not supply services itself and where the agent does not:

- contribute to the costs relating to the supply/purchase of the contract goods or services, including the cost of transport
- maintain at its own cost or risk stocks of the contracts goods
- undertake responsibility towards third parties for damage caused by the products sold
- take responsibility for customers' non-performance of the contract
- have to invest in sales promotion
- make market-specific investments in equipment, premises or training of personnel
- undertake other activities within the same product market required by the principal, unless these activities are fully reimbursed by the principal.

Paragraph 17 provides that the list in paragraph 16 is not exhaustive and that, where the agent does incur one or more of the costs or risks listed, Article 101(1) may apply as it would do to any other vertical agreement. Paragraph 17 states that the question of risk must be assessed on a case-by-case basis and with regard to economic reality rather than legal form. The Commission explains that, for practical reasons, the analysis may start

---

[23] See ch 16 n 18 above; on this point see Korah and O'Sullivan *Distribution Agreements under the EC Competition Rules* (Hart Publishing, 2002), pp 101–103.

[24] See eg Case T-325/01 *DaimlerChrysler AG v Commission* [2005] ECR II-3319, [2007] 4 CMLR 559, paras 110–111; the General Court held that the obligations imposed on German dealers of Mercedes-Benz cars to provide after-sales servicing and to acquire and stock spare parts did not give rise to 'meaningful economic risks'.

with the assessment of the contract-specific risks since, if they are incurred by the agent, it will be sufficient to conclude that the agent is an independent distributor.

(ii) Application of Article 101(1) to agency agreements

Paragraph 18 of the *Vertical guidelines* provides that, where an agency agreement does not fall within Article 101(1), all obligations on the agent will fall outside that provision, including limitations on the territory in which or the customers to which the agent may sell the goods or services and the prices and conditions at which the goods or services will be sold or purchased. The *Guidelines* indicate, in paragraphs 19 and 20, two situations in which there could be an infringement of Article 101(1) in the case of an agency agreement. The first is where there are exclusivity provisions: either that the principal will not appoint other agents or that the agent will not act for other principals. The Commission says that the former are unlikely to infringe Article 101(1), but that single branding provisions and post-term non-compete provisions, which concern inter-brand competition[25], could infringe Article 101(1) if they lead to foreclosure of the market: the Commission refers to the later provisions of the *Guidelines* in Section VI.2.1 (paragraphs 129 to 150) on this. The idea that non-compete provisions in an agency agreement could infringe Article 101(1) was noted with approval by the Court of Justice in the *CEPSA* case[26], although they may be block exempted where they satisfy the terms of Regulation 330/2010; and otherwise they may satisfy Article 101(3) on an individual basis.

Paragraph 20 deals with the second situation in which Article 101(1) might be infringed, which is where the agency agreement facilitates collusion: this could occur where a number of principals use the same agents whilst collectively excluding others from using these agents; or where they use agents for collusion on marketing strategy or to exchange sensitive market information between the principals.

Paragraph 21 states that, where the agent bears one or more of the risks described in paragraph 16, the agreement between agent and principal does not constitute an agency agreement. Instead the agent will be treated as an independent dealer, and the agreement with it is capable of infringing Article 101(1)[27].

5. Vertical Agreements: Competition Policy Considerations

(A) Introduction

In this section the competition policy considerations raised by vertical agreements will be examined. Section 6 of this chapter will consider the application of Article 101(1) to vertical agreements in the light of the jurisprudence of the EU Courts and the Commission's *Guidelines*. Section 7 will examine the provisions of the block exemption for vertical agreements under Regulation 330/2010. Section 8 will consider the possibility that a vertical agreement that falls outside the block exemption might nevertheless satisfy the criteria of Article 101(3). Regulation 461/2010 on the distribution of motor cars will be considered in section 9.

---

[25] This expression is explained at 'Inter-brand and intra-brand competition', pp 624–625 below.

[26] Case C-217/05 *Confederación Española de Empresarios de Estaciones de Servicio v Compañía de Petróleos SA* [2006] ECR I-11997, [2007] 4 CMLR 181, para 62; see also the Commission's decision of 12 April 2006 under Article 9 of Regulation 1/2003 in the case of *Repsol CPP*, paras 20–24 identifying a possible foreclosure effect which was addressed by accepting legally-binding commitments offered by Repsol.

[27] See eg *Souris/Topps* Commission decision of 26 May 2004, paras 97–104.

(B) **Vertical agreements: possible detriments to competition**[28]

(i) Inter-brand and intra-brand competition

The application of Article 101 to vertical agreements has long been controversial. It is fairly obvious that horizontal agreements, for example to fix prices or to limit output, should be prohibited: in this situation firms combine their market power to their own advantage[29]; vertical agreements do not involve a *combination* of market power[30]. Vertical agreements are likely to raise competition concerns only where there is a degree of market power at the level of the supplier or the buyer or at both levels. Where this is the case competition with other firms' products – 'inter-brand competition' – may be limited; as a result it may be desirable to ensure that there is competition between distributors and retailers in relation to the products of the firm with market power – so-called 'intra-brand competition'[31].

Suppose that A is the brand owner of Wonder Widgets and B is the brand owner of Beautiful Blodgets.

A requires its retailers to purchase Wonder Widgets only from it and not to buy the competing products of M, N and O – a so-called 'single branding agreement' also known as an exclusive purchasing agreement[32]. The diagonal line means that the retailers and M, N and O have no access to each other.

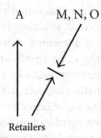

Fig.16.5

The question in this case would be whether the single branding agreement has an effect on inter-brand competition, that is to say on competition between the brands of A and those of its competitors, M, N and O; this will depend on how much market power A has.

Suppose now that B requires its retailers X, Y and Z not to sell Beautiful Blodgets at less than the recommended price of €100, and not to sell to customers who live in an area allotted to one of the other retailers.

Fig.16.6

---

[28] For further discussion of the arguments in favour of and against vertical agreements see Motta *Competition Policy: Theory and Practice* (Cambridge University Press, 2004), part VI; Van den Bergh and Camesasca *European Competition Law and Economics: A Comparative Perspective* (Sweet & Maxwell, 2nd ed, 2006), ch 6; Bishop and Walker *The Economics of EC Competition Law* (Sweet & Maxwell, 3rd ed, 2010), paras 5.034–5.054.

[29] *Vertical guidelines*, para 98.   [30] Ibid, para 98.
[31] Ibid, para 102.   [32] See 'Single branding agreements', pp 637–639 below.

The question in this case is whether the agreements have a significant effect on intra-brand competition between the three retailers X, Y and Z. They do not restrict competition between B and its competitors; however the extent of inter-brand competition in the relevant market will affect the extent to which a restriction of intra-brand competition is a cause for concern.

(ii) *Consten* and *Grundig v Commission*

It was argued in *Consten and Grundig v Commission*[33] that Article 101(1) should not apply to vertical agreements at all as that provision was simply concerned with horizontal arrangements between undertakings. The Court of Justice rejected this argument[34] and concluded that the exclusive agreement in that case which conferred absolute territorial protection upon a distributor was caught by Article 101(1) and did not satisfy the criteria of Article 101(3)[35].

(iii) The single market imperative and intra-brand competition

As a general proposition competition law has less concern with restrictions of intra-brand competition than with restrictions of inter-brand competition: a restriction of intra-brand competition is likely to raise concerns only where inter-brand competition is weak. However to this must be added a further concern of EU competition law, which has been mentioned several times in this book already: the integrity of the single market. The EU Courts and the Commission have, from the earliest days, been concerned about vertical agreements that lead to a division of national markets, even where the restrictions relate to intra-brand rather than to inter-brand competition. The strict treatment of export bans, the determination to maintain parallel imports and the reluctance to allow distributors to enjoy absolute territorial protection are all issues affecting intra-brand rather than inter-brand competition. The law on vertical agreements in the EU therefore has a component – single market integration – that will not be found in other (domestic) systems of competition law[36]. Two judgments in 2011 demonstrate that the single market imperative remains in place[36a].

(iv) The commentary in the *Vertical guidelines* on the negative effects of vertical restraints

In determining whether a vertical agreement has a restrictive effect on competition, it is necessary to consider what the market situation would have been in the absence of the vertical restraints in the agreement[37]. Useful guidance on analysing the anti-competitive effects of an agreement can be found in the Commission's *Guidelines on the application of Article [101(3)] of the Treaty* ('the *Article [101(3)] Guidelines*')[38]. Those guidelines make clear that negative effects are likely to occur when at least one of the parties has or obtains some degree of market power and the agreement contributes to the creation, maintenance

---

[33] Cases 56 and 58/64 [1966] ECR 299, [1966] CMLR 418.

[34] [1966] ECR 299, pp 339–340 and [1966] CMLR 418, p 470; see further ch 3, 'Horizontal and vertical agreements', p 117.

[35] Absolute territorial protection may be permitted in exceptional circumstances, as in Case 262/81 *Coditel II* [1982] ECR 3381, [1983] 1 CMLR 49: see ch 3, 'Cases in which agreements containing contractual restrictions were found not to have anti-competitive effects', pp 128–129.

[36] See the *Vertical guidelines*, para 7.

[36a] See Cases C-403/08 and C-429/08 *Football Association Premier League Ltd v QC Leisure*, [2011] ECR I-000 and Case C-439/09 *Pierre Fabre Dermo-Cosmétique SAS v Président de l'Autorité de la Concurrence*, [2011] ECR I-000.

[37] Ibid, para 97.

[38] OJ [2004] C 101/97, paras 24–27; on agreements that have as their effect the restriction of competition see ch 3, 'Agreements that have as their effect the prevention, restriction or distortion of competition', pp 125–137 of this book.

or strengthening of that market power or allows the parties to exploit it, a point repeated in paragraph 97 of the *Vertical guidelines*. Paragraph 100 of the Commission's *Vertical guidelines* notes four possible negative effects arising from vertical restraints which EU competition law aims at preventing:

- anti-competitive foreclosure of other suppliers or buyers by raising barriers to entry
- softening of competition between the supplier and its competitors and/or facilitation of both explicit and tacit collusion, often referred to as a reduction of inter-brand competition[39]
- softening of competition between the buyer and its competitors and/or facilitation of collusion, commonly referred to as a reduction of intra-brand competition between distributors of the same brand
- the creation of obstacles to market integration.

Paragraph 101 of the *Guidelines* explains that foreclosure, softening of competition and collusion in the upstream or downstream market may harm consumers in particular by raising wholesale prices, depriving consumers of choice, lowering quality or reducing the level of innovation. Paragraphs 103 to 105 consider the circumstances in which vertical restraints are more likely to have negative effects: for example exclusive arrangements are generally more anti-competitive than non-exclusive arrangements since they result in one firm sourcing all or practically all of its demand from another. Paragraph 105 states that a combination of vertical restraints will usually increase their individual negative effects; however certain combinations may have the reverse effect: for example a maximum resale price used to prevent an exclusive distributor from raising price beyond a certain level. Paragraph 105 also points out that the negative effects arising from vertical restraints are reinforced when several suppliers and their respective buyers organise their trade in a similar way, leading to so-called 'cumulative effects' within the market leading to a restriction of competition.

(C) **Vertical agreements: possible benefits to competition**

Having set out the Commission's views as to the possible detriments to competition arising from vertical agreements, it is important to stress that there are also significant arguments in their favour. Some theorists argue that vertical restraints are not a suitable target for competition authorities at all[40]; a more realistic view is that they should be investigated only where at least one of the parties has market power[41]. Paragraph 106 of the *Vertical guidelines* states that vertical restraints often have positive effects, in particular by promoting non-price competition and improved quality of service. Paragraph 107 sets out nine situations in which vertical restraints may help to realise efficiencies and the development of new markets; the Commission says that it does not claim that the list is complete or exhaustive[42].

---

[39]   On practices, including vertical agreements, that may facilitate tacit collusion see ch 14, 'Article 101(1), the exchange of information and other facilitating practices', pp 569–570.

[40]   See eg Bork *The Antitrust Paradox* (The Free Press, 1993), chs 14 and 15.

[41]   See eg White 'Vertical Restraints in Antitrust Law – a Coherent Model' (1981) 26 Antitrust Bulletin 327; Easterbrook 'Vertical Arrangements and the Rule of Reason' (1984) 53 Antitrust Law Journal 135; Bock 'An Economist Appraises Vertical Restraints' (1985) 30 Antitrust Bulletin 117; for criticism of the permissive view of vertical restraints adopted by many commentators see Comanor 'Vertical Price Fixing, Vertical Market Restrictions and the New Antitrust Policy' (1985) 98 Harv L Rev 983 and Pitofsky 'Can Vertical Arrangements Injure Consumer Welfare?' in Pitofsky (ed) *How the Chicago School Has Overshot the Mark* Whinston *Lectures on Antitrust Economics* (MIT Press, 2008), ch 4.

[42]   See further *Vertical guidelines*, paras 108–109.

(i) The free-rider problem

One distributor may take a free ride on the investment of another. For example a retailer may invest in a particular brand and create a demand for it: it has an obvious interest in preventing another retailer from making sales in circumstances where it made no contribution to the creation of that demand. The Commission states that free-riding between buyers can occur only on pre-sales services and not on after-sales services; it adds that free-riding is usually only a problem where the product is relatively new or complex and of reasonably high value. Exclusive distribution agreements may be used to prevent the problem of free-riding: for example if A appoints B as the exclusive distributor for France, this will provide some degree of immunity from intra-brand competition. Absolute territorial protection will not usually be countenanced in vertical agreements, because of the wider EU objective of achieving an integrated internal market. A term conferring exclusivity on a distributor might not infringe Article 101(1), in particular where parallel imports into the exclusive territory are possible[43]. A free-rider issue can arise where a supplier invests in promotion at a retailer's premises which a competing supplier takes advantage of: a non-compete provision may be justified to prevent this type of free-riding.

(ii) Opening up and entering new markets

A 'special case of the free-rider problem' is where a manufacturer wants to enter a new geographic market and this requires its distributor to make 'first time investments'. It may be necessary to protect the distributor from competition so that it can recoup its investment by temporarily charging a higher price; this may mean that distributors in other markets should be restrained for a limited period from selling in the new market.

(iii) The certification free-rider issue

In some sectors certain retailers have a reputation for stocking only 'quality' products. In such a case a manufacturer must limit its sales to such retailers, since otherwise its products may be delisted. Exclusive or selective distribution may be justified for a period of time in these circumstances.

(iv) The hold-up problem

This refers to a situation in which a supplier or buyer needs to make client-specific investments, and will not commit to these until supply agreements have been concluded. It may be that an undertaking making an investment will require a long-term supply agreement, so that it knows that it will recoup its costs. Where the supplier makes the investment, it may wish the buyer to agree to a non-compete, or to an analogous, provision; a buyer may seek the benefit of an exclusive distribution, customer allocation or exclusive supply provision[44].

(v) The hold-up problem where know-how is transferred

Where know-how is supplied by one firm to another it may be necessary to impose a non-compete provision on the recipient of the know-how to ensure that it is not used by competitors of the owner of it.

---

[43] See further 'The single market imperative and intra-brand competition', p 625 above and 'Article 4(b): territorial and customer restrictions', pp 665–668 below.

[44] For an example of the 'hold-up problem' under UK law see *Lucite International (UK) Ltd and BASF plc* OFT decision of 29 November 2002 [2003] UKCLR 176, paras 44–46.

(vi) The 'vertical externality issue'

Vertical restraints can be used to align the incentives of the parties so that one party does not act in a way that would harm the interests of the other. There may be situations where the manufacturer needs the retailer to improve sales levels or not to price too high in order to obtain benefits. The negative externality of too high pricing by a retailer can be avoided by imposing a maximum resale price on the retailer[45].

(vii) Economies of scale in distribution[46]

Economies of scale on the part of distributors may lead to lower retail prices. Various vertical agreements might contribute to this, including exclusive distribution and exclusive purchasing.

(viii) Capital market imperfections

In some cases banks or equity markets may be unwilling to provide sufficient capital for the needs of the business of a supplier or a buyer. In such cases the supplier may lend to the buyer or vice versa. An obvious example is a brewer which makes a loan available to the operator of a public house or a café. A supplier in such a case may wish to impose a non-compete, or an analogous, provision; and a buyer may insist, for example, on exclusive supply.

(ix) Uniformity and quality standardisation

Vertical restraints may help to promote the brand image of a product and increase its attractiveness to consumers by bringing about uniformity and quality standardisation. This is typical of selective distribution and franchising systems.

6. Vertical Agreements: Article 101(1)[47]

(A) Introduction

This section will consider the application of Article 101(1) to vertical agreements. Given the breadth of the new block exemption for vertical agreements, in many cases it is not necessary, in practical terms, to decide whether an agreement infringes Article 101(1) in the first place: if an agreement is within the 'safe haven' of Regulation 330/2010 and therefore satisfies the criteria of Article 101(3) the parties may have little interest in arguing, or even knowing, that the agreement did not infringe Article 101(1) in the first place. Paragraph 110 of the Commission's *Vertical guidelines* suggests, at indents (1) and (2), that there is no need to consider the application of Article 101(1) to agreements that are within the safe haven of the block exemption. This is a sensible and pragmatic point, and one with which the Court of Justice agrees[48]. However it would be intellectually incorrect to conclude that, *because* an agreement benefits from block exemption, it *therefore* infringes Article 101(1); and in some cases an agreement may not benefit from the block exemption, for example because the market share of one of the parties exceeds 30 per cent,

---

[45] This is sometimes known as the 'double marginalisation problem', see *Vertical guidelines*, para 107(f).

[46] On economies of scale see ch 1, 'Economies of scale and scope and natural monopolies', p 10.

[47] For more detailed discussion of this topic readers are referred to Filipponi, Peeperkorn and Woods in Faull and Nikpay *The EC Law of Competition* (Oxford University Press, 2nd ed, 2007), ch 9 and Robertson *Distribution Agreements Under EC Competition Law: An Analytical Review* (m-press, 2008).

[48] See Case C-260/07 *Pedro IV Servicios SL v Total España SA* [2009] ECR I-2437, [2009] 5 CMLR 1291, para 36.

in which case the parties may wish to argue that Article 101(1) is not infringed. This is exemplified by the Commission's finding that Interbrew's agreements, which imposed a single branding provision on cafés and bars in Belgium, did not infringe Article 101(1), once they had been modified to its satisfaction[49].

(B) The *de minimis* doctrine

Paragraphs 8 to 11 of the Commission's *Vertical guidelines* point out that agreements of minor importance usually fall outside Article 101(1) altogether. These paragraphs refer to the Commission's 2001 *Notice on Agreements of Minor Importance*[50]; it is described in chapter 3 of this book[51]. Vertical agreements entered into by non-competing undertakings whose individual market share does not exceed 15 per cent are usually regarded as *de minimis*, although a 'hard-core' restriction such as an export ban might infringe Article 101(1) even below this threshold[52].

(C) The combined effect of the *de minimis* doctrine and the block exemption

The combined effect of the *de minimis* doctrine and the block exemption is that most vertical agreements where the market share of each of the parties is below 15 per cent fall outside Article 101(1) altogether; and that most vertical agreements, even if they are caught by Article 101(1), will be block exempted under Regulation 330/2010, provided that the supplier's and the buyer's market share is below 30 per cent and that the agreement does not contain any of the 'hard-core' restrictions in Article 4 of that Regulation[53]. As a consequence a very large number of vertical agreements will enjoy the benefit of one of these two 'safe havens'. Individual examination of vertical agreements will be necessary only where none of the safe havens is available, for example because the supplier's market share exceeds 30 per cent or because the parties wish to include a blacklisted provision in their agreement. Where the market share of one of the parties exceeds 30 per cent it may be that it has a dominant position, in which case restrictions in its vertical agreements may amount to an abuse of a dominant position contrary to Article 102 TFEU: firms have been found to be dominant where they had a market share in the region of 40 per cent, and they are presumed to be dominant at 50 per cent[54]. However in the case of Interbrew's single branding agreements the Commission concluded that, even though Interbrew had a market share of around 56 per cent, the agreements did not appreciably restrict competition once the extent of the exclusivity had been reduced[55]. Agreements containing hard-core restrictions are unlikely to satisfy the criteria of Article 101(3), since these are restrictions to which the Commission generally takes exception. It follows that individual examination of vertical agreements under Article 101(1) and Article 101(3) is likely to be relatively rare: it is most likely to be necessary where the supplier or the buyer

---

[49] See Commission Press Release IP/03/545, 15 April 2003.

[50] OJ [2001] C 368/13, [2002] 4 CMLR 699.

[51] See ch 3, 'The *De Minimis* Doctrine', pp 140–144.

[52] *Vertical guidelines,* para 10 states that the applicable case law of the EU Courts is relevant in this respect, referring in particular to Case 5/69 *Völk v Vervaecke* [1969] ECR 295, [1969] CMLR 273; see further ch 3, 'Part II of the Notice: the threshold', pp 141–142.

[53] See 'Article 4: hard-core restrictions', pp 663–669 below.

[54] See ch 5, 'The AKZO presumption of dominance where an undertaking has a market share of 50 per cent or more', pp 182–183.

[55] See ch 16 n 49 above.

has a market share in excess of 30 per cent but does not have a dominant position in the sense of Article 102.

	Market shares and vertical agreements
50%	An undertaking with a market share of more than 50% is presumed to be dominant
40%	An undertaking with a market share of more than 40% may be dominant
30%	An undertaking with a market share of more than 30% will not benefit from the block exemption. If an agreement is caught by Article 101(1) it will benefit from block exemption if the supplier's and the buyer's market share is below 30% and the agreement does not contain Article 4 hard-core restrictions
15%	An agreement will benefit from the *de minimis* doctrine where the market share of each of the parties is below 15% and the agreement does not contain any Article 4 hard-core restrictions

(D) The case law of the EU Courts on vertical agreements

The Court of Justice and the General Court have repeatedly made clear that, except in those cases where the *object*[56] of an agreement is plainly anti-competitive, for example because of the imposition of an export ban, the application of Article 101(1) to an agreement cannot be ascertained simply by taking into account its formal terms; rather it has to be assessed in its economic context in order to determine whether it could have an effect on competition in the relevant market. This case law is discussed in chapter 3 of this book[57]. Of particular importance in the context of vertical agreements are the judgments in *Société Technique Minière v Maschinenbau Ulm*[58], *Brasserie de Haecht v Wilkin*[59], *Pronuptia de Paris v Schillgalis*[60] and *Delimitis v Henninger Bräu*[61], each of which makes clear that, in 'effect' rather than 'object' cases under Article 101(1), a detailed examination of all the relevant facts is required before a conclusion can be reached as to whether competition is restricted by a vertical agreement.

Notwithstanding these important judgments there was a tendency on the part of the Commission over many years to adopt a formalistic approach to the application of Article 101(1) to vertical agreements, and a reluctance to follow the lead suggested by the EU Courts; the result was that large numbers of vertical agreements required exemption under Article 101(3) and, in particular, under the block exemptions adopted by the Commission. However it is clear from the *Vertical guidelines* that the Commission now adopts a flexible and economics-oriented approach to the application of Article 101(1). Paragraphs 110 to 127 of the *Guidelines* establish the methodology of analysis for determining whether vertical agreements infringe Article 101(1) and whether they might satisfy the terms of Article 101(3). The footnotes in the *Guidelines* contain helpful references to the case law of the Courts: due to constraints of space not all of these judgments are mentioned in the text that follows, but the reader should be aware of this useful reference point.

---

[56] See ch 3, 'Object', pp 118–120.
[57] See ch 3, 'The "object or effect" of preventing, restricting or distorting competition', pp 117–121.
[58] Case 56/65 [1966] ECR 235, [1966] CMLR 357.
[59] Case 23/67 [1967] ECR 407, [1968] CMLR 26.
[60] Case 161/84 [1986] ECR 353, [1986] 1 CMLR 414.
[61] Case C-234/89 [1991] ECR I-935, [1992] 5 CMLR 210.

(E) **The methodology for the analysis of vertical agreements in the Commission's *Vertical guidelines***

(i) The four steps involved in assessing vertical agreements under Article 101

Paragraph 110 of the *Vertical guidelines* suggests that four steps should be taken when assessing vertical agreements under Article 101. First, the relevant market should be defined in order to determine the supplier's and the buyer's market share; secondly, where the market share of each of the parties is below 30 per cent the block exemption will usually be applicable, provided that there are no hard-core restrictions contrary to Article 4 of Regulation 330/2010[62]; the third step is that, where the market share of 30 per cent is exceeded at the level of the supplier or the buyer, it will be necessary to consider whether the agreement falls within Article 101(1); lastly, where Article 101(1) is infringed, it will be necessary to consider whether the agreement benefits from the exception conferred by Article 101(3).

(ii) Relevant factors for the assessment under Article 101(1)

Paragraphs 111 to 121 set out the factors that are relevant to the analysis of agreements under Article 101(1). Paragraph 111 refers to nine particular factors that are relevant to this assessment:

- the nature of the agreement
- the market position of the parties
- the market position of competitors
- the position of the buyers of the contract products
- entry barriers
- the maturity of the market
- the level of trade affected by the agreement
- the nature of the product
- 'other factors'.

Each of these factors is expanded upon in the succeeding paragraphs. Paragraph 117 discusses the issue of entry barriers and emphasises the significance of sunk costs in determining how high the entry barriers are in a particular industry[63]. Paragraph 121 deals with 'other factors' that may be relevant to the analysis: these include whether there is a 'cumulative effect' within the market of similar vertical agreements leading to a restriction of competition, the regulatory environment and behaviour that may indicate or facilitate horizontal collusion.

(iii) Relevant factors for the assessment under Article 101(3)

Paragraphs 122 to 127 discuss the application of Article 101(3) to vertical agreements. They should be read in conjunction with the Commission's *Article [101(3)] Guidelines*[64]. Paragraph 123 states that it is necessary to take into account the investments made by any of the parties and the time needed and the restraints required to commit and recoup an efficiency-enhancing investment. Paragraphs 124 to 127 rehearse the conditions of Article 101(3). Paragraph 127 states that, in the absence of rivalry between undertakings, a dominant undertaking will lack adequate incentives to continue to create and pass on efficiency gains to consumers: in other words that such agreements are unlikely to satisfy Article 101(3).

---

[62] See 'Article 4: hard-core restrictions', pp 663–669 below.
[63] On barriers to entry see ch 1, 'Potential Competitors', pp 44–45.
[64] OJ [2004] C 101/97; for discussion of the *Article [101(3)] Guidelines* see ch 4, 'The Article 101(3) Criteria', p 151ff.

(iv) Application of the methodology to particular types of agreement

Having set out this methodology the Commission's *Vertical guidelines* proceed to consider the application of Article 101 to a series of particular types of vertical agreement: these are considered in section G below[65]. The *Vertical guidelines* do not contain a specific section dealing with the application of Article 101(1) to direct and indirect export bans, other than the commentary on Article 4(b) of the block exemption[66]. However there is a wealth of precedent on this subject and, as has been stressed throughout this book, the single market imperative is a dominant feature of EU competition law. For this reason section F below will consider the approach of the EU Courts and the Commission to direct and indirect export bans before the discussion in the *Vertical guidelines* of other types of vertical agreement is considered in section G.

(F) Direct and indirect export bans

(i) Direct export bans

Export bans in vertical agreements will be held to infringe Article 101(1), and will not be permitted under Article 101(3) except in exceptional circumstances. Such agreements will be found to have as their object the restriction of competition; anti-competitive effects do not need to be demonstrated. In *General Motors BV v Commission*[67] the Court of Justice held that this was so even if an agreement does not have the restriction of competition as its sole aim but also pursues other legitimate objectives[68], adding that the same was true if the restriction of exports happened as a result of indirect rather than direct measures[69]. In *GlaxoSmithKline v Commission* the General Court rejected the Commission's view that Glaxo's dual pricing system involved an indirect export ban that had as its object the restriction of competition[70]. On appeal the Court of Justice reaffirmed its case law that agreements aimed at prohibiting or limiting parallel trade have as their object the restriction of competition; that this applies to the pharmaceutical sector as to any other; that, for an agreement to restrict competition by object, it was not necessary that final consumers be deprived of advantages; and that Article 101 protects 'competition as such'[71]. However the Court of Justice agreed with the General Court that the Commission had failed to deal appropriately with Glaxo's arguments and evidence under Article 101(3)[72]. The Court of Justice's judgements in *Football Association Premier League*[72a] and *Pierre Fabre Dermo-Cosmétique SAS*[72b] are also emphatic that agreements that impede single market integration are prohibited unless there are exceptional circumstances.

Export bans are blacklisted by Article 4(b) of Regulation 330/2010, and their inclusion prevents the application of the block exemption to the agreement in question[73]. Examples

---

[65] See 'Application of Article 101(1) to other types of vertical agreements', pp 637–649 below.

[66] See 'Article 4(b): territorial and customer restrictions', pp 665–668 below.

[67] Case C-551/03 P [2006] ECR I-3173, [2006] 5 CMLR 9.   [68] Ibid, para 64.

[69] Ibid, para 68.

[70] Case T-168/01 *GlaxoSmithKline Services Unlimited v Commission* [2006] ECR II-2969, [2006] 5 CMLR 29, paras 114–147.

[71] Cases C-501/06 P etc *GlaxoSmithKline Services Unlimited v Commission* [2009] ECR I-9291, [2010] 4 CMLR 50, paras 54–67.

[72] Case T-168/01 *GlaxoSmithKline Services Unlimited v Commission* [2006] ECR II-2969, [2006] 5 CMLR 29, paras 214–316; and Cases C-501/06 P etc *GlaxoSmithKline Services Unlimited v Commission* [2009] ECR I-9291, [2010] 4 CMLR 50, paras 68–118.

[72a] Cases C-403/08 and C-429/08 [2011] ECR I-000, paras 134–146.

[72b] Case C-439/09 [2011] ECR 000, paras 37-47.

[73] See 'Article 4(b): territorial and customer restrictions', pp 665–668 below.

of export bans which the Commission and the EU Courts have objected to are legion[74], and the competition authorities of the Member States ('NCAs') have been equally opposed to them[75]. It is highly likely that the Commission or an NCA will impose a fine where it discovers an export ban, although reluctant distributors which accepted the ban under duress may not themselves be fined[76]; alternatively it may be that the fine on unwilling participants will be reduced[77]. In a serious case the fine for imposing export bans could be very substantial: in *VW*[78] the fine on Volkswagen amounted to €102 million, at the time one of the largest penalties to have been imposed by the Commission on one undertaking for infringing the competition rules; the fine was reduced to €90 million on appeal[79]. When determining the level of fines, and in particular ensuring that they have a sufficiently deterrent effect, the Commission is entitled to take into account the central position within a distribution system of the manufacturer, which must display special vigilance and ensure that it observes the competition rules when concluding distribution agreements[80].

All of the vertical cases that the Commission prosecuted to the stage of adopting an infringement decision[81] in the 2000s, with the exception of *VW II*[82] which concerned resale price maintenance, involved direct or indirect export bans[83]. For example in *Nintendo*[84] the Commission condemned the prevention of parallel trade in video games and their consoles and imposed a fine of €167.8 million on the manufacturer and its dis-

---

[74] See ch 16 n 83 below for examples of such cases since 2000; for a list of cases in the preceding 20 years or so see p 623 n 102 of the sixth edition of this book and the online Resource Centre that accompanies this book, www.oxfordtextbooks.co.uk/orc/whish7e/.

[75] See eg the UK *Tobacco*, OFT decision of 15 April 2010, on which see 'Decisional practice of the OFT', pp 679–680 below; *Consumer Electronics*, decision of the French Conseil de la Concurrence of 5 December 2005 (imposing total fines of €34.4 million for resale price maintenance): the decision has been annulled twice on appeal by the Cour de Cassation, judgments of 3 June 2008 and 7 January 2011, available at www.autoritedelaconcurrence.fr; *Witt Hvidevarer*, decision of the Danish Competition Council of 24 November 2010, available at www.kfst.dk.

[76] See eg *Kawasaki* OJ [1979] L 16/9, [1979] 1 CMLR 448; *Johnson and Johnson* OJ [1980] L 377/16, [1981] 2 CMLR 287; *John Deere* OJ [1985] L 35/58, [1985] 2 CMLR 554.

[77] See eg *BMW Belgium* OJ [1978] L 46/33, [1978] 2 CMLR 126; *Hasselblad* OJ [1982] L 161/18, [1982] 2 CMLR 233.

[78] OJ [1998] L 124/60, [1998] 5 CMLR 33.

[79] Case T-62/98 *Volkswagen AG v Commission* [2000] ECR II-2707, [2000] 5 CMLR 853, upheld on appeal to the Court of Justice in Case C-338/00 *Volkswagen AG v Commission* [2003] ECR I-9189, [2004] 4 CMLR 351.

[80] Case T-13/03 *Nintendo Co Ltd v Commission* [2009] ECR II-947, [2009] 5 CMLR 1421, paras 79–80.

[81] The Commission also settled some vertical cases informally: see eg *OMV/Gazprom* Commission Press Release IP/05/195, 17 February 2005 (involving gas supply contracts which prevented OMV from reselling the gas outside Austria: however the offending provisions were dropped, and OMV agreed to increase capacity in the gas pipeline that transports Russian gas through Austria).

[82] OJ [2001] L 262/14, annulled on appeal in Case T-208/01 *Volkswagen v Commission* [2003] ECR II-5141, [2004] 4 CMLR 727; on appeal to the Court of Justice the Court agreed that the Commission's decision should be annulled, but on different grounds from those of the General Court: Case C-74/04 P *Commission v Volkswagen AG* [2006] ECR I-6585, [2008] 4 CMLR 1297.

[83] See *Nathan-Bricolux* OJ [2001] L 54/1; *Opel* OJ [2001] L 59/1, [2001] 4 CMLR 1441, substantially upheld on appeal to the General Court Case T-368/00 *General Motors Nederland BV v Commission* [2003] ECR II-4491, [2004] 4 CMLR 1302 and on appeal to the Court of Justice Case C-551/03 P *General Motors BV v Commission* [2006] ECR I-3173, [2006] 5 CMLR 9; *JCB* OJ [2002] L 69/1, upheld in part on appeal to the General Court Case T-67/01 *JCB Service v Commission* [2004] ECR II-49, [2004] 4 CMLR 1346 and on appeal to the Court of Justice Case C-167/04 P *JCB Service v Commission* [2006] ECR I-8935, [2006] 5 CMLR 1337; *GlaxoSmithKline* OJ [2001] L 302/1: see ch 16 n 72 above; *DaimlerChrysler* OJ [2002] L 257/1, annulled on appeal Case T-325/01 *DaimlerChrysler AG v Commission* [2005] ECR II-3319, [2007] 4 CMLR 559; *Yamaha*, Commission decision of 16 July 2003 (fine of €2.56 million); *Souris/Topps*, Commission decision of 26 May 2004 (fine of €1.59 million).

[84] OJ [2003] L 255/33, [2004] 4 CMLR 421.

tributors; this was the largest fine ever to have been imposed by the Commission for an unlawful vertical agreement under Article 101; on appeal to the General Court two of the fines[85] were slightly reduced, but the substance of the Commission's decision was upheld. What is noticeable is the dearth of cases brought by the Commission in relation to vertical agreements in recent years: indeed there has not been one Commission decision finding an infringement of Article 101 in the case of a vertical agreement since *Peugeot* in October 2005[86]. The Commission's enforcement activities in recent years have been overwhelmingly geared to detecting and penalising hard-core horizontal cartels and to enforcing Article 102[87].

The lack of enforcement action on the Commission's part in relation to vertical agreements ought not, however, to be interpreted as a downgrading, on its part, of the importance of the internal market, nor of an increased tolerance of restrictions of parallel trade[88]. One explanation for the reduced enforcement action on the part of the Commission against vertical restraints under Article 101 in recent years is that there have been numerous cases at national level, both on the part of the NCAs and the national courts[89]. This is hardly surprising: while the Commission grapples with large, often EU-wide (or even global), cartels and major cases of abuse of dominance, problems in relation to distribution systems, which are often arranged along national lines, are resolved at the level of the Member States. A further explanation for the lack of enforcement action on the part of the European Commission – which cannot be proven empirically, but which is plausible – is that the EU regime for vertical agreements is well understood by undertakings and their legal advisers and has worked well in practice.

(ii) Indirect export bans

The EU Courts, the Commission, the NCAs and national courts will condemn indirect measures that might have the same effect as an export ban. Indirect export bans are blacklisted by Article 4(b) of Regulation 330/2010, and their inclusion in an agreement would prevent the application of the block exemption[90]. An example of an indirect export ban would arise if a producer provides that its guarantees are available to consumers in a particular Member State only if they buy the product from a distributor in that State; this obviously acts as a strong disincentive to purchase elsewhere. In *Zanussi*[91] the Commission condemned such an arrangement, and it has taken similar action on several occasions since[92]. As a general

---

[85] See Case T-13/03 *Nintendo Co Ltd v Commission* [2009] ECR II-947, [2009] 5 CMLR 1421 and Case T-18/03 *CD-Contact Data GmbH v Commission* [2009] ECR II-1021, [2009] 5 CMLR 1469, upheld on appeal in Case C-260/09 P *Activision Blizzard Germany GmbH (formerly CD-Contact Data GmbH) v Commission* [2011] ECR I-000, [2011] 4 CMLR 964; see also Case T-12/03 *Itochu Corp v Commission* [2009] ECR II-883, [2009] 5 CMLR 1375, where the appeal was dismissed in its entirety.

[86] Decision of 5 October 2005, upheld as to substance on appeal Case T-450/05 *Peugeot v Commission* [2009] ECR II-2533; the fine was reduced from €49.5 million to €44.55 million as the Commission had failed sufficiently to take into account the impact of currency fluctuations on the volume of parallel trade.

[87] See eg Communication from the Commission to the European Parliament and the Council *Report on the functioning of Regulation 1/2003* COM(2009) 206 final, paras 3 and 13, available at www.ec.europea.eu

[88] On the continuing importance of the 'single market imperative' see *Vertical guidelines*, para 7 and Commission Press Release IP/10/1175, 25 September 2010 in which the Commission announced that, following a preliminary assessment, Apple had taken action to make it easier for consumers to exercise their warranty rights in relation to iPhones purchased in a Member State other than their home country.

[89] For examples of cases brought by NCAs see ch 16 n 75 above.

[90] See 'Article 4(b): territorial and customer restrictions', pp 665–668 below.

[91] OJ [1978] L 322/26, [1979] 1 CMLR 81.

[92] See *Matsushita Electrical Trading Company* Commission's XIIth *Report on Competition Policy* (1982), point 77; *Ford Garantie Deutschland* XIIIth *Report on Competition Policy* (1983), points 104–106; *Fiat* XIVth *Report on Competition Policy* (1984), point 70; XVIth *Report on Competition Policy* (1986), point 56; *Sony* XVIIth *Report on*

proposition customer guarantees should be available for products no matter where they are marketed in the single market. The Commission's approach was endorsed by the Court of Justice in *ETA Fabriques d'Ebauches v DK Investments SA*[93], in which it held that the partitioning of national markets by denying the benefit of guarantees to imported goods infringed Article 101(1). However it may be legitimate to provide that the guarantee should extend only to services that a local representative is bound to provide in accordance with local safety and technical standards[94], and it is permissible to withhold the guarantee from products sold by a dealer who is not an authorised member of a selective distribution system[95]. A requirement that a distributor that exports goods into the territory of another distributor should pay a service fee to the latter as compensation for the after-sales service that it is required to provide may be treated as an export ban where the fee does not relate to the value of the service to be provided; so may the provision to distributors of financial support conditional on products supplied being used only within a distributor's allotted territory[96].

Another way of indirectly affecting exports is through the use of monitoring clauses in contracts, whereby a producer requires information as to the destination of its products, and by the imposition on products of serial numbers which enable their movement from one territory to another to be traced. While these practices are not objectionable in themselves, they will be condemned where they are used by a producer in order to prevent or control parallel importing[97].

Exports may be impeded in numerous other ways. Price discrimination devised to prevent exports would be caught[98]; the withdrawal of discounts previously granted to a French dealer in so far as it exported the products in question to Italy attracted fines in *Gosmé/ Martell*[99]. In *Konica*[100] Konica's policy of buying up supplies of its film imported from the UK into Germany in order to protect its German distributors from cheap imports was condemned under Article 101(1): this did not prevent parallel imports in itself, but it did deprive consumers in Germany of the possibility of buying cheaper film. Restrictions on cross-supplies between distributors would be caught, as they may prevent parallel imports

Competition Policy (1987), point 67; Mathiak 'The Commission persuades Saeco to implement an international guarantee for its products and closes the complaint file' *Competition Policy Newsletter*, October 2000, 48.

[93] Case 31/85 [1985] ECR 3933, [1986] 2 CMLR 674.

[94] See *Zanussi* (ch 16 n 91 above, para 14).

[95] Case C-376/92 *Metro v Cartier* [1994] ECR I-15, [1994] 5 CMLR 331, paras 32–34.

[96] *JCB* OJ [2002] L 69/1, [2002] 4 CMLR 1458, paras 155–167, on appeal the General Court confirmed the Commission's approach on this point but annulled its finding of infringement for lack of evidence: Case T-67/01 *JCB Service v Commission* [2004] ECR II-49, [2004] 4 CMLR 1346, paras 136–145.

[97] See eg *Victor Hasselblad AB* OJ [1982] L 161/18, [1982] 2 CMLR 233: its cameras had serial numbers on them and the Commission considered that this afforded an opportunity to Hasselblad to discover whether there had been any parallel importing; *Sperry New Holland* OJ [1985] L 376/21, [1988] 4 CMLR 306; *Newitt/ Dunlop Slazenger International* OJ [1992] L 131/32, [1993] 5 CMLR 352, paras 59–60.

[98] See eg *Pittsburgh Corning Europe* JO [1972] L 272/35, [1973] CMLR D2; *Kodak* JO [1970] L 147/24, [1970] CMLR D19; Case 30/78 *Distillers v Commission* [1980] ECR 2229, [1980] 3 CMLR 121; the Commission considered that Glaxo had failed to demonstrate that its dual pricing policy satisfied the requirements of Article 101(3) in *GlaxoSmithKline* OJ [2001] L 302/1, [2002] 4 CMLR 335: the Commission's decision was annulled on this point in Case T-168/01 *GlaxoSmithKline Services v Commission* [2006] ECR II-2969, [2006] 5 CMLR 29, paras 233–317, and that aspect of the General Court's judgment was upheld on appeal to the Court of Justice in Cases C-501/06 P etc *GlaxoSmithKline Services Unlimited v Commission* [2009] ECR I-9291, [2010] 4 CMLR 50, paras 68–168; see ch 3, 'Refinement of the range of agreements within the object box', pp 124–125.

[99] OJ [1991] L 185/23, [1992] 5 CMLR 586; see similarly *Newitt/Dunlop Slazenger International* OJ [1992] L 131/32, [1993] 5 CMLR 352, paras 54–57; *Ford Agricultural* OJ [1993] L 20/1, [1995] 5 CMLR 89, paras 13–14 (discounts dependent on non-export and penalties for exporting infringed Article 101(1)).

[100] OJ [1988] L 78/34, [1988] 4 CMLR 848; see similarly *Newitt/Dunlop Slazenger International* OJ [1992] L 131/32, [1993] 5 CMLR 352, para 58.

between Member States[101]. A requirement that coffee beans be resold only in a roasted form could affect exports: the Commission required agreements to be amended so that the beans could also be sold in their raw form[102]. Reducing supplies to a distributor in a particular territory so that there are none available for export could be caught, provided that this is done by agreement or concerted practice[103]. In *Bayo-n-ox*[104] the supply of a product for a customer's own use was held to entail an export ban contrary to Article 101(1) and in *Bayer Dental*[105] the Commission condemned a clause forbidding the resale of Bayer's dental products in a repackaged form since it regarded this as an indirect ban on exports.

In *Zera/Montedison*[106] the Commission concluded that an agreement to differentiate agrochemical products between one national market and another, with the consequence that a German distributor enjoyed absolute territorial protection, infringed Article 101(1)[107]. In *DaimlerChrysler*[108] the Commission considered that the requirement that only foreign customers should pay a 15 per cent deposit for a new vehicle unjustifiably hindered cross-border car sales[109].

An important point to bear in mind is that the Commission will take a wide view of the term 'agreement' for the purpose of establishing whether an export ban infringes Article 101(1) and, in particular, that conduct that may appear to be unilateral may be characterised as sufficiently consensual to be caught by that provision[110]. Furthermore in some cases it may be relatively easy to establish a concerted practice between a supplier and its distributors to divide up the internal market[111]. However, as pointed out in chapter 3, there have been several occasions on which Commission findings of a vertical agreement have been overturned on appeal[112]. A different point to note is that in *Activision Blizzard*[113], an appeal in the *Nintendo* case, the Court of Justice held that the standard of proof for demonstrating the existence of a vertical agreement is not higher than in the case of a horizontal agreement[114].

(iii) Export bans falling outside Article 101(1) or satisfying Article 101(3)

There have been several occasions on which the Court of Justice has concluded that an export ban, in the context of a specific type of agreement, did not have as its object the restriction of competition and could fall outside Article 101[115]. An example can be found in

---

[101] *German Spectacle Frames* [1985] 1 CMLR 574; *JCB* OJ [2002] L 69/1, [2002] 4 CMLR 1458, paras 174–178.

[102] *Colombian Coffee* OJ [1982] L 360/31, [1983] 1 CMLR 703; see similarly the 'green banana' clause in Case 27/76 *United Brands Co v Commission* [1978] ECR 207, [1978] 1 CMLR 429.

[103] *Sandoz* OJ [1987] L 222/28, [1989] 4 CMLR 628, para 30, upheld on appeal Case C-277/87 *Sandoz Prodotti Farmaceutici SpA v Commission* [1990] ECR I-45; see also *Chanelle Veterinary Ltd v Pfizer Ltd (No 2)* [1999] Eu LR 723 (Irish Supreme Court): delisting not attributable to an agreement; see further ch 16 n 281 below.

[104] OJ [1990] L 21/71, [1990] 4 CMLR 930, upheld on appeal to the General Court in Case T-12/90 [1991] ECR II-219, [1993] 4 CMLR 30, and to the Court of Justice in Case C-195/91 P *Bayer v Commission* [1994] ECR I-5619.

[105] OJ [1990] L 351/46, [1992] 4 CMLR 61.   [106] OJ [1993] L 272/28, [1995] 5 CMLR 320.

[107] Ibid, paras 96–126.   [108] OJ [2002] L 257/1, [2003] 4 CMLR 95.

[109] Ibid, paras 173–175, upheld in part on appeal Case T-325/01 *DaimlerChrysler AG v Commission* [2005] ECR II-3319, [2007] 4 CMLR 559.

[110] See ch 3, '"Unilateral" conduct and Article 101(1) in vertical cases', pp 105–110.

[111] See in particular Cases 100–103/80 *Musique Diffusion Française SA v Commission* [1983] ECR 1825, [1983] 3 CMLR 221.

[112] See ch 3, 'Judgments since *Bayer v Commission* annulling Commission findings of an agreement', pp 109–110.

[113] Case C-260/09 P *Activision Blizzard Germany GmbH (formerly CD-Contact Data GmbH) v Commission* [2011] ECR I-000, [2011] 4 CMRL 964.

[114] Ibid, paras 71–72.

[115] See eg Case 27/87 *Erauw-Jacquery Sprl v La Hesbignonne Soiété Coopéative* [1988] ECR 1919, [1988] 4 CMLR 576.

Javico v Yves St Laurent[116], where an export ban was imposed on distributors *outside*, rather than within, the EU: obviously such cases do not trigger the same concerns about single market integration in the way that export bans imposed upon EU distributors do[117].

Paragraphs 60 to 64 of the *Vertical guidelines* state that there may be circumstances in which hard-core sales restrictions do not infringe Article 101(1) at all or may in an individual case satisfy Article 101(3):

- a prohibition on resale may fall outside Article 101(1) where there is an objective justification, for example, on grounds of health or safety[118]

- where a distributor makes substantial investments to enter a new market, restrictions of passive sales into its territory by other distributors during the first two years of it operating on the market do not infringe Article 101(1)[119]

- where a new product is genuinely being tested in a limited territory, restrictions of active sales outside that test area will not be caught by Article 101(1) for the period of the testing or introduction of the product[120]

- wholesalers within a selective distribution system may be prevented from actively selling to retailers in other territories, where this is necessary to protect the investment of wholesalers obliged to invest in particular promotional activities within their territories[121]

- a dual pricing policy, under which products intended for export are priced at a premium to equivalent products intended for the domestic market, may satisfy Article 101(3), in particular where higher prices correspond to substantially higher costs for the manufacturer[122].

These paragraphs demonstrate the extent to which the Commission has moved away from a prescriptive, formalistic approach to the application of Article 101 and towards a more effects-based approach.

(G) **Application of Article 101(1) to other types of vertical agreements**

Paragraphs 128 to 229 of the *Guidelines* provide guidance on the application of Article 101 to ten types of vertical agreements: single branding, exclusive distribution, exclusive customer allocation, selective distribution, franchising, exclusive supply, up-front access payments, category management agreements, tying and resale price restrictions. Each of these categories will be examined in this section; relevant cross-references to Regulation 330/2010 will be provided.

(i) **Single branding agreements**[123]
(A) *Possible detriments to inter-brand competition*
Single branding agreements have as their main element that the buyer is obliged or induced to concentrate its orders for a particular product on one supplier[124]. Exclusive purchasing and non-compete obligations are obvious examples of single branding agreements.

---

[116] Case C-306/96 [1998] ECR I-1983, [1998] 5 CMLR 172; on *Javico* see ch 3, 'Refinement of the range of agreements within the object box', pp 124–125.

[117] The Commission specifically refers to *Javico* in fn 5 of its *Vertical guidelines*.

[118] *Vertical guidelines*, para 60; see eg *Kathon/Biocide* OJ [1984] C 59/6, [1984] 1 CMLR 476.

[119] *Vertical guidelines*, para 61.　　　　[120] Ibid, para 62.　　　　[121] Ibid, para 63.

[122] Ibid, para 64; in such cases the Commission would investigate the extent to which such a pricing policy is likely to limit sales and hinder the distributor in reaching more and different customers.

[123] *Vertical guidelines*, paras 129–150.　　　　[124] Ibid, para 129.

In the Commission's view such agreements may restrict inter-brand competition; this could happen by foreclosing access on the part of other suppliers to the market, by softening competition, by facilitating collusion and by limiting in-store inter-brand competition[125].

(B) Application of the block exemption to single branding agreements

Regulation 330/2010 will apply to single branding agreements, provided that the market share of each of the parties is less than 30 per cent[126] and provided that the duration of the non-compete obligation is limited to five years or less[127]. Where the block exemption applies, it will not be necessary to consider further whether Article 101(1) is infringed or whether the requirements of Article 101(3) are satisfied on an individual basis; however the *Guidelines* provide guidance for those cases in which 'self-assessment' of agreements is necessary because the block exemption is not applicable[128].

(C) Factors to be considered in determining whether single branding agreements infringe Article 101(1)

The Commission sets out the factors that are to be considered in determining whether Article 101(1) is infringed in paragraphs 132 to 143 of the *Vertical guidelines*. The approach taken by the Commission is an economic one, and is consistent with the many judgments of the EU Courts (not referred to in the *Guidelines*) which have held that such agreements must be assessed in their economic context in order to determine whether they have an anti-competitive effect: single branding agreements do not have the *object* of restricting competition[129]. Judgments of particular note on this issue include *Brasserie de Haecht v Wilkin*[130], *Delimitis v Henninger Bräu*[131], *BPB Industries v Commission*[132] and *Neste Markkinointi v Yötuuli*[133]. Decisions in which the Commission has concluded that single branding agreements infringed Article 101(1) and did not satisfy Article 101(3) include *Spices*[134], *Bloemenveilingen Aalsmeer*[135] and *Langnese/Schöller*[136].

---

[125] Ibid, para 130.

[126] See 'Article 3: the market share cap', pp 660–662 below.

[127] See 'Article 5(1)(a): non-compete obligations', pp 669–670 below on Article 5(1)(a) of Regulation 330/10; as will be explained there, in certain, limited, circumstances a period of more than five years may be permitted.

[128] *Vertical guidelines*, para 139.

[129] See eg Case T-65/98 *Van den Bergh Foods v Commission* [2003] ECR II-4653, [2004] 4 CMLR 14, para 80.

[130] Case 23/67 [1967] ECR 407, [1968] CMLR 26.

[131] Case C-234/89 [1991] ECR I-935, [1992] 5 CMLR 210; see Lasok 'Assessing the Economic Consequences of Restrictive Agreements: A Comment on the Delimitis Case' (1991) 12 ECLR 194; Korah 'The Judgment in *Delimitis* – A Milestone Towards a Realistic Assessment of the Effects of an Agreement – or a Damp Squib' (1993) 8 Tulane European and Civil Law Forum 17; a shorter version is to be found at (1992) 5 EIPR 167.

[132] Case T-65/89 [1993] ECR II-389, [1993] 5 CMLR 32, para 66.

[133] Case C-214/99 [2000] ECR I-11121, [2001] 4 CMLR 993; the UK Competition Appeal Tribunal considered the application of the judgment in *Neste* to an exclusive purchasing agreement in Case No 1087/2/3/07 *Independent Media Support Ltd v Office of Communications* [2008] CAT 13, [2008] CompAR 161, paras 108–123, agreeing with the conclusion of OFCOM that the agreement in question did not infringe the Chapter I prohibition in the Competition Act 1998 or Article 101 TFEU; the Court of Appeal refused permission to appeal, [2008] EWCA Civ 1402.

[134] OJ [1978] L 53/20, [1978] 2 CMLR 116.   [135] OJ [1988] L 262/27, [1989] 4 CMLR 500.

[136] OJ [1993] L 183/19, [1994] 4 CMLR 51, substantially upheld on appeal Cases T-7/93 and T-9/93 *Langnese-Iglo GmbH etc v Commission* [1995] ECR II-1533, [1995] 5 CMLR 602 and [1995] ECR II-1611, [1995] 5 CMLR 659 and Case C-279/95 P [1998] ECR I-5609, [1998] 5 CMLR 933; see also the Commission's decision on Article 101 in *Van den Bergh Foods Ltd* OJ [1998] L 246/1, [1998] 5 CMLR 530, upheld on appeal Case T-65/98 *Van den Bergh Foods Ltd v Commission* [2003] ECR II-4653, [2004] 4 CMLR 14: the same dispute was the subject of an Article 267 reference by the Irish Supreme Court to the Court of Justice in Case C-344/98 *Masterfoods Ltd v HB Ice Cream Ltd* [2000] ECR I-11369, [2001] 4 CMLR 449.

As far as Article 101(1) is concerned the *Guidelines* explain that single branding agreements with one supplier may result in anti-competitive foreclosure where they prevent an important competitive constraint from being exercised by existing and future competitors; this may be the case in particular where the supplier is an unavoidable trading partner, for example because its brand is a 'must stock item'. It follows that the market position of the supplier is particularly important for the analysis of single branding agreements[137]. The duration of a single branding agreement will also be relevant[138]. The higher the market share and the longer the duration, the more likely it is that there will be a significant foreclosure of the market[139]. Paragraph 133 of the *Vertical guidelines* states that agreements on the part of non-dominant undertakings of less than a year are unlikely to infringe Article 101(l)[140]; between one and five years they may do; and agreements of more than five years would normally be caught. Single branding agreements are more likely to result in anti-competitive foreclosure when entered into by dominant undertakings[141].

Where there are parallel networks of single branding agreements, their cumulative effect may be to foreclose access to the market[142]; this would be unlikely where the largest supplier in the market has a market share of less than 30 per cent and the market share of the five largest suppliers is below 50 per cent[143]. Other relevant factors are the level of entry barriers[144], countervailing power[145] and the level of trade affected[146].

(D) The application of Article 101(3)

Article 101(3) issues are discussed in paragraphs 144 to 148 of the *Vertical guidelines*: this is considered below[147].

(ii) Exclusive distribution agreements[148]

(A) Possible detriments to intra-brand competition and to market integration

A supplier will often grant exclusive distribution rights to a distributor for a particular territory: for example it might appoint X as the exclusive distributor for France and Y as the exclusive distributor for Germany. The supplier may also agree that it will not sell its products directly into the territories granted to X and Y. The Commission's main concern in relation to exclusive distribution agreements is that intra-brand competition will be reduced and that the market will be partitioned[149]. A separate concern arises when most or all suppliers in a particular market adopt exclusive distribution systems since this may soften competition and facilitate collusion, both at the suppliers' and the distributors' level of the market; this would entail harm to inter-brand competition. The Commission

---

[137] *Vertical guidelines*, para 132; see similarly *DSD* OJ [2001] L 319/1, [2002] 4 CMLR 405, paras 121–140, upheld on appeal in Case T-289/01 *Duales System Deutschland GmbH v Commission* [2007] ECR II-1691, [2007] 5 CMLR 356.

[138] Ibid, para 133.   [139] Ibid.

[140] See Case C-214/99 *Neste Markkinointi Oy v Yötuuli* [2000] ECR I-11121, [2000] 4 CMLR 993, where the Court of Justice concluded that exclusive purchasing agreements for petrol of not more than one year's duration did not infringe Article 101(1); see also Case E-7/01 *Hegelstad Eiendomsselskap Arvid B Hegelstad v Hydro Texaco AS* [2003] 4 CMLR 236, where the EFTA Court held that a 15-year fixed term exclusive purchasing agreement for petrol was permissible where it only made an insignificant contribution to the foreclosure of the market.

[141] See ch 17, 'Could the tie have an anti-competitive foreclosure effect?', pp 649–695.

[142] *Vertical guidelines*, para 134.   [143] Ibid, para 135.   [144] Ibid, para 136.

[145] Ibid, para 137.   [146] Ibid, paras 138–141.

[147] See 'The Application of Article 101(3) to Agreements that do not Satisfy the Block Exemption', pp 672–674 below.

[148] *Vertical guidelines*, paras 151–167.   [149] Ibid, para 151.

also notes that exclusive distribution may lead to foreclosure of other distributors and thereby reduce competition at that level.

(B) Application of the block exemption to exclusive distribution agreements

The block exemption for vertical agreements will apply to exclusive distribution agreements, provided that the market share of the supplier and the buyer is less than 30 per cent and that there are no 'hard-core' restrictions contrary to Article 4[150]. In particular there should be no restrictions on passive sales (sales in response to unsolicited orders)[151] to other territories; where there is a combination of exclusive distribution and selective distribution, there must be no restrictions even of active sales by retailers to end users[152], and there must be no restrictions on sales between authorised distributors[153]. The *Guidelines* provide guidance for those cases in which individual assessment of agreements is necessary because the block exemption is not applicable[154].

(C) Factors to be considered in determining whether exclusive distribution agreements infringe Article 101(1)

The Commission sets out the factors that are to be considered in determining whether Article 101(1) is infringed in paragraphs 153 to 160 of the *Vertical guidelines*. There is no reference to the judgment of the Court of Justice in *Société Technique Minière v Maschinenbau Ulm*[155], where the Court held that an exclusive distribution agreement does not have as its object the restriction of competition, but must be considered in its market context to determine whether it has this effect. The reason that the Court of Justice took a stricter line in *Consten and Grundig v Commission*[156] was that in that case the distributor, Consten, was given absolute territorial protection against parallel imports[157]: because of the single market imperative in EU competition law, absolute territorial protection almost always infringes Article 101(1) and only rarely would benefit from Article 101(3)[158]. It is important however to bear in mind that an exclusive distribution agreement may not infringe Article 101(1) at all where there is not the additional element of absolute territorial protection.

As far as Article 101(1) is concerned the Commission states that the market position of the supplier and its competitors is of 'major importance', since the loss of intra-brand competition is problematic only if inter-brand competition is limited[159]. The stronger the position of the supplier, the more serious is the loss of intra-brand competition[160]. Where there are strong competitors, the restriction of intra-brand competition will generally be outweighed by inter-brand competition[161], although there may be a risk of collusion and/or softening of competition where the number of competitors is 'rather small'[162]. The *Guidelines* also discuss the possibility of exclusive distribution agreements having a foreclosure effect, which is considered unlikely unless the exclusive distributor has buyer

---

[150] On Article 4 of Regulation 330/10 see 'Article 4: hard-core restrictions', pp 663–669 below.
[151] Regulation 330/2010, Article 4(b).
[152] Ibid, Article 4(c); see also *Vertical guidelines*, para 152.   [153] Ibid, Article 4(d).
[154] *Vertical guidelines*, para 152.
[155] Case 56/65 [1966] ECR 235, [1966] CMLR 357.
[156] Cases 56 and 58/64 [1966] ECR 299, [1966] CMLR 418.
[157] See ch 3, 'Cases in which agreements containing contractual restrictions were found not to have anti-competitive effects', pp 128–129; see also the discussion of the two US cases, *Schwinn* and *Sylvania* at ch 3 n 390.
[158] See ch 3, 'Cases in which agreements containing contractual restrictions were found not to have anti-competitive effects', pp 128–129.
[159] *Vertical guidelines*, para 153.   [160] Ibid, para 153.   [161] Ibid, para 154.
[162] Ibid, para 154.

power in the downstream market[163]; the *Guidelines* also discuss the relevance of the maturity of the market[164] and of the level of trade affected[165].

(D) *The application of Article 101(3)*

Article 101(3) issues are discussed in paragraphs 161 to 164 of the *Vertical guidelines*; this is considered below[166].

(iii) **Exclusive customer allocation agreements**[167]

Exclusive customer allocation refers to the situation in which a supplier agrees to sell its products to a distributor who will resell only to a particular class of customers. Exclusive customer allocation is discussed in paragraphs 168 to 173 of the *Vertical guidelines*, and is treated in much the same way as exclusive distribution, although the Commission makes a few specific comments on this particular type of vertical restraint[168]; in particular it says that the allocation of final consumers is unlikely to satisfy the criteria of Article 101(3)[169].

(iv) **Selective distribution agreements**[170]

Selective distribution agreements are often deployed by producers of branded products. The producer establishes a system in which the products can be bought and resold only by authorised distributors and retailers. Non-authorised dealers will not be able to obtain the products, and the authorised dealers will be told that they can resell only to other members of the system or to the final consumer[171]. The *Vertical guidelines* state that selective distribution systems may restrict intra-brand competition, may foreclose access to the market, and may soften competition and/or facilitate collusion between suppliers or buyers[172]. In determining the application of Article 101 to selective distribution agreements, a distinction must be made between a 'purely qualitative' system and a 'quantitative' system; a purely qualitative selective distribution system will not infringe Article 101(1) at all even though, by its very nature, it may involve the restrictions just mentioned.

(A) *Purely qualitative selective distribution systems*[173]

The Court of Justice held in *Metro v Commission*[174] that:

> the Commission was justified in recognising that selective distribution systems constituted, together with others, an aspect of competition which accords with Article [101(1)], provided that resellers are chosen on the basis of objective criteria of a qualitative nature relating to the technical qualifications of the reseller and its staff and the suitability of its trading premises and that such conditions are laid down uniformly for all potential resellers and are not applied in a discriminatory fashion. It is true that in such systems of distribution price competition is not generally emphasised either as an exclusive or indeed as a principal factor...However, although price competition is so important that it can never be eliminated it does not constitute the only effective form of competition or that to which absolute priority must in all circumstances be afforded[175].

---

[163] Ibid, paras 155 and 156.   [164] Ibid, para 158.
[165] Ibid, paras 159 and 160.
[166] See 'The Application of Article 101(3) to Agreements that do not Satisfy the Block Exemption', pp 672–674 below.
[167] *Vertical guidelines*, paras 168–173.   [168] Ibid, paras 169–172.   [169] Ibid, para 172.
[170] Ibid, paras 174–188.   [171] Ibid, para 174.   [172] Ibid, para 175.
[173] Ibid, para 175.   [174] Case 26/16 [1977] ECR 1875, [1978] 2 CMLR 44.
[175] Ibid, para 21.

The judgment in *Metro* confirmed that the Commission's approach in earlier decisions had been correct[176] and provided the basis for subsequent cases. The Court of Justice has itself repeated the *Metro* test on several occasions[177], as has the General Court[178]; the Commission has relied on the *Metro* doctrine on various occasions[179]. Three criteria must be satisfied for a system to be treated as purely qualitative and therefore outside Article 101(1).

First, the product in question must be of a type that necessitates selective distribution. It is only in the case of such goods that the suppression of price competition – inherent in selective distribution – in favour of non-price competition is objectively justifiable. It is not only complex equipment such as cars and electronic equipment that has benefited from the *Metro* doctrine. From the judgments of the EU Courts and the decisions of the Commission it is possible to identify three categories of goods that may come within it, although it should be pointed out that this is not a formal classification that they themselves have adopted. The most obvious category consists of products that are technically complex, so that specialist sales staff and a suitable after-sales service are needed. In this category may be placed cars[180], cameras[181], electronic equipment such as hi-fis[182], consumer durables[183], clocks and watches[184] and computers[185]. The second category consists of products the brand image of which is particularly important, such as perfumes and

---

[176] The Commission had Concluded to various aspects of the selective distribution networks in *Kodak* JO [1970] L 147/24, [1970] CMLR D19 and *Omega Watches* JO [1970] L 242/22, [1970] CMLR D49, did not infringe Article 101(1) and found that Article 101(3) applied to other terms.

[177] See eg Case 99/79 *Lancôme SA v Etos BV* [1980] ECR 2511, [1981] 2 CMLR 164, paras 20–26; Case 31/80 *L'Oréal NV v de Nieuwe AMCK* [1980] ECR 3775, [1981] 2 CMLR 235, paras 15–21; Case 126/80 *Maria Salonia v Giorgio Poidomani* [1981] ECR 1563, [1982] 1 CMLR 64; Case 210/81 *Demo-Studio Schmidt v Commission* [1983] ECR 3045, [1984] 1 CMLR 63; Case 107/82 *AEG-Telefunken v Commission* [1983] ECR 3151, [1984] 2 CMLR 325; Case 75/84 *Metro v Commission (No 2)* [1986] ECR 3021, [1987] 1 CMLR 118.

[178] Case T-19/91 *Vichy v Commission* [1992] ECR II-415; Case T-19/92 *Groupement d'Achat Édouard Leclerc v Commission* [1996] ECR II-1851, [1997] 4 CMLR 995; Case T-88/92 *Groupement d'Achat Édouard Leclerc v Commission* [1996] ECR II-1961, [1997] 4 CMLR 995.

[179] *Junghans* OJ [1977] L 30/10, [1977] 1 CMLR D82; *Murat* OJ [1983] L 348/20, [1984] 1 CMLR 219; *SABA (No 2)* OJ [1983] L 376/41, [1984] 1 CMLR 676; *IBM Personal Computers* OJ [1984] L 118/24, [1984] 2 CMLR 342; *Villeroy Boch* OJ [1985] L 376/15, [1988] 4 CMLR 461; *Grundig* OJ [1985] L 233/1, [1988] 4 CMLR 865; *Yves Saint Laurent Parfums SA* OJ [1992] L 12/24, [1993] 4 CMLR 120, mostly upheld on appeal Case T-19/92 *Groupement d'Achat Édouard Leclerc v Commission* [1996] ECR II-1851, [1997] 4 CMLR 995, and given further approval in 2001, Commission Press Release IP/01/713, 17 May 2001; *Parfums Givenchy System of Selective Distribution* OJ [1992] L 236/11, [1993] 5 CMLR 579, mostly upheld on appeal Case T-88/92 *Groupement d'Achat Édouard Leclerc v Commission* [1996] ECR II-1961, [1997] 4 CMLR 995; *Kenwood Electronics Deutschland GmbH* OJ [1993] C 67/9, [1993] 4 CMLR 389; *Schott-Zwiesel-Glaswerke* OJ [1993] C 111/4, [1993] 5 CMLR 85; *Grundig* OJ [1994] L 20/15, [1995] 4 CMLR 658; *Sony España SA* OJ [1993] C 275/3, [1994] 4 CMLR 581; Case C-439/09 *Pierre fabre Dermo-cosmétique SAS* [2011] ECR I-000, paras 40–41; the Commission's decision of 3 October 2007 in *Morgan Stanley/Visa International and Visa Europe* provides an interesting application of the *Metro* doctrine by analogy to a horizontal agreement: the decision was upheld on appeal to the General Court in Case T-461/07 *Visa Europe v Commission* [2011] ECR II-000.

[180] *BMW* OJ [1975] L 29/1, [1975] 1 CMLR D44; note that there is a specific block exemption for the distribution of cars: see 'Regulation 461/2010 on Motor Vehicle Distribution', pp 674–669 below.

[181] *Kodak* JO [1970] L 147/24, [1970] CMLR D19.

[182] *Grundig* OJ [1985] L 223/1, [1988] 4 CMLR 865 and again OJ [1994] L 20/15, [1995] 4 CMLR 658.

[183] Case 107/82 *AEG-Telefunken v Commission* [1983] ECR 3151, [1984] 3 CMLR 325; it was only when AEG's system was applied in a discriminatory way that it came within Article 101(1).

[184] *Omega Watches* JO [1970] L 242/22, [1970] CMLR D49; *Junghans* OJ [1977] L 30/10, [1977] 1 CMLR D82; note however that the Court of Justice in Case 31/85 *ETA Fabriques d'Ebauches SA v DK Investment SA* [1985] ECR 3933, [1986] 2 CMLR 674 doubted that mass-produced Swatch watches would qualify for selective distribution under the *Metro* doctrine: ibid, para 16.

[185] *IBM Personal Computers* OJ [1984] L 118/24, [1984] 2 CMLR 342.

luxury cosmetic products[186], ceramic tableware[187] and gold and silver jewellery[188]. A third category is newspapers, the special characteristic of which is their extremely short shelf-life which necessitates particularly careful distribution[189]. The Commission has doubted whether plumbing fittings qualify for such treatment[190].

The second requirement for the *Metro* doctrine to apply is that the criteria by which a producer may limit the retail outlets through which its products are resold must be purely qualitative in nature, laid down uniformly for all potential resellers and applied in a non-discriminatory manner[191]. Where this is the case, any dealer that can satisfy the qualitative criteria should be able to obtain the products in question: there is no restriction on the number of dealers in the system. A producer may require that its goods be sold only to retail outlets which employ suitably trained staff, have suitable premises in an appropriate area, use a suitable shop name consistent with the status of the brand, and provide a proper after-sales service; also a restriction on sales to non-authorised distributors and retailers is permitted, as is a restriction not to advertise products at 'cash-and-carry prices'. A problem is that it is not always obvious whether a particular requirement is 'qualitative' or not. Criteria that do not relate to the technical proficiency of outlets[192] but extend to such matters as the holding of minimum stocks, stocking the complete range of products, the achievement of a minimum turnover or a minimum percentage of turnover[193] in the products in question and the promotion of products have sometimes been treated as quantitative, although they have often been found to satisfy the criteria of Article 101(3)[194].

The third requirement of the *Metro* doctrine is that any restrictions that are imposed on appointed distributors and retailers must go no further than is objectively necessary to protect the quality of the product in question[195]: this is a manifestation of the principle

---

[186] Case 99/79 *Lancôme SA etc v Etos BV* [1980] ECR 2511, [1981] 2 CMLR 164; Case T-19/92 *Groupement d'Achat Édouard Leclerc v Commission* [1996] ECR II-1851, [1997] 4 CMLR 995, paras 113–123; Case T-88/92 *Groupement d'Achat Édouard Leclerc v Commission* [1996] ECR II-1961, [1997] 4 CMLR 995, paras 105–117.

[187] *Villeroy Boch* OJ [1985] L 376/15, [1988] 4 CMLR 461.

[188] *Murat* OJ [1983] L 348/20, [1984] 1 CMLR 219.

[189] See eg Case 126/80 *Maria Salonia v Giorgio Poidomani* [1981] ECR 1563, [1982] 1 CMLR 64; Case 243/83 *Binon v Agence et Messageries de la Presse* [1985] ECR 2015, [1985] 3 CMLR 800; Commission's Notice *Agence et Messageries de la Presse* OJ [1987] C 164/2; Commission's XXIXth *Report on Competition Policy* (1999), pp 161–162.

[190] *Grohe* OJ [1985] L 19/17, [1988] 4 CMLR 612; *Ideal Standard* OJ [1985] L 20/38, [1988] 4 CMLR 627.

[191] For an example of the discriminatory application of a purely qualitative selective distribution system see Case 107/82 *AEG-Telefunken v Commission* [1983] ECR 3151, [1984] 3 CMLR 325, in particular at para 39; where a producer refuses to supply to certain distributors or retailers, the problem arises of whether this refusal is attributable to an agreement or concerted practice, or whether it is a unilateral act and therefore outside Article 101(1): see ch 3, ' "Unilateral" conduct and Article 101(1) in vertical cases', pp 105–110.

[192] *Vichy* OJ [1991] L 75/57, upheld on appeal Case T-19/91 [1992] ECR II-415 (restriction on the sale of Vichy products except to officially appointed pharmacists was quantitative).

[193] *Yves St Laurent* OJ [1992] L 12/24, [1993] 4 CMLR 120, mostly upheld on appeal Case T-19/92 *Groupement d'Achat Édouard Leclerc v Commission* [1996] ECR II-1851, [1997] 4 CMLR 995, paras 148–155; Case T-88/92 *Groupement d'Achat Édouard Leclerc v Commission* [1996] ECR II-1961, [1997] 4 CMLR 995, paras 141–148.

[194] See eg *Parfums Givenchy* OJ [1992] L 236/11, [1993] 5 CMLR 579; *Grundig* OJ [1994] L 20/15, [1995] 4 CMLR 658; in *Sony Pan-European Dealer Agreement (PEDA)*, Commission's XXVth *Report on Competition Policy* (1995), pp 135–136 the Commission approved a selective distribution system which contained a formal procedure for determining whether a particular undertaking qualifies for admission.

[195] See eg *Grohe* OJ [1985] L 19/17, [1988] 4 CMLR 612; *Ideal Standard* OJ [1985] L 20/38, [1988] 4 CMLR 627.

of proportionality. In *Hasselblad*[196] objection was taken by the Commission to provisions which enabled the producer to exercise supervision of the advertising of its distributors and retailers, as this would mean that control could be exercised over advertisements indicating cuts in prices. In *AEG-Telefunken v Commission*[197] the Court of Justice made clear that restrictions would not be permitted simply in order to guarantee dealers a minimum profit margin. In *Pierre Fabre*[197a] the Court of Justice held that a restriction on Internet selling of non-prescription cosmetic products could not be justifed by the need to provide individual advice to the customer or by the protection of brand image.

(B) Selective distribution systems that are not purely qualitative

Where a selective distribution system is not purely qualitative in the sense of the *Metro* doctrine it may be caught by Article 101(1), although it may also benefit from the block exemption conferred by Regulation 330/2010[198] or satisfy Article 101(3) on an individual basis[199]. In determining whether Article 101(1) is infringed the Commission will look at the market position of the supplier and its competitors, since the loss of intra-brand competition is problematic only where inter-brand competition is weak[200]. A further issue is whether, in a particular market, there is a number of selective distribution systems in operation: where this is the case the Commission is anxious that there may be a lack of intra-brand competition, a foreclosure of certain types of distributors and retailers (for example those that sell only online) and that collusion may be facilitated[201]. In *Metro v Commission (No 2)*[202] the Court of Justice held that where, in a particular market, the existence of a number of selective distribution systems leaves no room for other methods of distribution or results in a rigidity in price structure which is not balanced by other types of competition, Article 101(1) may apply after all[203].

(C) Application of the block exemption to selective distribution systems

Selective distribution agreements may benefit from the block exemption conferred by Regulation 330/2010. To do so the market share held by each of the parties must be below 30 per cent[204], and the requirements of Articles 4(a), 4(c), 4(d) and 5(c)[205] must be respected. Where a selective distribution system benefits from the block exemption, but there are minimal efficiency-enhancing effects, for example because the product is not suitable for this form of distribution, the block exemption could be withdrawn where appreciable anti-competitive effects occur[206]. The Commission has indicated that the benefit of the block exemption may be withdrawn from selective distribution systems where there is a 'cumulative effect' problem; however it says that such a problem is unlikely to arise when the share of the market covered by selective distribution is below 50 per cent, or

---

[196] OJ [1982] L 161/18, [1982] 2 CMLR 233.

[197] Case 107/82 [1983] ECR 3151, [1984] 3 CMLR 325, para 42.

[197a] Case C-439/09 [2011] ECR I-000, paras 42–46.

[198] See 'Vertical Agreements: Regulation 330/2010', pp 649–672 below.

[199] See 'The Application of Article 101(3) to Agreements that do not Satisfy the Block Exemption', pp 672–674 below.

[200] *Vertical guidelines*, para 177.

[201] Ibid, para 178.   [202] Case 75/84 [1986] ECR 3021, [1987] 1 CMLR 118.

[203] [1986] ECR 3021, [1987] 1 CMLR 118, paras 41 and 42; a similar argument was considered, but rejected, in Case T-19/92 *Groupement d'Achat Édouard Leclerc v Commission* [1996] ECR II-1851, [1997] 4 CMLR 995, paras 178–192 and in Case T-88/92 *Groupement d'Achat Édouard Leclerc v Commission* [1996] ECR II-1961, [1997] 4 CMLR 995, paras 170–184.

[204] See 'Article 3: the market share cap', pp 660–662 below.

[205] See *Vertical guidelines*, para 182; these provisions are explained at 'Article 4: hard-core restrictions', pp 663–669 below.

[206] *Vertical guidelines*, para 176.

where this figure is exceeded but the aggregate market share of the five largest suppliers is below 50 per cent[207]. An individual supplier with a market share of less than 5 per cent is unlikely to be considered as making a contribution to the cumulative effect[208].

In its decision in *Yamaha*[209] the Commission imposed a fine of €2.56 million on Yamaha for operating a selective distribution system in a way that led to the partitioning of the single market and to the fixing of resale prices. The Commission objected to a series of restrictions imposed on its dealers[210], including obligations on official distributors to sell only to final customers, since this amounted to a restriction on cross-supplies within the network; obligations on official distributors to purchase exclusively from the Yamaha national subsidiary, as this could inhibit cross-border trade; and obligations on official distributors to contact Yamaha before exporting via the Internet, in relation to which sales there should have been no restriction. Yamaha's selective distribution system failed to benefit from the block exemption partly because in several markets its market share exceeded 30 per cent[211] and partly because there were violations of Article 4(a), (b) and (d)[212]. In *Pierre Fabre*[212a] the Court of Justice held that a clause prohibiting, de facto, Internet selling in a selective distribution agreement will cause the agreement to lose the benefit of the block exemption under Article 4(c)[212b].

In some systems of domestic law a selective distribution system is binding on unauthorised third parties, who can be sued for unfair competition if they obtain and attempt to sell the products; in German law there is a requirement on the producer which uses such a system to ensure that it is 'impervious', that is to say that its products are kept within the system; however the imperviousness ('lückenlosigkeit') of the system is not a requirement for its validity under EU competition law[213].

(v) Franchising agreements[214]

(A) *Pronuptia v Schillgalis*

The application to franchising agreements of Article 101 was explored by the Court of Justice in *Pronuptia de Paris v Schillgalis*[215]. Mrs Schillgalis, the franchisee for Hamburg, Oldenburg and Hanover, was in dispute with Pronuptia, the franchisor, over her royalty payments and in the course of litigation pleaded that the agreement was void as it contravened Article 101. The Court identified the crux of a franchise system: that it enables a franchisee to operate as an independent business whilst using the name and know-how of the franchisor. The transfer of intellectual property rights from the franchisor to the franchisee is the feature of franchises that distinguishes them from more conventional distribution systems. In a franchise, the franchisee pays a fee to the franchisor for the right to use the know-how, trade marks, designs, logos and other intellectual property rights ('IPRs') of the franchisor. In order for the franchise system to work effectively it is essential that each franchisee should conform with the uniform commercial methods

---

[207] Ibid, paras 75 and 179.

[208] Ibid, para 179, final sentence; see also the Commission's *Notice on Agreements of Minor Importance* OJ [2001] C 368/13, [2002] 4 CMLR 699, para 8.

[209] Commission decision of 16 July 2003.

[210] Ibid, para 88; each of the offending restrictions is analysed in the paragraphs following para 88.

[211] Ibid, para 168; the Commission considered the application of the old block exemption, Regulation 2790/99, which applied only where the supplier's market share was below 30 per cent.

[212] Ibid, paras 169–174.   [212a] Case C–439/09 [2011] ECR I–000.   [212b] Ibid, paras 57–59.

[213] Case C–376/92 *Metro-SB-Großmärkte GmbH v Cartier* [1994] ECR I-15, [1994] 5 CMLR 331, para 28; see also Case C–41/96 *VAG-Händlerbeirat eV v SYD-Consult* [1997] ECR I-3123, [1997] 5 CMLR 537.

[214] *Vertical guidelines*, paras 189–191.

[215] Case 161/84 [1986] ECR 353, [1986] 1 CMLR 414; see Dubois 'Franchising Under EC Competition Law: Implications of the *Pronuptia* Judgment and the Proposed Block Exemption' [1986] Fordham Corporate Law Institute ch 6; Waelbroeck 'The *Pronuptia* Judgment – A Critical Appraisal' [1986] Fordham Corporate Law Institute ch 9; Venit '*Pronuptia*: Ancillary Restraints or Unholy Alliances' (1986) 11 EL Rev 213.

laid down by the franchisor: from the consumer's point of view, it is important that all franchised outlets should achieve the same standard. Therefore it is essential that the franchisor should be able to impose common standards on all franchisees. Also, as the transfer of IPRs is vital to the whole exercise, it is legitimate for the franchisor to impose terms on the franchisee to protect these rights. The Court concluded that restrictions in these two categories, that is to maintain common standards and to protect IPRs, did not infringe Article 101(1). However restrictions that could divide the market territorially or which imposed resale price maintenance would be within Article 101(1), although they might satisfy Article 101(3) in certain circumstances[216].

(B) Application of the block exemption to franchising

Regulation 330/2010 will apply to franchising agreements, provided that the market share of each of the parties is below 30 per cent and that there are no Article 4 hard-core restrictions. Paragraph 190 of the *Vertical guidelines* refers to paragraphs 24 to 46, which deal specifically with the meaning of vertical agreements in the block exemption and the extent to which the licensing of IPRs, including franchise agreements, are covered by it[217].

(vi) Exclusive supply agreements[218]

Exclusive supply agreements have as their main element that the supplier is obliged or induced to sell the contract products only to one buyer, in general or for a particular use[219]. Exclusive supply agreements may benefit from the block exemption, provided that the supplier's and the buyer's market shares satisfy the 30 per cent cap[220]. Paragraphs 194 to 199 discuss the application of Article 101(1) to exclusive supply agreements that are not covered by the block exemption; paragraphs 200 to 201 consider the application of Article 101(3)[221]. In considering whether Article 101(1) applies to such agreements the buyer's market share in its downstream market will be of particular importance: the greater its market share there, the more likely there is to be an anti-competitive effect[222]; the duration of the supply obligation will also be of relevance[223]. Other matters, such as entry barriers[224], the countervailing power of suppliers[225] and the level of trade affected[226], are also discussed.

(vii) Up-front access payments[227]

Up-front access payments are fees paid by a supplier to a buyer to remunerate the latter for services supplied: for example 'slotting allowances' may be paid to a supermarket in return for access to shelf space, and pay-to-stay fees may be paid to ensure the continued presence of a product on the shelf for a longer period. Paragraph 203 of the *Guidelines* explains that, where the supplier's and buyer's market shares do not exceed 30 per cent, up-front access payments are block exempted. The *Guidelines* then explain the

---

[216] See *Vertical guidelines*, para 47.
[217] On Article 2(3) of Regulation 330/10 see 'Article 2(3) is applicable only where there is a vertical agreement', pp 659–657 below.
[218] *Vertical guidelines*, paras 192–202.
[219] Ibid, para 192.   [220] Ibid, para 193.
[221] See 'The Application of Article 101(3) to Agreements that do not Satisfy the Block Exemption', pp 672–674 below.
[222] *Vertical guidelines*, para 194.
[223] Ibid, para 195; the Commission considers that exclusive supply agreements of more than five years are unlikely to fulfil the criteria of Article 101(3).
[224] Ibid, para 197.   [225] Ibid, para 198.   [226] Ibid, para 199.
[227] Ibid, paras 203–208.

extent to which such payments might infringe Article 101(1), either by foreclosure of the downstream[228] or the upstream[229] market or by the facilitation of collusion[230]; the possibility that up-front access payments might lead to efficiencies is discussed in paragraphs 207 and 208, for example by improving the use of shelf space or by ensuring that the supplier shares the risk that the introduction of a new product might fail.

(viii) Category management agreements[231]

A category management agreement is an agreement between a supplier and a distributor whereby the latter entrusts the supplier with the marketing of a category of products, not only the marketing of the supplier's own products: for example a supplier might be appointed the 'category captain' for breakfast cereals or for non-alcoholic beverages within a chain of supermarkets. Paragraph 209 states that such agreements will benefit from the block exemption where both parties' market shares do not exceed 30 per cent. Paragraph 210 acknowledges that in most cases category management agreements do not raise competition concerns; however the possibility that they might have a foreclosure effect upstream in the market is noted in that paragraph, and the Commission suggests that any analysis should be conducted as it would be in the case of single branding agreements[232]. The possibility that category management might facilitate collusion between distributors or between suppliers is discussed in paragraphs 211 and 212 respectively, and their scope for improving efficiency in paragraph 213.

(ix) Tying agreements[233]

A tying agreement arises where a supplier makes the supply of one product (the 'tying product') conditional upon the buyer also buying a separate product (the 'tied product'). Tying may constitute an abuse of a dominant position contrary to Article 102[234]; however, a vertical agreement imposing a tie may also infringe Article 101(1) where it has a 'single branding' effect in relation to the tied product[235]. Tying agreements benefit from the block exemption when the market share of the supplier, on the markets both for the tying and for the tied products, and the market share of the buyer on the relevant upstream markets are below the 30 per cent cap[236]. Where the market share threshold is exceeded paragraphs 219 to 221 discuss the application of Article 101(1) to tying agreements: the market position of the supplier is the most important issue[237]; the position of its competitors and the entry barriers to the market for the tying product must also be considered[238]. Tying is less likely to be problematic where customers possess significant buyer power[239]. Paragraph 222 considers the possibility of tying practices benefiting from the exception conferred by Article 101(3)[240].

(x) Resale price restrictions[241]

(A) Minimum and fixed resale prices infringe Article 101(1)

The imposition upon distributors and retailers of minimum or fixed resale prices will be held to infringe Article 101(1): such agreements are considered to have as their object the

---

[228] Ibid, para 204.   [229] Ibid, para 205.
[230] Ibid, para 206.   [231] Ibid, paras 209–213.
[232] Ibid, paras 132 to 141; see 'Single branding agreements', pp 637–639 above.
[233] *Vertical guidelines*, paras 214–222.   [234] See ch 17, 'Tying', pp 688–696.
[235] *Vertical guidelines*, para 214.   [236] Ibid, para 218.   [237] Ibid, para 219.
[238] Ibid, para 220.   [239] Ibid, para 221.
[240] See 'The Application of Article 101(3) to Agreements that do not Satisfy the Block Exemption', pp 672–674 below.
[241] *Vertical guidelines*, paras 223–229.

restriction of competition[242]. The Commission has condemned resale price maintenance on various occasions[243]. Furthermore this practice amounts to a hard-core restriction contrary to Article 4(a) of the block exemption[244]; paragraph 48 of the *Guidelines* considers a range of practices that might be considered as having as their 'direct or indirect object', to use the words of Article 4, the imposition of minimum or fixed resale prices[245].

(B) Minimum and fixed prices under Article 101(3)

In recent years there has been a growing recognition that, in some cases, there may be efficiency arguments in favour of resale price maintenance[246]. On one occasion the Commission appeared to be sympathetic to the idea that a newspaper publisher should be allowed to impose a cover price on newspapers[247]. It should be recalled that the General Court in *Matra Hachette v Commission*[248] has ruled that the parties to any kind of agreement are entitled to defend it under Article 101(3)[249], and that the Commission has set out, in its *Article [101(3)] Guidelines*[250], the type of evidence that is required in support of a defence. Paragraph 225 of the *Vertical guidelines* acknowledges that resale price main-

---

[242] See ch 3, 'Agreements that have as their object the prevention, restriction or distortion of competition', p 119; minimum and fixed resale prices will also infringe the Chapter I prohibition in the UK Competition Act 1998: see 'UK Law', pp 677–680 below; in the US the maintenance of minimum resale prices was for many years illegal *per se* as a result of the Supreme Court decision in *Dr Miles Medical Co v John D Park & Sons Co* 220 US 373 (1911); however in *Leegin Creative Leather Products, Inc v PSKS, Inc* 551 US 877 (2007), the Supreme Court explicitly overruled *Dr Miles*, holding that resale price maintenance should be subject to a rule of reason standard henceforth; for discussion of *Leegin*, supportive of the majority approach, see Klein 'Competitive Resale Price Maintenance in the Absence of Free Riding' (2009) 76(2) Antitrust Law Journal 431; and for criticism see Brunell 'Overruling *Dr Miles*: The Supreme Trade Commission In Action' (2007) 52 Antitrust Bulletin 475.

[243] See eg *Deutsche Phillips* OJ [1973] L 293/40, [1973] CMLR D241; *Gerofabriek* OJ [1977] L 16/8, [1977] 1 CMLR D35; *Hennessey/Henkel* OJ [1980] L 383/11, [1981] 1 CMLR 601 where the Commission rejected the argument that setting resale prices was justified for the protection of the product's brand image; *Novalliance/ Systemform* OJ [1997] L 47/11, [1997] 4 CMLR 876; *Nathan-Bricolux* OJ [2001] L 54/1, [2001] 4 CMLR 1122, paras 86–90; *Volkswagen II* OJ [2001] L 262/14, [2001] 5 CMLR 1309, annulled on appeal to the General Court on the ground that the Commission had failed to demonstrate that there was an agreement between Volkswagen and its dealers in Case T-208/01 *Volkswagen v Commission* [2003] ECR II-5141, [2004] 4 CMLR 727; the Court of Justice agreed that the Commission's decision should be annulled, but on different grounds from those of the General Court: Case C-74/04 P *Commission v Volkswagen AG* [2006] ECR I-6585, [2008] 4 CMLR 1297; for discussion see ch 3, 'Judgments since *Bayer v Commission* annulling Commission findings of an agreement', pp 109–110; *JCB* OJ [2002] L 69/1, [2002] 4 CMLR 1458, paras 168–173; *CD prices* Commission Press Release IP/01/1212, 17 August 2001; *Yamaha*, Commission Press Release IP/03/1028, 16 July 2003.

[244] See 'Article 4(a): resale price maintenance', pp 664–665 below; see generally Iacobucci 'The Case for Prohibiting Resale Price Maintenance' (1995) 19(2) World Competition 71 and Gippini-Fournier 'Resale Price Maintenance in the EU: in statu quo ante bellum?' [2009] Fordham Corporate Law Institute (ed Hawk), pp 515–549.

[245] See 'Article 4(a): resale price maintenance', pp 664–665 below on para 47 of the *Vertical guidelines*.

[246] See eg Peeperkorn 'Resale Price Maintenance and Its Alleged Efficiencies' (2008) European Competition Journal 201; Jones 'Resale Price Maintenance: A Debate About Competition Policy in Europe' (2009) European Competition Journal 425; the series of essays in June 2010 (1) CPI Antitrust Journal, available at www.competitionpolicyinternational.com. For criticism see Gippini-Fournier (ch 16 n 244 above) and Lao 'Free Riding: An Overstated, and Unconvincing, Explanation for Resale Price Maintenance' in Pitofsky (ed) *How the Chicago School Overshot the Mark* (Oxford University Press, 2008), pp 196–232.

[247] See the Commission's XXIXth *Report on Competition Policy* (1999), pp 161–162 (although the Commission never revealed publicly what conclusion it reached on the matter); the Commission's Notice in *Agence et Messageries de la Presse* OJ [1987] C 164/2 had suggested that it might countenance resale price maintenance for newspapers and periodicals; see also Case 243/85 *Binon & Cie v SA Agence et Messageries de la Presse* [1985] ECR 2015, [1985] 3 CMLR 800, para 46.

[248] Case T-17/93 [1994] ECR II-595.   [249] See ch 4, 'The Article 101(3) Criteria', pp 155–166.

[250] OJ [2004] C 101/97.

tenance might lead to efficiencies in the sense of Article 101(3). Paragraph 225 gives, as a 'most notable' example, resale price maintenance imposed by a manufacturer that introduces a new product to the market, where this induces the distributor to increase its sales efforts for the new product, thereby expanding overall demand and making the launch a success, itself a benefit to consumers.

(C) Recommended and maximum resale prices

Paragraphs 226 to 229 of the *Vertical guidelines* consider the extent to which it is lawful to recommend a resale price to a distributor or retailer or to impose a *maximum* rather than a minimum price[251]. Article 4(a) of the block exemption provides that these practices are not 'hard-core' restrictions, 'provided that they do not amount to a fixed or minimum sale price as a result of pressure from, or incentives offered by, any of the parties'. Agreements containing recommendations or maximum prices would therefore be exempt, provided that the market share of each of the parties does not exceed the cap of 30 per cent[252]. Where the block exemption is not applicable the Commission states at paragraph 227 of the *Guidelines* that it will consider whether recommended or maximum prices might work 'as a focal point for the resellers and might be followed by most or all of them'[253]; it will also examine whether these practices could soften competition or facilitate collusion between suppliers[254]. The market power of the supplier is an important factor to be taken into consideration[255]; the stronger its power over the market, the greater the risk that a maximum or recommended price will lead to uniform pricing[256]. Paragraph 229 considers the possible application of Article 101(3) to maximum or recommended prices. In *Repsol CPP* the Commission accepted commitments from Repsol to modify its long-term exclusive supply agreements with service stations selling its fuel, but which explicitly allowed it to impose maximum or recommended prices[257].

7. Vertical Agreements: Regulation 330/2010[258]

(A) Introduction

It was explained above that the Commission over many years tended to adopt a formalistic (insufficiently economics-oriented) approach to the application of Article 101(1); as a result it was necessary for many agreements to be brought within the 'safe haven' of one of the Commission's block . It adopted Regulation 1983/83 for exclusive distribution agreements[259], Regulation 1984/83 for exclusive purchasing agreements[260] and Regulation

---

[251] In *Albrecht v Herald Co* 390 US 145 (1968) the US Supreme Court condemned *per se* the imposition of maximum resale prices; however it overruled itself in *State Oil v Khan*, substituting a rule of reason approach to this particular phenomenon: 522 US 3 (1997); see Steuer '*Khan* and the Issue of Dealer Power – Overview' (1997–98) 66 Antitrust Law Journal 531; Blair and Lopatka '*Albrecht* Overruled – At Last' ibid, 537; Grimes 'Making Sense of *State Oil Co v Khan:* Vertical Maximum Price Fixing under a Rule of Reason' ibid, 567.

[252] *Vertical guidelines*, para 226.   [253] Ibid.

[254] Ibid, para 227.   [255] Ibid, para 228.   [256] Ibid.

[257] Commission decision of 12 April 2006.

[258] Part of the text that follows is based on the authors' article 'Regulation 330/2010: the Commission's New Block Exemption for Vertical Agreements' (2010) 47 CML Rev 1757; on Regulation 330/2010 see also Wijckmans and Tuytschaever *Vertical Agreements in EU Competition Law* (Oxford University Press, 2nd ed, 2011), part II; Brenning-Louko, Gurin, Peeperkorn and Viertiö 'Vertical Agreements: New Competition Rules for the Next Decade', CPI Antitrust Journal June 2010(1), p 2; Subiotto and Dautricourt 'The Reform of European Distribution Law' (2011) 34(1) World Competition 11.

[259] OJ [1983] L 173/1.   [260] OJ [1983] L 173/5.

4087/88 for franchise agreements[261]. However dissatisfaction with the over-application of Article 101(1) and the formalistic nature of the block exemptions became widespread, and led to the publication in 1997 of the Commission's *Green Paper on Vertical Restraints in [EU] Competition Policy*[262] suggesting a range of possible options for reform. This document paved the way for the adoption in 1999 of Commission Regulation 2790/99[263]. The new block exemption was radical in various ways[264]: it was much broader in scope than its predecessors, applying to virtually all vertical agreements in both the goods and services sector; it was more economics-based, in particular by including a market share cap for determining which agreements would benefit from the block exemption; and it was less prescriptive than its predecessors, containing a relatively limited list of 'hard-core' restrictions that could not be included in an agreement. Regulation 2790/99 was a considerable improvement on the system it replaced and entered into force on 1 June 2000. The Regulation was accompanied by extensive *Guidelines on Vertical Restraints* and appears to have worked well in practice[265].

The Commission published in July 2009 a draft revised block exemption for vertical agreements together with draft guidelines and asked for comments within two months, noting when it did so that the main suggestions for amendment were prompted by the increased buyer power of retailers and the evolution of online sales on the Internet[266]. The two matters identified by the Commission generated the most extensive debate[267], and the issues involved, and the outcome, will be discussed in the context of the new Regulation below. With the exception of the change in the operation of the rules on market shares, the new Regulation represents a mild evolution of the law, as opposed to the revolution of Regulation 2790/99.

(B) **Brief description of the provisions of the block exemption**

The Commission adopted the block exemption on Vertical Agreements and Concerted Practices on 20 April 2010[268]. Regulation 330/2010 entered fully into force on 1 June 2010[269]. Article 9 provided transitional relief for agreements already in force on 31 May 2010 and which satisfy the terms of Regulation 2790/99, but not the new one, until 31 May 2011. The Regulation is without prejudice to the application of Article 102[270]. The Regulation should be read in conjunction with the accompanying *Vertical guidelines* which were published in the Official Journal in May 2010[271].

---

[261] OJ [1988] L 359/46.

[262] COM(96) 721 final, [1997] 4 CMLR 519; see the Commission's XXVIth *Report on Competition Policy* (1996), points 46–50. There was a *Follow-up to the Green Paper on Vertical Restraints* OJ [1998] C 365/3, [1999] 4 CMLR 281; see the Commission's XXVIIIth *Report on Competition Policy* (1998), points 34–53.

[263] Regulation 2790/99, OJ [1999] L 336/21; see the Commission's XXIXth *Report on Competition Policy* (1999), points 8–19.

[264] For a detailed description of the provisions of Regulation 2790/99 see the sixth edition of this book, pp 640–662 and Korah and O'Sullivan *Distribution Agreements under the EC Competition Rules* (Hart Publishing, 2002).

[265] See De Boer and Posthuma 'Ten Years On: Vertical Agreements under Article 81' (2009) 30(9) ECLR 424.

[266] Commission Press Release IP/09/1197, 28 July 2009.

[267] The responses to the Commission's consultation are available on DG COMP's website: www.ec.europa.eu/competition/index_en.html.

[268] OJ [2010] L 102/1.   [269] Regulation 330/2010, Article 10.

[270] On the relationship between Article 101(3) and Article 102 see ch 4, 'Fourth condition of Article 101(3): no elimination of competition in a substantial part of the market', pp 164–165.

[271] OJ [2010] C 130/1.

The Regulation consists of 16 recitals and 10 Articles. Article 1 defines certain key terms such as 'vertical agreements', 'vertical restraints', 'competing undertakings' and 'non-compete obligation'. Article 2 is the provision that actually confers block exemption upon certain vertical agreements pursuant to Article 101(3) TFEU; Article 3 imposes a market share cap of 30 per cent on both the supplier and the buyer. Article 4 sets out a list of hard-core restrictions that will prevent the block exemption from applying to an agreement. Article 5 sets out a list of 'excluded restrictions' that fail to benefit from the block exemption: it is important to note however that the inclusion of Article 5 obligations does not prevent the block exemption from applying to the remainder of the agreement.

Recital 15 of Regulation 330/2010 refers to Article 29 of Regulation 1/2003 which provides for the possibility of the Commission or the competent authority of a Member State to withdraw the benefit of the block exemption in certain circumstances. Article 6 gives the power to the Commission by regulation to disapply the block exemption to vertical agreements containing specific restraints in a relevant market more than 50 per cent of which is covered by parallel networks of similar vertical restraints. Articles 7 and 8 contain provisions on the application of market share and turnover thresholds. Articles 9 and 10 deal respectively with transitional matters and entry into force of the Regulation.

(C) **Article 1: definitions**

Article 1 contains important definitions. These will be explained below, in the specific context in which they are used in the Regulation. Of particular importance is Article 1(1)(a) which defines a 'vertical agreement' as:

> an agreement or concerted practice entered into between two or more undertakings each of which operates, for the purposes of the agreement or the concerted practice, at a different level of the production or distribution chain, and relating to the conditions under which the parties may purchase, sell or resell certain goods or services.

The Regulation applies to vertical agreements to the extent that they contain 'vertical restraints'. Article 1(1)(b) provides that 'vertical restraint' means a restriction of competition in a vertical agreement falling within Article 101(1). These key expressions will be discussed in the context of Article 2 below.

Article 1(2) of Regulation 330/2010 contains rules extending the expressions 'undertaking', 'supplier' and 'buyer' to include connected undertakings.

(D) **Article 2: scope of the block exemption**

(i) **Article 2(1): block exemption for vertical agreements**[272]
Article 2(1) confers block exemption on vertical agreements to the extent that they contain vertical restraints pursuant to Article 101(3) of the Treaty. Several points should be noted about Article 2(1).

(ii) **Many vertical agreements do not infringe Article 101(1)**
It is worth repeating that many vertical agreements do not infringe Article 101(1)[273]; where an agreement does not infringe Article 101(1) it follows that, no matter how generous and flexible the Regulation is, it will not be necessary to bring the agreement in

---

[272] *Vertical guidelines*, paras 23–25.
[273] See 'Vertical Agreements: Article 101(1)', pp 628–649 above.

question within its terms. Despite this, however, many undertakings endeavour to sat-isfy the block exemption, which provides a 'safe haven' for many vertical agreements: as explained earlier, most firms will have no interest in knowing whether their agree-ment infringes Article 101(1) if they know that they benefit from block exemption under Article 101(3) anyway[274]. Recital 9 of the Regulation states that there is no presumption that agreements infringe Article 101(1) or that it will fail to satisfy Article 101(3) where either of the parties' market shares exceeds the prescribed threshold in Article 3, a point repeated in paragraphs 23 and 96 of the *Guidelines*. Where the thresholds are exceeded an agreement requires individual analysis[275]. An example of a vertical agreement not infrin-ging Article 101(1) would be a purely qualitative selective distribution system[276]; only to the extent that it is not purely qualitative – for example because the product is not of the type that necessitates selective distribution[277] or because quantitative as well as qualita-tive criteria are applied[278] – is it necessary to have resort to the block exemption.

(iii) If it is not forbidden, it is permitted

A second point to stress about the Regulation is that, in relation to a vertical agreement as defined in Article 1(1)(a), if the Regulation does not prohibit something, it is permitted. This is the consequence of not stating what must be included in a vertical agreement, but only stating the hard-core restrictions which must not be in it, and is an essential feature of the Regulation. Block exemption is available under Regulation 330/2010 to all verti-cal agreements, as defined, subject to Articles 2(2), 2(4) and 2(5) on agreements made by associations of retailers, agreements between competing undertakings and agreements subject to other block exemptions, Article 3 on market share, and to Articles 4 and 5 which deal with particular vertical restraints that the Commission has concerns about.

(iv) The definition of a vertical agreement

Paragraph 25 of the *Vertical guidelines* discusses the meaning of 'vertical agreement'[279]. Indent (a) of that paragraph explains the distinction between an agreement and/or con-certed practice on the one hand and unilateral conduct, which is not caught by Article 101 but could be by Article 102, on the other. In particular, drawing on the judgments of the Court of Justice in *Commission v Volkswagen*[280] and the General Court in *Bayer v Commission*[281], the Commission sets out the circumstances in which an apparently uni-lateral act on the part of one party might, in fact, be characterised as an agreement and/or concerted practice due to the explicit or tacit acquiescence of the other[282].

---

[274] See 'Introduction', p 617 above.

[275] On the burden of proof in this situation see Article 2 of Regulation 1/2003, OJ [2003] L 1/1 and ch 4, 'The burden of proving that the conditions of Article 101(3) are satisfied', pp 152–153.

[276] See 'Selective distribution agreements', pp 641–645 above.

[277] See eg *Grohe* OJ [1985] L 19/17, [1988] 4 CMLR 612; note that, where it *is* necessary to apply the Regulation to a selective distribution system, the definition of this term in Article 1(1)(e) does not bring into account the nature of the product; this consideration is relevant only to the question of whether the system falls outside Article 101(1) altogether.

[278] See 'Purely qualitative selective distribution systems', p 641–644 above.

[279] The definition of a vertical agreement is identical to that in Council Regulation 1215/99, OJ [1999] L 148/1.

[280] Case C-74/04 P [2006] ECR I-6585, [2008] 4 CMLR 1297.

[281] Case T-41/96 [2000] ECR II-3383, [2001] 4 CMLR 126 upheld on appeal in Cases C-2/01 P etc *BAI and Commission v Bayer* [2004] ECR I-26, [2004] 4 CMLR 653.

[282] On the meaning of agreements and concerted practices see ch 3, 'Agreements, Decisions and Concerted Practices', pp 99–115.

(v) The exempted agreement may be multilateral

Article 2(1) confers block exemption on agreements between two *or more* undertakings[283]. However the Regulation applies only where each of the undertakings operates, for the purposes of the agreement, at a different level of the market[284]. Some illustrations may help:

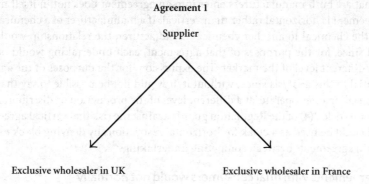

Agreement 1

Supplier

Exclusive wholesaler in UK   Exclusive wholesaler in France

Fig. 16.7

(a) The agreement is trilateral

(b) The supplier supplies goods to each wholesaler

(c) It is agreed that neither wholesaler will sell into the other's territory

The agreement is not vertical since there are two parties, the wholesalers, at the same level of the production and distribution chain.

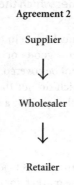

Agreement 2

Supplier

Wholesaler

Retailer

Fig. 16.8

(a) The agreement is trilateral

(b) The agreement sets out the mutual rights and obligations of each party

The agreement is vertical since each party operates at a different level of the production and distribution chain.

Where the agreement is in the form of Agreement 2, Article 3(2) provides that the market shares of the supplier and the wholesaler on their respective downstream markets and the market share of the wholesaler and the retailer on their respective purchase markets would have to be considered for the purpose of the market share cap in Article 3(1)[285].

---

[283] Pursuant to the power conferred on the Commission by Article 1(a) of Council Regulation 19/65, OJ [1965] L 36/533, as amended by Council Regulation 1215/99, OJ [1999] L 148/1.

[284] *Vertical guidelines*, para 25(c).

[285] Ibid, para 90.

(vi) 'For the purposes of the agreement'

The definition of a vertical agreement in Article 1(1)(a) refers to undertakings which operate, '*for the purposes of the agreement or concerted practice*, at a different level of the production or distribution chain' (emphasis added). It follows that the fact that two firms that are both manufacturers enter into an agreement does not in itself mean that the agreement is horizontal rather than vertical. If a manufacturer of a chemical were to supply the chemical to another chemical manufacturer, the relationship would still be vertical since, for the purposes of that agreement, each undertaking would be operating at a different level of the market. The expression 'for the purposes of the agreement' is essential to this analysis since, without it, it would not be possible to say that the two chemical companies operate 'at a different level of the production or distribution chain'. However Article 2(4) of the Regulation guards against the risk that vertical agreements as defined could be used as a cloak for horizontal restrictions by denying block exemption to certain agreements between competing undertakings[286].

(vii) Agreements with final consumers would not normally be vertical agreements

Agreements entered into with final consumers would not normally be vertical agreements, since they would not be entered into 'between two or more undertakings': a final consumer in the sense of a member of the public buying goods or services would not be carrying on an economic activity[287]. For the same reason, however, such agreements would not infringe Article 101(1) in the first place, and therefore would not need to be block exempted.

(viii) 'Relating to the conditions under which the parties may purchase, sell or resell certain goods or services'

To qualify as a vertical agreement it must relate to the conditions under which the parties may purchase, sell or resell certain goods or services. It appears, therefore, that rental and leasing agreements would not be covered[288]; nor would bartering agreements. Provisions in vertical agreements which do not themselves relate to purchase, sale or resale would not be covered: an example would be a covenant not to compete in research and development[289].

(ix) Interconnection agreements

In many industries undertakings require access to an infrastructure owned by someone else in order to be able to operate on the market: for example in the electronic communications sector access to, and interconnection of, all forms of communications networks may be crucial; in electricity access will be needed to the national grid. Where access is provided there will be an 'interconnection agreement' between the owner of the infrastructure and the service provider. It would seem that such an agreement would be vertical in the sense of Article 2(1), since it would relate to the 'conditions under which the parties may purchase, sell or resell...services'[290]. However in many (most?) such cases

---

[286] See 'Article 2(4): agreements between competing undertakings', p 658–659 below.

[287] *Vertical guidelines*, para 25(b): on the meaning of the term 'undertaking' see ch 3, 'Undertakings', pp 83–99; however the supplier would be an undertaking, and would infringe Article 102 if it held a dominant position and acted in an abusive manner and the other terms of that provision were satisfied: on Article 102 generally see ch 5.

[288] *Vertical guidelines*, para 26.   [289] Ibid, para 26.

[290] Note however that the agreement would not be vertical in so far as it is a rental or leasing arrangement: see above.

the owner of the infrastructure would have a market share in excess of 30 per cent, so that Article 3(1) of the Regulation would prevent the application of the block exemption[291].

(x) Agency

Many agency agreements fall outside Article 101(1); paragraphs 12 to 21 of the *Vertical guidelines* deal with this[292]. However those paragraphs suggest that some agency agreements could fall within Article 101(1), if they could foreclose access to the market or if they might facilitate collusion. It is necessary to consider whether an agency agreement that does fall within Article 101(1) would be eligible for block exemption. In such a situation the agent is operating at a different level of the market from the principal in the sense of Article 1(1)(a) of the Regulation. Therefore, to the extent that the agreement relates to the conditions under which the principal or the agent may purchase, sell or resell goods or services, the Regulation could apply: a point specifically noted in paragraph 19 of the *Vertical guidelines*. In such cases it will be necessary to avoid the inclusion of hard-core restrictions of the kind listed in Article 4[293]; paragraph 49 of the *Guidelines* states that an obligation on an agent preventing it from sharing its commission with its customers would be a 'hard-core' restriction under Article 4(a). Also it will be necessary to avoid non-compete provisions of the kind set out in Article 5[294].

(xi) Article 2(2): associations of retailers[295]

A common business phenomenon is that small retailers establish an association for the purchase of goods, which they then resell to final consumers[296]. This is necessary to enable the retailers to achieve some bargaining power in their dealings with large manufacturers and/or intermediaries. Consumers will benefit if the retailers are enabled to obtain lower prices which are transmitted on to them. Article 2(2) provides that *vertical* agreements entered into between such an association and (a) its suppliers or (b) its members can benefit from block exemption, provided that all its members are retailers of goods and provided that no individual member of the association, together with its connected undertakings[297], has a total annual turnover in excess of €50 million[298]. The Regulation does not define the term retailer, but paragraph 29 of the *Vertical guidelines* says that '[r]etailers are distributors reselling goods to final consumers'[299]. The concluding words of Article 2(2) provide that the block exemption for such vertical agreements is without prejudice to the application of Article 101 to the horizontal agreement between the members of the association

---

[291] Where the infrastructure is indispensable for a firm to operate on a downstream market Article 102 may be applicable: see ch 17, 'Refusal to supply a new customer', pp 697–711.

[292] See 'The application of the Commission's *Vertical guidelines* to agency agreements', pp 621–623 above.

[293] On Article 4 generally see 'Article 4: hard-core restrictions', pp 663–669 below.

[294] On Article 5 generally see 'Article 5: obligations in vertical agreements that are not exempt', pp 669–670 below.

[295] *Vertical guidelines*, paras 28 and 29.   [296] See ch 15, 'Purchasing Agreements', pp 603–605.

[297] Articles 1(2) and 8 deal of Regulation 330/2010 respectively with connected undertakings and the calculation of turnover.

[298] The final sentence of para 29 of the *Guidelines* states that where only a limited number of the members of the association have a turnover exceeding €50 million and where those members together represent less than 15 per cent of the aggregate turnover of all the members, 'the assessment under Article 101 will normally not be affected'; this presumably refers to the *individual* assessment under Article 101; if this is intended to mean that the block exemption would still be applicable, it does not provide any legal justification for this view.

[299] It presumably follows that if the association purchases for its own use, as for example a group of National Health Service hospitals in the UK, Article 2(2) would not be applicable since the group does not purchase in order to *sell* to final consumers.

or decisions of the association itself[300]. Paragraph 30 of the *Guidelines* explains that the lawfulness of a vertical agreement entered into by an association of retailers under Article 2(2) can be determined only after it has been concluded that any underlying horizontal agreement between the members of the association is itself lawful.

(xii) Article 2(3): ancillary provisions in relation to intellectual property rights[301]

Article 2(3) deals with the important question of the extent to which vertical agreements which contain provisions on intellectual property rights can benefit from Regulation 330/2010. The first sentence of Article 2(3) provides that the exemption shall apply to vertical agreements:

> containing provisions which relate to the assignment to the buyer or use by the buyer of intellectual property rights[302], provided that those provisions do not constitute the primary object of such agreements and are directly related to the use, sale or resale of goods or services by the buyer or its customers.

Essentially the policy is that Regulation 330/2010 will apply where any provisions relating to intellectual property rights are ancillary to the main purpose of the vertical agreement[303]; although the Regulation itself does not use the term, it is helpful to call such provisions 'IPR provisions'. The policy of Article 2(3) is simple to state; however the actual application of Article 2(3) is not without its difficulties. A number of points should be noted: the five headings (xiii–xvii) used below are based upon paragraph 31 of the Commission's *Guidelines*.

(xiii) Article 2(3) is applicable only where there is a vertical agreement

First, for Article 2(3) to apply to the IPR provisions – that is to say if they are to benefit from block exemption – there must be a vertical agreement; Article 1(1)(a) defines this as an agreement relating to the conditions under which the parties may purchase, sell or resell goods or services. It follows that 'pure' licences – for example of know-how or of a trade mark – would not be covered, since they would not relate to the conditions under which the parties purchase, sell or resell goods or services: rather, they would authorise the use of the know-how or of the trade mark. Pure know-how licences, however, would be able to benefit from the block exemption under Regulation 772/2004[304] on technology transfer agreements[305]. Paragraph 33 of the *Guidelines* gives five examples of agreements that would not benefit from block exemption:

- the provision of a recipe for the production of a drink under licence
- the production and distribution of copies from a mould or master copy
- a pure licence of a trade mark or sign for the purposes of merchandising

---

[300] On such agreements see ch 15, 'Purchasing Agreements', pp 603–605.

[301] *Vertical guidelines*, paras 31–45.

[302] Intellectual property rights are defined in Article 1(1)(f) to include 'industrial property rights, know-how, copyright and neighbouring rights'; know-how is defined in Article 1(1)(g) as 'a package of non-patented practical information, resulting from experience and testing by the supplier, which is secret, substantial and identified'.

[303] Although the term 'ancillary' does not feature in Article 2(3) itself, recital 3 states that the Regulation 'includes vertical agreements containing ancillary provisions on the assignment or use of intellectual property rights'.

[304] OJ [2004] L 123/11.

[305] See ch 19, 'Technology Transfer Agreements: Regulation 772/2004', pp 781–791.

- sponsorship contracts[306]
- copyright licensing such as broadcasting contracts concerning the right to record and/or the right to broadcast an event[307].

(xiv) The IPR provisions must be for the use of the buyer

Secondly, Article 2(3) applies only where the supplier transfers IPRs to the buyer; it does not apply where the buyer transfers IPRs to the supplier. It follows that a sub-contracting agreement, whereby one undertaking asks another to manufacture goods on its behalf, often with the use of its IPRs, would not be covered by the block exemption[308], since the IPRs are supplied by the buyer to the supplier, rather than the other way around. However many sub-contracting agreements do not infringe Article 101(1) at all, so that block exemption is unnecessary[309]; and the *Vertical guidelines* state that, where the buyer simply provides specifications to the supplier as to the goods or services to be supplied, the block exemption remains applicable[310]: in that case there are no IPR provisions, and Article 2(3) is irrelevant.

(xv) The IPR provisions must not be the object of the agreement

Thirdly, for Article 2(3) to apply the IPR provisions must not be the 'primary' object of the agreement: in the language of the *Guidelines*, '[t]he primary object must be the purchase, sale or resale of goods or services and the IPR provisions must serve the implementation of the vertical agreement'[311].

(xvi) The IPR provisions must be directly related to the use, sale or resale of goods or services by the buyer or its customers

A trade mark licence to a distributor is generally necessary for and ancillary to the distribution of goods or services, so that an exclusive licence would benefit from the block exemption, provided that it satisfies the other rules in the Regulation[312]. A sale of hard copies of software, where the reseller does not acquire a licence to any rights over the software, is regarded as an agreement for the supply of goods for resale[313]. Paragraphs 43 to 45 of the *Vertical guidelines* examine the application of the block exemption to franchise agreements. The Commission's view is that Regulation 330/2010 is capable in principle of application to franchise agreements, other than industrial franchise agreements: the latter would be subject, if at all, to Regulation 772/2004 on technology transfer agreements[314]. Paragraph 44 of the *Guidelines* states that most franchise agreements would be covered by Article 2(3), since the IPR provisions in them are directly related to the use,

---

[306] On sponsorship contracts see *Danish Tennis Federation Commission* OJ [1996] C 138/6, [1996] 4 CMLR 885, Commission's XXVIIIth *Report on Competition Policy* (1998), p 160 (comfort letter issued).

[307] See *Telenor/Canal+/Canal Digital* Commission decision of 29 December 2003, a case concerning the licensing of premium content channels, protected by copyright, to a pay-TV platform, where the Commission decided that Regulation 2790/99 was not applicable: see in particular para 196 of the Commission's decision.

[308] *Vertical guidelines*, para 34.

[309] Ibid, para 22 and the Commission's *Notice on Sub-contracting Agreements* OJ [1979] C 1/2, discussed at 'Sub-Contracting Agreements', pp 676–677 below.

[310] *Vertical guidelines*, para 34.   [311] Ibid, para 35.   [312] Ibid, para 39.

[313] Ibid, para 41; this would cover the sale of software subject to a 'shrink-wrap' licence, the conditions in which the end user is deemed to accept by opening the package.

[314] The Commission notes the difference between industrial franchise and non-industrial franchise agreements at para 43 of the *Vertical guidelines*; see ch 19, 'Technology Transfer Agreements: Regulation 772/2004', pp 781–791.

sale or resale of goods or services by the franchisee. It adds that, where a franchise agreement 'only or primarily concerns licensing of IPRs', it would not be covered by the block exemption; however the Commission will normally analyse such an agreement by analogy to the principles contained in the Regulation and *Guidelines*.

Where the franchisor franchises a business method, the franchisor must calculate its market share on the market where the business method is to be exploited for the purpose of the market share cap in Article 3 (see below)[315].

Paragraph 45 of the *Vertical guidelines* sets out a series of typical IPR-related obligations that are found in franchise agreements and which, if restrictive of competition, would be regarded as ancillary and therefore would benefit from block exemption. These are obligations on the franchisee:

(a) not to engage, directly or indirectly, in any similar business

(b) not to acquire financial interests in competing undertakings

(c) not to disclose secret know-how to third parties

(d) to grant a non-exclusive licence to the franchisor of know-how obtained from exploitation of the franchise

(e) to assist the franchisor in action to protect the IPRs

(f) only to use the franchisor's know-how for the purpose of the franchise

(g) not to assign the rights and obligations under the franchise agreement without the consent of the franchisor.

(xvii) The IPR provisions must not have an illegitimate object or effect[316]

The final sentence of Article 2(3) provides that the IPR provisions will be exempt only in so far as they 'do not contain restrictions of competition having the same object or effect as vertical restraints which are not exempted under this Regulation'. Thus it is not possible to avoid the provisions of Articles 4 and 5 of the Regulation (see below) by attaching the vertical restraints which they seek to prevent to the IPR provisions rather than to the vertical agreement itself.

Article 2(3) should also be understood in conjunction with Article 2(5), which prevents the application of the Regulation where another block exemption is applicable (below).

(xviii) Article 2(4): agreements between competing undertakings[317]

Article 2(4) provides that the block exemption does not apply to vertical agreements entered into between competing undertakings as defined in Article 1(1)(c) of the Regulation; this applies to agreements at any level of the market: for example the undertakings may be competing as manufacturers, wholesalers or as retailers. Article 1(1)(c) provides that undertakings compete where they are active on the same relevant market (actual competitors) and where, in the absence of the vertical agreement, they would realistically be able to enter and compete on the market 'within a short period of time' in response to a small but permanent increase in relative prices[318] (potential competitors). Paragraph 27 of the *Vertical guidelines* says that a 'short time' would normally not be longer than a year. The *Guidelines* also state that, where a distributor provides specifications to a manufacturer to produce particular

---

[315] *Vertical guidelines*, para 92.

[316] Ibid, para 37.

[317] Ibid, paras 27–28.

[318] The *Guidelines* do not state that the potential suppliers' response must have been triggered by a price rise by 'competing undertakings', but presumably this is what the spirit of Article 1(1)(c) is envisaging.

goods under the distributor's brand name, it is not to be considered a manufacturer of such own-brand goods.

Non-reciprocal vertical agreements between competing undertakings are permitted subject to conditions. Article 2(4) allows a non-reciprocal vertical agreement between competing undertakings where[319]:

- the supplier is a manufacturer and a distributor of goods, whilst the buyer is a distributor not manufacturing goods competing with the contract goods[320]. In this case the manufacturer conducts its own distribution, but also appoints other distributors which are, according to the definition in Article 1(1)(c), 'competing undertakings'. Paragraph 28 of the *Guidelines* describes this phenomenon as 'dual distribution' or

- the supplier is a provider of services at several levels of trade, whilst the buyer does not provide competing services at the level of trade where it purchases the contract services. This is the analogue of the previous situation, adjusted for the purposes of an agreement in the services sector.

Where a vertical agreement between competitors falls outside Article 2(4), it should be considered under the Commission's *Guidelines on Horizontal Cooperation Agreements*[321].

(xix) Article 2(5): agreements within the scope of another block exemption[322]

Article 2(5) of the Regulation provides that 'This Regulation shall not apply to vertical agreements *the subject matter of which* falls within the scope of any other block exemption regulation, unless otherwise provided for in such a regulation' (emphasis added). The italicised words are important: Article 2(5) does not say that the Regulation shall not apply to an agreement which is exempt under another regulation; rather, it says that it does not apply to agreements which, generically, are of a kind covered by another regulation. It follows that vertical agreements covered by the block exemptions for technology transfer agreements[323], the distribution of motor vehicles[324], R&D agreements[325] and specialisation agreements[326] would not be covered by Regulation 330/2010 except to the extent provided for in those specific Regulations. If an agreement fails to satisfy the criteria for exemption in any of these Regulations, Article 2(5) prevents the agreement from being exempted by Regulation 330/2010. Article 2(5) would also prevent Regulation 330/2010 from applying to any agreement within the scope of any future block exemption[327].

---

[319] Article 2(4)(a) of Regulation 2790/99 contained a further exception to the non-application of the block exemption to vertical agreements between competing undertakings, namely the situation where the buyer has a total annual turnover not exceeding €100 million; this was removed from Regulation 330/2010 as a company with a turnover of €100 million or less may be the main local or national producer, and thus a major competitor of the seller, in certain markets.

[320] At para 27 of the *Vertical guidelines* the Commission states that an 'own-brand' retailer would not be treated as a manufacturer for this purpose.

[321] The Commission specifically makes this point at para 12 of its *Guidelines on Horizontal Cooperation Agreements* OJ [2011] C 11/1; see ch 15, 'Purpose and scope of the *Guidelines on Horizontal Cooperation Agreements*', pp 588–590.

[322] *Vertical guidelines*, para 45.

[323] Regulation 772/2004, OJ [2004] L 123/11; see ch 19, 'Technology Transfer Agreements: Regulation 772/2004', pp 781–791.

[324] Regulation 461/2010, OJ [2010] L 129/52; see 'Regulation 461/2010 on Motor Vehicle Distribution', pp 674–676 below.

[325] Regulation 1217/2010, OJ [2010] L 335/36: see ch 15, 'The block exemption for research and development agreements: Regulation 1217/2020', pp 595–599.

[326] Regulation 1218/2010, OJ [2010] L 335/43; see ch 15, 'The block exemption for specialisation agreements: Regulation 1218/2010', pp 601–603.

[327] The Commission specifically says this in para 46 of the *Vertical guidelines*.

(E) Article 3: the market share cap[328]

(i) Why a market share test?

One of the key features of Regulation 2790/99 was the inclusion of a market share cap for determining which agreements would benefit from block exemption: at the time of the adoption of that Regulation concern was expressed as to the uncertainty that this would introduce. However the inclusion in the block exemption regulations of market share thresholds as proxies for the non-existence of market power is no longer controversial. If market power is at the heart of sensible analysis of such agreements (whether under Article 101(1) or 101(3)), the Commission can hardly be criticised for using a principled, economics-based approach in order to escape from the discredited and formalistic Regulations of the past. The inclusion of market share thresholds in Regulation 330/2010 was therefore not, in itself, controversial; what did cause considerable debate, however, was the Commission's decision to require, in all cases, that the buyer's as well as the supplier's market share should be below 30 per cent.

Recitals 8 and 9 of the Regulation discuss market share. Recital 8 states that it can be presumed that vertical agreements that do not contain hard-core restrictions of the kind listed in Article 4 will lead to an improvement in the production or distribution of products and allow consumers a fair share of the resulting benefits, provided that the parties' market shares do not exceed the prescribed threshold of 30 per cent: in other words that such agreements will satisfy Article 101(3). Recital 9 goes on to make two different, and important, points: first, that no such presumption can be made where either of the parties' market shares exceed 30 per cent; but, secondly, that there is no presumption that, where the thresholds are exceeded, an agreement infringes Article 101(1) or that it will fail to satisfy Article 101(3)[329]. Where the thresholds are exceeded an agreement requires individual analysis.

(ii) What market share?

Of course it is possible to argue about what the market share cap should be. The predecessor to Regulation 330/2010 set the fairly generous market share threshold of 30 per cent[330]: thousands, if not hundreds of thousands, of agreements will have benefited from the safe harbour provided by this figure. However some commentators would have liked the Commission in the new Regulation to raise the market share threshold, perhaps to 40 per cent, but the Commission resisted calls to do so. A market share cap of 40 per cent would have come close to saying that only vertical restraints, other than the hard-core restrictions set out in Article 4, imposed by dominant undertakings are problematic: perhaps it is not surprising that the Commission was unwilling to diminish the role of Article 101 to this extent.

In *JCB* the Commission held that block exemption was unavailable to JCB's distribution agreements since its market share was in the region of 40 to 45 per cent[331]. The 30 per cent cap prevented the application of the block exemption in *Telenor/Canal+/Canal Digital*[332].

---

[328] Section V of the *Vertical guidelines* deals with market definition and market share calculation issues. See generally ch 1, 'Market definition', pp 27–42.

[329] See similarly paras 23 and 96 of the *Guidelines*.

[330] See Article 3 of Regulation 2790/99, OJ [1991] L 336/21.

[331] OJ [2002] L 69/1, [2002] 4 CMLR 1458, para 198; the Commission also considered that block exemption was unavailable as a result of the presence of hard-core restrictions in the agreements: ibid, para 199; on hard-core restrictions see 'Article 4: hard-core restrictions', pp 663–669 below.

[332] Commission decision of 29 December 2003, para 196.

In the case of Interbrew's single branding agreements for bars and cafés in Belgium the Commission concluded that, notwithstanding Interbrew's market share of around 56 per cent, the agreements did not appreciably restrict competition once the extent of the exclusivity had been limited only to pils lager[333].

(iii) Whose market share?

Article 3(1) of Regulation 330/2010 requires that the market share of each of the parties must not exceed 30 per cent. Article 3(1) provides that the block exemption shall apply:

> on condition that the market share held by the supplier does not exceed 30% of the relevant market on which it sells the contract goods or services and the market share held by the buyer does not exceed 30% of the relevant market on which it purchases the contract goods or services.

Regulation 2790/99, the predecessor to Regulation 330/2010, applied only to vertical agreements that did not exceed a supplier's market share cap; apart from the case of an exclusive supply obligation[334], the buyer's market share was irrelevant under the old regime. When it was proposed in 2009, the extension of the market share cap to that of the buyer in all cases was controversial. Concerns were expressed at the complexity that might be involved in its application[335], in particular because of the inherent difficulty in assessing how the relevant market should be defined. However, a buyer's market share cap was included in Regulation 330/2010 for two reasons in particular. First, the Commission took into account the increase in large distributors' market power since the adoption of Regulation 2790/99[336]. Secondly, the new rule on the buyer's market share recognises that vertical restraints are not necessarily imposed by a supplier on a buyer: it is also possible that the restraint is 'buyer-led'[337]; the inclusion in the *Guidelines* of sections on up-front access payments and category management agreements can also be attributed to this fact.

Article 3(1) states that the relevant market share is that of the buyer on the market 'on which it purchases the contract goods or services'; block exemption does not depend on the (potentially) much larger number of market(s) in which a distributor sells or resells products[338]. The market on which a buyer buys will usually be wider than the market(s) on which it sells: for example it may procure internationally but sell nationally; or purchase nationally and sell regionally or locally[339]. However there is likely to be some relationship between the buyer's power in the purchasing and the selling markets, and the test adopted in Regulation 330/2010 may be seen as a compromise between the avoidance of undue complexity on the one hand and the desire of the Commission not to ignore the power of buyers on the other.

---

[333] Commission Press Release IP/03/545, 15 April 2003.

[334] See Article 3(2) of Regulation 2790/99 in conjunction with Article 1(c).

[335] For criticism of the new downstream threshold see RBB Economics 'Comments on Proposed Changes to EC Commission Guidelines on Vertical Restraints', September 2009, available at www.ec.europa.eu/competition/index_en.html.

[336] See speech by Commissioner Almunia, SPEECH/10/172, 20 April 2010; for further reading on the anti-competitive effects of buyer power see the OECD's Policy Roundtable *Monopsony and Buyer Power* (2008), available at www.oecd.org and the OFT Economic Discussion Paper (OFT 863) *The competitive effects of buyer groups* (RBB Economics, January 2007) and the literature there cited.

[337] On these vertical restraints see 'Up-front access payments' and 'Category management agreements', pp 646–647 above.

[338] The position would have been much more complex if the Commission had maintained the position it had adopted in its draft Regulation of 28 July 2009, which did depend on the buyer's market share in the market(s) in which it sold or resold the products acquired under the agreement.

[339] *Vertical guidelines*, para 89.

The application of the market share cap to include that of the buyer in all cases gives rise to obvious compliance issues for the parties to vertical agreements. The supplier will need to ask each buyer for information about, and assurances as to, its market share in its purchasing markets; obviously these may fluctuate over time; their veracity will need to be checked; the market share figure may be exceeded in the case of some buyers but not others; and different agreements may need to be used in the case of those that exceed the market share from those of others. Furthermore the supplier will need to negotiate with each of its buyers individually in order to avoid any possibility of being accused of participating in a 'hub and spoke' conspiracy of the kind that various competition authorities have been looking at in recent years[340].

Article 3(2) of Regulation 330/2010 deals with the position where there is a multipartite agreement. Article 3(2) provides that, where an undertaking that is party to an agreement both buys and sells the contract goods or services, it must respect both the seller's and the buyer's market share threshold. Paragraph 90 of the *Guidelines* gives the obvious example of an agreement between a manufacturer, a wholesaler and a retailer, where the wholesaler would have to have a market share of 30 per cent or less both in its buying and selling markets.

(iv) The vertical guidelines

Paragraph 23 of the *Guidelines* explains that competition concerns will arise for most vertical restraints only if there is market power at the level of the supplier or the buyer or at both levels. It then rehearses the terms of Article 3(1). Paragraphs 72 and 73 of the *Guidelines* deal with the situation where a supplier uses the same distribution agreement to distribute a portfolio of goods and/or services, and has a market share of more than 30 per cent for some of those products and less than 30 per cent for others: the Commission states that the block exemption will not apply in the former case but would in the latter.

Section V of the *Guidelines* (paragraphs 86 to 95) discusses various issues concerning market definition and market share calculation. Paragraph 89 examines questions concerning the relevant product market; the Commission states that in most cases the relevant market will be defined by examining the market from the buyer's perspective. Paragraph 90 deals with the position where there are more than two parties to the agreement[341]. Paragraph 91 discusses the position of original equipment manufacturer ('OEM') suppliers; and paragraph 92 deals with market shares in the context of franchising agreements. Paragraphs 93 to 95 deal specifically with the calculation of market shares under the Regulation.

(v) Article 6

It is worth noting in passing that the Regulation has a further market share test in Article 6, albeit one that will have only rare application. This provides that the Commission may disapply the block exemption where 50 per cent of a relevant market is covered by a network of similar vertical agreements. This is dealt with below[342].

---

[340] See eg, in the UK, *Argos Ltd v OFT* (the *Toys and Games* appeal) and *JJB Sports plc v OFT* (the *Football Shirts* appeal), [2006] EWCA Civ 1318, [2006] UKCLR 1135.

[341] See 'The exempted agreement may be multilateral', p 653

[342] See 'Article 6: disapplication of the block exemption by Commission Regulation', pp 671–672.

(F) **Article 4: hard-core restrictions**[343]

Recital 10 of the Regulation states that vertical agreements 'containing certain types of severe restrictions of competition such as minimum and fixed resale-prices, as well as certain types of territorial protection, should be excluded from the benefit of the block exemption established by this Regulation irrespective of the market share of the undertakings concerned'. Article 4 contains the list of 'hard-core' restrictions which lead to the exclusion of the entire vertical agreement – not just the provision in question – from the block exemption[344]. Article 4 is to be contrasted with Article 5, which denies block exemption to certain specific obligations, but which does not deprive the rest of the agreement of the benefit of the block exemption[345]. The Commission states specifically at paragraph 70 of the *Guidelines* that there is no severability for hard-core restrictions.

Each of the hard-core restrictions in Article 4 relates to a restriction of intra-brand competition[346], although the Commission's view is that in some cases restrictions of intra-brand competition can affect inter-brand competition by softening competition and/or facilitating collusion[347]. Paragraph 47 of the *Guidelines* states that an agreement that contains a hard-core restriction of the kind listed in Article 4 'is presumed to fall within Article 101(1)'. This is a reference to agreements that, in the terms of Article 101 TFEU, have the 'object' of restricting competition: paragraphs 23 and 96 of the *Guidelines* specifically refer to hard-core restrictions as restrictions of competition by object. Even hard-core restrictions might, as a matter of law, fall outside Article 101(1) where they could not have an appreciable effect on competition or on inter-state trade[348]. However the Commission's *Notice on Agreements of Minor Importance*[349] provides that, even below the 15 per cent market share threshold, it cannot be ruled out that vertical agreements that have as their object or effect to fix resale prices or to confer absolute territorial protection on the undertakings or third undertakings might infringe Article 101(1)[350]. Separately, paragraphs 60 to 64 of the *Vertical guidelines* acknowledge that there are situations in which hard-core restrictions may be objectively necessary for an agreement of a particular type and therefore fall outside Article 101(1) altogether, or fulfil the conditions of Article 101(3)[351]. Paragraph 47 of the *Guidelines* states that it is presumed that agreements containing hard-core restrictions are unlikely to satisfy Article 101(3), but continues that undertakings may be able to demonstrate pro-competitive effects in a particular case, and refers to paragraphs 106 to 109 of the *Guidelines* which discuss possible efficiencies related to vertical restraints generally and to Section VI.2.10 (paragraphs 223 to 229) which consider arguments against, but also possible justifications for, resale price maintenance specifically.

---

[343] See *Vertical guidelines*, paras 47–59.　　　[344] Ibid, para 47.

[345] See 'Article 5: obligations in vertical agreements that are not exempt', pp 669–670 below.

[346] Restrictions of inter-brand competition, or situations in which inter-brand competition is weak, are specifically dealt with in other parts of the Regulation, for example Article 2(4); Article 3; Article 5; and the provisions for withdrawal of the block exemption, as to which see 'Withdrawal of the block exemption by the Commission or by a Member State', p 671 below.

[347] For an example of a situation where the Commission was concerned that 'most-favoured nation' clauses might be causing price parallelism see its investigations of Hollywood studios, Commission Press Release IP/04/1314, 26 October 2004 and Commission Press Release IP/11/257, 4 March 2011.

[348] Case 5/69 *Völk v Vervaecke* [1969] ECR 295, [1969] CMLR 273; Case C-306/96 *Javico v Yves Saint Laurent* [1998] ECR I-1983, [1998] 5 CMLR 172; see ch 3, 'The *De Minimis* Doctrine', pp 140–144; Case C-506/07 *Lubricarga v Petrogal Española* [2009] ECR I-134.

[349] OJ [2001] C 368/13, para 11.　　　[350] See similarly *Vertical guidelines*, para 10.

[351] See 'Export bans falling outside Article 101(1) or satisfying Article 101(3)', pp 636–637 above.

Article 4 provides that block exemption will not be available to agreements which 'directly or indirectly, in isolation or in combination with other factors under the control of the parties, have as their object' the matters dealt with below, such as resale price maintenance and excessive territorial protection. Article 4 applies only according to the object, and *not* the effect, of an agreement. The word 'object' in Article 4 of the Regulation, and in Article 101(1) of the Treaty, does not refer to the subjective intention of the parties; rather to the aim of the agreement judged by objective standards[352]. The scope of the exclusion of the block exemption is nonetheless quite extensive as it will prevent the block exemption from applying where the agreement 'directly or indirectly, in isolation or in combination with other factors' has one of the forbidden objects.

(i) Article 4(a): resale price maintenance[353]

Block exemption will not be available where the object of the agreement is:

(a) the restriction of the buyer's ability to determine its sale price, without prejudice to the possibility of the supplier imposing a maximum sale price or recommending a sale price, provided that they do not amount to a fixed or minimum sale price as a result of pressure from, or incentives offered by, any of the parties.

This formulation explicitly recognises that the imposition of maximum[354] resale prices and the recommendation[355] of prices is permitted; this, however, is subject to the proviso that follows, which itself must be read in conjunction with the words 'directly or indirectly' in the opening part of Article 4. Paragraph 48 of the *Vertical guidelines* picks up on the idea that the agreement may have the direct *or indirect* object of resale price maintenance. A contractual restriction establishing a minimum price would be a simple example of an agreement the *direct* object of which is to fix prices. Paragraph 48 gives examples of price maintenance through indirect means:

fixing the distribution margin, fixing the maximum level of discount the distributor can grant from a prescribed price level, making the grant of rebates or reimbursement of promotional costs by the supplier subject to the observance of a given price level, linking the prescribed resale price to the resale prices of competitors, threats, intimidation, warnings, penalties, delay or suspension of deliveries or contract terminations in relation to the observance of a given price level.

Measures taken to identify price-cutting distributors might also amount to 'indirect pressure' to fix prices; paragraph 48 suggests that printing a recommended resale price or an obligation to apply a most favoured customer clause would reduce the incentive to cut price and so could be within the mischief of Article 4. The paragraph acknowledges that the use of a particular 'supportive' measure or the recommendation of prices is not, in itself, a hard-core restriction. In the case of domestic litigation, it is for the national court to determine, on the basis of the evidence before it, whether a resale price is recommended, fixed or a minimum one[356].

---

[352] See ch 3, 'Object', pp 118–120.

[353] See *Guidelines*, paras 48 and 49 and 'Recommended and maximum resale prices', p 649 above.

[354] The Court of Justice has never ruled on the imposition of maximum prices; for the position in the US see *State Oil Co v Khan* 522 US 3 (1997), see ch 16 n 251, p 638 above.

[355] The Court of Justice held in Case 161/84 *Pronuptia de Paris v Pronuptia de Paris Irmgard Schillgalis* [1986] ECR 353, [1986] 1 CMLR 414 that the recommendation of prices would not, in itself, infringe Article 101(1): see para 25.

[356] See Case C-260/07 *Pedro IV Servicios SL v Total España SA* [2009] ECR I-2437, [2009] 5 CMLR 1291, paras 79 and 80, citing Case C-279/06 *CEPSA Estaciones de Servicio SA v LV Tobar e Hijos SL* [2008] ECR I-6681, [2008] 5 CMLR 1327, paras 67, 70 and 71.

In the case of agency agreements Article 101(1) would normally not be applicable[357]. However where such an agreement falls within Article 101(1), paragraph 49 of the *Guidelines* states that a restriction on the agent preventing or restricting the sharing of commission with its customers, whether fixed or variable, would amount to a hard-core restriction. The agent should be left free to lower the effective price paid by the customer without reducing the income for the principal[358].

(ii) Article 4(b): territorial and customer restrictions[359]

This important provision deals with the extent to which it is possible to grant territorial or customer exclusivity. The opening words of Article 4(b) provide that the block exemption will not be available where the object of the agreement is:

> the restriction of the territory into which, or of the customers to whom, a buyer party to the agreement, without prejudice to a restriction on its place of establishment, may sell the contract goods or services.

Several points should be noted about Article 4(b). First, subject to Article 4(e) of the Regulation (below), Article 4(b) is concerned only with restrictions on the *buyer's* right to sell, and not to restrictions on the supplier's sales, which are not to be treated as hard-core. Secondly, paragraph 50 of the *Guidelines* explains that the expression 'without prejudice to a restriction on its place of establishment' in Article 4(b) means that the benefit of the block exemption will not be lost if it is agreed that the buyer will restrict its distribution outlet(s) and warehouse(s) to a particular address, place or territory. The same expression recurs in Article 4(c) in the context of selective distribution (below). Thirdly, paragraph 50 of the *Guidelines* picks up on the 'direct/indirect object' dichotomy in the opening words of Article 4. Indirect measures to restrict the buyer could include:

> refusal or reduction of bonuses or discounts, termination of supply, reduction of supplied volumes or limitation of supplied volumes to the demand within the allocated territory or customer group, threat of contract termination, requiring a higher price for products to be exported, limiting the proportion of sales that can be exported or profit pass-over obligations.

The withholding of a guarantee service could also amount to indirect means. These practices would be more likely to be considered indirect measures to restrict the buyer's freedom when operated in conjunction with a monitoring system for detecting parallel trade. Clearly this paragraph of the *Vertical guidelines* is based on the Commission's decisional practice, upheld by the EU Courts, over many years[360].

Paragraph 50 of the Guidelines specifically points out that an obligation on the reseller relating to the display of the supplier's brand names is not regarded as hard-core under Article 4(b)[361].

Four exceptions to the basic prohibition in Article 4(b) are set out; the first is particularly important, since it deals with the distinction between active and passive sales.

---

[357] See 'Commercial Agents', pp 621–623 above.

[358] See Case 311/85 *Vereniging van Vlaamse Reisbureaus v Sociale Dienst van de Plaatselijke en Gewestelijke Overheidsdiensten* [1987] ECR 3801, [1989] 4 CMLR 213, para 24.

[359] *Vertical guidelines*, paras 49–52.

[360] See 'Direct and indirect export bans', pp 632–637 above.

[361] This is presumably based on the judgment of the Court of Justice in Case 161/84 *Pronuptia de Paris v Pronuptia de Paris Irmgard Schillgalis* [1986] ECR 353, [1986] 1 CMLR 414.

Exception 1: it is permissible to have a restriction:

> of active sales into the exclusive territory or to an exclusive customer group reserved to the supplier or allocated by the supplier to another buyer, where such a restriction does not limit sales by the customers of the buyer.

The first point to note here is that, although a restriction of active sales to other territories or customers is permitted, there must remain the possibility of passive sales to them. This is not stated specifically in the Regulation; it is stated explicitly, however, in paragraph 51 of the *Vertical guidelines*. The second point is that the restriction must be on active sales into the territory or customer group 'reserved to the supplier or allocated by the supplier to another buyer'. Paragraph 51 explains that this means that the buyer must be protected against sales by all other buyers of the supplier within the EU, 'irrespective of sales by the supplier'. It follows that protection against active selling will not be lost because a vertical agreement does not impose a restriction on the supplier, but only on its buyers; to put the point another way, *sole* distributorships (which leave the supplier free to supply in the distributor's territory) can benefit from block exemption as well as *exclusive* distributorships, where the supplier agrees that it will not supply to customers in the latter's territory. It is apparently not possible to restrict active sales into an area reserved to a licensee of know-how or of a patent, although no explanation is given of why this should be so. Thirdly, exclusive distribution may be combined with exclusive customer allocation under Article 4(b), provided that passive selling is not restricted.

Paragraph 51 of the *Guidelines* deals with the distinction between active and passive sales and differs in certain respects from its predecessor. Active selling includes establishing a warehouse or distribution outlet in another's exclusive territory, approaching individual customers by sending unsolicited emails, and advertising to a specific customer group or customers in a particular territory through advertisements on the Internet. It adds that advertisement or promotion that is attractive for the buyer only if it reaches a specific group of customers or customers in a specific territory is active selling.

As to passive selling, paragraph 51 explains that this means responding to unsolicited requests from individual customers, including delivery of goods or services to such customers. 'General advertising or promotion' amounts to passive selling; paragraph 51 states that advertising that reaches customers in other territories or customer groups will be regarded as general if it would make sense for the buyer to invest in that advertising or promotion even if it would only reach customers in its own territory or customer group.

Paragraphs 52 to 54 of the *Guidelines* explain the Commission's thinking in relation to online sales on the Internet; as would be expected, given the exponential growth of e-commerce, they are much richer in detail than their predecessor. Paragraph 52 states that, in principle, every distributor must be allowed to use the Internet to sell products, and that, in general, the use of a website to sell products amounts to passive selling. It follows that, if a customer visits the website of a distributor and if such contact leads to a sale, that is treated as a passive sale. Paragraph 52 adds that offering different language options on the website does not, of itself, change the passive character of such selling. The Commission then gives four examples of hard-core restrictions of passive selling:

- an agreement that a distributor in one territory will prevent customers in another distributor's territory from viewing its website or will automatically re-route customers to other distributors' websites: however it is permissible for a website to have links to those of other distributors and/or the supplier

- an agreement that a distributor will terminate customers' transactions over the Internet if their credit card data reveal an address that is not within the distributor's territory

- an agreement that a distributor will limit its proportion of overall sales made over the Internet. However it is permitted to require that the distributor will sell at least a certain absolute amount (in value or volume) offline so as to ensure an efficient operation of its 'brick and mortar' shop, that is to say, its physical point of sale: the absolute amount may be the same for all distributors, or may be determined individually for each buyer on the basis of objective criteria

- an agreement that the distributor will pay a higher price for products intended to be resold by the distributor online rather than offline. However paragraph 64 of the *Guidelines* acknowledges that there may be circumstances in which dual pricing, though treated as hard-core under Article 4(b), may satisfy Article 101(3) on an individual basis. Such circumstances may be present where sales online lead to substantially higher costs for the supplier than offline sales.

Paragraph 53 of the *Guidelines* discusses the circumstances in which Internet sales might be regarded as active rather than passive, with the result that it would be permissible under the block exemption to restrict them. Advertising specifically addressed to certain customers would be considered to be active, as would paying a search engine or online advertisement provider to have advertisements displayed specifically to users in a particular territory. Paragraph 54 explains that the supplier may impose quality standards for the use of the Internet site to resell its goods, just as the supplier may do for selling in shops or by catalogue. In particular the supplier may require that its distributors have one or more brick and mortar shops or showrooms as a condition for becoming a member of the distribution system.

In *Yamaha*[362] the Commission considered that a restriction on Internet selling infringed Article 101(1)[363] and was not covered by the block exemption[364]. In *Pierre Fabre Dermo-Cosmétique*[365] the Court of Justice held that a general and absolute prohibition of online selling imposed on members of a selective distribution system is a 'hard-core' restriction under Article 4(c)[366].

Exception 2: it is permissible to have a restriction of sales – both active and passive – to end users by a buyer operating at the wholesale level of trade. Paragraph 55 of the *Guidelines* explains that this means that the supplier can keep the wholesale and retail levels of the market separate, with the result that buyers of its goods can specialise in their particular level of activity in the market; it adds that the supplier may, if it wishes, permit wholesalers to sell to some end users, for example large customers, though not to others.

Exception 3: it is permissible to have a restriction on sales – both active and passive – by members of a selective distribution system to unauthorised distributors in any territory where the system is currently operated or where the supplier does not yet sell the contract products[367]. A selective distribution system is defined in Article 1(1)(e) to mean a system where the supplier agrees to supply the contract goods or services only to distributors selected on the basis of specified criteria and those distributors agree not to sell to unauthorised distributors. It should be noted that this definition of a selective distribution system in the Regulation is not limited by reference to the nature of the goods or

---

[362] Commission decision of 16 July 2003.

[363] Ibid, paras 107–110.

[364] Ibid, para 171.

[365] Case C-439/09 *Pierre Fabre Dermo-Cosmétique SAS v Président de l'Autorité de la Concurrence and Ministre de l'Économie, de l'Industrie et de l'Emploi* [2011] ECR I-000.

[366] Ibdi, paras 54–59.

[367] This is the way para 55 of the *Vertical guidelines* interprets the phrase 'within the territory reserved by the supplier to operate that system' in Article 4(b)(iii) of the Regulation.

services in question; nor does it specify that the criteria should be qualitative rather than quantitative[368].

Exception 4: it is possible to restrict the buyer of components for use from selling them – both actively and passively – to a customer who would use them to manufacture goods that would compete with those of the supplier. Paragraph 55 of the *Guidelines* explains that the term 'component' includes any intermediate goods and the term 'incorporation' refers to the use of any input to produce the goods.

In *Souris-Topps*[369] the Commission concluded that Topps's distribution arrangements for its Pokémon stickers and cards failed to benefit from the block exemption since they violated Article 4(b) of Regulation 2790/99[370].

(iii) Article 4(c): the restriction of active or passive sales to end users by members of a selective distribution system operating at the retail level of trade[371]

Article 4(c) prevents the application of the block exception when there are restrictions on active or passive sales by selected distributors at the retail level of trade to end users. Paragraph 56 of the *Vertical guidelines* says that the end users may be a professional buyer or a final consumer. However there is a proviso to Article 4(c), which is that the distributor may be prohibited from operating out of an unauthorised place of establishment: without this proviso the distributor would not be complying with the 'specified criteria' that make the system selective, and would effectively be operating as an unauthorised distributor[372]. The Court of Justice has said that the Internet cannot be understood as a 'virtual' place of business in this context; the Internet is a method of selling and marketing goods.[372a]

Paragraph 56 of the *Guidelines* also explains that it is permitted to impose a restriction 'to protect an exclusive distribution system operated elsewhere', referring back to paragraph 51; paragraph 51 addresses Article 4(b)(i) of the Regulation, which permits restrictions on active, but not on passive sales. It presumably follows, therefore, that members of a selective distribution system can be prevented from actively selling to users in a territory or customer group allocated exclusively to another distributor, but cannot be prevented from passive selling. Paragraph 56 goes on to say that dealers within a selective distribution system should be free to sell to all end users, including with the help of the Internet. The Court of Justice agrees with this point.[372b] Paragraph 56 of the Guidelines explains that obligations which dissuade dealers from using the Internet to reach a greater number and variety of consumers by imposing criteria for online sales which are not overall equivalent to the criteria imposed for sales from the brick and mortar shop will be regarded as hard-core. This does not mean that the same criteria must be applied to online and offline sales, but that any differences in those criteria 'should pursue the same objectives and achieve comparable results and that the difference between the criteria must be justified by the different nature of these two distribution modes'.

Paragraph 57 of the *Guidelines* explains that, within the territory in which a selective distribution system is operated, there cannot be exclusive distribution, since this would violate the rule in Article 4(c) that there must be the possibility of both active and passive sales to end users. In other words, selective distribution may be combined with exclusive distribution under the block exemption if active or passive selling is not restricted[373].

---

[368] *Vertical guidelines*, para 176.   [369] Commission decision of 26 May 2004.
[370] Ibid, paras 136–140.   [371] *Vertical guidelines*, paras 56–57.
[372] On this point see para 57 of the *Vertical guidelines*.
[372a] Case C439/09 *Pierre Fabre* [2011] ECR I-000, paras 56–58.   [372b] Ibid, para 59.
[373] This is the way the point is expressed in para 152 of the *Vertical guidelines*.

(iv) Article 4(d): restrictions on cross-supplies within a selective distribution system[374]

Article 4(d) prevents the application of the block exemption where there is a restriction of cross-supplies between distributors within a selective distribution system, including distributors at different level of trade. Thus it is not possible to require a selected retailer to purchase solely from one source: it must be able to buy from any approved distributor[375].

(v) Article 4(e): restrictions on the supplier's ability to supply components to third parties[376]

Article 4(e) designates as hard-core a restriction on the ability of a supplier of components to sell them as spare parts to end users or to repairers or service providers not entrusted by the buyer with the repair or servicing of its goods. End users and independent service providers should be free to obtain spare parts; but the buyer can insist that repairers and service providers within its system should buy the spare parts only from him[377].

(G) Article 5: obligations in vertical agreements that are not exempt[378]

Recital 11 of the Regulation states that certain conditions are attached to the block exemption in order to ensure 'access to or to prevent collusion on the relevant market'. Where an agreement contains an obligation of the kind set out in Article 5, that obligation does not benefit from block exemption: this is true whether the parties' market shares is above or below the market share cap. However, as paragraph 65 of the *Vertical guidelines* states, the block exemption continues to apply to the remaining parts of the vertical agreement if they are 'severable' from the non-exempted obligation[379]. Neither the Regulation nor the *Guidelines* discuss the notion of 'severability' for the purpose of Article 5; whether a contractual obligation is 'severable' for the purpose of Article 101(2) is a matter for the applicable law of the contract[380].

Article 5 contains three exclusions.

(i) Article 5(1)(a): non-compete obligations[381]

Article 5(1)(a) excludes from the block exemption:

> any direct or indirect non-compete obligation, the duration of which is indefinite or exceeds five years.

Article 1(1)(d) provides that 'non-compete obligation' means an obligation not to manufacture, purchase, sell or resell goods or services which compete with the contract goods or services: this is what most people would understand by this expression. However Article 1(1)(d) goes on to provide that the term also includes any obligation on the buyer to purchase from the supplier or from an undertaking designated by the supplier more than 80 per cent[382] of the buyer's total purchases of the contract goods or services and their substitutes on the relevant market, calculated on the basis of the value or, where such is standard industry practice, the volume of its purchases in the preceding calendar year. The Commission's concern is not just that a 100 per cent requirements contract

---

[374] *Vertical guidelines*, para 58.   [375] Ibid.   [376] Ibid, para 59.
[377] Ibid, para 59.   [378] Ibid, paras 65–69.   [379] Ibid, para 71.
[380] See ch 8, 'Severance', pp 322–323.   [381] *Vertical guidelines*, paras 66–67.
[382] A literal interpretation would mean that an obligation to purchase 80 per cent of the buyer's total purchases would not amount to a non-compete obligation, but that an obligation to purchase 81 per cent would, since only the latter applies to 'more than 80 per cent'.

could foreclose access to the market, but that lesser commitments of 'more than 80 per cent' also might do so.

An agreement which is 'tacitly renewable' is treated as having an indefinite duration. Paragraph 66 of the *Vertical guidelines* states that non-compete obligations are block exempted where their duration is limited to five years or less and no obstacles exist that hinder the buyer from effectively terminating at the end of five years should it so wish. Article 5(2) contains a derogation from the rule contained in Article 5(1)(a): longer periods are block exempted when the contract goods or services are sold from land and premises owned by the supplier or leased from third parties: paragraph 67 of the *Guidelines* states that 'artificial ownership constructions' to take advantage of this derogation will not be permitted. These 'longer periods' mean that beer and petrol agreements in 'tied' houses and garages will be permissible for more than five years[383].

There have been many cases in the English courts in which the validity of beer ties has been considered[384].

(ii) Article 5(1)(b): post-term non-compete obligations[385]

Article 5(1)(b) excludes from the block exemption:

> any direct or indirect obligation causing the buyer, after termination of the agreement, not to manufacture, purchase, sell or resell goods or services.

Article 5(3) contains a derogation from Article 5(1)(b) for a post-term ban of not more than one year on sales of competing goods or services from the point of sale at which the buyer operated during the contract period where this is indispensable to protect know-how transferred from the supplier to the buyer. Article 5(3) also provides that Article 5(1)(b) is without prejudice to the possibility of imposing a restriction which is unlimited in time on the use and disclosure of know-how which has not entered the public domain. Know-how for this purpose is defined in Article 1(1)(g) of the Regulation, and must be 'substantial', that is to say significant and useful to the buyer for the use, sale or resale of the contract goods or services[386].

(iii) Article 5(1)(c): competing products in a selective distribution system[387]

Article 5(1)(c) excludes from the block exemption an obligation causing the members of a selective distribution system not to sell the brands of particular competing suppliers. It is permissible, subject to Article 5(1)(a), to require a selective distributor not to handle competing brands in general[388]; however Article 5(1)(c) prevents the exemption from applying where there is a boycott of particular competing suppliers. Paragraph 69 of the *Guidelines* explains that this is to prevent the exclusion of 'a specific competitor or certain specific competitors'.

---

[383] See eg *Whitbread* OJ [1999] L 88/26, [1999] 5 CMLR 118, upheld on appeal Case T-131/99 *Shaw v Commission* [2002] ECR II-2023, [2002] 5 CMLR 81; *Bass* OJ [1999] L 186/1, [1999] 5 CMLR 782, upheld on appeal Case T-231/99 *Joynson v Commission* [2002] ECR II-2085, [2002] 5 CMLR 123; Case T-25/99 *Roberts v Commission* [2001] ECR II-1881, [2001] 5 CMLR 828.

[384] See eg *Holleran v Thwaites* [1989] 2 CMLR 917; *Inntrepreneur Estates (GL) Ltd v Boyes* [1993] 2 EGLR 112; *Little v Courage Ltd* (1994) 70 P & CR 469; *Star Rider Ltd v Inntrepreneur Bub Co* [1998] 1 EGLR 53; *Greenall Management Ltd v Canavan (No 2)* [1998] Eu LR 507; *Gibbs Mew plc v Gemmell* [1998] Eu LR 588; *Trent Taverns Ltd v Sykes* [1998] Eu LR 492; *Passmore v Morland* [1999] Eu LR 501; *Crehan v Courage* [1999] Eu LR 409; the *Crehan* case was referred to the Court of Justice under Article 267 TFEU in Case C-453/99 [2001] ECR I-6297, [2001] 5 CMLR 1058, as to which see ch 8, 'Courage Ltd v Crehan', pp 298–299.

[385] *Vertical guidelines*, para 68.

[386] It is not necessary for the know-how to be 'indispensable' as had been required by Article 1(f) of Regulation 2790/99.

[387] *Vertical guidelines*, para 69.   [388] Ibid.

(H) Withdrawal of the block exemption by the Commission or by a Member State[389]

Regulation 330/2010 does not confer power on the Commission or Member States to withdraw the benefit of the block exemption for vertical agreements in an individual case, since this power is conferred by Article 29(1) and (2) of Regulation 1/2003[390]; it is worth noting in passing that this power has never been used. Recital 15 of Regulation 330/2010 refers to Article 29 of Regulation 1/2003 and states that, in determining whether the benefit of block exemption should be withdrawn pursuant to that provision, the anti-competitive effects that may derive from parallel networks of vertical agreements having similar effects and which significantly restrict access to a relevant market or competition therein are of particular importance: the recital says that selective distribution and non-compete obligations are examples of provisions that might lead to such cumulative effects. The power in Article 29 of Regulation 1/2003 is different from the power in Article 6 of Regulation 330/2010 (below), where the block exemption may be disapplied from all vertical agreements in a particular relevant market; under Article 29 the block exemption is withdrawn 'in a particular case'[391].

(i) Article 29(1) of Regulation 1/2003: withdrawal by the Commission

Article 29(1) provides that the Commission may withdraw the benefit of the block exemption in an individual case where an agreement has effects that are incompatible with Article 101(3). As noted above this could be so where there is a 'cumulative effect' within the market of similar vertical agreements leading to a restriction of competition[392]. Paragraphs 74 to 78 of the *Guidelines* discuss the withdrawal procedure. Paragraph 77 states that the Commission would have the burden of proving that Article 101(1) is infringed and that the agreement does not fulfil the conditions of Article 101(3). Paragraph 77 also states that a withdrawal decision can only have *ex nunc* effect, so that block exemption will persist until the time of the withdrawal.

(ii) Article 29(2) of Regulation 1/2003: withdrawal by a Member State

Article 29(2) confers power on the competition authorities of Member States to withdraw the benefit of the block exemption where agreements to which the Regulation applies have effects incompatible with Article 101(3) 'in the territory of a Member State, or in a part thereof, which has all the characteristics of a distinct geographic market'. Paragraph 78 of the *Guidelines* states that, where the geographic market is wider than a Member State, the Commission has the sole power to withdraw the block exemption. In other cases the power is concurrent.

(I) Article 6: disapplication of the block exemption by Commission Regulation[393]

Recital 16 of the Regulation introduces the idea of the Commission disapplying the block exemption from agreements in a given market. Article 6 provides that the Commission may by regulation declare that, where parallel networks of similar vertical restraints cover more than 50 per cent of a relevant market, the block exemption shall not apply to vertical agreements containing specific restraints in that market. Article 1a of Council Regulation 19/65 provides that such a regulation shall not become applicable earlier than

---

[389] See generally the *Verticle guidelines*, paras 74–78.
[390] See recitals 13 and 14 of Regulation 330/2010 and recital 10 of Regulation 1/2003.
[391] See recital 13 of Regulation 330/2010.
[392] Ibid, recital 15 and *Vertical guidelines*, paras 75–76.   [393] *Vertical guidelines*, paras 79–85.

six months following its adoption: as paragraph 84 of the *Vertical guidelines* says, time may be needed for the undertakings concerned to adapt their agreements. The Commission discusses the 'disapplication' of Regulation 330/2010 in paragraphs 79 to 85 of Part IV of the *Guidelines*. As it explains in paragraph 80, a regulation under Article 8 removes the benefit of the block exemption and restores the full application of Article 101(1) and (3). The Commission would have to decide how to proceed in relation to any individual agreements, and might take a decision in an individual case in order to provide guidance to undertakings in the market generally. The Commission may in some cases have a choice of whether it wishes to proceed under Article 29(1) of Regulation 1/2003 (against a particular undertaking or particular agreements) or under Article 6 of Regulation 330/2010: paragraph 82 of the *Guidelines* says that, in making this choice, the Commission would consider the number of competing undertakings contributing to the cumulative effect or the number of geographic markets within the Union that are affected. Paragraph 85 of the *Guidelines* states that a regulation under Article 8 would not affect the exempted status of the agreements in question prior to its entry into force.

(J) Articles 7 and 8: market share and turnover

Article 7 deals with the calculation of market share[394]. Article 7(a) provides that market share shall be calculated by reference to market sales value; where market sales value data are not available, estimates based on other reliable market information, including sales volumes, may be used. Article 7(b) provides that the market share data should be calculated by reference to the preceding calendar year. Article 7(d) to (g) provide some marginal relief for up to two years where the market share rises above 30 per cent but not beyond 35 per cent.

Article 8 explains how turnover is to be calculated for the purpose of the rules in Article 2(2).

(K) Articles 9 and 10: transitional provisions and entry into force

The Regulation entered into force on 1 June 2010. Transitional relief until 1 June 2011 was provided for agreements already block exempted under Regulation 2790/99. The new Regulation will expire on 31 May 2022.

8. The Application of Article 101(3) to Agreements that do not Satisfy the Block Exemption

Vertical agreements which infringe Article 101(1) and which are ineligible for block exemption under Regulation 330/2010 may nevertheless satisfy the terms of Article 101(3) on an individual basis.

As we have seen Section VI of the *Vertical guidelines* discusses at length the application of Article 101(1) to a series of different types of vertical agreement[395]. Guidance will also be found in Section VI on the application of Article 101(3) to vertical agreements where this is needed in individual cases because the block exemption is inapplicable. The positive effects of vertical restraints are described in paragraph 107[396], and some general

---

[394] See generally the *Vertical guidelines*, paras 93–95.
[395] See 'Vertical Agreements: Article 101(1)', p 628 above.
[396] See 'Vertical agreements: possible benefits to competition', pp 626–628 above.

comments on the application of Article 101(3) will be found at paragraphs 122 to 127[397]. There is a presumption that hard-core restrictions of the kind set out in Article 4 of the block exemption are unlikely to satisfy Article 101(3)[398], although undertakings may be able to demonstrate pro-competitive effects in an individual case[399]; as the General Court stated in *Matra Hachette v Commission*[400] the parties to any kind of agreement – including, therefore, an agreement containing hard-core restrictions – are entitled to defend it under Article 101(3). Individual assessment of agreements is most likely to be necessary where the 30 per cent market share cap is exceeded. What is unclear is whether the Commission will ever adopt a decision saying that it considers that an agreement satisfies Article 101(3): it could do this only by adopting a 'declaration of inapplicability' under Article 10 of Regulation 1/2003, something it has never done; of by providing informal guidance, again which has never occurred[401].

Specific guidance is given on the application of Article 101(3) to single branding agreements at paragraphs 144 to 148. Where a 'client-specific investment' is made, a non-compete obligation of more than five years may be allowed under Article 101(3)[402]: this is consistent with the Commission's past practice where, for example, 15-year exclusive purchase agreements have been allowed where an investment is made in the building of new power stations[403]. Where a non-compete clause is included in an exclusive distribution agreement this may be permitted for the duration of the agreement, even where this is for longer than the five years permitted by the block exemption[404]. In *DSD*[405] the Commission considered that the criteria of Article 101(3) were satisfied in relation to an agreement whereby DSD, an undertaking in Germany which operated a nationwide system for the collection and recovery of sales packaging, agreed to purchase collection and sorting services exclusively from one collector in each designated district: the exclusivity made it possible for the parties to plan the provision of services on a long-term basis and to organise it reliably, and this gave practical effect to a scheme intended to provide a high level of environmental protection[406].

The possible application of Article 101(3) to exclusive distribution agreements is considered at paragraphs 161 to 164 of the *Vertical guidelines*. The Commission states that, in the absence of a foreclosure effect, a non-compete obligation of more than five years may be allowed when it is part of an exclusive distribution agreement[407]. The Commission specifically notes that exclusive distribution is most likely to have efficiency-enhancing effects where the products involved are new, complex or have qualities that are difficult to assess prior to consumption[408]. Paragraph 172 of the *Guidelines* considers the possible improvements in efficiency attributable to exclusive customer allocation. Article 101(3) and selective distribution agreements are considered at paragraphs 185 and 186; exclusive supply is dealt with at paragraphs 200 to 201; up-front access payments at

---

[397] See 'Relevant factors for the assessment under Article 101(3)', pp 631–632 above.

[398] *Vertical guidelines*, para 47.

[399] See the discussion in 'Recommended and maximum resale prices', p 649 above.

[400] Case T-17/93 [1994] ECR II-595, para 85; see also para 46 of the Commission's *Guidelines on the application of [Article 101(3)]* OJ [2004] C 101/97.

[401] See ch 7, 'Article 10: finding of inapplicability', pp 253–255.

[402] *Vertical guidelines*, para 146.

[403] See eg *Isab Energy* [1996] 4 CMLR 889, Commission's XXVIth *Report on Competition Policy* (1996), pp 133–134; *REN/Turbogás* [1996] 4 CMLR 881, XXVIth *Report on Competition Policy* (1996), pp 134–135.

[404] *Vertical guidelines*, para 161.

[405] OJ [2001] L 319/1, [2002] 4 CMLR 405, upheld on appeal in Case T-289/01 *Duales System Deutschland GmbH v Commission* [2007] ECR II-1691, [2007] 5 CMLR 356.

[406] OJ [2001] L 319/1, [2002] 4 CMLR 405, paras 141–163.   [407] *Vertical guidelines*, para 161.

[408] Ibid, para 164.

paragraphs 207 and 208; category management at paragraph 213; and tying at paragraph 222. The circumstances in which, in an individual case, resale price maintenance might lead to efficiencies are discussed in paragraph 225[409].

9. Regulation 461/2010 on Motor Vehicle Distribution[410]

The single market in the sale and after-sale servicing of motor vehicles has been slow to develop: differing tax regimes and methods of distribution, fluctuating exchange rates and the fact that certain Member States drive on the 'wrong' side of the road, have meant that this market remains much less integrated than others. The Commission has, for years, monitored price differentials between Member States[411]. Over the years the Commission has had cause to examine a number of anti-competitive practices in the market for motor cars, in particular the partitioning of national markets to prevent sales of vehicles from low- to high-priced Member States, and has adopted numerous decisions finding infringements both of Article 101(1)[412] and, on a few occasions, of Article 102[413]. The Commission also closed its file on the basis of informal assurances in several cases[414] and accepted commitments under Article 9 of Regulation 1/2003 in four cases[415]. As far

---

[409] See 'Minimum and fixed prices under Article 101(3)', pp 648–649 above.

[410] OJ [2010] L 129/52; for commentary see Clark and Simon 'The New Legal Framework for Motor Vehicle Distribution: A Toolkit to Deal with Real Competition Breakdowns' (2010) 1(6) Journal of European Competition Law and Practice 491; Colino 'Recent Changes in the Regulation of Motor Vehicle Distribution in Europe – Questioning the Logic of Sector-Specific Rules for the Car Industry' (2010) 6(2) Competition Law Review 203–224.

[411] See eg Commission Press Release IP/10/913, 9 July 2010; DG COMP's website contains useful material on car distribution: www.ec.europa.eu/comm/competition.

[412] See eg *BMW Belgium* OJ [1978] L 46/33, [1978] 2 CMLR 126, upheld on appeal Case 32/78 *BMW v Commission* [1979] ECR 2435, [1980] 1 CMLR 370; *Ford Werke* OJ [1983] L 327/31, [1984] 1 CMLR 596, upheld on appeal Cases 25 and 26/84 *Ford Werke AG v Commission* [1985] ECR 2725, [1985] 3 CMLR 528; *Fiat* XIVth *Report on Competition Policy* (1984), point 70; *Alfa Romeo* ibid, point 71; *Peugeot* OJ [1986] L 295/19, [1989] 4 CMLR 371; *Citroen* Commission Press Release IP(88)778 [1989] 4 CMLR 338; *Peugeot* OJ [1992] L 66/1, [1993] 4 CMLR 42, upheld on appeal Case T-9/92 *Peugeot v Commission* [1993] ECR II-493 and on appeal to the Court of Justice Case C-322/93 P [1994] ECR I-2727; *Volkswagen* OJ [1998] L 124/60, [1998] 5 CMLR 33, substantially upheld on appeal Case T-62/98 *Volkswagen AG v Commission* [2000] ECR II-2707, [2000] 5 CMLR 853 and on appeal to the Court of Justice Case C-338/00 P *Volkswagen AG v Commission* [2003] ECR I-9189, [2004] 4 CMLR 351; *Opel* OJ [2001] L 59/1, [2001] 4 CMLR 1441, substantially upheld on appeal Case T-368/00 *General Motors Nederland BV v Commission* [2003] ECR II-4491, [2004] 4 CMLR 1302 and on appeal to the Court of Justice Case C-551/03 P *General Motors BV v Commission* [2006] ECR I-3173, [2006] 5 CMLR 9; *Peugeot*, Commission decision of 5 October 2005, substantially upheld on appeal to the General Court Case T-450/05 *Automobiles Peugeot v Commission* [2009] ECR II-2533; the Commission's decision in *Volkswagen II* [2001] L 262/14 was annulled on appeal Case T-208/01 *Volkswagen AG v Commission* [2003] ECR II-5141, [2004] 4 CMLR 727 and to the Court of Justice Case C-74/04 P *Commission v Volkswagen AG* [2006] ECR I-6585, [2008] 4 CMLR 1297; and the Commission's decision in *DaimlerChrysler* OJ [2002] L 257/1 was partially annulled on appeal Case T-325/01 *DaimlerChrysler v Commission* [2005] ECR II-3319, [2007] 4 CMLR 559.

[413] See eg Case 226/84 *BL v Commission* [1986] ECR 3263, [1987] 1 CMLR 185; Case 26/75 *General Motors Continental NV v Commission* [1975] ECR 1367, [1976] 1 CMLR 95.

[414] See eg *Audi* Commission Press Release IP/03/80, 20 January 2003; *General Motors* Commission Press Release IP/06/302, 13 March 2006; *BMW* Commission Press Release IP/06/303, 13 March 2006 (the Commission settled two cases in which complaints had been made against BMW and General Motors that they had raised unjustified obstacles for multi-brand distribution and servicing and had imposed unnecessary restrictions on garages to become members of the authorized networks).

[415] *DaimlerChrysler* OJ [2007] L 317/76; *Fiat* OJ [2007] L 332/77; *Opel* OJ [2007] L 330/44; *Toyota Motor Europe* OJ [2007] L 329/52.

as the system of block exemptions is concerned the distribution of motor vehicles has, since 1985, been subject to a legislative regime separate from that for vertical agreements generally[416]. There have been many cases brought before the General Court and the Court of Justice relating to the special regime for cars[417].

In May 2008 the Commission published a Report on the operation of the old block exemption, Regulation 1400/2002[418]. The Report noted that the new car sales markets are highly competitive, although competition was more limited in the markets for repair and maintenance and spare parts due to their brand-specific nature. In July 2009 the Commission published a Communication, *The Future Competition Law Framework applicable to the Motor Vehicle Sector*[419]. In this document the Commission concluded that a more flexible approach, drawing more closely on the general regime for vertical agreements, would have adequately protected competition while involving lower compliance costs and a more efficient enforcement system. Having published a draft Regulation for comment in December 2009, the Commission adopted Regulation 461/2010 on 27 May 2010[420].

Article 2 of Regulation 461/2010 provides that, from 1 June 2010 to 31 May 2013, agreements relating to the purchase, sale or resale of new motor vehicles which fulfil the requirements of Regulation 1400/2002 are block exempted. In such cases the supplier's market share must be below 30 per cent, although it is 40 per cent for quantitative selective distribution of new motor vehicles; the 'general conditions' contained in Article 3 of Regulation 1400/2002 must be met; the agreement must not contain any 'hard-core' restrictions contrary to Article 4 of Regulation 1400/2002; and specific obligations, in particular non-compete obligations and location clauses, which do not meet the conditions set out in Article 5 are not block exempted[421]. From 1 June 2013 vertical agreements relating to the purchase, sale or resale of new motor vehicles will come within the regime set out in Regulation 330/2010.

Article 3 of Regulation 461/2010 confers block exemption on vertical agreements relating to purchase, sale or resale of spare parts for motor vehicles or repair and maintenance services for motor vehicles, provided they satisfy the requirements of Regulation 330/2010 and do not contain any of the specified additional hard-core restrictions in Article 5 of Regulation 461/2010. In particular a supplier must be free to sell spare parts to authorised

[416] Prior to Regulation 461/2010 there were three earlier block exemption Regulations for motor vehicle distribution, Regulation 123/85 OJ [1985] L 15/16; it was replaced by Regulation 1475/95 OJ [1995] L 145/25 which in turn was replaced by Regulation 1400/2002 OJ [2002] L 203/30.

[417] In addition to the cases in fn 412 above, see Case 10/86 *VAG France v Magne* [1986] ECR 4071, [1988] 4 CMLR 98; Case C-70/93 *BMW v ALD* [1995] ECR I-3439, [1996] 4 CMLR 478; Case C-266/93 *Bundeskartellamt v Volkswagen AG* [1995] ECR I-3477, [1996] 4 CMLR 505; Case C-226/94 *Grand Garage Albigeois* [1996] ECR I-651, [1996] 4 CMLR 778; Case C-309/94 *Nissan France* [1996] ECR I-677, [1996] 4 CMLR 778; Case C-128/95 *Fontaine* [1997] ECR I-967, [1997] 5 CMLR 39; Case C-41/96 *VAG-Handlerbeirat eV v SYD-Consult* [1997] ECR I-3123, [1997] 5 CMLR 537; Case C-230/96 *Cabour SA v Automobiles Peugeot SA* [1998] ECR I-2055, [1998] 5 CMLR 679; Case C-125/05 *VW-Audi Forhandlerforeningen v Skaninavisk Motor Co A/S* [2006] ECR I-7037, [2007] 4 CMLR 1071; Cases C-376/05 and C-377/05 *A Brünsteiner GmbH v BMW* [2006] ECR I-11383, [2007] 4 CMLR 259; Case C-421/05 *City Motors Groep NV v Citroën Belux NV* [2007] ECR I-653, [2007] 4 CMLR 455; cf also in the EFTA Court Case E-3/97 *Jan and Kristia]ceger AS v Opel Norge AS* [1999] 4 CMLR 147 and, in the UK courts, *Cound v BMW* [1997] Eu LR 277 and *Clover Leaf Cars v BMW* [1997] Eu LR 535.

[418] *Evaluation Report on the operation of Commission Regulation (EC) No 1400/2002* SEC(2008) 1946, 28 May 2008.

[419] COM(2009) 388 final, 22 July 2009.

[420] OJ [2010] L 129/52; the expiry of an old block exemption and its replacement by a new Regulation does not of itself require that existing contracts be terminated: see to that effect Case C-125/05 *Vulcan Silkeborg A/S v Skandinavisk Motor Co A/S* [2006] ECR I-7637, [2007] 4 CMLR 1071.

[421] For detailed guidance on these provisions see *Explanatory brochure for Commission Regulation (EC) No 1400/2002 – Distribution and Servicing of Motor Vehicles in the European Union*, 31 July 2002.

distributors or independent repairers[422]; this is intended to ensure effective competition on the repair and maintenance markets[423]. Article 29 of Regulation 1/2003 enables the Commission or the competent authority of a Member State to withdraw the benefit of the block exemption in certain circumstances[424]. Article 6 of Regulation 461/2010 gives the power to the Commission by regulation to disapply the block exemption to vertical agreements containing specific restraints in a relevant market more than 50 per cent of which is covered by parallel networks of similar vertical restraints. The Commission is required to monitor the operation of Regulation 461/2010 and will prepare a report on its application by 31 May 2021. Agreements relating to motor vehicle aftermarkets are subject to Regulation 461/2010 until 31 May 2023.

The Commission has published *Supplementary guidelines* which deal not only with the interpretation of the block exemption itself, but also, in Section IV, with the application of Article 101(1) to single branding and selective distribution in the motor vehicle sector[425].

10. **Sub-Contracting Agreements**

Sub-contracting agreements are a common feature of the commercial world. A contractor often entrusts another undertaking – the sub-contractor – to manufacture goods, supply services or to perform work under the contractor's instructions. Where the sub-contractor simply supplies goods or services to the contractor, the agreement would be a vertical one and the agreement would be governed by the Commission's *Vertical guidelines* and by the block exemption for vertical agreements[426]. Where a sub-contracting agreement is entered into between competing undertakings it falls to be considered under the Commission's *Guidelines on Horizontal Cooperation Agreements*[427]. However in some cases the contractor transfers know-how to the sub-contractor in order for it to be able to perform the tasks entrusted to it. The Commission has adopted a *Notice on Subcontracting Agreements* to explain the application of Article 101(1) to this situation[428].

The Commission's view is that sub-contracting agreements of the kind just described do not infringe Article 101(1). Subject to the proviso explained below, clauses in such agreements which stipulate that any technology or equipment provided by the contractor to the sub-contractor may not be used except for the purpose of the agreement generally fall outside Article 101(1); so too are restrictions on making that technology or equipment available to third parties and a requirement that goods, services or work arising from the use of the technology or equipment will be supplied only to the contractor. The proviso referred to is that the technology or equipment must be necessary to enable the sub-

---

[422] See Article 5(b) of Regulation 461/2010, on which see *Supplementary guidelines on vertical restraints in agreements for the sale and repair of motor vehicles and for the distribution of spare parts for motor vehicles* OJ [2010] C 138/16, para 23.

[423] See recital 17 of Regulation 461/2010.

[424] See recitals 20 and 23 of Regulation 461/2010; on the powers to withdraw the benefit of the block exemption see 'Withdrawal of the block exemption by the Commission or by a Member State', p 671 above.

[425] OJ [2010] C 138/16.

[426] See the Commission's *Guidelines on Horizontal Cooperation Agreements* OJ [2011] C 11/1, para 154.

[427] Ibid, paras 150–153; on these *Guidelines* generally see ch 15, 'Production Agreements', pp 599–603.

[428] OJ [1979] C 1/2; see also *Vertical guidelines*, para 22; for further discussion of sub-contracting see Bellamy and Child *European Community Law of Competition* (Oxford University Press, 6th ed, 2008, eds Roth and Rose), paras 6-189–6-195; note also that in some cases an agreement might amount to a technology transfer agreement that benefits from block exemption under Regulation 772/2004: see ch 19, 'Technology Transfer Agreements: Regulation 772/2004', pp 781–791.

contractor to manufacture the goods, supply the services or carry out the work: where this is the case, the sub-contractor is not regarded as an independent supplier in the market. This proviso is satisfied where the sub-contractor makes use of intellectual property rights or know-how belonging to the contractor. However it would not be satisfied if the sub-contractor could have obtained access to the technology or equipment in question acting on its own.

The *Sub-contracting Notice* sets out other permissible clauses. In particular the contractor can require the sub-contractor to pass on to it on a non-exclusive basis any technical improvements made during the agreement; an exclusive licence may be acceptable where any improvements or inventions on the part of the sub-contractor cannot be made without use of the contractor's intellectual property rights. The sub-contractor must be free, however, to dispose of the results of its own research and development.

11. UK Law

(A) Vertical integration

It would be theoretically possible to investigate an industry in which the extent of vertical integration was considered to be problematic under the market investigation provisions of the Enterprise Act 2002[429]; in its guidance on these provisions[430] the Office of Fair Trading ('the OFT') specifically notes that vertical integration may foreclose competitors and add to entry barriers within an industry[431]. Under the now-repealed Fair Trading Act 1973 the Monopolies and Mergers Commission (the predecessor of the Competition Commission) recommended in the *Supply of Beer*[432] that the 'Big Six' brewers should not be permitted to own more than 2,000 retail outlets each: this would require them to divest themselves of 21,900 retail outlets. Radical changes to the UK beer industry were subsequently set in motion by the Supply of Beer (Loan Ties, Licensed Premises and Wholesale Prices) Order 1989[433] and the Supply of Beer (Tied Estate) Order 1989[434]. These Orders have since been revoked[435].

It is possible for vertical mergers to be referred to the Competition Commission where the value of the turnover of the enterprise to be acquired is more than £70 million[436].

(B) Commercial agents

There is no specific guidance in the UK on the treatment of agency agreements under the Competition Act 1998. However, as a result of section 60(3) of the Act, the OFT, in its application of the Chapter I prohibition, will have regard to paragraphs 12 to 21 of the

---

[429] See ch 11 for a description of the market investigation provisions in the Enterprise Act 2002.

[430] *Market investigation references*, OFT 511, March 2006, para 5.1, available on the OFT's website at www.oft.gov.uk.

[431] Ibid, para 5.8.

[432] Cm 651 (1989).

[433] SI 1989/2258.

[434] SI 1989/2390.

[435] See the Supply of Beer (Tied Estate) (Revocation) Order 2002, SI 2002/3204 and the Supply of Beer (Loan Ties, Licensed Premises and Wholesale Prices) (Revocation) Order 2003, SI 2003/52.

[436] Enterprise Act 2002, s 23(1)(b); on vertical mergers under the Act, see ch 22, 'Non-horizontal mergers', pp 937–938.

European Commission's *Vertical guidelines*[437]. In *Vodafone Ltd*[438] the Director General of Telecommunications (now OFCOM) did not accept that agreements between Vodafone and its distributors that fixed the retail prices of pre-pay mobile phone vouchers were agency agreements[439]; however it was concluded that Vodafone was not guilty of infringing the Chapter I prohibition since it was acting pursuant to a regulatory obligation[440].

(C) Vertical agreements under the Competition Act 1998

(i) The exclusion of vertical agreements from the Chapter I prohibition until 30 April 2005

Section 50(1) of the Competition Act 1998 gives a power to the Secretary of State to exclude vertical agreements from the Chapter I prohibition. The Competition Act 1998 (Land and Vertical Agreements Exclusion) Order 2000[441] excluded all vertical agreements, with the exception of those imposing minimum or fixed resale prices, from the Chapter I prohibition from March 2000 until 30 April 2005.

(ii) Repeal of the exclusion for vertical agreements

The adoption of Regulation 1/2003 meant that there was much to be said for aligning the domestic law on vertical agreements with the position under EU law. It was decided, therefore, that the exclusion from the Chapter I prohibition should be repealed, and that there should be consistency, where possible, in the application of domestic and EU competition law to vertical agreements. The statutory instrument was therefore repealed with effect from 1 May 2005 (allowing a period of one year from the entry into force of Regulation 1/2003 during which undertakings could adapt their agreements)[442], since when there has been no special treatment for vertical agreements under the Competition Act. The position is now that vertical agreements that affect trade between Member States are subject to Article 101 including, when applicable, Regulation 330/2010 or Regulation 461/2010; and that agreements that do not have an effect on trade between Member States are subject to the Chapter I prohibition, which will be interpreted consistently with EU law according to the provisions of section 60 of the Competition Act[443], and the EU block exemption by virtue of section 10 of the Act which provides for parallel exemption[444]. This means that many agreements are exempt from both EU and UK law, and that there is no need for the UK to adopt a block exemption of its own for vertical agreements.

(iii) The *OFT's Guidance on Vertical agreements*

The OFT has published *Guidance on Vertical agreements*[445], which discusses the application of Articles 101 and 102 TFEU and the Chapter I and Chapter II prohibitions to vertical agreements. The *Guidance* also deals with the (now repealed) Exclusion Order and briefly notes the possible application of the Enterprise Act to vertical agreements.

---

[437] See 'Commercial Agents', pp 621–623 above; on s 60 Competition Act 1998 see ch 9, '"Governing Principles Clause": Section 60 of the Competition Act 1998', pp 369–374.

[438] OFTEL decision of 5 April 2002.

[439] Ibid, paras 35–37.

[440] Ibid, para 47.

[441] SI 2000/310.

[442] See the Competition Act 1998 (Land Agreements Exclusion and Revocation) Order 2004, SI 2004/1260.

[443] For discussion of s 60 see ch 9, '"Governing Principles Clause": Section 60 of the Competition Act 1998', pp 369–374.

[444] For discussion see ch 9, 'Parallel exemptions', pp 359–360.

[445] OFT 419, December 2004.

The *Guidance* concludes with some discussion of the competitive assessment of vertical agreements.

(iv) Decisional practice of the OFT

The OFT has investigated a number of vertical agreements under the Competition Act 1998. In *DSG Retail Ltd*[446] the OFT considered that the exclusive distribution agreements between Compaq and Hewlett-Packard, manufacturers of desktop computers, and Dixons did not infringe the Chapter I and Chapter II prohibitions; Dixons did not have a dominant position for the purpose of the Chapter II prohibition, and, in the absence of significant market power on Dixons' part, there were insufficient grounds for using the power that existed at that time to withdraw the exclusion from the Chapter I prohibition[447]. In *Lucite International UK Ltd*[448] the OFT concluded that a long-term supply contract for the supply of hydrogen cyanide by BASF to Lucite International was a vertical agreement and therefore, at the time, excluded from the Chapter I prohibition[449]; it further decided that it would not be appropriate to withdraw the exclusion as it was possible that the agreement would have been granted an exemption: it conferred individual and collective benefits on users and consumers by lessening environmental pollution[450]. An investigation into allegations that record companies were taking steps to impede parallel imports of compact discs into the UK was concluded, as the OFT could not find evidence of continuing agreements against which it could take action, though it stated that it would continue to monitor the market in question[451].

On several occasions the OFT has found that vertical agreements involved the imposition of minimum resale prices. In *John Bruce UK Ltd, Fleet Parts Ltd and Truck and Trailer Components*[452] vertical price fixing between John Bruce and Fleet Parts was held to be outside the Exclusion Order and so an infringement of the Chapter I prohibition[453]: a relatively small fine of £33,737 was imposed in this case, for a combination of horizontal and vertical price fixing. In *Hasbro UK Ltd*[454] a fine of £4.95 million was imposed on Hasbro for imposing minimum resale prices on its distributors[455]. In *Toys and Games*[456] much larger fines, of £17.28 million on Argos and of £5.37 million on Littlewoods, were imposed for a mixture of horizontal and vertical price fixing[457]; Hasbro was given full immunity because of its cooperation with the OFT[458]. On appeal the findings of infringement were upheld by the Competition Appeal Tribunal ('the CAT'), although the fines were reduced to £19.50 million[459]. In *Lladró Comercial*[460] the OFT found minimum resale price maintenance provisions in *Lladró*'s standard-form documentation, but refrained from imposing a fine since the European Commission had sent to *Lladró* a comfort letter

---

[446] OFT decision of 18 April 2001.
[447] Ibid, paras 97–98 and 111 and 118.
[448] OFT decision of 29 November 2002 [2003] UKCLR 176.
[449] Ibid, paras 11–14.
[450] Ibid, paras 39–41.
[451] *Wholesale supply of compact discs*, OFT 391, September 2002.
[452] OFT decision of 17 May 2002 [2002] UKCLR 435.
[453] Ibid, paras 35–37.
[454] OFT decision of 28 November 2002 [2003] UKCLR 150.
[455] Ibid, para 47.
[456] OFT decision of 19 February 2003 [2003] UKCLR 553.
[457] On the finding of a multilateral agreement in this case see ch 9, 'Agreements', pp 337–340.
[458] On leniency under the Competition Act 1998 see ch 10, 'Whistleblowing: the leniency programme', pp 414–418.
[459] Case Nos 1014 and 1015/1/1/03 *Argos Ltd and Littlewoods Ltd v OFT* [2005] CAT 13, [2005] CompAR 834, upheld on appeal [2006] EWCA Civ 1318, [2006] UKCLR 1135.
[460] OFT decision of 31 March 2003 [2003] UKCLR 652.

that could be interpreted to mean that this practice did not infringe competition law[461]. In *Football Shirts* the OFT imposed fines totalling £18.6 million for a mixture of horizontal price fixing and resale price maintenance in relation to replica football kits[462]. Some of the findings of infringement were annulled on appeal to the CAT[463], and the fines were reduced to £14.92 million[464]. The OFT has closed its files on several cases concerning alleged resale price maintenance, often against assurances that the offending behaviour would be terminated[465]. In *Tobacco*[466] the OFT imposed fines totalling £225 million for a number of bilateral, vertical agreements whereby the prices of various tobacco brands were linked to those of competitors' brands. The OFT concluded that these 'price-matching' arrangements restricted each retailer's ability independently to set resale prices for cigarettes[467].

(D) **Enterprise Act 2002**

It is possible for vertical agreements to be investigated under the market investigation provisions in the Enterprise Act 2002: these have been described in chapter 11. They will not be used where use of the Competition Act is more appropriate[468]. However the OFT has recognised that in certain circumstances a market investigation reference might be appropriate, for example where vertical agreements are prevalent in a market and have the effect of preventing the entry of new competitors[469]. In *Movies on Pay TV*[470] the Office of Communications ('OFCOM') made a market investigation reference in relation to the supply of premium pay-TV movies. OFCOM was concerned that several features of the markets, in particular BSkyB's exclusive agreements with the major Hollywood studios, might restrict competition. This investigation was continuing when the book went to press.

---

[461] Ibid, paras 120–125.   [462] OFT decision of 1 August 2003 [2004] UKCLR 6.

[463] Case Nos 1021/1/1/03 etc *JJB Sports plc v OFT* [2004] CAT 17, [2005] CompAR 29, upheld on appeal [2006] EWCA Civ 1318, [2006] UKCLR 1135.

[464] Case Nos 1019/1/1/03 etc *Umbro Holdings Ltd v OFT* [2005] CAT 22, [2005] CompAR 1060, upheld on appeal [2006] EWCA Civ 1318, [2006] UKCLR 1135.

[465] See eg OFT Press Release 86/04, 18 May 2004 in the case of *Swarovski UK Ltd*; case closure summaries of other cases are available at www.oft.gov.uk.

[466] OFT decision of 15 April 2010.

[467] This case is on appeal to the CAT, Case Nos 1160–1165/1/1/10 *Imperial Tobacco Group plc v OFT*, not yet decided; the OFT commissioned research on arrangements of this kind: see *Can Fair Prices be Unfair? A Review of Price Relationship Agreements*, LEAR, April 2011.

[468] *Market investigation references*, OFT Guideline 511, March 2006, para 2.3; note that the Commission published various reports on vertical agreements under the now-repealed provisions of the Fair Trading Act 1973, including *The Supply of Beer* (above); *Carbonated Soft Drinks* Cm 1625 (1992); *Newspaper and Periodicals* Cmnd 7214 (1978) and Cm 2422 (1993); *Fine Fragrances* Cm 2380 (1993); *Electrical Goods* Cm 3675 and Cm 3676 (1997); *Foreign Packaged Holidays* Cm 3813 (1997); and *New Cars* Cm 4660 (2000).

[469] OFT Guideline 511, para 2.6; see also paras 5.9 and 6.15–6.18 and the *Market Investigation References: Competition Commission Guidelines* (June 2003, CC3), paras 3.41–3.45 and 3.76–3.77, available at www.competition-commission.org.uk.

[470] OFCOM decision of 4 August 2010, available at www.ofcom.org.uk; details of the Competition Commission's ongoing work in relation to the reference can be found at www.competition-commission.org.uk.

17

Abuse of dominance (1): non-pricing practices

1. Introduction

The previous four chapters have been concerned with the application of EU and UK competition law to horizontal and vertical agreements between undertakings. The focus of attention in this and the following chapters turns to a different issue: the extent to which the unilateral acts of dominant firms might infringe Article 102 TFEU and the Chapter II prohibition in the Competition Act 1998.

The main principles underlying Article 102 were discussed in chapter 5; the Chapter II prohibition was explained in chapter 9[1]. It may be helpful to recall that care must be taken in the application of Article 102 and the Chapter II prohibition not to prevent dominant firms from being able to compete 'on the merits'[2]; that Article 102 has been applied to exploitative abuses, to exclusionary practices and to actions that partition the internal market[3]; that the dominant position, the abuse and the effects of the abuse may arise on different markets[4]; that a distinction should be drawn between horizontal and vertical foreclosure of the market[5]; and that some limited defences based on objective justification and/or economic efficiency are available to dominant undertakings accused of abusing a dominant position[6].

This chapter is concerned with non-pricing practices; abusive pricing practices are considered in chapter 18. There is no legal significance in this division of the material: pricing and non-pricing practices can have the same anti-competitive effect. However analysis of pricing abuses requires an understanding of a number of cost concepts, and these are introduced at the beginning of chapter 18[7]. Abuses that involve the exercise, or non-exercise, of intellectual property rights are considered in chapter 19.

---

[1] See ch 9, 'The Chapter II Prohibition', pp 360–369.

[2] See ch 5, 'Introduction', pp 192–194.

[3] See ch 5, 'Exploitative, exclusionary and single market abuses', pp 201–210.

[4] See ch 5, 'The dominant position, the abuse and the effects of the abuse may be in different markets', pp 205–208.

[5] See ch 5, 'Horizontal and vertical foreclosure', pp 204–205.

[6] See ch 5, 'Defences', pp 210–213.   [7] See ch 18, 'Cost concepts', pp 716–718.

This chapter will deal in turn with exclusive dealing agreements; tying; refusals to supply; abusive practices that are harmful to the single market; and miscellaneous other practices which might infringe Article 102 or the Chapter II prohibition. Reference will be
made where appropriate to the Commission's *Guidance on the Commission's Enforcement
Priorities in Applying Article [102 TFEU] to Abusive Exclusionary Conduct by Dominant
Undertakings* ('*Guidance on Article 102 Enforcement Priorities*')[8]. The reader is reminded
that this document does not contain guidelines on the law of Article 102; however it does
provide valuable insights as to why the Commission thinks that some practices are more
likely than others to produce anti-competitive harm to consumers, and so to be more
appropriate for enforcement action[9].

2. Exclusive Dealing Agreements[10]

(A) EU law

The application of Article 101 to vertical agreements was considered in chapter 16[11].
Regulation 330/2010 on vertical agreements confers block exemption on vertical agreements where the supplier and the buyer each has a market share of 30 per cent or less[12],
provided that the agreement contains no hard-core restrictions contrary to Article 4[13].
As a general proposition Article 5 of the block exemption limits the permissible duration
of a non-compete clause to five years[14]. Where either party's market share exceeds 30 per
cent, an individual assessment of a vertical agreement is necessary to determine whether
it infringes Article 101(1)[15] and whether it satisfies the terms of Article 101(3)[16]. Article
101(3) cannot provide a defence to an agreement that amounts to an abuse of a dominant
position[17]; and the Commission has also said that it is unlikely that a dominant undertaking would be able to defend an agreement under Article 101(3), even if it is not abusive,
where it maintains, creates or strengthens a market position approaching monopoly[18].

It is clear that exclusive dealing agreements are capable of infringing Article 102: this
term can apply both to an exclusive supply obligation, whereby a supplier is restricted
from supplying to anyone other than a specific downstream customer; and to an exclusive

---

[8] OJ [2009] C 45/7.
[9] For a general discussion see ch 5, 'The Commission's *Guidance on Article 102 Enforcement Priorities*',
pp 174–177.
[10] For further reading on exclusive dealing see Motta *Competition Policy: Theory and Practice* (Cambridge
University Press, 2004), pp 363–372; O'Donoghue and Padilla *The Law and Economics of Article 82 EC* (Hart
Publishing, 2006), pp 352–374; section 7 of DG COMP's *Discussion paper on the application of Article [102] of
the Treaty to exclusionary abuses*, available at www.ec.europa.eu; on the position in the US see *US v Dentsply
International, Inc.* 399 F 3d 181 (3d Cir 2005); Jacobson 'Exclusive Dealing, "Foreclosure" and Consumer
Harm' (2002) 70 Antitrust Law Journal 311; Melamed 'Exclusive Dealing Agreements and Other Exclusionary
Conduct – Are There Unifying Principles?' (2006) 73 Antitrust Law Journal 375.
[11] See ch 16, 'Resale price restrictions', pp 647–649.
[12] Regulation 330/2010, Article 3: see ch 16, 'Article 3: the market share cap', pp 660–662.
[13] See ch 16, 'Article 4: hard-core restrictions', pp 663–669.
[14] See ch 16, 'Article 5: obligations in vertical agreements that are no exempt', pp 669–670.
[15] See ch 16, 'Vertical Agreements: Article 101(1)', pp 628–649.
[16] See ch 16, 'The Application of Article 101(3) to Agreements that do not Satisfy the Block Exemption',
pp 672–674.
[17] See para 127 of the Commission's *Guidelines on Vertical Restraints* OJ [2010] C 130/1, relying on Case
T-51/89 *Tetra Pak Rausing SA v Commission* [1990] ECR II-309, [1991] 4 CMLR 334 and para 106 of its
Guidelines on the application of Article [101(3)] of the Treaty OJ [2004] C 101/97.
[18] See para 127 of the Commission's *Guidelines on Vertical Restraints* OJ [2010] C 130/1.

purchasing obligation whereby a downstream customer is forbidden to acquire products except from a specific supplier. In practice the cases are predominantly concerned with exclusive purchasing obligations.

A difference between the application of Article 101 and Article 102 to such agreements is that, where an agreement infringes Article 101, both (or all) of the parties to the agreement will have committed an infringement and will be liable accordingly. In the case of Article 102, however, it is the dominant firm that infringes the competition rules, since Article 102 applies to a dominant firm's *unilateral* behaviour; the conclusion of an anti-competitive agreement can be an abusive unilateral act, so that the dominant firm can be fined and sued for damages, as well as being unable to enforce the offending provisions in the agreement[19].

(i) The application of Article 102 to exclusive purchasing agreements

The most obvious vertical agreement that could infringe Article 102 is one whereby a customer is required to purchase all or most[20] of a particular type of goods or services only from a dominant supplier. Various terminology can be used to describe such agreements – 'exclusive purchasing', 'single branding', 'requirements contracts' and 'non-compete obligations'. Each of these terms connotes the same idea: that the purchaser is prevented from purchasing competing products from anyone other than the dominant firm. The Commission, in its *Guidance on Article 102 Enforcement Priorities*, uses the term exclusive purchasing agreements, and this is the one that will be used in the text that follows. The extent to which pricing practices such as the grant of rebates might have the same effect as an exclusive purchasing agreement is considered in chapter 18[21].

(A) *Judgments of the EU Courts*

There is not a great deal of judicial precedent on the application of Article 102 to exclusive purchasing agreements; however it is clear that there is a strong possibility that Article 102 will be applied to such agreements when entered into by a firm in a dominant position. Once the Court of Justice had held in *Suiker Unie v Commission*[22] that it was contrary to Article 102 for a dominant firm to foreclose competition by offering loyalty rebates to customers that purchase only from it, it was inevitable that the same condemnation would apply to an exclusive purchasing commitment. This was confirmed in *Hoffmann-La Roche v Commission*[23]. The Court of Justice held that:

> An undertaking which is in a dominant position on a market and ties purchasers – even if it does so at their request – by an obligation or promise on their part to obtain all or most of their requirements exclusively from the said undertaking abuses its dominant position within the meaning of Article [102] of the Treaty, whether the obligation in question is stipulated without further qualification or whether it is undertaken in consideration of the grant of a rebate[24].

---

[19] On the final point see ch 8, 'Article 102', p 324.

[20] The Commission treats an agreement to purchase 80 per cent or more of a buyer's requirements of a particular product as analogous to an exclusive purchasing commitment: see eg para 129 of the *Guidelines on Vertical Restraints*.

[21] See ch 18, 'Rebates that have effects similar to single branding agreements', pp 728–737.

[22] Cases 40/73 etc [1975] ECR 1663, [1976] 1 CMLR 295.

[23] Case 85/76 [1979] ECR 461, [1979] 3 CMLR 211; see also Case T-65/89 *BPB Industries plc and British Gypsum v Commission* [1993] ECR II-389, [1993] 5 CMLR 32, paras 65–77, upheld on appeal Case C-310/93 P [1995] ECR I-865, [1997] 4 CMLR 238.

[24] Case 85/76 [1979] ECR 461, [1979] 3 CMLR 211, para 89.

This language suggests a *per se* approach on the part of the Court of Justice: that any exclusive purchasing agreement on the part of a dominant undertaking is abusive, irrespective of the actual or likely impact of the agreement on competition. The General Court used similarly formalistic language in its judgments in *Solvay SA v Commission*[25] and in *Imperial Chemical Industries Ltd v Commission*[26] in 2009 and 2010 respectively. However, in the author's view, it is questionable whether it is ever appropriate to apply *per se* rules under Article 102[27]. In its *Guidance on Article 102 Enforcement Priorities* the Commission discusses factors that it would take into account when deciding whether it would take enforcement action in relation to exclusive purchasing agreements; these will be considered below in the context of the Commission's decisional practice.

In *BPB Industries v Commission*[28] the General Court held that an exclusive purchasing agreement cannot, as a matter of principle, be considered to infringe Article 101, that is to say that it does not restrict competition by object: rather it is necessary to examine the effects of such an agreement in its specific context[29]. However the Court went on to say that those considerations:

> which apply in a normal competitive market situation, cannot be unreservedly accepted in the case of a market where, precisely because of the dominant position of one of the market operators, competition is already restricted[30].

The General Court did not go so far as to say that there is a *per se* rule against exclusive purchasing agreements on the part of a dominant firm, but at the very least it suggests a very strict standard.

An important point about the statement by the Court of Justice in *Hoffmann-La Roche* quoted above is that it is no defence that the customer willingly entered into the agreement, or even that it requested exclusivity: the issue in these cases is not whether the agreement is oppressive to the customer, but whether it could horizontally foreclose competition in the relevant market. In *Almelo*[31] the Court of Justice considered that an exclusive purchasing clause in a supply contract for electricity could infringe Article 102 if entered into by a dominant firm, even where the clause was requested by local distributors.

(B) The Commission's approach to exclusive purchasing agreements

The Commission discusses exclusive purchasing agreements at paragraphs 129 to 150 of its *Guidelines on Vertical Restraints*[32]: those *Guidelines* are predominantly concerned with the treatment of such agreements under Articles 101(1) and 101(3). As far as Article 102 is concerned, the Commission provides some insights into its thinking in paragraphs 33 to 36 and in paragraph 46 of its *Guidance on Article 102 Enforcement Priorities* (paragraphs 37 to 46 deal with the analogous case of conditional rebates[33]). At paragraph 34 of the *Guidance* the Commission acknowledges that a customer of a dominant undertaking may have no objection to an exclusive purchasing obligation, in particular if it is compensated in some way for accepting it; however this does not, in itself, mean that such obligations should be tolerated: the Commission will focus its attention on whether they are likely to

---

[25] Case T-57/01 [2009] ECR II-4621, [2011] 4 CMLR 9, paras 365–383; this judgment is on appeal to the Court of Justice, Case C-101/10 P *Solvay v Commission*, not yet decided.

[26] Case T-66/01 [2010] ECR II-000, [2011] 4 CMLR 162, paras 315–323.

[27] See ch 5, 'Are there or should there be any *per se* rules under Article 102?', pp 199–201.

[28] Case T-65/89 [1993] ECR II-389, [1993] 5 CMLR 32.   [29] Ibid, para 66.

[30] Ibid, para 67.   [31] Case C-393/92 [1994] ECR I-1477.

[32] OJ [2010] C 130/1: see ch 16, 'Factors to be considered in determining whether single branding agreements infringe Article 101(1)', pp 638–639.

[33] See ch 18, 'The Commission's approach to conditional rebates in its *Guidance on Article 102 Enforcement Priorities*', pp 735–736.

be harmful for consumers as a whole, which may be the case where they have the effect of preventing the entry or expansion of competing undertakings.

Paragraph 35 of the *Guidance* refers back to paragraph 20, which sets out a range of factors that the Commission will take into account when deciding whether to initiate enforcement proceedings in relation to a possibly anti-competitive foreclosure of the market[34]. Paragraph 36 discusses some additional factors that the Commission will look at in the case of exclusive purchasing obligations. In particular it will ask whether the dominant undertaking's competitors are unable to compete for an individual customer's entire demand. If a customer is bound to purchase a certain amount of its needs from the dominant undertaking – for example because a particular brand is a 'must-stock item' or because other suppliers lack the capacity to satisfy the whole of the customer's needs – a risk arises that competitors will be excluded from the market altogether. Because of this the Commission considers that in such a situation even an exclusive purchasing obligation of short duration can lead to anti-competitive foreclosure. Where, however, suppliers can compete for the customer's entire demand, the Commission says that exclusive purchasing is unlikely to hamper effective competition unless the dominant undertaking imposes a very long period of exclusivity: the longer the duration, the greater the likely foreclosure effect.

The Commission took action in relation to exclusive purchasing agreements in *Hoffmann-La Roche*, *BPB Industries*, *Solvay* and *ICI*: the appeals to the EU Courts in these cases were discussed above[35]. There have been various other interventions. In *Istituto/ IMC and Angus*[36] the Commission took action in a case where the dominant supplier of a raw material was refusing to supply a customer except on terms which would have foreclosed its competitors; the Commission persuaded IMC and Angus to offer supply contracts that would last two years with automatic renewal for one year unless terminated by six months' notice. The Commission brought an end to exclusive contracts entered into by AC Nielsen for the procurement of data in relation to fast-moving consumer goods in 1997[37]. The Commission proceeded against Nordiron in respect of exclusive, long-term supply clauses for Molybdenum 99, a base product for radiopharmaceuticals used in nuclear medicine; following the receipt of a statement of objections Nordiron dropped the clauses[38]. The Commission required Frankfurt Airport to abandon long-term contracts covering periods from three to ten years which it had entered into with airlines for the provision of ramp-handling services[39]; the Commission had required the termination of Frankfurt Airport's monopoly of such services and, not surprisingly, was unwilling to see this replaced by long-term exclusive terms that would have the same effect in practice of excluding third parties. Agreement was reached with the Commission that the contracts would be for a period of one year only, automatically renewable but terminable on six months' notice[40].

The Commission has accepted commitments under Article 9 of Regulation 1/2003[41] in a number of cases that resulted in dominant undertakings abandoning or modifying exclusive purchasing obligations. The Coca-Cola Company agreed that it would refrain from entering into exclusive purchasing commitments with customers in 2004; the company also agreed not to require customers to purchase a specified minimum percentage of

---

[34] See ch 5, 'Effects analysis', pp 208–210.
[35] See also Case T-155/06 *Tomra Systems ASA v Commission* [2010] ECR II-000, [2011] 4 CMLR 416, paras 55–67, on appeal to the Court of Justice Case C-549/10 P *Tomra Systems v Commission*, not yet decided.
[36] Commission's XVIth *Report on Competition Policy* (1986), point 76.
[37] Commission's XXVIIth *Report on Competition Policy* (1997), pp 144–148.
[38] Commission's XXVIIIth *Report on Competition Policy* (1998), pp 169–170.
[39] *Frankfurt Airport* OJ [1998] L 72/30, [1998] 4 CMLR 779.
[40] Commission Press Release IP/98/794, 8 September 1998.
[41] See ch 7, 'Article 9: commitments', pp 255–261 on Article 9 of Regulation 1/2003.

their requirements from it[42]. In the case of *Distrigas* the Commission announced in October 2007 that it had accepted Article 9 commitments from Distrigas, an undertaking that at one time was the only gas supplier on the Belgian wholesale market and that remained dominant on it, that it would limit the duration of future agreements for the supply of gas, and that it would reduce the volume of gas subject to long-term supply commitments[43]. A similar outcome was achieved in *EDF: Long-term contracts France*[44]. A notable feature of the decision in *Distrigas* is that the Commission recognised that long-term agreements may be justified where investments are made in the building of new power plants[45].

In *De Beers*[46] the Commission considered that long-term exclusive supply terms for rough diamonds agreed between Alrosa and De Beers could infringe Article 102. Alrosa and De Beers were competitors in the relevant market, and the Commission's concern was that the supply arrangement led to De Beers, *de facto*, acting as an exclusive distributor. De Beers offered commitments to bring the arrangements to an end, which the Commission accepted under Article 9 of Regulation 1/2003. Alrosa successfully appealed to the General Court against the Commission's decision, arguing that the commitments would impact disproportionately on its own business[47]; however the Court of Justice overturned the General Court's judgment and reinstated the Commission's decision[48].

(ii) Article 102 applies to de facto as well as to contractual exclusivity

In *Van den Bergh Foods*[49] the Commission concluded that it was an abuse of a dominant position for Van den Bergh to provide freezer cabinets free of charge to retail outlets on condition that they were to be used exclusively for the storage of its ice cream products[50]. The consequence of this practice was that, *de facto*, Van den Bergh achieved outlet exclusivity, since retailers were unlikely to, and in practice did not, maintain a second freezer in their shops; in effect, therefore, the retailers would purchase ice cream exclusively from Van den Bergh. This decision, which was upheld on appeal to the General Court[51] and to the Court of Justice[52], demonstrates that Article 102 can be applied to *de facto* as well as to contractual exclusivity[53]. The Commission notes in paragraph 33 of its *Guidance on Article 102 Enforcement Priorities* that 'stocking requirements', of which *Van den Bergh* is an example, may in practice lead to the same effect as exclusive purchasing agreements.

(iii) Is there an objective justification for a long-term agreement?

In some circumstances long-term supply agreements may be objectively justifiable, for example where the supplier has to make a client-specific investment in order to be able to

---

[42] Commission decision of 22 June 2005.

[43] Commission Press Release IP/07/1487, 11 October 2007.

[44] Commission decision of 17 March 2010; see also *Gas Natural/Endesa*, Commission Press Release IP/00/297, 27 March 2000, a case which preceded the Article 9 commitments procedure, where Gas Natural agreed to reduce the length of its supply agreement with its customer, Endesa, to 12 years and to allow it to purchase a proportion of its requirements elsewhere.

[45] See recital 37 of the Commission's decision and the final two paras of the Commission's MEMO/07/407, 11 October 2007.

[46] Commission decision of 22 February 2006.

[47] Case T-170/06 *Alrosa v Commission* [2007] ECR II-2601, [2007] 5 CMLR 494.

[48] Case C-441/07 P *Commission v Alrosa* [2010] ECR I-000, [2010] 5 CMLR 643.

[49] OJ [1998] L 246/1, [1998] 5 CMLR 530.

[50] Ibid, para 265.

[51] Case T-65/98 *Van den Bergh Foods Ltd v Commission* [2003] ECR II-4653, [2004] 4 CMLR 14.

[52] Case C-552/03 P *Unilever Bestfoods (Ireland) v Commission* [2006] ECR I-9091, [2006] 5 CMLR 1460.

[53] See para 94 of the Opinion by Advocate General Cosmas in Case C-344/98 *Masterfoods Ltd v HB Ice Cream Ltd* [2000] ECR I-11369, [2001] 4 CMLR 449.

supply[54]. It was noted in chapter 16 that this may result in Article 101(3) being satisfied in relation to an agreement that infringes Article 101(1); in the case of Article 102, the same reasoning may result in a finding that an agreement is not abusive. The Commission says at paragraph 46 of its *Guidance on Article 102 Enforcement Priorities* that it will consider evidence demonstrating that exclusive purchasing agreements result in advantages to particular customers if they are necessary for the dominant undertaking to make certain relationship-specific investments in order to be able to supply those customers[55].

(B) UK law

The Office of Fair Trading ('the OFT') has published a guideline on *Vertical agreements*[56] which sets out its thinking on the application of Article 101 TFEU and the Chapter I prohibition to vertical agreements[57], but which also sets out some general thoughts on the assessment of vertical restraints, including efficiencies that may be associated with them[58]. Specific guidelines have been published on the application of the competition rules, including Article 102 and the Chapter II prohibition, in the telecommunications[59], water and sewerage[60], energy[61] and rail[62] sectors. It should be pointed out that all these guidelines predate the Commission's *Guidelines on Vertical Restraints* and *Guidance on Article 102 Enforcement Priorities*.

The OFT has intervened on a few occasions in relation to exclusive agreements that it considered to be abusive. In *Bacardi* the OFT was concerned that Bacardi's agreements foreclosed the market by requiring pubs and bars to sell exclusively its white rum and thereby infringed the Chapter II prohibition[63]. The case was closed on Bacardi giving (non-binding) assurances that it would not insist on exclusive purchasing[64], although this was challenged on appeal before the Competition Appeal Tribunal ('the CAT') by a third party complainant[65]. This case was eventually settled[66]; the CAT suggested that in future a settlement of a case such as this should be made under the statutory procedure now set out in section 31A of the Competition Act 1998, a procedure that was not available at the time that the OFT was dealing with the case[67].

In *Calor Gas Northern Ireland* the OFT investigated five-year exclusive purchasing agreements entered into in Northern Ireland between Calor Gas and various retailers; it concluded that Calor Gas was dominant and that the effect of its network of agreements was to make entry into or expansion within the market more difficult. A negotiated settlement was achieved whereby Calor Gas agreed to reduce the length of the agreements to two years[68].

---

[54] See the Commission's *Guidelines on Vertical Restraints*, paras 107(d) and 146.
[55] See ch 17 n 45 above on the Commission's decision in *Distrigas*.   [56] OFT 419, December 2004.
[57] Ibid, paras 5.1–5.5.   [58] Ibid, paras 7.1–7.29.
[59] *The application of the Competition Act in the telecommunications sector*, OFT 417, February 2000.
[60] *The application of the Competition Act in the water and sewerage sectors*, OFT 422, March 2010.
[61] *Application in the energy sector*, OFT 428, January 2005.
[62] *Application to services relating to railways*, OFT 430, October 2005.
[63] OFT Press Release PN 38/02, 28 June 2002.
[64] OFT Press Release PN 10/03, 30 January 2003.
[65] Case No 1017/2/1/03 *Pernod Ricard SA and Campbell Distillers v OFT* [2004] CAT 10, [2004] CompAR 707.
[66] Case No 1017/2/1/03 *Pernod Ricard SA and Campbell Distillers v OFT* [2005] CAT 9, [2005] CompAR 894.
[67] Ibid, para 7; for discussion of s 31A of the Competition Act see ch 10, 'Commitments', pp 405–407.
[68] OFT case closure of 30 June 2003, available at www.oft.gov.uk; see also *Calor Gas Ltd v Express Fuels Ltd* [2008] CSOH 13, where the Outer House of the Court of Session in Scotland decided that exclusive purchasing agreements with a minimum duration of five years infringed Article 101 and were therefore void and unenforceable.

In *English Welsh & Scottish Railway Ltd*[69] the Office of Rail Regulation ('the ORR') found that EW&S had abused its dominant position in a number of ways, including by entering into exclusive agreements for the carriage of coal to various power stations: a fine of £4.1 million was imposed. In *National Grid*[70] the Gas and Electricity Markets Authority ('OFGEM') concluded that National Grid had abused its dominant position in the market for the provision of domestic gas meters by entering into long-term contracts with gas suppliers that rent meters from National Grid; its view was that the payment structure had the effect of preventing gas suppliers from acquiring less expensive and/or more technologically advanced meters from competing meter operators. National Grid was fined £41.6 million for this infringement. On appeal to the CAT[71] and the Court of Appeal OFGEM's decision on substance was upheld, though the fine was reduced to £15 million[72]. A consequence of the finding of infringement in this case was that National Grid's customers would be able to renegotiate their agreements with National Grid, since the existing ones would be void and unenforceable.

In *Claymore Dairies Ltd v OFT*[73] the Competition Appeal Tribunal was critical of the OFT's investigation into whether Robert Wiseman Dairies had entered into agreements with two customers in Scotland that, *de facto*, resulted in an exclusive purchasing arrangement[74] and therefore set the decision on this point aside[75]; no further order was made since, by the time of the CAT's judgment, the position in the market had changed.

In February 2011 the OFT announced that it had issued a statement of objections alleging that CH Jones had abused a dominant position by entering into exclusive agreements with customers in the market for bunker fuels card services[76].

3. Tying[77]

This section considers the extent to which tying may infringe Article 102 TFEU and/or the Chapter II prohibition in the Competition Act 1998.

---

[69] ORR decision of 17 November 2006 [2007] UKCLR 937; the agreements in question were void and unenforceable: see *English Welsh & Scottish Railway Ltd v E.ON UK plc* [2007] EWHC 599, [2007] UKCLR 1653.

[70] OFGEM decision of 21 February 2008 [2008] UKCLR 171.

[71] Case No 1099/1/2/08 *National Grid plc v Gas and Electricity Markets Authority* [2009] CAT 14, [2009] CompAR 282.

[72] [2010] EWCA Civ 114, [2010] UKCLR 386; the Supreme Court refused National Grid permission to appeal: Order of 28 July 2010.

[73] Case No 1008/2/1/02 [2005] CAT 30, [2006] CompAR 1.   [74] Ibid, paras 287–313.

[75] Ibid, para 318.

[76] OFT Press Release, 25 February 2011.

[77] For further reading on tying and bundling see Nalebluff *Bundling, Tying, and Portfolio Effects* (DTI Economics Paper No 1, 2003), available at www.bis.gov.uk/publications; Motta *Competition Policy: Theory and Practice* (Cambridge University Press, 2004), pp 460–483; O'Donoghue and Padilla *The Law and Economics of Article 82 EC* (Hart Publishing, 2006), ch 9; Van den Bergh and Camesasca *European Competition Law and Economics: A Comparative Perspective* (Sweet & Maxwell, 2nd ed, 2006), pp 264–276; Schmidt *Competition Law, Innovation and Antitrust: An Analysis of Tying and Technological Integration* (Edward Elgar, 2009); section 8 of DG COMP's *Discussion paper on the application of Article [102 TFEU] to exclusionary abuses*; Bishop and Walker *The Economics of EC Competition Law* (Sweet & Maxwell, 3rd ed, 2010), paras 6.63–6.83.

(A) **Terminology and illustrations of tying**

Tying is the practice of a supplier of one product, the tying product, requiring a buyer also to buy a second product, the tied product. Tying may take various forms[78]:

- **contractual tying:** the tie may be the consequence of a specific contractual stipulation: for example in the *Hilti* case Hilti required users of its nail guns and nail cartridges to purchase nails exclusively from it[79]

- **refusal to supply:** the effect of a tie may be achieved where a dominant undertaking refuses to supply the tying product unless the customer purchases the tied product

- **withdrawal or withholding of a guarantee:** a dominant supplier may achieve the effect of a tie by withdrawing or withholding the benefit of a guarantee unless a customer uses a supplier's components as opposed to those of a third party[80]

- **technical tying:** this occurs where the tied product is physically integrated into the tying product, so that it is impossible to take one product without the other: this is what happened in the *Microsoft* case, discussed below[81]

- **bundling:** this is closely related to the idea of tying. It refers to a situation in which two products are sold as a single package at a single price. Two types of bundling should be noted:

  - **pure bundling:** this occurs where it is only possible to purchase the two products together

  - **mixed bundling:** this occurs where the two products are sold separately; however, when they are sold together they are available at a discount to the price that would be charged if they were purchased separately.

The extent to which bundling might lead to an infringement of Article 102 is discussed in chapter 18 on pricing abuses, since it is necessary to analyse the price of the bundle to determine whether this is the case[82].

(B) **Policy considerations: arguments for and against tying**

A simple, and simplistic, objection to tying is that it involves the dominant firm 'leveraging' its position in relation to the tying product to achieve increased sales in the market for the tied product, thereby extending its market power. This would be an example of horizontal foreclosure of the market[83]. So powerful was this argument that, at one time, US law took a strict standard against the practice, holding it to be a *per se* infringement. However this approach was subjected to sustained criticism, in particular by 'the Chicago School'[84]: the central thrust of this criticism was that a monopolist can earn its monopoly

---

[78] Some of these are described in para 48 of the Commission's *Guidance on Article 102 Enforcement Priorities*.

[79] See '*Hilti*', pp 692–693 below.

[80] The Commission required an end to this practice in *Novo Nordisk*: XXVIth *Report on Competition Policy* (1996), pp 142–143.

[81] See '*Microsoft*', pp 693–694 below.

[82] See ch 18, 'Bundling', pp 737–739.

[83] See ch 5, 'Horizontal and vertical foreclosure', pp 204–205.

[84] See eg Bork *The Antitrust Paradox* (Basic Books, 1978), ch 19; Bowman 'Tying Arrangements and the Leverage Problem' (1967) 67 Yale Law Journal 67; Turner 'The Validity of Tying Arrangements under the Antitrust Laws' (1958) 72 Harvard Law Review 73; Ridyard 'Tying and Bundling – Cause of Complaint?' (2005) 26(6) ECLR 316; for a review of the different arguments see Scherer and Ross *Industrial Market Structure and Economic Performance* (Houghton Mifflin, 3rd ed, 1990), pp 565–569.

profit only once, and that if it has monopoly power over product A, it cannot increase its profit by leveraging its position into product B. The insights of the Chicago School were persuasive, and there is now general recognition that *per se* illegality is inappropriate for tying: it is now subjected in the US to the rule of reason[85], requiring a full analysis of the likelihood of competitive harm.

It is not only that tying is no longer thought to be eligible for *per se* illegality. There is now much better understanding that tying is a normal feature of commercial life, and not something that should be regarded as inherently suspicious. Tying involves the integration of components into one product and this can lead to significant economic efficiencies, resulting in lower costs of production and distribution and in improvements of quality. Manufacturing activity, by its very nature, involves the bringing together of different components, and it would be perverse to suggest that, when engaged in by a dominant firm, such behaviour should be stigmatised as presumptively unlawful: the presumption should be the other way[86].

A few illustrations of the benefits of tying may assist. Tying may be used to maintain the efficiency of the tying product: for example a piece of equipment may function at its best only if a particular chemical or material is used which is available solely from the manufacturer, because it has a patent or relevant know-how. Another reason for tying may be to enable economies of scale or scope to be achieved: a manufacturer of a photocopying machine which also supplies ink, paper and spare parts will be able to reduce costs if all these items are delivered to customers at the same time; tying these products may lead to lower prices. A third reason for tying is to enable a producer to discriminate between customers: the manufacturer of a photocopying machine may wish to charge high-volume users more than low-volume ones; this it can do by tying photocopying paper: the customer which uses the machine the most will pay the most and the tie operates as a substitute for putting a meter onto the machine[87]. A further example of a tying practice that may promote efficiency is where X produces game consoles and computer games that operate only with those consoles: as consumers buy more consoles of a particular type, software writers produce more games that are compatible with it. This, in due course, may lead to higher sales of consoles and, therefore, lower prices overall. In this case the network effect leads to efficiencies to the benefit of consumers[88].

However there may be circumstances in which tying might have a foreclosure effect on the market. Some 'post-Chicago' authors have identified some vitality in the 'leveraging' theory, for example where the firm with dominance over the tying product also has some market power in relation to the tied product and is able to raise barriers to entry in that market[89].

(C) **EU law**

Both Article 101(1)(e) and Article 102(2)(d) specifically state that tie-in agreements may amount to infringements. Although Article 101 may be applicable to such agreements[90],

---

[85] *US v Microsoft* 253 F 3d 34 (DC Cir 2001).

[86] For a discussion of efficiency explanations for the practice of tying and bundling see Nalebluff *Bundling, Tying, and Portfolio Effects* (DTI Economics Paper No 1, 2003), part 4.3, available at www.dti.gov.uk; Evans and Salinger 'Why Do Firms Bundle and Tie? Evidence from Competitive Markets and Implications for Tying Law' (2004) 22(1) Yale Journal on Regulation 38.

[87] See Bowman 'Tying Arrangements and the Leverage Problem' (1957) 67 Yale Law Journal 19.

[88] See ch 1, 'Network effects', pp 11–12.

[89] See Whinston 'Tying, Foreclosure and Exclusion' (1980) 80 American Economic Review 837; *Bundling, Tying, and Portfolio Effects* (DTI Economics Paper No 1, 2003), para 4.4.2; Nalebluff 'Bundling as an Entry Barrier' (2004) 119 Quarterly Journal of Economics 159; Elhauge 'Tying, Bundled Discounts, and the Death of the Single Monopoly Profit Theory' (2009) 123 Harvard Law Review 397.

[90] See the Commission's *Guidelines on Vertical Restraints* OJ [2010] C 130/1, paras 214–222.

most cases have been brought under Article 102, including the landmark decision in *Microsoft*[91]. Article 102(2)(d) gives as an example of abuse:

> making the conclusion of contracts subject to acceptance by the other parties of supplementary obligations which, by their nature or according to commercial usage, have no connection with the nature of such contracts.

The Court of Justice has established that tying practices may also be caught by Article 102 where they do not fall within the precise terms of Article 102(2)(d): in *Tetra Pak v Commission* the Court concluded that there was an unlawful tie even though the products in question were connected by commercial usage, a situation not covered by the express wording of paragraph (d)[92].

Issues of tying (and bundling) have also arisen in cases under the EU Merger Regulation, most noticeably in *Tetra Laval/Sidel*[93] and in *GE/Honeywell*[94], in each of which the Commission's findings that the merged entity would, in the future, be likely to engage in tying practices were overturned on appeal to the General Court[95]. The Commission's *Guidelines on the assessment of non-horizontal mergers*[96] explain the circumstances in which it might proceed against a merger on the basis of so-called 'conglomerate effects'[97].

In determining whether there is an infringement of Article 102, five issues must be addressed:

- does the accused undertaking have a dominant position?
- is the dominant undertaking guilty of tying two distinct products?
- was the customer coerced to purchase both the tying and the tied products?
- could the tie be detrimental to competition by foreclosing access to the market?
- is there an objective justification for the tie?

Each of these requirements will be considered in turn; the Commission's views, set out in its *Guidance on Article 102 Enforcement Priorities*, as to the circumstances in which it might consider it appropriate to take enforcement action in relation to tying practices will be incorporated into the text that follows.

(i) Does the accused undertaking have a dominant position?

Clearly there can be an infringement of Article 102 only if an undertaking has a dominant position, and this would be in the tying market; there is no need for there to be dominance in the tied market. Footnote 34 of the Commission's *Guidance on Article 102 Enforcement*

---

[91] Commission decision of 24 March 2004, upheld on appeal Case T-201/04 *Microsoft Corpn v Commission* [2007] ECR II-3601, [2007] 5 CMLR 846.

[92] Case C-333/94 P [1996] ECR I-5951, [1997] 4 CMLR 662, para 37; the General Court makes the same point at para 861 of its judgment in Case T-201/04 *Microsoft Corpn v Commission* [2007] ECR II-3601, [2007] 5 CMLR 846, although it concluded that the abuse in that case fell fully within Article 102(2)(d) anyway: ibid, para 862.

[93] Case M 2416, decision of 30 October 2001, OJ [2004] L 43/13.

[94] Case M 2220, decision of 3 July 2001, OJ [2004] L 248/1.

[95] Case T-5/02 *Tetra Laval v Commission* [2002] ECR II-4381, [2002] 5 CMLR 1182, upheld on appeal to the Court of Justice, Case C-12/03 P *Commission v Tetra Laval BV* [2005] ECR I-987, [2005] 4 CMLR 573; Case T-210/01 *General Electric v Commission* [2005] ECR II-5575, [2006] 4 CMLR 686.

[96] OJ [2008] C 265/6, available at www.ec.europa.eu/comm/competition/mergers/legislation/legislation.html.

[97] Ibid, paras 91–121; see ch 21, 'Conglomerate mergers', p 879.

Priorities states that, in the 'special' case of tying in aftermarkets[98], Article 102 could be infringed where an undertaking is dominant in either the tying or the tied market.

(ii) Is the dominant undertaking guilty of tying two distinct products?[99]

The notion of tying is, at first sight, simple enough; a customer is forced to purchase two distinct products that could have been bought individually. However a moment's reflection reveals that there is a real difficulty in determining when two or more products should be regarded as distinct so that their sale together should be regarded as a tie. A car is sold with wheels and tyres: clearly this does not involve a tie; there will also be a spare wheel: presumably this is not a tie; the car may be fitted with a radio: this perhaps does amount to a tie; if the purchaser is required to insure the car with an insurance company specified by the manufacturer or dealer, this presumably would be a tie. In the same way a pair of shoes would not be regarded as a tie; nor would the sale of shoes with laces; but a requirement to purchase a particular brand of polish with the shoes presumably would be. It is necessary to determine at what point a case becomes one of tying: the burden of proving that two products are the subject of a tie is on the competition authority or the claimant in proceedings before a national court.

According to the formulation in Article 102(2)(d) products are tied when they have no connection either 'by their nature or according to commercial usage'. The Commission says in paragraph 51 of its *Guidance on Article 102 Enforcement Priorities*[100], citing the judgment of the General Court in *Microsoft*, that it considers two products to be distinct if, in the absence of tying (or bundling), a substantial number of customers would purchase or would have purchased the tying product without also buying the tied product from the same supplier. It notes that there might be direct evidence that customers, when given a choice, purchase the tying and the tied products separately; or indirect evidence, such as the presence on the market of undertakings that manufacture or sell the tied product without the tying one.

The EU Courts have examined the 'distinct products' requirement in three high-profile cases.

(A) *Hilti*

In *Eurofix-Bauco v Hilti*[101] the Commission held that the requirement that users of Hilti's patented nail cartridges should also acquire nails from it was an abuse of a dominant position; a fine of €6 million was imposed for this and other infringements. Hilti appealed[102], including on the ground that the Commission had been wrong to find that the nail guns, the cartridge strips and the nails were three distinct product markets rather than forming one indivisible whole, a 'powder actuated fastening system' comprising the nail guns and their consumables. The General Court held that there were three markets, and that independent producers should be free to manufacture consumables intended for use in equip-

---

[98] See ch 1, 'Spare parts and the aftermarket', pp 37–38.

[99] For an interesting discussion of this issue in the Irish Supreme Court, concluding that a savings protection scheme was an integral part of the service provided by credit unions so that there was no tie, see *The Competition Authority v O'Regan and others* [2007] IESC 22, [2007] ECC 343; for comment see Gorecki 'The Supreme Court Judgment in the Irish League of Credit Unions Case: Setting New Standards or Misapplying Current Case Law?' [2008] 29 ECLR 499.

[100] See to similar effect para 215 of the Commission's *Guidelines on Vertical Restraints*.

[101] OJ [1988] L 65/19, [1989] 4 CMLR 677.

[102] Case T-30/89 *Hilti AG v Commission* [1990] ECR II-163, [1992] 4 CMLR 16, upheld on appeal Case C-53/92 P *Hilti AG v Commission* [1994] ECR I-667, [1994] 4 CMLR 614.

ment manufactured by others unless in so doing they would infringe intellectual property rights[103].

(B) *Tetra Pak*

In *Tetra Pak II*[104] Tetra Pak required customers to whom it supplied liquid packaging machines to purchase cartons from it; it also insisted that only it should provide the services of repair and maintenance. Tetra Pak argued that it supplied an integrated distribution system for liquid and semi-liquid foods intended for human consumption and could not therefore be guilty of an abuse in tying the supply of its filling machines to the supply of its cartons. The Commission stated at paragraph 119 of its decision that it was not customary to tie cartons to machines and concluded that the cartons formed a separate market upon which the dominant firm was trying to eliminate competition.

(C) *Microsoft*

The question of whether two distinct products were the subject of a tie was a key issue in *Microsoft*. The Commission found that Microsoft had tied its Media Player to its personal computer operating system[105]. On appeal to the General Court the Commission's decision was upheld[106]. The Court agreed that the operating software system and the media player were separate products[107]. The Court noted that the IT and communications industry was in constant and rapid evolution, so that what appear to be separate products may subsequently be regarded as forming a single one[108]; it then pointed out that its function was to consider whether the operating system and Media Player were separate products *in May 1999* when the conduct complained of was alleged to be harmful, rather than at the time of the judgment (September 2007) when a different answer might be given[109]. The Court said that the distinctness of the products had to be determined by reference to consumer demand[110]. In its view there was a functional difference between system software (the operating system itself) and applications software (word processing, media players etc)[111]; there were operators on the market that supplied the tied product (a media player) without the tying product (an operating system): the Court pointed out that case law had established that this was 'serious evidence' of there being separate products[112]; Microsoft supplied Media Player as a separate product to work with its competitors' operating systems[113]; it was possible to download Microsoft's media player independently

---

[103] Case T-30/89 *Hilti AG v Commission* [1990] ECR II-163, [1992] 4 CMLR 16, para 68.

[104] OJ [1992] L 72/1, [1992] 4 CMLR 551, upheld on appeal to the General Court Case T-83/91 *Tetra Pak International SA v Commission* [1994] ECR II-755, [1997] 4 CMLR 726 and on appeal to the Court of Justice Case C-333/94 P *Tetra Pak International SA v Commission* [1996] ECR I-5951, [1997] 4 CMLR 662; for comment see Korah 'The Paucity of Economic Analysis in the EEC Decisions on Competition: Tetra Pak II' (1993) 46 Current Legal Problems 148, pp 156–172.

[105] *Microsoft* Commission decision of 24 March 2004, upheld on appeal Case T-201/04 *Microsoft Corpn v Commission* [2007] ECR II-3601, [2007] 5 CMLR 846; for comment on the finding of a tie in the *Microsoft* decision see Art and McCurdy 'The European Commission's Media Player Remedy in its Microsoft Decision: Compulsory Code Removal Despite the Absence of Tying or Foreclosure' (2004) 11 ECLR 694 (the authors of this article were advisers to Microsoft during the proceedings in this case); Banasevic, Huby, Pena, Castellot, Sitar and Piffaut 'Commission adopts Decision in the Microsoft case' (2004) (Summer) *Competition Policy Newsletter* 46–47 (the authors of this article were officials at DG COMP at the time of the decision).

[106] Case T-201/04 *Microsoft Corpn v Commission* [2007] ECR II-3601, [2007] 5 CMLR 846; for discussion of the case by DG COMP officials see Kramler, Buhr and Wyns 'The judgment of the Court of First Instance in the Microsoft case' (2007) 3 *Competition Policy Newsletter* 39.

[107] Case T-201/04 *Microsoft Corpn v Commission* [2007] ECR II-3601, [2007] 5 CMLR 846, paras 912–944.

[108] Ibid, para 913.   [109] Ibid, para 914.   [110] Ibid, para 917.

[111] Ibid, para 926.   [112] Ibid, para 927.

[113] Ibid, para 928.

from its website[114]; Microsoft promoted MP as a standalone product[115]; it had a separate licence agreement for MP[116]; and customers did acquire media players from Microsoft's competitors[117].

In January 2008 the Commission announced that it had initiated fresh proceedings against Microsoft in relation to alleged tying[118]. In this case Opera, a producer of a competing browser, complained that Microsoft's inclusion of Internet Explorer in its Windows operating system amounted to an illegal tie, in particular since Microsoft had introduced proprietary technologies in its browser that would reduce compatibility with open Internet standards. The Commission announced in December 2010 that it had accepted commitments under Article 9 of Regulation 1/2003 from Microsoft that it would offer users of Windows choice among different web browsers[119].

(iii) Was the customer coerced to purchase both the tying and the tied products?

The language of Article 102(2)(d) suggests that a component of the abuse of tying is that the customer is coerced into acquiring the tied product: '*making* the conclusion of contracts subject to acceptance by the other parties of supplementary obligations' (emphasis added). A contractual stipulation obviously satisfies this test. However in *Microsoft* there was no contractual requirement to take Media Player; rather it was included in the operating software, whether customers wanted it or not: in the parlance of the subject, this was 'technical bundling'. The General Court concluded in *Microsoft* that there was coercion of customers to take Media Player because it was impossible to uninstall it from the operating software system[120]; the Court was unimpressed by the fact that there was no extra charge for the inclusion of Media Player[121]. In paragraph 53 of the Commission's *Guidance on Article 102 Enforcement Priorities* the Commission says that it considers that the anti-competitive foreclosure effect of technical tying is likely to be greater than contractual tying or bundling since it may be costly to reverse and may reduce the opportunities for resale of individual components.

(iv) Could the tie have an anti-competitive foreclosure effect?

To amount to an abuse of a dominant position tying must have, or be capable of having, an anti-competitive foreclosure effect. The Commission discusses factors that it would take into account when deciding whether tying might lead to anti-competitive foreclosure in paragraphs 52 to 58 of its *Guidance on Article 102 Enforcement Priorities*. It refers to the general factors set out in paragraph 20 of its *Guidance*[122], and then considers some additional ones of significance in tying cases. As noted above, paragraph 53 suggests that technical tying may have a greater anti-competitive foreclosure effect than contractual tying or bundling. Paragraph 55 expresses the concern that tying might result in less competition for customers interested only in buying the tied, but not the tying, product, leading to higher prices for the former. Paragraph 57 notes that, if prices for the tying product are regulated, the dominant undertaking may decide to raise prices in the tied market in order to compensate for the loss of revenue in the tying market. A further con-

---

[114] Ibid, para 929.   [115] Ibid, para 930.   [116] Ibid, para 931.
[117] Ibid, para 932.   [118] Commission MEMO/08/19, 14 January 2008.
[119] Commission decision of 16 December 2010; see Buhr, Wenzel Bulst, Foucault and Kramler 'The Commission's Decision in the Microsoft Internet Explorer Cases and Recent Developments in the Area of Interoperability' (2010) 1 *Competition Policy Newsletter* 28.
[120] Case T-201/04 *Microsoft Corp v Commission*, [2007] ECR II-3601, [2007] 5 CMLR 846, para 963.
[121] Ibid, para 967–969.
[122] See ch 5, 'Effects analysis', pp 208–210.

cern set out in paragraph 58 is that entry into the tying market alone may be made more difficult if there is a limited number of alternative suppliers of the tied product.

The Commission has applied Article 102 to several tying transactions because it considered that the practice could have a foreclosure effect. In *IBM*[123] it brought an end to IBM's practices of 'memory bundling' and 'software bundling', accepting an undertaking that IBM would offer its System/370 central processing units without a main memory or with only sufficient memory as was needed for testing[124]. In *London European-Sabena*[125] the Commission concluded that an attempt by Sabena to stipulate that access to its computer reservation system on the part of London European should be conditional upon London European using Sabena's ground-handling services was an abuse under Article 102. In *De Post/La Poste*[126] the Commission objected to the Belgian postal operator giving a more favourable tariff for its general letter mail service to those customers who also purchased its new business-to-business mail service.

In *Centre Belge d'Etudes de Marche-Télémarketing v CLT*[127] the Court of Justice held that it was an abuse of a dominant position for the Luxembourg radio and television station, which had a statutory monopoly, to insist that advertisers should channel their advertising through its advertising manager or an agency appointed by it. This amounted to an extension of its monopoly power from one market into a neighbouring one, a kind of 'tie-in' that prevented other advertising agencies from competing with it and which limited the commercial freedom of users. In *Napier Brown-British Sugar*[128] the Commission applied this principle when condemning British Sugar's refusal to allow customers to collect sugar at ex-factory prices, thereby reserving to itself the distribution function in respect of this product.

In *Microsoft* the General Court agreed with the Commission's finding that the tie led to a foreclosure of the market[129]. It considered that the inclusion of Media Player had appreciably altered the balance of competition in favour of Microsoft to the detriment of competitors[130]. The Court referred to the ubiquity of the Windows operating system which, in 2002, enjoyed a market share of more than 90 per cent[131]. It also said that users who find that Media Player is pre-installed on their operating system would be less likely to make use of an alternative media player[132]. The Court considered that the inclusion of Media Player created disincentives for manufacturers of computers to include the media player of a competitor in their computers[133]. The General Court also agreed with the Commission that the ubiquity of Windows was likely to have a strong influence upon content providers and software designers[134] and noted market surveys that demonstrated a trend towards the use of Media Player to the detriment of other media players[135].

---

[123] Commission's XIVth *Report on Competition Policy* (1984), points 94–95; see further on this matter XVIth *Report on Competition Policy* (1986), point 75 and XVIIth *Report on Competition Policy* (1987), point 85; for comment see Vickers 'A Tale of Two EC Cases: IBM and Microsoft' (2008) 4(1) Competition Policy International 3.

[124] Note that the Commission investigated complaints that IBM had tied its mainframe hardware to its mainframe operating system, but decided to close the case file: Commission Press Release IP/11/1044, 20 September 2011.

[125] OJ [1988] L 317/47, [1989] 4 CMLR 662.

[126] OJ [2002] L 61/32, [2002] 4 CMLR 1426.

[127] Case 311/84 [1985] ECR 3261, [1986] 2 CMLR 558.

[128] OJ [1988] L 284/41, [1990] 4 CMLR 196.

[129] Case T-201/04 *Microsoft Corpn v Commission* [2007] ECR II-3601, [2007] 5 CMLR 846, paras 1031–1090.

[130] Ibid, para 1034.   [131] Ibid, para 1038.   [132] Ibid, para 1041.

[133] Ibid, para 1043.   [134] Ibid, para 1060.   [135] Ibid, para 1078.

(v) Is there an objective justification for the tie?

A dominant undertaking may be able successfully to argue that tying is objectively justified or enhances efficiency: the burden of proof would be on the dominant firm[136]. In *Hilti* the Commission's concern was that the practice of tying would prevent producers of nails from supplying users of Hilti nail guns. Hilti argued that its behaviour was objectively justifiable as it was necessary to maintain safety standards, so that operators would not be injured by nail guns. The Commission rejected this argument, concluding that Hilti's primary concern was the protection of its commercial position rather than a disinterested wish to protect users of its products. The General Court upheld this finding, pointing out that in the UK, where the competitors were selling their nails, there were laws about product safety and authorities which enforced them. In those circumstances it was not the task of a dominant undertaking to take steps on its own initiative to eliminate products which, rightly or wrongly, it regarded as dangerous or inferior to its own products[137].

The General Court concluded in *Microsoft* that Microsoft had failed to show any objective justification for tying Media Player with its operating software[138].

In paragraph 62 of its *Guidance on Article 102 Enforcement Priorities* the Commission says that it will consider claims that tying (and bundling) may lead to savings in production or distribution that would benefit consumers. The Commission also notes that there might be a reduction in transaction costs if customers can save money by not having to purchase components separately; or if suppliers achieve savings in distribution or packaging. Another possibility mooted is that tying might be a way of bringing a new, integrated, product to the market to the benefit of consumers; or that it might enable the supplier to pass on efficiencies to its customers arising from the production or purchase of large quantities of the tied product.

(D) UK law

As in the case of Article 102(2)(d), section 18(2)(d) of the Competition Act 1998 specifically states that a tie-in agreement may constitute an abuse of a dominant position.

In *Pricing of BT Analyst*[139] the Office of Communications ('OFCOM') received a complaint that BT had tied a billing analysis product, BT Analyst, to the provision of business telephony services. OFCOM's conclusion was that the billing product was part of the telephony service, and that therefore there was no tie[140]. On two earlier occasions the Office of Telecommunications[141] ('OFTEL', now OFCOM) and the OFT[142] were asked to investigate allegations of tie-in practices, but in each case they concluded that there was one single market over which there was no dominance, rather than a dominated primary market and a separate, secondary, market[143].

---

[136] See ch 5, 'Defences', pp 210–213.

[137] See further para 29 of the Commission's *Guidance on Article 102 Enforcement Priorities* which refers specifically to the proposition in *Hilti* discussed in the text.

[138] Case T-201/04 *Microsoft Corpn v Commission* [2007] ECR II-3601, [2007] 5 CMLR 846, paras 1144–1167.

[139] OFCOM decision of 27 October 2004 [2005] UKCLR 15.   [140] Ibid, paras 46–53.

[141] *Swan Solutions Ltd/Avaya Ltd*, 6 April 2001.   [142] *ICL/Synstar*, 26 July 2001.

[143] On this point see ch 1, 'Spare parts and the aftermarket', pp 37–38.

4. Refusal to Supply[144]

There are some circumstances in which a refusal on the part of a dominant firm to supply goods or services can amount to an abuse of a dominant position[145]. Refusal to supply is a difficult and controversial topic in competition law. First, as a general proposition most legal systems in countries with a market economy adopt the view that firms should be allowed to contract with whomsoever they wish. At paragraph 56 of his Opinion in *Oscar Bronner GmbH & Co, KG v Mediaprint Zeitungs-und Zeitschriftenverlag GmbH & Co KG*[146] Advocate General Jacobs pointed out that:

the right to choose one's trading partners and freely to dispose of one's property are generally recognised principles in the laws of the Member States

and that:

incursions on those rights require careful justification.

The Commission begins the section on refusal to supply in its *Guidance on Article 102 Enforcement Priorities* by repeating these same points.

A second point about refusal to supply is that, irrespective of whether the law should sometimes require a dominant firm to supply to customers, there are many perfectly reasonable explanations for a refusal to do so: for example that a customer is a bad debtor, that there is a shortage of stocks or that production has been disrupted.

A third consideration is that forcing a dominant undertaking to supply may not be conducive to economic welfare if it means that 'free riders' can take advantage of investments that have been made by other firms in the market. At paragraph 57 of his Opinion in *Oscar Bronner*[147] Advocate General Jacobs pointed out very clearly to the Court of Justice that allowing competitors to demand access to the 'essential facilities'[148] of dominant firms, which might seem to be pro-competitive by enabling claimants to enter the market in the short term, might ultimately be anti-competitive, if the consequence would be to discourage the necessary investment for the creation of the facility in the first place. In the following paragraph the Advocate General stated that, in the long term, it is generally pro-competitive to allow an undertaking to retain its facilities for its own use, since granting access to a third party may remove the incentive to invest in the establishment of efficient facilities. At paragraph 58 the Advocate General stressed the importance of the fact that the primary purpose of Article 102 is to prevent distortions of competition, and not to protect the position of particular competitors[149]. While accepting that the case law

---

[144] For further reading on refusals to supply see Motta *Competition Policy: Theory and Practice* (Cambridge University Press, 2004), pp 66–68; O'Donoghue and Padilla *The Law and Economics of Article 82 EC* (Hart Publishing, 2006), ch 8; Van den Bergh and Camesasca *European Competition Law and Economics: A Comparative Perspective* (Sweet & Maxwell, 2nd ed, 2006), pp 276–280; section 9 of DG COMP's *Discussion paper on the application of Article [102] of the Treaty to exclusionary abuses*; Bishop and Walker *The Economics of EC Competition Law* (Sweet & Maxwell, 3rd ed, 2010), paras 6.119–6.135.

[145] The term 'refusal' in this context includes a constructive refusal, for example by charging unreasonable prices, by imposing unfair trading conditions for the supply in question or by unduly delaying or degrading the supply of the product in question; see para 79 of the Commission's *Guidance on Article 102 Enforcement Priorities*.

[146] Case C-7/97 [1998] ECR I-7791, [1999] 4 CMLR 112.

[147] Ibid.

[148] See 'Is the product to which access is sought indispensable to someone wishing to compete in the downstream market?', pp 701ff below for discussion of this, and related, expressions.

[149] See also the Order of the President of the General Court in Case T-184/01 R *IMS Health Inc v Commission* [2001] ECR II-3193, [2002] 4 CMLR 58, para 145.

did, in certain circumstances, impose a duty on dominant firms to supply, the Advocate General advised that the duty should be appropriately confined and should be invoked only where a clear detriment to competition would follow from a refusal.

The Commission notes in paragraph 75 of its *Guidance* that the existence of an obligation to supply – even for a fair remuneration – may undermine undertakings' incentive to invest and innovate, which could be detrimental to consumers; and that, where a competitor can take a 'free ride' on the investment of the dominant firm, it is unlikely itself to invest and innovate, again to the detriment of consumers. However it also notes, in paragraph 82, that these considerations would not apply where an obligation to supply has already been imposed by regulation compatible with EU law, in which case a public authority will already have undertaken a balance of the parties' incentives; or where the upstream market position of the dominant undertaking has been developed under the protection of special or exclusive rights financed by state resources[150]. In these circumstances the Commission would simply be concerned to identify whether a refusal to supply could result in anti-competitive foreclosure, without applying the stringent rules discussed below that would otherwise be applicable.

When considering the law of refusal to supply it is helpful to keep in mind the distinction between horizontal and vertical foreclosure of the market[151]. Most cases on refusal to supply involve harm to the downstream market, that is to say vertical foreclosure: this section will be primarily concerned with cases of this kind. However there have been some cases that were concerned with horizontal foreclosure, and these are noted towards the end of this section[152], as are cases where the refusal was motivated by discrimination on grounds of nationality[153] and where the withholding of sales was a way of preventing parallel exports to a higher-priced Member State[154].

EU case law will be considered first, then that of the UK.

(A) EU law[155]

(i) Vertical foreclosure: competitive harm in a downstream market

Most refusal to supply cases concern a vertically-integrated undertaking that is dominant in an upstream market and which refuses to supply an existing or a new customer in a downstream market on which it is also present. Paragraph 76 of the Commission's *Guidance on Article 102 Enforcement Priorities* explains that the section in that document that deals specifically with refusal to supply is concerned only with cases of this kind. Paragraph 84 of the *Guidance* suggests that a refusal to supply a new customer is capable of infringing Article 102 as well as the disruption of an existing relationship: case law supports this proposition[156]. However the Commission adds that it is more likely that termination of an existing relationship will be found to be abusive than a *de novo* refusal to supply: for eample if a

---

[150] On the meaning of special or exclusive rights see ch 6, 'Undertakings with "special or exclusive rights"', pp 224–226.

[151] See ch 5, 'Horizontal and vertical foreclosure', pp 204–205.

[152] See 'Horizontal foreclosure', pp 708–709 below.

[153] See 'Refusal to supply on the basis of nationality', p 708 below.

[154] See 'Refusal to supply to prevent parallel imports', p 708 below.

[155] Note that the Commission has given specific guidance on the application of Article 102, including on refusal to supply, in the electronic communications and postal services sectors: see ch 23, 'Application of EU competition law', pp 982–983 and 'Application of EU competition law', pp 986–988.

[156] For example the successful complainant in the *Magill* case was a new, rather than an existing, customer; see similarly Case T-301/04 *Clearstream v Commission* [2009] ECR II-3155, [2009] 5 CMLR 2677 and Telekomunikacja Polska Commission decision of 22 June 2011; in a case on margin squeeze the Court of Justice specifically stated that it should make no difference to a finding of abuse whether a customer is an existing or a new one: see Case C-52/09 *Konkurrensverket v TeliaSonera Sverige AB* [2011] ECR I-000, [2011] 4 CMLR 982 paras 90–95.

customer has made specific investment to use an input supplied by the dominant supplier, this might lead to the conclusion that the input has become indispensable[157].

It was established by the Court of Justice in *Commercial Solvents v Commission*[158] that a refusal to supply a downstream customer could amount to an abuse of a dominant position. Zoja was an Italian producer of a drug used in the treatment of tuberculosis; it was dependent upon supplies of a raw material, amino-butanol, the dominant supplier of which was Commercial Solvents. When the latter refused to make amino-butanol available to Zoja the Commission found that it had abused its dominant position and ordered it to resume supplies. The Commission's decision was upheld on appeal to the Court of Justice. Commercial Solvents was not only a dominant supplier of amino-butanol in the upstream market for the raw material; its refusal to supply Zoja coincided with the emergence of Commercial Solvent's own subsidiary, ICI, onto the downstream market for the anti-TB drug on which Zoja was operating: the refusal to supply would eliminate Zoja from the downstream market. The Court of Justice said that:

> [a]n undertaking which has a dominant position in the market in raw materials and which, with the object of reserving such raw material for manufacturing its own derivatives, refuses to supply a customer, which is itself a manufacturer of these derivatives, and therefore risks eliminating all competition on the part of this customer, is abusing its dominant position[159].

There have been many cases on refusal to supply of this kind since *Commercial Solvents*; *Magill*, *Oscar Bronner* and *Microsoft* are of particular note and will be discussed below and/or in chapter 19[160]. The quest for the Commission and the EU Courts has been to find the correct balance between upholding the right of undertakings, whether dominant or not, to choose their trading partners freely on the one hand and ensuring that vertically-integrated dominant undertakings do not exclude competitors from downstream markets to the detriment of consumers on the other. The case law appears to establish that, in determining whether a refusal to supply a customer in a downstream market amounts to an abuse of a dominant position, four issues must be addressed[161]:

- does the accused undertaking have a dominant position in an upstream market?
- is the product to which access is sought indispensable to someone wishing to compete in the downstream market?
- would a refusal to grant access lead to the elimination of effective competition in the downstream market?
- is there an objective justification for the refusal to supply?

(A) Does the accused undertaking have a dominant position in an upstream market?

It is a statement of the obvious that, for there to be an infringement in an Article 102 case, the accused must have a dominant position; and in cases of the kind under consideration in this section the dominant position will be in an upstream market. However there are three points about this that merit consideration. The first is that the way in which the upstream market is defined will inevitably be influenced by the definition of the downstream

---

[157] This could provide an explanation for the outcome in *Commercial Solvents*, discussed below.

[158] Cases 6 and 7/73 [1974] ECR 223, [1974] 1 CMLR 309.   [159] Ibid.

[160] See ch 19, 'Compulsory licences', pp 797–802.

[161] But note that the Commission would not apply such strict standards where an undertaking is already subject to a regulatory duty to deal or where its position has been derived from state resources: see 'Refusal to Supply', p 698 above.

market. For example in *Sealink/B&I–Holyhead*[162] a ferry operator, B&I, wished to have access to the port of Holyhead in north Wales in order to operate ferry services to and from Ireland. The port at Holyhead was owned by Sealink, which was also present on the downstream market for ferry services. The Commission noted that there were three 'corridors' for short-sea routes between Great Britain and Ireland: the northern corridor, served, for example, by Stranraer in Scotland; the central corridor, served predominantly by Holyhead; and the southern corridor, served by Fishguard, Pembroke and Swansea in south and west Wales. The Commission defined the upstream market as the provision of port facilities for passenger and ferry services on the central corridor route; however, had it considered that the downstream market was all short-sea crossings between Great Britain and Ireland, it could not have defined the upstream market so narrowly; in this case, Holyhead Harbour (or more precisely the services available there) would not have been indispensable for B&I to be able to compete in the downstream market.

A second point about market definition in refusal to supply cases is that the dominant firm may not be operating on an upstream market at all; it may not be in the business of supplying the input to which access is sought to anyone. This does not mean that, in competition law terms, it cannot have market power over the input in question: the Court of Justice has said that it is sufficient that there is a potential, or even a hypothetical, market[163]. The Commission notes this point in paragraph 79 of its *Guidance on Article 102 Enforcement Priorities*.

A quite different point is that many Member States have laws that impose obligations on undertakings, *whether dominant or not*, to supply customers which are in a position of 'economic dependency': examples are Article L420-2, paragraph 2 of the French Commercial Code and section 20 of the German Act against Unfair Restraints of Competition of 1957[164]. It should be recalled that Article 3(2) of Regulation 1/2003 permits the application of national legal provisions that are stricter than Article 102 to unilateral behaviour[165]. It can only be a matter of conjecture whether Commission officials and judges of the EU Courts, when deciding whether refusals to supply existing customers amounted to an abuse of a dominant position under Article 102, may have been influenced by domestic laws that consider such conduct to be reprehensible even, in some cases, where the supplier is not dominant. Such a consideration might make it easier to conclude that the same conduct amounts to an abuse where the supplier is dominant. However competition policy in the EU today is predominantly concerned with consumer welfare, and the protection of economically dependent firms is not necessarily consistent with this aim[166]. As we shall see, case law has made it clear that a duty to deal does not arise under Article 102 from 'mere' dominance; rather it turns on the *indispensability* of access to an upstream product or service for someone to be able to compete in a downstream market. The criterion of indispensability limits the scope of Article 102, and is a

---

[162] [1992] 5 CMLR 255; note that this highly-influential case was an interim measures decision of the Commission that was not appealed to the EU Courts.

[163] See Case C-418/01 *IMS Health GmbH & Co v NDC Health GmbH & Co* [2004] ECR I-5039, [2004] 4 CMLR 1453, para 44; this point is helpfully discussed in Pitofsky, Patterson and Hooks 'The Essential Facilities Doctrine under US Antitrust Law' (2002) 70 Antitrust Law Journal 443, pp 458–461; see also DG COMP's *Discussion paper*, para 227.

[164] A useful guide to such laws will be found in *Dominance: the regulation of dominant firm conduct in 35 jurisdictions worldwide* (Global Competition Review, 2011, eds Janssens and Wessely), which specifically addresses the question, in relation to each jurisdiction, whether there are any rules applicable to the unilateral conduct of non-dominant firms.

[165] See ch 2, 'Conflicts: Article 102', pp 77–78.

[166] For discussion of the aims of competition policy see ch 1, 'Goals of competition law', pp 19–24.

conscious attempt to link findings of abuse to anti-competitive foreclosure from down-stream markets to the detriment of consumers.

(B) Is the product to which access is sought indispensable to someone wishing to compete in the downstream market?

Case law has established that a vertically-integrated undertaking is not required to deal with customers with which it competes in a downstream market simply because it is dominant in relation to an upstream market. It is necessary that the product or service to which a customer seeks access is 'indispensable' if it is to be able to compete in the downstream market. The word indispensable is the one that the EU Courts have tended to use; alternative expressions for the input to which access is sought are 'essential facilities' and 'objectively necessary'. The former expression has its antecedents in US antitrust, and there is a vast amount of periodical literature on the essential facilities doctrine[167]; as we shall see, the Supreme Court has significantly limited the scope of the doctrine in recent years[168]. The term essential facilities is particularly apt where an undertaking seeks access to a physical infrastructure such as a port, airport, railway network or pipeline: it is a fairly natural use of language to regard such infrastructures as 'facilities', and 'essential' carries the same meaning as 'indispensable'. However the case law has demonstrated that there can also be an obligation, for example, to license intellectual property rights or to provide proprietary information to a third party[169], where the expression 'essential facility' is a less natural one. Perhaps because of this the Commission refers to inputs that are 'objectively necessary' in paragraphs 83 and 84 of its *Guidance on Article 102 Enforcement Priorities*. The text that follows will use the term indispensability in deference to the jurisprudence of the EU Courts, but it would seem that all three expressions can be used interchangeably.

The requirement for indispensability became clear in the judgment of the Court of Justice in *Oscar Bronner GmbH*[170]. Bronner was an Austrian publisher of a daily newspaper, *Der Standard*, and wished to have access to the highly developed home-delivery distribution system of its much larger competitor, Mediaprint; Bronner complained that a refusal to allow such access amounted to an infringement of the Austrian equivalent of Article 102. The Austrian court sought the opinion of the Court of Justice, under Article 267 TFEU, whether such a refusal would infringe Article 102. The entire tone of the judgment is sceptical towards Bronner's case.

---

[167] The following articles would capture much of the writing on this subject: Areeda 'Essential Facilities: An Epithet in Need of Limiting Principles' (1990) 58 Antitrust Law Journal 841; Temple Lang 'Defining Legitimate Competition: Companies' Duties to Supply Competitors and Access to Essential Facilities' (1994) 18 Fordham International Law Journal 439; Ridyard 'Essential Facilities and the Obligation to Supply Competitors under UK and EC Competition Law' (1996) 17 ECLR 438; Lipsky and Sidak 'Essential Facilities' (1999) 51 Stanford Law Review 1187; Korah 'Access to Essential Facilities under the Commerce Act in the Light of Experience in Australia, the European Union and the United States' (2000) 31 Victoria University of Wellington Law Review 231; Capobianco 'The Essential Facility Doctrine: Similarities and Differences between the American and European Approaches' (2001) 26 EL Rev 548; Doherty 'Just What are Essential Facilities?' (2001) 38 CML Rev 397; Pitofsky, Patterson and Hooks 'The Essential Facilities Doctrine under US Antitrust Law' (2002) 70 Antitrust Law Journal 443; Bavasso 'Essential Facilities in EC Law: the Rise of an "Epithet" and the Consolidation of a Doctrine in the Communications Sector' [2003] Yearbook of European Law (Oxford University Press, eds Eeckhout and Tridimas), ch 2.

[168] See below.

[169] See ch 19, 'Compulsory licences', pp 797–802 on the *Magill* and *Microsoft* cases.

[170] Case C-7/97 [1998] ECR I-7791, [1999] 4 CMLR 112; see Treacy 'Essential Facilities – Is the Tide Turning?' (1998) 19 ECLR 501; Bergman 'The *Bronner* Case – A Turning Point for the Essential Facilities Doctrine?' (2000) 21 ECLR 59.

The Court of Justice stated that the first task for the national court would be to determine whether there was a separate market for the home-delivery of newspapers in Austria, and whether there was insufficient substitutability between Mediaprint's nationwide system and other, regional, schemes. If the market was the nationwide delivery of newspapers to homes, the national court would be bound to conclude that Mediaprint had a monopoly, and, since this extended to the entire territory of Austria, that this monopoly would be held in a substantial part of the internal market[171].

The Court of Justice then moved on to the question of abuse. It pointed out that in *Commercial Solvents* the effect of the refusal to supply the raw material by the dominant firm was likely to eliminate all competition in the downstream market between its own subsidiary and anyone else[172]. The Court of Justice then referred to the *Magill* case[173], saying that the refusal by the owner of an intellectual property right to license it to a third party could, in exceptional circumstances, involve an abuse[174]; in the Court's view *Magill* was an exceptional case for four reasons. First, the information sought by Magill was *indispensable* to the publication of a comprehensive listings guide: without it Magill could not publish a magazine at all; secondly, there was a demonstrable potential consumer demand for the would-be product; thirdly, there were no objective justifications for the refusal to supply; and fourthly, the refusal would eliminate all competition in the secondary market for TV guides[175]. The Court of Justice said, therefore, that, for there to be an abuse, it would have to be shown that refusal to grant access to the home-delivery service would be likely to eliminate all competition in the daily newspaper market (the downstream market) on the part of the person requesting the service and that the home-delivery service was indispensable to carrying on business in the newspaper market[176]. In the Court of Justice's view, use of Mediaprint's home-delivery service was not indispensable, since there were other means of distributing daily newspapers, for example through shops, kiosks and by post[177]; furthermore there were no technical, legal or economic obstacles that made it impossible for other publishers of daily newspapers to establish home-delivery systems of their own[178]. Specifically on the question of whether access to the distribution system could be considered indispensable the Court of Justice said that:

45. It should be emphasised in that respect that, in order to demonstrate that the creation of such a system is not a realistic potential alternative and that access to the existing system is therefore indispensable, it is not enough to argue that it is not economically viable by reason of the small circulation of the daily newspaper or newspapers to be distributed.

46. For such access to be capable of being regarded as indispensable, it would be necessary at the very least to establish, as the Advocate General has pointed out at point 68 of his Opinion, that it is not economically viable to create a second home-delivery scheme for the distribution of daily newspapers with a circulation comparable to that of the daily newspapers distributed by the existing scheme.

In the Court of Justice's view, the behaviour of Mediaprint did not amount to an abuse of a dominant position.

The Court of Justice's judgment in *Oscar Bronner* established that the key to the law on refusal to supply a competitor in a downstream market is indispensability. The input to which access is sought must be something that is incapable of being duplicated, or which

---

[171] Case C-7/97 [1998] ECR I-7791, [1999] 4 CMLR 112, paras 32–36.[172] Ibid, para 38.
[173] Cases C-241/91 P etc *RTE and ITP v Commission* [1995] ECR I-743, [1995] 4 CMLR 718; for an analysis of this case see ch 19, 'The *Magill* case', p 798.
[174] Case C-7/97 [1998] ECR I-7791, [1999] 4 CMLR 112, para 39.   [175] Ibid, para 40.
[176] Ibid, para 41.   [177] Ibid, para 42.
[178] Ibid, para 44.

could be duplicated only with great difficulty. In some cases duplication may be physically impossible: for example there may be only one point on the coastline of a country where a deep-sea port can be established; and planning or environmental reasons may make it impossible to build a competing airport, a nationwide system of gas transportation or a second rail network. The impossibility of duplication may be legal, for example where an undertaking owns intellectual property rights, such as the copyright in *Magill*. It may also be that a facility cannot be duplicated for economic reasons, although the Court of Justice was careful to point out in *Bronner* that this should be determined by reference to a competitor in the position of Mediaprint, not Bronner: that is to say that it is not sufficient for a small firm to argue that, because of its smallness, it should be entitled to have access to its larger competitor's infrastructure; rather economic non-duplicability asks whether the market is sufficiently large to sustain a second facility such as Mediaprint's distribution system. The Court repeated this idea in *IMS Health GmbH & Co v NDC Health GmbH & Co*[179]. It should be noted that this presages the idea of the 'as efficient competitor' test that underlies the Commission's *Guidance on Article 102 Enforcement Priorities*[180].

The requirement of indispensability means that it is not sufficient that it would be *convenient* or *useful* to have access: access must be *essential*. In *Tiercé Ladbroke v Commission*[181] and in *European Night Services v Commission*[182] the General Court rejected arguments that the provision of sound and television pictures of horse races in the former case and the supply of train paths, locomotives and train crews in the latter were indispensable services. In the Commission's *Notice on the Application of the Competition Rules to Access Agreements in the Telecommunications Sector*[183] it states that:

> It will not be sufficient that the position of the company requesting access would be more advantageous if access were granted – but refusal of access must lead to the proposed activities being made either impossible or seriously and unavoidably uneconomic[184].

The Commission discusses the requirement of indispensability – or in its parlance 'objective necessity' – in paragraph 83 of its *Guidance on Article 102 Enforcement Priorities*. In paragraph 83 it refers to *Magill*, *Bronner* and *Microsoft* and says that, in determining whether an input is indispensable, it will normally make an assessment of whether it could be duplicated by competitors in the foreseeable future; duplication is taken to mean the creation of an alternative source of efficient supply capable of allowing competitors to exert a competitive constraint on the dominant undertaking in the downstream market.

It may be helpful to identify a number of facilities to which access has been mandated under Article 102:

- **ports**: the *Sealink/B&I–Holyhead* decision has been noted above; another example of access being mandated to a port is *Port of Rødby*[185]

---

[179] Case C-418/01 [2004] ECR I-5039, [2004] 4 CMLR 1543, paras 28–30.

[180] See ch 5, 'The Commission's *Guidance on Article 102 Enforcement Priorities*', pp 174–177.

[181] Case T-504/93 [1997] ECR II-923, [1997] 5 CMLR 309; see Korah 'The Ladbroke Saga' (1998) 19 ECLR 169; note that in this case the undertakings against which the complaint was made were not present on the downstream betting market.

[182] Cases T-374/94 etc [1998] ECR II-3141, [1998] 5 CMLR 718.

[183] OJ [1998] C 265/2, [1998] 5 CMLR 821, para 91(a).

[184] Ibid.

[185] OJ [1994] L 55/52, [1994] 5 CMLR 457; note that the Commission's interim measures decision in the case of *Irish Continental Group v CCI Morlaix*, reported in the Commission's XXVth *Report on Competition Policy* (1995), pp 120–121 and at [1995] 5 CMLR 177, was different from the *Sealink* case in that the port operator in the *Irish Continental* case was not active on the downstream ferry market; see also *Tariffs for Piloting in the Port of Genoa* OJ [1997] L 301/27.

- **airports:** in *Frankfurt Airport*[186] the Commission required that the airport authority should terminate its monopoly over ground-handling services and that it should grant access to third parties wishing to supply such services there[187]

- **rail networks:** in *GVG/FS*[188] the Commission concluded that Ferrovie dello Stato, the Italian state-owned railway company, had abused its dominant position by preventing Georg Verkehrsorganisation, a German railway operator, from providing rail transport from Germany to Milan. The abuses consisted of refusal to grant access to the Italian railway infrastructure[189]; a refusal to supply traction (a locomotive, driver and ancillary services)[190]; and a refusal to enter into an international grouping of the kind necessary for cross-border rail passenger services[191]

- **gas pipelines:** the Commission has taken action in relation to access to gas pipelines in a number of cases[192]. Of particular notice in the recent past are *Gaz de France*[193], *E.ON*[194] and *ENI*[195], in each of which the Commission was given legally-binding commitments, under Article 9 of Regulation 1/2003, some of which were structural, to address concerns about possibly abusive refusals to deal[196]

- **oil storage:** in *Disma* the Commission required access to equipment for storing jet fuel and transferring it to supply points at Milan's Malpensa Airport; this case was brought under Article 101 rather than Article 102, since a number of undertakings owned the infrastructure in question[197]

- **telecommunications wires and cables:** the essential facilities doctrine is capable of application to telecommunications networks[198]

- **set-top boxes:** it may be possible to invoke the essential facilities doctrine to obtain access to set-top boxes which are necessary, for example, for the provision of interactive television services[199]

- **computerised airline reservation system**[200]: the Commission has ordered that access be made available to a computerised reservation in the air transport sector

---

[186] OJ [1998] L 72/30, [1998] 4 CMLR 779; note that Council Directive 96/67/EC, OJ [1997] L 272/36 liberalises ground-handling at airports and prevents discriminatory fees.

[187] See 'The Commission's approach to exclusive pruchasing agreement', p 685 above on the termination of the long-term supply contracts.

[188] OJ [2004] L 11/17, [2004] 4 CMLR 1446.   [189] Ibid, paras 119–131.

[190] Ibid, paras 132–146.   [191] Ibid, paras 147–152.

[192] See eg *Gaz de France and Ruhrgas*, Commission Press Release IP/04/573, 30 April 2004, where those two gas companies agreed to grant the Norwegian subsidiary of US gas producer Marathon access to their gas networks: a comment on the case will be found by Fernández Salas, Klotz and Moonen (2004) (Summer) *Competition Policy Newsletter* 41.

[193] Commission decision of 3 December 2009.   [194] Commission decision of 4 May 2010.

[195] Commission decision of 29 September 2010.

[196] See ch 7, 'Article 9 commitments', pp 255–261; and on Commission interventions in gas markets see ch 23, 'Energy', pp 989–991.

[197] *Disma* Commission's XXIIIrd *Report on Competition Policy* (1993), pp 141–143.

[198] Commission *Notice on the Application of the Competition Rules to Access Agreements in the Telecommunications Sector* OJ [1998] C 265/2, [1998] 5 CMLR 821, paras 49–53 and 87–98; see Nikolinakos 'Access Agreements in the Telecommunications Sector – Refusal to Supply and the Essential Facilities Doctrine Under EC Competition Law' (1999) 20 ECLR 399.

[199] See eg Case JV.37 *BSkyB/KirchPayTV* (under the EU Merger Regulation), Commission Press Release IP/00/279, 21 March 2000; *British Interactive Broadcasting* OJ [1999] L 312/1, [2000] 4 CMLR 901, paras 173–181 (a case under Article 101).

[200] *London European-Sabena* OJ [1988] L 317/47, [1989] 4 CMLR 662; see also *Lufthansa* Commission Press Release IP/99/542, 20 July 1999, where the Commission imposed a fine of €10,000 under Council Regulation 2299/89 on a code of conduct for computerised reservation systems.

- **interlining:** in *British Midland/Aer Lingus* the Commission required Aer Lingus to provide 'interlining facilities' to a competing airline, so that passengers of the latter would be able, in certain circumstances, to fly on the aeroplanes of the former[201]

- **cross-border payment systems:** the Commission may insist that access be granted to a cross-border payment system[202]. In *Society for Worldwide International Financial Telecommunications* SWIFT controlled the only international network for transferring payment messages; it also operated the only network capable of supplying connections for banking establishments anywhere in the world. The Commission considered that the network constituted a 'basic infrastructure in its own right, since to refuse any entity access to such a network is tantamount to a *de facto* exclusion from the market for international transfers'[203]. The Commission's view was that it was a manifest abuse of a dominant position to lay down unjustified admission criteria and to apply them in a discriminatory manner[204]. SWIFT agreed to grant access to any entity meeting the criteria laid down by the European Monetary Institute for admission to domestic payment systems[205]

- **cross-border securities clearing and settlement services:** in *Clearstream (Clearing and Settlement)*[206] the Commission found that Clearstream had abused its dominant position in relation to clearing and settlement services for registered services by refusing to deal with Euroclear Bank; the Commission's decision was upheld on appeal to the General Court[207]

- **postal network:** the Commission's view is that there can be an obligation to provide access to postal networks[208]

- **premium TV content:** the Commission has regarded premium TV content as an essential input for pay-TV operators[209]

- **intellectual property rights and or proprietary information:** it may be that access may be obtained to intellectual property rights and/or proprietary information[210]

---

[201] OJ [1992] L 96/34, [1993] 4 CMLR 596.

[202] Commission *Notice on the Application of the Competition Rules to Cross-border Credit Transfers* OJ [1995] C 251/3; see also the Commission's XXVIth *Report on Competition Policy* (1996), point 109, on the ECU Banking Association.

[203] Commission's XXVIIth *Report on Competition Policy* (1997), point 68.   [204] Ibid.

[205] For details of the settlement see the Commission's XXVIIth *Report on Competition Policy* (1997), pp 143–145; it should be noted that Article 28(1) of Directive 2007/64/EC on Payment services in the internal market, OJ [2007] L 319/1, requires Member States to ensure that rules on access to payment systems shall be objective, non-discriminatory and proportionate, and that they should not inhibit access more than is necessary to safeguard against specific risks such as settlement risk, operational risk and business risk and to protect the financial and operational stability of the payment system; Article 28(2) of the Directive excludes certain types of payment systems (so-called three party, closed-loop schemes) from its scope.

[206] Commission decision of 2 June 2004 [2005] 5 CMLR 1302; see Martínez and Bufton 'The Clearstream decision: the application of Article 82 to securities clearing and settlement' (2004) (Summer) *Competition Policy Newsletter* 49.

[207] Case T-301/04 *Clearstream v Commission* [2009] ECR II-3155, [2009] 5 CMLR 2677.

[208] Commission *Notice on the Application of the Competition Rules to the Postal Sector* OJ [1998] C 39/9, [1998] 5 CMLR 108, paras 2.8–2.9.

[209] For a summary of the Commission's decisional practice see Géradin 'Access to Content by New Media Platforms: A Review of the Competition Law Problems' (2005) 30(1) EL Rev 68.

[210] See ch 19, 'Compulsory licences', pp 797–802 on the *Magill* and *Microsoft* cases.

- **spare parts:** it may be that spare parts necessary for the repair of a particular product could be regarded as indispensable[211], depending on how the relevant market is defined[212].

Before moving on to the next requirement for a finding of an abusive refusal to supply a competitor in a downstream market, it may be worth pausing to reflect on why there have been so many cases of this kind in the EU and why the Supreme Court in the US has retreated from the essential facilities doctrine in recent years. As far as the EU is concerned, from the 1980s onwards the Commission (and many Member States) developed a policy that favoured the demonopolisation and liberalisation of sectors that for much of the twentieth century were regarded as natural monopolies, or which were considered to be inappropriate for the market mechanism; often these sectors were under state control or in state ownership. Exposing sectors such as telecommunications, energy and transport to competition was considered desirable. However competition would be slow to emerge where service providers could compete only if they had access to important infrastructures such as telecommunication wires and cables, the electricity grid, gas and oil pipelines, ports, airports and railway lines owned and operated by vertically-integrated dominant undertakings. In many Member States this problem was overcome by the establishment of specific regulatory regimes that mandate access to such infrastructures on reasonable, non-discriminatory terms[213]; and in some systems of competition law there are specific rules requiring undertakings in particular sectors to supply[214]. It may be sensible in principle that situations of natural or persistent monopoly should be dealt with by a system of *ex ante* regulation rather than by competition law: a competition authority is likely to be ill-equipped to deal with the persistent disputes in relation to access, and the appropriate price for access, that arise in relation to essential facilities. However competition law has proved to be an important adjunct to *ex ante* regulation, as the cases in this section have demonstrated[215].

In the US the first case on the essential facilities doctrine is considered to have been *United States v Terminal Railroad Association of St Louis*[216], although the term was not used in that case. More recently, in *Verizon Communications Inc v Law Offices of Curtis Trinko*[217], the Supreme Court adopted a notably unenthusiastic approach to the essential facilities doctrine. A case was brought under section 2 of the Sherman Act asserting the right of third parties to have access to Verizon's local telecommunications network. The New York and federal telecommunications regulators had conducted investigations and

---

[211] See Case 22/78 *Hugin Kassaregister v Commission* [1979] ECR 1869, [1979] 3 CMLR 345; the Commission's decision in this case finding an abusive refusal to supply was annulled by the Court of Justice as it had failed to demonstrate an effect on trade between Member States: see ch 3, 'The Effect on Trade between Member States', pp 144–149.

[212] Market definition in the case of 'aftermarkets' is discussed in ch 1, 'Spare parts and the aftermarket', pp 37–38.

[213] See ch 23, 'Regulated Industries', pp 977ff.

[214] See para 53 of the Opinion of Advocate General Jacobs in Case C-7/97 *Oscar Bronner GmbH & Co, KG v Mediaprint Zeitungs-und Zeitschriftenverlag GmbH & Co KG* [1998] ECR I-7791, [1999] 4 CMLR 112; see also Part IIIA of the Australian Trade Practices Act 1974, inserted by the Competition Policy Reform Act 1995, and s 8(b) of the South African Competition Act 1998; on the provisions in Australian law see Kench and Pengilley 'Part IIIA: Unleashing a Monster?' in *Trade Practices Act: A Twenty-Five Year Stocktake* (Federation Press, 2001, eds Hanks and Williams).

[215] See also ch 6, 'Making sense of the case law on Article 102 in conjunction with Article 106(1)', pp 229–235 on the role of Article 102 TFEU in circumstances where a Member State is responsible for anti-competitive behaviour on the part of public undertakings and undertakings entrusted with exclusive or special rights and ch 18, 'Margin Squeezing', pp 754–759 on the phenomenon of a 'margin squeeze' on the part of vertically-integrated dominant undertakings which is closely related to refusals to supply.

[216] 224 US 383 (1912).

[217] 540 US 398 (2004); for comment see Géradin 'Limiting the Scope of Article 82 EC: What can the EU learn from the US Supreme Court's Judgment in *Trinko* in the wake of *Microsoft*, *IMS*, and *Deutsch Telekom*?' (2004) 41 CML Rev 1519.

concluded them; the plaintiff was not satisfied with the outcome, and therefore brought a claim based on competition law. The Supreme Court reviewed the case law on essential facilities, in particular the *Aspen Skiing* case[218], which it regarded as 'at or near the outer boundary of section 2 liability'. There is little doubt that the Supreme Court was reluctant to allow the plaintiff in *Trinko* to obtain, through private antitrust litigation, what it had failed to achieve by complaining to the public institutions with sector-specific responsibility for telecommunications. The US Federal Trade Commission has urged Congress to clarify that the *Trinko* judgment ought not to apply to the *public* enforcement of the antitrust rules in regulated sectors, since the incentives of private litigants to sue, perhaps vexatiously, are different from those of a public competition authority[219].

(C) Would a refusal to grant access lead to the elimination of effective competition in the downstream market?

In the *Commercial Solvents* judgment the Court of Justice spoke of the risk of the refusal to supply 'eliminating *all* competition' on the downstream market (emphasis added); but in an earlier part of the judgment it had noted that the refusal to supply Zoja would result in the elimination of *one* of the principal manufacturers of the downstream product – in other words it was not correct to say that the removal of Zoja from the market would eliminate *all* competition. To limit the scope of Article 102 in refusal to supply cases to those where *all* competition downstream would be eliminated would restrict it considerably. In *Microsoft v Commission*[220] the General Court said, at paragraph 563, that it was not necessary for the Commission to demonstrate that 'all' competition on the market would be eliminated; it was sufficient to show that the refusal to supply is liable, or likely, to eliminate all *effective* competition. The Commission, in paragraph 85 of its *Guidance on Article 102 Enforcement Priorities*, says that it thinks that a refusal to supply an indispensable input is liable to eliminate *effective*, rather than *all*, competition.

In the Commission's view, harm to competition in the downstream market is likely to be greater where the dominant undertaking has a higher rather than a lower market share in the downstream market. The Commission also discusses, in paragraphs 86 to 88 of the *Guidance*, whether any refusal to supply would be likely to have an adverse effect on consumer welfare. In paragraph 87 it specifically says that it would look to see whether the refusal would result in innovative products not being brought to the market or follow-on innovation being stifled. On this point it specifically refers to the General Court's judgment in *Microsoft*, where this was considered to be a relevant factor in the finding of abuse, and *IMS Health*; it might also have referred to *Magill*, where this was clearly an influential matter – Magill wished to produce a composite TV listings magazine which at the time did not exist. In paragraph 88 the Commission says that it also would be concerned about harm to consumer welfare where an upstream input price is regulated, the downstream price is not regulated, and the refusal to supply might lead to the extraction of more profits in the downstream market.

(D) Is there an objective justification for the refusal to supply?

A refusal to supply a downstream customer would not be unlawful where there is an objective justification for it[221]. An obvious example would be that the customer is a bad

---

[218] *Aspen Skiing Co v Aspen Highlands Skiing Corp* 472 US 585 (1985).

[219] See 'Is There Life After *Trinko* and *Credit Suisse*? The Role of Antitrust in Regulated Industries', Prepared Statement of the Federal Trade Commission to the US House of Representatives, 15 June 2010, available at www.ftc.gov/os/testimony/100615antitrusttestimony.pdf.

[220] Case T–201/04 [2007] ECR II–3601, [2007] 5 CMLR 846.

[221] See ch 5, 'Objective justification', pp 211–212.

debtor, has become a credit risk or has failed to observe its contractual obligations; in the UK OFCOM and the CAT have accepted that there is no obligation to supply an input to a customer who will use it for an illegal purpose[222]. The owner of the input might also be able to argue that there is a capacity constraint which makes it impossible for access to be provided[223]: for example the owner of a port might already be using it to full capacity, in which case it would not be possible for it to grant access to a third party. In paragraphs 89 and 90 of the Commission's *Guidance on Article 102 Enforcement Priorities* the Commission says that it would consider claims that a refusal is necessary to allow the dominant undertaking to realise an adequate return on investments required to develop its input business; and also that granting access might affect negatively both the dominant undertaking's incentive to innovate (why invest if I must give access to my competitors?) and that of the downstream competitor (why invest if I can take a free-ride on my upstream supplier?)

(ii) Horizontal foreclosure

(A) *Refusal to supply a distributor as a disciplining measure*

A refusal to supply may be abusive where a dominant firm does so as a disciplinary measure against a distributor who handles competitors' products: this would be an example of horizontal foreclosure, whereby the dominant supplier takes steps to exclude a competitor in the upstream market in which it is dominant. This happened in *United Brands v Commission*[224], where United Brands was trying to prevent its distributor, which was not subject to an exclusive purchasing obligation, from taking part in a competitor's advertising campaign. The Court of Justice held that it was abusive to stop supplying a long-standing customer which abides by normal commercial practice, and that orders should be met which were in no way out of the ordinary. United Brand's objective was to prevent the distributor from selling competitors' products; this was not a case in which United Brands was seeking to eliminate a competitor in a downstream market.

(B) *Refusal to supply a potential competitor in the supplier's market*

It may be an abuse to refuse supplies as an exclusionary tactic against a customer trying to enter an upstream market in competition with the supplier. In *BBI Boosey & Hawkes: Interim Measures*[225] the Commission found that Boosey & Hawkes had abused a dominant position by refusing to supply brass band instruments to a distributor which was intending to commence the manufacture of such instruments in competition with it. The Commission said that the dominant firm was entitled to take reasonable steps to protect its commercial interest, but that such measures must be fair and proportional to the threat[226]; in its view it was not reasonable 'to withdraw all supplies immediately or to take reprisals against that customer'[227].

(iii) Refusal to supply on the basis of nationality

Discrimination on grounds of nationality is contrary to Article 18 TFEU. In *GVL v Commission*[228] the Court of Justice held that it was abusive for a national copyright collecting society to refuse to admit to membership nationals of other Member States. The

---

[222] See 'UK case law', pp 709–711 below.
[223] The Commission rejected the airport authority's arguments on capacity constraints in *Frankfurt Airports* OJ [1998] L 72/30, [1998] 4 CMLR 779, paras 74–88.
[224] Case 27/76 [1978] ECR 207, [1978] 1 CMLR 429.
[225] OJ [1987] L 286/36, [1988] 4 CMLR 67.   [226] Ibid, para 19.   [227] Ibid.
[228] Case 7/82 [1983] ECR 483, [1983] 3 CMLR 645.

Commission's investigation of the ticketing arrangements in *Football World Cup 1998*[229] was prompted by the fact that they discriminated in favour of French residents.

(iv) Refusal to supply to prevent parallel imports and exports

Refusals to supply that are harmful to the internal market are discussed below[230].

(B) UK case law[231]

In *JJ Burgess & Sons v OFT*[232] the CAT concluded that W Austin & Sons had abused a dominant position by refusing to grant access to Harwood Park Crematorium for the purpose of conducting cremations; in doing so the CAT annulled a decision of the OFT[233] that there had been no abuse. This was the first occasion on which the CAT made its own finding of a substantive infringement of competition law[234]; subsequently JJ Burgess commenced a 'follow-on' action for damages against W Austin: this case was settled between the parties in February 2008[235]. The CAT's judgment surveyed the relevant case law on refusal to supply[236] and formulated three propositions that were sufficient to reach a finding on the facts of that case, while noting that these were not intended to contain an exhaustive statement of the law on refusal to supply[237]:

- an abuse may occur where a dominant undertaking, without objective justification, refuses supplies to an established existing customer who abides by regular commercial practice, at least where the refusal to supply is disproportionate and operates to the detriment of consumers (*United Brands*)

- such an abuse may occur if the potential result of the refusal to supply is to eliminate a competitor in a downstream market where the dominant undertaking is itself in competition with the undertaking potentially eliminated, at least if the goods or services in question are indispensable for the activities of the latter undertaking, and there is a potential adverse effect on consumers (*Commercial Solvents*)

- it is not an abuse to refuse access to facilities that have been developed for the exclusive use of the undertaking that has developed them, at least in the absence of strong evidence that the facilities are indispensable to the service provided, and there is no realistic possibility of creating a potential alternative[238] (*Oscar Bronner v Mediaprint*).

Problems of refusal to supply are sometimes settled informally following investigation by the OFT[239].

---

[229] OJ [2000] L 5/55, [2000] 4 CMLR 963; see Weatherill 'Fining the Organisers of the 1998 World Cup' (2000) 21 ECLR 275.

[230] See 'Non-Pricing Abuses That are Harmful to the Internal Market', pp 711–712 below.

[231] Note the guidelines on the application of the competition rules to telecommunications, water and sewerage, energy and railways, cited in ch 17 nn 59–62 above, each of which discusses the circumstances in which a refusal to supply might amount to an abuse.

[232] Case No 1044/2/1/04 [2005] CAT 25, [2005] CompAR 1151.

[233] OFT decision of 11 August 2004 [2004] UKCLR 1586.

[234] See ch 10, 'Successful appeals against explicit non-infringement decisions', pp 441–442.

[235] Case No 1088/5/7/07 *ME Burgess, JJ Burgess and SJ Burgess v W Austin and Sons Ltd*, order of the Tribunal of 18 February 2008.

[236] Case No 1044/2/1/04 [2005] CAT 25, [2005] CompAR 1151, paras 291–313.

[237] Ibid, para 312.

[238] Ibid, para 311.

[239] See eg the 2000 *Annual Report of the Director General of Fair Trading*, p 46 (assurances by cement producers to supply bulk cement for resale).

In *Disconnection of Floe Telecom Ltd's Services by Vodafone Ltd*[240] Floe complained to OFCOM that Vodafone was abusively refusing to supply it with certain services necessary for it to operate in the market for mobile telephony. OFCOM decided that Vodafone had an objective justification for the refusal, since Floe would have been acting unlawfully on the market. On appeal to the CAT the decision was quashed and remitted to OFCOM[241] which, in a second decision[242], maintained its position that there had not been an unlawful refusal to supply. Floe again appealed against OFCOM's decision; on this occasion the CAT agreed with OFCOM that there had been no infringement, albeit on different grounds from those given by OFCOM[243]. The CAT's judgment was set aside on appeal to the Court of Appeal[244].

There have been a number of cases before the courts concerning refusals to supply by dominant firms that allegedly infringed the Chapter II prohibition; most of these were unsuccessful[245]. In *Network Multimedia Television Ltd v Jobserve Ltd*[246] the defendant operated a website on which IT recruitment agencies advertised job vacancies; it refused to accept advertisements from agencies that had an interest in a competing 'job board'. The court, with which the Court of Appeal agreed, decided that there was a serious issue to be tried, and granted an injunction in the claimant's favour pending the trial of the action. In *Intel Corpn v VIA Technologies* Intel, a manufacturer of computer components, was alleged to have abused its dominant position by refusing to grant a patent licence to one of its competitors. Lawrence Collins J granted summary judgment in favour of Intel on the basis that the mere refusal to grant a licence of an intellectual property right was not an abuse[247]. The Court of Appeal disagreed. Having surveyed the relevant EU law it concluded that Intel's refusal to license might fall within the 'exceptional circumstances' found to exist in *Magill*[248] and thereby infringe the Chapter II prohibition. In any event, the Court of Appeal considered that the difficult questions of law and fact raised by the case were not suitable for summary judgment.

In *AAH Pharmaceuticals Ltd v Pfizer Ltd*[249] wholesalers of pharmaceuticals sought an interim injunction to require the defendant to maintain supplies of pharmaceutical products. The OFT had declined a request from the wholesalers for interim measures, and instead launched a market study[250]; the High Court decided that it was not appropriate to grant the relief sought in these circumstances. Interim relief was successfully obtained in a refusal to supply case in *Software Cellular Network Ltd v T-Mobile (UK) Ltd*[251].

---

[240] OFCOM decision of 3 November 2003.

[241] Case No 1024/2/3/04 *Floe Telecom Ltd v OFCOM* [2004] CAT 18, [2005] CompAR 290.

[242] OFCOM decision of 28 June 2005 [2005] UKCLR 914.

[243] Case No 1024/2/3/04 *Floe Telecom Ltd v OFCOM* [2006] CAT 17, [2006] CompAR 637; note that OFCOM reached similar non-infringement decisions in the case of a complaint by VIP Communications Ltd against T-Mobile in *Disconnection of VIP Communications Ltd's Services by T-Mobile Ltd*, OFCOM decision of 31 December 2003 [2004] UKCLR 637 and *Re-investigation of VIP Communications*, OFCOM decision of 28 June 2005 [2005] UKCLR 914.

[244] *Office of Communications v Floe Telecom Ltd* [2007] EWCA Civ 47, [2009] UKCLR 659.

[245] See eg *Claritas (UK) Ltd v Post Office and Postal Preference Ltd* [2001] UKCLR 2; *Land Rover Group Ltd v UPF (UK) Ltd* [2002] All ER (D) 323; *Getmapping plc v Ordnance Survey* [2002] UKCLR 410; *Intel Corpn v VIA Technologies* [2002] UKCLR 576, reversed on appeal [2002] EWCA Civ 1905, [2003] ECC 16; *Attheraces Ltd v British Horseracing Board Ltd* [2007] EWCA Civ 38, [2007] UKCLR 309; *Humber Oil Terminals Trustee Ltd v Associated British Ports* [2011] EWHC 352.

[246] [2002] UKCLR 184, upheld on appeal [2001] UKCLR 814.

[247] [2002] UKCLR 576, para 173.

[248] *Intel Corpn v VIA Technologies* [2002] EWCA Civ 1905, [2003] ECC 16, paras 50–51.

[249] [2007] EWHC 565, [2007] UKCLR 1561.

[250] *Medicines Distribution*, 11 December 2007.

[251] [2007] EWHC 1790, [2007] UKCLR 1663.

In *Purple Parking Ltd v Heathrow Airport Ltd*[252] the High Court was sceptical that Purple Parking would be able to demonstrate that the forecourts to various terminals at Heathrow Airport were 'essential' for the claimant that operated a 'meet and greet' service for passengers arriving there[253]; however the court did consider that the airport was guilty of abusive discrimination contrary to section 18(2)(c) of the Competition Act.

5. Non-Pricing Abuses that are Harmful to the Internal Market

As noted in chapter 5, the EU Courts and the Commission will condemn abusive practices that are harmful to the internal market[254]. In *BL v Commission*[255] the Court of Justice upheld the decision of the Commission that BL had abused a dominant position by refusing to supply type-approval certificates for Metro cars imported from the continent; this practice was part of a strategy of British Leyland aimed at discouraging parallel imports into the UK. In *United Brands v Commission*[256] one of the abuses committed by United Brands was to impose a restriction on its distributors against exporting green, unripened bananas: in practice this amounted to an export ban, since it would not be possible to export bananas that were already ripe. In *Amminstrazione Autonoma dei Monopoli dello Stato v Commission*[257] the General Court confirmed the Commission's conclusion that AAMS, which had a dominant position on the Italian market for the wholesale distribution of cigarettes, had abused its dominant position by imposing distribution agreements on foreign producers which contained terms limiting the access of foreign cigarettes to the Italian market; a fine of €6 million was imposed.

The suppression of parallel trade in the pharmaceutical sector may be treated differently. In *Syfait v GlaxoSmithKline plc*[258] the Court of Justice was asked by the Greek Competition Authority whether it could be an abuse of a dominant position for Glaxo to have ceased to supply wholesalers in Greece in order to prevent exports of pharmaceutical products from Greece to higher-priced Member States. Advocate General Jacobs reviewed the law on refusal to supply under Article 102[259]; he did not think that Glaxo's refusal to supply amounted to a *per se* abuse and considered that, given the specific characteristics of the pharmaceuticals market – pervasive and diverse state intervention in the pricing of pharmaceuticals, regulation of distribution, the adverse effect that parallel trade might have on the incentive to innovate and the fact that end consumers may not themselves benefit from parallel trade – it was not necessarily an abuse for Glaxo to have refused to supply. However the Court of Justice held that, as the Greek Competition Authority was not a court or tribunal for the purpose of Article 267 TFEU, the reference was inadmissible; it therefore abstained from expressing an opinion on the extremely important question referred to it.

---

[252] [2011] EWHC 987.

[253] Ibid, paras 143 and 144.

[254] See ch 5, 'Abuses that are harmful to the single market', p 210; see also the Commission's XXVIIth *Report on Competition Policy* (1997), point 63.

[255] Case 226/84 [1986] ECR 3263 [1987] 1 CMLR 185; see also Commission Press Release IP (87) 390 *Re Volvo Italia* [1988] 4 CMLR 423.

[256] Case 27/76 [1978] ECR 207, [1978] 1 CMLR 429.

[257] OJ [1998] L 252/47, [1998] 5 CMLR 186, upheld on appeal Case T-139/98 *Amminstrazione Autonoma dei Monopoli dello Stato v Commission* [2001] ECR II-3413, [2002] 4 CMLR 302.

[258] Case C-53/03 [2005] ECR I-4609, [2005] 5 CMLR 7.

[259] Opinion of 28 October 2004, paras 53ff.

Subsequently the same point was referred to the Court of Justice by the Athens Appeal Court[260]. On this occasion the Court of Justice held that Article 102 must be interpreted as meaning that an undertaking occupying a dominant position on the relevant market for medicinal products which, in order to put a stop to parallel exports carried out by certain wholesalers from one Member State to other Member States, refuses to meet 'ordinary' orders from those wholesalers, is abusing its dominant position. However it went on to say that it is for the national court to ascertain whether the orders are ordinary in the light of both the size of those orders in relation to the requirements of the market in the first Member State and the previous business relations between that undertaking and the wholesalers concerned. Without actually saying so, this judgment would appear to mean that Glaxo was not under any obligation to supply more of the products in question than were needed to meet domestic demand in Greece: in other words that, in the context of the pharmaceutical sector, it was legitimate to restrict supplies in such a way that parallel trade would be restricted.

6. Miscellaneous Other Non-Pricing Abuses[261]

There have been some applications of Article 102 to non-pricing practices that do not fit under any of the headings so far deployed in this chapter. Some are concerned with the exercise (or non-exercise) of intellectual property rights, and are discussed in chapter 19[262]. Some other cases are discussed below.

(i) Harming the competitive structure of the market

It was established in *Continental Can*[263] that Article 102 could be applied to mergers in certain circumstances, and there was one other decision that condemned a merger[264]. However the inadequacy of Article 102 as a tool for controlling EU mergers lay behind the Commission's eagerness for a specific regulation, which finally emerged in 1989 after a gestation period of 16 years[265]. The application of Article 102 to mergers after the EU Merger Regulation is dealt with in chapter 21.

Even though mergers would now be dealt with under the EU Merger Regulation, the Commission considers that the *Continental Can* case is authority for the proposition that it can be an abuse to alter the competitive structure of a market where competition on that market is already weakened as a result of the very presence of the dominant undertaking on it. This is demonstrated by *Tetra Pak 1 (BTG Licence)*[266], where the Commission objected to the acquisition, by merger, of an exclusive licence of patents and know-how which would prevent competitors from entering Tetra Pak's market. Another example of harming the structure of the market occurred in *Irish Sugar v Commission*[267], where the

---

[260] Cases C-468/06 and C-478/06 *Sot. Lélos kai Sia EE and others v GlaxoSmithKline AEVE Farmakeftikon Proionton* [2008] I-ECR 7139, [2008] 5 CMLR 1382.

[261] For further reading see O'Donoghue and Padilla *The Law and Economics of Article 82 EC* (Hart Publishing, 2006), ch 10.

[262] See ch 19, 'Compulsory licences', pp 797–802.

[263] Case 6/72 [1973] ECR 215, [1973] CMLR 199.

[264] *Warner-Lambert/Gillette* OJ [1993] L 116/21, [1993] 5 CMLR 559.

[265] Council Regulation 4064/89/EEC, OJ [1990] L 257/13; that Regulation has since been recast by Council Regulation 139/2004, OJ [2004] L 24/1.

[266] OJ [1988] L 272/27, [1988] 4 CMLR 881, upheld on appeal Case T-51/89 *Tetra Pak Rausing SA v Commission* [1990] ECR II-309, [1991] 4 CMLR 334.

[267] Case T-228/97 [1999] ECR II-2969, [1999] 5 CMLR 1300.

General Court upheld the decision of the Commission that it was an abuse of a dominant position for Irish Sugar, the dominant undertaking in the Irish sugar market, to purchase a competitor's sugar from a wholesaler and a retailer and to replace it with its own, a so-called 'product swap'[268].

The Commission's decision in *Trans-Atlantic Conference Agreement*[269] that TACA had abused a dominant position by inducing undertakings to join a liner conference, thereby harming the competitive structure of the market, was annulled on appeal by the General Court[270].

The Commission held in *Decca Navigator System*[271] that it is an abuse for an undertaking in a dominant position to enter into an agreement with an actual or potential competitor with the intention of sharing markets or stunting the efforts of competitors.

(ii) Vexatious litigation

In the course of the *Promedia* case[272] the Commission stated that entering into litigation, which is the expression of the fundamental right of access to a judge, is not an abuse; however it could be abusive if a dominant firm brings an action:

> (i) which cannot reasonably be considered as an attempt to establish its rights and can therefore only serve to harass the opposite party, and (ii) which is conceived in the framework of a plan whose goal is to eliminate competition.

The General Court's judgment, in which it upheld the decision of the Commission not to proceed against Belgacom following a complaint from Promedia, appears, at paragraphs 72 and 73, to have confirmed the Commission's view that vexatious litigation could amount to an abuse in the circumstances envisaged by it. The General Court also stated in this judgment that a claim for the performance of a contractual obligation could amount to an abuse where the claim 'exceeds what the parties could reasonably expect under the contract or if the circumstances applicable at the time of the conclusion of the contract have changed in the meantime'[273].

In *Compagnie Maritime Belge Transports SA v Commission*[274] Cewal, a liner conference, had concluded an agreement with the Zairean Maritime Freight Management Office (the so-called 'Ogefrem agreement') granting Cewal exclusive rights to the freight trade between Zaire and northern Europe. When Ogefrem allowed a third party, Grimaldi and Cobelfret, a small amount of the trade in question, Cewal repeatedly insisted that Ogefrem should strictly comply with the terms of the agreement. The Court of Justice upheld the finding of the Commission that it was abusive of Cewal to insist on its exclusive rights under the Ogefrem agreement in circumstances where the insistence was intended to remove its only competitor from the market and where Cewal had a discretion under the contract whether to insist on its performance or not[275].

---

[268] Ibid, paras 226–235.

[269] OJ [1999] L 95/1, [1999] 4 CMLR 1415.

[270] Cases T-191/98 etc *Atlantic Container Line AB v Commission* [2003] ECR II-3275, [2005] 4 CMLR 1283.

[271] OJ [1989] L 43/27, [1990] 4 CMLR 627.

[272] Case T-111/96 *ITT Promedia v Commission* [1998] ECR II-2937, [1998] 5 CMLR 491; see Preece '*ITT Promedia v EC Commission*: Establishing an Abuse of Predatory Litigation?' (1999) 20 ECLR 118.

[273] Case T-111/96 [1998] ECR II-2937, [1998] 5 CMLR 491, para 140.

[274] Cases C-395/96 P etc [2000] ECR I-1365, [2000] 4 CMLR 1076.

[275] Ibid, paras 84–88.

(iii) **Other cases**

The General Court upheld the Commission's rejection of a complaint that lobbying for the imposition of anti-dumping duties constituted an abuse of a dominant position in *Industrie des Poudres Sphériques v Commission*[276]. The General Court's judgment in *AstraZeneca v Commission*[277] will be discussed in chapter 19 in the context of intellectual property rights; however it should be noted that it establishes that misuse of regulatory procedures can amount to an abuse of a dominant position[278].

276   Case T-5/97 [2000] ECR II-3755, [2001] 4 CMLR 1020.
277   Case T-321/05 [2010] ECR II-000, [2010] 5 CMLR 1585; the case is on appeal to the Court of Justice, Case C-457/10 *AstraZeneca AB v Commission*, not yet decided.
278   See ch 19, 'Vexatious behaviour and abuse of process', pp 805–806.

18

Abuse of dominance (2): pricing practices

1. Introduction

This chapter will consider abusive pricing practices under Article 102 TFEU and the Chapter II prohibition in the Competition Act 1998. The chapter will begin with a discussion of various cost concepts used in determining whether a price is abusive. It will then deal in turn with exploitative pricing practices; rebates and other practices that have an effect similar to exclusive dealing agreements; bundling; predatory pricing; margin squeezing; price discrimination; and practices that are harmful to the single market. This taxonomy is over-schematic, in that the categories can blur into one another: for example discrimination may be both exploitative and exclusionary, and an excessively high price may in reality be a way of preventing parallel imports or of excluding a competitor from the market; nevertheless this division may provide helpful insights into the way in which the law is applied in practice. In each section the application of Article 102 by the European Commission and by the EU Courts will be considered first, followed by cases dealt with by the competition authorities and courts in the UK. Reference will be made where appropriate to the Commission's *Guidance on the Commission's Enforcement Priorities in Applying Article [102 TFEU] to Abusive Exclusionary Conduct by Dominant Undertakings* ('the *Guidance on Article 102 Enforcement Priorities*' or 'the *Guidance*')[1]. As noted in previous chapters, the *Guidance* is not an attempt to state the law of Article 102; however it does attempt to explain why the Commission would have a greater interest in prosecuting some types of alleged exclusionary abuses than others. In particular the Commission says that, as a general proposition, only undertakings that are 'as efficient' as the dominant undertaking should benefit from the rules on exclusionary pricing abuse[2]; this is an economics-oriented approach, and one with which the Court of Justice agrees[3].

---

[1] OJ [2009] C 45/7; for a general discussion see ch 5, 'The Commission's *Guidance on Article 102 Enforcement Priorities*', pp 174–177.

[2] Ibid, paras 23 and 27.

[3] See eg Case C-280/08 P *Deutsche Telekom v Commission* [2010] ECR I-000, [2010] 5 CMLR 1495, para 177 and Case C-52/09 *Konkurrensverket v TeliaSonera Sverige* [2011] ECR I-000, [2011] 4 CMLR 982, para 39.

The law on abusive pricing practices is complex and controversial. Dominant firms may infringe Article 102 where they raise their prices to unacceptably high levels; they may also be found to have abused their dominant position where they cut their prices, if such cuts can be characterised not as normal, competitive responses on the merits, but as strategic behaviour intended to eliminate competitors. Not unnaturally a dominant firm, or one that is anxious that it might be found to be dominant, may feel itself to be on the horns of a dilemma where both a price rise and a price cut might be considered to be abusive; the dilemma might become a trilemma if leaving prices where they are might be considered to be evidence of a concerted practice with the other operators on the market, and if the word trilemma were to exist.

2. Cost Concepts

Analysis of whether a dominant undertaking's pricing practices are abusive typically requires consideration of its costs: this is acknowledged in paragraph 25 of the Commission's *Guidance on Article 102 Enforcement Priorities*. A price may infringe Article 102 where the difference between the price charged and the costs incurred is excessive; discrimination may be abusive where it lacks a cost justification; and a price may be unlawful where the price charged is below cost. However it is important to understand at the outset that the apparently simple term 'cost' in fact raises serious problems in practice; it may be helpful therefore to begin this chapter by outlining some of the cost concepts that are deployed in competition analysis[4]. These concepts will be referred to quite often later in this chapter.

(A) Fixed costs and sunk costs

Fixed costs are costs that do not vary with the amount of goods or services that a firm produces; for example a manufacturing firm must buy or rent land on which to build a factory, and will probably incur property taxes as well: these costs are fixed, as they must be paid irrespective of the firm's output.

Sunk costs are a particular type of fixed cost: a sunk cost is one that a firm has already incurred and which cannot be recovered, for example if it were to exit the market. The reason that costs may be sunk is that certain assets cannot be used for more than one purpose, and so have no or very little second-hand value. A typical sunk cost is advertising expenditure (the 'asset' being the advertising campaign) incurred in promoting a new product: if the product fails, the expense involved cannot be recovered. Another example of a sunk cost would be expenditure incurred in designing and/or producing a product for a specific customer, for which no one else would have any use.

(B) Marginal cost

Marginal cost is the cost incurred by a firm when producing an additional unit of output; it does not include any element of a firm's fixed costs, since fixed costs do not vary with

---

[4] Further definitions of various cost concepts can be found in Black *Oxford Dictionary of Economics* (Oxford University Press, 3rd ed, 2003); the European Commission's *Glossary of terms used in EU competition policy*, available at www.ec.europa.eu; the Commission's *Guidance on Article 102 Enforcement Priorities* OJ [2009] C 45/7, n 18; Niels, Jenkins and Kavanagh *Economics for Competition Lawyers* (Oxford University Press, 2011), pp 189–197.

output. Marginal cost usually decreases as the scale of a firm's output expands, but increases as a firm's output reaches total capacity. Marginal cost is a theoretical measure of cost: it is not used in practice[5]. More useful are the concepts of variable costs and avoidable costs, described below.

(C) Variable costs

Variable costs are costs that vary with the amount of products (rather than each additional unit of output) that a firm produces: for example a firm's expenditure on items such as raw materials, fuel and maintenance will vary according to the amount of its output; variable costs do not include any element of a firm's fixed costs.

(D) Avoidable costs

Avoidable costs refer to those costs which a firm would avoid incurring (or to put the matter another way, the savings it would make) by ceasing a particular activity over a specified period of time; for example where a firm is accused of predatory pricing over an 18-month period, it may be relevant to ask what costs it would have avoided if it had not produced the units that were the subject of the predation. Avoidable costs include some **fixed**, depending on the period of time in question, and **variable** costs, but omit **common costs**, that is to say costs that arise where two or more products are produced together even though they could be produced separately.

(E) Average variable cost ('AVC')

A firm's **average variable cost** is calculated by dividing all its variable costs by the total of its actual output. This calculation indicates the average cost of each extra unit of output.

(F) Average avoidable cost ('AAC')

A firm's **average avoidable cost** is calculated by dividing all its avoidable costs by its output. Because some fixed costs may be included in average avoidable cost, it may be higher than a firm's average variable cost.

(G) Long-run incremental cost ('LRIC')

Long-run incremental cost is the sum of the fixed and variable costs that a firm incurs when deciding to produce a particular product, referred to as 'the increment'. Long-run incremental cost does not include any variable or fixed costs *other* than those of the increment.

(H) Long-run average incremental cost ('LRAIC')

Long-run average incremental cost is calculated by dividing all its long-run incremental costs by its output. LRAIC is the same as the average total cost of a firm producing a single

---

[5] Marginal cost determines the level of output a firm will produce under conditions of perfect competition; on perfect competition see ch 1, 'The benefits of perfect competition', pp 4–6.

product. It will be lower than the average total cost of a multi-product firm enjoying economies of scope[6] as it excludes costs that are common to several products.

(I) Average total cost ('ATC')

A firm's **average total cost** is calculated by dividing both its variable costs and its fixed costs by the total of its output. It will, of course, be higher than its average variable cost.

(J) Stand alone cost

The **stand alone cost** of a firm refers to the cost that it would incur if it were to produce just a single product, so that there would be no common costs as a result of its other activities.

3. Exploitative Pricing Practices[7]

Exploitative pricing raises interesting questions for competition law. To the extent that firms form a cartel in order to restrict output, raise prices and take larger profits, EU and UK law both intervene: the price-fixing cartel is the most obvious target for any system of competition law; this has been considered in chapter 13. The position is more complicated where oligopolists indulge in tacit coordination falling short of an agreement or concerted practice; this has been considered in chapter 14. Different problems arise where a monopolist or dominant firm individually exploits its position by charging excessive (that is supra-competitive) prices.

(A) Arguments against direct control

It might seem obvious that competition authorities should take direct steps under Article 102 and analogous provisions to control exploitative pricing[8], but the case for doing so is not as clear-cut as may at first appear. There are persuasive arguments against direct control of prices under competition law.

First, if normal market forces have their way, the fact that a monopolist is able to earn large profits should, in the absence of barriers to expansion and entry, attract new entrants to the market. In this case the extraction of monopoly profits will be self-defeating in the

---

[6] Economies of scope occur where it is cheaper to produce two products together than to produce them separately; see ch 1, 'Economies of scale and scope and natural monopolies', p 10.

[7] For further reading on exploitative pricing see Bishop and Walker *The Economics of EC Competition Law* (Sweet & Maxwell, 3rd ed, 2010), paras 6.14–6.19; Evans and Padilla 'Excessive Prices: Using Economics to Define Administrable Legal Rules' (2005) 1 Journal of Competition Law and Economics 97; O'Donoghue and Padilla *The Law and Economics of Article 82 EC* (Hart Publishing, 2006), ch 12; *The Pros and Cons of High Prices* (Swedish Competition Authority, 2007); Fletcher and Jardine 'Towards an Appropriate Policy for Excessive Pricing' in *European Competition Law Annual 2007: A Reformed Approach to Article 82 EC* (Hart Publishing, 2008, eds Ehlermann and Marquis); Niels, Jenkins and Kavanagh *Economics for Competition Lawyers* (Oxford University Press, 2011), pp 268–280; the periodical literature includes Furse 'Excessive Prices, Unfair Prices and Economic Value' (2008) 4(1) European Competition Journal 59–83; Akman and Garrod 'When are Excessive Prices Unfair?' (2011) 7(2) Journal of Competition Law and Economics 403; Liyang 'Excessive Prices within EU Competition Law' (2011) 7(1) European Competition Journal 47.

[8] Note that s 2 of the Sherman Act 1890 in the US does *not* apply to exploitative excessive pricing: see Gal 'Monopoly Pricing as an Antitrust Offense in the US and the EC: Two Systems of Belief about Monopoly' (2004) 49 Antitrust Bulletin 343.

long run and can act as an important economic indicator to potential entrants to enter the market. If one accepts this view of the way that markets operate, one should accept with equanimity periods during which a firm earns a monopoly profit: the market will in due course correct itself, and intervention by the competition authorities will have the effect of undesirably distorting this process.

Secondly, there are formidable difficulties in telling whether a price really is exploitative: by what standards can this be assessed? To compare a monopolist's price with a hypothetical 'competitive' price is as much an intuitive as a scientific matter; alternatively to establish what would be a 'reasonable' price by adding an acceptable profit margin to the actual cost of producing goods or providing services is fraught with difficulties. One is that it is unclear what the relevant 'cost' of producing goods or services is: should one look at the historic costs involved in establishing a production line for goods or the cost that it would take to establish one at today's prices? Another problem is that it is difficult to apportion the common costs of a multi-product firm between its different products in order to determine whether it is making an unreasonable profit in one particular market. Furthermore the fact that a firm is earning a large profit may be attributable to its superior efficiency over its rivals, rather than to its market power.

A third argument against price control is that a monopolist should be permitted to charge a monopoly price so that it will be able to earn sufficiently large profits to be able to carry out expensive and risky research and development[9]. The Supreme Court of the US stated in its judgment in *Verizon Communications Inc v Law Offices of Curtis Trinko* that[10]:

> The opportunity to charge monopoly prices – at least for a short period – is what attracts 'business acumen' in the first place; it induces risk taking that produces innovation and economic growth.

Another view is that there is no objection to a monopolist increasing its personal wealth at consumers' expense since this involves only a transfer of wealth from one part of the economy to another, rather than a threat to the wealth of society generally. An argument against this view is that, even if one is prepared to tolerate the accretion of wealth by monopolists, there is a welfare loss where output is restricted by a firm with market power[11]; further there may be a loss to consumer welfare if the prospect of making monopoly profits entails a use of resources for that very purpose which might otherwise have been better used elsewhere in the economy[12].

A fourth problem is that even if it is accepted, despite these arguments, that exploitative pricing should be controlled, there is the difficulty of translating this policy into a sufficiently realistic legal test. A legal rule condemning exploitative pricing needs to be cast in sufficiently precise terms to enable a firm to know on which side of legality it stands.

A fifth problem is that, if a competition authority determines that a dominant undertaking is charging an excessive price, it will have to decide what remedial action should be taken: it can impose a fine for past abuse, but what directions should it issue as to future behaviour, and will the issue of such directions require continuous surveillance? Crafting pro-competitive remedies to deal with excessive pricing abuses is complex.

---

[9] See eg Schumpeter *Capitalism, Socialism and Democracy* (1942) and see ch 1, 'Dynamic efficiency', pp 5–6.
[10] 540 US 398 (2004).
[11] See ch 1, 'The harmful effects of monopoly', pp 6–7.
[12] See Posner 'The Social Costs of Monopoly and Regulation' (1975) 83 J Pol Ec 807.

A final point is that price regulation requires a competition authority to have a considerable amount of information about the market, which it may lack; it is even less easy for courts to determine what the correct level of prices should be[13].

Given these problems, it is not surprising that competition authorities tend to prefer to deploy their resources by proceeding against exclusionary abuses rather than establishing themselves as price regulators.

Where there are natural monopolies that are not under the direct control of a government there is much to be said for the establishment of a system of *ex ante* regulation of prices: the sectoral regulators in the UK have such powers[14]. When the European Commission had concerns about the high cost of tariffs for international mobile roaming services, it dealt with the matter by legislation rather than enforcement under Article 102[15]. In other cases where a competition authority is concerned that prices in a particular market appear to be higher than they would be in competitive conditions it might wish to consider conducting a sectoral review, using powers, if available, in order to discover what features of the market are causing the high prices[16]. Such a review may enable an authority to deal with any problem of excessive pricing in ways other than through price regulation, for example by reducing problems for consumers in switching between suppliers[17]. Where 'public' restrictions of competition are responsible, a competition authority may be able to play an advocacy role by suggesting ways in which the market could function more competitively[18].

These are some of the arguments against the direct control of high prices by competition authorities[19]. It is clear that neither the European Commission[20] nor the Office of Fair Trading ('the OFT') in the UK have an appetite for investigating high prices under Article 102 or the Chapter II prohibition. However this is not to say that such cases never arise, and, as will be seen in the discussion of EU and UK case law below, there have been investigations of excessive prices in both jurisdictions. The Commission's *Guidance on Article 102 Enforcement Priorities* indicates that it may proceed against exploitative behaviour, in particular where the protection of consumers or of the internal market cannot otherwise be adequately ensured[21].

---

[13] The English Court of Appeal expressed this view in the *Attheraces* case discussed at 'Cases on excessive prices', pp 725–727 below.

[14] See ch 2, 'Sectoral regulators', pp 68–69 on these regulatory bodies.

[15] See ch 23, 'Regulatory systems in the UK for utilities', pp 978–979.

[16] On the powers of the European Commission under Article 17 of Regulation 1/2003 see ch 7, 'Article 17: investigations into sectors of the economy and into types of agreements', pp 267–268.

[17] The competition authorities in the UK have favoured this non-regulatory approach in the context of market studies and market investigations, see ch 11, 'Outcomes of market studies', pp 459–466 and 'The Market Investigation Provisions in Practice', pp 479–485.

[18] See ch 1, 'Competition advocacy and public restrictions of competition', pp 24–25.

[19] For an interesting discussion of the role of a competition authority when faced with a complaint of excessive prices see the judgment of the Competition Tribunal of South Africa in Case No 13/CR/FEB04 *Harmony Gold Mining Company Ltd v Mittal Steel South Africa Ltd*, judgment of 27 March 2007, paras 70–89, reversed on appeal in Case No 70/CAC/Apr 07, judgment of 29 May 2009, paras 30–55; for comment see Lewis 'Exploitative Abuses – A Note on the Harmony Gold v Mittal Steel Excessive Pricing Case' [2008] Fordham Corporate Law Institute (ed Hawk), ch 23 and Calagno and Walker 'Excessive Pricing: Towards Clarity and Economic Coherence' (2010) 6(4) Journal of Competition Law and Economics 891.

[20] The European Commission has often said that it has no desire to become a price regulator: see eg the Commission's Vth *Report on Competition Policy* (1975), points 3–7 and 76; XXVIIth *Report on Competition Policy* (1997), point 77.

[21] OJ [2009] C 45/7, para 7; for an argument in favour of giving greater attention to issues of exploitative abuse see Lyons 'The Paradox of the Exclusion of Exploitative Abuse' in *The Pros and Cons of High Prices* (Swedish Competition Authority, 2007); this paper is also available on the website of the Centre for Competition Policy, www.ccp.uea.ac.uk.

This concern may arise when a dominant firm fails to license its technology on FRAND (fair, reasonable, and non-discriminatory) terms[22].

(B) EU law

(i) Determining whether prices are excessive

Article 102(2)(a) gives as an illustration of abuse:

directly or indirectly imposing unfair purchase or selling prices or other unfair trading conditions[23].

A practice which is harmful to consumers can be abusive, notwithstanding that it is not harmful to the structure of competition on the relevant market[24]; furthermore it is not necessary to show that the firm that is guilty of the abuse derives a commercial advantage from it[25].

(A) General Motors and United Brands

In *General Motors*[26] the Commission adopted the first decision condemning the excessive pricing of a dominant firm and imposing a fine for that practice. There had been earlier indications from the Court of Justice, in Article 267 cases concerning the use of intellectual property rights, that such action could be taken under Article 102[27]. On appeal the decision in *General Motors* was quashed by the Court of Justice[28] because there was insufficient evidence to support it.

In *United Brands*[29] the Commission imposed a fine for excessive pricing, but again its decision was quashed by the Court of Justice[30] because the Commission had failed to make out a clear case. However the Court of Justice said that:

charging a price which is excessive because it has no reasonable relation to the economic value of the product supplied is...an abuse[31].

Clearly, therefore, excessive pricing can amount to an abuse of a dominant position. The difficulty is to know at what point a price is abusive because it bears no relation to the

---

[22] See eg *Microsoft* Commission decision of 27 February 2008 (imposing a penalty of €899 million on Microsoft for refusing to provide interoperability information on reasonable and non-discriminatory terms), on appeal Case T-167/08 *Microsoft Corpn v Commission*, not yet decided; *Rambus* Commission decision of 9 December 2009 (accepting commitments under Article 9 of Regulation 1/2003 to reduce Rambus's royalty rates for licensing its computer chips), on appeal Case T-148/10 *Hynix Semiconductor v Commission*, not yet decided.

[23] For examples of the imposition of unfair trading conditions, as opposed to unfair prices, see *1998 Football World Cup* OJ [2000] L 5/55, [2000] 4 CMLR 963; *Amministratzione Autonoma dei Monopoli di Stato* OJ [1998] L 252/47, [1998] 5 CMLR 786, paras 33–46, upheld on appeal Case T-139/98 *AAMS v Commission* [2001] ECR II-3413, [2002] 4 CMLR 302, paras 73–80.

[24] *Football World Cup*, ch 18 n 23 above, paras 99–100, citing Case 6/72 *Continental Can v Commission* [1973] ECR 215, [1973] CMLR 199, para 26.

[25] *Football World Cup*, paras 101–102.

[26] OJ [1975] L 29/14, [1975] 1 CMLR D20.

[27] Case 78/70 *Deutsche Grammophon GmbH v Metro-SB-Grossmärkte GmbH* [1971] ECR 487, [1971] CMLR 631; Case 40/70 *Sirena v Eda* [1971] ECR 69, [1971] CMLR 260.

[28] Case 26/75 *General Motors v Commission* [1975] ECR 1367, [1976] 1 CMLR 95.

[29] OJ [1976] L 95/1, [1976] 1 CMLR D28.

[30] Case 27/76 *United Brands v Commission* [1978] ECR 207, [1978] 1 CMLR 429.

[31] Ibid, para 250; see similarly Case C-52/07 *Kanal 5 Ltd v STIM upa* [2008] ECR I-9275, [2009] 5 CMLR 2175, para 28.

'economic value' of the product. Various methodologies have been used, but none is free from difficulty.

The Commission in *United Brands* inferred that the price of bananas in Germany was too high by looking at the price charged in Ireland: it concluded that, since UBC could charge a low price in Ireland and still make a profit, it must follow that the higher price charged in Germany was excessive. The Court of Justice annulled the decision on the ground that it was improperly reasoned. Having stated that a price is excessive if it has no reasonable relation to its economic value, it noted that a step in the analysis of economic value can be a comparison between price and costs of production[32]. The Court accepted that it might be difficult to apportion costs to particular products, but concluded that there were no such difficulties in the case of the market for bananas. The Commission therefore had at least to:

> require UBC to produce particulars of all the constituent elements of its production costs[33].

The burden was on the Commission to prove that UBC was charging excessive and unfair prices. Having undertaken a cost analysis, the Court of Justice said that the questions to be asked are:

> whether the difference between the costs actually incurred and the price actually charged is excessive, and, if the answer to this question is in the affirmative, to consider whether a price has been charged which is either unfair in itself or when compared to other competing products[34].

(B) Deutsche Post

In *Deutsche Post AG – Interception of cross-border mail*[35] the Commission considered that Deutsche Post's prices for the onward transmission of cross-border mail were excessive. In doing so the Commission said that, as it could not make a detailed analysis of Deutsche Post's costs, it would have to use an alternative benchmark to determine whether it was guilty of abuse[36]; this it did by comparing Deutsche Post's prices for cross-border mail with its domestic tariff[37], and it decided that there was indeed an abuse. It should perhaps be added that, although cost analysis may be difficult, it is certainly not impossible; many reports of the UK Competition Commission have involved complex cost analyses[38].

(C) The Scandlines case

In *Scandlines Sverige AB v Port of Helsingborg*[39] the Commission, after an extensive investigation, rejected a complaint that port charges at the port of Helsingborg were excessively high. The Commission did not simply look at the costs incurred by the port in order to determine whether the charges were excessive; its view was that a simple 'cost-plus' approach was insufficient to establish that the prices were abusive, since it was necessary

---

[32] Ibid, para 251.   [33] Ibid, para 256.

[34] Ibid, para 252; see similarly Case 226/84 *British Leyland v Commission* [1986] ECR 3263, [1987] 1 CMLR 185, para 27; Case C-323/93 *Crespelle* [1994] ECR I-5077, para 25.

[35] OJ [2001] L 331/40, [2002] 4 CMLR 598.

[36] Ibid, para 159.   [37] Ibid, paras 160–166.

[38] See eg *The Supply of Banking Services by Clearing Banks to Small and Medium Sized Enterprises* Cm 5319 (2002), paras 2.243–2.431 and *Market investigation into payment protection insurance* (2009), paras 6.99–6.138; see also OFT Economic Discussion Paper 6 (OFT 657), *Assessing profitability in competition policy analysis* (Oxera, July 2003), available at www.oft.gov.uk.

[39] Commission decision of 23 July 2004 [2006] 4 CMLR 1224; a second complaint against the port, by Sundbusserne, was also rejected.

also to look at the economic value of the service provided[40]. The Commission looked to see if the charges were unfair, and attempted to compare them with prices charged for other services provided in the same port, and with prices charged to ferry operators in other ports; it concluded that, in particular given that the burden of proving an abuse was upon it, there was no infringement of Article 102[41].

(D) Yardstick competition

The Court of Justice suggested in *United Brands* that there are various ways of proving that a price is excessive[42]. In an Article 267 reference from France, *Corinne Bodson v Pompes Funèbres*[43], one question before the Court of Justice was whether Pompes Funèbres, which had been given an exclusive concession to provide 'external services' for funerals in a particular French town, was guilty of charging excessive prices. The Court of Justice said that, given that more than 30,000 communes in France had not granted exclusive concessions such as that enjoyed by Pompes Funèbres, but instead had left the service unregulated or operated it themselves, it must be possible to make a comparison between the prices charged by undertakings with concessions and other undertakings:

> Such a comparison could provide a basis for assessing whether or not the prices charged by the concession holders are fair[44].

This technique can be described as 'yardstick competition': comparing the performance of one undertaking with that of other ones. The idea in *Bodson* was repeated in *Lucazeau v SACEM*[45], which concerned the level of royalties charged for the playing of recorded music in discotheques; the Court of Justice again suggested that a comparison should be made with the level of fees charged in other Member States. In *Standard & Poor* the Commission used a standard set by an international standard-setting body as a benchmark to investigate the prices S&P charged for using international securities identification numbers[46]. In May 2011 S&P proposed commitments to change its pricing policy[47].

(E) Excessive or disproportionate costs should be ignored

In *Ministère Public v Tournier*[48], another case concerning the level of royalties charged to discotheques by a French performing rights society, the Court of Justice said that excessive or disproportionate costs should not be taken into account in determining the reasonableness of prices. The society in question had a *de facto* monopoly and the Court of Justice suggested that it was the very lack of competition which had led to high administrative costs: the society had no incentive to keep them down.

---

[40] Note that the English Court of Appeal reached the same conclusion in the *Attheraces* case discussed at 'Cases on excessive prices', pp 725–727 below.

[41] See Lamalle, Lindström-Rossi and Teixeira 'Two important rejection decisions on excessive pricing in the port sector' (2004) (Autumn) *Competition Policy Newsletter* 40.

[42] Case 27/76 *United Brands v Commission* [1978] ECR 207, [1978] 1 CMLR 429, para 253.

[43] Case 30/87 [1988] ECR 2479, [1989] 4 CMLR 984.

[44] Ibid, para 31.

[45] Case 110/88 [1989] ECR 2811, [1991] 4 CMLR 248.

[46] Commission MEMO/09/508, 16 November 2009.

[47] Commission Press Release IP/11/571, 16 May 2011.

[48] Case 395/87 [1989] ECR 2521, [1991] 4 CMLR 248; a recent case on the level of royalties charged by a collecting society is Case C-52/07 *Kanal 5 Ltd v STIM upa* [2008] ECR I-9275, [2009] 5 CMLR 2175.

(ii) Excessive pricing that impedes parallel imports and exports

There have been some applications of Article 102 to excessive pricing that is harmful to the single market; they are discussed below[49].

(iii) Excessive pricing that is exclusionary

Quite apart from excessive prices being exploitative and/or detrimental to the single market, they may also be exclusionary. The most obvious example would be the situation in which the owner of an essential facility charges an excessive (or discriminatory) price for granting access to it: this could be regarded as a constructive refusal to supply, and may be an abuse of a dominant position[50]. The Commission specifically states at paragraph 97 of the *Notice on the Application of the Competition Rules to Access Agreements in the Telecommunications Sector*[51] that excessive prices for access to essential facilities can be abusive[52]; the Commission summarises the case law set out above at paragraphs 105 to 109 of this *Notice*. In practice it is immensely complex to determine what the appropriate price for access to an essential facility should be[53]; a particular problem is that a firm that controls such a facility and makes use of it in a downstream market may not make an internal charge to itself for the service in question; this makes it particularly difficult to determine what price it should charge to a third party for access. For this reason the Access Directive requires separate accounting for activities related to interconnection in the electronic communications sector[54].

Given the difficulties involved in access pricing, it is not surprising that a competition authority would prefer not to become too involved in what may result in a large amount of detailed regulation: this activity is better carried out by a regulator. However there have been some occasions on which the Commission has investigated access pricing issues. For example in 1997 it took action against Belgacom for charging excessive and discriminatory prices for access to data on its subscribers for voice telephony services[55]. In *Microsoft* the Commission imposed a periodic penalty payment of €899 million on Microsoft for charging unreasonable prices for interoperability information[56].

---

[49] See 'Excessive pricing that impedes parallel imports and exports', p 764 below.

[50] See ch 17, 'Refusal to supply', pp 697–711 on the so-called essential facilities doctrine.

[51] OJ [1998] C 265/2, [1998] 5 CMLR 821.

[52] Ibid, para 97; for examples of intervention by the Commission in this sector see the Commission's XXVIIth *Report on Competition Policy* (1997), paras 67 and 77 and the XXVIIIth *Report on Competition Policy* (1998), paras 79–81.

[53] See Baumol, Ordover and Willig 'Parity Pricing and Its Critics: a Necessary Condition for Efficiency in the Provision of Bottleneck Services to Competition' (1997) Yale Journal of Regulation 14; Armstrong, Doyle and Vickers 'The Access Pricing Problem: A Synthesis' (1996) 44(2) Journal of Industrial Economics 131; OFTEL *The Pricing of Conditional Access and Access Control Services* (May 1999); see also *Telecom Corpn of New Zealand v Clear Communications* [1994] UKPC 36, [1995] 1 NZLR 385, a case which reached the Privy Council in the UK on appeal from New Zealand, in relation to pricing for access to the telecommunications 'local loop' there: the case is discussed by Tollemache in (1994) 15 ECLR 43, (1994) 15 ECLR 236 and (1995) 16 ECLR 248.

[54] *Directive 2002/19/EC of the European Parliament and of the Council on access to, and interconnection of, electronic communications networks and associated facilities*, OJ [2002] L 108/7, Article 11, as amended by Directive 2009/140/EC, OJ [2009] L 337/37.

[55] See the Commission's XXVIIth *Report on Competition Policy* (1997), point 67: the terms on which the case was settled are set out at pp 152–153 of the Report; see also point 77 of the same Report on the Commission's action against Deutsche Telekom for charging excessive prices for access to its infrastructure, and points 79–86 of the XXVIIIth *Report on Competition Policy* (1998) on further action in relation to excessive and discriminatory prices in the telecommunications sector.

[56] Commission decision of 27 February 2008, on appeal Case T-167/08 *Microsoft Corpn v Commission*, not yet decided.

(iv) Excessive pricing and aftermarkets

The Court of Justice has held that a car manufacturer may refuse to grant licences to third parties to produce spare parts for its cars; however if it charges excessive prices for the spares which it produces itself, this may amount to an abuse of its dominant position[57]. It may be that the market will solve this problem itself. Although such customers appear to be 'locked in' to the manufacturer's spare parts, the original car will eventually need to be replaced; excessive prices for spare parts may deter buyers of new cars from buying from their existing manufacturer: this in turn may deter the manufacturer from charging excessive prices for parts in the first place[58].

(v) Buyer power – excessively low prices

In *CICCE v Commission*[59] the Court of Justice rejected a complaint that the Commission had refused to condemn unfairly low prices paid by a monopsonist on the buying side of the market, as there was insufficient evidence to support the allegation. The interest of the case is that it demonstrates that, just as charging an excessively high price can be abusive, so too can the extraction of an unfairly low one demanded by an undertaking in a dominant position on the buying side of the market; on the facts of this case, however, the complainant failed.

(C) UK law

As in the case of Article 102(2)(a), section 18(2)(a) of the Competition Act 1998 specifically states that an unfair purchase or selling price may constitute an abuse of a dominant position. Guidelines have been published on the application of the competition rules, including Article 102 and the Chapter II prohibition, in particular regulated sectors, namely telecommunications[60], water and sewerage[61], energy[62] and railways[63]. An OFT Economic Discussion Paper, issued in July 2003, explores the issue of how to determine profitability in competition cases[64].

(i) Cases on excessive prices

In *Napp Pharmaceutical Holdings Ltd*[65] the OFT concluded that Napp had abused a dominant position contrary to the Chapter II prohibition by operating a discriminatory discount policy, by predatory price cutting and by charging excessive prices. Napp supplied sustained release morphine (referred to by its trade name of MST) to hospitals and to patients in the community. The prices for sales to the community were typically more than ten times higher than to hospitals. The OFT considered that the margin between Napp's costs and its prices was excessive: it did this by comparing the profit margin Napp earned on community sales of MST and comparing it with the margins it earned on sales of other products and on the sale of MST to other markets. The OFT also considered the actual prices of MST and

---

[57] Case 53/87 *CICRA v Renault* [1988] ECR 6039, [1990] 4 CMLR 265; Case 238/87 *AB Volvo v Erik Veng* [1988] ECR 6211, [1989] 4 CMLR 122.

[58] For discussion of this issue see ch 1, 'Spare parts and the aftermarket', pp 37–38.

[59] Case 298/83 [1985] ECR 1105, [1986] 1 CMLR 486.

[60] *The application of the Competition Act in the telecommunications sector*, OFT 417, February 2000.

[61] *Guidance on the application of the Competition Act 1998 in the water and sewerage sectors*, OFT 422, March 2010.

[62] *Application in the energy sector*, OFT 428, January 2005.

[63] *Application to services relating to railways*, OFT 430, October 2005.

[64] OFT Economic Discussion Paper 6 (OFT 657) *Assessing profitability in competition policy analysis* (Oxera, July 2003), available at www.otf.gov.uk.

[65] OFT decision of 30 March 2001 [2001] UKCLR 597, paras 203–234.

compared them with what a competitive price for it would be likely to be. On appeal the Competition Appeal Tribunal ('the CAT') noted the difficulties involved in determining whether a price is excessive, and concluded that the various methods used by the OFT were 'among the approaches that may reasonably be used', adding 'there are, no doubt, other methods'[66]. The CAT upheld the OFT's finding of excessive pricing[67], but considered that there were certain mitigating factors in favour of Napp, not least the uncertainty of the law on this issue, and it therefore reduced the fine that the OFT had imposed from £3.21 million to £2.2 million[68]. In June 2011 the OFT published a report indicating that since its intervention in 2001 prices for sales to the community had been reduced significantly[69].

In *Thames Water Utilities Ltd/Bath House and Albion Yard*[70] the Office of Water Services ('OFWAT') decided that Thames Water had not abused its dominant position by charging an excessive amount for the carriage of water extracted by Enviro-Logic to the latter's customers.

The complexity of determining access prices in the case of essential facilities is vividly illustrated by *Albion Water Ltd v Water Services Regulation Authority*. The CAT handed down several judgments in an appeal against a finding by OFWAT[71] that Dŵr Cymru was not guilty of offering an excessive price for the transportation of water through its water pipelines. The CAT's judgment in October 2006 reviewed the position at great length; it included extensive discussion of relevant cost principles[72] and of the 'efficient component pricing rule' ('the ECPR') advocated by some commentators as a methodology for determining the access price to essential facilities: the ECPR deducts from the retail price of a product the cost that an undertaking would avoid if it did not provide an upstream service such as the carriage of water[73]. The CAT's view was that the ECPR, which has been the subject of much criticism and has actually been banned by legislation in New Zealand[74], should not be accepted 'without careful scrutiny'[75]. Later in its judgment the CAT decided that the ECPR was not a safe methodology to use in the case before it[76], and concluded that the evidence 'strongly suggested' that the price quoted by Dŵr Cymru was excessive[77]. Following a further investigation of the costs involved by OFWAT the CAT concluded[78] that Dŵr Cymru had indeed offered prices that were so excessive that they were unfair and therefore abusive: the quoted access price to the Ashgrove system materially exceeded the costs reasonably attributable to the distribution of water by Dŵr Cymru; it was exclusionary as well as exploitative.

---

[66] Case No 1000/1/1/01 *Napp Pharmaceutical Holdings Ltd v Director General of Fair Trading* [2002] CAT 1, [2002] CompAR 13, para 392.

[67] Ibid, paras 389–442; for comment on the finding of excessive pricing in this case see Kon and Turnbull 'Pricing and the Dominant Firm: Implications of the [Competition Appeal Tribunal's] Judgment in the *Napp* Case' (2003) 24 ECLR 70, pp 82–86.

[68] Ibid, paras 497–541.

[69] *Evaluating the impact of the OFT's 2001 abuse of dominance case against Napp Pharmaceuticals*, OFT 1332, June 2011.

[70] OFT decision of 31 March 2003 [2003] UKCLR 709.

[71] OFWAT decision of 26 May 2004 [2004] UKCLR 1317.

[72] Case No 1046/2/4/04 [2006] CAT 23, [2007] CompAR 22, in particular paras 448–637.

[73] Ibid, paras 638–836.

[74] This legislation followed litigation in the telecommunications sector culminating in the decision of the Privy Council in *Telecom Corporation of New Zealand v Clear Communications* [1994] UKPC 36, [1995] 1 NZLR 385.

[75] Case No 1046/2/4/04 [2006] CAT 23, [2007] CompAR 22, para 739.   [76] Ibid, para 835.

[77] Ibid, para 637.

[78] Case No 1046/2/4/04 [2008] CAT 31, [2009] CompAR 28; see also [2009] CAT 12, [2009] CompAR 223, on remedy and costs; subsequently Albion commenced a 'follow-on' claim for damages against Dŵr Cymru: see Case No 1166/5/7/10 [2010] CAT 30, [2011] CAT 1 and [2011] CAT 18 on applications to strike out the claim.

In *SSL International plc: contraceptive sheaths*[79] the OFT concluded that, although it was possible that the prices of SSL's male condoms were high, a substantial amount of time and expense would be needed to reach a view as to whether they were excessive. The OFT's view was that further investigation was unlikely to be a sensible use of resources; in particular the OFT considered that there was evidence of emerging competition and that, if the outcome of the case were to be the imposition of a price cap, this might stifle such entry.

An intervention by the OFT under the Financial Services and Markets Act 2000 led to the London Stock Exchange reducing its issuing fees in 2003[80].

A particularly interesting case on excessive pricing arose in *Attheraces Ltd v The British Horseracing Board Ltd*[81], a 'standalone' action by Attheraces with no involvement on the part of any competition authority. Attheraces, a broadcaster, required so-called 'pre-race data' about British horse races in the possession of the British Horseracing Board ('the BHB'), the administrator and regulator of British horseracing. Attheraces wanted to make these data available to overseas bookmakers. It complained, and the judge at first instance held[82], that BHB had abused a dominant position by threatening to refuse to supply Attheraces, by charging it unfair prices, and by discriminating against it. The Court of Appeal allowed the appeal by BHB. It is of interest to note that Mummery LJ stated at the outset that the nature of the issues under consideration were ones that might more satisfactorily be solved by arbitration or by a specialist body equipped with appropriate expertise and flexible powers, rather than within the adversarial procedures of an ordinary private action[83]. The Court of Appeal accepted the suggestion in paragraph 250 of the Court of Justice's judgment in *United Brands v Commission* that a price that significantly exceeds the economic value of the product supplied could be abusive, but pointed out that this formulation 'begs a fundamental question: what constitutes economic value?'[84]. The court concluded that it was not possible to conclude that a price was abusive simply on the basis of a 'cost-plus' approach: that is to say that it is not sufficient merely to show that a price exceeds cost by more than a 'reasonable' amount[85]. In so far as the judge had reached his conclusion on the basis of cost plus a reasonable return he had adopted too narrow an approach: in particular he was wrong to reject BHB's contention that, in considering the economic value of the data, the amount that the overseas bookmakers were willing to pay Attheraces was relevant[86]. The Court of Appeal specifically noted that the principal object of Article 102 was to protect consumers – in this case the ultimate punters who bet on horse races – and not competitors such as Attheraces: it said that there was little, if any, evidence of harm to competition[87].

(ii) Excessively low prices

The OFT has said that charging excessively low prices is likely to be an abuse only in exceptional circumstances[88]. In *The Association of British Travel Agents and British Airways plc*[89] the OFT concluded that BA was not guilty of paying excessively *low* prices to travel agencies by offering a commission that failed to cover their costs of selling tickets: in the

---

[79] OFT case closure of 11 May 2005, available at www.oft.gov.uk.

[80] See *London Stock Exchange issuer fees*, OFT 713, March 2004.

[81] [2007] EWCA Civ 38, [2007] UKCLR 309; the judgment was considered by the Chancellor of the High Court in *Humber Oil Terminals Trustee Ltd v Associated British Ports* [2011] EWHC 352, paras 17–21 and 33.

[82] *Attheraces Ltd v The British Horseracing Board Ltd* [2005] EWHC 3015, [2005] UKCLR 757.

[83] [2007] EWCA Civ 38, [2007] UKCLR 309, para 7.   [84] Ibid, para 204.

[85] Ibid, para 209.   [86] Ibid, para 218.   [87] Ibid, para 215.

[88] *BetterCare Group Ltd/North & West Belfast Health & Social Services Trust (remitted)*, OFT decision of 18 December 2003 [2004] UKCLR 455, para 56.

[89] OFT decision of 11 December 2002 [2003] UKCLR 136.

OFT's view it would have been possible for the agents to charge their clients a fee for the service of issuing tickets, and it was not incumbent on BA to pay them an amount that would cover their costs in doing so[90].

(iii) Section 13 of the Competition Act 1980

There is a provision in section 13 of the Competition Act 1980, which remains in force, whereby the Secretary of State may ask the OFT to investigate prices 'of major public concern': only a factual report may be made under this section, which has never been used[91].

4. Rebates that have Effects Similar to Exclusive Dealing Agreements[92]

In chapter 17 the application of Article 102 to exclusive agreements, and in particular exclusive purchasing agreements[93], was considered. The basic objection to such agreements is that they may horizontally foreclose competitors of the dominant firm. Article 102 may also apply to pricing practices that have the same effect as exclusive purchasing agreements. As we shall see, there have been many cases in which 'fidelity' or 'loyalty' rebates[94], 'target' rebates, discounts and bonuses have been found to be abusive. The text that follows will use the expression 'rebates' to include all these practices. It is perhaps worth saying at the outset that this is one of the least satisfactory areas of EU competition law. Three particular inter-connected problems can be identified.

First, the law has developed along formalistic lines, whereas the economics that inform the way in which firms charge for their products are complex: this complexity suggests that form-based rules are not sophisticated enough to deal with the phenomena under scrutiny. A second problem – which restates the first one in the language of competition law – is that some of the case law suggests that loyalty rebates are unlawful *per se*, whereas it is arguable that actual or potential anti-competitive effects ought to be demonstrated before a rebate is condemned as unlawful[95]. A variant of *per se* unlawfulness is that loyalty rebates are presumed to be unlawful unless they can be objectively justified.

---

[90] Ibid, paras 28–37.

[91] See *Halsbury's Laws of England*, vol 47, para 505, n 21.

[92] For further reading on exclusive dealing agreements and rebates see the OECD reports on *Loyalty and Fidelity Discounts and Rebates* (2002) and on *Bundled and Loyalty Discounts and Rebates* (2008), both available at www.oecd.org; section 7 of DG COMP's *Discussion paper on the application of Article [102] of the Treaty to exclusionary abuses*; Bishop and Walker *The Economics of EC Competition Law* (Sweet & Maxwell, 3rd ed, 2010), paras 6.28–6.59; O'Donoghue and Padilla *The Law and Economics of Article 82 EC* (Hart Publishing, 2006), pp 374–406; Van den Bergh and Camesasca *European Competition Law and Economics: A Comparative Perspective* (Sweet & Maxwell, 2nd ed, 2006), pp 254–264; Niels, Jenkins and Kavanagh *Economics for Competition Lawyers* (Oxford University Press, 2011), pp 223–238; there is also an abundance of periodical literature on this subject: see eg Ridyard 'Exclusionary Pricing and Price Discrimination Abuses Under Article 82 – An Economic Analysis' (2002) 19 ECLR 286; Temple Lang and O'Donoghue 'Defining Legitimate Competition: How to Clarify Pricing Abuses under Article 82 EC' (2002) 26 Fordham International Law Journal 83; Kallaugher and Sher 'Rebates Revisited: Anti-competitive Effects and Exclusionary Abuse Under Article 82' (2004) 21 ECLR 263; Gyselen 'Rebates, Competition on the Merits or Exclusionary Practice?' in *European Competition Law Annual 2003: What is an Abuse of a Dominant position?* (Hart Publishing, 2006, eds Ehlermann and Atanasiu), p 287; Bishop 'Loyalty Rebates, and "Merger Standards": A roadmap for the practical assessment of Article 82 investigations' in *European Competition Law Annual 2007: A Reformed Approach to Article 82 EC* (Hart Publishing, 2008, eds Ehlermann and Marquis).

[93] See ch 17, 'Exclusive Dealing Agreements', pp 682–688.

[94] These two terms can be used interchangeably.

[95] See ch 5, 'Are there or should there be any *per se* rules under Article 102?', pp 199–201.

Although this position is less extreme than outright *per se* unlawfulness, it is also questionable for two reasons. The first argument against this variant is that rebates are often pro-competitive, so that it makes little sense to presume the contrary. The second is that the burden of proving that a rebate is objectively justified would be on the dominant undertaking[96]: if it has to prove a precise cost justification for every rebate this might be impossible to achieve in practice, because some rebates are simply offered to retain customers rather than to reflect savings in costs: it follows that they could not be objectively justified, so that a presumed unlawfulness would increase the likelihood of prohibiting pro-competitive behaviour[97].

The final problem, which follows from formalism, is that the law on rebates has developed with little or no reference to the cost concepts described at the beginning of this chapter. Later in this chapter we will see that the case law on predation, for example, is built upon the concepts of average variable and average total cost. The case law on rebates, which developed from the rule against dominant firms entering into exclusive purchasing agreements, does not have an explicit cost component, other than that a rebate can be defended on efficiency grounds[98].

An attractive way of addressing these problems would be for the law to condemn rebates only where it can be shown that they are likely to have an exclusionary effect on competitors as efficient as the dominant undertaking[99]. This would be consistent with the approach taken by the Court of Justice in two cases on margin squeeze[100] and with the Commission's *Guidance on Article 102 Enforcement Priorities*[101]. Paragraph 25 of the *Guidance* says that, in determining whether a dominant firm's pricing should be condemned, it is appropriate to look at the relationship between that firm's costs and its sales prices. Should the law on rebates begin to focus more on 'as efficient' competitors it is likely that greater attention would be given to cost concepts.

(A) EU law

The case law on rebates began by condemning them where they were explicitly linked to the loyalty of a customer. Subsequently it has been extended to target rebates which, though not explicitly linked to loyalty, are likely to have an exclusionary effect. The Court of Justice has stated that the law that forbids exclusionary rebates is based on Article 102 as a whole: it is not based solely upon the wording of Article 102(2)(b), which refers to practices that limit production, markets or technical development to the prejudice of consumers[102].

(i) The case law on loyalty rebates
(A) Hoffmann-La Roche

The obvious starting point is the Court of Justice's judgment in *Hoffmann-La Roche v Commission*[103]. The Court of Justice held that Hoffmann-La Roche had abused its dominant position both by entering into exclusive purchasing agreements with some of its

---

[96] See ch 5, 'Burden of proof', p 213.   [97] See further 'Permissible rebates', p 736 below.

[98] See 'Permissible rebates', p 736 below.

[99] On the 'as efficient competitor' test see ch 5, 'Article 102 protects competition; and competition is for the benefit of consumers', pp 196–197.

[100] Case C-280/08 P *Deutsche Telekom v Commission* [2010] ECR I-000, [2010] 5 CMLR 1495 and Case C-52/09 *Konkurrensverket v TeliaSonera Sverige* [2011] ECR I-000, [2011] 4 CMLR 982.

[101] See 'The Commission's approach to conditional rebates in its Guidance on Artical 102 Enforcement Priorities', pp 735–736.

[102] Case C-95/04 P *British Airways plc v Commission* [2007] ECR I-2331, [2007] 4 CMLR 982, para 58.

[103] Case 85/76 [1979] ECR 461, [1979] 3 CMLR 211; loyalty rebates were condemned in an earlier case that was predominantly concerned with cartelisation of the sugar market: Cases 43/73 etc *Suiker Unie v Commission* [1975] ECR 1663, [1976] 1 CMLR 295, paras 517–528.

customers and by offering others loyalty rebates. In relation to the latter the Court of Justice said that it was unlawful for a dominant firm to tie a customer by an exclusive purchasing commitment and that:

> The same applies if the [dominant] undertaking, without tying the purchasers by a formal obligation, applies, either under the terms of the agreements concluded with these purchasers or unilaterally, a system of fidelity rebates, that is to say discounts conditional on the customer's obtaining all or most of its requirements – whether the quantity of its purchases be large or small – from the undertaking in a dominant position[104].

This passage makes clear that the prohibition of loyalty rebates is directly related to the law that prohibits exclusive purchasing agreements. Behaviour becomes abusive when the inducement caused by the promise of loyalty rebates to a customer to purchase all or most of its requirements from the dominant firm is so great that it has the same effect that a contractual stipulation to purchase exclusively would have done[105].

The test set out in paragraph 89 of *Hoffmann-La Roche* (and in subsequent cases) is expressed as a *per se* rule; however, as has been pointed out in chapter 5[106], it is highly questionable whether *per se* illegality is appropriate under Article 102: this is particularly so in the case of rebates. Most rebates are simply manifestations of the competitive process; customers obviously benefit from the lower price that a rebate necessarily results in: a point acknowledged by the Commission's *Guidance on Article 102 Enforcement Priorities*[107]. The *Guidance* should also mean that future cases will concern rebates which the Commission considers to have had, or to be likely to have, an anti-competitive foreclosing effect[108]. If this is the case, and if, for example, the Commission does consistently apply the 'as-efficient' competitor test to rebates, over time this should have a positive influence on the content of the law.

Paragraph 89 of the judgment in *Hoffmann-La Roche* states that it is abusive to offer rebates 'conditional on the customer's obtaining all or most of its requirements – whether the quantity of its purchases be large or small – from the undertaking in a dominant position'. As has been seen in chapter 16, the block exemption for vertical agreements defines a non-compete obligation as one which requires a customer to obtain 80 per cent or more of its requirements of goods or services from the supplier[109]; it is not unreasonable to suppose that a similar threshold applies under Article 102 when determining what is meant by 'most' of a customer's requirements.

The stipulation that loyalty rebates are unlawful even where the quantities involved are small imposes a strict standard: where the customer purchases small quantities, the anti-competitive foreclosure effect – if any – is likely to be insignificant; however the Court of Justice's formulation indicates that there would still be an abuse. The 2009 judgment of the General Court in *Solvay v Commission* points to the same conclusion, in which it rejected an argument that a rebate of 1.5 per cent on all purchases of soda-ash was

---

[104] Case 85/76 [1979] ECR 461, [1979] 3 CMLR 211, para 89; the Court of Justice also objected to the 'English clause' requiring the buyer to report any better offer it received to Hoffmann-La Roche and preventing it from accepting the offer unless Roche chose not to match it: ibid para 102–108.

[105] It should be noted that, where a dominant firm offers different rebates to different customers, this may result in an accusation of discrimination contrary to Article 102(2)(c) as well: see 'Price Discrimination', pp 759–764. below.

[106] Ch 5, 'Are there or should there be any *per se* rules under Article 102?', pp 199–201.

[107] OJ [2009] C 45/7, paras 37 and 46: see 'The Commission's approach to conditional rebates in its *Guidance on Article 102 Enforcement Priorities*', pp 735–736 below.

[108] Ibid, paras 20 and 38; note that the Commission applied the 'as efficient' competitor test in the *Intel* case see 'The *Intel* case', p 732 below.

[109] See ch 16, 'Article 5(1)(a): non-compete obligations', pp 669–670.

too small to have an anti-competitive effect[110]. However the Commission's *Guidance on Article 102 Enforcement Priorities* indicates that it will consider the percentage of sales affected by a rebate scheme when deciding whether to initiate proceedings[111].

(B) Further case law of the EU Courts

The strict treatment of loyalty rebates can be found in several further cases[112]. In the *Plasterboard* case the EU Courts substantially upheld a Commission decision[113] that British Gypsum Ltd and its parent, BPB Industries plc, had abused their dominant position by offering loyalty payments to builders' merchants in Great Britain who stocked only their plasterboard[114]. BPB and British Gypsum claimed that the payments were made in order to assist merchants with the cost of promotion and advertising. The General Court agreed with the Commission that, even if there was truth in this, the payments were also intended to induce loyalty on the part of merchants and so were abusive[115].

In *Irish Sugar*[116] the Commission condemned fidelity and target rebates. On appeal the General Court, upholding the decision, stated that:

> fidelity rebates granted by an undertaking in a dominant position are an abuse...where their aim is, by granting financial advantages, to prevent customers from obtaining their supplies from competing producers[117].

In the *Soda-ash* decisions[118] the Commission condemned the exclusionary practices, including loyalty rebates, of Solvay and ICI. The original decisions were set aside for procedural reasons[119]. The Commission re-adopted the decisions, concluding again that Solvay and ICI were guilty of abusive rebates[120]. On appeal against the second decisions the General Court upheld the Commission's finding that rebates targeted at customers' marginal, or 'top-slice', requirements for soda-ash were abusive[121], and rejected Solvay's argument that the rebates were based on an objective justification[122].

In *Compagnie Maritime Belge Transports v Commission*[123] the Court of Justice upheld the decision of the Commission that the granting of loyalty rebates by members of a liner conference amounted to an abuse of a collective dominant position[124]; it was irrelevant to

---

[110] Case T-57/01 *Solvay SA v Commission* [2009] ECR II-4621 [2011] 4 CMLR 9, paras 355, on appeal Case C-109/10 P, not yet decided; Advocate General Kokott gave her Opinion on 14 April 2011 that the General Court's finding was 'beyond legal reproach': para 86.

[111] OJ [2009] C 45/7, paras 20 and 38.

[112] As well as the cases mentioned in the text see *Deutsche Post* OJ [2001] L 125/27, [2001] 5 CMLR 99; *DSD* OJ [2001] L 166/1, [2001] 5 CMLR 609 (a pricing practice that was not concerned with rebates but was found to have the effect of excluding competitors), upheld on appeal Case T-151/01 *Duales System Deutschland v Commission* [2007] ECR II-1607, [2007] 5 CMLR 300, upheld on appeal Case C-385/07 P [2009] ECR I-6155, [2009] 5 CMLR 2215.

[113] OJ [1989] L 10/50, [1990] 4 CMLR 464.

[114] Case T-65/89 *BPB Industries plc and British Gypsum v Commission* [1993] ECR II-389, [1993] 5 CMLR 32, upheld on appeal Case C-310/93 P [1995] ECR I-865, [1997] 4 CMLR 238.

[115] Case T-65/89 [1993] ECR II-389, [1993] 5 CMLR 32, para 71.

[116] OJ [1997] L 258/1, [1997] 5 CMLR 666.

[117] Case T-228/97 *Irish Sugar v Commission* [1999] ECR II-2969, [1999] 5 CMLR 1300, para 197.

[118] *Soda-ash/Solvay* OJ [1991] L 152/21 and *Soda-ash/ICI* OJ [1991] L 152/40.

[119] Cases T-30/91 etc *Solvay SA v Commission* [1995] ECR II-1775, [1996] 5 CMLR 57, upheld on appeal Cases C-286/95 P etc *Commission v ICI* [2000] ECR I-2341, [2000] 5 CMLR 413.

[120] *Soda-ash/Solvay* OJ [2003] L 10/10 and *Soda-ash/ICI* OJ [2003] L 10/33.

[121] Case T-57/01 [2009] ECR II-4621, [2011] 4 CMLR 9, paras 314–341, on appeal Case C-101/10 P *Solvay SA v Commission*, not yet decided.

[122] Case T-57/01 [2009] ECR II-4621, [2011] 4 CMLR 9, paras 334–335.

[123] Cases C-395/96 P etc [2000] ECR I-1365, [2000] 4 CMLR 1076.

[124] Ibid, paras 129–137.

the finding of abuse under Article 102 that the rebates may have benefited from the block exemption on maritime transport[125].

(C) *The* Intel *case*

In May 2009 the Commission imposed a fine of €1.06 billion, the largest fine ever imposed on a single undertaking, on Intel for an abuse of a dominant position in the market for computer processing units ('CPUs') by offering rebates to computer manufacturers conditional upon them purchasing all or the great majority of their CPUs from it[126]. The Commission considered that its decision was consistent with the case law[127] and its *Guidance on Article 102 Enforcement Priorities*[128]. The Commission found that Intel's rebates were capable of anti-competitive fore-closure as an 'as efficient' competitor would have had to price its CPUs below average avoidable cost[129]. Intel argued that its rebates merely responded to competition and increased efficiency. The Commission's view was that Intel had gone beyond legitimate competition for business, and had failed to substantiate any efficiencies[130]. The Commission also considered that Intel was guilty of 'naked restrictions' by making payments to computer manufacturers to prevent or delay the launch of competitors' products[131]. Intel has appealed to the General Court[132].

(ii) Individualised target rebates

The cases just discussed were concerned with rebates explicitly granted in return for loy-alty. However it will take only a moment's reflection to recognise that a dominant firm may be able to achieve 'loyal' purchasing without specifically linking rebates to loyalty. One obvious method is to set customers a target, and to promise rebates – perhaps very generous ones – if the target is met. It is normal practice for firms – whether dominant or not – to want to increase sales, and there is nothing sinister in a pricing policy which is geared to the incentivisation of a customer to purchase more units in the future than in the past. The question under Article 102 is when such a practice should be condemned as abusive. It is important in such cases to distinguish two questions: first, whether a rebate could have a loyalty-inducing effect; and secondly, whether a loyalty-inducing rebate could have an anti-competitive foreclosure effect. The difference is reflected in the Commission's *Guidance on Article 102 Enforcement Priorities* which states that a rebate might have the effect of inducing loyalty without necessarily being harmful to competition[133].

There have been several cases in which target rebates have been condemned because of their loyalty-inducing effects, even though there was no explicit requirement of loyalty: in most cases the targets were individualised for each customer according to its particular procurement needs.

(A) Michelin I *and* Michelin II

In *Michelin I*[134] the Commission condemned rebates payable to customers for replacement tyres in the Netherlands that reached annual sales targets. The targets were set for each

---

[125] Ibid, para 130.
[126] Commission decision of 13 May 2009: see also Commission MEMO/09/400, 21 September 2009; for comment see Allibert, Bartha, Bösze, Hödlmayr, Kaminski and Scholz 'Commission finds abuse of domi-nance in the Intel case' (2009) 3 *Competition Policy Newsletter* 31.
[127] Commission decision of 13 May 2009, paras 920–1001.   [128] Ibid, para 916.
[129] Ibid, paras 1002–1576.   [130] Ibid, paras 1617–1639.
[131] Ibid, paras 1641–1681, citing the General Court's judgment in Case T-228/97 *Irish Sugar v Commission* [1999] ECR II-2969, [1999] 5 CMLR 1300, paras 226–234.
[132] Case T-286/09 *Intel Corp v Commission*, not yet decided.
[133] See 'The Commission's approach to conditional rebates in its *Guidance on Article 102 Enforcement Priorities*', pp 735–736 below.
[134] OJ [1981] L 353/33, [1982] 1 CMLR 643.

customer individually, and were usually higher than for the preceding year. The Court of Justice upheld the Commission's finding on this point[135], saying that:

> any system under which discounts are granted according to the quantities sold during a relatively long reference period has the inherent effect, at the end of that period, of increasing pressure on the buyer to reach the purchase figure needed to obtain the discount or to avoid suffering the loss for the entire period[136].

The case made clear that a lack of transparency in a system of rebates is an exacerbating factor, making a finding of abuse more likely[137]. However the opposite point should also be noted: if a rebate scheme is loyalty-inducing and otherwise abusive, it will not be saved by the fact that it is transparent[138].

In *Michelin II*[139] the Commission condemned various practices in the French (as opposed to the Dutch) replacement tyre market, including individualised annual volume targets. The Commission said that rebates operated by reference to a period of more than three months will always be unlawful[140], a statement that seems clearly to be incorrect. The General Court upheld the Commission's findings of abuse in this case[141]. The General Court said that the loyalty-inducing nature of a system increases in proportion to the length of the reference period: '[t]he longer the reference period, the more loyalty-inducing the quantity rebate system'[142]; however the General Court also said that the Court of Justice had never held that the reference point could not be for more than three months[143]. The General Court was satisfied that Michelin's scheme, which had a reference period of one year, and where the discount was fixed on the basis of total turnover, had an abusive loyalty-inducing effect.

(B) The Virgin/British Airways case

In *Virgin/British Airways*[144] the Commission imposed a fine of €6.8 million on British Airways for operating a system of commission payments[145] and other incentives with travel agents which it considered had the object or effect of excluding BA's competitors from UK markets for air transport, by rewarding loyalty and by discriminating between travel agents[146]. The level of commission payable increased as a new target was reached, and that increased amount was payable on *all* the tickets sold, not just on the *incremental* sales above the target. This meant that the loyalty-inducing effect was a powerful one which, in the Commission's view, affected the ability of other airlines to compete with BA. The

---

[135] Case 322/81 *NV Nederlandse Banden-Industrie Michelin v Commission* [1983] ECR 3461, [1985] 1 CMLR 282.

[136] Ibid, para 81.

[137] Ibid, para 83; the Commission announced in April 2004 that it had closed an investigation into Interbrew's practices towards Belgian wholesalers of its beer following changes introduced by Interbrew: one was that its rebate system in future would be entirely transparent: Commission Press Release IP/04/574, 30 April 2004.

[138] Case T-203/01 *Michelin v Commission* [2003] ECR II-4071, [2004] 4 CMLR 923, para 111.

[139] OJ [2002] L 143/1, [2002] 5 CMLR 388; for critical comment, see Sher 'Price Discounts and *Michelin 2*: What Goes Around, Comes Around' (2002) 23 ECLR 482.

[140] OJ [2002] L 143/1, [2002] 5 CMLR 388, para 216.

[141] Case T-203/01 *Michelin v Commission* [2003] ECR II-4071, [2004] 4 CMLR 923.

[142] Ibid, para 88.   [143] Ibid, para 85.   [144] OJ [2000] L 30/1, [2000] 4 CMLR 999.

[145] BA was a purchaser of services from travel agents, to which it paid a commission for tickets sold: the 'rebates' in this case refer to the level of commissions paid.

[146] On BA's discriminatory treatment of different travel agents contrary to Article 102(2)(c), see 'Is the dominant undertaking guilty of applying dissimilar conditions to equivalent transactions?', pp 761–762 below.

Commission's finding that BA's reward scheme was abusive was upheld on appeal to the General Court[147] and to the Court of Justice[148].

The Court of Justice noted that the important precedent was *Michelin* rather than *Hoffmann-La Roche*, since the BA reward scheme was not based on loyalty but rather targets[149]. The Court said that, in order to decide whether a scheme such as that of BA could be abusive:

> it first has to be determined whether those discounts or bonuses can produce an exclusionary effect, that is to say whether they are capable, first, of making market entry very difficult or impossible for competitors of the undertaking in a dominant position and, secondly, of making it more difficult or impossible for its co-contractors to choose between various sources of supply or commercial partners[150].

The Court noted that BA devised bonus schemes on an individualised basis, linked to travel agents' growth in turnover during a given period[151]. The Court referred to the very strong inducement effect that arose from the fact that the bonus was payable not simply by reference to the *growth* in turnover, but to the *whole* of the turnover:

> It could therefore be of decisive importance for the commission income of a travel agent as a whole whether or not he sold a few extra BA tickets after achieving a certain turnover[152].

The General Court was satisfied that the Commission had demonstrated exclusionary effects[153]; BA's appeal to the Court of Justice on this point was dismissed as inadmissible[154]. It is questionable whether there was convincing evidence that BA's reward schemes had anti-competitive effects on the market; indeed an appeal court in the US concluded that similar BA incentive schemes did not restrict competition[155].

The Court of Justice rejected the argument that BA's reward schemes were objectively justified[156].

(C) The Prokent-Tomra case

In *Prokent-Tomra* the Commission imposed a fine of €24 million on Tomra for entering into exclusivity agreements, quantity commitments and loyalty-inducing rebate schemes on the market for the supply of machines for the collection of used drink containers in return for a deposit[157]. The Commission's findings of abuse, and the fine, were upheld on appeal to the General Court in *Tomra v Commission*[158].

---

[147] Case T-219/99 *British Airways plc v Commission* [2003] ECR II-5917, [2004] 4 CMLR 1008, paras 241–249 and 270–300.

[148] Case C-95/04 P *British Airways plc v Commission* [2007] ECR I-2331, [2007] 4 CMLR 982; on the Court of Justice judgment see Odudu 'Case C-95/04 P *BA plc v Commission*' (2007) 44 CML Rev 1781; Bacon 'European Court of Justice Upholds Judgment of the European Court of First Instances in the *British Airways/Virgin* Saga' (2007) 3 Competition Policy International 227.

[149] Case C-95/04 P [2007] ECR I-2331, [2007] 4 CMLR 982, para 65.   [150] Ibid, para 68.

[151] Ibid, paras 71–72.   [152] Ibid, paras 73–74.

[153] Case T-219/99 *British Airways plc v Commission* [2003] ECR II-5917, [2004] 4 CMLR 1008, paras 293–298.

[154] Case C-95/04 P [2007] ECR I-2331, [2007] 4 CMLR 982, para 101.

[155] *Virgin Atlantic Airways Ltd v British Airways plc* 257 F 3d 256 (2nd Cir 2001); cf in South Africa Case No 18/CR/Mar01 *Competition Commission v South African Airways (Pty) Ltd*, judgment of 28 July 2005 and Case No 92/CAC/Mar10 *South African Airways (Pty) Ltd v Comair Air Ltd*, judgment of 11 April 2011 (both finding South African Airways' incentive schemes, similar to that of British Airways, infringed the equivalent of Article 102 in South Africa's Competition Act).

[156] See 'Permissible rebates', p 736 below.

[157] Commission decision of 29 March 2006; see Maier-Rigaud and Vaigauskaite 'Prokent/Tomra, a textbook case? Abuse of dominance under perfect competition' (2006) (Summer) *Competition Policy Newsletter* 19.

[158] Case T-155/06 *Tomra Systems ASA v Commission* [2010] ECR II-000, [2011] 4 CMLR 416; for (critical) comment, see Federico 'Tomra v Commission of the European Communities: Reversing progress on rebates?'

(iii) The Commission's approach to conditional rebates in its *Guidance on Article 102 Enforcement Priorities*

The Commission discusses the factors which it will take into account when deciding whether to intervene in relation to conditional rebates in paragraphs 37 to 46 of its *Guidance on Article 102 Enforcement Priorities*. Conditional rebates are granted as a reward for certain purchasing behaviour, such as attaining individual sales targets, and can have foreclosure effects similar to exclusive purchasing agreements[159]. At paragraph 37 of the *Guidance* it draws a distinction between conditional rebates applicable to all sales ('retroactive rebates') as opposed to rebates paid only on incremental sales ('incremental rebates'). The Commission notes that retroactive rebates may foreclose the market significantly as they may make it less attractive for customers to switch even small amounts of demand to competitors[160].

Paragraph 38 of the *Guidance* refers back to paragraph 20, which sets out the factors that the Commission will take into account when deciding whether to take action under Article 102[161]. Paragraphs 39 to 45 discuss additional factors that the Commission will consider in the case of conditional rebates. The Commission says that anti-competitive foreclosure is more likely in cases where competitors are not able to compete on equal terms for the entire demand of each individual customer[162]. This may be so when a customer is bound to purchase a certain amount of its needs from a dominant firm, for example because that firm is an unavoidable trading partner whose product is a 'must-stock item'. This was an important part of the reasoning of the General Court in *Tomra v Commission*[163] and of the Commission in *Intel*[164] in support of the conclusion that the loyalty-inducing rebates in those cases could have anti-competitive effects.

In order to assess whether a conditional rebate can lead to anti-competitive foreclosure the Commission intends to investigate the dominant firm's prices, rebates and costs, thereby responding to the criticism that analysis in this area is insufficiently costs-oriented. The Commission will seek to determine the 'effective price' a rival would have to offer a customer as a compensation for the loss of a conditional rebate if the latter would switch part of its demand from the dominant firm[165]. The Commission considers that:

- where a dominant firm is charging an effective price below AAC, the rebate is generally capable of foreclosing competitors as efficient as the dominant firm
- where a dominant firm is charging an effective price that is between AAC and LRAIC, other relevant factors, such as competitors' counterstrategies, should be taken into account to determine the possibility of anti-competitive foreclosure
- where a dominant firm is selling at an effective price above LRAIC, the rebate is normally not capable of anti-competitive foreclosure.

(2011) 32(3) ECLR 139; the judgment is on appeal to the Court of Justice, Case C-549/10 P *Tomra Systems ASA v Commission*, not yet decided.

[159] *Guidance on Article 102 Enforcement Priorities*, para 37; the Commission points out that conditional rebates can have foreclosure effects without the dominant undertaking having to sell at a loss.

[160] Ibid, para 40

[161] See ch 5, 'Effects analysis', pp 208–210.

[162] *Guidance on Article 102 Enforcement Priorities*, para 39.

[163] Case T-155/06 *Tomra Systems ASA v Commission* [2010] ECR II-000, [2011] 4 CMLR 416, paras 269–271, on appeal to the Court of Justice, Case C-549/10 P, not yet decided.

[164] See Commission decision of 13 May 2009, paras 870–874, 1005 and 1010, on appeal to the General Court Case T-286/09 *Intel Corp v Commission*, not yet decided.

[165] *Guidance on Article 102 Enforcement Priorities*, para 41; this is a specific application of the methodology for all exclusionary pricing abuses: ibid, paras 23–27.

Paragraphs 27 and 45 of the *Guidance* explain that the cost/price analysis will be integrated into a more general assessment of anti-competitive foreclosure, taking into account other relevant quantitative and qualitative evidence. An important consideration will be whether the rebate system is applied with an individualised or a standardised threshold since the former is more likely to create a loyalty-enhancing effect[166].

(iv) Permissible rebates

As already noted, rebates and similar practices are a normal part of commercial life. Rebates should be condemned only where they could have a detrimental effect on competition[167], for example because they operate as a surrogate for an exclusive purchasing agreement. In *Hoffmann-La Roche v Commission* the Court of Justice accepted that not all discounts should be treated as abusive: for example it said that quantity discounts linked solely to the volume of purchases, fixed objectively and applicable to all purchasers, would be permissible[168]. Rebates granted for prompt payment would presumably also be regarded as objectively justifiable. Payments for services rendered by a customer, such as participation in a special promotion or for providing shelf-space in a supermarket, should also be permissible, provided that they are not, in fact, loyalty payments for exclusivity[169]. In *British Airways v Commission*[170] the General Court rejected BA's argument that its travel reward scheme was objectively justified because of the contribution it made to the recovery of its fixed costs. Paragraph 46 of the *Guidance on Article 102 Enforcement Priorities* indicates that the Commission will consider whether a rebate system creates efficiencies which are passed on to customers.

(B) UK law[171]

In *Napp Pharmaceutical Holdings Ltd*[172] the OFT held that Napp had abused its dominant position in the market for sustained release morphine by offering very large discounts to hospitals while charging excessive prices to patients in the community; more particularly Napp had targeted particular competitors, offering larger discounts to hospitals where it faced or anticipated competition and by granting higher discounts for specific products which were under competitive threat[173]. The OFT considered that Napp's intention was to eliminate competitors, and rejected its argument that it was simply 'meeting competition';

---

[166] Ibid, para 45; on this point see *Coca-Cola* Commission decision of 22 June 2005 (accepting commitments under Article 9 of Regulation 1/2003 from The Coca-Cola Company to, *inter alia*, refrain from setting target rebates to customers conditional upon them reaching individually-set purchase thresholds during a prescribed reference period); on Article 9 see ch 7, 'Article 9: commitments', pp 255–261.

[167] For an example of a conditional rebate scheme that was found to have no anti-competitive foreclosure effects see Albaek and Claici 'The Velux case – an in-depth look at rebates and more' (2009) 2 *Competition Policy Newsletter* 44.

[168] Case 85/76 [1979] ECR 461, [1979] 3 CMLR 211, para 90; see similarly Case C-95/04 P *British Airways plc v Commission* [2007] ECR I-2331, [2007] 4 CMLR 982, para 84.

[169] *British Gypsum* OJ [1992] C 321/9–C 321/12, [1993] 4 CMLR 143, proposing to take a 'favourable view' of various rebating and pricing rebates in the plasterboard and related markets in the case of some of the rebates related to quantities purchased; others to sales promotion.

[170] Case T-219/99 [2003] ECR II-5917, [2004] 4 CMLR 1008, paras 279–291; the Court of Justice dismissed the appeal by British Airways on this point since, in effect, it was questioning the factual assessment of the General Court, which is not possible in appeals to the Court of Justice: see Case C-95/04 P *British Airways plc v Commission* [2007] ECR I-2331, [2007] 4 CMLR 982, paras 84–91.

[171] See OFT Economic Discussion Paper (OFT 804) *Selective price cuts and fidelity rebates*, (RBB Economics, July 2005), available at www.oft.gov.uk.

[172] OFT decision of 30 March 2001 [2001] UKCLR 597.   [173] Ibid, paras 144–202.

its reaction to its competitors was held to be unreasonable and disproportionate[174]. On appeal the CAT found that Napp's discounts meant that it was selling at less than cost, and that they were therefore predatory[175].

In *English Welsh & Scottish Railway Ltd*[176] the Office of Rail Regulation ('the ORR') found that EW&S had abused its dominant position in a number of ways, including by offering discounts having an exclusionary effect in relation to the carriage of coal to various power stations: a fine of £4.1 million was imposed.

The OFT closed two cases concerning discounts and rebates in 2007, deciding that they were no longer an administrative priority since significant consumer detriment was unlikely[177].

5. Bundling[178]

(A) EU law

The application of Article 102 to tie-in agreements was considered in chapter 17[179]. It may be possible to achieve the same effect as a tie-in agreement through pricing practices.

(i) Rebates having a tying effect

In *Eurofix-Bauco v Hilti*[180] the Commission held that it was an abuse of a dominant position to reduce discounts to customers for orders of nail cartridges without nails[181]; the Commission's decision was upheld on appeal[182]. In *Tetra Pak II*[183] the Commission held that Tetra Pak had adopted a pricing policy that was a means of persuading customers to use its maintenance services[184]. In *Michelin II*[185] the Commission found that Michelin had a bonus scheme that enabled it to leverage its position on the market in new tyres to preserve or improve its position on the neighbouring retreads market[186].

(ii) 'Across-the-board' rebates

In *Hoffmann-La Roche v Commission*[187] the Court of Justice condemned Hoffmann-La Roche's 'across-the-board' rebates, which were offered to customers which acquired the

---

[174] Ibid, paras 197–202.

[175] Case No 1000/1/1/01 *Napp Pharmaceutical Holdings Ltd v Director General of Fair Trading* [2002] CAT 1, [2002] CompAR 13, paras 217–352.

[176] ORR decision of 17 November 2006 [2007] UKCLR 937; see Part IIA of the decision.

[177] *British Airways* OFT case closure, 30 April 2007 and *Walkers Snacks Ltd* OFT case closure, 3 May 2007.

[178] For further reading on tying and bundling see section 8 of DG COMP's *Discussion paper on the application of Article [102] of the Treaty to exclusionary abuses*; Motta *Competition Policy: Theory and Practice* (Cambridge University Press, 2004), pp 460–483; O'Donoghue and Padilla *The Law and Economics of Article 82 EC* (Hart Publishing, 2006), ch 9; Van den Bergh and Camesasca *European Competition Law and Economics: A Comparative Perspective* (Sweet & Maxwell, 2nd ed, 2006), pp 264–276; Bishop and Walker *The Economics of EC Competition Law* (Sweet & Maxwell, 3rd ed, 2010), paras 6.63–6.83; Niels, Jenkins and Kavanagh *Economics for Competition Lawyers* (Oxford University Press, 2011), pp 249–261.

[179] See ch 17, 'Tying', pp 688–696. [180] OJ [1988] L 65/19, [1989] 4 CMLR 677.

[181] Ibid, para 75.

[182] Case T-30/89 *Hilti AG v Commission* [1990] ECR II-163, [1992] 4 CMLR 16, upheld on appeal Case C-53/92 P *Hilti AG v Commission* [1994] ECR I-667, [1994] 4 CMLR 614.

[183] OJ [1992] L 72/1, [1992] 4 CMLR 551, upheld on appeal Case T-83/91 *Tetra Pak International v Commission* [1994] ECR II-755, [1997] 4 CMLR 726, upheld on appeal Case C-333/94 P *Tetra Pak International v Commission* [1996] ECR I-5951, [1997] 4 CMLR 662.

[184] OJ [1992] L 72/1, [1992] 4 CMLR 551, paras 111–114; see also para 139.

[185] OJ [2002] L 143/1, [2002] 5 CMLR 388. [186] Ibid, paras 300–311.

[187] Case 85/76 [1979] ECR 461, [1979] 3 CMLR 211.

whole range of its vitamins; these rebates meant that customers were dissuaded from acquiring any particular vitamin from other suppliers[188]. The Court of Justice noted specifically that such rebates amounted to an unlawful tie-in, contrary to Article 102(2)(d)[189]. The Commission's *Guidance on Article 102 Enforcement Priorities* says that it will generally compare the incremental price that customers pay for each of the dominant firm's products in a bundle to the dominant firm's LRAIC; an incremental price below LRAIC suggests that an equally efficient competitor may be foreclosed from the market[190].

(iii) Delivered pricing as a tie-in

In *Napier Brown-British Sugar*[191] the Commission held that British Sugar's delivered pricing system constituted an abuse of a dominant position, although it did not impose a fine in respect of this offence as it was the first decision on this particular practice. Until 1986 British Sugar had refused to allow customers to collect sugar at an ex-factory price. The Commission, relying on the Court of Justice's judgment in *Centre Belge d'Etudes de Marche Télémarketing v CLT*[192], held that British Sugar had reserved to itself an ancillary market (the delivery of sugar) as part of its activity on a neighbouring but separate market (the sale of sugar). The Commission's view was that there was no objective justification for this conduct on the part of British Sugar.

(iv) Bundling[193]

A firm may sell two or more products together as a bundle and charge more attractive prices for the bundle than for the constituent parts of it. Bundling may have the same effect as a tie-in agreement. In *Digital* the Commission objected to the fact that Digital offered prices which were more attractive when the customer purchased software services in a package with hardware services than when purchasing software services alone[194]. In *De Poste-La Poste*[195] the Commission imposed a fine of €2.5 million on the Belgian Post Office for, in effect, offering lower prices to customers in the market for the delivery of letters if they also made use of a separate 'B2B' ('business-to-business') service that it provided.

(B) UK law

In *BSkyB*[196] the OFT was not satisfied that BSkyB's bundling of sports and film premium channels had produced an anti-competitive effect since competitors had not been foreclosed; it therefore found that the Chapter II prohibition had not been infringed[197]. The OFT reached a similar conclusion in respect of the discounts given by BSkyB on the rates charged to distributors of its premium television channels[198]. The *BSkyB* decision illustrates

---

[188] Ibid, para 110.

[189] Ibid, para 111; for a similar case under US law see *Le Page's v 3M* 323 F 3d 141 (3rd Cir 2003).

[190] OJ [2009] C 45/7, paras 59–60; in the case of competing bundles of products the Commission will investigate whether the price of the dominant firm's bundle is predatory: ibid, para 61.

[191] OJ [1988] L 284/41, [1990] 4 CMLR 196.

[192] Case 311/84 [1985] ECR 3261, [1986] 2 CMLR 558.

[193] For a detailed discussion of this topic see DTI Economics Paper No 1 *Bundling, Tying, and Portfolio Effects* (Nalebuff, 2003), available at www.bis.gov.uk/publications.

[194] Commission's XXVIIth *Report on Competition Policy* (1997), pp 153–154; see similarly the Commission's action against AC Nielsen to prevent the charging of bundled prices: XXVIth *Report on Competition Policy* (1996), pp 144–148.

[195] OJ [2002] L 61/32, [2002] 4 CMLR 1426.

[196] OFT decision of 17 December 2002 [2003] UKCLR 240.

[197] Ibid, paras 548–600.   [198] Ibid, paras 601–646.

the point that the behaviour of a dominant firm should be considered abusive only where it actually has an anti-competitive effect or where there is a realistic possibility of such an effect[199].

In *Genzyme Ltd*[200] the OFT imposed a penalty of £6.8 million on that company for two pricing abuses, one of which was to charge a price to the National Health Service for a drug that included the price of home delivery, thereby reserving to itself the ancillary, but separate, activity of providing home care services[201]. This part of the OFT's decision was annulled on appeal to the CAT[202].

6. Predatory Pricing[203]

This section considers the extent to which predatory price cutting – selling at a loss – can amount to an infringement of Article 102 or the Chapter II prohibition in the Competition Act; it also considers the rare circumstances in which selective price cutting to retain customers may amount to an abuse even though no loss is incurred.

(A) Introduction

The idea of predatory price cutting is simple enough: that a dominant firm deliberately reduces prices to a loss-making level when faced with competition from an existing competitor or a new entrant to the market; the existing competitor having been disciplined, or the new entrant having been foreclosed, the dominant firm then raises its prices again, thereby causing consumer harm. Attempts to eliminate an existing competitor may be more expensive and difficult to achieve than deterring a new one from entry, especially where the existing competitor is committed to remaining in the market. Where a dominant undertaking has a reputation for acting in a predatory manner, this in itself may

---

[199] An allegation of anti-competitive bundling was rejected for this reason in *Alleged cross-subsidy of BT's discounts* OFTEL decision of 28 May 2003 [2003] UKCLR 816.

[200] OFT decision of 27 March 2003 [2003] UKCLR 950.

[201] Ibid, paras 294–363; the second practice condemned was a margin squeeze: see 'Findings of a margin squeeze', p 758 below.

[202] Case No 1016/1/1/03 *Genzyme Ltd v OFT* [2004] CAT 4, [2004] CompAR 358, paras 546–548.

[203] For further reading on predatory pricing see section 6 of DG COMP's *Discussion paper on the application of Article [102] of the Treaty to exclusionary abuses*; Motta *Competition Policy: Theory and Practice* (Cambridge University Press, 2004), pp 412–454; O'Donoghue and Padilla *The Law and Economics of Article 82 EC* (Hart Publishing, 2006), ch 5; Van den Bergh and Camesasca *European Competition Law and Economics: A Comparative Perspective* (Sweet & Maxwell, 2nd ed, 2006), pp 280–298; Bishop and Walker *The Economics of EC Competition Law* (Sweet & Maxwell, 3rd ed, 2010), paras 6.84–6.118; Niels, Jenkins and Kavanagh *Economics for Competition Lawyers* (Oxford University Press, 2011), pp 198–214; for literature in leading periodicals see eg Areeda and Turner 'Predatory Pricing and Related Practices under Section 2 of the Sherman Act' (1975) 88 Harvard Law Review 697; Scherer 'Predatory Pricing and the Sherman Act: A Comment' (1976) 89 Harvard Law Review 869; Williamson 'Predatory Pricing: A Strategic and Welfare Analysis' (1977) 87 Yale Law Journal 284; Baumol 'Quasi-Permanence of Price Reductions: A Policy for Prevention of Predatory Pricing' (1979) 89 Yale Law Journal 1; Brodley and Hay 'Predatory Pricing: Competing Economic Theories and the Evolution of Legal Standards' (1981) 66 Cornell Law Review 738; Williamson *Antitrust Economics* (Blackwell, 1987), pp 328–338; Mastromanolis 'Predatory Pricing Strategies in the European Union: a Case for Legal Reform' (1998) 19 ECLR 211; Edlin 'Stopping Above-cost Predatory Pricing' (2002) 111 Yale Law Journal 941; Elhauge 'Why above-cost price cuts to drive out entrants are not predatory – and the implications for defining costs and market power' (2003) 112 Yale Law Journal 681; ICN Unilateral Working Group *Report on Predatory Pricing* (2008), available at www.internationalcompetitionnetwork.org.

deter new entrants: not only predatory pricing itself but also the reputation for predation may be a barrier to entry[204].

It is the essence of competition that firms should compete for custom by reducing prices. It has already been pointed out that rebates and similar practices are an essential component of the competitive process, and that the law should not condemn practices, even on the part of dominant firms, that are pro-competitive; in particular a dominant firm should not be deterred from passing on its efficiency to customers in the form of lower prices. The law on predatory price cutting has to tread a fine line between not condemning competitive responses on the part of dominant firms on the one hand and prohibiting unreasonable exclusionary conduct on the other: this takes us back to the debate on 'false positives' and 'false negatives'[205]. It would be perverse if the effect of competition law were to be that dominant firms choose not to compete on price for fear that, by doing so, they would be found guilty of an infringement[206].

There is some theoretical scepticism as to whether a monopolist would ever benefit from predatory price cutting. For example Bork argues that in practice predation is too expensive for the predator; that the predator will not earn monopoly profits until some distant future time when the new firm has disappeared; and that if it is easy to drive firms out, it will be correspondingly easy for new firms to enter when the predator begins to reap a monopoly profit in the future[207]; if one agrees with this view, competition authorities ought not to concern themselves at all with the issue. However that extreme position now has fairly few advocates. Economists today acknowledge that dominant firms are able to act in a predatory manner[208], and game theory can help to demonstrate this[209]. There is no doubt that predatory price cutting can amount to an infringement of Article 102 and the Chapter II prohibition in the Competition Act 1998.

(B) The Areeda and Turner test

Many attempts have been made to frame an economic test of when a price is predatory. Areeda and Turner[210] suggested that a price should be deemed predatory under US law where it was below a dominant firm's AVC[211].

The Areeda and Turner test relies exclusively on a cost/price analysis. Some commentators think that the test should be less strict, and that predation should be condemned only where it can also be demonstrated that a predator will be able to recoup any losses it has made through the exercise of its market power in the future: the Supreme Court

---

[204] On this point see para 68 of the Commission's *Guidance on Article 102 Enforcement Priorities*; see also Bolton, Broadley and Riordan 'Predatory Pricing: Strategic theory and legal policy' (2000) 88 Georgetown Law Journal 2239.

[205] See ch 5, 'False positives and false negatives', pp 193–194.

[206] See eg the Supreme Court in the US in *Matsushita v Zenith Radio* 475 US 574, p 594 (1986): 'mistaken inferences in cases such as this chill the very conduct that antitrust laws are designed to protect'.

[207] See eg Bork *Antitrust Paradox* (Basic Books, 1978), pp 148–155; see also Koller 'The Myth of Predatory Pricing: An Empirical Study' (1971) 4 Antitrust L Ec Rev 105; Easterbrook 'Predatory Strategies and Counterstrategies' (1981) 48 University of Chicago Law Review 263.

[208] For a helpful review of contemporary economic theory and empirical evidence on predatory pricing see Shapiro and Kaplow 'Antitrust' in *Handbook of Law and Economics*, vol 2 (Elsevier, 2008, eds Polinsky and Shavell), 1073, pp 1195–1197.

[209] See eg Philips *Competition Policy: A Game-Theoretic Perspective* (Cambridge University Press, 1995).

[210] See Areeda and Turner 'Predatory Pricing and Related Practices under Section 2 of the Sherman Act' (1975) 88 Harvard Law Review 697.

[211] See 'Cost Concepts', pp 716–718 above on the meaning of this and various other cost concepts; for case law in the US on the cost standard to be applied to predation in the airline industry see *US v American Airlines Inc* 355 F 3d 1109 (10th Cir 2003) and *Spirit Airlines Inc v Northwest Airlines Inc* 431 F 3d (6th Cir 2005).

of the US has required proof of recoupment as a key component of the offence of predation[212]. Others question whether the Areeda and Turner test is strict enough, arguing that pricing above AVC could be exclusionary in some circumstances, especially where there is evidence of an intention to discipline or deter competitors or where in practice it has this effect. However there are difficulties with a legal rule which requires specific proof of a predator's intention. In the ruthless process of competition any competitor that enters a race wishes to win, so that by necessary implication it must also have 'intended' that its competitors should lose; in this sense a requirement of intention is hardly meaningful[213]. In so far as a requirement of intention means that evidence of a 'smoking gun' should be adduced, for example in the form of written memoranda, minutes of meetings and emails documenting a settled policy of eliminating competitors, this may be difficult for a competition authority to find: well-advised companies will be perfectly aware that they should not generate incriminating documents of this kind and that they should destroy those that they do. A rule requiring evidence of intention to eliminate would make more sense where it has an objective quality based in economics, for example that a predator's conduct, by departing from short-term profit maximisation, makes commercial sense only as a way of eliminating a competitor; this variant of intention is very different from proving the subjective intention of the predator, but is extremely difficult to prove as a matter of economic analysis. This discussion demonstrates some of the problems involved in establishing a suitable test for cases on predatory price cutting.

As we shall see, proving intention is sometimes relevant to the EU law on pricing abuses. The Court of Justice in *AKZO v Commission*[214] decided that pricing above AVC but below ATC could be abusive where there was evidence of an intention on the part of the dominant firm to eliminate a competitor[215]. In *Compagnie Maritime Belge v Commission*[216] the Court of Justice held that a policy of selective price cutting to particular customers carried into effect with the intention of eliminating the dominant undertaking's only competitor was abusive in the particular circumstances of the market for the maritime transport of containerised cargo[217]. These judgments seem to be based on the 'smoking gun' variant of intention[218]. The Commission, in paragraph 66 of its *Guidance on Article 102 Enforcement Priorities*, says that it may rely on documentary evidence of a predatory strategy.

EU law will be considered first, then that of the UK.

---

[212] See *Brooke Group Ltd v Brown Williamson Tobacco* 509 US 209 (1993); *Weyerhaeuser Co v Ross-Simmons Hardwood Lumber Co Inc* 549 US 312 (2007) (applying a requirement of proof of recoupment to predatory bidding as well as to predatory selling cases); on recoupment in US law see Joskow and Klevorick 'A Framework for Analysing Predatory Pricing Policy' (1979) 89 Yale Law Journal 213; Elzinga and Mills 'Testing for Predation: Is Recoupment Feasible?' (1989) 34 Antitrust Bulletin 869; *Edlin* (see ch 18 n 203 above); OECD report on *Predatory Foreclosure* (2004), available at www.oecd.org; on recoupment in a number of jurisdictions see Table 4 of ICN Unilateral Working Group *Report on Predatory Pricing* (2008), available at www.internationalcompetitionnetwork.org; in EU law see 'Is it necessary to show the possibility of recoupment?', pp 745–746 below; in UK law see 'Is there a need to prove recoupment of losses?', p 753 below.

[213] For judicial scepticism in the US on the role of intent in a case of predation see *Barry Wright Corp v ITT Grinnell Corp* 724 F 2d 227, p 232 (1st Cir 1983) and *AA Poultry Farms Inc v Rose Acre Farms Inc* 881 F 2d 1396, pp 1401–1402 (1989).

[214] Case C-62/86 *AKZO v Commission* [1991] ECR I-3359, [1993] 5 CMLR 215.

[215] Ibdi, para 72 and see 'AKZO v Commission', pp 742–743 below; see also 'Average total cost', p 718 above.

[216] Cases C-395/96 P etc [2000] ECR I-1365, [2000] 4 CMLR 1076.

[217] See 'Compagnie Maritime Belge v Commission', pp 750–752 below.

[218] For argument against the use of evidence of intention when establishing an abuse under Article 102 see Bavasso 'The role of Intent Under Article 82 EC: From "Flushing the Turkeys" to "Spotting Lionesses in Regent's Park'" (2005) 26 ECLR 616.

(C) **EU law**

(i) *AKZO v Commission*

In *ECS/AKZO*[219] the Commission imposed a fine of €10 million on AKZO for predatory price cutting. ECS was a small UK firm producing benzoyl peroxide. Until 1979 it had sold this product to customers requiring it as a bleach in the treatment of flour in the UK and Eire. It then decided also to sell it to users in the polymer industry. AKZO, a Dutch company in a dominant position on the market, informed ECS that unless it withdrew from the polymer market it would reduce its prices, in particular in the flour additives market, in order to harm it. Subsequently AKZO did indeed reduce its prices. In holding that AKZO had abused its dominant position the Commission declined to adopt the Areeda and Turner test of predatory price cutting, according to which pricing above AVC should be presumed lawful[220]. While accepting that cost/price analysis is an element in deciding whether a price is predatory, the Commission considered that it was also relevant whether the dominant firm had adopted a strategy of eliminating competition, what the effects of its conduct would be likely to be and what a competitor's likely reaction to the conduct of the dominant firm would be. At paragraph 79 of its decision the Commission suggested that even a price above ATC might be predatory when assessed in its particular market context[221].

On appeal[222] the Court of Justice upheld the Commission's finding of predatory pricing, saying that not all price competition can be considered legitimate[223]. The Court of Justice held that where prices were below AVC predation had to be presumed, since every sale would generate a loss for the dominant firm[224]. The Court of Justice did not say that the presumption could never be rebutted; in *France Télécom v Commission*[225] the Court said that prices below AVC are 'prima facie abusive'[226], an important difference. It would be wrong to have a *per se* rule that selling below AVC is always illegal[227]. For example it is arguable that a dominant firm should sometimes be able to sell below cost: sales promotions sometimes involve below-cost selling; and the disposal of old stock at the end of the season at a price below cost would presumably not be unlawful.

The Court of Justice in *AKZO v Commission* went on to hold that where prices are above AVC but below ATC they will be regarded as abusive if they are part of a plan which is aimed at eliminating a competitor[228]; such a pricing policy might mean that a dominant firm drives from the market undertakings that are as efficient as it but which, because of their smaller financial resources, are incapable of withstanding the competition waged against them. The Court of Justice therefore upheld the Commission's rejection of the Areeda/Turner test.

---

[219] OJ [1985] L 374/1, [1986] 3 CMLR 273; see Merkin 'Predatory Pricing or Competitive Pricing: Establishing the Truth in English and EC Law' (1987) 7 OJLS 182.

[220] See 'The Areeda and Turner test', pp 740–741 above.

[221] See also the Commission's comments at point 82 of its XVth *Report on Competition Policy* (1985).

[222] Case C-62/86 *AKZO v Commission* [1991] ECR I-3359, [1993] 5 CMLR 215.

[223] Ibid, para 70.

[224] Ibid, para 71; the Court of Justice did not discuss the period of time over which the AVC should be calculated.

[225] Case C-202/07 [2009] ECR I-2369, [2009] 4 CMLR 1149.

[226] Ibid, para 109; Advocate General Mazák made the same point in para 95 of his Opinion in this case; cf Case C-333/94 P *Tetra Pak International SA v Commission* [1996] ECR I-5951, [1997] 4 CMLR 662, para 41, where the Court of Justice had said that prices below AVC must 'always' be considered abusive.

[227] In the UK the CAT considered that the presumption of abuse should be rebuttable in rare cases: see Case No 1009/1/1/02 *Aberdeen Journals Ltd v OFT* [2003] CAT 11, [2003] CompAR 67, para 357.

[228] Case C-62/86 *AKZO v Commission* [1991] ECR I-3359, [1993] 5 CMLR 215, para 72.

The rule in *AKZO v Commission* can be depicted as follows, where the dominant firm's prices range from 0 to 100:

100	Where a dominant firm is charging prices above ATC, it is not guilty of predation under the rule in *AKZO v Commission*; however consideration must be given to the rule on selective price cutting in *Compagnie Maritime Belge v Commission* (see below)
ATC	Where a dominant firm is selling at less than ATC, but above AVC, it is guilty of predation where this is done as part of a plan to eliminate a competitor
AVC	Where a dominant firm is selling at less than AVC, it is presumed to be acting abusively; this presumption may be rebuttable where there is an objective justification for below-cost selling
0	

Fig. 18.1

The Commission suggests, in paragraphs 26 and 64 of its *Guidance*, that a preferable standard to AVC might be AAC because, over a period of time, a firm might have to incur not just variable costs but additional fixed ones. Suppose that a firm is accused of predating over a period of three years: during that time some of its machinery might have to be replaced, and this would normally be regarded as a fixed cost. The AAC standard includes not only the average of the variable costs incurred over that period, but also adds in any fixed costs. It follows that, in some cases, AVC and AAC might be the same; but that in others – depending on the duration of the conduct under examination – AAC could be higher than AVC due to the inclusion of some fixed costs[229]. The expression 'avoidable cost' is used because it refers to the amount of money that the dominant firm would have saved if it had not been involved in the production of widgets during the period in question. Of course, the Commission is bound by the law as laid down by the EU Courts; on the other hand, the suggestion that AAC, as a matter of economics, is a sounder standard than AVC in a case such as this seems compelling, and this is one of those areas where the EU Courts might, in future, be prepared to defer to the compelling logic of the *Guidance*.

(ii) *Tetra Pak v Commission*

In *Tetra Pak II*[230] the Commission found Tetra Pak guilty of predatory pricing in relation to its non-asceptic cartons[231]; it considered that Tetra Pak was able to subsidise its losses from its substantial profits on the market for asceptic cartons, where it had virtually no competition[232]. The Commission said that in seven Member States the non-asceptic cartons had been sold at a loss[233]. However the Commission concentrated on the position

[229] *Guidance on Article 102 Enforcement Priorities*, fn 40.
[230] OJ [1992] L 72/1, [1992] 4 CMLR 551.   [231] Ibid, paras 147–153.
[232] This type of intervention is envisaged by fn 39 of the Commission's *Guidance on Article 102 Enforcement Priorities*.
[233] Ibid, para 147.

in Italy, where the cartons had been sold below AVC. The Commission did not merely rely on the *AKZO* presumption of predation where prices are below AVC, but said that it had 'gathered sufficiently clear and unequivocal data to be able to conclude that, in that country at least, sales at a loss were the result of a deliberate policy aimed at eliminating competition'[234]. The Commission continued by saying that, although it was difficult to believe that an efficient multi-national company could have indulged in behaviour so opposed to the logic of economic profitability through management error, it should be asked whether exceptional circumstances, independent of Tetra Pak's free will, forced it to make losses. The Commission concluded that there were no such circumstances and that the prices were simply part of an 'eviction strategy'[235]. The Court of Justice upheld the Commission's finding of abuse; the judgment is of interest to the issue of recoupment, which is discussed below[236].

(iii) *Wanadoo*: on appeal *France Télécom v Commission*

In *Wanadoo*[237] the Commission applied the rule in *AKZO v Commission* and imposed a fine of €10.35 million on the subsidiary of France Télécom for having priced residential broadband internet services at levels that, until August 2001, fell considerably below AVC, and which subsequently were approximately equivalent to variable cost, but were significantly below ATC. In the Commission's view Wanadoo's behaviour 'was designed to take the lion's share of a booming market'[238].

The Commission's decision was upheld on appeal to the General Court and to the Court of Justice in *France Télécom v Commission* (by the time of the appeals France Télécom had succeeded to the rights of Wanadoo)[239]. The judgments deal with France Télécom's objections to the Commission's cost methodology and treatment of costs and its argument that the Commission had applied the wrong test of predation.

(A) *Errors as to costs*

The EU Courts rejected France Télécom's appeal as to costs[240]. The General Court held that the analysis of costs involves a complex economic assessment, and that the Commission 'must be afforded a broad discretion'[241]. The General Court noted that, since the case concerned a new product in an expanding market, the Commission had spread the costs over a period of 48 months when determining whether France Télécom was selling at a loss[242]; this did not amount to a manifest error of assessment[243]. The Court also rejected the argument that there were methodological problems with the actual calculations of the Commission[244].

---

[234] Ibid, para 147.   [235] Ibid, para 149.

[236] Case C-333/94 P *Tetra Pak International SA v Commission* [1996] ECR I-5951, [1997] 4 CMLR 662; see Korah 'The Paucity of Economic Analysis in the [EC] Decisions on Competition: Tetra Pak II' (1993) 46 Current Legal Problems 148, pp 172–181; Jones 'Distinguishing Predatory Prices from Competitive Ones' (1995) 17 EIPR 252.

[237] Commission decision of 16 July 2006 [2005] 5 CMLR 120.

[238] Commission Press Release IP/03/1025, 16 July 2003.

[239] Case T-340/03 [2007] ECR II-107, [2007] 4 CMLR 919, on appeal Case C-202/07 P *France Télécom v Commission* [2009] ECR I-2369, [2009] 4 CMLR 1149; for comment on the General Court's judgment see Gal 'Below-Cost Price Alignment: Meeting or Beating Competition? The *France Télécom* Case' (2007) 28 ECLR 382.

[240] Case T-340/03 [2007] ECR II-107, [2007] 4 CMLR 919, paras 122–169; France Télécom's appeal to the Court of Justice on this point was dismissed as inadmissible: Case C-202/07 P [2009] ECR I-2369, [2009] 4 CMLR 1149, paras 69–73.

[241] Case T-340/03 [2007] ECR II-107, [2007] 4 CMLR 919, para 129.   [242] Ibid, para 137.

[243] Ibid, para 155.   [244] Ibid, paras 162–169.

(B) The test of predation

The EU Courts also rejected France Télécom's argument that the Commission had applied the wrong test of predation[245]. The General Court, with whom the Court of Justice agreed, held that France Télécom did not have the right to align its prices on those of its competitors where this would mean that it was selling at below cost:

It is…not possible to assert that the rights of a dominant undertaking to align its prices on those of its competitors is absolute[246].

The General Court went on to say that, although a non-dominant undertaking would be allowed to match the prices of competitors, even by selling at below cost, dominant undertakings do not necessarily have the same right[247].

As to the question of a plan of predation, the General Court noted that the Commission had demonstrated such a plan for the period during which France Télécom was selling above AVC but below ATC[248].

The issue of recoupment is discussed in the next section.

(iv) Is it necessary to show the possibility of recoupment?

It was pointed out above that US law requires that an element of the offence of predatory price cutting is that it can be shown that the predator has the ability to recoup any losses incurred[249]. Many commentators have argued that a recoupment rule should be adopted under Article 102[250], although some argue to the contrary[251]. It is of interest to note that the Privy Council, a court in the UK that hears appeals from some countries in the British Commonwealth, said in *Carter Holt Harvey Building Products Group Ltd v The Commerce Commission*[252] that:

It is the ability to recoup losses because its price-cutting has removed competition and allows it to charge supra-competitive prices that harms competitors[253].

The EU Courts have not adopted a requirement of recoupment under Article 102; the most recent judgment on the point, that of the Court of Justice in *France Télécom v Commission*, states clearly that there is no such requirement in a case of pricing below AVC.

In *AKZO v Commission* the Court acknowledged the significance of recoupment in paragraph 71 of its judgment, where it noted that a dominant firm has no interest in applying prices below average variable cost:

except that of eliminating competitors so as to enable it subsequently to raise its prices by taking advantage of its monopolistic position.

However it did not expressly incorporate the need to prove recoupment as part of the abuse. In *Tetra Pak II* it was argued before the Court of Justice that the Commission should have to establish the possibility of recoupment as part of the offence of predation.

---

[245] Ibid, paras 170–230.
[246] Case T-340/03 [2007] ECR II-107, [2007] 4 CMLR 919, para 182, upheld on appeal Case C-202/07 P [2009] ECR I-2369, [2009] 4 CMLR 1149, paras 41-49.
[247] Ibid, para 186.   [248] Ibid, paras 195–218.
[249] On the view of the UK competition authorities on this issue see 'The *Aberdeen Journals* case', pp 752–753 below.
[250] See eg see Gal 'Below-Cost Price Alignment: Meeting or Beating Competition? The *France Télécom* Case' (2007) 28 ECLR 382 at p 383.
[251] See eg Ritter 'Does the Law of Predatory Pricing and Cross-subsidisation Need a Radical Rethink?' (2004) 27(4) World Competition 613.
[252] [2004] UKPC 37.   [253] Ibid, para 67.

The Court of Justice, upholding the finding that Tetra Pak was guilty of predatory pricing, remarked that:

> it would not be appropriate, *in the circumstances of the present case,* to require in addition proof that Tetra Pak had a realistic chance of recouping its losses. It must be possible to penalise predatory pricing whenever there is a risk that competitors will be eliminated[254] (emphasis added).

The *Tetra Pak* case was one in which the anti-competitive intention of Tetra Pak, manifested in a series of abusive acts contrary to Article 102, was particularly clear; furthermore its market power was considerable, so that may explain why the Court felt that 'in the circumstances of the present case' it was not necessary to impose a requirement to prove recoupment.

In *France Télécom v Commission*[255] the Court of Justice was invited to introduce a recoupment requirement into the test of predation. The Court cited the *AKZO* and *Tetra Pak* cases, and concluded that:

> it does not follow from the case-law of the Court that proof of the possibility of recoupment of losses suffered by the application, by an undertaking in a dominant position, of prices lower than a certain level of costs constitutes a necessary precondition to establishing that such a pricing policy is abusive[256].

The Court of Justice pointed out that the Commission is not precluded from finding that the possibility of recoupment is a relevant factor in assessing whether a pricing practice is abusive. This fits well with the approach adopted by the Commission in paragraph 71 of its *Guidance on Article 102 Enforcement Priorities*.

(v) The Commission's approach to predation in its *Guidance on Article 102 Enforcement Priorities*

The circumstances in which the Commission might consider it appropriate to take action in relation to predatory conduct are discussed in paragraphs 63 to 74 of the *Guidance on Article 102 Enforcement Priorities*. The Commission says that a dominant firm engages in predatory conduct when it deliberately incurs losses or forgoes profits in the short term and causes anti-competitive foreclosure[257]. The Commission's view is that pricing below AAC will generally be a clear indication of sacrificing profits[258], although it may also look at whether a dominant firm incurred a loss that it could have avoided[259]. The Commission adds that only pricing below LRAIC is capable of foreclosing as efficient competitors from the market[260]. Paragraph 68 of the *Guidance* then refers back to paragraph 20, which sets out a range of factors that the Commission will take into account

---

[254] Case C-333/94 P *Tetra Pak International SA v Commission* [1996] ECR I-5951, [1997] 4 CMLR 662, para 44; at paras 76–78 of his Opinion in this case Advocate General Ruiz-Colomer considered that proof of recoupment was not necessary; yet in Cases C-395 and 396/96 P *Compagnie Maritime Belge v Commission* [2000] ECR I-1365, [2000] 4 CMLR 1076 Advocate General Fennelly considered that recoupment should be part of the test for predatory pricing: ibid, para 136; see similarly the Opinion of Advocate General Mazák in Case C-202/07 P *France Télécom v Commission* [2009] ECR I-2369, [2009] 4 CMLR 1149, paras 68–76.

[255] Case C-202/07 P *France Télécom v Commission* [2009] ECR I-2369, [2009] 4 CMLR 1149.

[256] Ibid, para 110.

[257] *Guidance on Article 102 Enforcement Priorities*, para 63.   [258] Ibid, para 64.

[259] Ibid, para 65; fn 43 makes an important point that 'undertakings should not be penalised for incurring ex post losses where the ex ante decision to engage in the conduct was taken in good faith, that is to say, if they can provide conclusive evidence that they could reasonably expect that the activity would be profitable'.

[260] Ibid, para 67.

when deciding whether to intervene; the Commission must be satisfied that below-cost pricing results in anti-competitive foreclosure[261]. It is not necessary for a competitor to have exited the market: disciplining a rival to prevent it competing may suffice[262]. The Commission states that consumer harm warranting intervention may arise if a dominant undertaking can reasonably expect its market power after the predatory conduct to be greater than it otherwise would have been, for example by increasing its prices or by moderating a decline in prices[263]. The Commission says that predatory conduct is unlikely to create efficiencies[264].

(vi) Are the standards of AVC and ATC always appropriate?

A complicating factor in applying cost-based rules to determine whether prices are predatory is that it may not always be appropriate to apply the standards of AVC or ATC. In some industries fixed costs are very high but variable costs are low. An obvious example is telecommunications, where it is likely to have been very expensive to establish the original infrastructure of wires and cables; once they have been laid, however, the actual cost of carrying telephone calls is low, and may be as low as zero. The AVC of telephone calls is so low that there would hardly ever be predatory prices if the AVC standard were to be applied; and the ATC standard would require proof of the predator's intention to eliminate competition, following the judgment in *AKZO v Commission*, with the difficulties that this entails.

If the AVC and ATC standards in *AKZO v Commission* are inappropriate to determine whether prices are predatory in industries such as these, an alternative rule is needed. The Commission suggests, in its *Notice on the Application of the Competition Rules to Access Agreements in the Telecommunications Sector*[265], that the *AKZO* standards are not appropriate in a network industry such as telecommunications[266] and that a standard based on LRIC might be preferable[267]. Indeed, even a price above LRIC could be considered predatory, if it does not recover some of the common costs that are incurred where a firm supplies a range of different products: for this reason, a 'combinatorial' approach may be taken towards the assessment of cost, whereby a firm's LRIC is combined with its 'stand alone cost', that is to say the cost that it would incur if it had no other activities at all[268].

The Commission proceeded, for the first time in a formal decision, on the basis of LRIC in *Deutsche Post*[269]. UPS complained that Deutsche Post was using revenue from its profitable letter-post monopoly to finance a strategy of below-cost selling in the commercial parcels market, which was open to competition. The Commission's view was that Deutsche Post, in the period from 1990 to 1995, had received revenue from this business which did not cover the incremental cost of providing it[270]. By remaining in the market without any foreseeable improvement in revenue, Deutsche Post was considered to have restricted the activities of competitors which were in a position to provide the service at a price that would cover their costs[271]. The Commission therefore concluded that Deutsche

---

[261] Ibid, paras 67–73; para 68 describes situations in which a victim of predatory conduct may be foreclosed from the market.

[262] Ibid, para 69.   [263] Ibid, paras 70–71.   [264] Ibid, para 74.

[265] OJ [1998] C 265/2, [1998] 5 CMLR 821.   [266] Ibid, paras 113–115.

[267] See 'Long-run incremental cost', p 717 above.

[268] See 'Stand alone cost', p 718 above and *The Competition Act 1998: The application to the telecommunications sector*, OFT 417, February 2000, para 7.11.

[269] OJ [2001] L 125/27, [2001] 5 CMLR 99.

[270] Ibid, para 36; the Commission sets out the relevant cost concepts at paras 6 and 7 of the decision.

[271] OJ [2001] L 125/27, [2001] 5 CMLR 99.

Post was guilty of predatory pricing; however it did not impose a fine for this infringement, since this was the first time that it had applied the LRIC standard[272].

(vii) Predatory price cutting and cross-subsidisation[273]

An undertaking such as Deutsche Post, which enjoys a legal monopoly in relation to the basic letter service[274], is able to use the profits it makes there to support low prices in other markets where it faces competition: this was the essence of UPS's complaint[275]. Cross-subsidisation may facilitate abusive pricing practices such as predation and selective price cutting. This raises the interesting question of whether cross-subsidisation is an abuse of a dominant position in itself. There are no decisions of the Commission or judgments of the EU Courts finding that cross-subsidy is, in itself, an abuse of a dominant position, although the Commission in its *Notice on the Application of the Competition Rules to the Postal Sector*[276] suggests, at paragraph 3.3, that there could be circumstances in which it could be an abuse to subsidise activities open to competition by allocating their costs to those services in relation to which the postal operator enjoys a monopoly[277]. Despite this statement, however, in principle it would appear that the existing rules on abusive pricing practices, described in this chapter, are sufficient to control the behaviour of dominant firms; the adoption of a rule forbidding cross-subsidy itself is unnecessary. This was the view of the General Court in *UPS Europe SA v Commission*[278].

Where cross-subsidy is a problem there are other ways of dealing with it. In the case of regulated industries, specific rules are often imposed to prevent the practice[279]. Useful remedies that the Commission can deploy in Article 102 cases include a requirement to establish different legal entities, the maintenance of separate accounts and full financial transparency of dominant firms' pricing practices.

(viii) Selective price cutting but not below cost

One of the most contentious issues under Article 102 is whether it can be unlawful for a dominant firm to cut its prices selectively, but not to below cost, to customers that might desert to a competitor, while leaving prices to other customers at a higher level. Such a policy might amount to unlawful discrimination contrary to Article 102(2)(c) where it involves the application of dissimilar conditions to equivalent transactions, thereby placing other trading parties at a competitive disadvantage[280]. The specific issue under consideration in this section is whether selective price cutting could be held to be abusive irrespective of whether it infringes Article 102(2)(c) and, more specifically, where the undertaking harmed is a competitor operating at the same level of the market as the dominant firm rather than a trading party in a downstream market.

---

[272] Ibid, para 47; a fine of €24 million was imposed for the separate abuse of offering loyalty rebates: see 'Further case law on loyalty rebates under Article 102', pp 731–732 above.

[273] See Hancher and Buendia Sierra 'Cross-subsidisation and EC Law' (1998) 35 CML Rev 901; Abbamonte 'Cross-subsidisation and Community Competition Rules: Efficient Pricing Versus Equity?' (1998) 23 EL Rev 414; on the relationship between these concepts see Case No 1007/2/3/02 *Freeserve.com plc v Director General of Telecommunications* [2003] CAT 5, [2003] CompAR 202, paras 171–225.

[274] On the extent of the permissible monopoly in postal services under EU law see ch 23, 'Post', pp 984–989.

[275] OJ [2001] L 125/27, [2001] 5 CMLR 99, para 5.

[276] OJ [1998] C 39/2, [1998] 5 CMLR 108.

[277] See also the Opinion of Advocate General Mengozzi given on 24 May 2011 in Case C-209/10 *Post Danmark A/S v Konkurrencerådet*, not yet decided.

[278] Case T-175/99 [2002] ECR II-1915, [2002] 5 CMLR 67, para 61.

[279] See ch 23, 'Regulated Industries', pp 977–980.

[280] See 'EU law', pp 760–763 below.

The position can be depicted as follows:

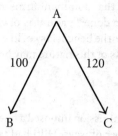

Fig. 18.2 Article 82(2)(c) discrimination

A charges B a price of 100 per widget, but charges C 120; B and C need widgets to manufacture blodgets, a market in which they compete. Clearly the discrimination puts C at a competitive disadvantage in the blodget market as against B. It may be, in a case such as this, that B is a subsidiary of A, or closely associated with it; this may help to explain why A practises discrimination in the first place. The detriment to competition occurs downstream from A's market: that is to say it amounts to vertical foreclosure, or to secondary-line injury, to be contrasted with the horizontal foreclosure, or primary-line injury, in the example that follows[281]:

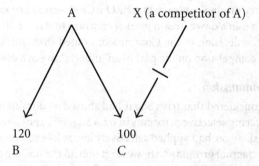

Fig. 18.3 Selective price cutting as an abuse

In this example A charges B 120 and C 100. B requires widgets for blodgets; C requires them for sprockets. Blodgets and sprockets do not compete, so that there is no harm to competition between B and C in the downstream market. The motivation for A's price cut to C is that A fears that it is going to lose C's business to X; X is able to supply a different input to C from which C could just as easily produce sprockets. The purpose of the selective price cut is to eliminate competition at A's level of the market: the case is one of horizontal foreclosure.

The question of whether selective price cutting such as this is abusive is controversial[282]. Provided that the dominant firm is not making a loss, it is not guilty of predatory price cutting; has not offered exclusionary rebates; and for the reasons just given it may

---

[281] For discussion of this terminology see ch 5, 'Horizontal and vertical foreclosure', pp 204–205.

[282] See eg Elhauge 'Why Above-Cost Price Cuts To Drive Out Entrants Are Not Predatory – and the Implications for Defining Costs and Market Power' (2003) 112 Yale Law Journal 681; some commentators have written in defence of a rule that prohibits above-cost predatory pricing in certain circumstances: see

not be infringing Article 102(2)(c). It would appear that, in making selective price cuts, the dominant firm is competing 'on the merits' with X, and that it has not acted abusively. The EU Courts have often stated that dominant firms are allowed to 'meet' competition, which is what A appears to have done[283]; and it is obviously in C's interest, and in the interest of C's customers, that it is the beneficiary of lower prices. Despite this, however, it is possible that selective price cuts of this nature may be held to be abusive, albeit only in narrowly defined circumstances.

(A) Eurofix-Bauco/Hilti

In *Eurofix-Bauco/Hilti*[284] the Commission imposed a fine of €6 million on Hilti for abusing its dominant position in a number of ways. Hilti had taken action to prevent customers from purchasing nails from its competitors. Apart from entering into tie-in agreements with some customers[285], Hilti singled out competing firms' main customers and offered them particularly favourable conditions; it removed quantity discounts from long-standing customers who bought from its competitors; and it classified certain custom-ers as 'unsupported', which meant that they qualified for lower quantity discounts than 'supported' firms: it appeared to the Commission that the 'unsupported' firms were ones which had purchased nails and nail cartridges other than from Hilti. Hilti had also given away some products free of charge. The Commission said that the pricing abuses in this case did not hinge on whether the prices were below cost, but on whether Hilti could rely on its dominance to offer discriminatory prices to its competitors' customers with a view to damaging the competitors' business; in other words the Commission proceeded not on the basis of predatory pricing contrary to *AKZO v Commission* nor on the basis of a det-riment to competition in a downstream market contrary to Article 102(2)(c). The General Court, upholding the decision of the Commission, stated that Hilti's strategy was not a legitimate mode of competition on the part of an undertaking in a dominant position[286].

(B) Irish Sugar v Commission

The Commission considered that Irish Sugar had abused its dominant position contrary to Article 102 by offering selective price cuts in *Irish Sugar*[287]. The General Court annulled the finding that Irish Sugar had applied selectively low prices to potential customers of a competitor, ASI, on factual grounds[288]; however it upheld the finding that Irish Sugar had been guilty of granting selective rebates to particular customers[289].

(C) Compagnie Maritime Belge v Commission

In *Compagnie Maritime Belge v Commission*[290] the Commission investigated the policy of 'fighting ships', whereby members of a liner conference in the maritime transport sector, Cewal, reduced their charges to the level, or to below the level, of their one competitor, Grimaldi and Cobelfret; they also operated the fighting ships on the same route and at the

---

eg Edlin 'Stopping Above-Cost Predatory Pricing' (2002) 111 Yale Law Journal 941; Ritter 'Does the Law of Predatory Pricing and Cross-subsidisation Need a Radical Rethink?' (2004) 27(4) World Competition 613.

[283] See eg the judgment of the General Court in Case T-228/97 *Irish Sugar v Commission* [1999] ECR II-2969, [1999] 5 CMLR 1300, para 112 and the judgments referred to in the footnote to that paragraph; for a general discussion of 'meeting' rather than 'beating' competition see Springer '"Meeting Competition": Justification of Price Discrimination under EC and US Antitrust Law' (1997) 18 ECLR 251.

[284] OJ [1988] L 65/19, [1989] 4 CMLR 677.   [285] See ch 17, 'Hilti', pp 692–693.

[286] Case T-30/89 *Hilti AG v Commission* [1990] ECR II-163, [1992] 4 CMLR 16, para 100.

[287] OJ [1997] L 258/1, [1997] 5 CMLR 666.

[288] Case T-228/97 [1999] ECR II-2969, [1999] 5 CMLR 1300, paras 117–124.

[289] Ibid, paras 215–225.   [290] OJ [1993] L 34/20, [1995] 5 CMLR 198.

same time as Grimaldi's. The Commission concluded that the policy was one of selective price cutting intended to eliminate the competitor and that Article 102 was infringed. In *Compagnie Maintain Belge v Commission*[291] the Commission's decision was upheld by General Court. The Court of Justice agreed that there was an infringement of Article 102, although the fines were annulled for technical reasons[292].

Advocate General Fennelly, urging that the application of Article 102 to selective price cutting should be approached with reserve, remarked that:

> Price competition is the essence of the free and open competition which it is the objective of [EU] policy to establish on the internal market. It favours more efficient firms and it is for the benefit of consumers both in the short and the long run. Dominant firms not only have the right but should be encouraged to compete on price[293].

In the Advocate General's view, non-discriminatory price cuts by a dominant undertaking which do not entail below-cost sales should not normally be regarded as being anti-competitive:

> In the first place, even if they are only short lived, they benefit consumers and, secondly, if the dominant undertaking's competitors are equally or more efficient, they should be able to compete on the same terms. [EU] competition law should thus not offer less efficient undertakings a safe haven against vigorous competition even from dominant undertakings. Different considerations may, however, apply where an undertaking which enjoys a position of dominance approaching a monopoly, particularly on a market where price cuts can be implemented with relative autonomy from costs, implements a policy of selective price cutting with the demonstrable aim of eliminating all competition. In those circumstances, to accept that all selling above cost was automatically acceptable could enable the undertaking in question to eliminate all competition by pursuing a selective pricing policy which in the long run would permit it to increase prices and deter potential future entrants for fear of receiving the same targeted treatment[294].

In its judgment the Court of Justice followed the Advocate General, holding that the selective price cutting on the facts of this case was abusive[295]. After noting that the scope of the special responsibility of dominant undertakings must be considered in the light of the specific circumstances of each case[296], the Court of Justice noted that the maritime transport market is 'a very specialised sector'[297]; it declined to establish a general rule for selective price cutting on the part of liner conferences, but, upholding the Commission's finding of abuse, concluded that:

> It is sufficient to recall that the conduct at issue here is that of a conference having a share of over 90% of the market in question and only one competitor. The appellants have, moreover, never seriously disputed, and indeed admitted at the hearing, that the purpose of the conduct complained of was to eliminate [Grimaldi & Cobelfret] from the market[298].

As a result of this judgment it is clear that selective price cutting is capable of being abusive in its own right. However it is important to point out a number of features of the *Compagnie Maritime Belge* case that restrict the scope of this precedent and which should therefore limit its application in the future. First, maritime transport is, as the Court of Justice remarked, an unusual sector in which an incumbent dominant firm is able to target its

---

[291] Cases T-24/93 etc [1996] ECR II-1201, [1997] 4 CMLR 273.

[292] Cases C-395 and 396/96 P *Compagnie Maritime Belge v Commission* [2000] ECR I-1365, [2000] 4 CMLR 1076; for comment see Preece '*Compagnie Maritime Belge:* Missing the Boat?' (2000) 21 ECLR 388.

[293] Cases C-395/96 P etc [2000] ECR I-1365, [2000] 4 CMLR 1076, para 117.   [294] Ibid, para 132.

[295] See paras 112–121 of the Court of Justice's judgment.   [296] Ibid, para 114.

[297] Ibid, para 115.   [298] Ibid, para 119.

competitors and eliminate them by strategic behaviour with little regard to cost; secondly, the conference had 90 per cent or more of the market: it therefore was 'super-dominant', and subject to particularly close scrutiny under Article 102[299]; thirdly, the conference had only one competitor, Grimaldi and Cobelfret; and fourthly, there was a 'smoking gun', that is to say evidence of an intention on the part of the conference to eliminate Grimaldi from the market: indeed the smoke was seen by the judges of the Court of Justice, where the appellants admitted that they had this intention. The Court of Justice did not say, but may also have been influenced by the fact, that the liner conference itself was the product of a horizontal agreement amongst its members: there was, in effect, a horizontal collective boycott of Grimaldi, which would be a serious offence under Article 101(1)[300]. The case should be read with these special features in mind; this makes it a less menacing precedent than it might otherwise appear to be, with the consequence that other dominant firms, operating in less unusual circumstances, should be free to respond to competition by price cuts that are not contrary to any of the other pricing abuses under Article 102 described in this chapter.

(D) **UK law**

There have been four cases in which predatory pricing has been established by competition authorities in the UK, *Napp, Aberdeen Journals, EW&S* and *Cardiff Bus*; allegations of predation have been rejected on a number of occasions.

(i) **The *Napp Pharmaceutical* case**

In *Napp Pharmaceutical Holdings Ltd*[301] the OFT concluded that Napp was guilty of charging predatory prices for sustained release morphine by selling some products to hospitals at less than direct cost, which it considered, on the facts of the case, to be a proxy for AVC[302]. The OFT rejected Napp's argument that sales below cost to hospitals were objectively justified since Napp would be able to recover the full price from follow-on sales to patients in the community[303]; indeed the very reason that Napp was able to earn high margins on sales to the community was that it had been successful in stifling competition in relation to sales to hospitals[304]. On appeal the CAT held that Napp, as an undertaking which it considered to be 'super-dominant'[305], had abused its dominant position by charging prices below cost to hospitals in order to ward off a competitor[306]. The CAT held that, as Napp had offered prices below AVC to hospitals, it was not necessary to determine whether it had a plan to eliminate competition[307]; however the CAT found that such a plan existed in any event[308].

(ii) **The *Aberdeen Journals* case**

In *Aberdeen Journals Ltd*[309] the OFT imposed a penalty of £1,328,040 on Aberdeen Journals for predatory pricing by failing to cover its AVC from 1 March to 29 March 2000. This decision was set aside by the CAT as it was not satisfied by the way in which the OFT had

---

[299] See ch 5, 'The emergence of super-dominance', pp 187–189.

[300] See ch 13, 'Anti-Competitive Horizontal Restraints', pp 550–552.

[301] OFT decision of 30 March 2001 [2001] UKCLR 597.   [302] Ibid, paras 188–196.

[303] Ibid, paras 192–195.   [304] Ibid, para 195.

[305] Case No 1000/1/1/01 *Napp Pharmaceutical Holdings Ltd v Director General of Fair Trading* [2002] CAT 1, [2002] CompAR 13, paras 219 and 343; for comment on the finding of predatory pricing in this case see Ahlborn and Allan 'The Napp Case: A Study of Predation' (2004) 26(2) World Competition 233.

[306] Case No 1000/1/1/01 [2002] CAT 1, [2002] CompAR 13, para 352.   [307] Ibid, paras 228 and 307.

[308] Ibid, paras 310 and 333.   [309] OFT decision of 16 July 2001 [2001] UKCLR 856.

defined the relevant market[310]. The OFT adopted a second decision, concluding again that Aberdeen Journals was guilty of predatory pricing[311]. On appeal against the second decision the CAT held that Aberdeen Journals had sold advertising in one of its newspapers at less than AVC contrary to the Chapter II prohibition[312]. This judgment contains several important points on the cost-based rules relating to predatory pricing. First, the CAT emphasised that the rules are not an end in themselves and ought not to be applied mechanistically[313]. Secondly, the CAT drew attention to the significance of the time period over which costs are to be calculated[314]; the reason for this is that, the longer the timescale, the more likely costs will be assessed as variable rather than fixed, with the result that a failure to cover them will give rise to a presumption of predation[315]. Thirdly, the CAT recognised the possibility that a dominant firm could in certain circumstances objectively justify pricing below cost, though this would be particularly difficult when such pricing occurred in response to a new entrant or as part of a strategy to eliminate a competitor[316]. On the issue of intention the CAT said that, in the absence of exceptional circumstances, the longer a dominant firm prices below total costs, the easier it would be to draw an inference of intention to eliminate competition[317].

(iii) *EW&S*

In *English Welsh & Scottish Railway Ltd*[318] the Office of Rail Regulation found that EW&S had abused its dominant position in a number of ways, including by predatory pricing[319].

(iv) *Cardiff Bus*

In *Cardiff Bus*[320] the OFT concluded that Cardiff Bus engaged in predatory conduct intended to eliminate 2 Travel, a rival bus company, from the market[321]. The OFT did not impose a fine due to Cardiff Bus's small turnover[322]; subsequently the liquidator of 2 Travel and several of its former shareholders commenced a 'follow-on' action for damages against Cardiff Bus[323].

(v) Is there a need to prove recoupment of losses?

In *Napp*[324] and the second *Aberdeen Journals* case[325] the CAT held that it was a form of recoupment for a dominant firm to engage in predatory pricing in one market so that it could protect its market share or supra-competitive profits in another market and that, in the circumstances of those cases, further evidence of recoupment was unnecessary.

---

[310] Case No 1005/1/1/01 *Aberdeen Journals Ltd v Director General of Fair Trading* [2002] CAT 4, [2002] CompAR 167, paras 182–186.

[311] *Aberdeen Journals Ltd – remitted case*, OTF decision of 16 September 2002 [2002] UKCLR 740.

[312] Case No 1009/1/1/02 *Aberdeen Journals Ltd v OFT* [2003] CAT 11, [2003] CompAR 67.

[313] Ibid, paras 380 and 411.   [314] Ibid, paras 353–356 and 382–387.

[315] See the discussion of variable and fixed costs at 'Cost Concepts', pp 716–718 above.

[316] Case No 1009/1/1/02 [2003] CAT 11, [2003] CompAR 67, paras 357–358 and 371.   [317] Ibid, para 356.

[318] ORR decision of 17 November 2006 [2007] UKCLR 937.   [319] See Part IIC of the decision.

[320] OFT decision of 18 November 2008 [2009] UKCLR 332.   [321] See Chapter 7 of the decision.

[322] Cardiff Bus benefited from immunity under s 40 of the Competition Act 1998, on which see ch 10, 'Immunity for small agreements and conduct of minor significance', pp 413–414.

[323] Case Nos 1175–1178/5/7/11 *Francis v Cardiff City Transport Services Ltd.*

[324] Case No 1000/1/1/01 *Napp Pharmaceutical Holdings Ltd v Director General of Fair Trading* [2002] CAT 1, [2002] CompAR 13, para 261.

[325] Case No 1009/1/1/02 *Aberdeen Journals Ltd v OFT* [2003] CAT 11, [2003] CompAR 67, para 445.

(vi) Cases where predatory pricing was not established

There have been some cases in which a complaint of predatory pricing was not upheld[326]. In *The Association of British Travel Agents and British Airways plc*[327] the OFT concluded that BA was not guilty of abusing a dominant position by reducing the commission it paid to travel agents for the sale of tickets for its flights with the consequence that it could sell those same flights at lower fees through its own website: the sale of tickets online as opposed to through travel agents was cheaper, and there was an objective justification for this price differential[328].

In *Complaint against BT's pricing of digital cordless phones*[329] the Office of Communications ('OFCOM') dealt with a complaint that BT was guilty of charging predatory prices for digital cordless telephones. OFCOM concluded that BT was not dominant[330]. However it also conducted an extensive analysis of whether, if BT was dominant, it would have been guilty of predatory pricing and concluded that this was not so[331].

In *Claymore Dairies Ltd v OFT*[332] the CAT was critical of the OFT's investigation into whether Robert Wiseman Dairies was guilty of predatory pricing in relation to the sale of milk in Scotland: in particular it was not satisfied that the OFT had sufficiently investigated whether Wiseman's prices were above ATC[333], and it therefore set the finding on this point aside[334].

The OFT rejected a complaint about predatory prices in *First Edinburgh/Lothian*[335], as did the ORR in *DB Schenker Rail (UK) Ltd*[336].

In *Alleged abuse of a dominant position by Flybe Ltd*[337] the OFT concluded that there were no grounds for action against Flybe, which had been accused by Air Southwest of predatory pricing on the air route from Newquay to London Gatwick. The OFT's view was that there was no abuse on that particular route, since Flybe was not in a dominant position on it[338]. The OFT also stated that there was an objective justification for Flybe to expect and to incur initial losses on entering a new route[339].

7. Margin Squeezing[340]

(A) The economic phenomenon

A margin squeeze can occur where a firm is dominant in an upstream market and supplies a key input to undertakings that compete with it in a downstream market. In such a

---

[326] In addition to the cases mentioned in the text see the judgment of the High Court in *Chester City Council v Arriva Plc* [2007] EWHC 1373, [2007] UKCLR 1582.

[327] OFT decision of 11 December 2002 [2003] UKCLR 136.

[328] Ibid, paras 38–45.   [329] OFCOM decision of 1 August 2006 [2007] UKCLR 1.

[330] Ibid, paras 151–429.   [331] Ibid, paras 430–662.

[332] Case No 1008/2/1/02 [2005] CAT 30, [2006] CompAR 1.   [333] Ibid, para 256.

[334] Ibid, para 318.   [335] OFT decision of 9 June 2004 [2004] UKCLR 1554.

[336] ORR decision of 3 August 2010.   [337] OFT decision of 26 November 2010.

[338] Ibid, paras 5.12–5.20.

[339] Ibid, paras 6.97–6.99; the OFT referred to para 28 of the Commission's *Guidance on Article 102 Enforcement Priorities* on objective justification in fn 67 of the Decision.

[340] For further reading on margin squeezing see O'Donoghue and Padilla *The Law and Economics of Article 82 EC* (Hart Publishing, 2006), ch 6; Niels, Jenkins and Kavanagh *Economics for Competition Lawyers* (Oxford University Press, 2011), pp 239–250; Kavanagh 'Assessing Margin Squeeze under Competition Law' (2004) 3 Competition Law Journal 187; Crocioni 'Price Squeeze and Imputation Test – Recent Developments' (2005) 10 ECLR 558; Géradin and O'Donoghue 'The Concurrent Application of Competition Law and Regulation: The Case of Margin Squeeze Abuses in the Telecommunications Sector' (2005) 1 Journal of Competition Law and Economics 355; see Colley and Burnside 'Margin squeeze abuse' (2006) 2 European Competition Journal 185; Heimler 'Is a margin squeeze an antitrust or a regulatory violation?' (2010) 6 Journal of Competition Law and Economics 879.

situation the dominant firm may have a discretion as to the price it charges for the input, and this could have an effect on the ability of firms to compete with it in the downstream market. Suppose that A supplies widgets, essential for the manufacture of widget dioxide; that B is a subsidiary of A; and that C is an independent downstream competitor.

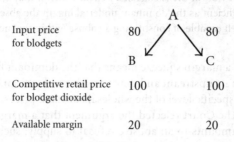

Input price for blodgets	80		80
Competitive retail price for blodget dioxide	100		100
Available margin	20		20

Fig. 18.4 Vertical margin squeeze: example 1

In this example C will be able to compete with B in the downstream market for widget dioxide only if C can transform the widgets into widget dioxide for a price of less than 20: if it cannot do so, it could not charge 100 in the retail market and make a profit. If, on the other hand, A had charged 60 for the widgets, the available margin would be 40, as in the following example:

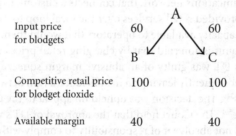

Input price for blodgets	60		60
Competitive retail price for blodget dioxide	100		100
Available margin	40		40

Fig. 18.5 Vertical margin squeeze: Example 2

In each situation the total revenue of the integrated undertaking AB amounts to 100, but A has 'squeezed' the margin available to C in example 1 in a way that makes it more difficult for C to remain in the market for widget dioxide than in example 2. However, it is a complex matter to determine when a squeeze becomes abusive. For example if, in example 1, B can transform widgets into widget dioxide for, say, 15, whereas C is less efficient and can perform the same task only for 25, there is no reason why C should be able to demand a lower input price: the fact is that it is not as efficient as B, and so does not merit protection from it. However if B's own cost of transformation is 25, and C's is 15, the input price is being manipulated to protect B from a more efficient competitor, C, and so there is an abusive margin squeeze, subject to any objective justification.

There may be other ways of addressing the pricing practices of the vertically-integrated entity AB. One is to inquire whether the input price charged by A to C is excessive; another is to determine whether the output price charged by B is predatory. Both of these issues were explored earlier in this chapter. If A were to charge higher prices to C than it charges to B, there might be a case of discrimination contrary to Article 102(2)(c), which is discussed towards the end of this chapter. However the focus of this section is whether A is guilty of manipulating the relationship of its upstream and downstream prices in order to eliminate its downstream competitor by a margin squeeze. This possibility does not exist in US law[341]. As far as EU law is concerned, the Court of Justice has established that A could be guilty of an independent abuse in its own right[342]. In *Konkurrensverket v TeliaSonera Sverige*[343] the Court said that:

> A margin squeeze, in view of the exclusionary effect which it may create for competitors who are at least as efficient as the dominant undertaking, in the absence of any objective justification, is in itself capable of constituting an abuse within the meaning of Article 102 TFEU[344].

The Court stated that a margin squeeze means that the dominant firm leaves an insufficient margin between its upstream and downstream products; and that it is this difference, rather than the specific level of the wholesale or retail prices, that is the essence of the infringement[345]. The Court rejected the argument that a margin squeeze can be an abuse only if it also amounts to an abusive refusal to supply: such an approach would unduly reduce the effectiveness of Article 102[346].

(B) **EU law**

(i) *Deutsche Telekom*

In *Deutsche Telekom* the Commission imposed a fine of €12.6 million on Deutsche Telekom ('DT') for imposing a margin squeeze in relation to access to its local networks[347]. DT had a dominant position in relation to the so-called 'local loop', that is to say the final section of the telecommunications network that connects a customer's premises to the local switching point. DT provided retail services over the local loop to its own customers, but also made wholesale capacity available to operators that would themselves like to provide retail services. The Commission said that by charging retail prices which were less than DT's wholesale prices DT was guilty of an abusive margin squeeze[348]. The Commission also objected to DT subsequently leaving an insufficient margin between its upstream and downstream products[349]. The decision was upheld on appeal to the General Court[350] and to the Court of Justice[351]. The Court held that the approval of DT's wholesale prices by a national regulator did not absolve it of responsibility to comply with Article 102 where it had the scope to adjust its retail prices to end the margin squeeze[352]. After stressing that Article 102 applies only to pricing practices which have exclusionary effects on competitors who are at least as efficient as the dominant firm[353], the Court concluded that such effects existed in this case[354].

[341] See *Pacific Bell Telephone Co v linkLine Communications Inc* 555 US 438 (2009); for comment, see the series of essays in the CPI Antitrust Chronicle Apr-09(1), available at www.competitionpolicyinternational.com.

[342] See eg Case C-280/08 P *Deutsche Telekom AG v Commission* [2010] ECR I-000, [2010] 5 CMLR 1495, para 183.

[343] Case C-52/09 P [2011] ECR I-000, [2011] 4 CMLR 982.

[344] Ibid, para 31.

[345] Ibid, para 34.

[346] Ibid, paras 54–58; this is a stricter approach than the one suggested in para 80 of the Commission's *Guidance on Article 102 Enforcement Priorities*: see p 757 below.

[347] OJ [2003] L 263/9, [2004] 4 CMLR 790.   [348] Ibid, paras 152–153.   [349] Ibid, paras 154–162.

[350] Case T-271/03 *Deutsche Telekom AG v Commission* [2008] ECR II-477, [2008] 5 CMLR 631.

[351] Case C-280/08 P *Deutsche Telekom AG v Commission* [2010] ECR I-000, [2010] 5 CMLR 1495.

[352] Ibid, paras 77–96.   [353] Ibid, paras 163–184.   [354] Ibid, paras 177–178 and 250–259.

(ii) TeliaSonera

In *Konkurrensverket v TeliaSonera*[355] the Swedish competition authority had brought proceedings alleging that TeliaSonera was guilty of a margin squeeze in relation to retail broadband services. The Swedish court sought the opinion of the Court of Justice, under Article 267 TFEU, on the criteria for establishing an abusive margin squeeze. The Court repeated its formulation in *Deutsche Telekom* of the test of when a margin squeeze is an abuse[356]. It also emphasised the need to demonstrate anti-competitive effects[357]. The Court continued by saying that the following factors are generally not relevant when establishing whether a margin squeeze infringes Article 102:

- the absence of any regulatory obligation on the dominant firm to supply the upstream product[358]
- the degree of dominance held[359]
- the absence of a dominant position on the downstream market[360]
- whether the customers to whom the pricing practice is applied are new or existing customers[361]
- the inability to recoup losses[362]
- the fact that the markets involve new as opposed to established technology[363].

(iii) **The Commission's decisional practice**

In its *Guidance on Article 102 Enforcement Priorities* the Commission discusses its approach to margin squeeze alongside refusal to supply; since the *Guidance* was issued, however, the Court of Justice has established that these practices are legally distinct. Paragraph 80 of the *Guidance* says that the Commission will generally rely on the LRAIC of the dominant firm's downstream operations to determine whether it has squeezed the margin available to an equally efficient competitor. The Commission may use the LRAIC of a downstream competitor in cases where it is not possible to allocate the costs of a vertically-integrated dominant firm[364]; something that is envisaged by paragraph 45 of the Court of Justice's judgment in *TeliaSonera*.

The Commission took action in relation to margin squeezing in *Napier Brown-British Sugar*[365], *Deutsche Telekom* and *Telefónica*[366]. The *Telefónica* decision is notable as the Commission imposed a fine of €151.8 million on Telefónica for engaging in a margin squeeze in relation to residential broadband access in Spain.

(C) **UK law**[367]

There have been a number of complaints about margin squeezing in the UK, two of which were successful.

---

[355] Case C-52/09 [2011] ECR I-000, [2011] 4 CMLR 982.   [356] Ibid, paras 31–35.   [357] Ibid, paras 60–67.
[358] Ibid, paras 47–59.   [359] Ibid, paras 78–82.   [360] Ibid, paras 83–89.
[361] Ibid, paras 90–95.   [362] Ibid, paras 96–103.   [363] Ibid, paras 104–111.
[364] *Guidance on Article 102 Enforcement Priorities*, fn 55.
[365] *Napier Brown–British Sugar* OJ [1988] L 284/41, [1990] 4 CMLR 196; see also *National Carbonising* OJ [1976] L 35/6 and the Commission's *Notice on the Application of the Competition Rules to Access Agreements in the Telecommunications Sector* OJ [1998] C 265/2, paras 117–119.
[366] Commission decision of 4 July 2007; see Le Meur, Gurpegui and Vierti 'Margin squeeze in the Spanish broadband market: a rational and profitable strategy' (2007) 3 *Competition Policy Newsletter* 22; the decision is on appeal to the General Court, Case T-336/07 *Telefónica and Telefónica España v Commission*, not yet decided and Case T-398/07 *Spain v Commission*, not yet decided.
[367] *The Application of the Competition Act in the Telecommunications Sector*, OFT 417, February 2000, para 7.26.

(i) Findings of a margin squeeze

In *Genzyme Ltd*[368] the OFT imposed a fine of £6.8 million on that company for abusing its dominant position in two ways, one of which was to have imposed a margin squeeze[369]. The finding of a margin squeeze was upheld on appeal to the CAT[370]. Genzyme was the producer of a drug, Cerezyme, used in the treatment of Gaucher's disease. Genzyme delivered the drug to patients in their homes; a competitor in the downstream market, Healthcare at Home, provided the same service. Genzyme was found guilty of squeezing the margin available to Healthcare at Home. In September 2005, following protracted but unsuccessful negotiations as to the price that Genzyme should charge for Cerezyme in order to avoid a margin squeeze, the CAT handed down a judgment on remedy[371]. Subsequently Healthcare at Home brought a 'follow-on' action for damages in the CAT[372]. An award of interim damages was made[373], but the case was settled late in 2006 and the action was withdrawn[374].

In *Albion Water/Dŵr Cymru* the Court of Appeal[375] upheld a judgment of the CAT overturning a non-infringement decision by OFWAT[376], and finding that Dŵr Cymru was guilty of margin squeezing[377].

(ii) Rejections of complaints about margin squeezes

The OFT concluded that there was no margin squeeze in *Companies House*[378]. In *BSkyB*[379] the OFT investigated complaints that BSkyB was guilty of a margin squeeze by setting its wholesale prices for the provision of premium channels at a level that would mean that distributors with the same efficiency as BSkyB would have to operate at a loss[380]. Following an extensive economic analysis, the conclusion was reached that there were insufficient grounds for believing that there was an abusive margin squeeze.

The Office of Telecommunications ('OFTEL'), and its successor OFCOM, have investigated a number of cases of margin squeezing, and have always reached the conclusion that there was no abuse[381]. In these decisions OFCOM has used various methodologies to determine whether there was a margin squeeze. In each case OFCOM concluded that, even if there was a margin squeeze, there was insufficient evidence of an anti-competitive

---

[368] OFT decision of 27 March 2003 [2003] UKCLR 950.   [369] Ibid, paras 364–385.
[370] Case No 1016/1/1/03 *Genzyme Ltd v OFT* [2004] CAT 4, [2004] CompAR 358; the Tribunal reviewed the case law at paras 489–493 of its judgment.
[371] *Genzyme Ltd v OFT* [2005] CAT 32, [2006] CompAR 195.
[372] Case No 1060/5/7/06 *Healthcare at Home v Genzyme Ltd.*
[373] Ibid [2006] CAT 29, [2007] CompAR 474.   [374] See the Order of the CAT of 11 January 2007.
[375] *Dŵr Cymru Cyfyngedig v Water Services Regulation Authority* [2008] EWCA Civ 536, [2008] UKCLR 457.
[376] OFWAT decision of 26 May 2004 [2004] UKCLR 1317.
[377] Case No 1046/2/4/04 *Albion Water Ltd v Water Services Regulation Authority* [2006] CAT 36, [2007] CompAR 328, paras 896–919; see also the Interim Judgment in this case of 22 December 2005 [2005] CAT 40, [2006] CompAR 269, paras 385–419.
[378] OFT decision of 25 October 2002 [2003] UKCLR 24, paras 29–36.
[379] OFT decision of 17 December 2002 [2003] UKCLR 240, paras 341–547.
[380] Ibid, paras 341–547.
[381] *BT/UK-SPN*, OFTEL decision of 22 May 2003 [2003] UKCLR 794, paras 21–53; *Alleged anti-competitive practices by BT in relation to BTOpenworld's consumer broadband products*, OFCOM decision of 20 November 2003 [2004] UKCLR 496, paras 6.1–6.162; *Investigation against BT about potential anti-competitive behaviour*, OFCOM decision of 12 July 2004 [2004] UKCLR 1695, paras 108–128; *BT 0845 and 0870 retail price change*, OFCOM decision of 19 August 2004 [2005] UKCLR 31, paras 3.24–3.100; *Suspected margin squeeze by Vodafone, O2, Orange and T-Mobile*, OFCOM decision of 26 May 2004 [2004] UKCLR 1639, paras 148–178; *Complaint from Gamma Telecom against BT about reduced rates for Wholesale Calls from 1 December 2004*, OFCOM decision of 16 June 2005 [2005] UKCLR 882, paras 47–120; *NCCN 5000*, OFCOM decision of 1 August 2008 [2008] UKCLR 501, paras 6.8–6.219.

effect. In *Investigation into BT's residential broadband pricing*[382] OFCOM conducted a detailed analysis of BT's financial performance and concluded that, while certain measures of profitability indicated that BT's margin on residential broadband products was negative during the relevant period, there was insufficient evidence of an abuse.

8. Price Discrimination[383]

This section considers the extent to which price discrimination may infringe Article 102 or the Chapter II prohibition of the Competition Act 1998. The extent to which other types of discrimination, in particular on the grounds of nationality, might lead to an infringement of Article 102 is discussed in chapter 17 on non-pricing abuses[384].

(A) The meaning of price discrimination

Price discrimination may be defined as the sale or purchase of different units of a good or service at prices not directly corresponding to differences in the cost of supplying them. There can be discrimination both where different, non-cost-related prices are charged for the sale or purchase of goods or services of the same description and also where identical prices are charged in circumstances in which a difference in the cost of supplying them would justify their differentiation.

There are many costs involved in supplying goods or services which may result in the charging of differentiated yet non-discriminatory prices. For example, apart from the cost of transporting goods, a manufacturer may incur heavier costs where it has to handle a series of small orders from a particular customer rather than a single, annual one. Orders for large quantities of goods may mean that a producer can plan long production runs and achieve economies of scale which lead to lower unit costs. The incidence of different contractual terms and conditions, payment of local taxes and duties, the different costs involved in operating distributorship networks from one area to another, may all explain the charging of different prices. However it can be difficult to determine whether differences in the cost of supplying goods or services justify, objectively, the charging of differentiated prices; and even more difficult to calculate the justifiable differentiation.

It is important to appreciate that price discrimination can be positively beneficial in terms of allocative efficiency, since it may result in an *increase* in output[385]: a theatre might be able to sell 80 per cent of its tickets to the public at £40 each, or alternatively 100 per cent of its tickets by charging 70 per cent of its customers £50 and the remaining 30 per cent £10 each (for example to impoverished students). Through such discrimination more theatre tickets will have been sold than would otherwise have been the case: resources have been more efficiently allocated. A specific example of efficient price discrimination is so-called 'Ramsey pricing'. This

---

[382] OFCOM decision of 2 November 2010, Section 4; an appeal to the CAT in Case No 1026/2/3/04 *Wanadoo UK plc v OFCOM* which had been adjourned pending the adoption of this decision was subsequently withdrawn: see Order of the CAT of 16 December 2010.

[383] For further reading on price discrimination see Scherer and Ross *Industrial Market Structure and Economic Performance* (Houghton Mifflin, 3rd ed, 1990), ch 13; Motta *Competition Policy: Theory and Practice* (Cambridge University Press, 2004), pp 491–511; O'Donoghue and Padilla *The Law and Economics of Article 82 EC* (Hart Publishing, 2006), ch 11; Van den Bergh and Camesasca *European Competition Law and Economics: A Comparative Perspective* (Sweet & Maxwell, 2nd ed, 2006), pp 254–264; Bishop and Walker *The Economics of EC Competition Law* (Sweet & Maxwell, 3rd ed, 2010), paras 6.29–6.36; Niels, Jenkins and Kavanagh *Economics for Competition Lawyers* (Oxford University Press, 2011), pp 215–223.

[384] See ch 17, 'Non-Pricing Abuses That are Harmful to the Internal Market', pp 711–712.

[385] See eg Schmalensee 'Output and Welfare Implications of Third Degree Price Discrimination' (1981) 71 American Economic Review 242.

occurs where a company supplies different products which share common costs[386]. It may be that customers for product A are highly price sensitive, but that customers for product B are not; if customers for product B are charged high prices and customers for product A low ones – that is to say if prices are marked up in inverse proportion to customers' respective price sensitivities – output will be increased and economic efficiency will therefore be maximised. The principle of Ramsey pricing has been accepted by regulators and competition authorities in some sectors[387], although it was rejected by the UK Competition Commission in its investigation of call-termination charges in the mobile telephony sector[388].

In practice the allocative effects of discrimination will vary from one market situation to another: the question is ultimately an empirical rather than a theoretical one. There is no case for a *per se* prohibition of price discrimination, even on the part of a dominant firm. It may be that preventing discrimination has the effect of redistributing income from poorer consumers to richer ones[389]. This can be illustrated by imagining what might happen if discrimination is prevented. A producer may charge £10 per widget in a prosperous area and £5 per widget in a poorer one. If this discrimination is prevented the producer may sell at a uniform price of, say, £7 in both areas. It is reasonable to assume that as a result fewer people in the poorer area will buy widgets, and that those that do will pay a higher proportion of their income than those in the prosperous one. The net effect therefore is to transfer wealth from poorer consumers with the result that more prosperous ones will be better off.

(B) EU law

Article 102(2)(c) specifically gives as an example of abuse:

> applying dissimilar conditions to equivalent transactions with other trading parties, thereby placing them at a competitive disadvantage.

Clearly therefore price discrimination may infringe Article 102; so too could other types of discrimination, such as refusals to supply and preferential terms and conditions. Price discrimination may be exploitative of customers, for example where higher prices are charged to 'locked-in' customers unable to switch to alternative suppliers; it can also be harmful to the competitive process, where it leads to a distortion of competition in markets downstream of the dominant undertaking. The case law appears to establish that, in determining whether there is an infringement of Article 102(2)(c), five issues must be addressed:

- does the accused undertaking have a dominant position?
- has the dominant undertaking entered into equivalent transactions with other trading parties?
- is the dominant undertaking guilty of applying dissimilar conditions to equivalent transactions?
- could the discrimination place other trading parties at a competitive disadvantage?
- is there an objective justification for the discrimination?

Each of these requirements will be considered in turn.

---

[386] On the meaning of common costs see 'Avoidable costs', p 717 above.

[387] See Pflanz 'What Price is Right? Lessons from the UK Calls-to-Mobile Inquiry' (2000) 21 ECLR 147.

[388] See *Mobile phone charges inquiry* Report of 18 February 2003, paras 2.213–2.215, available at www.competition-commission.org.uk; the report was unsuccessfully challenged in *R v Competition Commission, Director General of Telecommunications, ex p T-Mobile (UK) Ltd, Vodafone Ltd, Orange Personal Communication Services Ltd* [2003] EWHC 1555.

[389] See Bishop 'Price Discrimination under Article 86: Political Economy in the European Court' (1981) 44 MLR 282.

(i) Does the accused undertaking have a dominant position?

Clearly there can be an infringement of Article 102 only if an undertaking has a dominant position, and this would be in the upstream market; there is no need for the firm to be present, still less dominant, in the downstream market.

(ii) Has the dominant undertaking entered into equivalent transactions with other trading parties?

Article 102 does not require that all trading partners of a dominant undertaking must have the benefit of the same prices. According to the formulation in Article 102(2)(c) different treatment must be examined only where compared transactions are 'equivalent'. Factors to be considered in determining whether one transaction is equivalent with another include the nature of the product supplied and the costs of supply. In *United Brands v Commission*[390] the Court of Justice recognised that a dominant firm may charge different prices to reflect the different economic and competitive conditions in the different markets on which it operates[391]. In *Irish Sugar*[392] the Commission found that Irish Sugar had infringed Article 102(2)(c) in several ways, in particular by practising discrimination against sugar packers in Ireland. This part of the decision was upheld on appeal[393]: the General Court rejected the argument that Irish Sugar's dealings with sugar packers were not comparable to those with its other customers[394]. In *Clearstream v Commission* the General Court confirmed the Commission's decision that there had been an infringement of Article 102(2) (c)[395]. The General Court considered that Clearstream had provided equivalent primary clearing and settlement services for cross-border transactions to two groups of comparable customers[396].

(iii) Is the dominant undertaking guilty of applying dissimilar conditions to equivalent transactions?

To amount to an abuse of a dominant position the dominant firm must have applied dissimilar conditions. In *Michelin I*[397] the Court of Justice quashed the Commission's finding of an infringement of Article 102(2)(c), as it was not satisfied that Michelin had applied dissimilar conditions[398]. In *Virgin/British Airways*[399] the Commission concluded that BA was not only guilty of abuse by offering travel agents loyalty rebates; there was discrimination contrary to Article 102(2)(c), since travel agents in the same circumstances received different levels of rebates[400]. This finding was upheld on appeal to the General Court[401] and to the Court of Justice[402]. The General Court of Justice noted that BA's reward scheme led to different rates of commission being applied to an identical amount of revenue generated by the sale of BA tickets by two travel agents, and that

---

[390] Case 27/76 [1978] ECR 207, [1978] 1 CMLR 429.

[391] Ibid, para 227.

[392] OJ [1997] L 258/1, [1997] 5 CMLR 666.

[393] Case T-228/97 *Irish Sugar plc v Commission* [1999] ECR II-2969, [1999] 5 CMLR 1300, paras 125–149 (sugar export rebates to industrial customers) and 150–172 (higher prices charged to competing sugar packers).

[394] Ibid, para 164.

[395] Case T-301/04 *Clearstream Banking AG v Commission* [2009] ECR II-3155, [2009] 5 CMLR 2677.

[396] Ibid, paras 169–190.

[397] OJ [1981] L 353/33, [1982] 1 CMLR 643.

[398] Case 322/81 [1983] ECR 3461, [1985] 1 CMLR 282, paras 87–91.

[399] OJ [2000] L 30/1, [2000] 4 CMLR 999.

[400] Ibid, paras 108–111.

[401] Case T-219/99 *British Airways plc v Commission* [2003] ECR II-5917, [2004] 4 CMLR 1008, paras 233–240.

[402] Case C-95/04 P *British Airways plc v Commission* [2007] ECR I-2331, [2007] 4 CMLR 982, paras 133–141.

this distorted the level of remuneration received by them[403]. In the General Court's view the Commission was right to hold that BA's reward schemes were abusive:

> in that they produced discriminatory effects within the network of travel agents established in the UK, thereby inflicting on some of them a competitive disadvantage within the meaning of subparagraph (c) of the second paragraph of Article [102 TFEU][404].

In *Portuguese Airports*[405] the Commission adopted a decision establishing that Portugal was in breach of Article 106 read in conjunction with Article 102 in respect of a system of discounts on landing charges at the airports of Lisbon, Oporto, Faro and the Azores. Discounts were offered to airlines according to the number of flights that landed at Portuguese airports. As a result of this discounting structure Portuguese airlines enjoyed the highest discounts on their flights; airlines from beyond the Iberian peninsular received meagre discounts. On appeal the Court of Justice acknowledged that quantity discounts linked solely to the volume of purchases may be permissible, but said that the rules for calculating the discounts must not result in the application of dissimilar conditions to equivalent transactions contrary to Article 102(2)(c)[406]. It went on to say that:

> where, as a result of the thresholds of the various discount bands, and the levels of discount offered, discounts (or additional discounts) are enjoyed by only some trading parties, giving them an economic advantage which is not justified by the volume of business they bring or by any economies of scale they allow the supplier to make compared with their competitors, a system of quantity discounts leads to the application of dissimilar conditions to equivalent transactions.

> In the absence of any objective justification, having a high threshold in the system which can only be met by a few particularly large partners of the undertaking occupying a dominant position, or the absence of linear progression in the increase of the quantity discounts, may constitute evidence of such discriminatory treatment[407].

The Court of Justice noted that the highest discount rate was enjoyed only by the two Portuguese airlines, that the discount rate was greatest for the highest band and that the airports concerned enjoyed a natural monopoly; it concluded that in these circumstances the discounts were discriminatory[408].

(iv) Could the discrimination place other trading parties at a competitive disadvantage?

The wording of Article 102(2)(c) specifically requires that one component of the abuse is the infliction of 'competitive disadvantage'[409]. In some cases little attention was given to this issue. In *Corsica Ferries*[410] the Court of Justice said that Article 102(2)(c) applied to 'dissimilar conditions to equivalent transactions with trading partners', without mentioning

---

[403] Case T-219/99 *British Airways plc v Commission* [2003] ECR II-5971, [2004] 4 CMLR 1008, paras 235–236.

[404] Ibid, para 240.

[405] OJ [1999] L 69/31, [1999] 5 CMLR 103, paras 24–40; Article 102(2)(c) has been applied to discriminatory practices at a number of EU airports: see eg *Alpha Flight Services/Aéroports de Paris* OJ [1998] L 230/10, [2001] 4 CMLR 611, upheld on appeal Case T-128/98 [2000] ECR II-3929, [2001] 4 CMLR 1376, upheld on appeal Case C-82/01 P [2002] ECR I-9297, [2003] 4 CMLR 609; *Brussels National Airport (Zaventem)* OJ [1995] L 216/8, [1996] 4 CMLR 232, paras 12–18; *Ilmailulaitos/Luftfartsverket* OJ [1999] L 69/24, [1999] 5 CMLR 90, paras 38–56; *Spanish Airports* OJ [2000] L 208/36, [2000] 5 CMLR 967, paras 45–56.

[406] Case C-163/99 *Portugal v Commission* [2001] ECR I-2613, [2002] 4 CMLR 1319, para 50.

[407] Ibid, paras 52–53.   [408] Ibid, paras 54–57.

[409] See Case 85/76 *Hoffmann-La Roche v Commission* [1979] ECR 461, [19791 3 CMLR 211, paras 122–123 (specifically finding competitive disadvantage).

[410] Case C-18/93 *Corsica Ferries Italia Srl v Corporazione dei Piloti del Porto di Genoa* [1994] ECR I-1783.

the requirement of competitive disadvantage at all[411]. In the Commission's decisions on EU airports[412] scant attention was given to the need for competitive disadvantage. The same was true in *Deutsche Post AG – Interception of cross-border mail*[413]. It may be that this element of the offence will be applied in a particularly liberal manner where, as in those decisions and as in *Corsica Ferries*, the discrimination is practised on national lines, to the detriment (though not the competitive disadvantage) of undertakings in other Member States.

In *British Airways v Commission*[414] the Court of Justice gave some consideration to the requirement of competitive disadvantage in Article 102(2)(c)[415]. The Court of Justice was explicit that it is necessary in a case under this provision to show that competition is distorted: the distortion may be between the suppliers or between the customers of the dominant undertaking[416]. There must be a finding that the discriminatory behaviour in question:

> tends to distort that competitive relationship, in other words to hinder the competitive position of some of the business partners of that undertaking in relation to others[417].

The Court of Justice held that it is sufficient that the behaviour 'tends' to distort competition; there is no need to adduce evidence of an actual quantifiable deterioration in the competitive position of the business partners taken individually[418]. The Court of Justice concluded that the General Court had sufficiently satisfied itself that the test of Article 102(2)(c) was met[419].

In *Clearstream v Commission*[420] the General Court concluded that the discrimination against a trading partner continuously over a period of five years 'could not fail' to cause that partner a competitive disadvantage[421].

(v) Is there an objective justification for the discrimination?

A dominant firm may be able successfully to argue that discrimination is objectively justified or enhances efficiency. As already noted, differential pricing may increase a dominant firm's output and enable customers to obtain a product which they might not otherwise be able to afford. The Court of Justice concluded in *Portugal v Commission* that Portugal had failed to show any objective justification for its discriminatory discounts[422].

(C) UK law

In *BT/BSkyB broadband promotion*[423] OFTEL concluded that any discrimination on BT's part in relation to the promotion of its broadband services did not have a material effect on competition, and in *BT TotalCare*[424] OFTEL rejected an allegation that BT had been guilty of discrimination towards it in relation to the provision of certain broadband services.

In *English Welsh & Scottish Railway*[425] the ORR found that EW&S had abused its dominant position in a number of ways, including by discriminating between customers[426].

---

[411] Ibid, para 43.   [412] See ch 18 n 405 above.

[413] OJ [2001] L 331/40, [2002] 4 CMLR 598, paras 121–134.

[414] Case C-95/04 P *British Airways plc v Commission* [2007] ECR I-2331, [2007] 4 CMLR 982.

[415] Ibid, paras 142–148.   [416] Ibid, para 143.   [417] Ibid, para 144.

[418] Ibid, para 145.

[419] Ibid, paras 146–148; see also paras 104–112 of the Opinion of Advocate General Kokott given on 14 April 2011 in Case C-109/10 P *Solvay SA v Commission* which criticises the General Court for failing to analyse the competitive relationships between Solvay's customers.

[420] Case T-301/04 [2009] ECR II-3155, [2009] 5 CMLR 2677.   [421] Ibid, para 194.

[422] Case C-163/99 [2001] ECR I-2613, [2002] 4 CMLR 1319, paras 67–78.

[423] OFTEL decision of 19 May 2003.   [424] OFTEL decision of 10 June 2003.

[425] ORR decision of 17 November 2006 [2007] UKCLR 937.   [426] See Part IIB of the decision.

In *Purple Parking v Heathrow Airport*[427] the High Court concluded that Heathrow Airport was guilty of abusive discrimination in relation to the provision by it of access to the forecourts of Terminals 1, 3 and 5.

9. Pricing Practices that are Harmful to the Single Market

The Commission and the EU Courts will condemn pricing practices on the part of dominant firms that are harmful to the single market[428]. High prices that are charged in order to prevent parallel imports will infringe Article 102.

(A) Excessive pricing that impedes parallel imports and exports

In *BL*[429] the Commission condemned that firm for charging £150 to any importer of BL cars from the continent requiring a type-approval certificate to enable the cars to be driven in the UK. The interest of this case is that the purpose of the excessive pricing was not to exploit a monopoly situation by earning excessive profits, but to impede parallel imports into the UK: the Commission's action was motivated by single-market considerations, and not by a desire to establish itself as a price regulator; the circumstances in the *General Motors* case were the same[430]. The Commission's decision in *BL* was upheld on appeal by the Court of Justice, which accepted that the price charged by BL was disproportionate to the value of the service provided[431]. In *Deutsche Post AG – Interception of cross-border mail*[432] the Commission decided that, by charging an excessive amount for the onward transmission of cross-border mail, Deutsche Post was preventing users of the mail system from taking advantage of the developing single market for postal services.

(B) Geographic price discrimination

In *United Brands v Commission*[433] the Court of Justice held that UBC had abused its dominant position by charging different prices for its bananas according to the Member State of their destination. It sold bananas to distributors/ripeners at Rotterdam and Bremerhaven, and charged the lowest price for bananas destined for Ireland and the highest for those going to West Germany. The different prices were not based on differences in costs: in fact transport to Ireland, for which UBC itself paid, cost more than to other countries so that, if anything, prices should have been higher there. UBC was also condemned for including clauses in contracts with distributors which had the effect of preventing parallel imports from one country to another by prohibiting the export of unripened bananas[434].

---

[427] [2011] EWHC 987, [2011] UKCLR 492.

[428] See eg Case 7/82 *GVL v Commission* [1983] ECR 483, [1983] 3 CMLR 645.

[429] OJ [1984] L 207/11, [1984] 3 CMLR 92.

[430] OJ [1975] L 29/14, [1975] 1 CMLR D20, annulled on appeal for want of evidence Case 26/75 *General Motors v Commission* [1975] ECR 1367, [1976] 1 CMLR 95.

[431] Case 226/84 [1986] ECR 3263, [1987] 1 CMLR 185.

[432] OJ [2001] L 331/40, [2002] 4 CMLR 598.   [433] Case 27/76 [1978] ECR 207, [1978] 1 CMLR 429.

[434] See ch 17, 'Non-Pricing Abuses That are Harmful to the Internal Market', pp 711–712.

The decision is curious[435]. UBC claimed that it was being required to achieve a common market by adopting a uniform pricing policy for all Member States and that this was an unreasonable requirement on the part of the Commission. The Court of Justice retorted that it was permissible for a supplier to charge whatever local conditions of supply and demand dictate, that is to say that there is no obligation to charge a uniform price throughout the EU. However it added that the equation of supply with demand could be taken into account only at the level of the market at which a supplier operates. In *United Brands* this would mean that only a retailer in a given Member State could consider what price the market could bear; UBC could not do so since it did not sell bananas at retail level in Member States: it supplied distributors/ripeners at Rotterdam and Bremerhaven. In the Court of Justice's view, therefore, it was entitled to take into account local market conditions only 'to a limited extent'. The reasoning has been questioned: supply and demand at retail level would inevitably exert a backward influence on UBC, and anyway it, rather than retailers, employed the staff who carried out market research and monitored the level of demand throughout the EU. A different criticism of the case is that the judgment could have undesirable redistributive effects. The logical response of UBC would be to charge a uniform price higher than that in Ireland but lower than that in Germany; it would seem therefore that the judgment would benefit the Germans at the expense of the Irish. It is therefore arguable that the discrimination in *United Brands* should not have been condemned; the practice which was rightly found to be abusive was the prohibition on the export of unripened (green) bananas, since this is what had the effect of harming the single market. In the absence of this practice, bananas could have moved from low- to high-priced parts of the EU.

The Commission also condemned geographical price discrimination in *Tetra Pak II*[436]. The Commission's view was that the relevant geographic market was the EU as a whole, and yet Tetra Pak had charged prices that varied considerably from one Member State to another. The Commission said that the price differences could not be explained in economic terms and lacked objective justification. They were possible because of Tetra Pak's policy of market compartmentalisation which it maintained by virtue of its other abusive practices.

(C) Rebates that impede imports and exports

The Commission will condemn rebates and similar practices which have the effect of impeding imports and exports. Pricing practices that were intended to dissuade customers from importing from other Member States were held to be abusive in *Plasterboard*[437] and in *Michelin II*[438]. The Commission's decision in *Irish Sugar*[439] was prompted by single market considerations. Irish Sugar had a share of the Irish sugar market in excess of 90 per cent and was found to have acted abusively by seeking to restrict competition from other Member States. In particular Irish Sugar was found to have offered selectively low

---

[435] For criticism see Bishop 'Price Discrimination under Article 86: Political Economy in the European Court' (1981) 44 MLR 282; Zanon 'Price Discrimination under Article 86 of the EEC Treaty: the *United Brands* Case' (1982) 31 ICLQ 36.

[436] OJ [1992] L 72/1, [1992] 4 CMLR 551, paras 154, 155 and 160, upheld on appeal Case T-83/91 *Tetra Pak International SA v Commission* [1994] ECR II-755, upheld on appeal Case C-333/94 P *Tetra Pak International SA v Commission* [1996] ECR I-5951, [1997] 4 CMLR 662.

[437] Case T-65/89 *BPB Industries plc and British Gypsum v Commission* [1993] ECR II-389, [1993] 5 CMLR 32, paras 117–122.

[438] OJ [2002] L 143/1, [2002] 5 CMLR 388, paras 240–247, 271 and 312–314.

[439] OJ [1997] L 258/1, [1997] 5 CMLR 666.

prices to customers of an importer of French sugar and to have offered 'border rebates' to customers close to the border with Northern Ireland and who were therefore in a position to purchase cheaper sugar from the UK. On appeal to the General Court the Court annulled the former finding[440], but agreed that the border rebates were unlawful[441]. The General Court stressed the importance in EU competition law of the competitive influence on one national market from neighbouring markets, the very essence of an internal market[442].

[440] Case T-228/97 *Irish Sugar v Commission* [1999] ECR II-2969, [1999] 5 CMLR 1300, paras 117–124.

[441] Ibid, paras 173–193.

[442] Ibid, para 185.

19

The relationship between intellectual property rights and competition law

This chapter considers the relationship between intellectual property rights and competition law. After a brief introduction, section 2 will deal in general terms with the application of Article 101 to licences of intellectual property rights; section 3 will examine the provisions of Regulation 772/2004[1], the block exemption for technology transfer agreements. Section 4 will consider the application of Article 101 to various other agreements concerning intellectual property rights such as technology pools and settlements of litigation. This will be followed by a section on the possible application of Article 102 to the way in which dominant undertakings exercise their intellectual property rights, including an examination of the controversial subject of refusals to license intellectual property rights which are sometimes found to be abusive. Section 6 of this chapter will look at the position in UK law.

1. Introduction

(A) Definitions

It is not possible to deal with the substantive law of intellectual property here in detail[2]. For present purposes the term 'intellectual property' includes patents, registered and

---

[1] OJ [2004] L 123/11.

[2] For a general account of the law see Bently and Sherman *Intellectual Property Law* (Oxford University Press, 3rd ed, 2008); Torremans and Holyoak *Intellectual Property Law* (Oxford University Press, 6th ed, 2010); Cornish and Llewellyn *Intellectual Property: Patents, Copyrights, Trademarks and Allied Rights* (Sweet & Maxwell, 7th ed, 2010); Cook *EU Intellectual Property Law* (Oxford University Press, 2010); for specific discussion of the relationship between intellectual property rights and EU competition law see Rothnie *Parallel Imports* (Sweet & Maxwell, 1993); Govaere *The Use and Abuse of Intellectual Property Rights in EC Law* (Sweet & Maxwell, 1996); Maher 'Competition Law and Intellectual Property Rights: Evolving Formalism' in Craig and de Búrca (eds) *The Evolution of EU Law* (Oxford University Press, 1999); Korah *Intellectual Property Rights and the EC Competition Rules* (Hart Publishing, 2006); *European Competition Law Annual: The Interaction between Competition Law and Intellectual Property Law* (Hart Publishing, 2007, eds Ehlermann and Atanasiu);

unregistered designs, copyrights including computer software, trade marks and analogous rights such as plant breeders' rights. It should also be taken to include know-how, defined for the purpose of the block exemption on technology transfer agreements as 'a package of non-patented practical information, resulting from experience and testing': such information must be secret, substantial and identified in a sufficiently comprehensive manner that it is possible to verify that it is secret and substantial[3]; although not strictly speaking an intellectual property right[4], know-how may be extremely valuable and may be sold or 'licensed' for considerable amounts of money.

(B) Intellectual property rights and the single market

Generally speaking intellectual property rights are the product of, and are protected by, national systems of law, although the growth of international commerce has resulted in an increasing measure of international cooperation[5]. The existence of different national laws on intellectual property presents particular difficulties in the European Union in so far as this may be detrimental to the goal of single market integration. The Court of Justice developed the 'exhaustion of rights' doctrine to prevent an undertaking that has consented to the sale of goods on the market within the European Union from using a national intellectual property right to prevent the free movement of those goods around the EU[6]; the exhaustion of rights doctrine does not apply to goods placed on the market outside the EU[7]. Article 118(1) TFEU provides for the creation of European intellectual property rights by the European Parliament and the Council. Various harmonisation measures have been adopted to reduce the differences between different national systems of law; an obvious example is the Trade Mark Directive[8], implemented in the UK by the Trade Marks Act 1994. The adoption of the 'Community Trade Mark' Regulation[9] takes matters a step further, by creating an intellectual property right that is itself a creature of EU rather than national law; there is also a

---

Anderman (ed) *The Interface Between Intellectual Property Rights and Competition Policy* (Cambridge University Press, 2007); Faull and Nikpay *The EC Law of Competition* (Oxford University Press, 2nd ed, 2007), ch 10; Stothers *Parallel Trade in Europe: Intellectual Property, Competition and Regulatory Law* (Hart Publishing, 2007); Bellamy and Child *European Community Law of Competition* (Oxford University Press, 6th ed, 2008, eds Roth and Rose), ch 9; *Oliver on Free Movement of Goods in the European Union* (Hart Publishing, 5th ed, 2010, ed Oliver); Turner *Intellectual Property Law and EU Competition Law* (Oxford University Press, 2010); Leslie *Antitrust Law and Intellectual Property Rights: Cases and Materials* (Oxford University Press, 2010); Ghidini *Innovation, Competition and Consumer Welfare in Intellectual Property Law* (Edward Elgar, 2010); Anderman and Schmidt *EU Competition Law and Intellectual Property Rights: The Regulation of Innovation* (Oxford University Press, 2nd ed, 2011); Tritton *Intellectual Property in Europe* (Sweet & Maxwell, 4th ed, 2011).

[3] Regulation 772/2004, Article 1(1)(i); the Regulation is considered at 'Technology Transfer Agreements: Regulation 772/2004', pp 781–791 below.

[4] Know-how is protected by the law of obligations: see generally on confidential information *Cornish and Llewellyn*, ch 8.

[5] See *Cornish and Llewellyn*, paras 1.30–1.34.

[6] See Coates, Kyølbye and Peeperkorn in Faull and Nikpay *The EC Law of Competition* (Oxford University Press, 2nd ed, 2007), paras 10.36–10.49.

[7] Ibid, paras 10.50–10.54.

[8] Council Directive 89/104, OJ [1989] L 40/1; see also the Directives on computer software, Directive 2009/24, OJ [2009] L 111/16; on rental rights, Directive 2006/115, OJ [2006] L 376/28; on the duration of copyright, Directive 2006/116, OJ [2006] L 372/12; on satellite broadcasting and cable transmissions, Directive 93/83, OJ [1993] L 248/15; on databases, Directive 96/9, OJ [1996] L 77/20; on biotechnology, Directive 98/44, OJ [1998] L 213/3; on designs, Directive 98/71, OJ [1998] L 289/28; and on copyright and related rights, Directive 2001/29, OJ [2001] L 167/10.

[9] Regulation 40/94, OJ [1994] L 11/1, as amended by Regulation 3288/94, OJ [1994] L 349/83 and Regulation 422/2004, OJ [2004] L 70/1.

'Community Designs' Regulation[10] and there are plans for an enhanced cooperation regime for a unified EU patent[11]. Much of this chapter is concerned with the problem that intellectual property rights may be used in a way that compartmentalises the single market.

(C) Is there an inevitable tension between intellectual property rights and competition law?

The essential characteristic of intellectual property rights is that they confer upon their owners an exclusive right to behave in a particular way. For example the UK Patents Act 1977 grants the owner of a patent the right to prevent others from producing the patented goods or applying the patented process for a period of 20 years; patents may be granted where a product or process is technically innovative[12]. A patent does not necessarily make the patentee a monopolist in an economic sense: there may be other products that compete with the subject-matter of the patent; however the patent does afford a degree of immunity from the activities of rival firms. The owner of a registered trade mark can prevent anyone else applying that name to goods or services where this would be confusing to consumers.

Because intellectual property rights confer exclusive rights upon their owners on the one hand, whereas competition law strives to keep markets open on the other, it is easy to suppose that there is an inherent tension between these two areas of law and policy[13]. However it has increasingly been recognised that this is simplistic and wrong[14]. As paragraph 7 of the European Commission's *Guidelines on the application of Article [101 TFEU] to technology transfer agreements*[15] ('the *Technology Transfer Guidelines*') says:

> Indeed, both bodies of law share the same basic objective of promoting consumer welfare and an efficient allocation of resources. Innovation constitutes an essential and dynamic component of an open and competitive market economy.

Clear statements to the same effect will be found in an invaluable document issued by the Department of Justice and the Federal Trade Commission in the US in April 2007 entitled *Antitrust Enforcement and Intellectual Property Rights: Promoting Innovation and Competition*[16]. It begins with the following very clear statement:

> Over the past several decades, antitrust enforcers and the courts have come to recognize that intellectual property laws and antitrust laws share the same fundamental goals of

---

[10] Regulation 6/2002, OJ [2002] L 3/1.

[11] See the Commission's *Proposal for a Regulation of the European Parliament and of the Council implementing enhanced cooperation in the area of the creation of unitary patent protection*, COM(2011) 215/3, 13 April 2011.

[12] On the law of patents see *Cornish and Llewellyn*, chs 3–7.

[13] For general discussion of the relationship between intellectual property and competition law and policy see the publications cited in ch 19 n 2 above.

[14] See eg Tom and Newberg 'Antitrust and Intellectual Property: From Separate Spheres to Unified Field' (1997–98) 66 Antitrust Law Journal 167 on the 'marked reduction in antitrust hostility toward intellectual property' in the US in the last 50 years; see also Kobak 'Running the Gauntlet: Antitrust and Intellectual Pitfalls on the Two Sides of the Atlantic' (1995–96) 64 Antitrust Law Journal 341; Commission's *Evaluation Report on the Transfer of Technology Block Exemption Regulation No 240/96*, December 2001, para 29; Report for the European Commission on *Multi-Party Licensing* (Charles River Associates, April 2003), pp 58–59; Kovacic and Reindl 'An Interdisciplinary Approach to Improving Competition Policy and Intellectual Property Policy' (2005) 28 Fordham International Law Journal 1062; Lianos 'Competition Law and Intellectual Property Rights: Is the Property Rights' Approach Right?', chapter 8 in *Cambridge Yearbook of European Legal Studies* (Hart Publishing, 2006, eds Bell and Kilpatrick); Hovenkamp, Janis, Lemley and Leslie *IP and Antitrust: An Analysis of Antitrust Principles Applied to Intellectual Property Law* (Wolters Kluwer, 2nd ed, 2010).

[15] OJ [2004] C 101/2.   [16] This document can be accessed at www.ftc.gov.

enhancing consumer welfare and promoting innovation. This recognition signaled a significant shift from the view that prevailed earlier in the twentieth century, when the goals of antitrust and intellectual property law were viewed as incompatible: intellectual property law's grant of exclusivity was seen as creating monopolies that were in tension with antitrust law's attack on monopoly power. Such generalizations are relegated to the past. Modern understanding of these two disciplines is that intellectual property and antitrust laws work in tandem to bring new and better technologies, products, and services to consumers at lower prices.

Many of the issues discussed in this chapter are analysed in the DoJ/FTC document, which will be cited at various points in the text that follows. In the same spirit as that document, the current block exemption in force in the EU for technology transfer agreements, Regulation 772/2004[17], and the accompanying *Technology Transfer Guidelines* adopt a much less grudging attitude towards such agreements than used to be the case: indeed recital 5 of the Regulation notes that such agreements 'will usually improve economic efficiency and be pro-competitive'; the same point is made at several points in the *Guidelines*[18]. The complex matter in modern competition policy is to determine at what point, if at all, the exercise of an intellectual property right could be so harmful to consumer welfare that competition law should override the position as it would be on the basis of intellectual property law alone.

2. Licences of Intellectual Property Rights: Article 101

(A) **Introduction**

A patentee may decide, instead of producing the patented goods or applying the patented process itself, to grant a licence to another firm enabling it to do so. The same may be true of any other intellectual property right. There are many reasons why a firm may choose to grant a licence. A patentee may lack the resources to produce in quantity; it may wish to limit its own production to a particular geographical area and to grant licences for other territories; or it may wish to apply a patented process for one purpose and to allow licensees to use it for others. A patentee may wish to impose various restrictions upon its licensees, for example as to the quantity or quality of goods that may be produced or the price at which they may be sold; these provisions relate to the patentee's own products and so can be restrictive only of intra-technology competition[19].

The argument for controlling restrictions of intra-technology competition in patent licences is weak. Given that a patentee has an exclusive right to produce and sell the patented goods, it is not obvious why it should not be able to impose whatever restrictions it chooses upon its licensees; the ability to do so is a manifestation of the right conferred by statute. Indeed the grant of a licence can be seen as increasing competition, by introducing a licensee onto the market which, without the licence, would not be there at all; even if the patentee imposes restrictions of intra-technology competition, these are likely to be compensated for by the stimulation of inter-technology competition[20]. However Article 101(1) has been applied to intra-technology restrictions in patent (and other) licences, in particular where they divide the single market: the 'single market imperative' is as influential in this area of EU competition law as it is elsewhere[21].

---

[17] OJ [2004] L 123/11.   [18] See eg paras 8, 9, 17 and 146ff.

[19] For discussion of this expression see the *Technology Transfer Guidelines*, paras 11–12.

[20] Ibid.

[21] See ch 1, 'The single market imperative', pp 23–24 and ch 2, 'The single market imperative', p 51.

Some terms in patent licences may affect inter-technology competition: examples are tie-in clauses requiring a licensee to acquire particular technology or products solely from the patentee and non-competition clauses forbidding the licensee to compete or to handle technology or products which compete with the patentee's: provisions such as these may foreclose the opportunities of other producers. Objection might be taken to terms which are perceived to be an attempt to extend a patentee's monopoly power beyond the protection afforded to it by the law and/or which might be considered to be oppressive to a person in a weak bargaining position.

(B) Typical terms in licences of intellectual property rights

It will facilitate an understanding of EU law on licensing agreements to have some knowledge of typical clauses that may be found in them. In the absence of legal controls it would be a matter for the parties to the agreement to settle the terms of the licence through the bargaining process. It would be wrong to assume that it is always the patentee that is in the more powerful bargaining position: a patentee may be an individual inventor and his prospective licensee a powerful company, in which case the former's position may be weak.

(i) Territorial exclusivity[22]

In EU law territorial exclusivity is the most critical aspect of licensing agreements because of the overriding determination of the Commission and the EU Courts to prevent the isolation of national markets. A licensee may consider that the risk involved in exploitation of a patent is that the high level of capital investment required is so great that it would not be worth taking a licence at all unless it is given immunity from intra-technology competition from the licensor, other licensees and their customers: these issues have been discussed already in relation to vertical agreements[23]. A licensee will often be taking a greater risk than a 'mere' distributor, since it has to invest in production as well as distribution, and so may require more protection against free riders than a distributor needs. The extent of the exclusivity required will be a calculation for the licensee; the amount actually given, apart from any limiting legal constraints, will be a matter for bargaining between the licensor and licensee.

Often the licensor will grant to the licensee an exclusive right to manufacture and sell the goods in a particular territory and agree to refrain from granting similar rights to anyone else there; in this situation the licensor retains the right to produce the goods in the territory itself: this is known as a 'sole' licence. A sole licence may be distinguished from an 'exclusive' licence, where the licensor also agrees not to produce the goods in the licensee's territory itself; this of course gives the licensee more protection than in the case of a sole licence. The licensee's position may be further reinforced by the licensor agreeing to impose export bans on its other licensees preventing them, or requiring them to prevent their customers, from selling into the licensed territory. Apart from the imposition of export bans, there are indirect ways of achieving the same end: for example a maximum quantities clause can limit the amount that a licensee can produce to the anticipated level of demand on its domestic market. As we shall see, the mere grant of territorial exclusivity in a licence of an intellectual property right does not necessarily infringe Article 101(1); this will depend on the effect that this would have on the market. However, where a licensor grants a licensee absolute territorial protection against any

---

[22] See further the *Technology Transfer Guidelines*, paras 161–174.
[23] See ch 16, 'Vertical agreements: possible benefits to competition', pp 626–628.

form of intra-technology competition there will almost certainly be an infringement of Article 101(1) and it is unlikely that the terms of Article 101(3) will be satisfied.

(ii) Royalties[24]

A licensor will usually require the licensee to pay royalties for use of the patent. The licensee may be required to make lump-sum payments, and in some situations the parties may agree upon a profit-sharing scheme. The licensor may ask for a payment 'up-front' before production begins. A licensor may stipulate that the licensee must pay a minimum amount of royalties in a given period in order to encourage it to exploit the patented process.

(iii) Duration

A licensor will specify what the duration of the agreement should be. It may decide to grant only a limited licence which will expire before the patent itself, after which it can reconsider its position. On the other hand it may attempt to tie the licensee even after the patent has expired, for example by requiring it to continue to pay royalties or to take licences of newly discovered technology.

(iv) Field of use restrictions[25]

A common clause is a 'field of use' restriction whereby a licensor limits the licensee's authority to produce goods to a particular purpose: a chemical protected by a patent may be useful both medicinally and industrially and the licensee could be limited to production for one purpose only. Field of use clauses are normally seen as a reasonable exploitation of the patentee's position, although the Commission may object where the restriction appears to be partitioning the single market[26].

(v) Best endeavours and non-competition clauses[27]

To ensure that the licensee does exploit the patent (and that the patentee receives adequate royalties) the licensee may be required to produce minimum quantities or to use its best endeavours to do so. A non-competition clause, whereby the licensee is forbidden to compete by using its own or rival technology, may encourage it to concentrate on producing the patented goods, although such a clause may have an anti-competitive foreclosure effect.

(vi) No-challenge clauses

The licensor may insist upon a no-challenge clause whereby the licensee agrees not to challenge the validity of the intellectual property right in question. A licensee with intimate knowledge of, say, a patented process may be in the best position to show that it lacks originality, and a licensor may be unwilling to grant a licence at all if it knows that the licensee might undermine its position by successfully applying for the patent to be revoked.

(vii) Improvements

A licensor may be fearful that the licensee will build upon the knowledge that becomes available from using the patent and emerge as a strong competitor; it may therefore require

---

[24] See further the *Technology Transfer Guidelines*, paras 156–160.   [25] Ibid, paras 179–185.
[26] See *Windsurfing International* OJ [1983] L 229/1, [1984] 1 CMLR 1, substantially upheld on appeal Case 193/83 *Windsurfing International Inc v Commission* [1986] ECR 611, [1986] 3 CMLR 489.
[27] See *Technology Transfer Guidelines*, paras 196–203.

the licensee to grant back to it any know-how or intellectual property rights acquired and not to grant licences to anyone else. Objection may be taken to this practice if the licensor requires the licensee to grant it exclusive access to such know-how, since this deprives the licensee of the opportunity to pass on the technology to third parties.

(viii) Tying and bundling[28]

The licensor may make the licensing of technology conditional upon the licensee taking a licence for another technology or purchasing a product from the licensor or a designated third party; or may bundle two technologies or a technology and a product together. These practices are capable of foreclosing access to the market, but may also lead to economic efficiencies.

(ix) Prices, terms and conditions

The licensor may wish to fix the prices at which the licensee sells or the terms and conditions on which it does so. The Commission, however, takes the view that the licensee should be free to determine its own policy when it brings the patented products to the market.

(C) The application of Article 101(1) to licences of intellectual property rights[29]

(i) The Commission's evolving policy in relation to patent licences in the 1960s and 1970s

In the early 1960s the Commission took the view that most provisions in patent licences did not infringe Article 101(1) at all, since restrictions of intra-brand competition simply emanate from the exclusive right of the patentee. The Commission's *Notice on Patent Licensing Agreements*[30] of 1962 reflected this approach. However the Commission's abstentionist view began to alter towards the end of the decade; the change can be traced back to the judgment of the Court of Justice in *Consten and Grundig v Commission*[31]. There the Court established that vertical agreements could fall within Article 101(1) and, of particular importance in this context, that the use of intellectual property rights could contribute to an infringement where it enabled a distributor to enjoy absolute territorial protection in its allotted territory; in *Consten and Grundig* it was the assignment to Consten of the GINT trade mark for France that enabled Consten to repel parallel imports from other Member States[32]. The distinction drawn by the Court of Justice in this case – between the existence of an intellectual property right on the one hand and its

---

[28] Ibid, paras 191–195.

[29] See the *Technology Transfer Guidelines*, paras 10–17 and paras 130ff; on the position in the US see the DoJ/FTC *Antitrust Guidelines for the Licensing of Intellectual Property* of 6 April 1995, available at www.justice.gov; the *Guidelines* state at para 2.0 that there is no presumption that intellectual property creates market power, a point with which the US Supreme Court agreed in *Illinois Tool Works Inc v Independent Ink Inc* 547 US 28 (2006); the *Guidelines* also say that licences of intellectual property rights are generally pro-competitive; the approach in the *Guidelines*, which suggests that terms in licences should be subject to a 'rule of reason' standard, was endorsed by the DoJ/FTC report on *Antitrust Enforcement and Intellectual Property Rights* of April 2007: see in particular chapter 4 of the report.

[30] JO [1962] 2922; this Notice was withdrawn in 1984, OJ [1984] C 220/14.

[31] Cases 56 and 58/64 [1966] ECR 299, [1966] CMLR 418; for discussion of this case see ch 3, 'Cases in which agreements containing contractual restrictions were found not to have anti-competitive effects', p 128; on the Commission's change of policy see *Anderman*, ch 2.

[32] See ch 3, 'Cases in which agreements containing contractual restrictions were found not to have anti-competitive effects', p 128.

improper exercise on the other – provided the foundation of much of the law in this area including, in particular, the exhaustion of rights doctrine.

In a series of decisions from the early 1970s the Commission applied Article 101(1) to various clauses found in patent licences, and in particular to territorial restrictions, although in some cases it decided that the criteria in Article 101(3) were satisfied[33]. In a series of block exemptions, beginning with Regulation 2349/84 in 1984[34] up until Regulation 240/96 in 1996[35], the Commission maintained a fairly formalistic approach to the application of Article 101(1), applying that provision to a wide variety of contractual restrictions but then exempting them according to the terms of the relevant Regulation. The latest block exemption, Regulation 772/2004, is noticeably less formalistic and, in conjunction with the *Technology Transfer Guidelines*, provides a more benign treatment of the transfer of technology. The *Technology Transfer Guidelines* explain both the ways in which licences of technology containing restrictive terms may have negative[36] and positive[37] effects on competition.

(ii) Territorial exclusivity and the *Maize Seeds* case

In many of the decisions referred to above the Commission held that manufacturing and sales licences granting territorial exclusivity to the licensee infringed Article 101(1); it also considered that export bans and provisions having similar effects such as maximum quantities clauses were caught. Having concluded that many patent licences were caught by Article 101(1), the Commission proceeded to grant them block exemption. However, as we have seen in chapter 3, Article 101(1) applies only to agreements 'which have as their object or effect the prevention, restriction or distortion of competition'[38]. It was explained there that the mere grant of exclusive territorial rights does not have as its object the restriction of competition[39]; such cases infringe Article 101(1), therefore, only where they can be shown to have appreciable effects on competition[40] and on trade between Member States[41]. The reason for the strict treatment of the agreement in *Consten and Grundig v Commission* was that it went beyond the mere grant of exclusive distribution rights in France by conferring upon Consten absolute territorial protection against parallel imports from other Member States. The application of Article 101(1) to territorial exclusivity in licence agreements follows the same contours.

---

[33] In chronological order the Commission's decisions on patent licences are *Burroughs AG and Deplanque & Fils Agreement* OJ [1972] L 13/50, [1972] CMLR D67; *Burroughs AG and Geha-Werke GmbH Contract* OJ [1972] L 13/53, [1972] CMLR D72; *Davidson Rubber Co Agreements* OJ [1972] L 143/31, [1972] CMLR D52; *Raymond and Nagoya Rubber Ltd Agreement* OJ [1972] L 143/39, [1972] CMLR D45; *Kabelmetal/ Luchaire* OJ [1975] L 222/34, [1975] 2 CMLR D40; *Zuid-Nederlandsche Bronbemaling en Grondboringen BV v Heidemaatschappij Beheer NV* OJ [1975] L 249/27, [1975] 2 CMLR D67; *AOIP v Beyrard* OJ [1976] L 6/8, [1976] 1 CMLR D14; *Vaessen BV v Moris* OJ [1979] L 19/32, [1979] 1 CMLR 511; *IMA AG Windsurfing International Inc* OJ [1983] L 229/1, [1984] 1 CMLR 1, substantially upheld on appeal Case 193/83 *Windsurfing International Inc v Commission* [1986] ECR 611, [1986] 3 CMLR 489; *Velcro/Aplix* OJ [1985] L 233/22, [1989] 4 CMLR 157; the Commission has reached decisions on other types of licences in which it has applied similar principles: see below.

[34] OJ [1984] L 219/15.   [35] OJ [1996] L 31/2, [1996] 4 CMLR 405.

[36] *Technology transfer guidelines*, paras 141–145.   [37] Ibid, paras 146–152.

[38] See ch 3, 'The "object or effect" of preventing, restricting or distorting competition', pp 117ff.

[39] See ch 3, 'Cases in which agreements containing contractual restrictions were found not to have anti-competitive effects', p 128; see in particular the discussion of Case 56/65 *Société Technique Minière v Maschinenbau Ulm* [1966] ECR 235, [1966] CMLR 357.

[40] See ch 3, 'The *De Minimis* Doctrine', pp 140–144.

[41] On the requirement for an appreciable effect on trade between Member States see ch 3, 'The Effect on Trade Between Member States', pp 144–149.

The first case on the licensing of intellectual property rights to come before the Court of Justice was *Nungesser v Commission*[42] (often referred to as the *Maize Seeds* case). One issue for the Court was whether an exclusive licence of plant breeders' rights[43] by its very nature infringed Article 101(1): in other words, whether such agreements had as their object the restriction of competition[44]. The Court distinguished between an 'open exclusive licence', whereby a licensor agrees not to license anyone else in the licensee's territory, and not to compete there itself; and an exclusive licence which confers absolute territorial protection, so that all competition from third parties is eliminated[45]. This, of course, is the difference between the facts of *Société Technique Miniere v Maschinenbau Ulm*[46] and *Consten and Grundig v Commission*. As to the open exclusive licence, the Court of Justice noted that a licensee of new technology might be deterred from accepting the risk of cultivating and marketing a new product unless it knew that it would not encounter intra-technology competition from other licensees in its territory[47]. It followed that an open licence which does not affect the position of third parties such as parallel importers does not have as its object the restriction of competition; a detailed analysis would be required to determine the effects of the agreement[48]. Absolute territorial protection however would be caught by Article 101(1)[49] and did not benefit from Article 101(3)[50].

The *Maize Seeds* judgment showed some sensitivity to the commercial and economic context of licensing agreements. It means that open exclusivity does not necessarily infringe Article 101(1); in particular where a licensee accepts risk and markets a new product the licence would not be caught.

(iii) The case law of the EU Courts on territorial exclusivity after *Maize Seeds*

In chapter 3 we have seen that the Court of Justice has, in a number of judgments, refrained from concluding too readily that agreements containing contractual restrictions necessarily restrict competition: these two ideas should not be confused with one another[51]. Some agreements – for example to fix prices or to share markets – are so obviously reprehensible that they are considered to have as their object the restriction of competition[52]; other agreements, however, infringe Article 101(1) only where it can be demonstrated that they will produce appreciable anti-competitive effects on the market[53]. In various judgments since *Maize Seeds* the Court of Justice has concluded that provisions involving territorial exclusivity did not infringe Article 101(1). In *Coditel v Ciné Vog Films*[54] the Court acknowledged that, in the special circumstances of a performance

---

[42] Case 258/78 [1982] ECR 2015, [1983] 1 CMLR 278.

[43] Plant breeders' rights are analogous to patents.

[44] See ch 3, 'Agreements that have as their object the prevention, restriction or distortion of competition', pp 121–125 for a discussion of agreements that have as their object the restriction of competition.

[45] Case 258/78 [1982] ECR 2015, [1983] 1 CMLR 278, para 53.

[46] Case 56/65 [1966] ECR 235, [1966] CMLR 357.

[47] Case 258/78 [1982] ECR 2015, [1983] 1 CMLR 278, para 57.   [48] Ibid, para 58.

[49] Ibid, paras 60–63; see similarly Cases C-403/08 etc *Football Association Premier League Ltd v QC Leisure* [2011] ECR I-000, paras 134–136.

[50] Ibid, paras 68–79; note that in the *Coditel* case even absolute territorial protection was found not to infringe Article 101(1) in the case of a performing copyright: see 'The case law of the EU Courts on territorial exclusivity after *Maize Seeds*', pp 775–776 below.

[51] See ch 3, 'Cases in which agreements containing contractual restrictions were found not to have anti-competitive effects', pp 128–130.

[52] See ch 3, 'Agreements that have as their object the prevention, restriction or distortion of competition', p 125.

[53] See ch 3, 'Agreements that have as their effect the prevention, restriction or distortion of competition', pp 121–125.

[54] Case 262/81 [1982] ECR 3381, [1983] 1 CMLR 49.

copyright, a licensee may need absolute territorial protection from re-transmissions of films from neighbouring Member States. In *Louis Erauw-Jacquery Sprl v La Hesbignonne Société*[55] the Court held that a prohibition on the export of so-called 'basic seeds' did not infringe Article 101(1), but rather was a manifestation of Erauw-Jacquery's plant breeders' rights and necessary for their protection[56]. In *Pronuptia de Paris v Schillgalis*[57] the Court suggested that the grant of exclusive territorial rights to a franchisee for a particular territory might not infringe Article 101(1) where the business name or symbol of the franchise was not well known[58].

Collectively these cases demonstrate that it is wrong to assume that all territorial exclusivity in licences of intellectual property rights infringes Article 101(1); a more nuanced approach is required than this, and even absolute territorial protection and export bans may not infringe Article 101(1) in particular circumstances.

(iv) Non-territorial restrictions caught by Article 101(1)

The Commission's decisions have sometimes applied Article 101(1) to non-territorial restrictions in licences of intellectual property rights, as have some judgments of the EU Courts, in particular the judgment of the Court of Justice in *Windsurfing International Inc v Commission*[59]. The treatment of non-territorial restrictions will be considered below in the context of Articles 4 and 5 of Regulation 772/2004[60].

(v) Know-how licences

The Commission applied the principles that it had developed in its decisions on patent licences to licences of know-how[61]. This culminated in the adoption of Regulation 556/89[62] granting block exemption to know-how licences. As was noted at the beginning of this chapter, know-how is not an intellectual property right as such: it is protected by the law of obligations. An anxiety for the Commission was that spurious claims to exclusivity might be made for agreements that do not in practice improve economic efficiency; this is why successive block exemption regulations have stipulated that know-how must be secret and substantial[63]. In practice the licensing of know-how is as important and as common as patent licensing, so that the extension of the protection of block exemption to this category of agreements was important for industry.

(vi) Copyright licences

There is not a great deal of authority specifically on the application of Article 101(1) or Article 101(3) to copyright licences. As we have seen, the Court of Justice held that

---

[55] Case 27/87 [1988] ECR 1919, [1988] 4 CMLR 576.

[56] See 'Licences of plant breeders' rights', pp 779–780 below.

[57] Case 161/84 [1986] ECR 353, [1986] 1 CMLR 414.

[58] [1986] ECR 353, [1986] 1 CMLR 414, para 24.

[59] Case 193/83 [1986] ECR 611, [1986] 3 CMLR 489.

[60] See 'Article 4: hard-core restrictions', pp 786–789 below.

[61] In chronological order the Commission's decisions on know-how licences are *Boussois/Interpane* OJ [1987] L 50/30, [1988] 4 CMLR 124; *Mitchell Cotts/Sofiltra* OJ [1987] L 41/31, [1988] 4 CMLR 111; *Rich Products/Jus-Rol* OJ [1988] L 69/21, [1988] 4 CMLR 527; *Delta Chemie/DDD Ltd* OJ [1988] L 309/34, [1989] 4 CMLR 535; see also *ICL/Fujitsu* XVIth *Report on Competition Policy* (1986), point 72 (case dealt with by comfort letter).

[62] Corrected version at OJ [1990] L 257/15; this Regulation was replaced by Regulation 240/96, which in turn has been replaced by Regulation 772/2004: see 'Technology Transfer Agreements: Regulation 772/2004', pp 781–791 below.

[63] See now Regulation 772/2004, Article 1(1)(i).

absolute territorial protection was not contrary to Article 101(1) in the specific context of a performance copyright in *Coditel v Ciné Vog Films*[64]. However in *Football Association Premier League Ltd v QC Leisure*[65] the Court of Justice concluded that the terms of the English Premier League's licences with foreign broadcasters, which prohibited the import into the UK from Greece of satellite broadcasts of live Premier League soccer games, conferred absolute territorial protection contrary to Article 101(1) and did not benefit from Article 101(3)[66].

The Commission has taken action in relation to copyright licences on a few occasions and in doing so it has applied the principles developed in relation to patent and know-how licences. In *Neilson-Hordell/Reichmark*[67] the Commission gave details of its objections to clauses in a licence of technical drawings and the products they represent; in particular it required the abandonment of a no-challenge clause, a royalties clause extending to products not protected by any copyright of the licensor, a non-competition clause which was to continue after the agreement and an exclusive grant-back to the licensor of the improvements. In *Ernest Benn Ltd*[68] the Commission took objection to a standard contractual term which prevented the export of books from the UK. In *Knoll/Hille-Form*[69] the Commission intervened in the case of an exclusive licence of a design right relating to furniture and closed its file after the parties agreed to remove export bans and to allow direct sales into each other's territories.

In *Film Purchases by German Television Stations*[70] the Commission investigated exclusive licence agreements entered into between MGM/UA, a major US film production and distribution company, and ARD, an association of public broadcasting organisations in Germany. The agreements granted ARD exclusive television rights to a large number of MGM/UA's feature films in most cases for a period of 15 years. The Commission's view was that the agreements restricted competition, in particular because of the large number of the licensed rights and the duration of the exclusivity[71]. However the Commission decided that the criteria of Article 101(3) were satisfied following modifications to the agreements, for example so that ARD would license the films to third parties at certain periods known as 'windows'.

There is no specific block exemption for copyright licences, although it may be possible to take the benefit of Regulation 330/2010 on vertical agreements or of Regulation 772/2004 on technology transfer agreements where the licensing of copyright is ancillary to an agreement covered by one of those Regulations[72]. The Commission will as a general rule apply the principles set out in Regulation 772/2004 to copyright licences[73], although not necessarily in the case of performance copyright[74].

---

[64] Case 262/81 [1982] ECR 3381, [1983] 1 CMLR 49; see 'The case law of the EU Courts on territorial exclusivity after *Maize Seeds*', pp 775–776 above.

[65] Cases C-403/08 etc *Football Association Premier League Ltd v QC Leisure* [2011] ECR I-000.

[66] Ibid, paras 134–146.

[67] Commission's XIIth *Annual Report on Competition Policy* (1982), points 88–89.

[68] Commission's IXth *Report on Competition Policy* (1979), points 118 and 119; see also *The Old Man and the Sea* VIth *Report on Competition Policy* (1976), point 164; *STEMRA* XIth *Report on Competition Policy* (1981), point 98.

[69] Commission's XIIth *Report on Competition Policy* (1983), points 142–146.

[70] OJ [1989] L 284/36, [1990] 4 CMLR 841; the decision is criticised by Rothnie 'Commission Re-runs Same Old Bill' (1990) 12 EIPR 72.

[71] OJ [1989] L 284/36, [1990] 4 CMLR 841, paras 41–46.

[72] See 'Article 1: definitions', p 782 below.   [73] *Technology Transfer Guidelines*, para 51.

[74] Ibid, para 52.

(vii) Software licences[75]

In *Sega and Nintendo*[76] the Commission required the deletion of clauses in licences of computer software with publishers of video games which, in the Commission's view, enabled Sega and Nintendo to control the market for video games[77]. In *Microsoft Internet Explorer*[78] the Commission required Microsoft to remove clauses from its software licences providing for minimum distribution volumes for its Internet Explorer browser technology and imposing a prohibition on advertising competitors' browser technology. A minimum quantities clause is normally considered not to be restrictive of competition at all; the Commission's concern here, however, was that the two clauses in question could have a foreclosure effect on competitors. A comfort letter was sent after these amendments had been made; the Commission did not give a ruling on whether Microsoft's behaviour overall might amount to an abuse of a dominant position[79]. Microsoft's refusal to make interoperability information, assumed to be protected by intellectual property rights, available to third party competitors was found to be an abuse of a dominant position in March 2004[80].

There are some typical clauses in software licences which have no analogies in the general law, for example prohibiting decompilation of a computer program and restrictions on copying[81]. Software licences are now covered by the Technology Transfer Regulation[82].

(viii) Trade mark licences[83]

The Commission has applied Article 101(1) to exclusive trade mark licences but decided that, where there was no absolute territorial protection, the criteria of Article 101(3) were satisfied. In *Davide CampariMilano SpA Agreement*[84] the Commission considered that Article 101(3) applied in the case of a standard form of agreement whereby firms were licensed to use the Campari trade mark and were given exclusive rights in their own territory to apply that mark and required not to pursue an active sales policy elsewhere.

In *Moosehead/Whitbread*[85] an exclusive licence of a trade mark with associated know-how was investigated by the Commission. The licensee wished to manufacture and to promote the Moosehead brand, a popular Canadian beer, in the UK. The licence prohibited active selling outside the UK. The Commission concluded that the exclusive trade mark and

---

[75] See Forrester 'Software Licensing in the Light of Current EC Competition Law Considerations' (1992) 13 ECLR 5; Darbyshire 'Computer Programs and Competition Policy: A Block Exemption for Software Licensing?' (1994) 16 EIPR 374.

[76] See the Commission's XXVIIth *Report on Competition Policy* (1997), point 80 and pp 148–149; see also, on the similar *Sony* case, the XXVIIIth *Report on Competition Policy* (1998), pp 159–160.

[77] Cm 2781 (1995).

[78] See the Commission's XXIXth *Report on Competition Policy* (1999), points 55 and 56 and p 162: details of Microsoft's notification in this case can be found at OJ [1998] C 175/3; for a separate investigation of Microsoft's licensing terms, following a complaint by Santa Cruz Operation in relation to the UNIX operating system, see the Commission's XXVIIth *Report on Competition Policy* (1997), point 79 and pp 140–141.

[79] Commission's XXIXth *Report on Competition Policy* (1999), point 56.

[80] See 'The *Microsoft* case', pp 800–802 below.

[81] It may be arguable that, by analogy from the *Erauw-Jacquery* judgment on the propagation of seeds, a restriction on copying software is outside Article 101(1).

[82] See 'Article 1: definitions', p 782 below.

[83] See Joliet 'Territorial and Exclusive Trade Mark Licensing under the EC Law of Competition' [1984] IIC 21.

[84] OJ [1978] L 70/69, [1978] 2 CMLR 397; see similarly *Goodyear Italiana SpA's Application* OJ [1975] L 38/10, [1975] 1 CMLR D31.

[85] OJ [1990] L 100/32, [1991] 4 CMLR 391; see Subiotto '*Moosebead/Whitebread*: Industrial Franchises and No-challenge Clauses Relating to Licensed Trade Marks in the EEC' (1990) 11 ECLR 226.

the restriction on active sales infringed Article 101(1), as did a non-competition clause[86]. The know-how was considered by the Commission to be ancillary to the trade mark, so that the block exemption for know-how licensing in force at that time, Regulation 556/89, was not applicable[87]; presumably the same conclusion would be reached under Regulation 772/2004[88]. However the Commission decided that Article 101(3) applied to the agreement as consumers would have the benefit of another beer from which to choose[89]. The agreement contained a no-challenge clause in respect of the trade mark, but the Commission held this to be outside Article 101(1) because the mark was not well known and its non-availability to competitors was not a barrier to entry[90].

Where a trade mark is ancillary to a vertical agreement or to a technology transfer agreement, it may benefit from the block exemption conferred by Regulation 330/2010 or Regulation 772/2004[91].

(ix) Licences of plant breeders' rights

In *Louis Erauw-Jacquery Sprl v La Hesbignonne Société*[92] the Court of Justice was asked to rule on the application of Article 101(1) to two clauses in a licence for the propagation and sale of certain varieties of cereal seeds. Erauw-Jacquery had licensed La Hesbignonne to propagate 'basic seeds' and to sell seeds reproduced from them ('reproductive seeds'). Clause 2(f) of the licence prohibited the export of basic seeds; clause 2(i) required the licensee not to resell the reproductive seeds below minimum selling prices. The Court's view was that the export ban in relation to basic seeds did not infringe Article 101(1): a plant breeder is entitled to reserve the propagation of basic seeds to institutions approved by him and an export ban is objectively justifiable to protect this right[93]. Basic seeds are not intended for sale to farmers for sowing, but are intended solely for the purpose of propagation; it follows that an export ban of this kind arises from the existence of the plant breeders' rights and is not an improper exercise of it[94]. The Court concluded that the provision on minimum pricing for reproductive seeds had as its object and effect the restriction of competition[95] but that the national court must decide on the facts whether it had an effect on trade between Member States[96].

In *Sicasov*[97] the Commission applied the Court's judgment in the *Erauw-Jacquery* case to the standard licences of Sicasov, a French cooperative of plant breeders. The Commission explains in more detail than the judgment in *Erauw-Jacquery* the distinction between basic seeds, which are intended only for propagation, and 'certified' seeds, intended for sale to farmers for sowing[98]. The breeder is entitled to control the destination of basic seeds by virtue of its plant breeders' rights[99], but cannot control certified seeds that have been put onto the market with its consent[100]. It followed that obligations not to entrust basic seeds to a third party, not to export them and related provisions did not infringe Article 101(1)[101].

---

[86] OJ [1990] L 100/32, [1991] 4 CMLR 391, para 15(1).
[87] Ibid, para 16(1); a corrected version of Regulation 556/89 will be found at OJ [1990] L 257/15.
[88] See 'Article 1: definitions', p 782 below.
[89] OJ [1990] L 100/32, [1991] 4 CMLR 391, para 15(2).   [90] Ibid, para 15(4).
[91] See 'Article 1: definitions', p 782 below.
[92] Case 27/87 [1988] ECR 1919, [1988] 4 CMLR 576.
[93] Ibid, para 10.
[94] This was the view of Advocate General Mischo in this case, and of the Commission: Case 27/87 [1988] ECR 1919, [1988] 4 CMLR 576, para 9.
[95] Case 27/87 [1988] ECR 1919, [1988] 4 CMLR 576, para 15.   [96] Ibid, para 19.
[97] OJ [1999] L 4/27, [1999] 4 CMLR 192.   [98] Ibid, paras 21–27.
[99] Ibid, para 50, citing *Erauw-Jacquery*.   [100] Ibid, para 51.   [101] Ibid, paras 53–61.

However a restriction on the export of certified seeds did infringe Article 101(1)[102] but was found to satisfy the terms of Article 101(3)[103].

In *Roses*[104] the Commission condemned two clauses in a standard licence of plant breeders' rights. The first was an exclusive grant-back clause, which effectively removed the sub-licensee from the market for mutations which it discovered. The second was a no-challenge clause: the fact that plant breeders' rights are conferred only after a national authority's involvement does not mean that there might not have been an error of appreciation that could be challenged by a licensee.

(x) Sub-contracting agreements

Sub-contracting agreements typically involve a licence from the principal to the sub-contractor. Horizontal sub-contracting agreements have been considered in chapter 15 and vertical ones in chapter 16[105].

(D) The application of Article 101(3) to licences of intellectual property rights[106]

Licensing agreements which are not covered by Regulation 772/2004 and which contain provisions which are not ancillary to an agreement covered by that Regulation or by Regulation 330/2010 on vertical agreements[107] may still fulfil the conditions of Article 101(3). When assessing the validity of their licences under the competition rules, firms will derive guidance from the Commission's block exemptions. The Commission has said that the restrictions listed as 'hard core' in Article 4 of the Technology Transfer Regulation would be likely to satisfy the criteria of Article 101(3) only in exceptional circumstances[108]; however it also says that there is no presumption that agreements that fall outside the block exemption are caught by Article 101(1) or fail to satisfy the terms of Article 101(3)[109].

In *Telenor/Canal+/Canal Digital*[110] the Commission decided that the criteria of Article 101(3) were satisfied and therefore permitted for five years agreements concerning the distribution of pay-TV premium content channels on the satellite platform of Canal Digital in the Nordic region. The agreements involved in this case concerned the licensing of material protected by artistic copyright, and fell outside the block exemption for vertical agreements because the licences were not ancillary to a vertical agreement[111]. Similarly the licences were not ancillary to a technology transfer agreement, as artistic copyright is not regarded as technological. The interesting issue raised by a case such as this is whether a licence is more analogous to a vertical agreement or to a transfer of technology: this will determine whether the principles of Regulation 330/2010 or Regulation 772/2004 provide better guidance for firms having to conduct a self-assessment under Article 101(3). As a general proposition Regulation 772/2004 permits more restrictions than

---

[102] Ibid, paras 62–64.

[103] Ibid, paras 73–77; note that the block exemption Regulation on technology transfer agreements at the time did not apply since the standard licence did not correspond with any of the provisions listed in Article 1(1) thereof: ibid, para 72.

[104] OJ [1985] L 369/9, [1988] 4 CMLR 193; see Harding 'Commission Decision on Breeders' Rights in Relation to Roses: Hard Line on Breeders' Rights Maintained' (1986) 9 EIPR 284.

[105] See ch 15, 'Production Agreements', p 799 and ch 16, 'Sub-Contracting Agreements', pp 676–677.

[106] See the *Technology Transfer Guidelines*, para 18 and paras 130ff.

[107] On ancillary provisions see 'Article 1: definitions', p 782 below.

[108] *Technology Transfer Guidelines*, para 18.   [109] Ibid, para 37.

[110] Commission decision of 29 December 2003.

[111] On Article 2(3) of the vertical block exemption see ch 16, 'Article 2(3): ancillary provisions in relation to intellectual property rights', p 656.

Regulation 330/2010: for example the former allows (limited) restrictions on passive sales which the latter does not[112].

3. Technology Transfer Agreements: Regulation 772/2004

Acting under powers conferred on it by Council Regulation 19/65[113] the Commission has adopted Regulation 772/2004[114] conferring block exemption on technology transfer agreements pursuant to Article 101(3) of the Treaty. Regulation 772/2004 replaced Regulation 240/96[115]. The adoption of Regulation 772/2004 followed the publication by the Commission in December 2001 of an *Evaluation Report*[116] on the previous block exemption, which was followed by a public debate which was generally in favour of reform of the law. The Commission recognises in the recitals of Regulation 772/2004 that technology transfer agreements usually improve economic efficiency and are pro-competitive, but notes that this depends on the degree of market power that the parties have or, to put the point another way, the extent to which they face competition from undertakings owning substitute technologies or undertakings producing substitute products[117].

The Commission adopted Regulation 772/2004 on 27 April 2004. It entered into force on 1 May 2004 and will expire on 30 April 2014[118]. Regulation 772/2004, the format of which is similar to Regulation 330/2010 on vertical agreements, consists of 20 recitals and 11 Articles. Article 1 contains a series of definitions. Article 2 confers block exemption on certain technology transfer agreements. Article 3 imposes market share caps, which differ depending on whether an agreement is horizontal or vertical, the former being treated more strictly. Article 4 contains a list of hard-core restrictions, the inclusion of which in an agreement will prevent the block exemption from applying: the list is stricter for horizontal than for vertical agreements. Article 5 sets out certain restrictions that are not block exempted, but which do not prevent the application of the Regulation to the rest of the agreement. Articles 6 and 7 provide for the block exemption to be withdrawn from agreements in certain circumstances. Subsequent provisions deal with matters such as the calculation of market share thresholds and transitional arrangements. Regulation 772/2004 should be read in conjunction with the Commission's *Technology Transfer Guidelines*.

(A) Article 1: definitions

Article 1 of the Regulation contains a series of definitions. Some of these will be explained in the text that follows, in the specific context in which they are used in the Regulation.

---

[112] Note however that paras 60–64 of the Commission's *Guidelines on Vertical Restraints* discuss situations in which hard-core sales restrictions may be objectively necessary for an agreement of a particular type and therefore fall outside Article 101(1) altogether, or fulfil the conditions of Article 101(3); see ch 16, 'Export bans falling outside Article 101(1) or satisfying Article 101(3)', pp 636–637.

[113] JO [1965] 533, OJ Sp Ed [1965–66] 87.

[114] OJ [2004] L 123/11; for detailed commentary on Regulation 772/2004 see Dolmans and Piilola 'The New Technology Transfer Block Exemption: A Welcome Reform After All' (2003) 27(3) World Competition 351; Anderman and Kallaugher *Technology and the New EU Competition Rules: Intellectual Property Licensing after Modernisation* (Oxford University Press, 2006); Korah *Intellectual Property Rights and the EC Competition Rules* (Hart Publishing, 2006); Coates, Kyølbye and Peeperkorn in Faull and Nikpay *The EC Law of Competition* (Oxford University Press, 2nd ed, 2007), paras 10.58–10.125.

[115] OJ [1996] L 31/2.　　[116] COM(2001) 786 final, available at www.ec.europa.eu.

[117] Regulation 772/2004, recitals 5 and 6.　　[118] Ibid, Article 11.

Of particular importance is Article 1(1)(b), which defines what is meant by a technology transfer agreement. This term includes licences[119] of:

- patents[120]
- know-how, meaning a package of non-patented information that is secret, substantial and identified[121]
- software copyright[122]
- a mixture of patents, know-how and software copyright
- provisions in a technology agreement that do not constitute the primary objective of such agreements, but are directly related to the application of the licensed technology (sometimes referred to as 'ancillary provisions')[123].

Recital 7 of the Regulation explains that it applies only to agreements whereby a licensor permits a licensee to exploit the licensed technology for the production of goods or services: it therefore does not apply to an agreement that sub-contracts research and development to another party, since in that case the sub-contractor, to whom some technology may be transferred by the principal, will not exploit the technology itself[124]. Recital 7 also explains that the Regulation does not apply to technology pools[125].

Article 1(2) of the Regulation explains that the terms 'undertaking', 'licensor' and 'licensee' include 'connected undertakings', as defined therein.

(B) **Article 2: exemption**

Article 2 of the Regulation confers block exemption on certain technology transfer agreements pursuant to Article 101(3). It provides that, subject to the provisions of the Regulation, Article 101(1) shall not apply:

> to technology transfer agreements entered into between two undertakings permitting the production of contract products[126].

Several points should be noted about Article 2(1).

(i) **Many technology transfer agreements do not infringe Article 101(1)**

It is worth recalling that many technology transfer agreements do not infringe Article 101(1) at all, and therefore do not need to be block exempted. It has already been

---

[119] Regulation 772/2004 can also apply to assignments where part of the risk associated with the exploitation of the technology remains with the assignor: ibid, Article 1(1)(b); and the Regulation can apply to sub-licensing whereby a licensee, with authority of the licensor, sub-licenses to a third party for the exploitation of the technology: *Technology Transfer Guidelines*, para 48; the Regulation does not apply to a 'master licence' where sub-licensing is the primary object of the agreement: ibid, para 42.

[120] The term patents includes numerous rights, including utility models, designs, topographies of semiconductor products, supplementary protection certificates for medicinal products and plant breeder's rights: ibid, Article 1(1)(h).

[121] Ibid, Article 1(1)(i); see also the *Technology Transfer Guidelines*, para 47.

[122] Note that copyright, other than software copyright, would not be included in this term; see 'Copyright licences', pp 776–777 above on the Commission's approach to copyright licences in the *Technology Transfer Guidelines*; see also the Commission's decision in *Telenor/Canal+ Canal Digital* discussed at 'The application of Article 101(3) to licences of intellectual property rights', pp 780–781 above.

[123] See further the *Technology Transfer Guidelines*, paras 49–53.

[124] See further ibid, paras 44–45; on horizontal sub-contracting agreements see ch 15, 'Production Agreements', p 599 and on vertical ones see ch 16, 'Sub-Contracting Agreements', pp 676–677.

[125] On pooling agreements see 'Technology pools', pp 791–794 below.

[126] On the meaning of 'product' and 'contract products' see Article 1(1)(e) and (f) of the Regulation.

noted that recital 5 of the Regulation acknowledges that such agreements usually improve economic efficiency and are pro-competitive, a point which is picked up in paragraph 9 of the *Technology Transfer Guidelines*, which states that there is no presumption that licence agreements give rise to competition concerns. Indeed paragraph 17 of the *Guidelines* goes as far as to say that licence agreements 'have substantial pro-competitive potential'; it continues that 'the vast majority of licence agreements are pro-competitive'. Recital 12 of the Regulation states that there is no presumption that agreements above the market share thresholds in Article 3 infringe Article 101(1), a point repeated in paragraph 37 of the *Technology Transfer Guidelines*. It is almost unthinkable that the Commission would have said such things in, say, the 1970s and 1980s, and this shows how far the Commission has moved in wanting to take a more economics-oriented, less regulatory approach to the application of the competition rules.

(ii) If it is not forbidden, it is permitted

The Commission's less regulatory approach, specifically stated in recital 4 of the Regulation, is reflected in the removal from the Regulation of a 'white list', stating what must be in a technology transfer agreement[127]; instead there are market share caps in Article 3, and the 'black list' of what must not be included in Article 4. These two are the Articles of key importance. Provisions in an agreement that are not blacklisted in Article 4 are permitted, subject to the 'excluded restrictions' of Article 5 and the possibility of withdrawal of the block exemption by the Commission or a Member State (see below). Other than that the maxim 'If it is not forbidden, it is permitted', applies under Regulation 772/2004[128].

(iii) The exempted agreement must be bilateral

An interesting distinction between the vertical block exemption and the one for technology transfer is that the latter is applicable only in the case of bilateral agreements, whereas the former is capable of application to multilateral ones[129]. Council Regulation 19/65 does not provide a legal basis for block exemption of multilateral technology transfer agreements[130]. However recital 19 of that Regulation explains that the Regulation can apply to an agreement between a licensor and licensee where the licensor makes stipulations for more than one level of trade. For example the licensor may impose conditions and obligations on the licensee not only in relation to its own production and sales; it may also require the licensee to impose conditions and obligations on its own distributors, for example requiring them to maintain a selective distribution system. The agreement between the licensor and licensee is still a bilateral agreement, and so capable of being covered by the block exemption; however the agreement(s) between the licensee and any distributor would not be covered by Regulation 772/2004, but might satisfy the block exemption for vertical agreements[131].

Where a technology transfer agreement is multilateral, but of the same nature as one covered by Regulation 772/2004, the Commission will analyse the agreement by analogy to the principles contained in the Regulation[132].

---

[127] Regulation 772/2004, recital 8.
[128] The same maxim applies under the vertical block exemption: see ch 16, 'If it is not forbidden, it is permitted', p 652.
[129] Ch 16, 'The exempted agreement may be multilateral', p 653.
[130] Specific provision for the block exemption of multilateral vertical agreements was made by Council Regulation 1215/99, OJ [1999] L 148/1.
[131] See further the *Technology Transfer Guidelines*, para 39 and paras 61–64.
[132] Ibid, para 40.

(iv) Duration

The block exemption will run until 30 April 2014. However Article 2 contains a further relevant provision as to the duration of block exemption in relation to any particular agreement. It provides that the exemption lasts only as long as the intellectual property right in the licensed technology has not expired, lapsed or been declared invalid; or, in the case of know-how, that the exemption lasts only as long as the know-how remains secret. The block exemption will cease to apply on the date of the last intellectual property right to expire, become invalid or enter the public domain[133].

(v) Relationship with other block exemptions

Paragraphs 56 to 64 of the *Technology Transfer Guidelines* explain how the Technology Transfer Regulation relates to other block exemptions, in particular the Regulations for Research and Developments Agreements[134], for Specialisation Agreements[135] and Vertical Agreements[136].

(C) Article 3: the market share cap

The Regulation applies only to technology transfer agreements that do not exceed a market share cap. Recital 12 states that there is no presumption that an agreement above the thresholds infringes Article 101(1) or that it is incapable of satisfying the terms of Article 101(3) on an individual basis. Article 3(1) of the Regulation requires that the combined market share of the parties does not exceed 20 per cent of the affected relevant technology and product market for horizontal agreements; Article 3(2) provides that, in the case of vertical agreements, the market share of each of the parties must not exceed 30 per cent.

(i) Horizontal agreements

In order to determine whether an agreement is a horizontal agreement it is necessary to ask whether the parties to an agreement are 'competing undertakings' as defined in Article 1(1)(j) of the Regulation[137]. Undertakings may compete on a technology market or on a product market.

(A) Technology markets

Article 1(1)(j)(i) provides that undertakings compete on the relevant technology market where they license out competing technologies without infringing each others' intellectual property rights. The relevant technology market includes technologies which are regarded as interchangeable with or substitutable for the licensed technology, by reason of the technologies' characteristics, their royalties and their intended use. This definition captures only *actual* competitors in the technology market: it does not apply to potential competitors[138].

(B) Product markets

Article 1(1)(j)(ii) provides that undertakings compete on the relevant product market where, even without a technology transfer agreement, they are both active on the relevant product and geographic markets on which the contract products are sold without

[133] Ibid, para 55.

[134] Regulation 1217/2010: see ch 15, 'The block exemption for research and development agreements: Regulation 1217/2010', pp 595–599.

[135] Regulation 1218/2010: see ch 15, 'The application of Article 101(3) to production agreements', pp 601–603.

[136] See ch 16, 'Vertical Agreements: Regulation 330/2010', pp 649–672.

[137] See further the *Technology Transfer Guidelines*, paras 26–33.   [138] Ibid, para 66.

infringing each others' intellectual property rights (actual competitors) and where they might realistically be able to enter and compete on the market within 'a period of one to two years'[139] in response to a small but permanent increase in product prices (potential competitors). The relevant product market includes products which are regarded as interchangeable with or substitutable for the contract products by reason of the products' characteristics, their prices and their intended use.

(ii) Vertical agreements

Where an agreement is not horizontal, because it is not between competing undertakings as defined in Article 1(1)(j), it is vertical, and so the higher market share cap of 30 per cent is applicable. An agreement will not be horizontal where one party can use its intellectual property to prevent the other entering the market, or where both parties need the other's technology to operate on the market: these are referred to as 'one-way' and 'two-way' blocking positions, as to which the Commission will require objective evidence, for example court judgments and the opinions of independent experts[140]. It can be the case that two undertakings compete in relation to existing products, but that a licence by A to B is not between competitors because A's technology is so innovative that B's current products are now obsolete or uncompetitive: such an agreement would be regarded as vertical and therefore subject to the higher market share cap (and the more lenient list of hard-core restrictions)[141].

Where the parties are not competing undertakings at the time of the agreement, but subsequently become so, they will usually continue to be considered to be non-competing: Article 4(3) of the Regulation provides that this means that the less strict list of hard-core restrictions for vertical agreements will continue to apply[142].

(iii) Technology markets

Paragraphs 19 to 25 of the *Technology Transfer Guidelines* discuss market definition for the purpose of analysing technology transfer agreements. In particular they explain that such agreements can have an effect on competition both in the upstream technology market and in the downstream product market[143]. Article 3(3), in conjunction with paragraph 23 of the *Technology Transfer Guidelines*, explains that a licensor's share of a technology market is to be calculated by reference to the value of the licensed technology on the relevant product market; this figure is calculated on the basis of both the licensor's and its licensee's sales[144]. Where a new technology has yet to generate any sales a market share of zero is assigned[145].

(iv) Product markets

A licensee's market share of a product market is calculated on the basis of its sales of products incorporating the licensor's technology and competing products, that is to say the total sales of the licensee on the product market in question; sales by other licensees are not taken into account[146].

---

[139] Ibid, para 29.   [140] Ibid, para 32.   [141] Ibid, para 33.

[142] See 'Article 4: hard-core restrictions', pp 786–789 below.

[143] *Technology Transfer Guidelines*, para 20.

[144] See the final sentence of Article 3(3) of Regulation 772/2004 and the *Technology Transfer Guidelines*, para 70.

[145] Ibid.   [146] Ibid, para 71.

(v) Article 8: calculation of market share and marginal relief

Article 8(1) of the Regulation deals with the calculation of market share, which should be done by reference to market sales value data. Where such data are not available, estimates based on other reliable information, including sales volumes, may be used to establish the market share of the undertaking concerned. Market shares should be calculated on the basis of data relating to the preceding calendar year.

Article 8(2) provides some marginal relief for up to two years where the market share caps of 20 or 30 per cent are subsequently exceeded.

(vi) Examples

The *Technology Transfer Guidelines* provide examples of how the market share figures operate, both in relation to horizontal and vertical licensing agreements[147].

(D) Article 4: hard-core restrictions

Recital 13 of the Regulation states that technology transfer agreements should not enjoy block exemption when they contain 'severely anti-competitive restraints such as the fixing of prices charged to third parties…irrespective of the market shares of the undertakings concerned'. The block exemption ceases to apply to the entire agreement, not just to the offending provisions[148]. The Commission considers that the hard-core restrictions are restrictions by object in the sense of Article 101[149]. The Regulation contains one set of hard-core restrictions for agreements between competing agreements in Article 4(1) and a different set for agreements between non-competing undertakings in Article 4(2). As one would expect the provisions are stricter in the case of agreements between competing undertakings than between non-competing undertakings[150]. Article 4(3) provides that, where the parties were non-competing at the time that they entered into an agreement, Article 4(2) applies to their agreement throughout its lifetime unless the agreement is subsequently amended in any material respect; in other words the agreement does not metamorphose into a horizontal one, and so become subject to the stricter standard of Article 4(1), simply because the firms subsequently become competitors.

(i) Agreements between competing undertakings: horizontal agreements[151]

The concern of the Commission is that a technology transfer agreement between competing agreements might be a cloak for, or have the effect of, a cartel. Article 4(1) therefore provides that block exemption is not available for agreements that, directly or indirectly, in isolation or in combination with other factors, have as their object restrictions concerning prices, output, the allocation of markets or customers, and the exploitation by the licensee of its own technology: such restrictions are regarded as hard-core. The provisions on price and output are simple, but those on markets and customers can be complex. In some cases restrictions are treated as hard-core only where an agreement is reciprocal, that is to say where each undertaking grants a licence to the other and where the licences concern competing technologies or can be used for the production of competing products[152]; the same restriction in a non-reciprocal agreement[153] is not regarded as hard-core[154]. Where a non-reciprocal agreement becomes a reciprocal one due to the conclusion of a second licence

---

[147] Ibid, para 73.   [148] Ibid, para 75.
[149] Ibid, para 14.
[150] Ibid, para 26.   [151] See generally the *Technology Transfer Guidelines*, paras 77–95.
[152] Regulation 772/2004, Article 1(1)(c).   [153] Ibid, Article 1(1)(d).
[154] See the *Technology Transfer Guidelines*, para 78.

between the same parties, they may have to revise the first licence in order to avoid the inclusion of a hard-core restriction[155].

(A) Prices

Article 4(1)(a) provides that the block exemption is not applicable to an agreement between competing undertakings that restricts a party's ability to determine its prices to third parties. It is immaterial whether the agreement concerns fixed, minimum, maximum or recommended prices[156]. Where there are cross licences between two undertakings that have no pro-competitive purpose and where the parties agree to pay running royalties to one another the Commission might treat the case as sham and tantamount to a price-fixing agreement[157]. Article 4(1)(a) (and Article 4(1)(d)) may be infringed where royalties are based on the sales of products irrespective of whether the licensed technology was used in the production of those products[158].

(B) Output

Article 4(1)(b) provides that the block exemption is not applicable to an agreement between competing undertakings that has as its object the limitation of output, other than a limitation on the output of contract products imposed on the licensee in a non-reciprocal agreement or imposed on only one of the parties in a reciprocal agreement. Non-reciprocal agreements are treated more favourably than reciprocal ones since they are less likely to lead to a restriction of output and they are more likely to lead to an improvement in economic efficiency[159].

(C) The allocation of markets and customers

Article 4(1)(c) provides that the block exemption does not apply to an agreement between competing undertakings that allocates markets or customers[160]. However there are seven exceptions to this:

- an obligation on the licensee(s) to produce with the licensed technology only within one or more technical fields of use or one or more product markets. The field of use restriction must not go beyond the scope of the licensed technology[161]. It does not matter whether, in a reciprocal agreement, the field of use restrictions are symmetrical or asymmetrical[162]
- an obligation on the licensor and/or the licensee in a non-reciprocal agreement not to produce with the licensed technology within one or more technical fields of use or one or more product markets or one or more exclusive territories reserved for the other party
- an obligation on the licensor not to license the technology to another licensee in a particular territory

---

[155] Ibid; the Commission will take into account the time lapsed between the conclusion of the first and the second licence.

[156] Ibid, para 79.　　　[157] Ibid, para 80.　　　[158] Ibid, para 101; see also paras 156–160.

[159] Ibid, para 102; see also paras 175–178.

[160] The terms 'exclusive territory' and 'exclusive customer group' are defined in Articles 1(1)(l) and 1(1)(m) of the Regulation; for further discussion of exclusive licensing and sales restrictions see the *Technology Transfer Guidelines*, paras 161–174.

[161] *Technology Transfer Guidelines*, para 90; see also paras 179–185.

[162] Ibid, para 91.

- the restriction in a non-reciprocal agreement of active and/or passive sales by the licensee and/or the licensor into the exclusive territory or to the exclusive customer group reserved for the other party[163]

- the restriction in a non-reciprocal agreement of active sales by the licensee into the exclusive territory or to the exclusive customer group allocated by the licensor to another licensee provided the latter was not a competing undertaking of the licensor at the time of the conclusion of its own licence. An agreement between licensees not to sell, actively or passively, into each others' territories would be regarded as a cartel agreement between them and would fall outside the scope of the block exemption[164]

- an obligation on the licensee to produce the contract products only for its own use provided that the licensee is not restricted in selling the contract products actively and passively as spare parts for its own products: these are known as 'captive use restrictions'[165]

- an obligation on the licensee in a non-reciprocal agreement to produce the contract products only for a particular customer where the licence was granted in order to create an alternative source of supply for that customer.

(D) *Exploitation by the licensee*

Article 4(1)(d) provides that the block exemption does not apply to an agreement between competing undertakings that restricts the licensee's ability to exploit its own technology or that prevents any of the parties to the agreement from carrying out research and development, unless such a provision is indispensable to prevent the disclosure to a third party of the licensed know-how. Where such a restriction is found in an agreement between non-competing undertakings it is not regarded as hard-core but is excluded from the block exemption under Article 5[166].

(ii) Agreements between non-competing agreements: vertical agreements[167]

Article 4(2) of the Regulation provides that block exemption is not available for agreements between non-competing undertakings that, directly or indirectly, in isolation or in combination with other factors, have as their object restrictions concerning prices, territories and customer groups or sales within a selective distribution system[168].

(A) *Prices*

Article 4(2)(a) provides that the block exemption does not apply to an agreement between non-competing undertakings that restricts a party's ability to determine its prices when selling products to third parties. However it is permissible to impose a maximum price or to recommend a price provided that this does not amount to a fixed or minimum price as a result of pressure from, or incentives offered by, any of the parties. Paragraph 97 of the *Technology Transfer Guidelines* provides examples of agreements that would be considered to fix prices indirectly, for example fixing a licensee's margin, fixing the maximum

---

[163] For a definition of active and passive sales see para 51 of the Commission's *Guidelines on Vertical Restraints*; see further ch 16, 'Article 4(b): territorial and customer restrictions', pp 665–668.

[164] *Guidelines on Vertical Restraints*, para 89.

[165] Ibid, para 92; see also paras 186–190.

[166] See 'Article 5: excluded restrictions', pp 789–790 below.

[167] See generally the *Technology Transfer Guidelines*, paras 96–106.

[168] This term is defined in Article 1(1)(k) of the Regulation.

level of discounts and making threats or intimidating a licensee as to a particular price level.

(B) Territories and customer groups[169]

Article 4(2)(b) provides that the block exemption does not apply to an agreement between non-competing undertakings that restricts the territory into which, or the customer group to whom, the licensee may passively sell the contract goods. Paragraph 98 of the *Technology Transfer Guidelines* provides examples of indirect methods of preventing passive sales, such as financial incentives, monitoring mechanisms to identify the final destination of the contract products and, in some cases, quantity limitations. Article 4(2)(b) provides six exceptions to the prohibition on restrictions on passive sales by the licensee:

- a restriction of passive sales into an exclusive territory or to an exclusive customer group reserved for the licensor
- a restriction of passive sales into an exclusive territory or to an exclusive customer group allocated by the licensor to another licensee during the first two years that the other licensee is selling the contract products in that territory or to that group
- an obligation to produce the contract goods only for its own use provided that the licensee is not restricted in selling the contract products actively and passively as spare parts for its own products
- an obligation to produce the contract products only for a particular customer where the licence was granted in order to create an alternative source of supply for that customer
- a restriction of sales to end users by a licensee operating at the wholesale level of trade
- a restriction of sales to unauthorised distributors by the members of a selective distribution system.

It should be noted that Article 4(2)(b) does not prohibit sales restrictions on the licensor; nor restrictions on active sales by the licensee, except in the case of selective distribution systems (see below)[170]. Furthermore there is no restriction on active or passive sales by licensees to territories or customer groups reserved to the licensor[171].

(C) Restrictions in selective distribution systems

Article 4(2)(c) provides that the block exemption does not apply where an agreement between non-competing undertakings restricts active or passive sales to end users by a licensee which is a member of a selective distribution system and which operates at the retail level, without prejudice to the possibility of prohibiting a member of the system from operating out of an unauthorised place of establishment.

(E) **Article 5: excluded restrictions**[172]

Recital 14 of the Regulation states that, in order to protect incentives to innovate, certain restrictions should be excluded from the block exemption, in particular exclusive grant-back obligations for severable improvements; however the inclusion of an Article 5

---

[169] The terms 'exclusive territory' and 'exclusive customer group' are defined in Articles 1(1)(l) and 1(1)(m) of the Regulation.

[170] See the *Technology Transfer Guidelines*, para 99.   [171] Ibid, para 100.

[172] Ibid, paras 107–116.

restriction does not prevent the application of the block exemption to the remaining parts of the agreement if they are 'severable' from the excluded restriction[173].

Article 5(1) lists three excluded restrictions:

- **exclusive grant back:** an obligation on the licensee to grant an exclusive licence to the licensor or a third party designated by the licensor in respect of its own severable improvements[174] to or its own new applications of the licensed technology
- **assignments back:** an obligation to assign back such technology
- **no-challenge clauses:** an obligation on the licensee not to challenge the validity of intellectual property rights held by the licensor in the internal market, without prejudice to the right of the licensor to terminate the licence in the event of such a challenge.

Article 5(2) also excludes a restriction, in an agreement between non-competing undertakings, that imposes an obligation limiting the licensee's ability to exploit its own technology or limiting either of the party's ability to carry out research and development, unless the latter restriction is indispensable to prevent the disclosure of the licensed technology to third parties.

(F) Article 6: withdrawal in individual cases[175]

Recital 16 of the Regulation states that the provisions of Articles 3 to 5 mean that agreements to which the block exemption applies normally will not eliminate competition in respect of a substantial part of the products in question, with the result that the fourth requirement of Article 101(3) will be satisfied. However, as a safety net, the possibility exists of either the Commission or the national competition authorities ('the NCAs'), in certain circumstances, withdrawing the benefit of the block exemption. The authority doing so bears the burden of proving that an agreement falls within the scope of Article 101(1) and that the terms of Article 101(3) are not satisfied[176]. It is worth noting in passing that this power has never been used.

(i) Article 6(1): withdrawal by the Commission in individual cases

Article 6(1) provides that the Commission may withdraw the benefit of the block exemption in an individual case where an agreement has effects that are incompatible with Article 101(3). Recital 16 states that this may happen in particular where incentives to innovate are reduced or where access to markets is hindered, and Article 6(1) gives examples of when this could be so.

(ii) Article 6(2): withdrawal by an NCA of a Member State

Article 6(2) provides that an NCA may withdraw the benefit of the block exemption under the same circumstances specified in Article 6(1) where a technology transfer agreement has effects incompatible with Article 101(3) in the territory of a Member State or a part thereof that has all the characteristics of a distinct geographic market. Recital 17 states that, in exercising this power, 'Member States must ensure that they do not prejudice the uniform application of the [EU] competition rules throughout the common market or the full effect of the measures adopted in implementation of those rules'.

---

[173] Ibid, para 107.
[174] This term is defined in Article 1(1)(n) of the Regulation.
[175] See generally the *Technology Transfer Guidelines*, paras 117–122.
[176] Ibid, para 119.

(G) Article 7: non-application of the Regulation[177]

Article 7(1) of the Regulation provides that the Commission may by regulation declare that the block exemption does not apply to technology transfer agreements containing specific restraints relating to a market where parallel networks of similar technology transfer agreements cover more than 50 per cent of the relevant market. Article 7(2) adds that a regulation adopted pursuant to Article 7(1) will not become applicable earlier than six months following its adoption. Where the Commission exercises the power conferred on it by Article 7 it may make a decision in an individual case to provide guidance on the application of Article 101 to the agreements that will have lost the benefit of the block exemption[178].

(H) Article 8: application of the market share thresholds

This provision was dealt with in the context of Article 3 above[179].

(I) Articles 9 to 11: repeal, transitional period and period of validity

Article 9 repealed Regulation 240/96, the previous technology transfer regulation. Article 10 granted transitional relief to agreements that satisfied Regulation 240/96 until 31 March 2006. Article 11 provides that Regulation 772/2004 will expire on 30 April 2014.

4. The Application of Article 101 to Other Agreements Relating to Intellectual Property Rights

The previous two sections of this chapter considered the application of Article 101 to agreements to license intellectual property rights, with particular reference to technology transfer agreements and the block exemption conferred by Regulation 772/2004. In this section the application of Article 101 to other agreements relating to intellectual property rights will be examined.

(A) Technology pools[180]

It is not uncommon for two or more undertakings to 'pool' their technology. Regulation 772/2004 explicitly states that it does not apply to technology pools, that is to say to:

> agreements for the pooling of technologies with the purpose of licensing the created package to third parties[181].

However the licences granted by the pool to a third party may not infringe Article 101(1) at all[182]; or they may be block exempted, provided that the conditions of Regulation 772/2004 are satisfied[183].

---

[177] See generally the *Technology Transfer Guidelines*, paras 123–129.
[178] Ibid, para 124.
[179] See 'Article 8: calculation of market share and marginal relief', p 786 above.
[180] See generally the report prepared for the European Commission on *Multi-Party Licensing* (Charles River Associates, April 2003).
[181] Regulation 772/2004, recital 7; see also the *Technology Transfer Guidelines*, para 210.
[182] See *Philips/Sony CD Licensing program*, Commission Press Release IP/03/1152, 7 August 2003.
[183] *Technology Transfer Guidelines*, para 212.

Sometimes a pooling arrangement is fairly simple and informal; however it is not unknown for the pool to have an elaborate structure, the management of which may be entrusted to a separate entity. In some cases a technology pool may be linked to an industry standard. Industry standards are sometimes established by law ('*de jure*'); in others they may become a standard as a matter of fact ('*de facto*'). It may be that, in order to comply with a standard, access is needed to intellectual property rights, and these rights might be managed through a technology pool. It follows that, just as agreements to establish standards might sometimes infringe Article 101[184], so too might the creation and operation of a pool where it is the product of an agreement between undertakings and where it could have the effect of foreclosing access to the market[185]. A related point is that undertakings that participate in the setting of a standard may own essential patents, a licence of which is needed by anyone wishing to comply with the standard. A deliberate concealment of this fact by a dominant undertaking during the standard-setting procedure, or a refusal to license the patents on reasonable, non-discriminatory terms, might infringe Article 102[186].

It may also be the case that, within a particular industry, there may be more than one technology pool, and that the different pools may compete with one another. There may be considerable benefits for a firm or firms which control a standard or a technology pool if the industry 'tips' towards that standard or technology as the industry norm. Obvious industries in which one witnesses this phenomenon are mobile telephony[187], high-density television and digital broadcasting, where the 'battle of the standards' may be fierce. The example of the video cassette industry tipping to the VHS standard, away from Betamax, 20 years ago was matched, in 2008, by the market opting for Sony's Blu-Ray technology for the next generation of DVD players rather than Toshiba's HD DVD platform.

Technology pools may have both pro-competitive and anti-competitive effects[188]. The Commission's *Technology Transfer Guidelines* provide guidance on the application of Article 101 to technology pools[189]. The Commission explains that pools may be restrictive of competition in two ways. First, the pooling of technology implies joint selling: if the pooled technologies are substitutes for one another this amounts to a price-fixing cartel[190]. Secondly, technology pools may, in particular when they support an industry standard or establish a *de facto* industry standard, reduce innovation by foreclosing alternative technologies from obtaining access to the market[191]. However the Commission also notes that technology pools may be pro-competitive; for example firms that need access to the technology in the pool will get the benefit of a 'one-stop shop', dealing only with the pool, instead of having to negotiate individually with a number of different owners; this can lead to a reduction in costs[192]. The Commission authorised a technology

---

[184] See ch 15, 'Standardisation Agreements', pp 607–611.

[185] The Commission condemned a patent pooling scheme in *Video Cassette Recorders Agreements* OJ [1978] L 47/42, [1978] 2 CMLR 160; see also *Concast-Mannesman* Commission's XIth *Report on Competition Policy* (1981), point 93; *IGR Stereo Television* ibid, point 94 and XIVth *Report on Competition Policy* (1984), point 92.

[186] See 'Miscellaneous cases concerning intellectual property rights', pp 804–806 below.

[187] See Commission Press Release IP/02/1651, 12 November 2002 dealing with pooling arrangements in relation to third generation ('3G') mobile telephony standards; for discussion see Choumelova 'Competition law analysis of patent licensing arrangements—the particular case of 3G3P' (2003) (Spring) *Competition Policy Newsletter* 41.

[188] See generally the DoJ/FTC report on *Antitrust Enforcement and Intellectual Property Rights: Promoting Innovation and Competition*, ch 3, available at www.justice.gov.

[189] See also Piesiewcz and Schellingerhout on the issue of setting standards in 'Intellectual property rights in standard setting from a competition law perspective' (2007) (Summer) *Competition Policy Newsletter* 36.

[190] *Technology Transfer Guidelines*, para 213.   [191] Ibid.   [192] Ibid, para 214.

pool in the case of *MPEG-2*[193]. MPEG-2 is a technology that improves the quality of video signals; to apply the technology it is necessary to have access to a number of patents. These were pooled by their respective owners, who agreed that access to the pool would be permitted on a non-exclusive and non-discriminatory basis. This meant that the pool, far from foreclosing the market to third parties, would enable them to gain access to the technology with a beneficial effect on technical and economic progress.

The *Technology Transfer Guidelines* examine three issues: the nature of the pooled technologies; the assessment of individual restraints; and the institutional framework governing the pool.

(i) The nature of the pooled technologies

The Commission makes a distinction between the situation where the pooled technologies are substitutes for one another and where they are complements to each other[194].

(A) *Substitute technologies*

Where the pooled technologies are substitutes for one another the Commission's prime concern is that the royalties payable will be higher than they would otherwise be[195] and that this amounts to price fixing between competitors; this would violate Article 101(1) and be unlikely to satisfy the criteria of Article 101(3)[196].

(B) *Complementary technologies*

Where the pooled technologies are complements the arrangement is likely to reduce transaction costs and to lead to lower overall royalties[197]; this means that the creation of the pool is likely to fall outside Article 101, irrespective of the market position of the parties[198]. However the conditions on which any licence is granted may be caught by Article 101[199]. In particular the Commission has a concern where a licensee is required to take a licence of 'non-essential' technology as a condition of gaining access to 'essential' technology[200], as this amounts to a bundling practice, and may have a foreclosure effect depending on the market power of the pool[201]. The Commission will be less concerned about pools where, for example, technologies which, over time, become non-essential are excluded from the pool; where licensors remain free to license their technologies independently of the pool, so that a licensee could put together its own technology package; and where it is possible to take a licence of part only of the pooled technology at a lower royalty rate[202].

(ii) Assessment of individual restraints

Where a technology pool has a dominant position on the market, the royalties and other licensing terms that it offers should be fair and non-discriminatory and the licences granted should be non-exclusive; this is to ensure that there is no anti-competitive foreclosure effect[203]. However it is permissible to charge different royalty rates for different uses and in different product markets[204]. The Commission is also concerned to ensure that a technology pool does not foreclose third party technologies from the market: licensors

---

[193] See OJ [1998] C 229/6 and the Commission's XXIXth *Report on Competition* Policy (1999), points 55 and 56 and p 162; see similarly *Philips/Matsushita—D2B* OJ [1991] C 220/2, [1991] 4 CMLR 905; *Philips International—DCC* OJ [1992] C 333/8, [1993] 4 CMLR 286; see also *European Telecommunications Standards Institute's Intellectual Property Rights Policy* OJ [1994] C 76/5, [1995] 5 CMLR 352.

[194] *Technology Transfer Guidelines*, para 215.   [195] Ibid, para 217.

[196] Ibid, para 219.   [197] Ibid, para 217.   [198] Ibid, para 220.   [199] Ibid.

[200] These expressions are discussed in para 216 of the *Guidelines*.   [201] Ibid, para 221.

[202] Ibid, para 222.   [203] Ibid, para 226.   [204] Ibid, para 227.

and licensees must therefore be free to develop competing products and standards and must be free to grant and obtain licences outside the pool[205]. Any grant-back obligations towards the pool should be non-exclusive and limited to developments that are essential or important to the use of the pooled technology[206]. In the event that a licensee challenges the validity of a patent, the pool's right to terminate the licensee's licence is limited to the patent in question, and cannot apply to the licence of other (non-challenged) technology: this is to prevent the 'shielding' of invalid patents[207].

(iii) The institutional framework governing the pool

The Commission considers that the way in which a pool is created, organised and operated can reduce the risk of it restricting competition[208]. A restriction of competition is less likely when the process of setting a standard and creating a pool is open to all interested parties representing different interests[209]; and the involvement of independent experts may be a helpful factor, for example where they help to ensure that only essential technologies are included in the pool[210]. The Commission is anxious that the operation of a pool does not lead to the exchange of sensitive commercial information that could lead to parallel behaviour, particularly in oligopolistic markets, and will look to see what safeguards have been put in place to prevent this[211]. The Commission also has a preference for there to be dispute resolution mechanisms that are independent of the pool and its members[212].

(B) Copyright pools

Closely related to technology pools are copyright pools. In *IFPI 'Simulcasting'*[213] the Commission authorised an agreement under Article 101(3) whereby two collecting societies, acting on behalf of record companies, established a 'one-stop shop' whereby an international licence could be granted to radio and television broadcasters wishing to 'simulcast' programmes to the public both by conventional radio and television and also, at the same time, via the Internet. The Commission required the deletion of territorial restrictions[214]. The Commission concluded that the joint fixing by the societies of the simulcasting royalty fee infringed Article 101(1)[215]. However, it considered that the agreement met the requirements of Article 101(3) as it would enable a collecting society to grant a 'one-stop shop' licence for simulcasting across the EU which would give consumers a wider access to audio and video music programmes through the Internet[216]. The Commission required the parties to charge for their administrative costs separately from the royalties[217], which were the subject of the horizontal agreement: this meant that broadcasters could exercise a competitive choice on the basis of different societies' costs.

---

[205] Ibid.
[206] Ibid, para 228.   [207] Ibid, para 229.   [208] Ibid, para 230.
[209] Ibid, para 231.   [210] Ibid, paras 232–233.   [211] Ibid, para 234.
[212] Ibid, para 235.
[213] OJ [2003] L 107/58; for comment on this decision see Pereira 'From discothéques to websites, a new approach to music copyright licensing: the *Simulcasting* decision' (2003) (Spring) *Competition Policy Newsletter* 44.
[214] OJ [2003] L 107/58, para 3 and paras 27–28.   [215] Ibid, paras 69–80.
[216] Ibid, paras 86–87.   [217] Ibid, paras 99–107.

(C) **Settlements of litigation**[218]

(i) **Patent settlements**

The Commission has been concerned for many years about the possibility that settlements of patent disputes might have resulted in producers of generic drugs being delayed from entering, or even being excluded from, markets for pharmaceuticals. Essentially the concern is that the owner of a patent (known as the 'originator') might enter into an agreement with a would-be entrant to the market once the patent has expired (the 'generic' company) that encourages or induces the generic firm not to enter the market: direct payments or other commercial advantages might be offered by the originator that lead to an agreement that violates Article 101(1). In its inquiry into the pharmaceutical sector the Commission identified this as a possible problem[219]; it subsequently opened investigations against *Les Laboratoires Servier*[220] and *Lundbeck*[221]: these investigations were continuing as at 20 June 2011.

As a separate initiative the Commission announced that it would keep patent settlements under review, and launched a monitoring exercise in January 2010. In July 2010 the Commission published a *Report on the monitoring of patent settlements in the pharmaceutical sector*[222]. The Commission's view was that the number of 'potentially problematic' patent settlements during this period had declined; it is possible that this decline was due to a greater awareness within the pharmaceutical sector that patent settlements might give rise to competition law scrutiny as a consequence of the Commission's sectoral inquiry. The Commission is continuing to monitor patent settlements in the sector[223].

(ii) **Trade mark settlements**

The Commission will carefully scrutinise trade mark delimitation agreements whereby owners of independent trade marks accept restrictions on the exercise and use of their respective marks[224]. This means that legal advisers must be careful when advising clients as to the terms on which they should settle a trade mark dispute, since it may be that the settlement itself will contravene Article 101(1)[225]. In *BAT v Commission*[226] the Court of

---

[218] On the position in the US see the DoJ/FTC report on *Antitrust Enforcement and Intellectual Property Rights: Promoting Innovation and Competition*, pp 88–91; see also Willig and Bigelow 'Antitrust Policy Toward Agreements That Settle Patent Litigation' (2004) XLIX Antitrust Bulletin 655; Robert and Falconi 'Patent Litigation Settlements in the Pharmaceutical Industry: Marrying the Innovation Bride and the Competition Groom' (2006) 27 ECLR 524; Manogue 'Patent Settlements and Authorized Generics – Legal and Practical Issues' in [2009] Fordham Corporate Law Institute (ed Hawk), ch 14.

[219] See Commission Communication *Pharmaceutical Sector Inquiry Report* of 8 July 2009; see also Commission Press Release IP/09/1098 of the same date.

[220] See Commission MEMO/09/322, 8 July 2009.

[221] See Commission Press Release IP/10/8, 7 January 2010.

[222] See www.ec.europa.eu; see also the Commission Press Release IP/10/887, 5 July 2010.

[223] See Commission Press Release IP/11/40, 17 January 2011 and Commission Press Release 1P/11/840, 6 July 2011.

[224] See *Sirdar and Phildar Trade Marks* [1975] 1 CMLR D93; *Re Penney's Trade Mark* OJ [1978] L 60/19, [1978] 2 CMLR 100 (Article 101 inapplicable to a trade mark agreement which was a genuine attempt to settle litigation and not an attempt to partition the market); *Syntex/Syntbelabo* [1990] 4 CMLR 343 (Commission required modification of trade mark agreement that unjustifiably partitioned markets); *Toltecs and Dorcet Trade Marks* OJ [1982] L 379/19, [1983] 1 CMLR 412 (this decision was the subject of the appeal in *BAT v Commission* below); *Hershey/Herschi* XXth *Report on Competition Policy* (1990), point 111; *Chiquita/Fyffes plc* XXIInd *Report on Competition Policy* (1992), points 168–176 (agreement by Fyffes not to use the Fyffes trade mark in continental Europe contrary to Article 101; also an abuse of a dominant position under Article 102); see *Fyffes plc v Chiquita Brands International Inc* [1993] ECC 193 on the litigation in the English High Court in this case.

[225] See generally Singleton 'IP Disputes: Settlement Agreements and Ancillary Licences' (1993) 15 EIPR 48.

[226] Case 35/83 [1985] ECR 363, [1985] 2 CMLR 470; see Alexander (1985) 22 CML Rev 709.

Justice established that trade mark delimitation agreements are permissible and fall outside Article 101(1) where they serve to avoid confusion or conflict; however there must be a genuine dispute between the parties and the agreement must be no more restrictive than necessary to overcome the problem of confusion.

The Commission's *Technology Transfer Guidelines* discuss licensing as a means of settling disputes. Where the parties to a dispute agree, as part of a settlement, to license, or to cross-license, the terms of the licence(s) may be covered by Regulation 772/2004 subject, of course, to compliance with its terms. The Commission makes the point that where the undertakings agree to license one another in circumstances where their technologies do not block one another[227] – in other words where they are actual competitors – an agreement between them would be a hard-core restriction contrary to Article 4(1) of the Regulation[228]. On the other hand if one party had the ability to exclude the other from the market by virtue of its technology, a licence would be likely to be pro-competitive[229]. Cross-licences that impose restrictions on the parties' use of their technologies, including restrictions on licensing to third parties, may infringe Article 101, in particular where the parties have significant market power and where the agreement imposes restrictions that clearly go beyond what is required to give access to the disputed technology[230]. The Commission will be concerned to ensure that any settlement between the parties does not inhibit their future opportunity to innovate and thereby gain a competitive advantage over each other[231]. No-challenge agreements in a settlement would generally be regarded as falling outside Article 101, since this is regarded as an inherent aspect of any such agreement[232].

In *Chiquita/Fyffes plc*[233] the Commission took the view that an agreement between Chiquita and Fyffes whereby Fyffes agreed not to use the Fyffes trade mark in continental Europe for a period of 20 years infringed both Articles 101 and 102. The alleged infringement of Article 102 lay in the fact that the inability of Fyffes to use that mark diminished its ability to compete vigorously with Chiquita in Europe. Following the Commission's intervention, Chiquita abandoned the agreement.

5. Article 102 and Intellectual Property Rights

The law of intellectual property confers exclusive rights; Article 102 prohibits the abuse of a dominant position. The question arises of whether Article 102 can be applied in such a way as to limit the exclusive rights given by intellectual property law[234]. The Court of Justice has made clear that mere ownership of intellectual property rights cannot be attacked under Article 102[235]; however Article 102 may apply to an improper exercise of

---

[227] See 'Vertical agreements', p 785 above on one-way and two-way blocking positions.

[228] *Technology Transfer Guidelines*, para 205.   [229] Ibid, para 206.

[230] Ibid, para 207.

[231] Ibid, para 208.   [232] Ibid, para 209.

[233] Commission's XXIInd *Report on Competition Policy* (1992), points 168–176.

[234] For further discussion of this subject see Govaere *The Use and Abuse of Intellectual Property Rights in EC Law* (Sweet & Maxwell, 1996), ch 5; Coates, Kyølbye and Peeperkorn in Faull and Nikpay *The EC Law of Competition* (Oxford University Press, 2nd ed, 2007), paras 10.209–10.255; Tritton *Intellectual Property in Europe* (Sweet & Maxwell, 3rd ed, 2008), ch 11; Anderman and Schmidt *EU Competition Law and Intellectual Property Rights: The Regulation of Innovation* (Oxford University Press, 2nd ed, 2011), chs 3–11; Kjølbye 'Article 82 EC as Remedy to Patent System Imperfections: Fighting Fire with Fire?' (2009) 32(2) World Competition 163; Vickers 'Competition Policy and Property Rights' (2010) 120 Economic Journal 375.

[235] Article 345 TFEU provides that the TFEU and TEU 'shall in no way prejudice the rules in Member States governing the system of property ownership'.

the right in question[236]. Article 8(2) of the WTO agreement on Trade-Related Aspects of Intellectual Property Rights (the so-called 'TRIPS Agreement') says much the same:

> Appropriate measures, provided that they are consistent with the provisions of this Agreement, may be needed to prevent the abuse of intellectual property rights by holders or the resort to practices which unreasonably restrain trade or adversely affect the international transfer of technology.

(A) Compulsory licences

A question that has been much debated is the extent to which the owner of an intellectual property right can be compelled to grant a licence of it to a third party under Article 102. As a general proposition the owner of an intellectual property right is entitled to determine how it should be exploited and a compulsory licence should be imposed only in exceptional circumstances.

(i) The *Renault* and *Volvo* judgments

In *Renault*[237] and in *Volvo v Erik Veng*[238] third parties wished to be granted licences of the car manufacturers' intellectual property rights in order to produce spare parts, and claimed that a refusal to grant such licences was an abuse of a dominant position under Article 102. The Court of Justice adopted an orthodox approach to the application of Article 102 to compulsory licensing and held that, in the absence of EU harmonisation of laws on designs and models, it was a matter for national law to determine the nature and extent of protection for such matters. In *Volvo* the Court stated at paragraph 8 that:

> the right of the proprietor of a protected design to prevent third parties from manufacturing and selling or importing, without its consent, products incorporating the design constitutes the very subject-matter of its exclusive rights. It follows that an obligation imposed upon the proprietor of a protected design to grant to third parties, even in return for a reasonable royalty, a licence for the supply of products incorporating the design would lead to the proprietor thereof being deprived of the substance of its exclusive right, and that a refusal to grant such a licence cannot in itself constitute an abuse of a dominant position.

The Court added, however, that a car manufacturer might be guilty of abusing its dominant position where it refused to supply spare parts to independent repairers in an arbitrary manner, charged unfair prices for spare parts[239] or decided no longer to produce spare parts for models still in circulation.

---

[236] See Case 24/67 *Parke, Davis & Co v Probel* [1968] ECR 55, [1968] CMLR 47 where the Court of Justice said that ownership of a patent is not an abuse in itself although 'the utilisation of the patent could degenerate into an improper exploitation of the protection'; the ownership of intellectual property is a factor to be taken into account in assessing whether a firm has a dominant position: see ch 5, 'Legal barriers', p 184.

[237] Case 53/87 *Conzorzio Italiano della Componentistica di Ricambio per Autovericoli and Maxicar v Regie National des Usines Renault* [1988] ECR 6039, [1990] 4 CMLR 265.

[238] Case 238/87 [1988] ECR 6211, [1989] 4 CMLR 122; see Korah 'No Duty to Licence Independent Repairers to Make Spare Parts: the *Renault*, *Volvo* and *Bayer* Cases' (1988) 12 EIPR 381; Groves 'The Use of Registered Designs to Protect Car Body Panels' (1989) 10 BLR 117.

[239] In Case T-198/98 *Micro Leader Business v Commission* [1999] ECR II-3989, [2000] 4 CMLR 886 the General Court held that the Commission, before rejecting a complaint against Microsoft concerning the exercise of its copyright protection, should have investigated whether its prices were discriminatory contrary to Article 102(2)(c): ibid, paras 49–59.

(ii) The *Magill* case

A less orthodox approach was taken by the Commission in *Magill TV Guide/ITP, BBC and RTE*[240], variously known as the *Magill* case or the *TV Listings* case. Mr Magill wished to publish the listings of three television companies broadcasting in the UK and Ireland in a single weekly publication. At the time there was no publication which contained the details of all three companies' programmes for a week in advance; this information was available only in daily newspapers for the day in question, or on a Saturday for the weekend. There was an obvious public demand for listings magazines, which were widely available in continental countries. Copyright protection was available for TV listings under UK and Irish law, which is why Magill required a licence. The Commission concluded that the three television companies had abused their individual dominant positions in relation to their own TV listings by refusing to make them available to Magill and required that advance information be supplied in order to enable comprehensive weekly TV guides to be published. The Commission's decision was appealed to the General Court and the Court of Justice, each of which upheld it[241]. The Court of Justice stated that the abuse consisted of the refusal to provide basic information by relying on national copyright provisions, thereby preventing the appearance of a new product, a comprehensive guide to television programmes, which the television companies did not offer and for which there was a potential consumer demand[242]; the Court also noted that there was no objective justification for the refusal[243] and that the result of the refusal was to reserve to the television companies the downstream market for television guides[244].

The case was immensely controversial and led to numerous comments and articles, mainly adverse[245]. It appeared to sit oddly with the earlier judgments of the Court of Justice in *Renault* and *Volvo*; it meant that the possibility of compulsory licensing had been introduced under Article 102; and it could be seen to be an application of the so-called 'essential facilities doctrine' to intellectual property rights[246]. A particular anxiety was that the precedent might be applied to intellectual property rights that were the consequence of substantial risk-taking and investment – for example patents and computer software – as opposed to a mere list of television programmes, though this did not happen in practice. There is little doubt that the Commission and the EU Courts were influenced in *Magill* by the fact that information as prosaic as TV listings was entitled to copyright protection: most systems of law in the Member States would not have conferred intellectual property protection at all in such circumstances[247]. However this was not an explicit part of the reasoning in the Commission's decision or the Courts' judgments.

---

[240] OJ [1989] L 78/43, [1989] 4 CMLR 757.

[241] Cases T-69/89 etc *RTE v Commission* [1991] ECR II-485, [1991] 4 CMLR 586, upheld by the Court of Justice Cases C-241/91 P etc *RTE and ITP v Commission* [1995] ECR I-743, [1995] 4 CMLR 718.

[242] Ibid, para 54.   [243] Ibid, para 55.   [244] Ibid, para 56.

[245] For comment on the Court of Justice's judgment see eg Pombo 'Intellectual Property and Intra-Community Trade' [1996] Fordham Corporate Law Institute (ed Hawk), 491–505; Crowther 'Compulsory Licensing of Intellectual Property Rights' (1995) 20 EL Rev 521; Anderman and Schmidt *EU Competition Law and Intellectual Property Rights: The Regulation of Innovation* (Oxford University Press, 2nd ed, 2011), pp 102–109.

[246] See ch 17, 'Is the product to which access is sought indispensable to someone wishing to compete in the downstream market?', pp 701–707; see generally Cotter 'Intellectual Property and the Essential Facilities Doctrine' (1999) 44 Antitrust Bulletin 211 on the question of whether intellectual property rights can be regarded as essential facilities.

[247] Directive 96/9 on the legal protection of databases, OJ [1996] L 77/20 adopts criteria for originality which differ from UK and Irish copyright laws at the time of the *Magill* case.

(iii) *Oscar Bronner*

In *Oscar Bronner v Mediaprint*[248] the Court of Justice stressed the exceptional circumstances in *Magill*: in paragraph 40 of its judgment it referred to four factors in particular: the information sought by Magill was indispensable to the publication of a comprehensive listings guide; there was a demonstrable potential consumer demand for the would-be product; there were no objective justifications for the refusal to supply; and the refusal would eliminate all competition in the secondary market for TV guides.

(iv) *IMS Health*

In the next case to deal with this matter, *IMS Health GmbH & Co v NDC Health GmbH & Co*[249], the Court of Justice repeated the formulation of the Court in *Bronner*. The *IMS* case was an Article 267 reference from a German court[250]. NDC Health was seeking a licence from IMS, the world leader in data collection on pharmaceutical sales and prescriptions, that would give it access to IMS's copyrighted format for processing regional sales data in Germany, the so-called '1,860 brick structure'. After considering whether the brick structure might be an indispensable requirement for NDC, as required by the *Bronner* judgment[251], the Court went on to consider the questions of whether a refusal to license NDC might exclude all competition in a secondary market[252], and whether it might prevent the emergence of a new product[253]. On the latter point the Court agreed with Advocate General Tizzano that, in achieving a balance between the need to protect the economic freedom of the owner of an intellectual property right on the one hand and the protection of competition on the other:

> the latter can prevail *only where refusal to grant a licence prevents the development of the secondary market to the detriment of consumers*[254] (emphasis added).

In seeking some limitation to what might be meant by 'exceptional circumstances', this last statement of the Court of Justice in *IMS* was helpful: even if one acknowledges that there is room for debate as to what is meant by 'the development of the secondary market' – what, for example, is a 'new' product – nevertheless the Court establishes clearly that there is no

---

[248] Case C-7/97 [1998] ECR I-7791, [1999] 4 CMLR 112.

[249] Case C-418/01 [2004] ECR I-5039, [2004] 4 CMLR 1543; for comment see Sufrin 'The IMS Case' (2004) 3 Competition Law Journal 18; Brinker 'Essential Facility Doctrine and Intellectual Property Law: Where does Europe Stand in the Aftermath of the *IMS Health* Case?' [2004] Fordham Corporate Law Institute (ed Hawk), 137; Eilmansberger 'The Essential Facilities Doctrine under Art. 82: What is the State of Affairs after IMS Health and Microsoft?' (2005) 16 King's College Law Journal 329; Fox 'A Tale of Two Jurisdictions and an Orphan Case: Antitrust, Intellectual Property, and Refusals to Deal' (2005) 28 Fordham International Law Journal 952; Ahlborn, Evans and Padilla 'The Logic & Limits of the "Exceptional Circumstances Test" in *Magill* and *IMS Health*' (2005) 28 Fordham International Law Journal 1109.

[250] Note that the Commission had adopted interim measures against IMS in *NDC Health/IMS: (Interim Measures)* OJ [2002] L 59/18, [2002] 4 CMLR 111; for comment see Korah 'The Interface between IP and Antitrust: The European Experience' (2001–02) 69 Antitrust Law Journal 801; Fine 'NDC/IMS: In Response to Professor Korah' (2002) 70 Antitrust Law Journal 247; the Presidents of the General Court and the Court of Justice suspended the Commission's decision pending the General Court's final judgment; both noted that there was a serious dispute as to whether the circumstances in *IMS* were exceptional: Case T-184/01 R [2001] ECR II-3193, [2002] 4 CMLR 58 (President of General Court Order), upheld on appeal Case C-481/01 P (R) [2002] ECR I-3401, [2002] 5 CMLR 44 (President of the Court of Justice Order); in due course the Commission withdrew the interim measures decision, so that the appeal to the General Court was itself withdrawn: see Commission Press Release IP/03/1159, 13 August 2003.

[251] See ch 17, 'Is the product to which access is sought indispensable to someone wishing to compete in the downstream market?', pp 701–707 on the meaning of indispensability in this context.

[252] Case C-418/01 [2004] ECR I-5039, [2004] 4 CMLR 1543, paras 40–47.

[253] Ibid, paras 48–50.   [254] Ibid, para 48.

right to a licence simply to duplicate what the owner of the intellectual property right in question is already doing[255].

(v) The *Microsoft* case

The *Magill* and the *IMS* cases established the possibility of a claim to a licence under Article 102 in exceptional circumstances, in particular where the licensee intended to produce a new product for which there was a potential consumer demand. The potential significance of this approach was dramatically revealed in the Commission's decision in the *Microsoft* case of 24 March 2004[256]. The Commission held that Microsoft was dominant in two markets, one for personal computer operating systems and the other for work group server operating systems. The Commission held that Microsoft had abused its dominant position by refusing to supply competitors with interoperability information to enable them to develop and distribute products that would compete with Microsoft's on the market for servers. The Commission also found Microsoft guilty of an abuse by tying its operating system with its Windows Media Player[257]. For the two abuses Microsoft was fined €497 million. The Commission's findings of abuse, and the fine, were upheld on appeal to the General Court in *Microsoft v Commission*[258]. A number of points should be noted about the abusive refusal to supply.

(A) The Commission and the General Court assumed that Microsoft enjoyed intellectual property protection

The first point is that the Commission and the General Court proceeded on the assumption that Microsoft's interoperability information was protected by the law of intellectual property, without actually reaching a conclusion on the point[259]. The Court noted that, in making this assumption, the Commission had imposed upon itself the strictest legal test, that is to say the one most favourable to Microsoft[260].

(B) The General Court's summary of the applicable law

The General Court then proceeded to analyse the relevant case law, referring in particular to *Magill*, *Bronner* and *IMS Health*, from which it drew the following conclusion:

> 331 It follows from the case law cited above that the refusal by an undertaking holding a dominant position to license a third party to use a product covered by an intellectual property right cannot in itself constitute an abuse of a dominant position within the meaning of Article [102 TFEU]. It is only in exceptional circumstances that the exercise

---

[255] Ibid, para 239.

[256] OJ [2007] L 32/23; see Banasevic, Huby, Pena, Castellot, Sitar and Piffaut 'Commission adopts Decision in the Microsoft case' (2004) (Summer) *Competition Policy Newsletter* 44–46; Lévêque 'Innovation, Leveraging and Essential Facilities: Interoperability Licensing in the EU Microsoft Case' (2005) 28(1) *World Competition* 71; O'Donoghue and Padilla *The Law and Economics of Article 82 EC* (Hart Publishing, 2006), pp 430–433; Dolmans, O'Donoghue and Loewenthal 'Are Article 82 and Intellectual Property Interoperable? The State of the Law Pending the Judgment in *Microsoft v Commission*' (2007) 3 Competition Policy International 107; Vesterdorf 'Article 82 EC: Where do we stand after the Microsoft judgment?' (2008) 1 ICC Global Antitrust Review 1.

[257] See ch 17, 'Tying', pp 688–696 for discussion of the tying infringement; see also McMahon 'Interoperability: "Indispensability" and "Special Responsibility" in High Technology Markets' (2007) 9 Tulane Journal of Technology and Intellectual Property 123.

[258] Case T-201/04 [2007] ECR II-3601, [2007] 5 CMLR 846; for discussion of the case by Commission officials see Kramler, Buhr and Wyns 'The judgment of the Court of First Instance in the Microsoft case' (2007) 3 *Competition Policy Newsletter* 39; see also Howarth and McMahon ' "Windows has Performed an Illegal Operation": The Court of First Instance's Judgment in Microsoft v Commission' (2008) 29 ECLR 117.

[259] Case T-201/04 [2007] ECR II-3601, [2007] 5 CMLR 846, paras 283–290.

[260] Ibid, para 284.

of the exclusive right by the owner of the intellectual property right may give rise to such an abuse.

332 It also follows from that case law that the following circumstances, in particular, must be considered to be exceptional:

- in the first place, the refusal relates to a product or service indispensable to the exercise of a particular activity on a neighbouring market;

- in the second place, the refusal is of such a kind as to exclude any effective competition on that neighbouring market;

- in the third place, the refusal prevents the appearance of a new product for which there is potential consumer demand.

333 Once it is established that such circumstances are present, the refusal by the holder of a dominant position to grant a licence may infringe Article [102 TFEU] unless the refusal is objectively justified.

334 The Court notes that the circumstance that the refusal prevents the appearance of a new product for which there is potential demand is found only in the case law on the exercise of an intellectual property right.

(C) The General Court's benign application of the 'new product' requirement

The Court concluded that the requirement of indispensability was satisfied[261] and that all effective competition would be eliminated on a secondary market[262]. A notable feature of the General Court's judgment is its treatment of the 'new product' requirement[263]. The Court began by noting that this consideration was one that should be understood in the context of Article 102(2)(b) which prohibits abusive conduct which consists of 'limiting production, markets or technical development to the prejudice of consumers'[264]. However the Court did not make a finding, nor did it require the Commission to have made a finding, that any specific new product – such as the composite TV listings magazine in *Magill* – would have resulted from the provision of interoperability information; rather the Court said that the new product criterion should be read to include a restriction of technical development[265], and that the Commission's emphasis on this factor was not manifestly incorrect[266]. In the Court's view Microsoft's refusal meant that consumers were increasingly locked into Microsoft's platform at the work group server level[267]; and that competitors were prevented from developing operating systems distinguishable from the Windows systems already on the market[268]. The Court concluded with the rather bizarre statement that Microsoft had 'impaired the effective competitive structure on the work group server operating systems market by acquiring a significant market share on that market'[269]. The General Court rejected Microsoft's claim that its behaviour was objectively justified[270].

The Court seems to have taken a somewhat benign approach to the 'new product' rule in this judgment[271]. It can be anticipated that future cases will have to examine further the scope of the new product rule, both as to the 'newness' of the product and the possibility that a restriction of technical development may suffice[272].

---

[261] Ibid, paras 369–436.　　[262] Ibid, paras 479–620.　　[263] Ibid, paras 643–665.
[264] Ibid, para 643.　　[265] Ibid, para 647.　　[266] Ibid, para 649.
[267] Ibid, paras 650–652.　　[268] Ibid, paras 653–659.　　[269] Ibid, para 664.
[270] Ibid, paras 688–712.
[271] See Vickers 'A Tale of Two EC Cases: *IBM* and *Microsoft*' (2008) 4 Competition Policy International 3.
[272] On this point see para 62 of the Advocate General's Opinion in Case C-418/01 *IMS Health GmbH & Co OHG v NDC Health GmbH & Co KG* [2004] ECR I-5039, [2004] 4 CMLR 1543; see also O'Donoghue and Padilla *The Law and Economics of Article 82 EC* (Hart Publishing, 2006), pp 445–450.

(D) Remedy

An obvious difficulty with a case such as *Microsoft* is to determine an appropriate remedy, and to ensure that there is proper compliance. Courts in the US are reluctant to make positive orders that require supervision[273]. After the Commission's decision in *Microsoft* in March 2004 there were protracted negotiations between the Commission and Microsoft as to whether the latter was making the necessary interoperability information available to the market on 'RAND' terms (reasonable and non-discriminatory). The Commission appointed a Trustee to provide technical advice on compliance[274], although the General Court subsequently ruled that the Commission lacked the legal power to have done so[275]. The Commission decided in July 2006 that Microsoft had been guilty of failing to provide interoperability information, as required by its decision, from 16 December 2005 to 20 June 2006, and therefore imposed a daily periodical payment penalty of €1.5 million on Microsoft which totalled €280.5 million[276]. In February 2008 the Commission imposed a further penalty of €899 million for charging unreasonable prices for the information from 21 June 2006 until 21 October 2007[277]. In October 2007 the Commission announced that it had finally reached agreement with Microsoft on compliance with its decision[278].

(B) The Commission's Guidance on Article 102 Enforcement Priorities

The Commission provides some insights into its thinking on refusal to license intellectual property or to provide proprietary information in paragraphs 75 to 90 of its *Guidance on Article 102 Enforcement Priorities*[279]. The *Guidance* does not purport to state the law under Article 102; rather it explains the factors that inform the Commission's enforcement activity. Refusals to supply will be an enforcement priority if the Commission is satisfied that:

- the refusal relates to a product or service that is objectively necessary to be able to compete effectively on a downstream market
- the refusal is likely to lead to the elimination of effective competition on the downstream market[280] and
- the refusal is likely to lead to consumer harm.

It is noticeable that the Commission applies the same factors to a refusal to license intellectual property rights as to other types of refusal to supply, although it may well be more difficult to establish them in such cases. In deciding whether a refusal is likely to lead to consumer harm the Commission specifically says that it would look to see whether a refusal would result in innovative products not being brought to the market or follow-on

---

[273] See ch 17, 'Is the product to which access is sought indispensable to someone wishing to compete in the downstream market?', pp 701–707, discussing the *Trinko* case.

[274] See eg Commission Press Release IP/05/1215, 5 October 2005.

[275] Case T-201/04 *Microsoft Corp v Commission* [2007] ECR II-3601, [2007] 5 CMLR 846, paras 1251–1279.

[276] Commission decision of 12 July 2006.

[277] Commission decision of 27 February 2008, on appeal Case T-167/08 *Microsoft Corp v Commission*, not yet decided.

[278] Commission Press Release IP/07/1567, 22 October 2007; see also Commission MEMO/08/106, 21 February 2008.

[279] OJ [2009] C 45/7; for a general discussion see ch 5, 'The Commission's *Guidance on Article 102 Enforcement Priorities*', pp 174–177.

[280] On this point the *Guidance on Article 102 Enforcement Priorities* does not refer to, but is consistent with, paras 332 and 563 of the General Court's judgment in Case T-201/04 *Microsoft Corp v Commission* [2007] ECR II-3601, [2007] 5 CMLR 846.

innovation being stifled[281]. The onus is on the dominant firm to demonstrate any negative impact which an obligation to supply is likely to have on its own level of innovation[282].

(C) Collecting societies

Article 102 may be applied to the activities of collecting societies, that is to say organisations that manage copyright on behalf of authors and publishers; in particular they collect royalties from the media, nightclubs and other users on behalf of their members and distribute them in return for a fee. Article 102 has been invoked both by the Commission[283] and before domestic courts, several of which have referred matters to the Court of Justice under Article 267 TFEU[284].

The Court of Justice has indicated that there is nothing intrinsically objectionable about the establishment of collecting societies, which may be necessary in order that individual artists can obtain a reasonable return for their endeavours[285]. However the activities of a society may amount to a breach of Article 102 in various ways. Of particular significance in EU law terms will be the tendency of national societies to discriminate against undertakings from other Member States[286]. In *CISAC* the Commission prohibited the International Confederation of Authors and Composers and 24 collecting societies from restricting competition by limiting their ability to offer services outside the domestic territory of each collecting society[287]. The Commission rejected arguments that the restrictive practices were justified by the territorial nature of copyright[288] or by a need for geographical proximity between the collecting society which grants the licence and the commercial user[289]; it concluded that the practices did not satisfy Article 101(3)[290].

Other aspects of collecting societies' activities have been condemned, such as clauses in the constitution which unreasonably restrict an author's right to act unilaterally and

---

[281] *Guidance on Article 102 Enforcement Priorities*, para 87, which specifically cites the judgments of the Court of Justice and General Court in respectively *IMS* and *Microsoft* in support of this approach.

[282] Ibid, para 90.

[283] *GEMA* JO [1971] L 134/15, [1971] CMLR D35; *Interpar v GVL GmbH* OJ [1981] L 370/49, [1982] 1 CMLR 221; *GEMA Statutes* OJ [1982] L 94/12, [1982] 2 CMLR 482; *BIEM-FPI* XIIIth *Report on Competition Policy* (1983), points 147–150; *GEMA* XVth *Report on Competition Policy* (1985), point 81; *GVL* OJ [1981] L 370/49, upheld on appeal to the Court of Justice Case 7/82 *GVL v Commission* [1983] ECR 483, [1983] 3 CMLR 645; the Commission's decision not to proceed with complaints against SACEM, a French collecting society, was unsuccessfully challenged in Case T-114/92 *BEMIM v Commission* [1995] ECR II-147, [1996] 4 CMLR 305 and in Case T-5/93 *Roger Tremblay v Commission* [1995] ECR II-185, [1996] 4 CMLR 305, on appeal to the Court of Justice Case C-91/95 P [1996] ECR I-5547, [1997] 4 CMLR 211; for comment see Torremans and Stamatoudi 'Collecting Societies: Sorry, the Community is No Longer Interested!' (1997) 2 EL Rev 352.

[284] Case 127/73 *Belgische Radio en Televisie v SABAM* [1974] ECR 313, [1974] 2 CMLR 238; Case 22/79 *Greenwich Film Production v SACEM* [1979] ECR 3275, [1980] 1 CMLR 629; Case 402/85 *Basset v SACEM* [1987] ECR 1747, [1987] 3 CMLR 173; Case 395/87 *Ministère Public v Tournier* [1989] ECR 2521, [1991] 4 CMLR 248; Case 110/88 *Lucazeau v SACEM* [1989] ECR 2811, [1991] 4 CMLR 248; Case C-52/07 *Kanal 5 Ltd and TV 4 AB v Föreningen Svenska Tonsättares Internationella Musikbyrå (STIM) upa* [2008] ECR I-9275, [2009] 5 CMLR 2175.

[285] See Case 127/73 *BRT v SABAM* [1974] ECR 313, [1974] 2 CMLR 238, paras 8–15.

[286] Re *GEMA* JO [1971] L 134/15, [1971] CMLR D35; Case 7/102 *GVL v Commission* [1983] ECR 483, [1983] 3 CMLR 645.

[287] Decision of 16 July 2008 [2009] 4 CMLR 577, on appeal Cases T-422/08 etc *CISAC v Commission*, not yet decided; the President of the General Court rejected applications for interim measures in Case T-411/08 R *Artisjus Magyar Szerzői Jogvédő Iroda Egyesület v Commission* [2008] ECR II-270, [2009] 4 CMLR 353.

[288] Decision of 16 July 2008 [2009] 4 CMLR 577, paras 159–160.

[289] Ibid, paras 171–199, note that the Commission's finding was confined to exploitations by satellite, Internet and cable transmission, for which local presence was not necessary to monitor the use of a licence; 'offline' forms of exploitation (concerts, radio, discotheques, bars, etc) were not the subject of that part of the decision.

[290] Ibid, paras 233–255.

provisions which are unreasonable vis-à-vis the media or which attempt to extend the protection of copyright to non-copyrighted works[291].

(D) Miscellaneous cases concerning intellectual property rights

(i) Unlawful acquisition of technology

In *Tetra Pak Rausing v Commission*[292] the General Court upheld the Commission's decision[293] that it was an abuse of Tetra Pak's dominant position in the market for cartons and machines for packaging milk to acquire Liquipak and thereby obtain the benefit of an exclusive licence relating to technology for a new method of sterilising cartons suitable for long-life milk. This finding was despite the fact that the licence complied with the provisions of the block exemption in force at the time on patent licensing agreements.

(ii) Demanding excessive royalties

In *Eurofix-Bauco v Hilti*[294] the Commission held that it was an abuse to demand an 'excessive' royalty with the sole object of blocking, or at any rate unreasonably delaying, a licence of right which was available under UK patent law. This was seen as part of Hilti's strategy of preventing competition in respect of its nail cartridges.

In *Duales System Deutschland*[295] the Commission concluded that it was an abuse of a dominant position for DSD, an undertaking that operated a comprehensive system for the collection and recycling of waste in Germany, to contain a provision in its trade mark agreement that its clients would pay a royalty for sales packaging bearing its 'Green Dot' trade mark, irrespective of whether the client actually used the services of DSD. This could dissuade those clients from using the services of competitors. The Commission's decision was upheld on appeal to the General Court[296] and again on appeal to the Court of Justice[297].

In *Qualcomm* the Commission investigated complaints that Qualcomm, the owner of patents in the European standard for third generation (3G) mobile telephony technology, had failed to license its technology on FRAND (fair, reasonable, and non-discriminatory) terms[298], but decided that the case was no longer an administrative priority[299].

---

[291] The most thorough decision on these issues remains the Commission's decision in *Re GEMA* JO [1971] L 134/15, [1971] 1 CMLR D35; on the lawfulness of 'supplementary mechanical reproduction fees' see Case 402/85 *Basset v SACEM* [1987] ECR 1747, [1987] 3 CMLR 173.

[292] Case T-51/89 [1990] ECR II-309, [1991] 4 CMLR 334.

[293] *Tetra Pak I (BTG Licence)* OJ [1988] L 272/27, [1990] 4 CMLR 47.

[294] OJ [1988] L 65/19, [1989] 4 CMLR 677, para 78, upheld on appeal Case T-30/89 *Hilti AG v Commission* [1991] ECR II-1439, [1992] 4 CMLR 16, para 99.

[295] OJ [2001] L 166/1, [2001] 5 CMLR 609, paras 111–113.

[296] Case T-151/01 *Duales System Deutschland GmbH v Commission* [2007] ECR II-1607, [2007] 5 CMLR 300; for comment see Gremminger and Miersch 'The Court of First Instance confirms Duales System Deutschland's abuse of dominance in the packaging recycling system' (2007) 3 *Competition Policy Newsletter* 47.

[297] Case C-385/07 P *Duales System Deutschland GmbH v Commission* [2009] ECR I-6155, [2009] 5 CMLR 2215.

[298] See Commission MEMO/07/389, 1 October 2007; see also Piesiewcz and Schellingerhout on the issue of setting standards in 'Intellectual property rights in standard setting from a competition law perspective' (2007) (Summer) *Competition Policy Newsletter* 36; and Commission MEMO/09/549, 10 December 2009: following its acquisition of Robert Bosch's mobile telephony patent portfolio and discussions with the Commission, IPCom agreed to take over Bosch's commitment to grant irrevocable patent licences on FRAND terms.

[299] See Commission MEMO/09/516, 24 November 2009.

(iii) Vexatious behaviour and abuse of process

In *BBI/Boosey and Hawkes: Interim Measures*[300] the Commission seems to have regarded it as an aspect of Boosey and Hawkes' abusive behaviour to have brought vexatious litigation against an undertaking for 'slavish imitation' of its products[301]. On one occasion the Commission intimated that it might be an abuse for a firm in a dominant position to register a trade mark knowing that a competitor already uses that mark[302].

In *AstraZeneca*[303] the Commission imposed a fine of €60 million on AstraZeneca for misuse of regulatory procedures. AstraZeneca had a patent for a highly successful drug, Losec. When a patent expires, it is normal for so-called 'generic' manufacturers to enter the market and to sell the drugs in question at considerably lower prices than were charged during the period of patent protection. AstraZeneca was found by the Commission to have abused regulatory procedures in two ways. First, it had succeeded in persuading various patent authorities to grant it 'supplementary protection certificates', extending the period of patent protection, on the basis of misleading information. Secondly, AstraZeneca held a market authorisation that allowed the drug to be sold in a capsule form. AstraZeneca withdrew the capsules from the market, selling them in tablet form instead. This meant that the generics companies could no longer market their capsules. On appeal the General Court largely upheld the Commission's decision[304].

A fundamental disagreement between AstraZeneca and the Commission concerned the concept of abuse. AstraZeneca argued that an abuse can exist only when a dominant undertaking has wilfully acquired or enforced the patent knowing that it is invalid. The General Court rejected this[305]. In paragraph 355 of its judgment the General Court held:

> the submission to the public authorities of misleading information liable to lead them into error and therefore to make possible the grant of an exclusive right to which an undertaking is not entitled, or to which it is entitled for a shorter period, constitutes a practice falling outside the scope of competition on the merits which may be particularly restrictive of competition.

The Court stated that a dominant firm has a 'special responsibility' not to impair undistorted competition that requires it, at the very least, to inform the public authorities of any errors in information it provides to them[306]. Further disagreements between AstraZeneca and the Commission arose as to whether the misleading representations were capable of restricting competition; and as to whether the Commission had based its findings upon adequate evidence and drawn correct conclusions from that evidence. The judgment of the General Court went against AstraZeneca on all these points.

---

[300] OJ [1987] L 286/36, [1988] 4 CMLR 67, para 19.

[301] See further ch 17, 'Vexatious litigation', p 713.

[302] *Osram/Airam*, XIth *Report on Competition Policy* (1981), point 97.

[303] Commission decision of 15 June 2005; see De Souza 'Competition in Pharmaceuticals: the challenges ahead post AstraZeneca' (2007) (Spring) *Competition Policy Newsletter* 39; Gunther and Breuvart 'Misuse of Patent and Drug Regulatory Approval Systems in the Pharmaceutical Industry: an Analysis of US and EU Converging Approaches' (2005) 26 ECLR 669; Murphy 'Abuse of regulatory procedures – the AstraZeneca case: Parts 1, 2 and 3' (2009) 30 ECLR 223, 289 and 314.

[304] Case T-321/05 *AstraZeneca AB v Commission* [2010] ECR I-000, [2010] 5 CMLR 1585, paras 239–294 (dominance), paras 352–381 (legal analysis of the first abuse) and paras 474–613 (proof of the first abuse) and paras 666–696 (legal analysis of the second abuse) and paras 757–865 (proof of the second abuse).

[305] Ibid, para 356: 'proof of the deliberate nature of the conduct and of the bad faith of the undertaking in a dominant position is not required for the purposes of identifying an abuse of a dominant position'; see also paras 493 and 814; the Commission may, nevertheless, take into account evidence of anti-competitive intention: ibid, para 359.

[306] Ibid, para 358.

The Court overturned some of the findings of the second abuse for lack of evidence[307], but it did not question the principle that such behaviour can be abusive[308]. The General Court rejected a claim by AstraZeneca that it was being made subject to an obligation to protect the interests of generics manufacturers or parallel importers by maintaining the marketing authorisations[309]. The case has been appealed to the Court of Justice[310].

In *Rambus* the Commission sent a statement of objections alleging that Rambus had infringed Article 102 by conducting a so-called 'patent ambush'. This refers to the phenomenon of an undertaking participating in the setting of an industry standard, but doing so in a deliberately deceptive manner by not disclosing the existence of patents that would be necessary for anyone making use of the standard. This means that, once the standard is set, the owner of the patents will be able to demand unreasonable royalties from licensees that need access to the technology in question[311]. The Commission subsequently focused on whether Rambus was charging too much for its technology. In the end the Commission accepted commitments from Rambus to bring an end to the Article 102 proceedings against it: Rambus agreed to a worldwide cap on its royalty rates for five years[312]. The commitments therefore addressed a symptom of the patent ambush rather than the alleged ambush itself. The Commission's intervention in this case followed an earlier action in the US, where the Federal Trade Commission required Rambus to license its technology for computer memory subject to maximum royalty rates[313].

6. UK Law

(A) Licences of intellectual property rights: the Chapter I prohibition

The Chapter I prohibition in the Competition Act 1998 applies to agreements that have as their object or effect the prevention, restriction or distortion of competition[314]. There are no specific provisions in the legislation on licences of intellectual property rights, and

---

[307] Ibid, paras 824–861; the fine on AstraZeneca was reduced to €52.5 million for this reason.

[308] Ibid, para 672.   [309] Ibid, paras 815–817.

[310] Case C-457/10 P *AstraZeneca AB v Commission*, not yet decided.

[311] See Commission MEMO/07/330, 23 August 2007; the Commission closed an investigation of whether Boehringer, a pharmaceutical company, had infringed Article 102 by exclusionary 'misuse of the patent system': see Commission Press Release 1P/11/842, 6 July 2011.

[312] Commission decision of 9 December 2009, on appeal in Case T-148/10 *Hynix Semiconductor v Commission*, not yet decided; for comment see Schellingerhout and Cavicchi 'Patent ambush in standard-setting: the Commission accepts commitments from Rambus to lower memory chip royalty rates' (2010) 1 *Competition Policy Newsletter* 32.

[313] See *In the Matter of Rambus Inc* FTC's Final Order of 2 February 2007, reversed on appeal *Rambus Inc v FTC* (DC Cir 2008), certiorari denied 129 S Ct 1318; details of these proceedings are available at www.ftc. gov; see also *Broadcom Corporation v Qualcomm Incorporated* 501 F 3d 297 (3d Cir 2007); for discussion of issues arising from the adoption of standards and intellectual property rights see Ohana, Hansen and Shah 'Disclosure and Negotiation of Licensing Terms Prior to Adoption of Industry Standards: Preventing Another Patent Ambush?' (2003) 24 ECLR 644; on patent ambushing more generally see Naughton 'The Antitrust Risks of Unilateral Conduct in Standard Setting, in the Light of the FTC's Case Against Rambus' (2004) XLIX Antitrust Bulletin 699; Petritsi 'The Case of Unilateral Patent Ambush Under EC Competition Rules' (2005) 28(1) World Competition 25; Farrell, Hayes, Shapiro and Sullivan 'Standard Setting, Patents and Hold-Up' (2007) 74 Antitrust Law Journal 603.

[314] For a general account see ch 9, 'The Chapter I Prohibition', pp 333–360.

the Office of Fair Trading ('the OFT') has not published a guideline on the subject[315]. As a general proposition it can be anticipated that the Chapter I prohibition will be applied to agreements in the same way as Article 101 TFEU[316]. The possibility exists that some of the jurisprudence of the EU Courts might not be applied to a purely domestic agreement in so far as that jurisprudence reflects single market considerations that need not be applied within the UK[317].

Perhaps the most important provision of the Competition Act as far as licences of intellectual property rights are concerned is section 10, which provides for so-called parallel exemption[318]. This section means that any agreement that is exempt under Regulation 772/2004, or that would be if the agreement in question were to have an effect on trade between Member States, is also exempt from the Chapter I prohibition. This means that many agreements are exempt from both EU and UK law, and that there is no need for the UK to adopt a block exemption of its own for technology transfer agreements.

(B) Other agreements relating to intellectual property rights

It is reasonable to assume that domestic law will, subject to the point about single market considerations, be interpreted consistently with the jurisprudence and decisional practice under Article 101; and that the UK institutions will have regard to the Commission's *Technology Transfer Guidelines*[319].

(C) Anti-monopoly control of intellectual property rights: the Chapter II prohibition and market investigations

The Chapter II prohibition could apply to abusive behaviour in relation to intellectual property rights; the decisional practice of the Commission and the judgments of the EU Courts would of course be relevant to the application of this prohibition[320]. The OFT has said that a firm's conduct is not immune from the Chapter II prohibition purely on the basis that its market power stems from the holding of intellectual property rights[321]. In the case of *Capita Business Services Ltd and Bromcom Computers plc*[322] Capita gave the OFT voluntary assurances that it would provide 'interface information' to a third party to enable it to have access to data on Capita's server; the case was therefore closed.

The market investigation provisions of the Enterprise Act 2002 may also be relevant where features of a market have an adverse effect on competition as a result of intellectual property rights. These provisions have been described in chapter 11. The Competition Commission has published some reports under the now-repealed

---

[315] A draft Guideline was published in November 2001, OFT 418, but it was not published in final form.

[316] See 'The application of Article 101(1) to licences of intellectual property rights', pp 773 ff above.

[317] See ch 9, ' "Governing Principles Clause": Section 60 of the Competition Act 1998', pp 369–374.

[318] See ch 9, 'Parallel exemptions', pp 359–360.

[319] See 'The Application of Article 101 to Other Agreements Relating to Intellectual Property Rights', pp 791–796 above.

[320] See 'Article 102 and Intellectual Property Rights', pp 796–806 above.

[321] *BSkyB* OFT decision, 17 December 2002, paras 331–340.

[322] Weekly Gazette of the OFT, Competition case closure summaries, 26 April–2 May 2003, available at www.oft.gov.uk; see also *British Standards Institution agrees to grant online licence*, OFT Press Release PN 94/03, 7 July 2003.

monopoly provisions of the Fair Trading Act 1973 dealing with intellectual property issues, including *Exhaust Gas Analysers*[323], *Recorded Music*[324], *Historical On-line Database Services*[325], *Video Games*[326] and *Performing Rights*[327].

In *Reckitt Benckiser*[328] Reckitt admitted infringing Article 102 and the Chapter II prohibition by withdrawing and delisting a drug, Gaviscon Original Liquid, from the NHS prescription channel in 2005. The Government commenced an action in 2011 against Reckitt for damages[329].

---

[323] Cm 2386 (1993).   [324] Cm 2599 (1994).   [325] Cm 2554 (1994).
[326] Cm 2781 (1995).   [327] Cm 3147 (1996).
[328] OFT decision of 13 April 2011, see also OFT Press Release 53/11 of the same date.
[329] *Secretary of State for Health and others v Reckitt Benckiser Group plc*, not yet decided.

20

Mergers (1) – introduction

CHAPTER CONTENTS

1. Introduction

This chapter briefly introduces the subject of merger control. This book so far has been concerned essentially with two issues: anti-competitive agreements and abusive conduct. Merger control is an important third component of most, though not all, systems of competition law. The EU Merger Regulation ('the EUMR') will be described in chapter 21 and the merger provisions in the UK Enterprise Act 2002 in chapter 22. Before doing so it may be useful to make some brief preliminary observations about the subject of mergers generally and about systems of merger control in particular. The issues introduced in this chapter will be discussed in more depth in the two that follow.

2. Terminology

(A) The meaning of 'merger' and 'concentration'

A true merger involves two separate undertakings merging entirely into a new entity: a high-profile example of this was the fusion in 1996 of Ciba-Geigy and Sandoz to form the major pharmaceutical and chemical company Novartis[1]; a further example in 2000 was the creation of GlaxoSmithKline as a result of the merger of Glaxo Wellcome and SmithKline Beecham[2]. However it is important to understand that the expression 'merger' as used in competition policy includes a far broader range of corporate transactions than full mergers of this kind. Where A acquires all, or a majority of, the shares in B, this would be described as a merger if it results in A being able to control the strategic business decisions of B; even the acquisition of a minority shareholding may be sufficient, in particular circumstances, to qualify as a merger: under the EUMR the question

---

[1] Case M 737, decision of 17 July 1996, OJ [1997] L 201/1; the Commission's decisions are available on DG COMP's website at www.ec.europa.eu/competition/mergers/cases.

[2] Case M 1846, decision of 8 May 2000.

is whether A will acquire 'the possibility of exercising decisive influence' over B[3]; under the Enterprise Act the question is whether A would at least have 'material influence' over B[4]. The acquisition of assets – for example a well-known brand name – can amount to a merger[5]. Two or more undertakings which merge part of their businesses into a newly-established joint venture company, 'Newco', may be found to be parties to a merger[6]. In each case the essential question is whether previously independent businesses have come or will come under common control with the consequence that, in the future, the market will function less competitively than it did prior to the merger. For the sake of convenience the term 'merger' will be used in this and the following chapters to encompass all these phenomena unless the context requires a different usage. When discussing the EU system an alternative expression, 'concentration' will also sometimes be used, since that is the word used in the EUMR itself.

(B) The horizontal, vertical and conglomerate effects of mergers

Competition law is concerned about the possibility that a merger will lead to the market being less competitive in the future than it currently is, leading to adverse effects for consumers. The main concern of competition authorities when assessing a merger is whether it will have adverse *horizontal* effects; there may also be concerns about *vertical* and *conglomerate* effects, but these concerns are much rarer. It is possible that the same case can give rise to horizontal, vertical and conglomerate concerns[7].

(i) Horizontal effects

Horizontal effects occur where a merger takes place between actual or potential competitors in the same product and geographic markets and at the same level of the production or distribution cycle. As a general proposition the horizontal effects of mergers present a much greater danger to competition than vertical (or conglomerate) ones, in the same way that horizontal agreements are treated more strictly than vertical agreements. Horizontal mergers may be scrutinised both for their 'unilateral' or 'non-coordinated' effects and for their 'coordinated' effects[8].

(ii) Vertical effects

Vertical effects may be experienced where a merger occurs between firms that operate at different, but complementary, levels of the market for the same final product: for example A might produce a raw material (an 'upstream' product) for a product produced by B (a 'downstream' product). Often such mergers will enhance, or be neutral, in terms of economic efficiency, but there is a possibility that vertical integration may have a harmful effect on competition, either because it gives rise to a risk of the market becoming

---

[3] See ch 21, 'The concept of control', pp 834–836.

[4] See ch 22, 'Enterprises ceasing to be distinct', pp 919–920.

[5] See eg Case M 890 *Blokker/Toys 'R' Us*, decision of 26 June 1997, OJ [1998] L 316/1.

[6] See in particular ch 21, 'Joint ventures – the concept of full-functionality', pp 837–838 on the application of the EUMR to so-called 'full-function' joint ventures.

[7] See eg the European Commission's decision in Case M 2220, *General Electric/Honeywell*, decision of 3 July 2001, OJ [2004] L 48/1; on appeal to the General Court the Commission's finding on horizontal effects was upheld but the findings of vertical and conglomerate effects were annulled: see Case T-210/01 *General Electric v Commission* [2005] ECR II-5575, [2006] 4 CMLR 686.

[8] See further 'Unilateral or non-coordinated effects', pp 818–819 below; on horizontal effects under the EUMR see ch 21, 'Horizontal mergers', pp 868–876; for their treatment under UK law see ch 22, 'Horizontal mergers', pp 935–937.

foreclosed to third parties or because it could lead to collusion between the merged entity and third parties[9].

(iii) Conglomerate effects

There have been a few occasions on which competition authorities have had concerns about mergers not on the basis of horizontal or vertical effects, but because of possible conglomerate effects: for example that a merger between A and B who are neither horizontal competitors, nor functionally related vertically, might enable the merged entity AB to use its market power in two different but related, or even unrelated, markets to foreclose competitors. Whether conglomerate mergers should be controlled at all is a matter of controversy: the Department of Justice and the Federal Trade Commission in the US long ago abandoned any interest in the conglomerate effects of mergers[10]; however the European Commission has expressed concern about the 'portfolio' or 'range' or 'conglomerate' effects of mergers on various occasions, though its adverse findings on conglomeracy in both *Tetra Laval/Sidel*[11] and in *General Electric/Honeywell International*[12] were annulled on appeal by the General Court[13].

3. Merger Activity

In the corporate world there are frequent bouts of 'merger mania' when the level of merger activity is very high[14]; enormous fees are earned by financial and legal (including competition law) advisers during these periods. For example there was a very high degree of merger activity in the second half of the 1980s[15], and again in the mid-1990s[16]. From 1998 to 2001 there was a period of frenetic merger activity, although this then declined markedly as the global economy slowed. Another upswing commenced in 2005 and continued through to 2007, not least as private equity firms became involved in ever-larger acquisitions of well-established firms. In a speech in June 2007 Commissioner Kroes spoke of a 'tsunami' of mergers which she welcomed since it involved the cross-border restructuring of markets in many sectors from energy to banking and from air transport to telecommunications[17]. The financial crisis that erupted in 2008 led to a sharply reduced amount of merger activity in the following years. The European Commission's Table of Statistics, reproduced in chapter 21[18], shows clearly the peaks and troughs of merger notifications under the EUMR: from 211 in 2003 up to 402 in 2007 and down to 259 in 2009.

---

[9] See further 'Vertical effects', pp 819–820 below; on vertical effects under the EUMR see ch 21, 'Vertical mergers', pp 878–879; for their treatment under UK law see ch 22, 'Non-horizontal mergers', pp 937–939.

[10] See Scherer and Ross *Industrial Market Structure and Economic Performance* (Houghton Mifflin, 3rd ed, 1990), pp 188–190.

[11] Case M 2416 *Tetra Laval/Sidel*, decision of 30 October 2001, OJ [2004] L 43/13.

[12] See Case M 2220, *General Electric/Honeywell*, decision of 3 July 2001, OJ [2004] L 48/1.

[13] Case T-5/02 *Tetra Laval v Commission* [2002] ECR II-4381, [2002] 5 CMLR 1182, upheld on appeal Case C-12/03 P *Commission v Tetra Laval* [2005] ECR I-987, [2005] 4 CMLR 573; Case T-209/01 *Honeywell v Commission* [2005] ECR II-5527, [2006] 4 CMLR 652; Case T-210/01 *General Electric v Commission* [2005] ECR II-5575, [2006] 4 CMLR 686.

[14] See Scherer and Ross *Industrial Market Structure and Economic Performance* (Houghton Mifflin, 3rd ed, 1990), pp 153–159.

[15] See eg the 1986 *Annual Report of the Director General of Fair Trading*, pp 27–28.

[16] See eg the 1995 *Annual Report of the Director General of Fair Trading*, p 13.

[17] Neelie Kroes speech of 5 June 2007, available at www.ec.europa.eu/competition/speeches.

[18] See ch 21, 'Table of EUMR statistics', p 899.

A notable feature of mergers in recent years has been their increasing complexity, size and geographical reach. Very large mergers have taken place in many sectors as companies have sought to restructure and consolidate their place in an increasingly global market. For example in the pharmaceuticals industry Pfizer and Warner-Lambert merged to become the largest pharmaceutical company in the world[19]. Major mergers have taken place in the car industry, for example between Daimler-Benz and Chrysler[20], between Ford and Volvo[21], between Renault and Nissan[22], between General Motors and Saab[23] and between Fiat and Chrysler[24]. In the oil industry Exxon merged with Mobil to become the largest oil company in the world[25], and BP Amoco merged with Arco[26]. Many other industries have seen a high degree of merger activity, not least the legal profession. Several times in 1999 the *Financial Times* announced 'the biggest deal in corporate history'. For example the merger of America Online and Time-Warner[27], announced in January 1999, enjoyed 'biggest deal' status until the VodaphoneAirTouch/Mannesmann merger was announced in February[28]; the latter case was also of interest in that it was the first successful hostile bid for a German company.

4. The Proliferation of Systems of Merger Control

A particularly noticeable feature of competition policy in the last 20 years or so has been the proliferation of systems of competition law around the world. More than 110 countries now have competition law, and at least 100 of these laws include merger control[29]. The profusion of systems of merger control has a greater impact on most firms than rules against cartels and abusive behaviour, not because these firms disregard the latter but because their transactions are often subject to mandatory pre-notification under the former. This means that any sizable transaction with an international dimension – of which there are many – may have to be notified to 10, 20 or even more competition authorities. Law firms advising on international transactions must be able to obtain access to all the relevant merger laws and guidelines in order to determine where filings must be made[30]. Many competition lawyers in firms handling such cases will spend a substantial amount of time overseeing and coordinating a number of national filings; the initial enthusiasm of junior competition lawyers for such work often fades when it becomes apparent that the coordination of filings in Australia, Europe and the US entails an 18-hour working day or longer. It is important for lawyers to manage the expectations

---

[19] Case M 1878, decision of 22 May 2000.
[20] Case M 1204, decision of 22 July 1998.   [21] Case M 1452, decision of 26 March 1999.
[22] Case M 1519, decision of 12 May 1999.   [23] Case M 1847, decision of 28 February 2000.
[24] Case M 5518, decision of 24 July 2009.
[25] Case M 1383, decision of 29 September 1999, OJ [2004] L 103/1.
[26] Case M 1532, decision of 29 September 1999, OJ [2001] L 18/1, [2001] 4 CMLR 774.
[27] Case M 1845, decision of 11 October 2000, OJ [2001] L 268/28, [2002] 4 CMLR 454.
[28] Case M 1795, decision of 12 April 2000.
[29] Online access to information about countries with competition (including merger) laws can be obtained through the *Competition Law Toolkit* of the Asian Development Bank, available at www.adb.org/Documents/Others/OGC-Toolkits/Competition-Law/default.asp.
[30] Some helpful sources are Rowley and Baker *Merger Control: International Mergers* (Sweet & Maxwell looseleaf); Dabbah and Lasok *Merger Control Worldwide* (Cambridge University Press, 2005); White and Case *2009 Survey of Worldwide Antitrust Merger Notification Requirements* which can be ordered on the Internet at www.whitecase.com; *Worldwide Competition Filing Requirements* (Howrey, 2010); *The Global Merger Control Manual* (Cameron May, 9th ed, 2010, eds Laing and Gómez); *Merger Control 2011* (Global Legal Group, 2011); *Merger Control: The International Regulation of Mergers and Joint Ventures* (Global Competition Review, 2011).

of clients who may not fully appreciate how long and tortuous the regulatory road may be ahead of them before the transaction is able to proceed.

The problems that multiple notification can cause to the merging firms themselves – for example the cost of multiple filing, the workload involved in generating the data necessary for each filing, the delay involved in obtaining clearances from numerous jurisdictions, the differing procedural and substantive laws from one jurisdiction to another – are obvious. One of the major issues facing the 'world' of competition law – using this term both in its physical sense and to refer to the constituency of interested parties affected by merger control consisting of competition authorities, legal and business advisers, politicians, economists and the merging firms themselves – is to devise a sensible mechanism for investigating and adjudicating upon mergers having an international dimension in a way that minimises the administrative burden on businesses and competition authorities while at the same time ensuring that mergers do not escape scrutiny which could have detrimental effects upon competition[31]. These issues are under active consideration within various international fora, notably the International Competition Network ('the ICN')[32]: the subject of international cooperation has been discussed in chapter 12[33], while attempts in the EU to avoid multiple filing in the Member States by introducing the idea of the 'one-stop shop' of notifying the European Commission will be discussed in chapter 21[34].

5. Why Do Firms Merge?[35]

There are many reasons why firms merge, most of which are beneficial to, or at least not harmful to, the economy; there are others that are more problematic.

(A) Economies of scale and scope

An obvious explanation for some mergers is the achievement of economies of scale and scope[36]. A firm will produce goods at the lowest marginal cost where it is able to operate at the minimum efficient scale. If it operates on a smaller scale than this, marginal cost will increase and there will be a consequent loss of allocative efficiency. Economies of scale may be *product-specific*, where they enable a product to be produced more cheaply; *plant-specific*, where they mean that the overall use of a multi-product plant is made more rational; or *firm-specific*, where they result in lower overall costs. The globalisation of markets in recent years, as tariff and other barriers to trade have come down and as astonishingly rapid technological changes have altered the nature and structure of markets, has given opportunities to firms to grow into larger geographical markets. It may be that a firm can achieve economies of scale by internal growth; equally, however, it may be that this can most easily be achieved by external growth, that is by merging with other firms.

---

[31] See Hamner 'The Globalisation of Law: International Merger Control and competition law in the United States, the European Union, Latin America and China' (2002) 11(2) *Journal of Transnational Law and Policy* 385, accessible at www.law.fsu.edu/journals/transnational.

[32] The ICN website is www.internationalcompetitionnetwork.org.

[33] See in particular ch 12, 'The Internationalisation of Competition Law', pp 506–511.

[34] See ch 21, 'Article 21: one-stop merger control', pp 844–846.

[35] See further Scherer and Ross *Industrial Market Structure and Economic Performance* (Houghton Mifflin, 3rd ed, 1990), pp 159–167; Andrade, Mitchell and Stafford 'New Evidence and Perspectives on Mergers' (2001) 15(2) *Journal of Economic Perspectives* 103.

[36] These concepts are discussed in ch 1, 'Questioning competition itself', pp 9–15.

Whereas economies of scale arise from carrying on more of the same activity, economies of scope are the economic benefits generated from carrying on related activities; an obvious example would be lowering overall administrative expenditure through the operation of different lines of production.

Whether mergers actually lead to the achievement of the economies of scale and scope expected of them is another matter: some commentators have argued that in practice the gains anticipated tend to prove illusory[37].

(B) **Other efficiencies**

Apart from economies of scale and scope a merger may lead to efficiencies in other ways. For example it may be cheaper to take over a distributor than to set up a distribution network on a contractual basis; backward integration may guarantee supplies to a firm concerned about the availability of raw materials; a merger might mean that a firm will have improved access to loan and equity capital than it had when operating alone. A merger may result in a firm that is better able to carry out research and development and with access to a greater pool of industrial technology; quite often a merger is motivated by a desire to acquire the patents and know-how of a particular firm. Another possibility is that a merged firm may be able to make better use of the management skills of its constituent parts.

(C) **National champions**

Firms within one nation state – or within one political grouping such as the European Union – may wish to merge in order to become a 'national champion' (or a 'European champion'). Governments may positively encourage mergers that will create larger domestic firms more capable of competing on international markets, although 'national champions' free from the disciplining effect of competition on their domestic markets may lack the skills necessary to succeed in the wider world[38].

(D) **Management efficiency and the market for corporate control**

An explanation for some mergers is that one firm competes to run another. The threat of a successful takeover bid acts as an important influence upon the existing management of a firm to ensure that it functions as efficiently as possible. Where shareholders are satisfied with the current management's performance they will not sell their shares to another bidder, unless it is overbidding: the new regime would not be capable of generating greater profits than the existing one. If shareholders are dissatisfied, they may prefer to sell at the price offered and to reinvest the proceeds elsewhere; the result is likely to be that the old management will be replaced by the bidder. According to this argument the 'market for corporate control' is a crucial element in the promotion of economic

---

[37] See Scherer and Ross *Industrial Market Structure and Economic Performance* (Houghton Mifflin, 3rd ed, 1990), pp 167–174; Meeks *Disappointing Marriage: A Study of the Gains from Merger* (Cambridge University Press, 1977); see also the speech by Monti 'Review of the EC Merger Regulation—Roadmap for the Reform Project' 4 June 2002, available at www.europa.eu/competition/speeches, and the empirical studies referred to therein; Röller, Stennek and Verboven 'Efficiency Gains from Mergers', The Research Institute of Industrial Economics, Working Paper 543 (2000), available at www.ec.europa.eu/competition/speeches.

[38] The European Commission is resolutely opposed to the creation by Member States of 'national champions': see ch 21, 'Outright prohibitions', p 902; for interesting discussion of the issue see OECD Roundtable *Competition Policy, Industrial Policy and National Champions* 19 October 2009, available at www.oecd.org/competition.

efficiency[39]. It is particularly attractive if one agrees with the view that shareholders' influence over directors through the Annual General Meeting has been seriously diminished in listed companies with dispersed share ownership; at least the ability to sell to a bidder exercises some influence on the management of the company's affairs. If the threat of takeovers is considered to have this significant role, this has implications for merger policy: an interventionist approach to mergers on the part of a public authority in itself distorts the market for corporate control and thus weakens its disciplining effect on management.

(E) Exiting an industry

Mergers present firms that wish to do so with an opportunity of exiting an industry. In a free market it is important to encourage entrepreneurs to invest their money and skills in setting up new businesses and in entering new markets. Just as it is desirable to prevent the erection of barriers to entry and expansion that prevent new firms from competing on the market, so too it is necessary to avoid barriers to exit that make it difficult to leave the market. The incentive to set up a firm, invest risk capital and develop new products may be diminished if it is not possible to sell the enterprise in question as a valuable going concern. It is quite common, for example, for firms to acquire small undertakings which possess useful know-how or intellectual property rights and, from the perspective of the innovator of such technology, the freedom to sell may be an important element in the reward for the risks taken. A strict approach to mergers could have an undesirable effect if it were to make exit unduly difficult.

(F) Greed, vanity, fear and drugs

Having rehearsed some of the arguments in favour of mergers, and therefore against too strict a system of merger control, some opposing views should be mentioned. A sceptical view is that many mergers cannot be explained in the rational economic terms outlined above, but that instead they are fuelled by the speculative greed of individuals or companies or the personal vanity of a particularly swash-buckling senior executive; it will not take a great deal of imagination to think of certain high-profile entrepreneurs that might answer this description. Some mergers seem to be motivated by simple fear: if every other undertaking in a particular sector appears to be involved in mergers, it may be considered important not to be left behind in the process of industry consolidation. For some individuals 'deal-making' has the same stimulating effect as mood-changing drugs, altogether more exciting than the mundane task of managing a firm well. Even if one shares these sceptical explanations of why firms merge, however, it does not follow that merger control is the appropriate tool to deal with the 'problem'.

---

[39] See eg Manne 'Mergers and the Market for Corporate Control' (1965) 73 Journal of Political Economy 110; Easterbrook and Fischel 'The Proper Role of a Target's Management in Responding to a Tender Offer' (1981) 94 Harvard Law Review 1161; Coffee 'Regulating the Market for Corporate Control: a Critical Assessment of the Tender Offer's Role in Corporate Governance' (1984) 84 Columbia Law Review 1145; Rock 'Antitrust and the Market for Corporate Control' (1989) 77 California Law Review 1367; Bradley 'Corporate Control: Markets and Rules' (1990) 53 MLR 170; Wright, Wong and Thompson 'The Market for Corporate Control: an Economic Perspective' in Miller (ed) *The Monopolies and Mergers Yearbook* (Blackwell Business, 1992), pp 32–42.

(G) **Increasing market power**

Of course it might be that the real reason why firms wish to merge is that this will eliminate competition between them, increase their market power and give them the ability to restrict output and raise price. It would be very foolish in today's world of vigorous merger control for merging firms to make such a claim for their merger, although it is sometimes surprising what firms do say in press releases, intended to impress shareholders, as to the expected economic benefits of a merger: for example a claim that a merger will 'eliminate wasteful capacity' and return an industry to greater profitability is unlikely to charm a competition authority into submission; even less charming is a press release that announces that 'this merger will create the dominant world player in the market for widgets'[40]. Competition authorities routinely ask for copies of firms' documents (both internal and from external advisers) setting out the business rationale for a particular transaction, and these sometimes contain statements and data that are unhelpful to the prospect of unconditional clearance. The systems of merger control in place in the EU, the UK and elsewhere presumably inhibit the incidence of cases in which firms nakedly seek to achieve market power, but it is important to bear in mind that, in the absence of a system of merger control, firms would be able to do precisely this.

6. **What is the Purpose of Merger Control?**

This brings us to the central question: what is the purpose of merger control? There are many reasons why Governments, firms, shareholders, and individuals might object to mergers. A Government may object to a merger on a number of grounds: for example it might disapprove of a foreign firm taking over a native one, or of a merger that does not fit with its own industrial policy, or of a transaction that would lead to production facilities being closed down leading to unemployment. A firm might object to being the target of a hostile bid, or to a merger between two rivals that might give them a competitive edge. Shareholders (whether legal or natural persons) might be concerned that corporate transactions will have an adverse effect on the value or effectiveness of their shares. Company law is concerned with issues such as the oppression of minority shareholders, and complex regulatory systems also exist to protect shareholders generally. Reference should be made to standard works on the laws and regulations that deal with these matters; in particular in the UK the City Code on Takeovers and Mergers[41] provides an important system of protection. An individual might have qualms about foreign ownership of indigenous firms or the possibility that a takeover might lead to redundancy. These are perfectly understandable concerns, but they are not issues with which competition policy is concerned. Competition policy and competition authorities are predominantly concerned with maintaining the process of competition in the marketplace, not as an end in itself, but as a way of maximising consumer welfare[42].

Some systems of merger control do allow broader 'public interest' criteria to be taken into account in the overall assessment of a merger, a matter that will be discussed below. However for the most part competition authorities are concerned with just one issue, namely the assessment of the competitive effects of mergers.

---

[40] See ch 5, 'Evidence of managers', pp 186–187 on the probative value of statements made by an undertaking.
[41] For further information see www.takeoverpanel.org.uk.
[42] See ch 1, 'Consumer protection', pp 20ff.

(A) Is merger control necessary?

Competition law forbids the abuse of market power: Article 102 TFEU is an obvious example of this. It can reasonably be asked, therefore, why there needs to be a power to prevent the creation or strengthening of market power before it occurs ('*ex ante* control') given that there are legal controls to prevent the abuse of market power when it happens ('*ex post* control'). One answer to this is that merger control is not simply about preventing future abuses: it is also about maintaining competitive market structures which lead to better outcomes for consumers[43]. Another is that Article 102 investigations (and their domestic equivalents) are lengthy, complex and cumbersome, and that competition authorities lack the resources to police every alleged infringement; exclusive reliance on Article 102 would be unlikely to be effective. In the UK both the Office of Fair Trading ('the OFT') and the Competition Commission have attempted in recent times to evaluate the gains to consumers from merger control in specific cases and have found them to be significant[44].

(B) Assessing the competitive effects of mergers

Assessing the competitive effects of mergers is far from simple. A very helpful starting point when considering this issue is the *ICN Merger Guidelines Workbook* produced by a Subgroup of the ICN ('the *Workbook*')[45]. This was produced as a tool for countries that are new to or in the early years of merger control; however it is commended to anyone interested in the subject. In particular the *Workbook* contains a series of eight 'Worksheets' on key matters that are of importance when conducting a substantive assessment of mergers, for example market definition, market structure and concentration, unilateral and coordinated effects, and market entry and expansion; these Worksheets set out the economic principles that are relevant to each subject and provide illustrative case studies. Some of the issues dealt with in the Worksheets, such as market definition and market structure, are relevant to all competition analysis, and have been discussed in chapter 1 of this book. Others, such as unilateral and coordinated effects, are specific to merger control and are considered further below.

A complicated feature of merger control is that it is necessarily forward-looking: a competition authority is called upon to consider whether a merger will lead to harmful effects on competition in the future[46]. Most mergers must be notified to the competition authority and cleared before they are put into effect, in which case the substantive analysis is entirely forward-looking. Even in those few jurisdictions, such as the UK and Australia, where a merger can be implemented prior to approval by the competition authority, because there is no duty to pre-notify[47], the assessment is still essentially about predicting the future effects of the merger on the market. The predictive nature of merger

---

[43] On this point see Case T-102/96 *Gencor v Commission* [1999] ECR II-753, [1999] 4 CMLR 971, para 106.

[44] See ch 22, 'Evaluation of the value of the CC's actions', pp 955–956; see further Nelson and Sun Su 'Consumer Savings from Merger Enforcement: A Review of the Antitrust Agencies' Estimates' (2002) 69 Antitrust Law Journal 921.

[45] The *Workbook* is available at www.internationalcompetitionnetwork.org; see also OECD *Substantive Criteria used for Assessment of Mergers* (2003), available at www.oecd.org.

[46] See Case C-12/03 P *Commission v Tetra Laval BV* [2005] ECR I-987, [2005] 4 CMLR 573, at para 42: 'A prospective analysis of the kind necessary in merger control must be carried out with great care since it does not entail the examination of past events...or of current events, but rather a prediction of events which are more or less likely to occur in future if a decision prohibiting the planned concentration or laying down the conditions for it is not adopted.'

[47] On the voluntary nature of pre-notification in UK law see ch 22, 'OFT procedure', pp 912–914.

control is different from the assessment of agreements and conduct under Articles 101 and 102 TFEU and the Competition Act 1998, where the competition authority will usually be investigating behaviour that has already taken place and trying to verify, for example, whether and when the members of an alleged cartel met or whether the pricing practices of a dominant firm amounted to a margin squeeze.

The fact that merger control is about predicting future behaviour means, necessarily, that it must be in part theoretical: a competition authority that decides to challenge a merger must have a *theory of competitive harm* as to why the market will work less well for consumers in the future than it does at the moment. However it would not be acceptable for the authority to be able to proceed against a merger purely on the basis of theory. There is nothing unlawful about merger activity, and the market for corporate control, in which firms compete for the right to acquire and manage businesses, is an important feature of a free-market economy. Intervention on the part of public authorities should not be permissible on the basis of mere speculation. It follows that the competition authority should be required to produce *evidence* that supports its theory of competitive harm. Furthermore the competition authority should also have to demonstrate that the market, after the merger has been consummated, will be less competitive than if there had been no merger: in other words the authority will need not only to predict the likely outcome of the merger, but also to consider the *counterfactual*, that is to say the position if the merger were not to occur.

(i) Theories of competitive harm

Most mergers cause no harm to competition. However there may be cases where it can be predicted that the changed structure of the market will provide the merged entity with the incentive and the ability to exercise market power in a way that will be harmful to consumer welfare. A competition authority concerned about a particular merger will need to articulate its theory as to how competition will be harmed. Various theories of competitive harm have been developed.

(A) *Unilateral or non-coordinated effects*[48]

Unilateral effects occur where A merges with B and the merged entity, AB, will be able, as a result of the merger, to exercise market power. The most obvious manifestation of the exercise of market power is the ability to increase price, but there are other possibilities: for example a reduction of output, quality, variety or innovation. It is helpful to think of the expression 'price increase' as shorthand which includes all these different manifestations of the exercise of market power. The ability to exercise market power is particularly likely if, prior to the merger, an increase in price on the part of A would have been likely to cause a substantial number of customers to divert their purchases to B: post-merger AB would not lose any profits as a result of such a shift, since AB would benefit from the increased sales of B's products.

It may even be that, after the merger, C, a competitor of AB, will also be able to exercise market power because, if AB was to raise its prices, some customers would divert to C, which in turn could raise its own prices. C may be able to do this without coordinating its behaviour with that of AB, in which case C's behaviour can itself be characterised

---

[48] See the *Workbook*, Worksheet C; unilateral effects are sometimes referred to as non-coordinated effects, in order to differentiate them from the coordinated effects discussed in the next section.

as unilateral or non-coordinated. This is the phenomenon sometimes known as 'non-collusive oligopoly'[49].

(B) *Coordinated effects*[50]

Coordinated effects occur where A merges with B and this results in a situation where AB will be able, or more able than when A and B were independent, to coordinate their competitive behaviour on the market with other firms, for example with C and D, and thereby exercise collective market power. As the *Workbook* suggests, three conditions must be met for coordination to be successful[51]. First it must be possible for AB, C and D to coordinate their behaviour in some way, for example by charging the same prices or, perhaps, by aligning their behaviour on output and capacity expansion. Secondly, it must be costly for those firms to deviate from coordination, for example because 'cheats' will be punished. Third, AB, C and D must be free from competitive constraint from other participants in the market, for example E and F.

(C) *Vertical effects*[52]

As a general proposition it is unlikely that a merger will produce adverse vertical effects. Indeed a merger between an upstream firm, A, with a downstream firm, B, is likely to be neutral in terms of economic efficiency or even highly beneficial. For example if A and B are independent each will need to earn a margin on its operation – perhaps A as a producer and B as a distributor. The merged AB will need to earn only one margin: the elimination of 'double marginalisation' may lead to lower costs, and therefore to lower prices for the customers of AB. However there may be circumstances in which a vertical merger could produce adverse effects, first, where the possibility of foreclosure of a third party arises and, secondly, where the vertical integration of AB makes it more likely that there will be coordinated effects on the market.

An example of foreclosure could arise where A, a firm in an upstream market, acquires access through a merger with B, a firm in a downstream market, to an important downstream product, for example a distribution system such as a gas pipeline that is difficult to duplicate. The merged entity AB may have the incentive to deny competitors in the upstream market access to the distribution system, thereby foreclosing them from the downstream market. Similarly where B, a firm in a downstream market, merges with A, a firm that has substantial market power in relation to an important raw material or input in an upstream market, the merged entity AB may have the incentive to deny competitors in the downstream market access to that input. The concern here is that competitors in the downstream market will be unable to obtain supplies of the raw material or input, or that they will be able to do so only on discriminatory terms, with the result that they will be unable to compete effectively. These two examples of foreclosure can be depicted diagrammatically as follows, where the diagonal lines represent the foreclosure effect that arises from the merger of A and B:

---

[49] On the treatment of non-collusive oligopoly under the EUMR see ch 21, 'The non-collusive oligopoly gap', pp 864–866 and under UK law see ch 22, 'Unilateral effects', pp 935–936; an example of such a case in the US is *FTC v HJ Heinz Company and Milnot Corpn* 246 F 3d 708 (DC Cir 2001).

[50] See the *Workbook*, Worksheet D.   [51] Ibid, para D.6.   [52] Ibid, Worksheet H.

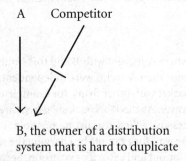

A   Competitor

B, the owner of a distribution
system that is hard to duplicate

Fig. 20.1 Foreclosure of access to a downstream distribution system

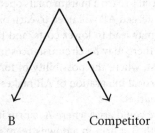

A, the owner of an important raw material or other input

B   Competitor

Fig. 20.2 Foreclosure of access to an important input

A merger of vertically-related firms might also increase the possibility of the merged entity, AB, being able to coordinate its behaviour with other competitors if, for example, it will lead to increased price transparency or if it will make it easier to detect firms that deviate from the coordinated behaviour.

In considering whether a merger could give rise to adverse vertical effects a competition authority should not only consider whether the merged entity would have the ability and the incentive to exercise market power; it should also consider carefully whether this would lead to harm to consumers, taking into account in particular the possibility that the merger may give rise to significant economic efficiencies that might be passed on to them in lower prices.

(D) *Conglomerate effects*[53]

As a general proposition conglomerate mergers are unlikely to give rise to adverse competitive effects. They do not involve the removal of actual or potential competitors from the market as in the case of horizontal mergers; nor do they bring together firms that have a vertical relationship in relation to the same final product, where there may be incentives

---

[53] Ibid, Worksheet H; see also OECD *Portfolio Effects in Conglomerate Mergers* (2002), available at www.oecd.org.

to foreclose competitors from the upstream or downstream market. Furthermore, as in the case of vertical mergers, conglomerate mergers often result in efficiency gains, for example where the merged entity AB is able to offer complementary products that do not compete with one another to a customer desiring both: if A produces widgets and B blodgets, a 'one-stop shop' may be highly beneficial to a customer that requires both products. The theory of harm in the case of conglomerate effects is particularly speculative – for example that AB might decide to 'tie' the two complementary products together in a way that will foreclose competitors, or to price a bundled package of both of them to similar effect. It is possible that tie-in transactions and bundling practices would violate laws that forbid the abuse of a dominant position or, in the case of US law, monopolization, although the law on this subject is controversial in itself[54]. It is even more controversial that a merger should be prohibited on this ground, and the US authorities do not normally challenge mergers on this basis. Intervention on conglomerate grounds is a possibility in EU and UK law, but would require very convincing evidence in support of the theory of harm[55].

(ii) Evidence

Having identified a theory (or theories) of competitive harm, a competition authority must then search for evidence in support of that theory: its case must be based on empirical facts. The ICN produced, in 2005, a helpful *Investigative Techniques Handbook*[56], chapter 3 of which identifies five types of evidence that may be of use in merger reviews: evidence that was produced before the merger was contemplated, such as corporate strategy documents, planning documents and sales reports; documents produced for the purpose of the merger, such as surveys, reports and economic analyses; descriptive evidence from participants in the market, such as customers, suppliers and competitors; written responses to requests for information from the competition authority; and expert and quantitative evidence, for example from industry experts and economists. Chapter 4 of the *Investigative Techniques Handbook* discusses various types of quantitative analyses, such as the measurement of critical loss[57] and price correlations, that may be helpful when predicting whether a merger might lead to anti-competitive effects. The Worksheets already referred to in the ICN's *Merger Guidelines Workbook* also provide summaries of evidence of value when assessing, for example, whether a merger might lead to adverse unilateral[58] or coordinated[59] effects[60].

An emerging development, in unilateral effects cases, is the use of so-called 'merger simulation models' which attempt to predict, using a set of quantitative techniques, the effect that a merger will have on the post-merger level of prices[61]. If such an exercise could produce entirely reliable evidence the traditional analysis of defining the relevant market, assessing market power and then considering unilateral effects could be considerably abbreviated, perhaps with no need for market definition at all. However the science of

---

[54] See ch 17, 'Tying', pp 688–696 and ch 18, 'Bundling', pp 737–739.

[55] On the position under the EUMR see ch 21, 'Recent cases on non-horizontal mergers', pp 879–880 and under UK law see ch 22, 'Non-horizontal mergers', pp 937–938.

[56] The *Handbook* is available at www.internationalcompetitionnetwork.org.

[57] See also Langenfeld and Li 'Critical loss analysis in evaluating mergers' (2001) 46 Antitrust Bulletin 299.

[58] See Worksheet C – *Unilateral Effects*, para C.10.

[59] See Worksheet D – *Coordinated Effects*, paras D.9–D.16.

[60] See also the OECD Roundtable *Managing Complex Mergers*, 29 October 2008, available at www.oecd.org.

[61] A well-known case in the US in which merger simulation was used is the *Staples/Office Depot* case, *FTC v Staples Inc* 970 F Supp 1066, District of Columbia, as to which see Baker 'Econometric Analysis in FTC v Staples' (1999) 18 Journal of Public Policy & Marketing 11.

merger simulation is not yet sufficiently robust for this, and the technique, at most, can form only part of the overall body of evidence in a particular case[62].

The Court of Justice has made clear that, where a merger is challenged on conglomerate grounds, the evidence on which the Commission relies must be particularly convincing, given that the chains of cause and effect between the merger and the predicted adverse effects 'are dimly discernible, uncertain and difficult to establish'[63].

An important issue in relation to evidence is to decide what standard of proof a competition authority should have to attain before it can take action to block or require the modification of a merger: should it have to prove its case that a merger would be harmful to competition 'on the balance of probabilities', or should it have to go further and show 'beyond reasonable doubt' that the merger would have detrimental effects? If a competition authority can intervene too easily, on the basis of weak evidence, the possibility exists that 'false positives' might arise: that is to say that some innocuous mergers might be blocked; however, if the criteria for intervention are too demanding, or if the standard of proof is set at a very high level, 'false negatives' might occur: some harmful mergers might be cleared[64]. Being realistic, it is inevitable that some errors of both kinds will be made by competition authorities: it is a matter of public policy to decide which of the two types of error is the more troubling.

(iii) The counterfactual

Merger assessment involves predicting the effect on competition in the market if a particular transaction is consummated. This necessarily involves a comparison between the situation if the merger goes ahead and the position if it did not happen: the competitive situation without the merger is often referred to as the counterfactual[65]. The counterfactual will usually be the prevailing conditions before the merger, although there may be cases in which it is necessary to take into account conditions as they would be in the near future if, for example, it is known that other firms are about to enter or exit the market or to expand capacity; another example would be that one of the merging firms was on the point of failing, so that it would not be present on the market in the future anyway. The Competition Commission in the UK explicitly states the counterfactual in each of its merger inquiry reports[66].

(C) The substantive test: SLC, dominance, SIEC

Any system of merger control must set a substantive test against which to determine whether a particular merger should be modified or prohibited. When the EUMR was in

---

[62] On merger simulation see Werden and Froeb 'Simulation as an Alternative to Structural Policy in Differentiated Products Industries' in *The Economics of the Antitrust Process* (Kluwer, 1996, eds Coate and Kleit); Epstein and Rubinfeld 'Merger Simulation: A Simplified Approach with New Applications' (2002) 69 Antitrust Law Journal 883; Werden, Froeb and Scheffman 'A Daulbert Discipline for Merger Simulation' February 2004, available at www.ftc.gov/be/daubertdiscipline.pdf; Walker 'The Potential for Significant Inaccuracies in Merger Simulation Models' (2005) 1 Journal of Competition Law and Economics 473.

[63] Case C-12/03 P *Commission v Tetra Laval BV* [2005] ECR I-987, [2005] 4 CMLR 573, para 44.

[64] These phenomena are also referred to as Type I and Type II errors: see Black *Oxford Dictionary of Economics* (Oxford University Press, 3rd ed, 2003), and ch 5, 'False positives and false negatives', pp 193–194.

[65] See the *Workbook*, paras 2.9 and 2.10.

[66] See eg *Deutsche Börse AG, Euronext NV and London Stock Exchange plc*, paras 5.125–5.130, available at www.competition-commission.org.uk/rep_pub/reports/2005.

the process of being reformed in the years leading up to 2004 there was an interesting and important debate as to the most appropriate formulation[67]. Many systems, such as the US and the UK, permit the prohibition of a merger which will 'substantially lessen competition' ('SLC')[68]; the original Merger Regulation of 1989 required intervention where a merger would 'create or strengthen a dominant position as a result of which effective competition would be significantly impeded'[69]. Many Member States of the EU use the same formulation; some, for example France and Greece, have both substantial lessening of competition and dominance tests. The test in the EUMR was changed in 2004: the question now to be asked is whether the merger would 'significantly impede effective competition' ('SIEC'), in particular (but not exclusively) as a result of the creation or strengthening of a dominant position[70].

(D) **Guidelines**

There are abundant guidelines on the substantive assessment of mergers. Reference has already been made to the ICN's *Merger Guidelines Workbook* and *Investigative Techniques Handbook*[71]. Many competition authorities have also published guidelines on substantive assessment. Of particular importance are the 2010 *Horizontal Merger Guidelines* in the US[72] and the joint guidelines of the OFT and Competition Commission in the UK[73]. The European Commission has published *Guidelines on the assessment of horizontal mergers*[74] and *Guidelines on the assessment of non-horizontal mergers*[75]. Guidelines must strike an appropriate balance between providing guidance for firms and their advisers as to what might be expected of a system of merger control and avoiding too much speculation, which can lead to a loss of certainty.

A specific problem in systems of merger control is whether a merger which reduces competition but which would lead to gains in efficiency should be permitted: the US Guidelines address this issue specifically in paragraph 4 and do, in very limited circumstances, recognise efficiency arguments[76]. In the UK section 30 of the Enterprise Act 2002 allows the OFT and the Competition Commission to take into account 'relevant customer benefits'

---

[67] See eg OECD Roundtables *Substantive Criteria used for the Assessment of Mergers* 11 February 2003, and *Standard of Merger Review*, 10 May 2010, available at www.oecd.org; the European Commission's *Green Paper on the Review of Council Regulation (EEC) No 4064/89* COM(2001) 745/6 final, paras 159–169.

[68] See, eg, s 7 Clayton Act 1914 in the US; s 50 Trade Practices Act 1974 in Australia; s 92 Competition Act 1985 in Canada; s 12A Competition Act 1998 in South Africa.

[69] EUMR, Articles 2(2) and 2(3).

[70] For further discussion of this issue see ch 21, 'Adoption of the "significant impediment to effective competition" test', pp 863–867.

[71] The ICN has also published 'Recommended Practices' on matters such as remedies, notifications and merger procedures; these are all available at www.internationalcompetitionnetwork.org.

[72] These are available at www.justice.gov.atr/public/guidelines, on which see Shaprio 'The 2010 Horizontal Merger Guidelines: From Hedgehog to Fox in Forty Years' (2010) 77 Antitrust Law Journal 701.

[73] *Merger Assessment Guidelines*, CC2 (revised) and OFT 1254, September 2010, available at www.oft.gov.uk.

[74] OJ [2004] C 31/5.   [75] OJ [2008] C 265/6.

[76] The complexity of allowing efficiencies as a defence in a merger case is vividly illustrated by the *Superior Propane* case in Canada: see *The Commissioner of Competition v Superior Propane Inc* [2003] 3 FC 529, judgment of 31 January 2003 (Federal Court of Appeal), available at www.fca-caf.gc.ca/index_e.shtml; see also the European Commission's (2003) (Summer) *Competition Policy Newsletter* 43–49; Williamson 'Economies as an Antitrust Defense: The Welfare Trade-off' (1968) 58 American Economic Review 158; Kolasky and Dick 'The Merger Guidelines and the Integration of Efficiencies into Antitrust Review of Horizontal Mergers' (2003) 71 Antitrust Law Journal 207; Gerard 'Merger Control Policy: How to Give Meaningful Consideration to Efficiency Claims?' (2003) 40 CML Rev 1367.

in certain circumstances[77]; while the European Commission's *Horizontal Guidelines* take efficiencies into account within the overall assessment of a merger[78]. Another issue that sometimes arises is whether a merger should be allowed in order to save a 'failing firm', even though there will be less competition in the market after the merger than before. A failing firm defence does exist in US law[79], has been applied under the EUMR[80] and is recognised in an appropriate case under the guidelines of the UK competition authorities[81].

(E) Remedies

It is quite often the case that most aspects of a particular merger give rise to no competition concerns. However it may be, for example, that there are certain parts of the businesses of A and B that overlap horizontally, in which case a competition authority, rather than prohibiting the entire transaction, may look for a remedy whereby its competition concern is assuaged and the rest of the deal is allowed to proceed. The most obvious remedy is the divestiture of one or other of the overlapping businesses so that there will be no accretion of market power. Some cases may require more complex remedies, for example a right of access to an essential facility or the licensing of technology to competitors on reasonable and non-discriminatory terms. Devising and implementing satisfactory remedies is often a complex matter. The OECD published *Merger Remedies* in 2004 following roundtable discussions in which a number of recommendations as to best practice were made[82]. In 2005 the ICN published a *Merger Remedies Review Project*[83] that provides a practical guide as to the key principles and range of tools available in the establishment of suitable remedies. In 2005 the European Commission published a *Merger Remedies Study*[84] in which it reviewed the effectiveness of 96 remedies accepted in 40 cases in the five-year period from 1996 to 2000. This *Study* had an important bearing on the Commission's revised *Notice on remedies acceptable under the EUMR*[85] of 2007. In the UK the OFT and the Competition Commission have given careful attention to remedies when deciding cases under the Enterprise Act 2002, and conduct a rolling programme for the review of the success of past remedies[86].

(F) Merger control and the public interest[87]

As noted at the start of this chapter, numerous arguments may be made against mergers that have nothing to do with the maintenance of competitive markets. It would be possible to devise a system of merger control that allows intervention for non-competition reasons;

---

[77] See ch 22, 'Efficiencies', p 939; note in particular *Merger Assessment Guidelines*, CC2 (revised) and OFT 1254, September 2010, section 5.7.

[78] See the *Horizontal Guidelines*, paras 76–88; see further ch 21, 'Efficiencies', pp 874–876.

[79] See the *Horizontal Merger Guidelines*, section 11.

[80] See ch 21, 'The "failing firm" defence', p 876 and the Commission's *Horizontal Merger Guidelines*, paras 76–88.

[81] *Merger Assessment Guidelines*, CC2 (revised) and OFT 1254, September 2010, paras 4.3.8–4.3.18 (using the expression 'exiting firm scenario').

[82] Available at www.oecd.org.   [83] Available at www.internationalcompetitionnetwork.org.

[84] Available at www.ec.europa.eu/competition/index_en.html.

[85] See ch 21, 'Remedies', pp 884–890.

[86] OJ [2008] C 267/1; see ch 22, 'Undertakings in lieu of a reference', pp 927–928 and ' "Final powers" or "remedies" ', pp 944–948.

[87] For useful discussion of mergers and the public interest see Chiplin and Wright *The Logic of Mergers* (Hobart Paper 107, 1987); Fairburn and Kay (eds) *Mergers and Mergers Policy* (Oxford University Press, 1989); *Merger & Competition Policy in the European Community* (Blackwell, 1990, ed Jacquemain); Neven, Nuttall and Seabright *Mergers in Daylight: The Economics and Politics of European Merger Control* (CEPR, 1993); Lewis 'The Political Economy of Antitrust' [2001] Fordham Corporate Law Institute, ed Hawk, pp 617ff; Bishop and

in so far as it does so the law in question can hardly be called 'competition' law; indeed prohibiting mergers on social grounds or for reasons of industrial policy may be directly antagonistic to the process of competition. Some of the arguments sometimes heard are listed below.

(i) Loss of efficiency and 'short-termism'

Some commentators would argue that mergers, far from promoting economic efficiency, have a disruptive effect upon the management of one or both of the merged firms and may be detrimental to their long-term prospects. This claim is made in particular of contested takeover bids, where it is possible that the management of the target company will either be removed by the new shareholders or will resign rather than stay on in the new conditions. Sceptics of the way in which the market for corporate control functions would argue that it is not inevitable that the decisions of shareholders will produce the best result in the public interest, although it may yield the best financial deal for the shareholders themselves. In particular many would argue that a problem with takeovers is that they are motivated more by short-term profit-taking on the stock exchange than by serious analysis of the long-term prospects of companies. This may be particularly true of institutional investors in the market which are in the habit of regularly turning over their investments in pursuit of short-term gains.

(ii) Concentration of wealth

Mergers may be objected to on the ground that they lead to firms of such size and with such power as to be antithetical to a balanced distribution of wealth. This of course is a socio-political argument, but one which has become more widely accepted as aggregate industrial concentration has increased. In the US the merger control provisions laws were strengthened at a time when this problem was a dominant concern[88].

(iii) Unemployment and regional policy

Another objection to mergers is that they may lead to the closure of factories and result in serious unemployment. Mergers that savour of 'asset-stripping' and which appear to have no regard for the social problems that may follow attract particular opprobrium from sceptics of the free market. Opposition to acquisitions by private equity funds in the course of 2007 was partly inspired by this concern. Similarly the market operating in its unfettered form may not attach much weight to the desirability of maintaining a balanced distribution of wealth and job opportunities; the market has no reason to be sentimental about such matters. Governments can choose to adopt a regional policy, however, and it is possible to give expression to this issue in mergers policy as well as in laws on tax, planning and state aids.

(iv) Overseas control

Mergers may result in the control of indigenous firms passing to overseas companies, in which case any economic advantages of the merger may be thought to be outweighed by the desirability of maintaining the decision-making process and profits at home. Strong opposition was expressed in the US in 2006 when the possibility of sea ports there coming under the control of Dubai Ports became known. Many UK firms have expanded

Walker *The Economics of EC Competition Law* (Sweet & Maxwell, 3rd ed, 2010), chs 7 and 8; speech by Lewis at the sixth Annual ICN Conference in Moscow, 2006 available at www.internationalcompetitionnetwork.org.

[88] See eg *Brown Shoe Co v United States* 370 US 294, 344 (1962).

abroad, in particular into the US, and this makes it somewhat difficult to argue that UK firms should themselves be shielded from hostile foreign takeover bids. However the case for intervention may be more compelling where there is a lack of reciprocity[89] between the laws of the two countries: if the law of country A *prevents* inward invest- ment, whereas country B permits it, there may be a case for blocking a takeover by a firm from A of a firm in B.

(v) Special sectors

Some sectors of the economy – for example the electronic and print media – are espe- cially sensitive and this may mean that concentration of ownership within them requires special consideration. In the UK, as in several other countries, media mergers are sub- ject to special provisions[90] and mergers in industries such as oil, banking[91] and defence may be particularly closely scrutinised; the UK also has a special regime for mergers in the water industry[92] and the Communications Act 2003 contains special provisions on change of control[93]. Article 21(4) of the EUMR specifically recognises that Member States may have a 'legitimate interest' in investigating a merger other than on grounds of harm to competition[94].

7. Designing a System of Merger Control

Where a country decides, as a matter of policy, to adopt a system of merger control, a number of issues have to be addressed. In chapters 21 and 22 the EU and UK systems will be described; most cases would probably result in the same outcome, irrespective of which of these two laws is applied: the dominant consideration in each jurisdiction is the impact of a merger on competition, and the analysis will be conducted in much the same way in each of them. Despite this, however, it will be seen that the provisions them- selves – for example on jurisdiction, notification and substantive analysis – are actually quite different.

The following are some of the issues that must be confronted in designing a system of merger control.

- Which transactions should be characterised as mergers? How should the acquisition of minority shareholdings and of assets be dealt with? Will joint ventures be consid- ered as a matter of merger control or under the legal provisions that prohibit cartels and other anti-competitive agreements?

- How should the jurisdictional test be framed for determining those mergers that can be investigated? Should the test be based on turnover, the value of assets acquired, market share or some other criterion?

- To what extent should a system of merger control apply to transactions consum- mated outside a country but which have effects within it?

- Should mergers be subject to a system of mandatory pre-notification, or should it be a matter for the parties to decide whether to notify? In the latter case, in what

---

[89] Or, to put the matter more colloquially, where the 'playing fields' are not even.
[90] See ch 22, 'Public interest cases', pp 956–961.
[91] See the discussion of the *Lloyds TSB/HBOS* merger in ch 22, 'Public interest cases', pp 956–961.
[92] See ch 22, 'Mergers in the water industry', pp 960–961.
[93] Communications Act 2003, ss 351–354.
[94] See ch 21, 'Article 21(4): legitimate interest clause', pp 851–854.

circumstances and for how long after a merger has been completed should a competition authority be allowed to review a case?

- What should be the time period within which a merger investigation must be completed?

- What should be the substantive test for reviewing mergers? Should it be based solely on competition criteria, or should any or all of the other issues discussed above (for example unemployment, regional policy and overseas control) also be taken into account?

- How should the specific issues of (a) efficiency and (b) failing firms be dealt with?

- What mechanism should be put in place for the negotiation of remedies that would overcome any problems identified by the competition authority?

- Who should make decisions in merger cases? A Commission, in which case who should appoint the Commissioners? A court? A Minister in the Government?

- What checks and balances should there be to guarantee due process within merger control? What system of judicial review or appeals should be put in place to test the findings of the decision-maker in merger cases? How quickly will any judicial review or appeal be completed?

These are just some of the many interesting and important issues that arise in relation to the control of mergers. With these preliminary observations in mind, this book will now describe the systems in force in the EU and UK.

21

Mergers (2) – EU law[1]

1. Introduction

The EU rules on the control of mergers or, to use an alternative term often used in the parlance of EU law, 'concentrations', are contained in the EU Merger Regulation, Regulation 139/2004[2] ('the EUMR'). The terms 'merger' and 'concentration' are used interchangeably throughout this chapter. The EUMR has been applicable since 1 May 2004; prior to that date Regulation 4064/89[3] had been in effect since 21 September 1990. Regulation 139/2004 amended the rules of merger control in a number of respects, in particular by making the allocation of jurisdiction as between Member States and the European Commission more flexible and by amending the substantive test for the analysis of mergers. Section 2 of this chapter provides an overview of EU merger control. Section 3 sets out the jurisdictional rules which determine whether a particular merger should be investigated by the European Commission in Brussels or by the national competition authorities ('the NCAs') of the Member States. Section 4 deals with a number of procedural matters such as the mandatory pre-notification to the Commission of mergers that have a Community dimension and

---

[1] For further reading on the EU Merger Regulation readers are referred to Levy *European Merger Control Law: A Guide to the Merger Regulation* (LexisNexis, 2003); Navarro, Font, Folguera and Briones *Merger Control in the EU* (Oxford University Press, 2nd ed, 2005); Lindsay *The EC Merger Regulation: Substantive Issues* (Sweet & Maxwell, 3rd ed, 2009); Faull and Nikpay *The EC Law of Competition* (Oxford University Press, 2nd ed, 2007), ch 5; Bellamy and Child *European Community Law of Competition* (Oxford University Press, 6th ed, 2008, eds Roth and Rose), ch 8; Cook and Kerse *EC Merger Control* (Sweet & Maxwell, 5th ed, 2009); Schwalbe and Zimmer *Law and Economics in European Merger Control* (Oxford University Press, 2009); as to mergers under the EEA Agreement see ch 2, 'European Economic Area', pp 57–58 and Broberg *The European Commission's Jurisdiction to Scrutinise Mergers* (Kluwer International, 3rd ed, 2006), ch 7; on international merger control see *Merger Control: The International Regulation of Mergers and Joint Ventures in 65 Jurisdictions Worldwide* (GCR, 2011, ed Davies).

[2] OJ [2004] L 24/1.

[3] OJ [1989] L 395/1; Regulation 4064/89 was repealed by Article 25 of Regulation 139/2004. Note that the TFEU does not contain any specific provisions on merger control, and that the legal basis for the EUMR is Article 103 and Article 353 TFEU. Mergers in the coal and steel sectors that would once have been investigated under Article 66(7) of the ECSC Treaty are now dealt with under the EUMR.

the procedural timetable within which the Commission must operate. Section 5 discusses the substantive analysis of mergers under the EUMR and section 6 explains the procedure whereby the Commission may authorise a merger on the basis of commitments, often referred to as remedies, offered by the parties to address its competition concerns. The chapter then contains sections on the Commission's powers of investigation and enforcement, on judicial review of Commission decisions by the EU Courts and on international cooperation, both within the EU and with the competition authorities in third countries. Section 10 considers how the merger control provisions work in practice.

2. Overview of EU Merger Control

(A) Brief description of the EU system of merger control

The Commission first proposed a merger control regulation as early as 1973[4]. The issue was controversial as opinions differed substantially between Member States on the extent to which mergers should be controlled at the EU level as opposed to domestically. It was not until 21 December 1989 that the Council of Ministers adopted Regulation 4064/1989; it entered into force on 21 September 1990. Regulation 4064/1989 was amended quite significantly by Regulation 1310/97[5], and was repealed and replaced by the current EUMR in 2004[6].

In essence the EU system of merger control is as follows. Mergers that have a Community dimension must be pre-notified to the Commission; it is an offence to consummate a merger without a prior clearance from the Commission (there are some minor exceptions to this proposition). Whether or not a merger has a Community dimension is determined by reference to the turnover of the undertakings concerned in a transaction. Where a merger has a Community dimension the Commission has sole jurisdiction in relation to it: this is the principle of 'one-stop merger control'. However there are some circumstances in which the Commission might allow jurisdiction (wholly or in part) over a merger having a Community dimension to be ceded to one or more Member States; and in certain situations it is obliged to do this. There are also some circumstances in which Member States may transfer jurisdiction to the Commission over mergers that do not have a Community dimension. Once the Commission has jurisdiction it is required, within fixed time limits, to determine whether a merger could significantly impede effective competition in the common market or a substantial part of it; in conducting this assessment the Commission asks, in particular, whether the merger could create or strengthen a dominant position. Most cases are completed within 25 working days of the notification, known as a Phase I investigation. In approximately 3 per cent of cases the Commission finds, at the end of its Phase I investigation, that it has serious doubts as to the compatibility of the merger with the common market and so it proceeds to an in-depth Phase II investigation; this may take an additional 90 working days, and there are provisions for this period to be extended for up to an additional 35 working days.

---

[4] *Commission Proposal for a Regulation of the Council of Ministers on the Control of Concentrations between Undertakings* OJ [1973] C 92/1; for successive drafts see OJ [1982] C 36/3; OJ [1984] C 51/8; OJ [1986] C 324/5; OJ [1988] C 130/4.

[5] OJ [1997] L 180/1.

[6] For discussion of the changes introduced by Regulation 139/2004 see González Diaz 'The Reform of European Merger Control: *Quid Novi Sub Sole*?' (2004) 27(2) World Competition 177.

The Commission has wide-ranging powers under the EUMR, including the power to prohibit a merger in its entirety. This is rare – there have been only 21 prohibitions in the entire lifetime of EU merger control, four of which were overturned by the General Court on appeal[7]. However there have been numerous occasions on which the Commission has authorised a merger only after the parties had offered commitments to remedy its competition concerns: this has happened in roughly 5 per cent of cases. When the parties offer commitments in this way they become legally binding upon them[8]. The Commission works closely both with the NCAs of the Member States and with competition authorities in other jurisdictions – for example the US, Canada and Japan – when exercising its powers under the EUMR[9].

(B) Institutional arrangements

The full College of Commissioners takes the most important decisions under the EUMR, for example to prohibit a merger or to clear it subject to commitments at the end of a Phase II investigation. The fact that the full Commission is sometimes involved in decisions of considerable economic and political importance means that there may be a degree of lobbying of individual Commissioners, not just of the Commissioner for competition[10].

Some powers are delegated by the Commission to the Commissioner for competition. For example decisions at the end of a Phase I investigation can be taken by the Commissioner for competition, who in turn may delegate certain functions to the Director General of the Directorate General for Competition ('DG COMP'). Within DG COMP there is a Deputy Director General with special responsibility for mergers. Unit 2 of Directorate A of DG COMP deals with policy and scrutiny in relation to mergers and antitrust. Case work is handled by merger units within Directorates B to F, each of which has specific sectoral responsibilities[11]. DG COMP has a Chief Competition Economist who reports directly to the Director General to provide independent economic advice on cases and policy[12]. The Commission also has two Hearing Officers with a range of functions including overseeing the fairness of the Commission's proceedings and arranging and conducting oral hearings[13].

The Advisory Committee on Concentrations[14] has an important role in EU merger control: it provides the Member States with the opportunity of input into the decision-making process. Appeals against decisions of the Commission are taken to the General Court[15]. Provision has been made for appeals to the General Court in merger cases to be handled under the so-called 'expedited procedure' where appropriate[16].

---

[7] See 'Comment', pp 902–906 below.

[8] On commitments, or 'remedies' as they are often referred to, see 'Remedies', pp 884–890 below.

[9] See 'International Cooperation', pp 897–898 below.

[10] See Marsden 'Lobbying for climate change in EU Competition Policy–just don't talk about the weather' 2009 (1) Concurrences 11; McLeod 'Brussels' hamstrung press corp and the dumbing down of news' 2009 (1) Concurrences 18.

[11] See ch 2, 'European Commission', pp 53–54.

[12] On the Chief Competition Economist see further www.ec.europa.eu/dgs/competition/economist/role_en.html.

[13] On the Hearing Officers see further www.ec.europa.eu/competition/hearing_officers/index_en.html.

[14] See 'International Cooperation', pp 897–898 below.

[15] Prior to the Nice Treaty applications by a Member State were made to the Court of Justice, as in Cases C-68/94 etc *France v Commission* [1998] ECR I-1375, [1998] 4 CMLR 829.

[16] On judicial review under the EUMR and the expedited procedure see 'Judicial Review', pp 891–897 below.

(C) The Implementing Regulation and the Commission's Notices and Guidelines

In addition to the EUMR anyone interested in EU merger control will require a number of other texts, in particular the Implementing Regulation and a series of Commission Notices and Guidelines, including the Guidelines on Best Practices. The General Court has stated that the Commission is bound by the notices it issues in the area of the supervision of mergers, provided that they do not depart from the rules in the Treaty or from the EUMR[17]; however the Commission retains 'great freedom of action' where a notice allows it to choose the types of evidence or the economic approach most appropriate to a particular case[18]. All of the materials set out below can be accessed on DG COMP's website[19]; the Commission has also published a helpful compendium of materials, *EU Competition Law: Rules Applicable to Merger Control*, available electronically on the same website.

(i) The Implementing Regulation

The Implementing Regulation, Regulation 802/2004 (which replaced earlier legislation), contains rules on notifications to the Commission, time limits, the right to be heard and hearings, access to the file and the treatment of confidential information and remedies[20]. Regulation 802/2004 has been amended[21] in order to provide the format for Form RM, a form that has to be used when undertakings offer commitments to the Commission in order to remedy competition concerns that it may have identified[22].

(ii) Commission Notices and Guidelines

The Commission has published numerous Notices and Guidelines on matters both of procedural and substantive concern, each of which will be referred to where appropriate in the text that follows:

- *Notice on the definition of the relevant market*[23]
- *Guidelines on the assessment of horizontal mergers*[24]
- *Notice on a simplified procedure for treatment of certain concentrations*[25]
- *Notice on restrictions directly related and necessary to concentrations*[26]
- *Notice on Case Referral in respect of concentrations*[27]
- *Notice on access to the file*[28]
- *Consolidated Jurisdictional Notice*[29]
- *Guidelines on the assessment of non-horizontal mergers*[30]
- *Notice on remedies acceptable under the EUMR*[31].

---

[17] See Case T-282/06 *Sun Chemical Group BV v Commission* [2007] ECR II-2149, [2007] 5 CMLR 483, para 55 and the judgments referred to therein.

[18] See Case T-210/01 *General Electric v Commission* [2005] ECR II-5575, [2006] 4 CMLR 686, para 519.

[19] See www.ec.europa.eu/competition/index_en.html.   [20] OJ [2004] L 133/1.

[21] See Commission Regulation 1033/2008, OJ [2008] L 279/3.

[22] See 'Remedies', pp 884–896 below.   [23] OJ [1997] C 372/5.   [24] OJ [2004] C 31/5.

[25] OJ [2005] C 56/32.   [26] OJ [2005] C 56/24.   [27] OJ [2005] C 56/2.

[28] OJ [2005] C 325/7.

[29] OJ [2008] C 95/1; this Notice replaces four previous Notices adopted by the Commission in 1998 dealing with each of full-function joint ventures (OJ [1998] C 66/1), the concept of a concentration (OJ [1998] C 66/5), undertakings concerned (OJ [1998] C 66/14) and the calculation of turnover (OJ [1998] C 66/25).

[30] OJ [2008] C 265/6.   [31] OJ [2008] C 267/1.

(iii) Best Practice Guidelines

The Commission has also published Guidelines setting out 'Best Practices' on various aspects of merger control:

- *DG Competition Best Practices on the conduct of EC merger control proceedings*
- *Best Practice Guidelines: the Commission's model texts for divestiture commitments and the trustee mandate*
- *Market Share Ranges in Non-confidential Versions of Merger Decisions*
- *Best practices for the submission of economic evidence and data collection concerning the application of Articles 101 and 102 TFEU and in merger cases.*

(D) **Access to the Commission's decisions**

DG COMP's website is an important source of material about the operation of the EUMR. As well as the legislation and guidance just referred to, the website also carries a large amount of information about both completed cases and current investigations; these can be searched for by reference to the case number, a company's name, decision type or by industry sector. The website also contains interesting statistical information, regularly updated, about the EUMR in practice (for example the number of notifications each year and the number of conditional clearances or prohibitions) and useful studies and reports on matters such as unilateral effects, tacit coordination and the impact of vertical and conglomerate mergers on competition[32].

Each notification received by the Commission is given a case number, which will be prefixed with an 'M' (as in Case M 4600 *TUI/First Choice*). The practice of giving full-function joint ventures a prefix of 'JV' was abandoned in 2002; cases that occurred under the now-expired European Coal and Steel Community Treaty were prefixed 'ECSC'. When a merger is notified a summary of it will appear on DG COMP's website and a provisional deadline for the decision will be given; the website is updated as the investigation progresses.

The Commission's decisions can be accessed in various ways. A press release summarising the Commission's finding in cases other than those for which the simplified procedure is available[33] will usually be published in English, French, German and in the language of the notification. The press release is normally issued at noon on the day following adoption of the decision. It can be obtained on the Rapid database of the Commission's website[34]. Phase I decisions – that is to say cases that do not require 'in-depth' investigation – are not themselves published in the Official Journal, other than a brief statement of the outcome. Phase I decisions are published on DG COMP's website, but only in the language in which the parties notified. Decisions following an in-depth, Phase II investigation are more widely available. Summaries of Phase II decisions are published in the Official Journal together with the final report of the Hearing Officer and the opinion of the Advisory Committee on Concentrations. The non-confidential version of the full decisions are published on the Commission's website; there may be a lengthy delay between the adoption of a decision and its appearance on the website while

---

[32] See www.ec.europa.eu/competition/mergers/studies_reports/studies_reports.html.
[33] On this procedure see 'Notifications', p 857 below.
[34] The website of the Rapid database is www.europa.eu/rapid.

agreement is reached between the parties and the Commission as to what confidential information should be omitted from the published version.

3. Jurisdiction

This section will deal with the following matters:

(A) **Article 3: meaning of a concentration:** the EUMR applies to mergers or, more precisely, to 'concentrations', a term defined in Article 3 and further explained in the case law of the EU Courts and in the Commission's *Consolidated Jurisdictional Notice*[35] ('the *Jurisdictional Notice*').

(B) **Articles 1 and 5: concentrations having a Community dimension:** the EUMR applies to concentrations that have a 'Community dimension'. The meaning of this term is found in Article 1, and is further explained in the *Jurisdictional Notice*. It is determined by reference to the turnover of the 'undertakings concerned', including their affiliated undertakings as set out in Article 5.

(C) **One-stop merger control:** as a general proposition concentrations that have a Community dimension should be investigated only by the Commission and not by the Member States; this is the principle of 'one-stop merger control'.

(D) **Article 4(4) and Article 9: referral of concentrations having a Community dimension to the competent authorities of the Member States:** in certain cases Article 4(4) and Article 9 provide a mechanism whereby concentrations that have a Community dimension can be reviewed by the competent authorities of the Member States, either because the undertakings concerned or a Member State make a request to that effect. The Commission's *Notice on Case Referral in respect of concentrations* ('the *Case Referral Notice*') provides important guidance on this topic.

(E) **Article 4(5) and Article 22: referral of concentrations not having a Community dimension by Member States to the Commission:** in certain cases Article 4(5) and Article 22 provide a mechanism whereby concentrations that do not have a Community dimension can be investigated by the Commission, either because the undertakings concerned or a Member State make a request to that effect. Again the *Case Referral Notice* provides important guidance.

(F) **Article 21(4): legitimate interest clause:** Member States are not allowed to apply their domestic competition law to concentrations that have a Community dimension except in the circumstances in which Article 4(4) or Article 9 are applicable. However provision is made by Article 21(4) for Member States to investigate a concentration having a Community dimension where it threatens to harm some 'legitimate interest' of the State other than the maintenance of competition.

(G) **Defence:** Member States retain jurisdiction to examine the national security aspects of mergers as a result of Article 346 TFEU.

Each of these propositions will be examined in turn.

---

[35] For an overview of the *Jurisdictional Notice* see Lübking 'Commission adopts Jurisdictional Notice under the Merger Regulation' (2007) 3 *Competition Policy Newsletter* 1.

(A) Article 3: meaning of a concentration

Part B of the *Jurisdictional Notice* deals with the meaning of a concentration. The foot-notes in the *Jurisdictional Notice* contain many references to the decisional practice of the Commission and the judgments of the EU Courts, and the reader should be aware of these useful reference points. Article 3(1) of the EUMR provides that:

> A concentration shall be deemed to arise where a change of control on a lasting basis results from:
>
> (a) the merger of two or more previously independent undertakings or parts of under-takings, or
>
> (b) the acquisition, by one or more persons already controlling at least one undertak-ing, or by one or more undertakings, whether by purchase of securities or assets, by contract or by any other means, of direct or indirect control of the whole or parts of one or more other undertakings.

(i) Article 3(1)(a): mergers

Mergers in the sense of Article 3(1)(a) are dealt with in paragraphs 9 and 10 of the *Jurisdictional Notice*, which provides examples of cases covered by it such as *AstraZeneca/ Novartis*[36] and *Chevron/Texaco*[37]. Paragraph 10 explains that there can be factual ('*de facto*') mergers where, in the absence of a legal merger, activities of previously inde-pendent entities are combined with the result that a single economic unit is created under a permanent, single economic management; examples given are *Price Waterhouse/ Coopers&Lybrand*[38] and *Ernst & Young/Andersen Germany*[39].

(ii) Article 3(1)(b): acquisition of control

In practice most cases are concerned with the acquisition of control in the sense of Article 3(1)(b) of the EUMR: the *Jurisdictional Notice* deals with this concept from paragraphs 11 to 123. It begins by discussing the concept of control; it then deals in turn with the acqui-sition of sole control and of joint control.

(A) *The concept of control*

Article 3(2) of the EUMR defines control for the purpose of determining whether there is a concentration[40]:

> Control shall be constituted by rights, contracts or any other means which, either separately or in combination and having regard to the considerations of fact or law involved, confer the possibility of exercising decisive influence on an undertaking, in particular by:
>
> (a) ownership or the right to use all or part of the assets of an undertaking;
>
> (b) rights or contracts which confer decisive influence on the composition, voting or decisions of the organs of an undertaking.

---

[36] Case M 1806, decision of 26 July 2000. [37] Case M 2208, decision of 26 January 2001.
[38] Case M 1016, decision of 20 May 1998. [39] Case M 2824, decision of 27 August 2002.
[40] It would seem that the notion of control in Article 3(2) of the EUMR is broader than the one used when applying the single economic entity doctrine under Article 101 TFEU: see ch 3, 'The test of control', pp 94–95.

Clearly this is a very broad concept[41], and control can exist on a legal ('*de jure*') or a factual ('*de facto*') basis[42]. The most common means for the acquisition of control is the acquisition of shares, sometimes in conjunction with a shareholders' agreement, in the case of joint control, or the acquisition of assets[43]. However it is also possible for control to be acquired on a contractual basis[44]. A franchise agreement is not normally sufficient to establish control[45]. In exceptional cases a situation of economic dependence resulting from, for example, long-term supply agreements, could give rise to control[46]. It is important to understand that the concept of control as used in the EUMR may be different from the one used in other EU or national laws on matters such as taxation or the media[47]. It should be added that, when deciding under Article 5(4) whether the turnover of affiliated companies should be included within group turnover, a stricter notion of control is applied than in the case of Article 3.

The acquisition of control of assets – for example the transfer of the client base of a business or of intangible assets such as brands, patents or copyrights – will be considered a concentration only if they amount to a business with a market presence to which a market turnover can be clearly attributed[48]. To amount to a concentration the acquisition of control must be on a lasting basis, resulting, as recital 20 of the EUMR notes, in a change in the structure of the market[49]. Where several undertakings acquire a company, with the intention of dividing up the assets at a later stage, the first acquisition may be regarded as purely transitory with the result that it would not amount to a concentration: the subsequent division of the assets in question would however have to be investigated, and could give rise to more than one concentration[50]. The same analysis could be applied where an operation envisages the joint control of a new operation for a start-up period followed by a conversion to sole control: where the joint control does not exceed a year there would not be a concentration during that period[51].

Where an interim buyer, such as a bank, acquires an undertaking on the basis of an agreement in the future to sell it on to an ultimate buyer, the Commission will examine the case as one of acquisition by the ultimate buyer[52]: this is sometimes referred to in practice as a 'warehousing' arrangement. Several transactions may be regarded as a single concentration in the sense of Article 3 where they are unitary in nature, that is to say where they are interdependent in such a way that one transaction would not have

---

[41] Note however that, under the UK Enterprise Act 2002, the concept of 'material influence' is broader than 'the possibility of exercising decisive influence' under Article 3(2) EUMR with the result that some transactions that might not be caught under EU merger control could be under the UK system: see ch 22, 'Enterprises ceasing to be distinct', pp 919–921, and paras 21, 49 and 64 of the General Court's judgment in Case T-411/07 *Aer Lingus Group plc v Commission* [2010] ECR-000, [2011] 4 CMLR 358. Note also that it is possible that the acquisition by A of a shareholding in B, although insufficient to provide the possibility of exercising decisive influence in the sense of Article 3(2) of the EUMR, may give rise to the possibility of coordinated behaviour between A and B and so require consideration under Article 101 TFEU: see Cases 142 and 156/84 *BAT v Commission* [1987] ECR 4487, [1988] 4 CMLR 24, in particular paras 37–39; see also *Warner-Lambert/Gillette* OJ [1993] L 116/21, [1993] 5 CMLR 559, paras 33–39; *BT-MCI* OJ [1994] L 223/36, [1995] 5 CMLR 285; *BiB* OJ [1999] L 312/1, [2000] 4 CMLR 901; see further Struijla 'Minority Share Acquisitions Below the Control Threshold of the EC Merger Regulation: An Economic and Legal Analysis' (2002) 25 World Competition 173; Caronna 'Article 81 as a tool for controlling minority cross-shareholdings between competitors' (2004) 29 EL Rev 485; Ezrachi and Gilo 'EC Competition Law and the Regulation of Passive Investments Among Competitors' (2006) 26(2) OJLS 327.

[42] *Jurisdictional Notice*, para 16.   [43] Ibid, para 17.   [44] Ibid, para 18.

[45] Ibid, para 19.   [46] Ibid, para 20.   [47] Ibid, para 23.   [48] Ibid, para 24.

[49] Ibid, para 28.   [50] Ibid, paras 29–33.   [51] Ibid, para 34.   [52] Ibid, para 35.

been carried out without the other and if they ultimately lead to control by the same undertaking(s)[53].

Article 5(2) of the EUMR establishes a rule that allows the Commission to consider successive transactions occurring within a two-year period to be treated as a single concentration: this is an 'anti-avoidance' rule to ensure that the same persons do not break a transaction down into a series of sales of assets over a period of time with the aim of avoiding the application of the EUMR[54]. The internal restructuring of an undertaking that does not result in a change of control is not covered by the EUMR[55].

(B) Sole control

Sole control may be enjoyed on a legal or a factual basis. Legal control is normally acquired where an undertaking acquires a majority of the voting rights of a company, but could also occur, for example, where a minority shareholder owns shares that confer special rights to determine the strategic direction of the company to be acquired[56]. Factual control can occur where a minority shareholder is able to veto the strategic decisions of an undertaking: although it cannot impose decisions, the fact that it can block decisions means that it has the possibility of exercising decisive influence in the sense of Article 3(2) of the EUMR. This is often referred to as negative control[57]. Factual control can also exist where a minority shareholder is likely to be able at shareholders' meetings to achieve a majority: the Commission will look at past voting behaviour to try to predict what the position is likely to be in the future[58]. In *Electrabel/Compagnie Nationale du Rhone*[59] the Commission concluded that Electrabel had acquired sole control over CNR, despite being a minority shareholder, on the basis of a number of different considerations, including that it was assured of a *de facto* majority at CNR's General Meeting; as the concentration had not been implemented, but sole control had been acquired, Electrabel was fined €20 million for 'gun jumping'[60]. Depending on the facts of the case, a shareholding of less than 25 per cent can be found to provide the possibility of exercising decisive influence: for example in *CCIE/GTE*[61] CCIE acquired 19 per cent of the voting rights in EDIL and was found to have acquired control, the remaining shares being held by an independent investment bank whose approval was not needed for important commercial decisions.

An option to purchase or convert shares does not in itself confer control unless the option will be exercised in the near future according to legally binding agreements[62].

(C) Joint control

Joint control occurs where two or more undertakings have the possibility of exercising decisive influence over another undertaking. Joint control typically arises from the fact that the undertakings in question enjoy negative control, that is to say the power to reject strategic decisions, which means that they have to act in common in order to determine the joint venture's commercial policy[63]. Joint control can be established both on a legal and a factual basis[64]. The simplest form of joint control arises where there are only two

---

[53] Ibid, paras 36–47.   [54] Ibid, paras 49–50.   [55] Ibid, para 51.
[56] Ibid, paras 56–58.   [57] Ibid, para 54.   [58] Ibid, para 59.
[59] Case M 4994, decision of 10 June 2009.
[60] On gun-jumping see 'Suspension of concentrations', p 858 below; the case is on appeal to the General Court, Case T-332/09 *Electrabel v Commission*, not yet decided.
[61] Case M 258, decision of 25 September 1992; similarly in *Mannesmann/Vallourec*, Case M 906, decision of 3 June 1997, a shareholding of 21 per cent was found sufficient to confer sole control; see further ch 22, 'Enterprises ceasing to be distinct', p 920 on *BSkyB/ITV* where BSkyB was to have found to have 'material influence', the test in the Enterprise Act 2002, over ITV with a shareholding of 17.9 per cent.
[62] *Jurisdictional Notice*, para 60.   [63] Ibid, para 62.   [64] Ibid, para 63.

parent companies each with the same number of voting rights[65]. Joint control can also occur where, despite inequality of voting rights, parent companies enjoy veto rights, either by virtue of the statute of the joint venture or a shareholders' agreement between the parents[66]. The veto rights must be related to strategic decisions of the joint venture that go beyond the protection accorded to minority shareholders to protect their investment: examples of veto rights giving rise to joint control would be decisions on issues such as the budget, business plan, major investments or the appointment of senior management[67]. Joint control can also arise even where there are no veto rights if it is likely, in fact or in law, that the parents will act jointly in the exercise of their voting rights, whether as a result of a legally binding agreement[68] or as a matter of fact, because of 'strong common interests'[69].

(iii) Changes in the quality of control

A concentration can occur where there is a change in the quality of control of an undertaking: there may be a change from sole to joint control; a change in the identity of the parent companies so that there is a change in the nature of the joint control; and a change from joint to sole control[70]. However a change from negative to positive control is not regarded as a concentration[71]. A short-form notification may be made in the case of a change from joint to sole control[72].

(iv) Joint ventures – the concept of full-functionality

Article 3(4) of the EUMR provides that:

> The creation of a joint venture performing on a lasting basis all the functions of an autonomous economic entity shall constitute a concentration within the meaning of Article 3(1)(b).

Concentrations in the sense of Article 3(4) are known as 'full-function joint ventures'. It is important to know whether a joint venture is full-function or not since this determines whether the EUMR is capable of application; if the joint venture is not full-function the possibility remains that it might be subject to Article 101 TFEU and/or national merger control. A full-function joint venture having a Community dimension is subject to mandatory pre-notification to the Commission; a partial-function joint venture would not be notifiable under Article 101, the process of notification of agreements under Article 101 having been abolished by Regulation 1/2003[73]. In the case of *BHP Billiton/Rio Tinto* the parties abandoned a full-function joint venture in relation to which the Commission had opened a Phase II investigation[74]; a subsequent partial-function joint venture between the same parties became the subject of a Commission investigation under Article 101 TFEU, and it was also abandoned[75].

The *Jurisdictional Notice* provides considerable detail on the concept of full-functionality. It begins by explaining that the requirement of autonomy in Article 3(4) refers to operational autonomy: its parents will be responsible for its strategic decisions, which is precisely why they will be considered to be in joint control in the first place[76]. To be operationally autonomous the joint venture must have sufficient resources to operate independently on a market: this means that it must have a management dedicated to its

---

[65] Ibid, para 64.   [66] Ibid, para 65.   [67] Ibid, paras 67–73.   [68] Ibid, para 75.
[69] Ibid, paras 76–80.   [70] Ibid, paras 83–90.   [71] Ibid, para 83.
[72] See Annex II of the Implementing Regulation.
[73] See ch 4, 'Regulation 1/2003', pp 166–168.
[74] See Commission Press Release IP/08/1798, 6 December 2008.
[75] See Commission Press Release IP/10/45, 25 January 2010.   [76] *Jurisdictional Notice*, para 93.

day-to-day operations and access to sufficient resources including finance, staff and assets to carry on the business activities provided for in the joint-venture agreement[77]. A joint venture will not be full-function where it takes over one specific function of its parents' activities, such as R&D or production; similarly a joint sales company would not be full-function[78]. An example of a joint venture found not to be full-function will be found in *Electrabel/Energia Italia/Interpower*[79]. Such cases would need to be analysed under Article 101 and/or national merger control.

A joint venture may not be sufficiently autonomous where its parents have a strong presence as suppliers to or purchasers from it; however the Commission recognises that the joint venture might be dependent on sales to or purchases from its parents during its 'start-up' period, which should normally not exceed three years[80]. Where sales are made to the parents on a lasting basis the Commission will consider whether the joint venture is geared to play an active role on the market independently of its parents: the proportion of sales made to the market will be an important consideration, and if the joint venture sells more than 50 per cent of its output to the market it would normally be considered to be full-function[81]. The Commission is more sceptical about long-term purchases from the parents, which might mean that the joint venture is closer to being a sales agency[82]; however it recognises that, where the joint venture operates on a 'trade market', it may be full-function even though it purchases from its parents[83]. A trade market is one where undertakings specialise in the selling and distribution of products without being vertically integrated and where different sources of supply are available for the products in question. In such a case a joint venture could be considered to be full-function provided that it has the necessary facilities and is likely to obtain a substantial proportion of its supplies not only from its parents but also from competing sources.

To be full-function a joint venture must be established on a lasting basis; the fact that the parents provide for dissolution of the joint venture, for example in the event of its failure or fundamental disagreement between them, does not mean that it is not established on a lasting basis[84]. If the joint venture is established for a short, finite period – for example in order to construct a specific project such as a power plant – it would not be considered to be long-lasting[85]. An enlargement of the activities of a full-function joint venture may amount to a new concentration, as will a change from being partial-function to being full-function[86].

As a matter of substantive analysis, agreements between the parents of a full-function joint venture and the joint venture itself may amount to ancillary restraints; or they may require independent assessment under Article 101 TFEU[87].

(v) Exceptions

Article 3(5) of the EUMR provides that certain operations will not amount to a concentration: the acquisition of securities by credit or other financial institutions on an investment basis where the voting rights are not exercised other than to protect the investment; the acquisition of control according to the law of a Member State relating to liquidation, winding up and similar matters; and acquisition by financial holding companies in relation to such matters. The *Jurisdictional Notice* explains that these provisions are

---

[77] Ibid, para 94.   [78] Ibid, para 95.   [79] Case M 3003, decision of 23 December 2002.
[80] *Jurisdictional Notice*, para 97.   [81] Ibid, para 98.   [82] Ibid, para 101.
[83] Ibid, para 102.   [84] Ibid, para 103.   [85] Ibid, para 104.
[86] Ibid, paras 106–109; for an example of a joint venture changing from partial-function to full-function see Case M 5241 *American Express/Fortis/Alpha Card*, decision of 3 October 2008.
[87] See further 'Contractual restrictions directly related to and necessary for a merger: "ancillary restraints"', pp 882–884 below.

construed narrowly, and they have rarely been applied in practice[88]. They did apply, however, in *Lagardère/Natexis/VUP*[89]; this finding by the Commission was unsuccessfully challenged before the General Court by a third party[90].

(B) Article 1: concentrations having a Community dimension

Part C of the Commission's *Jurisdictional Notice* deals with the notion of Community dimension. As a general proposition concentrations having a Community dimension are investigated exclusively by the Commission; concentrations that do not do so are subject to the merger laws of the Member States[91]. Given that 26 of the 27 Member States have a system of merger control[92], and that one transaction might be subject to investigation under a number of them, there may be significant regulatory advantages in being subject to EU rather than Member State law: this is discussed further below in the context of one-stop merger control[93].

(i) Thresholds

Turnover is used as a proxy for the economic resources that would be combined as a result of a concentration, and it is allocated geographically in order to reflect the geographical distribution of those resources[94]. Turnover thresholds are used in order to provide a relatively simple and objective mechanism for determining the allocation of jurisdiction; they are not intended in any sense to act as a way of predicting the market power of the undertakings concerned: that is a matter of substantive assessment, to be conducted by the competition authority (or authorities) that have jurisdiction[95]. Article 1 of the EUMR sets out the numerical thresholds to establish Community jurisdiction: it should be noted that the EUMR does not require that the undertakings concerned should be domiciled within the EU, nor that the transaction in question should take place there[96]. The method of calculating turnover is set out in Article 5.

Article 1(1) provides that the EUMR shall apply to all concentrations having a Community dimension as defined in Article 1(2) or Article 1(3). The criteria set out in Articles 1(2) and 1(3) of the EUMR are *alternative* grounds on which a concentration may have a Community dimension.

(A) Article 1(2)

Article 1(2) provides that a concentration has a Community dimension where:

(a) the combined aggregate worldwide turnover of all the undertakings concerned is more than €5,000 million; and

(b) the aggregate Community-wide turnover of each of at least two of the undertakings concerned is more than €250 million,

unless each of the undertakings concerned achieves more than two-thirds of its aggregate Community-wide turnover within one and the same Member State.

---

[88] *Jurisdictional Notice*, paras 110–116   [89] Case M 2978, decision of 7 January 2004.

[90] Case T-279/04 *Éditions Odile Jacob SAS v Commission* [2010] ECR II-000.

[91] See Case C-170/02 P *Schlüsselverlag JS Moser GmbH v Commission* [2003] ECR I-9889, [2004] 4 CMLR 1522, at para 34: 'the [EU] legislature intended to lay down a clear division between the activities of the national authorities and those of the Community authorities, by avoiding successive definitions of positions by those different authorities on the same transaction…'.

[92] Luxembourg is the only Member State not to do so.

[93] See 'Article 21: one-stop merger control', p 844–845 below.

[94] *Jurisdictional Notice*, para 124.   [95] Ibid, para 127.

[96] On the territorial scope of the EUMR see ch 12, 'The jurisdictional criteria in the EUMR', p 499.

Article 1(2) is intended to reflect the overall size of the undertakings concerned on a worldwide basis; to establish that there is a minimum level of activities within the EU; and to exclude purely domestic transactions. It is not unusual for very substantial transactions to fall outside the EUMR as a result of the two-thirds rule where two undertakings from the same Member State are involved: this is particularly likely to happen in the case, for example, of banks, insurance companies and undertakings in the energy sector that operate predominantly in their domestic market. For example the *Lloyds TSB Group plc/ Abbey National plc* case in 2001 was not subject to the EUMR, since at least two-thirds of the turnover of each of those banks arose in the UK; however the case was investigated, and prohibited, under the UK's domestic system of merger control[97]. In the later case of *Lloyds TSB plc/HBOS plc* the merger again fell outside the jurisdiction of the Commission because of the two-thirds rule, but on this occasion the merger was permitted by the UK Government on the ground of 'exceptional public interest' due to the financial crisis, and in particular the perilous state at that time of the banking system[98].

A controversial case arose in 2005 when Gas Natural, a Spanish company active in the energy sector, notified its intention to make a hostile public bid for Endesa, another Spanish company primarily active in the electricity sector, to the Spanish Competition Authority; Gas Natural claimed that the two-thirds rule was applicable with the consequence that the Commission lacked jurisdiction. Endesa lodged a complaint with the Commission, arguing that the two-thirds rule did not apply. The Commission rejected Endesa's argument[99]; Endesa appealed to the General Court but its appeal was dismissed[100].

In June of 2009 the Commission published a *Report on the functioning of Regulation No 139/2004* in which it concluded that 'the present form of the two-thirds rule merits further consideration'[101], noting that some mergers that fell outside its jurisdiction because of this rule gave rise to competition concerns and yet were permitted under national law on 'public interest' grounds. The Commission invited the Council to 'take note' of this information; as at 20 June 2011 the Council had not indicated whether it intends to pursue this matter.

(B) *Article 1(3)*

Article 1(3) provides an alternative basis of jurisdiction to Article 1(2). A concentration that does not meet the Article 1(2) thresholds nevertheless has a Community dimension where:

(a) the combined aggregate worldwide turnover of all the undertakings concerned is more than €2,500 million; and

(b) in each of at least three Member States, the combined aggregate turnover of all the undertakings concerned is more than €100 million;

(c) in each of the three Member States included for the purpose of (b), the aggregate turnover of each of at least two of the undertakings concerned is more than €25 million; and

(d) the aggregate Community-wide turnover of each of at least two of the undertakings concerned is more than EUR €100 million;

unless each of the undertakings concerned achieves more than two-thirds of its aggregate Community-wide turnover within one and the same Member State.

---

[97] Cm 5208 (2001).   [98] See ch 22, 'Public interest cases', p 958.

[99] See Press Release IP/05/1425, 15 November 2005.

[100] Case T-417/05 *Endesa v Commission* [2006] ECR II-2533, [2008] 4 CMLR 1472.

[101] *Communication from the Commission to the Council: Report on the functioning of Regulation No 139/2004* COM(2009) 2101 final; the Report should be read in conjunction with the accompanying Commission Staff Working Paper containing a more detailed review.

The purpose of Article 1(3) is to give jurisdiction to the Commission in cases where a concentration does not have a Community dimension in the sense of Article 1(2), but nevertheless could be expected to have a substantial impact in at least three Member States[102]. In practice there have not been a large number of concentrations filed under Article 1(3), although it is interesting to note that jurisdiction in the *Ryanair/Aer Lingus* case, which the Commission prohibited in 2007, was based on Article 1(3)[103]. What is more common in practice is that parties to a concentration that does not have a Community dimension make use of the procedure provided by Article 4(5) of the EUMR to request that their transaction be reviewed by the Commission on a one-stop shop basis[104]. In the Commission's *Report on the functioning of Regulation No 139/2004* of June 2009 it noted that, despite the addition of Article 1(3) to the EUMR, there continue to be a number of transactions with significant cross-border effects which remain outside its jurisdiction, concluding that 'there is further scope for "one-stop-shop" review'[105]. As noted above, the Council has yet to indicate whether it intends to take any action in pursuance of the Commission's *Report*.

(ii) Notion of undertaking concerned

The first step in determining whether a concentration has a Community dimension is to identify the 'undertakings concerned', an expression that is used in Article 1 of the EUMR. Having done so, turnover is calculated in the manner set out in Article 5; Article 5(4) identifies those other entities that form part of the same group as the undertakings concerned and whose turnover should therefore be included in the calculation. Where the concentration is a merger in the sense of Article 3(1)(a) of the EUMR the undertakings concerned are the merging entities[106]. In cases of the acquisition of control under Article 3(1)(b) it can be a complicated matter to determine who are the undertakings concerned. The *Jurisdictional Notice* gives extensive guidance on this:

- where A acquires sole control of B, the undertakings concerned will be A and B[107]
- however if A acquires part of B, the undertakings concerned will be A and the part of B to be acquired, in accordance with Article 5(2) of the EUMR: after the concentration has been effected the economic strength of the rest of B would be irrelevant to the position of the merged entity[108]
- where A and B jointly control C and A acquires B's interest in C, the undertakings concerned are A and C: as in the previous example, once the transaction has been put into effect the position of B is irrelevant to the economic strength of A and C[109]
- where A and B establish a new entity, C, the undertakings concerned are A and B[110]
- however if A and B acquire joint control of an existing entity, C, each of A, B and C is an undertaking concerned[111].

If a joint venture, C, acquires D, the question arises of whether C, or its parents A and B, should be regarded as the undertakings concerned. The answer to this question may have a decisive effect on jurisdiction: if A and B are undertakings concerned and their group

---

[102] *Jurisdictional Notice*, para 126.

[103] Case M 4439 *Ryanair/Aer Lingus*, decision of 27 June 2007, upheld on appeal Case T-342/07 *Ryanair v Commission* [2010] ECR II-000, [2011] 4 CMLR 245.

[104] See 'Pre-notification referrals: Article 4(5)', p 849 below.

[105] *Communication from the Commission to the Council: Report on the functioning of Regulation No 139/2004* COM(2009) 2101 final, para 13.

[106] *Jurisdictional Notice*, para 132.   [107] Ibid, para 134.   [108] Ibid, para 136.

[109] Ibid, para 138.   [110] Ibid, para 139.   [111] Ibid, para 140.

turnover is added into the calculation of turnover, it is more likely that the transaction will be found to have a Community dimension:

- if C is a full-function joint venture and is already operating on the market, it will be regarded as an undertaking concerned, along with D[112]
- if C is a mere vehicle for the acquisition by A and B of D the Commission will consider each of A and B to be undertakings concerned, along with D[113].

(iii) Relevant date for establishing jurisdiction

The relevant date for determining whether a concentration has a Community dimension is the date when a final agreement was concluded or a public bid was announced or a controlling interest was acquired, whichever date is earlier[114].

(iv) Turnover[115]

Article 5(1) of the EUMR defines turnover as the amounts derived by undertakings in the preceding financial year 'from the sale of products and the provision of services falling within the undertakings' ordinary activities'. Sales rebates, VAT and other taxes directly related to turnover (for example taxes on alcoholic drinks and cigarettes) are deducted from any turnover figure, as is internal turnover within a group of companies. Article 5(5)(a) of the EUMR provides that turnover between a joint venture and its parents should be excluded from the calculation of turnover; but Article 5(5)(b) provides that turnover between a joint venture and third parties should be apportioned equally between its parents.

The *Jurisdictional Notice* explains that the Commission will usually base its findings on turnover on the most recent audited accounts of the undertakings concerned; it will rely on management or other provisional accounts only in exceptional circumstances[116]. Where there are major differences between the EU's accounting standards and those of a non-Member State the Commission may consider it necessary to ask for the accounts to be restated according to EU standards[117]. The *Notice* explains the circumstances in which the Commission will accept an adjustment to the figures in the audited accounts, for example where there has since been a divestiture of part of the business of an undertaking concerned[118].

In determining jurisdiction it is necessary not only to take into account the turnover of the undertakings concerned but also that of other undertakings within the same group. This can be problematic where undertakings such as private equity funds do not have consolidated accounts: care must be taken to ensure that all relevant turnover is brought into the calculation. Article 5(4) of the EUMR provides that the aggregate turnover of an undertaking concerned shall be calculated by adding together the respective turnovers of the following, where (b) refers to subsidiaries, (c) to parents and (d) to affiliates:

(a) the undertaking concerned;

(b) those undertakings in which the undertaking concerned directly or indirectly:

(i)   owns more than half the capital or business assets, or

(ii) has the power to exercise more than half the voting rights, or

(iii) has the power to appoint more than half the members of the supervisory board, the administrative board or bodies legally representing the undertakings, or

---

[112] Ibid, para 146.   [113] Ibid, para 147.   [114] Ibid, paras 155–156.
[115] Several points relating to the calculation of turnover are referred to in the General Court's judgment in Case T-417/05 *Endesa SA v Commission* [2006] ECR II-2533, [2008] 4 CMLR 1472.
[116] *Jurisdictional Notice*, paras 169–170.   [117] Ibid, para 171.   [118] Ibid, paras 172–174.

(iv) has the right to manage the undertaking's affairs;

(c) those undertakings which have in an undertaking concerned the rights or powers listed in (b);

(d) those undertakings in which an undertaking as referred to in (c) has the rights or powers listed in (b);

(e) those undertakings in which two or more undertakings as referred to in (a) to (d) jointly have the rights or powers listed in (b).

The *Jurisdictional Notice* provides fairly extensive guidance on these provisions[119]. An important point is that the criteria in Article 5(4), such as 'the power to exercise more than half the voting rights' or 'the right to manage the undertakings' affairs', are considerably stricter than the concept of 'control' set out in Article 3(2); Article 5(4) provides 'bright-line' criteria for determining which group turnover should be added to that of the individual undertakings concerned in a transaction[120]. The Commission's decision in *SoFFin/Hypo Real Estate* considers the application of the EUMR, and in particular the calculation of group turnover, where a state-owned body (in that case the German Special Fund Financial Market Stabilisation) acquires a distressed financial institution[121].

(v) Geographic allocation of turnover

It is important to be able to determine where turnover arises, since Article 1(2) and (3) of the EUMR refer to global, Community and Member State turnover. The general rule is that turnover should be attributed to the place where the customer is located[122]; the *Jurisdictional Notice* explains how this principle is applied in practice to the sale of goods[123] and the provision of services[124].

(vi) Conversion of turnover into Euros

For the purposes of the EUMR turnover must be calculated in Euros: for many undertakings this will require conversion from another currency. The annual turnover should be converted at the average European Central Bank rate for the 12 months concerned; and this average can be obtained from DG COMP's website[125].

(vii) Provisions for credit and other financial institutions and insurance undertakings

Article 5(3) of the EUMR provides specific rules for the calculation of turnover of credit and other financial institutions. Their operation is explained in the Commission's *Jurisdictional Notice*[126].

(viii) Illustrations

A few examples may help to illustrate how the jurisdictional rules just outlined operate in practice. See Fig. 21.1.

---

[119] Ibid, paras 175–194.   [120] Ibid, para 184.

[121] Case M 5508, decision of 14 May 2009; see also recital 22 of the EUMR.

[122] *Jurisdictional Notice*, para 196.   [123] Ibid, paras 197–198.

[124] Ibid, paras 199–202; for an example of a case in which the geographical allocation of turnover was crucial to jurisdiction see Case M 4439 *Ryanair/Aer Lingus*, decision of 27 June 2007, upheld on appeal Case T-342/07 *Ryanair v Commission* [2010] ECR II-000, [2011] 4 CMLR 245.

[125] *Jurisdictional Notice*, para 204; the website is www.ec.europa.eu/comm/competition/mergers/exchange_rates.html.

[126] *Jurisdictional Notice*, paras 206–220.

Example 1

A acquires B: A is the wholly-owned subsidiary of X

Undertakings concerned: A and B (Article 5(1))

Turnover to be taken into account: A and B (undertakings concerned) and X (X's turnover is included as a result of Article 5(4)(c)).

Example 2

A acquires B, a division of Y; A is a part of X, and has a wholly-owned subsidiary, Z

Undertakings concerned: A and B (Article 5(1))

Turnover to be taken into account: A and B (undertakings concerned: disregard the turnover of Y, as A is acquiring B only, a part of Y: Article 5(2)); X (Article 5(4)(c)) and Z (Article 5(4)(b)).

Example 3

A acquires B. A is jointly controlled by X, Y and Z.

Undertakings concerned: A and B

Turnover to be taken into account: A and B (undertakings concerned); X, Y and Z (this is based on the language of Article 5(4)(c) of the EUMR and is supported by paragraph 182 of the Commission's *Consolidated Jurisdictional Notice*).

Example 4

A acquires B; A has joint control of X with Y

Undertakings concerned: A and B

Turnover to be taken into account: A and B (undertakings concerned); but is the turnover of X relevant? The answer to this question could determine whether the concentration has a Community dimension if A and B's combined turnover falls below the Community dimension thresholds. The Commission states at paragraph 187 of its *Consolidated Jurisdictional Notice* that it would allocate a 50% share of the joint venture's turnover to A in these circumstances.

Fig. 21.1 Illustrative examples.

(C) Article 21: one-stop merger control

(i) The benefits of one-stop merger control

As a general proposition it is undesirable, both for businesses and for competition authorities, if a particular concentration has to be investigated under two or more systems of law. Multiple investigation leads to administrative inefficiency, duplication, delay, expense, uncertainty and the possibility of conflicting decisions. A central principle of the EUMR is the idea of one-stop merger control: that is to say that concentrations having a Community dimension should be investigated within the EU only by the Commission. This policy is given expression in Article 21 of the EUMR. Article 21(2) provides that, subject to review by the EU Courts, only the Commission may take decisions in respect of concentrations having a Community dimension; Article 21(3) adds that no Member State shall apply its national legislation on competition to such concentrations[127]. However, as explained below, there are some circumstances in which cases can be 'reattributed' from and to the Commission. A different point is that Article 21(4) of the EUMR provides that, in defined circumstances, a Member State may be able to apply non-competition legislation to a concentration where this is necessary to protect a 'legitimate interest'; this provision is discussed in section F below.

Article 21(1) of the EUMR adds that Regulation 1/2003, the Regulation that gives the Commission the power to enforce Articles 101 and 102 TFEU, shall have no application to concentrations as defined in the EUMR[128]. However Article 21(1) makes clear that the Commission retains the right to use its powers under Regulation 1/2003 in relation to joint ventures that do not have a Community dimension and which have as their object or effect the coordination of the competitive behaviour of undertakings that remain independent.

(ii) The benefits of more flexible jurisdictional rules

Notwithstanding the principle of one-stop merger control the EUMR makes provision for 'case referral', that is to say for the reattribution, in defined circumstances, of cases to and from the Commission. The Commission's *Notice on Case Referral in respect of concentrations* ('the *Case Referral Notice*')[129] provides detailed guidance on the reattribution of jurisdiction under the EUMR, both on the guiding principles[130] and on the mechanics of the system[131]. It also contains helpful flow charts[132]. The case referral rules were 'flexibilised' by the 2004 Regulation to make reattribution easier than under the original Merger Regulation; it was felt that more flexibility was desirable in order to enable the more appropriate competition authority or authorities to conduct the investigation of cases[133].

In certain cases a concentration that has a Community dimension can be referred by the Commission to Member States under the provisions of Article 4(4) and Article 9: this is described in section D below; and a concentration that does not have a Community dimension can be referred under Article 4(5) and Article 22 by Member States to the

---

[127] It is arguable that a national court could apply Articles 101 and 102 to concentrations having a Community dimension, in so far as those provisions are capable of applying to concentrations, on the basis that they are directly effective, though there would appear to be no example of this having happened since the entry into force of the original Merger Regulation in September 1990: for discussion of the point see Cook and Kerse *EC Merger Control* (Sweet & Maxwell, 5th ed, 2009), pp 19–22; Levy *European Merger Control Law: A Guide to the Merger Regulation* (LexisNexis, 2003), ch 21.

[128] Theoretically the Commission may be able to proceed under Articles 101 and 102, in so far as they are capable of application to a concentration, under Article 105 TFEU; at the time of the adoption of the original Merger Regulation the Commission said that it would do so only rarely, and in practice it has never done so; see the Commission's statement entered in the minutes of the Council [1990] 4 CMLR 314; see also Cook and Kerse *EC Merger Control* (Sweet & Maxwell, 5th ed, 2009), pp 21–22; Levy *European Merger Control Law: A Guide to the Merger Regulation* (LexisNexis, 2003), ch 21.

[129] OJ [2005] C 56/2; see also *Joint Statement of the Council and the Commission on the functioning of the network of Competition Authorities* available at www.ec.europa.eu/competition/ecn/documents. html; for discussion of the referral system see Rakovsky, Godhino de Matos, Kopke, Ohrlander and Shiels 'EC Merger Regulation contributes to more efficient merger control in EU' (2009) 2 *Competition Policy Newsletter* 19.

[130] *Case Referral Notice*, Section II (paras 8–45).

[131] Ibid, Section III (paras 46–82).

[132] Ibid, pp 20–23.

[133] Ibid, paras 4–7.

Commission: this is dealt with in section E below. The idea of reattribution is consistent with the principle of subsidiarity[134]. The case referral procedures in the EUMR are carried out by the Commission in close and constant liaison with the national competition authorities[135]. A notable feature of the 2004 changes is that the parties themselves can now attempt to precipitate a reallocation of jurisdiction before a formal filing has been made either to the Commission or to the national competition authority or authorities: this is a result of Articles 4(4) and 4(5) of the EUMR, described below. The Commission notes that in applying the rules on reattribution of jurisdiction due account should be taken of the need for legal certainty, so that case referral should normally be made only where there is a compelling reason for departing from the 'original jurisdiction'[136].

(D) Article 4(4) and Article 9: referral of concentrations having a Community dimension to the competent authorities of the Member States

The starting point is that concentrations that have a Community dimension benefit from a one-stop shop; the Commission acknowledges that the fragmentation of such cases, that is to say the partial referral of aspects of a concentration having a Community dimension to one or more Member States, is undesirable in principle even though possible as a matter of law[137].

Case referrals of concentrations having a Community dimension may be made following a request from the parties to a concentration prior to a notification having been made ('pre-notification referrals') or following a request from a Member State (or Member States) after a notification ('post-notification referrals'). The Commission's decision to refer a case to a Member State is capable of being challenged by a third party that would prefer the Commission to investigate the case[138]; the reverse may not be true[139].

(i) Pre-notification referrals: Article 4(4)[140]

Article 4(4) was an innovation in the 2004 Regulation. It allows the parties to a transaction to make a 'reasoned submission' to the Commission that a concentration will significantly affect competition in a market within a Member State which presents all the characteristics of a distinct market and therefore that it should be examined, in whole or in part, by that Member State. The parties do not have to demonstrate that the effect on competition is likely to be adverse[141]. The submission must be made on Form RS, the format of which is set out in Annex III of the Implementing Regulation[142].

Having made a request the Commission will transmit it to all Member States without delay. The Member State referred to in the Form RS must express its agreement or disagreement with the request within 15 working days; if it does not do so it is deemed to have agreed. Unless the Member State disagrees with the request the Commission has a discretion to refer whole or part of the case to the Member State in question for it to be investigated under that State's national competition law; this decision must be made within

---

[134] Ibid, para 8.   [135] Ibid, paras 53–58.
[136] Ibid, paras 13–14.   [137] Ibid, paras 11–12.
[138] See Case T-119/02 *Royal Philips Electronics v Commission* [2003] ECR II-1433, [2003] 5 CMLR 53, paras 252–300; Cases T-346/02 and 347/02 *Cabeleuropa SA v Commission* [2003] ECR II-4251, [2004] 5 CMLR 1216, paras 100–157.
[139] See Case T-224/10 *Association belges des consommateurs test-achats ASBL v Commission* [2011] ECR II-000, paras 74–85.
[140] *Case Referral Notice*, paras 16–23.
[141] Ibid, para 17.
[142] Regulation 802/2004, OJ [2004] L 133/1, available at www.ec.europa.eu/competition/mergers/legislation/regulations.html#impl_reg; as to Form RS see the *Case Referral Notice*, paras 59–64.

25 working days of receipt of the Form RS. If the Commission does not take a decision within this period it is deemed to have referred the case. The Commission is most likely to make a referral where the effects of a concentration are likely to be felt within a national market, or a market that is narrower than national, and where the markets are likely to be within one and the same Member State[143]. Where a concentration might affect competition in a number of national markets the Commission might consider it appropriate to retain jurisdiction: this would avoid the need for coordinated investigations by a number of competition authorities and the danger of conflicting outcomes. However referral to a number of Member States might occur, especially where competitive conditions vary from one State to another; fragmentation of jurisdiction is less of a concern where the parties themselves have made a request under Article 4(4)[144]. The final paragraph of Article 4(4) provides that, where the whole of the case is referred to a Member State, the duty to notify the case to the Commission ceases to apply.

(ii) Post-notification referrals: Article 9[145]

Article 9 of the EUMR provides a mechanism whereby Member States may make a request that a concentration having a Community dimension should be referred to them. The powers of the Office of Fair Trading ('the OFT') in the UK in relation to such cases are set out in a statutory instrument[146]. Article 9(2) establishes two situations in which a Member State may make such a request.

(A) Article 9(2)(a)

The first is where a concentration threatens to affect significantly competition in a market within a Member State which presents all the characteristics of a distinct market. Where the Commission considers that these criteria are fulfilled it has a discretion to refer the whole or part of the case to the Member State that made the request[147].

(B) Article 9(2)(b)

The second is where a concentration affects competition within a Member State which presents all the characteristics of a distinct market and which does not constitute a substantial part of the common market: the latter expression is likely to refer to a geographical market that is narrow in scope and within a single Member State[148]. Where the Commission considers that these criteria are fulfilled it has an obligation to refer the whole or part of the case relating to the distinct market concerned[149]: the Commission would not be able to take action against a concentration that does not impede competition in a substantial part of the common market anyway[150].

As a general rule the decision to refer must be taken within 35 working days of the working day following receipt of the notification[151]. Once a referral has been made the competent authority of the Member State must decide upon the case 'without undue delay'. Within 45 working days of the referral the Member State must inform the undertakings concerned of the preliminary competition assessment and what further action, if any, it proposes to take[152]; other than this the only time constraints on the Member State are those imposed by national law. Member States may take only the measures strictly

---

[143] Ibid, para 20.   [144] Ibid, para 22.   [145] Ibid, paras 33–41.
[146] EEC Merger Control (Distinct Market Investigations) Regulations 1990, SI 1990/1715, as amended by the EC Merger Control (Consequential Amendments) Regulations 2004, SI 2004/1079.
[147] EUMR, Article 9(3).   [148] *Case Referral Notice*, para 40.
[149] EUMR, Article 9(3), final paragraph.
[150] Ibid, Article 2(3).   [151] Ibid, Article 9(4)(a).   [152] Ibid, Article 9(6).

necessary to safeguard or restore effective competition on the market concerned[153]. Where the Commission refuses a request a Member State may appeal to the General Court[154].

(iii) Statistics

The statistics on Article 4(4) and Article 9 are of interest[155]. In the years immediately preceding 1 May 2004, when the current EUMR became applicable, Member States were making quite a large number of Article 9 requests – in 2003 the figure was ten. Refusals are rare: out of a total of 98 Article 9 requests to have been made by 30 September 2011 only six were refused, and the only refusals in the last three years were in the cases of *EDF/Segebel*, where the Commission considered that commitments offered by EDF would address the competition concerns that it had identified in the Belgian electricity market[156], and *Crédit Agricole/Cassa di Risparmio Della Spezia/Agences Intesa Sanpaolo*[157], where the Commission refused an Article 9 request from Italy in relation to Crédit Agricole's purchase of bank branches in Italy. Since 1 May 2004 the number of Member State requests under Article 9 has tended to be fewer than it had been, from ten in 2003 to just three in 2009; however that tendency was reversed in 2010, when seven cases were referred to Member States, and several of those were to two Member States rather than one. Undertakings have made use of the Article 4(4) procedure on quite a number of occasions: by 30 September 2011 there had been 65 requests under Article 4(4), and none had been refused.

(iv) Article 4(4) and Article 9 in practice

Referrals to a Member State can give rise to problems for the undertakings concerned. In *Interbrew/Bass* the European Commission referred part of the case to the UK[158]. The Competition Commission in the UK recommended that the transaction should be prohibited in its entirety[159], a particularly unfortunate outcome given that the sale agreement had been entered into without a condition that approval from the UK authorities was required. Following a judicial review the transaction was permitted to go ahead in an amended form[160]. In *Tesco/Carrefour*[161] the concentration was approved by the European Commission in December 2005; however the intended acquisitions in Slovakia were prohibited following an Article 9(2)(b) referral of that part of the transaction[162]. In *Foster Yeoman/Aggregate Industries*[163] the UK requested a referral which led to the OFT accepting undertakings in lieu of a reference to the Competition Commission to overcome concerns about both unilateral and coordinated effects that would arise from the transaction there[164]. It is possible for a third party to appeal against a Commission decision to make a referral under Article 9[165].

---

[153] Ibid, Article 9(8).   [154] Ibid, Article 9(9).

[155] See 'Table of EUMR statistics', p 899 below for a statistical table of merger notifications.

[156] Case M 5549, decision of 12 November 2009, on appeal Case T-224/10 *Test-Achats v Commission* [2011] ECR II-000; see Kadar '*EDF/Segebel* – A Member State's issue?' [2010(4)] Revue de la Concurrence Belge 23; Asbo, De Coninck, Kecsmar, Panayides and Van Haasteren 'EDF/Segebel (SPE): More power to boost competition in Belgian energy markets' (2010) 1 *Competition Policy Newsletter* 56.

[157] Case M 5960, decision of 11 November 2010.   [158] Case M 2044, decision of 22 August 2000.

[159] *Interbrew SA/Bass plc* Cm 5014 (2001).

[160] *Interbrew SA and Interbrew UK Holdings Ltd v Competition Commission and Secretary of State for Trade and Industry* [2001] EWHC Admin 367, [2001] UKCLR 954.

[161] Case M 3905, decision of 22 December 2005.

[162] See www.antimon.gov.sk, decision of 17 January 2007.

[163] Case M 4298, decision of 6 September 2006.   [164] OFT decision of 22 December 2006.

[165] See 'Appeals against Article 9 references', pp 895–896 below.

In its *Report on the functioning of Regulation No 139/2004* of June 2009[166] the Commission concluded that the Article 4(4) (and Article 4(5)) pre-notification referral mechanisms had considerably enhanced the efficiency and jurisdictional flexibility of merger control in the EU, although it noted that some stakeholders had expressed concern about the overall timing and cumbersomeness of the referral process; the same comment was made in relation to the Article 9 and Article 22 procedures[167].

(E) Article 4(5) and Article 22: referral of concentrations not having a Community dimension by Member States to the Commission

The starting point in the case of concentrations not having a Community dimension is that they are subject to the national systems of merger control of the Member States. With the exception of Luxembourg every Member State has provisions on merger control, and it can happen that one transaction may be reviewable in numerous jurisdictions: in its *Report on the functioning of Regulation No 139/2004* of June 2009[168] the Commission noted that in 2007 there were at least 100 transactions that were notifiable in three or more Member States. As noted already multiple filings can be undesirable both for businesses and for competition authorities. The EUMR makes provision for concentrations not having a Community dimension to be referred to the Commission, in which case they may benefit from the principle of one-stop merger control. As the statistics in the text that follows show these provisions, and in particular Article 4(5), are used quite often.

(i) Pre-notification referrals: Article 4(5)[169]

Article 4(5), like Article 4(4), was an innovation in the 2004 Regulation. Article 4(5) allows the parties to a concentration that is capable of being reviewed under the national competition laws of at least three Member States to make a reasoned submission that it should be examined by the Commission. They must do so on Form RS, and the Commission must transmit the submission to the Member States without delay.

Member States competent to examine the concentration must disagree with the request within 15 working days. If one Member State expresses disagreement, the case will not be referred (in other words the case referral process under Article 4(5) can be vetoed by a single Member State, although this is not the case under Article 22). However if there is no disagreement within the stipulated period the concentration is deemed to have a Community dimension[170] and falls to be dealt with under the provisions of the EUMR; Member States can no longer apply their national competition law to the case, which proceeds on the basis of one-stop merger control. In the Commission's view the most appropriate cases for referral under Article 4(5) are those where the potential impact on competition will be felt in markets that are wider than national in geographic scope; the Commission is likely to be in the best position to investigate such cases[171]. It might also be best-placed to investigate where the markets affected are national or narrower, but competition concerns arise in a number of Member States; this may lead to a more coherent and consistent outcome[172]. It might also be appropriate for a referral to the Commission to take place under Article 4(5) even where there are no competition concerns at all, simply to avoid the burden of multiple Member State filings[173].

---

[166] *Communication from the Commission to the Council* COM(2009) 2101 final.
[167] Ibid, paras 17–21.   [168] Ibid, para 12.   [169] *Case Referral Notice*, paras 24–32.
[170] Note that under Article 22 the Commission has a discretion whether to accept a request, whereas under Article 4(5), in the absence of a veto by a Member State, the Commission must accept jurisdiction.
[171] *Case Referral Notice*, para 28.   [172] Ibid, para 29.   [173] Ibid, para 32.

(ii) Post-notification referrals: Article 22[174]

Article 22 of the EUMR provides a mechanism whereby Member States may refer concentrations that do not have a Community dimension to the Commission for it to investigate: the concentration in question must affect trade between Member States[175] and must threaten to affect competition significantly within the territory of the Member State or States making the request[176]. In 2010 the Commission accepted a request from six Member States to investigate the acquisition by Proctor & Gamble of Sara Lee's 'Ambi Pur' air-freshener: the interesting point about this is that the transaction was not notifiable under the merger control provisions of five of the six referring Member States, and yet the Commission still accepted the referral. There is nothing in the wording of the EUMR to prevent a request in such circumstances, and when the original Merger Regulation was introduced in 1989 one of the justifications for the Article 22 procedure was that some Member States did not have a system of merger control: it seemed sensible in those circumstances to allow references to the Commission of mergers that could be harmful to competition and that would have an effect on trade between Member States[177]. However the interesting point about the *Sara Lee* case is that the referring Member States *did* have systems of merger control, but the transaction in question was below the national jurisdictional thresholds.

When the Commission receives an Article 22 request it must inform the competent authorities of the Member States without delay; other Member States may join the request within 15 working days of being informed of the initial request, and national time limits as to merger control are suspended until the jurisdictional question has been decided[178]. Silence on the part of a Member State does not mean that it is deemed to have joined the request. If a Member State decides not to join the request its national time limits revive[179]. That Member State can then apply its own law, even if the Commission accepts the request from other Member States: to put the point another way, the principle of one-stop merger control does not necessarily apply in an Article 22 case, since Member States retain the right to disagree with a request and to apply their own law. The Commission must decide, within a further ten working days from the end of the period given to Member States to decide whether to join the request, whether to examine the concentration[180]. If the Commission does not take a decision it is deemed to have accepted the request[181]. If the Commission does decide to examine the case it may request the parties to make a formal notification[182]. Once the Commission has taken jurisdiction the case proceeds in accord-

---

[174] Ibid, paras 42–45.

[175] The Commission's *Notice on the notion of effect on trade concept contained in Articles [101] and [102] of the Treaty* OJ [2004] C 101/81, may, by analogy, provide helpful guidance on the application of this expression; see the *Case Referral Notice*, fn 36.

[176] EUMR, Article 22(1).

[177] Three prohibitions under the EUMR were of mergers referred by Member States that had no merger control provisions: see Case M 553 *RTL/Veronica/Endemol*, decision of 17 July 1996, upheld on appeal Case T-221/95 *Endemol Entertainment Holding BV v Commission* [1999] ECR II-1299, [1999] 5 CMLR 611; Case M 784 *Kesko/Tuko*, decision of 20 November 1996, OJ [1997] L 110/53, upheld on appeal Case T-22/97 *Kesko Oy v Commission* [1999] ECR II-3775, [2000] 4 CMLR 335; Case M 890 *Blokker/Toys 'R' Us*, decision of 26 June 1997, OJ [1998] L 316/1.

[178] EUMR, Article 22(2).   [179] Ibid.

[180] For an example of a decision not to examine a concentration following an Article 22 request see *Gas Natural/Endesa*, Commission Press Release IP/05/1356, 27 October 2005.

[181] EUMR, Article 22(3).

[182] Ibid; the parties in an Article 22 case will already have made a notification to the national competition authority or authorities, and it is possible that the Commission will be able to glean the information it requires from those notifications.

ance with the provisions of the EUMR[183]. The Commission may invite Member States to make a request under Article 22[184].

(iii) Statistics

The statistics on Article 4(5) and Article 22 are of interest, and demonstrate in particular that undertakings have found the Article 4(5) procedure to be a useful provision[185]. In the early years of EU merger control Article 22 requests were rare; three were made by Member States that had no system of merger control at all at the relevant time, and each of them led to an outright prohibition by the Commission[186]. All the Member States now have a system of merger control, with the exception of Luxembourg, so that cases such as these would no longer happen except in relation to that one Member State. More recently Article 22 requests have become a little more common, usually where a number of Member States were willing to transfer jurisdiction to the Commission. Article 4(5) requests have become common: 23 requests were made in 2008 and the same number in 2009; none was refused. In 2010 there were 26 requests and one refusal.

(iv) Article 4(5) and Article 22 in practice

As already noted, three early Article 22 requests led to outright prohibitions of the concentrations in question. More recently Article 4(5) and Article 22 requests have continued to lead to problems for the undertakings concerned. For example an Article 4(5) request in the case of *Metso/Aker Kvaerner* led to a Phase II investigation and was cleared only subject to commitments[187]. Commitments were required following Article 22 requests in *Promatech/Sulzer Textil*[188], *GE/AGFA NDT*[189], *AREVA/Urenco/ETC*[190], *Omya/J.M.Huber*[191], *ABF/GBI Business*[192] and *Syngenta/Monsanto*[193]. The case of *Glatfelter/Crompton Assets*[194] was taken into a Phase II investigation, but was cleared unconditionally. As noted above, the Commission's *Report on the functioning of Regulation No 139/2004* of June 2009[195] reported that Article 4(5) and Article 22 have worked well in practice, albeit that they are sometimes perceived to be slow and cumbersome[196].

(F) Article 21(4): legitimate interest clause

The principle of one-stop merger control means that a Member State cannot apply its competition law to a concentration having a Community dimension except where Article 4(4) or Article 9 apply. However there may be circumstances in which a Member State wishes to investigate and perhaps to prohibit a concentration for some other reason: for example because it objects to a domestic undertaking being acquired by a foreign one; because the concentration might lead to unemployment and social disruption; or because the sector in question is a sensitive one in which the Member State wishes to maintain a strong influence which might be undermined by wider participation. Some interventions by a Member

---

[183] EUMR, Article 22(4). [184] Ibid, Article 22(5).

[185] See 'Table of EUMR statistics', p 899 below for a statistical table of merger notifications.

[186] See ch 21 n 177 above.

[187] Case M 4187, decision of 12 December 2006; see similarly Case M 4209 *Thule/Schneekten*, subsequently abandoned by the parties.

[188] Case M 2698, decision of 24 July 2002.   [189] Case M 3136, decision of 5 December 2005.

[190] Case M 3099, decision of 6 October 2004.

[191] Case M 3796, decision of 19 July 2006, OJ [2007] L 72/24.

[192] Case M 4980, decision of 23 September 2008.   [193] Case M 5675, decision of 17 November 2010.

[194] Case M 4215, decision of 20 December 2006, OJ [2007] L 151/41.

[195] *Communication from the Commission to the Council* COM(2009) 2101 final.

[196] Ibid, paras 17–21.

State to prevent a concentration involving an undertaking from another Member State might infringe primary provisions of the Treaty, for example Article 49 TFEU on the right of establishment or Article 63 TFEU on the free movement of capital; in such a situation the Commission may proceed against the Member State in question by bringing proceedings before the Court of Justice under Article 258 TFEU. In other cases the Commission might bring proceedings against a Member State that tries to block a concentration having a Community dimension on the basis that this involves a violation of the EUMR itself since Article 21 confers exclusive competence on the Commission in relation to concentrations having a Community dimension (see below). The Commission made a declaration to the European Parliament in March 2006 stressing its determination to use these legal provisions to ensure that the principles of the single market are upheld[197], and the former Commissioner for Competition, Neelie Kroes, expressed her strong opposition to national protectionist measures contrary to the principles of the internal market in a speech in St Gallen in May 2007[198]. The Commission does not believe that the creation of 'national champions' justifies non-compliance with, or exemption from, competition law[199].

Article 21(4) of the EUMR provides that Member States may take appropriate measures to protect legitimate interests other than those taken into consideration by the EUMR that are compatible with the general principles and other provisions of EU law. Public security, plurality of the media and prudential rules – that is to say rules designed to ensure the stability and financial adequacy of banks, insurance companies and similar undertakings – are regarded as legitimate interests for this purpose. Any other legitimate interest must be communicated to the Commission which must inform the Member State in question of its decision within 25 working days of the communication.

(i) Authorised applications of Article 21(4)

Decisions to allow a Member State to proceed on the basis of Article 21(4) are rare: by 31 May 2011 only eight had been granted[200]. As Article 21(4) involves a derogation from the general principles of the EUMR, that concentrations having a Community dimension should be subject to a one-stop shop, the Commission will apply it strictly.

In *Lyonnaise des Eaux SA/Northumbrian Water Group*[201] the Commission accepted that the UK was entitled to investigate the regulatory aspects of a transaction whereby Lyonnaise des Eaux acquired a UK water undertaking, while the Commission considered the competition issues. The UK also investigated the *Independent Newspaper* case under the (now-repealed) newspaper merger provisions of the Fair Trading Act 1973[202]. In *Sun Alliance/Royal Insurance*[203] the Commission acknowledged that the UK could consider whether the merger would be in accordance with the Insurance Companies Act 1982,

---

[197] Commission Declaration of 15 March 2006, available at www.europarl.europa.eu/.

[198] 'European competition policy facing a renaissance of protectionism – which strategy for the future?', 11 May 2007, available at www.ec.europa.eu/comm/competition/speeches/index_2007.html; for a more general account of legal provisions intended to inhibit protectionism in the context of mergers see Nourry and Jung 'EU State Measures against Foreign Takeovers: "Economic Patriotism in All But Name"' (2006) 2 Competition Policy International 99.

[199] See the Commission's contribution to the OECD Best Practices Roundtable on *Competition Policy, Industrial Policy and National Champions* (2009), pp 145–147, available at www.oecd.org.

[200] See 'Table of EUMR statistics', p 899 below for a statistical table of merger notifications.

[201] Case M 567, decision of 21 December 1995, OJ [1995] C 11/3; the Monopolies and Mergers Commission, as it was then called, subsequently published a report *Lyonnaise des Eaux SA and Northumbrian Water Group plc* Cm 2936 (1995) identifying possible public interest detriments: see 1999 *Annual Report of the DGFT*, p 35.

[202] Case M 423, decision of 14 March 1994, OJ [1994] C 85/6.

[203] Case M 759, decision of 18 June 1996, OJ [1996] C 225/12.

but said that this would be done in close liaison with it. In *Electricité de France/London Electricity*[204] the UK requested a referral under Article 9 of the EUMR and claimed a legitimate interest under Article 21(4); the Commission did not accept either request: the regulatory concerns of the Director General of Electricity Supply were not with the concentration itself but with the conduct of the merged undertakings after it would have taken place, to which the regulatory authority could apply national regulatory provisions. In *Thomson-CSF/Racal* the UK investigated the public security aspects of the proposed transaction under the merger provisions of the now-repealed Fair Trading Act 1973[205]. In *MBDA/SNPE/JV* the European Commission cleared the concentration under the EUMR, and the UK accepted behavioural undertakings in lieu of a reference to the Competition Commission to alleviate public security concerns[206]. In *News Corp/BSkyB*[207] the Commission cleared the concentration, but acknowledged the right of the UK to consider its potential effects on the plurality of the media in the UK[208].

(ii) Prohibited applications of Article 21(4)

In *Banco Santander Central Hispano/A Champalimand*[209] a concentration in the financial services sector having a Community dimension was notified to the Commission. The Portuguese Minister of Finance opposed the concentration, claiming to have anxieties about the prudential supervision of Mundial Confianga, an insurance undertaking, and also because he considered that the concentration would interfere with Portuguese national interests; further it would prejudice an integral sector of the Portuguese economy and financial system. The concerns of the Minister were increased by the parties' procedural impropriety in failing to notify the Minister of Finance. The Commission rejected these arguments and required the Minister to suspend his opposition to the transaction[210].

The Commission took a similar view in *Secil/Holderbank/Cimpor*. The Portuguese Minister of Finance objected to the proposed acquisition of a Portuguese cement company, Cimpor, which the Portuguese Government was in the process of privatising. The proposed acquisition had a Community dimension and therefore fell within the Commission's exclusive jurisdiction[211]. The Commission adopted a decision requiring Portugal to withdraw the decisions it had taken opposing the acquisition on the ground that Portugal had failed to show that it had a legitimate interest in the sense of Article 21(4) of the EUMR[212]. The Government of Portugal challenged the Commission's decision, but in *Portugal v Commission*[213] the Court of Justice held that the Commission was entitled to adopt an Article 21 decision to preserve the 'effet utile' of that provision;

[204] See the Commission's XXIXth *Report on Competition Policy* (1999), paras 193 and 197–198.

[205] Commission Press Release IP/00/628, 16 June 2000.

[206] See DTI Press Release P/2002/754, 27 November 2002 and DTI Press Release P/2002/802, 17 December 2002.

[207] Case M 5932, decision of 21 December 2010. [208] See ch 22, 'European mergers', pp 959–960.

[209] Case M 1616, decision of 3 August 1999, OJ [1999] C 306/37; see Mohamed 'National Interests Limiting EU Cross-border Mergers' (2000) 21 ECLR 248.

[210] Commission decisions of 20 July 1999 and 20 October 2000: see the Commission's XXIXth *Report on Competition Policy* (1999), paras 194–196.

[211] The notification in this case was withdrawn by the parties before the Commission had reached a decision: Case M 2054.

[212] See Commission Press Release IP/00/1338, 22 November 2000; in Case C-367/98 *Commission v Portugal* [2002] ECR I-4731, [2002] 2 CMLR 1213 the Court of Justice ruled that the law under which the Portuguese Government had proceeded was itself in violation of Article 63 TFEU.

[213] Case C-42/01 [2004] ECR I-6079, [2004] 5 CMLR 363; see Mäkel 'The Court of Justice rules for the first time on Article 21(3) of the merger regulation in Case C-42/01 *Portuguese Republic v Commission*' (2005) (Spring) *Competition Policy Newsletter* 19.

that the Commission can conclude that a decision of a Member State on the public interest is incompatible with EU law even where that interest has not been communicated to it by the Government asserting it; and that the Commission is entitled to require by an Article 21 decision that the state measure in question should be withdrawn.

In *UniCredito/HVB*[214] the Commission cleared the proposed acquisition by UniCredito of Italy of HVB. However Poland required UniCredito to divest itself of shares in a Polish bank, BPH, which was indirectly controlled by HVB; it considered that the retention by UniCredito of these shares would violate the terms of an earlier agreement, in 1999, whereby UniCredito had purchased another bank, Pekao, as part of the process of bank privatisation in Poland. The Commission subsequently notified the Polish Government that it considered that the Government had violated both Article 21 of the EUMR[215] and Articles 49 and 63 TFEU[216], on the right of establishment and the free movement of capital respectively; however these cases were subsequently closed.

In *E.ON/Endesa*[217] the Commission approved the proposed acquisition by E.ON of Germany of a Spanish undertaking in the energy sector, Endesa. Spain took steps to impede the acquisition leading to two decisions of the Commission finding violations of Article 21 of the EUMR[218]. In March 2007 the Commission made a formal request to Spain to comply with these decisions[219]. Spain failed to satisfy the Commission with the result that the Commission referred the matter to the Court of Justice; the Court ruled in March 2008 that Spain had acted in breach of its obligations under EU law[220]. The Commission also came to a preliminary conclusion that Italy was in breach of Article 21 of the EUMR in *Abertis/Autostrade*[221], a transaction which the Commission cleared[222] but which Italy objected to on the basis that it was concerned that Abertis, of Spain, would not be able to carry out the investment required to maintain and improve the motorway network in Italy. In November 2006 Italy withdrew the obstacles to the merger and offered to cooperate fully with the Commission[223]. In January 2007 Italy made a submission to the Commission fully explaining the public interest criteria that were relevant to the case[224]. The Commission, after expressing its frustration at the late reply on the part of Italy, sent a new preliminary assessment again finding Italy in breach of Article 21 of the EUMR[225]. In July 2007 Italy took steps towards addressing the Commission's concerns[226], and the Commission closed the infringement proceedings in October 2008[227].

---

[214] Case M 3894, decision of 18 October 2005; see Busa and Cuadrado 'Application of Article 21 of the Merger Regulation in the E.ON/Endesa case' (2008) 2 *Competition Policy Newsletter* 1.

[215] Commission Press Release IP/06/277, 8 March 2006.

[216] Commission Press Release IP/06/276, 8 March 2006.

[217] Case M 4110, decision of 25 April 2006.

[218] See Commission Press Release IP/06/1265, 26 September 2006 and Commission Press Release IP/06/1853, 20 December 2006.

[219] Commission Press Release IP/07/296, 7 March 2007.

[220] Case C-196/07 *Commission v Kingdom of Spain* [2008] ECR I-41; see similarly the Commission's decision in Case M 4685 *Enel/Acciona/Endesa*: Spain appealed against this decision in Case T-65/08 *Spain v Commission*, but withdrew its appeal in June 2010.

[221] See Commission Press Release IP/06/1418, 18 October 2006.

[222] Case M 4249, decision of 22 September 2006.

[223] See Commission MEMO/06/414, 7 November 2006.

[224] See Commission MEMO/07/01, 5 January 2007.

[225] See Commission Press Release IP/07/117, 31 January 2007.

[226] See Commission Press Release IP/07/1119, 18 July 2007.

[227] See Commission Press Release IP/08/1521, 16 October 2008.

(G) **Defence**

Article 346(1)(b) TFEU provides that a Member State 'may take such measures as it considers necessary' in matters of security connected with its defence industry; such measures must not adversely affect the conditions of competition in the internal market regarding products which are not intended for specifically military purposes. This means that a Member State may investigate the military aspects of a concentration and the Commission the civilian aspects; this distinction in itself inevitably raises the problem of how to deal with products that have a 'dual-use', that is to say that can be used both for military and for civilian purposes. The UK Government successfully invoked Article 346(1)(b) in relation to the proposed takeover of VSEL by British Aerospace[228], where both companies produced military equipment for the British defence forces; it required British Aerospace not to notify the military element of the takeover to the Commission. Subsequent to this the *GEC/Thomson-CSF(II)*[229], *British Aerospace/Lagardère*[230] and *British Aerospace/GEC Marconi*[231] cases all involved the exercise of Article 346 by the UK. In the case of *GEC/Marconi* it was reported that the Competition Commissioner at the time, Karel van Miert, was concerned that the Commission in the past had been too generous in allowing the UK to assert jurisdiction in defence matters: at the least the Commission would wish to look at the civilian aspects of the case and might in future be more sceptical on how 'dual-use' products should be investigated. More recently it seems that the Commission has been taking a stricter view in relation to the application of Article 346; since late 1999 several mergers involving the defence industry in Europe have been fully notified to the Commission[232].

4. Notification, Suspension of Concentrations, Procedural Timetable and Powers of Decision

This section will deal with the following matters:

(A) **Notification:** concentrations that have a Community dimension are required by Article 4 to be notified on Form CO to the Commission.

(B) **Suspension of concentrations:** Article 7 provides that concentrations that have a Community dimension are automatically suspended until they are declared compatible with the common market; this period may be waived in appropriate cases.

(C) **Procedural timetables and powers of decision of the Commission:** strict time limits are imposed on the Commission's decision-making in order to disturb the operation of the market as little as possible: the EU Courts have stressed the importance of speedy procedures under the EUMR on several occasions[233]. The Commission can make a range of decisions when reviewing concentrations.

---

[228] DTI Press Notice P/94/623 of 19 October 1994: see Case M 528, Commission decision of 24 November 1994; see also Case M 529 *VSEL/GEC*, decision of 7 December 1994.

[229] Case M 724, decision of 15 May 1996.   [230] Case M 820, decision of 23 September 1996.

[231] Case M 1438, decision of 25 June 1999.

[232] These cases can be accessed at www.ec.europa.eu/competition/mergers/cases.

[233] See eg Case C-170/02 P *Schülsselverlag JS Moser and others v Commission* [2003] ECR I-9889, [2004] 4 CMLR 1522, paras 33 and 34; Case C-42/01 *Portuguese Republic v Commission* [2004] ECR I-6079, [2004] 5 CMLR 363, paras 51 and 53.

(A) **Notification**

Article 4(1) of the EUMR provides that concentrations with a Community dimension must be notified to the Commission following the conclusion of the agreement, the announcement of the public bid, or the acquisition of a controlling interest but prior to their implementation. Notification may also be made where undertakings demonstrate to the Commission a good faith intention to conclude an agreement or to make a public bid: this means that they can begin the investigative procedure, with the benefit of the fixed time limits, before the formal legalities of the transaction have been completed. The Commission publishes a notice of concentrations having a Community dimension in the Official Journal. Articles 4(4) and 4(5) make provision for the parties to make reasoned submissions for the reallocation of cases to or from the Commission: this has already been discussed in the section on jurisdiction[234]. Fines can be imposed for providing incorrect or misleading information in a notification or in response to a Commission request for information and for implementing a concentration without prior approval[235].

The Commission may declare a notification to be incomplete – for example because it omits information which ought to have been included – in which case the time limits for reaching a decision will not have begun to run. Rejection of a notification may have serious consequences for the undertakings concerned which, for a variety of reasons, may wish to conclude the transaction by a certain date. DG COMP has published *Best Practices on the conduct of EC merger control proceedings*[236] which seek to clarify the day-to-day conduct of proceedings under the EUMR; compliance will make it less likely that a notification is rejected as incomplete. The *Best Practices Guideline* suggests that, even in the simplest of cases, there should be pre-notification contact with DG COMP: the discussions should be commenced at least two weeks prior to notification and will be held in strict confidence[237]. Pre-notification discussions can cover a range of matters from jurisdictional questions and waivers of informational requirements to substantive analysis and possible remedies. The Commission prefers there to be business representatives present at meetings who have knowledge of the relevant markets as well as legal advisers[238]. The *Guideline* goes on to explain that a memorandum should be submitted to DG COMP to facilitate its initial contact with the parties, followed by more detailed submissions or a draft Form CO[239]. The *Guideline* explains that there may be 'state-of-play' meetings between the notifying parties and officials from DG COMP at key stages of the investigation; DG COMP may also meet with interested third parties, and it may even hold 'triangular meetings' if it would be helpful to hear everyone concerned in a single forum[240]. The *Guideline* also discusses access to the Commission's file following the opening of a Phase II investigation[241], the review of 'key documents' and issues of confidentiality[242]. Officials from DG COMP meet on Mondays to allocate new cases to a particular case team.

The Commission has adopted Regulation 802/2004[243] which sets out the format in which a notification (or a reasoned submission) is to be made.

---

[234] See 'Pre-notification referrals: Article 4(4)', pp 846–847 and 'Pre-notification referrals: Article 4(5)', p 849 above.

[235] See 'Powers of Investigation and Enforcement', pp 890–891 below.

[236] Available at www.ec.europa.eu/competition/mergers/legislation/legislation.html.

[237] *Best Practices Guideline*, paras 5–8.   [238] Ibid, para 9.   [239] Ibid, paras 10–23.

[240] Ibid, paras 30–39.

[241] See also the Commission's *Notice on access to the file* OJ [2005] C 325/7.

[242] Ibid, paras 42–47.

[243] OJ [2004] L 133/1; this Regulation replaces the earlier Regulation 447/98, OJ [1998] L 61/1.

(i) Notifications

Notifications are made in the format known as Form CO. An original, signed version of the Form CO, on paper, must be submitted to the Commission together with a further five paper copies with annexes and 32 copies of the notification in CD- or DVD-ROM format[244]; the notification is sent to a registry (known as the Greffe) which registers its time of arrival, at which point the merger review timetable begins to run. Form CO requires the notifying firms to provide substantial information: Annex I of Regulation 802/2004 explains the information that must be provided. The pre-notification meetings required by DG COMP's *Best Practices Guideline* provide an opportunity for the parties, their advisers and the officials from DG COMP dealing with the case to satisfy themselves that the Form CO, when it is eventually submitted, contains all the information needed for the Commission to commence its investigation.

In certain circumstances a 'Short Form' notification may be made, relieving the parties from some of the informational burden that they would otherwise bear. The circumstances in which this procedure can be used, and the information required in the short-form notification, are set out in Annex II of Regulation 802/2004. The procedure is available for:

- joint ventures that have no, or negligible, activities in the EEA
- concentrations where the parties are not engaged in business activities in the same product and geographical markets or in markets that are vertically related to one another
- transactions where the parties' combined market shares are below 15 per cent in the case of a horizontal concentration or, in the case of a vertical concentration, where the parties do not have an individual or combined market share in excess of 25 per cent at any level of the market
- cases where a party is to acquire sole control of an undertaking over which it already has joint control.

When a short-form notification is permitted the Commission will usually adopt a short-form clearance decision within 25 working days from the date of notification: this procedure is described in the Commission's *Notice on a simplified procedure for treatment of certain concentrations under Council Regulation 139/2004*[245]. A significant proportion of cases are dealt with under the simplified procedure. For example of 274 merger notifications in 2010, 143 were dealt with under the simplified procedure[246]. Cases dealt with under the short-form procedure are still subject to the suspension rule contained in Article 7 of the EUMR, but the undertakings concerned could apply for a derogation under Article 7(3)[247].

(ii) Reasoned submissions

Annex III of Regulation 802/2004 sets out the requirements for a Form RS where the parties seek a reallocation of jurisdiction to or from the Commission.

---

[244] See the Commission's *Communication pursuant to Regulation 802/2004 on the format in which notifications should be delivered to the Commission* OJ [2006] C 251/2, updated to take into account the accession of Bulgaria and Romania.

[245] OJ [2005] C 56/32.

[246] See 'Table of EUMR statistics', p 899 below for a statistical table of merger notifications.

[247] See below.

(B) Suspension of concentrations

Article 7(1) of the EUMR requires automatic suspension of a concentration that the Commission has jurisdiction to investigate before notification and before it has been declared compatible with the common market: this provision has been described by the General Court as one of the 'founding principles' of the EUMR in *Aer Lingus v Commission*[248]. Article 7(2) provides that, in the case of a public bid, the bid may be implemented provided that the concentration is notified to the Commission without delay and that the acquirer does not exercise the voting rights attached to the shares in question[249]. Article 14 provides penalties for 'gun-jumping' – that is to say implementing the transaction before receiving the Commission's approval – in breach of Article 7(1): infringement of Article 7 could lead to a fine of as much as 10 per cent of the worldwide turnover of the undertakings concerned. There have been three fines imposed for gun-jumping[250].

Article 7(3) provides that the Commission may grant a derogation from the provisions on suspension, subject to conditions where appropriate. A request for derogation from the automatic suspension must be reasoned, and the Commission will take into account the effects of the suspension on the undertakings concerned by a concentration or on a third party, and the threat to competition that the concentration poses. A few Article 7(3) derogations are allowed each year, as the Table of EUMR Statistics demonstrates[251].

(C) Procedural timetable and powers of decision of the Commission

(i) Phase I investigations

(A) Possible decisions at the end of Phase I

The Commission is required by Article 6 to examine a concentration that has been notified by the parties in accordance with the EUMR as soon as the notification is received. It must then make a decision either that the concentration:

- is outside the EUMR (Article 6(1)(a)) or

- is compatible with the common market (Article 6(1)(b)): this finding extends to any restrictions directly related and necessary to the concentration ('ancillary restraints')[252] or

- as modified by the parties no longer raises serious doubts and so may be declared compatible with the common market: such a decision may be subject to conditions and obligations ('commitments')[253] (Article 6(1)(b) in conjunction with Article 6(2)) or

- raises serious doubts as to its compatibility with the common market (Article 6(1) (c)); in this situation the Commission must initiate a Phase II investigation[254].

A decision under Article 6(1)(a) or (b) can be revoked where it is based on incorrect information for which one of the undertakings is responsible or where it has been obtained by

---

[248] Case T-411/07 [2010] ECR II-000, [2011] 4 CMLR 358, para 80.

[249] This was the position in Case M 2283 *Schneider/Legrand*, decision of 10 October 2001, OJ [2004] L 101/1 and Case M 2416 *Tetra Laval/Sidel*, decision of 30 October 2001, OJ [2004] L 43/13 where unconditional bids for shares on the Paris Stock Exchange had been made.

[250] See 'Powers of Investigation and Enforcement', pp 890–891 below.

[251] See 'Table of EUMR statistics', p 899 below.

[252] On ancillary restraints see 'Contractual restrictions directly related and necessary to a merger: "ancillary restraints"', pp 882–884 below.

[253] See 'Remedies', pp 884–890 below.

[254] An Article 6(1)(c) decision cannot be challenged before the General Court: Case T-48/03 *Schneider Electric v Commission* Order of 31 January 2006; an appeal to the Court of Justice was dismissed by Order, Case C-188/06 P [2007] ECR I-35.

deceit[255], where there has been a breach of an obligation attached to a decision[256], or where the decision is illegal in accordance with general principles of EU law[257].

(B) Timetable

In general Phase I decisions must, in accordance with Article 10(1) of the EUMR, be made within 25 working days at most of the day following notification; if the notification is incomplete the period begins on the day following receipt of complete information. The Phase I period may, in accordance with the second indent of Article 10(1), be extended to 35 working days where a Member State makes a request for a reference under Article 9, or where the undertakings concerned offer commitments pursuant to Article 6(2).

The Phase I timetable of 25, sometimes extended to 35, working days can place great strain on all the relevant parties – the business people, the professional advisers and the staff at DG COMP – which is why pre-notification meetings are so important. The overwhelming majority of cases are dealt with within the Phase I time limit, a not inconsiderable achievement given the complexity and size of many of the transactions notified.

(ii) Phase II investigations

(A) Possible decisions at the end of Phase II

Where a concentration raises serious doubts about compatibility with the common market the Commission will commence proceedings in accordance with Article 6(1)(c) of the EUMR. An Article 6(1)(c) decision inaugurates an in-depth Phase II investigation.

The decisions the Commission may make at the end of Phase II are set out in Article 8. It may decide that the concentration:

- is compatible with the common market, having regard to the provisions of Article 2(2) and, in some cases, Articles 2(4) and 2(5)[258] (Article 8(1)): this finding extends to any ancillary restraints or

- is compatible with the common market, subject to commitments to ensure compliance with modifications proposed by the parties (Article 8(2)): again this extends to any ancillary restraints or

- is incompatible with the common market (Article 8(3)) or

- in so far as it has already been implemented, or implemented in breach of a condition attached to an Article 8(2) decision, must be reversed, or modified in an appropriate way (Article 8(4))[259].

---

[255] EUMR, Article 6(3)(a): see Case M 1397 *Sanofi/Synthélabo*, Commission Press Release IP(99)255, 23 April 1999, [1999] 4 CMLR 1178 where the Commission revoked its decision as the notifying parties had failed to produce information about activities in a particular market; the Commission reopened its examination of the case, but allowed a partial exemption from the Article 7(3) suspension that would otherwise have automatically occurred, since the parties were preparing to offer suitable undertakings to overcome any competition concerns and because of the significant prejudice that a delay could have caused to the parties and their shareholders.

[256] Article 6(3)(b): see Case M 1069 *World Com/MCI*, decision of 8 July 1998, OJ [1999] L 116/1.

[257] Case T-251/00 *Lagardère SCA and Canal SA v Commission* [2002] ECR II-4825, [2003] 4 CMLR 965, paras 130 and 138–141.

[258] See 'Articles 2(4) and 2(5) of the EUMR: full-function joint ventures and "spillover effects"', pp 880–882 below.

[259] Note that the power in Article 8(4) cannot be used to order the divestiture of shares in a company that do *not* confer control: Case T-411/07 *Aer Lingus Group plc v Commission* [2010] ECR II-000, [2011] 4 CMLR 358, para 66.

Further the Commission may order such interim measures as may be appropriate (Article 8(5)) or revoke a decision taken under Article 8(2) where the Commission based its decision of compatibility on incorrect information or where the undertakings concerned have acted in breach of an obligation attached to the Commission's decision (Article 8(6)).

(B) Timetable

Article 10 lays down the timetable within which the Commission must reach any of the decisions provided for in Article 8. The basic rule contained in Article 10(3) is that decisions under Articles 8(1) to 8(3) must be taken within 90 working days of the date on which proceedings were initiated; the second sentence of Article 10(3) provides that this period may be extended to 105 working days where the undertakings concerned offer commitments pursuant to Article 8(2) provided that they are offered within 55 working days of the commencement of Phase II. The second indent of Article 10(3) makes further provision for an extension of the Phase II time limit, at the request of the parties, for a period of up to 20 further working days.

Article 10(4) provides that the Phase II time limits may exceptionally be suspended where the Commission has had to obtain additional information owing to circumstances for which one of the undertakings involved is responsible. This provision is not invoked very often; in the case of *Oracle/PeopleSoft*[260] the Commission did 'stop the clock' pursuant to this provision in circumstances where it may have suited all the parties concerned, given that it meant that the decision under the EUMR could be taken after the proceedings instituted by the Department of Justice in the US had been concluded[261]. However in the case of *Omya/J.M.Huber*[262] the Commission stopped the clock to the annoyance of Omya; Omya's appeal against the Commission's decision was rejected by the General Court[263].

Where the Commission fails to reach a decision within the prescribed time scale, whether in Phase I or Phase II, the concentration will be deemed to be compatible with the common market[264].

(C) Phase II procedure

A Phase II investigation is usually an exhausting and exhaustive exercise for all concerned. The timetables are tight, given that the investigation is 'in depth'. During the 90 working day period there will normally[265] be:

- a detailed market investigation by the Commission, including the sending of questionnaires to the parties, competitors and customers
- a peer review panel within DG COMP, to test the strength of the case
- a statement of objections sent by the Commission to the undertakings concerned

---

[260] Case M 3216, decision of 26 October 2004, OJ [2005] L 218/6.
[261] *US and Plaintiff States v Oracle Corporation*, available at www.justice.gov/atr/cases/oracle.htm.
[262] Case M 3796, decision of 19 July 2006, OJ [2007] L 72/24.
[263] Case T-145/06 *Omya v Commission* [2009] ECR II-145, [2009] 4 CMLR 826; see Gatti, (2009) 2 *Competition Policy Newsletter* 59.
[264] EUMR, Article 10(6).
[265] It is not inevitable that the full procedure will be followed: for example it may be that the parties offer suitable commitments during the beginning of the Phase II procedure, thereby obviating the need for a statement of objections and/or the completion of the in-depth investigation; sometimes the parties choose not to have an oral hearing, not least because this can provide an occasion for third parties that object to the transaction to address their concerns orally to the Commission and the national competition authorities that attend the hearing.

- a period for them to reply
- access for the parties to the files of the Commission[266]
- an oral hearing which may last for one or two days
- a meeting (or meetings) of the Advisory Committee on Concentrations
- a period within which commitments can be discussed and an opportunity for interested third parties to comment on any such commitments[267]
- consultation of other Directorates General
- the preparation of a draft decision for the College of Commissioners to consider the adoption by the full Commission of the final decision.

Achieving all these steps within the Phase II time limits can be extremely difficult, especially since many of the cases that come to the Commission are immensely complex. The Chief Competition Economist and his team may play an important part in Phase II cases where in-depth economic analysis is called for[268].

(iii) 'Phase III'

Even when a final decision, whether under Phase I or II, has been made there may be a further period of uncertainty and delay for the undertakings concerned. Where the parties have offered commitments as a condition of clearance it may take a considerable period of time to implement them: practitioners sometimes use the expression 'Phase III' to describe this phase of some merger investigations[269]. Further delay may occur where there are appeals to the EU Courts, either by the undertakings concerned, or by third parties dissatisfied with the outcome of the Commission's investigation[270].

5. Substantive Analysis

Once the Commission has jurisdiction in relation to a concentration its task is to determine whether it is 'compatible with the common market'. The burden of proof is on the Commission which must produce convincing evidence that a merger is incompatible with the common market[271]. In *Bertelsmann AG v Independent Music Publishers and Labels Association*[272] the Court of Justice held that there is no presumption that a

---

[266] On access to the file see Case T-221/95 *Endemol Entertainment Holding BV v Commission* [1999] ECR II-1299, [1999] 5 CMLR 611, para 68 and Durande and Williams 'The practical impact of the exercise of the right to be heard: A special focus on the effect on Oral Hearings and the role of the Hearing Officers' (2005) (Summer) *Competition Policy Newsletter* 22.

[267] See 'Remedies', pp 884–890 below.

[268] On the role of the Chief Economist see Neven and de la Mano 'Economics at DG Competition, 2008-2009' (2009) 35 Rev Ind Org 317, available at www.ec.europa.eu/dgs/competition/economist/publications.html.

[269] On commitments see 'Remedies', pp 884–890 below.

[270] On judicial review of Commission decisions see 'Judicial Review', pp 891–897 below.

[271] See eg Case T-342/99 *Airtours v Commission* [2002] ECR II-2585, [2002] 5 CMLR 317, para 63; Case T-5/02 *Tetra Laval v Commission* [2002] ECR II-4381, [2002] 5 CMLR 1182, para 155, upheld on appeal Case C-12/03 P *Commission v Tetra Laval BV* [2005] ECR I-987, [2005] 4 CMLR 573, paras 37–51; Case T-210/01 *General Electric Company v Commission* [2005] ECR II-5575, [2006] 4 CMLR 686, paras 60–64; for discussion of issues concerning evidence generally see Levy 'Evidentiary Issues in EU Merger Control' in [2008] Fordham Corporate Law Institute (ed Hawk), ch 5.

[272] Case C-413/06 P [2008] I-4951, [2008] 5 CMLR 1073.

merger is compatible with, or incompatible with, the internal market[273]. The Commission is required to adopt a decision in accordance with its assessment of the economic outcome attributable to the merger which is most likely to ensue[274].

Article 2(1) sets out certain criteria which the Commission must take into account when making its appraisal: these criteria are described and explained below[275]. Compatibility with the common market turns on the issue of whether the concentration will significantly impede effective competition. Article 2(2) provides that:

A concentration which would not significantly impede effective competition in the common market or in a substantial part of it, in particular as a result of the creation or strengthening of a dominant position, shall be declared compatible with the common market.

Article 2(3) provides that:

A concentration which would significantly impede effective competition in the common market or in a substantial part of it, in particular as a result of the creation or strengthening of a dominant position, shall be declared incompatible with the common market.

The Commission has published three texts of particular importance to the substantive assessment of mergers, the *Notice on the definition of the relevant market*[276], the *Guidelines on the assessment of horizontal mergers*[277] and the *Guidelines on the assessment of non-horizontal mergers*[278].

(A) Market definition

The substantive assessment of mergers under the EUMR begins with a definition of the relevant product and geographic markets, the main purpose of which, as the Commission's *Notice on Market Definition*[279] says, is 'to identify in a systematic way the competitive constraints that the undertakings involved face'[280]. Some commentators believe that too much emphasis is placed on market definition in EU merger control, not least because techniques are being developed that make it possible to predict whether a particular merger would lead to an increase in prices without a formal determination of the relevant market or of market power[281]. Whatever the merits of this opinion may be, current practice assigns an important role to market definition: indeed notifying parties are required to identify any 'affected markets' in their Form CO (see below), and the Court of Justice held in *France v Commission*[282] that a proper definition of the relevant market is a necessary precondition for any assessment of the effect of a concentration on competition under the EUMR[283]. Market definition, including the Commission's *Notice on Market Definition*, has been discussed in detail in chapter 1 to which the reader is referred[284]. A few specific points about market definition under the EUMR follow.

---

[273] Ibid, para 48; see similarly Case T-210/01 *General Electric v Commission* [2005] ECR II-5575, [2006] 4 CMLR 686, para 61.

[274] Ibid, para 52; see also Advocate General Kokott's Opinion, para 208.

[275] See 'Article 2(1): the appraisal criteria', p 867 below.

[276] OJ [1997] C 372/5.   [277] OJ [2004] C 31/5.

[278] OJ [2008] C 265/6.

[279] OJ [1997] C 372/5.   [280] Ibid, para 2.

[281] See ch 20, 'Evidence', pp 821–822, on merger simulation.

[282] Cases C-68/94 and C-30/95 etc [1998] ECR I-1375, [1998] 4 CMLR 829, para 143.

[283] Ibid, para 55; subsequent judgments have regularly repeated this point: see eg Case T-151/05 *Nederlandse Vakbond Varkenshouders (NVV) etc v Commission* [2009] ECR II-1219, [2009] 5 CMLR 1613, para 51.

[284] See ch 1, 'Market definition', pp 27–42.

(i) Form CO: 'affected markets'

Sections 6 to 8 of Form CO require the notifying parties to provide information in relation to 'affected markets'. Affected markets are defined to mean, in the case of horizontal relationships, relevant markets where two or more parties to a concentration have a combined market share of 15 per cent or more at the national or EU level; and, in the case of vertical relationships, where their individual or combined market share is more than 25 per cent at one or more levels of the market. The information required in relation to these affected markets is substantial, including an estimate of the total size of the market, the parties' market shares for each of the last three financial years, the Herfindahl-Hirschman Index ('HHI') before and after the merger[285], the structure of supply and demand and details of barriers to entry. The *quid pro quo* for the supply of such extensive information is that the Commission should be able to make a speedy assessment of the case. As noted earlier the information contained in Form CO must be accurate and complete[286]; if it is not the notification may be declared incomplete, in which case the time within which a decision must be made will not have begun to run. This is why extensive preparation in advance of notification, including contact with DG COMP, is so crucial[287]. It is important to understand that one merger might involve a number of affected markets: multi-product firms may have many overlapping products. For example in the case of *Bayer/Aventis Crop Science*[288] the Commission considered that there were in the region of 130 affected markets for crop protection, professional pest control and animal health products.

(ii) Commission decisions

In the period up to 20 June 2011 the Commission had adopted more than 4,000 decisions under the EUMR, and these contain many useful insights into its likely definition of the relevant market. Practitioners therefore, quite apart from conducting SSNIP (and other) tests to define the relevant market, will have recourse to the decisional practice of the Commission for guidance. The point should perhaps be added that in many clearance decisions the Commission does not reach a finding on market definition, since it is clear that to do so would not materially affect its assessment; the Commission will say that, however the market is defined, it is satisfied that the concentration would not be incompatible with the common market.

(iii) Effect of decisions on market definition

In *Coca-Cola Co v Commission*[289] the General Court stated clearly that a market definition in an earlier decision of the Commission could not be binding in the case of a subsequent investigation, either by the Commission itself or a national court or competition authority: each case must turn on the particular facts and circumstances prevailing at the time.

(B) Adoption of the 'significant impediment to effective competition' test

The Commission will declare a merger to be incompatible with the common market where it would significantly impede effective competition, in particular as a result of the

---

[285] See 'Concentration levels', p 869 below on the HHI.

[286] See 'Notification', p 856 above.   [287] Ibid.

[288] Case M 2547, decision of 17 April 2002, OJ [2004] L 107/1; see similarly Case M 3465 *Syngenta CP/Advanta*, decision of 17 August 2004.

[289] Cases T-125/97 and T-127/97 [2000] ECR II-1733, [2000] 5 CMLR 467; it follows that notifying parties should not expect that the Commission will define a relevant market in the way it did in a previous decision: see Case T-151/05 *Nederlandse Vakbond Varkenshouders v Commission* [2009] ECR II-1219, [2009] 5 CMLR 1613, paras 136–140.

creation or strengthening of a dominant position. This formulation is subtly different from the test in the original Merger Regulation of 1989, which asked whether the merger would create or strengthen a dominant position as a result of which effective competition would be significantly impeded. The change in the substantive test was made in 2004 following a protracted debate which focused, in particular, on the respective merits of a test based on dominance, on the one hand, and on a substantial lessening of competition ('SLC'), on the other; and on the specific question of whether the dominance test left a 'gap' which meant that some mergers that could be harmful to competition could not be challenged under the EUMR. The compromise that emerged from this debate was the significant impediment to effective competition ('SIEC') test.

(i) The dominance/SLC debate

By the time that the original Merger Regulation was adopted there was a reasonable amount of jurisprudence on the meaning of dominance under Article 102, in particular in cases such as *Continental Can v Commission*[290] and *United Brands v Commission*[291]; it was obviously attractive to deploy that jurisprudence for the purpose of merger control. In the years that followed the adoption of the Merger Regulation the Commission was able to adapt the dominance test and to apply it successfully to cases on single-firm dominance[292] and to collective dominance[293]; it also prohibited some vertical mergers under the dominance test[294]. For the most part the EU system of merger control developed very successfully, with one exception: the possibility that it could not be used to deal with problems of 'non-collusive oligopoly'.

(ii) The non-collusive oligopoly gap[295]

The perception that there could be a 'gap' in the coverage of the Merger Regulation arose as a result of the *Airtours/First Choice* decision[296]. Airtours' proposed acquisition of First Choice would reduce the number of major tour operators in the UK from four to three. No firm would be individually dominant after the merger. The Commission prohibited the transaction on the basis that it would create a collective dominant position: however the language it used, in particular in paragraph 54 of its decision, suggested that each firm remaining on the market would be able *unilaterally* to exercise market power, without any need to act in a *coordinated* manner. The General Court, on appeal, handed down a judgment that clearly associated collective dominance with coordinated effects and annulled the Commission's decision[297]. It followed that, if the Commission did think that the

---

[290] Case 6/72 *Europemballage and Continental Can v Commission* [1973] ECR 215, [1973] CMLR 199.

[291] Case 27/76 *United Brands Co v Commission* [1978] ECR 207, [1978] 1 CMLR 429.

[292] See eg Case M 53 *Aerospatiale-Alenia/de Havilland*, decision of 2 October 1991, OJ [1991] L 334/42, [1992] 4 CMLR M2: this was the first prohibition decision under the Merger Regulation.

[293] See eg Case M 308 *Kali und Salz* OJ [1994] L 186/38, on appeal Cases C-68/94 and C-30/95 *France v Commission* [1998] ECR I-1375, [1998] 4 CMLR 829; Case M.619 *Gencor/Lonrho*, decision of 24 April 1996, OJ [1997] L 11/30, [1999] 4 CMLR 1076, upheld on appeal Case T-102/96 *Gencor v Commission* [1999] ECR II-753, [1999] 4 CMLR 971: this was the first prohibition decision based on collective dominance.

[294] See eg Case M 490 *Nordic Satellite Distribution*, decision of 19 July 1995, OJ [1996] L 53/20.

[295] See generally Kokkoris *Merger Control in Europe: The Gap in the ECMR and National Merger Legislations* (Routledge, 2011).

[296] Case M 1524, decision of 22 September 1999, OJ [2000] L 93/1.

[297] Case T-342/99 *Airtours plc v Commission* [2002] ECR II-5761, [2002] 5 CMLR 317: see 'Coordinated effects', pp 871–873 below; or comment on the *Airtours* case see eg O'Donoghue and Feddersen (2002) 39 CML Rev 1171; Stroux 'Collective Dominance under the Merger Regulation: a Serious Evidentiary Reprimand for the Commission' (2002) 27 EL Rev 736; Overd 'After the Airtours Appeal' (2002) 23 ECLR 375; Haupt 'Collective Dominance under Article 82 EC and EC Merger Control in the Light of the Airtours

problem in *Airtours/First Choice* was one of unilateral as opposed to coordinated effects, there appeared to be a gap in the Merger Regulation's coverage; if such a gap did exist it was because of the word 'dominance' which was not applicable in some situations.

A few examples may shed some light on the conundrum. In the following we assume that A, B and C produce high-quality products that are differentiated from one another; in other words the market is not one that is particularly conducive to coordinated behaviour[298]. In each case the proposal is that A will merge with B.

Example 1
Before the merger

A	B	C
50	30	20

After the merger

AB	C
80	20

After the merger AB will probably be individually dominant. The merger can be challenged under the dominance test.

Example 2
Before the merger

A	B	C
20	25	55

After the merger

AB	C
45	55

After the merger AB will certainly not be individually dominant since its market share will be less than C's; if the market is not conducive to coordination AB and C will not be collectively dominant either. The merger cannot be challenged under the dominance test.

Example 3
Before the merger

A	B	C
35	20	45

After the merger

AB	C
55	45

judgment' (2002) 23 ECLR 434; Nikpay and Houwen 'Tour de Force or a Little Local Turbulence? A Heretical View on the Airtours Judgment' (2003) 24 ECLR 193.

[298] See 'Coordinated effects', pp 871–873 below.

After the merger AB will be larger than C, but it is unlikely that, with these market shares, it would be found to be individually dominant; as in Example 2 if the market is not conducive to coordination AB and C will not be collectively dominant either. The merger cannot be challenged under the dominance test.

The key question is whether, in Examples 2 and 3, AB and C might be more able, on an individual basis, to exercise market power after the merger than they were before it; if so there is clearly a case for intervention, but intervention is not possible on the basis of individual or collective dominance.

(iii) The solution: 'SIEC'

Given the uncertainty raised by *Airtours*, some commentators raised the question of whether the dominance test was really an appropriate one to use: an alternative would be to adopt the test used in several Anglo-Saxon countries and to ask whether a merger would 'substantially lessen competition'[299]: this is the test in the UK[300]. However other commentators were far from convinced that a move to a substantial lessening of competition test was necessary or desirable: the dominance test was firmly established, had worked well in practice, and it was unclear that there really was a non-collusive oligopoly gap or that dominance could not be adapted to deal with it[301].

The solution adopted by the Council in the EUMR of 2004 was disarmingly simple: it retains the vocabulary of the old Regulation but rearranges it in a way that retains the existing law of dominance while at the same time endeavouring to close the gap. The wording within each of Articles 2(2) and 2(3) was simply reversed. The test is now whether a merger would lead to an SIEC, in particular by creating or strengthening a dominant position; it used to be whether the merger would create or strengthen a dominant position thereby leading to an SIEC[302]. The revised formulation envisages that most cases will be dealt with under the dominance standard as a result of the inclusion of the words '*in particular*': this responds to the concern that a repeal of the dominance test would lead to uncertainty and 'undo' 13 years of know-how and decisional practice of the Commission: recital 26 of the EUMR specifically refers to the desirability of preserving the existing jurisprudence of the EU Courts and the decisional practice of the Commission under the old Regulation, as does paragraph 4 of the Commission's *Guidelines on the assessment of*

---

[299] See eg Whish 'Substantive analysis under the EC Merger Regulation: should the dominance test be replaced by "substantial lessening of competition"?' in *EC Competition Law & Policy Developments & Priorities* (Hellenic Competition Commission, 2002), pp 45–62; speech by Whish 'Substantial lessening of competition/creation or strengthening of dominance' 28 September 2002, available at www.internationalcompetitionnetwork.org; speech by Vickers 'How to reform the EC merger test?' 8 November 2002, available at www.oft.gov.uk; Fingleton 'Does Collective Dominance Provide Suitable Housing for All Anti-competitive Oligopolistic Mergers' [2002] Fordham Corporate Law Institute (ed Hawk), pp 181–199; Biro and Parker 'A New EC Merger Test? Dominance v Substantial Lessening of Competition' (2002) 1 Competition Law Journal 157.

[300] See ch 22, 'The "Substantial Lessening of Competition" Test', pp 932–946.

[301] See eg Böge and Muller 'From the Market Dominance Test to the SLC Test: Are there any reasons for a change?' (2002) 23 ECLR 495; speech by Ulf Böge 'Analytical Framework of Merger Review' 28 September 2002, available at www.internationalcompetitionnetwork.org; Levy 'Dominance vs SLC: A Subtle Distinction' 8 November 2002, available at www.ibanet.org.

[302] See Schmidt 'The new ECMR: "Significant impediment or significant improvement?"' (2004) 41 CML Rev 1555; Fountoukakos and Ryan 'A New Substantive Test for EC Merger Control' (2005) 26 ECLR 277; Röller and de la Mano 'The Impact of the New Substantive Test in European Merger Control' (2006) 2 European Competition Journal 8; Maier-Rigaud and Parplies 'Five Years After The Introduction Of The SIEC Test: What Explains the Drop in Enforcement Activity? (2009) ECLR 565; Levy 'The SIEC Test Five Years On: Has it Made a Difference? (2010) 6 European Competition Journal 211.

horizontal mergers[303]. However the new test does not make dominance the exclusive test, and would enable the Commission to prohibit or require the modification of a merger that would not create or strengthen a dominant position but would 'significantly impede effective competition'. Recital 25 of the Regulation makes clear that this formulation is intended to provide jurisdiction to deal with the 'gap', that is to say the problem of non-collusive oligopoly. The application of the substantive test to cases of non-collusive oligopoly since 2004 will be considered below, in particular the Commission's decision in *T-Mobile/tele.ring*[304].

(iv) The need for a causal link between the concentration and the SIEC

The judgment of the Court of Justice in *France v Commission*[305] established that there must be a causal link between the concentration and the deterioration of the competitive structure of the market for the EUMR to apply. In that case the Court of Justice was considering whether a 'failing firm' defence existed under the EUMR[306]. It held that a concentration should not be blocked where the firm would have failed anyway and its market share would have accrued to the acquirer, since the concentration did not cause the harm to competition. In *De Beers/LVMH*[307] the Commission's clearance was specifically based on the absence of any causal link between the creation of the joint venture and the strengthening of De Beer's dominant position in the market for rough diamonds.

(v) Article 2(1): the appraisal criteria

Article 2(1) of the EUMR sets out a list of 'appraisal criteria' which the Commission must take into account when investigating concentrations. It provides that:

> In making this appraisal, the Commission shall take into account:-
> (a) the need to maintain and develop effective competition within the common market in view of, among other things, the structure of all the markets concerned and the actual or potential competition from undertakings located either within or outwith the Community;
> (b) the market position of the undertakings concerned and their economic and financial power, the alternatives available to suppliers and users, their access to supplies or markets, any legal or other barriers to entry, supply and demand trends for the relevant goods and services, the interests of the intermediate and ultimate consumers, and the development of technical and economic progress provided that it is to consumers' advantage and does not form an obstacle to competition.

The information required in relation to affected markets by Form CO reflects the appraisal criteria set out in Article 2(1). The list of factors in Article 2(1) is not exhaustive: the Commission must consider all matters relevant to the assessment of a merger. Article 2(1) does not establish a hierarchy, giving greater weight to one assessment factor than another; the impact that the different appraisal criteria have on the Commission's determination will vary from case to case.

---

[303] OJ [2004] C 31/5.

[304] See 'Non-coordinated effects', pp 870–871 below.

[305] Cases C-68/94 and C-30/95 [1998] ECR I-1375, [1998] 4 CMLR 829; this case was decided under the original Merger Regulation: there is no reason to suppose that the requirement of a causal link would not apply in the case of the reformulated substantive test.

[306] See 'The "failing firm" defence', p 876 below.

[307] Case M 2333, decision of 25 July 2001, paras 112–114; see similarly Case M 2816 *Ernst & Young France/Andersen France*, decision of 5 September 2002, paras 75 and 90; Case M 4381 *JCI/VB/FIAMM*, decision of 5 October 2007, paras 708ff.

(C) **Horizontal mergers**

The Commission's *Guidelines on the assessment of horizontal mergers*[308] ('the *Horizontal merger guidelines*' or 'the *Guidelines*') provide guidance as to how the Commission assesses concentrations when the undertakings concerned are actual or potential competitors on the same relevant market[309]. The *Guidelines* deal in turn with market shares and concentration thresholds; the likelihood that a merger would have anti-competitive effects; countervailing buyer power; the possibility of entry into the market as a competitive constraint; efficiencies; and failing firms. This sequence will be retained in the text that follows. Paragraph 13 stresses that the *Guidelines* are not to be applied in a mechanical manner in each and every case; rather the competitive analysis in a particular case will be based on an overall assessment of the foreseeable impact of the merger in the light of the relevant factors and conditions. The judgment of the General Court in *Sun Chemical Group BV and others v Commission*[310] endorses this approach by the Commission, noting that the Commission enjoys a discretion enabling it to take into account or not to take into account particular factors[311].

(i) **Market shares and concentration levels**

The *Horizontal merger guidelines* note that market shares and concentration levels provide useful first indications of the market structure and of the competitive importance of the merging parties and their competitors[312]. The reference to 'useful first indications' is important: market shares and concentration levels are simply a device for conducting a first screening of a merger: they could never be determinative in themselves of the outcome of a case.

(A) *Market shares*

The Commission usually looks at current market shares, although it may adjust them if it is certain that changes are about to occur because of exit, entry or expansion[313]; and in some industries, for example where there are 'large, lumpy' orders – for example irregular purchases of major capital equipment – it may be necessary to look at historical data[314]. Very large market shares of 50 per cent or more may in themselves be evidence of the existence of a dominant position, although they are not conclusive[315]; and the Commission may find a dominant position in the case of market shares between 40 and 50 per cent,

---

[308] OJ [2004] C 31/5; note that prior to the adoption of the *Horizontal merger guidelines* the Commission had published two reports on the topic, *The Economics of Unilateral Effects* and *The Economics of Tacit Collusion*, each prepared by Ivaldi, Julien, Seabright and Tirole: the reports can be accessed on DG COMP's website; for discussion of the *Guidelines* see Voight and Schmidt 'The Commission's guidelines on horizontal mergers: Improvement or deterioration?' (2004) 41 CML Rev 1583.

[309] *Horizontal merger guidelines*, para 5.

[310] Case T-282/06 [2007] ECR II-2149, [2007] 5 CMLR 438.

[311] Ibid, para 57.

[312] *Horizontal merger guidelines*, para 14.

[313] Ibid, para 15; a point not made in the *Horizontal merger guidelines* is that sometimes the Commission will, when investigating one merger, take into account the fact that a subsequent notification has been received in relation to a different merger in the same sector that will have an impact on the future competitive structure of the market: see eg Case M 938 *Price Waterhouse/Coopers & Lybrand*, decision of 15 October 1997, OJ [1997] L 50/27, [1999] 4 CMLR 665, paras 108–111 and Case M 2389 *Shell/DEA*, decision of 20 December 2001, para 21; see also Schmidt 'Spotting the Elephant in Parallel Mergers: First Past the Post, or Combined Assessment?' (2003) 24 ECLR 183.

[314] *Horizontal merger guidelines*, para 15.

[315] On this point see Case T-342/07 *Ryanair Holdings plc v Commission* [2010] ECR II-000, [2011] 4 CMLR 245, para 41 and the judgments cited therein.

and even sometimes of less than 40 per cent, depending on the other factors relevant to the case[316]. In *Ryanair Holdings plc v Commission*[317] the General Court rejected Ryanair's argument that the Commission had placed 'excessive weight' on the market shares that the merged entity would have had on some air routes[318]. The *Horizontal merger guidelines* state that a merger may be presumed to be compatible with the common market where the market share of the undertakings concerned does not exceed 25 per cent[319].

(B) Concentration levels

The *Horizontal merger guidelines* state that the overall concentration level in a market may provide useful information about the competitive situation, and that it may use the HHI in order to measure it[320]. The Commission is unlikely to be concerned about a market with a post-merger HHI of less than 1,000[321]. The Commission is also unlikely to be concerned where there would be a post-merger HHI between 1,000 and 2,000 and a delta[322] below 250, or a post-merger HHI above 2,000 and a delta below 150, unless there were special circumstances such as:

- the merger involves a potential entrant or a recent entrant with a small market share
- one or more of the parties are important innovators in ways not reflected in market shares
- there are significant cross-shareholdings among the market participants
- one of the merging firms is a maverick firm with a high likelihood of disrupting coordinated conduct
- indications of past or ongoing coordination or facilitating practices are present
- one or more of the merging parties had a pre-merger market share of 50 per cent or more[323].

The *Horizontal merger guidelines* say that HHIs below the thresholds set out above may be used as an indicator of the absence of competition concerns, but that they do not give rise to a presumption either of the existence or the absence of such concerns[324]. The General Court in *Sun Chemical Group BV and others v Commission*[325] has added, however, that 'the greater the margin by which those thresholds are exceeded, the more the HHI values will be indicative of competition concerns'[326].

(ii) Possible anti-competitive effects of horizontal mergers

The *Horizontal merger guidelines* discuss the possible anti-competitive effects of horizontal mergers from paragraphs 22 to 63, dealing in turn with non-coordinated effects[327] and

---

[316] *Horizontal merger guidelines*, para 17.
[317] Case T-342/07 [2010] ECR II-000, [2011] 4 CMLR 245.
[318] Ibid, paras 41–60.
[319] Ibid, para 18, referring to recital 32 of the EUMR; note however that this 'safe harbour' does not exist in the case of a collective dominant position involving the undertakings concerned and other third parties.
[320] *Horizontal merger guidelines*, para 16; the HHI is explained in ch 1, 'Market concentration and the Herfindahl-Hirschman Index', pp 43–44.
[321] *Horizontal merger guidelines*, para 19.
[322] The delta refers to the change in the HHI as a result of the merger.
[323] *Horizontal merger guidelines*, para 20.
[324] Ibid, para 21.
[325] Case T-282/06 [2007] ECR II-2149, [2007] 5 CMLR 438.
[326] Ibid, para 138.
[327] Note that the expression 'unilateral' effects is sometimes used as an alternative for non-coordinated effects: see fn 27 of the *Horizontal merger guidelines*.

coordinated effects; there is also a brief discussion of mergers with potential competitors. The footnotes in the *Guidelines* contain many references to the case law of the EU Courts and the decisional practice of the Commission: due to constraints of space these judgments and decisions are not reproduced in the text that follows, but the reader should be aware of this useful reference point.

(A) Non-coordinated effects

Paragraph 24 of the *Horizontal merger guidelines* explains that a horizontal merger may remove important competitive constraints on one or more firms in the market, thereby enhancing their market power and leading to significant price increases. Paragraph 25 notes that generally this will happen as a result of the creation or strengthening of a dominant position on the part of one firm whose market share, after the merger, will be appreciably larger than its next competitor. However the same paragraph also refers to the possibility of non-collusive oligopoly, that is to say a situation in which the firms remaining in the market after the merger will be able to exercise market power, and therefore increase prices, even though there is little likelihood of coordination among them and even though they are not individually dominant.

Paragraph 26 explains that a number of factors are relevant to a determination of whether non-coordinated effects might occur, but explains that not all of them must be present in a particular case and that the factors set out in the *Guidelines* are not an exhaustive list. The following factors are listed:

- **the merging firms will have large market shares:** the larger the addition of market share, the more likely it is that the merger will produce an SIEC[328]

- **the merging firms are close competitors:** the higher the degree of substitutability between the merging firms' products, the more likely it is that the merger will produce an SIEC[329]

- **customers of the merging parties will have limited possibilities of switching to other suppliers**[330]

- **competitors are unlikely to increase supply if prices increase:** in this case the merging parties will have an incentive to reduce output to less than the levels prior to the merger, thereby increasing price[331]

- **the merging firms will be able to hinder expansion by competitors:** for example they may control patents or other types of intellectual property that would make expansion or entry by rivals more difficult[332]

- **the merger would remove an important competitive force:** for example the removal of a particularly innovative firm as a competitor[333], or a merger between two particularly innovative firms, may change the competitive dynamics of the market considerably[334].

The most common ground for intervention on the part of the Commission is the possibility of non-coordinated effects arising from horizontal mergers. The most recent prohibition

---

[328] Ibid, para 27.

[329] Ibid, paras 28–30; paragraph 29 discusses various methods of evaluating cross-substitutability eg through customer preference surveys, estimating cross-price elasticities and diversion ratios.

[330] Ibid, para 31.   [331] Ibid, paras 32–35.   [332] Ibid, para 36.

[333] Ibid, para 37; see eg Case M 5650 *T-Mobile/Orange*, decision of 1 March 2010, where the Commission's concerns included the possible elimination of the mobile operator H3G from the market.

[334] *Horizontal merger guidelines*, para 38; see eg Case M 5675 *Syngenta/Monsanto sunflower seed business*, decision of 17 November 2010, where the Commission's concerns included the elimination of one of the most important innovators in the market for sunflower seeds.

decisions, *Ryanair/Aer Lingus*[335] and *Olympic Airways/Aegean Airlines*[336], were adopted on this basis. The Commission has required remedies because of non-coordinated effects in several Phase II cases in recent years[337]. The case of *T-Mobile/tele.ring*[338] was of interest since the Commission required a remedy as a result of non-coordinated effects in an oligopolistic market where the number of mobile telephony operators in Austria would be reduced from five to four, and the merging parties would not become the market leader: in other words this was a case of non-collusive oligopoly that the adoption of the SIEC test was designed to address[339]. A further example of a 'gap' case is *BASF/CIBA*[340] where the Commission accepted commitments within a Phase I investigation.

(B) Coordinated effects

Paragraph 39 of the *Horizontal merger guidelines* explains that in some markets the structure may be such that firms will consider it possible, economically rational, and hence preferable, to adopt on a sustainable basis a course of action aimed at selling at increased prices. Some mergers might lead to an SIEC by increasing the likelihood that firms will be able to behave in a coordinated manner without entering into an agreement or resorting to a concerted practice contrary to Article 101 TFEU. Such coordination might concern prices, but it could also occur in relation to levels of production, the expansion of capacity, the allocation of markets or contracts in bidding markets[341].

Paragraph 41 says that coordination is more likely to occur where it is fairly simple to reach a common understanding on the terms of coordination. It adds that three further conditions must be satisfied for coordination to be sustainable: these are taken from paragraph 62 of the General Court's judgment in *Airtours v Commission*[342]. First it must be possible for the coordinating firms to monitor whether the terms of coordination are being adhered to; secondly, there must be some credible deterrent mechanism to maintain the discipline of the coordinating firms and to keep it internally stable; and thirdly there must be no constraint from outsiders that could jeopardise the results expected from coordination and make it externally unstable. The Court of Justice has said that these three conditions should not be applied in a mechanical way: they should be looked at taking into account 'the overall economic mechanism of a hypothetical tacit coordination'[343]. The conditions for coordination are then explored in succeeding paragraphs of the *Guidelines*. They point out that a reduction in the number of firms in the market may be a factor that facilitates coordination; but also that other factors, such as the removal of a 'maverick' firm likely to disrupt an oligopoly, need to be examined[344]. In deciding

---

[335] Case M 4439 *Ryanair/Aer Lingus*, decision of 27 June 2007, upheld on appeal Case T-342/07 *Ryanair Holdings plc v Commission* [2010] ECR II-000, [2011] 4 CMLR 245.

[336] Case M 5830, decision of 26 January 2011, an appeal Case T-202/11 *Aeroporia Aigaiou Aeroporik: AE v Commission*, not yet decided.

[337] See 'Clearances subject to commitments', pp 905–906 below.

[338] Case M 3916, decision of 26 April 2006; see Lübking '*T-Mobile Austria/tele.ring*: Remedying the loss of a maverick' (2006) (Summer) *Competition Policy Newsletter* 46.

[339] See 'The non-collusive oligopoly gap', pp 864–866 above; findings of non-collusive oligopoly are rare: another one is Case M 3687 *Johnson & Johnson/Guidant*, decision of 25 August 2005, paras 312–325 in relation to endovascular stents.

[340] Case M 5355, decision of 12 March 2009.   [341] *Horizontal merger guidelines*, para 40.

[342] Case T-342/99 [2002] ECR II-2585, [2002] 5 CMLR 317.

[343] Case C-413/06 P *Bertelsmann AG v Independent Music Publishers and Labels Association* [2008] ECR I-4951, [2008] 5 CMLR 1073, para 125.

[344] *Horizontal merger guidelines*, para 42.

whether coordination is likely to result from the merger the Commission will look at evidence of past coordination or evidence of coordination in similar markets[345].

The *Guidelines* discuss the following factors:

- **reaching terms of coordination:** this is more likely to occur if it is easy to arrive at a common perception as to how the coordination should occur[346]. A number of matters are relevant when determining whether coordination would be easy, though these should not be applied in a mechanistic way[347]:

  - is the economic environment simple and stable?

  - are there a few, rather than many, firms in the market?

  - are the products homogeneous rather than complex?

  - are price and demand conditions stable rather than constantly changing?

  - is the market one in which there is little innovation?

  - in the case of coordination by way of market division would it be easy to allocate customers, for example on the basis of geography?

  - do other factors in the market increase transparency and so make it easier to coordinate prices?

  - are the firms symmetric in terms of cost structures, market shares, capacity levels and levels of vertical integration?

- **monitoring deviations:** coordination will work only if the coordinating firms are able to monitor one another to ensure that no one is cheating, for example by lowering price, expanding output or improving quality. Markets must be sufficiently transparent to prevent this happening[348]. Paragraphs 50 and 51 of the *Guidelines* discuss factors relevant to a determination of transparency: for example transparency is higher where transactions take place on a public exchange than where they are negotiated privately on a bilateral basis

- **deterrent mechanisms:** coordination will work only if there is a sufficient threat that there will be retaliation against a firm that deviates[349]. Paragraphs 53 to 55 of the *Guidelines* discuss the credibility of deterrent mechanisms: the coordinating firms must have an economic incentive to retaliate against any firms that deviate; and the deviation does not necessarily have to be in the same market as the coordination

- **reactions of outsiders:** coordination will work only if there is no competitive constraint from non-coordinating actual or potential competitors[350].

In *Impala v Commission*[351] the Commission originally had concerns about a merger that it thought might lead to coordinated effects, but, during its Phase II investigation, reached

---

[345] Ibid, para 43; in Case T-464/04 *Impala v Commission* [2006] ECR II-2289, [2006] 5 CMLR 1049 the General Court said that the close alignment of prices over a significant period of time might, together with other factors, be sufficient to prove evidence of past coordination: ibid, paras 252–254.

[346] *Horizontal merger guidelines*, para 44.   [347] Ibid, paras 45–48.   [348] Ibid, para 49.

[349] Ibid, para 52.   [350] Ibid, paras 56–57.

[351] Case T-464/04 [2006] ECR II-2289, [2006] 5 CMLR 1049; for comment see Völcker and O'Daly 'The Court of First Instance's *Impala* Judgment: a Judicial Counter-reformation in EC Merger Control?' (2006) 27 ECLR 589; Brandenburger and Janssens 'The *Impala* Judgment: Does EC Merger Control Need to be Fixed or Fine-Tuned?' (2007) 3(1) Competition Policy International 301; Ysewyn and Tajana 'The *Sony/BMG* Judgment of the Court of First Instance: Its Main Legal Implications and Impact on the Merger Control Process' (2007) 2 European Business Law Journal 233.

the conclusion that the merger should be cleared unconditionally. A third party success-fully challenged the Commission's clearance decision before the General Court, which considered that the market was a transparent one in which coordination was possible[352]. However the merging parties successfully appealed to the Court of Justice against the General Court's judgment[353]; the Court of Justice considered that the General Court had committed a number of errors of law and that, specifically in relation to tacit coordina-tion, it had failed to consider the transparency of the recorded music market 'by refer-ence to a postulated monitoring mechanism forming part of a plausible theory of tacit co-ordination'[354]. The Court therefore set aside the judgment of the General Court and referred the matter back to it; because of a subsequent alteration in the market the appeal was eventually dropped as it had become devoid of purpose[355].

The Commission was concerned about coordinated effects in *Areva/Urenco/ETC*[356], where it required various commitments, including a cessation of the flow of commercially sensitive information between a joint venture and its parents, as a condition of clearance. Commitments were also required as a condition of clearance in *Linde/BOC*[357], including the divestment of various wholesale supply contracts for helium and the termination of structural links, through a series of Asian joint ventures, between the merged entity and a competitor, Air Liquide. In *Travelport/Worldspan*[358] the Commission concluded, follow-ing a Phase II investigation, that a 'four to three' merger in the market for global distribu-tion services would not give rise to coordinated effects since the complexity of the pricing structure and product offerings in that case limited the transparency of the market and therefore the possibility of successfully monitoring coordinated behaviour. In *ABF/GBI Business*[359] remedies were required to address the reduction from three to two competi-tors on the Spanish and Portuguese markets for yeast.

(C) Mergers with a potential competitor

Paragraphs 58 to 60 of the *Horizontal merger guidelines* discuss mergers with potential competitors. Such a merger could lead to non-coordinated, or coordinated, effects where the potential competitor significantly constrains the behaviour of the firms active on the market. This is the case if the potential competitor possesses assets that could easily be used to enter the market without incurring significant sunk costs. Paragraph 60 states that for a merger with a potential competitor to give rise to significant anti-competitive effects two conditions must be satisfied: first, the potential competitors must already exert a significant constraining influence; and second, there must be a lack of other potential competitors which could maintain competitive pressure after the merger.

---

[352] Ibid, paras 288–294.

[353] Case C-413/06 P *Bertelsmann AG and Sony Corporation of America v Impala* [2008] ECR I-4951, [2008] 5 CMLR 1073.

[354] Ibid, paras 117–134; for comment on this case see Golding 'The Impala case: a quiet conclusion but a lasting legacy' (2010) 31(7) ECLR 261 and Luebking and Ohrlander 'The Joint Venture Sony/BMG: final rul-ing by the European Court of Justice' (2009) 2 *Competition Policy Newsletter* 68.

[355] Case T-464/04 *Impala v Commission*, order of 30 June 2009; note that, while the litigation in the EU Courts was proceeding, the Commission adopted a second decision clearing the *Sony/Bertelsmann* merger, Case M 3333, decision of 3 October 2007: see Lübking, Kijewski, Dupont, Jehanno and Eberl (2007) 3 *Competition Policy Newsletter* 85; that decision was also appealed to the General Court, Case T-229/08 *Impala v Commission*, but the Court declared that the action had become devoid of purpose; order of 30 September 2009.

[356] Case M 3099, decision of 6 October 2004.   [357] Case M 4141, decision of 6 June 2006.

[358] Case M 4523, decision of 21 August 2007.

[359] Case M 4980, decision of 23 September 2008; for comment see Amelio, de la Mano, Maximiano and Porubsky 'ABF/GBI Business: coordinated effects baked again' (2009) 1 *Competition Policy Newsletter* 91.

(iii) Countervailing buyer power

Paragraph 64 of the *Horizontal merger guidelines* explains that the competitive pressure on a supplier can come not only from competitors but also from a customer if it has countervailing buyer power, that is to say bargaining strength vis-à-vis a seller due to its size, commercial significance and its ability to switch to alternative suppliers. The Commission will consider to what extent a buyer could immediately switch to other suppliers, credibly threaten to integrate vertically (and therefore self-supply) or sponsor upstream expansion or entry; it is more likely that large and sophisticated customers will have this kind of countervailing buyer power than smaller firms in a fragmented industry[360]. In *Sun Chemical Group BV and others v Commission*[361] the General Court rejected an argument by a third party objecting to the clearance of a merger that the Commission had failed to apply the *Guidelines* on countervailing power correctly[362].

(iv) Entry

Paragraph 68 of the *Horizontal merger guidelines* explains that if entry into a market is sufficiently easy a merger is unlikely to lead to an SIEC: for entry to amount to a sufficient competitive constraint it must be shown to be likely, timely and sufficient:

- **likelihood of entry:** entry must be sufficiently profitable taking into account the price effects of injecting additional output into the market and the potential responses of the incumbents on the market; the amount of sunk costs will be relevant to the analysis[363]. Barriers to entry include:

  - legal advantages such as regulatory rules limiting the number of market participants or tariff and non-tariff trade barriers

  - technical advantages such as access to essential facilities, natural resources, R&D and intellectual property rights

  - incumbency advantages such as brand loyalty, established relationships with customers and other reputational advantages[364]

- **timeliness:** entry will be regarded as a competitive constraint only where it would be sufficiently swift and sustained to deter or defeat the exercise of market power; what constitutes an appropriate time period for entry will depend on the characteristics and dynamics of the market, but it should normally occur within two years[365]

- **sufficiency:** entry must be of sufficient scope and magnitude to deter or defeat the anti-competitive effects of the merger[366].

(v) Efficiencies[367]

Recital 29 of the EUMR says that, when determining the impact of a merger on competition, it is appropriate to take account of any substantiated and likely efficiencies put

---

[360] Ibid, para 65.

[361] Case T-282/06 [2007] ECR II-2149, [2007] 5 CMLR 438, para 57.

[362] Ibid, paras 209–217; the merger is question was Case M 4071 *Apollo/Akzo Nobel IAR*, decision of 29 May 2006.

[363] *Horizontal merger guidelines*, para 69.

[364] Ibid, para 71.

[365] Ibid, para 74.

[366] Ibid, para 75.

[367] Compare the *Horizontal merger guidelines* on efficiencies with the Commission's *Guidelines on the application of Article [101(3)] of the Treaty* OJ [2004] C 101/97, paras 48–72, which are clearly motivated by

forward by the undertakings concerned; the recital adds that the Commission should publish guidance on the conditions under which it may take efficiencies into account. This it has done in paragraphs 76 to 88 of the *Horizontal merger guidelines*. In *Ryanair Holdings plc v Commission*[368] Ryanair complained to the General Court that the Commission had made a manifest error in assessing Ryanair's claim that the concentration would lead to efficiencies; the Court rejected the claim, and was content to cite the Commission's *Horizontal merger guidelines* and to determine whether it had applied them correctly[369]. The Commission explains in paragraph 76 that efficiencies brought about by a merger may counteract the effects on competition and the potential harm to consumers that would otherwise have occurred. In making its appraisal of a merger the Commission takes all relevant factors into account including the development of technical and economic progress, as set out in the appraisal criteria in Article 2(1) of the EUMR. It is important to understand that this approach means that there is no 'efficiency defence' – if the merger will lead to an SIEC it cannot be saved by a finding of efficiency: rather the Commission will factor any possible efficiencies into its overall assessment of whether the merger will lead to an SIEC. Paragraph 78 explains that, for efficiencies to be taken into account, they must produce a benefit to consumers, be merger-specific and be verifiable; these conditions are cumulative:

- **benefit to consumers:** efficiencies should be substantial and timely and should benefit consumers in the relevant markets where it is likely that competition problems might occur[370]. The efficiency gain might be lower prices, though cost reductions that simply follow from a reduction in output would not qualify[371]; new or improved products or services could also amount to an efficiency gain[372]. Efficiency gains may enable a firm in an oligopolistic market to increase output and reduce prices, thereby reducing the incentive to act in a coordinated manner[373]. There must be an incentive to pass efficiency gains on to consumers, and the Commission will be more sceptical where the merger will lead to a monopoly or a very high degree of market power[374]

- **merger specificity:** the efficiencies must be a direct result of the notified merger and must not be capable of being achieved by less anti-competitive alternatives; the burden of proof is on the notifying parties[375]

- **verifiability:** the efficiencies must be verifiable such that the Commission can be reasonably certain that they are likely to materialise, and it is incumbent on the parties to produce the relevant information in due time to demonstrate that the efficiencies are merger-specific and likely to be realised[376].

In *Inco/Falconbridge*[377] the Commission considered, but rejected, arguments that the merger would generate efficiencies; in the Commission's view the parties had failed to demonstrate that the efficiencies were not attainable by less anti-competitive means and

---

similar considerations; the *Article [101(3)] Guidelines* are discussed in ch 4, 'The Commission's approach to the Article [101(3)] Guidlines', pp 160ff; see further Gerard 'Merger control policy: How to give meaningful consideration to efficiency claims?' (2003) 40 CML Rev 1367; Colley 'From "Defence" to "Attack"? Quantifying Efficiency Arguments in Mergers' (2004) 25 ECLR 342; Kocmut 'Efficiency Considerations and Merger Control – Quo Vadis, Commission?' (2006) 27 ECLR 19; Ilzkovitz and Meiklejohn (eds) *European Merger Control: Do We Need an Efficiency Defence?* (Edward Elgar, 2006); see also OECD Best Practice Roundtable on Competition Policy *Dynamic Efficiencies in Merger Analysis* (15 May 2008), including a European Commission contribution discussing different types of efficiencies and OECD Policy Brief *Mergers and Dynamic Efficiencies* (September 2008), available at www.oecd.org.

[368] Case T-342/07 [2010] ECR II-000, [2011] 4 CMLR 245. [369] Ibid, paras 386–443.
[370] *Horizontal merger guidelines*, para 79. [371] Ibid, para 80. [372] Ibid, para 81.
[373] Ibid, para 82. [374] Ibid, para 84. [375] Ibid, para 85. [376] Ibid, paras 86–88.
[377] Case M 4000, decision of 4 July 2006.

that consumers would benefit[378]. The parties were more successful in advancing efficiency arguments in *Korsnäs/Assidomän Cartonboard*[379], albeit in a case which it seems the Commission would have cleared unconditionally anyway.

(vi) The 'failing firm' defence[380]

Paragraph 89 of the *Horizontal merger guidelines* explains that the Commission may decide that an otherwise problematic merger is nevertheless capable of being found compatible with the common market where one of the parties is a failing firm. Three criteria are relevant:

- the allegedly failing firm would in the near future be forced out of the market because of financial difficulties if not taken over by another firm
- there is no less anti-competitive alternative than the notified merger
- in the absence of the merger the assets of the failing firm would inevitably exit the market[381].

It is for the notifying parties to provide in due time the relevant information to support a failing firm defence[382]. The Commission rejected a failing firm defence in *JCI/VB/ FIAMM*[383].

(D) Non-horizontal mergers

The Commission also investigates whether a merger could have vertical or conglomerate effects: its particular concerns are the possibilities of foreclosure and tacit collusion. These concerns were introduced in chapter 20[384]. For many years there was a lack of clarity about the Commission's practice in relation to vertical and conglomerate cases, and its findings in *Tetra Laval/Sidel*[385] and in *GE/Honeywell*[386] were reversed on appeal. In 2003 DG COMP commissioned a report on the competitive effect of vertical and conglomerate mergers which was published on its website in 2005[387]. In 2007 the Commission published

---

[378] Ibid, paras 529–550.
[379] Case M 4057, decision of 12 May 2006: see paras 57–64; see also Case M 4854 *TomTom/Tele Atlas*, decision of 14 May 2008, paras 238–250.
[380] See Cases C-68/94 and C-30/95 *France v Commission* [1998] ECR I-1375, [1998] 4 CMLR 829; for further discussion see Baccaro 'Failing Firm Defence and Lack of Causality: Doctrine in Europe of Two Closely Related Concepts' (2004) 25 ECLR 11 and the Note by the services of the European Commission for the OECD Competition Committee Meeting of 21 October 2009 *Roundtable on Failing Firm Defence*, available at www.ec.europa.eu/competition/international/multilateral/ec_submission.pdf.
[381] *Horizontal merger guidelines*, para 90.   [382] Ibid, para 91.
[383] Case M 4381, decision of 5 October 2007.
[384] See ch 20, 'Vertical effects', pp 819–820 and 'Conglomerate effects' pp 820–821.
[385] Case M 2416, decision of 30 October 2001, OJ [2004] L 38/13, on appeal Case T-5/02 *Tetra Laval v Commission* [2002] ECR II-4381, [2002] 5 CMLR 1182, on further appeal Case C-12/03 P *Commission v Tetra Laval BV* [2005] ECR I-987, [2005] 4 CMLR 573.
[386] Case M 2220, decision of 30 October 2001, OJ [2004] L 48/1, on appeal Cases T-209/01 *Honeywell International Inc v Commission of the European Communities* [2005] ECR II-5527, [2006] 4 CMLR 652 and T-210/01 *General Electric Company v Commission* [2005] ECR II-5575, [2006] 4 CMLR 686; for comment see Grant and Neven 'The Attempted Merger Between General Electric and Honeywell: A Case Study of Transatlantic Conflict' (2005) 1(3) Journal of Competition Law and Economics 595.
[387] See Church *Impact of Vertical and Conglomerate Mergers* (2004), available at www.ec.europa.eu; for discussion see Cooper, Froeb, O'Brien and Vita 'A Critique of Professor Church's Report' (2005) 1(4) Journal of Competition Law and Economics 785; Church 'A Reply to Cooper, Froeb, O'Brien and Vita' (2005) 1(4) Journal of Competition Law and Economics 797.

Guidelines on the assessment of non-horizontal mergers[388] ('the *Non-horizontal guidelines*' or 'the *Guidelines*') which provide valuable guidance as to how the Commission assesses concentrations where the undertakings concerned are active on different relevant markets. The *Guidelines* deal in turn with vertical mergers and with conglomerate mergers[389]. The *Guidelines* draw on the decisional practice of the Commission and the jurisprudence of the EU Courts since the EUMR entered into force in 1990. The text below does not cite this case law, but the reader should be aware that the *Guidelines* contain many useful references to relevant precedents. The *Guidelines* begin with an overview; they then discuss the significance of market shares and concentration levels; thereafter the specific issues arising in relation to vertical and conglomerate mergers are dealt with in turn. This sequence will be retained in the text that follows.

(i) Overview

The *Guidelines* acknowledge that non-horizontal mergers are less likely to significantly impede effective competition than horizontal ones[390]. First, they do not entail the loss of direct competition between the merging firms in the same relevant market[391]. Secondly, they provide substantial scope for efficiencies, for example by integrating complementary activities which may lead to lower prices and higher output[392] or by enabling a broader portfolio of products to be offered to customers, thereby giving them the benefit of 'one-stop-shopping'[393]. However the *Guidelines* point out that non-horizontal mergers may harm competition where they would alter the ability and incentive of the merged entity and its competitors in a way that could be harmful to consumers[394]. The Commission considers that (as in the case of horizontal mergers) non-horizontal mergers should be scrutinised for possible non-coordinated and possible coordinated effects[395]. Non-coordinated effects could accrue where a merger could lead to foreclosure of competitors[396]; coordinated effects if the merger would make it possible, or make it easier, for firms to act in a coordinated manner[397]. The Commission takes into account possible efficiencies that would arise from a merger as part of its assessment[398].

(ii) Market shares and concentration levels

The *Guidelines* state that the Commission is unlikely to have competition concerns where the market share of the new entity after the merger would be below 30 per cent and where the post-merger HHI would be below 2,000[399]. However it does say that there may be some cases where 'special circumstances' might lead it to investigate a merger below these thresholds, for example where a merger involves a company that is likely to expand significantly in the near future, for example because of a recent innovation: in this case its market share would not reflect its likely competitive impact on the market in the future; or where there are factors at play that suggest that the merger could facilitate coordination, for example the removal of a firm 'with a high likelihood of disrupting coordinated conduct' (often referred to as a 'maverick')[400]. There is no presumption *against* a merger above the 30 per cent and 2,000 thresholds[401].

---

[388] OJ [2008] C 265/6; see also *Non-Horizontal Mergers Guidelines: Ten Principles*, a note by the Commission's Economic Advisory Group for Competition Policy of 17 August 2006, available at www.ec.europa.eu/dgs/competition/economist/eagcp.html.

[389] For a discussion of the differences see ch 20, 'The horizontal, vertical and conglomerate effects of mergers', pp 810–811.

[390] *Non-horizontal guidelines*, para 12.　　[391] Ibid, para 12.　　[392] Ibid, para 13.
[393] Ibid, para 14.　　[394] Ibid, para 15.　　[395] Ibid, para 17.　　[396] Ibid, para 18.
[397] Ibid, para 19.　　[398] Ibid, para 21.　　[399] Ibid, para 25.
[400] Ibid, para 26.　　[401] Ibid, para 27.

(iii) **Vertical mergers**

(A) Non-coordinated effects: foreclosure

The *Guidelines* distinguish two types of foreclosure: **input foreclosure** and **customer foreclosure**.

Input foreclosure occurs where the merged entity would be likely to restrict access to products or services by competitors in a downstream market, thereby raising their costs and making it harder for them to compete in that market. The *Guidelines* say that it is not necessary to show that any competitor would be forced to leave the market, only that the higher input cost would lead to higher prices for consumers[402]. The assessment requires an analysis of whether the merged entity would have:

- the **ability to foreclose** access to inputs, which requires a 'significant degree of market power'[403]

- an **incentive to foreclose**, which requires an analysis of whether the foreclosure would be profitable[404]

- an **overall likely impact on effective competition**, because it would lead to increased prices in the downstream market, for example by raising rivals' costs or raising barriers to entry[405].

Likely efficiencies will be taken into account as part of the assessment[406].

Customer foreclosure occurs where a supplier integrates with an important customer in a downstream market: this may mean that potential rivals in the upstream market no longer have access to a sufficient customer base downstream[407]. As in the case of input foreclosure, the *Guidelines* require an analysis of:

- the **ability to foreclose** access to downstream markets[408]

- whether there is an **incentive to foreclose** access to downstream markets[409]

- whether there is an **overall likely impact on competition**[410].

(B) Other non-coordinated effects

The *Guidelines* briefly suggest other possible non-coordinated effects that might be problematic, for example obtaining access to commercially sensitive information about the activities of rivals in upstream or downstream markets leading to less aggressive pricing in the downstream market[411].

(C) Coordinated effects

The *Guidelines* discuss the possibility that a non-horizontal merger might lead to a situation in which coordination becomes possible, or more possible, than it previously was: as in the case of horizontal mergers, discussed above, the *Guidelines* explain that it is necessary to consider four issues:

- **reaching terms of coordination**

- **monitoring deviations**

- **deterrent mechanisms**

- **reactions of outsiders**[412].

---

[402] Ibid, para 31. [403] Ibid, paras 33–39. [404] Ibid, paras 40–46.
[405] Ibid, paras 47–51. [406] Ibid, paras 52–57. [407] Ibid, para 58.
[408] Ibid, paras 60–67. [409] Ibid, paras 68–71. [410] Ibid, paras 72–77.
[411] Ibid, para 78. [412] Ibid, paras 79–90.

(iv) Conglomerate mergers[413]

The *Non-horizontal guidelines* also discuss the possibility that a conglomerate merger could cause competitive harm, although they note that usually there will be no problem[414]; as in the case of vertical mergers they consider first non-coordinated effects and then coordinated effects.

(A) Non-coordinated effects

The *Guidelines* explain that the primary concern is that a conglomerate merger could lead to a foreclosure effect, for example by enabling the merged entity to indulge in tying, bundling or other exclusionary practices[415]. As in the case of vertical mergers, the *Guidelines* explain that it is necessary to consider:

- the **ability to foreclose**[416]
- the **incentive to foreclose**[417]
- the **overall likely impact** on prices and choice[418].

(B) Coordinated effects

The *Guidelines* also explain that the possibility exists of coordinated effects arising from conglomerate mergers, for example by reducing the number of effective competitors[419].

(v) Recent cases on non-horizontal mergers[420]

In *Thales/Finmeccanica/AAS/Telespazio*[421] the Commission went into a Phase II investigation because of vertical concerns, but concluded that the merged entity would not have the ability or incentive to restrict access to a critical component for the production of telecommunications satellites. In *SFR/Télé 2*[422] the Commission had vertical concerns about a merger that would bring together SFR, part of the Vivendi group that has a strong position in attractive television content, and Télé 2 with a presence in the downstream pay-TV distribution market. A number of commitments were given, including the provision of access to other pay-TV operators to the Vivendi group's content on non-discriminatory terms. In *Google/DoubleClick*[423] the Commission considered that the existence of strong competitors, such as Microsoft, meant that the merged firm would have neither the ability nor incentive to foreclose them and therefore concluded that the transaction did not give

---

[413] For further reading see Völcker 'Leveraging as a Theory of Competition Harm in EC Merger Control' (2003) 40 CML Rev 581; Koponen 'The Long and Winding Road: The European Commission's Path to a Framework for the Analysis of Conglomerate Mergers' (2007) 1 European Business Law Journal 241; Nalebluff; OECD Roundtable on *Portfolio Effects in Conglomerate Mergers*, available at www.oecd.org; Neven 'The analysis of conglomerate effects in EU merger control' in *Advances in the Economics of Competition Law* (MIT Press, 2005), available at www.ec.europa.eu/dgs/competition/economist/publications.html.

[414] *Non-horizontal guidelines*, para 92.

[415] Ibid, para 93; on tying and bundling see ch 17, 'Tying', pp 688–696 and ch 18, 'Bundling', pp 737–739.

[416] *Non-horizontal guidelines*, paras 95–104.   [417] Ibid, paras 105–110.

[418] Ibid, paras 111–118.   [419] Ibid, paras 119–121.

[420] See also Lahbabi and Moonen 'A closer look at vertical mergers' (2007) 2 Competition Policy Newsletter 11.

[421] Case M 4403, decision of 4 April 2007.   [422] Case M 4504, decision of 18 July 2007.

[423] Case M 4731, decision of 11 March 2008; see Brockhoff, Jehano, Pozzato, Buhr, Eberl and Papandropoulos 'Google/DoubleClick: The first test for the Commission's non-horizontal merger guidelines' (2008) 2 *Competition Policy Newsletter* 53.

rise to vertical concerns. In *Tom-Tom/Tele-Atlas*[424] and *Navteq/Nokia*[425] the Commission concluded that foreclosure of the input market for navigable digital maps would not be profitable to the merged firms; both mergers were cleared without conditions. Remedies were required to address vertical concerns in *Thomson/Reuters*[426].

In *Pepsico/The Pepsico Bottling Group*[427] the Commission rejected concerns about conglomeracy, concluding that the merged entity would not have the ability to foreclose competitors by bundling its soft drinks with its savoury snacks[428]. Conglomerate concerns were also rejected in *Proctor & Gamble*[429], *Pernod Ricard/Allied Domecq*[430] and *News Corp/BSkyB*[431]. However the Commission did have concerns about conglomerate effects in *Intel/McAfee* which led to Phase I commitments[432].

(E) Articles 2(4) and 2(5) of the EUMR: full-function joint ventures and 'spillover effects'

Where a full-function joint venture has a Community dimension it falls to be analysed within the procedural framework of the EUMR. In so far as it would bring about a change in the structure of the market it will be investigated in accordance with the provisions of Article 2(1) to (3) that have just been discussed. However there is a further possibility that needs to be considered in relation to full-function joint ventures, which is whether the creation of the joint venture could lead to a coordination of the behaviour of undertakings that remain independent of one another: this is sometimes referred to as a 'spillover effect'. This is tested according to the provisions of Articles 2(4) and 2(5) of the EUMR which are based upon Article 101 TFEU and the decisional practice of the Commission.

Article 2(4) provides that:

> To the extent that the creation of a joint venture constituting a concentration pursuant to Article 3 has as its object or effect the coordination of the competitive behaviour of undertakings that remain independent, such coordination shall be appraised in accordance with the criteria of [Article 101(1) and (3)] of the Treaty, with a view to establishing whether or not the operation is compatible with the common market.

Article 2(5) provides that:

> In making this appraisal, the Commission shall take into account in particular:
>
> – whether two or more parent companies retain, to a significant extent, activities in the same market as the joint venture or in a market which is downstream or upstream from that of the joint venture or in a neighbouring market closely related to this market,
> – whether the coordination which is the direct consequence of the creation of the joint venture affords the undertakings concerned the possibility of eliminating competition in respect of a substantial part of the products or services in question.

---

[424] Case M 4854, decision of 14 May 2008.
[425] Case M 4942, decision of 2 July 2008; on the *TomTom* and *Navteq* decisions see Esteva Mosso, Mottl, De Coninck and Dupont 'Digital maps go vertical: TomTom/Tele Atlas and Nokia/NAVTEQ' (2008) 3 *Competition Policy Newsletter* 70; De Coninck 'Economic analysis in vertical mergers' (2008) 3 *Competition Policy Newsletter* 48.
[426] Case M 4726, decision of 19 February 2008.   [427] Case M 5633, decision of 26 October 2009.
[428] Ibid, paras 29–40.   [429] Case M 3732, decision of 15 July 2005.
[430] Case M 3779, decision of 24 June 2005.   [431] Case M 5932, decision of 21 December 2010.
[432] Case M 5984, decision of 26 January 2011.

(i) A practical example

The operation of these provisions is best understood with the benefit of an example.

Example of a full-function joint venture

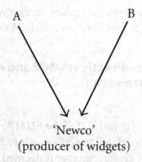

'Newco'
(producer of widgets)

Suppose that two producers of widgets, A and B, decide to merge their widget production into a joint venture, 'Newco'. Suppose further that both A and B will continue to produce widget dioxide, a raw material essential for the production of widgets, and that they will supply this raw material to Newco. In this case A and B will retain a presence in the 'upstream' market for widget dioxide[433].

The merger of the two widget businesses will be tested according to the criteria in Article 2(1) to (3) of the EUMR and the *Horizontal merger guidelines*:

- what will Newco's market share and market power be?
- will there be countervailing buyer power?
- would the merger lead to merger-specific efficiency gains?

However the additional question that has to be asked of this joint venture is whether the participation of A and B in the affairs of Newco will lead to them acting in a coordinated manner in the upstream market, for example because they will get to know about one another's pricing policy or capacity-expansion plans in relation to widget dioxide. This is the question that will be appraised in accordance with the criteria of Articles 2(4) and 2(5) of the EUMR.

(ii) Articles 2(4) and 2(5) in practice

In practice Articles 2(4) and 2(5) have not given rise to many difficult cases. The first Phase II investigation where possible spillover effects were considered was in the case of a joint venture between the telecommunications operators BT and AT&T[434]. The Commission identified certain 'candidate markets' in which coordination was a possibility and then considered, first, whether that coordination would happen as a result of the joint venture and, secondly, whether any restriction of competition would be appreciable. The joint venture was approved subject to commitments to eliminate the risk of parental coordination, including a divestiture of ACC, a wholly-owned subsidiary of AT&T[435]. In another

---

[433] It is equally possible that the spillover effects might occur in a downstream or a horizontally neighbouring market.

[434] Case JV 15 *BT/AT&T*, decision of 30 March 1999; a Phase II investigation into spillover effects was ended when the concentration in Case JV 27 *Microsoft/Liberty Media/Telewest* was abandoned; the first decision in a Phase I case was Case JV 1 *Schibsted Multimedia AS/Telenor AS/Telia AB*, decision of 27 May 1996 [1999] 4 CMLR 216; commitments have been accepted in some Phase I cases, eg Case M 1327 *NC/Canal+/CDPQ/Bank America*, decision of 3 December 1998; Case JV 37 *BSkyB/KirchPay TV*, decision of 21 March 2000.

[435] See the Commission's XXIXth *Report on Competition Policy* (1999), para 185.

Phase II investigation, *Areva/Urenco/ETC JV*[436], the Commission was concerned that a joint venture would lead to coordination between Areva and Urenco as a result of the increased scope for the exchange of information through the joint venture in relation to uranium enrichment. Commitments were given to reinforce firewalls between the parties and the joint venture and between the parties themselves[437]. The Commission investigated possible spillover effects in *Sony/BMG* but decided that they were not a concern[438].

(F) Contractual restrictions directly related and necessary to a merger: 'ancillary restraints'

(i) Introduction

Recital 21 and Articles 6(1)(b), 8(1) and 8(2) of the EUMR recognise that certain contractual restrictions may be directly related to and necessary for the successful implementation of a merger; a decision that clears a merger is deemed also to clear such restrictions. An obvious example would be where two undertakings merge their widget businesses into a joint venture 'Newco' and agree not to compete with the widget business of Newco since to do so would undermine the very purpose of the transaction. The question is whether clauses of this kind, often referred to for the sake of simplicity as 'ancillary restraints', are cleared at the same time as the merger. The Commission has published a series of notices on this subject, the most recent of which is the 2005 *Notice on restrictions directly related and necessary to concentrations* (the '*Notice on ancillary restraints*')[439]. Although the EUMR provides that a clearance decision will clear any ancillary restraints, it is for the undertakings concerned to conduct a self-assessment of which restrictions are ancillary (as in the case of Article 101 TFEU generally since the adoption of Regulation 1/2003). The Commission will not state in a clearance decision which restraints are ancillary: it will provide guidance only in the case of specific novel or unresolved issues giving rise to genuine uncertainty, other disputes having to be resolved before national courts[440]. Where a restriction is not ancillary this is not in itself prejudicial to it: rather it is then subject to independent examination under Articles 101 and 102 TFEU and national competition law[441].

(ii) General principles

Paragraph 11 of the *Notice* explains that the criteria of direct relation and necessity are objective in nature: it is not sufficient simply that the parties regard them as such. A restriction will be 'necessary' only where, without it, the merger could not be implemented or could be implemented only under considerably more uncertain conditions, at substantially higher cost, over an appreciably longer period or with considerably greater difficulty[442]. Examples given are restrictions necessary to protect the value of the business transferred, to maintain the continuity of supply after the break-up of a former economic entity or enabling the start-up of a new entity, regard being had to the duration, subject-matter and geographical field of application of the restriction in question[443].

---

[436] Case M 3099, decision of 6 October 2004.   [437] Ibid, paras 222–225 and 231–232.
[438] Case M 3333, decision of 19 July 2004, OJ [2005] L 62/30, paras 176–182.
[439] OJ [2005] C 56/24, replacing the previous *Notice*, OJ [2001] C 188/5.
[440] *Notice on ancillary restraints*, paras 2–6; in practice disputes as to whether a restriction is ancillary are quite often dealt with in arbitration proceedings: on the arbitration of competition law see ch 8, 'Arbitration', pp 325–326.
[441] *Notice on ancillary restraints*, para 7.   [442] Ibid, para 13.   [443] Ibid.

(iii) Principles applicable in cases of the acquisition of an undertaking

Paragraph 17 of the *Notice on ancillary restraints* explains that, as a general proposition, it is the acquirer that may need protection, for example to ensure that it acquires the full value of the business it has paid for; greater scepticism is shown to restrictions providing protection to the vendor. The *Notice* examines three types of restriction, non-compete clauses, licence agreements and purchase and supply obligations:

- **non-compete clauses:** these may be necessary to guarantee the transfer to the acquirer of the full value of the assets transferred including both the physical assets and the intangible ones such as goodwill and know-how[444]. Their duration, geographical field of application and subject-matter and personal scope must be limited to what is needed to implement the concentration[445]. As a general proposition a period of up to three years is justifiable where goodwill and know-how are transferred, and two years where only goodwill is included[446]. The geographical scope of the clause should be limited to the area in which the vendor has offered the relevant products or services prior to the transfer[447], and the clause should similarly be limited to the products or services forming the economic activity of the undertaking transferred[448]. Non-solicitation and confidentiality clauses have a comparable effect and are therefore evaluated in the same way[449]

- **licence agreements:** it may be that the vendor retains intellectual property rights in order to exploit them for activities other than those transferred to the acquirer, but licenses them to the acquirer for its purposes. Such licences – for example of patents or know-how – can be ancillary, but territorial limitations on the buyer as to the place of manufacture will not be; nor will restrictions protecting the licensor rather than the licensee[450]

- **purchase and supply agreements:** these may be needed in order to avoid the disruption of traditional lines of purchase and supply within the business transferred, in favour of both the acquirer and the purchaser, for up to five years; however exclusivity provisions and similar clauses would not be regarded as ancillary[451].

(iv) Principles applicable in cases of full-function joint ventures

Paragraphs 36 to 44 examine the same types of restriction in the case of full-function joint ventures:

- **non-compete obligations:** in the case of joint ventures an obligation not to compete with the joint venture is necessary to ensure good faith during negotiations, to fully utilize the joint venture's assets and to enable the joint venture to assimilate the know-how and goodwill transferred to it; obligations of this kind can be regarded as ancillary for the entire lifetime of the joint venture, not just for the period of two or three years envisaged in the case of the acquisition of a business from another

---

[444] Ibid, para 18.   [445] Ibid, para 19.

[446] Ibid, para 20; longer periods may exceptionally be permitted: see fn 21 of the *Notice*.

[447] Ibid, para 22.   [448] Ibid, para 23.   [449] Ibid, para 26.

[450] Ibid, paras 27–31; note however that licences that go beyond ancillarity in the terms of the *Notice* may be block exempted under Regulation 772/2004 on technology transfer agreements: see ch 19, 'Technology Transfer Agreements: Regulation 772/2004', pp 781–791.

[451] *Notice on ancillary restraints*, paras 32–35; note however that vertical agreements that go beyond ancillarity in terms of the *Notice* might be block exempted under Regulation 330/2010 on vertical agreements: see ch 16, 'Vertical Agreements: Regulation 330/2010', pp 649–672.

undertaking[452]. Non-solicitation and confidentiality clauses are evaluated in the same way[453]

- **licence agreements:** the principles are the same as for the acquisition of an undertaking[454]

- **purchase and supply obligations:** again the same principles apply as in the case of the acquisition of an undertaking[455].

6. Remedies

It is rare for the Commission to prohibit a merger in its entirety: by 20 June 2011 this had happened in only 21 cases, and four of those prohibitions were annulled on appeal. However there have been many cases in which the Commission permitted mergers to go ahead only after the parties had offered commitments to modify notified transactions that addressed competition concerns that it had identified: the Commission refers to such modifications as 'remedies'[456]. By 31 May 2011 the Commission had accepted commitments in 207 Phase I cases and 93 Phase II cases. This means that something in the region of 5 per cent of notifications of mergers having a Community dimension required modification before approval was forthcoming from the Commission[457]. The Commission calculated that in 2008 savings to customers as a result of merger remedies may have amounted to €3,100 million[458].

The Commission published a revised *Notice on remedies* in October 2008[459], replacing an earlier one of 2001[460]. The Commission has also published *Best Practice Guidelines: the Commission's model texts for divestiture commitments and the trustee mandate*[461] setting out model texts for divestiture commitments and for the trustee mandate.

(A) The legal basis for commitments

The legal basis for commitments as a way of settling merger cases is provided by Article 6(2) of the EUMR in the case of Phase I investigations and Article 8(2) for Phase II investigations. Each of Articles 6 and 8 provides that the Commission may attach conditions and obligations to a decision to clear a merger; such conditions and obligations are intended to ensure that the undertakings concerned comply with the commitments that they make to the Commission to modify their transaction. Recital 30 of the EUMR states that Phase I commitments are appropriate where the competition problem is easily identifiable and can easily be remedied: it adds that transparency and effective consultation of Member States and interested third parties should be ensured throughout the procedure[462]. Recital

---

[452] *Notice on ancillary restraints*, para 36.   [453] Ibid, para 41.   [454] Ibid, paras 42–43.
[455] Ibid, para 44.
[456] See para 2 of the Commission's *Notice on remedies* OJ [2008] C 267/1, available at www.ec.europa.eu/competition/mergers/legislation/legislation.html.
[457] The statistics in this paragraph can be accessed at www.ec.europa.eu/comm/competition/mergers/statistics.pdf.
[458] See DG COMP's Annual Management Plan 2009, available at www.ec.europa.eu/competition/publications.
[459] OJ [2008] C 267/1.   [460] OJ [2001] C 68/3.
[461] Available at www.ec.europa.eu/competition/mergers/legislation/best_practice.html.
[462] See also para 81 of the *Notice on remedies*.

31 explains the various consequences of failure to comply with conditions and obligations. These include:

- the possibility of the Commission ordering that a merger that has already been carried into effect, but in breach of a condition given in Phase I (Article 6(3)) or Phase II (Article 8(4)), should be dissolved
- the power to take interim measures to restore or maintain conditions of effective competition in the event of a breach of a Phase I or Phase II condition (Article 8(5))
- the power to revoke a decision where undertakings commit a breach of an obligation attached to a decision (Article 8(6)).

Article 14(2) of the EUMR provides for fines of up to 10 per cent of the aggregate turnover of the undertakings concerned to be imposed in the event of failure to comply with a condition or obligation attached to a decision; Article 15(1)(c) provides for periodic penalty payments to be imposed in the event of a failure to comply with an obligation.

(B) **The Commission's Notice on remedies**

The Commission published its revised *Notice on remedies* in October of 2008. The Commission also adopted Regulation 1033/2008[463] which amended the Implementing Regulation in order to provide the format for a new form, Form RM, which undertakings must submit to the Commission when offering remedies; Regulation 1033/2008 also clarifies that an independent trustee or trustees may be appointed to assist the Commission in overseeing the parties' compliance with the commitments that they give. The revised *Notice* reflects the insights resulting from DG COMP's 2005 *Merger Remedies Study*[464] in which it looked at the design, implementation and effectiveness of 96 remedies that it had accepted in 40 cases under the EUMR from 1996 to 2000. The study concluded that care is needed to define the right scope of a divested business; to ensure its interim preservation until divestiture; to approve adequate purchasers; and to ensure effective monitoring of the implementation of the remedies.

(i) **General principles**

Section II of the *Notice on remedies* discusses the general principles relevant to remedies. Most of the discussion is about the need for remedies to address the possibility that a merger might significantly impede effective competition in the sense of Article 2(3) of the EUMR, but paragraph 4 states that the *Notice* is also relevant to remedies required to address possible spillover effects under Article 2(4). Paragraph 6 of the *Notice* acknowledges that the Commission is not in a position to impose unilaterally conditions on the clearance of a merger: it can do so only pursuant to commitments offered by the parties[465]. Paragraph 7 explains the Commission's need to introduce Form RM. Only the parties to a transaction have the relevant information necessary to demonstrate that a remedy would address the Commission's competition concerns: they therefore must provide that information to the Commission so that it can conduct an assessment. However paragraph 8 of the *Notice* notes that the Commission retains the burden of proving that

---

[463] OJ [2008] L 279/3.

[464] Available at www.ec.europa.eu/competition/mergers/studies_reports/studies_reports.html; see also Davies and Lyons *Mergers and Merger Remedies in the EU* (Edward Elgar, 2008).

[465] See Case T-210/01 *General Electric v Commission* [2005] ECR II-5575, [2006] 4 CMLR 686, para 52; Case T-87/05 *EDP v Commission* [2005] ECR II-3745, [2005] 5 CMLR 1436, para 105.

a merger, as modified by the commitments proposed, would nevertheless significantly impede effective competition[466].

The amended Implementing Regulation established a new Annex, Annex IV, which sets out the information that must be contained in Form RM. It requires the notifying parties to submit detailed information concerning the commitments offered and, in particular, to provide specific information if the commitments offered consist of the divestiture of a business. The Commission may waive the provision of certain information if it considers that it is not necessary in a particular case. Form RM is divided into five sections dealing respectively with:

- a description of the commitment
- its suitability to remove competition concerns
- an explanation of any deviation from the Commission's Model Texts for divestiture commitments and the trustee mandate
- a summary of the commitments
- information on any business to be divested.

The last of these five sections requires a considerable amount of information about the nature of the business to be divested including:

- the assets (including IP rights and brands) to be transferred
- an organisational chart identifying the personnel currently working for the business concerned
- the customers of the business
- financial data including turnover for the last two years of the business involved and a prediction for the next two years
- an explanation of why the business will be acquired by a suitable purchaser within the time-frame proposed in the commitments offered.

The collection and presentation of this information will sometimes be a complex task and yet it will have to be supplied to the Commission within the tight timetables of the EUMR, whether the case is a Phase I or a Phase II one. The parties and their professional advisers will therefore need to begin the process of designing possible remedies and preparing a draft Form RM at quite an early stage of the investigation, very probably at a time when they are still arguing that the case is not one that gives rise to a significant impediment to effective competition or a spillover effect.

The *Notice* places considerable emphasis on the need for commitments to be effectively implemented and monitored. Paragraph 14 states that where the parties submit remedies that are extensive and complex it is unlikely that they will be acceptable, citing the cases of *ENI/EDP/GDP*[467] and *Volvo/Scania*[468] as examples. The Commission has a wide discretion as to the form that the commitments in question may take[469]. Paragraphs 15 to 17 make clear that there is a strong preference for structural remedies, such as divestitures and granting access to key infrastructure, over behavioural ones, although the use of the lat-

---

[466] See Case T-87/05 *EDP v Commission* [2005] ECR II-3745, [2005] 5 CMLR 1436, paras 62ff.

[467] Case M 3440, decision of 9 December 2004, OJ [2005] L 302/69, upheld on appeal Case T-87/05 *EDP v Commission* [2005] ECR II-3745, [2005] 5 CMLR 1436, para 102.

[468] Case M 1672, 15 March 2000, OJ [2001] L 143/74.

[469] Case T-177/04 *easyJet v Commission* [2006] ECR II-1931, [2006] 5 CMLR 663, para 197 and the cases cited therein.

ter cannot automatically be ruled out[470]. There are various disadvantages to behavioural remedies: pre-merger competition is preferable to post-merger regulation; remedies may increase transparency in the market, making tacit coordination easier; and they require monitoring and enforcement. In the Commission's view a commitment as to future behaviour would be acceptable 'only exceptionally in very specific circumstances'.

(ii) Different types of remedies

Section III of the *Notice* discusses different types of remedies. Paragraphs 22 to 57 deal with divestiture of a business to a suitable purchaser; paragraphs 58 to 60 discuss the removal of links with competitors; and paragraphs 61 to 69 consider 'other remedies'. The final part of Section III is concerned with review clauses.

(A) Divestiture of a business to a suitable purchaser

Paragraph 23 of the *Notice* explains that divested activities must consist of a viable business that, if operated by a suitable purchaser, can compete effectively with the merged entity on a lasting basis; the business should be divested as a going concern. Paragraphs 25 to 31 discuss the importance of determining the correct scope of the business to be divested. Paragraph 30 states that the business to be divested must be viable as such, so that the resources of a possible purchaser will not be taken into account at the stage of assessing the remedy. An exception to this is discussed at paragraphs 56 and 57 of the *Notice*: where a specific purchaser is identified during the investigation itself and the parties enter into a legally-binding agreement to sell, the Commission will decide in its final decision whether the purchaser is suitable; if it is there will be no need for commitments. The Commission welcomes 'fix it first' remedies of this kind, in particular where the identity of the purchaser is crucial for the effectiveness of the proposed remedy.

Paragraphs 32 and 33 of the *Notice* say that the Commission has a clear preference for the divestiture of an existing business that can operate on a standalone basis, that is to say independently of inputs from or cooperation with the merged entity. Paragraphs 35 and 36 discuss the situation where it is necessary to 'carve-out' a business from the merged entity's other businesses, that is to say to put a set of assets together capable of being divested that did not previously exist as a separate entity[471]; the Commission is not in favour of carve-outs, although it recognises that it would be disproportionate to rule them out altogether. The Commission would be more sympathetic to the sale of a standalone business with a 'reverse carve-out' of any business to be retained by the merged entity. Paragraph 37 expresses scepticism about the divestiture of assets such as brands that have not been a uniform and viable business in the past. Paragraph 43 states that, when the parties commit to a divestiture, they would normally be expected to agree not to reacquire influence over the divested business for a period of ten years.

Paragraphs 47 to 57 contain a detailed discussion of the need to transfer the business to a suitable purchaser, that is to say a purchaser who is independent of the parties, who has the financial resources, expertise, incentive and ability to maintain and develop the divested business, and who will be in a position to acquire the business without regulatory problems. The *Notice* deals in turn with cases where the Commission requires the business to be divested within a fixed time-limit (paragraph 52), or requires the identification of an 'up-front' buyer before the transaction can be completed (paragraphs 53

---

[470] The possibility of behavioural remedies has been confirmed by the EU Courts in a number of judgments, eg Case C-12/03 P *Commission v Tetra Laval* [2005] ECR I-987, [2005] 4 CMLR 573, paras 85–89; for further discussion see Ezrachi 'Behavioural Remedies in EC Merger Control – Scope and Limitations' (2006) 29(3) World Competition 459.

[471] On carve-out remedies see DG COMP's 2005 *Merger Remedies Study*, pp 74–80.

to 55), or accepts a 'fix-it-first' solution (see above). Paragraphs 44 to 46 explain that in some cases it may be possible to offer alternative commitments consisting of a preferred option but also a second one in case the first is not achieved. Sometimes this is referred to as a 'Crown Jewel' commitment: examples can be found in *Nestlé/Ralston Purina*[472] and *Johnson & Johnson/Guidant*[473].

(B) Removal of links with competitors

The removal of links with competitors – for example by divesting a minority shareholding in a joint venture or by terminating a distribution agreement – is discussed in paragraphs 58 to 60. Paragraph 59 explains that, in exceptional cases, it may be sufficient to agree to waive voting rights attached to shares rather than actually to sell them.

(C) Other remedies

Paragraphs 61 to 69 deal with other remedies, in particular commitments to grant access to key infrastructure, networks and key technology such as patents. Remedies of this kind have been accepted in many cases, which are helpfully cited in footnotes to the main text. Considerable emphasis is placed, in paragraph 66, on the need for there to be effective monitoring of remedies of this kind; this may include separation of accounting so that the cost of operating a key infrastructure can be ascertained and a fast-track dispute resolution mechanism to determine disputes about access. Paragraph 69 repeats the point made earlier that the Commission considers that behavioural remedies as to future behaviour will be acceptable only in exceptional circumstances. Paragraph 70 states that there may be cases in which a non-divestiture remedy is acceptable for a limited period of time.

(D) Review clauses

Commitments should normally contain a review clause that allows the Commission to grant an extension of time or to waive, modify or substitute the commitments. This issue is discussed in paragraphs 71 to 76.

(iii) Procedural issues

Section IV of the *Notice* is concerned with procedure, dealing in turn with Phase I and Phase II commitments. Article 19(1) of the Implementing Regulation requires that Phase I commitments be submitted within 20 working days of the date of receipt of the notification; Article 10(1), second sub-paragraph of the EUMR provides that the deadline for the Commission to make a Phase I decision is extended from 25 to 35 working days where commitments are offered. Paragraph 82 emphasises the need for Phase I commitments to be offered in a timely manner, given the tight timetables involved. Article 19(2) of the Implementing Regulation requires that Phase II commitments be submitted within 65 working days of the date on which the Commission decided to conduct a Phase II investigation; this deadline can be extended by a further 15 working days. Paragraphs 88 to 94 discuss timing issues, including the 'exceptional circumstances' in which it may be possible to offer commitments after the deadline has expired.

(iv) Implementation of commitments

Section V of the *Notice* discusses the implementation of commitments. It deals in turn with the divestiture process, the approval of purchasers, the obligations of the parties during the interim period, the role of the monitoring and divestiture trustees, and the

---

[472] Case M 2337, decision of 27 July 2001.
[473] Case M 3687, decision of 25 August 2005.

obligations of the parties following implementation of the divestiture. Paragraph 97 explains that the divestiture process can be divided into two periods. In the 'first divestiture period' the parties look for a suitable purchaser. If they are unsuccessful there follows the 'trustee divestiture period' when a divestiture trustee is appointed to divest the business. Paragraph 98 states that the Commission's experience is that short divestiture periods contribute to the success of the divestiture, and that it would normally expect the first divestiture period to last around six months and the trustee divestiture period around three months. A further period of three months is foreseen for closing the transaction.

As paragraphs 101 to 106 explain, the Commission will require to be satisfied that the purchaser is a suitable one, and if it thinks that this is not the case it will adopt a decision to that effect: such a decision could be challenged before the General Court, for example by a potential purchaser rejected by the Commission[474]. In *Éditions Odile Jacob SAS v Commission*[475] a monitoring trustee had approved a prospective purchaser, Wendel Invetissmement, for various publishing assets owned by Editis: the sale was a condition of the clearance of the *Lagardère/Natexis/VUP* transaction[476]; a competing purchaser of the assets, Editions Odile, successfully challenged the approval of Wendel as the trustee, who sat on the Board of Directors of Editis, the vendor, was insufficiently independent[477]. It is not unknown for the sale to a purchaser itself to amount to a merger having a Community dimension, with the result that it has to be notified to the Commission under the EUMR[478].

Paragraphs 107 to 116 discuss the obligations of the parties pending the divestiture of the business, dealing in turn with three points: safeguards for the interim preservation of the viability of the business; the necessary steps for a carve-out process if relevant; and the necessary steps to prepare the divestiture of the business. The parties will be required to hold the business separate from any retained business and a 'hold separate manager' will normally be required to be appointed.

Paragraphs 117 to 127 contain a helpful discussion of the respective roles of the monitoring and divestiture trustees. Five main tasks of the monitoring trustee are:

- to ensure that the business to be divested is not degraded during the interim period
- in carve-out cases to monitor the splitting of assets and the allocation of personnel between the divested and retained businesses
- to oversee the parties' efforts to find a potential purchaser and to transfer the business
- to act as a contact point for any requests by third parties
- to report on these issues to the Commission in periodic compliance reports.

The divestiture trustee – described in paragraph 118 of the *Notice* as the 'eyes and ears' of the Commission – will be given an irrevocable and exclusive mandate to dispose of the business within a specific deadline to a suitable purchaser; a minimum price will not be specified. The monitoring and divestiture trustees may be, but do not have to be, the same person or institution. In the Commission's experience auditing firms and other

---

[474] See the (unsuccessful) appeal by a potential purchaser in Case T-342/00 *Petrolessence v Commission* [2003] ECR II-1161, [2003] 5 CMLR 498; cf, under UK law, Case No 1081/4/1/07 *Co-operative Group Ltd v OFT* [2007] CAT 24, [2007] CompAR 899: see ch 22, 'Undertakings in lieu of a reference', pp 927–928.

[475] Case T-452/04 [2010] ECR II-000, on appeal Cases C-553/10 *Commission v Éditions Jacob* and C-554/10 P *Lagardère v Éditions Jacob*, not yet decided.

[476] Case M 2978, decision of 7 January 2004.

[477] Case T-452/04 [2010] ECR II-000.

[478] See para 104 of the *Notice* and the example given in fn 2 thereof.

consulting firms may be particularly well placed to act as a monitoring trustee; investment banks seem to be particularly suitable for the role of divestiture trustee.

Paragraph 128 states that the Commission will wish to be able to monitor compliance with commitments for a period of ten years after the adoption of its decision and will reserve the right to request information from the parties for that period.

(C) Remedies in practice

Remedy-setting sometimes involves extensive cooperation with competition authorities in other jurisdictions such as the US[479]. In several cases third parties have appealed to the General Court in relation to cases in which (in their opinion) the Commission had been too generous to the parties to a merger in accepting commitments[480]. Some cases in which the Commission has accepted commitments in recent Phase II cases are discussed in the final section of this chapter[481].

7. Powers of Investigation and Enforcement

The Commission is given wide powers of investigation and the ability to impose fines for transgression of the EUMR; these powers are broadly in alignment with the rules contained in Regulation 1/2003[482], although there is no power to conduct a 'dawn raid' on the homes of natural persons under the EUMR. To enable the Commission to carry out its functions the EUMR gives it powers to request information (Article 11), to carry out on-the-spot investigations (Article 13)[483] and to impose fines and periodic penalties (Articles 14 and 15) for breach of the Regulation's provisions. Article 11 requests for information are a standard feature of almost all investigations, and may be sent both to the notifying parties and to other undertakings – for example competitors, suppliers and customers – which might be able to supply DG COMP with relevant information. Fines for providing incorrect or misleading information or for breaking seals affixed to premises, books or records during an inspection can be up to one per cent of the aggregate group worldwide turnover of the undertakings concerned in the preceding financial year[484]. Fines for implementing a merger without notifying it and without the Commission's authority pursuant to Article 7 of the EUMR, for implementing a merger in breach of an Article 8 decision or for failing to comply with a condition or obligation attached to a decision can be as much as ten per cent of the aggregate group worldwide turnover in the preceding financial year[485]. In determining the amount of a fine the Commission is required by Article 14(3) to bear in mind the nature and gravity of the infringement. Article 15 provides the Commission with the power to impose periodic penalty payments of up to five per cent of average daily turnover where firms continue, for example, to fail to supply correct information or to submit to an inspection. Clearly the possibility of a heavy fine, in association with the power under Article 8(4) to require the reversal of a concentration

---

[479] See ch 12, 'The cooperation agreements in practice', pp 511.
[480] See 'Appeals against conditional clearances', p 896 below.
[481] See 'The EUMR in Practice', pp 905–906 below.
[482] OJ [2003] L 1/1.
[483] See Case M 1157 *Skanska/Scancem*, decision of 19 December 1997, OJ [1999] L 183/1, [2000] 5 CMLR 686, para 11; see also the Commission's MEMO/07/573 of 13 December 2007.
[484] EUMR, Article 14(1); under the original Merger Regulation the maximum fine for such infringements was much smaller, €50,000.
[485] EUMR, Article 14(2).

already effected, means that it is highly unwise to proceed without complying with the requirements of the EUMR. The EU Courts are given unlimited jurisdiction by Article 16 to review decisions imposing fines or periodic penalty payments.

The first fine (of €33,000), for failure to notify and for carrying out an operation without the prior approval of the Commission, was imposed in 1998 in *Samsung*[486]; in the US this phenomenon is often referred to as 'gun-jumping'[487]. In *AP Møller*[488] a larger fine, of €219,000, was imposed for failure to notify and for putting into effect three concentrations which were discovered in the course of an investigation of a notified concentration. In setting the level of the fine the Commission noted that the failure to notify was not intentional but that there had been 'qualified negligence'. AP Møller was a large European undertaking that could be expected to have a good knowledge of the EUMR, and the concentrations had been operated for a considerable time before they were brought to the Commission's attention. A mitigating factor was that there had been no damage to the competitive process. A much larger fine of €20 million was imposed in the case of *Electrabel/Compagnie Nationale du Rhone*[489] in June of 2009: the Commission concluded that Electrabel had acquired *de facto* control of CNR several years earlier, in December 2003, without having received prior approval from the Commission.

Fines were also imposed for the provision of incorrect information in 1999 in the cases of *Sanofi/Synthélabo*, *KLM/Martinair* and *Deutsche Post*[490]. In the case of *Mitsubishi*[491] the Commission for the first time imposed a fine on a third party, rather than the parties to the notified concentration; Mitsubishi had failed to provide information in response to requests from the Commission under Article 11 of the EUMR. The fines imposed in this case totalled €950,000. In *BP/Erdölchemie* the Commission imposed a fine of €35,000 for the provision of misleading information in a Form CO[492]; and a fine of €90,000 in the case of *Tetra Laval/Sidel*[493] for supplying incorrect or misleading information about its technology in the Form CO and for providing incorrect information in reply to a request for information.

8. Judicial Review

Decisions of the Commission under the EUMR are subject to judicial review by the EU Courts on the grounds set out in Article 263 TFEU, that is to say lack of competence, infringement of an essential procedural requirement, infringement of the Treaty or of any rule of law or misuse of powers[494]. Fines and periodic penalty payments are also subject to review, by virtue of Article 261 TFEU and Article 16 of the EUMR. In the early days of EU merger control appeals were relatively few, although there were some

---

[486] Case M 920, decision of 18 February 1998, OJ [1999] L 225/12.

[487] On gun-jumping see Modrall and Ciullo 'Gun-Jumping and EU Merger Control' (2003) 24 ECLR 424; Alomar, Moonen, Navea and Redondo 'Electrabel/CNR: the importance of the standstill obligation in merger proceedings' (2009) 3 *Competition Policy Newsletter* 58.

[488] Case M 969, decision of 10 February 1999, OJ [1999] L 183/29.

[489] Case M 4994, decision of 10 June 2009; the decision is on appeal to the General Court, Case T-332/09 *Electrabel v Commission*, not yet decided.

[490] See the Commission's XXIXth *Report on Competition Policy* (1999), Box 9, pp 73–74; the *Deutsche Post* decision will be found at OJ [2001] L 97/1.

[491] Case M 1634, decision of 14 July 2000, OJ [2001] L 4/31; see the Commission's (2000) (October) *Competition Policy Newsletter* 62–63.

[492] Case M 2624, decision of 19 June 2002, OJ [2004] L 91/40.

[493] Case M 3255, decision of 7 July 2004.

[494] See generally ch 7, 'Judicial Review', pp 290–294.

landmark judgments, for example on the meaning of collective dominance[495]. However in the second half of the 1990s anxiety grew that the Commission, acting as prosecutor, judge and jury in merger cases (as in cases under Articles 101 and 102 TFEU) possessed too much power; or, to put the matter another way, that there was insufficient judicial control of the Commission by the EU Courts. It was during this period that prohibition decisions under the EUMR began to increase in number, culminating in a record number of five prohibitions in 2001[496]. As if in response to this criticism there followed a dramatic series of annulments by the General Court of Commission prohibition decisions in June and October 2002: *Airtours v Commission*[497], *Schneider Electric v Commission*[498] and *Tetra Laval v Commission*[499]. In these judgments the General Court, while acknowledging that the Commission enjoys a considerable margin of appreciation when dealing with complex economic matters, nevertheless demonstrated that it was prepared to look quite deeply into both the Commission's findings on primary facts and into the inferences drawn from them when determining whether its analysis was vitiated by manifest errors of assessment. While each of these three judgments necessarily turned on its own facts, collectively they sent a strong signal to the Commission that it needed to be more rigorous in its investigations, and they succeeded in assuaging some of the concerns about the excessive power of the Commission and weak supervision by the General Court.

A different complaint about judicial review has been that, even if the General Court is prepared to exercise effective judicial control over the Commission, the time taken to obtain a judgment from the General Court is so long that the process is essentially without purpose. This has been addressed, to some extent, by the introduction of the so-called 'expedited procedure', discussed below. More radical solutions, such as the introduction of a specialist competition court at a lower level than the General Court[500], or even changing the role of the Commission to that of a prosecutor only, the actual decision to be taken by the General Court, seem, for the time being, to be in abeyance.

Appeals against decisions of the Commission have, in recent years, become more common, both on the part of the parties to the merger under scrutiny and on the part of third parties with objections to the way in which the Commission has handled a case. Advisers therefore need to explain to clients not only the time limits of Phase I and Phase II investigations under the EUMR, but also that a real possibility exists of protracted litigation in the EU Courts after the Commission has reached its final decision. The *Sony/Bertelsmann* case discussed below is particularly instructive in this respect[501].

(A) Acts

Only acts that produce binding legal effects may be appealed under Article 263 TFEU[502]. In the context of the EUMR the General Court has ruled that a decision under Article 6(1)

---

[495] See Cases C-68/94 etc *France v Commission* [1998] ECR I-1375, [1998] 4 CMLR 829, paras 169–178; Case T-102/96 *Gencor v Commission* [1999] ECR II-753, [1999] 4 CMLR 971, paras 148–158.

[496] See the statistical table of notifications at 'Table of EUMR statistics', p 899 below.

[497] Case T-342/99 *Airtours v Commission* [2002] ECR II-2585, [2002] 5 CMLR 317.

[498] Case T-310/01 *Schneider Electric v Commission* [2002] ECR II-4071, [2003] 4 CMLR 768.

[499] Case T-5/02 *Tetra Laval v Commission* [2002] ECR II-4381, [2002] 5 CMLR 1182, upheld on appeal Case C-12/03 P *Commission v Tetra Laval* [2005] ECR I-987, [2005] 4 CMLR 573; for comment on *Schneider* and *Tetra Laval* see Temple Lang 'Two Important Merger Regulation Judgments: The Implications of *Schneider-Legrand* and *Tetra Laval-Sidel*' (2003) 28 EL Rev 259.

[500] See ch 2, 'Court of Justice', pp 55–56.

[501] See 'The standard of review', p 894 below.

[502] See ch 7, 'Acts', pp 291–292.

(c) to take a case into a Phase II investigation is not an appealable act[503]; nor was a letter from the Commission expressing an opinion about the nature of commitments offered in an earlier case[504] and a decision not to take proceedings against Italy in relation to the *Abertis/Autostrade* case[505].

(B) Standing

Article 263 TFEU allows any natural or legal person to institute proceedings against a decision which is addressed to it or which is addressed to another person but which is of direct and individual concern to it.

(i) The parties to the transaction

It is obvious that the parties to the transaction have standing, for example where a merger is prohibited: examples of successful appeals were given above; there have also been several unsuccessful appeals against prohibition decisions[506]. An interesting question is whether parties that offer commitments to the Commission as a condition of being allowed to proceed with a transaction can then appeal to the General Court that the Commission had no right to insist on remedies. On the one hand it can be argued that offering commitments is a voluntary act on the part of the parties, so that they ought not to be able to challenge the Commission[507]; on the other hand the parties can argue that they were effectively 'forced' into offering a commitment in order to save what they could from the transaction, not least because the time limits imposed by the EUMR were soon to be reached. The General Court rejected an appeal of this kind in *Cementbouw Handel Industrie BV v Commission*[508].

(ii) Third parties

Third parties also have the right to appeal against merger decisions of the Commission provided that they can demonstrate that the decision is of direct and individual concern to them. Article 18(4) of the EUMR provides that natural or legal persons showing a sufficient interest have a right to be heard during the Commission's administrative procedure, and the General Court has held that such persons have standing to appeal[509]. In some cases third parties that were not involved in the administrative procedure have also been found to have standing to appeal[510]. However a third party that is in liquidation has been held not to have an interest in the final judgment of the court[511]. Many third

---

[503] Case T-48/03 *Schneider Electric v Commission*, order of 31 January 2006, appeal dismissed by order of the Court of Justice of 9 March 2007, Case C-188/06 P [2007] ECR I-35.

[504] Case T-57/07 *E.ON Ruhrgas International AG v Commission*, order of 2 September 2009.

[505] Case T-58/09 *Schemaventotto SpA v Commission*, order of 2 September 2010.

[506] See eg Case T-102/96 *Gencor Ltd v Commission* [1999] ECR II-753, [1999] 4 CMLR 971; Case T-87/05 *EDP v Commission* [2005] ECR II-3745, [2005] 5 CMLR 1436; Case T-210/01 *General Electric v Commission* [2005] ECR II-5575, [2006] 4 CMLR 686; Case T-342/07 *Ryanair Holdings plc v Commission* [2010] ECR II-000, [2011] 4 CMLR 245.

[507] See the Opinion of Advocate General Kokott in Case C-202/06 P *Cementbouw Handel Industrie BV v Commission*, [2007] ECR I-12129, [2008] 4 CMLR 1324, para 69.

[508] Case T-282/02 [2006] ECR II-319, [2006] 4 CMLR 1561, paras 293–321, upheld on appeal Case C-202/06 P [2007] ECR I-12129, [2008] 4 CMLR 1324.

[509] See Case T-2/93 *Air France v Commission* [1994] ECR II-323, paras 42–47; the General Court has held that the appellants lacked standing in Case T-350/03 *Wirtschaftskammer Kärnten v Commission*, order of 18 September 2006, [2006] ECR II-68 and in Case T-224/10 *Association belges des consommateurs test-achats ASBL v Commission* [2011] ECR II-000, paras 74–85.

[510] Case T-342/00 *Petrolessence SA v Commission* [2003] ECR II-1161, [2003] 5 CMLR 498, paras 36–42.

[511] Case T-269/03 *Socratec v Commission* [2009] ECR II-88; see similarly Case T-145/03 *Festival Crociere v Commission*, order of 31 March 2006.

party appeals have been unsuccessful, but this may be of little comfort to undertakings that have received a clearance from the Commission but then have to undergo a period of further uncertainty while the appeal process plays out. It is arguable that the rules on standing should be somewhat stricter in relation to third parties, at least where the appellant is a competitor of the merging parties whose objection to the transaction has nothing to do with consumer welfare considerations; objections from customers and consumers are likely to be much more meritorious[512]. Further discussion of third party appeals will be found below.

(C) **The standard of review**[513]

It is well established that the Commission enjoys a margin of appreciation when assessing mergers and that the EU Courts should not substitute their own views for those of the Commission. The standard of review to be applied was succinctly stated by the General Court in *Sun Chemical Group BV and others v Commission*[514]:

> [A]ccording to settled case law, review by the [EU] judicature of complex economic assessments made by the Commission in the exercise of the power of assessment conferred on it by the Merger Regulation is limited to ascertaining compliance with the rules governing procedure and the statement of reasons, the substantive accuracy of the facts and the absence of manifest errors of assessment or misuse of powers...In that respect, it should be borne in mind that not only must the [EU] judicature ascertain whether the evidence relied on is factually accurate, reliable and consistent but also whether that evidence contains all the information which must be taken into account in order to assess a complex situation and whether it is capable of substantiating the conclusions drawn from it.

In *Bertelsmann AG and Sony Corporation of America v Impala*[515] the Court of Justice ruled that the General Court had erred in law by expecting the Commission to apply 'particularly demanding requirements' to the notifying parties' evidence and arguments in response to the statement of objections[516].

(D) **The expedited procedure**

The expedited procedure entered into force on 1 February 2001[517]. Under this procedure certain cases can be dealt with by the General Court more quickly than is usual; this is particularly important in the case of a decision prohibiting a merger, since a prolonged appeal may mean that market conditions change so substantially between the

---

[512] Third parties in the US have standing only where they can show that they would suffer direct antitrust injury: see *Cargill Inc v Monfort of Colorado Inc* 479 US 104 (1986); in a case on state aids the Court of Justice took a stricter view on the rights of third parties to appeal in Case C-260/05 P *Sniace SA v Commission* [2007] ECR I-10005, [2008] 1 CMLR 1035, paras 49–61.

[513] See Bailey 'Standard of Proof in EC Merger Proceedings: a Common Law Perspective' (2003) 40 CML Rev 845; Reeves and Dodoo 'Standards of Proof and Standards of Judicial Review in EC Merger Law' [2005] Fordham Corporate Law Review (ed Hawk), ch 6; Vesterdorf 'Standard of Proof in Merger Cases: Reflections in the Light of Recent Case law in the Community Courts' (2005) 1(1) European Competition Journal 3.

[514] Case T-282/06 [2007] ECR II-2149, [2007] 5 CMLR 438, para 60.

[515] Case C-413/06 P [2008] ECR I-4951, [2008] 5 CMLR 1073.

[516] Ibid, paras 87–96.

[517] OJ [2000] L 322/4; on this procedure see Fountoukakos 'Judicial Review and Merger Control: The General Court's Expedited Procedure' (2002) (October) *Competition Policy Newsletter* 7; Chibnall 'Expedited Treatment of Appeals against EC Competition Decision under the EC Merger Control Regulation' (2002) 1 Competition Law Journal 327.

Commission's prohibition decision and the General Court's eventual judgment that, even after a successful appeal, it is no longer possible to proceed with the deal. The pleadings in a case under the expedited procedure are simplified and greater emphasis is placed on the oral hearing; this procedure is not suitable for a case involving a substantial number of points of appeal. Requests for an expedited procedure have sometimes been refused[518].

By 20 June 2011 the General Court had given judgments in ten merger cases in which the expedited procedure had been used[519].

The shortest period between the lodging of an appeal and the judgment in an expedited procedure case was seven months in the case of *EDP v Commission*[520] and the longest was 21 months in the case of *Impala v Commission*[521]. Judgments in cases under the expedited procedure are likely to be shorter than in a 'normal' appeal[522]. In the *Impala* case the General Court was critical of the fact that Impala, having asked for the expedited procedure to be used, was itself responsible for slowing the progress of the case; as a result, although Impala was successful in persuading the General Court to annul the Commission's decision clearing the merger, it was awarded only three-quarters of its costs against the Commission[523].

(E) Examples of third party appeals

(i) Appeals against the Commission's refusal to take jurisdiction

In *Schlüsselverlag JS Moser GmbH v Commission*[524] a merger was cleared by the relevant competition authority in Austria. Schlüsselverlag complained to the Commission that the merger in question had a Community dimension, and that therefore the Commission should have investigated it, not the domestic authority in Austria. The Court of Justice rejected the Commission's argument that it was not obliged to define its position when asked to do so by the appellant: the Court of Justice considered that it was vital, given that the Commission has sole jurisdiction in relation to concentrations having a Community dimension, that it should be required to take a decision if asked to do so[525]. However the appeal was rejected as the appellant had unduly delayed the making of its complaint to the Commission[526]. In *Endesa v Commission*[527] the General Court rejected Endesa's argument that a hostile bid for it by Gas Natural had a Community dimension and therefore fell within the jurisdiction of the Commission.

(ii) Appeals against Article 9 references

In *Cableuropa SA v Commission*[528] the General Court held that a third party that objected to the Commission's decision to refer a merger to the Spanish competition authorities

---

[518] An example is Case T-145/06 *Omya AG v Commission* [2009] ECR II-145, [2009] 4 CMLR 826, para 12.

[519] A Table of Expedited Procedure cases will be found at the website that accompanies this book: see www.oxfordtextbooks.co.uk/orc/whishandbailey7e.

[520] Case T-87/05 [2005] II-3745, [2005] 5 CMLR 1436.

[521] Case T-464/04 [2006] ECR II-2289, [2006] 5 CMLR 1049.

[522] Case T-87/05 *EDP v Commission* [2005] ECR II-3745, [2005] 5 CMLR 1436, para 39.

[523] Ibid, paras 544–554.

[524] Case C-170/02 P [2003] ECR I-9889, [2004] 4 CMLR 1522.

[525] Ibid, paras 25–30.

[526] Ibid, paras 31–40.

[527] Case T-417/05 [2006] ECR II-2533, [2008] 4 CMLR 1472

[528] Cases T-346/02 and T-347/02 [2003] ECR II-4251, [2004] 5 CMLR 1216; see similarly Case T-119/02 *Royal Philips Electronics v Commission* [2003] ECR II-1433, [2003] 5 CMLR 53, paras 254–300.

under Article 9 of the EUMR had the standing to challenge that decision[529], but upheld the Commission's decision on the merits.

(iii) Appeals against unconditional clearances

There have been several unsuccessful appeals by third parties against unconditional clearance decisions of the Commission[530]. However in one particularly striking case, *Impala v Commission*[531], a third party successfully persuaded the General Court that the Commission had wrongly cleared a merger with the result that the clearance decision in *Sony/Bertelsmann* was annulled[532]. This meant that the Commission had to re-investigate the case, leading to a second clearance decision in September 2007, more than three years after the original decision[533].

(iv) Appeals against conditional clearances

There have been several appeals by third parties against conditional clearance decisions, usually unsuccessful[534]. A successful case was *BaByliss v Commission*[535] where the Commission required commitments in relation to certain national markets, for example Germany and Austria, but not in relation to others, for example Spain and Italy, in order to clear a merger[536]. BaByliss appealed to the General Court claiming among other things that the Commission should not have authorised the concentration without commitments in relation to markets with serious competition problems. The General Court accepted the argument and annulled the Commission's decision in so far as it concerned the markets in the countries not covered by the commitments[537]. This led to a second decision again clearing the merger subject to conditions[538].

A different point arose in *Petrolessence SA v Commission*[539] where the Commission required certain assets to be divested as a condition of approving a merger[540]. A potential purchaser of the assets was rejected by the Commission on the basis that it would not be an effective competitor and was therefore an unsuitable purchaser. The General Court held that Petrolessence had standing to appeal[541], but it was unsuccessful on the merits[542].

---

[529] Ibid, paras 47–82.

[530] See eg Case T-2/93 *Air France v Commission* [1994] ECR II-323; Case T-290/94 *Kayserberg v Commission* [1997] ECR II-2137, [1998] 4 CMLR 336; Case T-282/06 *Sun Chemical Group BV and others v Commission* [2007] ECR II-2149, [2007] 5 CMLR 438; Case T-151/05 *Nederlandse Vakbond Varkenshouders and others v Commission* [2009] ECR II-1219, [2009] 5 CMLR 1613.

[531] Case T-464/04 [2006] ECR II-2289, [2006] 5 CMLR 1049.

[532] Case M 3333 *Sony/BMG*, decision of 19 July 2004, OJ [2004] L 62/30.

[533] Commission Press Release IP/07/1437, 3 October 2007; note that, on appeal to the Court of Justice, the General Court's judgment was reversed: Case C-413/06 P *Bertelsmann AG v Impala* [2008] ECR I-4951, [2008] 5 CMLR 1073.

[534] See eg T-119/02 *Royal Philips Electronics BV v Commission* [2003] ECR II-1433, [2003] 5 CMLR 53; Case T-158/00 *ARD v Commission* [2003] ECR II-3825, [2004] 5 CMLR 681; Case T-177/04 *easyJet v Commission* [2006] ECR II-1931, [2006] 5 CMLR 663; Case T-48/04 *Qualcomm Wireless Business Solutions Europe BV v Commission* [2009] ECR II-2029, [2009] 5 CMLR 2121, Case T-224/10 *Test-achats v Commission* [2011] ECR II-000.

[535] Case T-114/02 *BaByliss v Commission* [2003] ECR II-1279, [2004] 5 CMLR 21.

[536] Case M 2621 *SEB/Moulinex*, decision of 8 January 2002.

[537] Case T-114/02 *BaByliss v Commission* [2003] ECR II-1279, [2004] 5 CMLR 1, paras 308–411.

[538] Case M 2621 *SEB/Moulinex II*, decision of 11 November 2003, see the Commission's *Annual Report on Competition* (2003), paras 259–262.

[539] Case T-342/00 [2003] ECR II-1161, [2003] 5 CMLR 498.

[540] Case M 1628 *TotalFina/Elf*, decision of 9 February 2000, OJ [2001] L 143/1.

[541] Case T-342/00 [2003] ECR II-1161, [2003] 5 CMLR 498, paras 36–42.

[542] Ibid, paras 100–123; see similarly in the UK Case No 1081/4/1/07 *Co-operative Group Ltd v OFT* [2007] CAT 24, [2011] CompAR 899, discussed in ch 22, 'Undertakings in lieu of a reference', pp 927–928.

(v) Appeals seeking access to information

In various cases applicants have successfully appealed to the General Court seeking access to information in the Commission's possession[543].

(F) Damages claims against the Commission[544]

Two (unsuccessful) applications for damages have been made to the General Court for harm suffered as a result of a prohibition decision of the Commission which had been annulled on appeal. In *Commission v Schneider Electric SA*[545] the Commission's prohibition of the *Schneider/Legrand* merger had been annulled on appeal to the General Court[546]. Schneider sued the Commission for damages, and was successful before the General Court[547]; however the Court of Justice reversed the General Court's judgment since it considered that Schneider's financial loss was not actually caused by the Commission's prohibition decision[548].

In *MyTravel Group plc v Commission*[549] MyTravel, formerly Airtours, sued the Commission for damages arising from its decision in *Airtours/First Choice*[550] which was annulled on appeal by the General Court[551]. The Court held that it cannot be ruled out in principle that manifest and grave defects underlying the Commission's substantive analysis could constitute breaches that are sufficiently serious to give rise to a claim for damages. However, taking into account the complexity of merger control and the Commission's margin of appreciation, the Court concluded that the Commission had not committed a sufficiently serious error in either its assessment of collective dominance or of the remedies offered by MyTravel to justify the award of damages against it.

9. International Cooperation

(A) Close and constant liaison with Member States

Article 4(3) TEU establishes the principle of cooperation between Member States and the institutions of the EU. In the context of the EUMR Article 19 sets out detailed provisions to establish liaison between the Commission and the Member States. Notifications under the EUMR must be transmitted to the competent authorities of Member States, which must be able to express their views on the Commission's treatment of cases; and the Advisory Committee on Concentrations must be consulted before important

---

[543] See Case T-111/07 *Agrofert Holding v Commission* [2010] ECR II-000, on appeal to the Court of Justice Case C-477/10 P *Commission v Agrofert Holdings*, not yet decided; Case T-237/05 *Éditions Jacob v Commission* [2010] ECR II-000, on appeal to the Court of Justice Case C-404/10 P *Commission v Editions Odile SAS*, not yet decided; Case T-403/05 *MyTravel v Commission* [2008] ECR II-2027, [2008] 3 CMLR 1517, annulled on appeal to the Court of Justice Case C-506/08 P *Sweden v Commission*, [2011] ECR I-000, [2011] 5 CMLR 575, paras 72–103 and 109–119.

[544] See generally Bailey 'Damages Actions under the EC Merger Regulation' (2007) 44 CML Rev 101.

[545] Case C-440/07 P *Commission v Schneider Electric SA* [2009] ECR I-6413, [2009] 5 CMLR 2051.

[546] Case T-310/01 *Schneider Electric SA v Commission* [2002] ECR II-4071, [2003] 4 CMLR 768.

[547] Case T-351/03 *Schneider Electric SA v Commission* [2007] ECR II-2237, [2008] 4 CMLR 1533.

[548] Case C-440/07 P *Commission v Schneider Electric SA* [2009] ECR I-6413, [2009] 5 CMLR 2051, paras 205 and 218–223; Schneider was awarded damages for the cost of having to undergo a second investigation of its transaction as a result of the annulment of the first Commission decision.

[549] Case T-212/03 [2008] ECR II-1967, [2008] 5 CMLR 1429.

[550] Case M 1524, decision of 22 September 1999, OJ [2000] L 93/1.

[551] Case T-342/99 *Airtours v Commission* [2002] ECR II-2585, [2002] 5 CMLR 317.

decisions – for example at the end of Phase II, or imposing fines – are taken. The Advisory Committee's opinion is not binding on the Commission, but considerable importance is attached to it. The General Court in *Kayserberg SA v Commission*[552] rejected a claim by a third party objecting to the Commission's clearance of the *Procter & Gamble/VP Schickedanz* transaction[553]; the third party was arguing that the Advisory Committee had not been properly consulted.

The Commission also cooperates with the EFTA Surveillance Authority pursuant to the provisions of the EEA Agreement[554]. This cooperation is provided for by Articles 57 and 58 of the EEA Agreement and Protocol 24.

(B) Relations with non-EU countries

(i) Reciprocity

Article 24 addresses the issue of reciprocity of treatment of mergers by non-EU countries. Some systems of law make it difficult, if not impossible, for foreign firms to take over local ones. Not surprisingly resentment is felt where, for example, a British firm is prevented from taking over a foreign one in circumstances in which, were the roles reversed, there would be no obstacle to the merger under UK law. Article 24(1) of the EUMR requires Member States to inform the Commission of any difficulties encountered by their undertakings in the case of concentrations in non-EU countries. Where it appears that a non-EU country is not affording reciprocal treatment to that granted by a Member State, the Commission may seek a mandate from the Council of Ministers to negotiate comparable treatment.

(ii) The international dimension

It is possible that a transaction might fall within the merger control systems of the EU, the US, Canada and many other countries. The problems associated with the international dimension – the burden on companies of multiple filings, the need for cooperation between competition authorities and the desirability of an expeditious and harmonious outcome – are considerable. These have been discussed in chapter 12, including the territorial reach of the EUMR and cooperation agreements between the EU, the US, Canada, Japan and Korea[555].

10. The EUMR in Practice

(A) Statistics

From 21 September 1990, when the original EUMR entered into force, until 31 May 2011 the number of notifications received and decisions reached by the Commission were as follows:

---

[552] Case T-290/94 [1997] ECR II-2137, [1998] 4 CMLR 336, paras 57–58.
[553] Case M 430 OJ [1994] L 354/32.
[554] See ch 2, 'European Economic Area', pp 57–58.
[555] See ch 12, 'EU Merger Regulation', pp 499–500 and 'The EU's dedicated cooperation agreements on competition policy', pp 509–511.

Table 21.2 Table of EUMR statistics

I.) NOTIFICATIONS

	90	91	92	93	94	95	96	97	98	99	00	01	02	03	04	05	06	07	08	09	10	May 11	Total
Number of notified cases	11	64	59	59	95	110	131	168	224	276	330	335	277	211	247	313	356	402	347	259	274	128	4676
Cases withdrawn - Phase 1	0	0	3	1	6	4	5	9	5	7	8	8	3	0	3	6	7	5	10	6	4	2	102
Cases withdrawn - Phase 2	0	0	0	1	0	0	1	0	4	5	5	4	1	0	2	3	2	2	3	2	0	1	36

II.) REFERRALS

	90	91	92	93	94	95	96	97	98	99	00	01	02	03	04	05	06	07	08	09	10	May 11	Total
Art 4(4) request (Form RS)															2	14	13	5	9	8	6	5	62
Art 4(4) referral to Member State															2	11	13	5	9	6	7	4	57
Art 4(4) partial referral to Member State															0	0	0	1	0	0	0	1	2
Art 4(4) refusal of referral															0	0	0	0	0	0	0	0	0
Art 4(5) request (Form RS)															20	28	38	51	23	23	26	10	219
Art 4(5) referral accepted															16	24	39	50	22	25	24	9	209
Art 4(5) refusal of referral															2	0	0	2	0	0	1	0	5
Art 22 request	0	0	0	1	0	1	1	1	0	0	0	0	2	1	1	4	4	3	2	1	3	1	26
Art 22(3) referral (Art 22. 4 taken in conjunction with article 6 or 8 under Reg. 4064\89)	0	0	0	1	0	1	1	1	0	0	0	0	2	1	1	3	3	2	3	1	2	2	24
Art 22(3) refusal of referral																1	1	0	0	0	0	0	2
Art 9 request	0	1	1	1	1	0	3	7	4	9	4	9	8	10	4	7	6	3	5	3	11	1	98
Art 9.3 partial referral to Member State	0	0	1	0	1	0	0	6	3	2	3	6	7	1	1	3	1	1	2	0	3	0	41
Art 9.3 full referral	0	0	0	1	0	0	3	1	1	3	2	1	4	8	2	3	1	1	2	1	4	1	39
Art 9.3 refusal of referral	0	1	0	0	0	0	0	0	0	1	0	0	0	1	0	0	0	1	0	1	1	0	6

III.) FIRST PHASE DECISIONS

	90	91	92	93	94	95	96	97	98	99	00	01	02	03	04	05	06	07	08	09	10	May 11	Total
Art 6.1 (a) out of scope Merger Regulation	2	5	9	4	5	9	6	4	4	1	1	1	1	0	0	0	0	0	0	0	0	0	52
Art 6.1 (b) compatible	5	47	43	49	78	90	109	118	196	225	278	299	238	203	220	276	323	368	307	225	253	104	4054
Art 6.1(b) compatible, under simplified procedure (figures included in 6.1(b) compatible above)	0	0	0	0	0	0	0	0	0	0	41	141	103	110	138	169	211	238	190	143	143	71	1698
Art 6.1 (b) in conjunction with Art 6.2 (compatible w. commitments)	0	3	4	0	2	3	0	2	12	16	26	11	10	11	12	15	13	18	19	13	14	3	207

IV.) PHASE II PROCEEDINGS INITIATED

	90	91	92	93	94	95	96	97	98	99	00	01	02	03	04	05	06	07	08	09	10	May 11	Total
Art 6.1 (c)	0	6	4	4	6	7	6	11	11	20	18	21	7	9	8	10	13	15	10	5	4	5	200

V.) SECOND PHASE DECISIONS

	90	91	92	93	94	95	96	97	98	99	00	01	02	03	04	05	06	07	08	09	10	May 11	Total
Art 8.1 compatible (8.2 under Reg. 4064/89)	0	1	1	1	2	2	1	1	3	0	3	5	2	2	2	2	4	5	9	0	1	1	48
Art 8.2 compatible with commitments	0	3	3	2	2	3	3	7	4	7	12	9	5	6	4	3	6	4	5	3	2	0	93
Art 8.3 prohibition	0	1	0	0	1	2	3	1	2	1	2	5	0	0	1	0	0	1	0	0	0	1	21
Art 8.4 restore effective competition	0	0	0	0	0	0	0	2	0	0	0	0	2	0	0	0	0	0	0	0	0	0	4

VI.) OTHER DECISIONS

	90	91	92	93	94	95	96	97	98	99	00	01	02	03	04	05	06	07	08	09	10	May 11	Total
Art 6.3 decision revoked	0	0	0	0	0	0	0	0	0	0	1	0	0	0	0	0	0	0	0	0	0	0	1
Art 8.6 decision revoked	0	0	0	0	0	0	0	0	0	0	0	0	0	0	0	0	0	0	0	0	0	0	0
Art 14 decision imposing fines	0	0	0	0	0	0	0	0	1	4	0	1	0	1	0	0	0	0	1	0	0	0	9
Art 7.3 derogation from suspension (7.4 under Reg. 4064/89)	1	1	2	3	3	2	4	5	13	7	4	7	14	8	10	6	2	3	6	5	1	3	110
Art 21	0	0	0	0	0	1	0	1	0	1	1	0	1	0	0	0	2	1	0	0	0	0	8

(B) Table of Phase II investigations

The following Table contains a list of cases in which a Phase II investigation was initiated since the sixth edition of this book was published in 2008 and completed by 20 June 2011[556].

---

[556] A complete list of all Phase II cases can be found at www.ec.europa.eu/competition/mergers/cases.

Table 21.3 EUMR Table of Phase II investigations

Name of case	Cleared?	Cleared with commitments?	Prohibited?
Case No COMP/M.4799 *OMV/MOL* **NB: abandoned by the parties**			
Case No COMP/M.4854 *TomTom/TeleAtlas*	Yes		
Case No COMP/M.4874 *BarcoVision/Itema*	Yes		
Case No COMP/M.4919 *StatoilHydro/ConocoPhillips*		Yes	
Case No COMP/M.4942 *Nokia/NAVTEQ*	Yes		
Case No COMP/M.4956 *STX/AkerYards*	Yes		
Case No COMP/M.4980 *ABF/GBI*		Yes	
Case No COMP/M.4985 *BHP Billiton/Rio Tinto* **NB: abandoned by the parties**			
Case No COMP/M.4989 *ALO/MX* **NB: abandoned by the parties**			
Case No COMP/M.5046 *Friesland/Campina*		Yes	
Case No COMP/M.5141 *KLM/Martinair*	Yes		
Case No COMP/M.5153 *Arsenal/DSP*		Yes	
Case No COMP/M.5262 *Bonnier/Schibsted/Retriever Sverige* **NB: abandoned by the parties**			
Case No COMP/M.5335 *Lufthansa/SN Airholding*		Yes	

Name of case	Cleared?	Cleared with commitments?	Prohibited?
Case No COMP/M.5440 *Lufthansa/Austrian Airlines*		Yes	
Case No COMP/M.5454 *DSV/Vesterhavet/DFDS* **NB: abandoned by the parties**			
Case No COMP/M.5529 *Oracle/Sun Microsystems* **Appeal by a third party, Case T-292/10** *Monty Program AB v Commission,* **not yet decided**	Yes		
Case No COMP/M.5658 *Unilever/Sara Lee Body Care*		Yes	
Case No COMP/M.5675 *Syngenta/Monsanto's sunflower seed business* **NB: Article 22 reference from Spain and Hungary**		Yes	
Case No COMP/M.5969 *SC Johnson/Sara Lee* **NB: abandoned by the parties; Article 22 reference from Spain, Belgium, France, Italy, the Czech Republic and Greece**			
Case No COMP/M.5830 *Olympic Air/Aegean Airlines* **On appeal Case T-202/11** *Aeroporia Aigaiou Aeroporiki and Marfin Investment Group Symmetochon v Commission,* **not yet decided**			Yes
Case No COMP/M.5907 *Votorantim/Fischer/JV*	Yes		

(C) Comment

(i) Outright prohibitions

Outright prohibitions are rare: by 20 June 2011 there had been only 21 examples, of which four were annulled on appeal to the General Court[557]. Since 2001 there have been only three prohibitions[558].

The first concentration to be blocked, in 1991, was *Aerospatiale-Alenia/de Havilland*[559]. Aerospatiale and Alenia intended to purchase the De Havilland division of Boeing. The Commissioner responsible for Industry disagreed violently over the decision with Sir Leon Brittan, the Competition Commissioner, in particular as industrial policy considerations were not taken on board. However the language of Article 2(3) of the EUMR does not provide for industrial policy to be taken into account, and the decision set an important precedent in demonstrating that the test of the compatibility of a concentration with the common market was its impact on competition[560].

The second concentration to be blocked, in 1994, was *MSG Media Service*[561]. Three companies intended to establish a German pay-TV joint venture, MSG. In the Commission's view the joint venture would give MSG a lasting dominant position on the pay-TV market for administrative and technical services; it would give Bertelsmann and Kirch a dominant position on the German-speaking pay-TV market; and it would protect and strengthen the dominant position of Deutsche Telekom for cable infrastructure. It is of interest that this was the first of several concentrations in the media sector to be prohibited outright: the very rapid changes in technology in this sector, and the possibility that concentrations could have serious foreclosure effects on third parties, particularly through vertical integration, help to explain the Commission's cautious approach[562].

Three of the outright prohibitions – *RTL/Veronica/Endemol*[563], *Kesko/Tuko*[564] and *Blokker/Toys 'R' Us*[565] – were requests from Member States under Article 22 of the EUMR. That these requests led to prohibitions is perhaps not surprising: at the time the Member States making the requests (the Netherlands and Finland) had no domestic system of merger control and had obviously concluded that there was a very serious threat to competition, so that the cases were always likely, at the very least, to raise serious doubts.

---

[557] See 'Prohibition decisions annulled on appeal', p 904 below.

[558] Case M 3440, *ENI/EDP/GDP*, decision of 9 December 2004, OJ [2005] L 302/69, upheld on appeal Case T-87/05 *EDP v Commission* [2005] ECR II-3745, [2005] 5 CMLR 1436; Case M 4439 *Ryanair/Aer Lingus*, decision of 27 June 2007, upheld on appeal Case T-342/07 *Ryanair v Commission* [2010] ECR II-000, [2011] 4 CMLR 245: for comment on the latter case by DG COMP officials see Gadas, Koch, Parplies and Beuve-Méry 'Ryanair/Aer Lingus: Even "low-cost" monopolies can harm consumers' (2007) *Competition Policy Newsletter* 65; DeLa Mano, Pesaresi and Stehman 'Econometric and survey evidence in the competitive assessment of the Ryanair-Aer Lingus merger' (2007) *Competition Policy Newsletter* 73.

[559] Case M 53, decision of 2 October 1991, OJ [1991] L 334/42.

[560] See Fox 'Merger Control in the EEC—towards a European Merger Jurisprudence' [1991] Fordham Corporate Law Institute (ed Hawk), 738–9.

[561] Case M 469, decision of 9 November 1994, OJ [1994] L 364/1.

[562] See also Case M 490 *Nordic Satellite Distribution*, decision of 19 July 1995, OJ [1996] L 53/20; Case M 553 *RTL/Veronica/Endemol*, decision of 17 July 1996, OJ [1996] L 134/32 (this concentration was subsequently cleared in an amended form: OJ [1996] L 294/14); Case M 993 *Bertelsmann/Kirch/Premiere*, decision of 27 May 1998, OJ [1999] L 53/1; Case M 1027 *Deutsche Telekom/BetaResearch* OJ [1999] L 53/31.

[563] Case M 553 *RTL/Veronica/Endemol*, decision of 17 July 1996, OJ [1996] L 134/32, upheld on appeal Case T-221/95 *Endemol Entertainment Holding BV v Commission* [1999] ECR II-1299, [1999] 5 CMLR 611.

[564] Case M 784 *Kesko/Tuko*, decision of 20 November 1996, OJ [1997] L 174/47, upheld on appeal Case T-22/97 *Kesko v Commission* [1999] ECR II-3775, [2000] 4 CMLR 335.

[565] Case M 890 *Blokker/Toys 'R' Us*, decision of 26 June 1997, OJ [1998] L 316/1.

Of the other outright prohibitions *Gencor/Lonrho*[566] was an important case on the meaning of collective dominance or, to use more modern language, coordinated effects[567]. In *Saint-Gobain/Wacker-Chemie/NOM*[568] the Commission found that the merged entity would enjoy very high market shares in relation to silicon carbide, substantially higher than its competitors, that potential competition and countervailing power were weak and that the case could not be 'saved' by an efficiency or a failing firm defence. In *Volvo/Scania*[569] the Commission prohibited a merger that would lead to high market shares for buses and trucks in a series of national markets, Sweden, Finland, Denmark, Norway and Ireland: the delimitation of national markets, rather than a European-wide one, was a crucial feature of this case. In the countries where the Commission identified a problem the evidence showed that Volvo and Scania were each other's closest competitors. The concentration in *SCA/Metsä Tissue*[570] was prohibited as it would have led to very high market shares in hygienic tissue products in Scandinavia and Finland. The Commission blocked the concentration in *CVC/Lenzing*[571] as a result of the high market shares that the merged entity would enjoy in the man-made fibre sector and because CVC already controlled Lenzing's main rival.

The prohibition decision in *GE/Honeywell*[572] was particularly controversial. This was an agreed merger between two US undertakings which had been cleared by the US authorities. The Commission prohibited it, predominantly because of its vertical and conglomerate effects, on grounds that were anathema to the Department of Justice in the US. On appeal to the General Court the Commission's reasoning on both vertical and conglomerate effects was severely criticised; nevertheless GE's appeal was unsuccessful, because the General Court accepted that there were some horizontal effects that justified the prohibition of the merger[573].

In *ENI/EDP/GDP*[574] the Commission prohibited a proposed acquisition by EDP, the incumbent electricity company in Portugal, of GDP, the incumbent gas company. The Commission was concerned both at the horizontal and vertical implications of the transaction, and resisted suggestions that a Portuguese 'national champion' should be created. An expedited appeal was made to the General Court which upheld the Commission's decision[575]. The most recent prohibitions occurred in *Ryanair/Aer Lingus*[576], where the Commission was particularly concerned that the merged airline would have accounted for around 80 per cent of intra-European air traffic from and to Dublin airport: an appeal by Ryanair to the General Court was unsuccessful[577]; and in *Olympic Airways/Aegean*

---

[566] Case M 619, decision of 24 April 1996, OJ [1997] L 11/30, upheld on appeal Case T-102/96 *Gencor v Commission* [1999] ECR II-753, [1999] 4 CMLR 971.

[567] See 'Coordinated effects', pp 871–873 above.

[568] Case M 774, decision of 4 December 1996, OJ [1997] L 247/1.

[569] Case M 1672, decision of 15 March 2000, OJ [2001] L 143/74.

[570] Case M 2097, decision of 31 January 2001, OJ [2002] L 57/1.

[571] Case M 2187, decision of 17 October 2001, OJ [2004] L 82/20.

[572] Case M 2220, decision of 3 July 2001.

[573] Case T-210/01 *General Electric Company v Commission* [2005] ECR II-5575, [2006] 4 CMLR 686.

[574] Case M 3440, *ENI/EDP/GDP*, decision of 9 December 2004, OJ [2005] L 302/69.

[575] Case T-87/05 *EDP v Commission* [2005] ECR II-3745, [2005] 5 CMLR 1436.

[576] Case M 4439, decision of 27 June 2007.

[577] Case T-342/07 *Ryanair v Commission* [2010] ECR II-000, [2011] 4 CMLR 245; Aer Lingus failed in a separate appeal against the Commission's decision not to require Ryanair to divest itself of all its shares in Aer Lingus, Case T-411/07 *Aer Lingus Group v Commission* [2010] ECR II-000, [2011] 4 CMLR 358, see further ch 22, 'Time limits and prior notice', p 923 on this issue.

Airlines[578] where there would have been very high market shares (and in some cases a monopoly) on various air routes within Greece.

(ii) Prohibition decisions annulled on appeal

Four of the Commission's prohibition decisions were annulled on appeal. In *Airtours/ First Choice*[579] the Commission had prohibited the proposed hostile acquisition by Airtours of First Choice on the basis of collective dominance[580]. The General Court, in an excoriating judgment, annulled the decision on the basis of manifest error of assessment: it was particularly critical of the Commission's assessment of the evidence and of its reasoning[581]. The mergers in *Schneider Electric/Legrand*[582] and *Tetra Laval/ Sidel*[583] were both prohibited by the Commission, but each decision (together with additional decisions requiring the mergers to be reversed) was annulled on appeal to the General Court[584]; an appeal by the Commission in the case of the *Tetra Laval/Sidel* case was unsuccessful[585]. In the case of *Schneider/Legrand* the General Court subsequently awarded Schneider damages for some of the economic loss it had suffered[586]. The Commission's prohibition decision in *MCI WorldCom/Sprint*[587] was annulled by the General Court in *MCI Inc v Commission*[588] since the parties had terminated their agreement by the time of the Commission's decision; the mere fact that they were continuing to negotiate an agreement in a modified form did not entitle the Commission to adopt a decision[589].

(iii) Unconditional clearances

It is not inevitable that a case that is taken to a Phase II investigation will lead to a prohibition or require a remedy. Some Phase II cases culminate in an unconditional clearance: indeed the merger in *Sony/Bertelsmann* was cleared by the Commission twice[590]. This contradicts the view sometimes expressed that, by the time a case reaches Phase II, the Commission has already made up its mind about the outcome; it is possible at the 'in-depth' phase of an investigation to demonstrate to the Commission that a merger will not significantly impede effective competition. By 31 May 2011 this had happened in 48

---

[578] Case M 5830, decision of 26 January 2011; on appeal to the General Court Case T-202/11 *Aeroporia Aigaiou Aeroporiki and Marfin Investment Group Symmetochon v Commission*, not yet decided.

[579] Case M 1524 *Airtours/First Choice*, decision of 22 September 1999, OJ [2000] L 93/1.

[580] See 'The non-collusive oligopoly gap'; pp 864–865.

[581] Case T-342/99 [2002] ECR II-2585, [2002] 5 CMLR 317.

[582] Case M 2283, decision of 10 October 2001, OJ [2004] L 101/1.

[583] Case M 2416, decision of 30 October 2001, OJ [2004] L 43/13.

[584] Case T-310/01 *Schneider Electric v Commission* [2002] ECR II-4071, [2003] 4 CMLR 768 (annulment of prohibition decision); Case T-77/02 *Schneider Electric v Commission* [2002] ECR II-4201, (annulment of divestiture decision); Case T-5/02 *Tetra Laval v Commission* [2002] ECR II-4381, [2002] 5 CMLR 1182 (annulment of prohibition decision); Case T-80/02 *Tetra Laval v Commission* [2002] ECR II-4519, [2002] 4 CMLR 1271 (annulment of divestiture decision).

[585] Case C-12/03 P *Commission v Tetra Laval* [2005] ECR I-1113, [2005] 4 CMLR 573 (appeal seeking annulment of the General Court's prohibition decision); Case C-13/03 P *Commission v Tetra Laval* [2005] ECR I-987, [2005] CMLR 667 (appeal seeking annulment of the General Court's divestiture decision).

[586] See 'Damages claims against the Commission', p 897 above.

[587] Case M 1741, decision of 28 June 2000, OJ [2003] L 300/1; see the Commission's XXXth *Report on Competition Policy* (2000), point 249 and Box 6.

[588] Case T-310/00 [2004] ECR II-3253, [2004] 5 CMLR 1274.

[589] See further 'Withdrawal of notifications', p 906 below.

[590] See 'Coordinated effects', pp 871–873 above.

cases out of a total of 162, and it is noticeable that it has occurred on a number of occasions in recent years[591].

In *Oracle Corporation/Sun Microsystems Inc*[592] the Commission was concerned about the possible elimination from the market of Sun's MySQL open-source database, given that Oracle was the owner of the leading proprietary brand. The Commission decided to give the concentration unconditional clearance, and in doing so it took into account public pledges by Oracle to continue to release new versions of MySQL[593]. It is unusual for the Commission to proceed on the basis of such pledges without incorporating them as a legally binding commitment as a condition of clearance: the General Court has been asked to rule on the lawfulness of the Commission's approach in the appeal against the clearance decision[594].

(iv) Clearances subject to commitments

A notable feature of the EUMR is that a majority of Phase II decisions have resulted in clearances subject to commitments. This is shown both in the statistical Table and in the Table of Phase II investigations above. The Commission's approach to remedies in merger cases was discussed above, and its preference for structural rather than behavioural commitments was noted[595]. There are several recent examples of structural remedies at the end of Phase II. In *Sonoco/Ahlstrom*[596] the parties agreed to divest themselves of a plant in Norway that manufactured paper core to an 'up-front' buyer. In *Inco/Falconbridge*[597] the parties agreed to the divestment of a nickel refinery in Norway to an up-front buyer; interestingly in this case the Commission required that the merged entity should agree to provide important input materials to the buyer on a long-term basis. In *Gaz de France/ Suez*[598] the parties agreed to divest various assets in order to overcome the Commission's concerns about horizontal overlaps at both the wholesale and retail levels of the gas and electricity markets in France and Belgium; the remedy included a termination of the link between the operator of gas network infrastructure and the supply of gas, effectively an unbundling remedy, as well as an agreement to invest in enhancing the capacity and functioning of the gas network[599]. In *Kronospan Group/Constantia*[600] the Commission was concerned that Kronospan's acquisition of three companies owned by Constantia that produced raw particle board used in the manufacture of furniture would lead to a significant impediment to effective competition; the simple remedy in this case was that Kronospan would acquire only two of the three companies: the third one, Fundermax of Austria, would remain with Constantia. In *Lufthansa/SN Holding (Brussels Airlines)*[601] and *Lufthansa/Austrian Airlines*[602] the Commission accepted commitments that would

[591] For comment see Maier-Rigaud and Parplies 'EU Merger Control Five Years After the Introduction of the SIEC Test: What Explains the Drop in Enforcement Activity?' (2009) 11 ECLR 565.

[592] Case M 5529, decision of 21 January 2010, on appeal to the General Court Case T-292/10 *Monty Program v Commission*, not yet decided; for comment see Buhr, Lübbert, Simon and Thomas 'Oracle/Sun Microsystems: The Challenge of Reviewing a merger Involving Open Source Software' (2010) 2 *Competition Policy Newsletter* 20.

[593] Ibid, paras 176–185, 627–658 and 737–759.

[594] See ch 21 n 592 above.

[595] See 'Remedies', pp 884–880 above.

[596] Case M 3431, decision of 6 October 2004.   [597] Case M 4000, decision of 21 July 2006.

[598] Case M 4180, decision of 14 November 2006.

[599] See Bachour and others '*Gaz de France/Suez*: Keeping energy markets in Belgium and France open and contestable through far-reaching remedies' (2007) (Spring) *Competition Policy Newsletter* 83.

[600] Case M 4525, decision of 19 September 2007.   [601] Case M 5335, decision of 22 June 2009.

[602] Case M 5440, decision of 28 August 2009, on appeal to the General Court Case T-162/10 *Niki Luftfahrt GmbH v Commission*, not yet decided.

lead to take-off and landing slots becoming available at various European airports: this would enable competitors to compete with the merged entities on routes such as Brussels to Munich and Brussels to Vienna; ancillary remedies, on matters such as participation in Lufthansa's Frequent Flyer Programme, were also accepted. Structural remedies were also given in *Unilever/Sara Lee Body Care*[603] and *Syngenta/Monsanto's sunflower seed business*[604].

There have also been some cases in which behavioural commitments have been accepted. For example in *Deutsche Bahn/English Welsh & Scottish Railway Holdings*[605] (a Phase I case) the Commission accepted commitments by Deutsche Bahn to fulfil EW&S's expansion plans for rail freight transport in France by investing in locomotives and personnel and to provide fair and non-discriminatory access to EW&S's driver training schools. In *SFR/Télé 2*[606] a series of remedies was offered to ensure that Vivendi, the owner of valuable television content, would not discriminate against competitors in the downstream pay-TV market; nor that it would weaken competitors in the upstream market for the acquisition of television content.

It is a notable feature of some cases, particularly in the energy and telecommunications sectors, that the package of remedies may be very complex: obvious examples of this are *E.ON/MOL*[607], a merger impacting on the gas sector in Hungary, where the Commission required a divestment on the part of MOL, a release of gas to the wholesale market and access to storage facilities for customers that succeeded in buying the gas; *Gaz de France/ Suez*, referred to above; *T-Mobile/tele.ring*, a case that was discussed in the context of non-collusive oligopoly[608]; and *Friesland Foods/Campina*[609] where, apart from structural remedies, a complex set of commitments were accepted to ensure that competitors downstream from the merged entity would have access to raw milk in the Netherlands and that, over a period of time, a competitor to the merged entity might emerge.

(v) Withdrawal of notifications

It is important to note that there have been many cases in which the parties to a merger subject to a Phase II investigation have chosen to withdraw the notification. Out of 201 cases to have gone to a Phase II investigation by the end of September 2011 36 were then withdrawn. It would be reasonable to assume that at least some of these withdrawals were made because it seemed inevitable that the Commission would otherwise have prohibited the merger outright. In this sense the total of 21 prohibitions referred to above may understate the number of cases that might, but for withdrawal, have led to an outright prohibition.

Article 6(1)(c) of the EUMR provides that the Commission shall conclude a Phase II investigation with a decision, unless it is satisfied that the parties have abandoned the merger. The Commission's *Consolidated Jurisdictional Notice* explains, at paragraphs 117 to 121, the procedure to be followed in such circumstances.

---

[603] Case M 5658, decision of 17 November 2010.   [604] Case M 5675, decision of 17 November 2010.
[605] Case M 4746, decision of 7 November 2007.   [606] Case M 4504, decision of 18 July 2007.
[607] Case M 3696, decision of 21 December 2005, OJ [2006] L 253/20.
[608] See 'Non-coordinated effects', p 871 above.
[609] Case M 5046, decision of 17 December 2008; see de la Mano and others (2009) 1 *Competition Policy Newsletter* 84.

22

Mergers (3) – UK law[1]

1. Introduction

UK law on the control of mergers is contained in Part 3 of the Enterprise Act 2002, which entered into force on 20 June 2003. This legislation involved a major overhaul of the domestic system of merger control. Merger control was first introduced in the UK by the Monopolies and Mergers Act 1965 which was replaced by the Fair Trading Act 1973. In July 2001 Government proposed a number of changes to the system of merger control in its White Paper *Productivity and Enterprise – A World Class Competition Regime*[2]. A central feature of the Government's proposed reform was that responsibility for making decisions in merger cases should be given to the Office of Fair Trading ('the OFT')[3] and the Competition Commission ('the CC')[4], and that the Secretary of State should become involved only in cases which raise exceptional public interest issues[5]; the decisions to be adopted by the OFT and CC would be made against a 'substantial lessening of competition' ('SLC') test, rather than the public interest test set out in the Fair Trading Act. These changes were put into effect by Part 3 of the Enterprise Act 2002, with which this chapter is predominantly concerned. However there are some specific rules for 'public interest cases', including media mergers, for 'other special cases' and for certain mergers between water companies; these will be briefly described at the end of the chapter.

In reading this chapter it should be recalled that, as a general proposition, a 'concentration' that has a 'Community dimension' under the EU Merger Regulation (the 'EUMR')

---

[1] For more detailed texts on the merger control provisions of the Enterprise Act 2002 readers are referred to Parr, Finbow and Hughes *UK Merger Control: Law and Practice* (Sweet & Maxwell, 2nd ed, 2005); Bankes and Hadden *UK Merger Control: Law and Practice* (LexisNexis Butterworths, 2006); Scott, Hviid, Lyons and Bright *Merger Control in the United Kingdom* (Oxford University Press, 2006); Parker and Majumdar *UK Merger Control* (Hart Publishing, 2011).

[2] Cm 5233, ch 5; see also the Government's *Response* (December 2001).

[3] See ch 2, 'The OFT', pp 63–69.   [4] See ch 2, 'Competition Commission', pp 69–72.

[5] *Mergers: The Response to the Consultation on Proposals for Reform* URN 00/805, October 2000, paras 4.10–4.12.

cannot be investigated under domestic law[6], although exceptions to this are to be found in Article 4(4)[7], Article 9[8] and in Article 21(4)[9] of that Regulation.

2. Overview of UK Merger Control

(A) Part 3 of the Enterprise Act 2002

Part 3 of the Enterprise Act 2002 consists of five chapters; the Government's *Explanatory Notes* to the Bill as introduced into Parliament on 26 March 2002 are a helpful adjunct to the Act itself; the Competition Appeal Tribunal ('the CAT') has noted that they may be used as an aid to ascertaining the intention of Parliament[10]. Chapter 1 of Part 3 of the Act is entitled 'Duty to make references': it deals both with jurisdictional matters, such as the meaning of 'relevant merger situations', and with the substantive assessment of mergers under the SLC test. The overwhelming majority of mergers will be considered under Chapter 1. However Chapter 2 contains provisions on 'public interest' cases and Chapter 3 addresses 'other special cases': these provisions will be invoked only rarely, except perhaps in relation to media mergers following amendments made by the Communications Act 2003; the provisions on public interest and other special cases, and on water mergers, are described briefly in section 9 of this chapter[11]. Chapter 4 of Part 3 of the Enterprise Act contains rules on enforcement, which set out the various undertakings that can be accepted by the OFT and the CC in the course of merger investigations and the orders that they may make, as well as certain automatic restrictions on the integration of firms during the currency of an investigation. Chapter 5 deals with numerous supplementary matters such as merger notices, investigatory powers, review by the CAT and the payment of fees.

Section 3 of this chapter explains the procedures of the OFT when determining whether a merger should be referred to the CC and when deciding to accept undertakings in lieu of a reference. Section 4 describes the procedures of the CC and section 5 discusses the way in which the OFT and the CC apply the SLC test in practice. Section 6 explains the enforcement powers in the Act, including the remedies that the CC can impose in merger cases. Various supplementary matters are dealt with in section 7 and section 8 considers how the merger control provisions work in practice. Section 9 contains a brief account of the provisions on public interest cases, other special cases and mergers in the water industry.

(B) Brief description of the system of merger control in the UK

In essence the system of control for 'ordinary' mergers (as opposed to public interest or other special cases) in the Enterprise Act is as follows. The OFT has a duty to refer certain mergers to the CC; in some circumstances it has a discretion not to refer, and some mergers cannot be referred at all. There is no obligation on firms to pre-notify mergers to the OFT, although provision is made for them to do so on a voluntary basis either by making

---

[6] See ch 21, 'Article 21: one-stop merger control', pp 844–845.

[7] See ch 21, 'Pre-notification referrals: Article 4(4)', pp 846–847.

[8] See ch 21, 'Post-notification referrals: Article 9', pp 847–848.

[9] See ch 21, 'Article 21(4): legitimate interest clause', pp 851–854.

[10] See para 222 of the final judgment in Case No 1023/4/1/03 *IBA Health Ltd v OFT* [2003] CAT 27, [2004] CompAR 235; the *Explanatory Notes* are available at www.legislation.gov.uk.

[11] See '"Public Interest Cases", "Other Special Cases" and Mergers in the Water Industry', pp 956–961 below.

an informal submission or by submitting a more formal 'merger notice' for which there is a legislative basis: the difference between the two lies in the timetable that each triggers. In practice many firms voluntarily have pre-merger discussions with the OFT, not least because power exists to refer a merger to the CC after it has been consummated and, where appropriate, to require a merger to be reversed: a highly undesirable outcome for the firms concerned. Provision is made for the OFT to accept legally binding undertakings to modify a merger in lieu of a reference to the CC.

In cases where the OFT is concerned that there is a realistic prospect of an SLC and where it is not possible to agree a remedy the matter will be referred to the CC: there is an obvious analogy here with the procedure under the EUMR, where cases that raise 'serious doubts' as to the compatibility of a merger with the common market are taken to an in-depth Phase II investigation; however a significant difference is that, in the UK system, Phase II is conducted by a separate body from Phase I. The CC, when conducting an investigation under the Act, must determine whether there is a 'relevant merger situation' which qualifies for investigation and, if so, whether that merger would lead to an SLC within any market or markets in the UK for goods or services; it must also decide on appropriate remedies. The CC has available to it a number of final powers following its investigation including, where necessary, the power to prohibit a merger outright and to require the reversal of a merger that has already been consummated.

(C) Institutional arrangements

An important feature of the merger provisions in the Enterprise Act is that the Secretary of State is not involved at all, unless there is a public interest consideration: such cases are rare. In the overwhelming majority of cases decisions are taken by the OFT[12]; a relatively small number of mergers are referred to the CC, and in those cases the CC will be responsible for the final decision. Decisions of the OFT and the CC are subject to review by the CAT. Sectoral regulators do not have concurrent powers in relation to mergers in the way that they do under the Competition Act 1998 and the market investigation provisions in the Enterprise Act[13]; however they are asked to provide input into the deliberations of the OFT and the CC where appropriate[14].

Within the OFT the Mergers Group has specific responsibility for mergers. It has a director and two deputy directors for casework, and three assistant directors – two for economics and one for law. The Group also has more than 30 case officers to enable the OFT to perform its functions under the Act. The case officers are divided into a number of teams, each of which has responsibility for particular industry sectors; there is also a Head of EU Merger Regulation post which deals with policy and the coordination of OFT input into cases arising from the EUMR. The OFT's website[15] contains a considerable amount of information about mergers under the Enterprise Act such as decisions, case lists and a register of undertakings; it also discusses procedures, facilitates consultation on undertakings in lieu of a reference to the CC and gives details of people to contact and of speeches and OFT publications.

The CC has about 40 part-time members. In each case referred to it a group will be appointed to carry out the investigation, usually consisting of four or five members; legal and economics staff as well as accountants and business advisers support the work of the groups.

---

[12] The reference of *BSkyB/ITV* was made by the Secretary of State under the public interest provisions in the Enterprise Act: see 'Public interest cases', pp 956–958 below.

[13] See ch 10, 'Concurrency', pp 437–439.

[14] *Mergers – Jurisdictional and procedural guidance* OFT 527, June 2009, para 1.10.

[15] See www.oft.gov.uk.

(D) Guidelines, rules of procedure and other relevant publications

In addition to Part 3 of the Enterprise Act various guidelines, rules and other publications seek to explain the operation of the UK system of merger control. Section 106 of the Act requires the OFT and the CC to prepare and publish general advice and information about the making of merger references and, in the case of the CC, about the way in which relevant customer benefits may affect the taking of enforcement action. Section 107 of the Act imposes additional publicity requirements on the OFT, the CC and the Secretary of State: for example references, undertakings and orders must all be published.

(i) OFT publications

The OFT has published the following guidance in relation to mergers under the Enterprise Act:

- *Mergers – Jurisdictional and procedural guidance*[16]
- *Mergers – Exceptions to the duty to refer and undertakings in lieu of reference guidance*[17]
- *Merger fees*[18]
- *Merger notice*[19]
- *Prior notice of publicly proposed mergers*[20]
- *Enquiry letter template*[21]

The OFT has also published two reports, prepared for it, the CC and the Secretary of State, on *Ex post evaluation of mergers*[22] and *Review of merger decisions under the Enterprise Act 2002*[23].

(ii) CC publications

Acting under Schedule 7A to the Competition Act the CC has adopted the *Competition Commission Rules of Procedure 2006* which superseded the earlier rules of 20 June 2003[24]. The CC has published four sets of guidelines under section 106(3) of the Enterprise Act of relevance to merger investigations[25]:

- *General Advice and Information*[26]
- *Statement of Policy on Penalties*[27]
- *Merger Remedies: Competition Commission Guidelines*[28]
- *Water Merger References: Competition Commission Guidelines*[29].

The Chairman of the CC has published three further documents of relevance:

- *Guidance to Groups*[30]
- *Disclosure of Information in Merger and Market Inquiries*[31]
- *Disclosure of Information by the Competition Commission to Other Public Authorities*[32].

---

[16] OFT 527, June 2009.   [17] OFT 1122, December 2010.
[18] September 2009.   [19] June 2003.   [20] June 2003.
[21] Available at www.oft.gov.uk/OFTwork/mergers/publications.
[22] OFT 767, March 2005.   [23] OFT 1073, March 2009.
[24] Available at www.competition-commission.org.uk.   [25] Ibid.
[26] CC4, March 2006.   [27] CC5, June 2003.   [28] CC8, November 2008.
[29] CC9, December 2004.   [30] CC6, March 2006.   [31] CC7, July 2003.
[32] CC12, April 2006.

The CC has also published some other guidance documents[33]:

- *Template Interim Undertakings for Completed Mergers*
- *Suggested Best Practice for Submissions of Technical Economic Analysis from Parties to the CC*
- *Notice of Variation of Procedure – Adoption of Undertakings.*

(iii) Joint OFT and CC publications

When the Enterprise Act first entered into force the OFT and CC each published their own guidance on how they assess the competitive impact of mergers[34]. A joint review of their respective guidelines was launched by the OFT and the CC in 2008[35]: this led to the publication in September 2010 of their joint *Merger Assessment Guidelines*[36]. The OFT and CC have also published *A Quick Guide to UK Merger Assessment*[37].

(iv) Department for Business, Innovation and Skills delegated legislation[38]

The Secretary of State has made the following orders under the Enterprise Act of relevance to merger investigations:

- The Enterprise Act 2002 (Merger Fees and Determination of Turnover) Order 2003[39]: this establishes how turnover is to be calculated when determining whether a merger qualifies as a 'relevant merger situation' for jurisdictional purposes[40] and the amount of any merger fee that may be payable to the OFT[41]. The level of fees has been raised by the Enterprise Act (Merger Fees) (Amendment) Orders 2005[42] and 2009[43]

- The Competition Commission (Penalties) Order 2003[44]: this establishes the maximum levels of penalties that the CC can impose for offences under section 110 of the Act[45]

- The Enterprise Act (Merger Pre-notification) Regulations 2003[46]: this makes provision for the serving of merger notices by parties who pre-notify a merger to the OFT

- The Competition Appeal Tribunal Rules 2003[47]: this governs the way in which the CAT deals with applications for review of decisions under Part 3 of the Act

- The OFT Registers of Undertakings and Orders (Available Hours) Order 2003[48]

- The Enterprise Act (Protection of Legitimate Interests) Order 2003[49]: this enables the Secretary of State to issue a 'European intervention notice' and to take appropriate measures to protect legitimate interests which may be adversely affected by a merger

- The Enterprise Act (Supply of Services) Order 2003[50]: this sets out the situations in which permission to use land will be regarded as a supply of services

---

[33] The documents referred to in the text that follows are available at www.competition-commission.org.uk.
[34] *Mergers: substantive assessment guidance* OFT 516, May 2003 and *Merger References: Competition Commission Guidelines* CC 2, June 2003.
[35] Details of the joint review are available at www.competition-commission.org.uk.
[36] CC 2 (Revised), OFT 1254, September 2010.   [37] CC 2 (Summary), OFT 1313, March 2011.
[38] The documents referred to in the text that follows are available at www.legislation.gov.uk.
[39] SI 2003/1370, as amended by the Enterprise Act 2002 (Merger Fees and Determination of Turnover) (Amendment) Order 2004, SI 2004/3204.
[40] See 'Relevant merger situations', pp 918–923 below.   [41] See 'Fees', pp 928–929 below.
[42] SI 2005/3558.   [43] SI 2009/2396.   [44] SI 2003/1371.
[45] See 'Investigation powers and penalties', p 949 below.   [46] SI 2003/1369.
[47] SI 2003/1372.   [48] SI 2003/1373.   [49] SI 2003/1592.   [50] SI 2003/1594.

- The Enterprise Act (Anticipated Mergers) Order 2003[51]: this makes provision for the aggregation of two or more transactions which take place between the same parties within a two-year period
- The Enterprise Act 2002 and Media Mergers (Consequential Amendments) Order 2003[52]
- The EC Merger Control (Consequential Amendments) Regulations 2004[53]
- The Enterprise Act 2002 (Enforcement Undertakings and Orders) Order 2004[54]
- The Water Mergers (Modification of Enactments) Regulations 2004[55]: this makes provision for the modified application of Part 3 of the Act to mergers in the water industry
- The Water Mergers (Determination of Turnover) Regulations 2004[56]
- The Enterprise Act 2002 (Enforcement Undertakings) Order 2006[57]
- The Enterprise Act 2002 (Enforcement Undertakings and Orders) Order 2006[58]
- The Enterprise Act 2002 (EEA State) (Amendment) Regulations 2007[59]
- The Enterprise Act 2002 (Specification of Additional Section 58 Consideration) Order 2008[60].

3. The OFT's Duty to Make References

Chapter 1 of Part 3 of the Enterprise Act is entitled 'Duty to make references', and is central to the domestic system of merger control. Chapter 1 contains both jurisdictional rules, explaining what is meant by a merger and which mergers can be investigated under the Act, and substantive rules, setting out the test to be applied by the OFT and the CC when investigating mergers. Chapter 1 also defines the respective roles of the OFT and the CC in relation to merger investigations: the OFT conducts the preliminary analysis of mergers, analogous to a Phase I investigation under the EUMR; cases that raise serious competition concerns and that cannot be resolved at the stage of the OFT's investigation are referred to the CC for an in-depth analysis, analogous to a Phase II investigation under the EUMR. The procedures of the OFT and the CC in merger investigations will be explained in the text that follows[61].

Sections 22 to 32 of the Enterprise Act deal with the position of the OFT in relation to mergers that have already been consummated ('completed mergers') and sections 33 to 34 set out the relevant provisions in relation to mergers that have yet to be completed ('anticipated mergers'). Unlike the position under the EUMR, there is no duty under UK law to pre-notify mergers to the OFT. In practice many firms bring their transactions to the attention of the OFT on a voluntary basis prior to completion, although in recent years there has been a noticeable increase in the number of completed mergers that have been investigated by the OFT and CC, sometimes leading to the forced divestiture of assets already acquired[62]. There is evidence to suggest that quite a few mergers that might

---

[51] SI 2003/1595. [52] SI 2003/3180. [53] SI 2004/1079. [54] SI 2004/2181.
[55] SI 2004/3202. [56] SI 2004/3206. [57] SI 2004/354. [58] SI 2004/355.
[59] SI 2007/528. [60] SI 2008/2645.
[61] See 'OFT procedure', pp 923–929 and 'Determination of references by the CC', pp 929–931 below.
[62] See 'Completed mergers', p 954 below.

be harmful to competition escape the scrutiny of the OFT and CC[63]. To deal with this problem the OFT has a Mergers Intelligence Officer who monitors merger activity which has not been brought to its attention[64].

Sections 35 to 41 of the Act are concerned with the determination of references by the CC.

(A) Duty to make references: completed mergers

(i) Duty to refer

Section 22(1) of the Enterprise Act provides that the OFT has a duty to make a reference to the CC if it believes that it is or may be the case that a 'relevant merger situation'[65] has been created and that the creation of that situation has resulted, or may be expected to result, in an SLC within any market or markets in the UK, or a part of the UK, for goods or services[66]. It is important to note that the Act imposes a duty, rather than conferring a discretion, on the OFT to refer mergers of the kind set out in section 22(1): this means that it is possible for a firm that is opposed to a particular merger, for example the victim of a hostile bid, a customer or a competitor, to apply to the CAT for a review of the decision of the OFT not to refer that merger to the CC[67]. The fact that a decision not to refer a merger can be challenged, as well as a decision to refer one, has resource implications for the OFT, which has to take care to ensure that it publishes a decision setting out the primary evidence and the reasoning that led to its decision in a manner which is clear to all interested parties.

(A) The IBA Health case

The first application by a third party for a review concerned a proposed acquisition by iSOFT Group plc of Torex plc, two direct competitors in the supply of software applications to hospitals; the merger would result in the merged entity having a significant market share. This case led to an important judgment of the Court of Appeal which examined the nature of the duty of the OFT under the Act to make a reference. The OFT decided that it would not refer the iSOFT/Torex merger to the CC. IBA Health, a competitor, challenged the decision not to make a reference before the CAT; the CAT concluded that the OFT's decision should be quashed and that the matter should be reconsidered[68]. In reaching this conclusion the CAT considered the scheme of the merger control provisions in the Act and noted that the OFT's role is to act as a 'first screen' in relation to mergers, but not to be a decision-maker: that is the function of the CC. Section 33[69] imposes a duty on the OFT to refer a merger where it believes that 'it is or *may be*' the case that a merger '*may be* expected to result' in an SLC (emphasis added). In the CAT's view this formulation (and in particular the appearance in section 33(1) of the word 'may' in two places (the so-called 'double may')) meant that if the OFT itself did not consider that a merger would result in an SLC, but if it was possible that the CC might credibly have that view, the OFT was obliged to refer:

If there is room for two views, the statutory duty of the OFT is to refer the matter[70].

---

[63] See *The deterrent effect on competition enforcement by the OFT: a report prepared for the OFT by Deloitte* OFT 962, November 2007, paras 4.48–4.61.

[64] *Mergers – Jurisdictional and procedural guidance* OFT 527, June 2009, para 4.9.

[65] This term is defined in s 23 of the Act: see 'Relevant merger situations', pp 918–923 below.

[66] On the meaning of 'markets in the UK for goods and services' see Enterprise Act 2002, s 22(6).

[67] See 'Review of decisions under Part 3 of the Enterprise Act', pp 950–951 below.

[68] Case No 1023/4/1/03 *IBA Health Ltd v OFT* [2003] CAT 27, [2004] CompAR 235.

[69] Because the *iSOFT/Torex* merger was anticipated rather than completed, the relevant section was s 33(1) rather than s 22(1); the wording under consideration in the case is identical in each section.

[70] Case No 1023/4/1/03 *IBA Health Ltd v OFT* [2003] CAT 27, [2004] CompAR 235, para 192.

The CAT considered that, as the OFT had not asked whether there was a significant prospect that the CC might consider that the merger would give rise to an SLC, it had failed to ask itself the correct question and so had erred in law[71]; the CAT also held that the OFT's decision was defective because it was not based on sufficient evidence and was insufficiently reasoned[72]. In the OFT's view the CAT's formulation of the duty upon it would significantly lower the threshold for referring mergers to the CC and might lead to many more mergers being referred: this raised important policy questions, as a result of which the OFT appealed to the Court of Appeal. The Court of Appeal upheld the decision of the CAT to quash the decision and refer the matter back to the OFT on the facts of the case, but concluded that the CAT's formulation of the duty on the OFT was incorrect[73]. The Vice-Chancellor (as he then was) was of the opinion that the CAT's 'two part' test was wrong and that it would make various provisions in the Act unworkable:

> the relevant belief is that the merger may be expected to result in a substantial lessening of competition, not that the Commission may in due course decide that the merger may be expected to result in a substantial lessening of competition. Further, the body which is to hold that belief is OFT not the Commission[74].

The Vice-Chancellor went on to say that the words in section 33 should be applied in accordance with their ordinary meaning.

(B) Guidance

Part 2 of the OFT/CC *Merger Assessment Guidelines*[75] provides guidance on the OFT's duty to refer in the light of this judgment and of some specific guidance that the Vice-Chancellor provided on the proper application of section 33(1) in paragraphs 44 to 49 of his judgment. The OFT must form a reasonable belief, objectively justified by relevant facts, as to whether a merger will lessen competition substantially. The OFT must make a reference to the CC where it believes that a merger is more likely than not to result in an SLC, that is to say, that it believes there is more than a 50 per cent chance that an SLC will occur. The *Guidelines* go on to say that a reference to the CC can be made at lower ranges of probability than 50 per cent: if the OFT believes that the degree of likelihood is not fanciful, but has less than a 50 per cent chance of occurring, the OFT has a wide margin within which to exercise its judgment as to whether it may be the case that the merger would result in an SLC[76]. In such cases the OFT will have a duty to refer when it believes there to be a 'realistic prospect' that the merger will result in an SLC.

(C) The UniChem case

In *UniChem v OFT* UniChem objected to the fact that the OFT had not referred a proposed acquisition by Phoenix Healthcare Distribution Ltd of East Anglian Pharmaceuticals Ltd to the CC. The CAT considered that much of the OFT's decision was soundly based, but nevertheless quashed it since the OFT had made primary findings of fact about

---

[71] Ibid, para 232.

[72] When the OFT reconsidered the case it found that there could be an SLC in relation to the supply of laboratory information management systems to NHS hospitals, but did not refer the merger to the CC as iSOFT offered undertakings in lieu: see OFT Press Release 56/04, 24 March 2004.

[73] *OFT v IBA Health Ltd* [2004] EWCA Civ 142, [2004] UKCLR 683; for comment see Parr 'Merger Control in the Wake of *IBA Health*' (2007) 6 Competition Law Journal 282.

[74] *OFT v IBA Health Ltd* [2004] EWCA Civ 142, [2004] UKCLR 683, para 38.

[75] CC2 (Revised), OFT 1254, September 2010, paras 2.2–2.7; this replaces the OFT's *Guidance note revising Mergers – substantive assessment guidance* OFT 516a.

[76] Case No 1049/4/1/05 *UniChem v OFT* [2005] CAT 8, [2005] CompAR 907, para 172 (distinguishing the term 'margin of judgment' from the broader concept of discretion).

UniChem's position on the market on the basis of information provided by the merging parties but without any reference to UniChem itself. In the CAT's view a 'balanced and fair procedure' would have been for the OFT to have checked these important facts with UniChem[77]. On reconsideration of the matter the OFT again cleared the merger without a reference to the CC[78].

(D) *The Celesio case*

In *Celesio AG v OFT*[79] Celesio unsuccessfully challenged the decision of the OFT not to refer a proposed acquisition by the Boots Group plc of Alliance UniChem plc; the CAT rejected a submission by Celesio that the OFT is always under a duty to refer a merger where the prospect of there being an SLC is greater than fanciful[80].

(E) *Other points about the duty to refer*

The OFT may by notice under section 31 require information from the merging parties for the purpose of deciding whether to make a reference under section 22. The OFT is likely to proceed in this manner in cases where a completed merger has not been pre-notified to it[81]. However it has no powers to force the parties to provide this information, nor to require information from third parties[82]. The lack of such powers can be a handicap to the OFT, and might even mean that, in some cases, it has to make a reference to the CC since it cannot satisfy itself that a merger would not result in an SLC. It would be a criminal offence for notifying parties or third parties to provide the OFT with false or misleading information[83].

The duty imposed on the OFT by section 22(1) must be read subject to the provisions of section 22(2) and (3), which provide a discretion not to refer certain mergers and which prevent the reference of some others.

(ii) **Discretion not to refer**

Section 22(2) provides the OFT with a discretion not to make a reference in two situations.

(A) *Markets of insufficient importance*

The first is where the OFT believes that the market or markets concerned are not of sufficient importance to justify the making of a reference to the CC[84]. The primary purpose of this provision is to avoid references where the costs involved would be disproportionate to the size of the market concerned. The OFT's original guidance on this issue had been taken to suggest that this '*de minimis*' exception would apply only rarely, where the value of the market affected was less than £400,000, and in practice quite a few 'small' mergers were referred to the CC. The OFT therefore launched a consultation in June 2007 which led to the publication of revised guidance in November 2007[85] that raised the threshold

---

[77] Ibid, paras 268–269.

[78] www.oft.gov.uk/advice_and_resources/resource_base/Mergers_home/decisions/2005/phoenix-healthcare.

[79] Case No 1059/4/1/06 [2006] CAT 9, [2006] CompAR 515.   [80] Ibid, para 74.

[81] See *Mergers – Jurisdictional and procedural guidance*, para 4.17.

[82] Enterprise Act 2002, s 31; see further *Mergers – Jurisdictional and procedural guidance*, para 6.3.

[83] Enterprise Act 2002, s 117.

[84] Ibid, s 22(2)(a), on which see Christian 'The OFT's Discretion Not to Refer – Where do We Stand?' (2010) 9(1) Competition Law Journal 29 and Mackenzie 'The OFT's De Minimis Exception – When Size Really Doesn't Matter' (2010) 31(8) ECLR 331.

[85] *Exception to the duty to refer: markets of insufficient importance* OFT 516b.

from £400,000 to £10 million, albeit subject to certain qualifications[86]. The 2007 guidance was itself amended in 2010 to reflect the OFT's experience of applying the exception in practice, and will now be found in *Mergers – Exceptions to the duty to refer and undertakings in lieu of reference guidance* ('the *Exceptions guidance*')[87]. Chapter 2 of the OFT's *Exceptions guidance* stresses that the OFT will apply the *de minimis* exception by carrying out a 'broad cost-benefit analysis' in the light of all relevant factors[88]. The *Exceptions guidance* does not provide a mechanical 'safe harbour' below which the *de minimis* exception will always be applied[89]; however it does provide guidance on when the OFT is likely to consider that the exception does, or does not, apply:

- where the annual value of the market(s) concerned is, in aggregate, more than £10 million, the OFT will generally consider the case to be of sufficient importance to justify a reference[90]

- where the annual value of the market(s) concerned is, in aggregate, less than £3 million, the OFT will generally consider that a reference is not justified[91].

In cases where the annual value of the market(s) concerned is between £3 million and £10 million the OFT will typically consider three points:

- whether clear-cut undertakings in lieu of a reference could, in principle, be offered by the parties[92]

- whether the expected customer harm resulting from the merger is materially greater than the cost of a reference to the public purse (currently around £400,000)[93]

- the wider implications of the OFT's decisions for its treatment of future cases[94].

Separately, the OFT's *Exceptions guidance* also explains how the exception is used to reduce the costs of a first phase review[95]. The OFT has cleared several mergers on *de minimis* grounds since its guidance was first revised in 2007[96], including one that it considered might lead to a monopoly[97].

(B) Customer benefits

The second situation in which there is a discretion not to make a reference is where any 'relevant customer benefits' in relation to the creation of the merger concerned outweigh the expected SLC and any adverse effects of it[98]. The meaning of relevant customer benefits for this purpose is set out in section 30 of the Act: there must be a benefit for 'relevant customers'[99] in the form of lower prices, higher quality or greater choice of goods

---

[86] Ibid, para 7.6.   [87] OFT 1122, December 2010.

[88] *Exceptions guidance*, paras 2.21–2.27.   [89] Ibid, fn 3.   [90] Ibid, para 2.14.

[91] Ibid, para 2.15 (assuming that a clear-cut undertaking in lieu of a reference is not available).

[92] Ibid, paras 2.18–2.27; see also *Dunfermline Press Ltd/Trinity Mirror plc*, 4 February 2008.

[93] *Exceptions guidance*, paras 2.9–2.12, 2.16, and 2.28–2.29.

[94] Ibid, paras 2.40–2.43; this point is specifically based on the findings in *The deterrent effect on competition enforcement by the OFT: a report prepared for the OFT by Deloitte* OFT 962, November 2007.

[95] *Exceptions guidance*, paras 2.44–2.53.

[96] See eg three mergers arising from the award of railway franchises: OFT Press Release 180/07, 20 December 2007, *Exceptions guidance*, OFT Press Release 15/08, 4 February 2008 and OFT Press Release 16/08, 4 February 2008; see also *FMC/ISP Holdings*, 30 July 2008, paras 63–76; *Stagecoach/Cavalier Contracts*, 18 September 2008, paras 93–111; *Ocean Park/Orbital Marketing Services Group*, 14 November 2008; paras 68–86; and *Lochard/Spectris*, 29 January 2009, paras 114–131.

[97] *Ordnance Survey/Local Government Improvement and Development*, 23 February 2011, paras 102–118.

[98] Enterprise Act 2002, s 22(2)(b).

[99] On the meaning of relevant customers see Enterprise Act 2002, s 30(4); the term includes customers in a chain of customers beginning with the immediate customers of the merging parties, and includes future customers.

or services in any market in the UK (which need not be the market in which the SLC has occurred or would occur) or greater innovation in relation to such goods or services[100]; and the benefit must have accrued, or be expected to accrue within a reasonable period, as a result of the merger, and be unlikely to have accrued without the merger or a similar lessening of competition[101]. The notion of relevant customer benefits occurs elsewhere in the Act, in particular in relation to the CC's investigations[102]. However, whereas the OFT is asked by section 22 to consider whether any relevant customer benefits would outweigh an SLC and any adverse effects of the SLC arising from the merger as a whole[103], the CC is asked to consider the effect that any remedial action it might take would have on any relevant customer benefits[104].

The OFT's *Exceptions guidance* cautions that cases in which relevant customer benefits are established are likely to be rare[105]. The parties must adduce detailed and verifiable evidence of anticipated relevant customer benefits[106]. The parties must also demonstrate that they will have the incentive to pass on these benefits to customers and that the merger will leave customers better off than they would otherwise have been[107]. It is important to appreciate that the OFT (and the CC) is asked to consider only whether there will be a *customer* benefit rather than a benefit to consumers generally, which would be a very difficult thing to demonstrate. It would presumably be a matter for the judgment of the OFT (or the CC) to determine how to proceed in circumstances where some customers would benefit from a merger but others would not[108]. Even where such benefits can be established the OFT has a discretion whether to refer a merger; in exercising its discretion the OFT will have regard to the benefits of a CC investigation, including the possibility of remedies that could preserve any relevant customer benefits[109].

A separate point is that there may be cases in which predicted customer benefits would increase the rivalry in a market, in which case this fact could be taken into account as part of the SLC test, rather than as a subsequent counterweight to a possible SLC[110].

(iii) Circumstances in which a reference cannot be made

Section 22(3) sets out various circumstances in which a reference cannot be made: for example where the OFT is considering whether to accept an undertaking in lieu of a reference[111]; where the merger has been, or is being, considered under the provisions on anticipated mergers[112]; in certain public interest cases[113]; and where the European

---

[100] Enterprise Act 2002, s 30(1)(a); these benefits are not limited to efficiencies affecting rivalry: see *Exceptions guidance*, para 4.3.

[101] Enterprise Act 2002, s 30(2) and (3): note that these subsections set out the test for completed mergers and for anticipated mergers respectively.

[102] See 'Efficiencies', p 939 below.   [103] *Exceptions guidance*, para 4.4.

[104] The CC considered the effect of possible remedial action on relevant customer benefits in *Mid Kent Water/ South East Water*, paras 8.108–8.152, available at www.competition-commission.org.uk and *Macquarie UK Broadcast Ventures/National Grid Wireless Group*, paras 10.8–10.19, available at www.competition-commission. org.uk.

[105] Ibid.   [106] *Exceptions guidance*, para 4.9.

[107] Ibid, para 4.12.

[108] This may be the case where a merger gives rise to relevant customer benefits in one market but causes an SLC in another market: see *Exceptions guidance*, paras 4.3 and 4.13.

[109] Ibid, para 4.5.

[110] *Exceptions guidance*, para 4.2 and fn 36; see also section 5.7 of the OFT/CC *Merger Assessment Guidelines*.

[111] Enterprise Act 2002, s 22(3)(b): see 'Undertakings in lieu of a reference', pp 927–928 below.

[112] Ibid, s 22(3)(c): see below on anticipated mergers.

[113] Ibid, s 22(3)(d): see 'Public interest cases', pp 956–958 below.

Commission is deciding whether to exercise jurisdiction under Article 4(5) or Article 22 of the EUMR[114].

(B) Duty to make references: anticipated mergers

In practice most mergers are brought to the attention of the OFT on a voluntary basis prior to their consummation; there is a statutory basis for pre-notification, though its use is not obligatory[115]. Section 33(1) of the Enterprise Act imposes a duty on the OFT to make a reference of anticipated mergers where it believes that it is or may be the case that arrangements are in progress or in contemplation which, if carried into effect, would result in the creation of a relevant merger situation and the creation of that situation may be expected to result in an SLC within any market or markets in the UK for goods or services[116]. The OFT will generally consider that 'arrangements are in progress or in contemplation' where the merger has been publicly announced[117]. A merger may be 'in contemplation' without there being a binding agreement: in the *London Stock Exchange* case the CC said that there must be 'genuine consideration' on the part of the acquirer to enter into the transaction; its interest in the transaction must be real; there must be an intention to enter into the transaction within a reasonable time; and the acquirer must be capable of bringing the transaction about[118].

As in the case of section 22 for completed mergers the OFT has a duty, rather than a discretion, to refer anticipated mergers. However, as in the case of completed mergers, the OFT has a discretion not to refer markets of insufficient importance or mergers where relevant customer benefits would outweigh the SLC concerned[119]. An additional discretionary ground for non-reference exists for anticipated mergers, where the arrangements are not sufficiently advanced, or are not sufficiently likely to proceed, to justify the making of a reference to the CC[120]. Section 33(3) sets out circumstances in which a reference cannot be made, which mirror the provisions of section 22(3)[121]. Pursuant to section 34, provision has been made for the aggregation of two or more transactions which take place between the same parties within a two-year period[122].

(C) Relevant merger situations

Section 23 of the Enterprise Act defines what is meant by 'relevant merger situations'. For there to be a relevant merger situation, two or more enterprises must have ceased to be distinct, and the merger must satisfy either the turnover or the share of supply test.

---

[114] Ibid, ss 22(3)(e) and 22(3)(f): on the Article 4(5) and Article 22 procedure in the EUMR see ch 21, 'Article 4(5) and Article 22: referral of concentrations not having a Community dimension by Member States to the Commission', pp 849–851.

[115] See 'Notifying mergers to the OFT', pp 924–925 below.   [116] Enterprise Act 2002, s 33(1).

[117] *Mergers – Jurisdictional and procedural guidance*, para 3.6.

[118] See the Final Report, para 3.26, available at www.competition-commission.org.uk.

[119] Enterprise Act 2002, s 33(2)(a) and (c).

[120] Ibid, s 33(2)(b); see *Exceptions guidance*, paras 3.1–3.5.

[121] See 'Duty to make references: completed mergers', pp 913–918 above.

[122] The Enterprise Act 2002 (Anticipated Mergers) Order 2003, SI 2003/1595.

(i) Enterprises ceasing to be distinct

A merger occurs where two or more enterprises 'have ceased to be distinct'[123]. For this purpose enterprise means the activities, or part of the activities, of a business[124]. There is no requirement that the activities transferred should generate a profit[125]. The question whether the activities transferred constitute an enterprise is one of substance, not form, taking into account all the circumstances of the case[126]. The transfer of physical assets could amount to an enterprise where this enables a business activity to be continued[127]; and intellectual property rights could be considered to be an enterprise where a turnover can be attributed to them that could be transferred to a buyer[128]. Paragraph 3.10 of the OFT's *Jurisdictional and procedural guidance* states that the transfer of customer records, the application of the Transfer of Undertakings (Protection of Employment) Regulations 2006[129] and a payment for goodwill relating to a transferred business are likely to be important factors in assessing whether an enterprise has been transferred[130]. The fact that a business is no longer trading does not prevent it from being treated as an enterprise[131]. An outsourcing agreement will not normally result in enterprises ceasing to be distinct[132]. In *Project Canvas* the OFT concluded that the contribution of know-how and temporary staff, in particular from the BBC, and finance to a joint venture in the Internet protocol television sector did not amount to an enterprise[133].

Enterprises cease to be distinct if they are brought under common ownership or control[134]. Control for this purpose is defined broadly in section 26 of the Act: it includes legal control[135]; however the definition also covers a situation in which one person is able to control the policy of another, though without having legal control ('*de facto* control'), or has the ability to influence the policy of another ('material influence')[136]. The 'policy' of a company means the management of its business, in particular in relation to its competitive conduct[137]. The expression 'material' influence is wider than 'decisive' influence in Article 3(2) of the EUMR, with the result that some transactions that would not amount to mergers under EU law would do under UK law[138]. The effect of the provisions in section 26 of the Enterprise

---

[123] Enterprise Act 2002, s 23(1)(a) and (2)(a); see Parker and Pritchard 'Jurisdictional Frontiers in UK Merger Control: "Enterprises Ceasing to be Distinct"' (2010) 9(1) Competition Law Journal 90.

[124] Enterprise Act 2002, s 129(1); the reference to 'part of the activities' of a business means that the sale of a division of a company may be investigated, provided that the other requirements of s 23 are satisfied.

[125] *Mergers – Jurisdictional and procedural guidance*, para 3.8 and OFT/CC *Merger Assessment Guidelines*, para 3.2.2.

[126] *Mergers – Jurisdictional and procedural guidance*, para 3.9 and OFT/CC *Merger Assessment Guidelines*, para 3.2.3.

[127] See eg the CC's Final Report in *Arcelor SA/Corus UK Ltd*, para 3.8, available at www.competition-commission.org.uk.

[128] *Mergers – Jurisdictional and procedural guidance*, para 3.10 and OFT/CC *Merger Assessment Guidelines*, para 3.2.4; on this point see *Home Retail Group plc/Focus (DIY) Ltd*, OFT decision of 15 April 2008, paras 4–8 and *Cineworld/Holywood Green*, OFT decision of 17 March 2008; see further, under similar provisions in the (now repealed) Fair Trading Act 1973, *AAH Holdings plc/Medicopharma NV* Cm 1950 (1992) paras 6.101–6.102; *William Cook Acquisitions* Cm 1196 (1990) paras 6.5–6.6; *Stagecoach Holdings plc/Lancaster City Transport Ltd* Cm 2423 (1993) para 6.21.

[129] SI 2006/246.

[130] On this point see *Buzz Asia Ltd/Club Asia London Ltd*, OFT decision of 22 December 2009.

[131] *Mergers – Jurisdictional and procedural guidance*, paras 3.11–3.12.   [132] Ibid, para 3.13.

[133] OFT decision of 19 May 2010, paras 10–28; see, by contrast, the CC's Final Report in *Project 'Kangaroo': BBC Worldwide/Channel 4/ITV*, paras 3.52–3.63, available at www.competition-commission.org.uk.

[134] Enterprise Act 2002, s 26(1).   [135] Ibid, s 26(2) and s 129(1) and (2).

[136] Ibid, s 26(3).

[137] *Mergers – Jurisdictional and procedural guidance*, para 3.15 and OFT/CC *Mergers Assessment Guidelines*, para 3.2.8.

[138] On Article 3(2) of the EUMR see ch 21 'Article 3: meaning of a concentration', pp 834–839; for an example of a transaction that the OFT considered gave rise to material influence under the Enterprise Act, though not to decisive influence under the EUMR, see *Centrica plc/Lake Acquisitions Ltd*, OFT decision of 25 August 2009.

Act is that a person who acquires a shareholding in a company of much less than 51 per cent may have control for the purpose of UK merger control. There can be material influence where the shareholding is less than 25 per cent, and the OFT has said that it will examine any shareholding greater than 15 per cent to determine whether this is the case; even a share-holding of less than 15 per cent might attract scrutiny in exceptional cases[139]. The OFT's *Guidance* states that an assessment of material influence will require a case-by-case analysis and sets out various factors which may be relevant, such as the ownership and distribution of other shareholdings in a company, the pattern of attendance at recent shareholder mee-tings, the power to appoint members of the board of directors and any agreements that may have been made between the shareholders[140]. The key question for the OFT is not whether the acquiring party has the right to block special resolutions, but whether, given these other factors, it is able to do so as a practical matter[141].

In *BSkyB Group plc/ITV plc* the OFT considered that BSkyB's acquisition of a 17.9 per cent stake in ITV gave it the ability materially to influence the policy of ITV and that the test for making a reference to the CC was met[142]; the CC agreed with this finding[143]. The CC noted that BSkyB's holding of 17.9 per cent of the shares in ITV made it the largest shareholder by some margin; the CC also looked at the voting behaviour at past general meetings of ITV, and considered that a holding of 17.9 per cent would have enabled BSkyB to block any special resolutions[144]. The CC also considered that BSkyB's industry know-ledge and standing were of relevance and concluded that, in combination with its share-holding of 17.9 per cent, it did have material influence over ITV[145]. An appeal against this finding by BSkyB to the CAT was unsuccessful[146]. The CAT held that once the CC finds that there is material influence over a company's policy there will be little scope for the exercise of any discretion under section 26(3) to decline to treat that influence as giving rise to common control[147].

The OFT's *Jurisdictional and procedural guidance* says that, since a shareholding of 25 per cent or more generally enables the shareholder to block special resolutions, it is likely to be seen as presumptively conferring the ability materially to influence policy[148]. It is possible that one person may have the ability materially to influence the policy of a company even though another has a controlling interest[149].

A transition from one level of control to another (for example from material influence to *de facto* control) would itself amount to a merger for the purposes of the Act[150]. As a result, if Company A acquires Company B in stages, this could give rise to several differ-ent mergers: first when A acquires material influence over B; secondly when A acquires *de facto* control; and finally when it achieves *de jure* (or legal) control[151]. The OFT has

---

[139] *Mergers – Jurisdictional and procedural guidance*, para 3.20; the OFT is likely to investigate such cases only where they concern one business taking a stake in a direct competitor: ibid.

[140] *Mergers – Jurisdictional and procedural guidance*, paras 3.17–3.28; see similarly paras 3.2.8–3.2.12 of the OFT/CC *Merger Assessment Guidelines*.

[141] *Mergers – Jurisdictional and procedural guidance*, para 3.21.

[142] See the OFT's Report to the Secretary of State for Trade and Industry *Acquisition by British Sky Broadcasting Group plc of a 17.9 per cent stake in ITV plc* of 27 April 2007, available at www.oft.gov.uk.

[143] See the Final Report, paras 3.29–3.67, available at www.competition-commission.org.uk.

[144] Ibid, paras 3.39–3.57.   [145] Ibid, paras 3.58–3.62.

[146] Case No 1095/4/8/08 *British Sky Broadcasting Group plc v Competition Commission* [2008] CAT 25, [2008] CompAR 223, paras 110–145.

[147] Ibid, paras 97–105.   [148] *Mergers – Jurisdictional and procedural guidance*, para 3.19.

[149] Ibid, para 3.32.

[150] Enterprise Act 2002, s 26(4); for an example of the OFT finding no change of control when a company increased its minority shareholding to 50–60 per cent see *Fresh Trading Ltd/Coca-Cola Company*, decision of 11 May 2010.

[151] *Mergers – Jurisdictional and procedural guidance*, paras 3.33–3.36.

recognised that, in its substantive assessment of a merger, it should not treat the acquisition of material influence in the same way that it would treat *de facto* or *de jure* control[152]. Section 29 of the Act provides that, where a person acquires control in stages within a two-year period, those stages can be regarded as having occurred simultaneously on the date when the last of them occurred.

The Act does not define the period of time that a merger should last in order for it to qualify as a relevant merger situation. The OFT's *Jurisdictional and procedural guidance* provides guidance on temporary merger situations, such as 'break-up bids' and cases where a person incrementally builds up a stake in a target company[153].

When deciding whether enterprises have come under common control or ownership, 'associated persons' and any companies which they control will be treated as one person; section 127(4) defines associated persons broadly and includes any individual, their partners, trustees and business partners[154]. Shareholders of a new joint venture are not necessarily treated as 'associated persons'; for this to be the case there must be evidence that they acted together to secure or exercise control of an enterprise[155].

The award of a rail franchise under the provisions of the Railways Act 1993 qualifies as the acquisition of control for the purposes of section 23 of the Enterprise Act[156].

(ii) The turnover test

A merger can be investigated under the Enterprise Act only where it satisfies either the turnover test or the share of supply test. Section 23(1)(b) of the Act provides that a relevant merger situation has been created where the value of the turnover in the UK of the enterprise being taken over exceeds £70 million: the requirement that there must be turnover in the UK provides the jurisdictional nexus for the application of the Act. The OFT will keep the turnover threshold under review and advise the Secretary of State from time to time whether it is still appropriate[157]; the Secretary of State has power to amend the figure[158]. Section 28(2) provides that an enterprise's turnover shall be determined in accordance with an order to be made by the Secretary of State: the Enterprise Act 2002 (Merger Fees and Determination of Turnover) Order 2003[159] explains how turnover is to be calculated for the purpose both of the turnover test and the calculation of any merger fees payable[160]. The OFT has published specific guidance on the application of the turnover test[161]. Turnover is calculated by adding together the turnover of the enterprise being taken over and that of any associated enterprises. The period by reference to which turnover is calculated is the business year preceding the date of completion of a merger or, in the case of anticipated mergers, the date of the OFT's decision whether to make a reference to the CC[162].

---

[152] See paras 63 and 64 of the OFT's Report to the Secretary of State on *Acquisition by British Sky Broadcasting Group plc of a 17.9 per cent stake in ITV plc* of 27 April 2007; see further OFT/CC *Merger Assessment Guidelines*, fn 34.

[153] *Mergers – Jurisdictional and procedural guidance*, paras 3.37–3.41.

[154] Enterprise Act 2002, s 127(1); see further *Mergers – Jurisdictional and procedural guidance*, paras 3.42–3.43, OFT/CC *Merger Assessment Guidelines*, paras 3.2.18–3.2.19 and the CC's report on *Icopal Holding A/S/Icopal a/s*, paras 2.31–2.39, available at www.competition-commission.org.uk.

[155] *Project Canvas*, 19 May 2010, paras 39–42.

[156] See the Final Report in *Firstgroup plc/Scotrail*, para 3.12, available at www.competition-commission.org.uk; several instances of the award of rail franchises have led to CC references: see 'Table of merger references to the Competition Commission' at pp 952–953 below.

[157] Enterprise Act 2002, s 28(5). [158] Ibid, s 28(6). [159] SI 2003/1370.

[160] On merger fees see 'Fees', pp 928–929 below.

[161] See Annexe B to the OFT's *Mergers – Jurisdictional and procedural guidance*.

[162] *Mergers – Jurisdictional and procedural guidance*, Annexe B, paras B.7–B.10.

(iii) The share of supply test

Section 23(2)(b) of the Enterprise Act provides that a relevant merger situation has been created where the merged enterprises supply or acquire 25 per cent or more of a particular description of goods[163] or services[164] in the UK or a substantial part of it; the supply of services includes permitting or making arrangements to permit the use of land for various purposes such as caravan sites or car parks[165]. The share of supply test requires an *increment* in the share of supply, no matter how small that increment may be[166]. An obvious corollary of this is that the share of supply test does not apply to non-horizontal mergers[167]. The share of supply test enables a merger to be investigated which could give rise to competition problems even though the turnover threshold of £70 million is not achieved: this may be necessary in the case of narrowly-defined product markets or small geographic markets. The OFT (and the CC) has a discretion in determining whether goods or services are of the same description and whether the 25 per cent threshold is achieved[168], in relation to which it can use value, cost, price, quantity, capacity, number of workers or any other criteria considered appropriate[169].

To determine whether the share of supply test is met the OFT will have regard to any reasonable description of a set of goods or services[170]; this will often be a standard recognised by the industry in question, although this will not always be the case. The OFT may also consider different forms of supply, for example the wholesale or resale of goods[171]. When deciding whether the share of supply test is satisfied the OFT is not required to define the relevant product or geographic markets in accordance with the small but significant non-transitory increase in price ('SSNIP') test[172]: the share of supply test is jurisdictional, and does not require a full market analysis. The OFT has stated that it does not believe that it is necessary to show a nexus between the area in which an SLC is identified and the area in which the share of supply test is satisfied[173]. A review of the OFT's case lists of merger decisions on its website reveals that there are quite a large number of cases in which jurisdiction over a particular merger arises from the parties' share of supply[174].

In determining whether the share of supply test is satisfied in relation to a substantial part of the UK the OFT (and the CC) will be guided by the judgment of the House of Lords (now the Supreme Court) in *South Yorkshire Transport v Monopolies and Mergers Commission*[175] which held (under analogous provisions in the Fair Trading Act 1973) that the part must be of such size, character and importance as to make it worth consideration for the purpose of merger control. According to the OFT, among the factors to be taken into account in deciding whether the merger is 'worth' consideration and can therefore be referred are the size of the specified area, its population, its social, political, economic, financial and geographic significance, and whether it has any particular characteristics that might render it special or significant[176]. The CC applied the *South Yorkshire* test in

---

[163] Enterprise Act 2002, s 23(3).   [164] Ibid, s 23(4).

[165] The Enterprise Act 2002 (Supply of Services) Order 2003, SI 2003/1594.

[166] *Mergers – Jurisdictional and procedural guidance*, para 3.53.

[167] Ibid, para 3.55, fourth indent.

[168] Enterprise Act 2002, s 23(5).   [169] Ibid, s 23(5)–(8).

[170] *Mergers – Jurisdictional and procedural guidance*, para 3.55, second indent.

[171] Enterprise Act 2002, s 23(6) and (7).

[172] *Mergers – Jurisdictional and procedural* guidance, para 3.55, first indent; on the SSNIP test see ch 1, 'Market definition', pp 27–42.

[173] See *Vue Entertainment Holdings (UK) Ltd/A3 Cinema Ltd*, 23 September 2005, para 4.

[174] See eg www.oft.gov.uk/OFTwork/mergers/Mergers_Cases.

[175] [1993] 1 All ER 289, [1993] 1 WLR 23; see also *Stagecoach Holdings v Secretary of State for Trade and Industry* 1997 SLT 940.

[176] *Mergers – Jurisdictional and procedural* guidance, para 3.56.

Archant/Independent News and Media in determining that the acquisition of some local newspapers, in different localities that were not contiguous, occurred in a substantial part of the UK[177], and in *Arriva/Sovereign Bus and Coach Company*[178] when reaching the same conclusion in relation to bus services in Hertfordshire.

(iv) Time limits and prior notice

A reference of a completed merger cannot be made if the enterprises ceased to be distinct more than four months prior to the reference to the CC[179] or, if later, more than four months before notice was given to the OFT of the merger or the fact of the merger became publicly known[180]. In certain circumstances these time limits can be extended[181]. In January 2011 the OFT considered that the time limits for reaching a decision on the acquisition of Ryanair's minority shareholding in Aer Lingus during 2006 did not begin to run until appeals against the European Commission's decisions relating to Ryanair's bid for Aer Lingus had been concluded[182]. The CAT dismissed an appeal by Ryanair against this finding[183].

Section 27 deals with the question of when enterprises cease to be distinct, in particular where ownership or control is obtained over a period of time. Section 27(2) provides that mergers are treated as having been completed when all the parties to a transaction became contractually bound to proceed: the existence of options or other conditions are irrelevant until the option is exercised or the condition satisfied[184]. Where ownership or control has been acquired incrementally over a period of time through a series of transactions they can be treated as having occurred on the date of the last transaction, subject to a two-year cut-off period[185]. In *Archant/Independent News and Media* the CC rejected Archant's argument that the reference had been made outside the four-month statutory period; it also concluded that two successive transactions should be regarded as having occurred on the date of the later of the two[186].

(D) OFT procedure

Having explained the OFT's functions in relation to completed and anticipated mergers, it is important to consider how it exercises its functions up to the point of making a reference to the CC. There is no duty to pre-notify mergers under UK law, although there is a legal basis for making a notification using a 'statutory merger notice'[187]; alternatively the parties may make an 'informal submission' to the OFT. In practice many firms do approach the OFT prior to a transaction in order to discuss the application of the Act to it. If the parties to a transaction go ahead without discussing the matter with the OFT

---

[177] See the Final Report, Appendix C, paras 23–31, available at www.competition-commission.org.uk.

[178] See the Final Report, paras 3.10–3.14, available at www.competition-commission.org.uk; see similarly the Final Report in *Tesco/Co-Op store acquisition in Slough*, para 4.6, available at www.competition-commission.org.uk.

[179] Enterprise Act 2002, s 24(1)(a).

[180] Ibid, s 24(1)(b), (2) and (3).   [181] Ibid, s 25.

[182] Ibid, s 122; see OFT Press Release 1/11, 4 January 2011.

[183] Case No 1174/4/1/11 *Ryanair Holdings plc v OFT* [2011] CAT 23; Ryanair has appealed to the Court of Appeal.

[184] Enterprise Act 2002, s 27(3).

[185] Ibid, ss 27(5) and 27(6); on this point see *Mergers – Jurisdictional and procedural* guidance, para 3.47 and the decisional practice cited therein.

[186] See the Final Report, Appendix C, paras 17–22, available at www.competition-commission.org.uk.

[187] Enterprise Act 2002, s 96; see 'Notification using a statutory merger notice', pp 924–925 below.

they run the risk that their completed merger might be detected by the OFT and referred to the CC; this does happen fairly frequently, and on some occasions the CC has required a divestiture of assets that had already been acquired[188]. Useful guidance on the OFT's procedures will be found in its *Jurisdictional and procedural guidance*[189].

(i) Notifying mergers to the OFT

(A) The OFT's market intelligence function[190]

The OFT gathers intelligence about merger activity from monitoring the press, liaising with other public bodies and listening to third party complainants. In cases where a merger is not notified, but the OFT learns about it by other means, it will send an 'enquiry letter' if there is a reasonable prospect that it is under a duty to make a reference. A copy of a standard enquiry letter is available on the OFT's website[191].

(B) Informal advice[192]

The OFT will provide informal advice only where the parties can demonstrate a good faith intention of proceeding with a transaction: hypothetical advice will not be given; nor will informal advice be given in the case of a transaction that is already in the public domain. Informal advice will be given only where there is a genuine competition issue that could give rise to a reference to the CC: the OFT cannot be used to endorse the advice of professional advisers that a transaction gives rise to no competition problem. Parties seeking informal advice should submit an application to the OFT explaining why the transaction qualifies for such advice, the theory of harm and the issues on which advice is sought. When the OFT provides informal advice in relation to a genuine competition issue it may provide advice on jurisdictional issues as well.

(C) Pre-notification discussions[193]

The OFT encourages pre-notification discussions, which it considers to be beneficial both to the parties and to the OFT. Among the benefits are that the OFT team can be educated where markets are complex and/or unfamiliar and that the discussions can help to identify the information needed by the OFT. A draft notification document should be submitted to the OFT to facilitate pre-notification discussions, which are held in confidence.

(D) Notification using a statutory merger notice[194]

Sections 96 to 100 of the Enterprise Act make provision for mergers that qualify for investigation under the Act to be pre-notified to the OFT: the advantage to the parties of a 'statutory merger notice' is that the OFT must make a decision whether to refer the case to the CC within 20 working days, with a maximum extension of a further ten working days if the filing is incomplete or a request for information is not complied with. There are no statutory time limits where the parties make an 'informal submission': in a case where time is of the essence, therefore, it may be attractive to invoke the statutory procedure. The OFT gives priority to dealing with cases notified under the statutory procedure because of its obligation to comply with the deadlines: in the case of a merger notice a merger is cleared if the OFT has not referred it to the CC within the statutory period. The procedure

---

[188] See 'Completed mergers', p 954 below.   [189] OFT 527, June 2009.
[190] *Mergers – Jurisdictional and procedural guidance*, paras 4.6–4.24.
[191] www.oft.gov.uk/shared_oft/business_leaflets/general/enquirysampleletter.pdf.
[192] *Mergers – Jurisdictional and procedural guidance*, paras 4.28–4.41.
[193] Ibid, paras 4.42–4.48.
[194] Ibid, paras 4.52–4.62.

may be used only to notify anticipated mergers in the public domain[195]. The OFT has the power to request a person who gives a merger notice to provide it with information[196]. A fee must be paid in advance when using this procedure, and the clock does not start until this has occurred[197]. Statutory merger notices must be made in the prescribed form[198]. The Enterprise Act 2002 (Merger Pre-notification) Regulations 2003[199] make further provision in relation to merger notices, and the procedure is explained in Annexe A of the OFT's *Jurisdictional and procedural guidance* and in an OFT leaflet *Prior notice of publicly proposed mergers*.

(E) Informal submissions[200]

Notwithstanding the fact that there is a system of statutory merger notices, companies and their professional advisers tend to make so-called informal submissions in relation to transactions that may give rise to competition concerns; unless time is of the essence, there is no particular advantage in the statutory procedure which, in practice, the OFT regards as best suited to straightforward cases. The OFT considers that informal submissions are equally acceptable as statutory ones. Although there is no statutory time limit for dealing with informal submissions[201], in practice the OFT has an administrative timetable of 40 working days which it meets in most cases. In more complex cases the parties prefer the OFT to extend its administrative timetable beyond the 40-day period if this makes it possible to avoid a reference to the CC. The OFT will stop the administrative timetable where important information is not provided or is provided late[202]. The *Jurisdictional and procedural guidance* provides for an extension of time, at the request of the parties, for a period of up to ten working days. There is no prescribed form for making an informal submission; however the OFT's *Jurisdictional and procedural guidance* contains advice on the kind of information that should be submitted (below).

(F) Fast track reference cases[203]

Under a 'fast track' procedure certain cases can be dealt with by the OFT more quickly than is usual. The OFT may, at the request of the parties, accelerate the making of a reference to the CC in cases where it is satisfied that a reference must be made. This was done for the first time in 2011 in the case of *Thomas Cook/Cooperative Group/Midlands Cooperative Society*, a joint venture that the European Commission had referred back to the UK under Article 9(3)(b) of the EUMR[204].

(ii) Content of submissions

Chapter 5 of the OFT's *Jurisdictional and procedural guidance* discusses the type of information that an informal submission should contain. This information falls broadly into three categories: general background information; jurisdictional information; and information that is necessary for a substantive assessment of the merger.

---

[195] Completed mergers can be notified only by filing an informal submission.
[196] Enterprise Act 2002, s 99(2).   [197] See 'Fees', pp 928–909 below on the payment of fees.
[198] A copy can be downloaded from the OFT's website, www.oft.gov.uk.   [199] SI 2003/1369.
[200] *Mergers – Jurisdictional and procedural guidance*, paras 4.63–4.70.
[201] There is a statutory time limit for the reference of completed mergers to the CC: Enterprise Act 2002, s 24; see 'Time limits and prior notice', p 923 above.
[202] *Mergers – Jurisdictional and procedural guidance*, paras 4.76–4.77.
[203] Ibid, paras 4.71–4.75.
[204] See OFT Press Release 28/11, 2 March 2011, the joint venture was cleared by the CC: see CC News Release 44/11, 16 August 2011.

(iii) **The assessment process**

Chapter 6 of the OFT's *Jurisdictional and procedural guidance* explains how it goes about its assessment of mergers. The *Guidance* begins by discussing the gathering of supplementary information and the verification of it, which involves consultation with third parties[205]. The OFT's website lists the cases on which the OFT is inviting third party comments and names the responsible case officer[206]. Paragraphs 6.17 to 6.22 of the *Jurisdictional and procedural guidance* explain the OFT's rights and obligations as regards confidentiality. The circumstances in which the OFT may seek an initial undertaking or make an order to prevent pre-emptive action that might prejudice a reference to the CC are also explained[207].

The *Jurisdictional and procedural guidance*[208] explains that in all cases there may be 'state-of-play' meetings between the parties and officials from the OFT; the purpose of these meetings is to inform the parties about the OFT's possible competition concerns. Cases that do not raise serious concerns are usually decided within the Mergers Group, although a clearance decision paper is prepared and circulated to other staff of the OFT. In complex or more problematic cases, where a reference might be made to the CC, the parties are sent an 'issues letter' setting out the relevant evidence and the core arguments for a reference; an issues letter is not a provisional decision or a statement of objections[209]. The parties are given an opportunity to respond, in writing or at an 'issues meeting', and in practice usually do both. It is not the OFT's practice to provide third parties with an opportunity to comment on the issues letter given time constraints and confidentiality. Thereafter a case review meeting ('CRM') will take place within the OFT: it is usually chaired by the Director of Mergers, and will be attended by those officials present at the issues meeting, potentially also with a representative from the Office of the Chief Economist, and, where appropriate, individuals in the Market Group with relevant expertise in a particular sector. An individual within the review group will be charged specifically with acting as a 'devil's advocate' at the CRM, to test the soundness of the case team's assessment and to argue the contrary position. After the CRM there is a separate decision meeting: the person who chaired the CRM will act as a rapporteur when briefing the person responsible for making the final decision: this is generally the Chief Executive of the OFT or a Senior Director. A provisional decision is taken at this meeting; the decision is then drafted, and becomes final when signed by the decision-maker. Notifying parties are contacted one hour before the public announcement of the decision and are informed of the timing and the nature of the decision. The decision is then publicly announced.

If an issues letter has been sent, but the OFT then decides not to make a reference to the CC, the Court of Appeal has said that it must be shown that the likelihood of an SLC has been removed and that the material relied on by the OFT can reasonably be regarded as dispelling the uncertainties highlighted by the issues letter[210].

All decisions on public merger cases must be published; the text of the decision, once any business secrets have been removed, is placed on the OFT's website. The OFT informs the CC of cases that might be referred so that the CC is aware of potential work that is 'in the pipeline' and can prepare accordingly. Once a decision to refer is made the CC

---

[205] *Mergers – Jurisdictional and procedural guidance*, paras 5.2–5.11.

[206] See www.oft.gov.uk/OFTwork/mergers/Mergers_Cases/.

[207] *Mergers – Jurisdictional and procedural guidance*, paras 6.23–6.45; on the OFT's enforcement powers see 'Enforcement', pp 941–949 below.

[208] Ibid, paras 5.16–5.21.

[209] *Mergers – Jurisdictional and procedural guidance*, para 6.50, third indent.

[210] *OFT v IBA Health Ltd* [2004] EWCA Civ 142, [2004] UKCLR 683, paras 73 and 100; see also the CAT in Case No 1049/4/1/05 *UniChem Ltd v OFT* [2005] CAT 8, [2005] CompAR 907, para 201.

receives relevant documentation from the OFT; the staff of the two institutions meet at an early stage to discuss the handing-over of the case.

(iv) Ancillary restraints[211]

Mergers and 'any provision directly related and necessary to the implementation of the merger provisions' are excluded from the Competition Act 1998[212]. The OFT's treatment of ancillary restrictions generally follows the approach of the European Commission under the EUMR. It is for the parties to conduct a self-assessment of which restraints are ancillary. The OFT will not normally state in a clearance decision which restraints are ancillary: it will provide guidance only on novel or unresolved questions giving rise to genuine uncertainty.

(v) Undertakings in lieu of a reference

Section 73 of the Act gives power to the OFT to accept an undertaking in lieu of making a reference to the CC[213]. In doing so the OFT must have regard to the need to achieve as comprehensive a solution as is reasonable and practicable to the SLC and any adverse effects resulting from it[214], taking into account any relevant customer benefits[215]. The OFT's *Guidance on undertakings in lieu*[216] contains a number of important insights on the law and practice of undertakings in lieu of a reference and is much more detailed than the previous guidance. The OFT considers that undertakings in lieu of a reference are appropriate only where 'the competition concerns raised by the merger and the proposed remedies to address them are clear cut'[217]. In *Co-operative Group (CWS) Ltd v OFT* the CAT held that the OFT cannot be expected to conduct a detailed investigation when exercising its power to accept undertakings in lieu of a reference[218]. The OFT's starting point is to seek undertakings that restore competition to the level that would have existed without the merger, although there may be cases in which it accepts a different outcome[219]. The *Guidance on undertakings in lieu* makes clear that the OFT has a strong preference for structural remedies[220], such as divestitures, over behavioural ones, although the latter may be acceptable where a divestiture is clearly impractical or in mergers raising vertical concerns[221]. In some cases the OFT may insist on the parties securing a purchaser who has agreed to acquire the business to be divested before it accepts undertakings in lieu[222]; the OFT has required 'up-front buyers' in several cases[223]. The OFT will always bear in mind the proportionality of remedies[224].

Useful guidance on the OFT's procedures for considering, accepting and implementing undertakings in lieu of a reference can be found in its *Jurisdictional and procedural guidance*. In many cases undertakings in lieu will be offered before or immediately after the issues meeting; the OFT may invite undertakings at this meeting[225]. In 'near miss'

---

[211] *Mergers – Jurisdictional and procedural guidance*, paras 4.79–4.82.

[212] Competition Act 1998, Sch 1; on this exclusion see ch 9, 'Schedule 1: mergers and concentrations', pp 349–351.

[213] See *Mergers–Exceptions to the duty to refer and undertakings in lieu of reference guidance*, OFT 1122, December 2010, ch 5.

[214] Enterprise Act 2002, s 73(3).   [215] Ibid, s 73(4).

[216] OFT 1122, December 2010, available at www.oft.gov.uk.

[217] *Guidance on undertakings in lieu*, paras 5.6–5.9 and 8.5.

[218] Case No 1081/4/1/07 [2007] CAT 24, [2007] CompAR 899, paras 179–180.

[219] *Guidance on undertakings in lieu*, para 5.11.   [220] Ibid, paras 5.20 and 8.2.

[221] Ibid, para 5.43.   [222] Ibid, paras 5.31–5.37.

[223] See eg *Home Retail Group plc/Focus (DIY) Ltd*, OFT decision of 15 April 2008; *Global Radio UK/GCap Media plc*, OFT decision of 8 August 2008; and *Co-operative Group Ltd/Somerfield Ltd*, OFT decision of 20 October 2008.

[224] *Guidance on undertakings in lieu*, paras 5.14–5.19.

[225] *Mergers – Jurisdictional and procedural guidance*, para 8.10.

cases the OFT may ask the parties to reconsider their proposed remedies[226]. Where the OFT considers that undertakings are suitable, there will normally be a period of consultation of at least 15 days; a further period of consultation may take place in the event that the undertakings are modified[227]. If an undertaking in lieu is not accepted it is still possible for the OFT to refer the merger to the CC; the OFT did this for the first time in *Tesco/Slough Co-op store*[228]. If an undertaking in lieu has been accepted, it is not possible to make a reference to the CC, although the position is different if the OFT was not in possession of material facts at the time the undertaking was accepted. The OFT has power to make an order where the undertaking in lieu is not being fulfilled or where false or misleading information was given prior to the acceptance of the undertaking. There is also a power to make a supplementary interim order while the main section 75 order is being prepared; the same power is available to the CC.

Undertakings in lieu of a reference have been accepted by the OFT on a number of occasions: details of cases dealt with in this way are available on the OFT's website[229]. In most cases the undertaking was structural, typically to divest assets[230]. In *Aggregate Industries Ltd/Foster Yeoman Ltd* the OFT accepted undertakings in lieu that were intended to address not only non-coordinated but also coordinated effects, the first case of this kind[231]. The OFT accepted its largest ever remedies package in *Co-operative Group Ltd/Somerfield Ltd*, consisting of divestitures in 133 local areas in which the OFT had identified competition concerns[232]. There has been one occasion on which the OFT has accepted a quasi-structural remedy: in *Tetra Laval Group/Carlisle Process Systems* an undertaking was given to grant an irrevocable EEA-wide licence of a package of intellectual property rights to a third party, approved 'up-front' by the OFT, that would enable it to compete on the market for equipment used in the industrial manufacture of cheddar cheese[233]. An unusual remedy was accepted in *IVAX International GmbH/3M*, where the OFT was given a behavioural undertaking to limit the price of asthma inhalers until such time as competitive products emerged onto the market[234].

(vi) Fees

Pursuant to section 121 of the Enterprise Act provision is made by the Enterprise Act 2002 (Merger Fees and Determination of Turnover) Order 2003[235] for the payment of fees in connection with the exercise of the functions of the OFT (and, exceptionally, the Secretary of State) in relation to mergers. Article 3 sets out the circumstances in which fees are payable, and Article 4 specifies certain cases in which fees are not payable. The level of fees – from £30,000 to £90,000, depending on the turnover of the enterprise taken over or to be

---

[226] Ibid, paras 8.18–8.23.

[227] Ibid, paras 8.24–8.30; the procedure varies in cases involving 'up-front buyers': see paras 8.31–8.35.

[228] OFT decision of 19 April 2007.

[229] See www.oft.gov.uk.

[230] See eg *Boots plc/Alliance UniChem plc*, OFT decision of 7 February 2006; note that the OFT's decision not to refer this case to the CC was the subject of an unsuccessful judicial review: Case No 1059/4/1/06 *Celesio AG v OFT* [2006] CAT 9, [2006] CompAR 515.

[231] OFT decision of 3 January 2007.   [232] OFT decision of 15 January 2009.

[233] OFT decision of 20 November 2006.   [234] OFT decision of 9 January 2004.

[235] SI 2003/1370.

taken over[236] – is set out in Article 5. Article 6 explains who must pay the fee[237], and Article 7 provides an exemption for small and medium-sized enterprises. Article 8 provides that the fees are payable to the OFT and Article 9 establishes when the fees are payable. Provision is made for the repayment of fees in certain cases. Part 3 of the Order explains how turnover is to be calculated for the purpose of determining the appropriate level of the fee[238]. Further guidance on merger fees can be found in chapter 7 of the OFT's *Jurisdictional and procedural guidance.*

4. Determination of References by the CC

Once a reference has been made by the OFT to the CC section 35 of the Enterprise Act sets out the questions to be decided in relation to completed mergers and section 36 the questions in relation to anticipated mergers. Sections 38 and 39 deal with the reports of the CC and the time limits within which they must be produced. Section 41 requires the CC to take action to remedy any loss of competition.

(A) **Questions to be decided in relation to completed mergers**

Section 35(1) of the Enterprise Act requires the CC to decide, first, whether a merger situation has been created[239] and secondly, whether, if so, the creation of that situation has resulted, or may be expected to result, in an SLC within any market or markets in the UK for goods or services[240]. The CC will always try to identify how the market would look if the merger were not to happen: in other words it will attempt to establish the 'counterfactual' in order to determine the extent of any SLC[241]. The CAT has endorsed the use of a 'counterfactual' as an analytical tool used to assist in answering the statutory questions[242]. The way in which the CC is likely to apply the SLC test is considered in section 5 below[243]. If the CC considers that there is an 'anti-competitive outcome'[244], it must decide three additional questions: first, whether it should take remedial action[245]; secondly, whether it should recommend that anyone else should take remedial action[246]; and thirdly, if remedial action should be taken, what that action should be[247]. When considering remedial action the CC must have regard to the need to achieve as comprehensive a solution as is reasonable and practical to the SLC and any adverse effects resulting from it[248], and may in particular have

---

[236] Note that the figures in the 2003 Order were increased by the Enterprise Act 2002 (Merger Fees) (Amendment) Order 2005, SI 2005/3558 and again by the Enterprise Act 2002 (Merger Fees) (Amendment) Order 2009, SI 2009/2396; in September 2009 the OFT published a leaflet, *Merger fee information*, available at www.oft.gov.uk.

[237] Note that Article 6(5) of the 2003 Order was repealed by Article 2(8) of the Enterprise Act 2002 (Merger Fees) (Amendment) Order 2005, SI 2005/3558.

[238] See 'The turnover test', p 921 above.

[239] Enterprise Act 2002, s 35(1)(a).   [240] Ibid, s 35(1)(b).

[241] See eg *Ticketmaster/Live Nation*, paras 6.1–6.102, available at www.competition-commission.org.uk.

[242] Case No 1095/4/8/08 *British Sky Broadcasting Group plc v Competition Commission* [2008] CAT 25, [2008] CompAR 223, para 91, upheld on appeal [2010] EWCA Civ 2, [2010] UKCLR 351, para 55; see similarly Case No 1145/4/8/09 *Stagecoach Group plc v Competition Commission* [2010] CAT 14, [2010] CompAR 267, paras 19–20.

[243] See 'The "Substantial Lessening of Competition" Test', pp 932–940 below.

[244] This term is defined in Enterprise Act 2002, s 35(2).   [245] Ibid, s 35(3)(a).

[246] Ibid, s 35(3)(b).   [247] Ibid, s 35(3)(c).   [248] Ibid, s 35(4).

regard to the effect of any action on any relevant customer benefits[249]. If the CC finds that there is no anti-competitive outcome, no question of considering remedies arises.

(B) **Questions to be decided in relation to anticipated mergers**

Section 36 requires the CC to decide similar questions in relation to anticipated mergers, with the necessary linguistic adjustments to address the fact that such mergers are yet to be completed.

(C) **Investigations and reports**

Section 37 of the Enterprise Act contains provisions for the cancellation and variation of references by the OFT or the CC, for example where a referred merger has been abandoned: as will be seen from the Table of merger references later in this chapter, a significant number of mergers are abandoned following reference to the CC[250]. Section 38(1) of the Act requires the CC to prepare and publish a report within the period permitted by section 39. Section 39(1) requires the CC to do so within 24 weeks of the date of the reference, a longer period than the 90 working days available to the European Commission in a Phase II case under the EUMR[251]. The 24-week period may be shorter where this is necessary to comply with Article 9(6) of the EUMR[252]; and may be extended by no more than eight weeks where there are 'special reasons' for doing so[253], or where there has been a failure to comply with a requirement of a notice under section 109[254]. The CC has extended the inquiry period on several occasions[255]; for example it extended the period in the case of two bids for the London Stock Exchange in 2005 due to the 'exceptional complexity' of the inquiry[256].

The time limits in section 39 may be reduced by the Secretary of State[257]. The report must contain the decisions of the CC on the questions to be decided under section 35 or 36, its reasons for those decisions and such information as the CC considers appropriate for facilitating a proper understanding of those questions and its reasons for its decisions[258]. In the CAT's view the duty to give reasons has three main purposes: to allow interested persons to know the justification for the decision; to enhance public confidence in the decision-making process; and to concentrate the mind of the decision-maker[259].

The implementation of remedies following the CC's report does not have to be completed within the statutory period for the investigation, and may be quite protracted; the

---

[249] Ibid, s 35(5); see 'Customer benefits', pp 916–917 above.

[250] See 'Merger references to the Competition Commission', pp 952–953 below.

[251] See ch 21, 'Phase II investigations', pp 859–866.

[252] Enterprise Act 2002, s 39(2); on Article 9 EUMR see ch 21, 'Post-notification referrals: Article 9', pp 847–848.

[253] Ibid, s 39(3): special reasons might be the illness or incapacity of a member of the group of members investigating the case or an unexpected merger of competitors: *Explanatory Notes*, para 132; only one such extension is possible: s 40(4).

[254] Enterprise Act 2002, s 39(4); the CC used this power in *Project 'Kangaroo': BBC Worldwide/Channel 4/ITV*, available at www.competition-commission.org.uk and in *Sports Direct/JJB Stores*, available at www. competition-commission.org.uk.

[255] See eg the Final Reports in *Railway Investments Ltd/Marcroft Holdings Ltd*, Appendix A, paras 9–10; *Stonegate Farmers Ltd/Deans Food Group Ltd*, Appendix A, paras 11–12; *Tesco plc/Cooperative Group*, Appendix A, para 11, available at www.competition-commission.org.uk.

[256] See the Final Report Appendix A, para 6, available at www.competition-commission.org.uk.

[257] Enterprise Act 2002, s 40(8).   [258] Ibid, s 38(2).

[259] Case No 1051/4/8/05 *Somerfield plc v Competition Commission* [2006] CAT 4, [2006] CompAR 390, para 62.

group of CC members conducting an inquiry will be discharged only when the remedies have been finally accepted.

(D) **Duty to remedy the anti-competitive effects of completed or anticipated mergers**

Where the CC has prepared and published a report under section 38 within the time limits established by section 39 and has concluded that there is an anti-competitive outcome section 41(2) requires it to take such action as it considers to be reasonable and practicable to remedy, mitigate or prevent the SLC and any adverse effects of it[260]. In doing so the CC must be consistent with the decisions in its report on the questions it is required to answer, unless there has been a material change of circumstances since the preparation of the report or the CC has a special reason for deciding differently[261]. In making its decision under section 41(2) the CC must have regard to the need to achieve as comprehensive a solution as is reasonable and practicable to the SLC and any resulting adverse effects[262].

(E) **CC procedure**

The procedures of the CC during merger references are set out in its *Rules of Procedure*[263] and the *Chairman's Guidance to Groups*[264]. When a reference is made the Chairman will appoint members of the CC to a group, consisting of a minimum of three, though usually four or five, who will carry out the inquiry. Rule 6 of the *Rules of Procedure* requires the CC to draw up an administrative timetable for its investigation. The CC has wide-ranging investigatory powers to enable it to carry out its investigation effectively[265], and can impose penalties for non-compliance[266]. The major stages of an investigation include the gathering and verification of evidence; providing a statement of issues; notifying provisional findings[267]; notifying and considering possible remedies; the publication of the final report; and deciding on remedies. Hearings will be held with third parties and with the main parties to the proceedings; where appropriate there will also be hearings on remedies. Often the CC visits appropriate facilities of the merging parties in order better to understand the context of the merger. Each investigation has its own home page on the CC's website, and it is a simple matter to follow the progress of the investigation in this way. This accords with the CC's aim to be open and transparent in its working[268]. The home page sets out the core documents of the inquiry; contains the CC's announcements, for example on its provisional findings, possible remedies and its final report; and makes available the parties' responses to the CC's questionnaires, third party submissions, consumer reports and comments on draft remedies.

---

[260] Enterprise Act 2002, s 41(2). [261] Ibid, s 41(3).
[262] Ibid, s 41(4). [263] CC1, March 2006. [264] CC6, March 2006.
[265] Enterprise Act 2002, s 109. [266] Ibid, s 110.
[267] It can happen that the CC changes its assessment of a merger between its provisional findings report and its final report: see eg *British Salt Ltd/New Cheshire Salt Works*; *Stagecoach/Eastbourne Buses*; and *Ticketmaster/Live Nation*, all available at www.competition-commission.org.uk.
[268] See *Chairman's Guidance on Disclosure of Information in Merger and Market Inquiries* CC7, July 2003, paras 1.5 and 1.6, available at www.competition-commission.org.uk.

5. The 'Substantial Lessening of Competition' Test

The Enterprise Act subjects mergers to an SLC test. This section considers how the OFT and the CC apply the SLC test in practice.

(A) Publication of merger guidelines

Section 106(1) of the Enterprise Act requires the OFT and the CC to publish general advice and information about the making and assessment of merger references. When the Act entered into force in June 2003 the OFT and CC each published their own guidance on the substantive assessment of mergers[269]; these were replaced in September 2010 by a single publication, *Merger Assessment Guidelines*[270] ('the *Assessment Guidelines*'): a welcome development. The *Assessment Guidelines* discuss the approach of the OFT and the CC to the SLC test, including an explanation of the concepts of 'theories of harm' and the 'counterfactual'[271]. The *Guidelines* then deal in turn with market definition; measures of concentration; unilateral and coordinated effects of horizontal mergers; non-horizontal mergers; efficiencies; barriers to entry and expansion; and countervailing buyer power. This section will follow the same sequence. The OFT and CC say that they will have regard to the *Assessment Guidelines* but will apply them flexibly, departing from them where appropriate.

(B) A substantial lessening of competition

(i) What is an SLC?

The Act does not define an SLC. The *Assessment Guidelines* explain that a merger gives rise to an SLC when it has a significant effect on rivalry over time, thereby reducing the competitive pressure on firms to improve their offer to customers or become more efficient or innovative[272]. There are three main reasons why mergers may lead to an SLC: unilateral effects; coordinated effects; and vertical or conglomerate effects: these theories of harm were explained in chapter 20[273]. A merger that gives rise to an SLC will be expected to lead to an adverse effect for customers[274].

(ii) Theories of harm

The OFT and CC devise a theory or theories of harm in order to provide a framework for assessing the effects of a merger[275]. A theory of harm describes possible changes arising from the merger and compares any impact on rivalry and expected harm to customers as compared with the situation likely to arise without the merger[276]. The CC's assessment of the effects of a merger is not limited by the OFT's conclusions on a theory (or theories) of harm[277].

---

[269] *Mergers – Substantive assessment guidance* OFT 516, May 2003 and *Merger References: Competition Commission Guidelines* CC2, June 2003.
[270] CC2 Revised, OFT 1254, September 2010.
[271] Part 3 of the *Guidelines* also briefly discuss the concept of a relevant merger situation.
[272] *Assessment Guidelines*, para 4.1.3.
[273] See ch 20, 'Theories of competitive harm', pp 818–821.
[274] *Assessment Guidelines*, para 4.1.3.   [275] Ibid, para 4.2.1.   [276] Ibid.
[277] Ibid, para 4.2.6.

(iii) The counterfactual

(A) The approach to the counterfactual

The application of the SLC test involves a comparison of the prospects for competition with the merger against the situation without the merger: the 'counterfactual'[278]. The counterfactual is affected by the extent to which events and their consequences are foreseeable, but does not suppose infringements of competition law will occur. The OFT generally adopts the prevailing conditions of competition as the counterfactual, whereas the CC selects the most likely future situation in the absence of the merger[279]. The need to examine the counterfactual was emphasised by the CAT in *Stagecoach Group v Competition Commission*[280], where it held that a CC decision finding that a merger would create a monopoly for local buses in Preston as the CC's choice of counterfactual was not supported by the evidence[281]. Paragraph 4.3.6 of the *Assessment Guidelines* describes three situations in which the OFT and the CC may use a counterfactual other than the prevailing conditions of competition; they are 'the exiting firm scenario', commonly referred to as the so-called 'failing firm defence'; 'the loss of potential entrant scenario'; and the situation where there are competing bids and parallel transactions[282].

(B) The exiting firm scenario

If a firm were to exit the market, irrespective of the merger under consideration, that merger would not be the cause of any SLC. Paragraph 4.3.8 of the *Assessment Guidelines* says that three considerations are relevant to an assessment of the exiting firm scenario:

- first, whether the firm would have exited the market either because of financial difficulties or for another reason, such as, for example, a change in the corporate strategy of the selling firm

- secondly, whether there would have been an alternative purchaser for the firm or its assets and

- thirdly, what would have happened to the sales of the firm in the event of it leaving the market?

The exiting firm scenario has been accepted by the OFT in a small number of cases[283]; the OFT requires compelling evidence that the acquired firm would leave the market and that there is no less anti-competitive purchaser for the firm or its assets[284].

The CC will generally consider the three 'exiting firm' considerations as part of its SLC analysis[285]: in *British Salt Ltd/New Cheshire Salt Works* the CC concluded that British Salt's acquisition of New Cheshire Salt Works would not result in an SLC since the latter would have closed in the foreseeable future due to large increases in actual and projected

---

[278] Ibid, paras 4.3.1–4.3.29; for further discussion see Davis and Cooper 'On the Use of Counterfactuals in Merger Inquiries', 28 April 2010, available at www.competition-commission.org.uk.

[279] *Assessment Guidelines*, paras 4.3.5–4.3.6.

[280] Case No 1145/4/8/09 [2010] CAT 14, [2010] CompAR 267.   [281] Ibid, paras 37–133.

[282] See further *Assessment Guidelines*, paras 4.3.8–4.3.27; the award of rail franchise awards is a further example: ibid, para 4.3.28–4.3.29.

[283] See eg the OFT decisions in *First West Yorkshire/Black Prince Buses*, 26 May 2005; *Tesco/Kwik Save stores*, 11 December 2007; *CDMG/Ferryways and Searoad Stevedores*, of 24 January 2008; *Home Retail Group plc/Focus DIY stores* (one store only), 15 April 2008; *HMV plc/Zavvi*, 28 April 2009; for comment see Broadhurst 'Succeeding to Fail: HMV/Zavvi and Other Stories' (2010) 9(1) Competition Law Journal 65.

[284] *Assessment Guidelines*, para 4.3.10.

[285] See eg *Stagecoach/Scottish Citylink*, paras 5.9–5.56; *Thermo Electron Manufacturing Ltd/GV Instruments Ltd*, paras 6.1–6.25; *Holland & Barrett/Julian Graves*, paras 4.4–4.14, available at www.competition-commission.org.uk.

energy prices: an interesting point about this case is that the CC changed its position between its provisional and its final determination[286]. Similarly, in *Long Clawson Dairy Ltd/Millway* the CC found that Millway was a failing firm and that if Long Clawson had not purchased the business, Dairy Crest would have closed it down[287]. In *STS/Butlers* the CC accepted arguments that the merger would not result in an SLC because the vendor would have closed the acquired business in any event for commerical and strategic reasons (rather than financial difficulties)[287a].

(C) Market definition

The *Assessment Guidelines* explain that market definition, though not an end in itself, provides a framework for the analysis of the competitive effects of the merger[288]. Market definition and the assessment of effects should not be viewed as distinct analyses and may overlap in practice[289]. The *Guidelines* say that in defining markets the OFT will usually make an initial assessment but may not reach a conclusion; whereas the CC will usually reach a conclusion: this difference reflects their respective roles under the Act[290]. The *Guidelines* explain that the relevant market contains the most significant competitive alternatives available to the customers of the merged firms and includes the sources of competition to the merging firms that are the immediate determinants of the effects of the merger[291]. The *Guidelines* explain the methodology for market definition and in particular the 'hypothetical monopolist test'[292]; among the factors that will be considered are the 'closeness' of substitution, that is to say the intensity of competition between products, the variable profit margins of the products and the sensitivity of customers to changes in price.

(D) Measures of concentration

The *Assessment Guidelines* explain that, as part of their assessment of the effects of a merger, the OFT and the CC may use measures of concentration[293]. There are several ways in which concentration can be measured: market shares; number of firms; concentration ratios; and the Herfindahl-Hirschman Index ('HHI')[294]. When interpreting these measures the OFT and the CC may have regard to the extent to which products are differentiated; changes in concentration over time; how widely the market is defined; and the level of variable profit margins[295]. The OFT says that it may have regard to the following market share and concentration thresholds[296]:

- it is unlikely to be concerned about unilateral effects in a market where products are undifferentiated and where the post-merger market share is less than 40 per cent

---

[286] See the Final Report, paras 5.28 and 6.1, available at www.competition-commission.org.uk.
[287] See the Final Report, paras 6.26–6.76, available at www.competition-commission.org.uk.
[287a] See the Final Report, paras 5.8–5.45, available at www.competition-commission.org.uk.
[288] *Assessment Guidelines*, paras 5.2.1–5.2.2.   [289] Ibid, para 5.1.1.
[290] Ibid, para 5.2.4; the term 'definition of the relevant market' should be understood with this difference in mind.
[291] *Assessment Guidelines*, para 5.2.1.
[292] Ibid, paras 5.2.9–5.2.20; on the tests for defining the relevant market see ch 1, 'Market definition', pp 27–42.
[293] Ibid, paras 5.3.1–5.3.6.
[294] Ibid, para 5.3.4; for further discussion see ch 1, 'Market concentration and the Herfindahl-Hirschman Index', pp 43–44.
[295] *Assessment Guidelines*, para 5.3.2.   [296] Ibid, para 5.3.5.

- it is unlikely to be concerned about mergers that reduce the number of firms from five to four (or above)

- a market with a post-merger HHI of more than 2,000 may be regarded as highly concentrated; however horizontal mergers that result in a change of the concentration level of less than 150 are unlikely to give rise to competition concerns

- a market with a post-merger HHI of more than 1,000 may be regarded as concentrated; horizontal mergers that result in a change of less than 250 are unlikely to be problematic.

The OFT adds that the HHI thresholds may be most informative for mergers in a market where the product is undifferentiated and where firms compete on output; this is based on the insights of an economic model of oligopolistic markets[297]. The OFT also says that it may have regard to the thresholds used by the European Commission in its *Guidelines on the assessment of non-horizontal mergers*[298].

(E) Horizontal mergers

(i) Unilateral effects

The *Assessment Guidelines* discuss the problem of unilateral effects arising from mergers[299]. Unilateral effects may arise where a merged firm finds it profitable to increase prices (or reduce output or quality) as a result of the loss of competition between the merged parties[300]. The *Guidelines* deal in turn with four theories of harm giving rise to unilateral effects: loss of existing competition[301]; the elimination of potential competition[302]; increased buyer power[303]; and the vertical effects arising from horizontal mergers[304].

The *Guidelines* explain the theory of harm relating to the loss of existing competition separately for mergers with undifferentiated products and differentiated products[305]; this distinction is based on economics and reflects the importance of product differentiation – for example by brand or quality – for the way in which competition concerns may arise[306]. There is an extensive literature on this subject[307] and a common criticism has been that market shares are an imperfect proxy for competition concerns in markets where products are highly differentiated. The more important issue in such markets is the 'closeness of substitution' between products: the higher the degree of substitutability between the merging firm's products, the closer the competition between them would

---

[297] Ibid, para 5.3.5, third indent.

[298] *Assessment Guidelines*, para 5.3.5, first indent; on the Commission's *Non-horizontal guidelines* see chapter 21, 'Commission Notices and Guidelines', p 831.

[299] *Assessment Guidelines*, paras 5.4.1–5.4.21; the expression 'non-coordinated effects' is sometimes used as an alternative for unilateral effects.

[300] *Assessment Guidelines*, para 5.4.1.   [301] Ibid, paras 5.4.4–5.4.12.

[302] Ibid, paras 5.4.13–5.4.18.   [303] Ibid, paras 5.4.19–5.4.21.   [304] Ibid, paras 5.4.22–5.4.23.

[305] The distinction between differentiated and undifferentiated products is one of degree and ought not to be treated too literally.

[306] See similarly the US *Horizontal Merger Guidelines*, August 2010, section 6.1, available at www.justice. gov; for further discussion see Bishop and Walker *The Economics of EC Competition Law* (Sweet & Maxwell, 3rd ed, 2010), paras 7-017–7-036.

[307] See eg Chamberlin 'Product Heterogeneity and Public Policy' (1950) American Economic Review 86; Farrell and Shapiro 'Horizontal Mergers: An Equilibrium Analysis' (1990) 80 American Economic Review 107; Werden 'A Robust Test for Consumer Welfare Enhancing Mergers Among Sellers of Differentiated Products' (1996) 44(4) Journal of Industrial Economics 409; Werden and Froeb 'Unilateral Competitive Effects of Horizontal Mergers' in Buccirossi (ed) *Handbook Of Antitrust Economics* (MIT Press, 2008) and Shapiro 'The 2010 Horizontal Merger Guidelines: From Hedgehog to Fox in Forty Years' (2011) 77 Antitrust Law Journal 701.

have been without the merger and the more likely it will be that the merger will give rise to unilateral effects[308]. It may be necessary for the OFT and the CC to analyse the change in the pricing incentives of the merged firms resulting from bringing their products under common control[309]. The potential response of other suppliers to any attempt by the merged firm to increase price can also have an effect on pricing incentives. In some cases not only the merging parties, but also their rivals, may be able to share the benefit of greater post-merger profitability: this is a reference to the 'problem' of non-collusive oligopoly referred to in chapter 21[310].

The *Assessment Guidelines* adopt a different approach to mergers involving undifferentiated or homogenous products and set out a series of factors which make unilateral effects more likely in such cases[311]:

- the market is concentrated

- there are a few firms in the affected market after the merger

- the merged firm has a large market share

- there are weak competitive constraints from rivals

- the merger eliminates a significant competitive force in the market and

- customers have little choice of alternative supplier perhaps as a result of switching costs or network effects.

Most of the CC's investigations have been concerned with the unilateral effects of horizontal mergers. In *Game Group plc/Games Station Ltd* the CC concluded that the merged firm would not be able unilaterally to raise prices profitably as it would face competition from a number of alternative retailers; two of the four CC members entered a dissenting opinion in this case[312]. The CC required remedies because of unilateral effects in several cases in 2009 and 2010[313].

(ii) Coordinated effects

The *Assessment Guidelines* discuss the problem of coordinated effects arising from mergers[314]. They begin by explaining the differences between explicit and tacit coordination, both of which can be germane to the substantive analysis[315]. It is necessary to consider evidence of pre-existing coordination and the characteristics of the market[316]. Paragraph 5.5.9 of the *Assessment Guidelines* says that there are three necessary conditions for coordination to be possible:

- first, firms must be able to reach and monitor the terms of coordination

- secondly, coordination needs to be 'internally sustainable': firms must have the incentive to coordinate and the existence of an effective mechanism to punish and deter cheating and

---

[308] *Assessment Guidelines*, para 5.4.6.   [309] Ibid.

[310] Ibid, para 5.4.11; see further ch 21, 'The non-collusive oligopoly gap', pp 864–866.

[311] *Assessment Guidelines*, paras 5.4.4–5.4.5; the importance of these factors will depend on the particular facts of each case.

[312] www.competition-commission.org.uk.

[313] See 'Table of merger references to the Competition Commission', pp 952–953 below.

[314] *Assessment Guidelines*, paras 5.5.1–5.5.19.

[315] Ibid, para 5.5.3; the problem of tacit coordination in oligopolistic markets was discussed in detail in chapter 14, to which the reader is referred.

[316] *Assessment Guidelines*, paras 5.5.5–5.5.9.

- thirdly, coordination needs to be 'externally sustainable', implying the absence of effective competitive constraints.

Each of these conditions is explored further in succeeding paragraphs of the *Guidelines*[317]. The OFT and the CC will consider the impact of the merger on the likelihood and effectiveness of coordination[318]. There have not been many cases under the Enterprise Act in which the OFT and/or the CC have considered coordinated effects in detail. As already noted, the OFT accepted undertakings in lieu of a reference to the CC in *Aggregate Industries Ltd/Foster Yeoman Ltd*, partly because of concerns about coordinated effects[319]; it did so for the same reason in *Lloyds Pharmacy Ltd/ Independent Pharmacy Care Centres plc*[320]. The CC was primarily concerned with the possibility that the merger in *DS Smith/LINPAC Containers* might lead to coordinated effects but concluded that, even though the conditions for achieving coordination might be present on the market, smaller suppliers would have the incentive to respond to any increase in the price of corrugated cardboard sheet by expanding output through existing and new capacity; the CC also rejected the suggestion that the acquisition of LINPAC would remove a maverick from the market[321]. The CC found in *Napier Brown Foods plc/James Budgett Sugars Ltd* that coordinated effects probably were occurring in the market for industrial sugar in Great Britain prior to the merger, but that the merger would not make any coordinated effects more sustainable or effective[322]. In *Wienerberger Finance Service BV/Baggeridge Brick plc* the OFT was concerned about a merger in the market for the supply of clay bricks that would reduce the number of major firms from four to three, but the CC decided that the conditions for coordination were not met and that the merger would not make coordination more likely[323]. The OFT was worried about a three to two merger in the wholesale supply of books to independent book retailers in *Woolworths Group plc/ Bertram Group Ltd*; the CC decided to give the merger unconditional clearance[324]. In *BOC/Ineos* the OFT considered that the merger could facilitate tacit coordination between the merged firm and its only remaining competitor[325]; the CC blocked the merger on other grounds[326].

(F) **Non-horizontal mergers**

Section 5.6 of the *Assessment Guidelines* discusses vertical and conglomerate mergers. The *Guidelines* acknowledge that non-horizontal mergers can lead to efficiencies which may result in the merged firm competing more vigorously[327]. They state that it is a 'well-established principle' that most non-horizontal mergers do not raise competition concerns[328], although they may weaken rivalry and result in an SLC under certain conditions.

---

[317] Ibid, paras 5.5.10–5.5.18.
[318] Ibid, para 5.5.19.
[319] OFT decision of 3 January 2007.
[320] OFT decision of 8 June 2007.
[321] See the Final Report, paras 5.50–5.99, available at www.competition-commission.org.uk.
[322] See the Final Report, paras 5.44–5.63, available at www.competition-commission.org.uk.
[323] See the Final Report, paras 7.9–7.114, available at www.competition-commission.org.uk.
[324] See the Final Report, available at www.competition-commission.org.uk.
[325] OFT decision of 29 May 2008.
[326] www.competition-commission.org.uk.
[327] *Assessment Guidelines*, para 5.6.4.   [328] Ibid, para 5.6.1.

The theories of how rivalry may be weakened by non-horizontal mergers typically involve the merged firm harming the ability of its competitors to compete[329]. Paragraph 5.6.6 of the *Guidelines* provides that the OFT and the CC will typically frame their analysis by asking:

- Would the merged firm have the ability to harm its rivals, for example through raising prices or refusing to supply them?
- Would the merged firm find it profitable to behave in this manner?
- Would the overall effect of the merged firm's behaviour give rise to an SLC?

The analysis of the above questions may overlap in practice as relevant factors may affect the answer to more than one question. The *Guidelines* explain, by way of illustration, how these questions might be answered in relation to a vertical merger where the theory of harm relates to partial input foreclosure[330].

The *Assessment Guidelines* briefly discuss other possible theories of harm arising from total foreclosure, customer foreclosure, conglomerate mergers, diagonal mergers[331] and coordinated effects. In particular they explain that a conglomerate merger could raise concerns if the merged entity were to sell complementary products at a price which, owing to the discounts that apply across the product range, is lower than the price charged when they are sold separately, thereby foreclosing competitors[332]. As in the case of vertical mergers, the OFT and the CC would consider the merged firm's ability and incentive to foreclose access to a market. In practice conglomeracy does not appear to have been a significant concern either for the OFT or the CC in cases under the Enterprise Act[333].

The CC identified possible vertical issues in the case of *Deutsche Börse AG/London Stock Exchange plc*[334] and concluded that the acquisition of LSE by either Deutsche Börse or Euronext may be expected to lead to an SLC in the market for the provision of on-book trading services within the UK because of the ability and incentive to foreclose entry or expansion to other providers of trading services. Vertical problems were identified in *Railway Investments Ltd/Marcroft Holdings Ltd* which were remedied by a divestiture of some of Marcroft's freight wagon maintenance business[335]. In the case of *Ticketmaster/Live Nation* the CC investigated a merger between Ticketmaster, the largest ticket agent in the UK, and Live Nation, one of the largest promoters of live music events. The CC provisionally found that the merger would result in the loss of a new entrant, CTS Eventim, as an effective competitor in the ticketing market, but changed its mind in light of new evidence and arguments[336]. Eventim was dissatisfied with the clearance decision and applied to the CAT for a review; however the CC decided that it would reconsider the matter and asked the CAT to quash the final report

---

[329] Ibid, para 5.6.5.

[330] Ibid, paras 5.6.9–5.6.12.

[331] For an explanation of diagonal mergers see *Assessment Guidelines*, para 5.6.13, fourth indent.

[332] *Assessment Guidelines*, para 5.6.13, third indent; on the concept of mixed bundling see ch 17, 'Terminology and illustrations of tying', p 689.

[333] On the question of whether a merger might lead to behaviour that might be abusive under Article 102 TFEU and/or the Chapter II prohibition of the Competition Act 1998, see 'Relationship with Article 102', p 955 below.

[334] See the Final Report, paras 5.136–5.170, available at www.competition-commission.org.uk.

[335] See the Final Report paras 7.74–7.133, available at www.competition-commission.org.uk.

[336] www.competition-commission.org.uk.

and refer the matter back to the CC[337]. The CC subsequently cleared the merger unconditionally[338].

(G) Efficiencies

Efficiencies may be relevant to merger analysis in two distinct ways: first, as part of the assessment of whether a merger gives rise to an SLC; secondly, in determining whether a merger generates 'relevant customer benefits' for the purpose of section 30 of the Act sufficient to offset any SLC. The *Assessment Guidelines* discuss the former[339] but not the latter[340]. For efficiencies to be considered as part of the competitive assessment the OFT and the CC consider that they must increase rivalry among the remaining firms in the market so that the merger does not result in an SLC[341]. The OFT requires the parties to prove, on the basis of compelling evidence, that the efficiencies are timely, likely and sufficient to prevent an SLC from arising and are merger-specific[342]. The CC expects the parties to demonstrate that the same criteria are met on the balance of probabilities. The *Guidelines* describe different types of supply-side efficiencies, such as cost savings, and demand-side efficiencies, such as pricing effects which arise when lowering the price of one product increases demand for it and other products that are used with it.

In *Global Radio UK Ltd/GCap Media plc*[343] the OFT took into account efficiency arguments in considering a merger between two radio stations and relied, for the first time, on evidence of efficiencies to conclude that there would not be an SLC in London advertising markets[344]. The OFT noted in particular that the evidential burden for demonstrating efficiencies should not be so high that it is impossible to meet, nor be so rigid and immutable as to be incapable of variation according to the context[345]. The OFT incorporated purchasing efficiencies into its analysis of unilateral effects in *Asda Stores Ltd/Netto Foodstores Ltd*, although this did not alter the number of markets in which an SLC was identified[346]. The CC concluded in *Ardagh International Holdings Ltd/Redfearn Glass Ltd* that the positive effect of the merger on rivalry would not offset the loss of a competitor[347].

(H) Barriers to entry and expansion[1]

The *Assessment Guidelines* point out that an important part of the analysis of a merger is a consideration of any barriers to entry or expansion faced by competitors[348]. Market power is unlikely to exist where there are low barriers to entry into and exit from the market[349]. In deciding whether entry or expansion might prevent an SLC the OFT and the CC will consider whether it would be likely, timely and sufficient[350]. Barriers to entry and expansion include[351]:

---

[337] Case 1150/4/8/10 *CTS Eventim AG v Competition Commission* [2010] CAT 7, [2010] CompAR 22.

[338] See the Final Report, available at www.competition-commission.org.uk.

[339] *Assessment Guidelines*, paras 5.7.1–5.7.18.

[340] See 'Customer benefits', pp 916–917 above.   [341] *Assessment Guidelines*, para 5.7.4.

[342] Ibid.

[343] OFT decision 8 August 2008; for comment see Didierlaurent and Stephanou 'UK Merger Control: Tuning into Efficiencies' (2010) 9(1) Competition Law Journal 55.

[344] OFT decision of 8 August 2008, paras 139–189; the OFT specifically relied on demand-side efficiencies as it was not satisfied that the cost savings were sufficient.

[345] Ibid, para 145.   [346] OFT decision of 23 September 2010, paras 65–76.

[347] See the Final Report, paras 8.59–8.63, available at www.competition-commission.org.uk.

[348] *Assessment Guidelines*, para 5.8.1.   [349] See further ch 1, 'Market power', pp 42–45.

[350] *Assessment Guidelines*, para 5.8.3.   [351] Ibid, para 5.8.5.

- **absolute advantages:** these exist where an incumbent firm owns or has access to important assets or resources which are not accessible to another firm: this could be the case, for example, where a system of regulation limits the number of firms that can operate on a market or where an existing firm has preferential access to essential facilities or owns intellectual property rights

- **intrinsic or structural advantages:** these arise from the technology, production or other factors required to establish an effective presence in the market

- **economies of scale:** the fact that a firm may need to enter or expand on a large scale can constitute a barrier to entry; even large-scale entry or expansion will generally be successful only if that firm expands the total market significantly or replaces an existing firm

- **strategic advantages:** these arise from being first into the market and may be a particular problem in markets which exhibit network effects.

The *Guidelines* provide insights into the way in which the OFT and the CC will assess the likelihood, timeliness and sufficiency of entry or expansion[352]. The OFT and the CC may consider entry or expansion within two years as timely, although they regard this issue as one that must be assessed on a case-by-case basis. In *Zipcar/Streetcar* the CC acknowledged that the merger would enable the merged firm to increase prices in the short term, but concluded that entry and expansion would be likely, timely and sufficient to prevent the merged firm from exercising market power in the medium to longer term and thus prevent an SLC[353].

(l) **Countervailing buyer power**

The *Assessment Guidelines* consider that countervailing buyer power could exist where a customer is able to use its negotiating strength to constrain the ability of a merged firm to increase prices; this is a factor that makes an SLC finding less likely[354]. An SLC is unlikely to arise where all the customers of the merged firm possess countervailing buyer power after the merger. In cases where only some customers have countervailing power, the OFT and the CC will look at the extent to which that power can be relied on to protect all customers[355]. The *Guidelines* set out various factors that affect the ability of buyers to constrain the power of a supplier, such as their ability to switch, the existence of alternative suppliers and the ability of buyers to either sponsor new entry or enter the supplier's market itself[356]. Any buyer power must remain effective following the merger[357].

The buyer power of major retailers of carbonated soft drinks was a significant factor in the CC's clearance of the merger in *Cott Beverages Ltd/Macaw (Holdings) Ltd*[358]. However this argument did not succeed in the case of a merger between the UK's two principal suppliers of eggs in *Stonegate Farmers Ltd/Deans Food Group Ltd*[359]; rather, the CC was concerned that the merger would result in an SLC between the merging parties in the procurement of shell eggs[360].

[352] Ibid, paras 5.8.8–5.8.13.
[353] Final Report, paras 7.29–7.57, available at www.competition-commission.org.uk.
[354] *Assessment Guidelines*, para 5.9.1.   [355] Ibid.   [356] Ibid, paras 5.9.2–5.9.7.
[357] Ibid, para 5.9.8.
[358] See the Final Report, paras 5.34–5.46, available at www.competition-commission.org.uk.
[359] See the Final Report, paras 6.64–6.73, available at www.competition-commission.org.uk.
[360] Ibid, paras 6.93–6.102.

6. Enforcement

Chapter 4 of Part 3 of the Enterprise Act deals with the issue of enforcement. It begins by describing the initial undertakings and orders that the OFT may accept or impose and undertakings in lieu of a reference to the CC; it then sets out certain interim restrictions on dealings during the course of a merger inquiry, and concludes with the powers of the CC. Undertakings and orders are legally binding and enforceable in the courts[361]; section 89 of the Act makes clear that undertakings[362] may contain provisions that go beyond the order-making powers in Schedule 8.

Section 90 of the Act provides that Schedule 10 shall have effect when accepting 'enforcement' undertakings or making orders other than initial and interim orders. Schedule 10 establishes the procedural requirements that the OFT and CC must satisfy when they intend to accept, vary or release an undertaking or, as the case may be, make, vary or revoke an order; paragraphs 1 to 5 of the Schedule deal with the acceptance of undertakings and the making of orders; paragraphs 6 to 8 with their termination. The purpose of Schedule 10 is to require the OFT or the CC to set out clearly what they are proposing to do and the reasons for it[363].

The OFT is required to maintain a register of undertakings and orders made under the merger provisions in the Enterprise Act; it is accessible to the public on the OFT's website[364].

(A) Initial undertakings and orders

(i) Initial undertakings and orders to prevent pre-emptive action

Under section 71 of the Act the OFT may accept an initial undertaking from the parties to a completed merger for the purpose of preventing 'pre-emptive action', that is to say action which might prejudice a merger reference or impede the taking of any action which may be justified by the CC's decision on the reference[365]. Such an undertaking can be accepted only where the OFT has reasonable grounds for suspecting that a 'relevant merger situation' has been, or may be, created[366]. There are provisions for such undertakings to cease to be in force[367], and for their variation and release[368]. Provision also exists for the OFT to make an initial enforcement order where it has reasonable grounds for suspecting that a relevant merger situation has been created and that pre-emptive action is in progress or in contemplation[369]. An initial enforcement order may prohibit the doing of things that the OFT considers would constitute pre-emptive action; may impose obligations as to the carrying on of any activities or the safeguarding of assets; may appoint a trustee to conduct or supervise matters; and may require the provision of information[370].

The OFT's *Mergers – Jurisdictional and procedural guidance*[371] explains its approach to initial undertakings and orders. The OFT will seek undertakings where the merger raises or is likely to raise competition concerns and where the circumstances of the case mean that initial undertakings are appropriate to prevent pre-emptive action[372]. Among the

---

[361] See 'Enforcement functions of the OFT', pp 948–949 below.
[362] 'Undertakings' includes undertakings in lieu of a reference, initial undertakings, interim undertakings and final undertakings.
[363] See further the CC's *General Advice and Information* CC4, March 2006, paras 7.23–7.31.
[364] Enterprise Act 2002, s 91; the OFT's website is www.oft.gov.uk.   [365] Ibid, s 71(8).   [366] Ibid, s 71(3).
[367] Ibid, s 71(5) and (6).   [368] Ibid, s 71(4) and (7).   [369] Ibid, s 72.
[370] Ibid, s 72(2) and para 9 of Sch 18.   [371] OFT 527, June 2009, paras 6.23–6.45.
[372] Ibid, para 6.30.

matters which the OFT will consider when determining the risk of pre-emptive action are the risk of loss of critical know-how and key staff, the risk that key assets will be rendered inoperable and the risk of exchange of sensitive information[373]. The OFT has made clear that the fact that it considers initial undertakings are necessary does not preclude unconditional clearance of a merger[374].

The OFT will seek initial undertakings as soon as the statutory test in section 71(3) is met, which may be at the time that an enquiry letter is sent out or immediately following notification[375]. The OFT has a standard form for initial undertakings and will not generally engage in lengthy discussions about them[376]. The OFT will consider imposing an initial order only where it has already given the merging parties a reasonable opportunity to provide initial undertakings, but they have not been forthcoming[377].

(ii) Undertakings in lieu of a reference to the CC

The ability of the OFT to accept undertakings in lieu of a reference to the CC has already been discussed[378].

(B) Interim restrictions and powers[379]

(i) Statutory restrictions on dealings

Sections 77 and 78 of the Enterprise Act impose automatic restrictions on certain dealings in relation to completed and anticipated mergers when a reference has been made to the CC; these are imposed in order to prevent any further integration of the businesses concerned. Section 77 provides that, when a reference has been made of a completed merger and no undertaking has been given in relation to it, no one may, without the consent of the CC, complete any outstanding matters in relation to that merger or transfer the ownership or control of any enterprises to which the reference relates[380]; any consent of the CC may be general or special, and may be revoked[381]. Section 78 provides that, when a reference is made of an anticipated merger, no one may, without the consent of the CC, directly or indirectly acquire an interest in shares in a company if any enterprise to which the reference relates is carried on by or under the control of that company[382]; again any consent of the CC may be general or special, and may be revoked[383]. These provisions are quite technical and section 79 deals with numerous points of interpretation, in particular to make clear what is meant by a share acquisition for the purposes of section 78. The CC gave consent to Heinz for the disposal of its ethnic foods business during the course of its investigation in *Heinz/ HP Foods Group* which otherwise would not have been possible due to the statutory restriction on share dealings and due to the subsequent interim undertakings that had been given to the CC under the provisions described in the following paragraph[384]. Section 78 does not apply to the transfer of assets; the CC may therefore put in place interim measures to deal with this issue[385].

---

[373] Ibid, para 6.32.   [374] Ibid, para 6.29.   [375] Ibid, para 6.29.

[376] Ibid, paras 6.37–6.39; the template is available on the OFT's website, www.oft.gov.uk; the OFT will consider subsequent waiver requests: ibid, para 6.39.

[377] Ibid, para 6.44.   [378] See 'Undertakings in lieu of a reference', pp 927–928 above.

[379] See *Merger Remedies: Competition Commission Guidelines* CC8, November 2008, Appendix A, available at www.competition-commission.org.uk.

[380] Enterprise Act 2002, s 77(2).

[381] Ibid, s 77(5).   [382] Ibid, s 78(3).   [383] Ibid, s 78(3).

[384] See the Final Report, paras 3.17–3.21, available at www.competition-commission.org.uk/inquiries/ref2005/heinz/index.htm.

[385] See *Remedies Guidelines*, Appendix A, para 16.

(ii) Interim undertakings and orders to prevent pre-emptive action

Just as the OFT can accept initial undertakings and make final orders to prevent pre-emptive action, section 80 (dealing with undertakings) and section 81 (dealing with orders) of the Act give the CC the same powers[386]; pre-emptive action means action which might prejudice the reference or impede the taking of any action that the CC might consider to be justified as a result of its decision on the reference[387]. Section 80(3) enables the CC to adopt an undertaking that has already been given to the OFT within seven days of the reference to it; section 80(4) provides that the OFT undertaking may be continued in force, varied, released or superseded by a new undertaking. Section 81(3) provides that the CC[388] may adopt an order of the OFT. It is common practice for the CC to adopt OFT undertakings on the basis of section 80(3), although it may then go on to accept undertakings directly from the parties concerned: an example of this can be found in the case of *Greif Inc/Blagden Packaging Group*[389]. Undertakings and orders may be varied[390]. In *Bucher Industries AG/Johnstone Sweepers Ltd* the CC was concerned that Bucher appeared not to be complying with its interim undertaking to prevent the integration of the Bucher and Johnstone businesses pending the completion of the investigation and required both an apology from Bucher and the appointment of a monitoring trustee to ensure compliance with the undertaking[391]. A monitoring trustee was also appointed in relation to a completed joint venture in the case of *Stagecoach/Scottish Citylink*[392]. Interim orders had been made in three cases by 20 June 2011. The *Stericycle* case[393] is discussed below. In the case of *Tesco/Co-op Store*[394] the CC gave directions to prevent Tesco from carrying out any further work on a store in Slough that could impede any remedial action. In *Sports Direct/JJB Sports*[395] the CC made an interim order to ensure both that the stores purchased by Sports Direct remained viable and that it had options for divestment after it had completed its investigation.

There is no duty to pre-notify mergers to the OFT under UK law, and quite a large percentage of the cases referred by the OFT to the CC are of completed mergers[396]. This gives rise to a concern that the CC might investigate a case in which it considers that there is an SLC, only to find that the merging businesses have become so intermingled that it is very difficult in practice to reverse the process and to restore conditions of

---

[386] See the CC's *General Advice and Information*, paras 7.1–7.8 and 7.11–7.13.

[387] Enterprise Act 2002, s 80(10).

[388] The Chairman, or a Deputy Chairman, of the CC may perform this function: see *Notice of Variation of Procedure*, 16 March 2010, available at www.competition-commission.org.uk.

[389] See www.competition-commission.org.uk; more recent examples are *Holland & Barrett/Julian Graves* (2009) and *Brightsolid/Friends Reunited* (2010).

[390] See eg the consent given to Deans to process liquid egg on behalf of Stonegate in *Stonegate Farmers Ltd/Deans Food Group Ltd*, available at www.competition-commission.org.uk.

[391] See the Final Report, para 9.3, available at www.competition-commission.org.uk.

[392] See the Final Report, para 8.56, available at www.competition-commission.org.uk; see similarly *Capita/IBS*, available at www.competition-commission.org.uk.

[393] See below.

[394] See the Final Report, paras 3.44–3.49, available at www.competition-commission.org.uk.

[395] See the Final Report, para 3.6, available at www.competition-commission.org.uk.

[396] For statistics on this point see 'Completed mergers' and following sections pp 954–956 below; see French and Scola 'How Risky is Buying in the UK without Merger Clearance?' (2007) 1 European Business Law Journal 196.

effective competition[397]. Obviously it is important for the OFT, which will have reviewed the merger prior to the CC, also to consider what measures should be put in place during its (the OFT's) period of investigation so that the CC's position will not be prejudiced. In 2008 the CC issued *Merger Remedies: Competition Commission Guidelines*[398] ('*Remedies Guidelines*'), replacing earlier guidance of 2006. The CC will normally expect to receive interim undertakings from the acquirer in the case of a completed merger to clarify or supplement the statutory restrictions on dealing[399]; the CC may also seek to restrict the flow of commercially valuable information between the parties pending the outcome. The CC explains that it might find it necessary to appoint a 'hold separate' manager to operate the business separately from that of the acquirer, and that a monitoring trustee might have to be appointed as well[400]. The CC has published a template set of interim undertakings for completed mergers[401].

In *Stericycle International LLC/Sterile Technologies Group Ltd* Stericycle had purchased STG's clinical waste management business at auction; no notification had been made to the OFT. The OFT referred the case to the CC, which made an order to prevent any further integration of the two businesses, and issued directions for the appointment of a monitoring trustee; subsequently further directions were issued for the appointment of a hold separate manager[402]. Stericycle challenged the CC before the CAT[403]; the CAT upheld the action of the CC, holding that it was 'well within the CC's margin of appreciation to propose the appointment of a [hold separate manager] in this case'[404], and that Stericycle was well aware of the risk it was taking by completing the transaction without approval from the competition authorities[405]. The CC's view was that the fact that substantial integration of the two businesses had already taken place made it more, not less, important to appoint a hold separate manager[406]. The final outcome of this case was that Stericycle was required to sell off part of the business that it had acquired to a suitable purchaser[407].

(C) 'Final powers' or 'remedies'[408]

Sections 82 to 84 of the Enterprise Act deal with 'final powers', that is to say the remedial action that the CC may take after it has completed its inquiry and reached its conclusion. Section 82 provides for the acceptance of final undertakings and section 83 for the

---

[397] The CC has raised the question of whether pre-notification of mergers should become compulsory: see its *Annual Report and Accounts 2006/2007*, p 6, available at www.competition-commission.org.uk.

[398] See Appendix A of CC8, November 2008, available at www.competition-commission.org.uk.

[399] *Remedies Guidelines*, para 1.32 and Appendix A, para 7; on s 77 of the Act see 'Statutory restrictions on dealings', p 942 above.

[400] *Remedies Guidelines*, paras 12–15; the risk factors making the appointment of a hold separate manager more likely are listed in para 14.

[401] See www.competition-commission.org.uk.

[402] The order and directions will be found at www.competition-commission.org.uk.

[403] Case No 1070/4/8/06 *Stericycle International LLC v Competition Commission* [2006] CAT 21, [2007] CompAR 281; for comment see Freeman 'Stericycle: A Lifeline for the UK's Voluntary Merger Control Regime' (2007) 6 Competition Law Journal 298.

[404] Case No 1070/4/8/06, [2006] CAT 21, [2007] CompAR 281 para 140.

[405] Ibid, para 137.   [406] Ibid, para 158.

[407] For the final undertakings in this case see www.competition-commission.org.uk.

[408] See the CC's *General Advice and Information*, paras 7.1–7.8 and 7.14–7.16 and *Remedies Guidelines*, CC8, November 2008.

making of an order where an undertaking is not being fulfilled or where false or misleading information was given to the OFT or CC prior to the acceptance of an undertaking. Section 84 gives the power to the CC to make a final order. As a general rule the CC prefers to proceed by accepting undertakings rather than by making final orders: the CC had made only one final order in a merger (as opposed to a market investigation) reference as at 20 June 2011: *Tesco/Co-op Store*[409]. Nevertheless the CC has pointed out that, in the event of undue delay in obtaining suitable undertakings after the completion of an investigation, it could proceed to the making of an order[410]. Undertakings may contain provisions that go beyond the order-making powers in the Act[411]. Provision is made for the variation of remedies[412].

(i) Schedule 8 to the Enterprise Act

The orders that can be made are set out in Schedule 8 to the Act, and are extensive. They include 'general restrictions on conduct' (paragraphs 2 to 9); 'general obligations to be performed' (paragraphs 10 and 11); 'acquisitions and divisions' (paragraphs 12 to 14); and 'supply and publication of information' (paragraphs 15 to 19); supplementary provisions as to the making of orders are to be found in paragraphs 21 and 22 of Schedule 8. An order may not interfere with conditions in patent licences or licences of registered designs[413]. It is specifically provided that an order may prohibit the performance of an agreement already in existence[414]. An order may provide for the revocation or modification of conditions in the licences of regulated undertakings under legislation such as the Telecommunications Act 1984, the Airports Act 1986 and the Gas Act 1986[415]. Section 87 of the Act allows the person making an order to give directions to an individual or to an office-holder in a company or association to take action or to refrain from action for the purpose of carrying out or ensuring compliance with the order; failure to comply with such directions may lead to court action[416]. Section 88 sets out the minimum contents of any final order or order to replace an undertaking in lieu of a reference.

(ii) General restrictions on conduct

Paragraphs 2 to 9 of Schedule 8 provide for orders to impose restrictions on conduct. An order may prohibit the making or performance of an agreement or require the termination of one (paragraph 2)[417]; and may forbid refusals to supply (paragraph 3), tie-ins (paragraph 4), discrimination (paragraph 5), preferential treatment (paragraph 6) and deviation from published price lists (paragraph 7). Price regulation is also a possibility (paragraph 8). An order may prohibit the exercise of voting rights attached to shares, stocks or securities (paragraph 9).

---

[409] The CC published its Final Report on 28 November 2007 and made a Final Order on 23 April 2009, www.competition-commission.org.uk.

[410] See CC's *General Advice and Information*, para 7.6 and the Final Report in *Firstgroup plc/Scotrail*, para 14, available at www.competition-commission.org.uk.

[411] Enterprise Act 2002, s 89.

[412] Ibid, s 82(2)(b) (variation of undertakings) and s 83(5)(c) (variation of orders); for an example of several variations of a remedy see *Firstgroup plc/Scotrail*, www.competition-commission.org.uk.

[413] Enterprise Act 2002, s 86(2).   [414] Ibid, s 86(3).   [415] Ibid, s 86(5) and Sch 9, Part 1.

[416] Ibid, s 87(4)–(8).

[417] Such an order may not deal with terms and conditions in contracts of employment or the physical conditions in which workers work: Enterprise Act 2002, Sch 8, para 2(2).

(iii) General obligations to be performed

Paragraph 10 of Schedule 8 provides that an order may require a person to supply goods or services, and it can be specified that they should be of a particular standard or that they should be applied in a particular manner: for example a bus company could be required to maintain a certain frequency of service[418]. Paragraph 11 of the Schedule enables an order to require that certain activities should be carried on separately from other activities.

(iv) Acquisitions and divisions

Paragraph 12 of Schedule 8 provides that an order may prohibit or restrict the acquisition of the whole or part of an undertaking or the assets of another person's business. Paragraph 13 provides for the division of any business, whether by sale of any part of an undertaking or assets or otherwise; paragraph 13(3) deals with associated issues such as the transfer or creation of property, rights, liabilities and obligations, the adjustment of contracts, share ownership and other matters. Provision is made for the buyer of a business to be approved by the OFT[419], and for the appointment of a trustee to oversee the divestment of a business[420].

In *Somerfield plc/Wm Morrison* the CC required Somerfield to divest four grocery stores that it had acquired from Morrison[421]. Somerfield appealed to the CAT arguing that the CC's remedy was unreasonable, and that it (Somerfield) should be given the option of selling either the stores that it had acquired or the stores that it already owned: since it was the common ownership of the stores that was responsible for the SLC, the situation could be remedied by divesting either the new or the original stores. The CAT upheld the finding of the CC in *Somerfield plc v Competition Commission*[422]. In the CAT's view the CC was entitled to take as its starting point that the '*status quo ante*' would normally involve reversing the acquisition, which would represent a simple, direct and easily understandable approach; the onus was therefore on Somerfield to show why divestment of its original stores would be an equally effective remedy[423]. The CAT considered that Somerfield had failed to show that this was the case, in particular because the CC had been correct to think that Somerfield's existing stores were less attractive to a potential purchaser than the ones that it had acquired from Morrison, meaning that it was less likely that selling the existing stores would be an effective remedy.

(v) Supply and publication of information

Paragraph 15 of Schedule 8 provides that an order may require a person to publish price lists. Paragraph 16 allows a prohibition on the practice of recommending prices to dealers. Paragraph 17 enables an order to require a person to publish accounting information. Paragraph 18 provides that orders can specify the manner in which information is to be published. There is a general power in paragraph 19 to require a person to provide the competition authorities with information, and for that information to be published.

---

[418] See *Explanatory Notes* to the Enterprise Bill, para 225.

[419] Enterprise Act 2002, Sch 8, para 13(3)(k).   [420] Ibid, Sch 8, para 13(1).

[421] See the Final Report, paras 11.9–11.23, available at www.competition-commission.org.uk.

[422] Case No 1051/4/8/05 [2006] CAT 4, [2006] CompAR 390; for comment see Beale 'The *Somerfield* Decisions of the Competition Commission and Competition Appeal Tribunal and the Economics of Divestment Remedies' (2006) 5 Competition Law Journal 45; Jephcott and Mahtani 'The *Somerfield* Judgment: A Damp Squib?' (2006) 5 Competition Law Journal 56.

[423] Case No 1051/4/8/05 [2006] CAT 4, [2006] CompAR 390, paras 99–105.

(vi) National security, media and financial stability mergers

Paragraphs 20, 20A and 20B make provision for orders to be made in relation to 'public interest cases' under Chapter 2 of Part 3 of the Act[424].

(vii) The CC's approach to remedies

The CC has established a Remedies Standing Group whose functions include the adoption of interim undertakings from the OFT; enforcing undertakings and orders; varying or releasing undertakings; and overseeing the implementation of undertakings and orders in relation to divestiture. Details of the work of the Group and of its membership are available on the website of the CC[425]. The CC also has a rolling programme of reviewing past remedies in merger cases in order to capture important learning points and to feed them into current remedies policy and practice[426]. The CC's approach to remedies is described in its *Remedies Guidelines* which expand and clarify the guidance provided by the CC previously[427]. Part 1 of the *Remedies Guidelines* explains the objectives of remedial action: the CC will seek the least costly and intrusive remedies that it considers will be effective to address any SLC and its adverse effects[428]. Part 2 provides an overview of the types of remedies. The CC generally prefers structural remedies to behavioural ones[429], although the use of the latter cannot be ruled out[430]. Part 3 of the *Remedies Guidelines* explains the principles relevant to divestiture remedies, including the criteria for identifying a suitable purchaser. Part 4 discusses behavioural remedies and emphasises the need for there to be effective and adequately resourced arrangements for monitoring and enforcement. The use of trustees and third party monitors to assist in the monitoring and implementation of undertaking or orders is discussed in Part 5.

(viii) Examples of remedies

The CC has opted for structural remedies in the majority of cases that gave rise to an SLC under the Act[431]. In both *Hamsard 2786 Ltd/Academy Music Holdings Ltd*[432] and *SvitzerWijsmuller A/S/Adsteam Marine Ltd*[433] the CC was offered behavioural remedies, including price controls, but rejected them in favour of partial divestitures. In rare cases an outright prohibition of an anticipated merger may be preferable, as occurred in *Serviced Dispense Equipment Ltd (SDEL)/Coors Brewers Ltd*[434]. However behavioural remedies are possible: the CC accepted a retail price cap and other behavioural remedies in *Dräger Medical A&G Co KGaA/Hillebrand Industries Inc*[435] and undertakings on both fares and the level of service, frequency and configuration of bus routes in Scotland, in

---

[424] See 'Public interest cases', pp 956–958 below.   [425] www.competition-commission.org.uk.
[426] See *Understanding past merger remedies: report on case study research*, January 2007, available at www.competition-commission.org.uk.
[427] See *Merger References: Competition Commission Guidelines* CC2, June 2003, part 4 and *Guidelines on the application of divestiture remedies in merger inquiries* CC8, December 2004.
[428] *Remedies Guidelines*, para 1.8.   [429] Ibid, para 2.14.
[430] See the three situations described in ibid, para 2.16.
[431] See 'The Merger Provisions in Practice', pp 951–956 below.
[432] See the Final Report, paras 6.47–6.67, available at www.competition-commission.org.uk.
[433] See the Final Report, paras 9.13–9.17, available at www.competition-commission.org.uk.
[434] See the Final Report, paras 6.42–6.48, available at www.competition-commission.org.uk; see also *BOC Ltd/Ineos Chlor Ltd*, paras 11.14–11.85, available at www.competition-commission.org.uk.
[435] See the Final Report, paras 10.26–10.40, available at www.competition-commission.org.uk.

particular in the Glasgow and Edinburgh areas, in *Firstgroup plc/Scotrail*[436]. In *Nufarm/ AH Marks* the CC found that, while divestiture would not be disproportionate, a package of behavioural remedies would be more targeted in addressing its competition concerns. The CC may exceptionally accept behavioural remedies even though it considers divestiture would be more effective, as it did in *Macquarie UK Broadcast Ventures/National Grid Wireless*[437] given the unique circumstances of the digital switchover process in the broadcasting sector.

The CC will also consider whether it should recommend action by persons other than the merging parties[438]. For example it might suggest to the Government that it should amend legislation or regulations that inhibit entry into a particular market; the Government has given a commitment to give a public response to any such recommendation; this happened in *Dräger Medical A&G Co KGaA/Hillenbrand Industries Inc*[439].

(D) Enforcement functions of the OFT

The lead role in monitoring OFT and CC undertakings and orders is given to the OFT. Section 92(1) of the Act requires it to keep enforcement undertakings and enforcement orders under review and to ensure compliance with sections 77 and 78, which restrict certain dealings; in particular the OFT must consider whether undertakings or orders are being complied with and whether, by reason of a change of circumstances, there is a case for release, variation or supersession[440]. The CC may ask the OFT to assist in the negotiation of undertakings[441]. The OFT also has a responsibility to keep under review undertakings and orders arising from merger cases conducted under the now-repealed Fair Trading Act 1973[442]. The OFT has agreed a *Memorandum of Understanding*[443] with the CC which records the basis on which they will cooperate on the variation and termination of merger, monopoly and market undertakings and orders under the Fair Trading Act and the Enterprise Act.

Section 94 of the Enterprise Act provides that orders and undertakings can be enforced through the courts. There is a duty to comply with orders and undertakings, and that duty is owed to anyone who may be affected by a contravention of it[444]; any breach of the duty is actionable if such a person sustains loss or damage[445], though a defence exists if the person in question took all reasonable steps and exercised all due diligence to avoid a contravention of the order or undertaking[446]. The OFT maintains a register of undertakings and orders on its website; it is open to physical inspection between 10.00 and 16.30

---

[436] See the Final Report, paras 6.8–6.36, available at www.competition-commission.org.uk.

[437] See the Final Report, paras 10.68–10.88, available at www.competition-commission.org.uk.

[438] *Remedies Guidelines*, para 2.22.

[439] See the Final Report, paras 10.16–10.25, available at www.competition-commission.org.uk.

[440] Enterprise Act 2002, s 92(2); further information on cases in which undertakings or orders are being reviewed can be found on the CC website, www.competition-commission.org.uk.

[441] Enterprise Act 2002, s 93.

[442] See ibid, Sch 24 and the Enterprise Act 2002 (Enforcement Undertakings) Order 2006, SI 2006/354 and the Enterprise Act 2002 (Enforcement Undertakings and Orders) Order 2006, SI 2006/355.

[443] 17 February 2009, available at www.oft.gov.uk.

[444] Enterprise Act 2002, s 94(2) and (3).

[445] Ibid, s 94(4); as to whether a person injured by breach of an undertaking or order could bring an action for damages, see *MidKent Holdings v General Utilities plc* [1996] 3 All ER 132, [1997] 1 WLR 14, brought under s 93 of the (now-repealed) Fair Trading Act 1973.

[446] Enterprise Act 2002, s 94(5).

on working days. Compliance with an order or undertaking is enforceable by civil proceedings brought by the OFT[447] or the CC[448] for an injunction (or interdict in Scotland). Similar provisions apply in relation to breaches of the statutory restrictions on certain dealings provided for in sections 77 and 78[449].

7. Supplementary Provisions

Chapter 5 of Part 3 of the Enterprise Act contains a number of supplementary provisions. Some of these, such as the statutory merger notice procedure and the payment of fees, have already been considered[450]. Two issues of particular importance remain to be considered: the information powers of the CC and its ability to impose penalties, and the review of decisions on mergers by the CAT.

(A) Investigation powers and penalties

Sections 109 to 117 of the Enterprise Act deal with the CC's powers of investigation and with penalties. Section 109 gives the CC powers to require, by notice, the attendance of witnesses[451], the production of documents[452] and the supply of various information[453]. A notice given under this section must explain the consequences of non-compliance[454]. The CC can impose a penalty on a person who, without reasonable excuse, fails to comply with a notice given under section 109[455] or who obstructs or delays a person who is trying to copy documents required to be produced[456]. The maximum amounts that the CC may impose as a penalty under section 110(1) and (3) are specified in the Competition Commission (Penalties) Order 2003[457]. It is a criminal offence for a person intentionally to alter, suppress or destroy any document that he has been required to produce under section 109[458]: a person guilty of this offence could be fined or imprisoned for a maximum of two years[459].

Sections 111 to 116 set out the main procedural requirements which the CC must observe when imposing a monetary penalty; the factors which it will have regard to when determining the amount of a penalty are set out in the CC's *Statement of Policy on Penalties*[460]. There is a full right of appeal to the CAT against decisions of the CC to impose monetary penalties: the CAT may quash the penalty or substitute a different amount or different dates for payment[461]. On several occasions the CC has used or threatened to use its section 109 powers, both on parties to the transaction under consideration and third parties: these powers can avoid delays in the provision of information and ensure that the information provided is full and accurate.

---

[447] Ibid, s 94(6).　　　[448] Ibid, s 94(7).
[449] Ibid, s 95.　　　[450] See 'Notifying mergers to the OFT', pp 924–925 above.
[451] Enterprise Act 2002, s 109(1).
[452] Ibid, s 109(2).
[453] Ibid, s 109(3).
[454] Ibid, s 109(4).
[455] Ibid, s 110(1).
[456] Ibid, s 110(3).
[457] SI 2003/1371.
[458] Enterprise Act 2002, s 110(5).
[459] Ibid, s 110(7).
[460] CC5, June 2003, paras 17–21.
[461] Enterprise Act 2002, s 114.

(B) **Review of decisions under Part 3 of the Enterprise Act**

Section 120 of the Enterprise Act makes provision for review of decisions under Part 3 of the Act. Section 120(1) provides that any person aggrieved by a decision of the OFT, the Secretary of State or the CC may apply to the CAT for a review of that decision. The CAT considered it difficult to conceive of a situation where the merging parties objecting to the CC's finding of an SLC would not be persons aggrieved by that decision, even if they were prepared to comply with it[462]. An aggrieved person could also be a third party with sufficient interest[463].

The application must be made within four weeks of the date on which the applicant was notified of the disputed decision or of its date of publication, whichever is earlier[464]; the date of publication is the date when the parties receive the reasons for the OFT's decision, rather than an earlier Press Release stating the content of the decision but without its reasoning[465]. The CAT's view is that, as a general proposition, a main hearing in merger cases should be held within three months of the report of the CC[466]; the CAT has succeeded in dealing with reviews of merger decisions within a short time period, considerably shorter than the General Court when reviewing decisions under the EUMR.

When dealing with cases under section 120(1) the CAT must apply the same principles as would be applied by a court on an application for review[467]. The fact that the CAT is a specialist competition tribunal does not mean that it should apply different principles[468]; this point was put beyond doubt by the Court of Appeal in *BSkyB Group plc v Competition Commission*[469]. The CAT may dismiss the application or quash the whole or part of the decision to which it relates[470]; and, in the latter situation, it may refer the matter back to the original decision-maker for further consideration[471]. An appeal may be brought before the Court of Appeal, with permission, against the CAT's decision on a point of law[472]. Part 3 of the Competition Appeal Tribunal Rules[473] makes provision for appeals under section 120 of the Act.

There have been several applications for review to the CAT in relation to merger cases[474]. The challenges by third parties to the OFT's decisions not to refer the *iSOFT/Torex*, *Phoenix Healthcare/East Anglian Pharmaceuticals* and *Boots/Alliance UniChem* mergers have already been discussed in the context of the OFT's duty to refer mergers to the CC that may be expected to result in an SLC[475]. A third party successfully appealed against the CC's clearance decision in *Ticketmaster/Live Nation*[476], leading to a re-investigation

---

[462] See Case No 1145/4/8/09 *Stagecoach Group Plc v Competition Commission* [2010] CAT 1, [2010] CompAR 238, para 12.

[463] See Case No 1107/4/10/08 *Merger Action Group v Secretary of State for Business, Enterprise and Regulatory Reform* [2008] CAT 36, [2009] CompAR 167, paras 32–48.

[464] Competition Appeal Tribunal Rules 2003, SI 2003/1372, r 26.

[465] See Case No 1030/4/1/04 *Federation of Wholesale Distributors v OFT* [2004] CAT 11, [2004] CompAR 764, paras 22–26.

[466] See Case No 1075/4/8/07 *Stericycle International LLC v Competition Commission* [2007] CAT 9, [2007] CompAR 662, para 7.

[467] Enterprise Act 2002, s 120(4).

[468] See para 52 of the Vice-Chancellor's judgment and paras 88–106 of Carnwath LJ's judgment in *OFT v IBA Health Ltd* [2004] EWCA Civ 142, [2004] UKCRL 683.

[469] [2010] EWCA Civ 2, [2010] UKCLR 351, paras 28–41.   [470] Enterprise Act 2002, s 120(5)(a).

[471] Ibid, s 120(5)(b).   [472] Ibid, s 120(6) and (7).   [473] SI 2003/1372.

[474] For comment see Burrows 'Review of Merger Decisions by the CAT: A Question of Evidence' (2006) 5 Competition Law Journal 169.

[475] See 'Duty to make references: completed mergers', pp 913–918 above.

[476] Case No 1150/4/8/10 *CTS Eventim AG v Competition Commission* [2010] CAT 7, [2010] CompAR 221; the CAT also gave a ruling on costs in this case: [2010] CAT 8, [2010] CompAR 224.

and a second clearance decision in May 2010[477]. The CAT accepted the argument that the CC's choice of counterfactual was unreasonable and unsupported by the evidence in the case of *Stagecoach/Preston Bus*[478].

The OFT's decision in *Cooperative Group/Fairways Group* has been dealt with in the discussion of undertakings in lieu of a reference[479] and the CC's suggested remedy in *Somerfield/Morrisons* was discussed in the section on divestiture remedies[480]. The appeals by BSkyB and Virgin Media against the decisions of the CC and the Secretary of State in *BSkyB plc/ITV plc* will be discussed in the section on public interest cases[481], as will the challenge to the Secretary of State's decision not to refer *LloydsTSB/HBOS*. Two further cases, *Federation of Wholesale Distributors v OFT*[482] and *Stericycle v Competition Commission*[483], did not proceed to final judgment. The CAT rejected an application by Morrisons for interim relief against the CC's decision to approve Sainsbury's as the purchaser of a site that Tesco was required to divest by the decision in *Tesco/Co-op Store*[484].

When the OFT asked for costs against the unsuccessful applicant in *Celesio v OFT* the OFT suggested that where a horizontal competitor (as opposed, for example, to a customer) brings a challenge to the non-referral of a merger, that applicant should bear the risk of failure in costs; however the CAT declined to accept this suggestion, saying only that each case depends on its own circumstances[485]. In the *Celesio* case itself the CAT did not award costs against the unsuccessful applicant since it had not been able to understand the OFT's decision without the witness statement by the OFT's director of mergers produced for the purposes of the appeal[486].

8. The Merger Provisions in Practice

The merger provisions of the Enterprise Act entered into force on 20 June 2003. The following Table contains a list of mergers referred by the OFT to the CC since the sixth edition of this book was published in 2008 in which the investigations were completed by 20 June 2011. A list of all cases referred to the CC since the Enterprise Act entered into force in 2003 will be found at the Online Resource Centre that accompanies this book[487].

A number of interesting points that emerge from the cases referred by the OFT to the CC will be discussed in the text that follows.

---

[477] www.competition-commission.org.uk.

[478] Case No 1145/4/8/09 *Stagecoach Group plc Competition Commission* [2010] CAT 14, [2010] CompAR 267.

[479] See 'Undertakings in lieu of a reference', pp 927–928 above.

[480] See 'Acquisitions and divisions', p 946 above.

[481] See 'Public interest cases', pp 956–958 below.   [482] Case No 1030/4/1/04.

[483] Case No 1075/4/8/07.

[484] Case No 1144/4/8/09 (IR) *WM Morrison Supermarkets Plc v Competition Commission* [2009] CAT 33, [2010] CompAR 191.

[485] Case No 1059/4/1/06 *Celesio AG v OFT* [2006] CAT 20, [2007] CompAR 269, para 47; in the US the Supreme Court ruled in *Cargill, Inc v Monfort of Colorado, Inc* 479 US 104 (1986), that an antitrust plaintiff seeking injunctive relief in a merger case must 'allege and ultimately prove that it would suffer threatened loss or damage constituting an antitrust injury', which is 'injury of the type the antitrust laws were intended to prevent and that flows from that which makes defendants' acts unlawful'.

[486] Case No 1059/4/1/06 *Celesio AG v OFT* [2006] CAT 20, [2007] CompAR 269, para 50.

[487] See www.oxfordtextbooks.co.uk/orc/whishandbailey7e.

Table 22.1 Merger references to the Competition Commission under the Enterprise Act 2002

Title	Date of reference	Date of publication	Finding of substantial lessening of competition?	Remedy
BOC Ltd/Ineos Chlor ltd	29 May 2008	18 December 2008	Yes	Prohibition
Project 'Kangaroo'	30 June 2008	4 February 2009	Yes	Behavioural remedies
Nufarm/AH Marks **NB: completed merger**	29 August 08	10 February 2009	Yes	Behavioural remedies to facilitate entry
Hospedia/Premier **NB: abandoned by the parties**	7 October 2008			
Long Clawson/Millway **NB: completed merger**	8 October 2008	14 January 2009	No	
Capita/IBS **NB: completed merger**	19 November 2008	4 June 2009	Yes	Divestiture required
Holland & Barrett/Julan Graves **NB: completed merger**	20 March 2009	20 August 2009	No	
Stagecoach/Eastbourne Buses Ltd **NB: completed merger**	13 May 2009	22 October 2009	No	
Stagecoach Bus Holdings Ltd/ Preston Bus Ltd **NB: completed merger**	28 May 2009	11 November 2009	Yes	Divestiture required NB: CAT judgment of 21 May 2010[1] finding irrationality on the part of the CC
Ticketmaster/Live Nation	10 June 2009	22 December 2009 Second decision of 7 May 2010	No No	NB: CAT judgment of 11 February 2010 setting the decision aside[2]

Title	Date of reference	Date of publication	Finding of substantial lessening of competition?	Remedy
Sport Direct/JJB Stores NB: completed merger	7 August 2009	16 March 2010	No	On appeal to the CAT by a third party[3]; the CC then withdrew the procedural decision under appeal
Contract Rights Renewal	29 May 2009	Consultation on possible amendments to the undertakings given following the Carlton/ Granada investigation	Final decision 12 May 2010 Final undertakings accepted 17 September 2010	
RMIG Ltd/Ash&Lacy Perforators ltd NB: abandoned by the parties	26 August 2009			
Brightsolid Group Ltd/Friends Reunited Holdings Ltd	2 November 2009	18 March 2010	No	
Getty Images Inc/Rex Features Ltd NB: abandoned by the parties	8 July 2010			
Zipcar Inc/Streetcar Ltd NB: completed merger	10 August 2010	22 December 2010	No	
Dorf Ketal Chemicals AG (Dorf)Johnson Matthey plc NB: abandoned by the parties	19 November 2010			
MBL/Trigold Crystal NB: abandoned by the parties	17 March 2011			

---

[1] Case No 1145/4/8/09 *Stagecoach Group Plc v Competition Commission* [2010] CAT 14, [2010] CompAR 276.
[2] Case No 1150/4/8/10 *CTS Eventim AG v Competition Commission* [2010] CAT 7, [2010] CompAR 221.
[3] Note Case No 1116/4/8/09 *Sports Direct International Plc v Competition Commission* [2009] CAT 32, [2010] CompAR 175.

(A) **Basic statistical analysis**

Eighty mergers had been referred by the OFT to the CC by 20 June 2011. The largest number of references in one complete year was 17 in 2005; the smallest was five in 2010.

(B) **Abandoned mergers**

As the Table above demonstrates, quite a few mergers that are referred to the CC are then abandoned by the parties. This occurred in 22 cases out of the total of 80. There are various possible explanations for this. One is that the parties may consider that it is too expensive, in terms of professional fees, to undergo an in-depth investigation by the CC, especially where the value of the business acquired is fairly small. The concern that too many 'small' mergers could be referred to the CC led to the OFT revising its *de minimis* guidance[488].

Another explanation for the abandonment of a merger might be that the parties realise that there is such a strong likelihood that the outcome of the investigation will be substantial remedies, or even an outright prohibition, that it is not worth continuing with the transaction. A third explanation for some abandonments is that an acquisition agreement may have been conditional on the merger not being referred to the CC.

(C) **Completed mergers**

It is noticeable that a significant percentage of mergers referred to the CC were completed ones: a total of 35 out of 80 or, in percentage terms, 43.75 per cent. The UK system does not require pre-notification of mergers, and the parties are perfectly entitled to complete a transaction without prior clearance, although they need to be aware of the risks of doing so. The OFT and the CC will take care, in the case of a completed merger, to ensure that there is no further intermingling of assets once the matter has come to their attention and become the subject of an investigation[489].

It is important to note that in several cases of completed mergers the CC required substantial remedies, including, in some, the total reversal of a transaction.

(i) **Full unscrambling**

In *Emap/ABI*, *Stonegate/Deans*, *Thermo/GVI*, *Tesco/Co-op Store* and *Stagecoach/Preston Bus* the transactions had to be fully unscrambled.

(ii) **Substantial unscrambling**

In *EWS/Marcroft*, *Stagecoach/Scottish Citylink*, *Somerfield/Morrisons*, *Stericycle/STG* and *Capita/IBS* the CC required significant unscrambling of the transaction.

(iii) **Slight unscrambling**

In some cases the remedy required was quite limited: for example in *Vue Entertainment Holdings (UK) Ltd/A3 Cinema Ltd* the CC required Vue Entertainment Holdings to divest itself of one of the two cinemas that it operated in the town of Basingstoke to a cinema operator with the resources, expertise, incentive and business plan to operate it as a multiplex cinema showing mainstream films[490].

---

[488] See 'Markets of insufficient importance', pp 915–916 above.
[489] See 'Initial undertakings and orders', pp 941–942 above.
[490] See the Final Report, paras 7.19–7.72, available at www.competition-commission.org.uk.

(D) The number of findings of an SLC

The CC found an SLC in 26 out of the 80 mergers to have been investigated by 20 June 2011.

(E) The number of outright prohibitions

There have been some cases in which a merger was prohibited in its entirety. The completed mergers in section A have already been referred to. The first occasion on which the CC prohibited an anticipated merger in its entirety was in *Knauf Insulation Ltd/Superglass Insulation Ltd*; the CC rejected various remedies suggested by Knauf to address concerns over its ability, after the merger, to raise prices, including a proposal for a system of price control or for the monitoring of prices by the OFT[491]. The second merger to be blocked was *BOC/Ineos Chlor* as it would have led to higher prices and/or lower service levels than would otherwise be the case in the markets for the distribution of packaged chlorine[492]. In *BBC Worldwide/Channel 4/ITV* the CC blocked a joint venture that would lead to an SLC in the supply of UK TV video on demand content at both the wholesale and retail levels; the CC consulted on a number of remedy options but concluded that prohibition would be the only effective and proportionate remedy[493].

(F) Relationship with Article 102

In *Railway Investments Ltd/Marcroft Holdings Ltd*[494] the CC was concerned that English Welsh & Scottish Railways, the owner of Railway Investments, would be able either to reduce service quality or raise prices in the market for rail freight haulage services. EW&S argued that the behaviour that the CC feared might occur would entail an infringement of Article 102 TFEU and/or the Chapter II prohibition of the Competition Act, and that the sanctions associated with those provisions would deter it from behaving in that way. The CC concluded that the deterrent effect of the prohibitions was too uncertain to counteract the incentives to indulge in the behaviour predicted[495].

(G) Evaluation of the value of the CC's actions[496]

Every year since 2006 the CC has published a document on its website in which it estimates the value to UK consumers of its work[497]. The CC reviews the mergers in which it took remedial action in the previous year and then estimates the total costs to consumers if it had not taken action. In 2009 the CC revised its methodology in order to quantify the benefits it expects to flow to consumers rather than the detriment that has been identified as resulting from the SLC. The CC estimated that a three-year rolling average of consumer benefits from its remedies for merger inquiries that resulted in an SLC finding between 2007/08 and 2009/10 was £205 million. The OFT estimated that, over the same period, the OFT had avoided detriment to consumers of £106 million by accepting undertakings in lieu of a reference, so that the merger system as a whole had saved consumers £310 million.

---

[491] See the Final Report, paras 9.1–9.21, www.competition-commission.org.uk.
[492] See the Final Report, paras 10.1 and 11.14–11.16, available at www.competition-commission.org.uk.
[493] See the Final Report, paras 5.4–5.92, available at www.competition-commission.org.uk.
[494] See www.competition-commission.org.uk.
[495] See www.competition-commission.org.uk, paras 7.114–7.126.
[496] See also the OFT's *Consumer savings from merger control* OFT 917, April 2007, available at www.oft.gov.uk.
[497] www.competition-commission.org.uk.

9. 'Public Interest Cases', 'Other Special Cases' and Mergers in the Water Industry

(A) Public interest cases[498]

A key feature of the merger provisions in the Enterprise Act is that the Secretary of State should not be involved in individual cases, and that decisions should be taken by the OFT and the CC: competition analysis in normal merger cases should be carried out by specialist competition authorities[499]. However there may be situations in which the investigation of a merger may be justifiable on grounds of a wider public interest than its detrimental effect on competition: Article 21(4) of the EUMR recognises that Member States may have a 'legitimate interest' in investigating a merger other than for reasons of competition[500], and the Act makes provision for the issue of a European intervention notice in such cases. Chapters 2 and 3 of Part 3 of the Enterprise Act provide for the investigation of mergers in 'public interest cases' and 'other special cases' respectively. Such cases will be rare, and the provisions are deliberately drafted narrowly; they will be described here only briefly.

Chapter 2 of Part 3 of the Act consists of sections 42 to 58, which deal with public interest cases. The Secretary of State may give an 'intervention notice' to the OFT if he believes that one or more public interest considerations are relevant to a consideration of a relevant merger situation[501]. Section 58(1) of the Enterprise Act specifies national security as a public interest consideration: it is given the same meaning as in Article 21(4) of the EUMR[502]. Section 375 of the Communications Act 2003[503] adds several additional 'media public interest considerations' to section 58 of the Enterprise Act: the need for accurate presentation of news and free expression of opinion in newspapers[504]; the need for a sufficient plurality of views in newspapers in each market for newspapers in the UK[505]; the need for plurality of media ownership[506]; the need for a wide range of high-quality broadcasting, appealing to a wide variety of tastes and interests[507]; and the need for media owners to be committed to the objectives set out in section 319 of the Communications Act. In May 2004 the Department of Trade and Industry published a helpful Guidance document, *Enterprise Act 2002, Public Interest Intervention in Media Mergers*[508]. The Secretary of State is given power to add a new

---

[498] See the OFT's *Mergers: Jurisdictional and procedural guidance*, ch 9 and the OFT/CC *Merger Assessment Guidelines*, Part 6; see further McElwee 'Politics and the UK Merger Control Process: The Public Interest Exceptions and Other Collision Points' (2010) 9(1) Competition Law Journal 77.

[499] See DTI White Paper on *Productivity and Enterprise: A World Class Competition Regime* Cm 5233, (2001), para 5.23.

[500] See ch 21, 'Article 21(4): legitimate interest clause', pp 851–854.

[501] Enterprise Act 2002, s 42(2).

[502] Ibid, s 58(1) and (2).

[503] Note that s 373 of the Communications Act 2003 repeals the provisions in the Fair Trading Act 1973 that subjected newspaper mergers to a special regime; on the current law see Pryor 'The New Regime for the Regulation of Newspaper Mergers' (2003) 4 Competition Law Journal 63.

[504] Enterprise Act 2002, s 58(2A), as added by s 375 of the Communications Act 2003.

[505] Ibid, s 58(2B).

[506] Ibid, s 58(2C)(a).

[507] Ibid, s 58(2C)(b).

[508] Available at www.culture.gov.uk.

public interest consideration to section 58 of the Enterprise Act by statutory instrument, but this would require the approval of Parliament[509]. This was exercised by the Enterprise Act 2002 (Specification of Additional Section 58 Consideration) Order 2008[510] in order to add 'the interest of maintaining the stability of the UK financial system'.

Where an intervention notice has been given the OFT will give a report to the Secretary of State dealing with both the competition and the public interest considerations; in the case of a media merger the Office of Communications ('OFCOM') will also report on the media public interest considerations[511]. Following a review of the local and regional media regime[512] the OFT agreed a *Memorandum of Understanding* with OFCOM on the use of local media assessments in local media mergers[513]. The Secretary of State then has power to make a reference to the CC[514]; in exercising this discretion the Secretary of State is bound by the OFT's findings as to competition: his intervention is permitted only on public interest grounds[515].

The CC must decide whether a relevant merger situation has been created[516]; it must also report on any competition issues and on admissible public interest considerations, as well as possible remedies[517]. The CC's report must be given to the Secretary of State[518], and must contain its decisions on the questions it is required to answer together with reasons for those decisions[519]. As a general proposition the CC must report to the Secretary of State within 24 weeks of the reference, although in certain circumstances the period may be shorter or longer[520]. Where a 'new' public interest consideration is raised, requiring the approval of Parliament, there are restrictions on the action that can be taken if the public interest is not 'finalised' within 24 weeks of the serving of the intervention notice[521]. At the end of an investigation of a merger under the public interest provisions section 54 gives the Secretary of State power to make an 'adverse public interest finding'[522] within 30 days of receipt of the report from the CC[523]. The Secretary of State is not entitled to diverge from the finding of the CC on the competition issues[524]. Enforcement powers are conferred upon the Secretary of State to accept undertakings or to make orders to remedy, mitigate or prevent any of the effects adverse to the public interest which have resulted from, or may result from, the creation of any relevant merger situation. The powers available are set out in Schedule 7 to the Act[525], and include the ability to order anything permitted by Schedule 8[526]; paragraph 20 of Schedule 8 enables action to be taken in the interests of national security, and paragraphs 20A[527] and 20B[528] enable appropriate action to be taken following investigations of media mergers and mergers affecting the stability of the UK financial system respectively. Provision is made for cases to revert to the competition authorities where an intervention notice ceases to have effect, either because the Secretary of State decides that a public interest consideration should not be

---

[509] Enterprise Act 2002, s 58(3) and (4).

[510] SI 2008/2645, inserting s 58(2D) Enterprise Act 2002.

[511] Ibid, s 44, as amended by ss 376 and 377 Communications Act 2003.

[512] OFT 1091, June 2009, available at www.oft.gov.uk.

[513] 26 November 2010, available at www.oft.gov.uk; see also the OFT's *Jurisidictional and procedural guidance*, para 6.15 and OFCOM's *Local Media Assessment Guidance*, 1 December 2010, available at www.ofcom.org.uk.

[514] Enterprise Act 2002, s 45.   [515] Ibid, s 46(2).   [516] Ibid, s 47(1).

[517] Ibid, s 47(2)–(11).   [518] Ibid, s 50(1).   [519] Ibid, s 50(2).

[520] Ibid, s 51; see also s 52.   [521] Ibid, s 53.   [522] Ibid, s 54(2).

[523] Ibid, s 54(5).   [524] Ibid, s 54(7).   [525] Ibid, s 55(2).

[526] See 'Schedule 8 to the Enterprise Act', p 945 above.

[527] Inserted by s 389 of the Communications Act 2003.

[528] Inserted by para 4 of the Enterprise Act 2002 (Specification of Additional Section 58 Consideration) Order 2008, SI 2008/2645.

taken into account, or because parliamentary approval for a public interest consideration is not given[529]. The OFT has a function of advising the Secretary of State on mergers that might raise public interest considerations[530], and the OFT and CC must bring to his attention any representations about the exercise of his powers as to what constitutes a public interest consideration[531].

By 20 June 2011 two intervention notices have been issued under the public interest provisions (as opposed to the 'special' public interest provisions discussed below), *BSkyB/ITV* and *LloydsTSB/HBOS*. In the case of the acquisition by BSkyB of 17.9 per cent of the shares of ITV plc the Secretary of State issued an intervention notice on 26 February 2007[532]. A reference was made to the CC which considered that the acquisition would give rise to an SLC; however it did not consider that the acquisition endangered the plurality of the media[533]. The Secretary of State decided in January 2008 that BSkyB should reduce its shareholding in ITV to below 7.5 per cent[534]. On appeal the CAT dismissed BSkyB's application for review of the CC's assessment of the acquisition and its finding of an SLC, but upheld Virgin Media's challenge to the CC's interpretation of the media plurality provisions[535]. The Court of Appeal rejected a further appeal by BSkyB on the competition points, but allowed its appeal, and that of the Commission and the Secretary of State, on the media plurality point[536]. The Court of Appeal judgment contains valuable guidance on the media plurality provisions[537]. On 8 February 2010 the Secretary of State accepted final undertakings from BSkyB.

The second case, *LloydsTSB/HBOS*, arose against the background of exceptional instability in global financial markets. The Secretary of State issued an intervention notice in September 2008[538]; he subsequently decided not to refer the merger to the CC[539]. The CAT dismissed an application for review of the Secretary of State's decision[540].

(B) Other special cases

Chapter 3 of Part 3 of the Act consists of sections 59 to 70, which deal with 'other special cases'.

(i) 'Special public interest cases'

Sections 59 to 66 are concerned with an exceptional category of mergers that may be referred for investigation on public interest grounds, even though they do not meet either the turnover or the share of supply thresholds for reference contained in section 23 of the Act[541]. Two types of merger may be considered under the 'special public interest' provisions.

---

[529] Enterprise Act 2002, s 56.

[530] Ibid, s 57(1).   [531] Ibid, s 57(2).

[532] www.culture.gov.uk.

[533] See www.competition-commission.org.uk.

[534] See www.culture.gov.uk.

[535] Case Nos 1095/4/8/08 and 1096/4/8/08 *British Sky Broadcasting Group plc v Competition Commission and the Secretary of State for Business, Enterprise and Regulatory Reform* [2008] CAT 25, [2008] CompAR 223; the CAT also dismissed the appellants' mirror image challenges to the partial divestiture remedy.

[536] *British Sky Broadcasting Group plc v Competition Commission* [2010] EWCA Civ 2, [2010] UKCLR 351.

[537] Ibid, paras 78–123.

[538] The relevant public interest consideration, the stability of the UK financial system, was created by the Enterprise Act 2002 (Specification of Additional Section 58 Consideration) Order 2008, SI 2008/2645.

[539] See www.bis.gov.uk; see also the OFT's *Report to the Secretary of State on anticipated acquisition by Lloyds TSB plc of HBOS plc*, 24 October 2008, available at www.oft.gov.uk.

[540] Case No 1107/4/10/08 *Merger Action Group v Secretary of State for Business, Enterprise and Regulatory Reform* [2008] CAT 36, [2009] CompAR 133.

[541] See 'The turnover test', p 921 above.

The first is mergers involving certain government contractors or sub-contractors who may hold or receive confidential information or material relating to defence; the second type is certain mergers in the newspaper and broadcasting sectors that do not qualify for investigation under the general merger rules because they fall below the turnover or share of supply tests[542]. Such cases are not scrutinised on competition grounds, but against public interest considerations only. In such cases the Secretary of State serves a 'special intervention notice'[543]. The OFT will then conduct an initial investigation and give a report to the Secretary of State[544]; in media cases OFCOM will report on the media public interest considerations. The Secretary of State has power to refer the matter to the CC[545], but must accept the OFT's decision as to whether a special merger situation has been created[546]. The CC will then investigate the matter and report to the Secretary of State[547]; he has power to take enforcement action[548], but must accept the view of the CC as to whether a special merger situation has been created or may be expected[549]. The Secretary of State has similar enforcement powers to those in public interest cases[550].

There have been two cases under these provisions. In the first, *Insys Group Ltd/ Lockheed Martin UK Ltd*, the Secretary of State issued a special intervention notice in August 2005; he subsequently accepted undertakings in lieu of a reference to the CC[551]. The Secretary of State also issued, in May 2009, a special intervention notice in the case of *Altas Elektronik UK Ltd/QinetiQ*; that case was also settled by undertakings in lieu of a reference[552].

(ii) European mergers

Where a merger has been completed or is in contemplation which has a Community dimension under the EUMR but which gives rise to a public interest consideration the Secretary of State may give a 'European intervention notice' to the OFT[553], and has power to make an order to provide for the taking of action to remedy, mitigate or prevent effects adverse to the public interest which have resulted from, or may be expected to result from, the creation of the merger[554]. This provides a legal basis to proceed against mergers in relation to which the UK asserts a 'legitimate interest' under Article 21(4) of the EUMR[555]. Further provision is made in relation to European merger cases by the Enterprise Act (Protection of Legitimate Interests) Order 2003[556].

European intervention notices have been issued on five occasions. The first four cases were settled on the basis of undertakings accepted by the Secretary of State to safeguard UK national security[557]. The fifth European intervention notice was issued by the Secretary of State on 4 November 2010 in relation to News Corp's proposed acquisition

---

[542] Sections 378–380 Communications Act 2003, amending ss 59 and 61 of the Enterprise Act 2002.
[543] Enterprise Act 2002, s 59.   [544] Ibid, s 61.   [545] Ibid, s 62.
[546] Ibid, s 62(5).   [547] Ibid, ss 63 and 65.   [548] Ibid, s 66.   [549] Ibid, s 66(4).
[550] Ibid, Sch 7, paras 9 and 11.
[551] See   www.bis.gov.uk/policies/business-law/competition-matters/mergers/mergers-with-a-public-interest/national-security-mergers.
[552] Ibid.   [553] Enterprise Act 2002, s 67.   [554] Ibid, s 68.
[555] On Article 21(4) of the EUMR, see ch 21, 'Article 21(4): legitimate interest clause', pp 851–854.
[556] SI 2003/1592.
[557] See ch 22, n 551; note that the same website contains details of similar undertakings (and variations of undertakings) given under the now-repealed provisions of the Fair Trading Act 1973: see eg *British Aerospace plc/General Electric Company plc* where the undertakings were varied in 2007.

of the shares in BSkyB that it does not already own[558]; however, following considerable controversy, News Corp abandoned its proposal in July 2011[559].

(C) Mergers in the water industry[560]

The Water Industry Act 1991, as amended by section 70 of the Enterprise Act 2002, contains special rules for mergers between water enterprises in England and Wales. The relevant provisions are sections 32 to 35 of the Water Industry Act, as substituted by section 70 of the Enterprise Act 2002; these provisions must be read in conjunction with Schedule 4ZA to the 1991 Act, as inserted by Schedule 6 to the 2002 Act. The purpose behind this special regime is to ensure that mergers do not adversely affect the ability of the Water Services Regulation Authority (OFWAT) to carry out its regulatory functions effectively by reducing the number of companies whose performances can be compared: OFWAT should be able to make use of 'comparative' or 'yardstick' competition. The provisions inserted by the Enterprise Act align the special arrangements for assessing water mergers with the general mergers regime. Two changes in particular should be noted. First, a turnover test is used to determine whether a reference should be made: the threshold was formerly based on the value of the assets acquired. Secondly, the OFT and the CC are responsible for water mergers; the Secretary of State is not involved.

Under the Water Industry Act, as amended, mergers between water enterprises in England and Wales are subject to a mandatory reference by the OFT to the CC[561], unless the turnover of one or both of the enterprises is less than £10 million[562]. The CC must determine whether a water merger would prejudice the ability of OFWAT to make comparisons between water enterprises[563]. Part 3 of the Enterprise Act applies to water mergers, subject to any modifications that the Secretary of State might make by regulation: thus the powers that the OFT and the CC have in relation to mergers generally also apply in the case of water mergers[564]. The CC has published *Water Merger References: Competition Commission Guidelines* explaining its approach to mergers subject to these provisions[565].

There had been one reference to the CC of a water merger under these provisions by 20 June 2011, *Mid-Kent Water/South-East Water*[566]. The CC concluded that there was a possibility that OFWAT's ability to carry out comparisons might be prejudiced, but only to a limited degree; and the CC was satisfied in this case that the merger would generate customer benefits[567]. The CC required the merging parties to make a one-off price reduction to their customers totalling £4 million[568].

[558] See www.culture.gov.uk; on 21 December 2010 the European Commission had cleared the merger unconditionally under the EUMR: Case COMP/M.5932.

[559] See Competition Commission News Release 41/11, 25 July 2011.

[560] See further Weir 'Comparative Competition and the Regulation of Mergers in the Water Industry of England and Wales' (2000) XLV Antitrust Bulletin 811; Barnes 'Holding Back the Flow: Do the UK Water Merger Control Rules Risk Dampening Investment in the Sector?' (2007) 1 European Business Law Journal, 205.

[561] Water Industry Act 1991, s 32.   [562] Ibid, s 33(1).

[563] Ibid, Sch 4ZA, as inserted by Enterprise Act 2002, Sch 6; these provisions must be read in conjunction with the Water Mergers (Modification of Enactments) Regulations 2004, SI 2004/3202 and the Water Mergers (Determination of Turnover) Regulations 2004, SI 2004/3206.

[564] Ibid, Sch 4ZA, paras 1, 2 and 4(3).

[565] CC9, December 2004; see further OFT's *Mergers – Jurisdictional and procedural guidance*, paras 10.1–10.3.

[566] See www.competition-commission.org.uk.

[567] See the Final Report, paras 8.108–8.160.

[568] Note that the CC investigated eight mergers under the Water Industry Act 1991 prior to its amendment by the Enterprise Act 2002, three of which were prohibited outright: see *General Utilities plc/Colne Valley Water Company/Rickmansworth Water Co* Cm 1929 (1990); *General Utilities plc/Mid Kent Water Co* Cm 1125 (1990); *Southern Water plc/Mid Sussex Water Co* Cm 1126 (1990); *Lyonnaise des Eaux SA/*

Where a merger does not involve one water company acquiring another it will be subject to the general merger rules. In such a case the OFT will look to OFWAT for advice on those aspects of the offer which will impact upon its ability to regulate the water undertakings or which might impact upon its wider ability to regulate other licensed providers of water and sewerage services.

In April 2009 the Government published a report, *Independent Review of Competition and Innovation in Water Markets*[569]; among its recommendations were changes to the special regime for water mergers. It is expected that a Government White Paper on these (and other) matters will be published in late 2011.

Northumbrian Water Group plc Cm 2936 (1995); *Wessex Water plc/South West Water* Cm 3430 (1996) (prohibited outright); *Severn Trent plc/South West Water* Cm 3429 (1996) (prohibited outright); *Mid Kent Holdings and General Utilities/SAUR Water Services* Cm 3514 (1997) (prohibited outright); *Vivendi Water UL plc/First Aqua (JVCo) Ltd* Cm 5681 (2002).

[569] Available at www.archive.defra.gov.uk.

23

Particular sectors

1. Introduction

The final chapter of this book will deal with three issues. First it will examine those sectors of the economy that are wholly or partly excluded from EU competition law, namely nuclear energy, military equipment and agriculture; the special regime for coal and steel products under the ECSC Treaty, now expired, is briefly referred to. Secondly, it will describe how the EU competition rules apply to the transport sector. Finally the chapter will look at the specific circumstances of so-called 'regulated industries' such as electronic communications, post and energy markets and the way in which EU and UK competition law apply to them. Constraints of space mean that these matters can be described only in outline; references to specialised literature on the application of competition law to particular sectors will be provided where appropriate.

2. Nuclear Energy[1]

The Treaty establishing the European Atomic Energy Community ('Euratom') deals with agreements regulating the supply and price of various nuclear materials. Articles 101 and 102 are capable of application to agreements and to the abuse of a dominant position to the extent that the Euratom Treaty is not applicable[2]. In its decisions under Article 101(3)

---

[1] See further Faull and Nikpay *The EC Law of Competition* (Oxford University Press, 2nd ed, 2007), paras 12.12–12.16; Bellamy and Child *European Community Law of Competition* (Oxford University Press, 6th ed, 2008, eds Roth and Rose), ch 12, Part 3; Cusack 'A Tale of Two Treaties: An Assessment of the Euratom Treaty in Relation to the EC Treaty' (2003) 40 CML Rev 117.

[2] For example the Commission opened an investigation in June 2010 into whether non-compete clauses in agreements between Areva and Siemens in respect of civil nuclear technology infringe Article 101: see Commission Press Release IP/10/655, 2 June 2010.

the Commission has tended to adopt a sympathetic attitude towards cooperation agreements in the nuclear industry[3].

3. Military Equipment[4]

Article 346(1)(b) TFEU provides that a Member State may take such measures as it thinks necessary for the protection of the essential interests of its security which are connected with the production of or trade in arms, ammunitions and war materials; however these measures must not adversely affect the conditions of competition in the internal market regarding products which are not intended specifically for military purposes. The Council of Ministers has drawn up a list of the products to which Article 346(1) applies, although it has not been published; Article 346(2) provides that the Council may, acting unanimously on a proposal from the Commission, amend this list. There have been some concentrations in which the Commission's jurisdiction to apply the EU Merger Regulation ('the EUMR') was limited as a result of the operation of Article 346[5].

4. Agriculture[6]

Articles 38 to 44 TFEU subject agriculture to a special regime with its own philosophy[7]. Article 42 provides that 'the rules on competition shall apply to production of and trade in agricultural products only to the extent determined by the European Parliament and the Council'. The Commission has published a number of policy documents on competition policy and agriculture which are available on its website[8].

(A) Council Regulations 1184/2006 and 1234/2007

Article 1 of Regulation 1184/2006[9], which replaced Regulation 26 of 1962, provides that Articles 101 and 102 shall apply to the production of or trade in the products listed in Annex I to the TFEU except for those covered by Regulation 1234/2007[10], subject to the derogations set

---

[3] See eg *United Reprocessors GmbH* OJ [1976] L 51/7, [1976] 2 CMLR D1; *KEWA* OJ [1976] L 51/15, [1976] 2 CMLR D15; *GEC/Weir* OJ [1977] L 327/26, [1978] 1 CMLR D42; *Amersham International and Buchler GmbH Venture* OJ [1982] L 314/34, [1983] 1 CMLR 619; *Scottish Nuclear, Nuclear Energy Agreement* OJ [1991] L 178/31.

[4] See further Faull and Nikpay *The EC Law of Competition* (Oxford University Press, 2nd ed, 2007), paras 3.05–3.11; Bellamy and Child *European Community Law of Competition* (Oxford University Press, 6th ed, 2008, eds Roth and Rose), paras 11.057–11.059.

[5] See ch 21, 'Defence', p 855.

[6] See further Bellamy and Child *European Community Law of Competition* (Oxford University Press, 6th ed, 2008, eds Roth and Rose), paras 12.194–12.209; see also DG COMP's Staff Working Paper 'The interface between EU competition policy and the Common Agricultural Policy', February 2010, available at www.ec.europa.eu/competition/sectors/agriculture/working_paper_dairy.pdf.

[7] On agricultural policy in the EU see *Agricultural Law of the European Union* (Academy of European Law, Trier and Irish Centre for European Law, Trinity College Dublin, 1999, eds Heusel and Collins); Ackrill *The Common Agricultural Policy* (Sheffield Academic Press, 2000); Usher *EC Agricultural Law* (Oxford University Press, 2nd ed, 2002); Cardwell *The European Model of Agriculture* (Oxford University Press, 2004); McMahon *EU Agricultural Law* (Oxford University Press, 2007).

[8] See www.ec.europa.eu/competition/sectors/agriculture/overview_en.html.

[9] OJ [2006] L 214/7.

[10] OJ [2007] L 299/1.

out in Article 2. Article 2 provides that Article 101(1) shall *not* apply to agreements that form an integral part of a national market organisation or that are necessary for the attainment of the objectives set out in Article 39 TFEU[11]. These derogations are strictly construed, and the Commission must give adequate reasons in the event that it allows such a derogation[12]. The derogations provided for in Article 2 of Regulation 1184/2006 relate only to the application of Article 101; the Chapter I prohibition of the UK Competition Act 1998 does not apply where there is a derogation from Article 101 in relation to agricultural products[13]. There is no derogation from the application of Article 102 to the agricultural sector.

Regulation 1234/2007 establishes a common organisation of agricultural markets for a number of sectors included in Annex I to the TFEU; it adopts the same approach as Regulation 1184/2006 to the application of the competition rules in those sectors[14].

The monopoly powers of the Milk Marketing Board in the UK were the subject of various proceedings in the civil courts under Article 102[15]. Subsequently the Monopolies and Mergers Commission (now the Competition Commission) conducted an investigation under the now-repealed monopoly provisions of the Fair Trading Act 1973[16] which led to Milk Marque, a successor to some of the assets of the Milk Marketing Board, being voluntarily split into three separate companies; the Secretary of State asked the Office of Fair Trading ('the OFT') to continue to monitor the situation[17]. Following the Commission's report an Article 267 reference was made by the High Court to the Court of Justice on the relationship between national competition law and the EU rules on the agricultural sector[18]. The Court concluded that the existence of specific EU rules did not deprive national competition authorities of their right to apply national law to a milk producers' cooperative in a powerful position on the market; however they should refrain from any measure which might undermine or create exceptions to the common organisation of the market in milk or compromise the objectives of the common agricultural policy.

(B) **Annex I products**

If a product is *not* mentioned in Annex I of the TFEU, it cannot benefit from the derogations provided by Article 2 of Regulation 1184/2006. In *Coöperative Stremsel-en Kleurselfabriek v Commission*[19] the Court of Justice held that, as rennet was not specifically mentioned in Annex I, it was fully subject to the competition rules; the fact that rennet was used in the production of cheese, which is itself listed in the Annex, did not provide it with immunity from the application of Article 101(1). In *Pabst and Ricbarz/*

---

[11] On Article 39 see 'The second derogation: common market organisations', pp 966–967 below. Article 2 contains a sentence dealing with the activities of farmers' associations; this is not a further exception, but rather an embellishment of the policy expressed in that provision: see *Milchförderungsfonds* OJ [1985] L 35/35, [1985] 3 CMLR 101, paras 21–22; *Bloemenveilingen Aalsmeer* OJ [1988] L 262/27, [1989] 4 CMLR 500, paras 150–152.

[12] See Cases T-70/92 and T-71/92 *Florimex v Commission* [1997] ECR II-697, [1997] 5 CMLR 769, upheld on appeal Case C-265/97 P *VBA and Florimex v Commission* [2000] ECR I-2061, [2001] 5 CMLR 1343; see also Case T-77/94 *Vereniging van Groothandelaren v Commission* [1997] ECR II-759, [1997] 5 CMLR 812, upheld on appeal Case C-266/97 P *VBA and Florimex v Commission* [2000] ECR I-2135.

[13] Competition Act 1998, Sch 3, para 9.

[14] OJ [2007] L 299/1, Articles 175–176 and recital 83.

[15] See *Garden Cottage Foods v Milk Marketing Board* [1984] AC 130, [1983] 2 All ER 770; *An Bord Bainne Cooperative Ltd v Milk Marketing Board* [1984] 1 CMLR 519; affd [1984] 2 CMLR 584.

[16] *The Supply in Great Britain of Raw Cow's Milk* Cm 4286 (1999).

[17] DTI Press Release P/99/895, 5 November 1999; see also DTI Press Release P/2000/304, 2 May 2000.

[18] Case C-137/00 *R v Monopolies and Mergers Commission and the Secretary of State for Trade and Industry, ex p Milk Marque Ltd* [2003] ECR I-7975, [2004] 4 CMLR 293.

[19] Case 61/80 [1981] ECR 851, [1982] 1 CMLR 240.

BNIA[20] the Commission applied Article 101 to the French trade association responsible for armagnac, pointing out that, as this product did not appear in Annex I, it was to be treated as an industrial product. In *BNIC v Clair*[21] the Court of Justice held, for the same reason, that cognac was an industrial product and rejected an argument that it should be treated in a special way because of its importance to the economic welfare of a particular region of France.

In *BNIC v Yves Aubert*[22] the Court of Justice had to deal with the application of the competition rules to a demand by BNIC for a levy claimed against a wine grower for having exceeded a marketing quota. One issue was whether the competition rules could be applied to brandy. The Court, having observed that brandies are not listed in Annex I and so are industrial rather than agricultural products, added that the fact that some of the proceeds of levies raised by BNIC were intended for measures on wine and must, which do appear in Annex I, did not affect the application of Article 101(1). In *Dansk Pelsdyravlerforening v Commission*[23] the General Court rejected a claim that animal furs should be treated as an agricultural product; in *Gøttrup-Klim Grovvareforeninger v Dansk Landburgs Grovvareselskab AmbA*[24] the Court of Justice held that fertiliser and plant protection products were not agricultural products. In *Sicasov* the Commission acknowledged that seeds fell within Annex I, but concluded that neither of the derogations in Regulation 26 (now Regulation 1184/2006) was applicable[25].

(C) The first derogation: national market organisations

Article 2 of Regulation 1184/2006 and Article 176(1) of Regulation 1234/2007 provide that Article 101 shall not apply to agreements which form an integral part of a national market organisation. However Regulation 1234/2007 (and its predecessors) established a common organisation for many agricultural products, so that the majority of national marketing organisations have ceased to exist. The Commission has construed this derogation from the application of Article 101(1) strictly[26]. In *FRUBO v Commission*[27] the Court of Justice upheld the Commission's decision[28] that a Dutch fruit marketing organisation did not benefit from the immunity contained in Article 2(1) since it was not a national marketing organisation. In *Scottish Salmon Board*[29] the Commission found that, as there was a common organisation of the market in fishery products[30], the Scottish Salmon Board could not rely on the national market organisation defence.

In *New Potatoes*[31] rules were laid down by seven economic committees in France, acting under a French law of 1962, to organise and regulate the production and marketing of new potatoes. The rules were intended to deal with the problem of a slump in the market at a time

---

[20] OJ [1976] L 231/24, [1976] 2 CMLR D63.
[21] Case 123/83 [1985] ECR 391, [1985] 2 CMLR 430.
[22] Case 136/86 [1987] ECR 4789, [1988] 4 CMLR 331.
[23] Case T-61/89 [1992] ECR II-1931.
[24] Case C-250/92 [1994] ECR I-5641, [1996] 4 CMLR 191, paras 21–27.
[25] OJ [1999] L 14/27, [1999] 4 CMLR 192, paras 65–69.
[26] As well as the decisions mentioned in the text see *Cauliflowers* OJ [1978] L 21/23, [1978] 1 CMLR D66; *Bloemenveilingen Aalsmeer* OJ [1988] L 262/27, [1989] 4 CMLR 500; *Sugar Beet* OJ [1990] L 31/32, [1991] 4 CMLR 629; *Sicasov* OJ [1999] L 14/27, [1999] 4 CMLR 192; *British Sugar* OJ [1999] L 76/1, [1999] 4 CMLR 1316, paras 185–188.
[27] Case 71/74 [1975] ECR 563, [1975] 2 CMLR 123.
[28] *Geeves and Zonen v FRUBO* OJ [1974] L 237/16, [1974] 2 CMLR D89.
[29] OJ [1992] L 246/37, [1993] 5 CMLR 602, para 22.
[30] See Council Regulation 3796/81, OJ [1981] L 379/1.
[31] OJ [1988] L 59/25, [1988] 4 CMLR 790.

of over-production. The Commission was asked to declare that Article 101(1) was not applicable: as there was no common organisation of the market in question, the Commission
had to decide whether the system qualified as a national market organisation. It held that
this term must be defined in a way that would be consistent with the objectives of a common
organisation under the second exception of Article 2 of Regulation 26: thus the objectives of
the common agricultural policy, contained in Article 39 TFEU and referred to below, were
read into the first exception of Article 2. The Commission went on to hold that the decisions
and agreements of various producer groups did form an integral part of the national market
organisation in question and concluded that Article 101(1) was not infringed.

(D) **The second derogation: common market organisations**

Article 2 of Regulation 1184/2006 also permits agreements which are necessary for the
attainment of the objectives of the common agricultural policy. Article 39 sets out these
objectives under five heads:

- to increase agricultural productivity
- to ensure a fair standard of living for the agricultural community
- to stabilise markets
- to ensure the availability of supplies
- to ensure supplies to consumers at reasonable prices.

Article 39(2) provides that, in implementing the common agricultural policy, account
shall be taken, *inter alia*, of:

> the particular nature of agricultural activity, which results from the social structure of
> agriculture and from structural and natural disparities between the various agricultural
> regions.

The aims expressed in Article 39 are not necessarily consistent with the normal forces of
competition.

In *FRUBO v Commission*[32] the Court of Justice rejected a defence based on the second
derogation in Article 2. A noticeable feature of the judgment is that, although some of the
heads of Article 39 may have been satisfied, not all of them were: to put the matter another way, in order to come within this derogation it is necessary to satisfy all five heads of
Article 39[33]. In practice it is likely that the Commission and the EU Courts will hold that
the objectives of Article 39 are expressly or impliedly advanced by the provisions of any
particular regulation establishing a common organisation of an agricultural sector, with
the result that there is no remaining latitude for the parties to an agreement to argue that
their agreement will have this effect[34].

In *Bloemenveilingen Aalsmeer*[35] the Commission rejected an argument that exclusive
dealing agreements between auctioneers and flower traders in respect of live plants and
floricultural products could advance the objectives of Article 39. It published a decision
to this effect, not only as the rules in question were the subject of litigation in the Dutch

---

[32] Case 71/74 [1975] ECR 563, [1975] 2 CMLR 123, paras 22–27.
[33] See similarly Cases T-70/92 etc *Florimex v Commission* [1997] ECR II-697, [1997] 5 CMLR 769, para 153
and Case T-217/03 *FNCBV v Commission* [2006] ECR II-4987, [2008] 5 CMLR 406, para 206.
[34] See eg *Cauliflowers* OJ [1978] L 21/23, [1978] 1 CMLR D66; *Milchförderungsfonds* OJ [1985] L 35/35,
[1985] 3 CMLR 101.
[35] OJ [1988] L 262/27, [1989] 4 CMLR 500.

courts, but also as similar rules were being applied by other auction houses[36]. In *Scottish Salmon Board*[37] the Commission rejected an argument that the Board's conduct was permissible as the industry was in economic difficulties; the Commission's view was that, if this was so, EU initiatives should be taken to deal with the problem: it was not for the parties themselves to take action which was unlawful under Article 101. In *Sicasov*[38] the Commission held that an agreement for the licensing of seeds was not necessary for the attainment of the objectives in Article 39 TFEU[39].

The Commission rejected defences based on the second derogation in *French beef*[40], *Raw Tobacco Spain*[41], *Raw Tobacco Italy*[42] and *Bananas*[43].

5. Coal and Steel

Coal and steel were originally dealt with by the Treaty of Paris of 1951 establishing the European Coal and Steel Community. The ECSC Treaty contained rules on competition that were similar in many respects to Articles 101 and 102 TFEU, although there were some material differences. The ECSC Treaty expired on 23 July 2002 which means that the coal and steel sectors are now subject to Articles 101 and 102 TFEU and the EUMR. The Commission has published a Communication explaining the consequences of the expiry of the ECSC Treaty[44].

6. Transport[45]

The TFEU contains special provisions on transport in Articles 90 to 100. Article 90(1) provides that these provisions are applicable to road, rail and inland waterway transport; Article 90(2) provides that the European Parliament and the Council of Ministers may lay down appropriate provisions for sea and air transport. Thus the Treaty itself recognises a distinction between these two categories, the difficulty being that the latter are subject to numerous international arrangements and are of particular political sensitivity.

---

[36] Ibid, para 168.

[37] OJ [1992] L 246/37, [1993] 5 CMLR 602, para 22.

[38] OJ [1999] L 14/27, [1999] 4 CMLR 192.

[39] Ibid, para 68.

[40] OJ [2003] L 209/12, [2003] 5 CMLR 891, paras 135–149, upheld on appeal Cases T-217/03 etc *FNCBV v Commission* [2006] ECR II-4987, [2008] 5 CMLR 406, paras 197–209.

[41] Decision of 20 October 2004, paras 337–348, upheld on appeal Case T-33/05 *Compañía española de tobaco en rama, SA v Commission* [2011] ECR II-000, paras 153–164.

[42] Decision of 20 October 2005, paras 306–311.

[43] Decision of 15 October 2008, paras 344–349.

[44] Communication from the Commission concerning certain aspects of the treatment of competition cases resulting from the expiry of the ECSC Treaty, OJ [2002] C 152/5, [2002] 5 CMLR 1036, section 2; the General Court held in Case T-24/07 *ThyssenKrupp Stainless AG v Commission* [2009] ECR II-2309, [2009] 5 CMLR 1773, that, after the ECSC Treaty expired, the Commission was able to adopt a decision that Article 65 ECSC had been infringed in the 1990s on the legal basis of Regulation 1/2003: ibid, paras 63–90; upheld on appeal Case C-352/09 P *ThyssenKrupp Nirosta v Commission* [2011] ECR I-000.

[45] See further Ortiz Blanco and Van Houtte *EC Competition Law in the Transport Sector* (Clarendon Press, 1996); Faull and Nikpay *The EC Law of Competition* (Oxford University Press, 2nd ed, 2007), ch 14; Bellamy and Child *European Community Law of Competition* (Oxford University Press, 6th ed, 2008, eds Roth and Rose), paras 12.004–12.051.

Articles 101 and 102 do apply to the transport sector (including air transport[46]), but in 1962 Council Regulation 141[47] provided that Regulation 17, which gave the Commission the necessary powers to implement the competition rules, did not apply to transport. The procedural lacuna left by Regulation 141 was filled in three stages: first, Council Regulation 1017/68[48] adopted specific provisions on the application of the competition rules to transport by road, rail and inland waterway (that is to say inland transport); secondly, Council Regulation 4056/86[49] provided the Commission with powers in the maritime transport sector; last came Council Regulation 3975/87[50] to deal with air transport. Since 1 May 2004 the procedural rules for the enforcement of Articles 101 and 102 in the transport sector are contained in Regulation 1/2003[51]; this means that the jurisdictional problem exposed in *Union Internationale des Chemins de Fer v Commission*[52], where the General Court concluded that the Commission had proceeded under the wrong procedural regulation when applying Article 101 to arrangements for the sale of railway tickets by travel agents, would no longer occur.

(A) Inland transport

(i) Legislative regime

Council Regulation 1017/68 provided that certain technical agreements do not infringe Article 101, and that some cooperation agreements between small and medium-sized undertakings benefit from block exemption. That Regulation was repealed in 2009 by Council Regulation 169/2009[53] which entered into force in April of that year. The exception for technical agreements will now be found in Article 2 of Regulation 169/2009, and the block exemption for certain cooperation agreements in Article 3.

Several Council Directives were adopted in the first railway package of 1991 with the intention of opening up the rail sector to competition[54], although the development of a single market in rail transport has been slow to develop[55]. A second package was adopted

---

[46] See Cases 209/84 etc *Ministère Public v Asjes* [1986] ECR 1425, [1986] 3 CMLR 173 and Case 66/86 *Ahmed Saeed Flugreisen v Zentrale zur Bekämpfung Unlauteren Wettbewerbs* [1989] ECR 803, [1990] 4 CMLR 102.

[47] OJ (Sp ed, 1959–62) 291.

[48] OJ [1968] L 175/1; note that Regulation 1017/68 has now been repealed and replaced by Council Regulation 169/2009 (see ch 23 n 53 below).

[49] OJ [1986] L 378/4.

[50] OJ [1987] L 374/1.

[51] OJ [2003] L 1/1, [2003] 4 CMLR 551, Articles 36–43, see ch 7, 'Chapter XI: transitional, amending and final provisions', p 287.

[52] Case T-14/93 [1995] ECR II-1503, [1996] 5 CMLR 40; upheld on appeal Case C-264/95 P *Commission v Union Internationale des Chemins de Fer* [1997] ECR I-1287, [1997] 5 CMLR 49.

[53] OJ [2009] L 61/1.

[54] Council Directive 91/440/EEC on Development of the [EU's] Railways, OJ [1991] L 237/25, as amended by Directive 2001/12/EC of the European Parliament and of the Council OJ [2001] L 75/1; Council Directive 95/18/EC on Licensing of Railway Undertakings, OJ [1995] L 143/70, as amended by Directive 2001/13/EC of the European Parliament and of the Council OJ [2001] L 75/26; Council Directive 95/19 EC on Allocation of Railway Infrastructure Capacity and the Charging of Infrastructure Fees, OJ [1995] L 143/75, as amended by Directive 2001/14/EC of the European Parliament and of the Council, OJ [2001] L 75/29.

[55] See the Commission's XXXth *Report on Competition Policy* (2000), points 198–199; see also the Commission's White Paper on *European Transport Policy for 2010: Time to Decide* COM(2001) 370 final, 12 September 2001; Stehmann and Zellhofer 'Dominant Rail Undertakings under European Competition Policy' (2004) 10 European Law Journal 327; Elzinga, Jutten and Niels 'Essential or Nice to Have? A Competition-based Framework for "Rail-related Services"' (2008) 29 ECLR 50.

in 2004[56] and a third in 2007[57]. In September 2010 the Commission published its proposal for a Directive establishing a single European railway area which, if adopted, will amend and consolidate the three railway packages[58]. The rail sector is subject to a complex regulatory regime under UK law, and the Office of Rail Regulation ('ORR') enjoys concurrent powers to apply the provisions of the Competition Act 1998 and market investigation provisions of the Enterprise Act 2002 to this sector[59].

(ii) Practical application of the competition rules to inland transport

The Commission has adopted several decisions in relation to inland transport. In *EATE Levy*[60] it condemned an agreement between French waterway carriers and French forwarding agents imposing a levy of ten per cent on freight charges for boat charters to destinations outside France, as it discriminated in favour of French carriers; the Court of Justice upheld the Commission on appeal[61]. In *Tariff Structures in the Combined Transport of Goods*[62] the Commission considered that the criteria in Article 101(3) were satisfied in the case of a tariff structure agreement between the rail companies of the EU on the sale of rail haulage in the international combined transport of goods.

In *European Night Services*[63] the Commission concluded that a joint venture established by five rail operators to provide night sleeper services through the Channel Tunnel between a variety of cities in the UK and continental Europe satisfied the criteria of Article 101(3). Under the system of granting individual exemptions then in force, the Commission made its decision subject to conditions and obligations to which the parents of the joint venture objected; the Commission limited the exemption to a period of time, ten years, which the parties considered to be too short, given the level of risk that they were undertaking. On appeal against the decision the General Court held in *European Night Services v Commission*[64] that the Commission had abjectly failed to demonstrate that the agreement between the rail operators had the effect of restricting actual and/or potential competition, with the consequence that its decision should be annulled; the General Court went further, holding that, even if there was an appreciable effect on

---

[56] Council Directive 2004/49/EC of the European Parliament and the Council on Safety of the [EU's] railways, OJ [2004] L 164/44; Council Directive 2004/50/EC of the European Parliament and the Council on Interoperability of the trans-European high-speed rail system, OJ [2004] L 220/40; Council Directive 2004/51/EC of the European Parliament and the Council on Development of the Community's Railway, OJ [2004] L 164/164; Regulation 1371/2007 on Rail passengers' rights and obligations, OJ [2007] L 315/14.

[57] Directive 2007/58/EC of the European Parliament and of the Council Allocation of railway infrastructure capacity and the levying of charges for the use of railway infrastructure, OJ [2007] L 315/44; Directive of the European Parliament and of the Council Certification of train drivers operating locomotives and trains on the railway system in the [EU], OJ [2007] L 315/51.

[58] Commission Proposal for a Directive establishing a single European railway area, COM(2010) 475 and Communication concerning the development of a Single European Railway Area, COM(2010) 474.

[59] On concurrency under the Competition Act 1998 see ch 10, 'Concurrency', pp 437–439 and under the Enterprise Act 2002 see ch 11, 'Super-Complaints', pp 454–455 and 'The power of the OFT to make a reference', pp 467–468; see also *Competition Act 1998: Application to services relating to railways* OFT Guideline 430, October 2005.

[60] OJ [1985] L 219/35, [1988] 4 CMLR 698.

[61] Case 272/85 *ANTIB v Commission* [1987] ECR 2201, [1988] 4 CMLR 677.

[62] OJ [1993] L 73/38.

[63] OJ [1994] L 259/21, [1995] 5 CMLR 76.

[64] Cases T-374/94 etc [1998] ECR II-3141, [1998] 5 CMLR 718; see similarly the Commission's decision in *Eurotunnel* OJ [1994] L 354/66, [1995] 4 CMLR 801: the Commission had granted exemption to the operating agreement for the Channel Tunnel, but its decision was annulled on appeal by the General Court in Cases T-79/95 etc *SNCF v Commission* [1996] ECR II-1491, [1997] 4 CMLR 334 since the Commission had failed to demonstrate that the agreement would be restrictive of competition; for the eventual outcome of this case see the Commission's XXIXth *Report on Competition Policy* (1999), p 163.

competition, the Commission had failed to demonstrate that the exemption should be subject to the conditions and obligations imposed or should be granted for such a short period[65]. In another case relating to the Channel Tunnel, *ACI*[66], the Commission authorised, subject to conditions, the creation of a joint venture company to market intermodal rail services through the tunnel[67].

In *HOV SVZ/MCN*[68] the Commission imposed a fine on Deutsche Bahn of €11 million for imposing discriminatory rail transport tariffs for the inland carriage of sea-borne containers to and from Germany, depending on whether they were shipped through German ports on the one hand or Belgian and Dutch ones on the other. The decision was upheld on appeal to the General Court[69], and the Court of Justice ruled that Deutsche Bahn's appeal to it was inadmissible[70]. In *GVG/FS* the Commission concluded that the Italian rail operator, Ferrovie dello Stato, had abused a dominant position by refusing to provide access to the Italian rail infrastructure, to enter into negotiations for the formation of an international grouping and to provide traction[71].

In the UK the ORR imposed a fine of £4.1 million on a rail freight operator, EW&S, for abusing its dominant position in the market for the haulage of coal by rail, in particular by acting in a discriminatory and a predatory manner[72]. The ORR has adopted a number of non-infringement decisions in relation to the rail sector[73]. Under the market investigation provisions of the Enterprise Act 2002 the Competition Commission ('the CC') recommended that the Government should reform the rail passenger franchise process to address its concerns about the rolling stock leasing market[74].

(B) Maritime transport[75]

(i) Legislative regime

For many years maritime transport was subject to a special procedural and substantive regime of its own, set out in Council Regulation 4056/86[76]. The cumulative effect of the Regulation 1/2003 and of Council Regulation 1419/2006[77], which entered into force in October 2006, is that the special regime has been terminated and the sector is now subject to the same procedural and substantive rules as the rest of the economy.

---

[65] For further comment on this case see ch 3, 'Effect', p 120 and 'Actual and potential competition', pp 127–128.

[66] OJ [1994] L 224/28.

[67] More recently the Commission authorized a merger, subject to conditions, to a 'new Eurostar' joint venture: Case M 5655, decision of 17 June 2010.

[68] OJ [1994] L 104/34.

[69] Case T-229/94 *Deutsche Bahn AG v Commission* [1997] ECR II-1689, [1998] 4 CMLR 220.

[70] Case C-436/97 P [1999] ECR I-2387, [1999] 5 CMLR 776.

[71] OJ [2004] L 11/17, [2004] 4 CMLR 1446; for comment see Stehmann 'Applying essential facility reasoning to passenger rail services in the EU – the Commission decision in the GVG case' (2004) 25 ECLR 390.

[72] ORR decision of 17 November 2007, [2007] UKCLR 937; subsequent damages actions against EW&S arising out of this case are discussed in ch 8, 'Causation', p 311 and 'Severance', p 323.

[73] See 'Table of published decisions' in ch 9, pp 374–389 and on the website accompanying this book at www.oxfordtextbooks.co.uk/orc/whishandbailey7e/.

[74] Final Report, 7 April 2009, available at www.competition-commission.org.uk; see the discussion in ch 11, 'Market Investigation References' pp 466ff.

[75] See further Ortiz Blanco *Shipping Conferences under EC Antitrust Law* (Hart Publishing, 2008).

[76] OJ [1986] L 378/4.

[77] OJ [2006] L 269/1; see Benini and Bermig 'Milestones in maritime transport: EU ends exemptions' (2007) (Spring) *Competition Policy Newsletter* 20.

(A) Procedural rules

Regulation 17 of 1962[78], which gave the Commission power to enforce Articles 101 and 102, did not apply to the maritime transport sector. Council Regulation 4056/86[79] provided the Commission with power to enforce Articles 101 and 102 in relation to international maritime transport services from or to one or more [EU] ports with effect from 1987. Regulation 1/2003[80] repealed these special procedural rules with effect from 1 May 2004, since when maritime transport has been subject to the same procedural regime as the rest of the economy. Regulation 4056/86 did not empower the Commission to enforce the competition rules in the case of so-called 'cabotage', that is to say services between ports within the same Member State; also excluded were international tramp vessel services, that is to say the transport of goods in bulk where freight rates are negotiated on a case-by-case basis[81]. These exclusions were maintained by Article 32 of Regulation 1/2003 until October 2006, from when Article 2 of Regulation 1419/2006 repealed them: recital 12 of that Regulation described the exclusion of cabotage and tramp vessel services as a 'regulatory anomaly'[82]. These changes mean that the Commission now has the power to apply Articles 101 and 102 to the entire maritime transport sector.

(B) Substantive rules

Article 2 of Regulation 4056/86 excluded 'technical agreements' from the scope of Article 101. More controversially, Articles 3 and 4 of Regulation 4056/86 provided block exemption for 'liner conferences', that is to say agreements between carriers concerning the operation of scheduled maritime transport services, allowing them to fix prices and regulate capacity. Following a consultation these substantive rules have been abolished[83]: Regulation 1419/2006 repealed Regulation 4056/86 in its entirety; however Article 1 provided transitional relief until 18 October 2008 for liner conferences that benefitted from the block exemption. In order to provide guidance to interested stakeholders affected by the demise of the block exemption the Commission published *Guidelines on the application of Article [101 TFEU] to maritime transport services*[84]; in particular they discuss the extent to which the exchange of information between competitors may infringe Article 101.

(C) Block exemption for shipping consortia

The Commission was given power by Council Regulation 479/92[85] to grant block exemption to some shipping consortia, and the first block exemption to be adopted was Regulation 870/95[86]. Over the years the enabling legislation was amended a number of times, as was the block exemption. In 2009 the Council decided to codify the enabling legislation in the interests of clarity and rationality, and it therefore adopted

---

[78] JO [1962] 13/204.

[79] OJ [1986] L 378/4.

[80] OJ [2003] L 1/1.

[81] See Regulation 4056/86, Article 1(3)(a).

[82] The Commission closed an investigation into the transport of bulk liquids by sea in 2008, after having sent statements of objections to a number of undertakings, as it concluded that the services in question may have been tramp vessel services and therefore excluded from the scope of Regulation 4056/86; following the repeal of Regulation 4056/86 agreements in the tramp vessel sector would be subject to investigation: see Commission MEMO/08/297, 8 May 2008.

[83] See *Review of Council Regulation 4056/86* and the responses to the Consultation, available at www.ec.europa.eu/competition/sectors/transport/legislation_maritime_archive.html.

[84] OJ [2008] C 245/2.

[85] OJ [1992] L 55/3.

[86] OJ [1995] L 89/7.

Regulation 246/2009 which repeals and replaces earlier legislation[87]. Under the powers conferred upon it the Commission adopted Regulation 906/2009[88] which confers block exemption on shipping consortia in so far as they provide international liner shipping services from or to one or more EU ports[89]; the block exemption does not apply in the event that the consortium involves certain 'hard-core restrictions' such as price fixing to third parties[90], and there is a 30 per cent market share threshold above which a consortium would not benefit from the block exemption[91].

(ii) Practical application of the competition rules to maritime transport

The relationship between the Commission and certain operators in the maritime transport sector has not been particularly harmonious. There have been a number of decisions in which the Commission has found infringements of Articles 101 and 102. The first fine in this sector was imposed in *Secretama*[92], for supplying incorrect information in response to a request for information by the Commission under Article 16(3) of Regulation 4056/86. The Commission also imposed fines of €5,000 on *Ukwal*[93] and €4,000 on *Mewac*[94] for failing to submit to investigations under Article 18 of Regulation 4056/86.

The first decision of the Commission imposing a fine for a substantive infringement of Articles 101 and 102 in the maritime transport sector was *French-West African Shipowners' Committees*[95]. The Commission considered that the Committees had cartelised the entire trade in liner cargo between France and various West African ports; quotas had been established and procedures established to ensure compliance. The offences arose both under Article 101 and under the concept of collective dominance in Article 102. The result of the practices was to exclude third parties from the trade. Various defences (for example that the agreements were 'technical' under Article 2 of Regulation 4056/86, that the block exemption under Article 3 was applicable and that the Committees were subject to 'state compulsion'[96]), were rejected. In fixing the level of the fines, which exceeded €15 million, the Commission noted that usually when it applies the competition rules in new circumstances it proceeds with moderation; on this occasion however it saw no reason for moderation, since the parties were well aware of the illegality of their conduct and that the block exemption in Regulation 4056/86 was unavailable[97]. In *Cewal*[98] the Commission imposed fines totalling €10.1 million on members of a liner conference, Cewal, for abusing their collective dominant position by taking action designed to eliminate their principal independent competitors, for example by offering lower freight rates and by offering loyalty rebates. The Commission's finding of collective dominance and its condemnation of the abusive practices were upheld both by the General Court[99] and

---

[87] OJ [2009] L 79/1.
[88] OJ [2009] L 256/31; see Prisker (2010) 1 *Competition Policy Newsletter* 8.
[89] Ibid, Articles 1 and 3.
[90] Ibid, Article 4.
[91] Ibid, Article 5.
[92] OJ [1991] L 35/23, [1992] 5 CMLR 76.
[93] OJ [1992] L 121/45, [1993] 5 CMLR 632.
[94] OJ [1993] L 20/6, [1994] 5 CMLR 275.
[95] OJ [1992] L 134/1, [1993] 5 CMLR 446.
[96] See ch 3, 'State compulsion and highly regulated markets', pp 137–138.
[97] OJ [1992] L 134/1, [1993] 5 CMLR 446, para 74(g).
[98] OJ [1993] L 34/20, [1995] 5 CMLR 198; the treatment of collective dominance in this case is discussed in ch 14, 'The judgment of the Court of Justice in *Compagnie Maritime Belge Transports v Commission*', pp 577–579, and the condemnation of the lower freight rates is discussed in ch 18, '*Compagnie Maritime Belge v Commission*', pp 750–752.
[99] Cases T-24/93 etc *Compagnie Maritime Belge NV v Commission* [1996] ECR II-1201, [1997] 4 CMLR 273.

the Court of Justice[100]; however the fines on the appellants were annulled by the Court of Justice because the Commission's statement of objections had been addressed directly only to the conference, Cewal, and not to its individual members, who had merely received a copy. Thirty-seven months after the judgment of the Court of Justice, the Commission served a new statement of objections on Compagnie Maritime Belge, one of the members of the conference, informing it that the Commission intended to impose a fine upon it for the infringements that it had found in the original decision and that had been upheld on appeal; this led to the imposition of a fine of €3.4 million on CMB[101]. CMB's appeal to the General Court, which included pleas that the Commission's second decision was unreasonably delayed and infringed the limitation rules, was unsuccessful[102].

In *TAA*[103] and in *FEFC*[104] the Commission prohibited price fixing in relation to the land-leg of combined transport operations; even though Council Regulation 4056/86 conferred block exemption on price fixing in relation to the maritime element of the transportation of containers, the Commission did not consider that this should extend to the non-maritime part of a journey; the Commission's approach was upheld by the General Court on appeal[105]. The Commission imposed a fine in *Ferry Operators*[106] on five ferry operators who colluded with one another in order to overcome difficulties experienced in currency fluctuations following the devaluation of the pound sterling in September 1992. In *Europe Asia Trades Agreement*[107] the Commission held that agreements not to use capacity and to exchange information infringed Article 101(1) and failed to satisfy the criteria of Article 101(3). In *Trans-Atlantic Conference Agreement*[108] the Commission imposed fines totalling €273 million for infringement of Article 101 and for abusing a collective dominant position contrary to Article 102 by altering the competitive structure of the market and by placing restrictions on the availability and contents of service contracts. This decision was partially annulled on appeal: in particular the General Court disagreed with most of the findings of abuse contrary to Article 102; the fines in this case were annulled[109]. In *Greek Ferries*[110] the Commission imposed fines of €9.12 million for fixing ferry prices between Italy and Greece. In *Far East Trade and Tariff and Surcharges Agreement* it imposed fines totalling €6.932 million where the parties to the agreement in question had agreed not to discount from their published tariffs; however these fines were quashed on appeal to the General Court on the ground that the Commission had failed to give good reasons for their belated imposition[111].

---

[100] Cases C-395/96 and C-396/96 P [2000] ECR I-1365, [2000] 4 CMLR 1076.

[101] *Compagnie Maritime Belge* decision of 30 April 2004.

[102] Case T-276/04 *Compagnie Maritime Belge v Commission* [2008] ECR II-1277, [2009] 4 CMLR 968.

[103] OJ [1994] L 376/1.

[104] OJ [1994] L 378/17.

[105] Cases T-395/94 etc *Atlantic Container Line v Commission* [2002] ECR II-875, [2002] 4 CMLR 1008 (*TAA*), paras 142–178 and Cases T-86/95 etc *Compagnie Generale Maritime v Commission* [2002] ECR II-1011, [2002] 4 CMLR 1115 (*FEFC*) paras 230–277; on these judgments see Fitzgerald 'Recent judgments in the liner shipping sector' (2002) (June) *Competition Policy Newsletter* 41.

[106] OJ [1997] L 26/23, [1997] 4 CMLR 798.

[107] OJ [1999] L 193/23, [1999] 5 CMLR 1380.

[108] OJ [1999] L 95/1, [1999] 4 CMLR 1415; the Commission subsequently authorised an amended version of the liner conference in *Revised TACA* OJ [2003] L 26/53, [2003] 4 CMLR 1001; see Commission Press Release IP/02/1677, 14 November 2002 and Fitzgerald 'The Revised *TACA* Decisions – The end of the conflict?' (2003) (Spring) *Competition Policy Newsletter* 56–58.

[109] Cases T-191/98 etc *Atlantic Container Line v Commission* [2003] ECR II-3275, [2005] 4 CMLR 1283.

[110] OJ [1999] L 109/24, [1999] 5 CMLR 47, upheld on appeal to the General Court Cases T-56/99 etc *Marlines v Commission* [2003] ECR II-5225, [2005] 5 CMLR 1761; Marlines' appeal to the Court of Justice was dismissed in Case C-112/04 P *Marlines v Commission*, order of 15 September 2005.

[111] Case T-213/00 *CMA CGM v Commission* [2003] ECR II-913, [2003] 5 CMLR 268.

On a less hostile note, in *P&O Stena Line*[112] the Commission authorised, for three years, a joint venture to provide short cross-channel ferry services between the UK and France and Belgium. In 2001 the Commission renewed this authorisation for a period of six years[113]. The Commission was aware that there were some anxieties about price rises, but considered that they were understandable as the market adjusted to more normal competitive conditions following the abolition of duty-free sales on ferry crossings, as new capacity was absorbed and as fuel prices rose.

(C) Air transport

(i) Legislative regime[114]

A number of measures have been adopted in order to liberalise air transport in the EU. In the first liberalisation package of 1987[115] the Council of Ministers adopted a Directive on fares for scheduled air services between Member States[116] and a Decision on the sharing of passenger capacity between Member States[117]. The 1987 package was regarded as a first step towards the completion of the internal market in air transport. In 1990 Regulation 2343/90[118] on access for air carriers to scheduled intra-EU routes was adopted. In 1991 the Council adopted Regulation 249/91[119] on air cargo services between Member States and Regulation 295/91 on compensation to passengers denied boarding ('bumped') in air transport; the latter was replaced by Regulation 261/2004[120].

In 1992 a further liberalisation package was adopted. Regulation 2407/92[121] dealt with the licensing of air carriers. Regulation 2408/92[122] provides that all EU carriers should have access to intra-EU routes (cabotage). Regulation 2409/92[123] provides that EU air carriers shall freely set their own fares. In March 2003 the Commission proposed several revisions in the third liberalisation package[124]. Regulation 95/93[125] establishes common rules for the allocation of slots at EU airports in order to ensure that they are made available on a neutral, transparent and non-discriminatory basis. Council Regulation 2299/89 established a

---

[112] OJ [1999] L 163/61, [1999] 5 CMLR 682; see also the Commission's XXVIth *Report on Competition Policy* (1996), points 84–87; and the XXVIIth *Report on Competition Policy* (1997), points 81–84 and pp 134–138.

[113] Commission Press Release IP/01/806, 7 June 2001 and XXXIst *Report on Competition Policy* (2001), point 160.

[114] See *Guide to [EU] legislation in the field of civil aviation*, June 2007, available at www.ec.europa.eu/transport/air/internal_market/doc/acquis_handbook.pdf.

[115] The package is helpfully summarised in the Commission's XVIIth *Report on Competition Policy* (1987), points 43–45.

[116] Council Directive 87/601/EEC, OJ [1987] L 374/12.

[117] Council Decision 87/602/EEC, OJ [1987] L 374/19.

[118] OJ [1990] L 217/8.

[119] OJ [1991] L 36/1, as amended by Regulation 2408/92, OJ [1992] L 240/8.

[120] OJ [2004] L 46/1.

[121] OJ [1992] L 240/1.

[122] OJ [1992] L 240/8; on the application of Regulation 2408/92 see Case T-260/94 *Air Inter v Commission* [1997] ECR II-997, [1997] 5 CMLR 851.

[123] OJ [1992] L 240/15.

[124] Commission *Consultation paper with a view to revision of Regulations No 2407/92, 2408/92 and 2409/92*; see also Commission Press Release IP/03/281, 26 February 2003.

[125] OJ [1993] L 14/1, as amended by Regulation 894/2000, OJ [2002] L 142/3.

Code of Conduct for Computerised Reservation Systems[126]. The ground-handling sector was liberalised to allow greater access to the market by Directive 96/67[127].

Despite these liberalisation measures there remain impediments to free competition in air transport markets. The lack of slots at premier airports distorts the market, as do bilateral agreements between individual Member States and third countries governing access to air space and which discriminate in favour of national carriers: some of these agreements were successfully challenged by the Commission before the Court of Justice under Article 43 TFEU in the so-called '*Open Skies*' judgment[128]. Following that judgment Regulation 847/2004[129] requires Member States to notify the Commission of negotiations with third countries and to ensure that their agreements comply with EU law. An important step forward was the signature of the *Air Transport Agreement* between the US, the EU and the Member States on 30 April 2007[130] which authorises US and EU airlines to fly between any city in the US and any city in the EU; this agreement took effect on 30 March 2008 and was amended in June 2010[131].

For many years air transport was subject to a special competition law regime contained in Council Regulation 3975/87[132]. It conferred power on the Commission to enforce the competition rules in the air transport sector to air transport services *between EU airports*; air transport between EU airports and third countries could be investigated only under the procedure provided for in Articles 104 and 105 TFEU[133]. The position is now much simpler: the applicable procedural regime is that of Regulation 1/2003[134], and Council Regulation 411/2004[135] provides that the Commission's powers under that Regulation apply to *all* routes, not only those within the EU.

Council Regulation 3976/87[136], as subsequently amended, gave the Commission power to publish block exemptions in the air transport sector. For many years there were block exemptions for consultations between carriers on passenger tariffs on routes within the EU and for arrangements on slot allocation and airport scheduling: however these have

[126] OJ [1989] L 220/1, as amended by Council Regulations 3089/93/EEC, OJ [1993] L 278/1 and 323/99/EC, OJ [1999] L 40/1; a fine of €10,000 was imposed under this Regulation in the case of *Lufthansa*: Commission Press Release IP/99/542, 20 July 1999.

[127] OJ [1996] L 272/36; see Commission Consultation paper on *Issues to be addressed in the review of Council Directive 96/97/EC on access to the ground handling market at EU airports*, available at www.ec.europa.eu/transport/air/consultations/2010_02_12_directive_96_67_ec_en.htm.

[128] See Cases C-466/98 etc *Commission v United Kingdom* [2002] ECR I-9427, [2003] 1 CMLR 143; see Communication from the Commission on the consequences of the Court judgments of 5 November 2002 for European air transport policy, COM(2002) 649 final, 19 November 2002; Hefferman and McAuliffe 'External relations in the air transport sector: the Court of Justice and the open skies agreements' (2003) 28 EL Rev 601.

[129] OJ [2004] L 157/7; the Commission has adopted two decisions, C(2006) 3009 of 31 May 2006 and C(2006) 2010 of 20 June 2006 setting out the criteria used to assess agreements negotiated by Member States.

[130] OJ [2007] L 134/4; see Gremminger 'New EU–US cooperation agreement in air transport' (2007) (Summer) *Competition Policy Newsletter* 27.

[131] Commission Press Release IP/10/818, 24 June 2010.

[132] OJ [1987] L 374/1.

[133] For the use of these provisions specifically in relation to air transport prior to the adoption of Regulation 3975/87 see Cases 209/84 etc *Ministère Public v Asjes* [1986] ECR 1425, [1986] 3 CMLR 173; Case 66/86 *Ahmed Saeed Flugreisen v Zentrale zur Bekämpfung Unlauteren Wettbewerbs* [1989] ECR 803, [1990] 4 CMLR 102.

[134] OJ [2004] L 1/1.

[135] OJ [2004] L 68/1.

[136] OJ [1988] L 374/9.

now lapsed[137]. Council Regulation 3976/87 was replaced, in 2009, by Council Regulation 487/2009[138]; however there are currently no block exemptions in the air transport sector.

The UK Civil Aviation Authority enjoys concurrent powers to apply the provisions of the Competition Act 1998 to the supply of air traffic services[139].

(ii) Practical application of the competition rules to air transport

The Commission has reviewed several cooperation agreements in the air transport sector under Article 101, for example *Lufthansa/SAS*[140], *Austrian Airlines/Lufthansa*[141], *Société Air France/Alitalia Linee Aeree Italiane SpA*[142] and *Austrian Airlines/SAS*[143]. In cases that arose prior to Regulation 1/2003 the Commission sometimes granted individual exemptions to cooperation agreements, subject to conditions and obligations: that was true of the first three cases cited above. Since Regulation 1/2003 the Commission contemplated closing the *Austrian Airlines/SAS* case on the basis of commitments offered by the parties under Article 9[144]; however that case did not reach a final decision. The Commission is considering the possibility of accepting commitments in the case of the *SkyTeam* airline alliance[145]. In the case of *British Airways/American Airlines/Iberia* the Commission accepted commitments under Article 9 of Regulation 1/2003 that would lead to the divestment of slots at London Heathrow and Gatwick airports and associated remedies that would facilitate entry and/or expansion on air routes between London and various US cities such as New York, Boston, Dallas and Miami; as a consequence the Commission closed its investigation. The Commission worked closely with the US authorities in this case, in particular with the Department of Transportation[146].

In some cases an alliance between two airlines may fall to be considered under the EUMR rather than Article 101. This happened for example in *Alitalia/KLM* where the Commission regarded the alliance as a full-function joint venture, even though the parties did not create a corporate vehicle for the cooperation; the Commission cleared the merger after the parties agreed to modify the transaction to address its competition concerns[147]. The Commission cleared a merger subject to conditions in the case of *Air France/ KLM*[148]; the clearance was unsuccessfully challenged in the General Court by a third party, easyJet[149]. In the case of *Ryanair/Aer Lingus* the Commission prohibited the proposed acquisition of Aer Lingus by Ryanair[150], a decision that was upheld on appeal to

---

[137] See Beuve-Méry and Struk 'Commission brings air transport in line with other industries by phasing out the block exemptions that have existed in this sector since 1988' (2007) (Summer) *Competition Policy Newsletter* 45.

[138] OJ [2009] L 148/1.

[139] See *Concurrent application to regulated industries* OFT 405, December 2004; the CAA's concurrent powers may be extended to include services provided by airport operators, see Statement of the Secretary of State for Transport of 21 July 2010, available at www.dft.gov.uk.

[140] OJ [1996] L 54/28, [1996] 4 CMLR 845; see Crocioni 'The *Lufthansa/SAS* Case: Did the Commission Get the Economics Right?' (1998) 19 ECLR 116.

[141] OJ [2002] L 242/25, [2003] 4 CMLR 252.

[142] Commission decision of 7 April 2004, OJ [2004] L 362/117.

[143] See the Commission's *Market Test Notice*, OJ [2005] C 233/18.

[144] See ch 7, 'Article 9: commitments', pp 255–261 on the Article 9 procedure.

[145] See the Commission's *Market Test Notice* OJ [2007] C 245/46; see also Commission Press Release IP/07/1558, 19 October 2007.

[146] See Commission Press Release IP/10/936, 14 July 2010.

[147] Case JV 19, decision of 11 August 1999.

[148] See Case M 3280, Commission decision of 11 February 2004.

[149] Case T-177/04 *easyJet Co Ltd v Commission* [2006] ECR II-1931, [2006] 5 CMLR 663.

[150] Case M 4439, Commission decision of 27 June 2007.

the General Court[151]. The Commission also blocked the proposed acquisition by Olympic Airlines of Aegean Airlines which would have led to a quasi-monopoly on the Greek air transport market[152]. Mergers were cleared after Phase II investigations in the cases of *Lufthansa/SN Holding (Brussels Airlines)*[153] and *Lufthansa/Austrian Airlines*[154] on the basis of remedies offered to address the concerns about a reduction of competition on various routes: the remedies, centred on the divestment of slots at certain airports, resemble those in the *British Airways/American Airlines/Iberia* case. Another Phase II investigation, of *KLM/ Martinair*[155], culminated in an unconditional clearance. There have been several other mergers between airlines that have been reviewed, and cleared, by the Commission[156].

Quite apart from the cooperation agreements and mergers in the air transport sector just referred to, the Commission has also proceeded against cartels (or alleged cartels) in this sector. In the case of *SAS/Maersk Air*[157] the Commission imposed fines of €39.4 million on SAS and €13.1 million on Maersk for market sharing, in particular with the consequence that SAS acquired a *de facto* quasi-monopoly on the Stockholm to Copenhagen route. The Commission's decision was upheld on appeal[158]. In November 2010 the Commission imposed fines of €799 million on 11 airlines for participation in a cartel in the provision of air cargo services[159], and has carried out dawn raids in the international airline passenger sector[160].

In the UK the CC considered that BAA's ownership of seven UK airports was detrimental to competition and, using its powers under the Enterprise Act 2002, required BAA to divest itself of three airports[161].

7. Regulated Industries

(A) Demonopolisation, liberalisation and privatisation

One of the most dramatic economic developments in the final two decades of the twentieth century was the demonopolisation and liberalisation of industries which for many years had been the preserve of state-owned monopolies; in many cases this process was coupled with privatisation or partial privatisation of state-owned undertakings[162].

---

[151] Case T-342/07 *Ryanair Holdings plc v Commission* [2010] ECR II-000, [2011] 4 CMLR 245.

[152] Case M 5830, Commission decision of 26 January 2011; the decision is on appeal Case T-202/11 *Aeroporia Aigaiou Aeroporiki and Marfin Investment Group Symmetochon v Commission*, not yet decided.

[153] Case COMP/M.5335, Commission decision of 22 June 2009.

[154] Case M 5440, decision of 28 August 2009.

[155] Case M 5141, decision of 17 December 2008.

[156] See eg Case M 5889 *United/Continental* decision of 27 July 2010 and Case M 5403 *BMI/Lufthansa* decision of 14 May 2009.

[157] OJ [2001] L 265/15, [2001] 5 CMLR 1119.

[158] Case T-241/01 *SAS v Commission* [2005] ECR II-2917, [2005] 5 CMLR 922.

[159] Commission Press Release IP/10/1487, 9 November 2010; note that this decision has now been appealed to the General Court, Cases T-9/11 etc *Air Canada v Commission*, not yet decided, and there are several pending damages actions arising from this case both in England and Wales (see ch 8, 'Group litigation orders and representative actions', p 314) and in other jurisdictions.

[160] Commission MEMO/08/158 of 11 March 2008.

[161] Final Report, 19 March 2009, available at www.competition-commission.org.uk; BAA successfully challenged the CC decision in Case No 1110/6/8/09 *BAA v Competition Commission* [2009] CAT 35, [2009] CompAR 23; the CC's appeal against this judgment was partially upheld in *Competition Commission v BAA Ltd* [2010] EWCA Civ 1097. BBA subsequently appealed the CC decision that there were no material changes in circumstances since the 2009 Report: Case No 1185/618/11, not yet decided

[162] On privatisation see Vickers and Yarrow *Privatisation and Economic Analysis* (MIT Press, 1987); Veljanowski *Selling the State – Privatisation in Britain* (Weidenfeld and Nicolson, 1987); *Privatisation and*

Obvious examples are the so-called 'utilities' such as telecommunications, gas, electricity and water. The problems for competition policy that arise where former monopolists are 'released' into the free market are obvious: in so far as there is no effective competition, which is particularly likely to be the case in the early years, they may be able to charge excessive prices; and they may also be able to adopt tactics intended to foreclose new competitors from entering the market. At the same time it is necessary to ensure that former monopolists provide adequate services of an appropriate standard. A complicating factor is that utilities are often subject to a requirement that they comply with a 'universal service obligation', for example a duty to undertake the daily delivery of letters or to maintain an electricity or water supply to business and residential premises. Undertakings that are subject to a universal service obligation of this kind may need some immunity from competition so that they can make sufficient profits to enable them to perform it, which is why, for example, postal operators historically enjoyed a legal monopoly over the delivery of letters of less than a certain weight and size[163].

(B) **EU law and the liberalisation of markets**

In the EU considerable steps have been taken towards the liberalisation of utilities and the development of a single market, albeit with greater success in some sectors than in others. Directives have been adopted in the case of electronic communications, post and energy markets with a view to creating conditions in which competitive markets develop. At the same time the European Commission has been adapting the principles of competition law and applying them to these sectors; in particular the so-called 'essential facilities doctrine' may play an important role in enabling third parties to gain access to physical infrastructures where this is necessary for the provision of competitive services[164].

(C) **Regulatory systems in the UK for utilities**

In the UK detailed regulatory regimes were established for the industries that were privatised in the 1980s and 1990s, namely telecommunications, gas, electricity, water, aviation and rail transport; these regimes provide, *inter alia*, for price control where persistent market power means that the normal process of competition will not deliver competitive prices to consumers[165]. The sectoral regulators[166], such as the Office of Communications, act as a surrogate for competition, at least until effective competition develops, by imposing constraints on what the regulated undertakings can do; the regulators are charged with the responsibility of protecting consumers, promoting competition where possible and controlling prices. In a sense, regulators 'hold the fort' until competition arrives. Regulated undertakings operate subject to licences that impose obligations upon them

---

Competition: A Market Prospectus (Hobart Paperback 28, 1988, ed Veljanowski); Graham and Prosser *Privatising Public Enterprises* (Oxford University Press, 1991).

[163] On the permitted 'reserved area' for letters under EU law, see 'Legislation', pp 984–985 below.

[164] See ch 17, 'Is the product to which access is sought indispensable to someone wishing to compete in the downstream market?', pp 701–707 on the essential facilities doctrine, noting the need, discussed there, to impose constraints upon it; these constraints are not so important where a facility was developed by a state-owned monopolist as opposed to an undertaking operating in the private sector: see the Opinion of Advocate General Mazák given on 2 September 2010 in Case C-52/09 *Konkurrensverket v TeliaSonera AB*, paras 24–28.

[165] See generally Armstrong, Cowan and Vickers *Regulatory Reform: Economic Analysis and British Experience* (MIT Press, 1994); *Competition in Regulated Industries* (Oxford University Press, 1998, eds Helm and Jenkinson); Baldwin and Cave *Understanding Regulation: Theory, Strategy and Practice* (Oxford University Press, 1999), in particular chs 14–18.

[166] See ch 2, 'Sectoral regulators', pp 68–69.

and that attempt to prevent conduct, *inter alia*, that will be anti-competitive, discriminatory or exploitative. The regulators monitor these licences and have powers to enforce compliance with them; in the event of disputes with regulated undertakings as to the appropriate terms for inclusion in a licence, the regulators can make a so-called 'modification reference' to the CC which will decide whether the matters referred operate, or may be expected to operate, against the public interest, and, if so, whether the effects adverse to the public interest could be remedied by modifications to the licences[167]. The sectoral regulators also have concurrent powers, with the OFT, to apply Articles 101 and 102 TFEU and the Chapter I and Chapter II prohibitions in the Competition Act 1998 in the sectors for which they are responsible[168].

(D) Price caps

A particular problem in the regulated industries is the control of prices. A central proposition of competition policy is that price should be determined by the market, and not by the state or an agency of the state. Competition authorities take action against excessive prices only rarely[169]. However where there is monopoly or near-monopoly, in particular in relation to essential services such as voice telephony or the supply of electricity, price control may be necessary; where this is the case, various techniques can be deployed to determine what the price should be. One method of capping prices is to fix an upper limit on the rate of return permissible on the capital invested in an industry: this, however, may encourage regulated bodies to over-invest, in order to expand the base on which profit can be earned; furthermore this technique does nothing to encourage efficiency. In the UK the price control function has therefore been exercised through the 'RPI minus X' formula: regulated undertakings are allowed to increase their prices only by the increase in the Resale Prices Index, less a particular percentage as fixed by the relevant regulator[170]. Over a period of time this formula leads to a reduction in prices in real terms, thereby benefitting the consumer and forcing the privatised industries to increase efficiency in order to continue in profit. The 'RPI minus X' formula encourages firms to become more efficient since, if they can cut their costs, they will make a higher profit. A further benefit of the 'RPI minus X' formula is that it is relatively simple to apply: the regulator simply sets the figure, after which all that is necessary is to check that the price is not being exceeded. When deciding the value of X for the purpose of 'RPI minus X', the regulator is asked, in effect, to determine the extent to which added efficiency is possible within the industry in question[171].

In the text that follows relevant provisions of EU and UK law will be briefly discussed, so that the reader has an idea of the regulatory environment of the electronic communications, post, energy and water markets and of the possible application of competition law to them. However the text is intended as a mere introduction to subject-matter that

---

[167] For an example of a modification reference see *Stansted price control review*, 4 November 2008; summaries of these reports can be found at www.competition-commission.org.uk.

[168] On concurrency under the Competition Act 1998 see ch 10, 'Concurrency', pp 437–439.

[169] See ch 18, 'Exploitative Pricing Practices', pp 718–728.

[170] See generally *Incentive Regulation: Reviewing RPI-X and Promoting Competition* (Centre for the Study of Regulated Industries, 1992); Spring 'An Investigation of RPI-X Price Cap Regulation using British Gas as a Case-study' (CRI, 1992); Cave and Mill 'Cost Allocation in Regulated Industries' (CRI, 1992).

[171] For a review of the 'RPI minus X' in the energy sector see OFGEM document 13/09 'Regulating energy networks for the future: RPI-X@20 Principles, Process and Issues', 27 February 2009, available at www.ofgem.gov.uk.

is substantial and complex; references to more detailed literature will be provided where appropriate.

8. Electronic Communications[172]

(A) EU law

(i) Legislation

There are two 'streams' of Directives of relevance to the electronic communications sector. The first consists of Directives adopted by the Council of Ministers and the European Parliament under Article 114 TFEU to bring about harmonisation necessary for the establishment of an internal market. A series of Directives, dating back to 1990, had been adopted under Article 114; by the end of that decade[173] the convergence of the telecommunications, media and information technology sectors meant it was desirable that a single regulatory framework for electronic communications should cover all transmission networks and services. This led to the adoption of a package of five Directives and one Decision in 2002[174]. The package was amended in December 2009 by two further Directives[175]. Under this regulatory framework national regulatory authorities are required to impose regulatory obligations on undertakings in the electronic communications sector that have significant market power, which for this purpose is given the same meaning as 'dominance' in Article 102, in any relevant markets. The Commission published a Recommendation on *Relevant Product and Service Markets* to be regulated in accordance with the rules set out in the package[176]: a new Recommendation was published in November 2007[177]; and in July 2002 the Commission published its guidelines

---

[172] See further Gillies and Marshall *Telecommunications Law* (Butterworths, 2nd ed, 2003), ch 3; Geradin and Kerf *Controlling Market Power in Telecommunications* (Oxford University Press, 2003); Nihoul and Rodford *EU Electronic Communications Law* (Oxford University Press, 2004); Nikolinakos *EU Competition Law and Regulation in the Converging Telecommunications, Media and IT Sectors* (Kluwer Law International, 2006); Farr and Oakley *EU Communications Law* (Sweet & Maxwell, 2nd ed, 2006); Faull and Nikpay *The EC Law of Competition* (Oxford University Press, 2nd ed, 2007), ch 13; Bellamy and Child *European Community Law of Competition* (Oxford University Press, 6th ed, 2008, eds Roth and Rose), paras 12.087–12.168; Garzaniti *Telecommunications, Broadcasting and the Internet: EU Competition Law and Regulation* (Sweet & Maxwell, 3rd ed, 2010).

[173] Commission Working Document *Proposed New Regulatory Framework for Electronic Communications Networks and Services* COM(2001) 175 final, 28 March 2001.

[174] See Directive of the European Parliament and of the Council on a common regulatory framework for electronic communications networks and services, OJ [2002] L 108/33 (the 'Framework Directive'); Directive of the European Parliament and of the Council on the authorisation of electronic communications networks and services, OJ [2002] L 108/22 (the 'Authorisation Directive'); Directive of the European Parliament and of the Council on access to, and interconnection of, electronic communications networks and associated facilities, OJ [2002] L 108/7 (the 'Access Directive'); Directive of the European Parliament and of the Council on universal service and users' rights relating to electronic communications networks and services, OJ [2002] L 108/51 (the 'Universal Service Directive'); Directive of the European Parliament and of the Council concerning the processing of personal data and the protection of privacy in the electronic communications sector, OJ [2002] L 201/37 (the 'Data Protection Directive'); and the Radio Spectrum Decision, OJ [2002] L 108/1; see Bavasso 'Electronic Communications: A New Paradigm for European Regulation' (2004) 41 CML Rev 87.

[175] Directive 2009/136/EC of the European Parliament and of the Council of 25 November 2009 amending the Universal Service Directive and the Data Protection Directive, OJ [2009] L 337/11; Directive 2009/140/EC of the European Parliament and of the Council amending the Framework Directive, the Access Directive and the Authorisation Directive, OJ [2009] L 337/37.

[176] OJ [2003] L 114/45.

[177] Available at www.ec.europa.eu/information_society.

on *Market Analysis and the Calculation of Significant Market Power* to be followed by national authorities in reaching their conclusions[178]. A 'Body of European Regulators for Electronic Communications' has been established to ensure the consistent application of the regulatory package[179]. There is also a Council and Parliament Regulation of 2000 on *Unbundled Access to the Local Loop*[180]. The Commission reports each year to the Council, the Parliament, ECOSOC and the Committee of the Regions on progress achieved in implementing the EU's electronic communications policy.

The second stream of EU legislation consists of Directives adopted by the Commission pursuant to Article 106(3) TFEU[181]. The first of these was the Telecommunications Terminal Equipment Directive of 1988[182], which required Member States to withdraw special or exclusive rights granted to undertakings with respect to the importation, marketing, connection and bringing into service of telecommunications terminal equipment and the maintenance of such equipment. The Commission subsequently adopted the Telecommunications Services Directive of 1990[183], which began the process of opening up telecommunications markets themselves to competition. The Services Directive has been amended several times in order to expand its scope; it was successively extended to apply to the satellite[184], cable[185] and mobile telephony[186] sectors, and ultimately required full competition in telecommunications markets[187]. The Commission has also amended the original Services Directive to require that, where a single operator owns both a telecommunications and a cable network, they must be established as separate legal entities[188]. A consolidating Directive, bringing all these pieces of legislation into a single legal instrument, was adopted in September 2002[189].

In May 2010 the Commission launched its *Digital Agenda for Europe*[190], suggesting various ways in which to create a digital single market. As part of this *Agenda* the Commission adopted a Recommendation on regulated access to 'Next Generation Access Networks'[191] and two other measures[192] in order to facilitate the delivery of fast and ultrafast broadband.

---

[178] OJ [2002] C 165/6, [2002] 5 CMLR 989.

[179] Regulation 1211/2009/EC, OJ [2009] L 337/1.

[180] Regulation 2887/2000/EC, OJ [2000] L 336/00; on the issue of the local loop see Nikolinakos 'Promoting Competition in the Local Access Network: Local Loop Unbundling' (2001) 22 ECLR 266.

[181] On the Commission's powers to adopt directives under Article 106(3) see ch 6, 'Article 106(3)', pp 243–244.

[182] Commission Directive 88/301/EEC, OJ [1988] L 131/73, [1991] 4 CMLR 922; on the (mostly unsuccessful) challenge to this Directive see Case C-202/88 *France v Commission* [1991] ECR I-1223, [1992] 5 CMLR 552, and for comment see Naftel 'The Natural Death of a Natural Monopoly' (1993) 14 ECLR 105; on France's failure to implement the Directive correctly see Case C-91/94 *Tranchant v Telephone Store* [1995] ECR I-3911, [1997] 4 CMLR 74; see also Case C-146/00 *Commission v France* [2001] ECR I-9767.

[183] Commission Directive 90/388/EEC, OJ [1990] L 192/10, [1991] 4 CMLR 932; this Directive was unsuccessfully challenged in Cases C-271/90 etc *Spain v Commission* [1992] ECR I-5833, [1993] 4 CMLR 100.

[184] Commission Directive 94/46/EC, OJ [1994] L 268/15.

[185] Commission Directive 95/51/EC, OJ [1995] L 256/49.

[186] Commission Directive 92/1/EC, OJ [1996] L 20/59.

[187] Commission Directive 96/19/EC, OJ [1996] L 74/13.

[188] Commission Directive 99/64/EC, OJ [1999] L 175/39.

[189] Commission Directive 2002/77/EC, OJ [2002] L 249/21.

[190] COM(2010) 245 final, available at www.ec.europa.eu/information_society/digital-agenda/index_en.htm.

[191] OJ [2010] L 251/35.

[192] *Communication on investing in broadband networks* COM(2010) 472 a *Proposal for a Decision to establish the first radio spectrum policy programme* COM(2010) 471 final, available at www.ec.europa.eu/information_society/.

(ii) Application of EU competition law

The Commission has been active in applying the competition rules to the telecommunications sector for many years. In 1991 it published *Guidelines on the Application of EEC Competition Rules in the Telecommunications Sector*[193], and in 1998 it adopted the *Notice on the Application of the Competition Rules to Access Agreements in the Telecommunications Sector*[194]. The latter of these two instruments is of particular interest. Part I is entitled 'Framework', and discusses the relationship between the competition rules and sector-specific regulation. Part II deals with market definition, and Part III provides detailed analysis of the application of the principles of competition law to access agreements; the most extensive discussion is of the 'essential facilities doctrine' under Article 102, but the Notice also contains useful guidance on other types of abuse.

The Commission has adopted numerous favourable decisions on strategic alliances in the electronic communications sector, such as *BT/MCI*[195], *Atlas*[196], *Iridium*[197], *Phoenix/ GlobalOne*[198], *Uniworld*[199], *Unisource*[200], *Cégétel+4*[201] and *Télécom Développement*[202]. It also approved the *GSM MoU Standard International Roaming Agreement*, which enables GSM mobile telephone users in one country to use the network in another country[203]. In *T-Mobile Deutschland/O2 Germany* the Commission authorised an agreement that would enable the parties to roam on one another's 3G networks[204]. On appeal the General Court was critical of the Commission's analysis and partially annulled the decision[205].

Acting under Article 102 in conjunction with Article 106 the Commission took action against Italy and Spain as a result of their discriminatory treatment of the second operators of mobile telephony in those countries[206]; however it declined to take similar action against Austria, which had not discriminated in favour of the incumbent operator[207].

In 1998 the Commission initiated action in relation to possible excessive or discriminatory prices for calls to mobile telephones[208], which ended in May 1999 following significant price reductions[209]. In 1999 the Commission launched a sector inquiry into three issues, leased lines, mobile roaming services and the local loop[210]. The leased line investigation

---

[193] OJ [1991] C 233/2, [1991] 4 CMLR 946.

[194] OJ [1998] C 265/2, [1998] 5 CMLR 821.

[195] OJ [1994] L 223/36, [1995] 5 CMLR 285.

[196] OJ [1996] L 239/29, [1997] 4 CMLR 89.

[197] OJ [1997] L 16/87, [1997] 4 CMLR 1065.

[198] OJ [1996] L 239/57, [1997] 4 CMLR 147.

[199] OJ [1997] L 318/24, [1998] 4 CMLR 145.

[200] OJ [1997] L 318/1, [1998] 4 CMLR 105; this decision was subsequently withdrawn due to changes in the market: Commission Press Release IP/01/1, 3 January 2001.

[201] OJ [1999] L 218/14, [2000] 4 CMLR 106.

[202] OJ [1999] L 218/24, [2000] 4 CMLR 124.

[203] See the Commission's XXVIIth *Annual Report on Competition Policy* (1997), point 75 and pp 139–140.

[204] OJ [2004] L 75/32.

[205] Case T-328/03 *O2 (Germany) GmbH v Commission* [2006] ECR II-1231, [2006] 5 CMLR 258.

[206] See *Second Operator of GSM Radiotelephony Services in Italy* OJ [1995] L 280/49, [1996] 4 CMLR 700; *Second Operator of GSM Radiotelephony Services in Spain* OJ [1997] L 76/19.

[207] Case T-54/99 *max.mobil Telekommunikation Service GmbH v Commission* [2002] ECR II-313, [2002] 4 CMLR 1356, on appeal Case C-141/02 P *Commission v max.mobil* [2005] ECR I-1283, [2005] 4 CMLR 735.

[208] See the Commission's XXVIIIth *Report on Competition Policy* (1998), points 79–81.

[209] See Commission Press Release IP/99/298, 4 May 1999 and Commission's XXIXth *Annual Report on Competition Policy* (1999), pp 375–380.

[210] See the Commission's XXIXth *Report on Competition Policy* (1999), points 74–76; see further the XXXth *Report* (2000), points 157–160 and XXXIst *Report* (2001), points 125–131; speech by Sauter 'The Sector Inquiries into Leased Lines and Mobile Roaming: Findings and follow-up of the competition law investigations' 17 September 2001, available at www.ec.europa.eu/competition/speeches/.

ended in December 2002, as a result of substantial price decreases[211]. In September 2007 a Regulation of the Council and European Parliament was adopted with the intention of dealing with the problem of excessive prices for international mobile calls[212].

The Commission has taken action on four occasions against incumbent operators for impeding access to the market for the provision of residential broadband internet access: it concluded that Wanadoo of France[213] was guilty of predatory pricing contrary to Article 102; that Deutsche Telekom of Germany[214] and Telefónica of Spain[215] were guilty of margin squeezes; and that Telekomunikacja Polska of Poland[215a] had imposed unfair trading conditions. The Commission is investigating similar misconduct by the incumbent operator in the Slovak Republic[216].

The Commission has investigated many concentrations in the telecommunications sector under the EUMR. Of particular interest was *Telia/Telenor*[217], where the Commission granted conditional clearance, following a Phase II investigation, to a concentration between the public telecommunications operators of Sweden and Norway; having received the clearance, the parties decided not to proceed with the transaction. Subsequently, the Commission gave conditional clearance in *Telia/Sonera*[218], the incumbent operators of Sweden and Finland: this merger was consummated in December 2002. The Commission also granted conditional clearance, following a Phase II investigation, to *WorldCom/ MCI*[219]; in 2000, however, it prohibited the concentration in *MCI WorldCom/Sprint*[220] which, in its view, would have created a dominant firm in the market for 'top-level' Internet interconnectivity. In *T.Mobile/tele.ring*[221] the Commission required remedies to approve a merger that it considered would otherwise lead to a non-collusive oligopoly in the Austrian mobile telephony sector. The Commission approved the joint venture in *T-Mobile/Orange*[222], following a Phase I investigation, on condition that the parties amend a network sharing agreement with a competitor and agree to divest spectrum.

(B) **UK law**

The Telecommunications Act 1984 established the office of Director General of Telecommunications and the regulatory framework for the telecommunications sector;

[211] See Commission Press Release IP/02/1852, 11 December 2002.

[212] Regulation 717/2007, OJ [2007] L 171/32, as amended by Regulation 544/2009, OJ [2009] L 167/12; see the Commission's report on the operation of Regulation 712/2007, COM (2011) 407 final, available at www. ec.europa.eu/information_society.

[213] [2005] 5 CMLR 120, upheld on appeal to the General Court Case T-340/03 *France Télécom SA v Commission* [2007] ECR II-107, [2007] 4 CMLR 919, and on appeal to the Court of Justice Case C-202/07 P [2009] ECR I-2369, [2009] 4 CMLR 1149.

[214] OJ [2003] L 263/9, [2004] 4 CMLR 790, upheld on appeal to the General Court Case T-271/03 *Deutsche Telekom AG v Commission* [2008] ECR II-477, [2008] 5 CMLR 631, and on appeal to the Court of Justice Case C-280/08 P [2010] ECR I-000, [2010] 5 CMLR 1495.

[215] The case is on appeal to the General Court, Case T-336/07 *Telefónica and Telefónica España v Commission*, not yet decided.

[215a] See Commission Press Release IP/11/771, 22 June 2011.

[216] See Commission Press Release IP/10/1741, 17 December 2010.

[217] Case M 1439 OJ [2001] L 40/1, [2001] 4 CMLR 1226.

[218] Case M 2803 [2002] C 201/19.

[219] Case M 1069, OJ [1999] L 116/1, [1999] 5 CMLR 876.

[220] Case M 1741, annulled on appeal for technical reasons Case T-310/00 *MCI Inc v Commission* [2004] ECR II-3253, [2004] 5 CMLR 1274.

[221] Case M 3916, decision of 26 April 2006; on non-collusive oligopoly see ch 21, 'The non-collusive oligopoly gap', pp 864–866.

[222] Case M 5650, decision of 1 March 2010; the Commission cooperated closely with the OFT and OFCOM during its investigation.

the position of the Director General of Telecommunications has now been abolished, and his powers have been transferred to the Office of Communications ('OFCOM')[223]. OFCOM is a single regulator for the media and communications industries and has considerable regulatory powers under the Communications Act 2003. OFCOM is required by the EU regulatory framework to review certain markets to determine whether the market is 'effectively competitive'[224]. If OFCOM determines that a market is not effectively competitive, it must identify undertakings with significant market power on that market and impose on such undertakings appropriate specific regulatory obligations or maintain or amend such obligations where they already exist[225].

OFCOM has concurrent powers with the OFT to apply Articles 101 and 102 TFEU and the Chapter I and Chapter II prohibitions[226]. A Guideline has been adopted, *Competition Act 1998: The Application in the Telecommunications Sector*[227], to explain the application of the competition rules in this sector; in particular it discusses the approach that will be taken to determining costs in a network industry such as telecommunications[228].

OFCOM has adopted numerous decisions in which it concluded that there had been no infringement of the EU or the UK competition rules: these can be found in the Table of published decisions in chapter 9 and the accompanying website for this book[229]. Many disputes in the electronic communications sector are now being dealt with, not under competition law, but under sector-specific legislation[230]. In practical terms this may be a simpler and quicker way to address problems of market failure, with an obvious knock-on effect on the number of infringement decisions.

OFCOM also has concurrent powers with the OFT in relation to market investigation references under the Enterprise Act 2002[231]. OFCOM accepted extensive undertakings in lieu of a reference in *BT*[232] but made a reference to the CC in *Premium pay TV movies* in August 2010[233].

9. Post[234]

(A) EU law

(i) Legislation

Development of EU law and policy in the postal sector has come about partly through initiatives of the Council of Ministers and the Commission, and partly as a result of the very

---

[223] Office of Communications Act 2002, s 1.

[224] In identifying such markets, OFCOM is required to take the utmost account of recommendations and guidelines published by the Commission as to what product and service markets should be analysed: Article 16(1) of the Framework Directive.

[225] Communications Act 2003, s 45.

[226] Ibid, s 371.

[227] OFT 417 (2000).

[228] Ibid, paras 7.5–7.12.

[229] See ch 9, 'Table of published decisions', pp 374–389.

[230] See eg Communications Act 2003, ss 185–191 which contain OFCOM's duties and powers in relation to resolving certain regulatory disputes.

[231] Communications Act 2003, s 370; on market investigations see ch 11, 'Market Investigation References', pp 466ff.

[232] OFCOM, 22 September 2005, available at www.ofcom.org.uk.

[233] OFCOM, 4 August 2010, available at www.ofcom.org.uk.

[234] See further Bellamy and Child *European Community Law of Competition* (Oxford University Press, 6th ed, 2008, eds Roth and Rose), paras 12.004–12.051.

important judgment of the Court of Justice in the *Corbeau* case[235]. The Commission first began to take an interest in the postal sector, and the possibility of applying the competition rules to it, in the late 1980s. This culminated in the adoption of the Commission's Green Paper on *The Development of the Single Market for Postal Services*[236]. It proposed that all postal services, except ordinary internal letter deliveries, should be liberalised. In 1993 the Commission issued a communication setting out *Guidelines for the Development of [EU] Postal Services*[237]. The Council of Ministers asked the Commission to draft a proposal for a legislative framework; there are now two legislative instruments, the Directive of the European Parliament and of the Council on *Common Rules for the Development of the Internal Market of [EU] Postal Services and the Improvement of Quality of Service*[238] and the Commission *Notice on the Application of the Competition Rules to the Postal Sector*[239]. The Directive entered into force on 10 February 1998[240]. The Notice was adopted by the Commission on 17 December 1997. These two measures should be seen as part of a single package, the Directive intended to liberalise access to certain postal activities in the EU and the Notice to ensure that it is understood how the competition rules impact upon the sector.

The Directive establishes common rules throughout the EU on six matters:

- the provision of a universal service
- the extent of the permissible monopoly and the conditions governing the provision of non-monopolised services
- tariff principles and transparency of accounts for universal service provision
- the setting of quality standards for universal service provision
- the harmonisation of technical standards
- the creation of independent national regulatory authorities.

As regards the first two matters the Directive establishes *minimum* standards as to the universal standards and *maximum* limits to the permissible monopoly. Member States are entitled to confer lesser, but not broader, monopoly rights than those set out in the Directive. Article 7(1) provides essentially that the services 'which may be reserved' (that is which may remain a monopoly) shall be 'the clearance, sorting, transport and delivery of items of domestic correspondence, provided they weigh less than 350 grams'. The monopoly was reduced to letters weighing less than 50 grams by Directive 2002/39/EC[241]. A third postal directive, Directive 2008/06/EC, provides that all postal services in the EU should be opened to competition by 31 December 2010[242]. Directive 2008/06 also contains provisions relating to the universal service and the powers and role of independent national regulatory authorities.

---

[235] Case C-320/91 *Corbeau* [1993] ECR I-2533, [1995] 4 CMLR 621: see 'The *Corbeau* case and the universal service obligation', pp 986–987 below.

[236] COM(91) 476, June 1991.

[237] COM(93) 247.

[238] Directive 97/67/EC, OJ [1998] L 15/14.

[239] OJ [1998] C 39/2, [1998] 5 CMLR 108.

[240] The Directive was implemented in the UK by the Postal Services Regulations 1999, SI 1999/2107.

[241] Article 1 of Directive 2002/39/EC, OJ [2002] L 176/21, amending Article 7 of Directive 97/67/EC.

[242] OJ [2008] L 52/3, substantially amending Directive 97/96/EC; certain Member States (those which joined the EU in 2004 or which are very small) have the option to extend this deadline by a further two years.

(ii) Application of EU competition law

(A) The Corbeau case and the universal service obligation[243]

There is general agreement among Member States that there are societal benefits in the maintenance of a universal postal service, that is to say a right of access to a minimum range of postal services, of a specified quality, which must be provided in all Member States at affordable prices for the benefit of all users, irrespective of their geographical location. People living in remote rural areas should have access to these services on no less favourable terms than those living in major conurbations; there is an obvious benefit, in terms of social cohesion, if all members of society can communicate with one another through the postal system, no matter where they live. A complex policy issue is to determine whether, and if so how extensive, a legal monopoly needs to be granted to the undertaking charged with performing this universal service in order to enable it to perform its duties; this question turns in part on how costly the universal service obligation is to the undertaking that has to perform it. Clearly the maintenance of a universal service is likely to be expensive, and the relevant provider will need to be assured of sufficient profits to pay for it; competitors should not be able to 'pick the cherries' or, depending on taste, 'skim the cream' and earn profits from lucrative services, while leaving the unprofitable services to the undertaking charged with the universal service obligation.

These issues came before the Court of Justice in the *Corbeau case*[244]. Corbeau had been charged with infringing a Belgian criminal law which conferred a monopoly on the Regie des Postes to collect, carry and distribute post in Belgium. Corbeau offered local courier services, but not a basic postal service. The Belgian court sought a preliminary ruling on the compatibility of the monopoly conferred by Belgian law with Articles 102 and 106 TFEU. The task for the Court of Justice was to determine whether Belgium was in breach of Article 106(1) in maintaining in force a measure contrary to Article 102, or whether the rights conferred on Régie des Postes satisfied the terms of Article 106(2). This provision does permit a restriction of competition – or even the elimination of all competition – where this is necessary to enable an undertaking to carry on the task entrusted to it[245]. At paragraph 15 of its judgment the Court noted that it could not be disputed that Régie des Postes was entrusted with a service of general economic interest[246]; the question was the extent to which a restriction of competition was necessary to enable it to carry on that function[247]. The Court continued at paragraph 17:

> The starting point of such an examination must be the premise that the obligation on the part of the undertaking entrusted with that task to perform its services in conditions of economic equilibrium presupposes that it will be possible to offset less profitable sectors against the profitable sectors and hence justifies a restriction of competition from individual undertakings where the economically profitable sectors are concerned.

In the following paragraph the Court of Justice notes that, in the absence of a monopoly, it would be possible for individual undertakings 'to concentrate on the economically profitable operations' (in other words, to 'cherry pick'). But the Court went on, at paragraph 19:

> However, the exclusion of competition is not justified as regards specific services dissociable from the service of general interest which meet special needs of economic operators

---

[243] See also Case C-340/99 *TNT Traco SpA v Poste Italiane SpA* [2001] ECR I-4109.

[244] See ch 23, n 235 above.

[245] See ch 6, 'Article 106(2)', pp 235–242.

[246] *Corbeau* (ch 23 n 235 above), para 15.

[247] Ibid, para 16.

and which call for certain additional services not offered by the traditional postal service, such as collection from the senders' address, greater speed or reliability of distribution or the possibility of changing the destination in the course of transit in so far as such specific services, by their nature and the conditions in which they are offered, such as the geographical area in which they are provided, do not compromise the economic equilibrium of the service of general economic interest performed by the holder of the exclusive right.

At paragraph 20, the Court said that the application of the foregoing tests would be a task for the national court dealing with the case.

The importance of this carefully crafted judgment is clear: postal monopolies may be consistent with EU competition law, but subject to the important tests set out in paragraph 19. That paragraph makes clear that it is possible, as a matter of law, that a Member State may have conferred a monopoly that is wider than is legitimate for the purpose of maintaining the universal service, and that, where this is the case, the monopoly rights in question may be unenforceable. The first package of measures in the postal sector attempts on the one hand, in Directive 97/67, to determine the permissible limits of the legal monopoly and on the other, in the *Commission's Notice*, to explain the circumstances in which a legitimate monopolist might nonetheless be found guilty of infringing the competition rules. The Commission has itself taken action to strike down monopolies that go beyond what is justifiable under the *Corbeau* judgment[248].

(B) The Commission's Notice on competition in the postal sector[249]

This *Notice* sets out in some detail how the Commission expects to apply the competition rules in the postal sector. It is divided into nine parts. After a preface and a discussion of terminology, the *Notice* considers market definition in the postal sector. Part 3 considers the issue of cross-subsidisation in some detail; the position of public undertakings and the freedom to provide services are then looked at, followed by state measures and state aid. Part 8 discusses what are meant by services of general economic interest in Article 106(2) TFEU.

(C) Cases and decisions[250]

In *Spanish International Courier Services*[251] the Commission held that it was unlawful for Spain to reserve to the Spanish Post Office, which already had a monopoly of the basic postal service, the ancillary activity of international courier services. In practice the Spanish Post Office was unable to meet the demand for international courier services (for example it did not cover the whole territory of Spain, nor did it extend to all countries in the world), so that there was a limitation of supply and technical development in the sense of Article 102(2)(b) TFEU. A similar decision in *Dutch Express Delivery Services*[252] was annulled on appeal by the Court of Justice as the Commission had not followed the correct procedure in adopting its decision[253]. In *Slovakian postal legislation*[254] the Commission concluded that Slovakia had infringed Article 101 by extending

---

[248] On the Commission's infringement proceedings see below.

[249] OJ [1998] C 39/2, [1998] 5 CMLR 108.

[250] See Flynn and Rizza 'Postal Services and Competition Law – A Review and Analysis of the EC Case Law' (2002) 25 World Competition 475.

[251] OJ [1990] L 233/19, [1991] 4 CMLR 560.

[252] OJ [1990] L 10/47, [1990] 4 CMLR 947.

[253] Cases C-48/90 and 66/90 *Netherlands v Commission* [1992] ECR I-565, [1993] 5 CMLR 316.

[254] Commission decision of 7 October 2008; the decision is on appeal Case T-556/08 *Slovenská pošta v Commission*, not yet decided.

the Slovakian Post Office's monopoly over the basic letter service to hybrid mail services. In *Deutsche Post*[255] the Commission imposed a fine of €24 million on the incumbent operator in Germany for offering loyalty rebates to customers of its business parcels service, and it also concluded that it was guilty of predatory pricing[256]. In *New Postal Services with a Guaranteed Day- or Time-Certain Delivery in Italy*[257] the Commission concluded that an Italian Decree excluding competition for a specific type of hybridised electronic mail service was contrary to Article 106(1) in conjunction with Article 102. In *Reims II*[258] the Commission decided that the criteria of Article 101(3) were satisfied in the case of an agreement between the postal operators of the EU as to the amount that one operator would pay to another when a letter posted in the former's country had to be delivered in the territory of the latter, so-called 'terminal dues'. There has been a long-running battle between the Union Francaise de l'Express, La Poste of France and the Commission, in relation to international express mail[259]. In *De Post/La Poste*[260] the Commission imposed a fine of €2.5 million on the Belgian postal operator for giving a more favourable tariff for its general letter mail service to those customers who also used its new business-to-business mail service. In *UPS v Commission*[261] the General Court upheld the Commission's rejection of a complaint by UPS that Deutsche Post was guilty of an abuse of a dominant position by using income from its reserved letter market to finance the acquisition of a shareholding in the express parcels operator DHL.

A number of concentrations in the postal sector have been notified to the Commission under the EUMR. In the first case, *TNT/Canada Post*[262], the establishment of a joint venture between TNT and five postal administrations for the purpose of offering worldwide international express delivery services was cleared, subject to the offering of commitments by the four European postal administrations concerned that they would not discriminate in favour of the joint venture (the Canadian Post Office was not asked to give such a commitment). Similar commitments have been offered in subsequent cases[263]. The Commission granted conditional clearance in the cases of *Post Office/TPG/SPPL*[264] and *Posten/Post Danmark*[265].

---

[255] OJ [2001] L 125/27, [2001] 5 CMLR 99; see also *Deutsche Post AG II* OJ [2001] L 331/40, [2002] 4 CMLR 598 imposing a 'symbolic' fine of €1,000 on Deutsche Post for abusing its dominant position in relation to so-called 'A-B-A remail'.

[256] For discussion of the Commission's approach to predatory pricing in this case see ch 18, 'Predatory price cutting and cross-subsidisation', p 748.

[257] OJ [2001] L 63/59.

[258] OJ [1999] L 275/17, [2000] 4 CMLR 704: the Commission renewed the authorisation it had given in this case: OJ [2004] L 56/76, [2004] 5 CMLR 123; on the REIMS agreement see Reeves 'Terminal Problems in the Postal Sector' (2000) 21 ECLR 283; see also Cases C-147/97 and C-148/97 *Deutsche Post v GZS* [2000] ECR I-825, [2000] 4 CMLR 838, dealing with the right of Deutsche Post to impose charges for cross-border mail prior to the agreement on terminal dues.

[259] A helpful summary of the various decisions and appeals is provided in Case T-60/05 *UFEX v Commission* [2007] ECR II-3397, [2008] 5 CMLR 580, paras 1–24.

[260] OJ [2002] L 61/32, [2002] 4 CMLR 1426.

[261] Case T-175/99 [2002] ECR II-1915, [2002] 5 CMLR 67.

[262] Case M 102, decision of 2 December 2001.

[263] See eg Case M 787 *PTT Post/TNT-GD Net*, decision of 22 July 1996 and Case M 1168 *DHL/Deutsche Post*, decision of 26 June 1998.

[264] Case M 1915, decision of 13 March 2001.

[265] Case M 5152, decision of 21 April 2009.

(B) **UK law**

The Postal Services Act 2011 establishes the regulatory framework for the postal sector. The Postal Service Act Swept away much of the system that had been established over the precending 11 years. In particular it abolished the Postal Services Commission; its functions were transferred to OFCOM on 1 October 2011. OFCOM has concurrent powers with the OFT to apply Articles 101 and 102 TFEU and the Chapter I and Chapter II prohibitions in the Competition Act 1998[266]. OFCOM has proposed a number of changes to the domestic regulatory framework that seek to ensure Royal Mail satisfies its universal service obligations and becomes more efficient[267]. In June 2001 the OFT decided that the UK Post Office had not abused its dominant position in the postal services market by refusing to license its Royal Mail trade mark to an operator in the market for consumer lifestyle surveys[268].

10. ENERGY[269]

(A) **EU law**

(i) **Legislation**

Article 194 TFEU provides that EU policy on energy shall aim, in a spirit of solidarity between Member States, to ensure the functioning of the energy market; ensure security of energy supply in the EU; promote energy efficiency; and promote the interconnection of energy networks. However the accomplishment of an internal energy market has been a gradual process. The Council took the initiative in the 1990s by adopting Directives which established a procedure to improve the transparency of prices for gas and electricity in the EU[270]; which required Member States to take steps to ensure the possibility of transit of gas and electricity between Member States;[271] and which established common rules for the internal market in gas and electricity[272]. This was followed by a second wave of reform in 2003 when the Council adopted Directives establishing a new set of common rules for the internal market in gas and in electricity[273].

In 2007 the Commission conducted a sectoral inquiry under Article 17 of Regulation 1/2003 and concluded that energy markets in the EU were not functioning well: in particular many energy markets were highly concentrated; there is an absence of cross-border integration and cross-border competition; and there is insufficient unbundling of

---

[266] OFCOM's website is www.ofcom.org.uk.

[267] OFCOM consultation *Securing the Universal Postal Service*, 20 October 2011, available at www.ofcom.org.uk.

[268] See *Consignia/Postal Preference Service Ltd*, decision of 15 June 2001, available at www.oft.gov.uk; see also the interim High Court judgment in *Claritas v Post Office* [2001] UKCLR 2.

[269] See further Faull and Nikpay *The EC Law of Competition* (Oxford University Press, 2nd ed, 2007), ch 12; Bellamy and Child *European Community Law of Competition* (Oxford University Press, 6th ed, 2008, eds Rett and Rose), ch 12, Part 3, paras 12.073–12.083; Cameron *Competition in Energy Markets: Law and Regulation in the European Union* (Oxford University Press, 2nd ed, 2007).

[270] Council Directive 90/377/EEC, OJ [1990] L 185/16 (gas) and Council Directive 90/377/EEC, OJ [1990] L 185/16 (electricity).

[271] Council Directive 91/296/EEC, OJ [1991] L 147/37 (gas), as amended by Council Directive 95/49/EC, OJ [1995] L 233/86 and Council Directive 90/547/EEC, OJ [1990] L 313/30 (electricity).

[272] Council Directive 98/30/EC, OJ [1998] L 204/1, as amended by Council Directive 95/49/EC, OJ [1995] L 233/86 (gas) and Council Directive 96/92/EC, OJ [1997] L 27/20 (electricity).

[273] Council Directive 2003/55/EC, OJ [2003] L 176/57 (gas) and Council Directive 2003/54, OJ [2003] L 176/37 (electricity).

network and supply activities[274]. The Council and the European Parliament subsequently adopted a third package of legislative measures[275] which have as their objective a single EU gas and electricity market.

(ii) Application of EU competition law

The Commission has investigated a number of agreements in the energy sector. The privatisation of the electricity industry in Great Britain led to a decision that the criteria of Article 101(3) were satisfied in *Scottish Nuclear, Nuclear Energy Agreement*[276] and to two notices in the Official Journal dealing with numerous agreements that had been notified to the Commission under the system of notification for individual exemption in force at that time[277]. In 1995 the Commission gave its approval to a joint venture established by nine gas companies to construct and operate a gas interconnector between the UK and Belgium[278]. The Commission has also approved a number of long-term agreements for the supply of gas[279] and electricity[280]. However it has taken action (or is taking action) in a number of cases involving territorial restrictions and profit-sharing mechanisms in gas supply agreements[281]. In *IJsselcentrale*[282] the Commission held that an agreement between all the generators of electricity in the Netherlands and a joint subsidiary that only the latter could import and export electricity to and from that country entailed a restriction of competition that infringed Article 101(1).

Following the Commission's sectoral inquiry[283], it brought a number of cases under Article 102 in the energy sector. This enforcement action has led to a striking number of decisions under Article 9 of Regulation 1/2003, in which structural commitments were offered to, and accepted by, the Commission to address its concerns about exclusionary practices by vertically-integrated undertakings[284].

---

[274] COM(2006) 851 final; see also Wäktare, Kovács and Gee 'The Energy Sector Inquiry: conclusions and way forward' (2007) (Spring) *Competition Policy Newsletter* 55; Lowe, Pucinskaite, Webster and Lindberg 'Effective unbundling of energy transmission networks: lessons from the Energy Sector Inquiry' (2007) (Spring) *Competition Policy Newsletter* 23.

[275] Regulation 713/2009 establishing the EU Agency for co-operation of national energy regulators, OJ [2009] L 211/1; Regulation 714/2009 on conditions for access to the network for cross-border exchanges in electricity, OJ [2009] L 211/15; Regulation 715/2009 on conditions for access to the natural gas transmission networks, OJ [2009] L 229/29; Directive 2009/72/EC concerning common rules for the internal market in electricity, OJ [2009] L 211/55 and Directive 2009/73/EC concerning common rules for the internal market in natural gas, OJ [2009] L 211/94.

[276] OJ [1991] L 178/31.

[277] See OJ [1990] C 191/9 (dealing with ten notifications) and OJ [1990] C 245/9 (dealing with eight notifications). A joint venture to develop independent generators of electricity was the subject of a favourable notice in 1992, OJ [1992] C 92/4.

[278] See eg Commission's XXVth *Report on Competition Policy* (1995), point 82.

[279] See eg *Transgás/Turbogás* Commission's XXVIth *Report on Competition Policy* (1996), p 135 and *British Gas Network Code* XXVIth *Report on Competition Policy* (1996), pp 136–137.

[280] See eg *REN/Turbogás* OJ [1996] C 118/7, [1996] 4 CMLR 881 and *ISAB Energy* OJ [1996] C 138/3, [1996] 4 CMLR 889; see also Commission's XXXth *Report on Competition Policy* (2000), pp 154–155.

[281] See Wäktare 'Territorial restrictions and profit sharing mechanisms in the gas sector: the Algerian case' (2007) 3 *Competition Policy Newsletter* 19.

[282] OJ [1991] L 28/32, [1992] 5 CMLR 154; the decision was (eventually) partly annulled on appeal in Case T-16/91 *RV Rendo v Commission* [1996] ECR II-1827, [1997] 4 CMLR 453.

[283] See 'legislation', p 989 above.

[284] For a table of these and other decisions under Article 9 of Regulation 1/2003 see ch 7, 'Table of Article 9 Commitment Decisions', pp 259–260.

The Commission has investigated several mergers involving undertakings in the energy sector[285].

(B) **UK law**[286]

The regulatory regimes for the gas and electricity sectors are respectively contained in the Gas Act 1986 and Electricity Act 1989. Both sectors are regulated by the Gas and Electricity Markets Authority ('GEMA')[287], which is assisted by the Office of Gas and Electricity Markets ('OFGEM'). GEMA has concurrent powers with the OFT to apply Articles 101 and 102 TFEU and the Chapter I and Chapter II prohibitions in the Competition Act 1998. A *Guideline* has been adopted under the Act, *Competition Act 1998: Application in the Energy Sector*[288], and a *Guideline* on its application to the energy sector in Northern Ireland[289]. GEMA has adopted one infringement decision under its concurrent powers, imposing a fine of £46.1 million on National Grid plc for abusing its dominant position in the market for the supply of domestic gas meters[290]. On appeal GEMA's finding of abuse was upheld by the Competition Appeal Tribunal ('the CAT') and Court of Appeal, but the fine it had imposed was reduced to £15 million[291].

Concerns about energy prices led GEMA to launch an 'Energy Supply Probe' into the markets in gas and electricity for households and small businesses in February 2008[292]. GEMA concluded that in important respects the market worked well, but identified some areas of concern, such as unjustified price differentials. GEMA subsequently changed the energy companies' operating licences to address its concerns[293].

11. Water

The Water Industry Act 1991 provides a regulatory regime for water in the UK: the regulator is the Water Services Regulation Authority ('WSRA')[294], assisted by the Office of Water Services ('OFWAT')[295]. WSRA has concurrent powers with the OFT to apply Articles 101 and 102 TFEU and the Chapter I and Chapter II prohibitions in the Competition Act 1998. A Guideline has been adopted under the Act, *Competition Act 1998: Application in the Water and Sewerage Sectors*[296]. WSRA regulates prices for the provision of water to households; there is no competition in the UK for the supply of

---

[285] See Faull and Nikpay *The EC Law of Competition* (Oxford University Press, 2nd ed, 2007), paras 12.428–12.469.

[286] See Harker and Waddams 'Introducing Competition and Deregulating the British Domestic Energy Markets: a Legal and Economic Discussion' [2007] Journal of Business Law 244.

[287] Utilities Act 2000, s 1; the principal objective and general duties of the GEMA are contained in s 4AA of the Gas Act 1986 and s 3A of the Electricity Act 1989, as amended respectively by ss 16 and 17 of the Energy Act 2010.

[288] OFT 428, January 2005.

[289] OFT 437, July 2001.

[290] Decision of 25 February 2008.

[291] Case No 1097/1/2/08 *National Grid plc v Gas and Electricity Markets Authority* [2009] CAT 14, [2009] CompAR 282, on appeal in [2010] EWCA Civ 114, [2009] UKCLR 386; permission to appeal to the Supreme Court was rejected: see OFGEM Statement of 5 August 2010.

[292] See OFGEM Press Release of 21 February 2008, for details of this investigation see www.ofgem.gov.uk.

[293] See OFGEM Press Release of 23 March 2009 and OFGEM Information Note of 21 September 2009.

[294] Water Act 2003, s 34.

[295] OFWAT's website is www.ofwat.gov.uk.

[296] OFT 422, March 2010; see also Bailey 'The Emerging Co-existence of Regulation and Competition Law in the UK Water Industry' (2002) 25 World Competition 127.

residential customers. Theoretically it is possible for undertakings to compete for large industrial customers that use at least 50 megalitres of water a year, but competition has been slow to emerge[297]. There have been several complaints about exclusionary behaviour by incumbents in the water sector, but the WSRA has always concluded either that there was no infringement[298] or that the complaint was not one that it wished to pursue under competition law[299]. One case is particularly striking, *Albion Water v WSRA*[300], where the Authority had rejected two complaints against an incumbent water undertaking, Dŵr Cymru. On appeal the CAT concluded that Dŵr Cymru was guilty of a margin squeeze and annulled the Authority's decision to the contrary[301]. The judgment of the CAT was upheld on appeal to the Court of Appeal[302]. The CAT subsequently found Dŵr Cymru had proposed to charge Albion Water an excessive and unfair price for the transmission of water through its pipelines[303].

There are special rules requiring certain mergers between water companies to be referred to the CC; these have been amended, to bring the system more closely into alignment with the law on 'normal' mergers under the Enterprise Act 2002[304].

In April 2009 the Government published an *Independent Review of Competition and Innovation in Water Markets*, setting out various recommendations to increase competition in the upstream and retail levels of the 'value chain'[305]. A White Paper suggesting proposals for reform is expected in late 2011.

---

[297] See *Independent Review of Competition and Innovation in Water Markets: Final report*, April 2009, ch 5, available at www.defra.gov.uk.

[298] See ch 9, 'Table of published decisions' pp 374–389.

[299] See eg Case No 1058/2/4/06 *Independent Water Company Ltd v WSRA* [2007] CAT 6, [2007] UKCLR 614.

[300] Case No 1046/2/4/04 [2006] CAT 23, [2007] CompAR 22.

[301] Case No 1046/2/4/04 [2006] CAT 36, [2007] CompAR 328.

[302] *Dŵr Cymru Cyfyngedig v WSRA* [2008] EWCA Civ 536, [2008] UKCLR 457.

[303] Case No 1046/2/4/04 *Albion Water Ltd v WRSA* [2008] CAT 31, [2009] CompAR 28; Albion has brought a claim for damages under s 47A of the Competition Act 1998 in Case No 1166/5/7/10 *Albion Water Ltd v Dŵr Cymru Cyfyngedig*, not yet decided.

[304] See ch 22, 'Mergers in the water industry', pp 960–961.

[305] Available at www.defra.gov.uk.

Bibliography

There is a considerable body of literature on competition law. The following books are particularly recommended.

UK and EU competition law combined

Colino *Competition Law of the UK and EU* (Oxford University Press, 7th ed, 2011)

Graham *EU and UK Competition Law* (Longman, 2010)

Middleton, Rodger, MacCulloch and Galloway *Cases and Materials on UK and EC Competition Law* (Oxford University Press, 2nd ed, 2009)

Rodger and MacCulloch *Competition Law and Policy in the EC and UK* (Cavendish Publishing, 4th ed, 2008)

Slot and Johnston *An Introduction to Competition Law* (Hart Publishing, 2006)

EU competition law

Bellamy and Child *European Community Law of Competition* (Oxford University Press, 6th ed, 2008, eds Roth and Rose)

Buendia Sierra *Exclusive Rights and State Monopolies under EC Law* (Oxford University Press, 1999)

Competition Cases from the European Union (Sweet & Maxwell, 2nd ed, 2010, ed Kokkoris)

Competition Law: European Community Practice and Procedure (Sweet & Maxwell, 2007, eds Sacker, Hirsch and Montag)

EC Competition Procedure (Oxford University Press, 2nd ed, 2006, ed Ortiz Blanco)

Faull and Nikpay *The EC Law of Competition* (Oxford University Press, 2nd ed, 2007)

Gormesen *A Principled Approach to Abuse of Dominance in European Competition Law* (Cambridge University Press, 2010)

Goyder's *EC Competition Law* (Oxford University Press, 5th ed, 2009)

Goyder *EU Distribution Law* (Hart Publishing, 5th ed, 2011)

Jones and Sufrin *EU Competition Law: Text, Cases, and Materials* (Oxford University Press, 4th ed, 2010)

Jones and van der Woude *EU Competition Law Handbook* (Sweet & Maxwell, updated annually)

Kerse and Khan *EC Antitrust Procedure* (Sweet & Maxwell, 5th ed, 2005)

Komninos *EC Private Antitrust Enforcement: Decentralised Application of EC Competition Law by National Courts* (Hart Publishing, 2008)

Korah *Cases and Materials on EC Competition Law* (Hart Publishing, 3rd ed, 2006)

Korah *An Introductory Guide to EC Competition Law and Practice* (Hart Publishing, 9th ed, 2007)

Monti *EC Competition Law* (Cambridge University Press, 2007)

Nazzini *Concurrent Proceedings in Competition Law* (Oxford University Press, 2004)

O'Donoghue and Padilla *The Law and Economics of Article 82 EC* (Hart Publishing, 2006)

Odudu *The Boundaries of EC Competition Law* (Oxford University Press, 2006)

Prosser *The Limits of Competition Law: Markets and Public Services* (Oxford University Press, 2005)

Ritter, Braun and Rawlinson *European Competition Law: A Practitioner's Guide* (Kluwer Law International, 3rd ed, 2005)

Rousseva *Rethinking Exclusionary Abuses in EU Competition Law* (Hart Publishing, 2010)

Szyszczak *The Regulation of the State in Competitive Markets in the EU* (Hart Publishing, 2007)

Townley *Article 81 EC and Public Policy* (Hart Publishing, 2009)

Van Bael and Bellis *Competition Law of the European Community* (Kluwer Law International, 5th ed, 2010)

Wils *The Optimal Enforcement of EC Antitrust Law: Essays in Law and Economics* (Kluwer Law International, 2002)

Wils *Principles of European Antitrust Enforcement* (Hart Publishing, 2005)

Wils *Efficiency and Justice in European Antitrust Enforcement* (Hart Publishing, 2008)

UK competition law

Competition Litigation (Oxford University Press, 2010, eds Brealey and Green)

O'Kane *The Law of Criminal Cartels: Practice and Procedure* (Oxford University Press, 2009)

O'Neill and Sanders *UK Competition Procedure* (Oxford University Press, 2007)

Ten Years of UK Competition Law Reform (Dundee University Press, 2010, ed Rodger)

Mergers and concentrations

Bankes and Hadden *UK Merger Control: Law and Practice* (LexisNexis Butterworths, 2006)

Broberg *The European Commission's Jurisdiction to Scrutinise Mergers* (Kluwer Law International, 3rd ed, 2006)

Cook and Kerse *EC Merger Control* (Sweet & Maxwell, 5th ed, 2009)

Finbow and Parr *UK Merger Control: Law and Practice* (Sweet & Maxwell, 2nd ed, 2005)

Furse *The Law of Merger Control in the EC and the UK* (Hart Publishing, 2007)

Levy *European Merger Control Law: A Guide to the Merger Regulation* (LexisNexis, 2003)

Lindsay *The EC Merger Regulation: Substantive Issues* (Sweet & Maxwell, 2nd ed, 2006)

Parker and Majumdar *UK Merger Control* (Hart Publishing, 2011)

Schwalbe and Zimmer *Law and Economics in European Merger Control* (Oxford University Press, 2009)

Wilson *Globalization and the Limits of National Merger Control Laws* (Kluwer Law International, 2003)

Intellectual property

Anderman and Kallaugher *Technology and the New EU Competition Rules: Intellectual Property Licensing after Modernisation* (Oxford University Press, 2006)

Anderman and Schmidt *EU Competition Law and Intellectual Property Rights: The Regulation of Innovation* (Oxford University Press, 2nd ed, 2011)

Cornish, Llewellyn and Aplin *Intellectual Property* (Sweet & Maxwell, 7th ed, 2010)

Korah *Intellectual Property Rights and the EC Competition Rules* (Hart Publishing, 2006)

Turner *Intellectual Property and EU Competition Law* (Oxford University Press, 2010)

Economics

Bishop and Walker *The Economics of EC Competition Law: Concepts, Application and Measurement* (Sweet & Maxwell, 3rd ed, 2010)

Black, Hashimzade and Myles *Oxford Dictionary of Economics* (Oxford University Press, 3rd ed, 2009)

Carlton and Perloff *Modern Industrial Organization* (Addison Wesley, 4th ed, 2005)

Hylton *Antitrust Law: Economic Theory and Common Law Evolution* (Cambridge University Press, 2003)

Lipsey and Chrystal *Economics* (Oxford University Press, 12th ed, 2011)

Motta *Competition Policy: Theory and Practice* (Cambridge University Press, 2004)

Niels, Jenkins and Kavanagh *Economics for Competition Lawyers* (Oxford University Press, 2011)

Scherer and Ross *Industrial Market Structure and Economic Performance* (Houghton Mifflin, 3rd ed, 1990)

Sullivan and Harrison *Understanding Antitrust and Its Economic Implications* (LexisNexis, 4th ed, 2003)

Tirole *The Theory of Industrial Organization* (MIT Press, 1988)

Van den Bergh and Camesasca *European Competition Law and Economics: A Comparative Perspective* (Sweet & Maxwell, 2nd ed, 2006)

Whinston *Lectures on Antitrust Economics* (MIT Press, 2008)

Miscellaneous

Alese *Federal Antitrust and EC Competition Law Analysis* (Ashgate, 2008)

Amato *Antitrust and the Bounds of Power: The Dilemma of Liberal Democracy in the History of the Market* (Hart Publishing, 1997)

Bork *The Antitrust Paradox* (Free Press, 1993)

Broder *US Antitrust Law and Enforcement; A Practice Introduction* (Oxford University Press, 2010)

Elhauge and Geradin *Global Competition Law and Economics* (Hart Publishing, 2nd ed, 2011)

Gal *Competition Policy for Small Market Economies* (Harvard University Press, 2003)

Gerber *Law and Competition in Twentieth Century Europe* (Oxford University Press, 1998)

Gerber *Global Competition* (Oxford University Press, 2010)

Hovenkamp *The Antitrust Enterprise: Principle and Execution* (Harvard University Press, 2006)

Jones *Private Enforcement of Antitrust Law in the EU, UK and USA* (Oxford University Press, 1999)

Posner *Antitrust Law* (University of Chicago Press, 2nd ed, 2001)

Yeung *Securing Compliance with Competition Law* (Hart Publishing, 2003)

Statutes, treaties, EU regulations etc

Blackstone's UK and EU Competition Documents (Oxford University Press, 7th ed, 2011, ed Middleton)

Butterworths Competition Law Handbook (Butterworths, 17th ed, 2011)

Important websites

Competition Appeal Tribunal	www.catribunal.org.uk
Competition Commission	www.competition-commission.org.uk
Department for Business, Innovation and Skills	www.bis.gov.uk
European Commission, DG COMP	www.ec.europa.eu/competition
Court of Justice	www.curia.eu.int
EUR-Lex	www.eur-lex.europa.eu
International Competition Network	www.internationalcompetitionnetwork.org
Office of Fair Trading	www.oft.gov.uk
Organisation for Economic Co-Operation and Development	www.oecd.org
US Department of Justice	www.justice.gov/atr
US Federal Trade Commission	www.ftc.gov

Index